JUDICIAL REVIEW

JUDICIAL REVIEW

by

The Right Honourable The Lord Clyde, P.C.
A Lord of Appeal in Ordinary

and

Denis J. Edwards, LL.B., LL.M.
Assistant Professor of Law, City University of Hong Kong
Sometime Lecturer in Law, University of Strathclyde

Published under the auspices of
SCOTTISH UNIVERSITIES LAW INSTITUTE LTD

EDINBURGH
W. GREEN
2000

First published 2000

Published in 2000 by W. Green & Son Limited,
21 Alva Street,
Edinburgh, EH2 4PS

Phototypeset by LBJ Typesetting Ltd of Kingsclere

Printed in Great Britain by MPG Books Ltd
Bodmin, Cornwall

No natural forests were destroyed to make this product; only farmed timber
was used and replanted

A CIP catalogue record of this book is available from the British Library

ISBN 0 414 01173 2

© SCOTTISH UNIVERSITIES LAW INSTITUTE LTD 2000

The moral rights of the authors have been asserted

PREFACE

So much has already been published on the subject of judicial review that something of an apology may be required for the production of another volume. However, what we have endeavoured to present in this book is a systematic account of judicial review, primarily directed at the principles and practice of Scots law, but with some regard particularly to English law. Moreover, without attempting to embark upon a comparative study of the subject, we have also sought to find assistance from several other jurisdictions on particular issues. We have sought to set the subject of the work against a background not only of the origins and history of review in Scotland but also of its constitutional context. In that connection two recent developments may provide justification enough for a new book. These are the passing of the Human Rights Act 1998 and the creation of a Scottish Parliament under the Scotland Act 1998. These measures were still being debated when our work was in course of preparation and it is still too early to achieve a mature evaluation of their implications. But the consequences of each of these enactments will be of considerable significance for judicial review and we have tried to take account of each of them.

Co-authorships may give rise to a variety of problems. In our case we have been working in comparative isolation from each other, with one of us in London and the other in Hong Kong, corresponding by telephone, fax, and latterly e-mail. Inevitably the careful reader will be able to identify differences in style and language in the course of the text, but we have at least endeavoured to iron out any gross inconsistency in the substance of it.

Having aimed at a systematic study of the subject we have not attempted to include a comprehensive or exhaustive reference to all of the considerable case law on the subject. We have endeavoured to identify and illustrate the principles and provide something of a foundation for research or guidance. Our intention has been to provide a statement of the law which may be of use for professional practice as well as academic study. We have sought to state the law as at October 1, 1999.

We should record our gratitude to The Hon. Lord Reed, Christopher Himsworth and Robert McCreadie, Advocate, who read over the text in its nearly completed state on behalf of SULI. We have adopted nearly all of their many useful comments, while recognising that we retain responsibility for the substance of the text. We must also thank the staff of Greens for their work in processing our script and Professor George Gretton, the Director of SULI, for his patient supervision. Last, but not least, we must record our thanks to our respective wives, Ann and Kirstine, for their tolerating over a considerable period the distraction which the production of this volume has entailed.

Clyde
Denis Edwards

CONTENTS

PART I—THE CONTEXT OF JUDICIAL REVIEW

PART II—THE CHANGING WORLD OF JUDICIAL REVIEW

PART III—THE SCOPE OF JUDICIAL REVIEW

PART IV—THE GROUNDS OF JUDICIAL REVIEW

PART V—PROCEDURE AND REMEDIES

APPENDICES

TABLE OF CASES

TABLE OF STATUTES

TABLE OF STATUTORY INSTRUMENTS

TABLE OF TREATIES AND CONVENTIONS

PART I

THE CONTEXT OF JUDICIAL REVIEW

CHAPTER 1

INTRODUCTION

I   JUDICIAL REVIEW IN PERSPECTIVE
II   THE CONSTITUTIONAL NATURE OF JUDICIAL REVIEW
III THE CONTEXT AND SUBSTANCE OF JUDICIAL REVIEW

I JUDICIAL REVIEW IN PERSPECTIVE

This book is concerned with the power of a Supreme Court to ensure **1.01**
that all those vested with a legal authority exercise that authority lawfully
and properly. Historically, the supervisory jurisdiction of the Court of
Session has been the means by which the supreme court in Scotland has
achieved this objective. As elsewhere, the term "judicial review" is now
used to refer to this jurisdiction, the essential purpose of which is to
ensure that the law is observed. The existence of a supervisory jurisdiction is a fundamental element of a constitution which is based on respect
for the rule of law. It is an inherent jurisdiction of a supreme court and
cannot be taken away consistently with respect for the rule of law.[1]

Terminology

The supervisory jurisdiction is of considerable antiquity in Scotland but **1.02**
the use of the term "judicial review" as an equivalent is relatively
recent.[2] In many systems, notably the United States of America, the term
judicial review refers to the power of a supreme court under a supreme
written constitution to review all types of legislation and other governmental acts for consistency with the constitution. In Scotland, however,
as elsewhere in the United Kingdom, both the absence of a supreme
written constitution and the doctrine of Parliamentary supremacy have
traditionally confined the term judicial review to the Supreme Court's
power to review administrative action against the standards and values
which the law has developed for the lawful and proper exercise of legal
powers.[3] In 1985, the Rule of Court which introduced the new procedure
for cases of judicial review[4] gave an official recognition of the term
"judicial review" by providing that:

> "an application to the supervisory jurisdiction of the court which
> immediately before the coming into operation of this rule would

---

[1] For a discussion of the fundamental nature of judicial review in England & Wales, see
Laws, "Law and Democracy" [1995] P.L. 72; and Lord Woolf, "Droit Public–English
Style" [1995] P.L. 57. See also de Smith, Woolf and Jowell, *Judicial Review of Administra-
tive Action* (5th ed., Sweet & Maxwell, London, 1995), pp. 15–17.

[2] It was used by Prof. J.D.B. Mitchell in his *Constitutional Law* (1st ed., W. Green,
Edinburgh, 1964); but in Bennet Miller, *Administrative and Local Government Law* (1961),
the reference is to "judicial control".

[3] The development of these standards and values has produced what amounts to a
system of administrative law. See further para. 2.01.

[4] Rule of Court 260A, introduced by Act of Sederunt (Rules of Court Amendment No.
2) (Judicial Review) 1985, now Chapter 58 of the Rules of the Court of Session 1994.

have been made by way of summons or petition, shall be made by
way of an application for judicial review in accordance with the
provisions of this rule."

The identification of judicial review with the "supervisory jurisdiction"
underlines two important characteristics of the power of judicial review.
First, it indicates a distinction from the ordinary jurisdiction of a court so
as to point to the special quality of the power of review.[5] In particular,
judicial review is a power inherent in and unique to a supreme court.
Secondly, it emphasises the essential character of judicial review as being
supervisory. This consideration leads directly to the central limitation
upon judicial review to the effect that, while the court may express a
conclusion about the legal validity of a challenged act or decision, it will
not take on itself the task of making the correct decision or assume the
power of the person whose conduct is under review. This limitation on
the scope of judicial review is often drawn in terms of distinctions
between review and appeal, legality or validity and merits, and procedure
and substance. It must, however, be acknowledged that in practice none
of these distinctions offers a sure indication of the scope of judicial
review.

Review and appeal

1.03   The word "review" may be used by way of contrast with the word
"appeal". Whereas the former may be understood as indicating an
examination of the validity, that is to say the legality and propriety, of a
decision, the latter may be used to describe an examination of the merits
of a decision, an exercise which is beyond the scope of judicial review.[6]
This distinction between review and appeal was described by Lord Fraser
of Tullybelton in these words: "Judicial review is entirely different from
an ordinary appeal. It is made effective by the court quashing an
administrative decision without substituting its own decision, and is to be
contrasted with an appeal where the appellate tribunal substitutes its
own decision on the merits for that of the administrative officer."[7]
However, the terms review and appeal are not always so clearly
distinguished. As Lord Fraser pointed out in *Brown v. Hamilton District
Council*[8]: "The word 'review' is commonly used in Scottish cases to
describe a process which in England would be called 'appeal' and is not
restricted to procedure corresponding to the English procedure of
judicial review."[9]

    In England, the broad distinction between review and appeal is
generally recognised,[10] but on occasion the word "review" may be used

---

[5] As is noted later the word "jurisdiction" is open to misunderstanding; see para. 22.18
and para. 22.24.

[6] Although, of course, the scope of an "appeal" may be statutorily restricted to a point
of law; and obversely, some of the grounds of "review" may enter into the merits.

[7] *R. v. Entry Clearance Officer, ex parte Amin* [1983] 1 A.C. 818 at 829.

[8] 1983 S.C. (H.L.) 1.

[9] *ibid.* at 42. In the past the term "review" was regarded as inappropriate as a means of
reference to the supervisory jurisdiction. In *Ross v. Finlater* (1826) 4 S. 514 at 518, Lord
Pitmilly said of the Court's power to give redress: "it is not a power to review, but to quash
irregular proceedings contrary to statute". In *Perth General Station Committee v. Stewart*,
1924 S.C. 1004 at 1014, Lord President Clyde observed of an action of reduction: "it is in
no sense a proceeding for review; on the contrary its object is cassation, not review".

[10] See, for example, *R. v. Secretary of State for the Home Department, ex parte Brind*
[1991] 1 A.C. 696, *per* Lord Ackner at 762. See also Wade and Forsyth, *Administrative Law*
(7th ed, 1994), p. 38.

to refer to an appeal, as opposed to "supervision", which is the function of judicial review.[11] For present purposes, although the distinction may be questioned at least where irrationality or error are the grounds of review, the words "review" and "appeal" will be used in the distinct senses of review being concerned only with validity while appeal is concerned in addition with the merits.

Validity and merits

It is important to stress that, whatever language may be used to describe the supervisory jurisdiction, that jurisdiction does not allow the court to interfere with the merits of a discretionary decision where that decision has been lawfully and properly reached.[12] While, as will be seen, the power of the Court in the exercise of the supervisory jurisdiction may penetrate some distance into what may be considered the substance of a challenged decision,[13] the court cannot when exercising its power of judicial review simply substitute its own decision on the merits because it prefers a different construction of the facts.[14] In *Chief Constable of the North Wales Police v. Evans*,[15] Lord Brightman put the matter thus: "Judicial review is concerned, not with the decision, but with the decision-making process. Unless that restriction on the power of the court is observed, the court will in my view, under the guise of preventing the abuse of power, be itself guilty of usurping power".[16]

1.04

Procedure and substance

The attempt to find a workable distinction between procedure and substance is a recurring endeavour in discussions of judicial review.[17] Since judicial review is not an appeal, it focuses only on the way in which

1.05

---

[11] See, for example, *Anisminic v. Foreign Compensation Commission* [1969] 2 A.C. 147, *per* Lord Pearce at 195.

[12] This is a hallmark of judicial review in the common law tradition: see further, para 8.09. In contrast, in some civil law systems, the specialist administrative courts take a more activist approach to the "review" of exercises of administrative discretion. In Germany, for example, the courts have traditionally only conceded discretion (on the merits) to the administration where it is expressly conferred by law; in other cases, the court is prepared to enter into what a British lawyer would term the merits of decisions. See Nolte, "General Principles of German and European Administrative Law—A Comparison in Historical Perspective" (1994) 57 M.L.R. 191, especially at p. 196. Similarly, in France, the Conseil d'Etat does not traditionally draw a distinction between legality and merits or procedure and substance, at least not for the purposes of its jurisdiction as a judicial body: see Brown and Bell, *French Administrative Law* (4th ed., Clarendon Press, Oxford, 1993), pp. 237–251.

[13] See further paras 8–09 *et seq.*

[14] See *Stewart v. Monklands District Council*, 1987 S.L.T. 630.

[15] [1982] 1 W.L.R. 1155.

[16] *ibid.* at 1173.

[17] The distinction between procedure and substance provides the basis of a considerable volume of scholarship on what the proper scope of judicial review should be. Distinguished commentators have often attempted to build theoretical positions around distinctions between procedure and substance so as to formulate a philosophical position on what the proper role for judicial review, and more generally judicial power, should be. This has been especially true in the U.S. with reference to the great power of judicial review of legislation exercised by the U.S. Supreme Court under the U.S. Constitution. See, for example, Ely, *Democracy and Distrust: A Theory of Judicial Review* (1980); Sunstein, *The Partial Constitution* (Harvard U.P., 1993), esp. at pp. 133–153; and Tribe, "The Puzzling Persistence of process-based Constitutional Theories" (1980) 89 Yale L.J. 1037. More generally, see Bickel, *The Least Dangerous Branch: The Supreme Court at the Bar of Politics* (1962); and Wechsler, "Toward Neutral Principles of Constitutional Law" (1959) 73 Harv.L.R. 19. Although the issues raised in the U.S. context pertain to constitutional

a decision was reached without taking any notice of the substance, or merits, of the decision itself. So in Lord Diplock's famous formulation of the grounds of judicial review by reference to a threefold classification, it is "procedural" impropriety which provides the heading for those grounds of review related to the "fairness" of a decision.[18] Similarly, the ground of review known as legitimate expectation is traditionally understood as being procedural in nature, that is, concerning expectations of fair procedures, rather than protecting expectations, however "legitimate" they may be, of substantive decisions.[19] Nevertheless, a distinction between procedure and substance can be difficult to draw with precision. Inevitably, the terms are themselves uncertain, so that what on one view amounts to a "procedural" matter may on an equally valid alternative view amount to a "substantive" matter. Moreover, as has been noted above, some of the grounds of review themselves address the substance of the decision, notably irrationality and error. This leads the courts to seek other limiting devices in relation to such grounds, such as reviewing a decision only by reference to the material before the decision-maker, or classifying errors as "jurisdictional" or non-jurisdictional",[20] or distinguishing "soft" and "hard-edged" questions,[21] whereby the latter essentially focus on "jurisdiction in the narrow sense", or simple legality, which allows the court greater scope for intervention. Yet it may still be asked to what extent any of these devices allow the distinction between procedure and substance to hold firm.[22]

Statutory appeals on matters of validity

1.06 While the linguistic distinction between review and appeal has not always in the past been clearly drawn, the essential distinction between the court's power to intervene where a challenge is made to a decision-maker's excess of jurisdiction despite its inability to intervene in the merits of the decision has for long been recognised.[23] The distinction may be easier to identify if appeals are seen largely as the creatures of statute while the power of review is understood as a special provision of the common law. However, what are referred to as appeals under statutory provisions may involve grounds of challenge which are comparable with and may in some instances be identical to those which may be

---

review, the procedure–substance debate is also relevant to ascertaining the scope of judicial review in the U.K.: see Harlow and Rawlings, *Law and Administration* (2nd ed., Butterworths, 1997), esp. Chaps 2, 3 and 15.

[18] See *Council of Civil Service Unions v. Minister for the Civil Service* [1985] A.C. 374 at 410–411.

[19] Compare *R. v. Ministry of Agriculture, Fisheries and Food, ex parte Hamble Fisheries (Offshore) Ltd* [1995] 2 All E.R. 714 and *R. v. Secretary of State for the Home Department, ex parte Hargreaves* [1997] 1 W.L.R. 906. But see also *R. v. IRC, ex parte Unilever plc* [1996] C.O.D. 369. See further, Chap. 19.

[20] See further, Chap. 22.

[21] cf. *R. v. Monopolies and Mergers Commission, ex parte South Yorkshire Transport Ltd* [1993] 1 W.L.R. 23, *per* Lord Mustill at 32.

[22] For further discussion, see Craig, *Administrative Law* (3rd ed., Sweet & Maxwell, London, 1996), at pp. 12–16. See also, Fordham, "Surveying the Grounds: Key Themes in Judicial Intervention", in Leyland & Woods, *Administrative Law Facing the Future* (Blackstone Press, London, 1997), Chap. 8, esp. pp. 188–193.

[23] See Chap. 2.

open to an applicant in an application for judicial review.[24] For example, sections 238 and 239 of the Town and Country Planning (Scotland) Act 1997[25] allow an appeal on the grounds that the plan or the order in question is not within the powers of the Act or that there has been a failure to comply with the relevant statutory procedure. Furthermore, a statutory appeal may raise such questions as whether the particular tribunal was obliged to give reasons for its decision or whether the reasons given were adequate,[26] both of which questions may be canvassed in an application for judicial review. In many cases where statutory provision has been made for appeal against decisions taken or purported to be taken under the statute, the ground for appeal may simply be stated to be on a point of law. But even here, it has been held in England that a statutory appeal on the ground that a decision was "erroneous in point of law" includes the question whether a provision in regulations is within the scope of the enabling power.[27] In this regard, it should be noticed that section 11 of the Tribunals and Inquiries Act 1992[28] makes provision for an appeal to be taken from certain specified tribunals where a party is dissatisfied with a decision in point of law. While the present book is concerned only with the common law supervisory jurisdiction rather than statutory appeals, the scope of statutory appeals is at least of interest in casting some light on the scope of the common law power of judicial review.[29]

Indirect or collateral challenges in civil proceedings

While judicial review is only competent in the Court of Session and applications for judicial review not only must be raised in that court but must follow the statutory procedure,[30] it should not be forgotten that the validity of challengeable actings and decisions may be raised and resolved in a variety of other processes. Beyond the existence of statutory appeals, several examples of cases in which validity issues may arise collaterally, that is, outside of judicial review, may be noted. First, questions of the legality of proposed byelaws may require to be resolved by a sheriff in proceedings for their confirmation, and in that context, if they are found to be *ultra vires*, confirmation may be refused.[31] Secondly, an attempt to enforce by means of the civil law an obligation arising by virtue of the exercise of statutory powers may be defeated on the ground that the act or decision lying behind the obligation is *ultra vires*, provided

1.07

---

[24] This raises the question whether or not the existence of a statutory appeal in which "validity" issues may be canvassed operates to exclude recourse to the supervisory jurisdiction: see Rule of Court 58.3(2). See also *Crawford v. Lennox* (1852) 14 D. 1029; *Bovis Homes (Scotland) Ltd v. Inverclyde D.C.* 1982 S.L.T. 473; and *City Cabs (Edinburgh) Ltd v. City of Edinburgh D.C.* 1988 S.L.T. 184. For comment on the position in England & Wales, see Wade, "Judicial Review and Alternative Remedies", 1997 P.L. 589. See further, Chap. 12.

[25] c. 8.

[26] See *Carr v. UK Central Council for Nursing Midwifery*, 1989 S.L.T. 580.

[27] *Chief Adjudication Officer v. Foster* [1993] A.C. 754.

[28] 1992 c. 53.

[29] For further consideration of this, reference may be made to Professor Bradley's contribution on "Administrative Law" in the *Stair Encyclopaedia*, Vol.1, paras 337–344.

[30] The necessity for following the statutory procedure is considered later: see para. 8.14. For discussion of the position in England & Wales see Fredman, "Procedural Exclusivity: A Judicious Review" (1995) 111 L.Q.R. 591.

[31] See, for example, *Western Isles Islands Council v. Caledonian Macbrayne Ltd*, 1990 S.L.T. (Sh.Ct) 97.

that the point is raised in the pleadings and presented in argument.[32] Such a challenge on the grounds of validity may arise in the sheriff court or any inferior court or tribunal in Scotland and be taken to the point of decision, whether or not it is appealed to the Court of Session. So, for example, whether a minimum charge for electricity was within the power of an electricity board was determined through a summary cause in the sheriff court in a claim for £6.[33] But while such a decision may indirectly reflect a finding that there has been an excess of power, it is only by the course of judicial review that such a challenge can be directly raised. It is only in the Court of Session that a declarator of the invalidity, or a reduction, of the offending decision or order can be granted and thereby an effective remedy against the wrong be obtained.[34]

The raising of issues of validity incidentally in other proceedings can have its disadvantages and inconveniences. These include administrative inconvenience, uncertainty in the law, and sundry difficulties associated with the affairs of those who have relied on acts and decisions which are, possibly some considerable time later, impugned. Moreover, where regulations are challenged, it is far from satisfactory for the validity of regulations to be considered in proceedings in which their author may well not be a party and will not be represented.[35] In *Stornoway Town Council v. Macdonald*,[36] which came by way of appeal from the Sheriff Court, the defence to a claim for payment of a sum assessed as a proprietor's share of the cost of making up a private street was that the resolution to make up the street was *ultra vires*, since the street was not a "private street" for the purposes of the relevant statute. The defence failed since there was a statutory means of appeal against the resolution and the proprietor was in any event barred from his challenge; but the point was also made by Lord Kissen that such a challenge could not competently be raised when the other proprietors were not parties to the action. However, a different result was reached where the local authority had proceeded under the wrong statutory power.[37] It is clear that the rights of the citizen should not be prejudiced by the procedural exclusivity of judicial review. But it is not always easy to strike the balance between the right to plead invalidity of an act or decision in any proceedings and the collective interest in a stable administration and certainty which procedural exclusivity attempts to serve.[38]

Invalidity as a defence in criminal proceedings

1.08　The invalidity of subordinate legislation whereby an offence has been prescribed may be put forward as a defence to a prosecution brought under that legislation.[39] But the propriety of that course may, at least in

---

[32] See, for example, *Malloch v. Aberdeen Corporation* 1971 S.C. (H.L.) 85.

[33] *SSEB v. Elder* 1978 S.C. 132.

[34] It is thought that a reduction *ope exceptionis* is not competent in the sheriff court if it would amount to an exercise of the supervisory jurisdiction. The position in regard to arbitral awards is considered in the article on "Arbitration" in the *Stair Encyclopaedia*, Reissue, paras 75 *et seq*.

[35] *Sommerville v. Langmuir*, 1932 J.C. 55.

[36] 1971 S.C. 78.

[37] See *Magistrates and Town Council of the City of Edinburgh v. Paterson* (1880) 8 R. 197.

[38] See further, para. 8.14.

[39] See, for example, *M'Gregor v. Disselduff*, 1907 S.C.(J.) 21; *Shepherd v. Howman*, 1918 J.C. 78; *M'Lean v. Paterson*, 1939 J.C. 52; *Galloway v. Anderson*, 1928 J.C. 70 (whether the

England, depend upon the particular statutory provision in question.[40] In England, a distinction was sought to be drawn between substantive invalidity, where it is sufficient to show the invalidity itself, and procedural invalidity, where the complainer has also to show that he has been prejudiced. In the former case no evidence should be required. In the latter case, however, evidence might be required to show the procedural defect. Following this distinction, it was held in *Bugg v. Director of Public Prosecutions*[41] that a challenge to a byelaw on a point of procedural invalidity could not be made in a criminal prosecution in the Crown Court, although a challenge on its substantive validity could be made. The decision in *Bugg* was later overruled by the House of Lords in *Boddington v. British Transport Police*,[42] where it was held that in the absence of a clear parliamentary indication to the contrary a defendant in criminal proceedings was entitled to challenge the lawfulness of subordinate legislation, or an administrative decision made under that legislation, without any distinction between substantive and procedural invalidity.

In light of *Boddington*, the position in Scotland may now require some reconsideration. In *Hamilton v. Fyfe*,[43] where the question whether the summary complaint was a criminal or civil proceeding was waived, the complaint that the order was invalid on account of a defect in its preliminary procedure was held to have been rightly repelled by the sheriff. Lord Justice-Clerk Macdonald observed: "I do not think that a Court such as that which tried this case had any duty or right to enter upon any such matters at all, and I do not think that this Court could hold that the Sheriff in refusing to take up the matter was acting illegally in any way".[44] The case was distinguished from the situation where, as in *Eastburn v. Wood*,[45] a byelaw was challenged in criminal proceedings. In that case the court held that a power to make byelaws for the prevention of nuisances did not authorise a byelaw which sought to prevent affixing of bills to a hoarding; and in *Lord Advocate v. Sutherland*[46] it was held that a sheriff had erred in deserting charges against an accused on the ground that the defence had challenged the validity of an award for sequestration, the existence of which was an ingredient in the charges.

---

regulations were made by the proper Minister); *Drummond v. Pendreich*, 1972 J.C. 27 (power to alter a definition). In the U.K., challenges to rules of law themselves have historically been limited to challenges to the *vires* to make secondary legislation, the supremacy of the U.K. Parliament being a complete answer to any challenge to a provision in primary legislation. But it follows from E.C. law that all legislation, including Acts of the U.K. Parliament, is subject to challenge on the ground that it is incompatible with applicable rules of E.C. law. In the case of Acts of the Scottish Parliament, they may be challenged for inconsistency with the Scotland Act 1998: this includes challenges based on E.C. law and Convention rights. For example, provision made for criminal offences in Acts of the Scottish Parliament may be open to challenge on Convention rights grounds. Beyond E.C. law, however, U.K. primary legislation cannot be "struck down" for incompatibility with guaranteed Convention rights, the remedy being a declaration of incompatibility under s. 4 of the Human Rights Act 1998. The scope of judicial review involving E.C. law and Convention rights is discussed further in Chap. 5 on E.C. law, Chapter 6 on the Human Rights Act 1998, and Chapter 7 on the Scotland Act 1998.

[40] See *R. v. Wicks* [1998] A.C. 92; [1997] 2 W.L.R. 876. But see also *Boddington v. British Transport Police* [1998] 2 W.L.R. 639.

[41] [1993] Q.B. 473.

[42] [1998] 2 W.L.R. 639.

[43] 1907 J.C. 79.

[44] *ibid.* at 86.

[45] (1892) 19 R.(J.) 100.

[46] 1993 S.L.T. 404.

The High Court held that even although proceedings for suspension and reduction had been commenced in the Court of Session, the matter could be resolved in the course of a criminal trial.

Other remedies

1.09   It should also be noticed that where there is a grievance about administrative action, there may be opportunities for a remedy without recourse to the processes of the law and, in particular, judicial review. In some cases provision will be made for an express statutory remedy. As has been noticed above, the scope of a statutory appeal may be such as to include grounds which could also be grounds for an exercise of the supervisory jurisdiction.[47] In addition, recourse may in certain circumstances be had to an ombudsman, who may well provide a solution, perhaps necessarily less expeditious, but also less costly, than any remedy which may be available by way of judicial review.[48] Furthermore, there may be remedies available in the political process, such as an application to the Secretary of State, or the First Minister, or some other appropriate authority, even although there is no statutory provision which is being invoked. Alternatively, complaints may be made to members of one or other Parliaments, local councillors, pressure groups, or representative bodies of one kind or another, or even the media. Sometimes such avenues may provide preferable alternatives to judicial review.[49] The present study, however, is not concerned with the extra-judicial possibilities, but only with judicial review. In this regard, within the possibilities of alternative statutory procedures, it must be noticed that as a legal process judicial review is, in general, a remedy of last resort.[50]

II   THE CONSTITUTIONAL NATURE OF JUDICIAL REVIEW

The constitutional significance of judicial review

1.10   In a legal system committed to the rule of law, it is a fundamental principle that legal powers which affect the individual are defined, limited, and their exercise reviewable to ensure consistency with the law. The law for this purpose must be understood as including constitutional law and the ordinary law. Even in the absence of a codified constitution, it has always been possible to say that the United Kingdom has a constitution, at least in the sense of a system of constitutional values which the courts respect when deciding cases. These values have often emerged strongly when the courts exercise their power of judicial review.[51] The significant constitutional changes which have recently

---

[47] See, for example, *Allen & Sons Billposting Ltd v. Corporation of Edinburgh*, 1909 S.C. 70.

[48] For discussion of the various ombudsman procedures, and in particular the Parliamentary Commissioner for Administration, see Wade & Forsyth, *Administrative Law* (7th ed., Clarendon Press, Oxford, 1994), pp. 79–107.

[49] For a discussion, with some criticism, of the process of judicial review in England, see generally Richardson & Genn, *Administrative Law and Government Action: The Courts and Alternative Mechanisms of Review* (Clarendon Press, Oxford, 1994), and esp. Chap. 3 by Cranston: "Reviewing Judicial Review".

[50] For the recognition of this principle in England see Lord Woolf's Final Report to the Lord Chancellor on the civil justice system in England and Wales (HMSO): *Access to Justice* (1996), section IV, para. 7. See also Chap. 12.

[51] See, for example, *Anisminic Ltd v. Foreign Compensation Commission* [1969] 2 A.C. 147; *R. v. Secretary of State for the Home Department, ex parte Fire Brigades Union* [1995] 2 A.C. 513; and *R. v. Secretary of State for the Home Department, ex parte Simms and O'Brien* [1999] 3 W.L.R. 328 esp. at 336–340 *per* Lord Steyn.

occurred have strengthened the power of judicial review and given it some elements of the type of constitutional judicial review found in countries with a supreme constitutional instrument, such as the United States, Canada, Australia, India and Germany. The United Kingdom's membership of the European Union, the availability in the U.K. legal systems of the European Convention on Human Rights, and the establishment of regional legislatures in Scotland, Wales and Northern Ireland have produced a more formal set of constitutional instruments for the United Kingdom, albeit all owing their status to what may be seen as ordinary Acts of the U.K. Parliament. The important role which these Acts of Parliament give to the courts may now justify the view that U.K. courts possess a jurisdiction to ensure that legal powers are exercised in accordance with rules of law which may be termed superior constitutional laws. If not yet a fully fledged constitutional jurisdiction such as possessed by, for example, supreme or constitutional courts vested with the power to interpret a supreme constitutional instrument and invalidate primary legislation contrary to it, the point has now been reached where it may be said that U.K. courts have a jurisdiction which may be termed judicial review on constitutional grounds. But the constitutional significance of judicial review stretches far beyond its availability in cases of constitutional significance. Its very existence to challenge the exercise of any defined legal authority which affects an individual is of fundamental constitutional importance.

Judicial review as a constitutional jurisdiction

Even if courts in the United Kingdom now have a jurisdiction to review **1.11** the exercise of legal powers against the provisions of "constitutional" laws, the question arises about the extent to which the supervisory jurisdiction of the supreme court is to be regarded as a constitutional jurisdiction. Although there is no doubt about the constitutional nature and significance of judicial review, it cannot be said that judicial review is a general, far less exclusive, jurisdiction for matters of constitutional significance. Many cases which come before the court in the exercise of its supervisory jurisdiction will have constitutional significance.[52] This follows from the nature of the jurisdiction: where an applicant argues that a decision made by a government Minister in pursuance of statutory or prerogative powers has been made unlawfully, the case may have some constitutional significance depending on the nature of the challenged decision, the nature of the complaint and the nature of the remedy sought. But judicial review is by no means the only vehicle by which constitutional issues may be raised and determined.[53] Correspondingly, it is only a proportion of the cases that come to the court by way of judicial review which will have a constitutional character. Whether a case falls within the judicial review procedure depends on the scope of that procedure and not the "constitutional" dimensions of the case.[54] The United Kingdom does not have a separate constitutional court for distinct constitutional law questions, such as Germany or South Africa. It

---

[52] For example, *R. v. Secretary of State for the Home Department, ex parte Fire Brigades Union* [1995] 2 A.C. 513.

[53] For example, the compatibility of provisions in Acts of the U.K. Parliament (or Acts of the Scottish Parliament) with applicable E.C. law may arise before an Employment Tribunal.

[54] On the scope of the supervisory jurisdiction, see Chap. 8.

may be that the Judicial Committee of the Privy Council under the
devolution legislation could be seen as taking on the role of a constitutional court; but its jurisdiction ranges beyond the "devolution issues"
which may arise under, for example, the Scotland Act 1998. Moreover,
all "constitutional" cases will not come before the Privy Council: for
example, cases involving Convention rights may only come before it
where a "devolution issue" is raised; and not even all "devolution issues"
may come before it since its jurisdiction principally depends on references of such issues from other courts and only very exceptionally on
direct access.[55] In the future, perhaps prompted by reform of the House
of Lords, thought may be given to new arrangements for a British
supreme court. At present, however, it is too early to speculate on what
form any such arrangements might take.[56]

Judicial review of administrative action

1.12   As is discussed further in the following chapter, it is only recently that
the claim may be made that there now exists a developed system of
administrative law in the jurisdictions of the United Kingdom. That
"system" of administrative law has, for the most part, grown out of
ordinary legal principles and may well be regarded as one of the most
significant achievements of the common law in the latter part of the
twentieth century.[57] But even if the law has progressed as far as a system
of administrative law, the U.K. legal systems do not have separate
administrative courts to resolve disputes between natural and legal
persons and the government. Nor, as has already been mentioned, is
judicial review the exclusive process by which the validity of administrative action may come under challenge. Under the present Scottish
procedure applications for judicial review are directed to one or other of
the judges specially nominated for such work; but their judicial duties
are not confined to cases of judicial review and cases of judicial review
may on occasion be heard by judges other than those specifically
nominated. In some Commonwealth countries, of which New Zealand
may be taken as an example, a structural distinction is recognised for the
handling of cases of judicial review. There, an administrative division

---

[55] "Devolution issues" arising under the Scotland Act 1998 may only be brought before
the Privy Council directly in limited circumstances at the instance of defined office
holders—for example, the Lord Advocate or Attorney General: see s. 33 of the Scotland
Act 1998.

[56] In particular, thought may be given to establishing a separate constitutional court to
rule on "constitutional" issues. Experience elsewhere, however, suggests that such a body
can present difficult jurisdictional questions. In South Africa, for example, the new
Constitutional Court has been called on to decide cases on its jurisdiction (principally one
of reference from other courts and only exceptionally direct access) and how this relates to
that of other courts: see *S v. Mhlungu* 1995 (3) S.A. 867, esp. at 892–895; and *Transvaal
Agricultural Union v. Minister of Land Affairs*, 1997 (2) S.A. 621 at 628–630. For discussion
of the role of the new Constitutional Court in South Africa, see Sarkin, "The Political
Role of the South African Constitutional Court", (1997) 114 S.A.L.J. 134. Alternatively, it
may be thought preferable to retain a general final court of appeal, a purpose which,
subject to certain exceptions, particularly criminal appeals from Scotland, is presently
served by the House of Lords. Such is the position in the U.S., Australia and Canada. The
price, however, at least if the volume of "constitutional" cases is great, is for the court to
control its workload rigorously. Whatever reforms may be adopted, wider institutional
questions remain: for example (in relation to federal law) whether the court sits *en banc*,
who the judges are, and how they are appointed.

[57] *cf. R. v. IRC, ex parte National Federation of Self-Employed and Small Businesses Ltd*
[1982] A.C. 617, *per* Lord Diplock at 641.

was set up within the Supreme Court.[58] In continental Europe, matters of judicial review are processed through special administrative courts culminating in cases before, for example, in France the Conseil d'Etat or in Germany the Bundesverwaltungsgericht. In France, the Conseil d'Etat has an advisory as well as a judicial function. In Scotland, however, as elsewhere in the United Kingdom, neither the workload nor the specialty of the exercise of the supervisory jurisdiction have hitherto required the establishment of a separate administrative court.[59]

Luxembourg and Strasbourg

In understanding the context in which judicial review now operates, it is **1.13** necessary to recognise two major areas of influence. These are the jurisprudence of the European Union and the jurisprudence of the European Court of Human Rights. The influences of this European jurisprudence require to be taken into account in appreciating the context in which the practice of judicial review now operates. In recent times, several of the leading judicial review cases have had E.C. law dimensions, although it must be noticed that the modern growth of judicial review began before January 1, 1973 when the United Kingdom finally joined the then European Economic Community. Equally, the jurisprudence of the European Court of Human Rights, already spreading into areas of national law, has come more prominently to the attention of the courts since the passing of the Human Rights Act 1998, whereby alleged breaches of the European Convention on Human Rights may be raised directly in the courts of the United Kingdom without the immediate necessity of seeking a remedy in the European Court of Human Rights. The influence of the Luxembourg E.U. courts and the Strasbourg European Court of Human Rights has already been significant and it is improbable that the principles, concepts and approaches adopted in E.C. law and human rights law will remain exclusive to those areas. On the contrary, the probability is that the jurisprudence of these European institutions will merge with the common law and become indistinguishable.[60] Indeed, a perpetuation of distinctions between the European and national jurisdictions would be unacceptable in practice. In any event, the mutual interpenetration of ideas which is fostered by the developing jurisprudence of the European courts should cause no difficulty to those familiar with the law of Scotland. Its life, whether with regard to its civilian inheritance or its close relationship with the common law, has been characterised by the cross-fertilisation of ideas. And the exchange of ideas is also a two-way process: for example, the right to be heard before a decision is taken by

---

[58] See the Judicature Amendment Act 1968. See also, in New South Wales, the Supreme Court Act 1970 (NSW) and the Administration of Justice Act 1973 (NSW). Similar reforms have taken place in some Canadian jurisdictions. For discussion of current reform proposals to administrative law in New Zealand, see Justice Baragwanath, "Judicial Review: Tidying the Procedures" (1999) N.Z.L.J. 127.

[59] For discussion of the Conseil d'Etat in France, see Brown and Bell, *French Administrative Law* (4th ed., Clarendon Press, 1993), esp. Chap. 3. For a stimulating (and comparative) discussion of the French experience with administrative law, see Allison, *A Continental Distinction in the Common Law* (Clarendon Press, 1996). For an earlier view on what reforms U.K. administrative law needs, see Mitchell, "The Real Argument about Administrative Law" 1968 Pub. Admin. 167.

[60] See, for example, Craig, "Substantive Legitimate Expectations and the Principles of Judicial Review", in Andenas (ed.), *English Public Law and the Common Law of Europe* (1998).

a public authority affecting a person's interests may be seen to have passed from the legal traditions of the United Kingdom to the jurisprudence of the European Court of Justice and become a general principle of E.C. law[61]; and the concepts of legitimate expectation and of proportionality have already become familiar in the language, if not the reality, of judicial review in the United Kingdom.

Constitutional changes: new horizons for judicial review

1.14 The U.K. Constitution has undergone significant changes in recent years. Even before the enactment of the Human Rights Act 1998 and the three Acts of the same year granting devolved powers to Scotland, Northern Ireland and Wales, the constitutional landscape had been significantly altered by European Community (E.C.) law. Principles formerly considered sacrosanct, such as the supremacy of Parliament, have had to yield to the imperatives of membership of the European Union. Although the United Kingdom is not alone in the European Union in having had to reconcile its constitutional norms with E.U. membership, both the historical approach to the constitution and the traditions of the common law have combined to make the task of coming to terms with E.C. law more gradual and sometimes more apprehensive here than elsewhere. It may be that this can be explained by reference to the United Kingdom's absence of a public law tradition. In the twentieth century, the attachment to received wisdom about the absolute powers of a supreme Parliament has often meant that constitutional theory has not always been able to deal rationally with many of the changes that have taken place—especially, but not only, those relating to E.C. law. Yet coming to terms with change is perhaps a particular strength of the British constitution. To that end, one task of the present work has been to attempt to explain a system of judicial review which recognises grounds encompassing not only those well established in the common law but also those derived from E.C. law, human rights law and, most recently, those arising in relation to legislation passed under the Scotland Act 1998. Without doubt, E.C. law, human rights and devolution mean that the kinds of matters which may be subject to the supervisory jurisdiction now include to an increased extent matters of a constitutional nature. But, whatever the novelties may be from a traditional British perspective, the supervisory jurisdiction has a sound tradition on which to draw in order to address them.

III THE CONTEXT AND SUBSTANCE OF JUDICIAL REVIEW

1.15 It may be useful by way of conclusion to this introductory chapter to explain the pattern adopted not only for the consideration of the context of judicial review which forms the substance of Part I, but for the discussion of the various other aspects of the subject which form the rest of this book.

History and constitutionalism

1.16 The immediately following three chapters are concerned with the context in which judicial review has come to operate. With that end in view, attention is paid first to the history of the supervisory jurisdiction, then

---

[61] See Case C17/74 *Transocean Marine Paint v. Commission* [1974] E.C.R. 1063.

to its juridical context and finally to the constitutional setting. In endeavouring to find principle it is useful to explore the history of the supervisory jurisdiction. That forms the substance of the next chapter, where the idea can be discerned that no wrong should be without a remedy. But definition is then required of the particular kinds of wrong to which the principle should in the present context be applied. History may reveal that the old Scottish Privy Council picked up at least some of the cases of alleged injustice which slipped through the net of the other particular jurisdictions that operated in the earlier period of Scottish legal practice. The Court of Session, possessing from its outset the power to provide equitable remedies under its *nobile officium*, took over that responsibility and developed a single supervisory jurisdiction as a particular aspect of its residual equitable powers as a supreme court. Thus it is relevant to step aside briefly to consider the *nobile officium* of the Court of Session, as is done in Chapter 3. But with the development of a parliamentary democracy the power of Parliament has to be regarded and respected and the interrelation of the function of the court and the responsibilities of the legislative and executive branches of the government have to be considered. Here the rule of law plays a prominent part, and, as is discussed in Chapter 4, the supervisory jurisdiction operates as a constitutionally mandated check on any excess of power, providing a remedy where no other may be available. While some consideration is given to the Crown in that chapter, it has not been considered useful to dedicate a separate chapter on the specialities concerning the Crown; these are discussed within the context of the areas within which the specialities arise.

The emergence of constitutional review

Mention has already been made of the important developments, some **1.17** recent, whereby the opportunity has arisen for challenges to be made to the validity of legislation and to the actions of public authorities on what may be termed constitutional grounds. These even extend to the challenging of primary legislation which has been passed by a democratically elected body. These developments require to be explored not only because they are of considerable constitutional importance in themselves, but also because the likelihood is that they will come to play an important part in the development of judicial review in the coming years. Although the term is difficult in the absence of a supreme constitutional document, in the context of E.C. law, human rights and some elements of devolution, the exercise of the supervisory jurisdiction may be referred to as a form of "constitutional review". Accordingly, no further explanation should be needed for the space given to E.C. law, the Human Rights Act 1998 and the Scotland Act 1998 in the three chapters which form Part II of this book.

The scope and grounds of judicial review

The consideration of E.C. law, human rights and Scottish devolution sets **1.18** the background to a detailed consideration of the scope of the supervisory jurisdiction. This is the subject of Part III. In this Part an attempt is made to explore the possibility of finding guidance towards a definition of the extent of the supervisory jurisdiction,[62] with considera-

---

[62] Chapter 8.

tion thereafter being given in particular to the situations where the jurisdiction may not be exerciseable, either on account of the subject-matter under challenge, the lack of *locus standi* on the part of the person raising the challenge, an express exclusion of the jurisdiction, the existence of an alternative remedy, or a deficiency in respect of the reality of the issue or the timing of the application.[63] All of these matters may be seen as matters of the competency of an application, or as grounds on which a defence to an application for judicial review may be mounted.

Thereafter, in Part IV, the various grounds on which an application for judicial review may be made are considered, the order of treatment being explained in an introductory chapter, namely Chapter 14. Part V of the book is concerned with matters of practice and procedure.[64] In this connection, an attempt is made to discuss the nature of the remedies which may be available following a successful application for judicial review.

---

[63] Chapters 9–13.
[64] Chapters 23–26.

CHAPTER 2

THE HISTORICAL CONTEXT

I   INTRODUCTION
II THE ORIGINS OF REVIEW
III FROM THE UNION OF THE CROWNS TO THE UNION OF THE PARLIAMENTS
IV THE EIGHTEENTH CENTURY
V   THE GROWTH OF JUDICIAL CONTROL OF PUBLIC ADMINISTRATION
VI THE TWENTIETH CENTURY

I INTRODUCTION

General

It has already been noted that the supervisory jurisdiction and the **2.01** exercise of judicial review in Scotland are of very old standing.[1] But it is only relatively recently that there has been a lively consciousness of the existence of judicial review as a distinct area of law in its own right and of its availability as providing a useful means of redress in a wide variety of situations, especially those involving the citizen and the state. By way of introduction to a history of judicial review in Scotland two quotations may be made from English cases where the development of judicial review has been as recent and as rapid. In *Ridge v. Baldwin* Lord Reid stated[2]: "We do not have a developed system of administrative law, perhaps because until fairly recently we did not need it". Seven years later in *Breen v. Amalgamated Engineering Union* Lord Denning observed[3]: "It may truly now be said that we have a developed system of administrative law". Even the term "administrative law" has undergone some change. Earlier usage, developed in the universities, extended the term to matters of the substance of local government, health, education, local taxation and such concerns.[4] But the term has more recently been refined to refer to the exercise and control of the powers of administrative bodies at all levels of government.

England and Scotland

The development of judicial review in Scotland has followed a course **2.02** distinct from that which has occurred in England. In England its development was for a long time restrained by the technicalities of procedure, relating in particular to the use of the prerogative writs, later called prerogative orders, of certiorari, prohibition and mandamus.[5]

---

[1] para. 1.01.

[2] [1964] A.C. 40 at 77.

[3] [1971] 2 Q.B. 175 at 189. Lord Diplock recognised the speed of the development in *O'Reilly v. Mackman* [1983] 2 A.C. 237, 281.

[4] *Green's Encyclopaedia*, Vol. 9, para. 41.

[5] Administration of Justice (Miscellaneous Provisions) Act 1938 (c. 63); see also the earlier Administration of Justice (Miscellaneous Provisions) Act 1933 (c. 36), s. 5. Beyond the prerogative remedies, declaration and injunction also came to be available. An account of the former remedies in England can be found in the Law Commission Report No. 73 (1976).

More recently a liberal development both in substance and procedure has been achieved by the introduction in 1977 of the Order 53 procedure and by section 31 of the Supreme Court Act 1981.[6] The ordinary remedies of injunction and declaration have become available concurrently with the prerogative orders. But the English and the Scottish remedies do not precisely correspond with each other. Moreover the tendency to a more formalistic approach together with the influence of certain historical and constitutional differences may call for a degree of caution in the adoption of English precedents. The basis for judicial review in Scotland is a more generalised one which is not so dependent on specialised procedures or specific remedies.[7] The scope of the power of the Scottish court in matters of review has been defined by reference to the jurisdiction itself rather than the remedies which might be available or the forms of procedure necessary to obtain them, so that, in contrast with the older English procedure, a variety of remedies could be sought in the one process. In England the claim by the citizen would be taken up by the Crown, leaving the citizen in an *ex parte* position, but in Scotland the dispute remained as an issue to be contested directly between the party aggrieved and the authority against which he had brought his proceedings. Thus while considerable use may be made of English decisions on matters of substance, some care has to be taken with regard to matters of procedure or matters influenced by procedural considerations. Leave of the court is a necesary pre-condition to the making of an application for judicial review in England, but no leave is required in Scotland. The degree of discretion which controls the admission of an applicant to the possibility of a remedy enables the English court to give indications of the propriety or otherwise of bringing certain classes of case in a way which cannot be done, and has not needed to be done, in Scotland.[8]

II   THE ORIGINS OF REVIEW

The early stages

2.03   In the early period of Scottish legal history the distinction which is now familiar between appeal and review had not been formulated. The form of redress was more one of review[9] than of appeal, the court being unable to reconsider the case on its merits. Indeed it has been said that the process of appeal as known in modern practice did not exist before the sixteenth century.[10] Moreover the picture is further complicated by the fact that the various courts generally exercised privative jurisdictions.

---

[6] The reforms came into effect in 1978 by virtue of S.I. 1965 No. 1776, amended by S.I. 1977 No. 1955. The new rule provided for a single form of application for prerogative orders by way of an application for judicial review. The new Order 53 was given statutory backing by the Supreme Court Act 1981 (c. 54). See generally *O'Reilly v. Mackman* [1983] 2 A.C. 237. Similar procedural reforms were introduced into Northern Ireland by section 18 of the Judicature (Northern Ireland) Act 1978.

[7] The English prerogative remedies were only known in Scotland through the Exchequer court: see para. 2.21.

[8] *e.g. R. v. Hillingdon LBC, ex parte Puhlhofer* [1986] A.C. 404.

[9] A.D.C. III (1501–1503) p. xlviii. As suggested in the Preface to that work future references will simply be to "A.D.C. III".

[10] A.D.C. III p. xliv. In *Innes v. Dunbar* (1534) M. 7320, the Lords of Session affirmed their jurisdiction to reduce their own decrees like a judge of appeal at second instance.

In matters of feudal property the local feudal courts enjoyed a privative jurisdiction, but an appeal was available to Parliament.[11] Appeal processes existed from the church courts and from the burgh courts. The church courts allowed an appeal to the bishop or his representative, and a final appeal to Rome; but the process was slow and the fairness of the courts was questionable, despite attempts at reform.[12] Commercial causes were the preserve of the burgh courts. The growth of the burghs in the twelfth and thirteenth centuries led to the creation of the Court of the Four Burghs, which, under the presidency of the Lord Chamberlain heard appeals from the burghs until the lapse of that jurisdiction after the establishment of the Court of Session in 1532. From an early period the general procedure for obtaining redress, and eventually final redress, was by application for a falsing of doom.

The King's Council

The origins of the central civil courts in Scotland are to be found in the functions of the common council, which developed into the Parliament, and the King's Council, the *curia regis*. The latter body came to be referred to as the secret council and later the Privy Council. The King's Council exercised a judicial function from at least the twelfth century. But the Council was peripatetic in its practice and fluid in its constitution[13] and the practical advantages of a static and continuous body came to be recognised. By an Act of 1425 a committee was appointed to sit regularly for periods in each year to deal with such cases as might be determined by the King's Council.[14] The committee was composed of the Chancellor and members of the Estates appointed by the King. It came to be known as the Session to distinguish it from the peripatetic Council.[15] By an Act of 1457 the Lords of Session were reconstituted with a defined jurisdiction.[16] But that jurisdiction did not include advocations, which continued to to be brought to the King's Council.[17] After 1468 the Session, the Old Session as it has come to be called, fades from the scene, there being evidently no appointments made until the closing years of the century when regular sessions again appear to be appointed.[18] By that time James IV had succeeded to the throne and was promoting significant improvements in the administration of justice.[19]

2.04

---

[11] As in 1389, A.P.S. I, 535. See also Walker's *History*, Vol. III p. 563. Grants of regality took as much out of the Crown as the sovereign could give: Cosmo Innes, *Scottish Legal Antiquities*, p. 40. Appeal to the Privy Council in cases of error in inquests regarding heritable property was introduced by the Act 1471, c. 9.

[12] The older church courts faded into relative insignificance in the sixteenth century following on the Reformation, assisted by such measures as the Act against the Pope, 1560, A.P.S. II, 534, c. 2, and the Act on the Jurisdiction of the Church 1567, A.P.S. III, 24, c. 12. The new kirk sessions, the Presbyteries and the General Assembly thereafter exercised a jurisdiction in matters of ecclesiastical discipline.

[13] A general account is given in A.D.C. III, p. xviii.

[14] A.P.S. II, 11.

[15] Stair, *Inst.*, 4, 1, 8.

[16] A.P.S. II, 47.

[17] Kames, *Law Tracts*, 281, notes that the privilege of advocating causes was not communicated to the court of session instituted in 1425. Its procedure was confined to original actions founded on brieves.

[18] A.D.C. III, p. xxx. See the *Stair Encyclopaedia*, Vol. 6, para. 896 for a consideration of the reasons for the failure of the Old Session.

[19] By an Act of 1496 (A.P.S. II, 238, c. 3) it was provided that all barons and free men that were of substance should see that their sons attended school and received education in the law so that they might have knowledge of the laws and those that were sheriffs or judges ordinary might have the knowledge to do justice.

Parliament and Council

2.05   The Parliament was exercising judicial functions by the fourteenth
century and its judicial work, while the Parliament was not itself sitting,
came in time to devolve upon various committees of "auditors", one of
which, the auditors *ad judicata contradicta*, dealt with the falsing of
dooms.[20] But in the latter part of the fifteenth century the work of the
Parliamentary judicial committees came to be merged with the work of
the Lords of Council, the latter body establishing a judicial pre-
eminence.[21] In parallel with the early period of this development the
judicial work of the peripatetic council became merged with the work of
the Session,[22] leading to the eventual title of the supreme Scottish judges
as Lords of Council and Session. One step in this process was the
institution in 1503 of the so-called "Daily Council"[23] evidently necessi-
tated by pressure of work on the Lords of Session. It is, however, on the
work of the Privy Council that attention requires to be focused.[24]

The work of the Privy Council

2.06   The records of the Council disclose examples of what later developed
into a jurisdiction of review in matters of public administration. The
Council dealt with cases of misconduct and malversation of office by
judges and other officials of all kinds from an early date.[25] The records of
the Council contain examples of matters of burgh accounting and the
unorderly proceedings of magistrates being brought before the Council,
such as a dispute on the audit of the accounts of the burgh of
Aberdeen,[26] as well as a suspension of an attempt to secure a university
appointment contrary to the procedure laid down by statute.[27] In one
case the Council reduced the decisions of sheriff deputes on the ground
of a defect in procedure, namely the number of jurors sitting on an
inquest.[28] The Council's work can also be traced in the work of the
Parliament. An Act of 1449[29] recognises the suspension by the Council
from office of officials for misconduct. Acts of 1469 and 1475[30] provide
for an appeal from a judge to the Council. Of much greater significance,
however, for present purposes is the Act 1487, c.10.[31] This Act restricted

---

[20] A.D.C. III, p. xlix.

[21] In one Act of 1467 (A.P.S. II, 88), the Lords of Council were required to dispose of
cases not dealt with by the Parliament. In the Act 1491, c. 16 the Chancellor is instructed
to sit "with certain lords of council or else lords of session" for certain specified sittings.

[22] Council Ordinance of July 23, 1511, quoted by Hannay, *The College of Justice*, p. 21;
A.D.C. III, p. xxx.

[23] By the Act 1503, c. 2, A.P.S. II, 241 and 249, an Act which has been given undue
prominence in the mistaken belief that it superseded Council and Session and was the true
forerunner of the Court of Session. The point is discussed in A.D.C. (1501–1554) p. xxix,
and A.D.C. III, p. xxxi. Note may also be made of the Act 1503, A.P.S. II, 246, regulating
the process of the falsing of dooms.

[24] James Mackinnon, *The Constitutional History of Scotland* (1924), p. 253 observes that
the identities and composition of the various judicial bodies in the fifteenth century appear
to merge in their operation. The interrelation of work between the Council and the
Parliament may be hard to disentangle. R.S. Rait, *The Parliaments of Scotland*, p. 131,
refers to the falsing of dooms as a function of the Council in Parliament.

[25] A.D.C. III, p. xlv.

[26] *Acta Dominorum Concilii* 1501–1503, Stair Society, Vol. 8, 123; see also the discussion
at pp. xlv *et seq.*

[27] In 1593, Register of the Privy Council of Scotland (D. Masson, ed.), Vol. V, p. 58.

[28] A.D.C. I, 482.

[29] A.P.S. II, 35, c. 5.

[30] 1469 c. 2, A.P.S. II, 94; 1475 c. 3, A.P.S. II, 111.

[31] A.P.S. II, 177.

the jurisdiction of the Privy Council to, *inter alia*, complaints made against officials for fault of execution of their office or where "the officiar is parti himself". The Act provided that where the complaint was made on the official for wrongful and inordinate proceedings in any matter, if the complaint was made out, the proceedings should be reduced and annulled. The Privy Council was available to provide a remedy where, amid the various particular jurisdictions among which litigation in Scotland was distributed, no other remedy existed.[32]

The Institution of the College of Justice

The need for legal training and a professional judiciary had been **2.07** recognised by the early sixteenth century, as had the necessity for the establishment of a permanent civil court.[33] Of major importance in the history of the development of the legal system was the establishment by statute in 1532 of the College of Justice as the permanent supreme civil court in the country.[34] Both in matters of procedure and in the substance of the law the immense influence of the canon law and of the jurisprudence gathered from education in the Universities of Holland and France came to make itself felt. The initial significant ecclesiastical presence in the court began to give way following on the Reformation some 25 years later to a purely secular composition. But the links with the King and the Privy Council remained.

The jurisdiction of the Court of Session

The jurisdiction which was given to the Lords of Council and Session **2.08** was in Erskine's words[35] a jurisdiction "first, universal as to extent; and 2ly, supreme in degree".[36] The Court had the power "to set aside or suspend the sentences of all inferior courts in civil causes, unless where that power is denied them by special statute".[37] Erskine saw it as a court of equity as well as of law; and as such "may and ought to proceed by the rules of conscience in abating the rigour of the law, and in giving aid in the actions brought before them to those who can have no remedy in a court of law".[38] From its origins the Court of Session possessed the

---

[32] The distinction between the work of the Privy Council and the work of the Court of Session was pointed out by P.G.B McNeill, "Interference with the Court of Session by the Privy Council", 1961 J.R. 253, questioning the sub-title in the Stair Society edition (Vol. 4) of Hope's *Major Practicks*, Pt V, Title 2. An example can be found in *McDuff v. Doig* (1586) M. 7304, where the Court of Session held a decree of the Council on a matter not within the jurisdiction of the Council to be ineffective.

[33] The desirability of the appointment of particular persons to sit on judicial work is reflected by the appointment of certain named persons to be joined with the Lords of Council for the session starting in February 1526, A.D.C. (1501–1554), p. 238.

[34] For further detail see the *Stair Encyclopaedia*, Vol. 6, para. 904. Professor Hannay, in the *College of Justice*, p. 24, has warned of the misunderstanding about the alleged imitation of the Parlement de Paris which Erskine inherited and perpetuated.

[35] *Institutes*, 1, 3, 18, quoted by Lord Dunpark in *Brown v. Hamilton District Council*, 1983 S.L.T. 397 at 408.

[36] The universality did not, of course, operate at first instance since there were distinct original jurisdictions in the Commissary Court and the Admiralty Court. Erskine (1, 2, 5) explains that the jurisdiction of the Court of Session and the Court of Exchequer was supreme in the sense that their jurisdiction was universal over the whole kingdom.

[37] Erskine, *Institutes* 1, 3, 20. In *M'Creadie v. Thomson*, 1907 S.C. 1176 at 1183, Lord Justice-Clerk Macdonald observed: "The Supreme Courts have power to right wrongs done in the inferior Courts, their jurisdiction being universal, and their duty being to see justice done throughout the land. The other Courts have no jurisdiction beyond their own borders, and cannot review the conduct of any other Judge within their own border".

[38] Erskine *Institutes*, 1, 3, 22.

nobile officium, the equitable power which lies at the basis of the supervisory jurisdiction. There may have been less opportunity to develop that jurisdiction in the area of administrative matters while the Privy Council was itself exercising an equitable jurisdiction superior to the Court of Session.[39] But from an early period the Court was undertaking a supervisory jurisdiction over inordinate or unjust proceedings of lower courts, dealing with matters of legality rather than the merits.[40] Eventually the work of providing a remedy where no other remedy was available devolved upon the judges of the Court of Session, who as Lords of Council and Session combined both an equitable and a legal jurisdiction, or, as Stair described it,[41] an *officium ordinarium* and an *officium nobile*. As Lord Kames recognised, it was as a function of the *nobile officium* that the power of redress came to be exercised.[42]

Appeal and review

2.09   After the institution of the College of Justice in 1532 the new Court adopted the process of advocation as a procedure for providing remedies. The process of advocation, which superseded the earlier process of falsing of dooms,[43] served as a general means of obtaining a remedy in matters both of an administrative and of a judicial character.[44] It may be seen as the original formal expression of the power of review. It was a process of cassation, not of appeal. It did not touch on the merits of the matter nor did it alter the decision of the lower court. It covered a wide range of inferior judicatories. It was quicker than reduction and an easier remedy than suspension.[45] Reduction as a remedy peculiar to the Court of Session was developing in the early sixteenth century on a wide variety of grounds.[46] Suspension became available later. Suspension, which halted execution temporarily or permanently, was more properly a form of appeal. Advocation and suspension could be presented to the Court of Session or the Privy Council. Advocation in the Court of Session came to be competent not only on grounds of inequity but also on the ground of the importance of the matter[47] or even on any other reasonable ground.[48] The Court took the pragmatic attitude that inferior judges could economically deal with matters of small importance.[49] The remedy of protestation to Parliament for remeid of law which pre-dated the institution of the Court of Session

---

[39] See J. Irvine-Smith in *Introduction to Scottish Legal History*, The Stair Society, Vol. 20 at p. 28.

[40] For examples, see *Acta Dominorum Concilii et Sessionis*, The Stair Society Vol. 14 (ed. I.H. Shearer), and the editor's observations at p. xix.

[41] *Institutes*, 4, 3, 1.

[42] *Law Tracts* (5th ed.), p. 228. See Chap. 3 for a consideration of the *nobile officium*.

[43] Stair, *Institutions*, 4, 1, 31; but see the comment by Lord Kames, *Law Tracts*, pp. 279–280 that appeals did not fall into desuetude on the institution of the College of Justice.

[44] The opportunities for advocation in the mid-sixteenth century are noted in Balfour's *Practicks* pp. 340–342.

[45] *Wright and Graham* (1766) M. 375.

[46] Balfour, *Practicks*, pp. 268–299, and 405–411. According to Balfour (pp. 268–269) reduction of decrees was originally peculiar to the Lords of Council and reduction of actions of heritage was peculiar to the Lords of Session,

[47] *Cunninghame v. Drumquhassie* (1567) M. 7409.

[48] *Lairds v. Dick* (1630) M. 7411.

[49] *Marshal v. Blair* (1622) M. 7482.

continued to be used, albeit rarely, until the Union of the Parliaments.[50] In the sixteenth century there were some consultations and cross-references between the Parliament and the Lords of Session.[51]

Criminal cases

In criminal matters in the early period there was a considerable number **2.10** of officials exercising criminal jurisdictions, such as the ordinary judges, the justiciar, the chamberlain, the sheriff, the provost and bailies of burghs, the lords of regality and barony, and the higher ecclesiastics. The Parliament up to the sixteenth century also exercised a criminal as well as a civil jurisdiction. Justice Circuits were held from the thirteenth or fourteenth centuries[52] and on occasion the king would go personally on such circuits. Eventually in 1672, by the Courts Act of that year,[53] the High Court of Justiciary was established with a composition which remained until the reforms of 1887. After 1672 advocations in criminal matters came to be presented to the High Court of Justiciary. Parliament retained its original criminal jurisdiction until its demise. The Court of Session came by custom to review criminal sentences by inferior courts, at least in minor matters of policy, and continued to do so into the nineteenth century, because of the speedy and cheap method of review which suspension in particular offered. But more serious matters were not open to review by that route.[54]

III   FROM THE UNION OF THE CROWNS TO THE UNION OF THE PARLIAMENTS

The Union of the Crowns

In 1603 Queen Elizabeth of England died and the succession to the **2.11** throne in England passed to the King of Scotland, James VI.[55] The same individual monarch thus became the holder of two crowns.[56] The distinction between the two remained in some respects and may not be altogether lost. The doctrine that the King can do no wrong was recognised in England but not in Scotland. The Crown could always be sued in Scotland, initially directly against himself and later[57] through the Officers of State collectively, or through the King's advocate, or another officer representing the Crown in the matter of the action.[58] In 1539 it

---

[50] Balfour, *Practicks*, p. 268, recognises the legality of appeal to the Parliament from the Lords of Session and to reference to the Parliament by the Lords of Session in difficult cases. See Walker, *History*, III, pp. 225 and 543, and *Kennedy v. M'Lellan* (1534) M. 7320.

[51] *ibid.* 234. It is interesting to note that in one Act, A.P.S. III, 29, c. 22, Parliament declared that the Court could reduce infeftments even although they had been matters of grant or confirmation by Parliament.

[52] For the history, see *Stair Encyclopaedia*, Vol. 6, para. 852.

[53] A.P.S. VIII, 80, c. 40.

[54] Hume on *Crimes*, II, pp. 72 and 508. In *M'Intosh v. Sheriff of Inverness* (1660) M. 7411 the Court of Session advocated a case from the sheriff to the Justice-General.

[55] The consequences of this union on the legal systems of the two countries were in the event less radical than they might have been. The idea of a union of the laws proved to be abortive. See Brian Levack "The Proposed Union of English Law and Scots Law in the Seventeenth Century", 1975 J.R. 97.

[56] For the historical argument supporting an independant imperial Crown in Scotland, see Anderson's Historical Essay, reproduced in Stair Society, Vol. 39, Miscellany III.

[57] Walker's *History*, IV, 105–106.

[58] *Somerville v. Lord Advocate* (1893) 20 R. 1050, *per* Lord McLaren at 1075.

was laid down that actions against the King could be raised but only in the Supreme Court.[59] The King was not allowed to interfere in the administration of justice.[60] In the nineteenth century, however, the English doctrine came to be accepted into Scotland.[61] The view came to be held in the twentieth century that the Crown should be the same on each side of the Border.[62] While the doctrine was reversed by the Crown Proceedings Act 1947 it remains a rule of English common law.[63]

Appeal to Parliament

2.12   The struggles between the King and the English Parliament which led to the period of the Commonwealth and the subsequent restoration of the Stuart monarchy in 1661 had repercussions on the development of Scottish legal practice, not only in the administration of the courts during the Cromwellian period but in the bitter dispute which arose thereafter with regard to the availability of an appeal to Parliament from the Court, involving the disbarring of a considerable number of advocates who had insisted on the right of appeal. For a while the view of the Court of Session and the King was triumphant and appeal to Parliament was excluded.[64] But the Revolution of 1688 brought the opportunity of a reversal of the position and the right of appeal to the King in Parliament was again confirmed. It was of sufficient importance for the matter to be embodied in the Claim of Right.[65] The remedy was not strictly an appeal but a means of review where the Court of Session had acted unjustly or improperly.[66]

The Privy Council

2.13   The old Scottish Privy Council did not disappear after King James moved to England but continued to meet and work in Scotland.[67] During his reign it exercised the important function of putting into practice the royal decrees which the King granted in London and initially had much to occupy itself.[68] Its jurisdiction in the preservation of the public peace, in relation to riots, violent encroachments on private property and some civil matters remained. Its role continued throughout the century, except for the period of the Commonwealth, as agent of the monarch and as an executive of the Scottish Government. Critically (for present purposes) it continued to exercise its former supervisory jurisdiction: as in, for example, the nullifying of unlawful proceedings to obtain a lease, including a decree of the Presbytery of Arbroath.[69] It also intervened in

---

[59] (1539) M. 7321, 7323; see also *Hay v. Officers of State* (1832) 11 S. 196; *Somerville v. Lord Advocate* (1893) 20 R. 1050 at 1067.

[60] Balfour's *Practicks*, p. 267.

[61] *Smith v. Lord Advocate* (1897) 25 R. 112, 122 and *Wilson v. Edinburgh Royal Garrison Artillery Volunteers* (1904) 7 F. 168.

[62] *MacGregor v. Lord Advocate*, 1921 S.C. 847.

[63] *Trawnik v. Gordon Lennox* [1985] 2 All E.R. 368. See later on remedies, para. 23.36.

[64] See Fraser, *Constitutional Law*, p. 222.

[65] Stair, *Inst.*, 4, 1, 61, comments on the scope of the protest intended by the Claim of Right.

[66] Balfour, *Practicks*, p. 268 mentions appeals from the Lords of Session to Parliament.

[67] By Proclamation on 14 April 1603 the King entrusted the preservation of the public peace to the Privy Council: Register of the Council (Masson, ed.) Vol. VI, p. 563.

[68] Walker, *History*, Vol. IV, p. 134.

[69] *Laird of Guthrie v. Presbytery of Arbroath*, Register of the Council (Masson, ed.), p. 586.

criminal matters, as in one case regarding an overlong detention without trial.[70] Mackenzie records that it could mitigate a criminal sentence or quash a criminal conviction on the ground of a fundamental error or provide a remedy where the verdict was disconform to the libel.[71] It appears[72] that the Council could intervene where the justices erred in judging a matter of relevancy or where an assize found that proved which was not remitted to them, but that they could not intervene on the ground that the verdict was not sufficiently warranted by the sentence. It remained active after the Restoration, continuing to preserve public order and to secure compliance with religious observances, including the suppression of witchcraft. It was described in 1783 as an arbitrary and tyrannical court which had in 1606 assumed the prerogative of Parliament,[73] but it must also be recognised that it continued to exercise the royal prerogative of providing a remedy against the unlawful actings of administrative authorities.

The Supreme Court

The College of Justice continued during the seventeenth century to develop its jurisdiction. In 1611 it was decided that the Lords of Session alone could reduce all decrees of inferior judges.[74] The Lords of Session had not been competent to review decrees of the Lords of Council[75] and after the founding of the College they recognised that they could not review a decision of a supreme Court such as the Court of Justiciary.[76] Procedural irregularity was recognised as a ground for advocation.[77] The Court intervened in a case of palpable nullity,[78] reviewed alleged nullities in the baron court,[79] and in the sheriff court.[80] A recognition of the principle that review should not extend to the merits of a case is reflected in the 25th Act of the Articles of Regulation 1695 whereby reduction of a decree arbitral was not to proceed "upon any cause or reason whatsoever unless that of corruption, bribery or falsehood, to be alleged against the judges-arbitrators who pronounced the same". This measure was designed to check the tendency of the courts at that time to enter upon the substantial merits of an arbitral award and so enable the finality of the process of arbitration to be secured and preserved in the interests of those who sought such an expeditious remedy.[81]

2.14

---

[70] R.P.C. (2), IV, 152, 166.

[71] Mackenzie, *Matters Criminal* (1678), p. 382 (case of George Graham); the case is also noted in Hume on *Crime*, II, p. 449.

[72] Mackenzie, *Matters Criminal*, p. 383, expresses this as a conclusion which some might draw.

[73] *Sheriff-Clerk, Petr* (1783) Mor. 7393. Omond, *The Lord Advocates of Scotland*, I, 273 gives an account of its infamous history.

[74] *Leys v. Murray* (1611) M. 7495.

[75] *Touris v. Wemyss* (1545) M. 7414.

[76] *Strachen v. Commissioners of Justiciary* (1684) M. 7415.

[77] *Smith v. Miller* (1634) M. 7484.

[78] *Earl of Roxburgh v. A Minister* (1663) M. 7328.

[79] e.g. *Richardson v. Hay* (1624) M. 7496.

[80] *L. Bamff v. Chamberlain of Boyn* (1629) M. 7496. In 1696 the Court advocated a case from the Sheriff of Inverness to the Privy Council and not to themselves, evidently because the matter was within the exclusive jurisdiction of the Council: *Alexander v. Sheriff of Inverness* (1696) M. 7413.

[81] See Bell, *The Law of Arbitration in Scotland*, (2nd ed., 1877), p. 14.

Local government

2.15   By the seventeenth century the shape of local government in Scotland
had been established. The royal burghs had existed for a long time under
the government of their magistrates. The shires or sheriffdoms were by
the end of the seventeenth century well defined. The parishes had come
to be used as areas for local administration.[82] The care of the poor came
particularly to be their responsibility. The systematic appointment of
Justices of the Peace for the preservation of good order began after
1609[83] and they came to acquire a legal responsibility for such important
work as the development and maintenance of highways, bridges and
ferries. As local administration began to grow the occasion for review of
the actings of the authorities involved in it increased, so that by the
eighteenth century there was an evident and important part to be played
by a supervisory jurisdiction.

IV   THE EIGHTEENTH CENTURY

The Treaty and Act of Union

2.16   Article 18 of the Treaty and Act of Union sought to secure the
continued existence of certain Scottish institutions "with this difference
betwixt the Laws concerning publick Right, Policy and Civil Government, and those which cover Private Right; that the Laws which concern
publick Right, Policy and Civil Government may be made the same
throughout the United Kingdom: but that no alteration be made to Laws
which concern private Right, except for the evident utility of the subjects
within Scotland". There may be a question whether the former category
extends to those matters which are within the scope of judicial review;
but however that may be, although no formal harmonisation has been
made, at least the grounds for review have come to be recognised as
identical in the two countries.[84] By Article 19 of the Treaty and Act of
Union the continuation of the supreme Court in Scotland was secured,
thereby preserving the procedure and remedies which that court was
beginning to develop in matters of judicial review.

The demise of the Privy Council

2.17   The existence of the Privy Council was continued by Article 19 of the
Treaty and Act of Union "for preserving of public law and order until
the Parliament of Great Britain shall think fit to alter it or establish any
other effective method for that end". But shortly after the Union of
Parliaments it was provided[85] that there should only be the one Privy
Council and it was to have the powers of the English Council.[86] The
passing of the Scottish Privy Council left a hiatus which left open the way
for the development of an almost uncontrolled bureaucracy.[87] For
present purposes the hiatus was in the provision of a legal remedy for all

---

[82] The first step appears to have been by the Act 1556, A.P.S. II, 605, c. 10.

[83] By the Act 1609, A.P.S. IV, 434, c. 14. An earlier attempt had been made by the Act
1587, A.P.S. IV, 459, c. 57.

[84] see para. 14.02.

[85] By the Act 6 Anne c. 6.

[86] See *Green's Encyclopaedia*, Vol. 4, para. 944.

[87] P.G.B. McNeill, "The Passing of the Scottish Privy Council" 1965 J.R. 263 at p. 267.

the kinds of oppression and injustice which had fallen within the jurisdiction of the Privy Council; that hiatus the Court of Session, with hesitation, began to fill and it has come eventually to be occupied by the process of judicial review. In *Hamilton v. Boyd*[88] the Court of Session unanimously held that a judge ordinary had jurisdiction to try an alleged case of importing Irish victual although that crime had by an Act of 1672 been made privative to the Privy Council. Members of the Privy Council continued to be able to sit as extraordinary lords alongside the 14 ordinary senators of the College of Justice and to take part in the judicial work of the Court up until the time of George I.[89] The jurisdiction in review which the Court of Session inherited was a common law power and that is still its essential characteristic, although it has been embellished with the addition of a statutory power for ordering the performance of statutory duties[90] and a variety of statutory provisions giving appeal in particular matters to that Court. The grounds for review remain substantially common law grounds, and the common law jurisdiction possesses the flexibility to move with changes of time and attitude.

The Court and judicial review

The hesitation on the part of the Court of Session fully to take up the supervisory jurisdiction of the Privy Council and consolidate it with its own developing jurisdiction was noted by Lord Kames, writing in the early nineteenth century.[91] He recognised the growth of the jurisdiction in the Supreme Court but was conscious of a lack of principle, both in the theory and the practice. The former he was able to analyse and define. For the latter he could only look to the future. He expressed in his *Law Tracts* a real concern at the narrow approach sometimes adopted by the Court. He was critical of the decision of the Court in *Mackenzie of Highfield v. Freeholders of the Shire of Cromarty*[92] where the Court had dismissed as incompetent a claim by an aggrieved freeholder to have the Court interpose on his behalf against a failure to hold the statutory head count, thus preventing a person from being elected as a freeholder. Lord Kames commented[93]:

2.18

"It is the province of the sovereign and supreme court to redress wrongs of every kind when a peculiar remedy is not provided. Under the cognisance of the Privy Council in Scotland came many injuries which by the abolition of that Court are left without any peculiar remedy: and the Court of Session have with reluctance been obliged to listen to complaints of various kinds that belonged properly to the Privy Council while it had a being. A new branch of jurisdiction has thus sprung up in the Court of Session which daily increasing by new matter will probably in time produce a new maxim: That it is the province of this Court to redress all wrongs for which no other remedy is provided. We are however as yet far from

---

[88] (1741) M. 7335.
[89] Prof. R.K. Hannay, *The College of Justice*, p. 134, quotes the comment of Bankton (*Institutes*, 2, 509) on the advantage of having four of the nobility trained up in a knowledge of the law.
[90] see para. 26.10.
[91] The point was taken up by Erskine, *Institutes*, 1, 3, 23.
[92] (1753) M. 8830.
[93] *Law Tracts* (5th ed.), 228.

being ripe for adopting this maxim. The utility of it is perceived, but
perceived too obscurely to have any steady influence on the
practices of the Court, and for that reason their proceedings in such
matters are far from uniform."

It has been stated[94] that the flexible and adaptable general forms of
action used in Scotland and the use of interdicts evolved from the civil
law have enabled the Scottish courts to provide a remedy for nearly
every case.

The growth of review

2.19   Despite the criticisms of Lord Kames of the reluctance of the Court of
Session to take up the jurisdiction formerly exercised by the Privy
Council the institutional writers plainly recognised its importance. Stair,
as is noted later, warned of the need for restraint.[95] John More in his
Notes to Stair's Institutions[96] gives numerous examples of the range of
matters with which the Court in the eighteenth century considered they
could or could not deal. Indeed the Court, in the seventeenth and
eighteenth centuries, was prepared to make a number of regulations of
an administrative character.[97] Erskine recognises this ministerial power
of the Court[98] and Bankton gives "a memorable instance of the exercise
of this *nobile officium*, for which the court had the thanks of the
government", the making of an Act of Sederunt to compel the brewers
of Edinburgh to continue brewing.[99] More generally, the purpose of the
nobile officium, as Bankton saw it, was to interpose beyond the form of
the ordinary proceedings when the case required it, in order to bring out
the truth, to interpose in points necessary for the public good of society
or for making justice effectual in private cases, where the ordinary forms
could not reach the end.[1]

The cases

2.20   Furthermore the reports of the cases in the latter part of the eighteenth
century disclose a considerable exercise by the Court of its power of
review.[2] This was the period of that extraordinary flowering of talent in
all branches of the arts and sciences which has come to be known as the
age of enlightenment. The case law of that period provides many
examples of the Court of Session interfering with the decisions of a
variety of inferior bodies where it appeared that an excess of power had
been committed. One early example is in *Magistrates of Perth v. Trustees
on the Road from Queensferry to Perth*[3] where a finality clause was held
not to exclude the supreme jurisdiction of the Court of Session from
determining what it is which falls within the power of a body such as

---

[94] *Green's Encyclopaedia*, "Equity", para. 576 (the work of Sheriff A.G. Mackay and
Sheriff J.L. Wark).
[95] See para. 3.06.
[96] p. ccclxxiv.
[97] For examples, see More's *Notes, cit. sup.*, and *Green's Encyclopaedia*, "Nobile
Officium", Vol. 10, p. 325.
[98] *Institutes*, 1, 3, 22–23.
[99] Bankton's *Institutes*, 2, 517.
[1] *ibid.*
[2] The extent of this may invite a question as to the "reluctance" which Kames attributes
to the Court: see para. 2.18 above.
[3] (1756) Kilkerran's Notes, Brown's. Supp., Vol. 5, p. 318.

road trustees. Another early example is *Malcolm v. Commissioners of Supply for the Stewartry of Kircudbright*[4] where the Court of Session ordered a division of the valuation for tax purposes of an estate which had been split up into a number of separate parts but which the authority had insisted on valuing as a *unum quid*. Illustrations can be found in *Morrison's Dictionary* under the heading "Burgh Royal" of decisions in the eighteenth century prescribing the extent of the power of the local magistrates in a variety of functions. On occasion the Court took a somewhat robust view of their powers. In *Finlay v. Magistrates of Linlithgow*[5] the Court held that a measure which had been issued by the magistrates in Linlithgow for measuring malt and oats did not conform to the standard laid down by Parliament, instructed an intelligent tradesman to make a standard measure of the correct size, and ordered it to be used in the future. In another case the Court regulated the market hours for the buying of yarn.[6] In the eighteenth century the Court can be found to be reviewing, often by way of suspension, the decisions of magistrates in matters of buildings, such as the building of a new bridge,[7] of Justices of the Peace in such matters as the regulation of ferries,[8] and of statutory trustees.[9] The view was accepted that a right to review even in a case of the smallest excess of power was essential.[10] In one case a reduction of rates was ordered on the ground of a breach of natural justice.[11] The principle that officials could not be removed from office arbitrarily, but only for just and reasonable cause, was recognised in the eighteenth century.[12] The Court came to recognise and express the principle that every wrong must have a remedy and accordingly to accept that, failing other means of redress, the Court of Session had the jurisdiction to act on that principle.[13] Thus, for example, the Court recognised that while it was for the Dean of Guild to regulate matters of building in relation to risks of fire, nevertheless the Court could correct unsuitable regulations "upon the principle that every evil must have a remedy".[14] Moreover, as is later noted,[15] the Court under its *nobile officium* took a robust role in active participation in the prescribing as well as the enforcing of law. But in relation to the more particular exercise of the supervisory jurisdiction the distinction was recognised between matters of the merits of the case, into which the Court could not enter, and matters of the powers of the authority, which the Court could define and control.[16]

The Exchequer Court

By the Exchequer Court (Scotland) Act 1707[17] the Exchequer Court was established in Scotland with an adoption of the usage and practice of the English Exchequer Court. Thus the Court of Exchequer in Scotland was

2.21

---

[4] (1757) M. 8674.
[5] (1782) M. 7390.
[6] *Paterson v. Magistrates of Stirling* (1783) M. 1997, also at 7393.
[7] *Inhabitants of Sneddon v. Magistrates of Paisley* (1759) M. 7612 (a suspension).
[8] *Justices of the Peace of Midlothian and Fife v. Galloway* (1775) M. 7620 (a suspension).
[9] See *Morison's Dictionary* for examples under the title "Public Policy".
[10] *Countess of Loudoun v. Trustees on the High Roads in Ayrshire* (1793) M. 7398.
[11] *Swinzie v. Sutherland of Forse* (1751) M. 2436.
[12] *Magistrates of Montrose v. Robert Strachan* (1710) M. 13118.
[13] *M'Kenzie v. Stewart* (1752) M. 7443.
[14] *Proprietors in Carruber's Close v. William Reoch* (1762) M. 13175.
[15] see Chap. 3.
[16] See *West v. Secretary of State for Scotland*, 1992 S.C. 385 at 393 *et seq.*
[17] 6 Anne c. 53, s. 20.

given power to issue writs of certiorari in cases where they would have been issued under English law and thereby quash revenue proceedings, a practice which continued into the following century.[18] The practice of mandamus, permitted in the Exchequer Court, is not otherwise known in Scottish law.[19] But by the Exchequer Court (Scotland) Act 1850[20] the Scottish remedies of interdict, performance and appeal were substituted for the English remedies of injunction, mandamus, habeas corpus and certiorari in exchequer cases, and by the Court of Exchequer (Scotland) Act 1856[21] the Court of Exchequer was transferred to the Court of Session.

Appeal to Parliament

2.22   As has been noted, the early Scottish Parliament or its councils had provided a means of final redress from an early period and that had continued into the seventeenth century. It served as a means of review rather than an appeal in the modern sense. The availability of such redress from the Court of Session remained in the latter part of that century a matter of bitter controversy leading to the disbarring of a number of advocates who insisted on the right of appeal which the King and the Court considered should be excluded. Eventually, following upon the Claim of Right and the Revolution of 1688, the right to protest for remeid of law to the King in Parliament was confirmed. The right related only to civil cases and not to criminal cases. No express provision was made for the disposal of such matters on the Union of the Parliaments but the House of Lords, which was already exercising the appellate functions of the English Parliament, accepted a jurisdiction to hear appeals from Scotland, and since then the right of appeal to the House of Lords in civil matters from Scotland has been regular practice.[22]

The Bill Chamber

2.23   The Bill Chamber was created in 1532 by an Act of Sederunt of July 31 of that year ordaining such judges as were still in town during the season of the harvest to sit and deal with matters requiring acceleration and expedition. That function remained with it until it was superseded by the Vacation Court by the Administration of Justice (Scotland) Act 1933.[23] The Bill Chamber came at an early stage to deal with the preliminary stages in applications to the Court, which came in the form of Bills, such as advocations and suspensions. Something of the early roots of the judicial review process can be found here and it is of interest to note that

---

[18] Even long after the abolition of the separate Exchequer Court the Court of Session required to explore its scope: *Inland Revenue v. Barrs*, 1959 S.C. 273, 290. The matter is discussed by J. Bennett Miller in "Certiorari and the Scottish Courts" (1962) 25 M.L.R. 423. For habeas corpus, see McNeil, "Habeas Corpus in Scotland", 1960 S.L.T. (News) 46. An early Scottish provision to secure the freedom of the person may be found in the Act for Preventing Wrongous Imprisonment 1701, 1 William I, c. 6.

[19] *Lord Advocate v. Commissioners of Supply for the County of Edinburgh* (1861) 23 D. 933, 956. But a roughly corresponding remedy was introduced by the Court of Session Act 1868, s. 91. See para. 26.10.

[20] c. 56, ss. 14, 15 and 17. The Act 19 & 20 Vict. c. 26 merged the Exchequer Court with the Court of Session.

[21] 19 & 20 Vict. c. 56, s. 1.

[22] But not in criminal matters: *Mackintosh v. Lord Advocate* (1876) 3 R.(H.L.) 34.

[23] 23 and 24 Geo. 5, c. 41, s. 3.

affidavits could be produced to support factual averments[24] and that the Lord Ordinary on the Bills had the power to dismiss an application at the outset in the case of a manifest incompetence.[25] He could also refer difficult legal questions to the Inner House.[26] After the responsibility for judicial review passed to the Court of Session on the demise of the Scottish Privy Council the Bill Chamber was the appropriate forum for entertaining applications for review. It might have been that the Bill Chamber could have developed into an administrative court, and it had the required element of expedition in its procedures; but its abolition in 1933[27] prevented such a possibility.

V THE GROWTH OF JUDICIAL CONTROL OF PUBLIC ADMINISTRATION

Eighteenth and nineteenth century administration

In 1725 the office of Scottish Secretary was abolished and the Lord Advocate took on a general advisory function over the management and development of local and national administration of Scotland.[28] There was a brief revival of the office between 1741 and 1746 but it was not until 1885 that the office of Secretary for Scotland was created, to be superseded by a Secretary of State for Scotland in 1926.[29] In the eighteenth and nineteenth centuries various boards, trustees and commissioners came to be appointed for the management of particular undertakings and functions. Administrative duties came to be imposed on sheriffs, justices of the peace and quarter sessions. The church authorities had certain functions in the area of social welfare. Eventually a rationalisation was achieved in the system of local authorities which has developed to the present day. With the growth of local administration, the development of roads and other public facilities, the need grew for machinery to control and manage the facilities and resolve matters of dispute. By the Heritable Jurisdictions (Scotland) Act 1746[30] appeals were allowed not only in criminal matters but also in civil matters not exceeding twelve pounds in value from decrees of a variety of lower courts, service being made on the inferior judge where the complaint was of "wilful injustice, oppression or other malversation". While subordinate legislation began to grow it was only in the last decade of the nineteenth century that Lord Young came to identify the first instance of the making of local legislation to come before the Court.[31] **2.24**

Judicial review in the nineteenth century

The growth of judicial review which had occurred, at least as reflected in the reported cases, in the later part of the eighteenth century continued into the nineteenth and twentieth centuries. The principles on which the **2.25**

---

[24] Mackay, *Court of Session Practice*, II, 167.
[25] McLaren, *Bill Chamber Practice*, p. 11.
[26] *ibid*. p. 138.
[27] By s. 3 of the Administration of Justice (Scotland) Act 1933 (23 & 24 Geo. 5, c. 41). It may be noted that s. 3(2) preserved the rights of audience for solicitors which they had previously had in cases which required to be brought in the Bill Chamber.
[28] Omond, *The Lord Advocates of Scotland*, I, 273.
[29] By the Secretaries of State Act 1926.
[30] 20 Geo. II, c. 43, s. 34.
[31] *Eastburn v. Wood* (1892) 19 R.(J.) 100: the byelaw had been made under s. 57 of the Local Government (Scotland) Act 1889.

jurisdiction was to be exercised came to be more precisely formulated. They can be found set out in Baron Hume's lectures, delivered in the early part of the nineteenth century, in which he recognised that an excess of power can occur not only in the doing of something more than is allowed but also in a refusal to perform a statutory function, and he identified the limits of the Court's power to intervene, not only where the matter is one of a legitimate exercise of discretion within the scope of a statutory power, but also where the court has been effectively excluded or an alternative remedy is available.[32] In one case in 1801 the Court accepted that where there had been an excess of statutory power, although it occurred in matters where the Court had no power to review the judgment on the merits, it was nevertheless, under reference to many instances in the courts of both parts of the United Kingdom, still competent to superintend and control the inferior magistrates.[33] In the important case of *The Heritors of Corstorphine v. David Ramsay*[34] the Court affirmed its power to review a judgment of a presbytery of the Church which was protected by a statutory finality clause, where the presbytery had erred in law in holding a libel against a schoolmaster to be incompetent. The Lord President pointed out that the jurisdiction of a presbytery was only exclusive when it acted in matters committed to it. His observations[35] show the extent but also the limits to which the jurisdiction had developed.

> "In many cases of this kind, the Court has actually interfered; and the distinction they make is this, that so long as presbyteries keep to matters purely ecclesiastical, the Court cannot interfere; but when they touch on civil rights, then it may . . . In other cases of privative jurisdiction, the Court of Session, as the Supreme Court of this country, has been in use to interfere, and to control. Thus in the case of Commissioners of Supply refusing to split superiorities; - in the case of road trustees refusing to act; - and in the case of Courts of Lieutenancy exceeding their powers, - this Court has interfered. In the case of Road Trustees from Aberdeenshire, this was most completely exemplified. The trustees refused to act, and to assess the damages due to a person through whose property the road went. The Court compelled them to do so. They then proceeded; and the heritor, not satisfied, brought the case before the Court by advocation, complaining of the proceedings, in so far as they proceeded on no proper evidence. The Court refused to sustain the advocation. The Court could compel the trustees to act; but having once done so, they had no power to interfere with what was done".

Principles and practice

2.26   The basic principles were well recognised in the early part of the nineteenth century. In *Campbell v. Brown*,[36] in 1829, the Lord Chancellor observed: "There is in the Court of Session in Scotland, that supervisory

---

[32] Hume's *Lectures*, Stair ed., Vol. 5, pp. 270 *et seq*. While the lectures are not a work of institutional authority (*Fortington v. Lord Kinnaird*, 1942 S.C. 239) they nevertheless give a useful picture of the extent to which the principles of judicial review had developed.

[33] *Craig v. M'Colm*, Hume's *Decisions*, No. 198.

[34] Mar. 10, 1812, F.C.

[35] at p. 550 in the Faculty Collection.

[36] (1829) 3 W.&Sh. 441 at 448.

authority over inferior jurisdictions, which is requisite in all countries, for the purpose of confining those inferior jurisdictions within the bounds of their duty". But while the principle that bodies exercising statutory powers were required to confine themselves to acts which were within or incidental to the statutory provisions was established by the nineteenth century, there could still be room for dispute as to what was properly to be seen as incidental.[37] Moreover, the growth of administrative decision-making called for a growth in structure and machinery. In a number of administrative matters statutory provisions were made for appeal from the decision of the particular body entrusted with the particular administrative responsibility. Statutory processes for appeal in the civil courts were introduced in and after 1868 to take the place of advocation which was abolished.[38] Thereafter recourse to the supervisory jurisdiction of the Court of Session was obtained by the ordinary processes, such as actions of declarator, reduction, suspension and interdict.

Legality and merits

It was clearly recognised by the Court that statutory bodies had no **2.27** jurisdiction beyond what the statute gave them. In Lord Pitmilly's words, "if they go beyond it they act without jurisdiction; and in all such cases this Court . . . must have power to interfere, not to review, but to set aside irregular and illegal proceedings".[39] It was clearly established by 1843 that the Court of Session could review the actings of the heritors and kirk session of a parish. But in that year the more delicate question was decided, whether the Court could review the determination of the amount of aliment awarded by such a body.[40] By a majority of the whole court it was held that the Court could review an award not merely where it was elusory but where it was inadequate. The reasoning behind the decision may best be identified in the proposition that the sum awarded did not afford the "needful sustentation" which statute required to be provided.[41] An alternative analysis might be made on the ground of irrationality. But the case illustrates how close the Court was coming to the borderline between the legality of the decision and the substance of it.

Forbes v. Underwood

In 1886 the generality of the jurisdiction and the uniformity of its **2.28** application in principle were recognised in *Forbes v. Underwood* where the Court affirmed the application of the supervisory jurisdiction to arbiters.[42] Lord President Inglis observed:

"The position of an arbiter is very much like that of a Judge in many respects, and there is no doubt whatever that whenever an

---

[37] *Wakefield v. Commissioners of Supply of Renfrew* (1878) 6 R. 259.

[38] Court of Session (Scotland) Act 1868 (31 & 32 Vict. c. 100), ss. 64, 65 and 76. See also the Sheriff Courts (Scotland) Act 1853. Advocation remained as a remedy in the High Court of Justiciary.

[39] *Ross v. Findlater* (1826) 4 S. 514 at 518.

[40] *Pryde v. Heritors and Kirk-Sesson of Ceres* (1843) 5 D. 552.

[41] See the terms of the interlocutor at p. 578 of the report and the decision in the following year by the same court in *Halliday v. Heritors and Kirk-Session of Balmaclellan* (1841) 6 D. 1131.

[42] (1886) 13 R. 465 at 467.

inferior Judge, no matter of what kind, fails to perform his duty, or transgresses his duty, either by going beyond his jurisdiction, or by failing to exercise his jurisdiction when called upon to do so by a party entitled to come before him there is a remedy in this Court . . . The same rule applies to a variety of other public officers, such as statutory trustees and commissioners, who are under an obligation to exercise their functions for the benefit of the parties for whose benefit those functions are entrusted to them . . .''

The decision is a milestone in the development of judicial review in Scotland. It recognised that the supreme court was the only judicial body possessing the supereminent jurisdiction to supervise inferior judges, tribunals, statutory trustees and public officials. Review in the sheriff court was thus incompetent. But some problems remained. The Court felt some reservation about interfering where a new jurisdiction had been established and also as to the scope of its power.[43] The Court also required to develop an approach towards the understanding of the various forms of finality clauses which were often used in legislation of the period, or other forms of clause seeking to exclude the jurisdiction of the Court.[44] But the basic principle that no inferior judicatory could determine its own jurisdiction was recognised at an early stage and not forgotten.[45]

Examples

2.29   Alongside the growth in statutory means for redress in administrative matters which developed in the nineteenth century, the supervisory jurisdiction continued to be exercised over local authorities and a variety of other bodies including presbyteries. It was also used to challenge the legality of decisions of the statutory bodies set up to resolve disputes in the field of administration. The powers exercised by the magistrates of the burghs had for long been subject to the control of the Court and this came to be extended to the rural authorities on the creation of the system of county councils and town councils. The powers of the early burghs rested on charter and custom as much as any statutory provisions, and it was under reference to such sources that the Court required to determine the legality of the actings of magistrates.[46] The legality of expenditures out of the common good was also matter for review.[47] In addition, review was exercised over a variety of authorities established by statute for the operation of particular functions or undertakings. For example, the Poor Laws gave rise to some questions on the powers of those who administered them, such as the inspector of the poor.[48] With regard to roads, the Court intervened where the commissioners of supply exceeded their statutory powers in relation to the shutting up of roads[49]

---

[43] Indeed the suggestion was expressed that there might be no power in the Court to review a byelaw where it had been confirmed by the Secretary of State, since it might be thought that that had given the byelaw the authority of an Act of Parliament: *Crichton v. Forfar County Road Trustees* (1886) 13 R.(J.) 99, *per* Lord McLaren at 101.

[44] This is considered in more detail in Chap. 11.

[45] Thus in *Anisminic Ltd. v. Foreign Compensation Commission* [1969] 2 A.C. 147, Lord Reid observed (at 174): "It cannot be for the commission to determine its own powers".

[46] *e.g. Cowan v. Magistrates of Edinburgh* (1828) 6 S. 586 (on the levying of dues from fleshers); *Clapperton v. Magistrates of Edinburgh* (1846) 8 D. 1130 (levying of seat-rents).

[47] *e.g. Magistrates of Kilmarnock v. Aitken* (1849) 11 D. 1089.

[48] *Rankine v. Dempster* (1893) 20 R. 980.

[49] *Pollock v. Thomson* (1858) 21 D. 173.

and when commissioners sought to use their funds for financing opposition to proposed legislation.[50] In relation to ports and harbours the Court intervened to protect private interests against the *ultra vires* activities of statutory harbour trustees.[51] In relation to water undertakings it was held to be unlawful for water commissioners to charge against their trust funds the costs incurred in opposing a bill in Parliament, although it was observed that in some cases opposition to protect the interests of their undertaking might be a proper charge on their funds.[52] In one case regarding a schoolmaster it was held that a school board could require the schoolmaster to collect the school fees as he had been used to do, and there being nothing in the legislation to entitle his refusal.[53] The power of school boards to regulate and to dismiss schoolmasters under the Education Acts of the late nineteenth century also came before the Court.[54] Questions also arose on such matters as the duties of the commissioners of police in matters of public lighting[55] and the granting of public house licences.[56]

VI THE TWENTIETH CENTURY

The early twentieth century

The principles and practice in judicial review which had developed over the nineteenth century continued into the twentieth century. While there had come into being a considerable number of administrative bodies, pre-eminently the authorities comprising the system of local government, the Court of Session remained conscious of its power of control, but conscious also of the undesirability of interfering in administrative matters where no excess of jurisdiction could be identified.[57] In 1917 the position was summarised by Lord Shaw of Dunfermline in these words: "It is within the jurisdiction of the Court of Session to keep inferior judicatories and administrative bodies right in the sense of compelling them to keep within the limits of their statutory powers or of compelling them to obey those conditions without the fulfilment of which they have no powers whatsoever. It is within the power of the Court of Session to do that, but it is not within the power or function of the Court of Session itself to do work set by the legislation to be performed by those administrative bodies or inferior judicatories themselves".[58]

2.30

Criminal cases

The recognition of the developing distinction between civil and criminal matters in the context of review can be seen in Hume's *Lectures*.[59] The early remedies in criminal matters were advocation and suspension. The

2.31

---

[50] *Wakefield v. Commissioner of Supply of the County of Renfrew* (1878) 6 R. 259.
[51] *Milne Home and Others v. Allan and Others* (1868) 6 R. 189.
[52] *Perth Water Commissioners v. M'Donald* (1879) 6 R. 1050.
[53] *Buchanan v. Tulliallan School Board* (1875) 2 R. 793.
[54] e.g. *Robb v. Logiealmond School Board* (1875) 2 R. 417 and 698 (concerning a retiring allowance) and *Morrison v. Glenshiel School Board* (1875) 2 R. 715 (a dismissal).
[55] *Guthrie v. Miller* (1827) 5 S. 711.
[56] *Ashley v. Magistrates of Rothesay* (1873) 11 M. 708.
[57] *Walsh v. Magistrates of Pollockshaws*, 1907 S.C.(H.L.) 1.
[58] *Moss Empires v. Assessor for Glasgow*, 1917 S.C.(H.L.) 1 at 11.
[59] Stair Soc. ed., Vol. 5, 275.

former was available where judgment had not been carried into execution, and more strictly was available to the prosecutor before final sentence. The latter was available to the accused after the conclusion of the trial.[60] Review remained the only method of challenging a criminal proceeding until the establishment of a criminal appeal procedure by the Criminal Appeal (Scotland) Act 1926. At least by the nineteenth century it was seen to be incompetent for the Court of Session to review proceedings in the Court of Justiciary and a like view came to be developed in respect of the lower criminal courts. In *M'Caul v. Millar*[61] it was held to be incompetent for the Court of Session to review a criminal matter arising in the police court. But a problem could still arise in the identification of a matter as criminal or civil.[62]

The growth of tribunals

2.32   The twentieth century has seen the development of a considerable number of decision-making bodies, exercising powers delegated immediately or more remotely from Parliament. In *Brodie v. Ker*[63] the consulted judges commented on the history of the agricultural holdings legislation that "from first to last the policy of Parliament has been to narrow the ambit of the Court's functions and to expand that of various competing tribunals. It is not only in the field of agricultural law that this policy is manifest. There are now scores of statutes which remit justiciable issues to tribunals, subject only to an appeal to the Court by stated case on points of law. This policy we must of course accept". The development occurred without overall planning or system and the operation of the tribunals as well as of inquiries was seen as distinct from the Courts with little recourse from the one to the other. There was a hesitation on the part of the Court to move into the field of ministerial discretion. In *Pollock School v. Glasgow Town Clerk*[64] the Lord Ordinary held that it was open to him to explore the scope of the power in question and he held that what had been done was not within its scope. But the decision was reversed. Lord President Normand considered that the matter was a political question and that the exercise of the discretion was a matter for Parliament and could not be reviewed by a court of law. The inadequacy of the control over the growing body of tribunals was criticised in the Donoughmore Report in 1932[65] and the problem was further explored in the Franks Report of 1957. The Tribunals and Inquiries Act 1958, with its successors in 1966 and 1992, encouraged the recognition of the principles of openness and fairness in the procedures of the tribunals to which the Act applied, including provision being made for a duty to give reasons. Provision was also made for an appeal to the ordinary court on a point of law. But short of that level of appeal there has never been established any single coherent system for hearings or appeals.[66] The basic system has remained one built up by reference to the particular

---

[60] For an account of suspension and advocation in criminal matters, see *Renton & Brown's Criminal Procedure* (6th ed.), Chap. 33.
[61] (1838) 16 S. 617.
[62] See the cases referred to in para. 3.15.
[63] 1952 S.C. 216 at 222.
[64] 1946 S.C. 373.
[65] Cmd 4060.
[66] For a more unified system comparison may be made with Australia. See the Administrative Appeal Tribunal Act 1973 (c. 91), and in Victoria the Administrative Appeal Tribunal Act 1984 (Vict.) No. 10155.

subject-matter with which particular decision-making bodies are concerned, either by permanently established tribunals, such as the Medical Appeal Tribunals or the Employment Tribunals, each with their own appeal systems, or inquiries, such as planning inquiries, where a reporter may be appointed to consider and determine the issue.[67]

The sheriff court

An increasing number of administrative responsibilities has been **2.33** imposed on the sheriff court. The range of its "extrajudicial" functions has grown since the middle of the nineteenth century.[68] In addition, a number of statutes have allowed a means of appeal to the sheriff on specified grounds, which may extend to matters of error in law, breach of natural justice, unreasonableness[69] or even the appropriateness of the decision.[70] Problems can then arise whether the nature of the sheriff's determination is such that it can be subject to an appeal as a judicial determination within the framework of his ordinary judicial functions, or whether it is a special and particular function which is entrusted to him alone.[71]

The grounds for review

Intervention by the court on the ground of an excess of power had long **2.34** been accepted as had the basic ideas of natural justice. Both in England and in Scotland the two principles of *nemo judex in causa sua* and *audi alteram partem* had been recognised and applied in numerous cases in and before the twentieth century. But particularly in England the readiness which the courts had shown to apply the ideas of natural justice to administrative decision making[72] faded away particularly after the Second World War, despite, or perhaps accelerated by, the huge growth of administrative tribunals. The decisions in *Franklin v. Minister of Town and Country Planning*[73] and *Nakkuda Ali v. Jayaratne*[74] are prominent examples of the extent to which natural justice had been excluded. It could be argued that the inclination to concentrate on matters of procedure rather than the substance of an administrative decision, particularly in the face of a major expansion of discretionary power and of the processes for administrative decision making, was one cause of the evident decline in the scope of the supervisory jurisdiction in England. The courts plainly respected the intention of Parliament to vest decision making in a variety of new statutory bodies and hesitated to enforce the principles of natural justice too widely lest that came too close to the substance of the decision. The device used to contain the

---

[67] Town and Country Planning (Scotland) Act 1997 (c. 8), Sched. 4.

[68] *Glasgow Corporation v. Glasgow Churches' Council*, 1944 S.C. 97: see particularly the opinion of the Lord Justice-Clerk (Cooper). For example an appeal to the sheriff was allowed under section 143 of the Burgh Police (Scotland) Act 1892 where a proprietor wished to complain about the effect on his property of works on the road or the pavement.

[69] *e.g.* Licencing (Scotland) Act 1976 (c. 66), s. 39(4).

[70] *e.g.* Education (Scotland) Act 1980 (c. 44), s. 28F.

[71] *Arcari v. Dumbartonshire County Council*, 1948 S.C. 62. For a critical account of administrative appeals to the sheriff, see C.M.G. Himsworth, "Scottish Local Authorities and the Sheriff", 1984 J.R. 63. See also William Holligan, "Aspects of Appeals from the Sheriff Court", 1997 S.L.T. (News) 40.

[72] As in *Board of Education v. Rice* [1911] A.C. 179.

[73] [1948] A.C. 87.

[74] [1951] A.C. 66.

rules of natural justice was the concept of a "duty to act judicially". The rules of natural justice then could only apply where the decision-maker was acting in a capacity which could be described as "judicial". The practice also grew for the courts to apply the term "quasi-judicial" to decisions which were not judicial decisions but where the decision makers had to exercise judicial qualities, such as impartiality.

Ridge v. Baldwin

2.35 The decision of the House of Lords in *Ridge v. Baldwin*[75] marked a major turning-point in the development of the application of the rules of natural justice.[76] Following the decision in that case, attention came to be paid to the concept of a "duty to act fairly" which had to be established before decision makers would be required to observe at least some of the elements of natural justice. The requirement of a duty to act judicially had gone, but the idea of "quasi-judicial" actings lingered on. Subsequently, and in particular after the case of *O'Reilly v. Mackman*[77] and the introduction of Order 53, the debate in England has tended to be directed to a distinction between public and private matters.

Scots law

2.36 While the grounds for judicial review have long been regarded in practice as common between Scotland and England, it is not evident that the reluctance to interfere which overcame the English Courts during the middle of the twentieth century was significantly echoed in Scotland. The relatively smaller number of cases in the smaller jurisdiction may make it less easy to identify a trend, but if there was less reluctance in Scotland that may reflect a more robust attitude in the Scottish Courts. In *Magistrates of Ayr v. Lord Advocate*[78] Lord Birnam held that an inquiry into the amalgamation of police forces had erroneously been conducted as a departmental inquiry and not as an independent public investigation. He distinguished two English cases, one of which was the *Franklin* case, and held that the Secretary of State was not entitled to proceed with the proposed scheme. Of more importance was the decision in *Barrs v. British Wool Marketing Board*[79] where the Inner House decided that a board which was hearing appeals from wool producers was a quasi-judicial body which was bound to observe the principles of natural justice in reaching its decisions, and in particular that it had contravened those principles by allowing one of the parties to be present while it was deliberating on its decision but excluding the other. The Lord President (Clyde) observed:

> "Although quasi-judicial bodies such as this tribunal are not Courts of law in the full sense, it has always been the law of Scotland that they must conform to certain standards of fair play, and their failure to do so entitles a Court of law to reduce their decisions. Were this not so, such tribunals would soon fall into public disrepute, and confidence in them would evaporate".

---

75 [1964] A.C. 40.
76 See Wade & Forsyth, *Administrative Law* (7th ed.), p. 511.
77 [1983] 2 A.C. 257.
78 1950 S.C. 102.
79 1957 S.C. 72.

The case also affirmed the principle that justice must be seen to be done, whether or not injustice has in fact been done. Scotland has more recently sought to move away from an approach based on a classification of the nature of the power or the nature of the decision maker and looked rather to the question what the interests of the parties affected by the decision fairly require.[80]

Developments in case law

The later years of the twentieth century have seen a number of **2.37** significant cases in which the courts have developed and analysed what is now referred to as administrative law, so as to enable some systematic understanding to be available. A few of the leading cases may be noted at this stage. The cases of *Barrs v. British Wool Marketing Board*[81] in 1957 and *Ridge v. Baldwin*[82] in 1964 have already been mentioned. The standard and content of unreasonableness was discussed in *Associated Provincial Picture Houses Ltd v. Wednesbury Corporation*[83] in 1948; the extent of discretionary power was explored in *Padfield v. Minister of Agriculture, Fisheries and Food*[84] in 1968; the concept of error of law was redefined in *Anisminic Ltd v. Foreign Exchange Compensation Commission*[85] in 1969; a summary of the grounds of review was propounded in *Council of Civil Service Unions v. Minister for Civil Service*[86] in 1985; the basis and scope of Scottish law on judicial review was considered and restated in *West v. Secretary of State for Scotland*[87] in 1992. The subject-matter of judicial review has also been considerable, extending beyond the many instances of decisions in such fields as licensing, housing and immigration to such matters as, to take but a few examples, a non-statutory advisory circular, issued by a government department,[88] a decision of the Panel on Take-overs,[89] a decision of an ombudsman,[90] a decision by the Foreign Office on the refusal of a passport,[91] and a decision by the Scottish Legal Aid Board.[92]

The ombudsmen

A further reflection of the recognition of the growing need for control of **2.38** the actings of the administration and the executive can be found in the creation of ombudsmen at national and local level.[93] Consideration of this avenue for redress is not relevant to the present work beyond noticing the concern which the development sought to redress.

---

[80] See later para. 18.04.
[81] 1957 S.C. 72.
[82] [1964] A.C. 40.
[83] [1948] 1 K.B. 223.
[84] [1968] A.C. 997.
[85] [1969] 2 A.C. 147.
[86] [1985] 1 A.C. 374.
[87] 1992 S.C. 385.
[88] *Gillick v. West Norfolk Health Authority* [1986] A.C. 112.
[89] *R. v. Panel of Take-overs and Mergers, ex parte Datafin plc* [1987] Q.B. 815.
[90] *R. v. Commission for Local Administration, ex parte Eastleigh Council* [1988] 3 All E.R. 151. See 1988 P.L. 608.
[91] *R. v. Foreign Secretary, ex parte Everitt* [1989] 1 All E.R. 655.
[92] *K v. Scottish Legal Aid Board*, 1989 S.C.L.R. 144.
[93] The Parliamentary Commissioner Act 1967 (c. 13); the Parliamentary and Health Service Commissioners Act 1987 (c. 59); the Local Government (Scotland) Act 1975 (c. 30), Pt II.

Procedural reform in the Court of Session

2.39 With that concern in mind it remained for the Court to develop the procedural means of providing a remedy which it had for a long period exercised but the availability of which had not kept pace with the needs of the time. The equitable jurisdiction which forms the basis for the power of review is a jurisdiction peculiar to a Supreme Court, but until relatively recently it called for no pecular forms of action. Where a challenge was sought to be made against a decision made by a body that was subject to review the ordinary form of action was adopted, the remedies sought were remedies available in other kinds of cases, and the proceedings would follow the course of any other ordinary action. But the length of time which was involved in the pursuit of ordinary actions was excessive for the resolution of administrative disputes. Both the private citizen and the authority required an expeditious procedure and a rapid resolution of the issue between them. The initiative for reform was triggered by Lord Fraser of Tullybelton in *Brown v. Hamilton District Council*.[94] In that case the privative nature of the supervisory jurisdiction was discussed and affirmed in the House of Lords. Lord Fraser stated that there was no difference between the laws of Scotland and of England on the substance of the grounds for judicial review and suggested the development in Scotland of a special procedure for dealing with such matters. His suggestion was that there might be a revival in the civil context of what Lord President Cooper had described as "obsolete advocation and obsolescent suspension" as appropriate procedures for review. Through that initiative, and after a study of the matter under the guidance of Lord Dunpark, a new procedure for application for judicial review was brought into being and incorporated in Rule 260B, now Chapter 58, in the Rules of the Court of Session. The change thus effected was a change in procedure alone. No changes were proposed, nor effected, in the substance of the law.[95]

Since the introduction of the new procedures for judicial review there has been an increasing number of applications brought before the courts in Scotland and in England.[96] The procedure in Scotland is designed to achieve a rapid and flexible handling of the issues raised and the urgency of some of the issues combined with the desire of both parties to achieve an early resolution usually secures an expeditious determination. Cases of immigration and homelessness, which have formed a significant proportion of the cases coming before the Court, generally require and receive a rapid conclusion. While some delay can be caused where legal aid has to be sought, the new procedure has done much to improve access to the Court and may have contributed at least to some extent towards a greater consciousness on the part of administrative authorities of the necessity to observe the limitations on the powers which they exercise.[97] Studies continue towards the reform of administration and administrative procedures.[98]

---

[94] 1983 S.C. 1. His Lordship repeated the suggestion of an expeditious procedure in *Stephenson v. Midlothian District Council*, 1983 S.L.T. 433.

[95] The operation of the new procedure is considered later, in Chap. 23.

[96] An account of the position in England earlier on is given by Sunkin, "What is Happening to Applications for Judicial Review" (1987) 50 M.L.R. 432.

[97] See Bradley, "The Judge Over Your Shoulder", 1987 P.L. 485 and the article by Mullen *et al.* "Judicial Review in Scotland" (1997) 1 S.L.P.Q. 1.

[98] *e.g.* the Justice All Souls Review of Administrative Law, and the report of the Widdicombe Committee, both in 1988; see I.S. Dickinson, "Local Authorities and Administrative Law Reform, 1988 S.L.T. (News) 301.

Constitutional changes

This historical review should not close without mention of the three **2.40** major innovations which have already been noted in the previous chapter. The first in time has been the United Kingdom's membership of the European Economic Community, now the European Union. The latest are the two which have occurred during the preparation of the present book, namely the passing of the Human Rights Act 1998 and the passing of the Scotland Act 1998, together with the legislation on devolution for Northern Ireland and Wales. It can be predicted with some confidence that all of these changes will have a significant impact on the development of judicial review.

CHAPTER 3

THE JURIDICAL CONTEXT

I   GENERAL
II SCOPE IN CIVIL MATTERS
III CRIMINAL MATTERS
IV CONCLUSION

I   GENERAL

Principle

The great principle on which the supervisory jurisdiction of the Court of   **3.01**
Session is founded is the principle that every wrong should have a
remedy. This was recognised by Lord Kames both in his *Historical Law
Tracts*[1] and his work on Equity.[2] In the former work he wrote: "No
defect in the constitution of a state deserves greater reproach than the
giving licence to do wrong without affording redress. Upon this account
it is the province, one should imagine, of the sovereign, or supreme
court, to redress wrongs of every kind, when a peculiar remedy is not
provided". While, as he later in the same passage observes, the Court of
Session of his day still lacked uniformity in its proceedings he anticipated
the development of a new maxim "That it is the province of this court, to
redress all wrongs for which no other remedy is provided".

Basis

The basis for the Court of Session's jurisdiction in review is to be found   **3.02**
in the *nobile officium* of that Court.[3] To quote again from Lord Kames:
"This extraordinary process of redressing wrongs, far from a novelty, has
a name appropriated to it in the language of our law. For what else is
meant by the *nobile officium* of the Court of Session, so much talked of
and so little understood".[4] By the *nobile officium* is meant the extraordinary equitable power which is the prerogative of a Supreme Court.
The process of judicial review is thus one expression of the residual
power of a Supreme Court to provide a remedy where no other remedy
is available. Since its character is supervisory, this expression of the
nobile officium is conveniently referred to as the supervisory jurisdiction
of the Court of Session. Scots law has never required a distinct court of
equity for a variety of reasons related principally to the influence of the
Roman and Continental legal systems in its earlier development.[5] The
nobile officium expresses the recognition in the equitable system of

---

[1] (4th ed., 1817), pp. 228–229.

[2] (5th ed., 1825), Book 2, Chap. 3, p. 341.

[3] There is a continuing academic debate on the "basis" of judicial review which is noted
later in para. 4.03. For a consideration of the idea of the intention of the legislature as the
basis for judicial review in England, see Craig, "Ultra Vires and the Foundations of
Judicial Review" (1998) C.L.J. Vol. 57, Pt 1, p. 63.

[4] *Historical Law Tracts*, p. 231.

[5] Sheriff Mackay, "Equity", *Green's Encyclopaedia*, Vol. 6, p. 275.

jurisprudence that cases of necessity sometimes occur which call for exceptional remedies.[6]

Equity

3.03 Judicial review is an equitable remedy and the Court will only exercise its supervisory power when it is fair and equitable to do so.[7] The equitable character of the power which lies at the heart of the supervisory jurisdiction can be identified in a number of ways in the course of the exercise of the jurisdiction. While the formal consent of the Court is not required for the making of an application, nevertheless an application may be rejected at the outset if the Court considers that it is incompetent or plainly without merit.[8] While in general, as will be seen, an application cannot be made where there is another remedy available, there are cases where the Court may allow an application to proceed despite such an unexhausted alternative.[9] Equitable considerations will form an element in a decision whether or not an application should be excluded on the ground of delay. Where an application is held to be successful on its merits, the matter of the remedy to be given will again depend upon what may be considered appropriate in the circumstances.[10]

Meaning of the *nobile officium*

3.04 Some care has to be taken in using the expression *nobile officium*. It may be used in a somewhat general sense as a reference to the general jurisdiction of the Court in respect that that jurisdiction is nothing if not equitable.[11] But it is more usual for the expression to be adopted in relation to certain particular situations where the Court is prepared to provide an extraordinary remedy. Lord Justice-Clerk Ross said of it that it is "an extraordinary equitable jurisdiction in the Court of Session inherent in it as a supreme court: it enables it to exercise jurisdiction in certain circumstances which would not be justified except by the necessity of intervening in the interests of justice. Although the court tends to limit the exercise of its jurisdiction under the *nobile officium* to cases in which the power has already been exercised, it is neither possible nor desirable to define exhaustively or comprehensively all the circumstances in which resort may be had to the *nobile officium*".[12] As has been noted, the supervisory jurisdiction is to be seen as an expression of the *nobile officium*. The supervisory jurisdiction of the court is thus "narrower than and is encompassed within the privative jurisdiction of the court".[13]

The *nobile officium* and judicial review

3.05 The term "*nobile officium*" has come to be used in a narrow sense, in distinction to cases of review, whereby the reference is made to the particular series of situations where an exceptional remedy, not of a

---

[6] Craig's *Jus Feudale*, Stair Society, Introduction, p. xxii.
[7] *Ingle v. Ingle's Trustees*, 1999 S.L.T. 650.
[8] See para. 23–14.
[9] See para. 12.12 *et seq.*
[10] See later on Remedies, para. 23.32.
[11] *Gibson's Trustees*, 1933 S.C. 190 at 199.
[12] *The Royal Bank of Scotland v. Gillies*, 1987 S.L.T. 54 at 55.
[13] *Kyle & Carrick District Council v. A.R. Kerr & Sons*, 1992 S.L.T. 629, *per* Lord Penrose at 632.

supervisory character, is required in order to meet some extraordinary and unforeseen problem. This distinction between cases falling under the *"nobile officium"* and cases of review is recognised in modern terminology and in court practice, the procedure being in the one case by petition to the *nobile officium* and in the other by application for judicial review. However, whether the particular label is used or not may not be of consequence, provided that the underlying equitable power to provide a remedy in matters of review is recognised. As Lord President Inglis observed in *Forbes v. Underwood* with regard to the power of the Court of Session to order inferior bodies to perform their duty: "Now, all this belongs to the Court of Session as the Supreme Civil Court of this country in the exercise of what is called, very properly, its supereminent jurisdiction. It is not of much consequence to determine whether it is in the exercise of its high equitable jurisdiction, or in the performance of what is sometimes called its *nobile officium*. But of one thing there can be no doubt . . . that this Court is exercising an exclusive jurisdiction—a jurisdiction which cannot belong to any other Court in the country".[14]

II SCOPE IN CIVIL MATTERS

Scope of the *nobile officium*

It is nevertheless instructive to consider the scope of the *nobile officium* in approaching the problem of the scope of the supervisory jurisdiction. Stair saw the *nobile officium* as enabling the Supreme Court to go beyond the strict forms of law prescribed under the *officium ordinarium* to supply new cures in new cases where it was necessary to do so. But while the Lords were authorised to do that he warns that "if they might in other cases extend their *officium nobile*, it would render the subjects unsecure, and the power of the Lords too arbitrary".[15] It has been observed: "Amid much that is uncertain as to the exercise of the *nobile officium*, this may be laid down as a fixed principle,—that it will never be exercised except in cases of necessity, or very strong expediency, and where the ordinary procedure would provide no remedy".[16] As has been noticed in the preceding chapter, the Court came by the eighteenth century to exercise its powers under the *nobile officium* over a range of matters in the realm of public administration, providing a remedy where none else was available.[17] **3.06**

Development of the *nobile officium*

In the eighteenth century the court exercised what Erskine[18] called its ministerial powers in a variety of administrative problems where no other remedy was available. The development of administrative legislation and machinery in the nineteenth century made it less necessary for the Court to intervene to the extent to which it had previously done. The development of the processes and practices of the Court reduced the need for special remedies and the use of the *nobile officium* became in **3.07**

---

[14] (1886) 13 R. 465 at 468.
[15] Stair, *Institutions*, 4.3.1.
[16] Attributed by Lord Justice-Clerk Alness in *Gibson's Trustees*, 1933 S.C. 190 at 205 to More's *Notes on Stair*, but the quotation comes from Erskine's *Institutes* (Nicolson, ed.), 1.3.22 n.(6).
[17] See para. 2.19.
[18] *Institutes*, 1, 3, 23.

practice more restricted. The principal categories of case for its exercise came to be identified as those where it was necessary to make good omissions or defects in statutes or statutory procedure, particularly in matters of bankruptcy, where it was necessary to make good omissions or defects in deeds or writings, particularly in respect of trusts, and where some special appointment or special remedy was required.[19] There is no need to enlarge on the last of these three areas, but something more should be said of the other two.

Supplementing statutes

3.08 In relation to statutes the *nobile officium* may be used to supplement a remedy provided by statute[20] which may make the provision more effectual. It may provide a solution to a *casus omissus* in an Act of Parliament. Thus where it was found that the Succession (Scotland) Act 1964 provided no machinery for the formal recognition of the heir of a last surviving trustee as heir and so entitled to take up office as trustee, the Court provided a solution by way of a declarator.[21] "Where a formal step has been omitted and quite unnecessary delay and expense would be involved if the procedure had to be gone through all over again" then the *nobile officium* may enable justice to be done.[22] In *Ferguson, Petitioner*,[23] the registrar had acted *ultra vires* by deleting the name of the petitioners from the list of electors in that he had failed to intimate to them his proposal to omit them from the voting list. The regulations provided no remedy for such a situation and the Court under the *nobile officium* ordered the electoral registration officer to insert the names in the register as persons entitled to vote in the relevant constituency. In *Humphries, Petitioner*,[24] authority was granted to keep two children in places of safety for a period which was beyond that which could be achieved under the statutory provisions in order that a hearing before the sheriff on the grounds of referral could be held back to avoid prejudice to a criminal trial involving matter to which the grounds of referral related. It was considered that the extension in these special circumstances merely provided machinery to serve the underlying intention of Parliament. On that reasoning extensions of time have been granted in relation to various statutory procedures. The Court has appointed an interim Town Clerk in the public interest to secure the administration of the affairs of a burgh pending a dispute on the dismissal of the incumbent.[25] In *Sloan, Petitioner*,[26] the Court empowered a sheriff in Kirkwall to hold part of a hearing on the question whether grounds of referral to a children's panel were established in the chambers of a sheriff in Inverness, which was outwith his own sheriffdom, it being considered that it was desirable that certain of the child witnesses in the case should not in the circumstances be required to travel to Kirkwall for the hearing. In one case the Court discharged a bankrupt under the *nobile officium* where he had become insane and the

---

[19] Sheriff Mackay's article on the *"Nobile Officium"* in *Green's Encyclopaedia*, Vol. 10, p. 325. For examples, see McLaren, *Court of Session Practice*, pp. 101–104.
[20] *Ker v. Hughes*, 1907 S.C. 380.
[21] *Skinner, Petr*, 1976 S.L.T. 60.
[22] *Maitland, Petr*, 1961 S.C. 291 at 293.
[23] 1965 S.C. 16.
[24] 1983 S.L.T. 481.
[25] *Magistrates of Rothesay v. Carse* (1902) 4 F. 641.
[26] 1991 S.L.T. 527.

statutory procedure had become unavailable[27] and in another case the Court declared a late advertisement in the *London Gazette* to be equivalent to a timeous notice under the Bankruptcy (Scotland) Act 1913 where timeous notice had become impossible.[28]

Conformity with statutory intention

But the power will not go the length of solving problems which **3.09** Parliament ought to have solved.[29] Nor can it be used to extend the scope of an Act of Parliament.[30] It does not include a legislative power to alter statutes so as to give special statutory right to persons other than those for whom the statutory right has been created.[31] Nor can it be used to supplement the statutory procedure by what would in effect be an amendment of the statute[32] or to enable something to be done which has been expressly rendered ineffective by the Act.[33] In such a case the Act is to be regarded as finally determining the matter. Thus where the statutory scheme for children's hearings required that once the grounds for referral had been accepted or established the case should stand referred to the children's hearing, it was held to be incompetent to seek a rehearing of the grounds of referral where one of the children concerned had retracted the allegation previously made. It was observed that that would be supplementing the statutory procedure by what would in effect be an amendment to the statute. But the Court did indicate that if in exceptional circumstances by mistaken or incomplete information on a material point the grounds ought not to have been accepted or established, an exercise of the *nobile officium* might be appropriate; but the fact that a witness wished to withdraw or change his evidence was not an exceptional or unforeseen circumstance.[34] In *L, Petitioner*,[35] it was held that exceptional circumstances did exist and that it was competent for that case to be remitted to the sheriff for a rehearing. It was long ago recognised that the *nobile officium* cannot competently be used to supersede or override an express statutory provision.[36] More recently it has come to be accepted that a like restriction exists where the statutory provision is not express but is clearly implied.[37] In all of this the Court is plainly sensitive to the need to refrain from trespassing upon the province of Parliament.[38]

Alternative remedies

The *nobile officium* is only available in cases of necessity where no other **3.10** remedy is provided. It cannot be used "as a mere cloak for incompetence on the part of the applicant's representative".[39] It is well recognised that

---

[27] *Roberts* (1901) 3 F. 779.

[28] *Law Society of Scotland*, 1974 S.L.T. (Notes) 66.

[29] *Parochial Board of Borthwick v. Parochial Board of Temple* (1891) 18 R. 1190.

[30] *Smart v. Registrar General*, 1954 S.C. 81. *West Highland Woodlands Ltd, Petr*, 1963 S.C. 494.

[31] *Chrichton-Stuart's Tutrix, Petr*, 1921 S.C. 840.

[32] *Maitland, Petr*, 1961 S.C. 292. *London & Clydeside Estates Ltd v. Aberdeen District Council*, 1960 S.C.(H.L.) 1.

[33] *M'Laughlin, Petr*, 1965 S.C. 243.

[34] *R., Petr*, 1993 S.L.T. 910.

[35] 1993 S.L.T. 1310.

[36] *McGowan v. Cramb* (1897) 24 R. 481; *Adair v. Colville's & Sons*, 1922 S.C. 672.

[37] In *L, Petr*, 1993 S.L.T. 1310 at 1315 it was said that the first recognition of this was in *Anderson v. Lord Advocate*, 1974 S.L.T. 239.

[38] *cf. R. v. H.M. Treasury, ex p. Smedley* [1985] Q.B. 657, *per* Sir John Donaldson M.R. at 666.

[39] *Petr, Maitland*, 1961 S.C. 292 at 293.

the *nobile officium* may not be invoked where there is a statutory appeal available. Thus where the statute made provision for appeal on the merits of a conviction by way of stated case an application to the *nobile officium* on grounds which were concerned with the evidence and the facts was held not to disclose any extraordinary or unforeseen circumstance such as would admit recourse to the *nobile officium*.[40] The *nobile officium* may not be exercised where there is a statutory remedy which has not been taken timeously and some solution to the problem is available under the common law.[41] Where there was no other solution available the Court under the *nobile officium* authorised with some hesitation the removal of certain gravestones to allow room for the extension of a church.[42]

Delay

3.11   Finally, it is consistent with the necessity for having recourse to the *nobile officium* that the application should be made without delay.[43] Delay was held to be a factor to be taken into account in deciding whether a necessity existed to warrant the interference of the Court where a blunder had been committed in following out the provisions of a statute.[44]

Trusts

3.12   The most obvious occasion for resort to the *nobile officium* is probably the application for a *cy-près* scheme. There are many examples of cases where the court has intervened in the interest of charities. In this context the intention of the author is of critical importance. Thus the Court will be prepared to intervene where the truster has expressed a general charitable intention and the means or machinery for carrying it into effect are not indicated. In such a case the Court will simply be supplementing the omission in the constituting deed. The Court will also intervene where there is a general charitable intention and the stated means for its fulfilment are inadequately set out, such as where an institution is identified as the recipient but which is found never to have have existed. Here again the task is one of supplementing the deed. Where the failure occurs before the trust opens then, unless there is a general charitable intention evinced by the truster, the provision will lapse.[45] However, where a trust in favour of a charity has actually come into effect, the Court will not be concerned to look for a general charitable intention but will on the subsequent failure of the object apply the funds under a *cy-près* scheme.[46] Where a charitable scheme has failed the Court may under the *nobile officium* incorporate in an alternative scheme a power to the new trustees to sell heritage where that was necessary to make the scheme viable.[47] But the truster's intention is still paramount and if his intention was that on failure of the charitable

---

[40] *Anderson v. Lord Advocate*, 1974 S.L.T. 239.
[41] *Lord Macdonald's Curator*, 1924 S.C. 163; *Forth Shipbreaking Company*, 1924 S.C. 489.
[42] *Christie*, 1926 S.C. 750.
[43] *Robertson v. Tough's Trustee*, 1925 S.C. 234.
[44] *Tod v. Anderson* (1869) 7 M. 412; Lord Benholme, however, disagreed on the matter of delay as an element in the decision.
[45] *Burgess' Trustees v. Crawford*, 1912 S.C. 387.
[46] *e.g. Davidson's Trustees v. Arnott*, 1951 S.C. 42.
[47] *Stranraer Original Secession Congregation*, 1923 S.C. 722.

institution the fund was to revert to his estate, effect will be given to that intention.[48] It is only in cases of necessity that the *nobile officium* can be invoked, and accordingly the fact that the duties of the trustees have become more difficult or more arduous will not enable the Court to intervene,[49] but it has been held that in situations of strong expediency a *cy-près* scheme may be approved although the situation is not one of a failure of the trust.[50] The court may even give retrospective validation to *ultra vires* actings of trustees, but only in exceptional circumstances and for very compelling reasons, it not being usual to expand the the *nobile officium* beyond its accepted limits.[51]

Extent of intervention

In relation to trusts it may also be noticed that the power of the Court to **3.13** intervene extends not only to charitable trusts but also to the wider group of those which can be termed public trusts, that is to say those which are intended for the benefit of a section of the public and which may be enforced by a *popularis actio*.[52] Furthermore, it has been recognised that the *nobile officium* is available in the context of private as well as public trusts—one obvious example is the appointment of new trustees in situations of deadlock.[53] But here again the Court will only intervene where it is necessary to do so and in the context of private trusts there will be fewer opportunities for such a necessity to arise.[54] As Lord Justice-Clerk Thomson observed in *Coles, Petitioner*, where authorisation was sought for an assignation of part of an alimentary liferent in exchange for a capital payment: "I would be slow to think that it would be a proper exercise of the *nobile officium* so to interfere with the trust purposes, at any rate in a case where interference is not required to prevent the trust from becoming unworkable or to protect the trust estate from loss or the beneficiary from hardship".[55]

III   CRIMINAL MATTERS

General

The supervisory jurisdiction of the Court of Session in civil matters is **3.14** matched by a corresponding jurisdiction in the High Court of Justiciary in criminal matters.[56] Although Alison[57] refers to the power as a similar power "akin to the well-known *nobile officium* of the Court of Session",

---

[48] *e.g. Young's Trustees v. Deacons of the Eight Incorporated Trades of Perth* (1893) 20 R. 778.

[49] *Glasgow Domestic Training School*, 1923 S.C. 892.

[50] *e.g. The Provost, Magistrates and Councillors of Forfar and Others*, 1975 S.L.T. (Notes) 36.

[51] *Dow's Trustees*, 1947 S.C. 524; *Horne's Trustees*, 1952 S.C. 70.

[52] *Anderson's Trustees v. Scott*, 1914 S.C. 942 at 946.

[53] *e.g. Taylor*, 1932 S.C. 1.

[54] The sanction given to the conveyance of a trust to new trustees in the case of *Gray v. Gray's Trustees* (1877) 4 R. 378 occurred in a stated case, and since all the beneficiaries were known and consented it may not truly be an example of the *nobile officium*, although it is so presented in Mackenzie Stuart's *Law of Trusts*, p. 349.

[55] 1951 S.C. 608 at 617.

[56] Alison, *Criminal Law of Scotland*, Vol. II, p. 23. For a consideration of cases of error see P.W. Ferguson, "The Scope of the *Nobile Officium* to Review Appeal Court Decisions" (1993) 38 J.L.S.S. 439.

[57] *Practice of the Criminal Law of Scotland*, Vol. 2, paras 13–14.

Moncrieff[58] refers to the High Court's power as itself a *nobile officium*. He states:

> "In addition to its powers of review, the High Court of Justiciary, as the supreme court in criminal matters, has, in respect of its *nobile officium*, the power of interfering in extraordinary circumstances, for the purpose of preventing injustice or oppression, although there may not be any judgment, conviction or warrant brought under review".

The power to intervene in criminal cases is in practice regularly ascribed to the *nobile officium*.[59] In exceptional or unforeseen circumstances the *nobile officium* may be exercised in criminal cases, not to contradict a statutory provision on procedure, but to afford relief even in the face of an interlocutor which the statute has declared to be final.[60] Thus where the intention of the Act in a matter of criminal law was clear, but the machinery for its execution was set in terms appropriate to English procedure, the means for giving effect to the statute was provided by recourse to the *nobile officium*.[61] The Crown may seek a review of the legality of a sheriff's order by way of a Bill of Advocation.[62] The English Court has by way of declaration resolved a question whether a particular procedural management of an abortion would constitute an offence.[63]

Criminal and civil

3.15   Essentially the origin and nature of these two jurisdictions are the same. The boundary lines between them, however, has not always been clear. There was some uncertainty even as late as the nineteenth century on the extent to which the Court of Session could review what would certainly now be regarded as criminal matters, but which could then be distinguished as being merely matters of statutory offence.[64] It is now clearly settled that matters relating to the prosecution of crime should be raised in the High Court of Justiciary. But questions can still arise whether a matter is civil or criminal, as occurred in relation to the problem of a grant of criminal legal aid.[65] While matters relating to the apprehension of offenders, or their committal to prison, or the overlong detention of an accused person pending the processing of an application for bail,[66] or the detention of a witness,[67] where the judge is exercising a criminal jurisdiction, are matters for the High Court of Justiciary,

---

[58] *Review in Criminal Cases*, p. 264.

[59] *Reynolds v. Christie*, 1988 S.L.T. 68; *MacPherson, Petr*, 1990 J.C. 5 at 13. For a review of cases of the exercise of the *nobile officium* by the High Court of Justiciary for the purposes of liberation and other matters, see Stoddart "The *nobile officium* and the High Court of Justiciary", 1974 S.L.T. (News) 37. See also para. 2.31 (history).

[60] *McIntosh, Petr*, 1995 S.L.T. 796; *cf. Young, Petr*, 1994 S.L.T. 269.

[61] *Wan Pin Nam v. Minister of Justice of the German Federal Republic*, 1972 J.C. 48.

[62] *e.g. H.M. Advocate v. Law*, 1993 S.L.T. 435.

[63] *Royal College of Nursing of the U.K. v. Department of Health and Social Security* [1981] A.C. 800.

[64] *Phillips v. Steel* (1847) 9 D. 318; *Park v. Earl of Stair* (1852) J Shaw 532; *Bruce v. Linton* (1860) 23 D. 85, (1861) 24 D. 184; *Scott v. Muir and Annan* (1868) 7 M. 270. See also para. 2.31 (history). A comparison might perhaps be developed with the distinction drawn by the ECHR between criminal proceedings and disciplinary proceedings.

[65] *Reynolds v. Christie*, 1988 S.L.T. 68 and *K v. Scottish Legal Aid Board*, 1989 S.L.T. 617.

[66] *Gibbons, Petr*, 1988 S.L.T. 657.

[67] *Gerrard, Petr*, 1984 S.L.T. 108.

matters regarding the condition, detention, treatment, transfer and release of offenders, which are matters for the Secretary of State to control, fall within the jurisdiction of the Court of Session.[68] The recovery of shorthand notes of the evidence at a trial may be matter for the *nobile officium* of the High Court.[69] The grounds for review both in criminal and civil cases should be the same, but the procedures in the criminal court are different, being those of appeal, suspension and advocation.

Limitations

In relation to criminal matters the limits on the availability of the *nobile*   **3.16**
officium which have been noted in relation to the civil court will be found to apply. Thus in extraordinary circumstances where the intention of the legislature was clear the Court supplied the means for giving effect to it where the machinery provided by the legislation was by a procedure known in England but unknown in Scotland.[70] A clear and express declaration of finality may exclude recourse to the *nobile officium*,[71] but in a case of oppression, even although the statutory provision may be intended to be final,[72] the Court may nevertheless intervene.[73] The Court has refused to apply the *nobile officium* in a criminal case where the matter could have been dealt with by a statutory appeal.[74]

IV   CONCLUSION

The purpose of the foregoing consideration of the *nobile officium* is not   **3.17**
only to enlarge upon an understanding of the nature of the basis of the supervisory jurisdiction, but also to indicate the restrictions on its exercise outside the context of review. As will be seen, those restrictions have also come to be developed in relation to the supervisory jurisdiction, reflecting a consistency in principle between the various expressions of the fundamentally equitable power of the Supreme Court.

---

[68] *Newland, Petr*, 1994 S.L.T. 587.
[69] *Muirhead, Petr*, 1983 S.L.T. 208, where the application was refused.
[70] *Wan Ping Nam v. Minister of Justice*, 1972 J.C. 43.
[71] *Anderson v. Lord Advocate*, 1974 S.L.T. 239.
[72] *Heslin, Petr*, 1973 S.L.T. (Notes) 56.
[73] *Rae, Petr*, 1982 S.L.T. 233.
[74] *Berry, Petr*, 1985 S.C.C.R. 106.

CHAPTER 4

THE CONSTITUTIONAL CONTEXT

I   INTRODUCTION
II   CONSTITUTIONAL VALUES
III   THE RULE OF LAW AND JUDICIAL REVIEW
IV   THE LEGITIMACY OF JUDICIAL REVIEW
V   JUDICIAL INDEPENDENCE
VI   THE SUPREMACY OF PARLIAMENT
VII   EQUALITY BEFORE THE LAW

I INTRODUCTION

Constitutional review

This chapter attempts to discuss the constitutional context of judicial **4.01** review. Although it is beyond the scope of this work to present a complete survey of the United Kingdom's constitutional law,[1] it is necessary to place judicial review in its constitutional setting. This requires consideration to be given to the constitutional basis and constitutional implications of judicial review. In addition, it is important to consider the circumstances in which judicial review is available on what might be termed "constitutional grounds". At one level, this can be understood as referring to the extent to which judicial review protects the values of the constitution. More specifically, however, it refers to the extent to which the U.K. constitution now recognises a system of "constitutional review". It is true that the term "constitutional review", or "constitutional judicial review", is more apposite in a jurisdiction with a "written" or codified constitution, such as the United States of America or Germany, where the courts are empowered to measure provisions in primary legislation against the entrenched rules of the constitution.[2] Nevertheless, even under the United Kingdom's singular

---

[1] On which there are several outstanding works available: *e.g.* J.D.B. Mitchell, *Constitutional Law* (2nd ed., W. Green & Son/SULI, Edinburgh, 1968); Bradley & Ewing, *Constitutional & Administrative Law* (12th ed., Longman, 1997); Deans, *Scots Public Law* (T&T Clark, Edinburgh, 1995); Le Sueur & Sunkin, *Public Law* (Longman, 1997); Munro, *Studies in Constitutional Law* (Butterworths, London, 1987); and Turpin, *British Government and the Constitution: Text, Cases and Materials* (3rd ed., 1995). For a classical account of the U.K. Constitution from a Scottish perspective, see Fraser, *Constitutional Law* (1948), a work which pre-dates the modern E.C. and international developments.

[2] The distinction between "written" and "unwritten" constitutions is misleading. While some constitutions are more "written" than others, all constitutional arrangements have "written" and "unwritten" aspects. For example, the U.S. Constitution is not exclusively written, with many important constitutional concepts in that country not expressed in the constitutional text. Without mentioning numerous conventional practices, it is sufficient to note the following: the power of the federal courts to review and invalidate legislation (not stated explicitly in the Constitution but found to be implied, *inter alia*, by its written character, in the U.S. Supreme Court's landmark decision in *Marbury v. Madison* (1803) 1 Cranch 137); the power of the President to make "executive agreements" (treaties in all

51

constitutional arrangements a "modified form of judicial review of statutes" now exists,[3] where, for example, legislation is challenged under applicable E.C. law,[4] or under the Scotland Act 1998, or under the Human Rights Act 1998. Since the form of constitutional review which exists in the United Kingdom always follows from an Act of the supreme U.K. Parliament, it is not quite equivalent to constitutional review under a supreme constitutional instrument. In particular, since the jurisdiction is conferred by the U.K. Parliament, it does not arise independently under the "constitution" so as, for example, to be the equal in institutional terms of Parliament's power. Moreover, the scope and extent of the constitutional review which E.C. law, Convention rights and the devolution arrangements entail differ in important respects. Even so, it may be said that "in the UK we are already some way down the road of legislative review",[5] so that the U.K. Constitution now has enough of the characteristics of constitutional review to require its discussion in a work devoted to judicial review.

Although the emergence of a form of constitutional review in the United Kingdom poses interesting questions, these must not be allowed to overshadow the constitutional issues which relate to judicial review more generally. On the one hand, as was noted in Chapter 1,[6] not all cases involving an instance of constitutional review will arise under the supervisory jurisdiction. For example, the need to "review" statutes for consistency with E.C. law or Convention rights may arise in the context of ordinary actions or criminal proceedings.[7] On the other hand, while some cases arising under the supervisory jurisdiction will have some

---

but name but not for the purposes of "treaty" in Art. II of the Constitution); and the power of federal law (and by virtue of the so-called "dormant" commerce clause, also federal interests) to "pre-empt" state law. On the other hand, much of the U.K.'s Constitution is "written": *e.g.*, the Treaty and Acts of Union; the Bill of Rights and Claim of Right 1688/89; the Act of Settlement 1701; the European Communities Act 1972; the Human Rights Act 1998; the Scotland Act 1998. Rather than the misleading "written–unwritten" dichotomy, a preferable approach is to distinguish between codified and uncodified or flexible and rigid constitutions (on this latter distinction, see Bryce, *Studies in History and Jurisprudence* (1901)). Still not perfect, these classify constitutional arrangements according to their having a form of fundamental law set out in a text or texts, amendment of which invariably requires a special procedure: *e.g.* a 2/3rds majority in the legislature, and under which a supreme court resolves constitutional disputes. To this extent, the U.K.'s constitution is uncodified (and flexible) whereas that of most other countries (*e.g.* the USA, Canada, Australia, India, Germany, France) is more or less codified (and rigid). For further discussion, see Mitchell, *Constitutional Law*, at pp 10–14; and Barendt, "Is there a United Kingdom Constitution?" (1997) 17 O.J.L.S. 137 (answering "yes"): "From a formal perspective UK constitutional law is a hotchpotch of statutes, caselaw, and miscellaneous rules which are, it is said, made intelligible by reference to a number of conventions of uncertain scope and inconsistent application . . . Yet it seems unhelpful to withdraw from it the title 'Constitution'" (at p. 145).

[3] *Matadeen v. Pointu* [1999] A.C. 98, *per* Lord Hoffmann at 110.

[4] In this discussion European Community (E.C.) law will be preferred to European Union (E.U.) law since it is E.C. law which has most relevance for judicial review. For the distinction between E.C. law and E.U. law, see para. 5.01.

[5] Sir Stephen Sedley, "Human Rights: A Twenty-First Century Agenda" [1997] P.L. 386 at 394.

[6] See para. 1.11.

[7] For example, where a provision in U.K. or Scottish legislation is challenged for incompatibility with a provision in an E.C. Directive with direct effect: see *Webb v. EMO Cargo (U.K.) Ltd* [1995] 1 W.L.R. 1454; and *Pickstone v. Freemans* [1989] A.C. 66. Similarly, whether an Act passed by the Scottish Parliament is within the legislative competence of the Parliament or whether any rule of law violates a right guaranteed in the European Convention as given effect in the U.K. by the Human Rights Act 1998, may be raised in all types of proceedings.

"constitutional" significance,[8] many will be more routine. But in relation to all examples of the power of judicial review, whether it is an exercise of the supervisory jurisdiction or, more generally, an example of "constitutional review", it is important to appreciate both the constitutional basis of judicial review and the constitutional values on which it draws. With this in mind, the present chapter attempts to consider the constitutional basis of judicial review and how it relates to the values and principles of the U.K. constitution. Thereafter, the three chapters which make up Part II of the book deal respectively with the specific forms of "constitutional review" presented by E.C. law, Convention rights and the Scotland Act 1998.

Overview

Although it can be a controversial concept, if it is understood carefully **4.02** the rule of law can be said to provide both the constitutional basis and the leading constitutional values for judicial review. In order to serve as the basis for judicial review under the U.K. constitution, the rule of law must be understood as requiring four essential elements. First, all exercises of legal authority must be in accordance with the established law: that is, the principle of legality. Secondly, the exercise of all discretionary power which has been conferred by law is only valid if it is in accordance with established legal rules and principles: that is, the concept of limited government. Thirdly, disputes, particularly disputes between citizen and state, should ultimately be open to resolution in a court of law presided over by an independent judge: that is, the right of access to a court for a remedy at law and the institution of an independent judiciary. And fourthly, the state should have no privileges which are not open to justification in the public interest: that is, equality before the law and the need to respect democratic authority. These four elements of the rule of law provide the essential basis not only for the U.K. constitution's fundamental values but also for judicial review. Accordingly, part II of this chapter attempts to identify some of the U.K. constitution's values which give substantive meaning to the rule of law.

Thereafter, part III focuses on the elements of the rule of law which demand respect for the principle of legality and the need for limited government. This means that all decision makers must show not only a legal authority for their actions but also that their actions can be justified by reference to the established law, including the constitution's values. So, while an authority may be entrusted with wide discretionary powers, such powers are not to be exercised in a capricious, arbitrary or dictatorial manner, but fairly, honestly and properly in accordance with the law and in advancement of the purpose for which they are provided. Significantly, however, the role which judicial review has in supervising the exercise of legal powers leads inevitably to a consideration of the legitimacy of judicial review where it meets powers which have a democratic source. The unwritten nature of most of the U.K. constitution's values, taken with the judicially created substance of the grounds of judicial review, may be thought to underline problems associated with

---

[8] For example, *R. v. Secretary of State for Transport, ex p. Factortame (No. 2)* [1991] 1 A.C. 603; *R. v. Secretary of State for Employment, ex p. EOC* [1995] 1 A.C. 1; *R. v. Secretary of State for the Home Department, ex p. Fire Brigades Union* [1995] 2 A.C. 513; *Monckton v. Lord Advocate*, 1995 S.L.T. 1201; and *R. v. Secretary of State for Foreign and Commonwealth Affairs, ex p. Rees-Mogg* [1994] 2 W.L.R. 115.

the legitimacy of judicial review in the United Kingdom. However, by stressing the third and fourth identified elements of the rule of law, some attempt can be made to address such concerns. In particular, the means by which the law provides for the independence of the judiciary and the supremacy which the constitution gives to Acts of Parliament may be thought to strike a balance between judicial and political power. Accordingly, following a brief overview of the concerns about the legitimacy of judicial review in a democracy in part IV, parts V and VI of the chapter respectively address the means by which the independence of the judiciary is secured and the relationship between the courts and the supremacy of Parliament. Finally, part VII discusses the remaining aspect of the fourth identified element of the rule of law: namely, the need for equality before the law. While it is true that public officials should be given the respect and privileges which their responsibilities deserve, it is also essential that they should not be any less subject to the jurisdiction of the courts than a private citizen. In light of the development of judicial review in the United Kingdom, this aspect of the rule of law requires a consideration to be given to the nature and position of the Crown.

II CONSTITUTIONAL VALUES

Introduction

4.03 As has just been discussed, the fundamental concept on which judicial review proceeds is the rule of law. At a minimum this means that it is the province and duty of the courts to ensure that all those exercising legal powers do so properly and according to law[9]; and that all government powers must be limited by and have an ascertainable meaning according to law. But the full meaning of the rule of law under the U.K. constitution can only be understood in light of several constitutional values which give substance to it. In this regard, it may be that the differences which have emerged in recent years between various commentators on the proper basis of judicial review can be explained by a tendency to conceive of the constitution's values as a patchwork of single instances rather than as a whole.[10] While there are certainly difficulties with resting the whole basis of judicial review on the *ultra vires* rule,[11] it is necessary to see judicial review in constitutional terms. This may be achieved first by regarding judicial review as being based on the essential ingredient in the rule of law that all legal powers be limited by law and that the courts be available to ensure that all legal authority is exercised lawfully—in other words, that no wrong go without a remedy[12]; and secondly by understanding judicial review as serving to protect a range of

---

[9] If authority is required for this proposition, the leading case of *Anisminic v. Foreign Compensation Commission* [1969] 2 A.C. 147 demonstrates the fundamental nature of the court's power of judicial review. *cf.* Wade and Forsyth, *Administrative Law* (7th ed., Clarendon Press, Oxford, 1994) at pp. 737–738.

[10] *cf.* Lord Steyn, "The Weakest and Least Dangerous Department of Government" [1997] P.L. 84, especially at pp. 86–99.

[11] Although where the exercise of statutory powers is being reviewed this continues to be satisfactory. On the problem see, for example, Oliver, "Is the *Ultra Vires* Rule the Basis for Judicial Review" [1987] P.L. 543; and the authors cited at para. 4.16.

[12] A principle which was recognised at an early date in the history of judicial review; see paras 2.18 and 2.20.

constitutional values and principles which give substance to the rule of law beyond the essential of legality. Consideration must then be given to the idea of constitutionalism, which brings together all the values and principles concerning constitutionally limited government conducted according to law. In particular, constitutionalism requires that government be answerable for the exercise of its powers both to Parliament and to the courts. Further constitutional values which give substance to the rule of law in the United Kingdom are respect for democracy, human rights, the separation of powers and the supremacy of the law enacted by the U.K. Parliament. It may be said that judicial review respects all of these constitutional values and in doing so gives practical effect to the rule of law. But before saying a little more about these constitutional values, something should first be said about the form and nature of the U.K. constitution.

The Nature of the U.K. Constitution

The U.K.'s constitution is often discussed in terms of the United **4.04** Kingdom as a unitary state. Historically, however, it has been observed that the United Kingdom has always been a "union" state, following from the fact that the component nations of the United Kingdom, especially Scotland, have retained some distinct institutions.[13] The effect of the 1707 Treaty of Union was to preserve important differences between Scotland and England, notably the separate legal systems. Classifying the U.K. constitution as a unitary constitution therefore does not reflect its more complex nature. Indeed, in so far as the term "unitary" carries connotations of "centralised", it is inaccurate in view of the decentralisation of executive powers which has occurred during the twentieth century, so that in Scotland the vast majority of governmental powers have long been exercised by the Scottish Office.[14] But as with so much in relation to the U.K. constitution, the realities are often overshadowed by the dominance attributed to the supremacy of legislation enacted by the U.K. Parliament, which sits in London. The reality now, however, is that the U.K. Parliament's powers are less dominant, both in light of the U.K.'s membership of the European Union and the advent of the arrangements for legislative devolution. The creation of Parliaments in Scotland and Northern Ireland and an Assembly in Wales means that the United Kingdom's constitutional arrangements are now even less unitary. Nevertheless, it would still be erroneous to consider the United Kingdom as a federal state. Without entering the debate on the meaning of federalism,[15] it cannot be said that the various legislatures and governments in the United Kingdom are "co-ordinate and

---

[13] For a recent discussion of the nature of the U.K. constitution in light of the devolution reforms, see Brazier, "The Constitution of the United Kingdom" (1999) 58 Camb.L.J. 96.

[14] The office of Secretary for Scotland was created in 1885, becoming the Cabinet post of Secretary of State for Scotland in 1928. Since 1945, most executive powers in relation to Scotland have been exercised by the Scottish Office. Similarly, in 1964, the Welsh Office and post of Secretary of State for Wales were established., although the Welsh Office exercises a narrower range of powers than its Scottish counterpart. The Northern Ireland Office and the post of Secretary of State for Northern Ireland were created in 1974 following the suspension of the Government of Northern Ireland and the introduction of direct rule from London. For a discussion of these arrangements of executive devolution, see Bradley & Ewing, *Constitutional and Administrative Law* (12th ed., Longman, 1997), Chap. 3.

[15] For the classical account, see Wheare, *Federal Government* (4th ed., 1963). For a comparative study, see McWhinney, *Comparative Federalism* (1965).

equal", which is generally the threshold for a constitution to be considered "federal".[16] Even so, "federalism" comes in many forms and is often a matter of degree.[17] There can be little doubt that the devolution arrangements, at least in relation to Scotland and Northern Ireland, will entail some of the constitutional problems, such as inter-governmental disputes about allocation of powers, faced by federal systems elsewhere.[18]

Sources of the U.K. Constitution

4.05 It follows from the absence of a "written" constitution in the United Kingdom that many of the legal principles which may be characterised as reflecting constitutional values are not prescribed in a codified form. Rather, in Dicey's classical observation, "the constitution is the result of the ordinary law of the land".[19] Sir Stephen Sedley has neatly captured the position as follows: "British constitutional questions are answered not from a prior consensus of principle, written or unwritten, but by a body of descriptive law which functions by collapsing what ought to be into what is".[20] Although much of the U.K.'s constitutional law is contained in statutes,[21] it is often the common law which provides the values of the constitution—for example, many of the values, presumptions and principles concerning the protection of human rights.[22] Significantly, much of the U.K.'s constitution is contained in constitutional conventions. These identify many of the constitution's values which have been built up over time, such as the separation of powers and the democratic need for ministerial accountability to Parliament. Many constitutional conventions reflect the commitments and practices of the political system while others concern the relationship between the political system and the legal system.[23] The details of constitutional

---

[16] The U.K. Parliament remains the supreme law maker throughout the U.K. notwithstanding the provisions in the legislation establishing the Scottish and Northern Irish Parliaments and the Welsh Assembly: see, for example, s. 28(7) of the Scotland Act 1998.

[17] For a useful discussion of the degrees of federalism (especially in relation to the nature of the E.U.), see Barendt, *Introduction to Constitutional Law* (Clarendon Press, Oxford, 1998), Chap. 4.

[18] The issues which arise for judicial review in relation to the allocation of powers between the U.K. and Scottish Parliaments are discussed further in Chap. 7.

[19] A.V. Dicey, *Introduction to the Law of the Constitution* (10th ed., 1959, edited by E.C.S. Wade), at p. 203 (hereafter referred to as Dicey, *Law of the Constitution*).

[20] Sir Stephen Sedley, "The Sound of Silence: Constitutional Law without a Constitution" (1994) 110 L.Q.R. 270, at 273.

[21] For example, the Representation of the People Acts; the European Communities Act 1972; the Human Rights Act 1998; and the Scotland Act 1998.

[22] The main catalogue of human rights in the U.K. is now contained in the Human Rights Act 1998 which, subject to its terms, guarantees the human rights provided in the European Convention on Human Rights in U.K. law: see further, Chaps 6 and 16. For an example of the common law protecting human rights, see *Derbyshire County Council v. Times Newspapers Ltd* [1993] A.C. 534; and also *Singh, Petr*, 1988 G.W.D. 32–1377. For a discussion of the role of the common law in protecting human rights, see Allan, "Constitutional Rights and Common Law" (1991) 11 O.J.L.S. 453; and more generally the same author's *Law, Liberty, and Justice: The Foundations of British Constitutionalism* (Clarendon, Oxford, 1993), Chap. 6. In particular, it must be noted that the common law presumptions applicable in statutory interpretation are significant in protecting human rights: *cf.* Hunt, *Using Human Rights Law in English Courts* (Hart Publishing, Oxford, 1997).

[23] For example, relating to the appointment of judges, on which see para. 4.24 *et seq*. It is often thought that the British constitution is alone in having constitutional conventions

conventions may change, but the implications of their fundamental values, such as respect for democracy, remain firm.[24]

Conventions

The fact that so many of the British constitution's values are in practice **4.06** expressed in constitutional conventions has been a source of some difficulty for many constitutional lawyers.[25] Beginning with Dicey's conclusion that conventions "are not in reality laws at all since they are not enforced by the courts",[26] several commentators have stressed the political, non-justiciable nature of conventions.[27] Certainly, it can be accepted that, while not always inconceivable,[28] breaches of constitutional conventions will rarely be amenable to judicial review. Since they mostly concern the functioning of the political constitution—for example, relations between the Monarch, the Cabinet, civil servants and Parliament—it is difficult to imagine the circumstances in which the courts could be approached by an individual with standing seeking to complain about breach of a convention. The nature of constitutional litigation and the remedies available from a court, even a constitutional court, are rarely suitable to remedy breaches of political morality.[29] If there are difficulties for the courts in dealing with more or less legal subjects with political aspects, the difficulties would be greater in dealing with policies or political subjects which have some legal aspects.[30]

---

and that they are a unique feature of "unwritten" constitutional arrangements. It is true that some "written" constitutional orders, such as Germany and the E.U., do not rely heavily if at all on constitutional conventions. But many constitutional systems have conventions variously describing institutional customs, for example, governing relations between the legislature and executive or between the political and legal systems. In the U.S., for example, there are constitutional rules and practices in addition to the law contained in and built upon the constitution: see Foley, *The Silence of Constitutions* (Routledge, 1989); and Sedley, *supra*, n. 20 at pp. 273–274. Undoubtedly, however, the British constitution's reliance on conventions is greater than most.

[24] For a comprehensive discussion of the content and nature of constitutional conventions, see Marshall, *Constitutional Conventions* (Clarendon Press, Oxford, 1984). See also Bradley and Ewing, *Constitutional and Administrative Law*, pp. 20–31; and Munro, *Studies in Constitutional Law* (Butterworths, London, 1987).

[25] In particular, see Bentley, [1963] P.L. 401: ". . . the constitution is what happens" (at p. 402). See also Jennings, *The Law and the Constitution* (5th ed., 1959), at pp. 130 *et seq.*; and Mitchell, *Constitutional Law* (2nd ed., 1968), pp. 34–38. Beyond attempts to define the meaning and effects of recognised conventions of the constitution, a further problem is defining exactly what is meant by the term "convention": see Jaconelli, "The nature of constitutional convention" (1999) 19 L.S. 24.

[26] Dicey, *The Law of the Constitution*, p. 24. But see also his later comments at pp. 450–451: "The breach, therefore, of a purely conventional rule . . . ultimately entails upon those who break it in direct conflict with the undoubted law of the land".

[27] See Munro, "Laws and Conventions Distinguished" (1975) 91 L.Q.R. 218. *cf.* Allan, *Law, Liberty, and Justice* at pp. 238–240.

[28] *cf. Reference Re Amendment of the Constitution of Canada (Nos 1, 2 and 3)* [1981] 1 S.C.R. 753 (the *Patriation Reference*), esp. at 845; see also *Reference Re Manitoba Language Rights* [1985] 1 S.C.R. 721 at 752; and *Reference Re Secession of Quebec* [1998] 2 S.C.R. 217. In Australia, *cf. Nationwide News Ltd v. Wills* (1992) 177 C.L.R. 1, esp. *per* Brennan J. at 47.

[29] In Canada, where constitutional conventions have come before the courts on several occasions, it is the existence of the Supreme Court's reference jurisdiction which has generally allowed the issues to be litigated.

[30] The House of Lords decision in *Chandler v. DPP* [1964] A.C. 763 stands as a leading example of the difficulties posed for the courts in cases raising that most political of subjects, namely what is "in the interests of the state". Only Lord Devlin's speech in the case (at 811) demonstrates a willingness to supervise the validity of a ministerial assertion

Constitutional conventions are, however, relevant in litigation and particularly in judicial review.[31] Since the conventions often articulate the values of the constitution, such as the democratic value of ministerial responsibility to Parliament, the courts must draw on the conventions when deciding a case before them—for example, when interpreting a statute or understanding judicial dicta that only make sense in light of the constitutional conventions. An example is provided by *Adair v. Hill*,[32] where the Lord Justice-Clerk (Cooper) relied on the conventions surrounding the Lord Advocate's prosecutorial role to interpret an ambiguous statutory provision. In a case such as this, it is difficult to say conclusively that the relevant convention is not being "enforced" by the court.[33] Accordingly, although constitutional conventions may not be directly enforceable since they deal largely with non-justiciable subjects, it cannot be said that they are irrelevant in the courts. They may be drawn on in judicial review cases to view the constitutional background against which legislation must be construed and government action reviewed. To this limited extent, they are "enforceable". As the Supreme Court of Canada observed in the *Patriation Reference*: "The main purpose of constitutional conventions is to ensure that the legal frame-work of the Constitution will be operated in accordance with the prevailing constitutional values or principles of the period".[34] The Supreme Court added that on occasion "underlying constitutional principles" may have "full legal force".[35] Indeed, the conclusion that they can never do so amounts to "an impoverished sort of legal theory" about a constitution.[36] In this regard, it is likely that the development of "concordats" governing the relationship between the Scottish Executive and the U.K. government will be significant. Apart from the question of the extent, if any, to which concordats or anything done under them may be subject to judicial review, the courts are likely to refer to the concordats in order to understand the context and practice of Scottish devolution.[37]

Constitutionalism

4.07   The principle of constitutionalism brings together all of the concepts and ideals of a system of government limited by superior legal norms which have the dignity of human beings and the interests of society at their

---

of "interests of the state" or national security. Interestingly, in the *GCHQ* case [1985] A.C. 374, Lord Diplock considered Lord Devlin's speech in *Chandler* "difficult" (at 408) and Lord Roskill considered it "out of line" with the other speeches (at 421); but *cf.* Lord Scarman at 406, considering Lord Devlin's speech "sound law".

[31] One clear example of the relevance of conventions in litigation is *Att.-Gen. v. Jonathan Cape Ltd* [1976] Q.B. 752 (convention of Cabinet collective responsibility may be drawn on by the court to allow action for tort of breach of confidence the purpose of which was to preserve the secrecy of Cabinet deliberations). *Cf. R. v. H.M. Treasury, ex p. Smedley* [1985] Q.B. 657, per Donaldson M.R. at 666 (independence of judiciary from Parliament a "convention of the highest importance").

[32] 1943 J.C. 9.

[33] For further discussion of the extent to which conventions are "enforceable". albeit not directly at the instance of a private individual, see Mitchell, *Constitutional Law*, at pp. 38–39.

[34] [1981] 1 S.C.R. 753 at 845.

[35] *ibid*. See also *Reference Re Remuneration of Judges of the Provincial Court of PEI* [1997] 3 S.C.R. 3.

[36] Allan, *Law, Liberty, and Justice*, at p. 240.

[37] See para. 7.46.

core and with which all government action must comply. In a recent decision, the Supreme Court of Canada expressed the essential features of constitutionalism as being the rule of law, democracy, respect for human rights and a system of government kept within its limits by an independent judicial power, the decisions of which are binding.[38] Although constitutionalism and the rule of law are very close, the Supreme Court stressed that they should be distinguished:

> "The constitutionalism principle bears considerable similarity to the rule of law, although they are not identical . . . Simply put, the constitutionalism principle requires that all government action comply with the Constitution. The rule of law principle requires that all government action must comply with the law, including the Constitution".[39]

It might be said that constitutionalism requires a codified constitution. But this approach places too much emphasis on the nature of constitutional arrangements rather than the essential purposes of constitutional values.[40] In the United Kingdom, it is clear that both constitutionalism and the rule of law operate together to secure limited government conducted according to law. There is a body of values and principles against which all government action is measured for conformity with the constitution in addition to the requirement that all government action be justified by reference to the law.[41] For example, the courts ensure that the exercise of discretionary powers respects both human rights and the separation of powers.[42] The problems associated with placing emphasis on constitutionalism in the United Kingdom are derived from the received wisdom about the supremacy of the U.K. Parliament and the relationship between this supremacy and the constitution's commitment to the rule of law. While the implications of the supremacy of Parliament are attributed to Dicey, the richness of his analysis of the U.K. constitution has to be seen in the emphasis it places on the rule of law. In other words, the supremacy of Parliament is only one aspect of the Diceyan inheritance. In recent times several commentators have stressed a "different Dicey", namely: "The constitutional theorist struggling to escape the shackles of the Hobbesian authoritarianism he learned from Austin".[43] It is often forgotten that Dicey regarded the supremacy of

---

[38] *Reference Re Secession of Quebec* [1998] 2 S.C.R. 217. On the independence of the judiciary, see also *Reference Re Remuneration of Judges of the Provincial Court of PEI* [1997] 3 S.C.R. 3.

[39] [1998] S.C.R. 217 at 258.

[40] See generally, Allan, *Law, Liberty, and Justice*, esp. Chap. 1; and Alexander (ed.), *Constitutionalism* (1998).

[41] The House of Lords decision in *CCSU v. Minister for the Civil Service* [1985] A.C. 373 (*GCHQ* case) confirms that in general all governmental powers, whether deriving from statute or the prerogative, are subject to judicial review. It is not the nature of the power but the subject-matter of the decision which determines the extent to which it is reviewable.

[42] On human rights, see Laws, "Law and Democracy" [1995] P.L. 72; and Sedley, "Human Rights: A Twenty-First Century Agenda" [1997] P.L. 386. On separation of powers, consider *R. v. Secretary of State for the Home Department, ex p. Fire Brigades Unions* [1995] 2 A.C. 583.

[43] Allan, *Law, Liberty, and Justice*, at p. 2. See also Craig, "Formal and Substantive Conceptions of the Rule of Law: an Analytical Framework" [1997] P.L. 467; and Allan, "The Rule of Law as the Rule of Reason: Consent and Constitutionalism" (1999) 115 L.Q.R. 221.

Parliament and the rule of law as co-equal principles of the constitution. Given that Dicey's formulation of the rule of law entails much more than mere "rule by law", it is appropriate to affirm that constitutionalism has a sure foundation in the British constitutional arrangements.

Democracy

4.08 The exercise of political power in the United Kingdom, all its constituent parts, and all local governments, is based on respect for democracy.[44] Although democracy can come in many forms, some of which do not bear a close resemblance to the concept's essential idea, in the United Kingdom's political system democracy means regular popular elections to a legislative assembly from which the leading officers of the administration are chosen on the basis of their ability to command the confidence of a majority of the assembly to which they are accountable for their actions and decisions. In the United Kingdom, the assembly is Parliament, principally the House of Commons, and the administration is the U.K. government; in Scotland, the assembly is the Scottish Parliament and the administration the Scottish Executive; and in local government, the assembly will classically be the whole council, part of which will be the administration. The law makes provision for democracy at all the levels of government, extensive provision in the case of the Scottish Parliament and local councils and, perhaps curiously, somewhat less provision in relation to the U.K. Parliament, where law and convention interact to secure democracy and accountability. The courts have an important role in ensuring that the arrangements which the U.K. Parliament has made in relation to democracy throughout the United Kingdom are strictly observed, although it must be conceded that their role diminishes as matters move closer to the U.K. government and closer to the substance of democracy at that level. So, for example, the courts are involved in relation to the proper conduct of elections, including elections to the U.K. Parliament[45]; but they are not involved in ensuring the accountability of Cabinet ministers to Parliament. The latter is ultimately for Parliament to ensure.[46] In turn, the important role

---

[44] See Judge Edward, "Community Law: Integration and Diversity" (1986) 31 J.L.S.S. 51, describing the U.K. as a monarchy and a democracy with limited powers. Although the courts in this country have not frequently been called on to articulate the values of democracy, it is likely that the guarantee in U.K. law of Convention rights will require some attempts at identifying the essential values of a democratic society. See para. 16.08.

[45] See, for example, *Grieve v. Douglas-Home*, 1965 S.C. 315. Complaints about U.K. and Scottish Parliamentary elections are made to the Elections Court (in Scotland, consisting of two Court of Session judges) under Pt III of the Representation of the People Act 1983 (which is applied to the Scottish Parliament by virtue of s. 12(5) of the Scotland Act 1998). See also *Walker v. UNISON*, 1995 S.L.T. 1226; *DPP v. Luft* [1977] A.C. 962; and *cf. Wilson v. IBA*, 1979 S.C. 351.

[46] Under some constitutions the courts are more extensively involved in ensuring the accountability of government to the legislature. In the U.S., for example, the U.S. Supreme Court decision in *U.S. v. Nixon* 418 U.S. 683 (1974) requiring the errant President, in the interests of the "rule of law", to surrender all the relevant tapes to the Congressional committees investigating the Watergate affair, shows that the courts there can become involved in ensuring that the executive answers to the legislative branch for its misdeeds. It may be left an open question whether the courts here would underwrite relevant constitutional conventions on ministerial accountability in light of evidence of criminal acts by a government minister or ministers. In this regard, the controversy surrounding the Matrix-Churchill affair should be considered: see the Scott Report (H.C. 115 1995–96), discussed at [1996] P.L. 357–507. In any event, in the absence of a doctrine of separation

which Parliament has in securing the accountability of government must be respected by the courts when exercising the power of judicial review. In a democracy, Parliament and not the courts is the proper place for challenges to government policies on the ground of their political wisdom.[47]

The Supremacy of Parliament

Articulating the substantive values and standards which the rule of law **4.09** requires is made controversial in the United Kingdom by some assertions concerning the supremacy of Parliament.[48] However, both the rule of law and judicial review derive great benefit from the supremacy of Parliament. In an important respect, Parliament's supremacy means that there can be no conceptual problem about the courts supervising statutory bodies to ensure that they act in accordance with the powers which Parliament has conferred. Parliament's law is the highest law[49]; no "inferior judicatory" can act contrary to it.[50] But if the supremacy of Parliament means that an Act of Parliament is supreme in the sense that it demands subservience of the judges, who have no constitutional role beyond reflexively applying the statute, the rule of law would have a somewhat tenuous meaning. A government with a compliant majority in the House of Commons would be able to equip itself with any powers to do what it wished. Yet whatever may be the theoretical capacity of Parliament to enact anything it desires, the constitutional values which give meaning to the rule of law restrain Parliament's theoretical supremacy. The legal system's fundamental constitutional values mean that Parliament is not in practice supreme in an absolute sense. Instead, the U.K. constitution has: "a bi-polar sovereignty of the Crown in Parliament and the Crown in its courts, to each of which the Crown's ministers are answerable—politically to Parliament, legally to the courts".[51]

Separation of Powers

The doctrine of separation of powers is a prerequisite for a constitution **4.10** establishing a system of limited government.[52] The doctrine is seen in its classical form in the U.S. constitution, under which the federal govern-

---

of powers comparable with that under the US Constitution, and given that Parliament is also a court, it may be assumed that Parliament is in a better position to exercise both judicial and political powers over a minister accused of criminal acts.

[47] cf. *City of Edinburgh D.C. v. Secretary of State for Scotland*, 1985 S.L.T. 551; *Notts C.C. v. Secretary of State for the Environment* [1986] A.C. 240; *R. v. Secretary of State for the Environment, ex p. Hammersmith LBC* [1991] A.C. 521; and *R. v. Cambridge Health Authority, ex p. B* [1995] 2 All E.R. 129. See also *South Australia v. O'Shea* (1987) 163 C.L.R. 378, esp. *per* Mason C.J. at 388–389. But if the challenge is to the legality of a policy—for example, whether it has been applied lawfully to an individual case or whether it amounts to a fetter of discretion—the courts will review the lawfulness of the policy: see, for example, *R. v. Secretary of State for Defence, ex p. Smith* [1996] Q.B. 517.

[48] The implications of the supremacy of Parliament are discussed in part V of this chapter.

[49] See further Part VI below.

[50] But difficulty may arise with regard to some of the grounds of judicial review which the courts have developed, not to mention problems associated with the basis of judicial review of non-statutory powers and bodies. See further para. 4.16.

[51] Sedley, "Human Rights: a Twenty-First Century Agenda" [1995] P.L. 386 at 389.

[52] For a discussion of the importance of separation of powers for limited government, see Vile, *Constitutionalism and the Separation of Powers* (1967). *Cf.* Marshall, *Constitutional Theory* (1971), Chap. 5. For more recent discussion see Barendt, "Separation of Powers

ment's powers are expressly separated into legislative, executive and judicial compartments.[53] The U.S. constitution is not, however, the touchstone against which the existence of separation of powers in other systems is to be judged. Rather, a proper understanding of the purpose of separation of powers must be reached so that neither its unqualified presence nor its compromise in a constitution is exaggerated.[54] The main purpose of separation of powers is to prevent the fusion of government power in the same hands, so that the same part of government is not responsible for making the law, enforcing it and determining what its limits are. Such a development has long been recognised as leading to uncontrolled, arbitrary power and tyranny.[55] In light of the purpose of separation of powers, it may be said that the U.K. constitution does display a commitment to its ideals.[56]

The problem is that the institutions of the U.K. constitution allow for an overlap of personnel and powers. This is apparent from the ubiquity of the term "Crown" in the British constitution, with the Queen standing at the apex of all three branches of government. Likewise, the personnel of government often exercise more than one type of power, notably the Lord Chancellor who exercises all three.[57] But neither the terminology nor the personnel of the constitution should hide its acceptance of separation of powers in so far as the doctrine requires limited government. First, the U.K. constitution strongly affirms the separation of powers between the executive and the judiciary.[58] This separation is

---

and Constitutional Government" [1995] P.L. 599; and Allan, "Fairness, Equality, Rationality: Constitutional Theory and Judicial Review", in Forsyth and Hare (eds), *The Golden Metwand and the Crooked Cord* (OUP, Oxford, 1998), pp. 15, 22. On the interplay between legislative and executive power see *R. v. Secretary of State for the Home Department, ex p. Fire Brigades Union* [1995] 2 A.C. 513, and between executive and judicial power see *R. v. Secretary of State for the Home Department, ex p. Venables* [1997] 3 W.L.R. 23.

[53] On separation of powers in the U.S., see Gunther, *Constitutional Law* (12th ed., Foundation Press, New York, 1991), Chap. 6. Even in the U.S., however, the development of the modern state has placed the constitutional separation of powers under some strain, notably through the development of federal regulatory agencies that exercise legislative and judicial powers: see Strauss, "The Place of Agencies in Government: Separation of Powers and the Fourth Branch" (1984) 84 Columbia L.R. 573. For a broader comparison of constitutional values in the U.S. and in the U.K., see Craig, *Public Law and Democracy in the UK and the USA* (Clarendon Press, Oxford, 1991).

[54] *cf.* Mitchell, *Constitutional Law* (2nd ed., W. Green/SULI, Edinburgh, 1968), pp. 40–50. See also Allan, *Law, Liberty and Justice*, Chap. 3.

[55] See Locke, *Second Treatise of Civil Government*, Chap. XII, para. 143 (quoted in Bradley and Ewing, *Constitutional and Administrative Law* at p. 89); Montesquieu, *De l'Esprit des Lois*, Book XI, Chap. 6 (also quoted in Bradley and Ewing, at p. 90). See also Madison in *The Federalist*, No. XLVII.

[56] *cf.* Sedley, "The Sound of Silence: Constitutional Law without a Constitution" (1994) 110 L.Q.R. 270; and Allan, *Law, Liberty, and Justice*, Chap. 3. See also Lord Nolan & Sedley, *The Making and Remaking of the British Constitution* (Blackstone Press, London, 1997), pp. 58–65.

[57] But following a recent decision of the European Commission on Human Rights, there has been speculation that the Lord Chancellor's judicial functions may be inconsistent with Art. 6 of the European Convention: see *McGonnell v. U.K.*, App. No. 29488/95, Decision of 20/10/95.

[58] See *Hinds v. The Queen* [1977] A.C. 195, *per* Lord Diplock at 212; *Dupont Steels Ltd v. Sirs* [1980] 1 W.L.R. 142, *per* Lord Diplock at 157; *R. v. Secretary of State for the Home Department, ex p. Venables & Thomson* [1997] 3 W.L.R. 23, *per* Lord Steyn at 74. But consider s. 10 of the Human Rights Act 1998: the power to enact a Ministerial Order to remedy an incompatibility between legislation and Convention rights found by a court is accompanied by a discretion to give the order retrospective effect. The ministerial decision

essential for the independence of the judiciary. Secondly, in relation to legislative and executive powers in the United Kingdom, it is also clear that there is a separation of powers.[59] In a case deciding that the executive could not lawfully use its prerogative powers to legislate in an area covered by an Act of Parliament which the executive had decided in the exercise of its statutory discretion not to bring into force, Lord Mustill observed: "[It] is a feature of the peculiarly British conception of the separation of powers that Parliament, the executive and the courts each have their distinct and largely exclusive domain".[60] Accordingly, the visible fusion of the legislative and executive arms of government must be distinguished from the exercise of legislative and executive powers. Although the executive, more correctly the Queen in Council, possesses both primary and secondary legislative powers under the prerogative, and although ministers possess extensive powers to make delegated legislation, only the Queen in Parliament is the supreme legislature.[61] Only the Queen in Parliament has the power to enact and repeal Acts of Parliament.[62] In so far as some of the personnel of the legislature and executive coincide, the explanation is historical, namely that democracy and accountability of government to the people evolved from the historical relationships between Monarch, ministry and Parliament. As a parliamentary democracy the experience in the United Kingdom of overlapping legislative and executive bodies is shared with many other constitutional democracies.[63] As for the overlap of judicial and legislative power in the House of Lords, this is also explicable on historical grounds, Parliament always having been the High Court of Parliament. Although the judicial work of the House of Lords has been demonstrably independent from the House as legislature for more than a century, the question has recently arisen whether it is still appropriate.

It should also be noted that courts throughout the United Kingdom have looked to ideas of separation of powers in seeking to define their supervision of certain government powers, albeit with mixed results.[64] The old distinction between judicial and administrative powers for the purposes of the scope of judicial review can be understood by reference to the constitutional value of respecting the separation of powers. But the fact that the distinction between judicial and administrative powers operated to frustrate judicial supervision of expanding administrative powers shows that the separation of powers is not an end in itself but only one means to the end of limited government subject to the rule of

---

to give (or not to give) a s. 10 order such effect arguably amounts to an adjudication of the rights of the parties to the case in which the declaration of incompatibility was obtained under s. 4 of the Act (one or other of whom will ultimately win or lose according to whether or not a s. 10 order is given retrospective effect).

[59] *R. v. Secretary of State for the Home Department, ex p. Fire Brigades Union* [1995] 2 A.C. 513.

[60] *ibid*. at 567. The decision in *ex parte Fire Brigades Union* may be compared with the recent decision of the U.S. Supreme Court in *Clinton v. City of New York*, 118 S. Ct. 2091 (1998): in this case, the Supreme Court decided that the power granted to the President by Congress in the Line Item Veto Act 1996 allowing him unilaterally to repeal a law (or provision thereof) enacted by Congress violated the Presentment clause of the Constitution (Art. I, s. 7, cl. 2). See also *Loving v. U.S.*, 517 U.S. 748 (1996), esp. at 758.

[61] See *Bowles v. Bank of England* [1913] 1 Ch. 57.

[62] But Parliament may expressly confer power on the executive to make delegated legislation to the same extent as primary legislation. The leading example is the "Henry VIII" clause, which allows a minister to modify primary legislation by delegated legislation.

[63] For example, Germany, the Netherlands and Italy.

[64] See paras 8.20 *et seq*.

law. Indeed, the need to assert judicial supervision over all government powers, whether judicial, executive or legislative, required that the judicial/quasi-judicial/administrative distinctions of former times be abandoned as threshold criteria for judicial review.[65] The idea of the separation of powers has also operated by way of a conscious restraint on the part of the courts on the extent of their exercise of the supervisory power. Matters which are properly for the makers of policy, or which require the making of decisions of a political nature, will, at least as regards their substance, be recognised as outwith the competence of the court in judicial review.[66]

Respect for human rights

4.11 The protection of human rights is an integral part of the U.K.'s constitutional arrangements. In this regard, presumptions applicable in statutory interpretation have played a leading role. The most notable presumption is to the effect that all ambiguous statutory provisions are to be interpreted consistently with the UK's international obligations, in particular, those contained in international treaties protecting human rights.[67] More generally, however, the courts presume that Parliament does not intend to interfere with the citizen's rights unless it says so expressly. Accordingly, open-textured statutory provisions which confer wide discretionary powers are interpreted as not allowing interference with the citizen's rights beyond what is strictly necessary to give effect to the power. As Lord Browne-Wilkinson said in *R. v. Secretary of State for the Home Department, ex parte Pierson*[68]: "A power conferred by Parliament in general terms is not to be taken to authorise the doing of acts by the donee of the power which adversely affect the legal rights of the citizen or the basic principles on which the law of the UK is based unless the statute conferring the power makes it clear that such was the intention of Parliament".[69]

But none of this is to say that the law has always fulfilled the constitution's premises or anything like ideally protected human rights. While there are examples of the protection of human rights by the common law,[70] there are also examples of failures.[71] It is tempting to blame the supremacy of Parliament or the absence of a bill of rights for the problems but this is only part of the historical picture. Even in systems with bills of rights, the constitutional protection of human rights has low points as well as high points.[72] At all times a range of complex social and political factors affect human rights protection in every domestic legal system and these obviously bear on national legislatures and judiciaries. This fact alone is enough to justify the importance of

---

[65] See *Ridge v. Baldwin* [1964] A.C. 40. The matter is considered later in para. 8.21.
[66] See para. 9.19.
[67] See further, para. 6.10.
[68] [1998] A.C. 539.
[69] *ibid.* at 575. See also the speech of Lord Steyn.
[70] See, for example, *Derbyshire CC v. Times Newspapers Ltd* [1993] A.C. 534.
[71] A notable example of a failure is the House of Lords decision in *Liversidge v. Anderson* [1942] A.C. 206. But see the dissent of Lord Atkin and its subsequent vindication in *R. v. Inland Revenue Commissioners, ex p. Rossminster* [1980] A.C. 952, *per* Lord Diplock at 1011.
[72] Consider, for example, *Plessy v. Ferguson* 163 U.S. 537 (1896) compared with *Brown v. Board of Education* 347 U.S. 483 (1954). See also *Korematsu v. U.S.* 323 U.S. 214 (1944); and in Canada, under the 1961 Federal Bill of Rights, see *Bliss v. Att.-Gen. of Canada* [1979] 1 S.C.R. 183.

international supervision of human rights standards by international bodies.

Fundamental human rights are now guaranteed in U.K. law by the Human Rights Act 1998, which gives jurisdiction to the national courts with regard to the human rights guaranteed by the European Convention on Human Rights. This Act and the case law under it is likely to have very considerable importance in U.K. constitutional law. The importance and detail of the protection of human rights in terms of the 1998 Act justifies special treatment and this is given in subsequent chapters.[73] For present purposes, it is enough to note that the common law principles relating to human rights, notably the presumption that all ambiguous legislation be interpreted to be consistent with international human rights treaties, continue to be significant. It should also be noted in this context that many human rights are guaranteed in other legislation, notably the anti-discrimination legislation, and, significantly, by virtue of E.C. law.[74]

Judicial review and constitutional values

To a great extent, of course, every part of the present book is concerned with the judicial recognition, implementation and enforcement of the values of the constitution. The nature of the British constitutional arrangements gives judicial review of government powers a sense of being "the constitution in action".[75] Indeed, a recent discussion of developments in German administrative law can also describe the close relationship between constitutional values and judicial review in the United Kingdom: "The truth is that [leading principles of] German administrative law . . . [are] largely a product of recent impulses coming from constitutional law.[76] In the United Kingdom, the expansion of judicial review has been justified both by the rule of law and constitutionalism requiring the courts to make up for a perceived failure of the political process in making government accountable and also by the need to protect human rights from increasing encroachment by public power. The constitutional dimension of judicial review and its being a practical application of constitutional values has been noted by several judges both in court and extrajudicially. In a real sense, therefore, judicial review is constitutional values in practice.[77]

4.12

The question then arises about the nature of the role which the courts have in breathing life into the constitution's values. The answer according to past experience has been a varied one, progress being gradual,

---

[73] See Chaps 6 and 16.

[74] On human rights in E.C. law, see further para. 5.44.

[75] See an early description of German administrative law: "Verfassungsrecht vergeht, Verwaltungsrecht besteht" (constitutional law changes, administrative law remains), in Mayer, *Deutsches Verwaltungsrecht* (3rd. ed., Duncker & Humblot, Munich, 1924), Vol. 1 quoted by Nolte, "General Principles of German and European Administrative Law—A Comparison in Historical Perspective" (1994) 57 M.L.R. 190 at 198.

[76] Nolte, "General Principles of German and European Administrative Law—A Comparison in Historical Perspective" (1994) 57 M.L.R. 191 at 198. The article discusses the influence that leading principles of German administrative law, such as proportionality, legitimate expectation and equality, have had on E.C. law. It may be added that their influence has been greater still, coming into the grounds of judicial review in the U.K. itself.

[77] *cf.* Wade and Forsyth, *Administrative Law* (7th ed., OUP, Oxford, 1994), p. 24: "The British Constitution is founded on the rule of law, and administrative law is the area where this principle is to be seen in its most active operation".

cautious and by degree, characteristics which reflect both the nature of constitutional litigation everywhere and the common law nature of the U.K. constitution. On occasion the courts may assert the values of the constitution only to be countered by Parliament's intervention. The decision of the House of Lords in *Burmah Oil v. Lord Advocate*[78] stands as an example of constitutional values being recognised, applied and enforced by the courts,[79] in favour of a pursuer whose property had been destroyed by the exercise of public power in the public interest. But the decision was immediately evacuated by the enacting of retrospective legislation by Parliament on the utilitarian ground of protecting the public purse from possibly numerous claims for compensation. On the other hand, the first *Factortame* decision of the House of Lords,[80] deciding that injunctions were not available against a Minister of the Crown, because he enjoyed all the Crown's privileges and immunities, appeared to give the highest judicial approval to the erroneous nineteenth century fusion of the Crown and its officers, thereby ignoring the much older commitment to making the Crown's subordinates answerable in the courts for their unlawful actions.[81] The decision may be seen as a danger for the rule of law in so far as it raises the whole edifice of central government above the law of remedies.[82] But the case is undoubtedly complicated by the fact that it was the first time a U.K. court had faced an express contradiction of a fundamental principle of E.C. law by a provision in an Act of Parliament. The decision shows how difficult it is for a court to resolve a fundamental clash of constitutional norms—the supremacy of E.C. law and the supreme law-making power of Parliament—which neither society nor politicians have themselves clearly reconciled. This is equally difficult for a court guided by a constitutional charter, as the U.S. Supreme Court, the Canadian Supreme Court and the German Constitutional Court have found with the right to abortion.[83] In cases involving the most difficult constitutional choices, the risk is that the constitution's principles and values themselves become objects of contention, and the correct solution may be the harder to find.

Particular cases may often be resolved without the necessity to determine hard constitutional questions. The decision may be reached by reference to rules of standing, or of competency, or by reference to what the grounds of judicial review actually require in a particular case. One approach is the prospective articulation of the constitution's principles. In the *GCHQ* case,[84] for example, the House of Lords had an oppor-

---

[78] 1964 S.C. (H.L.) 117.

[79] More exactly by the House of Lords; the pursuer, Burmah Oil, in common with Mrs Donoghue, found the Court of Session less encouraging.

[80] *R. v. Secretary of State for Transport ex p. Factortame* [1990] 2 A.C. 65. For trenchant criticism, see Wade, "The Crown–Old Platitudes and New Heresies" (1992) New L.J. 1275 and 1315. The significance of the *Factortame* litigation and E.C. law generally in judicial review is discussed in Chap. 5.

[81] The first *Factortame* decision was explained in *M. v. Home Office* [1994] 1 A.C. 377 as not standing for approving the erroneous confusion of Crown with its officers. In *M*, the older tradition was reaffirmed. The Crown is discussed further in part VI of this chapter; and the availability of injunctions and interdicts against the Crown is discussed in para. 23.36.

[82] But see *M v. Home Office* [1994] 1 A.C. 377. For discussion of this important decision, see Sedley, "The Crown in its own Courts", in Forsyth and Hare (eds), *The Golden Metwand and the Crooked Cord* (OUP, Oxford, 1998).

[83] *cf. Roe v. Wade*, 410 U.S. 113 (1973); *Morgentaler v. The Queen* [1988] 1 S.C.R. 30; and *BVerfG*, 928.5.1993, *BVerfG.E*, 88, 203.

[84] *Council for Civil Service Unions v. Minister for the Civil Service* [1985] A.C. 374.

tunity to decide whether acts and decisions taken in pursuance of prerogative powers were amenable to judicial review to the same extent as those taken under statutory powers—a proposition which several lower court decisions had recently asserted and at which the law had been hinting for some time.[85] On the facts of the case, the House of Lords decided that the relevant decision was not reviewable because its substance concerned national security; but in extensive *obiter dicta* all the speeches made clear that as a matter of constitutional law, all government powers are subject to judicial review irrespective of their provenance.[86] Guidance is thus given for the future on what the rule of law expects and how the constitutional principles should be applied.

III THE RULE OF LAW AND JUDICIAL REVIEW

The Concept of the Rule of Law

The rule of law is the rock upon which constitutional government is **4.13** founded and the *sine qua non* of limited government. A legal system which does not subscribe to the rule of law cannot have an effective system of judicial supervision of government. As noted above, it may be said that the rule of law is the essential foundation of judicial review. But beyond these broad statements, what the rule of law means is the subject of a perennial debate.[87] At a minimum level, the rule of law is equated with the concept of Rechtsstaat, which in its attenuated form requires only that some form of legal authority exist for government actions.[88] At the broadest level, the rule of law incorporates a commitment to a vision of social justice.[89] In this sense, the rule of law tolerates only laws which are "good", in the sense of being in accordance with the commitment to social justice. It follows from these various meanings of the rule of law that the concept means different things to different people. Its meaning is rendered more subjective by depending on historical, political and cultural factors. As such, it is an unpredictable and sometimes unstable concept which poses great difficulty as a constitutional value. The problem is to avoid the rule of law meaning only the discredited minimum of a Rechtsstaat—that is, requiring only a showing of simple formal legality for government actions (something which many of the worst twentieth century regimes could satisfy), while at the same time avoiding the rule of law becoming a fully fledged political, social and economic philosophy.[90] This difficulty means that it is not possible to provide a universal definition of the rule of law.

---

[85] See *R. v. Criminal Injuries Compensation Board, ex p. Lain* [1967] 2 Q.B. 864; and *Laker Airways Ltd v. Department of Trade* [1977] Q.B. 643.

[86] The *GCHQ* case is discussed further in part III of this chapter in the context of judicial review of executive powers.

[87] For a recent exchange, see Craig, "Formal and Substantive Conceptions of the Rule of Law: An Analytical Framework" [1997] P.L. 467; and Allan, "The Rule of Law as the Rule of Reason: Consent and Constitutionalism" (1999) 115 L.Q.R. 221.

[88] See the discussion in Brewer-Carias: *Judicial Review in Comparative Law* (Cambridge UP, 1989), at pp. 7–85. The concept of Rechtsstaat became discredited because the Nazi regime was a Rechtsstaat according to the older, attenuated meaning of the term. But as Brewer-Carias demonstrates, the modern ideal of Rechtsstaat is richer, being imbued with the need for law to respect normative values such as fundamental human rights.

[89] For the leading (and different) approaches, see Hayek, *The Constitution of Liberty* (1960); Fuller, *The Morality of Law* (2nd ed., 1969); Dworkin, *Taking Rights Seriously* (Harvard UP, Cambridge MA, 1977); and *Law's Empire* (1986). For analysis and criticism of these approaches, see Loughlin, *Public Law and Political Theory*.

[90] See Raz, "The Rule of Law and its Virtue" (1977) 93 L.Q.R. 195.

The Rule of Law in the U.K. Constitution

4.14   In the United Kingdom the rule of law has a long and vivid tradition as a constitutional value. An important feature of the English Civil War was Parliament's insistence that the rule of law was the highest constitutional value in the state, higher than the King himself.[91] After this was firmly established following the Glorious Revolution in 1688/89, the principle was affirmed in several notable cases, most famously *Entick v. Carrington*.[92] In this case, with respect to an argument justifying the government's illegal actions by reference to a defence of state necessity, Lord Camden C.J. said:

> "And with respect to the argument of State necessity, or a distinction which has been arrived at between State offences and others, the common law does not understand that kind of reasoning nor do our books take notice of any such distinction".[93]

In short, if no legal authority can be found to justify a government act or decision, the act or decision is illegal. There are countless examples of this proposition in the cases, a leading Scottish example being *Glasgow Corporation v. Central Land Board*.[94] But it is also clear that the constitutional value of the rule of law in the United Kingdom means much more than that all government acts and decisions require legal authority. This meaning of the rule of law would be tenuous indeed, not least in the British system with a supreme legislature, where legal authority could easily be found or created to clothe any act or decision, however abhorrent. In light of this, Dicey emphasised the rule of law in terms of:

> "the absolute supremacy . . . of regular law as opposed to . . . arbitrary power . . . equality before the law and the equal subjection of all classes to the ordinary law of the land administered by the ordinary law courts . . . [and the constitution as] the consequence of the rights of individuals, as defined and enforced by the courts . . . ."[95]

Problematic as Dicey's approach may be,[96] it provides the germ of a more substantive conception of the rule of law than mere formal legality.[97] In the context of judicial review, making Dicey the starting point for the values carried by the rule of law means emphasising not only the supremacy of the law but also the need for equality before the law,[98] respect for individual rights, control of "arbitrary" and discretionary power, access to the ordinary courts, and implicitly independence of the judiciary. On this approach, the rule of law requires as a minimum the need for legal authority for all government activities. In addition,

---

[91] After the Glorious Revolution in 1688/89, which may be regarded as the culmination of the 17th century political strife, Parliament could at last say to the King, "L'Etat, ce n'est pas seulement Vous"!

[92] (1765) 19 St.Tr. 1029.

[93] *ibid.* at 1073. See also *Smith v. Jeffrey*, Jan. 24, 1817, F.C.

[94] 1956 S.C. (H.L.) 1.

[95] *The Law of the Constitution*, pp. 202–203.

[96] See Bradley and Ewing, *Constitutional and Administrative Law*, pp. 103–105.

[97] See Allan, *Law, Liberty, and Justice*, Chap. 2; and "The Rule of Law As the Rule of Reason: Consent and Constitutionalism" (1999) 115 L.Q.R. 221. *cf.* Craig, *supra*.

[98] *cf. Kruse v. Johnson* [1898] 2 Q.B. 91, *per* Lord Russell C.J. at 99–100.

however, it requires that primacy be given to both the laws and the legal institutions of the legal system. Every citizen irrespective of their office or status must owe obedience to the law and everyone must be subject equally to the jurisdiction of the courts. While officials may be entrusted with wide discretionary powers, such powers are not to be exercised in a capricious, dictatorial manner but fairly and honestly in the advancement of the purpose for which they were provided. And while public officials may be given the respect and privileges which their responsibilities deserve, they should not be any the less subject to the jurisdiction of the courts than any private citizen.

Beyond these essentials, it is also apparent that the rule of law requires minimum standards for the law and legal institutions. Among these are the need for minimum process rights, such as a right to a fair hearing, before the citizen's rights, interests, status and legitimate expectations are affected by government actions. Furthermore, laws must be clear, accessible and not retroactive, and so far as possible predictable, in the sense of being capable of guiding the citizen's conduct.[99] Although many of these values and standards are abstract, this does not make them any less real in an appropriate case. Many judicial review cases concern disputes about what these standards mean in practice in particular cases.

Judicial Review and Government Powers

It is an essential of the rule of law that all exercises of authority **4.15** conferred by law be reviewable by the courts to ensure that the law is observed. All government powers in the United Kingdom will be traceable to a statutory, prerogative or other common law source. Historically, the greatest problems for judicial review of government powers have been associated with the review of powers derived from the Royal Prerogative.[1] Increasingly, however, it is evident that limitations on the scope of judicial review also pose problems for review of government acts and decisions in pursuance of ordinary common law powers, such as entering contracts. Whether in the field of government employment contracts or public procurement contracts, the fact that government bodies are exercising ordinary contractual powers has sometimes obscured the public nature and public interest of the issues. As far as review of exercises of statutory powers is concerned, traditionally this has been least problematic. The existence of a supreme Parliament has meant that the courts have always been ready to ensure that the limit of statutory powers is respected by those vested with them. But as judicial review has grown and become more assertive, as the grounds of review have increased, as absolute discretions and attempts to exclude or limit review have been rejected by the courts, so analytical difficulties have also increased about the nature and basis of judicial review of statutory powers. Few conceptual problems arise with judicial review for *ultra vires* in its strictest sense—in other words, ensuring that statutory decision makers have "jurisdiction in the narrow sense" of power to enter on the decision; but when the supervision of the exercise of power extends to securing the observation of "jurisdiction in the wide

---

[99] On the latter, see *Robertson v. Minister of Pensions* [1949] 1 K.B. 227 (citizen entitled to rely on existence of official power and not required to investigate extent of the power held).

[1] See further para. 4.42.

sense", that is to say supervision of all of the judicially developed criteria for lawful and proper decision making, greater difficulties arise.

The Constitutional Basis of Judicial Review

4.16 The tension between the supremacy of Parliament and the substantive values of the rule of law resonates today in debates about the foundations of judicial review, and in particular in relation to the question whether the doctrine of *ultra vires* is the proper foundation for judicial review of government action. In some respects, these debates are about the legitimacy of judicial review and the extent to which its existence is protected from encroachment—or abolition—by Parliament. The problem here is whether judicial review implicitly rests on Parliament's intention that public powers be exercised in accordance with the common law's standards, such as the principles of fairness, or whether judicial review exists independently of Parliament's powers, beyond its reach as the highest institution of the common law and the expression of the legal system's commitment to the rule of law.[2]

As was observed earlier, it is necessary to envisage a broader, constitutional basis for judicial review.[3] This draws on the rule of law and the constitutional values which give it substance. First, it is an essential that all legal powers are limited by the law. This requires, in cases of dispute, a legal remedy whereby the powers can be defined and a decision made on whether their exercise is lawful. This is not only required where a body exercises statutory powers or where it can be classified as "public" but applies much more generally in respect of all exercises of legal authority which have effects for individuals and society. The way in which the courts steadily increased the scope of judicial review over prerogative powers demonstrates the commitment to the need for all government powers to be subject to review. But it may be that one danger of a public–private distinction is to exclude from judicial review decisions which require the court's supervisory powers.

Secondly, when a court is called upon to decide whether legal powers have been exercised lawfully, the grounds of review which it draws on are

---

[2] Although judicial review's basis in the *ultra vires* principle is much criticised, the principle remains a useful analysis in relation to review of exercises of statutory powers. For discussion, see Oliver, "Is the *ultra vires* rule the basis for judicial review" [1987] P.L. 543; Forsyth, "Of Fig Leaves and Fairy Tales: *Ultra Vires* Doctrine, The Sovereignty of Parliament and Judicial Review" (1996) C.L.J. 122: Craig, "*Ultra Vires* and the Foundations of Judicial Reviews" (1998) C.L.J. 63; Elliott, "The Demise of Parliamentary Sovereignty? The Implications for Justifying Judicial Review" (1999) 115 L.Q.R. 119. It has been suggested by Lord Irvine of Lairg that the basis of review is a constitutional imperative of judicial self-restraint in deference to the sovereignty of Parliament: "Judges and Decision-Makers: The Theory and Practice of *Wednesbury* Review" [1996] P.L. 59. But it may be important to recognise a distinction between the source and origin of the authority of the courts and the definition of the grounds on which the courts may exercise their authority in particular judicial review cases. See also *Boddington v. British Transport Police* [1992] 2 A.C. 143; and *cf. Kioa v. Minister for Immigration and Ethnic Affairs* (1985) 159 C.L.R. 550.

[3] *cf.* Hunt, "Constitutionalism and the Contractualisation of Government in the UK", in Taggart (ed.), *The Province of Administrative Law* (Hart, Oxford, 1997), Chap. 2 , at pp. 32–33 (arguing that the availability of judicial review rests on broader factors than whether a body is a "public" body or the statutory source of its powers, and rather on the nature of the power of a body in terms of how it affects others). Consider also developments in New Zealand: for example, *Finnigan v. NZRFU* [1985] 2 N.Z.L.R. 159; *Electoral Commission v. Cameron* [1997] 2 N.Z.L.R. 421; *Peters v. Davison* [1998] 2 N.Z.L.R. 164 and *RACS v. Phipps* [1999] 3 N.Z.L.R. 1 (all basically supporting the availability of judicial review where decisions have general or serious consequences). There may be a question whether there is room for ambiguity about what is meant by the basis of judicial review.

themselves expressions of higher constitutional values, many of them traceable to respect for human rights. The right to a fair hearing before a person's rights, interests and legitimate expectations are interfered with is perhaps the leading example. But the prohibition on improper purposes and the avoidance of irrationality where discretionary powers are concerned also have a human rights dimension. Similarly, the presumption that all discretionary powers must not be used to interfere with the citizen's rights more than is necessary to achieve the purpose of the power highlights the constitution's commitment to human rights. If Parliament wishes to provide stronger powers, it must express itself in the clearest terms. An independent judiciary mindful of its constitutional responsibility to uphold a meaningful conception of the rule of law will not fill Parliament's omissions where wide discretionary powers are relied on to limit individual rights.

The Grounds of Review

The principle that all decision makers must act in accordance with law **4.17** leads directly to a consideration of the grounds on which judicial review of their decisions may proceed. That topic forms the substance of Part IV of the present book. The point may simply be stressed at this stage that the grounds of review apply to all decisions whatever degree of discretion may be involved in the making of them. But it must also be acknowledged that both the grounds on which judicial review may be available and the intensity of review may differ according to the nature and substance of the particular decision challenged.

IV THE LEGITIMACY OF JUDICIAL REVIEW

Introduction

It is an essential condition of the rule of law that all exercises of power **4.18** by government bodies have their basis in pre-existing law. The constitution admits of no arbitrary power. Equally fundamental is that the courts have the power to judge on the validity and propriety according to the law of all exercises of public power. As expressed in Scrutton L.J.'s memorable phrase, "there must be no Alsatia in England where the King's writ does not run".[4] Accordingly, the purpose of judicial review is to ensure that the government has lawful authority to support its acts and decisions and that it has exercised this authority properly according to the law's standards for lawful decision making. Explained in this way, however, the purpose of judicial review immediately raises questions about the legal basis upon which it proceeds and the balance which must be struck between judicial power and political power in a democracy. These questions are made more pressing in light of the fact that the standards which the courts apply to judge the legality and propriety of government decision making are mostly judicially created. Consideration must therefore be given to the legitimacy of judicial review in a democracy.

The need for judicial review

Even in the 1960s as modern administrative law began to develop, **4.19** Professor John Mitchell wrote: "The place of the courts in the modern constitution is one of the major current issues . . . The rise of Parlia-

---

[4] *Czarnikow v. Roth Schmidt and Co.* [1922] 2 K.B. 478 at 488.

ment, both in stature and in scope of operation in regard to legislation and the control of administration, clearly has its effect, especially when coupled with the growth of ideas of democratic government in restraining courts".[5] The growth of judicial review, the possibility of primary as well as secondary legislation having to be declared invalid for violation of E.C. law or inconsistency with the Scotland Act 1998, and the advent of judicial review on the grounds of human rights, might be thought to have sharpened the tensions between the courts and the holders of democratically mandated political power. For some commentators, however, the strengthening of judicial power is necessary to make up for the failure of Parliament and the political system effectively to make government accountable, protect individual rights and redress grievances. According to Beloff: "the diminution in the power and effectiveness of political control over the Executive; the subservience of backbenchers disciplined by whips and ambition alike . . . It is for the political scientists to debate the relative significance of these factors. But that there has been a vacuum cannot be doubted; and the judges have filled it".[6] There is no doubt that a democracy committed to limited government and the rule of law requires a strong system of judicial review. The problem is deciding on the scope and parameters of judicial review and achieving a consensus on the standards which judicial review should apply in supervising legislative and governmental choices. More often than not, the most difficult questions concern whether judicial review should include the power to assess the constitutionality of primary legislation and if so, by reference to what standards and with a view to what remedies if the legislation is found to violate the constitution.[7] That is should the courts be able to invalidate or strike down legislative provisions in the face of a clear legislative will in their favour?

The uncodified nature of the U.K. constitution means that unlike in other systems, such as the United States of America, Australia or Germany, where the judicial power to uphold the constitution and more generally the law is either expressly conferred by or derived from the constitution, the power of judicial review in the United Kingdom derives either from authority conferred by Act of Parliament or from inherent powers of the court arising at common law.

The legitimacy of review

4.20 Judicial review and the values on which it draws are not without difficulties, not least in a democracy. In particular, many questions surround the legitimacy of judicial review. Although the supremacy of Parliament has allowed lawyers in the United Kingdom to avoid dealing with the legitimacy of judicial review, which is an ever present if not always pressing concern in legal systems with judicial review under a codified constitution, the frequently sensitive political nature of judicial review cases, the advent of enforceable human rights guarantees and the constitutional review posited by the Scotland Act 1998 now require that

---

[5] Mitchell: *Constitutional Law* (2nd ed., W. Green & Sons/SULI, Edinburgh, 1968), pp. 251 and 264.

[6] Michael Beloff, "Judicial Review—2001: A Prophetic Odessey" (1995) 58 M.L.R. 143 at 145.

[7] For a discussion of constitutional review of legislative choices in Germany, see Limbach, "The Law-Making Power of the Legislature and Judicial Review", in Markesinis (ed.), *Law Making, Law Finding and Law Sharing*.

the matter is addressed in the United Kingdom. A resolution of the difficulties must ultimately depend on value judgments about the nature of a constitution and the role of law in society, but the problem of legitimacy has to be considered if judicial review is properly to be placed in its constitutional context. In this regard, the concept of justiciability will require to be better understood as judicial review addresses ever more politically sensitive issues.

The difficulty for judicial review, and particularly for judicial review on constitutional grounds, is that it can involve a clash between judicial and political power where the latter derives its authority from popular election. There is no easy answer to this difficulty. A modern democratic constitution in which the legal system provides principles of good government and protects human rights inevitably makes the courts a forum before which the ancient struggle between the individual and society takes place. Outside Utopia this struggle will continue, probably with ever more intensity as the individual becomes more conscious of legal rights, while the domain of legal regulation simultaneously expands. The rule of law and the principle of constitutionalism demand that the courts should not retreat in the face of political power.[8] Although the courts must respect the proper place of political power in the constitutional order, their unavoidable constitutional duty is to uphold the law, including its fundamental values. When these authorise the exercise of government power, the courts are there to ensure that the government's and society's decisions are respected and enforced; but when the government acts without power, the constitution and society require that the judges say so and deny the validity of the government's actions.[9] While judicial review may seem to create a tension between the judiciary and the executive, the function of the former should be nothing more than to uphold the law and the tension should never become excessive.[10]

Judicial review and democratic legitimacy

T.R.S. Allan has captured the conflict that is at the centre of the debate on the legitimacy of judicial review. According to one constitutional model, which may be termed the "majoritarian" tradition: **4.21**

> "legislation should always be immune from judicial review because it carries the authority of the majority of elected representatives; and, by the same token, judges should be wary of substituting their own judgments of morality or political wisdom for those of ministers or officials, who enjoy discretionary powers conferred by the elected majority to whom such officials are ultimately accountable ... Obedience to parliamentary sovereignty, benignly construed, exhausts the requirements of the rule of law".[11]

The contrasting constitutional model, widely known as the counter-majoritarian model, puts respect for the individual as the highest value

---

[8] *cf.* Dyzenhaus, "Reuniting the Brain: The Democratic Basis of Judicial Review" (1998) 9 *Public Law Review* 98.

[9] *cf.* Allan: *Law, Liberty and Justice: The Legal Foundations of British Constitutionalism* (Clarendon Press, Oxford, 1993), at pp. 183–184.

[10] See Woolf, "Judicial Review—The Tensions between the Executive and the Judiciary" (1998) 114 L.Q.R. 579.

[11] Allan, "Fairness, Equality, Rationality: Constitutional Theory and Judicial Review", in Forsyth and Hare (eds), *The Golden Metwand and the Crooked Cord* (OUP, Oxford, 1998), at p. 17.

for the law to protect. Respect for the majority's freely expressed will is important, but:

> "the individual citizen's dignity and moral autonomy constitute essential components of the common good, which provides the ultimate touchstone for the validity of legislation and the legality of government action . . . Government has an obligation to identify and protect those rights and liberties fundamental to the citizen's dignity: its duty to treat all members of the polity with equal concern and respect, according to the community's reflective under-standing of what that means in practice, places firm limitations on the exercise of power".[12]

It follows that in terms of this model it falls to the courts to ensure that all exercises of public power stay within these "firm limitations" and respect them both in form and substance. This inevitably brings the courts into conflict with passing political majorities which seek to use their political powers in a way which may clash with the transcending "lasting values" of society. The conflict intensifies as the values protected by the courts move from forms or processes of decision making to substantive values such as "liberty", "privacy", "equality" and "prop-erty". Whereas ensuring proper procedures is usually a less controversial limitation on public power, procedures being seen as the natural province of the law, the limitations protecting substantive values and according them a high place in the hierarchy of values threatens to pit the court directly against the political majority which seeks to compro-mise the substantive limitation. The right of the judicial elite to make society's value judgments from time to time by reference to values appointed for an earlier time will be questioned and this questioning is the essence of the legitimacy debate surrounding judicial review. Although the debate is at its loudest where the judiciary interpret a written constitution, loudest of all in the U.S. where that constitution is more than 200 years old, it has echoes in the United Kingdom, particularly where statutory powers are challenged on the ground of "*Wednesbury* unreasonableness".[13]

The legitimacy of judicial review rests on the recognition that the preservation of the rule of law requires an independent judiciary capable of securing the legality of decision making. Thus, the independence of the judiciary becomes critical. The matter of their appointment and dismissal is considered below. But whatever mechanisms are used for those purposes, the independence of the judiciary remains paramount. Once the constitutional legitimacy of their position is recognised and acknowledged, what may be seen as conflict may in reality become more of a partnership between distinct elements in the constitution, each with their distinct functions and responsibilities, but each striving to secure a fair and ordered society in conformity with the rule of law. By means of legal rules, precedents and principled decision-making, the judiciary serve this partnership even when the political aspects of cases seem overwhelming.[14]

---

[12] *ibid.*, at pp. 17–18. Allan terms this constitutional model the "communitarian" theory.

[13] See Lord Irvine of Lairg, "Judges and Decision-Makers: The Theory and Practice of *Wednesbury* Review" [1996] P.L. 59. The subject of "unreasonableness" as a ground of judicial review is discussed further in Chap. 21.

[14] *cf.* Fiss, "Objectivity and Interpretation" (1982) 34 Stanford L.R. 739. For the perspective of a U.S. Supreme Court Justice, see Justice Breyer, "Judicial Review: A Practising Judge's Perspective" (1999) 19 O.J.L.S. 153.

The utility of a concept of justiciability

In the United Kingdom, as in many systems, there are constitutional **4.22** limits on the matters which are properly within the competence or the responsibility of the courts.[15] Recognition of the extent of this political reality may be more difficult in the United Kingdom, partly because there is no codified constitution, which means that law and political science share the constitutional terrain as equals, rather than under a codified constitution where law is invariably the senior partner. Moreover the courts have not until recently[16] in the field of judicial review sought to articulate a doctrine of justiciability, leaving it, by classical common law method, to be identified on a case to case, subject to subject basis.[17] Nevertheless a doctrine of justiciability has to be recognised. There is little difficulty in the concept of a principle of the admissibility of proceedings. It is indeed established in Scottish practice in the idea of the competency of an action. The problem is not with the idea of a concept of justiciability, or rather, non-justiciability, but with the formulation of the criteria for its definition.[18]

V JUDICIAL INDEPENDENCE

Introduction

Judicial independence is a fundamental element of the rule of law. Judicial review of government powers would not be transparent if the state's judicial power were not exercised by independent judges.

In all of the United Kingdom's jurisdictions the independence of the **4.23** judiciary is protected by statute and constitutional convention. While the separation of legislative and executive power is more difficult to discern under the U.K. constitution, the separation of judicial power from the other branches of government is an important, invariably respected and

---

[15] For example, whether the government's decision to ratify a treaty is "constitutional". It may be, however, that E.C. law could now be relied on to challenge the legality of the ratification of a treaty which violated E.C. law, *e.g.* where the treaty concerned the E.C.'s common commercial policy and therefore fell outside national treaty-making competence. For a U.S. example of non-justiciable constitutional values, consider Article IV of the Constitution guaranteeing to the states "a republican form of government". *Cf.* an attempt to challenge a decision of the Canadian federal Cabinet for breach of the Canadian Charter of Rights: *Operation Dismantle v. R.* [1985] S.C.R. 441.

[16] *cf. GCHQ; Notts C.C.;* See also *West v. Secretary of State for Scotland,* 1992 S.C. 385.

[17] *cf. Chandler v. DPP* [1964] A.C. 763; *Att.-Gen. v. Nissan* [1970] A.C. 179; *Blackburn v. Attorney-General* [1971] 1 W.L.R. 1037; *GCHQ* [1985] 1 A.C. 374; and *cf. J.H. Rayner Ltd v. Dept of Trade and Industry* [1990] 2 A.C. 418.

[18] The problem is mentioned later, at paras 9.18–9.19. Limits on justiciability may be termed a political question doctrine as in the USA; or "actes de gouvernement", as in France; or more generally acts of state, as in many systems, including the U.K. But the trend is in favour of rejecting non-justiciability of government acts: *cf. CCSU v. Minister for the Civil Service* [1985] A.C. 374; and *Operation Dismantle v. R.* [1985] 1 S.C.R. 441 (prerogative power to test weapons in principle not excluded from review under Canadian Charter of Rights). Nevertheless, in so far as the courts do not take jurisdiction over certain matters, whether these are termed political questions or "policy" matters, the difficulty is always ascertaining the limits of the matters excluded from judicial review: see the judgment of Wilson J. in *Operation Dismantle.*

valued feature of the constitution.[19] As ever, however, nothing is perfect.[20] But in recent times appointment to the higher judicial offices has not been motivated by political considerations. Attempts at political interference with the exercise of judicial power have been minimal.[21] Equally, public bodies' compliance with successful judicial review challenges to their decisions is very high. Overall, the constitutional tradition is vigorously to uphold the independence of the judiciary and to ensure it by appointing the best qualified persons to judicial office whose decisions will command the highest degree of respect and who will to the greatest extent be free from insecurity, suit or censure in the exercise of judicial office.

Legal basis for appointment and tenure of judges

4.24 Both in Scotland and elsewhere in the United Kingdom the law draws a distinction between supreme court judges and judges in inferior courts for the purposes of appointment to and tenure in office.[22]

In England and Wales all judges are appointed in the name of the Queen on the advice of the Lord Chancellor to all courts below the Court of Appeal and on the advice of the Prime Minister to the Court of Appeal, House of Lords and to head the Divisions in the High Court. Beyond this straightforward statement, matters are inevitably more complex and a range of factors, consultations and inquiries operate at all levels in reaching the decision on whom to appoint. The noteworthy point is that there is no independent Judicial Appointments Commission and no direct Parliamentary contribution to the appointment process. Although advertisements now invite applications from qualified persons for appointment to some judicial offices in England and Wales, the

---

[19] See, for example, the House of Commons Disqualification Act 1975, s. 1(1)(a), Sched. 1, Pt 1: full-time members of the judiciary are disqualified from membership of the House of Commons; see also s. 15 of the Scotland Act 1998 (similar exclusions from the Scottish Parliament). Even in relation to the judiciary, however, there are breaches of the principle of separation of powers. For example, the Lord Chancellor is Head of the Judiciary, a member of the Cabinet and of the House of Lords. As a member of the executive, the Lord Chancellor is responsible for appointing the vast majority of judges in England & Wales. And his direct involvement in the work of the House of Lords in its judicial capacity should not be regarded as minimal. For example, when he sits he chairs the appellate committee, which gives him some influence over the decision. Furthermore, the Lords of Appeal in Ordinary are also members of the House of Lords. But by convention they sit on the cross benches and remain independent of party politics, although this does not prevent them contributing, often actively, to House of Lords debates on current issues relevant to legal developments. In addition, the Lord Chief Justice and Master of the Rolls, the Lord Chief Justice of Northern Ireland, and the Lord President of the Court of Session are usually created Peers. Especially in Scotland, career developments (*e.g.* having been Lord Advocate or perhaps Advocate General for Scotland) often mean that several judges of the supreme courts are also Peers. The reform of the House of Lords and the advent of the Scottish Parliament may, however, alter the present pattern.

[20] In particular, concerns may be raised about the appointment of temporary judges to the supreme courts (in Scotland in terms of s. 35 of the Law Reform (Miscellaneous Provisions) (Scotland) Act 1990), and the appointment of temporary judges generally without security of tenure.

[21] But not non-existent: consider, *e.g.*, struggles between government and judiciary over sentencing powers.

[22] A full discussion of the appointment and tenure of judges in the U.K. is given in Wade & Ewing *Constitutional and Administrative Law* (12th ed., Longman, London, 1997). For a further discussion of the Scottish position, see *Stair Memorial Encyclopaedia*, Vol 5, paras 663–667. See also de Smith & Brazier, *Constitutional and Administrative Law* (7th ed., 1994,) pp. 397 *et seq.*

appointment process is closed and in all but the most general terms unaccountable.[23] As to security of tenure, there is a patchwork of legislation dealing with each level in the judicial hierarchy. All the higher court judges hold their offices during good behaviour.[24] If failing this standard, Lords of Appeal in Ordinary can only be removed by the Crown following an address by both Houses of Parliament,[25] and a similar procedure protects the security of tenure of judges of the High Court and Court of Appeal.[26] Judges of inferior courts enjoy less security, ranging from circuit judges who can be removed for incapacity or misbehaviour[27] to lay magistrates who hold their offices at the Lord Chancellor's pleasure until the age of 70.[28] Beyond removal from office, judicial salaries can only be reduced by Act of Parliament,[29] and Parliamentary procedures restrict ministers and members of Parliament from commenting either on the character of judges or on cases before the courts.[30] Finally, judicial independence is buttressed by a general common law immunity from civil liability enjoyed both by individual judges and the Crown for anything done in the discharge of judicial office.[31] But under the Human Rights Act 1998 a liability for judicial acts may now arise.[32]

---

[23] The Lord Chancellor's Department has more recently announced its policies in relation to judicial appointments: *cf. Judicial Appointments 1995* (Lord Chancellor's Department, 1995).

[24] A form of words deriving from the Act of Settlement; see now s. 11 of the Supreme Court Act 1981.

[25] Appellate Jurisdiction Act 1876, s. 6 (as amended).

[26] Supreme Court Act 1981, s. 11(3), which owes its origins to s. 3 of the Act of Settlement 1701.

[27] Courts Act 1971, s. 17(4). District judges hold office on the same conditions: County Courts Act 1984, s. 11(4) and (5). *cf.* the tenure of sheriffs in Scotland, discussed below.

[28] Justices of the Peace Act 1979, ss. 6, 8(2) and 10.

[29] For example, see Supreme Court Act 1981, s. 12(3) governing salaries of Supreme Court judges; Administration of Justice Act 1973, s. 9(1) in relation to the Lords of Appeal in Ordinary and the Courts Act 1971, s. 18(2) for circuit judges. Again, however, judges in inferior courts enjoy less security: see County Courts Act 1984, s. 6(1) (as amended) providing that district judges receive such salaries as the Lord Chancellor directs. Interestingly, the Lord Chancellor's own salary receives special treatment: the Ministerial and other Salaries Act 1975, s. 1(2) (as amended) provides that the Lord Chancellor is to receive a salary of an amount £2,500 greater than the salary from time to time paid to the Lord Chief Justice. The higher salary is designed to allow "headroom for proper payment of the judges" (see 327 HL Official Report (5th Series), 1 February 1972, col. 685); in practice it means that the Lord Chancellor is the highest paid Cabinet minister.

[30] Criticism of judges can only be made directly on a motion before either House of Parliament. See generally, Bradley & Ewing, *Constitutional & Administrative Law* (12th ed., Longman, London, 1997) at pp. 423–425.

[31] See *Re McC (A Minor)* [1985] A.C. 528 and the earlier Court of Appeal decision in *Sirros v. Moore* [1975] Q.B. 118. On the Crown's immunity, see the Crown Proceedings Act 1947, s. 2(5); but this matter is now more complicated in light of the decisions of the European Court of Justice in the *Francovich v. Italy* line of cases and generally on the meaning of Art. 5 of the E.C. Treaty. In short, as officers of the state, judges are bound by Art. 5 of the E.C. Treaty to advance the objectives of the E.C. and do nothing that hinders them. Subject to the ECJ accepting as reasonable some element of judicial immunity, it may follow from *Francovich* that if a judge violates this obligation the state may be liable in damages to any individual thereby caused loss. The E.C. law damages remedy is considered further in Chaps 5 and 26.

[32] See s.9 of the Act, and para. 6.68.

Scotland

4.25 In Scotland, the devolution arrangements have naturally had an impact on judicial appointments. Beyond being appointed by the Queen, the appointment of all Scottish judges has variously involved the Prime Minister, the Secretary of State for Scotland, the Lord Advocate and (if available) the existing Lord President of the Court of Session and the Lord Justice-Clerk.[33] Before the Scotland Act 1998 came into force, the Prime Minister nominated the Scottish Lords of Appeal in Ordinary, the Lord President and the Lord Justice-Clerk, on the advice of the Secretary of State and the Lord Advocate, who in turn consulted more widely. All other Court of Session judges, sheriffs principal and sheriffs were appointed by the Secretary of State for Scotland on the advice of the Lord Advocate and after consultations with the Lord President and Lord Justice-Clerk. Since the creation of the Scottish Parliament and Executive, the Scottish First Minister has the pre-eminent role in appointing judges in Scotland. Section 95 of the Scotland Act 1998 provides that the Prime Minister continues to recommend persons to be the Lord President and the Lord Justice-Clerk but only if that person has been nominated by the Scottish First Minister and after the latter has consulted the (existing) Lord President and Lord Justice-Clerk (if available).[34] In turn, the First Minister is responsible for recommending appointment of all other judges of the Court of Session, sheriffs principal and sheriffs, after consulting the Lord President of the Court of Session.[35] It may be assumed that the First Minister will continue to rely on the advice of the Lord Advocate, who will likely continue to be *de facto* the central figure in Court of Session and shrieval appointments. Equally, it is apparent that the Prime Minister will continue to consult the Secretary of State and also the Advocate General for Scotland in relation to the appointments which he recommends.[36] The appointment of Lords of Appeal in Ordinary, and of members of the judicial committee of the Privy Council do not appear to be touched by the changes that the Scotland Act 1998 has made.[37]

---

[33] See *Stair Memorial Encyclopaedia*, "Courts and Competency", Vol. 6, paras 929 *et seq.*; Bradley & Ewing, *Constitutional and Administrative Law* (12th ed., Longman, London, 1997). On the Scottish judiciary and the Scottish Court system generally, see Walker, *The Scottish Legal System* (7th ed., W. Green & Sons, Edinburgh, 1997).

[34] s. 95(1)–(3).

[35] s. 95(4).

[36] Although this is confined by s. 89(2) of the 1998 Act only to consult about persons already nominated by the First Minister.

[37] Appointment of judges has caused controversies in other constitutional systems. In Canada, for example, the absence of provision for any contribution from the provincial governments to the process of appointment of judges of the Supreme Court of Canada has been a continuing source of controversy. Indeed, the fact that the federal government appointed Supreme Court of Canada judges was one reason the provinces favoured appeals to the Privy Council in London. On the Canadian Constitution on this matter and recent attempts to give the provinces a role in appointing Supreme Court judges, see Hogg, *Constitutional Law of Canada* (3rd ed., 1992, Carswell, Toronto); see also Hogg, "Is the Supreme Court of Canada Biased in Constitutional Cases?" (1979) 57 Can. Bar Rev. 721. In the U.S., the Constitution theoretically gives the states a role in the appointment of the federal judiciary by requiring that federal judges are appointed by the President "by and with the advice and consent of the Senate": US Constitution, Art. II. Historically, the Senate was the states' House in the federal Congress and the place where state interests were furthered. Whether or not this remains so, there is a little evidence that regional representation (in addition to race and gender) plays some part in the appointment of U.S.

Beyond the mechanics of judicial appointment, as in England and Wales the appointment process is noted for its secrecy. Inevitably, this has led to speculation about the qualifications for judicial appointment beyond the rather minimal provision in the Act of Union that a Court of Session judge should be five years called as an advocate.[38] Historically, appointment as a Senator of the College of Justice, as judges of the Court of Session are formally styled,[39] occasionally involved overt political elements. Former Lord Advocates have tended to be appointed Court of Session judges, on more than one occasion effectively by their own hand, although there is no evidence of abuse in this regard. That there may be a conflict of interest reflects not on the office of the Lord Advocate but rather on the absence of an alternative process of appointing supreme court judges.[40]

Removal

The security of tenure enjoyed by Court of Session judges in Scotland is high, until recently in some measure by virtue of no clear procedure for removing them from office. When the College of Justice was founded in 1532, the Senators seem to have been appointed *ad vitam aut culpam*, that is, for life or until misconduct. This basis of tenure was confirmed by the Claim of Right[41] but no procedure was ever provided by which Court of Session judges could be removed.[42] The English Act of Settlement

4.26

Supreme Court judges. For discussion, see Abrahams. *The Judiciary: The Supreme Court in the Government Process* (3rd ed.), 1996, NYU Press, Chap. 2, especially pp. 67–69. In Germany Art. 94 of the Constitution (Basic Law) provides that the Bundestag and Bundesrat each appoint half of the judges of the Constitutional Court (Bundesverfassungsgericht). In the E.U., ECJ judges are appointed by the E.U. Council of Ministers having been nominated by a member state; all the member states are entitled to one judge carrying their nationality to serve on the ECJ. Whether this principle can continue in an E.U. with 25 or more states or whether, like the U.S. and Canadian Supreme Courts, there should be nine judges from around the Union, is one of the difficult issues surrounding reform of the E.U.'s institutions with a view to the widening of the E.U. to include CEE countries.

[38] Act of Union, A.P.S. XI, 406, Art. XIX. In practice, Court of Session judges in recent times have had considerably greater experience than the prescribed minimum. Deans suggests that the five-year qualification was set so that English lawyers would not be appointed to the Scottish courts following the Union (see Deans, *Scots Public Law* (T&T Clark, Edinburgh, 1995), p. 124). The Law Reform (Miscellaneous Provisions) (Scotland) Act 1990, s. 35 and Sched. 4 provides that Court of Session judges can also be appointed from those with at least five years' standing as a sheriff or as a solicitor with rights of audience before the Court of Session and the High Court. The qualifications for appointment of sheriffs are provided in the Sheriff Courts (Scotland) Act 1971, s. 5: at least 10 years' standing as an advocate or solicitor.

[39] The same judges are styled Lord Commissioners of Justiciary when sitting in the High Court of Justiciary.

[40] Several works have over the years discussed the nature of appointments to the Scottish judiciary, in particular to the supreme courts and the House of Lords: see Willock, "Scottish Judges Scrutinised", 1969 J.R. 193; Styles, "The Scottish Judiciary 1919–86", 1988 J.R. 41; and Paterson, "Scottish Lords at Appeal", 1988 J.R. 235. For discussion on the House of Lords as a court and on the judges who have served as Lords of Appeal in Ordinary, see Stevens, *Law and Politics* (1979). See also Paterson, *Law Lords* (1982).

[41] Claim of Right 1689, c. 28, A.P.S. IX, 38, Art. 13. Between the Restoration of Charles II and the Glorious Revolution there had been assertions that the Court of Session judges held their office at the King's pleasure.

[42] An age of retirement of 75 was introduced by the Judicial Pensions Act 1959, s. 2. See now the Judicial Pensions Act 1981, as amended by the Judicial Pensions Act 1993, s. 26(10) and Sched. 6, para. 3, which provides a retirement age of 70 for all appointments made after its provisions enter force. As will be seen, the Scotland Act 1998 now provides the grounds on and the procedure by which Court of Session judges can be removed.

procedure, now embodied in the Supreme Court Act 1981,[43] providing that the judges in the English Supreme Court could be removed by the Crown following an address by both Houses of Parliament, was never extended to Scotland. In the absence of a specified procedure for removal, it had always been thought that a similar procedure might apply.[44] The advent of devolution, however, required that a procedure be prescribed. The matter was the subject of considerable debate particularly in the House of Lords, during the passage of the Scotland Bill, with an original proposal that the Scottish First Minister supported by a majority of at least two-thirds of the total number of seats in the Scottish Parliament might recommend to the Queen that a Court of Session judge be removed from office. The eventual provision, contained in section 95 of the Act, requires the Scottish Parliament to provide for a tribunal to be constituted by the First Minister to investigate and report on the unfitness of the judge for office on certain specified grounds. The tribunal is required to give reasons for its conclusion that the judge is unfit. If, and only if, the tribunal reports to the First Minister that the judge is so unfit, and in the case of the Lord President or the Lord Justice-Clerk he has consulted the Prime Minister, and has complied with any other statutory requirement, the First Minister may make a motion to Parliament for a recommendation for removal. If, and only if, the Parliament resolves that a recommendation should be made, the First Minister is required to recommend to Her Majesty that the judge be removed.[45] Overall Scottish judges enjoy a strong security of tenure.[46] No Court of Session judge has ever been removed from office. Indeed the occasions on which a sheriff has been removed are few.[47] It must be hoped that this tradition will continue and that the stature of the higher

---

[43] s. 11.

[44] See *Haggart's Trustees v. Hope* (1824) 2 Shaw App. 125, *per* Lord Robertson at 135; *Cruichshank v. Gordon* (1843) 5 D. 963; and *McCreadie v. Thomson*, 1907 S.C. 1176 at 1182. See also Fraser, *Constitutional Law* (2nd ed., 1948) at p. 207. Again, however, judges in other courts do not enjoy the same security of tenure. The Sheriff Courts (Scotland) Act 1971, s. 12 provides that a sheriff or sheriff principal may be removed by the Secretary of State for Scotland on the ground of unfitness for office by reason of "inability, neglect of duty or misbehaviour" following a joint investigation by the Lord President of the Court of Session and the Lord Justice-Clerk which concludes that the sheriff is unfit for office on one of the stated grounds. Parliament has the final say, however: s. 12(3)(a) of the 1971 Act provides that the sheriff's removal is to be effected by statutory instrument made subject to the annulment procedure, that is, which can be annulled by resolution of either House of Parliament. Justices of the Peace in Scotland are appointed on the advice of the Secretary of State and may be removed by him.

[45] The final version of these provisions was introduced by an amendment made by the House of Commons and accepted by the House of Lords at the final stages of the Bill's course. The provision for a tribunal to consider the case for removal had already been secured at the Third Reading in the House of Lords in a form modelled on the provisions for the removal of sheriffs, but there were still questions about the precise composition of the body and the solution was found by leaving the matter to be worked out by the Scottish Parliament. By virtue of s. 95(11) the tribunal must have at least three persons and by virtue of s. 95(9) the chairman must be a member of the Judicial Committee as defined in s.103(2). The formula now enacted enables provision to be made for the tribunal to include at least one lay person.

[46] The independence of sheriffs is not directly relevant to the subject of judicial review, but it may be noted that so far as sheriffs are concerned the procedures in the Sheriff Courts (Scotland) Act 1971, involving the Lord President of the Court of Session, the Lord Justice-Clerk and the Secretary of State for Scotland continue to apply, there being no reason to alter those provisions on the occasion of the setting up of the Scottish Parliament.

[47] For a recent example, see *Stewart v. Secretary of State for Scotland*, 1998 S.L.T. 385.

judiciary is such that if a judge is involved in misbehaviour, he or she will opt to resign rather than wait to be removed.[48]

As in England and Wales, various other rules are designed to protect the independence of the judiciary: the salaries of Scottish judges are reserved to the U.K. Parliament and so immune from the Scottish Parliament[49]; the Scottish parliament is bound to observe a *sub judice* rule[50]; and supreme court judges are, as in England and Wales, absolutely immune from civil liability for acts done while discharging judicial office.[51] Sheriffs probably enjoy the same degree of immunity,[52] while inferior court judges are liable for *ultra vires* acts or acts done in bad faith.[53]

The mechanics of appointment and dismissal may not necessarily be a critical consideration, but the traditional approach in the United Kingdom which is not based on popular election has seemed secure. At the end of the day it may not be the forms which are crucial but the calibre and quality of the judges themselves, and there may be much to be said for a system which, despite its imperfections, aims to proceed on an objective assessment and a considerable knowledge of all of the particular circumstances.

VI THE SUPREMACY OF THE UNITED KINGDOM PARLIAMENT

INTRODUCTION

The supremacy of the U.K. Parliament is undoubtedly a key feature of **4.27** the U.K. constitution and of cardinal importance for judicial review. As was noted above,[54] both the rule of law and judicial review derive much support from Parliamentary supremacy, most notably through the authority and legitimacy it provides for judicial review of exercises of statutory powers. Nevertheless, a discussion of the Constitution is inadequate if its destination is merely the conclusion that the constitution can be summarised thus: whatever the Queen in Parliament enacts is law.[55] The United Kingdom Constitution must be understood against a range of values of which only one is the supremacy of Parliament. Accordingly, while it is true that the clearest words in an Act of

---

[48] In the controversy surrounding a Court of Session judge in 1989–90, the judge opted to resign rather than allow various allegations concerning his personal life to weaken the authority of the judiciary.

[49] Sched. 5, Pt II, head 11 of the 1998 Act.

[50] Sched. 3, para. 1(1)(b) of the 1998 Act. The *sub judice* rule concerns only restrictions on comments about cases before the courts; the Parliament itself will have to provide standing orders equivalent to those of the U.K. Parliament requiring that comment on any judge is only on a motion.

[51] *McCreadie v. Thomson*, 1907 S.C. 1176; see also *Hamilton v. Anderson* (1858) 3 Macq. 363.

[52] See *Harvey v. Dyce* (1876) 4 R. 265 (albeit a slander case, where the law on defamation obviously confers greater immunity on the sheriff); and *Watt v. Thomson* (1869) 8 M. (H.L.) 77.

[53] *McCreadie v. Thomson*, 1907 S.C. 1176.

[54] See para. 4.09.

[55] *cf.* Allan, "Parliamentary Sovereignty: Law, Politics, and Revolution" (1997) 113 L.Q.R. 443. See also Bogdanor, *Politics and the Constitution* (1996; Dartmouth); reviewed by Barendt (1997) 17 O.J.L.S. 137.

Parliament will be given effect by the courts, Parliament's failure, for whatever reasons, to set out with precision and clarity exactly what it wishes allows the courts to interpret Parliament's will against the background of the constitution's values.[56] These values are often expressed as presumptions applicable in statutory interpretation, such as the presumption against retrospective legislation or the presumption of non-interference with individual rights except to the extent strictly necessary to fulfil the statutory scheme. Accordingly, the courts have a critical role in giving meaning to Acts of Parliament and in giving effect to often ambiguous terms in the context of a "European liberal democracy founded on the principles and traditions of the common law".[57] In practice, therefore, Parliament's supremacy operates through the medium of the courts.

Although it is often justifiably criticised, there can be no doubt about the contribution which the United Kingdom Parliament has made to social and political reform everywhere in the United Kingdom. There should be no grudging acceptance of Parliament's importance nor of a properly understood concept of its supremacy. Parliament has its place and that place must be respected. The task, however, is always to find a balance between Parliament's supremacy and the rule of law. This was Dicey's task in his *Introduction to the Law of the Constitution*[58] and it remains the task of modern commentators. The problem continues to be to identify what is meant by Parliamentary supremacy while rejecting the theoretical extremes used to "prove" it. To this end, the present discussion attempts to note the emergence of the doctrine of Parliamentary supremacy in the United Kingdom, to discuss what it means in practice and to place it in the context of judicial review in modern circumstances. At the outset, however, it must be stressed that the supremacy of Parliament must be understood as only one pillar of the constitution. In addition, the constitution's other fundamentals include the values of the common law, not least as these emerge in the rules and presumptions applicable in statutory interpretation,[59] and the existence of the inherent supervisory jurisdiction of the supreme courts.[60] The supremacy of Parliament must be placed in the context of judicial review and judicial technique to show that neither legislative nor judicial power is absolute but rather that both draw support from each other to realise a stable constitutional balance. This is exemplified by the judicial respect for the privileges and prerogatives of Parliament (itself a court), by the judicial approaches to statutory interpretation, by differing approaches to primary and secondary legislation and by the basis of judicial review of statutory powers in the *ultra vires* principle.[61] Only by considering such

---

[56] For a recent analysis and application of this proposition, see the speech of Lord Steyn in *R. v. Secretary of State for the Home Department, ex parte Pierson* [1998] A.C. 539.

[57] *ibid.* at 587.

[58] (10th ed, 1959), ed. ECS Wade, hereafter Law of the Constitution.

[59] On the importance of the values of the common law in making up the U.K. Constitution, see Allan: *Law, Liberty and, Justice: The Legal Foundations of British Constitutionalism* (1993, Clarendon Press, Oxford). See also Sedley, "The Sound of Silence: Constitutional Law Without A Constitution" (1994) 110 L.Q.R. 270.

[60] *cf.* Lord Woolf, "Droit Public—English Style" [1995] P.L. 57; and Laws, "Law and Democracy" [1995] P.L. 72 (both suggesting that Parliament may not have power to abolish judicial review).

[61] The juridical basis of judicial review generally, as has been explained, lies in the constitutional principle that no wrong should be without a remedy: see para. 4.16 above. But as far as judicial review of statutory powers is concerned, the principle of *ultra vires* provides a satisfactory analysis of the grounds for intervention.

matters as a whole can a proper understanding of the relationship between judicial review and the United Kingdom Parliament be understood.

The United Kingdom Parliament

The present United Kingdom Parliament originates in the Parliament of **4.28** Great Britain established by the 1707 Treaty and Acts of Union between Scotland and England.[62] This legislature mutated into the Parliament of the United Kingdom of Great Britain and Ireland following the 1800 Treaty of Union between Great Britain and Ireland, only to contract following the independence of Ireland in 1922 to its modern form, in which it is properly styled the Parliament of the United Kingdom of Great Britain and Northern Ireland.[63]

As a matter of law, the U.K. Parliament is the supreme law maker in the United Kingdom.[64] Subject to applicable E.C. law, discussed elsewhere,[65] Acts of Parliament form the supreme law in the United Kingdom's legal order. A proper definition of Parliament's supreme legal power is, however, required. First, it is not Parliament alone that is the supreme law maker but the "Queen in Parliament"; an Act of Parliament requires not only the approval of both Houses of Parliament,[66] but also the Royal Assent before it is enacted.[67] Although the

---

[62] The Articles of Union were enacted into the two legal systems of Scotland and England by both countries' parliaments: see the Union with Scotland Act 1706 (6 Anne c. 11) and the Union with England Act (1706) c. 7, A.P.S. XI, 406. For discussion, see Riley, *The Union of England and Scotland* (1978); and Mitchell, *supra* n. 1, pp. 92–98. And see also Dicey and Rait, *Thoughts on the Union Between England and Scotland* (1920, MacMillan, London).

[63] Royal and Parliamentary Titles Act 1927, s. 2. By s. 2(2) of this Act, as amended by the Interpretation Act 1978, ss. 5, 22, Sched. 1 and Sched. 2, para. 4(1)(a), in every enactment passed after April 12, 1927, "the United Kingdom" means Great Britain and Northern Ireland. It does not include the Isle of Man and the Channel Islands. However, "Great Britain" is restricted only to England and Wales and Scotland. For a survey of the constitutional position of Northern Ireland see *Halsbury's Laws of England*, "Constitutional Law and Human Rights" Vol. 8(2), paras 67 *et seq.*; Hadfield, *The Constitution of Northern Ireland* (1968).

[64] But the qualification "as a matter of law" is crucial: see Munro, *supra*, n. 1, pp. 84–87. As a political matter, Dicey noted that the people are supreme: Dicey, *Introduction to the Law of the Constitution* (10th ed., 1959), 00. 73–74. As Munro observes, this is more than just true in theory; in a functioning democracy, Parliament does not enact abhorrent legislation not because it cannot legally do so but because it cannot do so politically.

[65] See chapter 5, especially para. 5.49.

[66] See *Stockdale v. Hansard* (1839) 9 Ad. & El. 1. This is now subject to the special procedures provided by the Parliament Acts 1911–1949, which in specified circumstances allow a public Bill to become an Act without the consent of the House of Lords—that is, only having passed its stages in the House of Commons in two sessions separated by a year and after receiving the Royal Assent: see Mitchell, *supra*, n. 1, at pp. 149–151, and for a rare but recent example, the War Crimes Act 1990.

[67] By a constitutional convention the Royal Assent cannot now be withheld: see *Halsbury's Laws of England*, Vol. 8(2), para. 20. The Royal Assent is also required for Acts of the Scottish Parliament to be enacted. Importantly, the continuing need for the Royal Assent for a Bill to become an Act implicates the executive in the legislative process. That is, the constitutional position must be that the Monarch gives her assent on the advice of her ministers and as such the Assent is an executive act rather than a personal act of the Monarch. If so, there must be a question about whether the giving (or theoretical refusal) of the Royal Assent is challengeable in court—for example, where it is alleged that the Bill, if enacted., would be unlawful (mention is made of this theoretical possibility by Heuston, "Sovereignty", in Guest (ed.), *Oxford Essays in Jurisprudence* (OUP, Oxford, 1961) Chap. VIII. The issue has arisen in Australia, where the federal constitution imposes

Queen in Parliament is not the only legislature empowered to pass primary legislation within the United Kingdom, only Acts of Parliament constitute supreme law.[68] Leaving aside the Scottish and Northern Irish Parliaments,[69] the Queen in Council may pass Orders in Council by virtue of prerogative powers. While these are sometimes the prescribed form subordinate legislation under Acts of Parliament,[70] when enacted under prerogative powers Orders in Council have the status of primary legislation. Although Orders in Council, passed under the prerogative are not used frequently in the United Kingdom,[71] there are some instances of their interaction with Acts of Parliament. Where this occurs, and perhaps more generally, the Crown's legislative powers under the prerogative are subject to judicial review.[72] In any event, the constitutional settlement brought about by the Glorious Revolution which culminated in the Bill of Rights 1688 and Claim of Right 1689 gave Acts of Parliament the ascendency over the Crown's prerogatives, so that any inconsistency between an Act of Parliament and prerogative Order is Council must be resolved in favour of the Act. Accordingly, there is no domestic body able to make higher law than that made by the Queen in Parliament in a duly enacted Act of Parliament.

The meaning of the supremacy of Parliament

4.29 Parliament's ability to make supreme laws means that it may be termed the legal sovereign in the United Kingdom.[73] Without entering the important debates on the nature and meaning of sovereignty, it is sufficient to note that a lawmaker who is sovereign is subordinate to no

---

limits on the powers of the state legislatures: see *Hughes & Vale Pty Ltd v. Gair* (1954) 90 C.L.R. 203. It is not inconceivable (albeit probably impracticable) that it could arise here too, *e.g.* where a Bill passed by both Houses is challenged before receiving the Royal Assent on the ground that it violates E.C. law (*cf. R. v. H.M. Treasury, ex parte Smedley* [1985] Q.B. 657); or where a Bill passed by the Scottish Parliament is alleged to be defective in some regard: see further para. 7.08. Alternatively, the fact that the executive is implicated in the legislative process by the Royal Assent could provide a theoretical basis for its liability in damages where legislation passed in violation of E.C. law causes loss to an individual, *i.e. Francovich* liability: see further para. 5.51.

[68] For example, Resolutions of the House of Commons do not have the supreme qualities of Acts of Parliament: *Bowles v. Bank of England* [1913] 1 Ch. 57. Following this case, Parliament passed the Provisional Collection of Taxes Act 1913, which allows existing taxes to be collected on the authority of Budget Resolutions.

[69] Acts of the Scottish Parliament may be regarded as primary legislation within Scotland; but in U.K. terms they are subordinate legislation. In particular, they are not supreme law, not even within Scotland, since they must comply with the powers given to the Scottish Parliament under the Scotland Act 1998. In this regard, the Scottish Parliament is comparable to a state or provincial legislature in a federal system. For discussion of the relationship between the Scottish Parliament and judicial review, see Chapter 7.

[70] For example, under s. 2(2) of the European Communities Act 1972. When Orders in Council are the form for subordinate legislation, they will usually be governed by the Statutory Instruments Act 1946.

[71] But it is used frequently to make laws for the U.K.'s overseas dependent territories, whereupon the Orders in Council are second only to applicable Acts of Parliament in the territory's legal system. For discussion of prerogative powers to legislate within the U.K., see *Grieve v. Edinburgh and District Water Trustees*, 1918 S.C. 700, *per* Lord Justice-Clerk Scott Dickson at 713.

[72] See *R. v. Secretary of State for Home Department, ex parte Fire Brigades Union* [1995] 2 A.C. 513.

[73] *cf. R. v. Criminal Injuries Compensation Board, ex parte Lain* [1967] 2 Q.B. 864; *CCSU Minister for the Civil Service* [1985] A.C. 374; and *R. v. Secretary of State for the Home Department, ex parte Fire Brigades Union* [1995] 2 A.C. 513.

other body, may make and unmake any law it pleases and suffers no questioning of its law-making power. A sovereign lawmaker is omnicompetent and omnipotent. Whether or not the United Kingdom Parliament is truly "sovereign" in this sense has been the subject of a long running debate among legal scholars.[74] At the risk of overly simplifying the theoretical issues, it may be said that the debates have tended to focus on two matters: first, the extent to which Parliament can bind its successors, for example, by prescribing a "manner and form" by which statutory provisions may be protected from inadvertent or implied repeal; and secondly, the extent to which the courts can refuse to apply abhorrent Acts of Parliament. Whatever the earlier views on the matter,[75] Parliament became designated a sovereign law-maker during the eighteenth century, and even more assertively during the nineteenth century.[76] Although the term Parliamentary "sovereignty" is still used, it often has a tendentious quality, particularly in debates about relations between the United Kingdom and the European Union. Indeed, the political nature of sovereignty, not to say the ever diminishing plausibility in light of European and international treaty obligations of regarding the United Kingdom Parliament as "sovereign", makes the term Parliamentary supremacy preferable in a discussion of the Parliament's ascendency in the legal order. If sovereignty was ever the accurate term, international and constitutional developments in the latter part of the twentieth century now gives the term a hollow ring.[77] Yet the doctrine of the supremacy of Parliament continues to generate abstract theories about what Parliament legally could do which work to give the doctrine an almost fantasy quality far removed from a consideration of what Parliament politically can do. Some part of the reason for this is a tendency in some quarters to misunderstand the work of Dicey, who sought not only to strike a balance between the supremacy of Parliament and the rule of law but also to show that the two were dependent; that they draw on each other to establish a constitution premised on the rule of law. Dicey wrote that:

> "By every path we come round to the same conclusion, that Parliamentary sovereignty has favoured the rule of law, and that the supremacy of the law of the land both calls forth the exertion of Parliamentary sovereignty, and leads to its being exercised in a spirit of legality".[78]

---

[74] In particular, see Jennings, *The Law and the Constitution* (5th ed.), 1957; Mitchell, *Constitutional Law* (2nd ed.), 1968, Chap. 4; Muro, *Studies in Constitutional Law* (London, Butterworths), 1987, Chap. 5; Wade, "The Basis of Legal Sovereignty" [1995] Camb. L.J. 172; Marshall, *Parliamentary Sovereignty and the Commonwealth* (1957); and Heuston, "Sovereignty," Chapter VIII in Guest (ed.). *Oxford Essays in Jurisprudence* Oxford, OUP, 1961. For a full discussion and survey of both the law and the literature, see Bradley and Ewing, *Constitutional and Administrative Law* (12th ed.) (Longman, 1997), Chapter 4. See also K.W.B. Middleton, "Sovereignty in Theory and Practice" (1952) 64 J.R. 135.

[75] On which, see below.

[76] It is Dicey who made the term Parliamentary "sovereignty" popular following the publication in 1885, of his hugely significant and still influential *Law of the Constitution* (10th ed., Wade, 1959), in particular pp. 39–85. On the terminology see G. Marshall, "Parliamentary Supremacy and the Language of Constitutional Limitation" (1955) 67 J.R. 62.

[77] The developments include membership of the E.U., the guarantee of Convention rights within the U.K. legal systems and devolution of legislative power. On the relationship between international human rights treaties and English law, see Hunt, *Human Rights Law in English Courts* (Hart, Oxford, 1997).

[78] *Law of the Constitution* (19th ed., 1959), p. 114.

Nevertheless, however instructive it may be, Dicey's undoubtedly distinguished late nineteenth century *Law of the Constitution*[79] should not be approached as if it were in fact the United Kingdom's written constitution.[80] While the U.K. Constitution continues to display many of the features Dicey discussed, it has also evolved in the light of more than 100 years of political and legal experience. The legal setting for the U.K. constitution and for the meaning of the rule of law today is very different from that of more than a century ago. It serves no practical purpose to continue to discuss the constitution and in particular the supremacy of Parliament only within the confines of Dicey's assumptions.[81]

In attempting to consider the nature and meaning of Parliament's supremacy at the beginning of the twenty-first century, it is useful to break down the issues under four headings: the historical record; Parliament's omnicompetence; Parliament and its successors; and Parliament and international law. Although it is necessary to touch on the particular matter of judicial review and of U.K. primary legislation here, this is discussed in more detail in the specific contexts in which it arises.[82]

PARLIAMENT'S SUPREMACY: THE HISTORICAL RECORD

4.30 The historical record on Parliament's claim to legal supremacy is ambiguous and made more so in the Scottish context by reflections on the effects of the Anglo-Scottish Treaty of Union on Parliament's genesis. In the early years before the Union the Court of Session did not hold the respect for parliamentary legislation which it came later to feel, and which had probably always been felt in England for the work of the English parliament. Craig noted this point of difference between the two countries, and observes that while in the first instance it was the duty of a lawyer to search in the Acts of Parliament for assistance since there was no other body of positive written law of comparable authority, nevertheless:

> "We do not attribute to our Scots acts the same sanctity as attaches in England to acts of the English parliament . . . The court has been jealous to preserve its jurisdiction intact in important affairs involving grave issues, and it has within my own experience often disregarded the act in question".[83]

English law had no parallel to the doctrine of desuetude.[84] Stair regarded ancient and immemorial custom, that is the common law, as anterior to

---

[79] (10th ed., Wade ed., MacMillan, London, 1959). All citations are to this 10th edition.

[80] *cf.* Harlow and Rawlings, *Law and Administration* (2nd ed.), p. 38.

[81] See E.C.S. Wade's reference to Dicey's theories as "purely lawyer's conceptions": *Law of the Constitution* (10th ed., 1959); and *cf.* Lord Cooper's reference to Dicey's theories as "earlier dogmas": *MacCormick v. Lord Advocate*, 1953 S.C. 396 at 412. Professor Sir William Wade has conceded that the U.K. Parliament is no longer supreme, at least not as long as the U.K. remains a member of the EU: Wade, "Sovereignty – Revolution or Evolution" (1996) 112 L.Q.R. 568 (1972 Act effective in binding Parliament's successors); and see reaction from Allan, "Parliamentary Sovereignty: Law, Politics and Revolution" (1997) 113 L.Q.R. 443. See also Munro, *supra*, n. 1, Chap. 5.

[82] para. 5.49 (E.C. law and U.K. Acts of Parliament); and Pt IV of Chap. 6 (Convention rights and Acts of Parliament). More generally on the relationship between judicial review and legislation, see Chap. 9.

[83] Craig, *Jus Feudale* (Stair Society ed.), 1, 8, 9.

[84] See *Johnstone v. Stotts* (1802) 4 Pat. 274, *per* Lord Eldon L.C. at 285.

statute law and superior to it, in that Acts of Parliament are liable to desuetude which never encroaches on the common law.[85] Even in the twentieth century it has been recognised that desuetude of a common law remedy would be a novelty in the law.[86] Even so, some support can be found for an argument that the Scottish Parliament enjoyed some supremacy.[87] The authority of the "positive laws of sovereigns" was recognised by Stair.[88] Bankton saw the doctrine of desuetude as being attributable to a tacit abrogation by the lawgiver through acquiescence.[89] Erskine similarly saw the will of the people to alter the law presumed by a contrary immemorial custom; their express declaration operated as strongly.[90]

It has been said that the idea of the sovereignty of Parliament had not developed in Scotland prior to the Union of the Parliaments although the idea had already been established in England.[91] On the other hand it is not clear that prior to 1707 even the English Parliament enjoyed legal supremacy in the modern sense. Take Blackstone's own contrasting views on (by then the U.K.) Parliament's powers: "What the parliament doth, no power on earth can undo"; but "the omnipotence of parliament [is] a figure rather too bold".[92] Both Coke and several early century decisions provide doubts about the freedom of the English Parliament to do anything it wished.[93] In any event, two considerations may suggest that the Scottish Parliament was no less powerful than its English counterpart before 1707. Both the English and Scottish Parliaments announced their triumph over the Crown in the 1688 Bill of Rights and 1689 Claim of Right and both considered themselves fully empowered to abolish themselves by their own enactments implementing the Treaty of Union.

The Anglo Scottish Treaty and Acts of Union

In *MacCormick v. Lord Advocate*[94] Lord President Cooper observed: **4.31**

---

[85] Stair, *Institutes*, 1, 1, 16, *cf. Minet v. Leman* (1855) 20 Beav. 269, at 278, *per* Sir John Romilly, M.R.

[86] *M'Kendrick v. Sinclair*, 1972 S.C. (H.L.) 25, *per* Lord Reid at 54.

[87] *cf.* Mitchell, *supra*, n. 1, pp. 82–85; and see *Queensberry v. Officers of State* (1807) Mor.App.Juris. 19; *Murray v. Bailie of Torwoodhead* (1683) Harc. 13. Mitchell quotes Balfour's *Practicks—Of Law* as noting, "No judges within this realm have power to make any laws or statutes except the Parliament alone".

[88] *Institutes*, 1, 1, 16.

[89] *Institute*, 1, 1, 60,

[90] *Institutes*, 1, 1, 45.

[91] Dicey and Rait, *Thoughts on the Union between England and Scotland* (1920) pp. 19–23. See also Smith, "The Union of 1707 as Fundamental Law" [1957] P.L. 99.

[92] Blackstone's *Commentaries* (14th Ed.), Vol. I, pp. 160–161. The *Commentaries* also show that Blackstone doubted the effect of statutes contrary to God's law, "impossible to be performed" or having "absurd consequences manifestly contradictory to common reason". To similar effect, see Erskine, *Institutes*, I, 1, 20: "What the law of nature hath commanded cannot be forbidden or even dispensed with by positive law"; also 1, 1, 23, against retrospective legislation.

But there are comments the other way: "Of the power and jurisdiction of Parliament for making laws in proceeding by Bill, it is so transcendent and absolute, as it cannot be considered either for causes or persons within any bounds" (4 Coke, *Inst.* 36); "It hath sovereign and uncontrollable authority in the making . . . and expounding of laws" (Blackstone, *supra*, p. 160).

[93] For challenges to Acts of the English Parliament, see: *The Prince's Case* (1606) 8 Co.Rep. 1a; *Bonham's Case* (1610) 8 Co.Rep. 113b at 118; and *R. v. Hampden, Ship Money Case* (1637) 3 State Tr. 826.

[94] 1953 S.C. 396 at 411.

"The principle of the unlimited sovereignty of Parliament is a distinctively English principle which has no counterpart in Scottish constitutional law. It derives its origin from Coke and Blackstone, and was widely popularised during the 19th Century by Bagehot and Dicey, the latter having stated the doctrine in its classic form in his *Law and the Constitution*. Considering that the Union legislation extinguished the Parliaments of Scotland and England and replaced them by a new Parliament, I have difficulty in seeing why it should have been supposed that the new Parliament of Great Britain must inherit all the peculiar characteristics of the English Parliament but none of the Scottish Parliament, as if all that happened in 1707 was that Scottish representatives were admitted to the Parliament of England. That is not what was done".[95]

These obiter comments have spawned a vibrant Scottish debate about the significance of the Treaty of Union for Parliament's supremacy.[96] In essence, the question is whether some provisions of the Articles of Union constitute fundamental law which the U.K. Parliament is not empowered to alter. On whether or not such a question, which did not have to be decided in MacCormick,[97] raised a justiciable issue, Lord President Cooper reserved his opinion. Where the issue has been aired in subsequent cases, again never having had to be decided, the Court of Session has continued to reserve its opinion.[98] Needless to say, this failure to dispose of the issue once and for all has continued to inspire the argument that the Treaty of Union is in some measure fundamental. Yet any claim that it is faces formidable difficulties. Even if the courts were prepared to accept a jurisdiction to review U.K. primary legislation against the provisions of the Treaty of Union, itself not an inconceivable proposition in light of judicial review of legislation on grounds of E.C. law and Convention rights, the antiquated terms of the Treaty, notably the concept of "evident utility" in Article XVIII of the Acts of Union, would clearly present problems of justiciability. Moreover, Parliament has on several occasions passed Acts which violated clauses in the Treaty of Union. Indeed, the equally "fundamental" Treaty of Union with Ireland, also declared to last "for ever", did not restrain Parliament in providing for Ireland's independence. And most recently, s. 37 of the Scotland Act 1998 expressly provides that the Acts of Union "have effect subject to this Act".[99] In any event, whether or not the U.K. Parliament

---

[95] *ibid.* at 411.

[96] For example, see Mitchell, *Constitutional Law* (2nd ed., 1968), Chap. 5 and pp. 92–98; *Stair Memorial Encyclopaedia*, "Constitutional Law", Vol. 5, paras 338–360; Smith, "The Union of 1707 as Fundamental Law" [1957] P.L. 99; MacCormick, "Does the UK have a Constitution? Reflections on MacCormick v. Lord Advocate" (1978) 29 N.I.L.Q. 1; Upton, "Marriage Vows of the Elephant: the Constitution of 1707" (1989) 105 L.Q.R. 79; and Edwards, "The Treaty of Union: More Hints of Constitutionalism" (1992) 12 L.S. 33. See also Munro, supra, n. 1, Chap. 4 and Himsworth and Walter, "The Poll Tax and Fundamental Law", 1991 J.R. 45.

[97] The case was disposed of on the grounds of relevancy and no title to sue; accordingly, what Lord President Cooper said about the Treaty and Acts of Union is *obiter*.

[98] See *Gibson v. Lord Advocate*, 1975 S.C. 136; *Pringle, Petr*, 1991 S.L.T. 330. *cf. R. v. The Lord Chancellor, ex parte the Law Society, The Times*, June 25, 1993.

[99] It might be argued that this provision cuts two ways: on the one hand, it demonstrates Parliament's power to alter the Treaty and Acts of Union; on the other, the need for express provision is desirable so as to avoid any potential challenge based on the Treaty of Union. Interestingly, however, Arts 4–6 of the Acts of Union "so far as they relate to

was "born free", Parliament's modern supremacy has to be understood in light of the nineteenth century political developments.

The U.K. Parliament's domestic legal supremacy must take account of the political supremacy that came from the electoral reforms after the Great Reform Act 1832. As the franchise for election to the House of Commons broadened, the role of the House of Commons in assuring the supremacy of Parliament increased. By the beginning of the twentieth Century, the advent of the Parliament Act 1911 confirms that whatever the legal definition might be, Parliamentary supremacy means the power of a majority in the House of Commons to insist on its will. Even if Dicey's later work reveals doubts about the consequences of democracy,[1] his assertion of the supremacy of Parliament must be understood against the background of a House of Commons elected by a broadening electorate and ensuring government accountable to that electorate. Mitchell captured the point well: "The place of Parliament in legal thinking cannot be divorced from the place of Parliament in current political thinking. Political decisions are as far as possible to be taken in Parliament, and the growth of the democratic process since 1832 has obviously affected the attitude of the courts".[2]

Post-Union legislation

By the end of the eighteenth century precedence had come to be accorded to statute law in place of custom. Legislation came to be seen as the direct expression of the will of the sovereign power and the implied will of the people identified through immemorial custom came to be no longer necessary or appropriate as a means of abrogating or qualifying statute law. At least in relation to Acts passed after the Union the Court will not apply the doctrine of desuetude. Thus, by the twentieth century the court, as guardian of customary or common law, has accepted the priority to be given to statute law.[3] As Lord Cooper observed: "We owe respect to previous decisions of superior or equal authority, but we also owe respect to Acts of Parliament; and if subsequent statutes have deprived a decision of its whole content, we have no duty to echo outmoded and superseded conceptions".[4] Parlia-

4.32

---

freedom of trade" are reserved from the competence of the Scottish Parliament by virtue of Sched. 4, para. 1(2)(a) to the Scotland Act 1998. It may therefore be (ironically?) that the courts will be called on to review Acts of the Scottish Parliament against some of the provisions of the Acts of Union—a power which arises by virtue of an enactment of the U.K. Parliament.

[1] *cf.* Heuston, *supra* (n. 67) who observes that Dicey's dilemma arose from trying to reconcile his strong Unionism (in relation to Ireland) with his views on the supremacy of Parliament.

[2] Mitchell, *supra*, n. 1, Chap. 4 at p. 89. He cites Lord Normand in *Pollok School v. Glasgow Town Clerk*, 1946 S.C. 373 at 386 by way of example of the judicial deference to democracy.

[3] That the courts accept Parliament's supremacy can be supported with abundant citation. See, for example, *British Railways Board v. Pickin* [1974] A.C. 765 (holding that private Acts also enjoy quality of supreme law); *Collco Dealings v. IRC* [1962] A.C. 1 (statute contrary to international law valid); *Cheney v. Conn* [1968] 1 All E.R. 779 (even if Act can be used for unlawful purpose, Act is not invalid). See also *Madzimbamuto v. Lardner-Burke & George* [1969] 1 A.C. 645, at 723; and, of course, the War Damage Act 1965 for an unusual example of retrospective legislation (overruling the House of Lords decision in *Burma Oil Co. v. Lord Advocate*, 1964 S.C. (H.L.) 117). But *cf. R. v. Secretary of State for Social Security, ex parte Joint Council for the Welfare of Immigrants* [1997] 1 W.L.R. 275 (regulations unlawful because contrary to fundamental human rights notwithstanding no protection thereof in parent statute or (at that time) in any Act of Parliament).

[4] *Beith's Trustees v. Beith*, 1950 S.C. 66 at 72.

ment will certainly alter the law in light of the decisions of the courts where it considers the position to require amendment.[5] On the other hand, in the interpretation of statutes there is a well-recognised presumption against alteration of the common law except in so far as the statute expressly provides.[6] Moreover it has been argued that the recognition of the superiority of statute law over the common law may not necessarily impose a qualification upon the power of the Supreme Court in matters of judicial review.[7]

Judicial support

4.33 During the twentieth century, commentators have increasingly noted that the supremacy of Parliament is in law a judicial creation. Its existence depends on recognition of the doctrine by the judges. Since Parliament cannot declare itself supreme, the constitutional doctrine of Parliamentary supremacy is a common law rule.[8] This means that parliamentary supremacy and what it entails are in the gift of the judges. Professor Sir William Wade is the leading proponent of this view which, in theoretical terms, has much to commend it.[9] Certainly it is not difficult to find dicta in judicial opinions showing judges attributing the quality of absolute supremacy to Parliament. In *Liversidge v. Anderson*, Lord Wright observed: "Parliament is supreme. It can enact extraordinary powers of interfering with personal liberty".[10] Although a controversial wartime decision and unlikely to be put so strongly today, not least in view of the United Kingdom's international human rights obligations, the strong approach to Parliament's supremacy still finds some judicial support.[11]

The European Union and human rights

4.34 Membership of the European Union carries with it a recognition of the supremacy of E.C. law.[12] The relationship between the supremacy of E.C. law is considered further in later chapters. But it must be noticed in the present context that in the area of matters over which the E.C. legislates the power of the U.K. Parliament is subordinate. Where there

---

[5] The passing of the Trade Dispute Act 1906 reversed the decision in *Taff Vale Ry Co. v. Amalgamated Society of Railway Servants* [1901] A.C. 426; the Scottish Land Court Act 1938 requiring members to retire at age 65 reversed the decision in *Mackay and Esslemont v. Lord Advocate*, 1937 S.C. 860 where it had been held that members of the Land Court held office *ad vitam aut culpam*; the Foreign Compensation Act 1969 was passed following the decision in *Anisminic Ltd v. Foreign Compensation Commission* [1969] 2 A.C. 147; the Education (Scotland) Act 1973 followed on the decision in *Malloch v. Aberdeen Corporation*, 1971 S.C.(H.L.) 85.

[6] Maxwell, *Interpretation of Statutes* (12th ed.). p. 116.

[7] See Lord Woolf, "Droit Public—English Style" [1995] P.L.; and Laws, "Law and Democracy" [1995] P.L. 72.

[8] A cogent argument that the doctrine of parliamentary sovereignty is not a dominant rule but the problem child of the constitution is presented by Chijoke Dike, "The case against Parliamentary Sovereignty" [1976] P.L. 283.

[9] see Wade, "The Basis of Legal Sovereignty" (1955) Camb.L.J. 172 at 187; and also *Constitutional Fundamentals* (1980 Hamlyn Lectures, Stevens, London, 1980). Professor Wade's approach to Parliament's supremacy has the support of Lord Denning M.R.: see *Blackburn v. Att.-Gen.* [1971] 2 All E.R. 1380 at 1383.

[10] [1942] A.C. 206 at 261.

[11] *cf. Madzimbamuto v. Lardner-Burke & George* [1969] 1 A.C. 645, *per* Lord Reid at 723 (PC); *R. v. Jordan* [1967] Crim. L.R. 483; *Cheney v. Conn* [1968] 1 All E.R. 779; but see also decisions involving E.C. law, most importantly, *R. v. Secretary of State for Transport, ex p. Factortame (No. 2)* [1991] 1 A.C. 603, esp. *per* Lord Bridge of Harwich at 658–659.

[12] See further para. 5.49.

is a conflict between applicable E.C. law and provisions in an Act of the U.K. Parliament, E.C. law demands that the national law be disapplied. For the most part, the U.K. courts now accept this conclusion.[13] In addition, further qualification on Parliament's supremacy may now be found to arise from the domestic effect given to the rights guaranteed by the United Nations Convention on Human Rights. These Convention rights are made directly accessible in the courts of the United Kingdom by the terms of the Human Rights Act 1998. While it is evident that in procedural terms the Act has been drafted to pay lip service to the idea of Parliamentary supremacy, the substantial reality is that the Convention rights as set out in the Act will govern the work of Parliament, the operation of government ministers, and the courts, most notably in the interpretation of legislation. The implications of the Human Rights Act 1998 for judicial review are considered in Chapter 6.

Conclusion on the historical record

The historical record provides some scope for debate for and against **4.35** Parliament's supremacy both as a legal and political matter. Today, however, the international, European and domestic legal context in which Parliament operates makes absolute law-making supremacy little more than a fiction.[14] While this is no answer to the question of what the courts would do if faced with immoral legislation such as that passed by the Nazis, it does require the constitution to be seen not only in terms of the theoretical plenitude of Parliament's powers but also against the background of a range of constitutional, international, legal and political values and realities which are equally supreme.[15] In other words, the U.K. constitution should be understood in terms of a "mutuality of respect between two constitutional sovereignties",[16] that of Parliament in creating the law, and that of the courts in upholding the rule of law. More generally, as Bradley and Ewing conclude: "A return to the U.K. to Diceyan orthodoxy would scarcely compensate for the disadvantages of an isolationist policy within Europe".[17]

PARLIAMENT'S OMNICOMPETENCE

It has been said to follow from Dicey's approach to the supremacy of **4.36** Parliament that Parliament's law-making power amounts to omnicompetence.[18] If it wished, Parliament could outlaw smoking on the streets of Paris or order that all blue-eyed babies be killed.[19] The fact that it did not do so was for Dicey not the result of any legal inhibition but rather because of political constraints.[20] Under Dicey's approach, Parliament's

---

[13] See *R. v. Secretary of State for Transport, ex parte Factortame Ltd (No. 2)* [1991] 1 A.C. 603; and *R. v. Secretary of State for Employment, ex parte EOC* [1995] 1 A.C. 1.

[14] *cf.* Bradley, "The Sovereignty of Parliament—in Perpetuity?" in Jowell and Oliver (eds), *The Changing Constitution* (3rd ed., London, Stevens, 1994).

[15] *cf.* Laws , "Law and Democracy" [1995] P.L. 72.

[16] *R. v. Parliamentary Commissioner for Standards, ex p. Al Fayed* [1998] 1 W.L.R. 669 at 670, *per* Sedley J.

[17] *Constitutional and Administrative Law* (12th ed., Longman, 1997), p. 85.

[18] See Dicey: *Law of the Constitution* (10th ed., 1959), pp. 87–91 and Chap. 2.

[19] The first example is from Jennings, *The Law and the Constitution* (5th ed., 1959), p. 171; the second that of Dicey's friend Leslie Stephen, *The Science of Ethics* (1882).

[20] The eventual restraint on legislation would be the active resistance of the people, but since the members of Parliament should be reflecting the views of other citizens it would be unlikely that measures which were such as to cause a general public outrage would be contemplated: see Fraser, *Constitutional Law*, p. 13.

powers were subject to internal and external limits; the former the result of what Parliament could not bring itself to do, and the latter what its electors would not allow it to do.[21] In any event, there were no enforceable legal constraints on Parliament's legislative powers. As noted above, however, Dicey balanced his belief in Parliament's sovereignty with the rule of law. The pre-eminence which the rule of law gives to the ordinary courts and the common law leads Dicey to notice the crucial role which the judges have in giving effect to Parliament's will.[22] It is tempting to conclude from this that even for Dicey, the absolute legal supremacy of Parliament was more imaginary than real.

Since Dicey's time, the ability of the U.K. Parliament "to make or unmake any law" has been significantly qualified. When Dicey was writing the U.K. Parliament's geographical powers, if not extending to the streets of Paris, were at their zenith. In the twentieth century, of course, the global reach of the Imperial Parliament's power has dwindled and this has produced legal limits on Parliament's powers whatever the theoretical purist may claim.[23] Originally, the limits on Parliament's powers to legislate for the Dominions such as Canada and Australia were the result of constitutional convention. In 1931, following an Imperial Conference, Parliament passed the Statute of Westminster 1931, section 4 of which expressly restricted Parliament's legislative power to extend a U.K. Act to a Dominion without the consent of the Dominion's own parliament.[24] The significance of the Statute of Westminster for Parliament's supremacy has since vexed commentators.[25] For some it is merely a political limit and can have no enforceable legal force in the United Kingdom. However, to insist that the U.K. Parliament may today unilaterally pass a law the effect of which is to repeal the New Zealand Bill of Rights Act 1990 or amend the Constitution of Australia Act 1900, in the expectation that these laws will be followed by U.K. judges irrespective of the views of other countries, is truly to believe in fairy tales. The absurdity of this position was forthrightly met by Lord Sankey L.C.: "It is doubtless true that the power of the Imperial Parliament to pass on its own initiative any legislation it thought fit extending to Canada remains in theory unimpaired: indeed the Imperial Parliament could, as a matter of abstract law, repeal or disregard s.4 of the Statute [of Westminster]. But that is theory and has no relation to realities".[26] Although this dictum may be criticised,[27] continuing to distinguish between what local courts would do (ignore the U.K. Parliament's legislation) and what U.K. courts would do (follow it) undermines the relationship between Parliamentary supremacy and the law. Indeed, Lord Sankey's choice of words, suggests an impatience with abstract theories on Parliament's potential powers and a preference for the realities of a constitutional system respecting the rule of law.

Be that as it may, the Statute of Westminster raises the question of whether Parliament can bind its successors. Other examples of Acts

---

[21] See Munro, *Studies in Constitutional Law* (1987, Butterworths), at p. 86.

[22] Dicey: *Law of the Constitution*, at pp. 413–414.

[23] *cf. British Coal Corporation v. R.* [1935] A.C. 500, *per* Lord Sankey L.C. at 520.

[24] A good example of s. 4 of the Statute of Westminster in operation is provided by the Australian High Court in *Copyright Owners' Reproduction Society Ltd v. EMI (Australia) Ltd* (1958) 100 C.L.R. 597, esp. at 612–613.

[25] *cf.* Mitchell, *supra*, n. 1, at pp. 78–80; and Munro, *supra*, n. 1, at pp. 94–97.

[26] *British Coal Corporation v. R.* [1935] A.C. 500 at 520.

[27] See Munro, *supra*, at pp. 95–96, describing it as "unhappy".

which are claimed to bind future Parliaments include the European Communities Act 1972, the Northern Ireland (Constitution) Act 1973, and no doubt also the Human Rights Act 1998 and the devolution legislation. Whether or not it may be said that these Acts show that Parliament can bind its successors, which is discussed further below,[28] mention of the European Communities Act 1972 and the devolution legislation allows the increasing use of referendums to be noted. Their use may suggest that at least on certain issues there may be a recognition that the mandate given by the people at a general election may not be sufficient to support the carrying through of particular measures and that direct resort to the ultimate source of power is appropriate in order to achieve their enactment. It may be arguable that both resort to referendums and the nature of legislation eventually enacted following them operates to qualify notions of Parliament's omnicompetence.

For Dicey, the main point about Parliament's omnicompetence was that the U.K. constitution knew of no higher form of law than an Act of Parliament. In strict legal terms this was and remains true. But to discuss any constitution, not least that of the United Kingdom, in strict legal terms is rather to miss the wood for the trees. In this respect, Dicey certainly concentrated on the wood: popular and practical controls on Parliament together with judicial interpretation of statutes operated to reconcile the "unlimited" supremacy of Parliament with the rule of law. As for the practical, the requirements of the United Kingdom's membership of the European Union, along with the Human Rights Act 1998, a variety of international treaties and the advent of other centres of legislative power within the United Kingdom, now give abstract discussions of Parliament's unlimited legislative powers an unreal air. Equally, the rules and presumptions applicable in statutory interpretation embodying as they do fundamental values and principles of the common law may be seen as effective limits on Parliament's omnicompetence. Having acknowledged their existence, it then becomes difficult to decide which is first: Parliament's enactments as the highest form of law known in the United Kingdom or the common law rules for giving practical effect to them.

PARLIAMENT AND ITS SUCCESSORS

Dicey observed that parliament's omnipotence is subject to only one, **4.37** though significant qualification. It cannot bind its successors. It follows, therefore, that parliament is simultaneously supreme and subordinate: it can do anything today except rule what it can do tomorrow. This conundrum has long fascinated constitutional theorists. More practically, the associated doctrine of implied repeal gives rise to several problems, although it is also an undeniably useful rule of statutory interpretation.

Detailed inquiries into Parliament's capacity to bind its successors is given in other works.[29] For present purposes, the main question is whether the courts agree that Parliament cannot bind its successors. Before the United Kingdom joined the EEC in 1973,[30] discussion of this

---

[28] See para. 4.37.
[29] In particular, see Bradley and Ewing, *Constitutional and Administrative Law* (12th ed., 1997, Longman), Chap. 4.
[30] Now the European Community, which is itself part of the broader European Union: see para. 5.04.

subject focused on several Commonwealth decisions,[31] the Statute of Westminster and the Treaty of Union, in the latter case particularly on the opinion of Lord Cooper in *MacCormick v. Lord Advocate*.[32] In light of the case law developments on the European Communities Act 1972, it is now difficult to deny that Parliament can bind its successors. Section 2(4) of the 1972 Act undoubtedly now has this effect. This leads to the question of whether the 1972 Act is confined to its own unique conditions or whether the policy underlying other enactments can also lead to a degree of entrenchment. In this respect, the Human Rights Act 1998 giving effect to the European Convention on Human Rights and the Scotland Act 1998 establishing a Scottish Parliament are significant. Although neither contains any terms entrenching their provisions, in the case of the Scotland Act 1998 not even any express term such as s. 2(4) of the European Communities Act 1972 to protect its provisions from the doctrine of implied repeal by subsequent Acts of the U.K. Parliament, some restriction on the freedom of future Parliaments must exist if the Convention rights and legislative devolution are to be effective.

PARLIAMENTARY SUPREMACY AND INTERNATIONAL LAW

4.38 A further restraint on the freedom of the legislature can be brought about by the obligation to honour international treaties into which the United Kingdom has entered. Domestic legislation may be required to incorporate the treaty provisions into domestic law and subsequent legislation may require to avoid conflict with obligations in the treaty.

International law may be divided into treaty law and customary international law.[33] Under the U.K. constitution as classically understood, international treaties are entered into by the Crown in right of the United Kingdom and its power to do so is not justiciable. When a treaty is signed and subsequently ratified by the government it operates in international law to bind the Crown. Compliance with and violation of the treaty is a matter exclusively for the international legal process. On this basis, ratified treaties can have no direct effect in the national legal systems until their terms have been implemented by an Act of Parliament and then only to the extent that they have been implemented. Until a treaty is implemented, therefore, no individual can rely directly on its terms in a U.K. court. In international law this constitutional tradition is termed "dualist", in contrast to the "monist" tradition under which treaties (and often rules of customary international law too) can be incorporated into the national legal order following ratification by the state. It has been convincingly argued that the United Kingdom cannot simply be termed "dualist" since national courts both draw on rules of customary international law and, more significantly, refer to a compliance presumption under which all enactments must be construed so as to comply with the United Kingdom's international obligations, such as those contained in ratified but unimplemented international treaties.[34] It

---

[31] In particular, *Att. Gen. for New South Wales v. Trethowan* [1932] A.C. 526 (P.O.) affirming (1931) 44 C.L.R. 394 (holding invalid a New South Wales Act repealing an entrenched provision in an earlier Act without the required referendum).

[32] 1953 S.C. 379. See further para. 4.31; and para. 9.10.

[33] *CCSU v. Minister for the Civil Service* [1985] 1 A.C. 374 at 418; *cf. Blackburn v. Att.-Gen.* [1971] 2 All E.R. 1380: see also *R. v. Secretary of State for Foreign & Commonwealth Affairs, ex p. Rees-Mogg* [1994] Q.B. 552.

[34] See Hunt, *Using Human Rights Law in English Courts* (Hart, Oxford, 1997). The compliance presumption is discussed further at para. 6.12 in the context of its role protecting human rights.

is therefore not so clear that the U.K. legal systems draw a rigid distinction between national law and international law as evidenced by the terms of treaties. Customary international law has also long been accepted as part of the common law, both in England and in Scotland.[35]

VII EQUALITY BEFORE THE LAW

Introduction

As was mentioned at the outset,[36] the fourth element which may be **4.39** derived from the concept of the rule of law is the idea that all should be equal before the law. In a just legal system, this is a principle of wide application, encompassing not only the need for institutions and rules to secure formal equality but also some attempt at achieving substantive equality between all persons. In the sense in which Dicey used equality as a precept of the rule of law,[37] it meant only that everyone, namely public officials and ordinary citizens, had to be subject to the same law and the same courts, in contradistinction to the implications of a separate system of administrative law and administrative courts such as in France, where public officials' conduct and liability were (and ultimately still are) exclusively the province of the Conseil d'Etat. For Dicey, perhaps unsurprisingly for a late nineteenth century legal scholar,[38] equality connoted little more than the formal meaning of the same law for everyone applied by the same courts. It certainly did not envisage courts, in pursuance of protecting the rule of law, formulating more substantive conceptions of equality, such as whether "equal" laws treated similarly situated persons similarly and, if not, whether the law's classifications were reasonable or impermissibly discriminatory.[39] Nevertheless, whatever may be the thinness of Dicey's conception of equality for the purposes of the rule of law, it at least identifies some idea of equality as being a central requirement of the rule of law. It is no criticism of Dicey to say that it is for subsequent generations to formulate what their times require equality to mean.

It is beyond the task of the present discussion to attempt to identify a conception of equality which ought to be part of a wide-ranging

---

[35] See *Halsbury's Laws*, Vol. 18, para. 1403, where the point is made that in some cases customary international law has been said to be incorporated into and to form part of the law, while in others (of which the Scottish case of *Mortensen v. Peters* (1906) 8 F.(J.) 93 is an example), it is only part of the national law in so far as the rules have been accepted as part of the law. In Vol. 8(2) of the same work (para. 236, n. 2), the view is stated that how far international law is a part of English law is a matter of some doubt.

[36] para. 4.02.

[37] *Law of the Constitution*, pp. 202–203.

[38] *cf.* the different approaches of the U.S. Supreme Court on the equal protection of the laws clause in the 14th Amendment to the U.S. Constitution in *Plessy v. Ferguson*, 163 U.S. 537 (1896)—holding that separate but equal treatment of the races is constitutional; and *Brown v. Board of Education*, 347 U.S. 483 (1954)—integration of the races required by the Constitution.

[39] But see *Kruse v. Johnson* [1898] 2 Q.B. 91, *per* Lord Russell C.J. at 99–100; *cf.* s. 15 of the Canadian Charter of Rights and Freedoms: guaranteed rights to be "equal before and under the law" and to "equal protection and equal benefit of the law". See *Andrews v. Law Society of British Columbia* [1989] 1 S.C.R. 143 for the early approach to s. 15; and *Eldridge v. Att.-Gen. of British Columbia* [1997] 3 S.C.R. 624 for a more recent application.

definition of the rule of law.[40] Instead, the present task is to stress the importance of equality as a feature of the rule of law for the purposes of judicial review of all governmental powers. On account of the way in which judicial review has developed throughout the United Kingdom, this gives rise to a consideration of the constitutional relationship between the executive and judicial review. As will be seen, the key problems have arisen around the definition of the Crown, the scope of review of its prerogative powers, and a variety of restraints on judicial review and the law of remedies where the Crown, or more generally the government, is concerned. More recent developments also raise issues about the implications of the deregulation and privatisation of government power for judicial review.[41] While these issues more often concern the scope of review and address wider concerns about the failure of the law to treat government bodies differently when they do things which everyone else does, such as make contracts,[42] there are also questions about the reach of the Crown's rights and privileges, in particular how many bodies may enjoy them. Of course, this raises the ever-present problem in discussions of British constitutional and administrative law, namely the absence of a definition of the "state". While it would be too ambitious in this context to attempt a theory of the state in the United Kingdom or, for that matter, an extensive discussion of the concept of the Crown,[43] it must be acknowledged that the ascertainment of what is "the Crown", and more generally, what is "public" and what "private", is made harder in the United Kingdom as a result of no conception of the state. In any event, the focus here is principally on the Crown as the embodiment of the executive government, on its position in judicial review, and on the reviewability of its powers. The specialities of remedies against the Crown are considered in a later context.[44]

The Crown and Equality Before the Law

4.40 Although Dicey asserted "equality before the ordinary law of the land" as an aspect of the rule of law, even in his own time the law did not truly satisfy this conception of equality. In particular, while it may have been true that the Prime Minister as an individual was subject to the same law as everyone else, in so far as government ministers came within the definition of the Crown, they enjoyed some privileges and immunities appertaining to the Crown. In effect these worked, and to the lesser extent to which they continue to apply, still work, an inequality in the law. Of course, it must be accepted that the government is in a special

---

[40] For further discussion, and comment on the literature, see Allan: *Law, Liberty, and Justice* (Clarendon Press, Oxford, 1993), Chap. 7. See also Craig, "Formal and Substantive Conceptions of the Rule of Law: An Analytical Framework" [1997] P.L 467; and Allan "The Rule of Law as the Rule of Reason: Consent and Constitutionalism" (1999) 115 L.Q.R. 221.

[41] This last subject is more graphically termed the "contractualisation" of government power: see Harden, *The Contracting State* (Open Uni. Press, Buckingham, 1992); and Hunt, "Constitutionalism and the Contractualisation of Government in the United Kingdom", in Taggart (ed.), *The Province of Administrative Law* (Hart, Oxford, 1997), Chap. 2.

[42] See Arrowsmith, "Judicial Review and the Contractual Powers of Public Authorities" (1990) 106 L.Q.R. 277.

[43] On theories of the state, see Dunleavy and O'Leary, *Theories of the State: The Politics of Liberal Democracy* (MacMillan, London, 1987); and on the Crown, Mitchell, *Constitutional Law*, pp. 167 *et seq.*

[44] See below, para. 23.36.

position. In order to perform its responsibilities effectively and efficiently
it has to be treated differently for some purposes. By way of example,
the conduct of foreign affairs, the defence of the realm, the ordering of
the public finances, the allocation of scarce resources, even the prosecution of those alleged to have violated the criminal law, all call for powers
which ordinary citizens neither possess nor need. But the important
questions are whether the extent of the special powers, privileges and
immunities the law confers on government is justifiable; whether their
exercise is lawful; and whether they strike a fair balance between the
government's (and society's) needs and the rights of the individual.[45]
Under a constitution committed to the rule of law, these are all
questions which are properly for the courts. As Nolan L.J. said in *M v.
Home Office*[46]: "The proper constitutional relationship of the executive
with the courts is that the courts will respect all acts of the executive
within its lawful province, and that the executive will respect all decisions
of the courts as to what its lawful province is".

Certainly, judicial review must recognise that the executive in all parts
of the United Kingdom is accountable to an elected legislature.[47] In
appropriate cases the court must show deference to the executive's
political responsibilities and the democratic source of the executive's
authority. But this cannot frustrate the constitutional duty of the courts
to ensure that the rule of law and the principles of constitutionalism are
observed by the executive. Indeed, failure to ensure that the executive
acts within the law would undermine the relationship between the
judiciary and the legislature.[48] In a constitutional democracy committed
to the rule of law, the executive's political accountability to the legislature and accountability in the courts for the legality of its actions operate
together to secure limited and lawful government.[49]

Judicial Review of Government Powers

As has been noticed above,[50] government powers traditionally fall into   **4.41**
two categories: those which have a statutory source and those which flow
from the Royal prerogative. In addition, of course, government bodies
also have all of the powers which everyone else has, such as the power to
enter contracts, rent property, employ people and tender for services

---

[45] So it might be asked., for example, whether such a balance was struck by the
traditional approach in Scotland under which judicial review was not available against
exercises of the Lord Advocate's prosecutorial discretion: *cf. McBain v. Crichton*, 1961 J.C.
25, esp. *per* Lord Justice-General Clyde at 29. See further para. 8.44; and compare *R. v.
DPP, ex p. C* [1995] 1 Cr.App.R. 136.

[46] [1992] Q.B. 270 at 314. The Court of Appeal's decision was affirmed on different
grounds by the House of Lords: [1994] 1 A.C. 377. This decision is discussed further at
para. 23.38 below.

[47] Of course, there are now several executive governments in the U.K.. Leaving aside
local government, there is the U.K. government, which is accountable to the U.K.
Parliament; the Scottish Executive, which is accountable to the Scottish Parliament; the
Welsh Executive, accountable to the Welsh Assembly; and the Northern Ireland Executive,
accountable to the Northern Ireland Parliament. How the law will develop to govern the
relationships between each of these executives will be an interesting aspect of the U.K.'s
devolution arrangements. Issues related to judicial review of the Scottish Executive are
discussed briefly in Chap. 7.

[48] This point arguably supports the *ultra vires* principle as the basis of judicial review of
statutory powers.

[49] *cf.* Sedley, "Human Rights: a Twenty-First Century Agenda" [1995] P.L. 386; and see
also Beloff, "Judicial Review—2001: A Prophetic Odyssey" (1995) 58 M.L.R. 143.

[50] See para. 4.15.

which they wish performed. Such powers will often be expressly conferred and expressly or impliedly limited by empowering statutes, but in
so far as these limits are observed, the exercise of ordinary common law
powers by government is subject to the ordinary law.

As regards statutory powers, subject to theoretical debates about the
basis of judicial review, the true nature of the courts' power to review the
exercise of statutory powers on some of the grounds of review and the
extent to which Parliament may exclude judicial review,[51] the courts'
jurisdiction to review exercises of statutory powers has been less
problematic in the development of the law. Once the modern development of judicial review began in the 1960s and freed itself from some
earlier precedents about "unfettered" or "absolute" discretions and
"subjective" powers, the courts' authority to ensure that Parliament's
expressed and implied intentions about how statutory powers are to be
exercised was easily recognised. At the very least, it could be assumed
that a supreme Parliament would tolerate no "inferior judicatory"
breaching the law both as Parliament had expressed it and, more
presumably, as it operated in general. More difficult, however, were the
sensitive subject-matters of some decisions. For example, to what extent
could the exercise of a statutory power framed in terms of a minister's
assessment of "the public interest" or "the interests of the state" be
challenged in judicial review[52]? In turn, this touched on the extent to
which the exercise of prerogative powers could be challenged in judicial
review.

Judicial Review of Prerogative Powers

4.42 Historically, judicial review of the exercise of prerogative powers was
restricted to ensuring the existence and proper definition of a prerogative power. Nothing done by the government in pursuance of prerogative
powers could be challenged in the courts. But the modern expression of
the courts' jurisdiction to review the lawfulness of exercises of prerogative powers began in 1920 with the House of Lords decision in *Att.-Gen.
v. De Keyser's Royal Hotel*.[53] In this case, the House of Lords decided that
where Parliament had legislated to provide statutory powers in areas
where powers previously derived from the prerogative, the statute
became the limit of the government's powers in that area. In other
words, the statute covered the field and the prerogative powers of the
government were removed; the government could only lawfully exercise
its powers in terms of the statute. Subsequent decisions in England,
however, have recognised that at least some prerogative powers are
susceptible to judicial review. The matter is considered later in Chapter
9, to which reference should be made.[54]

Definition of the Executive Government in the UK

4.43 A problem for judicial review is understanding what is meant by the
executive under the U.K. constitution. As already noticed, a problem for
constitutional and administrative law in the United Kingdom is that the

---

[51] See para. 4.16 above.
[52] See *Chandler v. DPP* [1964] A.C. 763, esp. the speech of Lord Devlin. *cf. GCHQ*
[1985] A.C. 374, esp. *per* Lord Diplock at 408.
[53] [1920] A.C. 508.
[54] See para. 9.14.

constitution has an awkward concept of the state.[55] Without doubt, this is the most negative aspect of Dicey's legacy to constitutional law and stunted the development of a Scottish and English system of judicial review of government power.[56] In Dicey's scheme, the government and its officers enjoyed no greater powers or privileges than an ordinary person since the rule of law required everyone to be subject to the same laws. Although this was more true at the end of the nineteenth century than it has been in most of the twentieth century, even in Dicey's time "the Crown" enjoyed immunities in the courts which made it misleading to say that the law applied to it equally.[57] As government and its legal powers increased, confusion about what is meant by "the Crown" and what are its limits also increased until after the Second World War when "Crown" had become coterminous with all of the executive government and all of its personnel.

Terminology: Crown and State

The terminology of "the Crown" is not difficult if "Crown" can simply be the British term for "state".[58] The difficulty is that the legal definition of "the Crown" has been expansive simultaneously embracing the Monarch personally, all the institutions of government, certainly executive and judicial institutions which all operate in the name of the Crown but also including aspects of legislative power, all government departments, government ministers, officials and possibly more.[59] Although there are always theoretical difficulties in conceptualising the state, British lawyers have conveniently avoided these in the course of the constitution's historical development by giving the Crown its ubiquitous nature at the head of all three branches of government.[60] The Crown's ubiquity was further asserted by its imperial dimensions and notions of the "indivisible Crown", notions which only gradually subsided as the old Dominions emerged out of the United Kingdom's shadow to become sovereign nations in their own rights on the international stage.[61] Without doubt, the problem of defining the Crown has posed significant problems for judicial review. Historically, the Scottish approach to the Crown was less expansive and less acquiescent than the English, with Scottish courts taking a more robust approach to the Crown's privileges and immu-

4.44

---

[55] See Allison, *A Continental Distinction in the Common Law: A Historical and Comparative Perspective on English Public Law* (Clarendon Press: Oxford, 1996), Chap. 2; Harlow, "The Crown: Wrong Once Again?" (1977) 40 M.L.R. 728; and Harlow and Rawlings, *Law and Administration* (2nd ed., London: Butterworths, 1997), pp. 4–7.

[56] See Mitchell, "The causes and effects of the absence of a system of public law in the United Kingdom" [1965] P.L. 95.

[57] For example, before the Crown Proceedings Act 1947, the Crown could not be sued at common law for tortious or delictual acts for which it was responsible directly or vicariously. A remedy was instead to be sought by means of a petition of right, submitted to the Lord Advocate or in England, the Attorney-General.

[58] *cf. Chandler v. DPP* [1964] A.C. 763, where the State is equated with the Crown, at least for the purposes of the (repealed) Official Secrets Act 1911, s. 1. But see Lord Devlin at 810–811, arguing that "interests of the State" is broader than "interests of the Crown".

[59] For example, the Post Office, the former nationalised industries.

[60] *cf.* Prosser, "The State, Constitutions and Implementing Economic Policy: Privatisation and Regulation in the UK, France and the USA" (1995) 4 *Social and Legal Studies* 507, esp. at 509–510; and Jacob, *The Republican Crown: Lawyers and the Making of the State in Twentieth Century Britain* (Dartmouth: Aldershot, 1996).

[61] The decisive evidence of this is usually considered to be the independent declarations of war that Australia, Canada, New Zealand and South Africa made in 1939.

nities.[62] In significant respects, however, the approach to the Crown throughout the United Kingdom is now the same and in at least one respect is more quiescent in Scotland than in England.[63]

The Crown

4.45 The simultaneous transformation and continuity of the British Constitution is most clearly observable in relation to the Crown. The Interpretation Act 1889 defined the Crown to mean "the Sovereign for the time being"[64] but in the Interpretation Act 1978, the equivalent provision, section 10, deals only with references to the Sovereign. The meaning of the Crown at the end of the nineteenth century is more limited than its meaning today, a reflection of the growth of the executive government which is the principal entity comprising the Crown as a concept rather than as a person.

Maitland described the Crown as "a convenient cover for ignorance [that] saves us from asking difficult questions".[65] The difficult questions concern who legally exercises government powers: the Monarch, the minister, the official or one or all of them for the Crown as a corporation.[66] Several attempts have been made to define the Crown as the figurative term for the government in the United Kingdom but, as Sedley has noted, the task is complicated by: "the theoretical unity of the Crown [which] keeps getting in the way of the notion of the separation of powers".[67]

One of the more useful definitions of Crown as executive government is given in the House of Lords decision in *Town Investments Ltd v. Department of the Environment*.[68] Lord Diplock spoke of the Crown in the sense of: "the 'Government'—a term appropriate to embrace both collectively and individually all the Ministers of the Crown and Parliamentary Secretaries under whose direction the administrative work of government is carried on by the civil servants employed in the various government departments".[69] While it is constructive to conflate Crown with government, so that the Crown describes the executive government in the United Kingdom and does not include the courts or Parliament,[70]

---

[62] So in *Bell v. Secretary of State for Scotland*, 1933 S.L.T. 519, an interdict was granted against the Secretary of State. See Fraser, *Constitutional Law* (2nd ed., 1948), Chaps 7 and 11; and Mitchell, *Constitutional Law*, pp. 167–172 and 304 *et seq*. See also Mitchell, "The Royal Prerogative in Modern Scots Law" [1957] P.L. 38; and Cameron, "Crown Exemption from Statute and Tax in Scotland" 1962 J.R. 191.

[63] Remedies against the Crown are now provided for throughout the U.K. in the Crown Proceedings Act 1947. Unlike in England, where injunctions are now available against ministers of the Crown in judicial review proceedings, interdict is not available against the Crown or its servants in Scotland: *McDonald v. Secretary of State for Scotland*, 1994 S.L.T. 692; *cf. Re M.* [1994] 1 A.C. 377 and see Edwards, "Interdict and the Crown in Scotland" (1995) 111 L.Q.R. 34.

[64] s. 30.

[65] Maitland, *Constitutional History* (1908), p. 418.

[66] Maitland considered that the Crown was a "corporation sole": F. W. Maitland, "The Crown as a Corporation", in *Selected Essays* (1936). In *Town Investments Ltd v. Department of the Environment* [1978] A.C. 359, Lord Diplock agreed with this characterisation but Lord Simon of Glaisdale considered the Crown a "corporation aggregate".

[67] Sedley, "The Crown in its Own Courts", in Forsyth and Hare (eds), *The Golden Metwand and the Crooked Cord* (OUP, Oxford, 1998), p. 253.

[68] [1978] A.C. 359.

[69] *ibid.*, at 397.

[70] *cf.* Fraser, *Constitutional Law* (2nd ed., 1948) at p. 91: "The Crown is the head of the Executive and many of the most important executive acts are done in the name of the Crown".

the error to be avoided is that this description of the Crown does not lead to everybody in the executive government enjoying the privileges and immunities which the law continues to extend to the Monarch personally and the Crown corporately. The decision in the *Town Investments* case points to the dangers of this error: as a matter of law, a lease signed by the minister in his official capacity for premises to be taken by the Department of the Environment meant that the Crown was the tenant. Lord Diplock held that "ministerial executive acts are acts done by the Crown", while Lord Simon considered a minister "an aspect or member of the Crown".[71] Although this identification of ministers with the Crown must now be reconsidered following the House of Lords decision in *Re M*,[72] the view that the Crown includes all its ministers and officers has some support in Scottish case law.[73] In light of the various privileges and immunities the Crown continues to enjoy in litigation and the number of bodies that the executive government embraces, many of which are at some remove from the central government, the present state of the law demands that the Crown is both carefully and narrowly defined.

Defining the Crown

Given that the Crown continues to enjoy some privileges and immunities **4.46** in litigation, it is crucial that it be defined properly. Ideally, this should be as narrowly as possible. Unfortunately, the courts have until recently been somewhat ambivalent in their approach to defining the Crown, especially to the question whether ministers are to be treated as indistinguishable from the Crown.

Like early English cases, earlier Scottish decisions clearly define the Crown as an entity in terms which distinguish it from its officers.[74] In *Somerville v. Lord Advocate*,[75] Lord M'Laren distinguishes the Crown from its officers, noting that Scots law never doubted that the Crown could be impleaded as a defender "in a proper action" through its officers.[76] The distinction is exemplified by *Russell v. Magistrates of Hamilton*,[77] where the Court of Session in substance granted an interdict against the Scottish Secretary in his official capacity as an officer of the Crown.[78] Significantly, the Crown Suits (Scotland) Act 1857 proceeds on the implicit distinction between the Crown and its officers, providing that

---

[71] *ibid*. See criticism of this decision in Wade & Forsyth, *Administrative Law* (7th ed., OUP, Oxford, 1994), p. 53.

[72] [1994] 1 A.C. 377.

[73] *cf. Somerville v. Lord Advocate* (1893) 20 R. 1050, esp. *per* Lord Kyllachy at 1065; *Macgregor v. Lord Advocate*, 1921 S.C. 847; and *McDonald v. Secretary of State for Scotland*, 1994 S.L.T. 692.

[74] Examples in the English cases are numerous: for example, in *Entick v. Carrington* (1765) 19 St.Tr. 1029, *Wilkes v. Lord Halifax* (1769) 19 St.Tr. 1046 (the *North Briton* case), *Benson v. Frederick* (1766) 3 Burr. 1845 and *Re Thomson* (1889) T.L.R. 565, Crown officers (including ministers) are given none of the Crown's immunities from suit or liability in tort. In *R. v. Commissioners of Woods, ex p. Budge* (1850) 15 Q.B. 761 and *R. v. Income Tax Special Commissioners* (1888) 21 Q.B.D. 313, the Prerogative Order of Mandamus is issued against officers of the Crown although it has always been clear that the Prerogative Orders do not lie against the Crown. For discussion, see Sedley, "The Crown in its own Courts", in Forsyth & Hare (eds), *The Golden Metwand and the Crooked Cord* (OUP, Oxford, 1998), pp. 257–259.

[75] (1893) 20 R. 1050.

[76] *ibid*. at 1075.

[77] (1897) 25 R. 350.

[78] See also *Bell v. Secretary of State for Scotland*, 1933 S.L.T. 519.

any action raised in Scotland by or against the Crown "or any Public Department" may be raised by or directed against the Lord Advocate.[79] By the end of the nineteenth century, however, the tendency to assimilate the Crown with its officers by characterising it in terms of the whole machinery of government had taken root in Scotland as well as in England. So in *Smith v. Lord Advocate*,[80] Lord Young has this to say:

> "Now, the action is directed against a public Department of Her Majesty's government, and in my opinion there is no rule, either of the statute law or of the common law, which entitles us to pronounce [declarator of entitlement to a military rank] against a Department of Her Majesty's Government . . . [Further] I know of no authority for a claim of damages against Her Majesty's Government, or any public Department of Her Majesty's Government . . . there is no authority for an action [in damages] against the Government or a public Department of the Government, which is the same thing, for all the Departments in the Government just constitute the Government as representing Her Majesty".[81]

Interestingly, however, Lord Young also notes that: "Any individual in the public service may so treat another as to subject himself personally in damages, and the damages may be recovered in a Court of law."[82]

Even in this "Crown means the government" approach, therefore, it is conceded that public officers may be liable personally for their misdeeds; but it is not clear if this means personally even when acting "in their official capacity". In *McGregor v. Lord Advocate*,[83] Lord Young's approach to defining the Crown is approved by Lord Justice-Clerk Scott Dickson who goes on to approve an approach which proceeds on the assumption that the Crown is indistinguishable from its officers. Quoting Glegg on *Reparation*, that "the maxim that the King can do no wrong . . . extends [protection from damages actions] to public departments [and] to officers of public departments when their action has been instructed by the State",[84] the Lord Justice-Clerk concludes that "the English decisions have been accepted as correctly expressing the law of Scotland".[85] Although Lord Salvesen is troubled by the conclusion,[86] by 1921 Scots law had begun to adopt an approach to defining the Crown in holistic terms—Crown includes government and its officers—similar to that which had by then prevailed in England. Although the Court of Session continued to distinguish between the Crown and its officers for some purposes before the Crown Proceedings Act 1947,[87] the approach taken by the Scottish courts to this Act confirmed the tendency to merge

---

[79] Under the Scotland Act 1998, amending the Crown Suits (Scotland) Act 1857, the Lord Advocate is now the law officer for the Scottish Administration and actions by or against it may stand in his name; actions by or against the U.K. government may now be raised by or directed against the Advocate General for Scotland.

[80] (1897) 25 R. 112.

[81] *ibid.* at 122–123. Note the use of the upper case for government and its public departments.

[82] *ibid.* at 123.

[83] 1921 S.C. 847.

[84] Glegg, *Reparation*, at p. 92.

[85] *McGregor v. Lord Advocate*, 1921 S.C. 847 at 852.

[86] *ibid.* at pp. 852–853.

[87] See *Bell v. Secretary of State for Scotland*, 1933 S.L.T. 519.

the Crown and its officers.[88] The position in this regard is discussed further, with particular reference to interdicts, in Chapter 23.[89]

Litigation and the Crown

The question can still be asked whether or not a particular body is or is not part of the Crown. It has been held in England that the British Broadcasting Corporation is not part of the Crown.[90] More recently, in *BMA v. Greater Glasgow Health Board*,[91] the House of Lords decided that a National Health Service health board could not be defined as part of the Crown. Even if a wide range of bodies are excluded from the definition of the Crown and if a clear distinction is drawn between the Crown and its officers, particularly ministers, even when acting in their official capacities, there remains the difficult relationship between the courts and the Crown corporately.[92] While the rule of law may tolerate the special privileges of the Monarch personally as Head of State,[93] a modern constitution committed to the principle of legality demands that the executive government as a whole be subject to legal remedies in the courts. There may be matters over which the courts' powers must be limited—for example, over decisions made in the interests of national security—but it is not altogether easy to see why in principle the executive government as a whole should not be amenable to legal process.

4.47

The Special Position of the Crown in Litigation

Among the Crown's privileges and immunities in litigation are the following: the presumption in statutory interpretation that statutes do not bind the Crown except where express words or necessary implication indicates that the Crown is bound; injunctions and interdicts are not available against the Crown directly or indirectly; money judgments cannot be enforced against the Crown; the Crown can claim special rights to prevent disclosure of information in its possession, a right formerly termed Crown privilege and now known as public interest immunity. For judicial review the most interesting special privileges of the Crown are the general immunity from statutes, the immunity from injunctions and interdicts and the concept of public interest immunity. As regards the Crown's liability to pay damages for its (or its servants') wrongful acts, this is now governed by the Crown Proceedings Act 1947.

4.48

Crown immunity from statutes

For some time it had been thought that the law in Scotland on the Crown's general immunity from statutes was the converse of the English position: that is, in Scots law statutes normally bind the Crown unless the

4.49

---

[88] Notably evidenced in *McDonald v. Secretary of State for Scotland*, 1994 S.L.T. 692, to be compared with *M. v. Home Office* [1994] 1 A.C. 377.

[89] See para. 23.36.

[90] [1965] Ch. 32.

[91] 1989 S.C. (H.L.) 65.

[92] In Scotland, the Crown Suits (Scotland) Act 1857 (as amended by the Scotland Act 1998) provides that the UK Crown may be impleaded in the Scottish courts by raising an action either against the Advocate General for Scotland or "any public department"; the 1857 Act allows actions against the Crown in right of the Scottish Administration to be raised against the Lord Advocate "or any public department" (of the Scottish Administration).

[93] Although, as the Pinochet litigation demonstrates, even the immunity of sovereigns may have limits: see *R. v. Bow Street Metropolitan Stipendiary Magistrate, ex p. Pinochet Ugarte (No. 3)* [1999] 2 W.L.R. 827.

contrary intention is expressed. This view derived much support from Lord Dunedin in *Magistrates of Edinburgh v. Lord Advocate*[94]: "While I do not doubt that there are certain provisions by which the Crown never would be bound—such, for instance, as the provisions of a taxing statute or certain enactments with penal clauses adjected—yet when you come to a set of provisions in a statute having for its object the benefit of the public generally there is not an antecedent unlikelihood that the Crown will consent to be bound." It may be that English law at one time adopted a similar approach to that summarised by Lord Dunedin for Scots law,[95] under which the presumption was that the Crown was only immune from taxing or penal statutes and probably also statutes affecting its prerogatives. In any event, the Privy Council in *Province of Bombay v. Municipal Corporation of Bombay*[96] shattered any illusion to this effect, disapproving Lord Dunedin's "unlikelihood" and affirming that the presumption is that the Crown is immune from all statutes unless express words or necessary implication indicate the contrary intention. The Crown would be bound by necessary implication only if "it is manifest from the very terms of the statute"[97] that Parliament intended to bind the Crown and only: "if it can be affirmed that, at the time when the statute was passed and received the royal sanction, it was apparent from its terms that its beneficent purpose must be wholly frustrated unless the Crown were bound".[98] When the court is asked to infer "necessary implication": "it must always be remembered that, if it be the intention of the legislature that the Crown shall be bound, nothing is easier than to say so in plain words".[99]

The presumption of the Crown's immunity from statutes has more recently been approved by the House of Lords in a Scottish appeal in which the Court of Session's adoption of the Dunedin dictum was overruled. In *Lord Advocate v. Dumbarton District Council*,[1] Lord Keith approved the general presumption of immunity and stressed that Acts of Parliament "should always state explicitly whether or not the Crown is intended to be bound". Lord Keith seems to have qualified the strictness of the *Bombay* dicta on what must be shown to establish a necessary implication that the statute binds the Crown, saying that the implication may be taken if the statutory purpose would "in a material" respect be frustrated if the Crown were not bound. As to a possible difference between Scots and English law on the presumption, however, Lord Keith states that constitutional policy requires that the presumption have the same meaning and effect in Scots law as it does in English law. Parliament cannot intend statutes applying throughout the United Kingdom to have different meanings in its various parts.[2] Only time will

---

[94] 1912 S.C. 1085, at 1091. This view was commended by Mitchell as being "rational": *Constitutional Law*, p. 183.

[95] Lord Dunedin says that he is only summarising the views of Lord Kyllachy in *Sommerville v. Lord Advocate* (1893) 20 R. 1050 at 1065, which were professed to be based on English law: see Mitchell, *Constitutional Law* at p. 183; *cf.* Fraser, *Constitutional Law*, at p. 176, n. 3. See also Wade & Forsyth, *Administrative Law*, p. 839, n. 14.

[96] [1947] A.C. 58.

[97] *ibid.* at 61.

[98] *ibid.* at 63.

[99] *ibid.*

[1] 1990 S.C.(H.L.) 1 at 26.

[2] *ibid.* at 16. This observation might influence arguments following *Glasgow Corporation v. Central Land Board*, 1956 S.C. (H.L.) 1 that the approach to the prerogative and even rules of statutory interpretation can be different in Scots and English law: see Mitchell, "The Royal Prerogative in Modern Scots Law" [1957] P.L. 304.

tell what the presumption is to be in relation to Acts of the Scottish Parliament.

The presumption of Crown immunity from statutes is not affected by the Crown Proceedings Act 1947.[3] The immunity appears to be enjoyed by the Crown in a wide sense, so that ministers and other Crown servants come within the definition of the Crown for this purpose.[4] This fact alone makes it difficult in a constitutional system based on the rule of law to justify a wide-ranging immunity for the executive government from the large part of the general law contained in statutes.[5] Leaving it to Parliament to indicate by express words if the statute binds the Crown is bound to lead to uncertainty where, deliberately or through oversight, the statute contains no provision for binding the Crown. The implicit unpredictability of the test for necessary implication makes matters worse.

New perspectives on Crown immunity from statutes

The High Court of Australia has recently reformulated the Crown immunity presumption, effectively turning the test of necessary implication on its head and adopting an approach redolent of Lord Dunedin's no "antecedent unlikelihood" that the Crown is normally bound by statutes. In *Bropho v. Western Australia*,[6] the High Court decided that in the modern constitutional system the presumption of Crown immunity from statutes should be more easily rebuttable. The Crown could be bound "notwithstanding that it could not be said that that intention was 'manifest from the very terms' of the statute or that the purpose of the statute would otherwise be 'wholly frustrated'.[7] Noting that the presumption of Crown immunity had hardened into an "inflexible and stringent rule" capable of defeating the legislature's intentions, the High Court said that the legislative intent "must be found in the provisions of the statute—including its subject matter and disclosed purpose and policy ... [which] must prevail over any judge-made rule of statutory construction".[8] This is not far from saying that the Crown should be considered bound by statutes unless the necessary implication from the purpose, content and structure of the statute leads to the Crown not being bound.

The decision in *Bropho* is interesting beyond what it says about the presumption of Crown immunity from statutes. The decision also demonstrates the complications of a federal system in which there is more than one Crown and more than one legislature. In the Australian and Canadian federal systems, the Crown is represented not only by the federal government but also by the various state and provincial govern-

4.50

---

[3] s. 40(2)(f).

[4] In *Lord Advocate v. Dumbarton D.C.*, 1990 S.C. (H.L.) 1, the Ministry of Defence was held to be immune from the Town and Country Planning Acts. Wade & Forsyth also accept that "The Crown" includes the Crown's ministers and servants: *Administrative Law* (7th ed., 1994), at p. 839.

[5] The continuing application of the presumption is severely criticised by scholars: see Hogg, *Liability of the Crown* (2nd ed., Carswell, Toronto, 1989), p. 201 *et seq.*

[6] (1990) 171 C.L.R. 1. See Kinley, "Crown Immunity: A Lesson from Australia" (1990) 53 M.L.R. 819 and Starke, "The High Court's New Approach to the Question whether the Crown is Bound by a Statute" (1990) 64 A.L.J. 527.

[7] *ibid.* at 21.

[8] *ibid.* at 21–22. The High Court accepted (at 22–23), however, that statutes passed before the new approach should be construed by reference to the former understanding of the presumption.

ments. Statutes are passed not only by the federal Parliament but also by the state and provincial legislatures. The scope of the various Crowns' immunities therefore has to be defined in a federal setting, which leads to conundrums such as whether the Crown in right of Western Australia is generally immune not only from statutes passed by the Western Australian legislature[9] but also from those passed by the federal Parliament[10]; and whether, for example, the Crown in right of Canada (the federal Crown) is immune from statutes passed by the federal Parliament and those passed by the various provincial legislatures. The answers provided by the Australian and Canadian courts to these questions have changed over time, but the modern tendency is to erode the presumption of Crown immunity from statutes, at least in respect of the state and provincial Crowns' immunity from federal statutes.[11] These developments are interesting in the United Kingdom now that there is a distinct Scottish Administration and a Scottish Parliament. Since the Scottish Administration forms a part of the Crown, *i.e.*, it represents the Crown in right of the Scottish Administration[12] there may be occasions when it will claim immunity from statutes passed by the U.K. Parliament, just as there may be occasions when the Crown in right of Her Majesty's government in the United Kingdom will seek immunity from statutes passed by the Scottish Parliament. On the face of it, s.99(1) of the Scotland Act 1998 seems to deal with this problem by providing that "rights and liabilities may arise" between the Crown in its various capacities: "by virtue of a contract, by operation of law, or by virtue of an enactment as they may arise between subjects".

But the catch is the effect to be attributed to the words "as they may arise between subjects". Where similar expressions have been used in statutory provisions in various contexts in other jurisdictions, they have not operated of their own force to effect a general removal of the presumption of Crown immunity from statutes.[13] In particular, in so far as it retains its privileges and immunities, the Crown in none of its capacities can be described as a "subject". Accordingly, the presumption of Crown immunity from statutes may have to be considered in light of an indivisible Crown and two co-ordinate legislatures within the United Kingdom. It must be hoped that the law will develop a narrow scope, if any at all, for continuing Crown immunity from statutes throughout the United Kingdom.

The Crown and interdicts and injunctions

4.51 The availability of interdict and injunction against the Crown is considered more fully in the context of remedies.[14] For present purposes, it is sufficient to note that subject to E.C. law interdict is available neither against the Crown nor against officers of the Crown acting in their

---

[9] Which was the issue in *Bropho*.

[10] See *Jacobsen v. Rogers* (1995) 127 A.L.R. 159: State government not immune from Commonwealth legislation (s. 10 of Federal Crimes Act 1914 authorising federal officers to enter premises of State government department to inspect and seize documents relating to a federal crime).

[11] See Hogg, *Liability of the Crown* (2nd ed., Carswell, Toronto, 1989).

[12] See the Scotland Act 1998, s. 99.

[13] *cf. Commonwealth v. Western Australia* (1999) 73 A.L.J.R. 345; and *Bass v. Permanent Trustee Co. Ltd* (1999) 73 A.L.J.R. 522.

[14] para. 23.36.

official capacity.[15] In a case involving E.C. law, there is no doubt that this procedural rule yields and interdict is available against both the Crown and its officers to enforce or protect rights and duties with an E.C. law source.[16]

The Crown and public interest immunity

The Crown Proceedings Act 1947 provides the general rule that docu- **4.52** ments in the possession of the Crown may be recovered for the purposes of any action.[17] This applies whether or not the Crown is a party to the action. The general rule is, however, subject to two significant qualifications: first, the Crown is not obliged to disclose the existence of a document if in the opinion of a minister of the Crown to do so would be injurious to the public interest; and secondly, the Crown has a right to withhold any document or (through its officers) refuse to answer any question if the court agrees with a minister of the Crown that on balance disclosure of particular information would be against the public interest. The second qualification has been variously termed Crown privilege, public interest immunity and public interest privilege.[18] The preservation of these qualifications reflects the typical compromise struck by the 1947 Act, on the one hand abolishing the (English) common law rule that the court has no power to order disclosure by the Crown in any action to which it is a party, while on the other preserving rules of law which confer special privileges on the Crown.[19] Historically, the Crown and bodies enjoying its privileges have sought to avoid disclosure not only of particular documents but also of whole classes of documents on the ground that disclosure would prejudice the public interest. This will have led to prejudice to litigants in particular cases, hopefully reducing as the gradual development of more open government and increasing consciousness of freedom of information have brought more judicial control

---

[15] *McDonald v. Secretary of State for Scotland*, 1994 S.L.T. 692, criticised by Edwards, "Interdict and the Crown in Scotland" (1995) 111 L.Q.R. 34. See also *Ayr Town Council v. Secretary of State for Scotland*, 1965 S.C. 394.

[16] *cf. Miller & Bryce Ltd v. Keeper of the Registers of Scotland*, 1997 S.L.T. 1000.

[17] s. 47—commission and diligence available against the Crown in Scotland; s. 28— discovery available against the Crown in England.

[18] *cf. R. v. Lewes Justices, ex p. Home Secretary* [1973] A.C. 388, *per* Lord Reid at 406– 407; and *Parks v. Tayside Regional Council*, 1989 S.L.T. 345, *per* Lord Sutherland at 347– 348. The fact that the term Crown privilege is retained in Scotland reflects the more limited understanding of the concept in Scots law.

[19] In England, the law used to be that only the Crown could claim "Crown Privilege". Further, the court possessed no power to order the Crown to produce a document in its possession: *Thomas v. R.* (1874) L.R. 10 Q.B. 31. In *Glasgow Corporation v. Central Land Board*, 1956 S.C. (H.L.) 1, Lord Normand noted (at 17) that in Scotland the court could always order the Crown to disclose documents in its possession. The Crown Proceedings Act 1947 makes clear that the Crown can seek to protect documents from disclosure even in actions to which it is not a party (therefore confirming the House of Lords decision in *Duncan v. Cammell Laird & Co. Ltd* [1942] A.C. 624). In addition, the House of Lords has clarified that anyone can refuse disclosure of information on the ground that it is protected by public interest immunity: *R. v. Lewes Justices, ex p. Home Secretary* [1973] A.C. 388, esp. *per* Lord Reid at 400 and Lord Simon of Glaisdale at 406. The development of Crown privilege and public interest immunity in England is discussed in Jacob, "Discovery and Public Interest" [1976] P.L. 134 and "From privileged Crown to interested public" [1993] P.L. 121. See also Lord Justice Simon Brown, "Public Interest Immunity" [1994] P.L. 579. The development of Scots law has been different: see McShane, "Crown Privilege in Scotland: The Demerits of Disharmony", 1992 J.R. 256 and 1993 J.R. 41; but *cf.* Wilkinson, *The Scottish Law of Evidence*, pp. 110–115; and discussion below.

to assertions of Crown privilege and public interest immunity.[20] The potential importance of public interest immunity in the context of judicial review requires that several issues which it raises receive some further discussion.

Ministerial certificates

4.53   An issue which has been canvassed both in England and in Scotland has been whether or not a ministerial certificate or statement to the effect that information is privileged and should not be disclosed is conclusive; and if it is not, what powers the court has to rule on admitting it. In *Duncan v. Cammell Laird & Co.*,[21] the House of Lords decided that even in an action to which the Crown was not a party, a properly submitted certificate from a minister of the Crown objecting that production of documents would injure the public interest should be treated as conclusive and not be subject to review by the court.[22] Both the wartime setting and the sensitive military facts of the case—dependents alleging negligence against a shipbuilder of a new submarine that sank on its trial dive—combined to produce a decision that tilted the law heavily in favour of the government.[23] Since the House of Lords reviewed Scottish and English cases in the course of its decision, it was thought that the decision also represented Scots law. In *Glasgow Corporation v. Central Land Board*,[24] however, the House of Lords decided that Scots law never extended finality to a ministerial certificate asserting privilege over documents or classes of documents, because in Scotland the Court of Session has always been able to overrule ministerial assertions of the public interest in the interests of justice.[25] This decision therefore affirmed an important difference "in matters of public right" between Scotland and England and it has frequently provided a good starting point for arguing that rules of public law, including the Crown's prerogative powers and possibly also rules of statutory interpretation, need not be the same throughout the United Kingdom.[26]

---

[20] In *Burmah Oil Co. Ltd v. Bank of England* [1980] A.C. 1090 at 1134, Lord Keith discusses the impact open government has had on the law in this area.

[21] [1942] A.C. 624.

[22] The decision meant that whole classes of documents could be kept secret, not only a particular document that contains sensitive information.

[23] See Viscount Simon at 642: "the interest of the state must not be put in jeopardy". Wade & Forsyth comment that the decision departs "from the current of earlier authority": *Administrative Law* at p. 846. For an example of the earlier law, see *Robinson v. South Australia (No. 2)* [1931] A.C. 704 (Privy Council favouring court inspection of documents to see if state government's privilege claim justified). On this basis, the earlier English law would have been the same as earlier Scots law: see *Sheridan v. Peel*, 1907 S.C. 577 and *Henderson v. McGown*, 1916 S.C. 821; but *cf. Admiralty v. Aberdeen Steam Trawling Co.*, 1909 S.C. 335. The development of the law (and the placing of this last case in its proper context) is explained by Lord Normand in *Glasgow Corporation v. Central Land Board*, 1956 S.C. (H.L.) 1 at 15–16.

[24] 1956 S.C. (H.L.) 1.

[25] In particular, see *Henderson v. McGown*, 1916 S.C. 821 and *Rogers v. Orr*, 1939 S.C. 492. A similar position is adopted by the courts in Australia, Canada and New Zealand: see *Sankey v. Whitlam* (1978) 21 A.L.R. 505 (Australia); *R. v. Snider* (1953) 2 D.L.R. (2nd) 9 (Canada); and *Corbett v. Social Security Commission* [1962] N.Z.L.R. 878. The U.S. also has a narrow understanding of what constitutes "executive privilege", the leading example being *U.S. v. Nixon*, 418 U.S. 683 (1974), the Watergate tapes decision.

[26] See Mitchell, "The Royal Prerogative in Modern Scots Law" [1957] P.L. 304, esp. at 314–315.

Developments

However, further developments in English law were launched some 12 **4.54**
years later in *Conway v. Rimmer*,[27] which overruled *Duncan v. Cammell
Laird*. Whilst the *Glasgow Corporation* decision affirmed that Scots law
did not regard ministerial assertions of the public interest as final, it did
not clearly provide the Scottish courts with a power to review those
assertions. The balancing process introduced by *Conway v. Rimmer* in
England, in which the court balances the interests of the government in
protecting sensitive information against the interests of private litigants
in pursuing their claims, may still not be part of Scots law.[28] Yet it is not
difficult to view the *Glasgow Corporation* decision as part of the line of
House of Lords decisions which led to the modern English approach to
public interest immunity and to more judicial review over government
decision making, so that there may now be no significant distinction to
be made between the Scottish and the English position, and in *Conway v.
Rimmer* Lord Reid observed that there was no rational justification for
the law on a matter of public policy being different in the two
countries.[29] Although the House of Lords in *Glasgow Corporation*
"narrowly" decided not to order production of the contested documents,
which were claimed to be privileged as part of a class of documents
disclosure of which would prejudice the public interest, Lord Radcliffe
considered that the case "comes very near to inviting an exercise of the
power".[30] He continued:

> "Most of the documents in question appear to be departmental
> minutes and they can hardly relate to anything else but questions as
> to the proper principles and methods to be followed in assessing
> development charges. Nothing of high politics, diplomatic relations
> or State secrets can be involved . . . But the Minister's certificate
> says no more than that he has formed the view that on grounds of
> public interest the documents ought not to be produced . . . I do not
> think that it will be a matter of surprise if some future Judge in
> Scotland finds himself obliged to disregard the Crown's objection
> and to hold that disclosure can do much less injury to the interest of
> the public than non-production of a particular document may do to
> that other public interest which is represented by the cause of
> justice. I am bound to say that I should myself have supposed
> Crown servants to be made of sterner stuff".[31]

Nothing is said about how a judge is to weigh the competing public
interests in an informed and judicious way. The "look-see" stage which
Conway v. Rimmer launched can be seen as the logical next step. Indeed,
the contribution of Lords Reid, Fraser and Keith of Kinkel to this
development in English law is of importance. Lord Reid stated that with
regard to a question whether something was or was not in the public
interest "I do not subscribe to the view that the Government or a
Minister must always or even as a general rule have the last word about
that".[32]

---

[27] [1968] A.C. 910.
[28] See McShane, *supra*, n. 4.
[29] [1968] A.C. 910 at 938.
[30] 1956 S.C. (H.L.) 1 at 19.
[31] *ibid.* at 19–20.
[32] *Chandler v. Director of Public Prosecutions* [1964] A.C. 763 at 790.

There can be little doubt that in many or even all cases if the Scottish court is to make an informed judgment overruling a ministerial claim for non-disclosure in the public interest, it must be able to see the contested documents and decide for itself if the minister's assessment of the public interest is lawful. That this development has not been expressly introduced into Scots law rests more on the fact that there have been no House of Lords decisions in the area in a Scottish context rather than Scots law being against the development. Indeed, the English developments follow from a meaningful understanding of the power of the Scottish court to overrule ministerial assessments of the public interest.

Terminology

4.55 The terminology in this area suggests apparent differences between Scots and English law. Whereas Crown privilege has been replaced in England with public interest immunity, reflecting Lord Reid's observations in 1972 that "there is no question of any privilege . . . the real reason is whether the public interest requires that the [information] not be disclosed",[33] the older term has been retained in Scotland.[34] This is also explained by the view that in Scotland only the Crown can claim the privilege whereas in England "it must always be open to any person interested to raise the question"[35] and claim that the disclosure of documents or information would be injurious to the public interest. In *Higgins v. Burton*,[36] Lord Avonside said that the privilege in the strict sense is limited to the Crown and the Lord Advocate and this view has been approved more recently by Lord Sutherland.[37]

Deregulation and Privatisation

4.56 But it may be doubtful if the privilege can now be limited to the Crown when so many government responsibilities have been deregulated or privatised. There are now many bodies exercising public powers which may possess information the disclosure of which would be injurious to the public interest but which cannot properly be designated as part of the Crown. They must be entitled to argue that information and documents in their possession should be protected from disclosure in the public interest. A modern approach reflecting how government has changed suggests that public interest immunity is the preferable term and that pleading it should be open to the Crown and any person who has in their possession information that deserves to be protected in the public interest.

It follows, however, that the court must have the final say on whether the disclosure of information or documents is against the public interest. It is necessary, therefore, for the Court of Session to have the same powers as the English courts to review claims for public interest immunity. If this review is to be meaningful, contested documents must be given to the trial judge to examine so that he may decide if the minister's assessment of their public interest implications is lawful. The English cases have provided for a balancing process under which the

---

[33] *R. v. Lewes Justices, ex p. Home Secretary* [1973] A.C. 388 at 400.
[34] But see Lord Sutherland's reference to "public interest privilege" in *Parks v. Tayside Regional Council*, 1989 S.L.T. 345.
[35] *R. v. Lewes Justices, ex p. Home Secretary* [1973] A.C. 388, *per* Lord Reid at 400.
[36] 1968 S.L.T. (Notes) 52.
[37] *Parks v. Tayside Regional Council*, 1989 S.L.T. 345.

courts decide if the information should be withheld in the public interest.[38] This approach involves two stages: in the first stage the judge must decide if he should examine the documents over which public interest immunity is claimed; then, having examined the documents, the second stage requires an assessment of whether or not they should be disclosed.

The contours of the tests at each stage are still unclear. In the first stage, the court must consider the prejudice to the party seeking disclosure if the documents are not disclosed in the public interest. The court must assess the relative interests and decide if the prejudice outweighs the need for secrecy. If so, the judge should apprise himself of the information. At the second stage, the judge must consider the interests of the party seeking non-disclosure. These include candour, the anonymity of the public service, confidentiality and privacy.

---

[38] See *Conway v. Rimmer* [1968] A.C. 910; *D v. NSPCC* [1978] A.C. 171; *Burmah Oil Co. v. Bank of England* [1980] A.C. 1090; *Air Canada v. Secretary of State for Trade* [1983] 2 A.C. 394; and *R. v. Chief Constable of the West Midlands Police, ex p. Wiley* [1995] 1 A.C. 274.

PART II

THE CHANGING WORLD OF JUDICIAL REVIEW

CHAPTER 5

EUROPEAN UNION LAW AND JUDICIAL REVIEW

I	INTRODUCTION
II	THE EUROPEAN UNION AND THE EUROPEAN INSTITUTIONS
III	SOURCES OF E.C. LAW
IV	DIRECT APPLICABILITY AND DIRECT EFFECT OF E.C. LAW
V	THE SUPREMACY OF E.C. LAW
VI	THE GENERAL PRINCIPLES OF E.C. LAW
VII	E.C. LAW IN THE U.K. LEGAL SYSTEMS
VIII	E.C. LAW AND JUDICIAL REVIEW
IX	JUDICIAL REVIEW IN THE E.U. COURTS

I INTRODUCTION

Outline

The operation in the United Kingdom of the law of the European Union 5.01 (E.U.) has significant implications for judicial review. One effect of European Community (E.C.) law, which is the most significant part of the law of the European Union,[1] is the emergence of the clearest form of constitutional judicial review so far known in the United Kingdom.[2] Beyond its impact on the constitution, E.C. law has also increased the prominence of judicial review generally by, for example, increasing the grounds on which acts and decisions may be challenged as illegal, such as where they interfere with the free movement of goods or services within the European Union[3]; by providing new grounds of judicial review such as proportionality and human rights[4]; by encouraging the further

---

[1] And the main focus of this chapter. The terms E.U. and E.C. and "E.U. law" and "E.C. law" are now being used interchangeably. But from a technical point of view they should be distinguished. As is discussed further in part II below (para. 5–03), the E.U. is the structural political entity within which the E.C. and E.C. law have the greatest scope.

[2] See *R. v. Secretary of State for Transport, ex p. Factortame Ltd (No. 2)* [1991] 1 A.C. 603; and *R. v. Secretary of State for Employment, ex p. EOC* [1995] 1 A.C. 1 (declaration (or declarator) against Secretary of State (or, presumably, as appropriate against the Attorney-General or the Advocate General for Scotland) is the appropriate remedy where provisions in an Act of the U.K. Parliament are found to be inconsistent with applicable E.C. law). Acts of the Scottish Parliament are also challengeable (and may be disapplied) to the extent that any of their provisions are inconsistent with E.C. law: Scotland Act 1998, s. 29. See also s. 106 of the Government of Wales Act 1998 and s.6 of the Northern Ireland Act 1998.

[3] See, for example, *Stoke-on-Trent City Council v. B & Q plc* [1993] A.C. 900; *R. v. Human Fertilisation and Embryology Authority, ex p. Blood* [1997] 2 W.L.R. 806; and *U v. W* [1997] 2 C.M.L.R. 431. See also the recent decision of the House of Lords in *R. v. Chief Constable of Sussex, ex p. International Trader's Ferry Ltd* [1998] 3 W.L.R. 1260.

[4] See, for example, *R. v. Minister of Agriculture, Fisheries and Food, ex p. Bell Line* [1984] 2 C.M.L.R. 502; *U v. W, supra*; and *Booker Aquaculture v. Secretary of State for Scotland* [1999] 1 C.M.L.R. 35; 1998 G.W.D. 21–1089. But *cf.* Hoffmann J. in *Stoke-on-Trent City Council v. B & Q plc* [1991] Ch. 48 (and in the House of Lords following a reference to the ECJ: [1993] A.C. 900).

113

development of grounds of review already recognised in national law, such as legitimate expectation[5]; and by creating new remedies against government: for example, state liability in damages for violation of rights conferred by E.C. law.[6] Although what is now called judicial review was already expanding before the United Kingdom joined the European Economic Community (EEC) in 1973 and although it has since developed impressively beyond the sphere of E.C. law, there can be little doubt that judicial review has been enhanced through the application of E.C. law and the reassessments of the U.K. constitution which this has required.

The great volume of E.U. law means that this chapter provides neither a full survey of it nor an extensive analysis of the effect it has on the U.K. constitution and public law generally. Both these tasks are beyond the scope of the present book and are well covered in many works devoted to E.U. law and constitutional and administrative law.[7] Subject to some brief references to "E.U. law", the focus of this chapter is on the implications of E.C. law for judicial review in U.K. courts.[8] Part II of the chapter provides a short introduction to the background, structure and instututions of the European Union and the European Community. Part

---

[5] In particular, by allowing judicial review of breach of legitimate expectations of substantive decisions: see Cases C–104/89 and C–37/90 *Mulder v. Council and Commission* [1992] E.C.R. I-3061; and in England, see *R. v. Ministry of Agriculture, Fisheries and Food, ex p. Hamble (Offshore) Fisheries* [1995] 2 All E.R. 714; but *cf. R. v. Secretary of State for the Home Department, ex p. Hargreaves* [1997] 1 W.L.R. 906 (CA). In Scotland, see *McPhee v. North Lanarkshire Council*, 1998 S.L.T. 1317, esp. *per* Lady Cosgrove at 1322C. For discussion, see Forsyth, "Wednesbury protection of substantive legitimate expectations" [1997] P.L. 375. Legitimate expectation as a ground of judicial review is considered in Chap. 19.

[6] See Cases C–6 and 9/90 *Francovich & Bonifaci v. Italy* [1991] E.C.R. I-5357; Cases C–46 and 48/93 *Brasserie du Pêcheur v. Germany* and *R. v. Secretary of State for Transport, ex p. Factortame Ltd (No. 3)* [1996] E.C.R. I-1029; Case C–392/93 *R. v. H.M. Treasury, ex p. British Telecommunications* [1996] E.C.R. I-1631; Case C–5/94 *R. v. Ministry of Agriculture, Fisheries and Food, ex p. Hedley Lomas* [1996] E.C.R. I-2553; and Cases C–178 and 179/94 *Dillenkofer v. Germany* [1996] E.C.R. I-4845. See also *R. v. Secretary of State for Transport, ex p. Factortame Ltd (No. 4)* [1998] 3 C.M.L.R. 192 (CA), before the House of Lords (at the time of writing).

[7] Among the many specialist works on E.C. law available in English are: Wyatt & Dashwood, *European Community Law* (3rd ed. 1993); Hartley, *The Foundations of EC Law* (3rd ed., Clarendon Press, Oxford, 1994); Edward & Lane, *European Community Law* (2nd ed., Butterworths, Edinburgh, 1995); Weatherill & Beaumont, *EC Law* (2nd ed., Penguin, London, 1997); and Craig & de Burca, *EU Law* (2nd ed., OUP, Oxford, 1998). For a U.S. perspective see Bermann, Goebel, Davey & Fox, *Cases and Materials on European Community Law* (West Publishing Co, St. Paul, 1993). An important looseleaf work is Vaughan, *Law of the European Communities* Service (Butterworths). For discussion of the effect of E.C. law on U.K. constitutional law, see Bradley & Ewing, *Constitutional & Administrative Law* (12 ed., Longman, London, 1997), Chap. 8; and also O'Neill, *Decisions of the ECJ and their Constitutional Implications* (1994, Butterworths, London). For the impact on judicial review, see de Smith, Woolf & Jowell, *Judicial Review of Administrative Action* (5th ed., 1995), Chap. 21. And for a work devoted to the effect of E.C. law on U.K. law generally, see Collins, *European Community Law in the UK* (5th ed., Butterworths, London, 1997). See also Lewis, *Remedies and the Enforcement of European Community Law* (Sweet & Maxwell, London, 1996) for analysis of the relationship between public law remedies and E.C. law in England & Wales.

[8] In any event, whatever may be thought to be the requirements of E.U. law, only those parts of the Treaty on European Union (TEU) which relate to E.C. law are formally part of U.K. law. That is, s. 1(2) of the European Communities Act 1972, as amended, does not incorporate those provisions in the TEU which relate only to the E.U. (for example, the provisions on the second and third pillars). Accordingly, any direct challenge to a U.K. law (or other measure) before a U.K. court must be based on E.C. law: see further para. 5.48 below.

III examines the sources of E.C. law while parts IV, V and VI look at the fundamental constitutional principles of the E.C. and their implications for judicial review in this country. Thereafter, part VII discusses the effect E.C. law has in the U.K. legal systems and part VIII examines the relationship between the European courts and national courts as it relates to judicial review. Finally, part IX provides a brief overview of the role of judicial review in the European Union's constitutional arrangements. Although this analytical structure often leads to a separate examination of the national and European dimensions of judicial review involving E.C. law, it is important to maintain a sense of unity between them. Too often the national and European aspects are seen in opposition, whereas in fact the purpose of both national courts and the European courts (namely the European Court of Justice (ECJ) and the Court of First Instance (CFI)) in their respective supervisory jurisdictions is to ensure that the law—European and national—is observed. This means that although the distinct functions of the ECJ and national courts must be stressed,[9] emphasis must also be placed on the obligations of national courts themselves under E.C. law, obligations which now allow national courts to be regarded as "E.C. courts" when interpreting and applying E.C. law.[10] At least in the context of judicial review there are several reasons why a rigid separation between the European courts and national courts is not appropriate. First, there are points at which national courts and the European Union's institutions meet. For example, national courts may be faced with challenges to E.C. legislation and national measures taken to implement it.[11] In such cases, a U.K. court must apply relevant decisions of the ECJ in the context of national legal procedures.[12] Secondly, the preliminary ruling procedure established by Article 234 (formerly 177) of the E.C. Treaty[13] means that the ECJ and national courts work together to ensure both the validity of E.C. legislation and the compatibility of national law with E.C. law. Thirdly, the law applied by the ECJ in interpreting both the E.C. Treaty and E.C. legislation is relevant in the United Kingdom, not only because national courts may be called on to apply it but also because principles developed by the ECJ in its case law—for example, legitimate expectation, propor-

---

[9] See MacCormick, "The Maastricht-Urteil: Sovereignty Now" (1995) 1 Eur.L.J. 259.

[10] *cf.* Maher, "National Courts as European Community Courts" (1994) 14 L.S. 226. See also Slaughter, Sweet and Weiler, *The European Courts of Justice and National Courts* (Hart, Oxford, 1997), esp. the Prologue and Chap. 13.

[11] See, for example, *R. v. Secretary of State for Health, ex p. Imperial Tobacco Ltd* [1999] C.O.D. 138 (attempt to challenge by way of judicial review validity of as yet unimplemented E.C. Directive).

[12] But as will be seen below (para. 5.36), national procedural rules may themselves be challenged on the ground that they are incompatible with E.C. law, for example, where their effect is to treat E.C. law rights less favourably than equivalent rights conferred by national law; where they render the enforcement of rights conferred by E.C. law impossible or excessively difficult; or more generally where they interfere with the full effectiveness of E.C. law. See, for example, Case 222/84 *Johnston v. Chief Constable of the RUC* [1986] E.C.R. 1651; and *cf.* Case C–120/97 *Upjohn Ltd v. The Licensing Authority Established By The Medicines Act 1968* [1999] 1 C.M.L.R. 825.

[13] The Treaty of Amsterdam has renumbered almost all the Articles of the Treaty on European Union (TEU) and the E.C.'s Treaty of Rome. To avoid confusion, the first citation of a Treaty article will include both the new and the old (and heretofore more familiar) article number: for example, Article 2 (formerly B) TEU; Article 234 (formerly 177) E.C.

tionality and a general duty to give reasons—are making an important contribution to judicial review in this country.[14]

Judicial Review and E.C. Law

5.02 European Community law has a pervasive presence in many areas of national law. In addition, the doctrine of supremacy (or primacy) of E.C. law means that applicable E.C. law has the force of supreme constitutional law in the national legal order. Although E.C. law issues will arise in many types of proceedings,[15] both the pervasive and constitutional effects of E.C. law may be demonstrated by considering two situations in which E.C. law can arise in judicial review. The first situation is where a challenge is brought against either E.C. legislation or a national measure, taken to implement it or in pursuance of it, and the ground of challenge is that the E.C. legislation violates a higher rule or principle of E.U. law.[16] In this case, it is the E.C. legislation which is alleged to violate E.C. (or E.U.) law. A U.K. court faced with such a challenge has to consider both jurisdictional issues and the substantive grounds of review in light of both E.C. and national law. For example, a court may have to decide if it is competent to determine the validity of a piece of E.C. legislation or whether the legality of an implementing national act or decision is to be reviewed against the standards of national law or E.C. law or both.[17] The second situation is where the challenge is brought against a national law or

---

[14] See, for example, de Burca, "Proportionality and Wednesbury Unreasonableness: The Influence of European Legal Concepts on U.K. Law" [1997] 3 E.P.L. 561; Craig, "Substantive Legitimate Expectations in Domestic and Community Law" (1996) 55 Camb.L.J. 289; and Thomas, "Reason-giving in English and European Community Administrative Law" [1997] 3 E.P.L. 213. On E.C. law's contribution to a duty to give reasons in national law, see also Neill, "The Duty to Give Reasons: The Openness of Decision-Making", in Forsyth and Hare (eds), *The Golden Metwand and the Crooked Cord* (OUP, Oxford, 1998). More generally, see Anthony, "Community Law and the Development of UK Administrative Law: Delimiting the 'Spill-Over' Effect" [1998] 4 E.P.L. 253; and Schwarze, "The Convergence of the Administrative Laws of the EU Member States" [1998] 4 Eur.P.L. 191. *Cf.* Loughlin, "Sitting on a fence at Carter Bar: In praise of JDB Mitchell", 1991 J.R. 135.

[15] Including criminal proceedings: see, for example, *Mehlich v. Mackenzie*; *Geweise v. Mackenzie*, 1984 S.L.T. 449 (before the ECJ, Case 24/83 [1984] E.C.R. 817); *Walkingshaw v. Marshall*, 1992 S.L.T. 1167. The general application of E.C. law means that many cases raising E.C. law issues can arise in the sheriff court. So, for example, the sheriff court may hear a (*Francovich*) action for damages against the Crown for breaches of E.C. law which are attributable to it.

[16] Such as the Treaty on European Union, the E.C. Treaty or a general principle of (E.C.) law. See, for example, *R. v. Ministry of Agriculture, Fisheries and Food, ex p. National Farmers Union* [1998] 2 C.M.L.R. 1125. This is an interesting example: the judicial review in the English High Court challenged the U.K. government's actions in implementation of an E.C. Commission decision which the applicants claimed was *ultra vires*; the High Court decided to refer the E.C. law issues to the ECJ under Art. 177 E.C. (Case C–157/96); separately, in *U.K. v. Commission* (Case C–180/96), the U.K. government had begun a direct action against the Commission under Art. 173 E.C. challenging the legality of the same decision (namely Decision 96/239). Before the ECJ, the two cases were joined.

[17] The ECJ has held that the supremacy and uniformity of E.C. law require that E.C. measures are only challengeable on the grounds offered by E.C. law: see Case 11/70 *Internationale Handelsgesellschaft mbH v. Einfuhr-und Vorratstelle fur Getreide und Futtermittel* [1970] E.C.R. 1125; [1972] C.M.L.R. 255. Further, as will be seen below (para. 5.53), a national court is not empowered to invalidate an E.C. measure. Where it has serious grounds for suspecting the validity of an E.C. measure, it must refer the matter to the ECJ under Art. 234 E.C.: Case 314/85 *Foto-Frost v. Hauptzollamt Lubeck-Ost* [1987] E.C.R. 4199. However, as regards national measures which implement E.C. measures, it is possible that they are reviewable on grounds available in both E.C. law and national law. See further para. 5.54 below.

other measure, such as an administrative decision, on the ground that *it* is inconsistent with an applicable rule or principle of E.C. law.[18] In this case, the challenge is to the effect that the national law or other measure is unconstitutional because it violates the higher norms of E.C. law. Where the challenge is successful, the inconsistent legislation, act or decision will be disapplied since no national law or exercise of authority under it can validly be inconsistent with applicable E.C. law.[19]

II   THE EUROPEAN UNION AND THE EUROPEAN INSTITUTIONS

The European Union and the European Community

Since the European Union was created by the Treaty on European   **5.03** Union (often known as the Maastricht Treaty) in 1993, the constitutional structure and accompanying acronymns of what was once known in the United Kingdom as the "Common Market" have become complex. The Treaty of Amsterdam, which amends the Treaty on European Union, has significantly added to the intricacy and it can be said that the institutional and legal arrangements underpinning the European Union have never been more complicated. One reason for this is that the European Union is organic and builds upon the European "project" which began after the Second World War with the founding of the

---

[18] See, for example, *R. v. Secretary of State for Employment, ex p. EOC* [1995] 1 A.C. 1; *R. v. Secretary of State for Transport, ex p. Factortame (No. 1)* [1990] 2 A.C. 85; and *(No. 2)* [1991] 1 A.C. 603. See also *Kincardine and Deeside D.C. v. Forestry Commissioners*, 1992 S.L.T. 1180; *R. v. Human Fertilisation and Embryology Authority, ex p. Blood* [1997] 2 W.L.R. 806; *U v. W* [1997] 2 C.M.L.R. 431; and *Booker Aquaculture v. Secretary of State for Scotland* [1999] 1 C.M.L.R. 35. But *cf. R. v. Ministry of Agriculture, Fisheries and Food, ex p. First City Trading Ltd* [1997] 1 C.M.L.R. 250 (national laws and other measures can only be reviewed against the general principles of E.C. law where they are adopted pursuant to or fall within the scope of E.C. law). Alternatively, the challenge may be that the absence of a national law or effective legal remedy conferred by national law violates E.C. law: see Case C–120/97 *Upjohn Ltd v. The Licensing Authority Established By The Medicines Act 1968* [1999] 1 C.M.L.R. 825; *cf.* Case C–185/97 *Coote v. Granada Hospitality Ltd* [1998] 3 C.M.L.R. 958.

[19] See Case 106/77 *Amministrazione delle Finanze dello Stato v. Simmenthal* [1978] E.C.R. 629; and the House of Lords' decision in *R. v. Secretary of State for Transport, ex p. Factortame (No. 2)* [1991] 1 A.C. 603. Throughout this chapter, the term "applicable E.C. law" is used to include rules and principles of E.C. law which have effects in national law. In traditional terms this includes both E.C. law provisions which are directly applicable in national law (that is, E.C. regulations) and provisions which have direct effect (that is, where the ECJ's criteria for direct effect are satisfied, provisions of the E.C. Treaty, provisions in other treaties to which the E.C. is a party, and provisions in all types of E.C. legislation): see further paras 5.23 *et seq.* below. But the neat categories of direct applicability and direct effect do not fully comprehend all of the relevance which E.C. law is capable of having in national law. For example, although the E.C. Treaty is not considered directly applicable, some of its provisions which do not have direct effect are still significant in national law. Most notably, although Art. 10 (formerly 5) E.C. has been held not to have direct effect (Case 44/84 *Hurd v. Jones* [1986] E.C.R. 29), it still creates obligations for national courts, for example, to interpret all national law consistently with all E.C. law, including directives which do not have direct effect, and more generally to ensure the full effectiveness of E.C. law rights in national law. Furthermore, the terms direct applicability and direct effect relate to the operation of the E.C.'s "written law" and do not fully explain the relevance for national courts of the general principles of E.C. law which the ECJ has found to be part of E.C. law. Accordingly, the broader term "applicable E.C. law" underlines that E.C. law has an impact on national law beyond the scope of the concepts of direct applicability and direct effect.

European Coal and Steel Community (ECSC) by the Treaty of Paris in 1951. This was followed in 1957 by the creation of the European Atomic Energy Community (EURATOM) and, most significantly of all, by the founding of the European Economic Community (EEC) by the Treaty of Rome signed on March 25, 1957.[20] There can be no doubt about the ambitious nature of the EEC since the Treaty of Rome speaks in its preamble about laying the foundations for "an ever closer union among the peoples of Europe".[21]

Although all three of the founding Communities are legally distinct,[22] their institutions were merged in 1965 by the Merger Treaty.[23] It was, however, the EEC Treaty which quickly acquired pre-eminence, an inevitable development in view of its broader nature. As the original six member states steadily increased, presently to number 15, the scope of the EEC increased dramatically, quickly reaching far beyond matters such as harmonisation of customs duties which might once have been considered as the limit of international "economic" co-operation. As a result of the expansion of the EEC's competences, together with broadening political horizons and the institutional pressures of more member states, it became clear that reform of the EEC's legal foundations and institutional structures was necessary. This led first to the Single European Act of 1986,[24] which (*inter alia*) expanded the subject areas over which the EEC could pass legislation, increased the scope of qualified majority voting in the Council of Ministers, and renamed the ECSC, EURATOM and EEC as the European Communities. Subsequently, in 1992, the European Communities' member states concluded the Maastricht Treaty on European Union.[25] This treaty established the European Union on the foundations of the European Communities, which now constitute one "pillar" of the European Union, and progressed efforts towards Europe's "ever closer union", most notably by creating the powers to establish the European single currency. Most recently, in 1997, the E.U. states concluded the Treaty of Amsterdam.[26]

---

[20] See Cmnd 4862 (1972). These Treaties are given effect in U.K. law by the European Communities Act 1972, which came into force on January 1, 1973 on the U.K.'s accession to the three Communities.

[21] The phrase may be compared with the ambition of creating a "more perfect union" in the preamble to the U.S. Constitution. There are, of course, other pan-European institutions but these should be clearly distinguished from the E.U. and its components. In particular, the Council of Europe, established in 1949, is a distinct international body and should not be confused with the European Union. The Council of Europe's most significant achievements are in the field of human rights, notably the European Convention on Human Rights and Fundamental Freedoms which it is ultimately responsible for supervising and enforcing. The Council of Europe is briefly discussed at para. 6.04.

[22] It should be emphasised that each has its own Treaty under which different law-making powers and instruments are provided. Accordingly, powers conferred on the E.U. Commission by the E.C.'s Treaty of Rome are not always replicated in the E.C.S.C.'s Treaty of Paris (and vice versa). See, for example, Case C–128/92 *Banks v. British Coal Corporation* [1994] E.C.R. I-1209.

[23] Art. 9 of the Treaty of Amsterdam repeals the Merger Treaty and makes new, more modern provision in similar terms.

[24] [1987] O.J. L169/1, published at [1987] 2 C.M.L.R. 741; given effect in U.K. law by the European Communities (Amendment) Act 1987.

[25] [1992] O.J. C224/1: in force, Nov. 1993; published at [1992] 1 C.M.L.R. 719; given effect in U.K. law in terms of the European Communities (Amendment) Act 1993 (on which a comprehensive annotation is available in 1993 *Current Law Statutes* (Beaumont & Junor)).

[26] [1997] O.J. C340/1: in force June 1, 1999, given effect in U.K. law in terms of the European Communities (Amendment) Act 1998. For comment see Langrish, "The Treaty of Amsterdam: Selected Highlights" (1998) 23 Eur.L.R. 3.

In addition to making a variety of important substantive amendments to the Treaty on European Union, it also renumbers the Treaty's articles. It is likely that further amendments to the Treaty on European Union will be required with the advent of economic and monetary union and the prospect of membership of more European states.[27]

The Treaty on European Union

The Treaty on European Union (TEU) is often described as creating a **5.04** structure resting on three pillars. The superstructure is the European Union itself, which, although not expressly established with its own legal personality, is a legal entity: for example, it is governed by several legal provisions in the TEU[28]; possesses some powers[29]; and possesses at least one international body, namely the European Council.[30] The three pillars represent the three areas of activity of the European Union: the first pillar comprises the three founding communities, the ECSC, EURATOM, and most significantly the EEC, which is renamed by the Maastricht Treaty the European Community (E.C.); the second and third pillars represent the two intergovernmental agreements on Foreign and Security Policy (second pillar) and Police and Judicial Co-operation in Criminal Matters (third pillar).[31] The legal processes of the three pillars are different and it is very important to be clear about the legal basis of any particular act emerging from the European Union.[32] While the law-making and nascent federal dimensions of the first pillar and especially the European Community are clear, the second and third pillars more resemble traditional international co-operation between states. In particular, there is less scope for making laws which can be directly applicable in the member states under the second and third pillars and the ECJ has only a limited jurisdiction over the activities pursued thereunder.[33] That the European Union's structure takes this form is explained by political factors and the current inability of all of the European Union's member states to agree that the areas governed

---

[27] A discussion of the institutional, economic and political pressures bearing on the E.U.'s future is contained in Grabbe & Hughes, *Enlarging the EU Eastwards* (RIIA Chatham House Papers, London, 1998).

[28] Mostly in Titles I and VIII (basically, the top and tail of the TEU).

[29] In terms of Titles V, VI and VII of the TEU.

[30] On which see para. 5.06 below.

[31] The third pillar, which was introduced by the Maastricht Treaty with the heading "Co-operation in the fields of Justice and Home Affairs", is given its new title by the Treaty of Amsterdam. The new heading more accurately reflects the scope of the third pillar. There are also proposals to introduce a fourth pillar covering defence co-operation, effectively subsuming the Western European Union (WEU). Such a move is heralded by the Treaty of Amsterdam giving the European Council the power to "integrate" the WEU into the E.U. by an unanimous vote (subject to ratification by the member states): Art. 17 TEU.

[32] This is important for two main reasons: first, in contrast to its jurisdiction under the E.C. Treaty, the powers of the ECJ are limited under the second and third pillars; secondly, by virtue of the definition of "Community Treaties" for the purposes of s. 1(2) of the European Communities Act 1972, acts and decisions of the E.U. under the second and third pillars can have no effects in U.K. law in terms of the 1972 Act itself.

[33] See, for example, Art. 46 (formerly L) TEU and more specifically, Art. 35 TEU. The restrictions on the ECJ's jurisdiction under the second and third pillars are now infecting the E.C. Treaty, at least in so far as the Treaty of Amsterdam has incorporated the Schengen Agreement to provide E.C. competence over immigration matters: see Art. 68 E.C. Although this part of the E.C. Treaty does not apply to the U.K. (by an opting out Protocol, the background being the U.K.'s not having signed the Schengen Agreement), the precedent of restrictions on the ECJ's jurisdiction and the binding effect of its judgments in national law in areas covered by the E.C. Treaty is regrettable.

by the second and third pillars be incorporated into the first pillar, specifically into the European Community's Treaty of Rome.[34] Except for the first pillar, therefore, the European Union has characteristics which give it an international hallmark in contrast to the European Community's distinctive supranational dimensions.

E.U. Law and E.C. Law

5.05   In comparison with the second and third pillars of the EU and, in particular, the more limited powers of the ECJ thereunder, the role of law and judicial review in the E.C. reinforces the European Community's supranational characteristics. The constitutional relationship between national law and E.C. law which membership of the European Union entails makes applicable E.C. law supreme over national law. Importantly, by virtue of their capacity for direct effect, E.C. laws often confer rights on individuals which are directly enforceable in national courts. The combination of the supremacy and direct effect of E.C. law means that national courts may be called on to review any national law for consistency with E.C. law and to apply E.C. law directly in cases arising before them. In appropriate cases, national courts must request the ECJ to rule on the meaning and effect of E.C. law and decisions of the ECJ on points of E.C. law are binding on all national courts. Moreover, there are several situations in which E.C. law can give rise to state liability to pay damages to individuals for losses caused by breaches of E.C. law which are attributable to the state. The pre-eminence which these factors give E.C. law, in addition to it being by far the largest part of the law of the European Union, makes it convenient to refer to E.C. law rather than E.U. law.[35] Indeed, while the terms "federalism" and "federal" are sensitive, at least in the United Kingdom, it is clear that the relationship between E.C. law and national law shares significant similarities with the relationship between federal and state or provincial law in a classical federation.[36]

---

[34] This is clearly demonstrated by the history and current position of the Schengen Agreement on the Free Movement of Persons and related efforts to create common visa and asylum policies: see now Arts 61–79 E.C., from which the U.K., Ireland and Denmark have opt outs.

[35] Technically, "E.U. law" may be the better general term; but at the present time, at least from the standpoint of judicial review in the U.K. legal systems, it is the E.C.'s Treaty of Rome (the E.C. Treaty) and the legislation passed and acts done under it which are of most interest. While there may be measures passed under the second and third pillars, and more properly called E.U. law, which could arise in judicial review cases, it is not clear to what extent these measures will be directly applicable or have direct effect: see para. 5.22 below. In any event, whatever "E.U. law" may require, E.U. measures are not given effect in U.K. law in terms of the European Communities Act 1972. Accordingly, unless the context otherwise demands, the remainder of this chapter will refer to E.C. law.

[36] On the emerging federal nature of the E.U. and of E.C. law in particular, see (from a large literature): Hartley, "Federalism, Courts and Legal Systems: The Emerging Constitution of the European Community" (1986) 34 Am.J. of Comp. Law 229; Mancini, "The Making of a Constitution for Europe" (1989) 26 C.M.L.R. 595; Laenerts, "Constitutionalism and the Many Faces of Federalism" (1990) 38 Am.J. of Comp. Law 205; Weiler, "The Transformation of Europe" (1991) 100 Yale L.J. 2403; Bermann, "Taking Subsidiarity Seriously" (1994) Colum.L.R. 331; and Edwards, "Fearing Federalism's Failure: Subsidiarity in the E.U." (1996) 44 Am.J. of Comp. Law 537. See also Barendt, *An Introduction to Constitutional Law* (Clarendon Press, Oxford, 1998). pp. 79–86. Of course, mention of the E.C.'s possible federal nature raises the question of what sort of federal relationship might exist between the E.U. institutions and the member states. Federalism comes in many forms and its implications may vary from time to time. For example, in the

The E.U./E.C. Institutions

The E.C. Treaty establishes five principal institutions for the European   **5.06**
Union's government: the Council of Ministers, the Commission, the
Parliament, the Court of Justice of the European Communities (the ECJ)
and the Court of Auditors.[37] In addition, the E.C. Treaty creates a
European Central Bank and the European System of Central Banks,
giving them broad powers over the single European currency and related
monetary and economic policies.[38] Article 7 E.C. establishes the institutions "to carry out the tasks entrusted to the Community" but adds the
important rule of law qualification that: "Each institution shall act within
the limits of the powers conferred upon it by this Treaty".[39] The TEU
provides that the institutions established by the E.C. Treaty are also
responsible for carrying out the European Union's responsibilities.[40] In
this regard, it expressly provides for the European Union to respect
human rights.[41] In addition, Article 4 TEU establishes the European
Council on a formal basis "to provide the Union with the necessary
impetus for its development". The European Council, which consists of
the member states' heads of government (and in the case of France, Head
of State), foreign ministers and the President of the E.U. Commission, is
to meet at least twice per year and is required to submit a report following
its meetings to the European Parliament. However, while the European
Council is a distinct E.U. body, it is not one of the European Community's
institutions.[42] In particular, it must be noted that the European Union, and
therefore presumably the European Council, is not vested with legal
personality, in contrast with the European Community and its institutions.[43] Yet, even if the European Council's lack of legal personality is

---

USA (with which the E.U. is often compared), recent decisions of the US Supreme Court
have increasingly stressed the limits on the powers of the federal government *vis-à-vis* the
states in terms which might seem surprising (or refreshing) to a European observer (*cf.*
New York v. U.S., 505 U.S. 144 (1992); and *Prinz v. U.S.* 521 U.S. 898 (1997)). In particular,
the US Supreme Court has recently taken a robust view of state "sovereignty", which has
led it to be strict about the extent to which the US Constitution allows a federal law to
expose state governments to damages liability to individuals who claim to have been
caused loss by the state's breach of the law: see *Seminole Tribe of Florida v. Florida* 517
U.S. 44 (1996); and *Alden v. Maine* 527 U.S. *cf.* Cases C–6 & 9/90 *Francovich and Bonifaci
v. Italy* [1991] E.C.R. I-5357.

[37] In addition, there is the Court of First Instance (CFI) created by the Single European
Act and established in 1989. However, the CFI is attached to the ECJ and should not be
regarded as a separate institution: see Edward and Lane, *European Community Law* (2nd
ed., Butterworths, Edinburgh, 1995), para. 94.

[38] Art. 8 E.C. The ECB's powers include the power to pass Regulations and make
Decisions: see Art. 110 E.C. The ECB is also given limited standing before the ECJ. The
ECB's most significant responsibilities are in the area of economic policy: for example, its
responsibility for supervising and enforcing the European Stability and Growth Pact
provided for in Council Regulations Nos 1466/97 and 1467/97. For discussion of the ECB,
see: Beaumont and Walker, *Legal Aspects of European Monetary Union* (1999).

[39] Art. 7 E.C. (formerly Art. 4). See also Art. 5 E.C. (formerly Art. 3b) on the principle
of subsidiarity in the E.C. The rule of law is given substantive content by other provisions
of the E.C. Treaty (*e.g.* Art. 12 (formerly 6) E.C. on the prohibition of discrimination) and
by the general principles of law (*e.g.* proportionality) which are part of E.C. law (on which
see paras 5.39–5.45 below).

[40] Art. 3 TEU provides for the E.U. to have "a single institutional framework"; see also
Art. 5 TEU.

[41] Art. 6 TEU (formerly Art. F). Some human rights are in any event part of E.C. law as
general principles of law: see para. 5–44 below.

[42] It should not be confused with the Council of Ministers.

[43] See Art. 281 (formerly Art. 210) E.C. Accordingly, the European Council cannot

sufficient to defeat any attempt to challenge its decisions before national courts, as a distinct E.U. body it may be asked whether the European Council is challengeable before the ECJ. Articles 46 and 47 (formerly L and M) TEU do not seem to prevent this.[44] But in *Roujansky v. Council*,[45] the ECJ decided that it had no jurisdiction over acts of the European Council.

Since the focus of the present work is on judicial review, it is the structure and role of the ECJ which holds greatest interest. But it must be understood that all of the European Union's institutions are juridical bodies and have defined roles under the E.C. Treaty which must be respected. This is often expressed by reference to a concept known as "institutional balance". Although not as such a doctrine of separation of powers,[46] it addresses the need for E.C. law to ensure that each of the institutions keeps within its allotted sphere. Accordingly, and if for no other reason than to inject some balance into the present discussion, a few words should be said about the functions of the principal E.U. institutions.

The Council of Ministers

5.07 The Council of Ministers is provided for in Articles 202–210 E.C. It is the principal part of the E.C. legislature and has a general co-ordinating role in the development of the policies of the European Community.[47] The Council consists of representatives of each member state "at ministerial level, authorised to commit the government" of their member state.[48] For most purposes this means that a departmental minister from a member state's national government will represent it in the Council. But in those decentralised states which have central (that is, national or federal) and regional governments—for example, Germany, Spain, and now the United Kingdom—it is possible for a member of the regional government to represent the whole member state, but only in so far as they can "commit the [national] government".[49]

---

conclude treaties in the name of the E.U. with third states. The member states in their own names would have to conclude treaties with third states in areas falling under the E.U.'s responsibilities. But there is an overlap between the E.C.'s powers in external relations (including the power to make treaties in its own name) and the E.U.'s powers under the second and third pillars: see Cremona, "The Common Foreign and Security Policy of the EU and the External Relations Power of the EC", in O'Keeffe & Twomey (eds), *Legal Issues of the Maastricht Treaty* (Wiley, London, 1994). *Cf.* Case C–124/95 *R. v. HM Treasury and Bank of England, ex p. Centro-Com* [1997] E.C.R. 81.

[44] See Curtin, "The Constitutional Structure of the Union: A Europe of Bits and Pieces" (1993) 30 C.M.L.R. 17 at 27.

[45] Case C–253/94P [1995] E.C.R. I-7.

[46] *cf.* Lenaerts, "Some Reflections on the Separation of Powers in the E.C." (1991) 28 C.M.L.R. 11.

[47] And even more significantly, the E.U. It must be noted that the Council is not only a legislative body; it also exercises executive (policy-making) and judicial (*e.g.* imposing anti-dumping duties) responsibilities in the E.C. Similarly, although the Commission may be termed the E.U.'s executive, it also possesses legislative and judicial powers. For discussion of the Council of Ministers and how it works, see Hayes-Renshaw and Wallace, *The Council of Ministers* (Macmillan, London, 1997).

[48] Art. 203 (formerly 146) E.C.

[49] Art. 203 E.C. was amended by the Maastricht Treaty at the instigation of the German government to allow the Council to consist of ministers in regional (in Germany, Laender) governments in addition to (and more usually) ministers in the German government. This provision arose during the Parliamentary debates on the Scotland Act 1998 since it would also allow ministers in the Scottish Executive to represent the U.K. government at the Council of Ministers. This could raise some accountability problems when a Scottish

The Council of Ministers consists of ministers responsible nationally (or subject to Article 203 E.C. regionally) for the subject-matter on the Council's agenda, for example, agriculture, transport or environment. There is also a General Affairs Council, consisting of the member states' foreign affairs ministers, and the ECOFIN Council, which consists of the member states' finance ministers. It is important to note that there is not just one Council: at any time, there can be various Councils sitting, deliberating and passing E.C. laws on various subjects; but every act or decision of the Council stands equally as a decision of the single Council of Ministers.[50] Voting in the Council may be by simple majority, by unanimity or, increasingly, by the system known as qualified majority voting. The E.C. (or E.U.) Treaty Article under which the Council acts determines which voting procedure applies. Failure to adopt either the correct legal basis for a measure or the appropriate voting or other required procedure will risk the Council's act being challenged and annulled by the ECJ.[51]

The Parliament

The European Parliament is provided for in Articles 189–201 E.C.[52] Since **5.08** 1979 it has been directly elected every five years by the voters eligible to vote in the member states.[53] The TEU now provides that the Parliament can consist of no more than 700 members.[54] The Parliament is given the traditional functions of a legislature, namely representation, ensuring the accountability of the European Union's administration,[55] passing the European Community's budget and law-making. But the Parliament's role in law-making, although expanding, is still significantly qualified by the

---

minister, although not a member of the U.K. Parliament, commits the U.K. government. It is, however, for the national government to decide when it will allow itself to be represented by a member of a regional government. It is not clear in the U.K. case how these decisions will be made, how open they will be or whether they will be challengeable in judicial review, for example, by a disappointed Scottish Executive. Assuming that experience in Germany's sophisticated federal polity is helpful here, the German experience may be instructive: see Kokott, "Federal States in Federal Europe: The German Laender and Problems of European Integration" [1997] 3 Eur.P.L. 607.

[50] Much of the preparatory and detailed work of the Council of Ministers is carried out by the COREPER committees (of which there are two), consisting of the member states' Ambassadors (COREPER II) and Deputy Ambassadors (COREPER I) acccredited to the E.U. In addition, considerable work is done by the Council's own committees, consisting of Council, Commission and national civil servants.

[51] But the jurisdiction of the ECJ under the E.C. Treaty to review acts of the Council of Ministers only extends to acts and decisions of the Council *qua* Council. The Court has held that it cannot review acts of the member states acting collectively as such (albeit "meeting in Council") but not under the auspices of the Council of Ministers: Cases C–181 & 248/91 *European Parliament v. Council and Commission* [1993] E.C.R. I-3685 (noted by Neville Brown at (1994) 31 C.M.L.R. 1347). But *cf.* Case C–316/91 *European Parliament v. Council* [1994] E.C.R. I-625 (ECJ's power to review binding acts of the Council of Ministers extends to acts adopted by the Council otherwise than in pursuance of Treaty provisions). In addition, the ECJ's jurisdiction is limited by Art. 46 TEU in relation to measures adopted by the Council of Ministers under the E.U.'s second and third pillars.

[52] Before the Single European Act amendments to the E.C. Treaty the Parliament was known as the Assembly.

[53] Also, as an incident of citizenship of the E.U. (created by Art. 17 E.C.), all nationals of the member states are entitled to stand as a candidate for the European Parliament and to vote for it in other member states in which they are resident: Art. 19(2) E.C.

[54] Art. 189 E.C.

[55] In which role it is assisted by the European Ombudsman whom it may appoint under Art. 195 (formerly 138e) E.C. Complaints may be made to the Ombudsman directly by individuals or referred to him by MEPs but only over E.U. (that is, not national) activities.

powers of the Council of Ministers. While the Parliament's importance as the only directly elected institution in the European Community's institutional system suggests an essential part in law-making, its role has been a continual source of tension in the European Community's constitutional arrangements.[56] Just as elected Parliaments everywhere struggle to assert their powers, the European Parliament has demanded more law-making powers in the European Community, including a right of legislative initiative so far predominantly possessed by the Commission.[57] The Parliament's powers have steadily increased but this has led to further tensions between the European Community's institutions and national Parliaments which are concerned that they will be eclipsed by a more powerful European Parliament.[58] More generally, the continuing restrictions on the Parliament's powers, along with qualified democracy and accountability at the E.C. level and the dominance of the Council of Ministers, are often referred to as the European Union's "democratic deficit".[59] Without doubt, this has led to an enhanced role for the law and the ECJ in ensuring accountability and limited government in the European Community and the Parliament as an institution has benefited from the ECJ's concern to ensure that the rule of law is upheld: notwithstanding the absence of an expressly conferred jurisdiction in such cases, the ECJ decided that the scheme of the E.C. Treaty demanded that the Parliament be able to sue under the E.C. Treaty to enforce and protect its prerogatives.[60] The Parliament's standing in appropriate cases is now expressly provided in the E.C. Treaty.[61]

The Commission

5.09 The European Commission may be considered the main element of the European Union's executive.[62] There are presently 20 Commissioners, at least one from each member state,[63] one of whom is appointed by the member states jointly with the European Parliament President of the

---

[56] Not least over its location and where it is to meet: see Case 230/81 *Luxembourg v. European Parliament* [1983] E.C.R. 255; Cases 358/85 and 51/86 *France v. European Parliament* [1988] E.C.R. 4821; and Case C–345/95 *France v. European Parliament* [1997] E.C.R. I-5215 (noted by de Zwaan at (1999) 36 C.M.L.R. 463). See also the Protocol to the TEU and E.C. Treaties on the Location of the seats of the Institutions.

[57] But see Art. 192 (formerly Art. 138b) E.C.

[58] See, for example, s. 6 of the European Parliamentary Elections Act 1978; and s. 2 of the European Communities (Amendment) Act 1998. The compromise seems to be acceptance of a dual role for the European Parliament and national Parliaments (including the Scottish Parliament) in ensuring accountability of the E.U. institutions, for example, by scrutinising proposals for E.C. legislation before they are enacted. See the Protocol to the TEU and the E.C. Treaties on the Role of National Parliaments in the E.U.

[59] For discussion, see Hayward, *The Crisis of Representation in Europe* (1995).

[60] Case C–70/88 *European Parliament v. Council* [1990] E.C.R. I-2041. Earlier, in Case 294/83 *Parti Ecologiste 'Les Verts' v. European Parliament* [1986] E.C.R. 1339, the ECJ decided that the Parliament could also be sued under Art. 230 (formerly 173) E.C. in its own name. See Bradley, "Maintaining the Balance: The Role of the Court of Justice in Defining the Institutional Position of the European Parliament" (1987) 24 C.M.L.R. 41.

[61] Arts 230 and 232 E.C.

[62] Several specialised works discuss the structure, role and functions of the E.U. Commission: see, for example, Cini, *The European Commission* (Manchester UP, 1996); and Edwards & Spence, *The European Commission* (Cartermill Publishing, London, 1994).

[63] The five larger member states (Germany, France, Italy, Spain and the U.K.) each have two Commissioners. However, on the enlargement of the E.U. to 20 member states (and subject to reforms to qualified majority voting) there will only be one Commissioner from each state: see Protocol to the TEU and E.C. Treaties on the Institutions with the Prospect of Enlargement of the E.U.

Commission. In consultation with the President, the member states nominate the remaining Commissioners. They are all then subject to confirmation by the European Parliament and once appointed serve for renewable terms of five years.[64] The members of the Commission are required by the E.C. Treaty to be independent and "shall neither seek nor take instructions from any government or from any other body".[65] They form a college and are bound by the principle of collective responsibility.[66] Each Commissioner is usually in charge of one of the Commission's Directorate Generals (basically departments) dealing with particular subjects such as environment, transport or competition. The responsibilities of the Commission are given in Article 211 of the E.C. Treaty. These include:

> "to ensure that the Treaty and measures taken under it are applied; to formulate recommendations or deliver opinions on matters dealt with in the Treaty as and when appropriate; to have its own power of decision and participate in the legislative processes provided in the Treaty; and to exercise the powers conferred on it by the Council".

Like administrations elsewhere the Commission also exercises plentiful legislative and judicial powers. Indeed, the extent of the Commission's judicial powers and the fact that it is often judge and prosecutor, for example, in competition investigations, is a source of criticism. In the legislative process the Commission has the power of initiation. All legislative proposals in the European Community must normally be initiated by the Commission.[67] In addition, the Council of Ministers has delegated legislative powers to the Commission in many areas.[68]

The Court of Justice

The E.C. Treaty vests judicial power in the ECJ and the Court of First **5.10** Instance (CFI).[69] Together, the ECJ and CFI are given jurisdiction by Article 220 E.C.: "to ensure that in the interpretation and application of

---

[64] Subject to being forced to resign en masse following a vote of censure passed by a two-thirds majority of the European Parliament: see Art. 201 (formerly 144) E.C.

[65] Art. 213(2) E.C.

[66] *cf.* Art. 210 E.C.

[67] In some cases, the Council may request the Commission to submit proposals: see Art. 208 E.C. (formerly Art. 152). The European Parliament also has a limited power of initiative where a majority of its members can request the Commission to submit a proposal for E.C. legislation: see Article 192 E.C. (formerly Art. 138b). The final decision, however, rests with the Commission and it may be assumed that the ECJ will be reluctant to exercise review of the Commission's power of initiative under the E.C. Treaty: *cf.* Case 247/87 *Star Fruit Co v. Commission* [1989] E.C.R. 291 and T–277/94 *AITEC v. Commission* [1996] E.C.R. II-351. The Commission's almost exclusive power of initiative under the E.C. Treaty must be contrasted with the position in the E.U.: under the second pillar, the power to initiate legislative proposals is possessed by the Council of Ministers (see Art. 14(4) TEU); under the third pillar, it is shared between the Council, the member states and the Commission (Art. 34(2) TEU). Compare also Art. 67 and Title IV of the E.C. Treaty: the member states share power of initiative with the Commission for the first five years following the entry into force of the Treaty of Amsterdam in those areas on free movement of persons related to the Schengen Agreement which are now incorporated into the E.C. Treaty (but with opt outs for the U.K. and Ireland).

[68] Several cases have concerned the legality of the Council's delegation of powers to the Commission: see, for example, Case 41/69 *ACF Chemiefarma NV v. Commission* [1970] E.C.R. 661.

[69] Before 1989, the E.C. had only one court, namely the ECJ. The volume of work

this [EC] Treaty the law is observed".[70] It follows that the power of the ECJ and CFI to exercise judicial review of E.C. legislation and other acts of the institutions to ensure consistency with the E.C. Treaty and other applicable laws is expressly conferred by the Treaty.[71] There can therefore be no doubt about the existence of the power of judicial review at the E.C. level.[72]

The ECJ and the CFI each have 15 judges. In addition, the ECJ is assisted by eight Advocates-General, whose duty, "acting with complete impartiality and independence", is to assist the Court in deciding cases brought before it by making "reasoned submissions".[73] Eligibility for

---

before the ECJ reached such a level that in 1986 the member states agreed in the Single European Act to the creation of a second court, namely the CFI. The CFI was brought into operation and given its first tranch of jurisdiction (mainly staff cases and direct actions in the area of competition law) by Decision 88/591 (O.J. L319). It commenced work in 1989. The CFI is not a separate Community institution and is often described as "attached" to the ECJ. Both courts are located in Luxembourg and share various facilities, although each has its own Registry. When a reference is made to the ECJ as an institution, it must be understood as including the CFI. But the CFI is a separate court with its own jurisdiction (which now includes all direct actions brought against an E.U. institution by natural and legal persons (see Decisions 93/350, O.J. L144 and 94/149, O.J. L66)). The Statute of the ECJ provides for the situation where an action is brought in the wrong court and Art. 225 E.C. allows appeals only on points of law to be taken from CFI decisions to the ECJ.

[70] Art. 220 E.C. (formerly Art. 164 E.C.) confers jurisdiction on the European Courts only under the E.C. Treaty. Jurisdiction under other pillars of the TEU must be expressly conferred by provisions of the TEU or subsequent agreements or other measures agreed by the E.U. member states thereunder, *cf.* Art. 46 TEU (formerly Art. L) and Art. 35 TEU; consider also Art. 68 E.C. The ECJ has also been given jurisdiction under other treaties agreed to by the E.U. states for example, the Brussels and Lugano Conventions on Jurisdiction and Recognition and Enforcement of Judgments; and the Rome Contracts Convention.

[71] It is clear from the words "the law is observed" that Art. 220 E.C. envisages E.C. law consisting of more than just the E.C. Treaty and E.C. legislation. For example, it must also include general principles of law such as at least some human rights. See Sir Jean-Pierre Warner, "The Relationship Between European Community Law and the National Laws of Member States" (1977) 93 L.Q.R. 349: " . . . the Treaty was not to be approached as if in a legal vacuum" (at 350).

[72] In contrast with the U.S. Constitution, with which the E.C. Treaty is often compared. The U.S. Constitution does not expressly provide for a power of judicial review. In the United States the U.S. Supreme Court derives its power of judicial review from the Supreme Court's famous early decision in *Marbury v. Madison*, 1 Cranch 137 (1803), in which Marshall C.J. decided that judicial review was inevitably implied by a (supreme) written Constitution, under which "it was the province and duty of the judicial branch to say what the law is". The U.S. Constitution does, however, expressly give the Constitution (and federal law) supremacy over state law and the potential to confer rights directly on individuals which can be enforced in state courts (see the 14th Amendment's Due Process Clause). But the E.C. Treaty does not expressly provide for the supremacy and direct effect of E.C. law, both of which follow from decisions of the ECJ. The literature on judicial review, the supremacy of the Constitution and constitutional rights in the U.S. is vast: see, for example, Tribe, *American Constitutional Law* (2nd ed., Foundation Press, New York, 1988), Chaps 3 and 4; and Redish, *Federal Jurisdiction: Tensions in the Allocation of Judicial Power* (1980). For comparisons with E.C. law, see Cappelletti, Seccombe and Weiler (eds), *Integration Through Law: Europe and the American Federal Experience* (de Gruyter, 1986).

[73] Art. 222 E.C. Treaty. An Advocate-General can also be called on by the Court of First Instance to assist it. Following the accession of Austria, Sweden and Finland on January 1, 1995, there have been nine Advocates-General; unless the Council of Ministers agrees with a request from the Court to increase the number of Advocates-General, their number will again be eight following the retirement of the ninth in October 2000. Obviously not all the member states have an Advocate-General. Each of the five larger states (France, Germany, Italy, the U.K. and Spain) have one, but the remaining three positions rotate around the

appointment as a judge or Advocate-General is restricted to "persons whose independence is beyond doubt and who possess the qualifications required for appointment to the highest judicial offices in their respective countries or who are jurisconsults of recognised competence".[74] In practice only nationals of the member states are eligible for appointment.[75] Article 223 E.C. provides that the judges of both the ECJ and CFI and the Advocates-General are appointed by "common accord of the Governments of the member states" for renewable terms of six years.[76] In practice, this means that each state nominates a qualified person and they are then appointed by "common accord" of all the member states. There is no further procedure on proposed appointments—for example, national or European Parliament hearings.[77]

Other institutions and bodies

The Court of Auditors is responsible for supervising the European Community's expenditure and ensuring that funds are allocated to their **5.11**

---

other member states. There is, therefore, the germ of a "federal supreme court" quality about the appointment of the Advocates-General which may point to possible future reform of the ECJ when the E.U.'s membership increases to a level at which it might be thought inefficient for the Court to have a judge from every member state. If it can be said as a general principle that all eight of the Advocates-General should as a whole represent the different legal traditions in the E.U., the same might one day be the basis for appointment of the judges to a Court with a maximum of nine, 11 or 13 judges. For discussion of future possible reforms to the ECJ in this regard, see *The Role and Future of the ECJ* (British Institute of International & Comparative Law, 1996), pp. 44–46.

[74] Art. 223 E.C.

[75] A member state could in theory nominate as a judge a person from another member state; or indeed from a non-member state (interestingly, a Canadian judge once sat on the European Court of Human Rights for Liechtenstein): see Kennedy, "Thirteen Russians! The Composition of the ECJ", in Campbell & Voyatzi (eds), *Legal Reasoning and Judicial Interpretation of European Law: Essays in honour of Lord Mackenzie Stuart* (Trenton Publishing, Hampshire, 1996) Chap. 4. Again in theory, it is possible for a member state to have more than one judge holding its nationality. Unlike the Commission, therefore, there is no express requirement that each state should have a national on the Court. In practice, however, each state's nationality will be represented since each state is likely to nominate one of its own nationals. But as the judges' and Advocates'-General independence is "beyond doubt", they must not be considered as representatives of their states or legal traditions. Their primary duty is coterminous with the ECJ's, to "ensure that in the interpretation and application of this Treaty the law is observed". This duty is ensured in their oath: see Brown & Kennedy, *The Court of Justice of the European Communities* (4th ed., Sweet & Maxwell, London, 1994), at p. 47.

So far, the judges appointed from the U.K. to the ECJ have been the Rt Hon. The Lord Mackenzie Stuart of Drem, the Rt Hon. The Lord Slynn of Hadley and Judge David Edward Q.C.; Judge Edward was previously a judge on the Court of First Instance and was succeeded there by Judge Christopher Bellamy Q.C.; the first Advocate-General from the U.K. was Sir Jean-Pierre Warner, succeeded by Sir Gordon (now Lord) Slynn, who in turn was succeeded by Professor Francis Jacobs Q.C.

[76] Art. 223 provides for the Judges and Advocates-General to be partially replaced (or reappointed) every three years.

[77] The Parliament has been lobbying for a role in the appointment of ECJ and CFI judges: see discussion and citations in Brown and Kennedy, *The Court of Justice of the European Communities* (4th ed., Sweet & Maxwell, London, 1994), at pp. 45–46. One suggested possibility for the Parliament is a role similar to that possessed by the Parliamentary Assembly of the Council of Europe (which elects the judges of the European Court of Human Rights from lists submitted by the member states); but since the Council of Europe's Parliamentary Assembly consists of delegates of national legislatures, such an approach begs the question of what role national parliaments should have, if any, in the appointment of ECJ judges, whose decisions often affect national legislative power. Significantly, the appointment of supreme court judges has been a sensitive point in several federal systems, notably the U.S., Canada and Germany: see para. 4.25.

proper purposes. As Article 246 of the E.C. Treaty succinctly says, it "shall carry out the audit". Other important bodies include the Economic and Social Committee and the Committee of the Regions, both of which the E.C. Treaty often gives a consultative role in the legislative process.[78] The European Community has also established various specialist bodies to administer policies which the member states have developed.[79] These bodies—for example, the European Environment Agency and the European Monitoring Centre for Drugs and Drug Addiction—are not institutions but they must work within the framework of E.C. law. It is likely that the ECJ will be able to review their activities against the standards of E.C. law.[80]

The Role of the European Court of Justice

5.12   There can be no doubt that decisions of the European Court of Justice (ECJ) have had an enormous influence on both the character of the European Community and the nature and effects of E.C. law. The creation of E.C. law as a new legal order, its supremacy over inconsistent laws of the member states and its capacity for direct effect are attributable to the approach which the ECJ has taken to the E.C. Treaty. Furthermore, the Court's decisions have given the rule of law pre-eminence in the European Community and resulted in a system of government based on law and respect for the rights of the citizen. By way of example of these achievements, mention need only be made of the Court's protection of some human rights values as general principles of E.C. law and of its decisions, later incorporated into E.C. Treaty provision, by which the European Parliament became capable of suing and being sued as an Institution. More generally, the Court is often recognised as having been an engine of European integration through law. In this regard, it is sometimes compared with the U.S. Supreme Court, which has also had a great influence on U.S. society by virtue of its power to interpret the US Constitution. But just as that Court's decisions have not always been received with universal acclaim, so too the ECJ's encouragement of the process of European integration through law has not always been approved.[81] Inevitably, the criticism has

---

[78] The Economic and Social Committee is provided for in Arts 257–262 E.C. and the Committee of the Regions in Arts 263–265 E.C. Both committees consist of 222 members. Where the E.C. Treaty requires, these committees are to be consulted by the Council before legislation is adopted. Basically, the Economic and Social Committee must be consulted in relation to all legislation in the social field (see, for example, Art. 141 on equal treatment of men and women in matters of employment and occupation); while the Committee of the Regions must be consulted where proposed legislation impacts on the national and regional diversity of the E.U. (for example, culture (Art. 151) and education (Art. 149, under which the Economic and Social Committee must be consulted too)).

[79] A useful discussion of some of the leading bodies is given in Edward & Lane, *European Community Law* (2nd ed., Butterworths, Edinburgh, 1995) at pp. 46–50.

[80] Following the principle established in the *Les Verts* case (Case 294/83 *Parti Ecologists 'Les Verts' v. European Parliament* [1986] E.C.R. 1339) that the E.C. Treaty establishes "a complete system of legal remedies and procedures" (at 1365), notwithstanding the absence of express provision for actions against particular bodies.

[81] See Rasmussen, *On Law and Policy in the ECJ: A Comparative Study in Judicial Policymaking* (Nijhoff, 1986) and *cf.* Cappelletti, "Is the European Court of Justice 'Running Wild'?" (1987) 12 Eur.L.R. 3. More recently, see Neill, *The ECJ – A Case Study in Judicial Activism*, published as evidence to the House of Lords Select Committee on the European Communities, 18th Report, 1994–95, pp. 218–245 and *cf.* Edward, "Judicial Activism – Myth or Reality" in Campbell and Voyatzi (eds), *Legal Reasoning and Judicial Interpretation of European Law* (1996), Chap. 3. And see also Lord Slynn of Hadley, "Critics of the Court: a Reconsideration", Chap. 1 in Ardenas and Jacobs, *E.C. Law in the English Courts* (Clarendon Press, Oxford, 1998).

been directed at the Court's legitimacy, raising issues which judicial review and constitutional interpretation must face in all contexts. Importantly, however, the ECJ's leading decisions on the relationship between E.C. law and national law have been made in the exercise of its jurisdiction under Article 234 of the E.C. Treaty.[82] For the most part, the ECJ has had frequent opportunities to exercise this jurisdiction because of the willingness of national courts to make references to the ECJ. Although not all national courts have always accepted the ECJ's rulings on the implications of E.C. law for national law,[83] it is evident that the extent to which national courts embrace both the jurisdiction and decisions of the ECJ not only demonstrates a "dialogue" between them, but also highlights the role which national courts themselves have had in creating the E.C. legal order. In particular, it may be arguable that in some cases, not least the United Kingdom, it has been easier for a national judge to give full effect to E.C. law over and above the hallowed strictures of national constitutional law with the benefit of a ruling of the ECJ in hand.[84] In any event, whatever may be thought about particular decisions or specific areas of the ECJ's jurisprudence, the historical absence of direct democratic accountability in the European Union has enhanced the Court's role. The approach which the Court has taken to giving meaningful effect to the E.C. Treaty and the laws passed under it, in addition to ensuring that the Community institutions strictly comply with the requirements of the Treaty, have been essential in creating a legal order in which the rule of law and constitutionalism are observed in and throughout the European Union.

This is not the place to enter an extensive discussion of how the ECJ functions. For the present, it is enough to note that the Court divides its decision-making powers between chambers of the Court, consisting of three, four or seven judges,[85] and plenaries, which can consist of nine, 11, 13 or all 15 judges.[86] The Court's Statute and decisions indicate how cases are allocated between chambers and plenaries, but unless a member state or a Community institution requests that a case be heard by a plenary court, it may be heard by a chamber.[87] Importantly, however, all decisions of the ECJ, whether rendered by a chamber or a plenary, stand in E.C. law as decisions of the Court. In other words, the ECJ is a collegiate court. But this does not necessarily put an end to questions about consistency in decision-making between various chambers, nor about whether decisions of a plenary court, especially of all the 15 judges, are more authoritative. Accordingly, although some may say that the ECJ has the potential to emerge as the European Union's supreme court, or rather its federal constitutional court,[88] the Court's management of its decision-making may make this problematic. In particular, since the ECJ's methods are more like those of a continental rather than a common law court, it may not be

---

[82] The details of Art. 234 are noted at paras 5.61 *et seq.* below.
[83] Notably the German Constitutional Court: see para. 5.32 below.
[84] *cf.* Craig, "Report on U.K.", in Slaughter, Sweet & Weiler, *The European Courts and National Courts* (Hart, Oxford, 1997), Chap. 7, esp. at pp. 220–222.
[85] Of whom three or five traditionally sit.
[86] See Art. 221 (formerly 165) E.C.
[87] See further, Edward & Lane, *European Community Law* (2nd ed., 1995), para. 87.
[88] *cf.* Rinze, "The Role of the ECJ as a Federal Constitutional Court" [1993] P.L. 426.

to everyone's satisfaction for the ECJ in its present form to emerge as a "constitutional court" for the E.U.[89]

III SOURCES OF E.C. LAW

5.13 Although the European Union itself now has potentially far-reaching legislative powers under the TEU,[90] it is E.C. law which has the greatest significance for the U.K. legal systems. Aside from a brief mention of distinct sources of E.U. law, the present discussion concentrates on the sources of E.C. law.

The New Legal Order

5.14 In its landmark decision in *Van Gend en Loos v. Netherlands* in 1963,[91] the ECJ declared that the E.C. Treaty "constitutes a new legal order in international law". In *Costa v. ENEL*[92] the following year, the ECJ underlined the distinctiveness of the legal order established by the E.C. Treaty: "As opposed to other international treaties, the Treaty instituting the EEC has created its own order which was integrated with the national order of the member states the moment the Treaty came into force: as such, it is binding on them". The subtle refinement of E.C. law from a "legal order in international law" to being "its own order . . . integrated with the national order" is enormously significant. Although the ECJ's decisions in *Van Gend en Loos* and *Costa*[93] are more famous for declaring the principles of direct effect and supremacy of E.C. law, the decisions are also notable for the Court's description of the nature of the European Community's legal order. While it is true at one level to say that E.C. law is an international legal order, the true nature of E.C. law is only observed in its penetration of the national laws of the member states. This means that E.C. law is a distinct source of law, of rights and duties, in the legal systems of the member states. Both its volume and its nature give it great potential to be the basis of an application for judicial review in the U.K. courts. It is therefore necessary to say something about the sources of the laws which comprise E.C. law.

The E.C. Treaty

5.15 In the European Community, the E.C. Treaty is the primary source of E.C. law.[94] It has been described by the ECJ as the European Community's "constitutional charter".[95] At the very least, this means that the

---

[89] From the common lawyer's viewpoint, the absence of dissenting opinions is often cast as a major deficiency (although it is only in recent times that dissents have become a feature of the Judicial Committee of the Privy Council; and many House of Lords decisions only contain one speech). For further discussion of reforms to the ECJ and the CFI, see *The Role and Future of the ECJ* (British Institute of International & Comparative Law, 1996); and Arnull, "Refurbishing the E.C.'s Judicial Architecture" (1994) 43 I.C.L.Q. 313. See also Lord Slynn of Hadley, *Introducing a European Legal Order* (1992), Chap. 4.

[90] Especially under the third pillar. See further para. 5.22 below.

[91] Case 26/62 [1963] E.C.R. 1.

[92] Case 6/64 [1964] E.C.R. 585.

[93] See the preceding two footnotes.

[94] The provisions of the E.C. Treaty include all the Protocols annexed to it (whether by the E.C. Treaty itself or by a subsequent Treaty, such as the TEU): Art. 311 (formerly 239) E.C. For discussion of the status of the Protocols, see *R. v. Secretary of State for Foreign Affairs, ex p. Rees-Mogg* [1994] 2 W.L.R. 115.

[95] Opinion 1/91 (EEA Opinion) [1991] E.C.R. I-6079, para. 21. See also Case 294/83 *Parti Ecologiste 'Les Verts' v. European Parliament* [1986] E.C.R. 1339, para. 3.

E.C. Treaty (along with the TEU) is the highest source of law in the European Community. No subordinate E.C. law or other act of the institutions can be inconsistent with the E.C. Treaty.[96] In relation to the member states, once the E.C. Treaty has been ratified by a state and, where more is necessary, as in the United Kingdom, implemented into national law according to the procedures prescribed in the state's constitutional law for giving effect to international treaties,[97] the provisions of the E.C. Treaty may be said to be applicable in the legal system of the member state, albeit not "directly applicable".[98] This means that the E.C. Treaty, in cases where it applies and according to the effect given to it by the ECJ, establishes rules of law which national courts must adopt in reaching their decisions.[99] Moreover, the supremacy or primacy of E.C. law means that E.C. Treaty articles will also be superior rules of law which, where they apply, override inconsistent rules of national law.[1] In addition, E.C. Treaty provisions can have direct effect—that is, the E.C. law concept which describes the capacity of E.C. laws to confer rights on individuals which are directly enforceable in national courts.[2] E.C. Treaty articles which meet the criteria established

---

[96] Accordingly, the E.C. has no power to enter an international agreement which would be in conflict with the terms and purpose of the E.C. Treaty: Opinion 1/91, *supra*. This much follows from the E.C. Treaty being seen as the E.C.'s constitution. But what happens if a provision in the TEU (or something done under it) is inconsistent with the E.C. Treaty? Art. 47 (formerly M) TEU provides that nothing in the TEU which does not amend the E.C. Treaty is to be taken to "affect" it. But some provisions of the TEU which do not in terms amend the E.C. Treaty may necessarily have priority over it: consider, for example, Art. 7 TEU (allowing for the rights of E.U. member states to be suspended where the Council concludes that the state is responsible for "serious and persistent" human rights violations); and Art. 46 (formerly L) TEU (restricting the ECJ's jurisdiction in relation to the second and third pillars of the TEU). It follows from Art. 46 TEU, however, that the ECJ has jurisdiction to explain what Art. 47 TEU means for the relationship between the TEU and the E.C. Treaty. So, for example, acts and decisions under the second and third pillars of the TEU may be challenged before the ECJ on the ground that they should properly have been enacted under the E.C. Treaty: see Case C–170/96 *Commission v. Council* [1998] ECR I-2763.

[97] For example, passage of an amendment to the national Constitution or, in the case of the U.K., enactment of the European Communities Act 1972. Amendments to the E.C. Treaty, for example, by the Maastricht Treaty, will usually also require national constitutional amendments or, in the U.K., enactment of a European Communities (Amendment) Act (such as the European Communities (Amendment) Act 1993) so as to include the new treaty within the definition of "Community treaty" for the purposes of s. 1(2) of the 1972 Act.

[98] The term "directly applicable" is reserved only for E.C. regulations, which are so described by Art. 249 (formerly 189) E.C. But once implemented into national law all of the E.C. Treaty may be considered as applicable "directly", at least in the sense of providing rules and principles of law which are binding on national courts. So, even although an E.C. Treaty article does not have direct effect, it can still be relevant in national litigation: for example, Art. 10 E.C.

[99] The operative phrases are "where it applies" and "according to the effect given to it by the ECJ". On the significance of the first, see *R. v. Chief Constable of Sussex, ex p. International Trader's Ferry Ltd* [1998] 3 W.L.R. 1260, esp. *per* Lord Hoffmann at pp. 1282 *et seq*. As to the second, it must first be noted that the ECJ's approach to interpretation of the Treaty emphasises its spirit over the limitations of its terms (see, for example, Case 34/79 *R. v. Henn and Darby* [1979] E.C.R. 3795; and [1982] A.C. 850); and secondly, it is for the ECJ to say whether provisions in the E.C. Treaty have direct effect.

[1] See, for example, *R. v. Secretary of State for Transport, ex p. Factortame (No. 2)* [1991] 1 A.C. 603 (provisions of Merchant Shipping Act 1988 which violate the Art. 12 (formerly 6, and before that 7) E.C. prohibition of nationality discrimination to be disapplied). See further para. 5.32 below.

[2] Case 26/62 *Van Gend en Loos v. Nederlandse Administratie der Belastingen* [1963] E.C.R. 1.

by the ECJ for direct effect have both "vertical" and "horizontal" direct effect—that is, they confer rights on individuals against the state and its "emanations" (vertical effect) and against other private natural and legal persons (horizontal effect).[3] The important concepts of direct applicability and direct effect are discussed further below.[4]

European Community legislation

5.16 The E.C. Treaty provides for several different types of E.C. legislation and several alternative procedures through which a legislative proposal may be enacted. European Community legislation falls into five categories, namely regulations, directives, decisions, recommendations and opinions.[5] Collectively these may be termed E.C. legislation. But since recommendations and opinions are said by Article 249 E.C. to have no binding force,[6] the most significant legislative acts are regulations, directives and decisions. Nevertheless, in relation to E.C. legislation the ECJ stresses substance over form: the difference between the various measures turns on their effects and not the name by which they go.[7] Similarly, how a measure is enacted turns not on its form but on the relevant E.C. Treaty article under which it is proposed. Where the E.C. Treaty confers legislative powers on the E.C. institutions, it will generally provide both for the type of legislative act permitted and the appropriate legislative procedure which must be followed. The E.C. Treaty provides for various alternative procedures by which E.C. legislation may be enacted.[8] In general, all legislation is initiated by a proposal from the European Commission. But the power to enact E.C. legislation is exercised by the Council of Ministers and increasingly by the Council jointly with the Parliament. In all cases, however, the Commission retains a consultative role in the legislative process. Although the technical details of the E.C. legislative procedures do not need to be discussed here, it is important to note from the standpoint of judicial

---

[3] Case 43/75 *Defrenne v. SABENA* [1976] E.C.R. 455, esp. at paras 30–31.

[4] See paras 5.24 *et seq*.

[5] Art. 249 E.C. (formerly Art. 189 E.C.). But there may also be a residual category of *sui generis* measures: see Case 22/70 *Commission v. Council (ERTA)* [1971] E.C.R. 263 (Council conclusions on how international treaties should be negotiated have some legislative force).

[6] They are also expressly not challengeable under Art. 230 (formerly 173) E.C. But just as departmental circulars in the U.K. may be reviewed in judicial review (*cf. Gillick v. DHSS* [1985] A.C. 112), E.C. recommendations and opinions are not irrelevant in litigation. The ECJ and national courts may have to take them into account, for example, when they are relevant to other provisions of E.C. law: see Case C–322/88 *Grimaldi v. Fonds des maladies Professionnelles* [1989] E.C.R. 4407.

[7] *cf.* Art. 230 E.C.; and see Edward & Lane, *European Community Law* (2nd ed., Butterworths, Edinburgh, 1995) at para. 143. As these authors note, there is in principle no "hierarchical ordering" between different types of E.C. legislation. Accordingly, a subsequent directive which may be inconsistent with an earlier regulation (or vice versa) should be reconciled with it rather than be taken as subordinate to it or impliedly repealed by it.

[8] The three main legislative procedures are known as the "Consultation Procedure", the "Co-operation Procedure" and the "Co-decision Procedure". They are provided for in Arts 250–252 E.C. (formerly Arts 189a–189c). Each, in ascending order, gives an increased role to the European Parliament in passing legislation. Following the Treaty of Amsterdam amendments, some two-thirds of E.C. legislation must be passed under the Co-decision procedure, which effectively gives to the European Parliament a power of veto. For further discussion, see Craig and de Burca, *EU Law* (2nd ed., 1998), pp. 129–142.

review that the ECJ is rigorous in ensuring that the correct legal basis and proper procedures for a measure are strictly complied with.[9]

The E.C. Treaty provides for the legal effects each of the principal legislative acts have in E.C. law and by implication in national law. The effects of regulations, directives and decisions will now be examined.

Regulations

Article 249 provides: "A regulation shall have general application. It shall be binding in its entirety and directly applicable in all Member States." E.C. regulations are expressly said to be directly applicable in the legal systems of the member states without the need for national implementing measures. Indeed, it is generally illegal under E.C. law for a member state to implement a regulation in national law by means of national legislation.[10] Once enacted by the European Community's legislature, a regulation operates of its own force directly in national law. In essence, this is what is meant by the principle of direct applicability. In addition, provisions in regulations can also have direct effect.[11] That is, where they meet the criteria for direct effect specified by the ECJ,[12] provisions in regulations can confer rights directly on individuals. As with Treaty articles, provisions in regulations which have direct effect are said to have both vertical and horizontal direct effect.

5.17

Directives

According to Article 249 E.C.: "A directive shall be binding, as to the result to be achieved, upon each Member State to which it is addressed, but shall leave to the national authorities the choice of form and

5.18

---

[9] See, for example, Case 242/87 *Commission v. Council* [1989] E.C.R. 1429 and Case C–84/94 *U.K. v. Council* [1996] E.C.R. I-5755 (both dealing with challenges to the legal basis of E.C. legislation); and the leading case of Case 138/79 *Roquette Freres v. The Council* [1980] E.C.R. 3333 (failure of the Council to wait for the Parliament's opinion when this was required by the E.C. Treaty rendered the legislative act void). Where there are doubts about the validity of a measure, it may be subject to challenge directly before the ECJ or CFI, for example, under Art. 230 E.C., or by way of defence in terms of Art. 241 E.C. Alternatively, an E.C. measure may be challenged before a national court: for example, in judicial review in the Court of Session where a national authority has implemented or otherwise relied on the E.C. measure—see Cases 133–136/85 *Walter Rau Lebensmittelwerke v. Bundesanstalt fur Landwirtschaftliche Marktordnung* [1987] E.C.R. 2289. But national courts cannot invalidate E.C. measures, which are presumptively valid until quashed by the ECJ (or CFI). Where a national court has (serious) grounds to suspect the invalidity of the E.C. measure, it must make a reference to the ECJ under Art. 234 E.C., since only the ECJ can quash E.C. laws: Case 314/85 *Foto-Frost v. Hauptzollamt Lubeck-Ost* [1987] E.C.R. 4199. But the national court may be able to grant an interim remedy suspending the effect of the national measure until the ECJ replies to the reference: see Cases 143/88 and C–92/89 *Zuckerfabriken Suderdithmarschen und Soest v. Hauptzollamter Itzehoe und Paderborn* [1991] E.C.R. I-415; and Case C–465/93 *Atlanta Fruchthandelsgesellschaft mbH v. Bundesamt fur Ernahrung und Forstwirtschaft* [1995] E.C.R. I-3761. The relationship between the powers of national courts and the ECJ in relation to the validity of E.C. measures is discussed further at para. 5.53 below.

[10] Case 50/76 *Amsterdam Bulb BV v. Produktschap voor Siergewassen* [1977] E.C.R. 137; Case 94/77 *Fratteli Zerbone v. Amministrazione delle Finanze dello Stato* [1978] E.C.R. 99. The rationale of this rule is that the E.C. source of the provisions in the regulation should not be disguised. *cf.* Case 230/78 *SpA Eridania-Zuccherifici Nazionale v. Minister of Agriculture and Forestry* [1979] E.C.R. 2749 at para. 34 (a regulation may provide for national measures to be adopted to implement it).

[11] Case 39/72 *Commission v. Italy* [1973] E.C.R. 101; and Case 41/74 *Van Duyn v. Home Office* [1974] E.C.R. 1337.

[12] On which, see pt IV below.

methods." In contrast with regulations, directives are not directly applicable in national law. They are "binding" on the member states "as to the result to be achieved" but leave the process of implementation into national law to the member states themselves.[13] However, this does not mean that member states have a discretion whether or not to implement directives. The member states' discretion is only as to how to implement a directive effectively into national law. In terms of Article 249, directives remain "binding" on the member states "as to the result" which they seek to achieve. Where a member state has failed to implement a directive or has only inadequately done so, the result to be achieved by the directive continues to bind the member state.[14] This conclusion has led the ECJ to decide that in some circumstances and subject to the usual criteria for direct effect, provisions in directives can have direct effect even though they are not directly applicable.[15] But where directives have direct effect, they only have "vertical" and not horizontal "direct effect", which means that they can only be relied on directly in cases against the state or an "emanation of the state" and not in cases between private individuals *inter se*.[16] However, the ECJ has made clear that Article 10 (formerly 5) of the E.C. Treaty imposes an obligation on all national authorities, including all courts and tribunals, to give effect to all national law so far as possible to comply with all E.C. law, and in particular directives.[17] The ECJ has decided that this obligation means that even in cases between two private individuals, a national court must interpret national legislation so far as possible to comply with directives which have not been implemented or have only been inadequately implemented into national law.[18] Provisions in directives may therefore be said to be capable of having direct effect in cases against the state and its "emanations" and "indirect effect" by

---

[13] On various techniques of implementation in the U.K., see Samuels, "Incorporating, Translating or Interpreting EU Law into UK Law" (1998) 19 Stat.L.R. 80. More generally, see Bates, "UK Implementation of EU Directives" (1996) 17 Stat.L.R. 27; and Ramsey, "The Copy Out Technique: More of a "Cop Out" Than a Solution" (1996) 17 Stat.L.R. 218.

[14] See Case 41/74 *Van Duyn v. Home Office* [1974] E.C.R. 1337, esp. para. 12, a decision which heralds the later development of direct effect for directives in actions against the State.

[15] Case 152/84 *Marshall v. Southampton & South West Hampshire Area Health Authority (Marshall I)* [1986] E.C.R. 723.

[16] But the defintion given by the ECJ to "emanation of the state" is a wide one: see Case 103/88 *Costanzo (Fratelli) SpA v. Milano* [1989] E.C.R. 1839 (directly effective provisions in directives may be relied on against a local government body). Accordingly, a directive may be relied on by an individual directly against the Scottish Administration. But do directives have direct effect as between public bodies? Could the Scottish Executive rely on a directly effective directive against the U.K. government? *Cf. R. v. Secretary of State for the Environment, ex p. Bury Metropolitan Borough Council* [1998] 2 C.M.L.R. 787. More generally, the identification of public bodies is for national law; *cf. Foster v. British Gas plc* (Case C–188/89 [1990] E.C.R. I-3313) in the Court of Appeal [1988] I.C.R. 584, *per* Donaldson M.R. at 588; and see further para. 5.29 below.

[17] Case 14/83 *Von Colson and Kamann v. Land Nordrhein-Westfalen* [1984] E.C.R. 1891. For a recent Scottish example of respect for this obligation, see *English v. North Lanarkshire Council*, 1999 S.C.L.R. 310.

[18] Case C–106/89 *Marleasing SA v. La Comercial Internacional de Alimentación SA* [1990] E.C.R. I-4135. For U.K. examples, see *Litster v. Forth Dry Dock Ltd*, 1989 S.C. (H.L.) 96; and *Webb v. EMO Cargo* [1993] 1 W.L.R. 49. The obligations of the court in this regard may be compared with the obligations flowing from s. 3 of the Human Rights Act 1998. That is, although the Convention rights do not in terms of s. 6 of the Act apply between private parties, a court must interpret all legislation so far as possible to be compatible with Convention rights, including in cases between private parties: see further, para. 6.57.

virtue of Article 10 E.C. in all other cases. Moreover, in its landmark decision in *Francovich v. Italy*,[19] the ECJ held that the state's failure to implement a directive or do so properly could give individuals who are caused loss by virtue of the state's violation of E.C. law a right to damages against the state which they can bring in national courts.[20] The issues which arise from the direct effect of directives require some more discussion and this is provided in part IV below.

Decisions

Article 249 provides that "a decision shall be binding in its entirety upon those to whom it is addressed". A decision having legislative effects may be made by the Council of Ministers[21] or by the Commission[22] in pursuance of a power to make decisions conferred by the E.C. Treaty or an E.C. regulation. A decision takes effect once it is notified to the person (often member state) to whom it is addressed.[23] A decision is directly applicable and can also have direct effect.[24] Significantly, decisions will often also affect the rights and interests of third parties.[25] More generally, the courts in the member states are bound by and must give effect to E.C. decisions.[26]

5.19

International treaties concluded by the European Community

The European Community has express and implied powers to conclude international treaties with third states and international organisations.[27] The European Community has concluded many such treaties.[28] Inter-

5.20

---

[19] Cases C–6 & 9/90 *Francovich & Bonifaci v. Italy* [1991] E.C.R. I-5357.

[20] In general, the remedy of damages against the state is only available for "sufficiently serious" violations of E.C. law: Cases C–46 and 48/93 *Brasserie du Pêcheur v. Germany* and *R. v. Secretary of State for Transport, ex p. Factortame Ltd (No. 3)* [1996] E.C.R. I-1029. Non-implementation of a directive (*a fortiori*, as in *Francovich*, following a decision of the ECJ holding the state in breach of its E.C. obligations) seems the classical example of a sufficiently serious breach: see Cases C–178 and 179/94 *Dillenkofer v. Germany* [1996] E.C.R. I-4845. But where the directive is to be treated as not having been properly implemented—for example, in light of an *ex post facto* interpretation of the directive by the ECJ—and the member state has acted reasonably and in good faith, its erroneous attempt to implement the directive may not sound in damages: see Case C–392/93 *R. v. H.M. Treasury, ex p. British Telecommunications PLC* [1996] E.C.R. I-1631.

[21] For example, a Council decision imposing anti-dumping or countervailing duties on imports into the E.U.

[22] For example, imposing fines on an undertaking following a competition investigation: see Art. 15 of Regulation 17/62.

[23] Art. 254(3) (formerly 191(3)) E.C. In contrast, regulations and most directives take effect on the date which they specify or, failing specification, on the 20th day following their publication in the *Official Journal of the European Communities* (Art. 254(1) and (2) E.C.).

[24] Where, for example, a decision is addressed to a member state, it may have direct effects *vis-à-vis* third parties who may be able to rely on it against the state or against other private persons. See, for example, Case 9/70 *Grad v. Finanzamt Traunstein* [1970] E.C.R. 825.

[25] Third parties are given limited standing to challenge decisions addressed to others before the Court of First Instance under Art. 230 E.C.: see pt IX below.

[26] See Art. 256 (formerly 192) E.C., providing that decisions which impose a pecuniary obligation on persons other than the state shall be enforceable in the relevant national legal system according to its rules of civil procedure.

[27] For express powers, see, for example, Arts 133 (formerly 113) and 310 (formerly 238) of the E.C. Treaty. The E.C.'s implied external relations powers are more extensive. Basically, they exist wherever the E.C. has internal legislative powers under E.C. law, in which case the external powers are shared with the member states; once such internal powers are exercised, the E.C. acquires exclusive external powers. See, for example, Case

national treaties concluded by the European Community will become part of E.C. law,[29] in which case they may be directly applicable in the laws of the member states and be capable of producing direct effect.[30] The powers of the European Community to enter into international treaties and the effect which international treaties have in the European Community and national legal systems are large subjects. In the present context it is necessary only to note that international treaties concluded by the European Community form part of E.C. law. Where they have direct effects, they have both vertical and horizontal direct effect and may therefore be relied on before national courts in actions against the state and private individuals.

European Community "common law"

5.21   At one level, the term E.C. "common law" refers to decisions of the ECJ and CFI. It only serves to indicate that these decisions are a crucial source of E.C. law.[31] The meaning and effect of the E.C. Treaty and E.C. legislation must be understood in light of the decisions and of the interpretive approach of the ECJ. In particular, the ECJ has often held that legal terms used in E.C. law have an "autonomous meaning" which it is for the ECJ to define.[32] Further, the "teleological" approach to interpreting E.C. law requires that: "every provision of Community law must be placed in its context and interpreted in the light of the provisions of Community law as a whole, regard being had to the

---

22/70 *Commission v. Council (The ERTA Case)* [1971] E.C.R. 263; Opinion 1/75 (local cost standard) [1975] E.C.R. 1355; Cases 3, 4 and 6/76 *Kramer* [1976] E.C.R. 1279; Opinion 1/76 (Laying-up fund for inland waterway vessels) [1977] E.C.R. 741. In more recent decisions on the E.C.'s implied external competence, the ECJ has been more cautious: see Opinion 1/94 (WTO Agreement) [1994] E.C.R. I-5267 and Opinion 2/94 (European Convention on Human Rights) [1996] E.C.R. I-1759. For discussion of the E.C.'s external relations powers, see Craig and de Burca, *EU Law*, at pp. 115–119. For a more extensive analysis, see McGoldrick, *International Relations Law of the EU* (Longman, London, 1997). Where the E.C.'s external powers are in some way deficient, it may enter into "mixed agreements", that is, international agreements entered into jointly with the member states: see, for example, Opinion 2/91 (ILO Convention No. 170) [1993] E.C.R. I-1061. It should be observed here that the E.C. and not the E.U. has the power to conclude international agreements with third states and international organisations in its own name; *cf*. Art. 24 TEU.

[28] The WTO Agreement (and its precursor the GATT) are often cited as the leading examples. In fact, the E.C. was not strictly speaking a party in its own right to the GATT but succeeded to the GATT (see Cases 21–24/72 *International Fruit Co. v. Produktschap* [1972] E.C.R. 1219). However, the E.C. in its own right is now a party to the WTO Agreement and acts in the WTO on behalf of its member states. But the ECJ decided in Opinion 1/94 [1994] E.C.R. I-5267 that the E.C. did not have exclusive competence to enter the General Agreement on Trade in Services or the World Intellectual Property Agreement, its powers being shared with the member states. On the status of GATT, GATS and the WTO Agreement in E.C. law, see generally Emiliou and O'Keeffe (eds), *The EU and World Trade Law – After the GATT Uruguay Round* (Wiley, London, 1996). The ECJ has held that the GATT does not normally produce direct effect: see Case C-280/93 *Germany v. Council* [1994] E.C.R. I-4973.

[29] See Art. 300(7) E.C. Although the provisions of an international treaty concluded by the E.C. may be incorporated into E.C. law—for example, by a regulation—this is not strictly necessary.

[30] See Case 104/81 *Hauptzollamt Mainz v. Kupferberg* [1982] E.C.R. 3641 and Case C-192/89 *SZ Service v. Staatssecretaris Van Justitie* [1992] 2 C.M.L.R. 57. See also *R. v. Secretary of State for the Home Department, ex p. Narin* [1990] 2 C.M.L.R. 233.

[31] And on points of E.C. law, these decisions are binding on all U.K. courts and tribunals: see s. 3 of the European Communities Act 1972.

[32] See, for example, Case 283/81 *Srl CILFIT v. Ministero della Sanita* [1982] E.C.R. 3415, para. 19.

objectives thereof and to its state of evolution at the date on which the provision in question is to be applied".[33] Importantly, however, the term E.C. common law has greater significance. It refers to the general principles of law which have been derived by the ECJ from the E.C. Treaty itself, from the national laws of the member states and, occasionally, international law.[34] These general principles are an independent source of E.C. law.[35] Many of the principles are so significant as to have a constitutional force in E.C. law, especially where, as most broadly are, they are concerned with fundamental rights.[36] To qualify as a general principle of E.C. law, it is not necessary that a legal principle is recognised in the laws of all member states.[37] Once recognised by the ECJ as part of E.C. law, the principle will have its own autonomous meaning in E.C. law which may not produce the same effects as the operation of the principle in national laws. Without doubt, general principles of law undoubtedly constitute an important source of E.C. law on which the ECJ will draw when assessing the validity of, and more generally interpreting, E.C. legislation and other acts of the institutions. Accordingly, the general principles of law are binding on all E.U. institutions. Moreover, in *ERT*[38] the ECJ confirmed that member states' actions and legislation may be measured against the standards of the general principles of law whenever the actions or legislation "fall within the scope of EC law".[39] It is unclear what limits are carried by the qualification "scope of EC law", since the potential scope of E.C. law extends over broad swathes of national authorities activities. In any event, a national court may have to consider whether relevant national measures comply with the general principles of E.C. law, at the very least where they are adopted to implement E.C. law or otherwise administer policies with an E.C. origin.[40] But the general principles of E.C. law do

---

[33] *ibid*. para. 20. *cf. James Buchanan & Co. Ltd v. Babco Forwarding & Shipping (U.K.) Ltd* [1977] Q.B. 208, *per* Lord Denning M.R. at 213 in the Court of Appeal; and *Buchanan v. Babco* [1978] A.C. 141 in the House of Lords. See also *Duke v. GEC Reliance Ltd* [1988] A.C. 618, *per* Lord Templeman at 638; and *Litster v. Forth Dry Dock Ltd*, 1989 S.C. (H.L.) 96.

[34] See, for example, Case C–260/89 *Elliniki Radiophonia Tileorassi AE v. Dimotiki Etairia Pliroforissis Sotirios Kouvelas* [1991] E.C.R. I-2925, hereafter *ERT* (concerning Art. 10 of the European Convention on Human Rights as a general principle of E.C. law).

[35] See, for example, Case 4/73 *Nold v. Commission* [1974] E.C.R. 491. For discussion of the development and content of the general principles of law in E.C. law, see Trindimans, *General Principles of Law* (Hart, Oxford, 1999); and Usher, *General Principles of Law* (Longman, Harrow, 1998). See also Usher's early article on one of the ECJ's leading cases articulating a general principle of law (the right to a fair hearing: Case 17/74 *Transocean Marine Paint Association v. Commission* [1974] E.C.R. 1063), "The Influence of National Concepts on Decisions of the European Court" (1976) 3 Eur. LR. 359. For more discussion, see de Smith, Woolf and Jowell, *Judicial Review of Administrative Action* (5th ed., 1995), Chap. 21.

[36] Such as respect for equality and the principle of effective remedies: see further paras 5.41 to 5.45 below.

[37] For example, the principle of proportionality became part of E.C. law by virtue of its prominence in continental systems of administrative law, particularly the German system, but at a time when it was not as such recognised as a principle of Scots and English law. It may be asked whether a general principle of E.C. law can be established where it enjoys no recognition in any of the member states' legal systems. For example, could a provision in an international treaty become part of E.C. law as a general principle of law where none of the E.U. states has ratified it?

[38] *supra*, n. 34.

[39] *ibid*. at para. 42.

[40] See *ERT, supra*; and *cf.* Cases 60 and 61/84 *Cinéthèque v. Federation Nationale des Cinemas Français* [1985] E.C.R. 2605.

not themselves provide grounds for challenging national measures which are clearly outside the scope of E.C. law.[41] The scope and content of the general principles of E.C. law are discussed further below.[42]

European Union measures

5.22   The TEU now provides for legislative acts to be passed under the two intergovernmental agreements which make up the European Union's second and third pillars. Under the second pillar, Articles 13–15 TEU provide for "common strategies", "joint actions" and "common positions" through which the Council of Ministers can implement the European Union's common foreign and security policy. Article 24 TEU provides for the Council to conclude "agreements" with third states and international organisations in pursuance of the European Union's responsibilities under both the second and third pillars. Under the third pillar, Article 34 TEU provides for the Council to adopt "common positions", "framework decisions", "decisions" and "conventions" to implement the European Union's policies in the area of Police and Judicial Co-operation in Criminal Matters. The effects these E.U. measures are intended to have in the national legal systems is uncertain. Article 34(2)(b) and (c) expressly provide that both "framework decisions" and "decisions" passed under the third pillar are "binding" but "shall not entail direct effect".[43] What this means for the other E.U. measures is not clear: are they not binding; if they are, can they produce direct effect? Indeed, just as E.C. directives are not directly applicable but in terms of the ECJ's jurisprudence can possess direct effect, it may be that in so far as it has jurisdiction under the second and third pillars the ECJ will seek to give E.U. measures some effects in national law.

IV   DIRECT APPLICABILITY AND DIRECT EFFECT OF E.C. LAW

Constitutional Fundamentals of the European Community

5.23   By way of introduction to this and the following two parts of the chapter, it may be noted that the ECJ has said that the E.C. Treaty "constitutes the constitutional charter of a Community based on the rule of law".[44] As such, the E.C. Treaty expresses and implies constitutional principles which are binding on both the European Union's institutions and the member states.[45] Both the Treaty on European Union (TEU) and the

---

[41] See *R. v. Ministry of Agriculture, Fisheries and Food, ex p. First City Trading Ltd* [1997] 1 C.M.L.R. 250.

[42] See paras 5.39–5.45.

[43] In particular, framework decisions are "binding upon the member states as to the result to be achieved but . . . leave to the national authorities the choice of form and methods", therefore making their binding effect on member states identical to E.C. directives in terms of Art. 249 E.C.

[44] See Opinion 1/91 [1991] E.C.R. 6079, para. 21.

[45] But, it may be asked, what if two parts of the E.C. Treaty appear to be inconsistent? The fact that the member states continue to amend and build on the original Treaty of Rome increases the scope for conflict between E.C. Treaty provisions. For example, the U.K.'s 1993–99 opt out from the Protocol on Social Policy could have been argued to put U.K. businesses (or workers) at an advantage (or disadvantage) *vis-à-vis* businesses (or workers) in other member states, thereby challenging the level playing field essential to the

E.C. Treaty expressly endow the European Union and the European Community with fundamental constitutional principles. The TEU provides that the European Union is to be based on respect for the rule of law, respect for the principle of subsidiarity and respect for the protection of human rights.[46] These principles are elaborated in more detail in the E.C. Treaty. For example, Article 5 E.C. provides for the principle of subsidiarity in the European Community while Article 12 provides for the fundamental principle of non-discrimination on the ground of nationality. The E.C. Treaty expresses further constitutional principles, such as the requirement in Article 7 that the institutions "shall act within the limits of the powers conferred" by the Treaty and the requirement in Article 253 (formerly 190) E.C. that E.C. legislation "state the reasons" on which it is based.[47]

But not all of the European Community's constitutional principles are expressed in the constituting treaties. As in other systems, the constitution's fundamental principles are identified and supplemented in decisions of the ECJ. It has already been noted that Article 220 E.C. provides for the power of the ECJ to exercise judicial review in the European Community to ensure that "in the interpretation and application of this Treaty the law is observed". This confirms the central role of judicial review and judicial remedies in the European Community, a point which has led the court more generally to emphasise the need for both E.C. law and national law to ensure effective legal remedies through which E.C. law can be observed.[48] Equally, in the exercise of its powers the ECJ has found several constitutional principles to be necessarily implied by the E.C. Treaty. The two pre-eminent constitutional principles which the ECJ has found are the principle of supremacy of E.C. law over all inconsistent national laws and the principle of direct effect by which E.C. law can create rights for individuals which they can directly enforce in national courts. The supremacy and direct effect of E.C. law have led the ECJ to establish and protect further constitutional principles, including, for example: a doctrine of pre-emption, under which valid E.C. legislation will displace (and prevent) inconsistent national law in areas in which legislative competence is shared concur-

---

common market established by the E.C. Treaty. At one level, of course, the function of constitutional interpretation is to resolve potential inconsistencies between two normatively equal provisions in the constitutional text. But the results are often difficult: consider the Supreme Court of Canada's decision in *Re Bill 30 (Ontario Separate School Funding Reference)* [1987] 1 S.C.R. 1148 (no conflict between some denominational school rights in Constitution Act, 1867 and general equality rights in s. 15 of the Charter of Rights and Freedoms guaranteed in the Constitution Act, 1982). The "variable geometry" now allowed between the European Union's member states under Arts 43–45 TEU and Art. 11 E.C. may present similar difficulties for the ECJ.

[46] See Arts 2 and 6 TEU. The implications of the principle of subsidiarity as provided for in Art. 5 (formerly 3b) of the E.C. Treaty have been the subject of extensive discussion: see, for example, Toth, "A Legal Analysis of Subsidiarity" in O'Keefe and Twomey (eds), *Legal Issues of the Maastricht Treaty* (Chancery, 1994) Chap. 3; and Emiliou, "Subsidiarity: Panacea or Fig Leaf?" (1992) 17 Eur.L.R. 383. For discussion of subsidiarity as a condition for the validity of E.C. law, see Craig and de Burca, *EU Law* (2nd ed., 1998), at pp. 124–129.

[47] The Court has interpreted this requirement strictly: see, for example, Case C–300/89 *Commission v. Council* [1991] E.C.R. I-2867; and Case C–187/93 *European Parliament v. Council* [1994] E.C.R. I-2857. See further Edward & Lane, *European Community Law* (2nd ed., 1995) at para. 144.

[48] See Case 222/84 *Johnston v. Chief Constable of the RUC* [1986] E.C.R. 1651.

rently by the E.C. and national legislatures[49]; principles associated with effective remedies to enable individuals to have the full benefit of rights conferred by E.C. law, including in appropriate cases and for sufficiently serious breaches of E.C. law a right to damages against the member states; and certain minimum guarantees of human rights which both European Community and related national measures must respect. Most of these rules and principles have been developed by the ECJ in response to the need to furnish the European Community with an effective legal order. In light of their importance for judicial review, some of these E.C. constitutional principles must now be examined.

The Concepts of Direct Applicability and Direct Effect

5.24 The distinct concepts of direct applicability and direct effect are central to the operation of E.C. law in the national legal order.[50] The term "directly applicable" is used in Article 249 of the E.C. Treaty to describe the relationship between E.C. regulations and national law but the term "direct effect" is not expressed in the E.C. Treaty.[51] It was created by the ECJ to describe the capacity of all types of E.C. law to create rights in favour of individuals which they can enforce directly before national courts over and above national law.[52] In light of their different implications and the fact that direct effect is a judicial creation, it is interesting that the ECJ has never distinguished the concepts and often uses them interchangeably. The concepts only came to be distinguished in the academic literature but even there are not always used consistently.[53] It is clear, however, that the concepts must be distinguished because they serve different purposes. Direct applicability is an institutional concept while direct effect is a remedial one. Direct applicability refers to the means by which some E.C. legislation comes to be operative in the national legal systems. Direct effect refers to the extent to which E.C. law, irrespective of its direct applicability, is directly enforceable before national courts. In other words, direct effect concerns the extent to which E.C. law is capable of producing rights—and sometimes also duties—which individuals can enforce directly before courts in the member states.

---

[49] See, for example, Case 111/75 *Officier van Justitie v. van den Hazel* [1977] E.C.R. 901; Case 83/78 *Pigs Marketing Board v. Redmond* [1978] E.C.R. 2347, esp. at para. 56; and Case 278/85 *Commission v. Denmark* [1987] E.C.R. 4069.

[50] The literature on the two concepts is enormous. For some of the leading articles see, for example, Winter, "Direct Applicability and Direct Effects" (1972) 9 C.M.L.R. 425; Steiner, "Direct Applicability in EEC Law—A Chameleon Concept" (1982) 98 L.Q.R. 229; Pescatore, "The Doctrine of 'Direct Effect': An Infant Disease of Community Law" (1983) 8 Eur.L.R. 155; and Craig, "Once Upon a Time in the West: Direct Effect and the Federalization of EEC Law" (1992) 12 O.J.L.S. 453.

[51] However, as noted above, it is now used in Art. 34 of the TEU: neither "framework decisions" nor "decisions" passed pursuant to the E.U.'s third pillar are to have direct effect although they are to be binding on the member states.

[52] The concept of direct effect was established by the ECJ in the landmark case of Case 26/62 *Van Gend en Loos v. Nederlandse Administratie der Belastingen* [1963] E.C.R. 1 (E.C. Treaty articles may have direct effect). In turn, the ECJ has found other E.C. measures to be capable of having direct effect: see Case 39/72 *Commission v. Italy* [1973] E.C.R. 101 (regulations); Case 9/70 *Franz Grad v. Finanzamt Traunstein* [1970] E.C.R. 825 (decisions); Case 104/81 *Hauptzollamt Mainz v. Kupferberg* [1982] E.C.R. 3641 (international agreements); and Case 148/78 *Pubblico Ministero v. Tullio Ratti* [1979] E.C.R. 1629 (directives).

[53] It was Winter who first sought to distinguish the concepts in his 1972 article, *supra*; but *cf.* Steiner (1982) 98 L.Q.R. 229, *supra*; and see also Collins, *European Community Law in the UK* (4th ed., Butterworths, London, 1990), Chap. 2.

Direct applicability

In terms of Article 249 E.C. only E.C. regulations, as distinct from **5.25** directives, are capable of being directly applicable. As already noted,[54] the main point about a regulation being directly applicable is that on its enactment as part of E.C. law, it is binding generally and normally operates directly in national law without the need for any national implementing measure. But if it follows that only regulations are directly applicable, it does not follow that regulations are always capable of producing direct effect. The two are not coterminous. As Advocate-General Warner lucidly explained: "Unquestionably every provision of every regulation is directly applicable, but not every provision of every regulation has direct effect, in the sense of conferring on private persons rights enforceable by them in national courts".[55]

Direct effect

Notwithstanding their lack of direct applicability in terms of Article 249 **5.26** E.C., the ECJ has found provisions in the E.C. Treaty, provisions in treaties concluded by the European Community with third states and provisions in directives and decisions, in addition to those in directly applicable regulations, to be capable of producing direct effect. The capacity for an E.C. law to have direct effect depends neither on its direct applicability nor on its form or character but on its substance satisfying the conditions for direct effect which the ECJ has identified. In countless decisions, the ECJ has formulated the criteria for the direct effect of a provision in E.C. law.[56] The essential requirement is that the provision must be such as to confer rights in favour of individuals. In addition, it must be sufficently clear and precise, it must be unconditional, and (*pace* directives) it must be complete in the sense that no element of discretion is left either to the E.C. institutions or to the member states for its implementation into the national legal system.[57] How these criteria apply to particular provisions is not always obvious.[58] And so, not least because E.C. law must have the same meaning and effect throughout the European Union, it is for the ECJ to decide whether a provision in an E.C. law fulfils the criteria for direct effect.[59] Where a national court is unsure if a provision has direct effect, this will be one consideration in the decision to make a reference to the ECJ for a preliminary ruling under Article 234 E.C.[60]

---

[54] See para. 5.17 above.

[55] Case 131/79 *R. v. Secretary of State for Home Affairs, ex p. Santillo* [1980] E.C.R. 1585 at 1608.

[56] See, for example, Case 26/62 *Van Gend en Loos* [1963] E.C.R. 1 at 13; and Case 152/84 *Marshall v. Southampton & South-West Hampshire Area Health Authority* [1986] E.C.R. 723.

[57] On the direct effect of directives, see paras 5.28 *et seq.* below.

[58] *cf. Griffin v. South West Water Services Ltd* [1995] I.R.L.R. 15, *per* Blackburne J. at 30.

[59] Which decision will thenceforth be binding on all national courts. Furthermore, a provision is normally deemed to have direct effect from the moment it became enforceable and not just from the date of the ECJ's judgment clarifying its direct effect. Exceptionally, however, the ECJ may limit the temporal (that is, retrospective) effects of a judgment which decides that a provision of E.C. law has direct effect. Since this matter is bound up with the relationship between E.C. law and national law, it is discussed below in the context of the supremacy of E.C. law: see para. 5.38.

[60] *cf. R. v. International Stock Exchange, ex p. Else* [1993] Q.B. 534, esp. *per* Bingham M.R. at 545.

Effects of E.C. Law Beyond Direct Applicability and Direct Effect

5.27 Although the concepts of direct applicability and direct effect are fundamental in E.C. law, it should not be concluded that all E.C. law falls neatly into one or other of the two categories. As the E.C. legal system develops and becomes more sophisticated, it is clear that the two concepts are no longer sufficient to capture the full implications which E.C. law has for national law.[61] For example, in a recent decision the ECJ held that whether or not an E.C. law provision is capable of conferring rights on individuals is distinct from the question whether it is sufficiently clear and precise so as to be enforceable before national courts.[62] This distinction emerges most clearly in relation to directives. Although directives are not directly applicable, the ECJ has held that some of their provisions are capable of producing direct effect. While directives do not through their own force operate in national law and depend on the national authorities to implement them before they can be fully effective in the national legal system,[63] where they are not implemented timeously or only inadequately implemented, the ECJ has found that they can still have direct effect.[64]

But the extent to which directives have direct effect is more limited than the extent to which other E.C. laws do so. Where they fulfil the criteria for direct effect, directives may only be relied on directly before national courts in cases against the state and its emanations.[65] That is, they have only vertical direct effect and not full or horizontal direct effect such that they could also be relied on directly in cases against private persons. But by virtue of Article 10 of the E.C. Treaty, in all cases which come before them national courts must interpret and apply national law so far as possible in light of all E.C. law irrespective of its direct applicability or direct effect.[66]

Since all E.C. law includes directives, the relevance of directives for national law is therefore greater than their capacity for direct effect suggests.[67] In turn, this poses an intersting question about the effect of

---

[61] In particular, the concepts are amenable only to describe the E.C.'s written law (that is principally, the Treaty and legislation) and not, for example, the effects of the E.C.'s general principles of law. As is discussed at paras 5–39 *et seq.* below, the general principles of law are relevant for national courts as grounds on which challenges can be made to E.C. measures and also national measures which fall within the scope of E.C. law.

[62] Case C–431/92 *Commission v. Germany* [1995] E.C.R. I-2189 (the point being that even if the E.C. law does not have direct effect so as to enable an individual to enforce it, the national court itself may be bound to "enforce" it against incompatible national law (by refusing to apply the latter). *Cf.* Case C–194/94 *CIA Security International SA v. Signalson SA and Securitel SPRL* [1996] E.C.R. I-2201, discussed further at para. 5.30 below.

[63] And once implemented, it is the national implementing measure which is relied on in national law. Even so, while the directive most clearly remains relevant where there is some inadequacy in its implementation, it is also relevant in interpreting the national implementing measure, *cf.* Bates, "The Impact of Directives on Statutory Interpretation: Using the Euro-Meaning (1986) Stat.L.R. 174.

[64] See para. 5.29 below.

[65] Case 152/84 *Marshall v. Southampton & South-West Hampshire Area Health Authority* (*Marshall I*) [1986] E.C.R. 723.

[66] Note that this obligation applies to all E.C. law: see, for example, Case C–165/91 *Van Munster v. Rijksdienst voor Pensioenen* [1994] E.C.R. I-4661.

[67] See further para. 5.30 below. See also Case C–126/96 *Inter-Environnement Wallonie ASBL v. Region Wallonne* [1998] All E.R. (E.C.) 155 (member states are obliged not to adopt national measures inconsistent with the result to be achieved by a directive even before the time by which the directive is to be implemented). *Cf. R. v. Secretary of State for Health, ex p. Imperial Tobacco Ltd* [1999] C.O.D. 138.

Article 10 of the E.C. Treaty. Although it has been held not to have direct effect[67a], and although the E.C. Treaty is not as such directly applicable, Article 10 still has significant effects for national law. In particular, it creates important obligations for national courts.[68] In a sense, therefore, it may be said that once the E.C. Treaty has been ratified and implemented into national law, all of its provisions are "applicable" as part of national law, that is, binding on national authorities including courts, even if it is not correct to describe the E.C. Treaty as "directly applicable".[69] In any event, E.C. law seems to be breaking out of the categories of direct applicability and direct effect: directives confirm that there is a world of direct effect beyond direct applicability and both Article 10 of the E.C. Treaty and directives show that there is a nebula between no direct effect and no effect at all.[70] Whether or not the concepts of "direct applicability" and "direct effect" might eventually be seen as sub-categories of a broader concept of "applicable E.C. law", the dimensions of E.C. law are now such that this all-inclusive broader term may be preferred.

Direct Effect of Directives

Although a full discussion of the complex issues surrounding the direct **5.28** effect of directives is not required here,[71] the fact that a national court may be called on to rule on the consistency between national law and rules of E.C. law contained in directives makes necessary a brief mention

---

[67a] See *Hurd v. Jones*, Case 44/86 [1986] E.C.R. 29.

[68] Article 10 expressly provides that national authorities—including for matters within their jurisdiction the courts—must further the aims of and do nothing to hinder E.C. law. In addition to requiring national courts to interpret national law consistently with all E.C. law, including provisions in directives, Article 10 has been referred to by the ECJ as one basis of its effective remedies case law, in particular, the *Francovich* damages remedy against member states for losses which their violations of E.C. law cause to others.

[69] Once it is properly implemented into national law, the E.C. Treaty is supreme over all inconsistent national law irrespective of the extent to which it is directly effective. Importantly, the E.C. Treaty provides rules of law which national courts must apply when deciding relevant cases. One such rule is the primacy of all E.C. law, which means that a national court faced with an incompatibility between national law and E.C. law, whatever its form, must prefer E.C. law. This applies to all cases including, in respect of directives, cases which are not against the state or its emanations. It may be that by looking at the effect of the E.C. Treaty in national law in this way, a solution may be found to some of the vexed questions surrounding the "horizontal" direct effect of directives said to arise from recent ECJ decisions such as Case C–194/94 *CIA Security International SA v. Signalson SA and Securitel SPRL* [1996] E.C.R. I-2201 and Case C–441/93 *Panagis Pafitis v. Trapeza Kentrikis Ellados AE* [1996] E.C.R. I-1347. In other words, the decisions in these cases follow from the supremacy of E.C. law—more particularly, the relationship between the E.C. Treaty and national law—rather than from the directives as such. See further para. 5.30 below.

[70] *cf.* Craig and de Burca, *EU Law* (2nd ed., OUP, Oxford, 1998), at pp. 174–175, who refer to a category of "direct enforceability" in addition (or in contrast) to direct effect. See also van Gerven, "The Horizontal Direct Effect of Directive Provisions Revisted: the Reality of Catchwords" in Heukels & Curtin (eds), *Institutional Dynamics of European Integration, Liber Amicorum for Henry Schermers* (Dordrecht, Boston, 1994).

[71] For analysis see, for example, Prechal, *Directives in EC Law* (OUP, Oxford, 1995); *Halsbury's Laws of England*, Vol. 51, paras 3.63 *et seq.*; Craig and De Burca, *EU Law* (2nd ed., OUP, Oxford, 1998), Chap. 4, esp. pp. 185 *et seq.*; and Edward & Lane, *European Community Law* (2nd ed., Butterworths, London, 1995), para. 148. For commentary, see also De Burca, "Giving Effect to EC Directives" (1992) 55 M.L.R. 215; Eleftheriadis, "The Direct Effect of Community Law: Conceptual Issues" (1996) 16 *Yearbook of Eur. Law* 205; and Craig, "Directives: Direct Effect, Indirect Effect and the Construction of National Legislation" (1997) 22 Eur.L.R. 519.

of the issues concerning the direct effect of directives. Basically, these may be separated under three headings: first, the extent to which directives have direct effect—in other words, the implications of the distinction between "vertical" and "horizontal" direct effect; secondly, the obligations which the E.C. Treaty imposes on national courts to give effect to directives in all cases which arise before them; and thirdly, the remedy in damages provided by E.C. law against the state for losses arising from the non-implementation or inadequate implementation of directives.

Directives have only "vertical" direct effect

5.29   As noted above, the ECJ has decided, albeit with increasing refinement, that directives only have "vertical" direct effect. In essence, this means that where provisions in directives are found to fulfil the criteria for direct effect and the time limit by which they should have been properly implemented has passed, they can only be relied on against the "state and its emanations". Directly effective provisions in directives cannot be relied on directly by one private person against another private person. This absence of horizontal direct effect for directives has been explained on various grounds. The principal ground is that allowing directives to be enforced against the state addresses the central problem of non-implementation or inadequate implementation of directives by member states. By carving out some scope for directives to have direct effect in national legal systems notwithstanding their lack of direct applicability, the ECJ has ensured that member states cannot escape their obligations under E.C. law. Having indicated throughout the 1970s that directives could have direct effect against the state,[72] the ECJ confirmed in *Marshall v. Southampton & South West Hampshire Area Health Authority*[73] that directives are capable of having direct effect after the date by which they should have been implemented,[74] subject to the usual conditions for direct effect,[75] but only as against the state and emanations of the state. In short, the direct effect of directives may be seen as a form of personal bar against a member state which has not (or not properly) implemented a directive. The state and its emanations are barred from relying on the state's own failure to implement a directive to defeat rights conferred on individuals by the directive.

   Yet the limitation on the direct effect of directives to "vertical" direct effect begets difficulties. The leading problem is defining the state and its emanations. Beyond the obvious government institutions, this is never an easy task, one made harder in the United Kingdom by the traditional absence either of a concept of "the state" or of the continental schema

---

[72] See, for example, Case 148/78 *Pubblico Ministero v. Ratti* [1979] E.C.R. 1629 at paras 22 and 23.

[73] *Marshall I*, Case 152/84 [1986] E.C.R. 723.

[74] But see Case C–126/96 *Inter-Environnement Wallonie ASBL v. Region Wallonne* [1998] All E.R. (E.C.) 155 (member states are obliged not to adopt national measures inconsistent with a directive even before the time by which the directive is to be implemented). For discussion see Kaczorowska, "New 'Right' Available to Individuals under Community Law" (1999) 5 E.P.L. 79.

[75] Except that, the condition for direct effect concerning the absence of member state discretion in the implementation of provisions does not apply to the same extent in the context of direct effect of directives; but the amount of discretion left by a directive to the member states may affect the extent to which directive provisions are capable of being "sufficiently clear and precise".

of "bodies governed by public law", on which E.C. law frequently draws. Not surprisingly, decisions of both the ECJ and national courts attempting to define "emanations of the state" have received a mixed reception. The leading ECJ decision is *Foster v. British Gas*,[76] where the Court ruled that British Gas, when still a nationalised industry, was an emanation of the state. As to the criteria by reference to which an "emanation of the state" was to be understood, the ECJ explained:

> "A body, whatever its legal form, which has been made responsible, pursuant to a measure adopted by the State, for providing a public service under control of the State and has for that purpose special powers beyond those which resulted from the normal rules applicable in relations between individuals is included among the bodies against which the provisions of a Directive capable of having direct effect may be relied upon".[77]

In *National Union of Teachers v. Governing Body of St Mary's Church of England (Aided) Junior School*,[78] the English Court of Appeal held that the (financial) relationship between a local authority and the governing body of a voluntary aided school was sufficient to make the latter an emanation of the state for the purposes of the direct effect of directives. Summing up the ECJ's approach to the matter, Schiemann L.J. said:

> "What emerges from the case law is a number of indicia which point to the appropriateness of treating the body in question as an emanation of the State, none of which indicia is conclusive . . . the Community case law indicates that a body may be an emanation of the State although it is not under the control of central government".[79]

But even if "emanation of the state" can be defined broadly,[80] the fact that directives cannot be relied on before national courts in actions between individuals may be criticised as a source of inequality and injustice.[81] Indeed, the lack of horizontal direct effect for directives has been criticised even within the ECJ[82]: in several opinions, the Court's own Advocates General have called for directives to be given horizontal direct effect.[82]

---

[76] Case C–188/89 [1990] E.C.R. I-3133.

[77] Case C–188/89 *Foster v. British Gas* [1990] E.C.R. I-3133 at para. 20 of the Court's Judgment. For discussion see Szyszczak (1990) 27 C.M.L.R. 859 *cf.* Sheimann L.J. in *St Mary's School* below.

[78] [1997] I.R.L.R. 242.

[79] *ibid.* at 247–248. See Spink "Direct effect: the boundaries of the state" (1997) 113 L.Q.R. 524; and Kvjatkovski, "What is an 'Emanation of the State'? An Educated Guess" (1997) 3 E.P.L. 329.

[80] See Case 222/84 *Johnston v. Chief Constable of the RUC* [1986] E.C.R. 1651 (the chief constable of a police force is an emanation of the state); and Case 103/88 *Costanzo SpA v. Milano*, [1989] E.C.R. 1839 (municipalities and decentralised government authorities are emanations of the state). *Cf. Doughty v. Rolls Royce plc* [1992] I.R.L.R. 126.

[81] See Curtin, "The Province of Government: Delimiting the Direct Effect of Directives in the Common Law Context" (1990) 15 Eur.L.R. 195; and Coppel, "Rights, Duties and the end of *Marshall*" (1994) 57 M.L.R. 859. See also Chalmers, "Judicial Preferences and the Community Legal Order" (1997) 60 M.L.R. 164.

[82] See, for example, Case C–91/92 *Faccini Dori v. Recreb Srl* [1994] E.C.R. I-3325.

Directives as a source of E.C. law beyond direct effect

5.30 Whether or not criticism of the limitation to vertical direct effect or the definitional problems inherent in defining the state and its emanations have influenced the ECJ, the Court has increasingly adapted its jurisprudence on the need for full effectiveness of E.C. law to the task of giving directives further effects in national law. In its landmark decision in 1984 in *Von Colson v. Land Nordrhein-Westfalen*,[83] the ECJ stressed the role which national courts have under the E.C. Treaty to ensure that national law complies with directives in all cases which come before them:

> "According to the third paragraph of Article 189 [now 249 E.C.]: 'a directive shall be binding as to the result to be achieved, upon each member state to which it is addressed, but shall leave to the national authorities the choice of form and methods'. Although that provision leaves member States to choose the ways and means of ensuring that the directive is implemented, that freedom does not affect the obligation imposed on all the member States to which the directive is addressed, to adopt, in their national legal systems, all measures necessary to ensure that the directive is fully effective, in accordance with the objective which it pursues . . .
>
> [T]he member States' obligation arising from a directive to achieve the result envisaged by the directive and their duty under Article 5 [now 10] of the Treaty to take all appropriate measures, whether general or particular, to ensure the fulfilment of that obligation, is binding on all the authorities of member States including, for matters within their jurisdiction, the courts. It follows that, in applying the national law and in particular the provisions of a national law specifically introduced in order to implement [a] directive . . . national courts are required to interpret their national law in the light of the wording and the purpose of the directive in order to achieve the result referred to in the third paragraph of Article 189."[84]

In *Marleasing*,[85] the ECJ reinforced this interpretive obligation on national courts as it arises in respect of directives from Articles 10 and 249 of the E.C. Treaty. The Court ruled: "It follows that, in applying national law, whether the provisions in question were adopted before or after the directive, the national court called upon to interpret it is required to do so, as far as possible, in the light of the wording and the purpose of the directive in order to achieve the result pursued by the latter."[86] In the context or unimplemented or improperly implemented directives, the general obligation incumbent on national courts and tribunals to interpret all national law "so far as possible" to comply with

---

[83] Case 14/83 [1984] E.C.R. 1891. *cf.* Case 80/86 *Kolpinghuis Nijmegen BV* [1987] E.C.R. 3969.

[84] *ibid.* paras 23 and 26. For application of this decision in the U.K., see *Litster v. Forth Dry Dock Co. Ltd*, 1989 S.C. (H.L.) 96, *per* Lord Templeman at 104; and *English v. North Lanarkshire Council*, 1999 S.C.L.R. 310.

[85] Case C–106/89 *Marleasing SA v. La Comercial Internacional de Alimentación SA* [1990] E.C.R. I-4156.

[86] *ibid.* at para. 8. See also Case C–334/92 *Wagner Miret v. Fondo de Garantia Salarial* [1993] E.C.R. I-6911. For discussion, see De Burca, "Giving Effect to EC Directives" (1992) 55 M.L.R. 215; and Maltby, "Marleasing: What is all the Fuss About?" (1993) 109 L.Q.R. 301.

all E.C. law may be termed "indirect" effect. Notably, however, all of the implications for national law of the interpretive obligation in relation to directives have not yet emerged. The contours of the obligation are still evolving. Meanwhile, the Court has so far held to its basic position that directives do not have "horizontal" direct effect so as to enable individuals to rely on their provisions directly against other private individuals.[87] But this is the essence of the limitation on direct effect of directives:—their provisions cannot be relied on directly against other private individuals. It does not follow from this formulation that directives can never be relied on against national law in cases involving private parties.[88] So where one private party is involved in an action against another private party and the issue comes down to an inconsistency between national legislation and a directive with direct effect, the supremacy of E.C. law means that the national court's obligation under Article 10 E.C. requires the inconsistent national rule to be either "interpreted" or, if necessary, set aside for the purposes of deciding the case.[89] On this basis, some ECJ decisions which have been argued to show creeping horizontal direct effect for directives may instead only be further evidence of the supremacy of E.C. law over all inconsistent national law. For example, in *CIA*,[90] the ECJ allowed a directive to be relied on before a national court in a case between two private parties. The issue was essentially whether the law which applied to the case was an E.C. directive with direct effect or a national law inconsistent with the directive.[91] The ECJ held that the pursuer could rely on the directive as against the inconsistent rule of national law. Accordingly, although it was a case between two private parties, the defender was restrained by virtue of the effect of the directive. Is this to be treated as an example of horizontal direct effect? On closer analysis, the directive was being relied

---

[87] See *Faccini Dori v. Recreb Srl*, Case C–192/94 *El Corte Ingles v. Cristina Blazques Rivero* [1996] E.C.R. I-1281; Case C–168/95 *Luciano Arcaro* [1996] E.C.R. I-4705. But see below.

[88] cf. Case C–194/94 *CIA Security International SA v. Signalson SA and Securitel SPRL* [1996] E.C.R. I-2201; Case C–168/95 *Luciana Arcaro* [1996] E.C.R. I-4705; Case C–129/94 *Rafael Ruiz Bernaldez* [1996] E.C.R. I-1829; and Case C–441/93 *Panagis Pafitis v. Trapeza Kentrikis Ellados AE* [1996] E.C.R. I-1347. For discussion, see Craig, "Directives: Direct Effect, Indirect Effect and the Construction of National Legislation" (1997) 22 Eur.L.R. 519; Coppel, "Horizontal Direct Effect of Directives" (1997) 28 I.L.J. 69; Chalmers, *supra*; and Lackoff & Nyssens, "Direct Effect of Directives in Triangular Situations" (1998) 23 Eur.L.R. 397.

[89] In the United Kingdom, the obligation on the courts to "construe national legislation so far as possible to be consistent with applicable E.C. law, including directives, follows from s. 2(4) of the European Communities Act 1972. This obligation has allowed the courts to "interpret" national legislation so as to be compatible with directives: see *Litster v. Forth Dry Dock Ltd*, 1989 S.C. (H.L.) 96 and *Webb v EMO Cargo Ltd* [1993] 1 W.L.R. 49; but cf. *Duke v. GEC Reliance* [1988] A.C. 618. It may be, however, that the obligation in E.C. law is stronger: that is to say that, in all cases which come before them, national courts must set aside national legislation which cannot be reconciled with directives. See further below.

[90] Case C–194/94 *CIA Security International SA v. Signalson SA and Securitel SPRL* [1996] E.C.R. I-2201.

[91] The effect of the ECJ's decision in CIA came up for discussion in *R. v. Secretary of State for Employment, ex p. Seymour Smith* [1997] 1 W.L.R. 473. But the real difficulty there was procedural: the employee could not first proceed against the Secretary of State in judicial review to have national legislation declared inapplicable for inconsistency with a directly effective directive so as to be able thereafter to sue her private employer. Rather, she should proceed directly against the employer, for example, in the employment tribunal, and there make the claim that national legislation should be set aside in favour of the directly effective directive.

on not as such against the defender but instead against the national law which was inconsistent with the directive. Similarly, in *Nils Drae-hmpaehl*,[92] once again proceedings between two private parties, the remedial provisions in the Equal Treatment Directive were not being relied on directly against a private party but rather directly against rules of national law which were argued to be inconsistent with the directive's requirements. The state was an omnipresent third party in the litigation by virtue of its legislation.[93] The task for the court was one of classical constitutional review, namely to say what the law is. Is it to be national law or E.C. law? The supremacy of E.C. law demands that it is E.C. law.

It follows that the limitation to vertical direct effect for directives means only that their provisions cannot be relied on directly against private parties so as, for example, to create obligations and burdens directly against them. But where the issue is inconsistency between directives with direct effect and national law, the directive may be relied on against the national rules even if the effect of setting aside national rules is to create obligations for private parties. In such a case, however, it is not actually the directive which is creating those obligations. Rather, it is the E.C. Treaty and its requirement for the supremacy of E.C. law. That directives with direct effect require inconsistent national law to yield was made clear by the ECJ early on. In *Ratti*,[94] the Court held that it follows from the direct effect of a directive that: "a national court requested by a person who has complied with the provisions of a directive not to apply a national provision incompatible with the directive . . . must uphold that request."[95] The contribution of the recent case law, such as *CIA*, may be only to highlight that this applies in every case before a national court, including cases between two private parties where the real problem is inconsistency between national law and directives with direct effect. In practical terms, therefore, a national lawyer advising on what "the law" is must always take account of what E.C. law provides, since inconsistency between E.C. law and national law requires to be resolved in favour of E.C. law. This is true also where the inconsistency is between national law and directly effective directives in cases between two private parties. More generally, the fact that directives can have direct effect at all is a manifestation of the ECJ's concern to ensure that rights conferred by E.C. law are fully effective. Accordingly, the direct and indirect ways in which E.C. directives can now be relied on before national courts is evidence of a more general principle of E.C. law to the effect that its full effectiveness must be ensured by national courts.

Directives and the damages remedy

5.31 The ECJ has established the E.C. law remedy of damages against the state for losses attributable to a state's failure to implement or properly implement E.C. directives.[96] In many ways, this remedy completes the

---

[92] Case C–180/95 *Nils Draehmpaehl v. Urania Immobilienservice ohG* [1997] E.C.R. I-2195, noted by Steindorff at (1997) 34 C.M.L.R. 1259; see also Ward, "New Frontiers in Private Enforcement of EC Directives" (1998) 23 Eur.L.R. 65.

[93] Or, alternatively, its failure to legislate properly to give effect to the directive: *cf.* Case C–215/97 *Coote v. Granada Hospitality Ltd* [1998] 3 C.M.L.R. 975. This case and *Nils Draehmpaehl* also highlight the application of the effective remedies principle which emerges from Art. 10 E.C.: on one view of these cases, it is this principle rather than the directive as such which is being relied on against a private party.

[94] Case 148/78 *Pubblico Ministero v. Tullio Ratti* [1979] E.C.R. 1629.

[95] *ibid.* at para. 23.

[96] Cases C–6 & 9/90 *Francovich & Bonifaci v. Italy* [1991] E.C.R. I-5357.

circle on the effects of directives for national law. If a directive is not properly implemented and does not have direct effect or, even if it does, cannot be relied on directly before national courts, then, assuming its provisions concern individual rights and the pursuer can show that the state's failure to effectuate those rights is "sufficiently serious" and has caused the losses, a remedy in damages against the state will lie. The remedy against the state for damages in this context is part of a wider E.C. law damages remedy for breaches of E.C. law attributable to the state.[97] As regards the condition that the remedy in damages will only be available for "sufficiently serious" breaches of E.C. law, the ECJ has said that the "decisive test" is whether the member state has "manifestly and gravely disregarded the limits on its discretion" under E.C. law.[98] It is clear that failure to implement a directive timeously is "sufficiently serious" for this purpose.[99] Equally, wilful or careless failure to give proper effect in national law to a directive also constitutes a sufficiently serious breach of E.C. law. There will, however, be cases in which a state has made a reasonable attempt at implementation of a directive which evidences good faith but is still deficient, for example, in light of a subsequent ECJ ruling on the meaning and effect of the directive. Accordingly, the ECJ has clarified that there will be situations in which the state's reasonable and good faith efforts at implementation of a directive, although incorrect, will not expose it to liability to pay damages.[1]

V THE SUPREMACY OF E.C. LAW

The supremacy of E.C. law over national law

It is a fundamental constitutional principle in the European Community 5.32 that E.C. law has supremacy or primacy over all inconsistent national law.[2] Although the E.C. Treaty does not say expressly that E.C. law is supreme,[3] the ECJ has affirmed on many occasions that this conclusion inevitably follows from the new "legal order" which the E.C. Treaty establishes.[4] While in *Van Gend en Loos*[5] the ECJ hinted at the

---

[97] See *Brasserie du Pecheur v. Germany* and *R. v. Secretary of State for Transport, ex p. Factortame Ltd (No. 3)*, Cases C–46 and 48/93 [1996] E.C.R. I-1029.

[98] *ibid.* at paras 51 and 55–57.

[99] See Cases C–178 and 179/94 *Dillenkofer v. Germany* [1996] E.C.R. I-4845.

[1] See Case C–392/93 *R. v. H.M. Treasury, ex p. British Telecommunications plc* [1996] E.C.R. I-1631; and Cases C–283, 291 and 292/94 *Denkavit International v. Bundesamt fur Finanzen* [1996] E.C.R. I-5063.

[2] It may be that some of the measures which may be passed under the second and third pillars of the TEU (particularly the latter) will also be endowed with supremacy over national law. In the United Kingdom, however, such measures will not be supreme over national law by virtue of the European Communities Act 1972, as amended. The definition of "Community Treaties" in s. 1(2) of the Act excludes the second and third pillars of the TEU. More generally, the ECJ's jurisdiction over the second and third pillars is more limited than under the E.C. Treaty, which clearly poses a problem for securing the supremacy of E.U. measures.

[3] Unlike, for example, other constitutional instruments, *cf.* Art. VI of the U.S. Constitution and s. 52 of the Canadian Constitution Act 1982.

[4] For recent affirmations, see Cases C–13 and C–113/91 *Debus* [1992] E.C.R. I-3617, at para. 32; and Case C–347/96 *Solred v. Administracion General del Estado* [1998] E.C.R. I-937 at para. 30.

[5] Case 26/62 [1963] E.C.R. 1. The supremacy conclusion also emerges in several of the ECJ's earlier decisions under the ECSC Treaty: see Judge Edward, "Judicial Activism – Myth or Reality" in Campbell and Voyatzi, *Legal Reasoning and Judicial Interpretation of European Law: Essays in honour of Lord Mackenzie Stuart* (Trenton Publishing, Hampshire, 1996), Chap. 3, at pp. 36–43.

supremacy of E.C. law, not only by observing that the member states had by entering the European Community limited "their sovereign rights" but also in declaring that E.C. law can create rights in favour of individuals which can be directly enforced over and above inconsistent national law, it was in *Costa v. ENEL*[6] that the ECJ clarified the constitutional relationship between E.C. law and the national laws of the member states:

> "The integration into the laws of each member state of provisions which derive from the Community, and more generally the terms and the spirit of the Treaty, make it impossible for the states, as a corollary, to accord precedence to a unilateral and subsequent measure over a legal system accepted by them on the basis of reciprocity. Such a measure cannnot therefore be inconsistent with that legal system. The executive force of Community law cannot vary from one state to another in deference to subsequent domestic laws . . . It follows . . . . that the law stemming from the Treaty, an independent source of law, could not, because of its special and original nature, be overridden by domestic legal provisions, however framed."[7]

Absent an express Treaty provision conferring supremacy on E.C. law, the ECJ relied on the purpose and "spirit" of the E.C. Treaty to establish its supremacy over national law. The requirement that E.C. law have a common meaning throughout the member states is emphasised by the Court to give E.C. law, by its "special and original nature", a constitutional force in the legal systems of the member states. Although the Court's judgment in *Costa* gives some opportunities to argue about the details of supremacy—for example, the Court only decided that E.C. law is supreme over a "unilateral and subsequent measure",—it was not practical for the Court to establish the supremacy of E.C. law over all inconsistent national law in one decision. The supremacy conclusion had to emerge gradually, not least because of the reluctance of the supreme courts in some member states, particularly Germany, to accept all of its consequences.[8] But from the standpoint of the ECJ, the logical con-

---

[6] Case 6/64 [1964] E.C.R. 585.

[7] *ibid.* at 593–594.

[8] The German, French and Italian constitutional courts refused to accept the primacy of E.C. law over some provisions of national law. In Germany, after the ECJ's decision in the *Internationale Handelsgesellschaft* case (Case 11/70 [1970] E.C.R. 1125; [1972] C.M.L.R. 255) returned to the German Constitutional Court, that court insisted that E.C. measures (or at least national measures implementing them) may still be reviewable against human rights as guaranteed by the German Basic Law: see [1974] 2 C.M.L.R. 540 (the decision being known as *Solange I*). That is, only so long as E.C. law was consistent with the German constitution would its supremacy in Germany be accepted. See also *Re Wunsche Handelsgesellschaft* [1987] 3 C.M.L.R. 225 (*Solange II*); and *Brunner v. The E.U. Treaty* [1994] 1 C.M.L.R. 57 (a potentially more far-reaching assertion of the German Constitutional Court's powers over the process of European integration). Consider also the German courts' resistance to the E.U.'s banana import arrangements on the ground that they violate GATT, now WTO, law: see Cases C–364 and 365/95 *T. Port GmbH v. Hauptzollamt Hamburg-Jonas* [1998] E.C.R. I-1023 (noted by Peers (1999) 24 Eur.L.R. 185); and Everling, "Will Europe Slip on Bananas? The Bananas Judgment of the Court of Justice and National Courts" (1996) 33 C.M.L.R. 401. As regards France, see *Syndicat Général de Fabricants de Semoules de France* [1970] C.M.L.R. 395; and *Raoul Georges Nicolo* [1990] 1 C.M.L.R. 173. And for Italy, see *Frontini v. Ministero delle Finanze* [1974] 2

sequences of the supremacy of E.C. law are clear and they were put beyond any shadow of doubt by the Court's judgment in *Simmenthal*.[9] The most important aspect of this case concerned a rule of Italian law to the effect that lower courts could not refuse to apply an unconstitutional law until the Constitutional Court had formally set aside the law. Did this rule also apply to laws which, following a reference from a lower Italian court to the ECJ, had been found to be inconsistent with E.C. law? Deciding that it could not, the ECJ clarified the relationship between E.C. law and national law in terms which deserve to be set out in full:

> "In accordance with the principle of the precedence of Community law, the relationship between provisions of the Treaty and directly applicable measures of the institutions on the one hand and the national law of the member states on the other is such that those provisions and measures not only by their entry into force render automatically inapplicable any conflicting provision of current national law but – in so far as they are an integral part of, and take precedence in, the legal order applicable in the territory of each of the member states – also preclude the valid adoption of new national legislative measures to the extent to which they would be incompatible with Community provisions.
>
> It follows . . . that every national court must, in a case within its jurisdiction, apply Community law in its entirety and protect rights which the latter confers on individuals and must accordingly set aside any provision of national law which may conflict with it, whether prior or subsequent to the Community rule.
>
> Accordingly, any provision of a national legal system and any legislative, administrative or judicial practice which might impair the effectiveness of Community law by withholding from the national court having jurisdiction to apply such law the power to do everything necessary at the moment of its application to set aside national legislative provisions which might prevent Community rules from having full force and effect are incompatible with those requirements which are the very essence of Community law . . .
>
> . . . [A] national court which is called upon, within the limits of its jurisdiction, to apply provisions of Community law is under a duty to give full effect to those provisions, if necessary refusing of its own motion to apply any conflicting provision of national legislation,

---

C.M.L.R. 372. For the relationship between U.K. and E.C. law, see further paras 5–49 *et seq.* below. For discussion of the supremacy of E.C. law from the standpoint of several member states, including the U.K., see Craig and de Burca, *EU Law* (OUP, Oxford, 1998), pp. 264–295. See also Weatherill and Beaumont, *EU Law* (2nd ed., Penguin, 1997), Chap. 5; and MacCormick, "The Maastricht-Urteil: Sovereignty Now" (1995) 1 Eur.L.J. 259. By way of comparison, it is interesting to note that although the U.S. Constitution expressly provides for its supremacy over state law, state resistance meant that it took time for the U.S. Supreme Court firmly to establish this conclusion in practice: see, for example, *Martin v. Hunter's Lessee* 14 U.S. (1 Wheat.) 304 (1816). Even in recent times, the Court has had to reaffirm the supremacy of its judgments over contrary state law and practice, *cf. Cooper v. Aaron*, 358 U.S. 1 (1958). For a discussion of the early U.S. experience and comparison with the German Constitutional Court's decision in Brunner, *supra*, see Boom, "The European Union After the Maastricht Decision: Will Germany be the 'Virginia of Europe?'" (1995) 43 Am. J. of Comp. Law 177.
[9] Case 106/77 *Amministrazione delle Finanze dello Stato v. Simmenthal SpA* [1978] E.C.R. 629.

even if adopted subsequently, and it is not necessary for the court to request or await the prior setting aside of such provision by legislative or other constitutional means".[10]

Accordingly, national rules which are in conflict with applicable E.C. law are "automatically inapplicable" and must be "set aside" by national courts. But, beyond the declaration that E.C. law is supreme over any inconsistent national law whatever its status and whenever adopted, the significance of *Simmenthal* lies in the emphasis the Court places on the duty of national courts to apply E.C. law "in its entirety" and to ensure the "full effect" of E.C. law. In other words, *Simmenthal* highlights the need to ensure full effectiveness of all E.C. law in the national legal system as a central feature of the supremacy of E.C. law. *Simmenthal* therefore provides the supremacy of E.C. law as the essential basis for both the direct and indirect effect of directives in national law.[11] More generally, the principle that national courts must ensure effective remedies for the protection of rights conferred by E.C. law is also rooted in the supremacy of E.C. law. Accordingly, when the ECJ was presented with rules of English law to the effect that the remedy of injunction is not available either against the Crown or to suspend the operation of an Act of Parliament, so that no interim injunction could issue against a minister ordering him not to apply provisions of an Act of Parliament challenged for inconsistency with the E.C. Treaty until the legal issues were resolved following a reference to the ECJ, the ECJ held that:

> "the full effectiveness of Community law would be just as much impaired if a rule of national law could prevent a court seised of a dispute governed by Community law from granting interim relief in order to ensure the full effectiveness of [an ECJ] judgment to be given on the existence of the rights claimed under Community law. It follows that a court which in those circumstances would grant interim relief, if it were not for a rule of national law, is obliged to set aside that rule."[12]

The implications of the supremacy of E.C. law

5.33 It emerges from the ECJ's decisions that membership of the European Community entails acceptance of the supremacy or primacy of applicable E.C. law over inconsistent national law. The nature of the Community established by the E.C. Treaty requires applicable E.C. law to have the same effect and meaning, in addition to full effectiveness, throughout the European Community, anything to the contrary in the member states' national laws notwithstanding. Without doubt, E.C. law's supremacy over national law underlines the federal nature of the relationship between the two legal orders, the European Community and the national. But as in other more or less federal systems in which two legal systems co-exist in a hierarchical relationship, the supremacy of the rules and principles of one system over the other poses a variety of

---

[10] *ibid.* at paras 17, 21, 22 and 24.
[11] See para. 5.30 above.
[12] Case C–213/89 *R. v. Secretary of State for Transport, ex p. Factortame Ltd* [1990] E.C.R. I-2433 at para. 21. When the case returned to the House of Lords, the supremacy of E.C. law was duly accepted: *ex parte Factortame (No. 2)* [1991] 1 A.C. 603.

interesting and difficult issues for judicial review.[13] Space only permits a few of these to be raised here. These are, first, the scope and effect of E.C. law over national law; secondly, when it can properly be said that national law is "inconsistent" with E.C. law; and thirdly, the consequences of conflict between E.C. law and national law.

The scope and effect of E.C. law over national law

Very basically, a national court faced with a challenge to the validity of a national measure on E.C. law grounds has to consider the implications of the supremacy of E.C. law from both the European and national perspectives. As far as the European perspective is concerned, the issues relate to the scope, validity and effect of E.C. law. Each of these three matters must be considered in turn. First, as regards the scope of E.C. law, it must be understood that not every national measure engages E.C. law. Where a national law or other measure is challenged on the ground of inconsistency with E.C. law, the national court must be clear that the E.C. law issues properly arise in the case. If the national measure concerns a matter which is unaffected by E.C. law—for example, there is either no relevant E.C. law on the matter, or the power to deal with the matter is exclusively retained by the national authorities because the European Community has no competence over the matter arising from the E.C. Treaty—then the national measure is not challengeable under E.C. law.[14] European Community law is simply not relevant to the case.

Secondly, once it is determined that E.C. law is relevant, the next issue is whether the particular rule of E.C. law is supreme over national law. Although it may be said in general that all E.C. law is supreme, it does not always follow that an inconsistency between a rule of E.C. law and a rule of national law automatically leads to the invalidity of the latter. Crucially, this conclusion depends on both the validity and the effect of the relevant E.C. law.[15] Any serious doubt that arises about either of these matters will have to be resolved by the ECJ on a preliminary ruling under Art. 234 E.C. Turning first to the validity of a rule of E.C. law, provisions of E.C. law will only be supreme if they themselves are valid. While the E.C. Treaty is in its own terms valid,[16] the validity of all E.C.

5.34

---

[13] The literature on judicial review in federal systems is extensive. For a detailed survey in various systems see, for example, Gunther, *Constitutional Law* (12th ed., Foundation Press, NY, 1991), Chaps 1–5 (USA); Hogg, *Constitutional Law of Canada* (4th ed., Carswell, Toronto, 1997), Chaps 5–16; and Hanks, *Constitutional Law in Australia* (2nd ed., Butterworths, Sydney, 1996), Chap. 8. For an excellent, if now dated, review of constitutional judicial review on federalism grounds in Germany, see Blair, *Federalism and Judicial Review in West Germany* (Clarendon Press, Oxford, 1981).

[14] cf. *R. v. Chief Constable of Sussex, ex p. International Trader's Ferry Ltd* [1998] 3 W.L.R. 1260. See also *R. v. Ministry of Agriculture, Fisheries and Food, ex p. First City Trading Ltd* [1997] 1 C.M.L.R. 250 (national measures are only reviewable against the general principles of E.C. law where they are adopted pursuant to or fall within the scope of E.C. law); and *R. v. H.M. Treasury, The Commissioners of Customs and Excise and the Attorney General, ex p. Shepherd Neame Ltd* [1999] 1 C.M.L.R. 1274 (power to raise excise duty still mostly unaffected by E.C. law). On the limits of the E.C.'s competence, see Dashwood, "The Limits of E.C. powers" (1996) 21 E.L. Rev. 113.

[15] The effect of E.C. law will, of course, also depend on being properly pleaded before the national court, unless it can be shown that national rules of procedure are making the enforcement of E.C. law rights impossible or excessively difficult: see further para. 5.36 below.

[16] By virtue of its supremacy. As the E.C.'s constitutional charter, the E.C. Treaty's validity as far as E.C. law goes is unimpeachable. As noted above (para. 5.32), however,

legislation depends on compliance with the substantive and procedural requirements for validity under the E.C. Treaty. For example, it must concern a subject over which the E.C. Treaty gives the E.C. competence, it must proceed on the correct legal basis under the E.C. Treaty and be supported by reasons, it must have been enacted properly and in addition be consistent with the principle of subsidiarity and respect the general principles of E.C. law.[17] Any defect in E.C. legislation may render it invalid, in which case it will not have any impact on national law.[18]

As regards the effect of E.C. law on national law, this may depend on both the nature of the particular rule of E.C. law relied upon and on the type of case in which the inconsistency between E.C. law and national law arises. As noted above,[19] provisions in E.C. law may be classified according to whether they are directly applicable or capable of producing direct effect. Where a conflict arises between national law and the E.C. Treaty or a directly applicable E.C. regulation, it is clear that national law must be disapplied. But whether or not an individual will be able to obtain this remedy may depend on whether the relevant provision in the E.C. Treaty or regulation has direct effect. Nevertheless, it is clear that the supremacy of E.C. law means that the duty of a national court to apply provisions in the E.C. Treaty and E.C. regulations is greater than the extent to which such provisions are capable of producing direct effect.[20] This emerges even more clearly in relation to the effect of directives on national law. Where national law is challenged for inconsistency with provisions in directives with direct effect, the nature of the case in which the challenge to national law arises is significant. The supremacy of a directive with direct effect over inconsistent national law may only be relied on directly in a case against the state or an emanation of the state because directives are not directly applicable and are said to

---

some national courts have suggested that they may not always accept the supremacy of the E.C. Treaty in the face of higher norms of national constitutional law (in particular, see *Brunner v. The E.U. Treaty* [1994] 1 C.M.L.R. 57). In any event, the authority to amend the E.C. Treaty (and wider TEU) is possessed only by the member states acting unanimously: Art. 48 (formerly N) TEU. Theoretically, questions could arise about whether the E.C. Treaty had been properly amended, or about whether what some member states had done under Title VII of the TEU (closer co-operation) required a Treaty amendment, or about whether amendments to the TEU have been properly implemented into national law. It may be presumed that whether the E.C. Treaty has been properly amended (or requires to be amended) is a matter for the ECJ. Interestingly, where issues have arisen in the U.S. about the validity of amendments to the U.S. Constitution, the U.S. Supreme Court has declined to get involved, regarding the matter as a non-justiciable "political question": see *Coleman v. Miller* 307 U.S. 433 (1939), especially at 449; but *cf.* Opinion 1/91 [1991] E.C.R. I-6079. On the other hand, the power to interpret national law is exclusively for national courts; accordingly, it is for them to decide whether national law has given the required effect to E.C. law.

[17] The ECJ has also held that E.C. measures must respect rules of customary international law too: see Case C–162/96 *A. Racke GmbH & Co v. Hauptzollamt Mainz,* [1998] E.C.R. I-3655.

[18] But only the ECJ has the power to declare E.C. measures invalid: see para. 5–53 below. In addition, an E.C. measure may be presumed valid until the ECJ sets it aside: Case C–137/92P *Commission v. BASF AG* [1994] E.C.R. I-2555. Once set aside, it will be "void" under Art. 231 E.C.; but "void" will not always mean invalid retrospectively, or "non-existent" in the ECJ's terminology. That is, while it was in force, the measure might attract valid consequences, for example, where third parties have relied on it in good faith. See further para. 5–69 below.

[19] See para. 5–24.

[20] This emerges clearly from *Simmenthal*: see para. 5–32 above. See also Case C–431/95 *Commission v. Germany* [1995] E.C.R. I-2189.

have only "vertical" direct effect.[21] Only in such a case must the inconsistent national law be held inapplicable. Where the case is between two private individuals, the obligation on national courts in terms of the directive and Art. 10 of the E.C. Treaty is to interpret national law as far as possible to comply with the directive.[22] This is an interpretive obligation which follows from the E.C. Treaty.[23] Yet, where it is not possible to interpret national law to be compatible with a directive in a case between two private parties, it is arguable that E.C. law now requires a national court to set aside the inconsistent national law.[24] Again, however, this follows from the E.C. Treaty and not directly from the directive. In so far as this highlights the greater scope for directives over national law, it confirms the broader obligations on national courts to apply all national law to be consistent with all E.C. law irrespective of the latter's capacity for direct effect.[25]

The meaning of inconsistency

As far as the national perspective on the supremacy of E.C. law is **5.35** concerned, the basic problem is what is to be understood by "inconsistency" between a national measure and applicable E.C. law. Focusing on the relationship between national rules of law and E.C. law, it may be said that two main points emerge: first, when can it truly be said that a national law is "inconsistent" with a rule of E.C. law; and secondly, how much "inconsistent" national law is subject to the supremacy of E.C. law. The answers to these points are not as straightforward as the supremacy of E.C. law over all inconsistent national law suggests. In particular, a distinction must be drawn between national provisions which are substantive in nature and those which are procedural in nature. In both cases, the problem is where the effects rather than the purposes of the national rule are said to be inconsistent with E.C. law. As will be seen, however, the ECJ's approach to the problem of challenged effects is basically one of proportionality and is broadly similar in relation to the impugned effects of both substantive and procedural rules.

Before dealing with this problem, it should first be said that in general a national court should be disposed to presume consistency between E.C. law and national law. The burden of showing the inconsistency of national law should normally rest on the party claiming it.[26] And in all

---

[21] See para. 5–29 above; *cf. R. v. Secretary of State for Employment, ex p. EOC* [1995] 1 A.C. 1 with *R. v. Secretary of State for Employment, ex p. Seymour-Smith* [1997] 1 W.L.R. 473.

[22] See Case C–106/89 *Marleasing SA v. La Comercial Internacionale de Alimentacion SA* [1990] E.C.R. I-4135.

[23] See para. 5–30 above.

[24] See Case C–194/94 *CIA Security International SA v. Signalson SA and Securitel SPRL* [1996] E.C.R. I-2201; and Case C–441/93 *Panagis Pafitis v. Trapeza Kentrikis Ellados AE* [1996] E.C.R. I-1347. But *cf.* Case C–91/92 *Faccini Dori v. Recreb Srl* [1994] E.C.R. I-3325; and Case C–192/94 *El Corte Ingles v. Cristina Blazques Rivero* [1996] E.C.R. I-1281.

[25] *cf.* Case C–165/91 *Van Munster v. Rijksdienst voor Pensioenen* [1994] E.C.R. I-4661. See also Case C–126/96 *Inter-Environnement Wallonie ASBL v. Region Wallonne* [1998] All E.R. (E.C.) 155.

[26] Unless, of course, either E.C. law or national law has shifted the onus to the party defending the challenged national law or other measure. For example, it may be that once a law is shown to be indirectly discriminatory contrary to E.C. law, the burden of establishing its objective justification falls on the party defending the law: see *R. v. Secretary of State for Employment, ex p. EOC* [1995] 1 A.C. 1. *Cf.* Directive 97/80 (which shifts the burden of proof in sex discrimination cases to the defender).

cases in which national law is challenged for inconsistency with E.C. law, the court should endeavour to interpret national law so far as possible to be consistent with E.C. law, if necessary "reading down" provisions in national legislation so that they have the minimum effects required to make them consistent with E.C. law.[27] Support for such an approach emerges from decisions of the ECJ and the House of Lords.[28] It may also be derived from the speech of Lord Goff of Chieveley in *R. v. Secretary of State for Transport, ex p. Factortame (No. 2)*.[29] Dealing with the availability of an interim injunction to restrain enforcement of a provision in an Act of Parliament challenged for inconsistency with E.C. law, Lord Goff said: "I respectfully doubt whether there is any rule that . . . a party challenging the validity of a law must . . . show a strong prima facie case that the law is invalid . . . [But] the court should not restrain a public authority by interim injunction from enforcing an apparently authentic law unless it is satisfied, having regard to all the circumstances, that the challenge to the validity of the law is, prima facie, so firmly based as to justify so exceptional a course being taken".[30]

In deciding whether there is a prima facie case of inconsistency the court will have to consider the respects in which the national law is said to be inconsistent. It may be that either the purpose or effects of a national law are argued to be inconsistent with E.C. law. This is where the distinction between substantive and procedural rules becomes important. Turning first to the relationship between E.C. law and substantive rules of national law,[31] it follows from *Simmenthal* that all inconsistent substantive rules of national law are "inapplicable". They are trumped (or pre-empted) by applicable E.C. law and must be "set aside". Where the purpose of a national law is shown to be inconsistent, this will normally be enough to vitiate the national law.[32] But where the problem is claimed to be the effects of a national law, the conflict with E.C. law may be less clear. For example, in *Torfaen Borough Council v. B & Q plc*,[33] the question was whether a national law requiring most shops to close on Sundays was inconsistent with Art. 28 (formerly 30) of the E.C. Treaty because it restricted the sale of imports from other member states, thereby constituting a prohibited "measure having equivalent effect" to a restriction on imports. From the standpoint of E.C. law, the purpose of a Sunday closing law was not objectionable. On the contrary, whatever the motives for the law may once have been, providing a rest

---

[27] This should follow for all cases in which national law is challenged on E.C. law grounds, that is, not only where the challenge is based on a directive in a case between private parties: *cf.* Craig, "Indirect Effect of Directives in the Application of National Legislation", Chap. 3 in Andenas and Jacobs (eds): *E.C. Law in the English Courts* (OUP, Oxford, 1998), especially at pp. 50–52.

[28] See, for example, Case 14/83 *Von Colson v. Land Nordrhein-Westfalen* [1984] E.C.R. 1891; Case 80/86 *Kolpinghuis Nijmegen BV* [1987] E.C.R. 3969; Case C–106/89 *Marleasing SA v. La Comercial Internacionale de Alimentacion SA* [1990] E.C.R. I-4135; *Litster v. Forth Dry Dock Ltd*, 1989 S.C. (H.L.) 96; *Webb v. EMO Cargo* [1993] 1 W.L.R. 49 and (No. 2) [1995] 1 W.L.R. 1454 (following a reference to the ECJ). *Cf. English v. North Lanarkshire Council*, 1999 S.C.L.R. 310.

[29] [1991] 1 A.C. 603.

[30] *ibid.* at 674.

[31] The relationship between E.C. law and national procedural rules is considered in the following paragraph.

[32] So the Merchant Shipping Act 1988 was arguably from the start of the *Factortame* litigation tainted by one of its purposes being to discriminate against the nationals of other member states in the ownership and management of fishing vessels.

[33] Case 145/88 [1989] E.C.R. 3851.

day for workers was a salutary objective. Equally, however, the fact that it was harder to buy Italian furniture on a Sunday meant that the law did have some effect on trade in goods imported from other member states. Of course, if it could be shown that the national law had a differential impact on imported goods which the state could not lawfully justify, the discriminatory effects on imported goods would be sufficient to condemn the law. But assuming equality of treatment between national and imported goods, did the existence of some dileterious effects on imported goods render the national law inconsistent with Art. 28 of the E.C. Treaty? The ECJ held that in this context the test for identifying the effects of national rules which cause them to be inconsistent with E.C. law is essentially one of proportionality: "the prohibition laid down in Article [28] covers national measures governing the marketing of products where the restrictive effect of such measures on the free movement of goods exceeds the effects intrinsic to trade rules".[34] This formulation may be adopted more generally. A national law which has some negative effects on E.C. law is not thereby rendered inconsistent with it. Assuming that the national law pursues an objective which is broadly consistent with E.C. law, its effects will only render it inconsistent with E.C. law if they are disproportionate in their impact on E.C. law and its values.[35] And in some circumstances, the ECJ will also concede a "margin of discretion" to member states when assessing the need for and proportionality of national measures.[36] Therefore, where a national law is challenged because of its effects on E.C. law, the effects must pass a threshold of severity before the national law can be said to be inconsistent with E.C. law.

The supremacy of E.C. law and national procedural rules

The need for a threshold of severity before the effects of national rules **5.36** can be said to breach E.C. law leads on to the problem posed by national procedural rules. The problem is where national procedural rules are argued to be inconsistent with E.C. law by virtue of the obstacles they pose to the full effectiveness of applicable E.C. law. The supremacy of E.C. law over national procedural rules is a source of some difficulty,[37] as it is in other federal systems where two legal systems are contingent, one supreme but operating for many purposes through the medium and

---

[34] *ibid.* at para. 15.

[35] In practice, of course, the balancing of interests involved is not easy. In the Sunday closing context, the ECJ in *Torfaen* left the balancing process to national courts, which inevitably reached different conclusions on the proportionality of various national Sunday trading laws. The proportionality (and validity) of Sunday trading laws under Art. 28 E.C. was only settled following a further ECJ ruling in Case C–169/91 *Stoke-on-Trent City Council v. B & Q plc* [1992] E.C.R. I-6635; [1993] A.C. 900 (in which the judge at first instance was Lord Hoffmann, whose commentary on the difficulties is instructive: see "A Sense of Proportion", Chap. 10 in Andenas and Jacobs (eds): *E.C. Law in the English Courts* (OUP, Oxford, 1998).

[36] As in *Torfaen* itself, *supra* at para. 14. See also Case 72/83 *Campus Oil Ltd v. Minister for Industry and Energy* [1984] E.C.R. 2727.

[37] See Prechal, "Community Law in National Courts: The Lessons from Van Schijndel" (1998) 35 C.M.L.R. 681; Hoskins, "Tilting the Balance: Supremacy and National Procedural Rules" (1996) 21 Eur.L.R. 365; and more generally, Jacobs, "Enforcing Community Rights and Obligations in National Courts: Striking the Balance" in Lonbay and Biondi (eds), *Remedies for Breach of EC Law* (1997).

institutions of the other.[38] If the doctrine of supremacy is to invalidate national rules of procedure by virtue of their effects hindering E.C. law on its incidental contact with them, vast areas of national law some way removed from the main scope of E.C. law will be endangered by the doctrine of supremacy. Many procedural rules relating to court jurisdiction, time-limits, standing, evidence and limits on damages would be challengeable where they interfered with the enforcement of E.C. law rights. Accordingly, the ECJ has moderated the implications of supremacy in relation to national procedural rules and focused attention on the need for national law to ensure the full effectiveness of E.C. law. The Court has accepted that in so far as E.C. law does not prescribe remedies or other procedures which national law must implement,[39] it is generally for national law to set the procedural context in which E.C. law operates.[40] European Community law must take national procedural rules as it finds them. But this principle of national procedural autonomy is accompanied by E.C. law requirements which national law must satisfy to ensure the full effectiveness of rights conferred by E.C. law.[41] These are, first, that national rules of procedure must not discriminate against rights conferred by E.C. law. That is, national law must not pose obstacles to the enforcement of E.C. law rights which are not posed for equivalent national law rights. This may be termed the principle of equivalence. Secondly, national law must be adequate to enable E.C. law rights to be enforced effectively; it must be "fit for the purpose" of enforcing E.C. law. And thirdly, national rules must not make "virtually impossible or excessively difficult" the enforcement of rights conferred by E.C. law in national courts. Together, these requirements may be termed the principle of effectiveness. Sometimes, the principles of equivalence and effectiveness are put more strongly as absolute requirements that national law must ensure the full effectiveness of E.C. law, if

---

[38] The problem is especially familiar in the U.S. To what extent are state procedural rules inapplicable where they impede the operation of constitutional (or other federal law) rights? Very basically, the answer is that state procedural rules which interfere with federal rights will only be invalid in so far as they do not show "adequate and independent state grounds" for a decision. But the problem is deciding what "adequate" means: see Hart & Wechsler, *The Federal Courts and the Federal System* (3rd ed., Foundation Press, New York, 1998), pp. 590–638. *Cf. Felder v. Casey*, 487 U.S. 131 (1988).

[39] Which it is increasingly doing: *cf. Directive* 92/28 (Advertising of Medicial Products) 1992, O.J. L113/13; Directive 92/59 (Product Safety) 1992, O.J. L228/4; and Directive 97/80 (Burden of Proof in Sex Discrimination) 1997 O.J. L14/6.

[40] The leading case on national procedural autonomy is Case 33/76 *Rewe-Zentralfinanz eG and Rewe-Zentral AG v. Landwirtschaftskammer fur das Saarland* [1976] E.C.R. 1989. But many subsequent cases have developed and qualified this concept. For an overview, see Craig and De Burca: *EU Law* (2nd ed., OUP, Oxford, 1998), Chap. 5.

[41] *cf.* Case 106/77 *Amministrazione delle Finanze dello Stato v. Simmenthal SpA* [1978] E.C.R. 629; Case C–213/89 *Factortame (No. 1)* [1990] E.C.R. 2433; Case C–208/90 *Emmott v. Minister for Social Welfare* [1991] E.C.R. I-4269; Case C–271/91 *Marshall v. Southampton and South-West Hampshire Area Health Authority (No. 2)* [1993] E.C.R. I-4367; Case C–410/92 *Johnson v. Chief Adjudication Officer* [1994] E.C.R. I-5483; Case C–312/93 *Peterbroeck, Van Campenhout & Cie SCS v. Belgium* [1995] E.C.R. I-4599; Cases C–430 and 431/93 *Van Schijndel & Van Veen v. Stichting Pensioenfonds voor Fysiotherapeuten* [1995] E.C.R. I-4705; Case C–66/95 *R. v. Secretary of State for Social Security, ex p. Sutton* [1997] E.C.R. I-2163; Case C–326/96 *R. v. Levez v. T.H. Jennings Ltd* [1999] 2 C.M.L.R. 363; and Case C–126/97, *Eco Swiss China Time Ltd v. Benetton International NV* [1999] 2 All E.R. (Comm.) 44. For discussion, see Lewis, *Remedies and the Enforcement of EC Law* (Sweet & Maxwell, London, 1996), Chap. 5; Prechal, "Community Law in National Courts: The Lessons from Van Schijndel" (1998) 35 C.M.L.R. 681 and Himsworth, "Things Fall Apart: The Harmonisation of Community Judicial Procedural Protection Revisted" (1997) 22 Eur.L.R. 291. See also Coppel, "Time up for Emmott" (1996) 25 I.L.J. 153.

necessary by creating adequate remedies to allow the effective enforcement of E.C. law rights. While there are ECJ decisions which could be
taken as supporting this formulation, and while the ECJ itself has also
created remedies which national law must provide, these relate to
remedies for losses arising as a result of violation of E.C. law by a
member state.[42] Beyond this important but specific context, the ECJ's
general approach to national procedural rules which neither discriminate
against E.C. law rights nor render virtually impossible their enforcement
seems to be to examine whether the national procedural rules make the
enforcement of E.C. law "excessively difficult" and, if not, whether they
are "adequate" in light of the nature of the E.C. law rights. The
standards "excessively" and "adequate" suggest that the essence of the
approach is that national rules must not have a disproportionate impact
on E.C. law rights such that the full effectiveness of those rights cannot
be secured. In other words, if the national rules have a disproportionate
impact on the enforcement of E.C. law rights their effects will be
"excessive", they will interfere with the full effectiveness of E.C. law and
be inconsistent with it. It follows from this, as it inevitably does with a
proportionality test, that some national procedural rules will *per se* be
invalid because of their inadequacy or the impact they have on the
effectiveness of E.C. law rights; but other rules will be valid because, for
example, they can easily be justified by the important purposes that they
serve in the context of the national legal order taken as a whole.[43]

The consequences of inconsistency: invalidity?

If it is established that there is an inconsistency between a national law **5.37**
or other measure and applicable E.C. law, what are the consequences of
the inconsistency? Does it follow from the duty of a national court to
hold "inapplicable" an inconsistent national rule that the national rule is
thereby rendered invalid? If so, what does "invalid" in this context
mean? For example, does invalidity mean that an inconsistent national
rule is of no force and effect generally, including in cases unaffected by
E.C. law? Is the invalidity of a national rule to be given retrospective
effect, so that a national rule found to be inconsistent with applicable
E.C. law is to be treated as void *ab initio*? Although it might be thought
that these matters are for national law, being essentially of a remedial
nature, it follows from what has just been said about the ECJ's
jurisprudence on the requirement of full effectiveness for E.C. law that
there are significant E.C. aspects here too. Moreover, the effect to be
attributed to E.C. law over national law may depend on a decision of the
ECJ, which may exceptionally vary the temporal effect of its decisions on
the implications of E.C. law.[44]

In *Simmenthal*,[45] the ECJ arguably draws a distinction between the
effects of "provisions of the Treaty and directly applicable measures of
the institutions" and "Community law in its entirety". Where national
rules are found to be inconsistent with Treaty provisions and directly
applicable E.C. law, the supremacy of E.C. law renders the national rules

---

[42] See Case 199/82 *Amministrazione delle Finanze dello Stato v. San Giorgio* [1983] E.C.R.
3595; and Cases C–6 & 9/90 *Francovich & Bonifaci v. Italy* [1991] E.C.R. I-5357.
[43] In this regard, see the ECJ's recent decision in Case C–126/97 *Eco Swiss China Time
Ltd v. Benetton International NV* [1999] 2 All E.R. (Comm.) 44.
[44] See para. 5–60 below.
[45] [1978] E.C.R. 629.

"automatically inapplicable". But where national rules are found to be inconsistent with the wider category of E.C. law "in its entirety", the obligation on the national court is to "set aside" the national rules. It may be therefore that the consequences for national rules of an inconsistency with E.C. law depend on the nature of the E.C. law relied upon. So, for example, where there is an inconsistency between national law and the E.C. Treaty or a regulation, the national law is "automatically inapplicable". Where the relevant provision also has direct effect, an individual will be able to rely on it to have the national law disapplied. The inapplicability of the national law will apply generally and will possibly also have retrospective effect.[46] In other words, all cases, whenever their facts arose, are not affected by the inconsistent national law.[47] But the same will be true in relation to directives only in so far as cases are against the state or an emanation of the state. Only in such cases will the remedy of inapplicability have general (and possibly retrospective) effect. Where an inconsistency between national law and a directive with direct effect arises in a case between two private parties, and it is impossible to construe the national law to be consistent with the directive, the obligation on national courts is to protect E.C. law "in its entirety" and "set aside" the inconsistent national law. That is, in cases between two private parties the inconsistency between national law and a directive will not render the national law "automatically inapplicable". The national law may only have to be "set aside" for the purposes of deciding the instant case.[48] Although the court's decision will be a precedent for future cases, the decision may not affect the validity of the national law generally as it applies to other cases. The court will leave it to the legislature to repeal or amend the national law so as to remove the inconsistency with E.C. law which does not have direct effect. Be that as it may, the point is that in some cases involving E.C. law which is not directly effective, the national court is still required to "set aside" national law so as to protect E.C. law "in its entirety".

The consequences of inconsistency: voidness?

5.38 Even where an inconsistent national rule is "automatically inapplicable" (or "set aside"), this will not necessarily mean that it is to be treated as invalid in the sense of void *ab initio*. As far as the ECJ is concerned, the important point is that inconsistent national rules do not interfere with the full effectiveness of E.C. law. If the full effectiveness of rights guaranteed by E.C. law requires the voidness of a national rule, the national court will be required to accept this conclusion. But voidness will not always be required. In *Simmenthal*, the ECJ said that national measures found to be inconsistent with applicable E.C. law are "inapplicable" or must be "set aside". But neither "inapplicable" nor, arguably even less, "setting aside" necessarily entail voidness. So, for example, procedural rules which hinder the full effectiveness of E.C. law need only be disapplied in so far as they

---

[46] See para. 5–38 below.
[47] *cf. Hammersmith and Fulham LBC v. Jesuthasan* [1998] I.C.R. 640.
[48] *cf.* Case C–194/94 *CIA Security International SA v. Signalson SA and Securitel SPRL* [1996] E.C.R. I-2201, discussed at para. 5–30 above. See also Case C–129/94 *Rafael Ruiz Bernaldez* [1996] E.C.R. I-1829; and Case C–441/93 *Panagis Pafitis v. Trapeza Kentrikis Ellados AE* [1996] E.C.R. I-1347.

hinder E.C. law.[49] They can remain in full force and effect in relation to national law. Similarly, in *R. v. Secretary of State for Employment, ex parte EOC*,[50] Lord Keith of Kinkel said of *Factortame*,[51] where provisions in the Merchant Shipping Act 1988 were held to be inconsistent with directly effective E.C. Treaty articles:

> "The effect was that certain provisions of U.K. primary legislation were held to be invalid in their purported application to nationals of member states of the E.C., but . . . [they] remained valid as regards nationals of non-member states".[52]

Furthermore, the ECJ has made clear that "inapplicable" does not always entail invalidity in the sense of void *ab initio*. In *Ministero delle Finanze v. IN.CO.GE '90 Srl*,[53] the ECJ held that:

> "It cannot . . . be inferred from the judgment in *Simmenthal* that the incompatibility with Community law of a subsequently adopted rule of national law has the effect of rendering that rule of national law non-existent. Faced with such a situation, the national court is, however, obliged to disapply that rule, provided always that this obligation does not restrict the power of the competent national courts to apply, from among the various procedures available under national law, those which are appropriate for protecting the individual rights conferred by Community law".

The distinction between "non-existent" and "inapplicable" recalls the ECJ's case law on the "voidness" of E.C. measures which are declared invalid following Article 230 E.C. annulment proceedings.[54] Although Article 231 E.C. provides that an E.C. measure successfully challenged under Article 230 is void, the ECJ has the power to vary the retrospective effect of the annulment of a measure. In addition to its power under Article 231 E.C. to allow annulled regulations to have some effect,[55] the ECJ has held that E.C. measures are generally to be presumed valid until they are annulled unless the breach of E.C. law which leads to the annulment is so severe as to justify holding them "non-existent", that is, void *ab initio*.[56] Accordingly, following IN.CO.GE,[57] inconsistent national rules are not normally rendered "non-existent" by virtue of inconsistency

---

[49] So, following the House of Lords decision in *R. v. Secretary of State for Transport, ex p. Factortame (No. 2)* [1991] 1 A.C. 603, injunctions became available against the Crown where E.C. law was being relied on. But s. 21 of the Crown Proceedings Act 1947 continued to restrict the availability of injunctions in cases against the Crown that were unaffected by E.C. law. Only following *M v. Home Office* [1994] 1 A.C. 377 did it become clear that injunctions could be granted against the Crown in England in all cases. In Scotland, following the Inner House decision in *McDonald v. Secretary of State for Scotland*, 1994 S.L.T. 692, interdict is not available against the Crown. However, in terms of E.C. law it will be available for the purposes of protecting and enforcing E.C. law rights.
[50] [1995] 1 A.C. 1.
[51] The relevant decisions are *R. v. Secretary of State for Transport, ex p. Factortame* [1991] 1 A.C. 603; and [1991] 3 C.M.L.R. 589.
[52] *R. v. Secretary of State for Employment, ex parte EOC* [1995] 1 A.C. 1, at 27.
[53] Cases C–10 to C–22/97 [1998] E.C.R. 569.
[54] See para. 5–69 below.
[55] The power also applies where directives have been annulled: see Case C–295/90 *European Parliament v. Council* [1992] E.C.R. I-4193.
[56] See Case C–137/92P *Commission v. BASF AG* [1994] E.C.R. I-2555.
[57] *supra*, n. 53.

with E.C. law, but only "inapplicable" to the extent of the inconsistency. Although they must be disapplied, or "set aside" by national courts, it does not necessarily follow that they are void *ab initio*. They, or some of their provisions, may retain some effect in national law, at least in so far as this is consistent with E.C. law, for example, to the extent necessary to ensure the full effectiveness of E.C. law. But if the seriousness of the violation of E.C. law or the need for the full effectiveness of E.C. law requires that a national measure be treated as "non-existent", or void *ab initio*, then the national court will be required to reach this conclusion.

This approach of relative "voidness" is consistent with other aspects of the ECJ's jurisprudence. For example, in *Amministrazione delle Finanze dello Stato v. Denkavit Italiana*,[58] the Court held that its decisions on the effect to be attributed to a provision of E.C. law are retrospective to the point at which the provision became effective. So, for example, the direct effect of a provision in an E.C. directive operates from when the directive entered force, not from the date of the ECJ's judgment clarifying the directive's direct effect. But this general rule is subject to the Court's power to vary the retrospective—or temporal—effect of its decisions.[59] So in *Defrenne v. Sabena*,[60] the Court decided that the direct effect of Article 119 E.C. only operated prospectively, save in the instant case and other cases in which proceedings had already been raised.[61]

Where a U.K. court concludes that a national measure is inconsistent with applicable E.C. law and holds it "inapplicable" or sets it aside, the effects of this decision may be informed by the ECJ's approach to the matter. As noted above,[62] in *ex parte EOC* Lord Keith of Kinkel observed that the effect of a declaration that provisions in Acts of the U.K. Parliament are incompatible with E.C. law does not render the provisions inapplicable generally.[63] But it may be that national legislation found to be inapplicable by virtue of inconsistency with directly effective E.C. law is to be treated as invalid retrospectively. So where the House of Lords granted a declaration to the effect that U.K. legislation is inapplicable by virtue of inconsistency with directly effective provisions of E.C. law, the Court of Appeal in England decided that the effect of this "judicial displacement" of legislation is to render the legislation inapplicable in all cases to which it applied, including not only cases not directly affected by E.C. law but also cases concerning events which took place before the House of Lords decision.[64] Whether this conclusion will always follow where national measures are disapplied because of inconsistency with E.C. law is not clear. Even if the conclusion is limited to cases affected by E.C. law, it may not always be required in terms of E.C. law.

---

[58] Case 61/79 [1980] E.C.R. 1205, at para. 16.

[59] See para. 5–60 below.

[60] Case 43/75 [1976] E.C.R. 547.

[61] See also Case 293/83 *Gravier v. Liege* [1985] E.C.R. 593; Case C–262/88 *Barber v. Guardian Royal Exchange Assurance Group* [1990] E.C.R. I-1889; and Case C–200/91 *Coloroll Pension Trustees v. Russell* [1994] E.C.R. I-4389. But note that only the ECJ has the power to vary the temporal effect of its decisions and it may only be asked to do so in the case in which the issues arise, not subsequently.

[62] See n. 52 above.

[63] *cf.* s. 102 of the Scotland Act 1998 *vis-à-vis* Acts of the Scottish Parliament: see para. 7–56.

[64] See *Hammersmith and Fulham LBC v. Jesuthasan* [1998] I.C.R. 640. Although this was a case against the state, the declaration which disapplied the legislative provisions (in *ex parte EOC*, n. 52 above) was based on an E.C. Treaty Art. and a directive. Accordingly, the inapplicability of the legislation was not limited to cases against the State, since E.C. Treaty Arts with direct effect have horizontal and vertical direct effect.

VI THE GENERAL PRINCIPLES OF E.C. LAW

Introduction

It has already been noted that the general principles of law which the   **5.39**
ECJ has identified as part of E.C. law form an important source of E.C.
law in their own right.[65] Their role in E.C. law is such that they may be
regarded as part of the E.C.'s constitutional law.[66] In particular, all E.C.
legislation is subject to review for consistency with the general principles
of law. Although not all of the general principles attract the same
importance, if the ECJ finds that a measure violates a general principle
of law it may invalidate the measure on this ground. From the
standpoint of judicial review before national courts, the importance of
the general principles of E.C. law goes beyond the grounds on which
E.C. measures may be challenged. Equally significant is that all national
measures which fall within the scope of E.C. law are also subject to being
reviewed for consistency with the general principles of law.[67] In other
words, where it is clear that E.C. law is applicable to the case, a national
measure whether in the form of legislation, executive act or decision,
may be challenged on the grounds that it is inconsistent with a general
principle of E.C. law.

Among the general principles of law which the ECJ has found to be
part of E.C. law are the principles of proportionality, legal certainty,
non-retrospectivity of laws, legitimate expectation, equality (or non-
discrimination), requirements of transparency in the E.C. institutions,
and some human rights—in particular, due process rights. Although the
development of general principles of law is necessary to furnish the
European Community's legal system with the essential values and
principles of an effective and working legal system to perform a role akin
to presumptions in statutory interpretation in the U.K., there are some
problems with the concept of general principles of law. The first problem
concerns the ascertainment of the general principles of law.[68] For
example, to what extent does recognition of a general principle of law
depend on its existence in national law? If existence in national law is a
criterion, how many of the national legal systems must have some form
of the principle before it can be recognised in E.C. law? Alternatively,
what limits are there on the ECJ's creativity in formulating general
principles of law? While the ECJ has been careful,[69] it is clear that the
general principles of law comprise legal principles drawn from a variety
of contexts, including the E.C. Treaty itself,[70] the laws of only some of
the member states,[71] and international law.[72] In turn, the fact that the

---

[65] See para. 5–21.

[66] For an extensive account, see Schwarze, *European Administrative Law* (1995), at pp.
938 *et seq.* For an overview of the general principles, see Usher, *General Principles of Law*
(Longman, London, 1997).

[67] See de Smith, Woolf and Jowell, *Judicial Review of Administrative Action* (5th ed.,
Sweet and Maxwell, London, 1995), Chap. 21, especially para. 21–119 *et seq.*

[68] See Usher, *General Principles of Law* (1997), Chap. 1.

[69] Some would argue too careful: see Coppel and O'Neill, "The European Court of
Justice: Taking Rights Seriously?" (1992) 12 Legal Studies 227; *cf.* Weiler & Lockhart,
"Taking Rights Seriously: The European Court and its Fundamental Rights Jurispru-
dence" (1995) 32 C.M.L.R. 51, 579 (two parts).

[70] *cf.* Art. 288 (formerly 215) E.C., providing for the E.C. institutions' non-contractual
liability, which has provided a reference point for the liability of the member states for
their breaches of E.C. law: see Cases C–46 and 48/93 *Brasserie du Pêcheur v. Germany* and
R. v. Secretary of State for Transport, ex p. Factortame Ltd (No. 3) [1996] E.C.R. I-1029.

[71] *cf.* Case 17/74 *Transocean Marine Paint Association v. Commission* [1974] E.C.R. 1063.

[72] *cf.* Case 4/73 *Nold v. Commission* [1974] E.C.R. 491.

general principles of law need not be recognised in the laws of every member state raises a second problem. In effect the judge-made general principles of E.C. law constitute a form of "common law" throughout the E.C. legal order. To the extent that this "common law" applies in the legal systems of the member states side by side with national legal rules, national courts could be faced with choice of law problems: first, it will be necessary to characterise a national act to determine whether it falls within the sphere of E.C. law; secondly, once so characterised, the national court will have to apply the autonomous E.C. law meaning of the relevant general principle, which may be foreign to the national court; and thirdly, the general principles of E.C. law will not apply in national cases untouched by E.C. law.[73] It may be that such problems will diminish if the grounds of review in E.C. law and national law converge.[74] But experience elsewhere with legal systems in a federal relationship, especially the United States of America, suggests that as the European Community's general principles of law proliferate and as the sphere of application of E.C. law grows, conflict of laws problems between E.C. "common law" and national law may arise and could lead to difficulty in particular cases.[75]

Although the ECJ has derived the general principles of E.C. law from particular provisions in the E.C. Treaty, or from legal concepts in national and international law, it must be stressed that any general principle of E.C. law has the meaning which the ECJ gives it in E.C. law. What the concept means in other legal contexts—in particular, how it is

---

[73] See *R. v. Ministry of Agriculture, Fisheries and Food, ex p. First City Trading Ltd* [1997] 1 C.M.L.R. 250.

[74] And there is evidence, at least in the U.K., that the grounds of judicial review are increasingly influenced by the E.C. jurisprudence: *cf.* de Burca, "Proportionality and Wednesbury Unreasonableness: The Influence of European Legal Concepts on U.K. Law" [1997] 3 E.P.L. 561; and Anthony, "Community Law and the Development of U.K. Administrative Law: Delimiting the 'Spill-Over' Effect" [1998] 4 EPL 253.

[75] Consider, for example, the history of the general common law applied by federal courts in the USA in cases coming before them under their "diversity jurisdiction"—that is, in cases between persons from different states. In such cases, where neither the Constitution nor any federal law provided a rule for decision, the U.S. Supreme Court in *Swift v. Tyson* 41, U.S. (16 Peters) 1 (1842) decided that the federal courts could apply a body of law to be developed by them and to be known as general common law. The main purpose of this general common law was to make the same common law apply to national commercial transactions. But in its landmark decision in *Erie Railroad Co. v. Tompkins* 304 U.S. 64 (1938), however, the Court overruled *Swift*. Among the grounds for doing so were that different common law rules were being applied in cases involving the same facts depending on which forum (state or federal) a plaintiff chose to sue a defendant. Clearly, the problem of forum-shopping leading to injustice does not arise in the E.C. But the problems of choice of law arising from a jurisdiction having two legal systems, one (the federal or E.C.) supreme and ever expanding over the other, do arise: wherefor the integrity of national law? It should be noted that the concept of a general common law is to be distinguished from federal common law in the sense of rules of law developed by the federal courts governing the federal government, *e.g.* in relation to contracts entered into by the federal government (see *Clearfield Trust Co. v. U.S.* (1943) 318 U.S. 363). Limited to this sense, the federal courts in Canada have not rejected the existence of a federal common law (see, for example, *R. v. Thomas Fuller Construction* [1980] 1 S.C.R. 695). But as in the U.S. following *Erie*, Canadian (and Australian) courts have rejected the existence of a system of generally applying common law separate from the state and provincial systems. For discussion of the U.S. experience, see Freyer, *Harmony and Dissonance: The Swift and Erie Cases in American Federalism* (NYU Press, New York, 1981); for Canada and Australia, see Hogg, *Liability of the Crown* (2nd ed., Carswell, Toronto, 1989), pp. 272–277. There is some evidence that the ECJ is sensitive to concerns about the expansion of the scope of the general principles of law: See Case C–2/92 *R. v. MAFF, ex p. Bostock* [1994] E.C.R. I-955.

understood in one or more of the member state legal systems—will not necessarily be how the ECJ has adopted and applied it.[76] Needless to say, the meaning and effects of a general principle of E.C. law depend on what the ECJ has said about it. So, for example, if a national court is faced with a challenge to a national measure which may be reviewed against the general principles of E.C. law, and the issue is whether a legitimate expectation has been honoured, the national court must apply the doctrine of legitimate expectation as it has been developed by the ECJ and not as it is understood in national law.

Scope of the General Principles of Law

It is clear that where an E.C. measure is challenged before the ECJ or **5.40** CFI, its validity may be questioned on the ground that it violates one of the general principles of law. Equally, in a judicial review before a U.K. court, it will be possible to argue that an E.C. measure is invalid by virtue of its breach of a general principle of law. Beyond E.C. measures proper, however, what scope do the general principles of E.C. law have as grounds on which national measures may be reviewed? In other words, when can it be said that the general principles of E.C. law apply to a case before a national court? The ECJ has not provided a clear answer to this question.[77] In the *Wachauf* case,[78] the ECJ confirmed the most obvious situation to which the general principles apply: where the national authorities are implementing E.C. measures. Accordingly, national laws and other acts which are adopted in implementation of E.C. measures fall within the scope of E.C. law and must be consistent with the general principles of law. Similarly, acts and decisions of national authorities pursuant to E.C. measures are covered. In the *ERT* case,[79] the ECJ decided that the general principles of E.C. law apply: "where a member state relies on [provisions of E.C. law] in order to justify [national] rules which are likely to obstruct the exercise of the freedom to provide services".[80] Accordingly, when national authorities are justifying their acts or decisions by reference to provisions in E.C. law, the general principles of law will apply. The matter will "fall within the scope of E.C. law".[81] Beyond the situations of implementation of E.C. measures and justification by reference to E.C. law, the reach of the general principles of E.C. law as grounds of review in national law is uncertain.[82]

The principle of proportionality

The principle of proportionality may be regarded as the pre-eminent **5.41** general principle of E.C. law. Well established in German administrative law, the ECJ adopted it as a general principle of E.C. law early on. It has

---

[76] *cf.* Case 90/74 *Deboeck v. Commission* [1975] E.C.R. 1123; and see discussion in Usher, *General Principles of Law* (1998), at pp. 124–127.

[77] For a fuller discussion, see Craig & de Burca, *EU Law* (2nd ed., OUP, Oxford, 1998), pp. 317–331. As the authors note, the lack of clear guidance on the scope of the general principles of E.C. law in national law may reflect the general lack of clarity about the scope of the legislative competence of the E.C. institutions.

[78] Case C–5/88 *Wachauf v. Bundesamt für Ernährung und Forstwirtschaft* [1989] E.C.R. 2609. See also Case C–2/92 *R. v. MAFF, ex p. Bostock* [1994] E.C.R. I-955.

[79] Case C–260/89 [1991] E.C.R. I-2925.

[80] *ibid.* at para. 43.

[81] *ibid.* at para. 42.

[82] See *Booker Aquaculture Ltd v. Secretary of State for Scotland* [1999] 1 C.M.L.R. 35; 1998 G.W.D. 21–1089.

been applied in a great number of ECJ decisions, although as is always the case in practice with the principle of proportionality, it does not always apply in the same degree. While it may be said in general that proportionality requires that the means adopted to achieve a particular aim must not exceed such means as are appropriate and necessary to achieve that aim, with a balance having to be struck between the importance of the aim and the nature and severity of the means, the discretion involved in assessing aims and means leads the ECJ to apply proportionality at times anxiously and at other times deferentially. Where fundamental human rights are involved, the ECJ will tend to apply proportionality more strictly, therefore requiring proof of the most important objectives to justify the most limited means to achieve them. In this regard, the ECJ will be influenced by the approach to proportionality of the European Court of Human Rights.[83] It is also clear that the ECJ will apply the principle of proportionality as it sees fit to national measures which fall within the scope of E.C. law. National courts are bound to do so too in cases to which E.C. law applies. Although U.K. courts have historically been doubtful about what proportionality entails, the principle has found its way into the jurisprudence of the United Kingdom. In that regard, it is considered in Part IV of the present book in the context of the grounds of review.[84]

The principle of legal certainty

5.42 The principle of legal certainty requires that legislation be clear and free from ambiguity, that it impose no burdens on individuals retrospectively, and that it state clearly its legal basis and the reasons on which it is based. More generally, the principle requires that the E.U. institutions give reasons for their decisions. In turn, this idea has led to a general requirement of transparency in the European Union's activities. Openness and accountability in E.C. decision-making, protection for the interests of third parties, consultation and other process rights may be enforceable before legislation is enacted by the European Community As far as the duty to give reasons is concerned, national authorities will also be bound by this general principle when they are acting pursuant to E.C. law.

The principle of legitimate expectation

5.43 The concept of legitimate expectation has also been found by the ECJ to be a general principle of E.C. law.[85] While it may be regarded as an aspect of a broader general principle of law relating to legal certainty, the principle of legitimate expectation in E.C. law involves more than maintaining legal certainty. More generally, the principle has a sufficient importance that it deserves to be regarded as a general principle of law in its own right. In particular, the principle encompasses enforceable expectations of substantive decisions. It is not only limited to expectations of procedures. But, as in the United Kingdom, the expectation must be lawful. No expectation is legitimate if it is founded on illegality or matters beyond the purview of the European Community's powers.

---

[83] See, for example, Case 222/84 *Johnston v. Chief Constable of the Royal Ulster Constabulary* [1986] E.C.R. 1651 at 1687.

[84] See Chap. 21.

[85] See, for example, Case 84/78 *Angelo Tomadini Snc v. Amministrazzione dello Finanze dello Stato* [1979] E.C.R. 1801 at 1815.

Fundamental human rights

In several decisions, the ECJ has affirmed that fundamental human **5.44**
rights are part of E.C. law to the extent that they are relevant to the
European Community's (and more broadly the European Union's)
activities.[86] At first, the Court found human rights to be protected as
general principles of E.C. law as a reaction to concerns in some national
courts that the European Community could violate national constitutional rights. Thereafter, the court emphasised many due process rights,
such as the rights of the defence, the right to a fair hearing, the
privileges against self incrimination and double jeopardy, and the right
to counsel as rights which the E.U. institutions were bound to respect in
their dealings with persons. More generally, the Court has drawn on the
several expressions in the E.C. Treaty regarding protection from non-
discrimination to establish more inclusive rights to equality. The general
principle here is that equality of treatment be afforded to similar
situations. But neither a right to equality nor the protection of all
fundamental human rights are free standing in E.C. law. They do not
enable individuals to challenge any national measure in circumstances
unaffected by E.C. law on the grounds that equality or other human
rights have been violated. The rights cannot be invoked in situations
which do not fall under E.C. law. Even where they can be invoked, they
are only relevant in so far as E.C. law reaches, which in general terms
means that the issues must have some relationship with economic
activity.[87] But where they do apply, their effect can be to render
inconsistent national measures inapplicable.

The principle of effective remedies

Although the ECJ has continually affirmed the principle of national **5.45**
procedural autonomy, which means that E.C. law does not generally
require harmonisation of national procedural rules or the creation of
new remedies just for E.C. law, the Court has also consistently emphasised the obligation of national law and national courts to ensure the full
effectiveness of E.C. law. This may be seen as a general principle of E.C.
law. It is most visible in relation to the effect the Court has carved out
for E.C. directives in national law.[88] More generally, the Court has
decided that national procedural rules must not discriminate against
rights conferred by E.C. law. Such rights must not be faced with
obstacles in national law not faced by equivalent national rights.
Furthermore, national law must not render virtually impossible or
excessively difficult the enforcement of E.C. law rights. National law
must also be adequate for the purposes of ensuring the effectiveness of
E.C. law. These requirements—equivalence, effectiveness and
adequacy—are cumulative.

In some cases, the ECJ has required national law to provide a remedy.
The most notable remedy is the remedy of damages against the state for
losses caused to persons by the state's violation of E.C. law.[89]

---

[86] Case 4/73 *Nold v. Commission* [1974] E.C.R. 491; Case C–44/79 *Hauer v. Land
Rheinland-Pfalz* [1979] E.C.R. 3727; Case C–5/88 *Wachauf v. Bundesamt für Ernährung und
Forstwirtschaft* [1989] E.C.R. 2609.
[87] *cf. SPUC v. Grogan* [1991] 3 C.M.L.R. 849.
[88] See para. 5–30 above.
[89] For discussion of the nature and extent of this remedy in E.C. law, see Heukels and
McDonnell (eds), *The Action for Damages in Community Law* (Kluwer, 1997). See also
para. 5–31 above and para. 5–51 below.

VII   E.C. LAW IN THE U.K. LEGAL SYSTEMS

Introduction

5.46   From the original standpoint of the national legal systems of the E.U. member states, E.C. law was international law. For E.C. law to have effect in a national legal system, it must be introduced into national law in accordance with each member state's constitutional arrangements for giving effect to international treaty obligations. Each of the member states has different traditions in this regard. Some states adopt a monist approach, which basically means that there is no strict separation between national and international law, with the result that individuals can derive rights and duties from international law notwithstanding the failure of national law directly to incorporate them. In contrast, other states adopt a dualist approach, which in its crude form means that rights and remedies created by an international treaty can have no direct effect in national law until implemented by a piece of national legislation. The U.K. constitution's tradition with respect to international treaties is more or less dualist. Accordingly, an Act of Parliament is required to implement legal provisions contained in international treaties if they are to be relied on directly before U.K. courts.[90] Since E.C. law possesses characteristics making it very different from traditional conceptions of international law—in particular, supremacy over national law, directly enforceable rights and remedies, and an active and powerful legislature—it presents some difficulties for a state which adopts a dualist approach to international law. For the United Kingdom, the principal difficulties follow from the supremacy of E.C. law and its continually evolving nature.[91] This means that the implementation of E.C. law must not only accord supreme effect to the E.C. Treaty over and above all national law, including subsequent Acts of Parliament, but also confer the same status on relevant legislation and legal rules and principles which arise or will arise under the E.C. Treaty. These tasks fall to the European Communities Act 1972.

E.C. law in the laws of the United Kingdom

5.47   The European Communities Act 1972 (the 1972 Act) gives applicable E.C. law the force of law in the United Kingdom. But although there are many areas in all of the U.K. legal systems which are now dominated by E.C. law or national legislation with an E.C. provenance, it is not correct to say that E.C. law is part of the laws of the United Kingdom. Rather, E.C. law has the force of law in the U.K.[92] Putting the matter in this way allows two implications of E.C. law to be highlighted. First, E.C. law has the force of supreme law. So, for example, if there is a conflict between an E.C. regulation and a provision in an Act of the U.K. Parliament, the

---

[90] See *J.H. Rayner (Mincing Land) Ltd v. Department of Trade and Industry* [1990] 2 A.C. 418. But the operation of the compliance presumption, namely, that ambiguous terms in statutes are to be construed consistently with the U.K.'s international obligations, modifies the rule: see further para. 6–12.

[91] See *Swan v. Secretary of State for Scotland* [1998] 2 C.M.L.R. 1192 at 1202: "European law does not stand still".

[92] *cf.* Sir Jean-Pierre Warner, "The Relationship Between European Community Law and the National Laws of the Member States" (1977) 93 L.Q.R. 349, at p. 351: "It is not quite true to say . . . that Community law 'has become part of English law' . . . though it would be true to say that it has become 'part of the law of England'".

U.K. enactment has to be disapplied to the extent of the inconsistency. Secondly, where U.K. legislation is passed to give domestic effect to an E.C. directive, thereby translating or incorporating the E.C. law into U.K. law, in some circumstances the E.C. directive can still be relied on directly before a national court if, for example, it has direct effect and the national legislation fails in some way to give full or proper effect to it.[93] European Community law therefore sits side by side with national law in the national legal order but with the potential to apply over and above it and to displace it in the event of inconsistency.

It follows from the provisions of the 1972 Act and from the requirements of E.C. law that rules and principles of E.C. law have the same scope and application everywhere in the United Kingdom. In particular, the Scottish Parliament has no powers to legislate contrary to E.C. law.[94] Furthermore, decisions of all U.K. courts and tribunals on the effect of the 1972 Act and E.C. law must be regarded as common jurisprudence within the United Kingdom, so that decisions of the House of Lords on the effect of the 1972 Act and E.C. law are binding on courts throughout the United Kingdom.[95] Moreover, decisions of the ECJ on points of E.C. law are also, by virtue of section 3 of the 1972 Act, binding on all courts and tribunals in the United Kingdom. Accordingly, although several Scottish cases have raised important E.C. law issues,[96] a complete understanding of the relationship between E.C. law and U.K. law requires consideration to be given not only, of course, to decisions of the ECJ but also to decisions of courts elsewhere in the United Kingdom.

European Communities Act 1972

The European Communities Act 1972 provides for the relationship **5.48** between E.C. law and U.K. law in five stages: first, in section 1, it designates what is meant by E.C. law; secondly, in section 2(1), it incorporates all applicable E.C. laws and gives effect to them in the United Kingdom according to the requirements of E.C. law from time to time; thirdly, in section 2(2), it confers powers on the U.K. government to have regard to and as required to implement U.K. obligations arising under the E.C. Treaty; fourthly, by section 3, it requires all national courts and tribunals to follow decisions of the European courts on questions of E.C. law where those questions are not referred to the ECJ under the E.C. Treaty; and fifthly, it seeks to provide that applicable E.C. laws have a measure of supremacy in the laws of the United Kingdom and, in particular, are protected from the doctrine of implied repeal.[97] In regard to the first point—that is, the definition of E.C. law—

---

[93] See para. 5–29 above.

[94] See s. 29 of the Scotland Act 1998.

[95] *cf. Dalgleish v. Glasgow Corporation*, 1976 S.C. 32, especially *per* Lord Justice Clerk Wheatley at 51–52.

[96] See, for example, Case 197/86 *Brown v. Secretary of State for Scotland* [1988] E.C.R. 3205; Case C–394/96 *Brown v. Rentokil Ltd* [1998] All E.R. (E.C.) 791; and *Litster v. Forth Dry Dock and Engineering Ltd* [1990] 1 A.C. 546. For discussion of some of the Scottish cases which have raised points of E.C. law, see Lord Clyde, "Scottish Cases and European Decision-making", Chap. 1 in Campbell and Voyatzi, *Legal Reasoning and Judicial Interpretation of European Law* (Trenton Publishing, 1996).

[97] For discussion of the effects of the 1972 Act in U.K. law, see Collins, *European Community Law in the U.K.* (5th ed., Butterworths, 1997). See also Mitchell, Kuipers and Gall, "Constitutional Aspects of the Treaty and Legislation relating to British Membership" (1972) 9 C.M.L.R. 134 (arguing that the 1972 Act delivers the supremacy of E.C. law over all inconsistent U.K. law, including Acts of Parliament).

it must be stressed that the 1972 Act, as amended,[98] effectively draws a distinction between E.C. law and E.U. law,[99] in so far as the latter is understood as referring to the Treaty on European Union (TEU) beyond the provision it makes for amendment of the E.C. Treaty. For the purposes of the 1972 Act, section 1(2) gives effect to the law contained in and arising under "the Community treaties" as defined. A close reading of this definition reveals that the second and third pillars of the TEU and any measures arising under them are not given effect in U.K. law by the operative provisions of the 1972 Act. Whatever may be thought about the requirements of membership of the European Union, domestic effect for the second and third pillars of the TEU and anything done under them does not flow from sections 1(2) and 2 of the 1972 Act but must depend on further specific enactment. Furthermore, it should not be thought that the 1972 Act implements all of E.C. law in the laws of the United Kingdom. Rather, section 2(1) of the Act only gives direct domestic effect to E.C. law which is directly applicable or has direct effect.[1] As has been noted elsewhere,[2] however, the increasing scope which E.C. directives have in national law operates to reduce the significance of this qualification.

The supremacy of E.C. law in the United Kingdom

5.49   Section 2(1) of the 1972 Act provides:

> "All such rights, powers, liabilities, obligations and restrictions from time to time created or arising by or under the Treaties, and all such remedies and procedures from time to time provided for by or under the Treaties, as in accordance with the Treaties, are without further enactment to be given legal effect or used in the U.K., shall be recognised and available in law, and be enforced, allowed and followed accordingly . . . "

This extensive implementation of E.C. law is then supported by sections 2(4) and 3 of the 1972 Act. Dealing first with section 3, it provides that for the purposes of "all legal proceedings", all questions of E.C. law, where they are not referred to the ECJ, are to be determined as questions of law in accordance with decisions of the ECJ and CFI. Where questions of E.C. law are referred to the ECJ under Article 234 E.C., the decision of the ECJ on the point of E.C. law referred will clearly also be binding on the referring national court or tribunal. In effect, therefore, decisions of the European courts on questions concerning the meaning and effect of E.C. law form binding precedents within the U.K. legal systems. Turning to section 2(4) of the Act, it provides in relevant part that: "any enactment passed or to be passed, other than one contained in this Part of this Act, shall be construed and have effect subject to the foregoing provisions of this section". Section 2(4) expresses the historic compromise which the U.K. Parliament accepted between its own and the E.C. Treaty's supremacy. For a variety of theoretical and political reasons, a straightforward provision for the

---

[98] By the European Communities (Amendment) Acts of 1987, 1993 and 1998.

[99] This distinction is discussed above at para. 5.05.

[1] But see *Re Westinghouse Uranium Contract* [1978] A.C. 547 at 564 *per* Lord Denning M.R.

[2] See para. 5.30.

supremacy of E.C. law over Acts of the U.K. Parliament was not practical. The orthodox approach to the supremacy of Parliament means that no Parliament can bind its successors; any attempt by Parliament to do so would be ineffective, so that the most that could be secured is an attempt to protect all E.C. law from the doctrine of implied repeal by subsequent Acts of Parliament. In practical terms, the implications of section 2(4) were left by Parliament to be worked out in the courts.[3] Now although section 2(4) certainly offers some scope for legal argument about what its terms mean—for example, what is meant by "enactment" and what effect is to be attributed to the phrase in parenthesis,[4]—and although earlier cases canvassed different views on the effect of section 2(4),[5] for all practical purposes it is now apparent that the effect of section 2(4) combined with section 2(1) and section 3 of the 1972 Act is to accord supremacy in the laws of the United Kingdom to applicable E.C. law over all inconsistent law, including provisions in subsequent Acts of the U.K. Parliament. In its landmark decision in *R. v. Secretary of State for Transport, ex parte Factortame Ltd (No. 2)*,[6] the House of Lords disapplied provisions in the Merchant Shipping Act 1988 which were inconsistent with directly effective provisions in the E.C. Treaty. Lord Bridge of Harwich said:

> "Some public comments on the decision of the Court of Justice, affirming the jurisdiction of the courts of member states to override national legislation if necessary to enable interim relief to be granted in protection of rights under Community law, have suggested that this was a novel and dangerous invasion by a Community institution of the sovereignty of the UK Parliament. But such comments are based on a misconception. If the supremacy within the EC of Community law over the national law of member states was not always inherent in the EEC Treaty it was certainly well established in the jurisprudence of the Court of Justice long before the UK joined the Community. Thus, whatever limitation of its sovereignty Parliament accepted when it enacted the European Communities Act 1972 was entirely voluntary. Under the terms of the 1972 Act it has always been clear that it was the duty of a UK court, when delivering final judgment, to override any rule of national law found to be in conflict with any directly enforceable rule of Community law".[7]

In *R. v. Secretary of State for Employment, ex p. EOC*,[8] the House of Lords clarified the remedy which is available in judicial review where it is shown that a provision in an Act of the U.K. Parliament is inconsistent with "directly enforceable" E.C. law, in this case comprising both

---

[3] See Winterton, "The British Grundnorm: Parliamentary Supremacy Re-Examined" (1976) 92 L.Q.R. 591.

[4] See Thomson, "The Supremacy of European Community Law?", 1976 S.L.T. (News) 273 (suggesting that "enactment" is limited to delegated legislation). As to the phrase "other than one contained in this part of this Act", does it mean that ss. 1–4 of the 1972 Act are themselves not to be construed and have effect subject to E.C. law?

[5] See, for example, *Felixstowe Dock and Railways Co. v. BTDB* [1976] 2 C.M.L.R. 655; *Shields v. E Coomes (Holdings) Ltd* [1978] 1 W.L.R. 1408; *Macarthys v. Smith* [1979] 1 W.L.R. 1189; and *Garland v. BREL* [1983] 2 A.C. 751.

[6] [1991] 1 A.C. 603.

[7] *ibid*. at 658–659.

[8] [1995] 1 A.C. 1.

Articles in the E.C. Treaty and provisions in directives with direct effect. In such a case, the proper course is to issue a declarator of the inconsistency—what may be termed a declarator of inapplicability. But as Lord Keith of Kinkel indicated, the effect of such a declarator is not to declare provisions in an Act of Parliament invalid for all purposes.[9] Commenting on the effect of the declaration eventually obtained in the *Factortame* case, his Lordship observed: "The effect was that certain provisions of UK primary legislation were held to be invalid in their purported application to nationals of member states of the EC, but without any prerogative order being available to strike down the legislation in question, which of course remained valid as regard nationals of non-member states".[10] Nevertheless, where an individual with standing seeks to rely on "directly enforceable" E.C. law which is inconsistent with provisions in an Act of the U.K. Parliament and the case is properly put,[11] the E.C. law "by virtue of s.2(1) of the Act of 1972 prevails over" the inconsistent Act of Parliament.[12] The duty of the national court is therefore to apply the applicable E.C. law instead of the inconsistent national rules.

It emerges from the decisions in the *Factortame* and *EOC* cases that the courts now accord supremacy to "any directly enforceable" E.C. law over all inconsistent national law, including provisions in Acts of the U.K. Parliament passed after the 1972 Act. While the term "directly enforceable" is broader than "directly applicable" or "directly effective" and encompasses not only provisions of the E.C. Treaty and regulations which create enforceable rights in favour of individuals but also provisions in directives which do so,[13] it must be acknowledged that problems remain concerning the relationship between E.C. directives and inconsistent Acts of the U.K. Parliament.[14] Nevertheless, at least as far as "directly enforceable" E.C. law is concerned, the practical result of the *Factortame* and *EOC* decisions on the effect of the 1972 Act is that if Parliament wishes to legislate inconsistently with such E.C. law, it must expressly provide that provisions in primary legislation are to have effect notwithstanding E.C. law.[15] It may even be arguable that the judicial approach to the 1972 Act effects a "constitutional revolution" which means that Parliament cannot even provide expressly for derogation from E.C. law as long as the United Kingdom remains a member state of the European Union, the only option being repeal of the 1972 Act.[16] In any event, although the *Factortame (No. 2)* decision may leave a variety

---

[9] But see *Hammersmith and Fulham LBC v. Jesuthasan* [1998] I.C.R. 640.

[10] *ibid*. at 27.

[11] That is, where the E.C. law is a treaty Article or a regulation with direct effect, in all cases; but where it is a directive with direct effect, only in cases against the state or an emanation of the state. *cf. R. v. Secretary of State for Employment, ex p. Seymour-Smith* [1997] 1 W.L.R. 473.

[12] *ex p. EOC* [1995] 1 A.C. 1 at 25 *per* Lord Keith of Kinkel. Similarly, where an inconsistency is found between "directly enforceable" E.C. law and subordinate legislation, and the case is properly put, the latter will be quashed as being *ultra vires*.

[13] And arguably beyond the capacity of directives to have direct effect: see para. 5.30 above.

[14] In particular, where the inconsistency arises in cases between two private parties: see para. 5.50 below.

[15] For discussion on the effect of the 1972 Act and the House of Lords decision in *Factortame (No. 2)* on the supremacy of Parliament, see Craig, "United Kingdom Sovereignty after *Factortame*" (1991) 11 *Yearbook of Eur. Law* 221.

[16] See Wade, "Sovereignty—Revolution or Evolution" (1996) 112 L.Q.R. 568; *cf.* Allan, "Parliamentary Sovereignty: Law, Politics, and Revolution" (1997) 113 L.Q.R. 443.

of theoretical questions about the status of the 1972 Act, the powers of the U.K. courts and the ultimate supremacy of the U.K. Parliament outstanding, for practical purposes the supremacy of E.C. law may now be said to be established in the laws of the United Kingdom.[17]

As regards the relationship between provisions in Acts of the Scottish Parliament and applicable E.C. law, matters are more straightforward. Section 29 of the Scotland Act 1998 expressly provides that the Scottish Parliament has no competence to enact laws which are inconsistent with E.C. law.[18] While section 101 of the 1998 Act requires Acts of the Scottish Parliament to be read "as narrowly as is required" to be within competence—that is, in this context to be compatible with E.C. law— where this is impossible, an Act of the Scottish Parliament is "not law" to the extent of its inconsistency with E.C. law.[19] Accordingly, a provision in an Act of the Scottish Parliament which cannot be interpreted consistently with a directive having direct effect, or with any other "directly enforceable" E.C. law, must be "set aside".

Direct effect of E.C. law in the United Kingdom

Section 2(1) of the 1972 Act means that all applicable E.C. law as it **5.50** arises "by or under" the E.C. Treaty has effect in U.K. law "as in accordance with" the E.C. Treaty and "without further enactment". Accordingly, all provisions in E.C. law, including, for example, the E.C. Treaty, regulations and directives, in addition to rules of law emerging from decisions of the ECJ in the exercise of its powers under the E.C. Treaty, have the same effect in the laws of the United Kingdom which they are given by E.C. law. Section 2(1) may therefore be thought sufficient to provide for the direct applicability and direct effect of E.C. law in the United Kingdom.

However, some problems have arisen concerning the effect to be given in U.K. law to directives. On one view the 1972 Act proceeds on a distinction between directly applicable and non-directly applicable E.C. law. While the former has effect in the United Kingdom in accordance with section 2(1) of the 1972 Act, the latter requires to be implemented under the powers conferred by section 2(2) of the Act. Although the terms of section 2(1) are certainly wide enough to give effect to all provisions of E.C. law which have direct effect, including non-directly applicable directives, s.2(4) arguably presents two problems in relation to

---

[17] As noted above (see para. 5.32), the U.K. is not alone in continuing to have constitutional problems with the supremacy of E.C. law. It may, however, be said that the absence of a written constitution means that the same issues do not arise here as, say, in Germany, where the Constitutional Court is concerned to maintain its jurisdiction to uphold the Basic Law. But it might be argued that as a body which in the U.K. derives its authority from statute (namely s. 3 of the 1972 Act), the ECJ is subject to the rationale of *Anisminic v. Foreign Compensation Commission* [1969] 2 A.C. 147 just as is any other statutory decision-maker. Thus, it is theoretically possible for the House of Lords to conclude that the ECJ has "asked itself the wrong question" and thereby made a jurisdictional error of law so as to give itself jurisdiction where it has none. In other words, there could be a theoretical *Kompetenz-Kompetenz* problem in the U.K. similar to that which exists in Germany. For further discussion of the implications of the supremacy of E.C. law in the U.K. see Craig, "Report from the U.K.", Chap. 7 in Slaughter, Sweet and Weiler, *The European Courts and National Courts* (Hart Publishing, Oxford, 1997).

[18] That is, E.C. law which has the force of law in the U.K. in terms of the European Communities Act 1972, as amended.

[19] See further, para. 7.21. Section 57(2) of the 1998 Act also provides that the Scottish Executive has no power to do any act which is incompatible with E.C. law.

directives. First, once directives are implemented properly into U.K. law, it is not clear that the rule of interpretation in section 2(4) requires all national law to be construed in accordance with the implementing national measure.[20] While the obligation to interpret the implementing measure itself consistently with the directive it purports to implement follows from the presumption of legislative compliance with international obligations, section 2(4) only provides a more general rule of interpretation by reference to section 2(1) of the 1972 Act. That is, section 2(4) only requires all enactments passed and to be passed to be construed and have effect in accordance with directly applicable E.C. law. This includes neither directives nor implementing enactments. But it may be that the effect of the compliance presumption can be understood more widely, to the effect that all ambiguous national legislation is to be construed consistently with all directives,[21] or alternatively that section 2(1) is to be understood more broadly as giving effect to all applicable E.C. law, including directives in so far as they have direct effect. In either way, the rule of interpretation established by section 2(4) can be given broader effect. In turn, however, this reveals a second problem. While the effect of directives with direct effect is clear in cases against the state or its emanations, and follows from section 2(1) of the 1972 Act, matters are less clear in the United Kingdom in cases in which directives have no, or no relevant, direct effect. Here, the obligation on national courts is to interpret all national law in accordance with directives (*a fortiori* where a directive is not implemented at all) in all cases which arise before them. This obligation emerges from decisions of the ECJ interpreting Articles 10 and 249 of the E.C. Treaty,[22] and applies in U.K. law in terms of sections 2(1) and 3 of the 1972 Act. But to what extent is a national court obliged to interpret inconsistent national legislation in accordance with directives where they do not have direct effect, that is, where the directive does not operate directly in national law by virtue of section 2(1) of the 1972 Act, for example, in cases between two private parties? Does the obligation only require ambiguous implementing legislation to be construed consistently with the directive, or does it require all national law to be construed consistently, even national legislation predating the directive[23]; does the obligation only apply where the directive has direct effect, albeit not relevant direct effect, or more generally for all directives; and to what extent is a national court, in pursuit of possible consistent interpretations, to interpret national law *contra legem*?[24] Whatever may be the device by which U.K. courts deal with the difficulties, there can be no doubt that E.C. law imposes an obligation on national courts to give effect to directives over and above inconsistent national law in all cases.[25]

---

[20] See Bates, "The Impact of Directives on Statutory Interpretation: Using the Euro-Meaning?" (1986) Stat.L.R. 174.

[21] *cf. Garland v. BREL* [1983] 2 A.C. 751, *per* Lord Diplock at 171.

[22] See para. 5.30, above. The obligation emerges most clearly in the ECJ's decisions in Case 14/83 *Von Colson v. Land Nordrhein-Westfalen* [1984] E.C.R. 1891 and Case C–106/89 *Marleasing v. La Comercial Internacional de Alimentación SA* [1990] E.C.R. I-4135.

[23] *cf.* Lord Slynn of Hadley, *Introducing a European Legal Order* (1991 Hamlyn Lectures; Stevens) at p. 124.

[24] See *Duke v. GEC Reliance Ltd* [1988] A.C. 618; and *Pickstone v. Freemans* [1989] A.C. 66. The ECJ has arguably suggested that a national court may have to interpret national legislation *contra legem* in order to achieve consistency between directives and national legislation, see Beltem, "The Principle of Indirect Effect of Community Law" (1995) 3 E.R.P.L. 1; *cf.* Case C–300/95 *Commission v. U.K.* [1997] E.C.R. I-2649.

[25] See para. 5.30 above.

In practice, the courts have accepted this obligation and striven to give effect to directives in national law.[26] In the end, however, where the court is unable to give effect to a directive, the appropriate course may be for individuals caused loss by the state's failure to implement or properly implement a directive to sue the state for compensation.[27]

The remedy of damages for violation of E.C. law in the United Kingdom

In its decision in *Francovich v. Italy*,[28] the ECJ ruled that the remedy of damages arising from losses caused by a member state's breach of E.C. law is to be provided "in accordance with the rules of national law on liability": "it is a matter for the internal legal order of each Member state to determine the competent courts and lay down the detailed procedural rules for [the] legal proceedings".[29] As long as the national law which provides for the E.C. law damages remedy complies with the general E.C. law requirement on effective remedies, namely equivalance and full effectiveness,[30] the detailed procedural issues are left for national law. In the United Kingdom, where there is traditionally no separate provision for state liability beyond that which arises from the ordinary law, this means that the *Francovich* damages remedy has to be fitted into a species of delictual liability. Although in the period before *Francovich* the English courts had rejected breach of statutory duty as a basis for state liability for violation of the E.C. Treaty,[31] following *Francovich* several commentators suggested that if breach of statutory duty was not the appropriate basis, then the liability would have to regarded as *sui generis*.[32] In any event, whatever may be the proper pigeon hole for the liability, recent case law confirms that a violation of the E.C. Treaty by the state, including by virtue of provisions in Acts of Parliament, gives rise to damages liability to those caused loss by the violation.[33]

Of course, several questions remain. For example, there are a variety of different situations in which state liability for breach of E.C. law can

5.51

---

[26] See *Litster v. Forth Dry Dock Co.*, 1989 S.C.(H.L.) 96; and *Webb v. EMO Cargo* [1993] 1 W.L.R. 49. For discussion, see Craig, "Indirect Effect of Directives in the Application of National Legislation", Chap. 3 in Andenas and Jacobs (eds), *E.C. Law in the English Courts* (OUP, Oxford, 1998).

[27] In particular, the House of Lords in England has held that the courts have no power to order the government by means of the prerogative order of *mandamus* to introduce legislation to implement or properly implement E.C. directives: see *R. v. Secretary of State for Employment, ex p. Seymour-Smith* [1997] 1 W.L.R. 473 at 478. *Cf. R. v. H.M. Treasury, ex p. Smedley* [1985] Q.B. 657 (Court of Appeal deciding that it has jurisdiction to grant a Declaration that draft subordinate legislation, if adopted, would violate E.C. law; but equally doubting any power to order Parliament not to consider or enact subordinate legislation).

[28] Cases C–6 & 9/90 *Francovich & Bonifaci v. Italy* [1991] E.C.R. I-5357.

[29] *ibid*. at para. 42.

[30] See para. 5.45 above.

[31] See *Bourgoin SA v. Ministry of Agriculture, Fisheries and Food* [1986] Q.B. 716; but *cf. Garden Cottage Foods v. Milk Marketing Board* [1984] A.C. 130.

[32] See Lewis and Moore, "Duties, Directives, and Damages in E.C. Law" [1993] P.L. 151.

[33] See *R. v. Secretary of State for Transport, ex p. Francovich (No. 5)* [1998] 3 C.M.L.R. 192, CA.

arise.[34] In a simple case, where the violation is alleged to follow from an act or decision of a U.K. government department, that department will be the defender. Where the Scottish Executive is to blame, it will be the appropriate defender. Alternatively, where the problem arises from an Act of the U.K. Parliament, it might first be necessary to have the Act declared inapplicable before questions of damages liability can arise, in which case it may be the U.K. government which will be the defender.[35] And where the problem is a provision in an Act of the Scottish Parliament, it may be the Parliament itself or the Scottish Executive, perhaps as represented by the Lord Advocate, which should be sued.[36] Trickier problems may arise where the breach of E.C. law is a failure to implement a directive, rather than improper implementation. While as a matter of E.C. law this is a state's most egregious breach of the law, it is not clear from the terms of the 1972 Act that a duty, as such, to implement E.C. law exists so that a failure to implement a directive can give rise to a breach of statutory duty.[37] Theoretically, an argument might be formulable to the effect that as long as the United Kingdom remains in the European Union and as long as the 1972 Act remains in force, the Crown's freedom in the field of legislation is circumscribed.[38] That is, in so far as the Crown's granting of Royal Assent to legislation which is in breach of E.C. law may be regarded as an act which violates E.C. law, it may be that the Crown's failure to secure the enactment of legislation which makes U.K. law compatible with E.C. law is an actionable failure to act. Indeed, in so far as the Crown's powers to propose legislation and grant the Royal Assent can be regarded as part of the Royal Prerogative, it is notable that in *Burmah Oil v. Lord Advocate*[39] the House of Lords decided that lawful use of prerogative powers which causes loss to others gives rise to a duty to compensate. This must be all the more so where there is an example of unlawful exercise of prerogative powers. In any event, any theoretical difficulties arising from national constitutional law must yield to the obligation to ensure the full effectiveness of rights conferred by E.C. law. It may be that the preferable general approach is to treat the state's liability arising from *Francovich* as a *sui generis* liability.[40]

---

[34] For discussion, see Lewis, *Remedies and the Enforcement of European Community Law* (Sweet & Maxwell, London, 1996), pp. 60–70. See also Lewis, "Damages and the Right to an Effective Remedy for Breach of EC Law", in Forsyth and Hare (eds), *The Golden Metwand and the Crooked Cord* (OUP, Oxford, 1998); Convery, "State Liability in the United Kingdom After Brasserie du Pêcheur" (1997) 34 C.M.L.R. 603; and Upton, "Crown liability in damages under Community Law", 1996 S.L.T. (News) 211.

[35] *cf. Kirkless B.C. v. Wickes Building Supplies* [1993] A.C. 227 *per* Lord Goff of Chieveley at 282; and *Factortame (No. 5)*, above.

[36] *cf.* s. 40 of the Scotland Act 1998.

[37] Consider, for example, the terms of s. 2(2) of the 1972 Act. Clearly, however, a duty to implement E.C. directives arises under the E.C. Treaty; accordingly, a statutory duty may be said to arise in terms of s. 2(1) of the Act.

[38] An approach that might build on *Att.-Gen. v. De Keyser's Royal Hotel* [1920] A.C. 508 and *R. v. Secretary of State for the Home Department, ex p. Fire Brigades Union* [1995] 2 A.C. 513.

[39] 1965 S.C. (H.L.) 117.

[40] For a broader analysis of the effect of E.C. law on civil remedies, see Brealey and Hoskins, *Remedies in E.C. law* (2nd ed., 1997); and D'Sa, *E.C. Law and Civil Remedies in England and Wales* (Sweet & Maxwell, London, 1994).

VIII E.C. LAW AND JUDICIAL REVIEW

European courts and national courts

There are no courts in the member states with exclusive jurisdiction over   **5.52**
cases raising E.C. law points. Unlike in, for example, Australia and the
United States of America, there is no separate system of federal or E.C.
courts in the European Union. Responsibility for interpreting and
applying E.C. law in the member states primarily rests with the ordinary
courts having jurisdiction in each member state according to national
law.[41] Since E.C. law often creates rights and duties which are enforceable in the national legal systems, many cases before national courts,
including judicial review cases, will necessarily involve giving effect to
E.C. law.[42] It follows, therefore, that the European Court of Justice
(ECJ) and the Court of First Instance (CFI) do not have jurisdiction
over all cases that involve E.C. law. As regards the administration of the
law in the European Union, it can be said that there is a high degree of
decentralisation.[43] What in other systems is sometimes termed "judicial
federalism" in the European Union means that most cases involving
E.C. law will be dealt with not by the European courts but by the
ordinary courts in the member states.[44] However, not all cases involving
E.C. law can be brought before national courts. For example, direct
actions under Article 230 (formerly 173) E.C. against an E.U. institution
must be brought before the European courts, in cases raised by an
individual, before the CFI. Furthermore, a key procedure is provided by
Article 234 (formerly 177) E.C. under which uniform interpretations of
E.C. law can be secured, albeit only on the initiative of national courts.[45]
This procedure is known as the preliminary ruling procedure under
which any national court or tribunal may and, subject to the E.C. law
doctrine of *acte clair*, all national courts of final appeal must, refer to the
ECJ points of E.C. law arising for decision in cases before them. The
ECJ's ruling on the point of E.C. law referred must be applied by the
national court and more generally constitutes a precedent binding on all
national courts and tribunals faced with the same point of E.C. law. It

---

[41] Albeit that national laws may be subject to some qualification from E.C. law, for
example, in the interests of ensuring the full effectiveness of E.C. law: see para. 5.45 above.
[42] For an instructive example of the interaction of national law and E.C. law in judicial
review, see *R. v. Human Fertilisation and Embryology Authority, ex p. Blood* [1997] 2 W.L.R.
806. *Cf. Kincardine and Deeside D.C. v. Forestry Commissioners*, 1992 S.L.T. 1180.
[43] The importance of national courts in giving effect to E.C. law may be regarded as an
implementation of the principle of subsidiarity, respect for which is one of the E.U.'s
constitutional fundamentals. Indeed, decentralisation is evident in several areas of the
administration of E.C. law. Consider, for example, the *Commission Notice on Co-operation
between National Courts and the Commission in Applying Arts 85 and 86 of the EC Treaty*,
O.J. 1993 C39/6; *cf.* Case T–24/90 *Automec v. Commission (No. 2)* [1992] E.C.R. II-2223.
See also *Commission Notice on Co-operation between the National Competition Authorities
and the Commission*, O.J. 1997 C313/3. For discussion, see Rhone (1998) 2 Edin.L.R. 345.
[44] But as E.C. law grows ever more voluminous, it may be that consideration will have to
be given to a new system of E.C. courts or a new relationship between national courts and
European courts. In the U.S., for example, the Constitution's original design gave pre-
eminence to state courts; but as the volume of federal law grew, more federal courts were
required and greater federal jurisdiction had to be conferred. For a discussion of the
E.U.'s existing judicial architechture and possible reforms of the structure including, for
example, a system of E.C. regional courts with the ECJ at the apex, see *The Role and
Future of the European Court of Justice* (British Institute of International and Comparative
Law: 1996).
[45] See further paras 5.55 *et seq.* below.

follows that the E.C. Treaty envisages a division of responsibility between the European courts and national courts in which the preliminary ruling procedure provides the crucial link.

Very basically, and subject to the Article 234 E.C. preliminary ruling procedure, national courts have a general jurisdiction over all cases involving E.C. law which properly come before them according to national law, whereas the ECJ (and CFI) have jurisdiction only over those cases given to them by the E.C. Treaty. While the jurisdiction of the ECJ and CFI is sometimes exclusive, for example, only the European courts can rule definitively on the validity of E.C. legislation, it can be said that even in respect of judicial review of the legality of E.C. measures, the jurisdiction of national courts is complementary. The grounds of jurisdiction which provide most of the European courts' work are direct actions and preliminary rulings. Both these types of case have their own detailed rules and a substantial body of case law has been built up on them. While national law obviously deals with threshold matters such as standing in cases which are referred by a national court to the ECJ,[46] in direct actions the relevant rules are set out in the E.C. Treaty and in greater, if not always lucid, detail in ECJ decisions. The purpose of this part of the Chapter is to identify the role which judicial review before national courts has in giving effect to E.C. law and to outline briefly the preliminary ruling procedure as it bears on judicial review. The subject of direct actions is dealt with in the following part.

Judicial review of E.C. measures before national courts

5.53　It may be noted that the E.U. institutions have no general immunity from proceedings in national courts.[47] However, where the E.C. Treaty confers jurisdiction on the ECJ and CFI, cases involving the institutions in respect of that jurisdiction must be taken to the European courts. Nevertheless, the division of responsibility between the European courts and national courts, taken with the restrictive admissibility and standing rules associated with Article 230 E.C.,[48] means that challenges to the legality of E.C. measures may arise before national courts.[49] Such challenges may be made before the Court of Session in judicial review proceedings. In such cases, it is clear from ECJ decisions,[50] whatever some national constitutional courts might think,[51] that the only grounds on which the validity of E.C. measures may be challenged are the grounds which are specified in E.C. law, notably in terms of Article 230 E.C. and in terms of the general principles of law. While a national court may consider a challenge to E.C. legislation and conclude that the

---

[46] But possibly with some E.C. law control, *e.g.* to ensure that national laws, in particular procedural rules, do not frustrate the "full effectiveness" of rights arising under E.C. law. See para. 5.45 above.

[47] In terms of the Protocol to the E.C. Treaty on the Institutions' Privileges and Immunities, they only have immunity from proceedings before national courts in respect of some defined matters; for example, the assets of the Commission cannot be attached. *Cf. Philipp Brothers v. Republic of Sierra Leone & E.C. Commission* [1995] 1 Lloyd's Reps 289; *R. v. Crown Court of Manchester, ex p. Huckfield* [1993] 1 W.L.R. 1524.

[48] See paras 5.64 *et seq.* below.

[49] For a recent example, see *R. v. Secretary of State for Health, ex p. Imperial Tobacco Ltd* [1999] C.O.D. 138.

[50] See Case 11/70 *Internationale Handelsgesellschaft mbH v. Einfuhr-und Vorratstelle für Getreide und Futtermittel* [1970] E.C.R. 1125; [1972] C.M.L.R. 255; and Case C–68/95 *T. Port GmbH v. Bundesanstalt für Landwirtschaft und Ernahrung* [1997] 1 C.M.L.R. 1.

[51] See para. 5.32 above.

legislation is valid, where a national court considers that there are serious grounds for suspecting the invalidity of E.C. legislation by reference to the rules and principles of E.C. law, it has no power itself to declare the E.C. legislation invalid.[52] Rather, it must refer questions about the possible invalidity of E.C. legislation to the ECJ under Article 234 E.C. and in the meantime exercise a discretion whether or not to supend the operation of the measure, or any national measure implementing it, pending the decision of the ECJ.[53] If the ECJ invalidates the E.C. legislation in the course of an Article 234 E.C. reference, it is clear that this decision has the effect of quashing the E.C. legislation and that the ECJ's decision in this regard is binding on all national courts.[54]

Given that an individual may challenge the validity of E.C. legislation either before a national court, most likely by means of judicial review, or before the European courts by means of a direct action under Article 230 E.C. in the CFI, the question arises as to how to decide which course to take.[55] The factors to be considered basically arise out of the terms and jurisprudence of Article 230 E.C.[56] These include the nature of the E.C. legislation challenged, by whom the challenge is raised, and the strict two-month time-limit within which an action under Article 230 E.C. must be commenced. It may also be suggested that practical considerations, such as expense and access to Luxembourg, are relevant. Be that as it may, it is clear that the ECJ is unhappy with the prospect of unrestricted challenges to the validity of E.C. measures before national courts.[57] The ECJ is understandably concerned that encouraging such challenges will undermine the need for legal certainty which lies behind the two-month time-limit and other restrictions built into the Article 230 E.C. procedure. Since a challenge to the validity of E.C. legislation brought before a national court will (if the national court considers that it is based on serious grounds) have to be referred to the ECJ, that Court will be able to assess the challenge and refuse to entertain it if it amounts to an abuse of process. Clearly, therefore, where a national court faces a challenge to an E.C. measure it should consider not only how serious the grounds for challenge are, but also the reasons why the matter was not taken directly to the CFI under Article 230 E.C. The position seems to be that those who clearly do have standing under

---

[52] Case 314/85 *Foto-Frost v. Hauptzollamt Lubeck-Ost* [1987] E.C.R. 4199.

[53] See Cases 143/88 and C–92/89 *Zuckerfabriken Suderdithmarschen und Soest v. Hauptzollamter Itzehoe und Paderborn* [1991] E.C.R. I-415; and Case C–465/93 *Atlanta Fruchthandelsgesellschaft mbH v. Bundesamt fur Ernahrung and Forstwirtschaft* [1995] E.C.R. I-3761.

[54] But the ECJ may vary the retrospective effects of any decision invalidating an E.C. measure: see para. 5.60 below.

[55] For discussion see Beloff, "Giving Effect to Community Law", Chap. 2 in Andenas and Jacobs (eds), *E.C. Law in the English Courts* (OUP, Oxford, 1989).

[56] Art. 230 E.C. is considered further at para. 5.64 below.

[57] See Case C–188/92 *TWD Textilwerke Deggendorf GmbH v. Germany* [1994] E.C.R. I-833, deciding that the ECJ will not allow an E.C. measure to be invalidated in a reference from a national court where one of the parties to the national proceedings had standing under Article 230 E.C. but did not avail of it within the two month time limit. Professor Wyatt, Q.C. argues that the decision does not establish a general principle but is focused on preventing abuse of process and prejudice to third parties and the public interest in particular types of cases (for example, state aid cases such as TWD itself concerned): "The Relationship between Actions for Annulment and References on Validity After TWD Deggendorf", Chap. 6 in Lonbay & Biondi, *Remedies For Breach of E.C. Law* (John Wiley & Sons, Chichester, 1997). See also Case C–241/95 *R. v. Intervention Board for Agricultural Produce, ex p. Accrington Beef* [1997] 1 C.M.L.R. 675.

Article 230 E.C. must proceed under that Article directly before the CFI. In other cases, proceedings may be launched before the national court or simultaneously before both the national court and the CFI.[58]

Judicial review of national measures on E.C. law grounds

5.54 The leading circumstances in which E.C. law issues can arise in judicial review are outlined at the beginning of this chapter.[59] As was noted, the supervisory jurisdiction does not have a monopoly over E.C. law issues. Indeed, the pervasive scope of E.C. law means that the majority of cases raising E.C. law will not arise in judicial review. Equally, however, the implications of the direct effect and supremacy of E.C. law mean that courts in many types of cases will be required to assess the consistency of national law with E.C. law. This task amounts to a form of constitutional judicial review and it is likely that the most notable cases in which national measures are challenged on the grounds of inconsistency with E.C. law will arise under the supervisory jurisdiction.[60]

While a challenge to the validity of E.C. legislation can only be made on grounds available in E.C. law and must, if the national court considers the challenge serious, be referred to the ECJ, it may be asked whether the validity of a national measure which implements an E.C. measure is also only challengeable on grounds available in E.C. law, or whether the validity of the national measure is also open to challenge on grounds which are only available in national law, such as, for example, irrationality or Convention rights.[61] On the one hand, it must be that a U.K. court has jurisdiction to ensure that the restrictions imposed on the power to make delegated legislation under section 2(2) of the European Communities Act 1972 are respected.[62] Equally, constitutional courts in some member states (notably Germany) have held that E.C. measures (or at least national measures implementing them) are reviewable on grounds available in national law.[63] On the other hand, if implementing national measures are reviewable on grounds available only in national law, there is a danger that differences between the constitutional and administrative laws of the member states will upset the uniform application of the E.C. legislation on which the national measure proceeds. But "choice of law" difficulties between E.C. law and national law in this regard may not be so severe: first, the grounds of review in E.C. law are influencing (and being influenced by) national law; and secondly, most defects in national implementing measures may be traceable back to the E.C. measure itself, so that questions about the latter's validity must be referred to the ECJ. In any event, the ECJ has decided that it is also competent in an Article 234 E.C. preliminary ruling to rule on the meaning of national measures based on E.C. legislation.[64] Accordingly, a

---

[58] *cf.* Beloff, *supra* at p. 24; and see *R. v. Ministry of Agriculture, Fisheries and Food, ex p. National Farmers Union* [1998] 2 C.M.L.R. 1125.

[59] See para. 5.02.

[60] *cf. R. v. Secretary of State for Transport, ex p. Factortame Ltd (No. 2)* [1991] 1 A.C. 603; and *R. v. Secretary of State for Employment, ex p. EOC* [1995] 1 A.C. 1.

[61] *cf.* Case C-212/91 *Angelopharm v. Hamburg* [1994] E.C.R. I-171; and see also *R. v. MAFF, ex p. Bell Lines* [1984] 2 C.M.L.R. 502.

[62] *cf. Hayward v. Cammell Laird Shipbuilders (No. 2)* [1988] A.C. 894, *per* Lord Mackay L.C. at 903; and see de Smith, Woolf and Jowell, *Judicial Review of Administrative Action* (5th ed., 1995), pp. 862–864.

[63] See para. 5.32 above.

[64] See Case C-28/95 *Leur Bloem v. Inspecteur Der Balastingdienst Ondernenemingen Amsterdam 2* [1998] 2 W.L.R. 27.

question about the validity of an implementing national measure in terms of E.C. law may be referred to the ECJ.

As was noted above,[65] it is also clear that national measures which "fall within the scope of E.C. law" are challengeable for consistency with the general principles of E.C. law. Accordingly, where national rules and measures do come within the scope of E.C. law, the grounds available to challenge them must at least include the general principles of E.C. law, such as the principle of proportionality and fundamental rights as guaranteed in E.C. law.[66]

The preliminary ruling procedure

The jurisdiction of ECJ under Article 234 (formerly 177) E.C. to provide 5.55 preliminary rulings on points of E.C. law arising in cases referred from national courts and tribunals is of great importance to the European Community's legal order. It provides the largest number of cases which come before the ECJ. From the point of view of national courts it is the most significant aspect of the ECJ's jurisdiction.[67] Article 234 E.C. provides:

"The Court of Justice shall have jurisdiction to give preliminary rulings concerning:

(a) the interpretation of this Treaty;
(b) the validity and interpretation of acts of the institutions of the Community and of the ECB;
(c) the interpretation of the statutes of bodies established by an act of the Council, where those statutes so provide.

Where such a question is raised before any court or tribunal of a Member State, that court or tribunal may, if it considers that a decision on the question is necessary to enable it to give judgment, request the Court of Justice to give a ruling thereon.

Where any such question is raised in a case pending before a court or tribunal of a Member State against whose decisions there is no judicial remedy under national law, that court or tribunal shall bring the matter before the Court of Justice."

Article 234 has provided the jurisdictional basis of most of the Court's decisions on the constitutional relationship between E.C. law and

---

[65] See para. 5.40.

[66] *cf. Booker Aquaculture v. Secretary of State for Scotland* [1999] 1 C.M.L.R. 35.

[67] One of the leading works in the U.K. on the preliminary ruling procedure is Anderson, *References to the European Court* (Sweet & Maxwell, London, 1995). See also Lewis, *Remedies and the Enforcement of E.C. Law* (Sweet and Maxwell, London, 1996), Chap. 11; and Edward, *Article 177 References to the European Court—Policy and Practice* (Butterworths, London, 1994). The ECJ has also been given an equivalent jurisdiction under other European Communities treaties, for example, the ECSC Treaty, and under other E.C. related Conventions, most notably the Brussels Convention on Jurisdiction and Recognition and Enforcement of Judgments and the Rome Contracts Convention. But the details of the jurisdiction vary depending on its source; for example, under the Brussels Convention only appeal courts can make references whereas under the E.C. Treaty any court or tribunal can make a reference. The present discussion focuses only on the ECJ's jurisdiction under the E.C. Treaty. For discussion on the procedure under other treaties, see Anton & Beaumont, *Private International Law* (2nd ed., SULI & W. Green & Sons, Edinburgh, 1990).

national law.[68] In light of its significant constitutional implications, the jurisdiction of the ECJ to give preliminary rulings on points of E.C. law is exclusive to the ECJ. The procedure highlights the dual nature of the institutional relationships in the European Community, namely, the European and the national, with the E.C. Treaty conferring the jurisdiction on the ECJ to make final interpretations of E.C. law to enable the law to apply uniformly in all the member states, but giving the national courts the gatekeeper role of deciding which points of E.C. law to refer to the ECJ. For various reasons, including the volume of references which the ECJ has received from national courts, the ECJ has itself reinforced the dual nature of the procedure. The Court has simultaneously underlined the supremacy of E.C. law and asserted the duties of national courts to refer while accepting and clarifying the discretion of national courts, including those of final appeal, to decide not to refer and instead decide points of E.C. law for themselves. But this discretion to make references cannot be understood without noticing other lines in the ECJ's jurisprudence, especially decisions interpreting Article 10 (formerly 5) E.C., which oblige all national courts to ensure full effectiveness of E.C. law rights irrespective of inconsistent national law. In effect these decisions make all national courts Community courts, thereby binding them to recognise the supremacy of E.C. law and to give effect directly in the national legal systems to all the rights and remedies E.C. law creates. In short, national courts' discretion to refer points of law to the ECJ does not detract from their obligations to apply E.C. law as the supreme law in the legal system. More generally, it is often said that the Article 234 E.C. procedure entails a dialogue between the ECJ and national courts. The procedure: "is based on co-operation which entails a division of duties between national courts and the ECJ in the interest of the proper application and uniform interpretation of Community law throughout all the member states".[69]

Article 234 of the E.C. Treaty has relevance for judicial review in various respects. In general, in any judicial review case in which a point of E.C. law arises it may be necessary for the national court to refer the point to the ECJ. Where, for example, the case turns on the meaning of E.C. legislation, it may be necessary to obtain the ECJ's ruling on the interpretation to be given to the legislation. Alternatively, if a case turns on whether a provision in E.C. legislation has direct effect, only the ECJ can rule on this matter. More specifically, where a challenge is made to the validity of E.C. legislation in a case before a national court, the matter will have to be referred to the ECJ if the national court suspects that the legislation is invalid, since only the ECJ has the power to invalidate E.C. legislation. For these reasons, it is necessary to say a little more about the preliminary ruling procedure established by Article 234 E.C. In particular, four matters should be considered: first, what issues can be referred to the ECJ; secondly, which bodies can make references to the ECJ; thirdly, when do references to the ECJ have to be made; and fourthly, what effect does the ECJ's decision on the reference have in national and E.C. law.

---

[68] For example, the ECJ's decisions in Case 26/62 *Van Gend en Loos* [1963] E.C.R. 1; Case 6/64 *Costa v. ENEL* [1964] E.C.R. 585; Case 106/77 *Simmenthal* [1978] E.C.R. 629; Case 152/84 *Marshall v. Southampton and South-West Hampshire Area Health Authority (No. 1)* [1986] E.C.R. 723; Case C–213/89 *R. v. Secretary of State for Transport, ex p. Factortame* [1990] E.C.R. I-2433; and Cases C–6 & 9/90 *Francovich v. Italy* [1991] E.C.R. I-5357.

[69] Case 244/80 *Foglia v. Novello (No. 2)* [1981] E.C.R. 3045 at para. 14.

What can be referred?

Article 234(1) is reasonably clear about what matters may be referred to **5.56**
the ECJ. Most significantly, these include questions concerning the
interpretation of the E.C. Treaty and questions concerning "the validity
and interpretation" of E.C. legislation and other acts of the institutions.
As noted above,[70] only the ECJ can rule definitively on the invalidity of
E.C. legislation. A national court which considers that E.C. legislation
may be invalid must refer this point to the ECJ. Questions arising under
the ECSC and EURATOM Treaties are governed by broadly similar
provisions in those treaties.[71] Questions concerning the interpretation of
the Treaty on European Union are, in general, not covered by Article
234 EC.[72] It is important to note that only questions of E.C. law may be
referred. That is, the preliminary ruling procedure does not enable the
ECJ to rule directly on the compatibility of national laws with E.C. law,[73]
nor on the acts and decisions of the member states outside the sphere of
E.C. law.[74] The distinction between interpretation of E.C. law and
application of the law to the instant case must be kept in mind: the
responsibility of the ECJ is to give final decisions on the meaning of E.C.
law, while it is for the national courts to apply the ECJ's ruling and other
case law to the facts of the case before them.[75]

It is for the national court to formulate the questions to be referred to
the ECJ. Although the ECJ may re-formulate the questions and will
invariably only answer those which it considers arise for decision in the
case referred, the Court only rarely refuses to accept a reference from a
national court.[76] So far, the ECJ has only refused to accept a reference
where no genuine dispute is disclosed by the case referred, where not
enough information has been provided to the Court, where the reference

---

[70] See para. 5.53.

[71] See ECSC Treaty, Art. 41; and EURATOM Treaty, Art. 150.

[72] See *Grau Gomis* [1995] I–E.C.R. 1023: the ECJ has no jurisdiction to interpret Art. 2
(formerly B) of the TEU in Art. 234 E.C. proceedings. But in Case C–170/96 *Commission
v. Council* [1998] E.C.R. I-2763, the ECJ made clear that acts and decisions under the
second and third pillars of the TEU may be challenged on the ground that they should
properly have been enacted under the E.C. Treaty. More generally, the ECJ may use TEU
provisions indirectly, for example, to interpret and understand the meaning of provisions
in the E.C. Treaty. Moreover, Art. 46 TEU now confers very limited jurisdiction on the
ECJ over some provisions in the TEU; see also Art. 35 TEU and compare Art. 68 E.C.

[73] See Case C–307/95 *Max Mara* [1995] E.C.R. I-5083. But *cf.* Case C–28/95 *Leur Bloem
v. Inspecteur Der Balastingdienst Ondernenemingen Amsterdam 2* [1998] 2 W.L.R. 27.

[74] See Case 44/86 *Hurd v. Jones* [1986] Q.B. 892: points of interpretation arising from
international treaties concluded by a member state outside the sphere of E.C. law cannot
be referred to the ECJ.

[75] Much is made of this distinction—that it is not for the ECJ to decide whether national
laws are valid or invalid, this decision being for the national court in applying the ECJ's
decision to the case before it. In practice, of course, the ECJ's decision on what E.C. law
means and requires will often to all intents and purposes signal the compatibility or
otherwise of a national law with E.C. law: consider, for example, the decision of the ECJ in
Case C–213/89 *R. v. Secretary of State for Transport, ex p. Factortame* [1990] E.C.R. I-2433
with the decision of the House of Lords following the ECJ's ruling: [1991] 1 A.C. 603. But
compare the experience in the cases on the validity of Sunday closing laws in light of Art.
30 E.C.: see Case 145/88 *Torfaen B.C. v. B & Q plc* [1989] E.C.R. 3851 and Case C–169/91
Stoke-on-Trent City Council v. B & Q plc [1992] E.C.R. I-6635; [1993] A.C. 900.

[76] But see Barnard and Sharpston, "The Changing Face of Art. 177 References" (1997)
34 C.M.L.R. 1113 (a thorough survey noting the increasing examples of the ECJ seeking to
control its jurisdiction under Art. 234 E.C., possibly evidencing the beginnings of docket
control). See also Kennedy, "First Steps Towards a European Certiorari" (1993) 18
Eur.L.R. 121.

was a device to obtain an advisory opinion or a ruling on hypothetical questions, or where accepting the reference would cause the Court to become involved in an abuse of process.[77] So in the case of *Foglia v. Novello*,[78] the ECJ refused to accept a reference from the Italian courts where the parties had apparently contrived a dispute so as to put in issue the compatibility of French legislation with the E.C. Treaty.[79] These cases raise several interesting issues, among them by what standards the ECJ is to assess whether a dispute in a case before a national court is "genuine" and whether or not the Court has competence to rule on the compatibility with E.C. law of rules of law in one member state in a reference made by the courts of another member state. In any event, the cases highlight that the ECJ's tradition of being "in principle, bound to give a ruling",[80] is subject to some, albeit not precisely clear, qualification.[81]

Who can refer

5.57 It is important to note that the ECJ is not a court of appeal on points of E.C. law from national courts. While the wishes of the parties to a national case are significant and should be taken into account by a national court, the decision on whether a point of E.C. law is to be referred to the ECJ is for the national court or tribunal before which the point arises. Article 234 E.C. provides that "courts and tribunals" may refer questions to the ECJ, with only courts and tribunals of final appeal being required to do so. But it is for the ECJ to decide whether a referring body is to be regarded as a court or tribunal for the purposes of Article 234 E.C. Beyond the requirement that the court or tribunal must belong to a member state,[82] the ECJ has said that the criteria indicating whether a body can refer include: "the absence, in practice, of any right of appeal to the ordinary courts . . . [the body operates] with the consent of the public authorities and with their co-operation . . . [and following] an adversarial procedure, [it] delivers decisions which are recognised as

---

[77] See Case 104/79 *Foglia v. Novello (No. 1)* [1980] E.C.R. 745; Case 244/80 *Foglia v. Novello (No. 2)* [1981] E.C.R. 3045 (no genuine dispute and abuse of process); Case 14/86 *Pretore di Salo v. Persons Unknown* [1987] E.C.R. 2545 (questions too general; not enough information for ECJ to give reference); Case C–186/90 *Durighello v. INPA* [1990] I–E.C.R. 5773 (E.C. law not relevant to action); *Meilicke v. ADV/ORGA FA Meyer AG* [1992] I–E.C.R. 4872 (no genuine dispute; case only academic and reference procedure not available where no real case to be decided). For a general discussion by the ECJ of some of the circumstances in which it will not accept a reference for a preliminary ruling, see Case C–343/93 *Lourenco Dias* [1992] E.C.R. I-4673.

[78] Case 104/79 [1980] E.C.R. 745 and Case 244/80 [1981] E.C.R. 3045.

[79] The ECJ's decisions in the *Foglia* cases have been criticised: see *Bebr*, 17 C.M.L.R. 525 and 19 C.M.L.R. 421; but *cf.* Wyatt, "Foglia No. 2: The Court denies it has jurisdiction to give advisory opinions" (1983) 7 Eur.L.R. 186.

[80] Case C–231/89 *Gmurzynska-Bscher v. Oberfinanzdirektion Koln* [1990] E.C.R. I-4003, para. 20.

[81] See further, Craig & de Burca, *EU Law* (2nd ed., OUP, Oxford, 1998), chapter 10; and also Barnard and Sharpston, "The Changing Face of Art. 177 References" (1997) 34 C.M.L.R. 1113.

[82] See Case C–355/89 *DHSS (Isle of Man) v. Barr and Montrose Holdings Ltd* [1991] E.C.R. I-3479 (courts of territories of member states to which not all provisions of the E.C. Treaty apply may make references).

final."[83] Although the nomenclature of national law is not conclusive,[84] it will be rarely that a dispute arises as to whether a national court or tribunal properly so called can make a reference.[85] In particular, a court hearing a judicial review application will be able to make a reference on a point of E.C. law arising before it notwithstanding that in the classical understanding of judicial review in the United Kingdom the court cannot disturb the merits of the challenged decision.[86] More complex issues surround the ability of arbiters to make references. That is, can arbitrations be termed "tribunals" for the purposes of Article 234 E.C.? Although on one view arbitrations operate "with the consent and co-operation" of the State, the ECJ has held that simple arbitrations are not courts or tribunals for the purposes of Article 234 E.C.[87] The ECJ decided in the *Nordsee* case[88] that there may be some types of arbitration which can make references to the ECJ but that in general the basis of arbitrations in law and their similarity with court proceedings were insufficient to allow arbitrations to refer.[89]

When a reference may be made

Article 234 E.C. proceeds on a distinction between courts and tribunals **5.58** of final appeal and other courts and tribunals. According to the literal terms of Article 234, only the former are required to refer points of E.C. law to the ECJ while the latter have a discretion to do so. As will be seen below,[90] the ECJ has clarified that in practice courts and tribunals of final appeal also have a discretion to decide certain points of E.C. law for themselves rather than refer them to the ECJ. As regards all other courts and tribunals, Article 234 means that any national court or tribunal faced with a point of E.C. law arising in a case before it may request a ruling from the ECJ on the point of E.C. law where this is

---

[83] Case 246/80 *C. Broekmeulen v. Huisarts Registratie Commissie* [1981] E.C.R. 2311 (deciding that the Netherlands Appeals Committee for General Medicine, which heard appeals from another body responsible for registering doctors of medicine, both bodies being established and run by a private association, could make references to the ECJ under Art. 234 E.C.).

[84] See Case C–24/92 *Corbiau v. Administration des Contributions* [1993] E.C.R. I-1277.

[85] Rather, problems more often arise with adjudicatory bodies which are less obviously "tribunals": see Case C–416/96 *Nour Eddline El-Yanini v. Secretary of State for the Home Department* [1999] 2 C.M.L.R. 32 (Immigration adjudicator may make a reference to the ECJ under Art. 234 E.C.).

[86] *cf.* Case C–120/97 *Upjohn Ltd v. The Licensing Authority Established by the Medicines Act 1968* [1999] 1 C.M.L.R. 825.

[87] See Case 102/81 *Nordsee Deutsche Hochseefischerei GmbH v. Reederei Mond Hochseefischerei Nordstern AG and Co. KG* [1982] E.C.R. 1095; for critical comment, see Friend (1983) 99 L.Q.R. 356. In this regard, *cf.* the definition of "public authority" in terms of s. 6(3) of the Human Rights Act 1998: does it include arbitrations?

[88] See n. 83 above.

[89] *cf.* Case C–126/97 *Eco Swiss China Time Ltd v. Benetton International NV* [1999] 2 All E.R. (Comm.) 44. The inability of arbiters to make references raises a variety of difficulties: for example, under the New York Convention on the Recognition and Enforcement of Arbitral Awards (1958), all international arbitration awards must be recognised and enforced in the legal systems of the contracting parties to that Convention (which includes all 15 states of the E.U.). A national court faced with an arbitral award rendered in another E.U. member state which is erroneous in point of E.C. law will be faced with a difficult choice between the New York Convention and its obligations under Art. 10 E.C. For discussion of the issues, see Murray, "Arbitrability in the E.U.", Chap. 6 in Campbell & Voyatzi, *Legal Reasoning and Judicial Interpretation of European Law* (Trenton Publishing, 1995).

[90] See para. 5.59.

necessary to enable judgment to be given in the case. While the ECJ has not definitively set out the criteria by which a national court should exercise its discretion to refer, several English cases have discussed the issues which should be considered. Most famous amongst these is Lord Denning's still useful judgment in *HP Bulmer Ltd v. Bollinger SA*,[91] but a more flexible statement of the factors to be considered is given by Bingham M.R. in *R. v. International Stock Exchange, ex parte Else*[92]:

> "If . . . the Community law issue is critical to the court's final decision, the appropriate course is ordinarily to refer the issue to the ECJ unless the national court can with complete confidence resolve the issue itself. In considering whether it can . . . the national court must be fully mindful of the differences between national and Community legislation, of the pitfalls which face a national court venturing into what may be an unfamiliar field, of the need for uniform interpretation throughout the Community and of the great advantages enjoyed by the ECJ in construing Community instruments. If the national court has any real doubt, it should ordinarily refer."[93]

When a reference must be made

5.59   According to the third paragraph of Article 234 E.C., a reference to the ECJ must be made where a point of E.C. law arises for decision before a court or tribunal from which there is no appeal. However, it is not in every case involving a point of E.C. law that a court of final appeal must make a reference to the ECJ. Rather, there are what may be termed a necessity condition and a classification condition which must be satisfied before a reference has to be made. The necessity condition is the same as applies to all courts and tribunals, namely that the point of E.C. law must be "necessary to enable" the court to give judgment. The classification condition emerges from the ECJ's landmark decision in *CILFIT*.[94] A national court of final appeal need not make a reference to the ECJ where the point of E.C. law is irrelevant to the case, or where the question has already been clearly decided by the ECJ in its previous decisions, or where the point of E.C. law is *acte clair*, that is, "the correct application of EC law is so obvious as to leave no scope for any reasonable doubt".[95] Some commentators have criticised the *acte clair* doctrine as disruptive to the uniformity of E.C. law and too unpredictable a discretion for national courts of final appeal.[96] Meanwhile, others have suggested that national courts of final appeal should have a greater discretion not to refer than *CILFIT* concedes.[97] In any event, if a national court is abusing the discretion which *CILFIT* provides to classify

---

[91] [1974] 2 W.L.R. 202.

[92] [1993] Q.B. 534.

[93] *ibid.* at 545 See also *Customs and Excise Commissioners v. ApS Samex* [1983] 1 All E.R. 1042 and *Booker Aquaculture v. Secretary of State for Scotland*, 1998 G.W.D. 21–1089.

[94] Case 283/81 *Srl CILFIT v. Ministry of Health (I)* [1982] E.C.R. 3415.

[95] *ibid.* at para. 21. In addition, a court of final appeal need not make a reference where the point of E.C. law arises in interim proceedings, given the need for expedition: see Case 107/76 *Hoffmann-La Roche v. Centrafarm* [1977] E.C.R. 957.

[96] See Arnull, "The Use and Abuse of Art. 177" (1989) 52 M.L.R. 622. *Cf. R. v. London Borough Transport Committee, ex p. Freight Transport Association* [1992] 1 C.M.L.R. 5.

[97] *cf.* Lord Slynn of Hadley, "Critics of the Court: A Reconsideration", Chap. 1 in Andenas and Jacobs (eds), *EC Law in the English Courts* (OUP, Oxford, 1998).

points of E.C. law so that references are not being made to the ECJ which should be, it will be for the E.U. Commission to raise the matter with the member state and, if necessary, pursue an enforcement action against the member state in terms of Article 226 E.C.

Effects of the ECJ's decision under Article 234 E.C.

Decisions of the ECJ in Article 234 proceedings are not only binding on **5.60** the national court making the reference but, in effect, provide precedents for all national courts before which similar points of E.C. law arise.[98] While E.C. law itself does not have a rigid doctrine of precedent, and although it is true that the ECJ will invariably follow at least the spirit of its previous decisions, the Court is not as such bound by its previous decisions and may overrule them. Accordingly, the Court has stressed on several occasions that it is prepared to receive references on points of E.C. law which it has already decided. That is, deciding to make a reference on a point of E.C. law which the Court has already decided is not an abuse of the reference procedure, although it might be thought that it is unlikely that a different result is going to be obtained in light of a more recent decision of the Court.[99]

Although the effect of an ECJ decision in an Article 234 E.C. preliminary ruling is generally retrospective, that is, the Court's decision on the meaning and effect of E.C. law operates from when the relevant rule of law became operative,[1] the Court has on several occasions varied the temporal effect of its decisions. However, only the ECJ has the power to vary the temporal effect of its decisions and it can only be asked to do so in the case in which the issues arise and not subsequently.[2] The reasons for its doing so must be exceptional and will generally relate to prior uncertainty about the effect and application of the particular rule of E.C. law, the effects of the decision on third parties, the financial consequences of the decision or some fault on the part of the E.U. institutions.[3]

IX JUDICIAL REVIEW IN THE E.U. COURTS

Jurisdiction of the ECJ and CFI

In so far as it has the final say on the meaning and effect of E.C. law, the **5.61** European Court of Justice (ECJ) has a role similar to that possessed by a supreme court in a federation. The ECJ's power to ensure uniformity in the application of E.C. law throughout the E.U. is exercised principally under the Article 234 preliminary ruling procedure, which is discussed above.[4] But the ECJ's role under Article 234 E.C. is only one,

---

[98] See Case 283/81 *Srl CILFIT v. Ministry of Health (I)* [1982] E.C.R. 3415; and Case 112/83 *Société de Produits de Mais v. Administration des Douanes* [1985] E.C.R. 719. For further discussion, see Toth, "The Authority of Judgments of the ECJ: Binding Force and Legal Effects" (1984) 4 *Yearbook of Eur.Law* 1.

[99] See *Trent Taverns Ltd v. Sykes, The Times*, March 5, 1999.

[1] See Case 61/79 *Amministrazione delle Finanze dello Stato v. Denkavit Italiana* [1980] E.C.R. 1205 at para. 16.

[2] See Case 293/83 *Gravier v. Liege* [1985] E.C.R. 593; Case C–262/88 *Barber v. Guardian Royal Exchange Assurance Group* [1990] E.C.R. I-1889; and Case C–200/91 *Coloroll Pension Trustees v. Russell* [1994] E.C.R. I-4389.

[3] *cf.* Case C–137/94 *R. v. Secretary of State for Health, ex p. Richardson* [1995] E.C.R. I-3407.

[4] See paras 5.55 *et seq.*

albeit an important, aspect of its jurisdiction under the E.C. Treaty. In addition, disputes may arise between the member states about the meaning and effect of their E.C. obligations between themselves. Accordingly, the E.C. Treaty expressly gives jurisdiction to the ECJ in such cases. More significantly, the E.C. Treaty's extensive provision for the powers, rights and duties of the E.U. institutions requires legal mechanisms by which the institutions' conduct can be supervised and enforced. Although each of the E.U. institutions jealously protects its own "privileges and prerogatives", institutional competition is not enough to ensure the rule of law and constitutionalism in the European Union. To this end, the E.C. Treaty gives the ECJ and the Court of First Instance (CFI) jurisdiction to resolve disputes involving the E.U. institutions.[5] The ECJ's jurisdiction includes exclusive jurisdiction over disputes involving E.C. law which arise between the European Union's institutions and between the member states and the E.U. institutions, both where an E.U. institution is challenged by a member state or a member state is "sued" by the Commission. In addition, Articles 230 and 232 of the E.C. Treaty provide the jurisdiction of the ECJ and CFI to hear challenges to the validity of the institutions' acts and failures to act. To some extent, this jurisdiction is comparable to the supervisory jurisdiction of a national court.

The jurisdiction and powers of the ECJ are set out in the E.C. Treaty.[6] The ECJ has also been said to have some inherent jurisdiction.[7] In addition to Article 234 E.C. preliminary rulings, the ECJ's jurisdiction principally comprises the following: first, direct actions, for example, between two E.U. institutions, between member states, between a member state and an E.U. institution, or between an individual and an institution; secondly, requests for opinions on the legality of international agreements the European Union proposes to enter with third states or international organisations; and thirdly, appeals on points of law from decisions of the CFI.[8] Some cases over which the ECJ has jurisdiction have become the responsibility of the CFI following its establishment in 1989. These include all direct actions between natural and legal persons and an E.U. institution. Further expansion of the CFI's jurisdiction is conceivable, even likely, but most cases involving member states and all references for preliminary rulings from national courts are likely to remain exclusively for the ECJ.[9]

---

[5] Unless the context otherwise indicates, general references to the powers and jurisdiction of the ECJ include references to the CFI.

[6] See Arts 220–245 and Art. 300(6) of the E.C. Treaty. The powers of the ECJ and CFI are given in more detail in the statutes of the courts, which are provided in two protocols to the E.C. Treaty (one for the ECJ and the other for the CFI), and also in the Court's Rules of Procedure (see O.J. L.176, July 4, 1991). In addition, the Treaty on European Union confers limited jurisdiction on the ECJ over some of its provisions: see Arts 35 and 46 TEU.

[7] See Arnull, "Does the Court of Justice have Inherent Jurisdiction?" (1990) 27 C.M.L.R. 683. The suggestion is based on the ECJ's decisions allowing the Parliament as an institution to sue and be sued notwithstanding the fact that there is no express provision in the original version of the E.C. Treaty allowing actions by or against the Parliament before the Court.

[8] These are only the principal heads of the ECJ's jurisdiction. Other cases over which the ECJ has jurisdiction are: staff cases, essentially comprising employment disputes between an E.U. institutions and their own employees, which cases come under the jurisdiction of the CFI; and actions against an E.U. institution to enforce its non-contractual liability.

[9] Although it must be noted that Art. 225 E.C. only expressly excludes references for preliminary rulings from the CFI's jurisdiction.

Direct actions

The E.C. Treaty provides several different categories of cases which may **5.62** be termed direct actions, by which is meant cases that must be brought directly before the ECJ or CFI. Leaving aside staff cases,[10] these actions are: enforcement actions, provided for in Articles 226–228 E.C.; actions for annulment, provided in Article 230 E.C.[11]; actions for failure to act, provided in Article 232 E.C.[12]; and actions for damages against an institution to enforce its non-contractual liability, provided in Article 288(2) E.C.[13] In addition, the ECJ's jurisdiction includes appeals on point of law from the CFI and the references concerning the legality of international agreements which the E.C. proposes to enter. The present discussion only seeks to identify and briefly explain the main forms of direct actions which may be raised against an E.U. institution.

Enforcement actions

Articles 226 and 227 E.C. allow the ECJ to hear actions brought by the **5.63** Commission or a member state against a member state that is alleged to have failed to fulfill an obligation under the E.C. Treaty.[14] In both cases the defendant member state is entitled to a prior administrative procedure, under which the Commission must deliver to the member state a reasoned opinion on the matter, give the member state an opportunity to be heard and subsequently an opportunity to correct the failure. If the Commission (or under Article 227 the complainant member state) considers that the member state continues to be in breach of its E.C. obligations, the case may be taken to the ECJ which can find the member state in breach of E.C. law. Under Article 228 E.C., the ECJ has powers to impose fines on member states that fail to comply with its judgments in enforcement actions.

Actions for annulment

Perhaps the most notable direct action is the action for annulment **5.64** provided in Article 230 E.C.[15] Five aspects of this action may be mentioned: first, what type of act can be challenged; secondly, the grounds on which reviewable acts may be challenged; thirdly, standing to challenge; fourthly, the time-limits within which the action must be brought; and fifthly, what effects annulment has.

Reviewable acts

The first paragraph of Article 230 E.C. provides the ECJ's jurisdiction in **5.65** actions for annulment: "The Court of Justice shall review the legality of acts adopted jointly by the European Parliament and the Council, of acts

---

[10] Provided for in Art. 236 E.C.
[11] Formerly Art. 173 A.C.
[12] Formerly Art. 175 E.C.
[13] Formerly Art. 215(2) E.C.
[14] Actions by one member state against another member state under Art. 227 have been rare. Only one has proceeded to a judgment of the ECJ: Case 141/78 *France v. U.K.* [1979] E.C.R. 2923. As Edward & Lane observe, the member states prefer to intervene in cases brought by the Commission against a member state, *European Community Law* (2nd ed., 1995), at para. 97.
[15] Formerly Art. 173 E.C. For discussion of actions for annulment, see Craig & De Burca, *EU Law* (2nd ed., OUP, Oxford, 1998), Chap. 11; and Edward & Lane, *European Community Law* (2nd ed., Butterworths, London, 1995), pp. 36–39. See also Usher, "Judicial Review of Community Acts and the Private Litigant", Chap. 7 in Campbell and Voyatzi, *Legal Reasoning and Judicial Interpretation of European Law* (1995).

of the Council, of the Commission and of the European Central Bank, other than recommendations and opinions, and of acts of the European Parliament intended to produce legal effects vis-à-vis third parties."[16] The "acts" subject to challenge have been defined widely by the Court. In its landmark *ERTA* judgment, the ECJ decided that the action for annulment must: "be available [against] all measures adopted by the institutions, whatever their nature or form, which are intended to have legal effects".[17]

The test for a reviewable act of an E.C. institution is almost certainly its capacity to have legal effects.[18] So in *Partie Ecologiste 'Les Verts' v. European Parliament*[19] the ECJ interpreted an earlier version of Article 230 E.C. which failed to include reference to the European Parliament as nevertheless permitting challenge to measures adopted by the Parliament which are "intended to have legal effects *vis-à-vis* third parties". Justifying the implication of jurisdiction over the Parliament by reference to an effective system of judicial review, the ECJ noted that the European Community is: "a Community based on the rule of law [and] neither its Member States nor its institutions can avoid a review of the question whether the measures adopted by them are in conformity with the basic constitutional charter, the [EC] Treaty".[20] In general, only acts of the institutions exercising powers conferred by the E.C. Treaty can be challenged. So, for example, decisions adopted by the member states collectively acting as such (that is, not acting as the Council of Ministers) are not subject to challenge under Article 230 E.C.[21] Moreover, the ECJ's jurisdiction is in general excluded from most areas of activity that fall within the European Union's domain, namely the matters provided

---

[16] Before the Maastricht amendments, Art. 230 (Art. 173) E.C. did not expressly provide for the Parliament to sue or be sued. But in Case 294/83 *Partie Ecologiste "Les Verts" v. European Parliament* [1986] E.C.R. 1339, the Court decided that "measures adopted by the European Parliament intended to have legal effects *vis-à-vis* third parties" could be challenged under Art. 173. And in Case C–70/88 *European Parliament v. Council* [1990] E.C.R. I-2041, the Court decided that the Parliament could also raise actions under Art. 173. In turn, what is now Art. 230 E.C. was amended at Maastricht to reflect the new reality.

[17] Case 22/70 *Commission v. Council (ERTA)* [1971] E.C.R. 263.

[18] Consider Case 60/81 *IBM Corporation v. Commission* [1981] E.C.R. 2639: a letter notifying the applicant that it was subject to competition proceedings under the E.C. Treaty was only "of a purely preparatory character" which could not be challenged in annulment proceedings; but defects in preparatory measures could provide grounds for challenge of the Commission's definitive decision in the case. But *cf.* Case C–39/93P *Syndicat Français de l'Express International v. Commission* [1994] E.C.R. I-2681: a letter from the Commission to a complainer who has alleged violations of E.C. competition law stating that the Commission does not intend to pursue the matter is reviewable since it is capable of having legal effects (namely, that the Commission does not intend to investigate the alleged breaches of E.C. law). In addition, some care should be taken to distinguish measures adopted by the institutions beyond the framework of the E.C. (or other Community) Treaties, for example, when acting as E.U. institutions under the second and third pillars. See below.

[19] Case 294/83 [1986] E.C.R. 1339.

[20] *ibid.*

[21] See Cases C–181 & 248/91 *European Parliament v. Council and Commission* [1993] E.C.R. I-3685, noted by Brown at (1994) 31 C.M.L.R. 1347. In that case, it did not matter that the member states were "meeting in Council"; they were acting collectively but not as the Council of Ministers as an E.C. institution. But *cf.* Case C–316/91 *European Parliament v. Council* [1994] E.C.R. I-625 (ECJ can review binding acts of the Council of Ministers where adopted by the Council otherwise than in pursuance of E.C. Treaty provisions (presumably as long as there is no express bar on the ECJ's jurisdiction, *cf.* Art. 46 TEU)).

for in the second and third pillars.[22] In this regard, particular note should be made of Article 35 of the Treaty on European Union. While the member states may expressly agree to the ECJ's jurisdiction in relation to aspects of the European Union's third pillar on Police and Judicial Co-operation in Criminal Matters, they do not have to do so. Further, even if they do so, it follows from Article 35(5) TEU that the ECJ does not have jurisdiction to assess the "validity or proportionality" of police and law enforcement actions "with regard to the maintenance of law and order and the safeguarding of internal security". Some care must therefore be taken in determining the legal basis of measures that could have a provenance in the Treaty on European Union.

Grounds of challenge

The grounds on which "the legality" of acts may be challenged are **5.66** specified in Article 230 E.C. as: "lack of competence, infringement of an essential procedural requirement, infringement of this Treaty or of any rule of law relating to its application, or misuse of powers". Very broadly, these co-relate to the grounds of judicial review in the United Kingdom. It must be noted, of course, that the grounds listed in Article 230 will be used by the ECJ to review the validity of E.C. legislation.[23] In addition, it follows from Article 6 taken with Article 46 of the Treaty on European Union that where the ECJ has jurisdiction in terms of the E.C. Treaty, the institutions must observe the human rights standards as guaranteed by the European Convention on Human Rights and as they result from the general principles of law which are part of E.C. law.[24] More generally, the general principles of law also constitute grounds against which E.C. legislation may be reviewed.[25] Finally, the application of the grounds of review listed in Article 230 E.C. to particular cases raises issues that are familiar in judicial review in this country, such as definition of the concept of jurisdiction, classification of misuse of power, the consequences of procedural irregularities and the appropriate intensity of review or the existence of tiers of scrutiny depending on the nature of the rights or interests infringed.

Standing to Challenge

Standing to bring what are essentially judicial review proceedings against **5.67** the E.U. institutions proceeds in terms of Article 230 E.C. on a distinction between privileged and non-privileged applicants. So called

---

[22] See Art. 46 TEU. In general the TEU does not confer jurisdiction on the ECJ outside the E.C. (and other Communities) Treaties. In the E.U. scheme, Art. 46 TEU only gives the ECJ jurisdiction over: Art. 6(2), requiring that the institutions comply with human rights; Arts 46–53 (the final provisions); under the third pillar (police & justice) according to the restrictions in Art. 35 TEU (basically, the member states may expressly agree in particular contexts (for example, specific Conventions) covered by the third pillar for the ECJ to have jurisdiction); and under Title VII (provisions on closer co-operation (or variable geometry)). Notably the ECJ is not given jurisdiction under the second pillar (common foreign and security policy). But the ECJ's traditional commitment to the rule of law and its case law on the need for effective judicial review may cause it to develop jurisdiction in some respects in regard to these areas: consider, for example, Case C–170/96 *Commission v. Council* [1998] E.C.R. I-2763.

[23] In so far as measures adopted under the Treaty on European Union may be challengeable, the grounds are identical to those in Art. 230 E.C.: see, for example, Art. 35(6) TEU.

[24] Article 6(2) TEU.

[25] See Case 4/73 *Nold v. Commission* [1974] E.C.R. 491; and Case 17/74 *Transocean Marine Paint v. Commission* [1974] E.C.R. 1063. For the general principles of E.C. law, see paras 5.39 *et seq.* above.

privileged applicants are the E.U. institutions themselves and the member states. As far as the member states and the E.U. institutions are concerned, they may raise actions of annulment as of right, albeit in the cases of the Parliament and the ECB subject to the qualification which Article 230 provides. For the purposes of Article 230 E.C., however, "member state" is limited to the fifteen national governments; it does not include regional or local governments.[26] Accordingly, the Scottish Executive is not a privileged applicant for the purposes of Article 230 E.C. As regards non-privileged applicants, that is, natural and legal persons, it is almost an understatement to describe their standing in terms of Article 230 E.C. as not privileged. Matters are simplest where a natural or legal person is actually addressed by an E.C. measure, invariably a decision. In such a case, an action of annulment can be raised in the CFI by that person. But where a person is not the addressee of a decision, or where the decision takes the form of a regulation, that is, it purports to have general application, then the test for standing is basically a showing that the person is "directly and individually concerned" by the measure. Established in the ECJ's landmark decision in *Plaumann v. Commission*,[27] this test has been applied strictly in the court's case law.[28] Most recently, for example, it was applied to deny Greenpeace standing under Article 230 E.C. because it could not be shown that as a representative body they were any more "directly and individually" affected by the challenged measure than anyone else.[29]

Time limits

5.68 Proceedings under Article 230 E.C. must be commenced within two months of the illegal measure being published or notified to the complainer or "of the day on which it came to the knowledge" of the complainer. The ECJ has interpreted this time-limit strictly, being clearly influenced by the need for legal certainty. But individual rights and the rule of law are preserved since E.C. acts and decisions can still be challenged in other proceedings not directly affected by Article 230 E.C.'s two-month time-limit. First, Article 241 E.C. provides that the ECJ (and in cases falling to it the CFI) has the power to review the legality of E.C. regulations outside the two-month time-limit on the same grounds specified under Article 230 where the issue of legality of the regulation arises in other proceedings before the Court—for example, an action for damages against the responsible E.C. institution. Secondly, national courts can hear challenges to E.C. measures outside the two-month time-limit, although no national court has the power under E.C. law to strike down any E.C. measure.[30] Where a national court considers that the challenge to the validity of E.C. legislation is based on serious grounds, the appropriate course is to make a reference of this E.C. law point to the ECJ.[31] This serves two purposes: first, it

---

[26] See Case C–129/96 *Region Wallone* [1997] E.C.R. I-1787, noted by Scott at (1999) 36 C.M.L.R. 227.

[27] Case 25/62 [1963] E.C.R. 95.

[28] See Case 106/63 *Toepfer v. Commission* [1965] E.C.R. 405.

[29] Case C–321/95P *Stichtung Greenpeace Council v. Commission* [1998] E.C.R. I-1651.

[30] See Case 314/85 *Foto-Frost v. Hauptzollamt Lubeck-Ost* [1987] E.C.R. 4199.

[31] The national court may, however, grant an interim remedy suspending the effect of the E.C. measure, or any national measure implementing it, pending the ECJ's ruling on the challenge: see Cases 143/88 and C–92/89 *Zuckerfabriken Suderdithmarschen und Soest v. Hauptzollamter Itzehoe und Paderborn* [1991] E.C.R. I-415.

ensures consistency throughout the European Union by allowing only the ECJ to rule definitively on the validity of E.C. legislation; and secondly, it allows the ECJ to supervise the propriety of challenges to E.C. legislation brought before national courts. The ECJ has not been prepared to tolerate all challenges to E.C. legislation brought before national courts—for example, where this would amount to an abuse of process in circumstances in which the challenge could properly have been brought under Article 230 E.C. before the CFI.[32]

Effects of annulment

Article 231 E.C. provides that if the action under Article 230 is **5.69** successful, the ECJ (or CFI) will declare the challenged measure "void". But this does not always mean that an annulled measure is void *ab initio*. First, Article 231(2) E.C. provides that the Court has a discretion to vary the retrospective effect of any decision annulling a measure.[33] More generally, the Court has indicated that E.C. measures are generally to be presumed valid until they are annulled unless the breach of E.C. law which leads to the annulment is so severe as to justify the measure being treated as "non-existent", which in effect means void *ab initio*.[34]

Actions for failure to act

Mention may also be made of Article 232 (formerly 175) of the E.C. **5.70** Treaty whereby member states and E.U. institutions as of right and individuals (in effect) under the same conditions applicable under Article 230 E.C. may bring an action before the ECJ to establish an infringement of E.C. law by an E.U. institution by virtue of a failure to act. Although in theory an important action, in practice it is used infrequently and with only rare success.[35]

Other actions

Actions may also be brought under Article 288 (formerly 215(2)) E.C. to **5.71** enforce the non-contractual liability of an E.C. institution.[36] It may also be noted that under Article 300(6) (formerly 228(6)) of the E.C. Treaty, the ECJ has an exclusive jurisdiction to rule on the legality of international agreements which the E.C. proposes to enter. This is the only true example of an advisory or reference jurisdiction possessed by the ECJ,[37] and has been the source of several significant decisions in E.C. law.[38] Finally, decisions of the CFI may be appealed to the ECJ on points of law.

---

[32] See Case C–188/92 *TWD Textilwerke Deggendorf GmbH v. Germany* [1994] E.C.R. I-833. For discussion, see Wyatt, "The Relationship between Actions for Annulment and References on Validity After *TWD Deggendorf*", chapter 6 in Lonbay & Biondi, *Remedies For Breach of EC Law* (John Wiley & Sons, Chichester, 1997).

[33] Although Art. 231(2) only refers to regulations, the ECJ has held that the power to vary the effects of annulment also applies where directives have been annulled: see Case C–295/90 *European Parliament v. Council* [1992] E.C.R. I-4193.

[34] See Case C–137/92P *Commission v. BASF AG* [1994] E.C.R. I-2555.

[35] See Edward and Lane, *European Community Law* (2nd ed., Butterworths, London, 1995), para. 103.

[36] For discussion, see Craig and De Burca, *EU Law* (2nd ed., OUP, Oxford, 1998), Chap. 12.

[37] Note that the Art. 234 E.C. preliminary ruling procedure under which national courts refer points of E.C. law for a ruling by the ECJ is not an advisory jurisdiction. The ECJ will only entertain a reference in so far as it is relevant to a real case properly before and to be decided by a national court: see para. 5.56 above.

[38] For example, Opinion 2/94 [1996] E.C.R. I-1759 (holding that the E.C. does not have competence to ratify the European Convention on Human Rights).

CHAPTER 6

THE HUMAN RIGHTS ACT 1998

I   INTRODUCTION
II THE CONVENTION RIGHTS PRIOR TO THE 1998 ACT
III INTERPRETATION OF THE HUMAN RIGHTS ACT 1998
IV THE HUMAN RIGHTS ACT 1998 AND LEGISLATION
V   SCOPE OF THE HUMAN RIGHTS ACT 1998
VI REMEDIES UNDER THE HUMAN RIGHTS ACT 1998
VII THE UNITED KINGDOM AND THE STRASBOURG COURT

I   INTRODUCTION

The purpose of the Human Rights Act 1998 is "to give further effect to   **6.01**
rights and freedoms guaranteed under the European Convention on
Human Rights"[1] in the United Kingdom. The Act makes extensive
provision for the operation of the European Convention in U.K. law
although it is not technically correct to say the Act "implements" or
"incorporates" the Convention.[2] The enactment of the Human Rights
Act 1998 marks the culmination of attempts to introduce into U.K. law
some form of "Bill of Rights" similar to that contained in many written
constitutions.[3] Although the protection of human rights has long been a
feature of the common law and also a focus of judicial review in recent
years, the judicial approach to Parliamentary supremacy operated to
restrict challenges to primary legislation and often also to discretionary
decisions where the grounds of challenge were fundamental human
rights.[4] Without doubt, the Human Rights Act confirms the importance
of the protection of human rights under the U.K. constitution and
significantly enhances the power of judicial review in the laws of the
United Kingdom.[5] In particular, the Act allows for what amounts to a

---

[1] Preamble to Human Rights Act 1998. The Act is reproduced in its entirety in
Appendix 1.

[2] See the comments of the Lord Chancellor, Lord Irvine of Lairg in the House of Lords,
Hansard, H.L. Vol. 583, cols 508–510 (Nov. 18, 1997): "The Convention rights will not . . .
in themselves become part of our domestic law". The distinction between "implementation" and "giving further effect" may be significant, particularly in view of the 1998 Act's
failure to give effect expressly to Article 13 of the Convention (the effective remedies
provision). This was a point of some contention in the House of Lords debates on the bill:
see *Hansard*, H.L. Vol. 87, cols 1264–1268 (Jan. 19, 1998). See further, para. 6.13 below.

[3] There is a large volume of literature debating the advantages and disadvantages of
introducing a bill of rights into U.K. law: in particular, see Zander, *A Bill of Rights* (4th ed.,
Sweet & Maxwell, London, 1997); and IPPR Consultation Paper No. 1, "A British Bill of
Rights" (1990). See also Chander, "Sovereignty, Referenda and the Entrenchment of a
U.K. Bill of Rights" (1991) 101 Yale L.J. 457. For a more doubtful look at the possibility
of a U.K. bill of rights, see Jaconelli, *Enacting a Bill of Rights* (OUP, 1980). In the late
1970s a select committee of the House of Lords considered whether the U.K. should adopt
a bill of rights but its members were "irreconcilably divided" on the arguments for and
against such a step: see Report of the House of Lords Select Committee on a Bill of
Rights, 1977–78, H.L. 176.

[4] *cf. R. v. Secretary of State for the Home Department, ex parte Brind* [1991] 1 A.C. 696.

[5] The constitutional nature of the Human Rights Act 1998 is noted by the Lord
Chancellor in the Second Reading debates on the Act in the House of Lords: see *Hansard*,
H.L., Vol. 582, col. 1227 (Nov. 3, 1997).

modified form of constitutional review of primary legislation enacted by the U.K. Parliament.[6] The contribution which the Act is likely to make to judicial review throughout the U.K. should not be underestimated.[7] The Act merits extensive discussion, not least because of its expansion of the scope of judicial review.[8]

Overview

6.02 Although the impact of the Human Rights Act 1998 (hereafter "the 1998 Act") is felt throughout the legal system, this chapter focuses on the issues which are most relevant to judicial review. Part II of the chapter discusses the background to the 1998 Act and considers the effect of Convention rights in the U.K. legal systems before the Act came into force. Part III explains the approach the courts must take to interpreting and applying the 1998 Act and the Convention rights it guarantees. Part IV focuses on the relationship between the 1998 Act and legislation, that is, primary legislation and delegated legislation. Acts of the Scottish Parliament are considered in a later chapter.[9] Part V discusses the scope of the 1998 Act and explains the significance of the Act's application only to public authorities. Part VI looks at the remedies the 1998 Act provides for violations of guaranteed rights and focuses on the important, albeit not exclusive, role judicial review is likely to play in the Act's operation. Finally, Part VII places the European Convention on Human Rights (hereafter "the Convention") in the context of the European institutions charged with its supervision and enforcement. It is always necessary to remember that the 1998 Act is the means chosen by the U.K. Parliament to give effect to the Convention in domestic law and that the Convention's own enforcement machinery remains important for the protection of human rights throughout the United Kingdom.

Substance of the Rights

6.03 This chapter considers only the 1998 Act's provisions for the effect to be given to Convention rights in U.K. law. Consideration of the Convention rights themselves is deferred until Chapter 16. Efficiency and clarity

---

[6] See s. 4 of the Human Rights Act 1998, discussed below at paras 6.34–6.37. Judicial review of legislation enacted by the Scottish Parliament also falls within the scope of the Human Rights Act 1998 (*cf.* s. 21(1) of the Act), but express provision is made for the relationship between Convention rights and the Scottish Parliament and Executive in the Scotland Act 1998 (see ss 29, 57 and 100 of that Act). In particular, it must be noted that the court's power over Acts of the Scottish Parliament is greater than over U.K. legislation in terms of s. 4 of the Human Rights Act 1998: provisions in Scottish Acts which are incompatible with Convention rights are *ultra vires* the Parliament and may be invalidated by the court. For further comment on the effects of the Scotland Act 1998 in these regards, see Chap. 7.

[7] This is generally confirmed by the experience of other Commonwealth legal systems following the introduction of bills of rights. The Canadian and New Zealand experiences are referred to on several occasions in the following discussion but emphasis is also placed on the Privy Council's own contribution interpreting the bills of rights in many other legal systems, not least Hong Kong before July 1, 1997.

[8] Judicial review is used here to mean cases coming under the supervisory jurisdiction. But the guarantee of Convention rights (along with the implications of devolution and the operation in the U.K. of E.C. law) extends to many other proceedings than those of judicial review: see Chap. 1. Indeed the guarantee of Convention rights means that all courts, including the criminal courts, will be required to enter into matters of legality and balancing of interests which are familiar in judicial review proper. But the effects of the decision of a criminal court ruling official conduct (or legislation) incompatible with Convention rights will be more limited than a decree of the Court of Session following a judicial review: see Chap. 8, on "Scope of the Supervisory Jurisdiction".

[9] See Chap. 7.

aside, this approach allows the broader constitutional aspects of the Human Rights Act, such as its scope and interpretation, to be considered here while the meaning of substantive Convention rights are considered as part of the grounds of judicial review, to which they properly belong. In addition, of course, it must be noted at the outset that the Convention rights do not exhaust human rights in the U.K. legal systems.[10] Common law human rights, international human rights guaranteed in various international treaties and according to customary international law, in addition to fundamental human rights which are part of E.C. law, remain significant.[11]

II THE CONVENTION RIGHTS PRIOR TO THE 1998 ACT

The European Convention on Human Rights

The European Convention for the Protection of Human Rights and **6.04** Fundamental Freedoms came into force on September 3, 1953.[12] The Convention was the first major achievement of the newly created Council of Europe, one of the post-war organisations established to ensure peace and security in Europe.[13] The Convention was signed by the U.K. government in November 1950 and was ratified by the United Kingdom in March 1951. The United Kingdom had provided a significant contribution to the preparatory work involved in drafting the Convention and it was thought that the rights to be guaranteed therein, especially the criminal procedure rights, represented the best of the British common law tradition.[14] Nevertheless, successive governments concluded that it should not be implemented into U.K. law.[15]

Convention Institutions

The Convention provides not only a catalogue of human rights but also **6.05** establishes a procedure for the enforcement of those rights.[16] Originally this procedure involved three institutions, namely the Commission on Human Rights and the Court of Human Rights set up by the Convention

---

[10] *cf.* s. 11 of the Act.

[11] See para. 16.06.

[12] UKTS 71 (1953), Cmd 8969.

[13] The Council of Europe was established by The Statute of the Council of Europe (UKTS 51 (1949) Cmd 7778) on May 5, 1949 and is located in Strasbourg, France. For further information see Council of Europe, *Manual of the Council of Europe. Its Structure, Functions and Achievements* (London, 1970). In addition to the European Convention on Human Rights, the Council of Europe is responsible for several trans-European human rights instruments—for example, the European Social Charter of 1961, in force since Feb. 26, 1965 (UKTS 38 (1965) Cmnd 2643) protecting economic and social rights (see Harris, *The European Social Charter* (Charlottesville, 1984)); the 1987 European Convention for the Prevention of Torture and Inhuman or Degrading Treatment or Punishment, in force since Feb. 1, 1989 (Council of Europe, ETS No. 126); and the European Convention on the Legal Status of Children Born Out of Wedlock (ETS No. 85). The Council of Europe is also active beyond the sphere of human rights: see, for example, the Council of Europe European Convention on Recognition & Enforcement of Decisions Concerning Custody of Children (implemented into U.K. law by the Child Abduction and Custody Act 1985, Sched. 2).

[14] See Marston, "The United Kingdom's Part in the Preparation of the European Convention on Human Rights" (1993) 42 I.C.L.Q. 796.

[15] On the ratification of treaties and their implementation into domestic law, see para. 4.38.

[16] The Convention institutions are discussed further in part VII of this Chapter.

and, thirdly, the Committee of Ministers of the Council of Europe. The role of the Committee of Ministers underlined the international nature of the enforcement procedure and the politically sensitive nature of human rights violations. The opportunity for human rights complaints to be resolved behind the closed doors of the Committee of Ministers reflected the early compromise struck by the Convention between state sovereignty and individual rights directly enforceable at the international level. Nevertheless, the Convention's distinct achievement is the pre-eminence which its legal processes have assumed over the political institutions. Although some cases have been resolved at the political level in the Committee of Ministers, its role quickly subsided and it is the decisions of the Court of Human Rights which have had an enormous impact and which have given the Convention both its international stature and relevance in domestic law. This has now been acknowledged by Protocol 11 to the Convention significantly amending the Convention enforcement machinery by abolishing the Commission on Human Rights, confining the Committee of Ministers to ensuring compliance with Court judgments and instituting the Court of Human Rights as the single Convention institution responsible for interpreting and applying the Convention.[17]

Export of the Convention rights to some Commonwealth jurisdictions

6.06 While in the United Kingdom the Convention languished for many years as an international treaty with only residual significance for U.K. courts,[18] the Convention was exported to a number of the colonies of the United Kingdom on their achieving independence. Often, the Acts of the U.K. Parliament establishing the constitutions of newly independent Commonwealth countries incorporated the Convention's human rights provisions into the constitution.[19] This is true of several Commonwealth constitutions: for example, the Bahamas, Jamaica, Mauritius and Zimbabwe. The Commonwealth experience with the Convention requires to be noted since many of these countries retained the Privy Council as their final court of appeal.

The Judicial Committee of the Privy Council

6.07 As the final appeal tribunal for many Commonwealth countries, the Judicial Committee of the Privy Council has had many opportunities to interpret and apply the Convention rights in cases brought before it. A hallmark of these Privy Council decisions is the need to bring "a generous and purposive construction" to constitutional provisions guaranteeing human rights and civil liberties.[20] In addition, between 1991 and

---

[17] For discussion of the reforms introduced by Protocol 11 to the Convention, see part VII below.

[18] See further paras 6.10 *et seq.* below.

[19] This point is noted with some irony by Lester, "Fundamental Rights: the United Kingdom Isolated" [1984] P.L. 46.

[20] *Att.-Gen. of The Gambia v. Jobe* [1984] A.C. 689, *per* Lord Diplock at 700. See also *Ministry of Home Affairs v. Fisher* [1980] A.C. 319, noted below. The Privy Council's approach to interpreting Commonwealth constitutional human rights guarantees has been exposed to critical comment: see Ewing, "A Bill of Rights: Lessons from the Privy Council", in Finnie, Himsworth and Walker, *Edinburgh Essays in Public Law* (Edinburgh UP, 1991), arguing that the approach is much more conservative than the words "generous and purposive construction" suggest; and Ghai, "Sentinels of Liberty or Sheep in Woolf's

1997 the Privy Council made several interesting decisions[21] interpreting the Hong Kong Bill of Rights which, although based on the United Nations International Covenant on Civil and Political Rights, has many similarities with the Convention.[22] There is no doubt that these decisions will be influential in the interpretation of the 1998 Act, providing as they do considerable U.K. judicial experience of construing constitutional guarantees of human rights based on or similar to the Convention.

Convention not implemented into U.K. law

Since the Convention is an international treaty, the traditional under- **6.08** standing of the U.K. constitution meant that it could have no direct effect in U.K. law unless and until it was incorporated by an Act of Parliament. But it has always been clear that the Convention is more than an ordinary international treaty. As the Court of Human Rights said in the *Ireland v. United Kingdom* case:

> "Unlike international treaties of the classic kind, the Convention comprises more than mere reciprocal engagements between con- tracting States. It creates, over and above a network of mutual, bilateral undertakings, objective obligations which . . . benefit from a 'collective enforcement' . . . By substituting the words 'shall secure' for the words 'undertake to secure' in the text of Article 1, the drafters of the Convention also intended to make it clear that the rights and freedoms set out in [the Convention] would be directly secured to anyone within the jurisdiction of the Contracting States".[23]

Clothing? Judicial Politics and the Hong Kong Bill of Rights" (1997) 60 M.L.R. 459, arguing that the approach is "lip service to rights, contradicted by a narrow statutory approach" (at 469). For a contentious example of a Privy Council human rights decision, see *Fisher v. Minister of Public Safety and Immigration and Others (No. 2)* [1999] 2 W.L.R. 349 (following on *Fisher (No. 1)* [1998] A.C. 673) in which the majority, in the face of a vigorous dissent, adopted a "strict construction" of the Bahamas constitution. Consider also *Reckley v. Minister of Public Safety and Immigration (No. 2)* [1996] A.C. 527 (and compare with *R. v. Secretary of State for the Home Department, ex p. Bentley* [1994] Q.B. 349).

[21] See in particular *Att.-Gen. of Hong Kong v. Lee Kwong-kut* [1993] A.C. 951 and *Ming Pao Newspapers Ltd v. Att.-Gen. of Hong Kong* [1996] A.C. 907.

[22] Before the resumption of sovereignty over Hong Kong by the People's Republic of China on June 30, 1997, Hong Kong was a British Crown Colony and the Privy Council was its final court of appeal. In 1991, the Hong Kong Legislative Council passed the Bill of Rights Ordinance (Laws of Hong Kong: Cap. 383) implementing the United Nations Covenant on Civil & Political Rights (ICCPR) which the U.K. ratified in 1976 (Cmnd 6702) and which was applied to Hong Kong at the same time. Many of the rights guaranteed in the ICCPR are in similar terms to the Convention rights and the ICCPR also guarantees some of its rights subject to limitations which are expressed in terms similar to those in Arts 8–11 of the Convention. Indeed, the Hong Kong courts have often referred to decisions of the European Court of Human Rights under the Convention. Since Hong Kong has a common law legal system very similar to English law, the Privy Council's interpretation of the Hong Kong Bill of Rights (in addition to the Hong Kong courts' own decisions) provides an important source of material on which U.K. courts can draw. For discussion of the Hong Kong Bill, see Chan & Ghai (eds), *The Hong Kong Bill of Rights: A Comparative Approach* (Butterworths, Singapore, 1993); and Ghai, "Sentinels of Liberty or Sheep in Woolf's Clothing? Judicial Politics and the Hong Kong Bill of Rights" (1997) 60 M.L.R. 459. For discussion of Hong Kong law and the (constitutional) Hong Kong Basic Law since the handover to China, see Ghai, *Hong Kong's New Constitutional Order: The Resumption of Chinese Sovereignty and the Basic Law* (2nd ed., Hong Kong University Press, 1998).

[23] European Court of Human Rights Judgment of Jan. 18, 1978, cited at (1979–80) 2 E.H.R.R. 25 at para. 239.

As to whether Convention States are under an obligation to incorporate the Convention directly into their national law, the Court has said that such an act is "a particularly faithful reflection" of the drafters' intentions but that it is not strictly required by the Convention.[24] Most states have, however, given effect to the Convention in their domestic laws.[25] In any case, as the Court noted in *Marckx v. Belgium*,[26] it is clear that the state's freedom on how to observe the Convention sits alongside its fundamental obligation to do so: "It is for the respondent State, and the respondent State alone, to take the measures it considers appropriate *to assure that its domestic law is coherent and consistent*".[27]

Article 13 of the Convention: effective remedies

6.09 Article 13 of the Convention has not been included within the definition of Convention rights contained in the Human Rights Act 1998,[28] but its provisions are of significance.[29] The Article provides: "Everyone whose [Convention] rights and freedoms are violated shall have an effective remedy before a national authority notwithstanding that the violation has been committed by persons acting in an official capacity". Article 13 has enabled the Court of Human Rights to focus on the existence and effectiveness of national law remedies for violations of Convention rights, thereby allowing it to concentrate on the substance rather than the form in which the Convention applies in particular cases.[30] In its decision in *Silver v. United Kingdom*[31] the Court set out what the Convention requires of a national legal remedy for it to be considered effective for the purposes of Article 13. Summarising its (then) case law, the Court said that a complainer of a violation of Convention rights should in light of all the remedies available in national law have some "remedy before a national authority in order both to have his claim decided and, if appropriate, to obtain redress", albeit that the national authority need not be a judicial body, although if it is not, "its powers and the guarantees which it affords are relevant in determining whether the remedy . . . is effective".[32] Several of the cases involving the United Kingdom have focused on the effectiveness of U.K. law and in particular of judicial review in providing for remedies for violations of Convention rights.[33] In *Vilvarajah v. United Kingdom*,[34] the Court concluded that

---

[24] *ibid*. See also *Silver v. U.K.* (1983) 5 E.H.R.R. 347 and *Lithgow v. U.K.* (1986) 8 E.H.R.R. 329.

[25] A good account of the domestic effect given to the Convention in the Council of Europe states is given by Drzemczewski, *European Human Rights Convention in Domestic law: A Comparative Survey* (OUP, Oxford, 1983).

[26] (1979) 2 E.H.R.R. 330.

[27] *ibid*. at para. 20 (emphasis added).

[28] Which was a source of some controversy in debates on the Bill: see *Hansard*, H.L. Vol. 87, cols 1264–1268.

[29] See para. 16.05.

[30] See, for example, *Klass v. Germany* (1979) 2 E.H.R.R. 214 and *Vilvarajah v. U.K.* (1991) 14 E.H.R.R. 248.

[31] (1983) 5 E.H.R.R. 347.

[32] *ibid*. at para. 113. Recent cases have focused on the independence of tribunals for the purposes of Art. 6 of the Convention: see *Cable v. United Kingdom* and *Hood v. United Kingdom* (ECHR, Feb. 18, 1999); consider also the decision of the European Commission on Human Rights in *McGonnell v. United Kingdom* (App. No. 28488/95, decision of Oct. 20, 1998).

[33] See *Soering v. United Kingdom* (1989) 11 E.H.R.R. 439 (deciding that judicial review is an effective remedy).

[34] (1992) 14 E.H.R.R. 248.

judicial review as understood in the United Kingdom is an effective remedy for a violation of Convention rights notwithstanding the absence of merits review. The Court was particularly impressed by the option of "heightened" scrutiny under *Wednesbury* principles where fundamental human rights are implicated in a challenged decision.[35] However, the Court has accepted that Article 13 of the Convention is subject to limits. In *Lithgow v. United Kingdom*,[36] the Court decided that the inability of complainers of violations of Convention rights to challenge primary legislation in the national courts did not violate Article 13. Since the Convention did not have to be directly accessible in national law, it followed that it did not have to be given an overriding effect. It probably follows from the Court's jurisprudence that neither the failure of the Human Rights Act 1998 expressly to guarantee Article 13 of the Convention nor the Act's lack of overriding effect in relation to primary legislation are in themselves breaches of the Convention.[37]

Use of the Convention in national law before the 1998 Act

Since the Convention was not incorporated into U.K. law by legislation, **6.10** no part of the Convention could operate directly in national law. The obligations under the Convention strictly remained obligations in international law and the rights and freedoms were not open to direct enforcement in the domestic courts. Nevertheless, the theoretically dualist tradition of the U.K. constitution did not prevent the indirect operation of the Convention in national law.[38] In a number of cases the Convention was used to assist in the interpretation of ambiguous legislation.[39] In *R. v. Secretary of State for the Home Department, ex parte Bhajan Singh*,[40] Lord Denning M.R. said: "What is the position of the Convention in our English law? . . . The court can and should take the Convention into account. They should take it into account whenever interpreting a statute which affects the rights and liberties of the individual . . . In addition, I would add that the immigration officers and the Secretary of State in exercising their duties ought to bear in mind the

---

[35] *ibid.* at paras 123–127 (understanding *Wednesbury* in terms of *R. v. Secretary of State for the Home Department, ex p. Bugdaycay* [1987] A.C. 415; see also *Singh v. Secretary of State for the Home Department*, 1998 S.L.T. 1370, *per* Lord Macfadyen at 1374). Compare, however, *Chahal Family v. United Kingdom* (1996) 23 E.H.R.R. 413. See generally Blake, "Judicial Review of Discretion in Human Rights Cases" [1997] E.H.R.L.R. 391. See now *Lustig-Prean und Becket v. U.K., The Times*, October 11, 1999, unreported.

[36] (1986) 8 E.H.R.R. 329.

[37] On the implications for U.K. courts of not guaranteeing Art. 13 in U.K. law, see part VI below.

[38] In the 1990s the Convention's residual importance increased as courts became more disposed to interpreting legislation and developing the common law to accord with Convention rights. A good discussion of the Convention's effects in English law (and generally on the relationship between international human rights and U.K. law) is given by Hunt, *Using Human Rights Law in English Courts* (Hart, Oxford, 1997), esp. Chap. 4. For an earlier, arguably pioneering, commentary, see Duffy, "English Law and the European Convention on Human Rights" (1980) 29 I.C.L.Q. 585. See also Lord Browne-Wilkinson, "The Infiltration of a Bill of Rights" [1992] P.L. 397. For a discussion of the earlier Scottish approach to the Convention, see Murdoch, "The European Convention on Human Rights in Scots Law" [1991] P.L. 40.

[39] See *R. v. Chief Immigration Officer, ex p. Salamat Bibi* [1976] 1 W.L.R. 979 at 984; and *R. v. Secretary of State for the Home Department, ex p. Bhajan Singh* [1976] Q.B. 198. *cf. Raymond v. Honey* [1983] 1 A.C. 1.

[40] [1976] Q.B. 198.

principles stated in the Convention".[41] In subsequent years, several
factors led to emphasising the Convention's relevance for litigation in
U.K. courts, among them the increasing effects of E.C. law in the United
Kingdom, greater awareness of human rights issues and greater use of
judicial review. In addition to using the Convention in developing the
common law,[42] the courts were able to use the Convention by reference
to the common law presumption applicable in statutory interpretation
that Parliament is presumed to legislate in conformity with the United
Kingdom's international obligations (the compliance presumption).[43]
Although this presumption normally only operates when legislative
provisions are ambiguous, so that Parliament can circumvent them either
expressly or with clear words,[44] the courts in England and Wales
increasingly became more willing to use the presumption in cases with
human rights implications, perhaps even beyond the confines of the
"compliance presumption".[45] In this way, the Convention has acquired
much significance in judicial review cases which raise human rights
issues.

The Convention and Scotland

6.11 Historically, the Scottish tradition was more restrained. In *Surjit-Kaur v.
Lord Advocate*,[46] Lord Ross felt unable to follow either the English cases
on the compliance presumption or a (then) novel argument on the
Convention's indirect effect in Scots law through the medium of E.C.
law. Holding to a view of the strictness of the U.K. constitution's dualist
distinction between international law and national law, Lord Ross said:
"So far as Scotland is concerned . . . the Court is not entitled to have
regard to the Convention either as an aid to construction or otherwise
. . . To suggest otherwise is to confer upon a Convention concluded by
the Executive an effect which only an Act of Parliament can achieve".[47]
Although it is now tempting to regard this position as old-fashioned, it
does at least have the benefit of constitutional orthodoxy on its side.

---

[41] *ibid*. at 207. But Lord Denning M.R. admitted that in an earlier unreported case (*Birdi
v. Secretary of State for the Home Department*, Feb. 11, 1975) he had gone "too far" when
he had said that he might be inclined to hold invalid an Act of Parliament which violated
the Convention.

[42] For examples, see *Att.-Gen. v. Guardian Newspapers Ltd (No. 2)* [1990] 1 A.C. 109, *per*
Lord Goff of Chieveley at 283–284; and *Derbyshire County Council v. Times Newspapers*
[1993] A.C. 534 (in which the Court of Appeal relied on the Convention (see [1992] Q.B.
770) but the House of Lords did not feel it necessary to do so since "the common law of
England is consistent with the obligations assumed by the Crown under the Treaty": *per*
Lord Keith of Kinkel at 551).

[43] For approval of this development see *Att.-Gen. v. BBC* [1981] A.C. 303, *per* Lord
Scarman at 354.

[44] The difference between expressly and with clear general words was highlighted in *R. v.
Secretary of State for the Home Department, ex p. Brind* [1991] 1 A.C. 696 (where the House
of Lords held that there must be a real ambiguity before the Convention may be referred
to). But see *R. v. Secretary of State for the Home Department, ex p. Leech* [1994] Q.B. 198,
per Steyn L.J. at 217. *cf. Leech v. Secretary of State for Scotland*, 1991 S.L.T. 910.

[45] See *ex parte Leech, supra. cf. R. v. Secretary of State for the Home Department, ex p.
Simms* [1999] 3 W.L.R. 328. See also Beloff & Mountfield, "Unconventional Behaviour:
Judicial Uses of the European Convention on Human Rights in England and Wales"
[1996] E.H.R.L.R. 467 (showing, for example, relevance of the Convention in developing
uncertain common law precepts). But *cf. Saunders* [1996] 1 Cr.App.R. 463, *per* Taylor C.J.
at 477–478 and *R. v. Morrissey* [1997] 2 Cr.App.R. 427, *per* Lord Bingham C.J. at 442–443
(Convention may only be referred to when English law unclear).

[46] 1980 S.C. 319.

[47] *ibid*. at 329. See also *Moore v. Secretary of State for Scotland*, 1984 S.L.T. 38.

Although the point is no longer often heard, sight should not be lost of the constitutional reasons for drawing a distinction between national and international law, namely the democratic basis of Parliament's authority to change the law.[48] In any event, the result of *Surjit-Kaur* was to discourage arguments that the effect of the compliance presumption should logically be the same in Scotland as in England, at least when interpreting U.K. legislation.[49] It took until 1996 for the Court of Session to confirm the English approach to the compliance presumption as part of Scots law. In *T, Petitioner*,[50] Lord President Hope said: "It is now clearly established as part of the law of England and Wales, as a result of decisions in the House of Lords, that in construing any provision in domestic legislation which is ambiguous in the sense that it is capable of a meaning which either conforms to or conflicts with the Convention, the Courts will presume that Parliament intended to legislate in conformity with the Convention, not in conflict with it".[51] This approach was confirmed in the High Court of Justiciary in *Anderson v. H.M. Advocate*,[52] where it was observed that while the provisions of Article 6(3)(a) to (c) of the Convention were not part of the domestic law, the principles which they describe have for a long time been established as part of the law of Scotland.

The compliance presumption

The compliance presumption is one of the common law presumptions applicable in statutory interpretation. In the present context, it is an aspect of a long-established approach to statutory interpretation which allows legislation to interfere with individual rights only if this is expressly provided for in the legislation or arises from it by necessary implication.[53] In *Metropolitan Asylum District Managers v. Hill*,[54] Lord

6.12

---

[48] The relationship between national and international law is not only controversial in the U.K. In the U.S., where the Constitution confers authority on the President by and with the advice and consent of the Senate to ratify (that is, implement into U.S. federal law) treaties, there has been a vigorous debate on the extent to which norms in unimplemented treaties can enter U.S. law by virtue of their becoming part of customary international law. The expressed concern of those against such incorporation is with its perceived absence of democratic legitimacy: if the constitutional process for incorporation of treaties has not occurred, why should the judiciary (for which, read "the elite") nevertheless give effect to the treaties? For discussion, see Bradley & Goldsmith, "Customary International Law as Federal Common Law: A Critique of the Modern Position" (1997) 110 Harv.L.R. 815; reply by Koh, "Is International Law Really State Law" (1998) 111 Harv.L.R. 1824; and response by Bradley & Goldsmith, "Federal Courts and the Incorporation of International Law" (1998) 111 Harv.L.R. 2260.

[49] Where the rules and principles of statutory interpretation should be the same, *cf. Lord Advocate v. Dumbarton D.C.* [1990] 2 A.C. 580, *per* Lord Keith at 591. For further analysis of the earlier Scottish position on the relevance of Convention rights, see Murdoch, "The European Convention on Human Rights in Scots Law" [1991] P.L. 40; and "Scotland and the European Convention", in Dickson (ed.), *Human Rights and the European Convention* (Sweet & Maxwell, London, 1997).

[50] 1997 S.L.T. 724. For discussion of the decision, see Lord Hope of Craighead, "Devolution and Human Rights" [1998] E.H.R.L.R. 367 and Brown, "The European Convention on Human Rights in Scottish Courts", 1996 S.L.T.(News) 267.

[51] The observations of Lord Ross in *Kaur* were held not to represent good law.

[52] 1996 S.C.C.R. 114 at 121.

[53] See *Pierson v. Secretary of State for the Home Department* [1998] A.C. 539, *per* Lord Browne-Wilkinson at 575; and *R. v. Secretary of State for the Home Department, ex p. Leech* [1994] Q.B. 198, *per* Steyn L.J. at 217 (referring to right of access to the courts as a "constitutional right"). *cf.* Cross, *Statutory Interpretation* (3rd ed.) at p. 166.

[54] (1881) 6 App. Cas. 193 (H.L.).

Blackburn said: "It is clear that the burden is on those who seek to establish that the legislature intended to take away the private rights of individuals to show that by express words or by necessary implication such an intention appears".[55]

The compliance presumption is to the effect that Parliament intends both primary and secondary legislation to comply with the international obligations of the United Kingdom. The presumption applies where the enactments are unclear or ambiguous and, as with all presumptions, it can be overcome by express words or necessary implication.[56] In *Salomon v. Commissioners of Customs & Excise*,[57] Diplock L.J. (as he then was) observed:

> "But if the terms of the legislation are not clear but are reasonably capable of more than one meaning, the treaty itself becomes relevant, for there is a prima facie presumption that Parliament does not intend to act in breach of international law, including therein specific treaty obligations; and if one of the meanings which can reasonably be ascribed to the legislation is consonant with treaty obligations and another or others are not, the meaning which is consonant is to be preferred. Thus, in case of lack of clarity in the words used in the legislation, the terms of the treaty are relevant to enable the court to make its choice between the possible meaning of these words by applying the presumption".[58]

Numerous cases have confirmed that courts make use of the compliance presumption when interpreting legislation.[59] It may now be said that use of the presumption is firmly established where a case concerns fundamental human rights.[60] The presumption can be seen as part of a wider disposition of the courts to refer to international legal materials when

---

[55] *ibid*. at 208. A contrary approach (allowing detention of the subject under words conferring a wide discretion) articulated by the majority in *Liversidge v. Anderson* [1942] A.C. 206 may be explained by the wartime context of that decision, and has in any event been disapproved by the House of Lords: see *R. v. IRC, ex p. Rossminster* [1980] A.C. 952, *per* Lord Diplock at 1011.

[56] For an example of overcoming the presumption, see *IRC v. Collco Developments Ltd* [1962] A.C. 1. But where human rights are at stake, it may be that even necessary implication is no longer enough to take away "constitutional rights"; only express words will suffice. *cf. R. v. Secretary of State for the Home Department, ex p. Leech* [1994] Q.B. 198; and *R. v. Secretary of State for the Home Department, ex p. Simms* [1999] 3 W.L.R. 328.

[57] [1967] 2 Q.B. 116.

[58] *ibid*. at 143–144.

[59] A more expansionist view of the presumption was presented by Lord Denning M.R. in *The Banco* (1971) P. 137; but greater restraint can be found in such cases as *The Atlantic Star* [1973] 2 W.L.R. 795 and *Federal Steam Navigation Co. v. Department of Trade and Industry* [1974] 1 W.L.R. 505. For a discussion of the mid-1970s approach to the construction of legislation implementing international treaties, see Collins, "Treaties and/or Statutes" (1974) Camb. L.J. 181. A narrower view of the relevance of treaties was taken in *British Airways v. Laker Airways* [1985] A.C. 58, where Lord Diplock (at 85–86) observed that the interpretation of treaties which have not been incorporated into English domestic law is not a matter within the interpretative jurisdiction of an English court.

[60] See, for example, *R. v. IRC, ex p. Rossminster Ltd* [1980] A.C. 952 at 1008; and *R. v. Secretary of State for the Home Department, ex p. Brind* [1991] 1 A.C. 696. *cf. Stefan v. GMC* [1999] 1 W.L.R. 1293 at 1302. But in *R. v. Brown* [1994] 1 A.C. 212, Lord Lowry suggested that the Convention could only be used to construe statutes enacted after it was ratified. This suggestion echos difficulties which have arisen in relation to E.C. directives and the obligation of national courts to interpret all national law to comply with directives, including statutes enacted prior to the directive: *cf. Duke v. Reliance Systems Ltd* [1988] A.C. 618; *Webb v. EMO Air Cargo (UK) Ltd* [1993] 1 W.L.R. 49; and see further para. 5.30.

seeking to ascertain the meaning of national legal rules and, in particular, legislation.[61]

Now that the Convention has effect in domestic law in terms of the 1998 Act, it may be asked whether the compliance presumption has less relevance in the context of the Convention rights. For several reasons, however, it is clear that the compliance presumption remains significant both in relation to the Convention and more generally to the operation of human rights standards in the United Kingdom. First, it is clear that it is not correct to say that the 1998 Act has implemented the Convention.[62] In particular, not all the Articles of the Convention have been given direct effect in domestic law and it is clear from section 2 of the 1998 Act that none of the decisions of the European Court of Human Rights are binding on U.K. courts. In many respects, U.K. courts will be able to develop their own jurisprudence under the Act, subject to it being tested in the European Court of Human Rights when a litigant takes a case to Strasbourg. But when deciding cases under the Act, U.K. courts must have regard to decisions of the European Court of Human Rights on the Convention rights and it is natural that they will also have regard to the Act's purpose in "giving further effect" to Convention rights in U.K. law. This must mean that the 1998 Act will be interpreted by reference to the Convention. To this extent, therefore, the compliance presumption retains a special importance in relation to the 1998 Act itself. Secondly, the compliance presumption remains highly relevant in the context of the many other international human rights treaties which the United Kingdom has ratified but which have not been implemented into national law by Act of the U.K. Parliament.[63] In so far as legislation may be ambiguous, it may be relevant to argue that it ought to be interpreted consistently with these other international treaties.[64] Thirdly, by virtue of section 101 of the Scotland Act 1998,[65] in relation to Acts of the Scottish Parliament the compliance presumption must apply in the process of their construction.[66] For these reasons, therefore, the scope of

---

[61] Particularly if the legislation is implementing the treaty—for example, by attaching it as a Schedule to the Act: see *Fothergill v. Monarch Airlines Ltd* [1981] A.C. 251.

[62] As s. 1(2) of the Act says, the Convention rights designated in s. 1(1) "are to have effect" for the purposes of this Act: see para. 6.01.

[63] For example, the UN Covenants on Civil and Political Rights; Economic, Social and Cultural Rights; Elimination of All Forms of Racial Discrimination; and Elimination of All Forms of Discrimination Against Women. There are also other Council of Europe human rights treaties and several treaties emerging from the International Labour Organisation which deal with human rights. For a detailed listing of some other international sources of human rights, see *Halsbury's Laws of England*, Vol. 8(2), para. 103. For judicial reference to the UN Covenant on Civil and Political Rights, see *Stefan v. GMC* [1999] 1 W.L.R. 1293 at 1302.

[64] A difficulty could arise where the meaning of Convention rights in terms of the Convention is less extensive than similar rights guaranteed by other international treaties binding on the U.K. but not implemented into U.K. law. Since the Human Rights Act 1998 is itself subject to the compliance presumption, and ECHR decisions are not binding on U.K. courts, it may be argued that the Act (and the Convention rights as they have effect in the U.K.) should be interpreted consistently with other international human rights treaties: see paras 6.14 *et seq.* below.

[65] And also Sched. 5, Pt I, para. 7(2).

[66] So that they should be interpreted consistently with international treaties, including human rights treaties, binding on the U.K. *Quaere* whether Sched. 5, Pt I, para. 7(2) of the Scotland Act 1998 would allow the Scottish Parliament to "implement" the U.N. Covenant on Civil and Political Rights (ICCPR) into Scots law; would an attempt to give rights under the ICCPR superiority over Convention rights in Scotland take the Scottish Parliament beyond its competence under s. 29 of the Act? Even if ICCPR rights were more generous than Convention rights?

the compliance presumption requires to be closely studied. In particular, the approach that the threshold for recourse to the Convention (or any international treaty obligation) is legislative ambiguity may have to be considered in light of some suggestions elsewhere that unimplemented treaty obligations have a greater influence in domestic law.[67] It may be that the threshold of textual ambiguity in legislation is no longer a precondition before reference can be made to unimplemented treaties, at least so far as treaties dealing with human rights are concerned.[68]

The Human Rights Act 1998

6.13 The government which came to power in May 1997 promised to incorporate the Convention into domestic law.[69] A White Paper was published on October 24, 1997[70] and the incorporation bill was introduced into the House of Lords some two weeks later. After the bill was enacted on November 9, 1998, sections 18, 20 and 21(5) of the Act entered force immediately. The remainder of the 1998 Act is to come into force on such day or days as the Secretary of State may by order appoint.[71] But the Convention rights have applied to the Scottish Parliament and Scottish Executive since their establishment by the Scotland Act 1998 in the same terms as the rights will apply after the Human Rights Act 1998 comes fully into force.[72]

The 1998 Act provides in some detail for the effect which the Convention rights are to have in U.K. law. Accordingly, the Act does not simply incorporate the Convention on its own terms but applies it subject to the provisions of the Act.[73] The 1998 Act cannot therefore be regarded as a "uniform statute".[74] Equally, however, the rights guaranteed in Articles 2–12 and 14 of the Convention, Articles 1–3 of the First Protocol and Articles 1 and 2 of the Sixth Protocol are annexed to the Act in Schedule 1. This device at least requires the courts to interpret

---

[67] In particular, consider the High Court of Australia's decision in *Minister for Immigration & Ethnic Affiars v. Teoh* (1995) 183 C.L.R. 273 (ratified but unimplemented international treaty may found legitimate expectation that discretionary powers will be exercised in accord with treaty), noted by Piotrowicz at [1996] P.L. 190. For criticism, see Taggart, "Legitimate Expectation and Treaties in the High Court of Australia" (1996) 112 L.Q.R. 50. *cf. R. v. Secretary of State for the Home Department, ex p. Ahmed, The Times,* July 30, 1998. See also the Court of Appeal of New Zealand's decision in *Tavita v. Minister of Immigration* [1994] 2 N.Z.L.R. 257.

[68] See Klug & Starmer, "Incorporation Through the Back Door?" [1997] P.L. 223.

[69] For example, see the article by Jack Straw and Paul Boateng, "Bringing Rights Home: Labour's Plans to Incorporate the European Convention on Human Rights" [1997] E.H.R.L.R. 71.

[70] Rights Brought Home: The Human Rights Bill (Cmnd. 3782), Oct. 1997.

[71] s. 22(2) and (3).

[72] See s. 129(2) of the Scotland Act 1998. For an example, see *H.M. Advocate v. Scottish Media Newspapers Ltd*, 1999 S.C.C.R. 599.

[73] See s. 1(2) of the 1998 Act.

[74] A uniform statute simply applies the provisions of an international treaty in domestic law without qualification, or subject only to minor modification. The Act merely directs the courts to the terms of the treaty attached in a Schedule to the Act. The emphasis of this approach is uniform interpretations of the treaty among the states parties to it. The Civil Jurisdiction and Judgments Act 1982 in so far as it applies the 1968 Brussels Convention on Jurisdiction and Recognition and Enforcement of Judgments to cases involving more than one E.U. state may be viewed as a uniform statute. On the interpretation of uniform statutes, see Mann, "Uniform Statutes in English Law" (1983) 99 L.Q.R. 376.

the Act in light of both the Convention rights and the Act's purpose of applying the Convention rights in U.K. law.[75]

III INTERPRETATION OF THE HUMAN RIGHTS ACT 1998

Interpretation of the Convention rights

The 1998 Act provides for "the Convention rights" to have effect "for **6.14** the purposes of this Act".[76] The Convention rights are defined in section 1(1) to mean: "(a) Articles 2 to 12 and 14 of the Convention, (b) Articles 1 to 3 of the First Protocol, and (c) Articles 1 and 2 of the Sixth Protocol, as read with Articles 16 to 18 of the Convention". The 1998 Act also provides some rules which U.K. courts must use to interpret the Convention rights. These may be termed the statutory provisions for interpretation.[77] They point U.K. courts to the European Convention's case law and this must be a logical starting point for interpreting and applying the Convention rights which the 1998 Act guarantees. Significantly, however, U.K. courts will be able to draw on the rich common law traditions of interpreting human rights instruments, and in particular the decisions of the Privy Council on constitutional and human rights issues.[78] The general approach in these decisions is likely to influence interpretation of the 1998 Act. Accordingly, the statutory provisions for interpretation, the approach of the European Court of Human Rights and the "traditional common law" approach to human rights guarantees will now be looked at in more detail.

Statutory provisions for interpretation

Section 2 of the 1998 Act requires a court or tribunal to take Convention **6.15** jurisprudence "into account" when interpreting Convention rights.[79] The Convention jurisprudence to which a court or tribunal must have regard

---

[75] *cf. Fothergill v. Monarch Airlines* [1981] A.C. 251. In addition, as noted above, the presumption applicable in statutory interpretation that statutory provisions are intended to comply with international obligations continues to apply to the interpretation of the 1998 Act. Accordingly, provisions in the text of the Act should be interpreted to accord with the Convention and the European Court of Human Rights' jurisprudence. Equally, of course, the Act must be interpreted in accordance with the U.K.'s other international obligations. This could present a difficulty where, for example, E.U. obligations are not consistent with the European Convention on Human Rights (but see Art. 307 (formerly Art. 234) of the E.C. Treaty and para. 6.000 below) or where another international human rights treaty— for example, the United Nations International Covenant on Civil and Political Rights (ICCPR)—imposes higher standards on its states parties (perhaps by virtue of an interpretation or decision of the Human Rights Committee which interprets and supervises the ICCPR). For discussion of the ICCPR, see Harris & Joseph (eds), *The International Covenant on Civil and Political Rights and UK law* (1995); and McGoldrick, *The Human Rights Committee* (1990).

[76] s. 1(2). This is "subject to any designated derogation or reservation" to the Convention made by the U.K., to which ss 14 and 15 apply.

[77] See s. 2 of the 1998 Act.

[78] See para. 6.07 above.

[79] This is the 1998 Act's equivalent of s. 3 of the European Communities Act 1972 which requires U.K. courts to follow decisions of the (Luxembourg) European Court of Justice and Court of First Instance on E.C. law. Section 3 of the 1972 Act is, however, more mandatory than s. 2 of the 1998 Act. Whereas s. 3 requires U.K. courts to follow decisions of the ECJ (and CFI) on points of E.C. law (which are established by s. 3 as questions of law), s. 2 of the 1998 Act only requires Convention jurisprudence, including decisions of the European Court of Human Rights, to be taken "into account". The effect of s. 3 of the 1972 Act is discussed at para. 5.49.

is defined as any: "(a) judgment, decision, declaration or advisory opinion of the European Court of Human Rights, (b) opinion of the Commission given in a report adopted under Article 31 of the Convention, (c) decision of the Commission in connection with Article 26 or 27(2) of the Convention, or (d) decision of the Committee of Ministers taken under Article 46 of the Convention."[80] The references in paragraphs (b) and (c) are to Articles of the Convention concerning the work of the Commission on Human Rights immediately before the 11th Protocol entered force on November 1, 1998.[81] Paragraph (d) refers to decisions of the Committee of Ministers under Article 46 of the (amended) Convention[82] and is defined as including reference to the Committee's decisions under Articles 32 and 54 of the Convention as they had effect immediately before the coming into force of the 11th Protocol.[83] There is now a large volume of jurisprudence under the Convention, particularly Commission opinions on the interpretation of the Convention and decisions on the admissibility of complaints brought under it.[84] Court of Human Rights and Commission decisions may be traced back to the mid-1950s but the first case involving the United Kingdom which reached the Court was in 1975.[85]

Extent of the duty to take account

6.16   Section 2(1) of the 1998 Act requires a court or tribunal dealing with a question concerning Convention rights to take the designated Convention jurisprudence into account: "so far as, in the opinion of the court or tribunal, it is relevant to the proceedings in which that question has arisen". Although the duty to take the designated Convention jurisprudence into account is expressed in mandatory terms, the duty is qualified by the court's discretion to take it into account only in so far as it is relevant. Two important points follow from this formulation. First, courts and tribunals have a discretion to determine the relevance of Convention jurisprudence presented to them before taking it into account. But there is a practical problem here. Since the relevance or otherwise of the material cannot be determined without the material being available to the court, the task of identifying and recovering it still remains. The quantity of the material referred to in section 2(1) is considerable, so that much labour may have to be spent in research. Secondly, even when, for example, a decision of the European Court of

---

[80] s. 2(1).

[81] s. 21(1) and (2). One effect of the 11th Protocol was to abolish the Commission on Human Rights and the decision-making role of the Committee of Ministers. The 11th Protocol and the Convention's institutions are discussed in part VII below: see paras 6.73 *et seq.*

[82] Article 46 of the Convention now limits the Committee of Ministers only to supervising the execution of decisions of the European Court of Human Rights.

[83] s. 21(3). Section 21(4) of the Act incorporates the 11th Protocol's transitional provisions in Art. 5, paras 3, 4 and 6 of the 11th Protocol. These provide for the Commission and Committee of Ministers to complete their work started under the (unamended) Convention but unfinished when Protocol 11 entered force. The effect of s. 21(4) is to include Commission opinions and decisions and Committee of Ministers decisions within the definition of Convention jurisprudence in s. 2.

[84] Under Arts. 26 and 27(2) of the original Convention.

[85] *Golder v. United Kingdom* 1979–80 1 E.H.R.R. 524. There are several sources of Commission and Court decisions. The most accessible source is likely to be the European Human Rights Reporter (E.H.R.R.), now published monthly. The official series is published by the Council of Europe.

Human Rights is relevant, a U.K. court or tribunal is not bound by it. If relevant, the obligation is only to take it into account. Section 2 of the 1998 Act is therefore some way short of the equivalent section 3 of the European Communities Act 1972 which requires U.K. courts to follow decisions of the ECJ on points of E.C. law which arise before them.[86] In any event, section 2 certainly imposes a duty on courts and tribunals to consider relevant Convention jurisprudence when interpreting Convention rights and it follows that legal advisers will have to accept the burden of identifying and recovering potentially considerable material.

Procedure for establishing interpretative material

Specific provision is made in section 2(2) of the 1998 Act for rules to establish the evidential authority of Convention jurisprudence. These rules are necessary because, unlike the official reports of the decisions of the Scottish Courts, the materials containing Convention jurisprudence are not within judicial knowledge and do not prove themselves in Scottish courts.[87] The rules are published as Rules of Court for the courts and by the Secretary of State for tribunals.[88]   **6.17**

The European Court's approach to Convention rights

Many decisions of the European Court of Human Rights exemplify its approaches to interpreting the Convention rights and examining the validity of limitations placed on the rights by states. The Court's general approach to the Convention must be understood in light of the fact that the Convention is an international treaty.[89] In *Golder v. United Kingdom*[90] the Court accepted the approach to treaty interpretation set out in the Vienna Convention on the Law of Treaties,[91] Article 31, which provides that a treaty: "shall be interpreted in good faith in accordance with the ordinary meaning to be given to the terms of the treaty in their context and in the light of its object and purpose".[92] The Court has accepted the primacy of the Convention text which this approach recommends but it does not follow that the Court necessarily accepts that the Convention must always be given its literal meaning. In practice the Court has adopted the full range of interpretive techniques. While the European Court of Justice has long been famed for its "teleological" approach to the E.C. Treaty, emphasising the object and purpose of the Treaty over its text, the case law of the Court of Human Rights is not hallmarked with one single approach to interpretation. While there are many cases in which the Court emphasises the object and purpose of a right,[93] or   **6.18**

---

[86] Where the point of E.C. law is clear. Where it is unclear, the court may (or in the case of a court of final appeal generally must) make a reference to the ECJ for a preliminary ruling under Art. 234 (formerly 177) of the E.C. Treaty.

[87] Walker & Walker, *Law of Evidence*, p. 48.

[88] In the latter case under s. 2(3) of the Act. The Lord Chancellor publishes the equivalent rules for tribunals in England & Wales.

[89] See Merrills, *The Development of International Law by the European Court of Human Rights* (2nd ed., Manchester U.P. Manchester, 1993), esp. Chaps 4, 5, 6 and 9.

[90] (1979–80) 1 E.H.R.R. 524.

[91] Which, although not yet in force, is taken as encapsulating the rules of customary international law on treaty interpretation.

[92] See also Arts 32–34 of the Vienna Convention, providing for use of *travaux préparatoires* and other language versions to interpret international treaties. For discussion of treaty interpretation, see Jennings & Watts, *Oppenheim's International Law* (9th ed., Longman, London, 1996) at pp. 1266–1284.

[93] See, for example, *Airey v. Ireland* (1979–80) 2 E.H.R.R. 305 (Art. 6 must be interpreted so as to be "practical and effective" and not "theoretical and illusory": at para. 24).

notes that the limitations which may be imposed on a right "must be narrowly interpreted",[94] or requires that the Convention be looked at as a whole,[95] or recalls that "the Convention is a living instrument which . . . must be interpreted in the light of present day conditions",[96] or accepts that rights may be implied by expressly guaranteed Convention rights,[97] there are some cases in which the Court resorts to a strictly literal interpretation of a guaranteed Convention right.[98] It is therefore difficult to describe the Court as "liberal" or "conservative" in its approach to the Convention rights.[99] While some cases display an organic, "living instrument" approach and reject restricting the Convention's meaning to the "original intent" of its drafters, other cases demonstrate a more literal or "strict constructionist" approach. The explanation for the Court's differing approaches partly lies in its international character and partly in the structure of the Convention: some Convention rights are guaranteed in absolute terms, such as the Article 3 right against torture[1]; while other rights are guaranteed subject to permissible limitations, such as the Article 10 right to freedom of expression. But the most significant explanation of the Court's approach to the Convention is the doctrine of margin of appreciation which the Court invariably adopts in the interpretation and application of the Convention.

The doctrine of margin of appreciation

6.19   The international nature of the Convention means that there are cases where a more gradualist, cautious approach is called for, perhaps because of an absence of consensus on what a right means throughout the Council of Europe. Indeed, this factor often underlies the Court of Human Rights' most famous doctrine, namely the margin of appreciation. The existence and flexibility of the doctrine of margin of appreciation means that it is not possible to reduce the Court's approach to the Convention to a neat formula. It is not possible to say in relation to any of the rights that the Court always adopts a logical two-stage process, such as first defining what the right means and secondly assessing whether any limit imposed is legitimate and proportionate.[2] Sometimes the Court may in effect follow such a process, but at other times it

---

[94] *Sunday Times v. U.K.* (1979–80) 2 E.H.R.R. 245, para. 65.

[95] See, for example, *Abdulaziz, Cabales and Balkandali v. U.K.* (1985) 7 E.H.R.R. 471 (immigration matters covered by Protocol No. 4 must be understood in light of the rights guaranteed in the Convention itself); and *Soering v. U.K.* (1989) 11 E.H.R.R. 439 (relationship between Art. 2 of Convention and Protocol No. 6 abolishing the death penalty).

[96] *Tyrer v. U.K.* (1979–80) 2 E.H.R.R. 1, para. 31.

[97] *Golder v. U.K.* (1979–80) 1 E.H.R.R. 524 (Art. 6(1) of Convention implies a right of access to the courts); *cf. Airey v. Ireland* (1979–80) 2 E.H.R.R. 305.

[98] *Johnston v. Ireland* (1987) 9 E.H.R.R. 203 (Art. 12 right to marry does not confer right to divorce so as to be able to remarry: the Court could not "by means of an evolutive interpretation, derive . . . a right that was not included [in the Convention] at the outset": at para. 53). *cf. Rees v. U.K.* (1987) 9 E.H.R.R. 56, esp. para. 49 of Court Judgment.

[99] Although some judges may be so described: see Jacobs & White, *The European Convention on Human Rights* (2nd ed., OUP, 1996) at pp. 36–38 on the contribution of Sir Gerald Fitzmaurice to the Court.

[1] *cf. Ireland v. U.K.* (1979–80) 2 E.H.R.R. 25. The flexibility, however, is found in defining torture: see para. 6.19 below.

[2] Compare the two-stage approach to rights and limits on rights of the Supreme Court of Canada under the Canadian Charter of Rights and Freedoms: see, for example, *Hunter v. Southam* [1984] 2 S.C.R. 145; and *R. v. Oakes* [1986] 1 S.C.R. 103.

emphasises its analysis of the limit which has been imposed on the right, while on other occasions it finds that the right itself does not carry the meaning for which the complainer has argued. In this regard, it is important to understand that the margin of appreciation applies generally in the interpretation of the Convention, not only for the purpose of assessing the permissibility of a limit imposed on a right but also in identifying the meaning of a right itself.[3] The danger, however, is that the Court's frequent use of the doctrine of margin of appreciation may allow it to avoid difficult questions concerning the appropriate scope or meaning which a right should be interpreted as having and to avoid articulating in detail the reasons why a particular limit on rights should be approached with more or less deference.[4] Nevertheless, whatever may be the criticisms against it,[5] the doctrine of margin of appreciation has limits. For the Court of Human Rights, the limit is summed up in the principle of effectiveness.[6] This means that: "The Convention is intended to guarantee not rights that are theoretical or illusory but rights that are practical and effective".[7] This conclusion on the object and purpose of the Convention has been adopted by the Court on numerous occasions and has informed the democratic values which permeate the Convention and to which the Court has referred many times.[8] It is, perhaps, the neatest encapsulation available of the Court's general approach to the Convention rights and the doctrine of margin of appreciation should be understood by reference to it.

---

[3] This is often (especially in the U.S.) termed "definitional balancing", which means that rights themselves have a limited meaning (for example, defining "speech" or "expression" to exclude certain categories of communication). In other words, rights are given a less generous meaning and the balancing of interests is not left to be done in the application of limitation clauses (for example, in deciding what is necessary in a democratic society). The European Court of Human Rights clearly engages in "definitional balancing" when applying those Convention rights guaranteed in absolute terms: for example, what is meant by "torture" under Art. 3 (on which, see *Tyrer v. U.K.* (1978) 2 E.H.R.R. 1; *Ireland v. U.K.* (1979–80) 2 E.H.R.R. 25; *Campbell & Cosans v. U.K.* (1980) 4 E.H.R.R. 293; and *Soering v. U.K.* (1989) 11 E.H.R.R. 439). See also *Johnston v. Ireland* (1987) 9 E.H.R.R. 203. But it is not apparent that the Court engages in definitional balancing in relation to rights which are qualified by a limitation clause, *cf. Handyside v. U.K.* (1979–80) 1 E.H.R.R. 737; and see Hovius, "The Limitation Clauses of the European Convention on Human Rights and Freedoms" (1986) 6 *Yearbook of Eur. Law* 1. For a positive argument that definitional balancing limits the volume of human rights litigation, see Hogg, *Constitutional Law of Canada* (4th ed., Carswell, Toronto, 1997), at paras 33.20–33.21.

[4] *cf.* the dissent in *Mathieu-Mohin v. Belgium* (1987) 10 E.H.R.R. 1 at 21, criticising the majority's approach to the Convention as "falling back on the margin of appreciation".

[5] Most famously made by Judge Rosalyn Higgins in "Derogations under Human Rights Treaties" (1977) 48 Brit.Y.B. of Int. Law 281 at 312 *et seq.* (arguing that the doctrine allows the state "two bites at the cherry"). For more recent discussion, see Jones, "The Devaluation of Human Rights under the European Convention" [1995] P.L. 430; and Lavender, "The Problem of the Margin of Appreciation" [1997] E.H.R.L.R. 380.

[6] See Merrills, *supra*, Chap. 5.

[7] *Airey v. Ireland* (1979–80) 2 E.H.R.R. 305 at para. 24. See also *Artico v. Italy* (1981) 3 E.H.R.R. 1 and *cf. Campbell & Cosans v. U.K.* (1982) 4 E.H.R.R. 293, esp. at para. 37.

[8] See, for example, *Golder v. U.K.* (1979–80) 1 E.H.R.R. 524, para. 34 (referring to the rule of law); *Handyside v. U.K.* (1979–80) 1 E.H.R.R. 737, para. 49 (referring to freedom of expression as one of the "essential foundations" of a democratic society based on "pluralism, tolerance and broadmindedness"); and *Lingens v. Austria* (1986) 8 E.H.R.R. 407, para. 41 (referring to freedom of political debate). *cf. Soering v. U.K.* (1989) 11 E.H.R.R. 439 at para. 87.

The European Court's approach to limitations on rights

6.20   The Court has stressed that limitations imposed on rights must not "impair their very essence and deprive them of their effectiveness".[9] In other words, every right has a core which is protected from limitation. Where a right is guaranteed subject to expressly stated permissible limitations, the limitation "must be narrowly interpreted".[10] Beyond these generalities, two doctrines stand out in the Court's jurisprudence on the validity of limitations placed on Convention rights. These are the doctrines of proportionality and margin of appreciation. While the Court's approach to proportionality is not always structured,[11] and while the application of margin of appreciation does not easily lend itself to legal analysis, both doctrines operate, if not always clearly, in the Court's assessment of the validity of limits on Convention rights. Although the two doctrines are usually treated as distinct, it may be argued that they are fused, or at least dependent on each other. That is, the nature of the proportionality analysis to which a limitation on a right will be subjected will depend on the scope of the margin of appreciation which the Court considers that the state retains. An example may be taken from one aspect of a traditional proportionality test, namely whether a limit on a right imposed by the government is "necessary" to achieve the desired objective or whether there is some reasonable and practicable alternative approach which would have less impact on the right. How this applies in a particular case will depend on how strictly or deferentially the Court applies the test, which will in turn depend on what margin of appreciation all the circumstances justify the government to be conceded. A "wide" margin of appreciation may mean that the court will more readily concede that the government had no alternative "practicable" means to achieve its objective. On the other hand, a "narrow" margin will cause the court to be more anxious about the government's priorities and how it chose the means to address them. As always with proportionality, there is a large amount of judicial discretion involved: for example, in the assessment of how important the reasons for limiting rights may be; or in the assessment of whether or not alternative means would be just as effective to achieve the objective. To some extent, the margin of appreciation is the means by which the European Court of Human Rights modulates the great discretion which proportionality gives it. By allowing a margin of appreciation in the application of the concept of proportionality, the Court may be able to counter concerns about the legitimacy of its judicial power. Such concerns are an inevitable part of human rights litigation and in one form or another, courts elsewhere have adopted techniques that are analogous with margin of appreciation.[12] Accordingly, while some commentators have suggested that the

---

[9] *Mathieu-Mohin v. Belgium* (1987) 10 E.H.R.R. 1, para. 52.

[10] *Sunday Times v. U.K.* (1979–80) 2 E.H.R.R. 245, para. 65.

[11] Unlike the approach of the Supreme Court of Canada set out by Dickson C.J. in *R. v. Oakes* [1986] 1 S.C.R. 106 at 136 *et seq.* and (at least as a structure for analysis) followed reasonably faithfully since.

[12] Consider, for example, the "tiers of scrutiny" which the U.S. Supreme Court applies to limits imposed on constitutional rights under the U.S. Bill of Rights. The approach is most famously articulated in footnote 4 to Stone J's opinion in *U.S. v. Carolene Products Co.* 304 U.S. 144 (1938): government regulation, particularly economic regulation, is to be presumed constitutional (and easily justified by showing a rational relationship between means and ends) unless it violates fundamental rights, impedes access to the political

doctrine of margin of appreciation is only to be adopted by an international court and is unsuitable to human rights litigation in domestic courts,[13] the relationship between proportionality and the margin of appreciation means that both doctrines may have their place before national courts, whatever different terms may be used to describe them.[14]

General approach to interpreting human rights guarantees

There are many decisions of the Privy Council and of courts in other parts of the Commonwealth which demonstrate what may be termed a general common law approach to interpreting human rights instruments. It has already been noted that the Privy Council has had many opportunities to interpret human rights guarantees in Commonwealth constitutions and more recently in relation to the Hong Kong Bill of Rights.[15] The experience of the Privy Council and also of the Supreme Court of Canada and Court of Appeal of New Zealand provides some indication of the general common law approach to interpreting human rights guarantees. **6.21**

Minister of Home Affairs v. Fisher

In *Minister of Home Affairs v. Fisher*[16] the Privy Council set out its general approach to instruments containing human rights guarantees. The Board had to decide if the word "child" included a child born out of wedlock for the purposes of a provision in the Constitution of Bermuda. The Privy Council decided that it did. Importantly, Chapter I of the Constitution was headed "Protection of Fundamental Rights and Freedoms of the Individual" and was based on the Convention. The Board's discussion of the conflicting approaches to interpreting the Constitution is instructive. Should the approach be that which would be taken to an ordinary statute, which the Constitution as an Act of the U.K. Parliament certainly was, or should it be animated by more dynamic considerations recognising the constitutional nature of the Act in the law of Bermuda? Reminiscent of Lord Sankey's metaphor that a constitution is a "living tree capable of growth and expansion" and should not be "cut **6.22**

---

process, or discriminates against "discrete and insular minorities" (in which case the measure is to attract "strict scrutiny", requiring a showing that the means are necessary to achieve a "compelling" government interest). The approach certainly reflects the difficulties the Court had with "substantive due process" under the 14th Amendment to the Constitution as understood in the line of cases launched by *Lochner v. New York*, 198 U.S. 45 (1905) but reversed by *West Coast Hotel v. Parrish*, 300 U.S. 379 (1937), so as to uphold the New Deal. Consider also the Supreme Court of Canada's approach to s. 1 of the Charter and the proportionality tests articulated in *R. v. Oakes* [1986] 1 S.C.R. 103: see, for example, *R. v. Edwards Books & Art* [1986] 2 S.C.R. 713; and cases cited at para. 6.24 below. For further discussion, see Hogg, *Constitutional Law of Canada* (4th ed., 1997), at para. 35.11(b).

[13] See Sir John Laws, *"Wednesbury"* in Forsyth & Hare (eds), *The Golden Metwand and the Crooked Cord"* (OUP, Oxford, 1998), at p. 201. See also Singh, Hunt and Demetriou, "Is There a Role for the 'Margin of Appreciation' in National Law after the Human Rights Act?" [1999] E.H.R.L.R. 15.

[14] *cf.* Pannick, "Principles of interpretation of Convention rights under the Human Rights Act and the discretionary area of judgment" [1998] P.L. 545. The possible relevance of the doctrine of margin of appreciation in the context of Convention rights and the Scottish Parliament is considered in para. 7.35.

[15] See para. 6.07 above.

[16] [1980] A.C. 319.

down" by a "narrow and technical construction",[17] Lord Wilberforce's analysis is worth setting out in full:

> "When therefore it becomes necessary to interpret 'the subsequent provisions of Chapter I—in this case section 11—the question must inevitably be asked whether the appellants' premise, fundamental to their argument, that these provisions are to be construed in the manner and according to the rules which apply to Acts of Parliament, is sound. In their Lordships' view there are two possible answers to this. The first would be to say that, recognising the status of the Constitution as, in effect, an Act of Parliament, there is room for interpreting it with less rigidity, and greater generosity, than other Acts, such as those which are concerned with property, or succession, or citizenship. On the particular question this would require the court to accept as a starting point the general presumption that "child" means "legitimate child" but to recognise that this presumption may be more easily displaced. The second would be more radical: it would be to treat a constitutional document such as this as *sui generis*, calling for principles of interpretation of its own, suitable to its character as already described, without necessary acceptance of all the presumptions that are relevant to legislation of private law.
>
> It is possible that, as regards the question now for decision, either method would lead to the same result. But their Lordships prefer the second."[18]

Human rights instruments require: "a generous interpretation, avoiding what has been called 'the austerity of tabulated legalism', suitable to give to individuals the full measure of the fundamental rights and freedoms referred to".[19] The Privy Council has endorsed this general approach in many subsequent cases.[20]

The generous and purposive construction

6.23 The recognition of the different approach required for instruments guaranteeing human rights is confirmed in later Privy Council decisions. In *Attorney-General of the Gambia v. Jobe*[21] Lord Diplock said: "A constitution, and in particular that part of it which protects and entrenches fundamental rights and freedoms to which all persons in the state are to be entitled, is to be given a generous and purposive construction".[22] The need to give a "generous and purposive construction" to human rights guarantees is also acknowledged by the Supreme Court of Canada and the New Zealand Court of Appeal when interpreting the Canadian Charter of Rights and Freedoms and the New

---

[17] *Edwards v. Att.-Gen. of Canada* [1930] A.C. 124 at 136.

[18] [1980] A.C. 319 at 329.

[19] *ibid. per* Lord Wilberforce at 328. This statement has been described by Lord Cooke of Thorndon as "now evidently destined for judicial immortality": *Ministry of Transport v. Noort* [1992] 3 N.Z.L.R. 260 *per* Cooke P. at 268.

[20] See, for example, *Att.-Gen. of the Gambia v. Jobe* [1984] A.C. 689, *per* Lord Diplock at 700; *Att.-Gen. of Hong Kong v. Lee Kwong-kut* [1993] A.C. 951, *per* Lord Woolf at 966; *Huntley v. Att.-Gen. for Jamaica* [1995] 2 A.C. 1, *per* Lord Woolf at 12; and *Matadeen v. Pointu* [1998] 3 W.L.R. 18, *per* Lord Hoffmann at 25.

[21] [1984] A.C. 689. See also *Vasquez v. The Queen* [1994] 1 W.L.R. 1304.

[22] *ibid.* at 700.

Zealand Bill of Rights respectively. In *Hunter v. Southam*[23] the Supreme
Court of Canada quoted with approval Lord Wilberforce's judgment in
Minister of Home Affairs v. Fisher.[24] In *R v. Big M Drug Mart*,[25] the
Supreme Court held that interpretation of the constitutional Charter of
Rights should be: "generous rather than legalistic . . . aimed at fulfilling
the purpose of the guarantee and securing for individuals the full benefit
of the Charter's protection".[26] Similarly, in *Ministry of Transport v.
Noort*,[27] Lord Cooke of Thorndon (then President of the New Zealand
Court of Appeal) said that the New Zealand Bill of Rights Act 1990
should receive: "such fair, large and liberal construction and interpretation as will best ensure the attainment of its object according to its true
intention, meaning and spirit".[28] Although the Canadian Charter is a
constitutional document, Lord Cooke's comments on the New Zealand
Bill indicate that there is no reason to deny the same generous and
purposive approach to the construction of an "ordinary" Act of Parliament such as the 1998 Act. The New Zealand Bill of Rights is an
"ordinary" statute but its provisions still attract a generous, even
dynamic, construction from the New Zealand courts.[29] Indeed, the need
to bring a generous and purposive interpretation to both types of human
rights instruments is highlighted both in Canada and New Zealand,
where emphasis is placed on the importance of striving for consistency
between domestic human rights guarantees and the state's international
human rights treaty obligations.[30]

The general approach to limitations on rights

The Privy Council, the Supreme Court of Canada and the Court of **6.24**
Appeal of New Zealand have generally demonstrated that whereas
guaranteed rights are to receive a "generous and purposive" construction, provisions allowing for limitations on rights are to be narrowly
construed. In particular, limits on rights have to be necessary, which
means that they must serve purposes which are "sufficiently important"
or "pressing and substantial"[31] in the interests of society, but which are
still consistent with the values of a free and democratic society.[32] The
burden of justifying limits on rights is generally on the government and
the burden will normally be high.[33] Although some differences have
emerged between their particular approaches, the Privy Council,

---

[23] [1984] 2 S.C.R. 145 at 156.
[24] *supra*.
[25] [1985] 1 S.C.R. 295.
[26] *ibid*. at 344.
[27] [1992] 3 N.Z.L.R. 260.
[28] *ibid*. at 271. But see *R. v. Grayson and Taylor* [1997] 1 N.Z.L.R. 399 at 409.
[29] In particular, see *Simpson v. Att.-Gen.* [1994] 3 N.Z.L.R. 667. Similarly, the Hong
Kong courts have adopted the "generous and purposive" approach to interpreting the
(statutory) Hong Kong Bill of Rights: see *R. v. Sin Yau-ming* (1991) 1 H.K.P.L.R. 88,
approved in *Att.-Gen. of Hong Kong v. Lee Kwong-kut* [1993] A.C. 951.
[30] *cf. R. v. Brydges* [1990] 1 S.C.R. 190 at 214 and *Simpson v. Att.-Gen.* [1994] 3 N.Z.L.R.
667.
[31] *R. v. Oakes* [1986] 1 S.C.R. 103, *per* Dickson C.J. at 138–139.
[32] *ibid*. where Dickson C.J. lists some of the values of a free and democratic society. See
para. 16.08.
[33] *cf. R. v. Oakes* [1986] 1 S.C.R. 103; but see *Hill v. Church of Scientology of Toronto*
[1995] 2 S.C.R. 1130 (where common law values are challenged for inconsistency with the
Charter of Rights, both the burden of proving a limitation of rights and the absence of
justification for any limitation are on the challenger).

Supreme Court of Canada and Court of Appeal of New Zealand all accept the need to apply principles of proportionality when balancing human rights guarantees against the need for and effects of limitations imposed on the rights.[34] But, as noted above, proportionality must be understood flexibly and incorporates elements of the European Court of Human Rights' doctrine of margin of appreciation.[35]

In particular, realism must be at the forefront of human rights jurisprudence. The desire that human rights guarantees receive "generous and purposive" interpretations must be seen in particular contexts. In *Attorney-General of Hong Kong v. Lee Kwong-kut*,[36] Lord Woolf explained the position as follows: "While the Hong Kong judiciary should be zealous in upholding an individual's rights under the Hong Kong Bill, it is also necessary to ensure that disputes as to the effect of the Bill are not allowed to get out of hand. The issues involving the Hong Kong Bill should be approached with realism and good sense, and kept in proportion. If this is not done the Bill would become a source of injustice rather than justice and it will be debased in the eyes of the public".[37] On this basis it should be desirable for the courts to keep a sense of proportion when interpreting guarantees of human rights. One limitation mechanism by which they do so is some form of public–private distinction built into most systems of domestic human rights protection.[38] Yet even in relation to "public" bodies, the policy concern of a "sense of proportion" sits uneasily with the desire to bring a "generous and purposive" interpretation to domestic guarantees of human rights. It reveals the inherent tension between judicial deference to legislative and executive choices, supported as they may be by democratically based authority, and the obligation on the judiciary to enforce and uphold

---

[34] See (in Canada) *R. v. Oakes* [1986] 1 S.C.R. 103, esp. at 138–139; but *cf. R. v. Edwards Books & Art* [1986] 2 S.C.R. 713; *Quebec v. Ford* [1988] 2 S.C.R. 712; *Irwin Toy v. Quebec* [1989] 1 S.C.R. 927; *Egan v. Canada* [1995] 2 S.C.R. 513; *RJR-McDonald Inc. v. Att.-Gen. of Canada* [1995] 3 S.C.R. 199; and *Thomson Newspapers Co. Ltd v. Att.-Gen. of Canada* [1998] 1 S.C.R. 877. In New Zealand, the *Oakes* approach was adopted in *Ministry of Transport v. Noort* [1992] 3 N.Z.L.R. 260; see also *R. v. Grayson & Taylor* [1997] 1 N.Z.L.R. 399, *cf.* however, the approach of the Privy Council in *Att.-Gen. of Hong Kong v. Lee Kwong-kut* [1993] A.C. 951, esp. *per* Lord Woolf at 975.

[35] In particular, compare the articulation of the Supreme Court of Canada's proportionality tests to be applied under s. 1 of the Charter in *Oakes*, *supra*, with the application of them in *R. v. Edwards Books & Art*, *supra*. See also *Libman v. Att.-Gen. of Quebec* [1997] 3 S.C.R. 569 at 605–606. For discussion of the Canadian position, see Trakman, Cole-Hamilton and Gatien, "*R v. Oakes* 1986–97: Back to the Drawing Board" (1998) 36 Os. Hall L.J. 83. On the doctrine of margin of appreciation in the Privy Council, see *Ming Pao Newspapers Ltd v. Att.-Gen. of Hong Kong* [1996] A.C. 907.

[36] [1993] A.C. 951.

[37] *ibid.* at 965. See also *R. v. Grayson & Taylor* [1997] 1 N.Z.L.R. 399, esp. at 409.

[38] See s. 6 of the Human Rights Act 1998. Interestingly, the public–private distinction generally only applies when the human rights protections have constitutional status, *cf.* the "state action" doctrine under the U.S. Bill of Rights and s. 32 of the Canadian Charter of Rights and Freedoms. Where human rights or "civil rights" are guaranteed in ordinary legislation, the distinction often does not apply: *e.g.* the U.S. Civil Rights Acts; the Ontario Human Rights Act. In the U.K., it may be noted that the Sex Discrimination Act 1975 and Race Relations Act 1976 apply in the "private" sector, albeit in the case of the 1975 Act only in the area of employment. The public/private distinction as it affects human rights guarantees receives extensive discussion in Clapham, *Human Rights in the Private Sphere* (OUP, Oxford, 1993).

fundamental human rights.[39] This tension is present for most exercises of judicial review but the value judgments demanded by human rights guarantees makes it more intense. As has been observed in the earlier chapter on the constitutional context of judicial review,[40] there is no easy way of avoiding the tension. But democratic processes themselves are not perfect and by passing the Human Rights Act 1998, Parliament has given its blessing to judicial review based on the fundamental human rights protected in the Convention. The courts cannot avoid what may now be termed their constitutional responsibility of giving effect to Convention rights in national law.

The Scottish courts

For the Scottish courts, particular attention will require to be paid to the **6.25** relationship between Convention rights and the Scottish Parliament and Executive. The interaction between the Human Rights Act 1998 and the Scotland Act 1998 is such that Convention rights are effectively entrenched as against legislation, acts and decisions of the Scottish Parliament and Executive. The implications of this are considered further in Chapter 7 (on judicial review and devolution).

More generally, it is likely that courts throughout the United Kingdom will adopt approaches similar to those of the Privy Council, the Supreme Court of Canada and the Court of Appeal of New Zealand when interpreting Convention rights and determining the validity of limitations placed on the rights.[41] The approach will to a great extent be influenced by the approach of the European Court of Human Rights under the Convention but in so far as there is any difference between the European Court's approach and the "common law approach", it is more in terminology than method. The essential point is that U.K. courts will require to develop techniques of interest balancing which will involve the articulation of standards to serve as thresholds for their intervention. They will have to go beyond the limits of irrationality to investigate the realities of each case and not merely the procedures in order to see if the degree of the limitation of rights is proportionate to the purpose it serves. In some cases, deference to legislative and administrative choices will be called for, while in others the importance of the right and the extent of its limitation will require stronger scrutiny. But the novelty of what is required should not be overstated. For some time the courts have accepted that review of discretionary decisions on the ground of irrationality requires different levels of scrutiny depending on the nature

---

[39] *cf.* s. 101 of the Scotland Act 1998, requiring that Scottish legislation (*i.e.* Acts of the Scottish Parliament and subordinate legislation made by the Scottish Executive) must be interpreted so far as possible "as narrowly as is required" so as to be within the powers of the Parliament and Executive. Convention rights, therefore, are to receive "generous and purposive" interpretations, while Acts of the Scottish Parliament are not to, at least in so far as they could be interpreted to violate (generously construed) Convention rights.

[40] See paras 4.20 *et seq.*

[41] In particular, of course, the Court of Session and all Scottish courts are bound by decisions of the House of Lords in civil cases concerning the interpretation of the Human Rights Act 1998 and the Convention rights it guarantees. It is likely that, although not bound, the High Court of Justiciary will regard House of Lords decisions on the Act in criminal cases as highly persuasive. But where "devolution" issues arise under Sched. 6 to the Scotland Act 1998, the Privy Council will be Scotland's highest court. Presumably its decisions will be binding on all Scottish courts—civil and criminal—on devolution issues, including *inter alia* decisions on Convention rights and Scottish criminal law in so far as this is enacted by the Scottish Parliament.

of the decision involved. As Lord Templeman has said: "Where the result of a flawed decision may imperil life or liberty a special responsibility lies on the court in the examination of the decision-making process".[42] The most significant contribution of the Human Rights Act 1998 will be to make this approach the norm. In doing so, it will reinforce the development of judicial review on human rights grounds in the United Kingdom.

IV THE HUMAN RIGHTS ACT 1998 AND LEGISLATION

Legislation and Conformity with the Convention

6.26 The relationship between the Human Rights Act 1998 and legislation is one of the central features of the Act.[43] It is also not without difficulty. In relation to primary legislation enacted by the U.K. Parliament,[44] the difficulty arises from the supremacy of Parliament. This supremacy is taken to mean that no Parliament can bind its successors, which leads to the doctrine of implied repeal. If the 1998 Act is not protected from this doctrine, for example, by a provision similar to section 2(4) of the European Communities Act 1972, the application of the Act to future legislation will be limited. Although the Act can in theory benefit from the doctrine of implied repeal in relation to prior legislation—for example, an earlier provision violating Convention rights is impliedly repealed by the later 1998 Act—this would only be significant if the Act did not expressly provide for its relationship with primary legislation. But sections 3 and 4 of the Act make express provision for the relationship between Convention rights and legislation whenever enacted. These provisions are of critical importance to the scope which the Convention rights are to have in relation to legislation enacted by the U.K. Parliament.

No Audit of Prior Legislation

6.27 In relation to legislation enacted before the Human Rights Act 1998, the government refused to "audit" the statute book before the Act entered force to ensure that all pre-existing legislation complied with Convention rights. Furthermore, subject to section 3 of the Act, it must be noted that the Act does not read in to all prior legislation a "compliance with the Convention" provision.[45] Whatever future legislation does, all legislation passed before the Act may infringe the Convention in some way.

Future Legislation: Pre-enactment Statements of Compatibility

6.28 Section 19 of the Act requires a minister of the Crown in charge of a bill in either House of Parliament before the Bill's second reading to make a statement on the Bill's compatibility or incompatibility with Convention

---

[42] *R. v. Secretary of State for the Home Department, ex p. Bugdaycay* [1987] A.C. 514 at 537. See later, para. 22.32.

[43] See Ewing, "The Human Rights Act and Parliamentary Democracy" (1999) 62 M.L.R. 79.

[44] The relationship between the Convention rights and Acts of the Scottish Parliament and subordinate Scottish legislation is governed by the Scotland Act 1998 and is discussed in Chap. 7.

[45] *cf.* s. 3 of the Hong Kong Bill of Rights (Laws of Hong Kong, Cap. 383).

rights.[46] Although section 6 of the Act means that proceedings in Parliament are not to be considered acts or failures to act for the purposes of section 6 of the Act,[47] it is arguable that a minister's failure to make a statement of compatibility or incompatibility as required by section 19 could be subject to judicial review.[48] In any event, it remains to be seen how much weight the courts give to a ministerial statement that a bill is compatible with the Convention if a challenge concerning the subsequent Act's provisions arises.[49]

Sections 3 and 4 of the 1998 Act: overview

The 1998 Act approaches the issue of its relationship with enacted **6.29** legislation in four ways. First, the Act conflates its application to prior and future legislation by providing an interpretive rule that all legislation, whenever enacted, must be "read and given effect" so far as possible to be compatible with Convention rights.[50] Secondly, the Act draws a distinction between its application to primary and subordinate legislation.[51] This has the effect of preserving the powers of a supreme court over secondary legislation but qualifying them where the problem stems from primary legislation. This leads to the third matter of the Act's relationship with primary legislation inconsistent with Convention rights. The Act provides only the declaratory remedy of a declaration of incompatibility where a supreme court finds inconsistency between Convention rights and a provision in primary legislation whenever enacted or a provision in subordinate legislation removal of which is barred by primary legislation.[52] Fourthly, this respect for Parliamentary supremacy is then addressed further by the Act: section 10 confers on a minister of the Crown the power to amend legislation by order following a declaration of incompatibility. It follows that the 1998 Act adopts a varied relationship with other legislation. This requires closer examination.

Interpretation of legislation: section 3

With regard both to all primary and subordinate legislation the general **6.30** requirement is prescribed in section 3(1) of the Act: "So far as it is possible to do so, primary legislation and subordinate legislation must be read and given effect in a way which is compatible with the Convention rights".[53] This obligation of interpretation is stated generally as universally applicable to anyone who reads legislation and anyone who gives effect to it. The requirement expressly applies to legislation whenever enacted.[54] But the obligation to "read and give effect" to legislation so far as possible to be compatible with Convention rights may be said not to be as strong an interpretive rule as that provided in section 2(4) of the

---

[46] *cf.* s. 7 of the New Zealand Bill of Rights Act 1990.

[47] See s. 6(3) and (6).

[48] See para. 6.46 below.

[49] For an argument that the court will pay close attention to compatibility statements made about a bill if the Act is subsequently challenged, see Lord Hoffmann, "Human Rights and the House of Lords" (1999) 62 M.L.R. 159 at 162.

[50] 1998 Act, s. 3(1).

[51] *ibid.* s. 3(2).

[52] s. 3(2)(b) and (c); s. 4.

[53] The terms "primary legislation" and "subordinate legislation" are defined in s. 21(1) of the Act: see further para. 6.32 below.

[54] s. 3(2)(a).

European Communities Act 1972, which provides that all legislation "shall be construed and have effect" subject to applicable E.C. law. In particular, the qualification "so far as possible" echoes a notable decision of the ECJ on the obligation of national courts to interpret and apply all national law in a way which gives effect to E.C. directives.[55] The qualification "so far as possible" has been a source of some controversy in this context: specifically, to what extent is it "possible" to distort the words of an enactment?[56] More generally, of course, section 2(4) of the European Communities Act 1972 draws its strength from the obligations incumbent on national courts directly under the E.C. Treaty, which requires national courts not only to give effect to E.C. law but also to accord it supremacy over inconsistent national law including, in the United Kingdom, primary legislation, even although section 2(4) may not clearly lead to this conclusion on its own terms.[57] In contrast, the Human Rights Act 1998 plainly recognises Parliamentary supremacy where U.K. primary legislation is directly or indirectly challenged. Furthermore, the 1998 Act does not give effect to Article 13 of the Convention, which provides for effective national remedies for Convention violations. However, the Act may itself fulfil Article 13 and must in any event itself be interpreted in accordance with the Convention.

The implications of section 3

6.31   The obligation to "read and give effect" in section 3(1) must be seen in light of the purpose of the Act. On this basis, it should be engaged in a similar manner to section 2(4) of the 1972 Act. In particular, the obligation created by section 3 applies generally to all legislation.[58] It is not limited to cases of ambiguity but rather requires the court to attempt to find in all legislation a possible meaning which will be compatible with Convention rights. This means that only the clearest form of words in primary legislation can operate to override Convention rights. Any ambiguous words must be interpreted to comply with the Convention. Further, general words which can have the effect of violating Convention rights—for example, words conferring a discretionary power—must be "read and given effect" so as to be compatible with Convention rights.[59] As Lord Steyn has said: "Traditionally the search has been for the true meaning of a statute. Now the search will be for a possible meaning that would prevent the need for a declaration of incompatibility. The questions will be (1) What meanings are the words capable of yielding? (2) And, critically, can the words be made to yield a sense consistent with Convention rights? In practical effect there will be a rebuttable presumption in favour of an interpretation consistent with Convention rights".[60] But exactly what section 3 requires in practice is less easy to

---

[55] Case C–106/89 *Marleasing v. La Comercial Internacional de Alimentación SA* [1991] E.C.R. I-4156.

[56] For discussion, see Maltby, "*Marleasing*: What is all the Fuss About?" (1993) 109 L.Q.R. 301. *cf. Duke v. GEC Reliance Ltd* [1988] A.C. 618; *Litster v. Forth & Clyde Dry Dock & Engineering Ltd*, 1989 S.C. (H.L.) 96 and *Webb v. EMO Air Cargo (U.K.) Ltd* [1993] 1 W.L.R. 49.

[57] *cf. R. v. Secretary of State for Transport, ex p. Factortame Ltd (No. 2)* [1991] 1 A.C. 603.

[58] *cf. R. v. Phillips* [1991] 3 N.Z.L.R. 175 at 176 where Cooke P. described s. 3's equivalent in the New Zealand Bill of Rights Act 1990 (s. 6) as "an important section".

[59] As far as the Convention rights are concerned, therefore, the House of Lords' decision in *ex p. Brind* [1991] 1 A.C. 696 is reversed by the 1998 Act.

[60] "Incorporation and Devolution" [1998] E.H.R.L.R. 153.

predict.[61] For example, to what extent is a presumption of compatibility to be recognised and if so, how can it be overcome: that is, only by express words or also by necessary implication? How easy will it be for a party to establish (or resist) the range of possible interpretations? To what extent are common law concepts (for example, the concept of marriage), on which statutes may proceed to be defined compatible with Convention rights.[62] As one commentator has argued, it may be in a party's interest to establish incompatibility, since if compatibility is demonstrated it may mean that the claim on the Convention right fails.[63] Only experience will reveal the full effect which section 3 is to have.

Primary and subordinate legislation

Section 21(1) of the 1998 Act defines primary and subordinate legisla- **6.32** tion for the purposes of the Act. Primary legislation means any public general Act, local and personal Act, private Act, Measure of the Church Assembly or of the General Synod of the Church of England, and Order in Councils made under section 38(1)(a) of the Northern Ireland Constitution Act 1973 or in exercise of the Royal Prerogative. It also includes "an order or other instrument made under primary legislation to the extent to which it operates to bring one or more provisions of that legislation into force or amends any primary legislation".[64] Subordinate legislation is defined to mean Orders in Council other than those defined as primary legislation, Acts of the Scottish Parliament, Acts of the Parliament of Northern Ireland, Measures of the Northern Ireland Assembly, any instrument made under primary legislation other than those which are included in the definition of primary legislation, and any instrument made under an Act of the Scottish Parliament, an Act of the Parliament of Northern Ireland or under a Measure of the Northern Ireland Assembly or under an Order in Council applying only to Northern Ireland. The distinction between primary and subordinate legislation is significant for the purposes of the Act. In particular, a provision in subordinate legislation which is incompatible with Convention rights may be invalidated by the court, unless the incompatibility is the result of primary legislation.[65] The power of the court in this regard is considered further below.

---

[61] See Marshall, "Interpreting interpretation in the Human Rights Bill" [1998] P.L. 167; see also Lord Lester, "The Art of the Possible—Interpreting Statutes under the Human Rights Act" [1998] E.H.R.L.R. 665.

[62] *cf. Quilter v. Att.-Gen. of New Zealand* [1998] 1 N.Z.L.R. 523, criticised by Butler, "Same-sex marriage and freedom from discrimination in New Zealand" [1998] P.L. 396; see also *Egan v. Canada* [1995] 2 S.C.R. 513.

[63] See Marshall, *supra.* At least it fails before U.K. courts; it is always possible that if the loser takes the case to Strasbourg, the European Court of Human Rights may take a different view.

[64] Accordingly, all orders bringing legislation into force are classified as primary legislation, *cf. R. v. Secretary of State for the Home Department, ex p. Fire Brigades Union* [1995] 2 A.C. 513.

[65] Therefore, since Acts of the Scottish Parliament are classified as subordinate legislation under the Human Rights Act 1998, they may be invalidated by the court for incompatibility with Convention rights contrary to the Act. But the relationship between the Convention rights and Acts of the Scottish Parliament is dealt with specifically in the Scotland Act 1998. It is thought that challenges to Acts of the Scottish Parliament on the grounds of Convention rights should be taken under the Scotland Act which, being enacted after the Human Rights Act, is the later statement of the U.K. Parliament's will. On the relationship between the Human Rights Act and the Scotland Act, see paras 7.31 *et seq.*

Incompatibility of primary legislation

6.33 If, in accordance with the requirement of section 3(1), it is possible to read and give effect to primary legislation in a way which is consistent with the Convention rights, then no question in this regard will arise about its compatibility.[66] If it is not possible for a provision in primary legislation to be read and given effect so as to be compatible with Convention rights, it follows that the provision will be incompatible with those rights in terms of the 1998 Act. However, this fact alone does not affect the validity, continuing operation or enforcement of the provision in primary legislation.[67] If it is not possible to read and give effect to primary legislation so as to be compatible with Convention rights under section 3(1) of the Act, the legislation remains valid and in full force and effect. Subject to section 10 of the Act, control over any amendment or repeal of primary legislation remains in Parliament's hands. Section 10 of the 1998 Act provides a particular remedy, which will be termed "the ministerial remedy", to deal with inconsistency between primary legislation and Convention rights. As will be seen, this remedy is available where the problem of inconsistency emerges from a declaration of incompatibility granted by a supreme court. But both in the absence of such a declaration and following the grant of one, primary legislation is not affected by any incompatibility; instead, it remains valid and enforceable.

Declarations of incompatibility

6.34 The road to the invalidity of primary legislation on the ground of its incompatibility with Convention rights passes through the court but does not end there. Section 4 of the Act provides for the making of a declaration of incompatibility. The circumstances in which a declaration of incompatibility can be obtained require to be noticed. First, there must be proceedings in which a court determines whether a provision of primary legislation (or secondary legislation controlled by it) is inconsistent with one or more of the Convention rights.[68] The proceedings in which this matter may arise are not confined to the judicial review procedure. The matter may arise in any proceedings, including proceedings before a criminal court. Secondly, however, the Act provides a definition of "courts" which are able to grant a declaration of incompatibility. Section 4(5) defines courts for this purpose as meaning the House of Lords, the Judicial Committee of the Privy Council, the Courts-Martial Appeal Court, the High Court of Justiciary sitting as a court of criminal appeal, the Court of Session and in England, Wales and Northern Ireland, the High Court or the Court of Appeal. Thirdly, before granting a declaration of incompatibility, one of these courts must be satisfied that the challenged provision in the legislation is incompatible with one or more of the Convention rights. Fourthly, the declaration of incompatibility will only relate to the provision or provisions that are found to be incompatible with Convention rights. It will not necessarily relate to the legislation as a whole nor to valid subordinate legislation

---

[66] But note that primary legislation may be challengeable for incompatibility with applicable provisions of E.C. law, which includes some human rights. If such incompatibility is established, the court may declare the legislation inapplicable: see *R. v. Secretary of State for Employment, ex p. EOC* [1995] 1 A.C. 1.

[67] s. 3(1)(b).

[68] s. 4(1).

passed validly under a power contained in incompatible primary legislation.

The effect of a declaration of incompatibility

When a court decides to grant a declaration of incompatibility, the court **6.35** simply declares an incompatibility. It does not reduce (or quash) the legislation nor even declare its invalidity. The declaration is, as its name suggests, of incompatibility between a provision in U.K. legislation and a Convention right or rights. It is expressly provided by section 4(6) of the 1998 Act that the declaration does not affect the validity, continuing operation or enforcement of the relevant provision in respect of which the declaration is given. Furthermore, section 4(6) also provides that the declaration is not binding on the parties to the proceedings in which it is made. In other words, as between the parties to the case, a declaration of incompatibility does not itself affect the result which the pre-existing law ordains. Rather, the validity or invalidity of the provision in legislation and the extent to which any invalidity is to be retrospective so as to affect the instant case lies in the hands of a minister of the Crown, not of the Court.[69] For practical purposes, where the parties to a dispute are looking for an effective and immediate solution and there are other grounds available than the possible incompatibility of primary legislation with a Convention right, they may be well advised to seek a decision at least initially on the other grounds, since even if a declaration of incompatibility was pronounced it may not necessarily lead to a retrospective order under section 10 which would apply to their case.

Procedure

Questions of incompatibility may arise in any proceedings but it is only **6.36** in proceedings before a court empowered by the 1998 Act that a declaration of incompatibility may be made.[70] An application for judicial review before the Court of Session will be among the proceedings in which a declaration of incompatibility may be made. Where the court is considering whether to make a declaration, the Crown is entitled to notice[71] and a minister of the Crown or person nominated by such a minister is entitled to be joined as a party to the proceedings.[72] Provision is made by Rules of Court[73] for the giving of notice to the Crown and for the application to be made to the court for joining the minister or the person nominated by him as a party to the proceedings. It is expressly provided by section 5(3) of the Act that the application to be joined may be made at any time during the proceedings. The existing procedure for judicial review has sufficient flexibility to enable notice to the Crown to be given whenever it is evident that a question of incompatibility may be in issue and a declaration may be made.

Discretion to issue declarations of incompatibility

If after hearing the arguments of the parties concerned about the issue, **6.37** the court is satisfied that the particular provision of the primary legislation (or subordinate legislation controlled by it) is incompatible

---

[69] See s. 10 and Sched. 2, para. 1.
[70] 1998 Act, s. 4(5).
[71] s. 5(1).
[72] s. 5(2).
[73] Act of Sederunt (Proceedings for Determination of Devolution Issues Rules) 1999 (S.I. 1999 No. 1347).

with one or more Convention rights, then in accordance with section 4(2) the court is empowered to make a declaration of that incompatibility. It should be noted that the court is not required to grant the declaration. The remedy is discretionary, making it the same as, for example, a declarator sought in an application for judicial review.

The section 10 ministerial remedy

6.38　In cases of an incompatibility between one or more of the Convention rights and a provision in primary legislation or subordinate legislation controlled by it, provision is made in section 10 of the 1998 Act for remedial action. The remedy provided is in the nature of a ministerial remedy, whereby the balancing of interests and reconciling of incompatible legislation with the Convention may be achieved by an order made under section 10 by a minister of the Crown.[74] There are two possible circumstances in which the ministerial remedy may be provided. The first is where there has been a declaration of incompatibility under section 4; the second is where it appears to a minister of the Crown or Her Majesty in Council that, having regard to a finding of the European Court of Human Rights, a provision of legislation is incompatible with one or more of the obligations of the United Kingdom arising under the Convention.[75] The remedy, which has been described as a "fast track" procedure, is by way of an order making amendments to primary or subordinate legislation.[76] The power to make remedial orders is conferred in the widest of terms: an order may amend any legislative provision, not only those in respect of which a declaration of incompatibility has been issued; it may have the same effect as the legislation which it affects; it may be given retrospective effect, although not so as to make a person guilty of an offence; and it may make "different provision for different cases".[77] A section 10 remedial order may extend to affect any legislation, primary or subordinate, and necessarily includes the power to repeal the incompatible provision or modify its application, including retroactively. If the incompatible legislation is an Order in Council, the equivalent power is exerciseable by Her Majesty in Council.[78] Finally, Schedule 2 to the Act makes provision for Parliamentary approval of any remedial order and also for the making of an order without prior Parliamentary approval.

Discretion to make remedial order

6.39　Section 10 of the 1998 Act does not require a remedial order to be made following a declaration of incompatibility. Rather, it empowers a minister of the Crown to issue a remedial order and to decide what effect such an order is to have. But the power conferred by section 10 is subject to

---

[74] s. 10(2) and (3) of the 1998 Act. But where the provision in U.K. legislation falls within the scope of the Scottish Executive's powers, it follows from s. 53(2)(c) and Sched. 4, paras 12 and 13 of the Scotland Act 1998 that a member of the Scottish Executive is empowered by s. 10 to remedy the incompatibility in the U.K. legislation.

[75] s. 10(1).

[76] Sched. 2, para. 1(2).

[77] Sched. 2, para. 1. So a minister could decide to give an order retrospective effect but limit such effect only so as to remove incompatibility with the Convention in the case in which the Declaration of incompatibility was issued. In substance, this amounts to a judicial function, the discretionary nature of which may lead to challenges in judicial review: see below.

[78] s. 10(5).

conditions: the minister must consider "that there are compelling reasons for proceeding under" section 10, in which case he "may by order make such amendments to the legislation as he considers necessary to remove the incompatibility". These conditions raise the question whether the discretionary powers conferred by section 10 are reviewable. It appears that the court has no jurisdiction to compel a minister of the Crown or Parliament to legislate in accordance with Convention rights, or to amend, repeal or modify legislation which has been declared to be incompatible with Convention rights. This follows from section 6 of the 1998 Act which provides that the bodies bound by the Act do not include "either House of Parliament or a person exercising functions in connection with proceedings in Parliament".[79] Moreover, although it is unlawful for a "public authority to act" in violation of Convention rights,[80] "act" is specifically defined not to include failure to: "introduce in or lay before Parliament a proposal for legislation; or make any primary legislation or remedial order".[81] In matters exclusively concerned with compatibility between national legislation and Convention rights, therefore, there is no enforceable obligation to legislate to remedy violations of Convention rights which have been found in incompatible legislation.[82] On this basis, it follows that the ministerial remedy does not create a statutory duty breach of which sounds in damages.[83] Nevertheless, it may be arguable that both the nature of "compelling reasons" and more particularly the way in which a minister exercises the power to make a remedial order under section 10—for example, whether or not to give it retroactive effect, or as regards "different provision for different cases"—may be subject to judicial review. Although some of the grounds of judicial review, notably irrationality, may not be available against subordinate legislation,[84] it is arguable that the assessment of what is "necessary" in terms of section 10 could be open to review on the ground of proportionality or possibly also fairness, where, for example, a person directly affected by a section 10 order is not given a right to be heard before the order is made.

Subordinate legislation where incompatibility irremoveable

The Act makes distinct but similar provision in relation to subordinate **6.40** legislation, permitting the making of a declaration of incompatibility by the court (as defined) where "the court is satisfied . . . that (disregarding any possibility of revocation) the primary legislation concerned prevents removal of the incompatibility".[85] In any proceedings before a defined court for example, in Scotland the Court of Session the court may make

---

[79] s. 6(3), discussed below.

[80] See s. 6(1) of the Act.

[81] s. 6(6), discussed in the next part of this chapter.

[82] In *R. v. Secretary of State for Employment, ex p. Seymour Smith* [1997] 1 W.L.R. 473, the House of Lords held that U.K. law recognises no such obligation arising from E.C. law either. But debate on whether or not E.C. law requires a judicial remedy to compel legislation compatible with it may well have inspired the exclusion of the Westminister legislative process from s. 6(1) of the 1998 Act: see para. 6.45 below.

[83] But a failure to act under s. 10 can still be challenged before the European Court of Human Rights as contrary to the Convention. In extreme cases, of course, the government may choose to make a reservation to the Convention, which as a State it has the sovereign right to do.

[84] *cf. Edinburgh D.C. v. Secretary of State for Scotland*, 1985 S.L.T. 551; and *Notts C.C. v. Secretary of State for the Environment* [1986] A.C. 240.

[85] s. 4(4)(b).

a declaration of incompatibility in respect of such subordinate legislation, if it is satisfied that there is an incompatibility and that, disregarding any possibility of revocation, the primary legislation under which the
subordinate legislation in question has been made prevents removal of
the incompatibility.[86] However, it must be noted that where the real fault
lies with primary legislation, the validity, continuing operation and
enforcement of subordinate legislation are not affected by the requirement in section 3(1) to read and give effect to it so far as possible in a
way which is compatible with the Convention,[87] nor by a declaration of
incompatibility.[88] In such cases, the remedy against the subordinate
legislation is the ministerial remedy provided by section 10.[89] But only
subordinate legislation made in the exercise of a power conferred by
primary legislation is affected by section 4 of the Act.[90] Further, it is not
that the court's powers over all subordinate legislation are limited by
section 4(4), only powers over subordinate legislation where the incompatibility with a Convention right cannot be "removed" because of
primary legislation.[91] The question, however, arises as to what is meant
by "removal". The purpose of the provision is presumably to preserve
what is seen as the supreme powers of Parliament and it is thought that
"removal" should be given a wide interpretation covering matters of
substance as well as procedure.

Other subordinate legislation

6.41   The making of future subordinate legislation may fall to be treated as an
act of a public authority and be open to challenge on that basis.[92] Apart
from that the question remains whether the 1998 Act operates to render
existing subordinate legislation open to challenge on the ground of
incompatibility with the Convention rights where the problem does not
truly lie with primary legislation. It has always been open to a court of
review—in Scotland the Court of Session—to reduce or declare invalid
ultra vires subordinate legislation. It is evidently intended by the 1998
Act that the court should have this power where subordinate legislation
is incompatible with Convention rights unless the incompatibility
requires amendment of primary legislation. The Act makes no express
provision in this regard, but the power to invalidate subordinate
legislation is implied.[93] The 1998 Act must mean that all empowering
legislation is not to be construed as enabling subordinate legislation to
be passed which would be incompatible with the Convention rights,
unless it is impossible so to construe the empowering legislation. This
follows from the obligation of interpretation imposed by section 3(1). It
should follow that if existing subordinate legislation is found to be

---

[86] s. 4(3) and (4).
[87] s. 3(1)(c).
[88] s. 4(6).
[89] See para. 6.38 above.
[90] s. 4(3). Subordinate legislation includes Orders in Council which are not classified as
primary legislation: s. 21. Basically, Orders in Council are primary legislation when made
under prerogative powers.
[91] See below. On the court's powers over subordinate legislation in general, see *F.
Hoffman-La Roche & Co. AG v. Secretary of State for Trade and Industry* [1975] A.C. 295
HL, and *Edinburgh D.C. v. Secretary of State for Scotland*, 1985 S.L.T. 551. See further
para. 9.12.
[92] This subject is considered in the next part of this chapter; but in relation to failures to
legislate compare s. 6 of the Human Rights Act 1998 with s. 100 of the Scotland Act 1998.
[93] See s. 10(4).

incompatible with a Convention right it can be challenged before the court and a judicial remedy obtained, thereby enabling the delegated legislator to exercise the powers afresh and enact a provision which conforms with the Convention.[94]

It must be noted that the definition of subordinate legislation in section 21(1) of the Human Rights Act 1998 includes Acts of the Scottish Parliament. Accordingly, Scottish Acts may be challengeable under section 6 of the Human Rights Act 1998. But the relationship between Acts of the Scottish Parliament and the Convention rights is also governed by the Scotland Act 1998. The issues in this regard are considered further in Chapter 7.[95]

V SCOPE OF THE HUMAN RIGHTS ACT 1998

Introduction

Among the issues raised by the 1998 Act few are as problematic as the meaning to be given to the Act's provisions on its scope of application.[96] The scope of guaranteed human rights, in particular the definition of public bodies bound by the rights and the extent to which human rights may bind private parties in situations traditionally considered private, has been a source of considerable difficulty in many systems with bills or charters of rights.[97] Although the issues must be viewed through the lens

6.42

---

[94] But see s. 6(2) on the effects of invalidity of subordinate legislation, discussed in the following part of the Chapter.

[95] See paras 7.31 *et seq.*

[96] This has become a controversial issue even before the Act enters force: see articles in Beatson *et al.* (eds), *Constitutional Reform in the United Kingdom: Practice & Procedure* (Hart Publishing, Oxford, 1998) by Wade, "The United Kingdom's Bill of Rights", at p. 61; Kentridge, "The Incorporation of the European Convention on Human Rights", at p. 69; and Lord Lester, "The Impact of the Human Rights Act on Public Law", at p. 105. See also Wade, "Human Rights and the Judiciary" (1998 Judicial Studies Board Annual Lecture) [1998] E.H.R.L.R. 520; Hunt, "The 'Horizontal Effect' of the Human Rights Act" [1998] P.L. 423; Singh, "Privacy and the Media after the Human Rights Act" [1998] E.H.R.L.R. 712; Sherlock, "The Applicability of the United Kingdom's Human Rights Bill: Identifying 'Public' Functions" [1998] 4 Eur. P.L. 593; and Leigh, "Horizontal Rights, the Human Rights Act and Privacy: Lessons from the Commonwealth?" (1999) 48 I.C.L.Q. 57. For a discussion of the scope of human rights under the German Basic Law and its relevance to the Human Rights Act 1998, see Markesinis, "Privacy, Freedom of Expression, and the Horizontal Effect of the Human Rights Bill: Lessons from Germany" (1999) 115 L.Q.R. 47. See also Markesinis (ed), *The Impact of the Human Rights Bill in English Law* (OUP, 1998).

[97] In particular, the USA, Canada and New Zealand. But in Ireland, the human rights guarantees in the Constitution can apply in the context of private activity by virtue of their applying to the common law: see, for example, *Re Tilson* [1951] I.R. 1; *Meskell v. Coras Eireann* [1973] I.R. 121; and *CM v. TM* [1988] I.L.R.M. 456; see also Walsh, "The Constitution: a view from the Bench", in Farrell (ed.), *De Valera's Constitution and Ours* (IPA, Dublin, 1988). In addition, the rights guaranteed in the new South African Constitution probably apply to private activity by virtue of their binding the Judiciary: s. 8(1), of the Constitution of the Republic of South Africa Act 108 of 1996, *cf.* s. 7(1) and Chap. 3 of the Interim Constitution, Constitution of the Republic of South Africa Act 200 of 1993, which did not apply the Bill of Rights to the Judiciary and which the South African Constitutional Court held could not directly apply to private activity (but could indirectly by virtue of the obligation on the courts in s. 35(3) to permeate the guaranteed rights through the common law): *Du Plessis v. De Klerk*, 1996 (3) S.A. 850. For discussion of the new Constitution on this matter, see "Private Litigation and Constitutional Rights under Sections 8 and 9 of the 1996 Constitution—Assistance from Ireland" (1999) 116 S.A.L.J. 77.

of relevant European Court of Human Rights decisions,[98] the approach that the 1998 Act takes to the scope of the guaranteed Convention rights seems destined to encounter at least some of the difficulties which have arisen elsewhere.

Section 6 taken with sections 7 to 9 of the 1998 Act define the violations of Convention rights which are made unlawful and provide for the remedies which may be sought for these violations and by whom. If the Act's provisions on its relationship with legislation may be considered its first pillar, sections 6 to 9 of the Act can be considered its second pillar.

Unlawful Acts

6.43 Section 6(1) of the 1998 Act provides: "It is unlawful for a public authority to act in a way which is incompatible with a Convention right". Section 6(6) clarifies that "an act" for the purposes of section 6(1) includes a failure to act. Accordingly, omissions by public authorities as well as their positive acts may be unlawful where they are incompatible with a Convention right.[99] Furthermore, section 7(1) effectively extends the definition of "act" in section 6(1) to include proposals to act. However, section 6(6) provides that a failure to act does not include a failure to propose legislation to be enacted by the U.K. Parliament or a failure to make primary legislation.[1] Since s. 7 of the Act allows the victim of an unlawful act by a public authority to bring proceedings against the authority, the definitions of "unlawful act" and "public authority" for the purposes of s. 6 are central.[2]

Legislation and Unlawful Acts

6.44 Section 6(2) provides that an act is not unlawful if: "(a) as the result of one or more provisions of primary legislation, the authority could not have acted differently; or (b) in the case of one or more provisions of, *or made under*, primary legislation which cannot be read or given effect in a way which is compatible with the Convention rights, the authority was

---

[98] The European Convention and decisions of the Court of Human Rights applying it are ambivalent on its application in the private sector. But this ambivalence may tend towards some "horizontal" effect for the Convention. First, cases which reach the Court always have a state as respondent, irrespective of how the alleged violation of Convention rights arises. As will be seen below, the Court has decided that the Convention can impose positive obligations on states: for example, by requiring them to introduce laws to protect private citizens *inter se*. Secondly, the codified nature of most of the legal systems over which the Court has jurisdiction means that it may not be sensitive to the distinction between (common) law governing private activity and other law in the same way as an Anglo-American court. See, for example, *Hoffmann v. Austria* (1993) 17 E.H.R.R. 293 at para. 29 (Art. 8 of Convention applies to judicial orders in custody dispute between private parties). For a brief discussion, see Janis, Kay and Bradley, *European Human Rights Law* (OUP, Oxford, 1995), at pp. 250–253.

[99] Even if the 1998 Act did not expressly include failures to act within the definition of unlawful acts, the guarantee of Convention rights would require it. Under the Convention the State can have a positive duty to act to protect Convention rights: see *X & Y v. Netherlands* (1986) 8 E.H.R.R. 235; *Costello-Roberts v. U.K.* (1995) 19 E.H.R.R. 112; *Lopez Ostra v. Spain* (1995) 20 E.H.R.R. 277; and *A v. U.K.* (1998) 5 B.H.R.C. 137. But see also *Botta v. Italy* (1998) 26 E.H.R.R. 241.

[1] Primary legislation is defined in s. 21 (discussed above). The implications of the exclusion of the Westminster legislative process from the 1998 Act are discussed below.

[2] s. 7, along with ss. 8 and 9, deal with *locus standi* and remedies for the purposes of acts made unlawful by s. 6. They are considered in the next part of the chapter.

acting so as to give effect to or enforce *those provisions*".[3] In essence, section 6(2) provides a public authority with a defence where its acts are challenged on the grounds of violation of Convention rights. The central principle is that a public authority is not to be liable for a violation of Convention rights where the fault truly lies with enacted legislation.[4]

At first sight section 6(2) reflects the Act's provisions on its relationship with legislation but a closer analysis reveals a difficulty. One problem relates to the application of section 6(2)(b) to secondary legislation. To clarify this problem, four propositions may be stated. First, under section 6(1) of the Act a public authority which gives effect to compatible legislation in a way which is incompatible with Convention rights acts unlawfully. So, for example, a local authority which acts under compatible primary legislation by making rules which violate a Convention right acts unlawfully under section 6(1). Secondly, where a public authority acts under incompatible primary legislation, its act is not unlawful by virtue of section 6(2)(a) where "the authority could not have acted differently" to achieve its purpose. There may, of course, be a question whether the authority could have used alternative means to achieve its purpose but if it could not, section 6(2)(a) provides that the authority's act under incompatible primary legislation is not unlawful.[5] So if a local authority committee is expressly required by primary legislation to make a licensing decision without hearing an applicant, its act will not be unlawful because the committee may be said not to have been able to act differently by virtue of primary legislation. Clearly this approach is consistent with the scheme of the 1998 Act; it would be unjust to treat a public authority as acting unlawfully when unavoidably following incompatible provisions in primary legislation which section 4 of the Act treats as continuing in full force and effect notwithstanding any declaration of incompatibility against them.

Thirdly, section 6(2)(b) proceeds on the same reasoning and means that a public authority does not act unlawfully when acting "to give effect to or enforce" incompatible provisions in primary legislation. When it is so acting, a public authority is not acting unlawfully irrespective of whether a court may issue a declaration of incompatibility against the provisions. So where a prison custody officer in a contracted-out prison uses reasonable force to perform a search on a prisoner, he is acting to enforce section 108 of the Criminal Justice and Public Order Act 1994 and even if that provision was incompatible with the Convention rights, he cannot be said to be acting unlawfully. Fourthly, however, problems may arise with regard to the proper construction to be given to section 6(2)(b) as regards secondary legislation. There is room for argument whether the word "which" refers to the "one or more provisions" or to the "primary legislation". On one view, section 6(2)(b) appears to mean

---

[3] Human Rights Act 1998, s. 6(2) (emphasis added). See also s. 57(3) of the Scotland Act 1998, which extends the benefit of s. 6(2) to the Lord Advocate when acting "to prosecute any offence" or "in his capacity as head of the systems of criminal prosecution . . . in Scotland". See para. 7.26.

[4] And in the case of secondary legislation which the court is empowered to invalidate, the defendant public authority is not responsible for making the legislation: see below.

[5] If the authority actually has an option either to achieve its purpose by acting under incompatible primary legislation or by another means which allows it to act consistently with Convention rights, only the latter course seems to be lawful. In other words, s. 6(2)(a) only allows the act to be treated as lawful if it is compelled by primary legislation. Of course, whether the purpose is itself lawful will depend on the interpretation to be given to the authority's legal powers.

that an authority which has acted "to give effect to or enforce" incompatible provisions in secondary legislation does not act unlawfully under section 6(1).[6] Alternatively, it may be that a public authority is only protected under section 6(2)(b) where it is giving effect to or enforcing subordinate legislation where the primary legislation under which it is made is incompatible.[7]

Consideration may also have to be given to the operation of section 6(2)(b) as it relates to subordinate legislation and to the effect of proceedings to challenge the validity of such legislation either at common law or under section 4. It is clear that a declaration of incompatibility made under section 4 against a provision in subordinate legislation controlled by incompatible primary legislation does not affect the validity of the provision.[8] But it is also arguable, depending on the preferred construction of section 6(2)(b) mentioned above, that where a provision in subordinate legislation is quashed at common law, the decision does not affect the validity of prior enforcement of the subordinate legislation. It may be therefore that in neither case is an act of a public authority made unlawful retroactively. So, for example, if the director of a contracted-out prison is acting to enforce provisions in the Prison Rules some of which, being rules which fall under section 6(2)(b), a court later invalidates as incompatible with Convention rights and against others of which the court issues a declaration of incompatibility under section 4(4), in neither case is the prison (as a public authority) liable for an unlawful act under section 6(1).[9] This touches on the difficult issue of what effects, if any, an *ultra vires* act can have, and it is not without complexity.[10] In any event, one way out of some of the complexity may be to distinguish the making of subordinate legislation from acting "to give effect to or enforce" it. So it follows from section 6(6) of the Act that the making of incompatible secondary legislation may be an unlawful act, at least in so far as it can be invalidated by a court,[11] even although "giving effect to or enforcing" it may not. Much may depend on the remedy which is sought against secondary legislation and against whom. In the last prison example above, judicial review

---

[6] Some support for this approach is derived from the language of s. 4(3).

[7] This approach may accord with a grammatical construction of the paragraph and avoid what may be considered too wide a protection for public authorities.

[8] See s. 4(6).

[9] It may therefore be said that the unlawful act (making the invalid secondary legislation) has some valid (that is, lawful) consequences. This approach of distinguishing between the valid consequences of "void" acts on which s. 6(2) may proceed is similar to Forsyth's approach to the effects to be attributed to *ultra vires* "void" administrative acts: see Forsyth, "'The Metaphysic of Nullity' Invalidity, Conceptual Reasoning and the Rule of Law", in Forsyth and Hare (eds), *The Golden Metwand and the Crooked Cord* (OUP, Oxford, 1998) at p. 141, esp. at pp. 146 *et seq.*

[10] See *Boddington v. British Transport Police* [1999] 2 A.C. 143; *R. v. Governor of Brockhill Prison, ex p. Evans (No. 2)* [1998] 4 All E.R. 993 (CA); *Percy v. Hall* [1996] 4 All E.R. 523. See also Forsyth, *supra*. The problem is discussed further at para. 14.16. A question could also arise about the propriety or irrationality of the public authority in enforcing the secondary legislation rather than staying its hand in the face of an obvious violation of Convention rights which is patently not authorised by the empowering primary legislation, therefore rendering the secondary legislation *ultra vires*.

[11] That is, there is nothing in primary legislation which prevents removal of the incompatibility: s. 4(4). But if the primary legislation compels the incompatible secondary legislation, the making of the latter is not unlawful in terms of s. 6(2)(a).

against the Secretary of State rather than an action against the prison may have to be considered.[12]

Failures to Act

Although section 6(6) generally includes a failure to act within the **6.45** definition of unlawful acts covered by section 6(1), section 6(6) expressly excludes any failure to: "(a) introduce in, or lay before, Parliament a proposal for legislation; or (b) make any primary legislation or remedial order". The effect of section 6(6) is therefore to exclude the operation of the Westminster legislative process from the definition of the unlawful acts caught by the 1998 Act.[13] Accordingly, the debate in the context of E.C. law whether U.K. courts are empowered to order the government to introduce legislation to implement E.C. directives and about the possible liability of Parliament for violations of E.C. law through the enactment of or failure to enact legislation has no direct counterpart under the Human Rights Act 1998.[14] This exclusion of Parliament's

---

[12] *cf. R. v. Secretary of State for the Home Department, ex p. Leech (No. 2)* [1994] Q.B. 198; and *R. v. Secretary of State for the Home Department, ex p. Simms & O'Brien* [1999] 3 W.L.R. 328. Section 6(2) also has important implications for the Scottish government exercising powers under the Scotland Act 1998. Section 57(2) provides that a member of the Scottish Executive "has no power to make any subordinate legislation, or do any other act so far as the legislation or act is incompatible with Convention rights". But what about when the Scottish Executive acts under U.K. legislation which is incompatible with Convention rights? Does it act unlawfully when "giving effect to or enforcing" a provision in U.K. legislation which is incompatible with Convention rights? Section 57(3) expressly gives the Lord Advocate the benefit of s. 6(2) in relation to his criminal justice responsibilities. Is this the limit to the benefit of s. 6(2) for the Scottish Parliament and Administration?

[13] But failures of the Scottish Parliament to legislate (or of the Scottish Executive to introduce legislation into the Scottish Parliament) may be challengeable under Convention rights: see s. 100(4) of the Scotland Act 1998 for the definition of "act" for the purposes of the relationship between the Scotland Act 1998 and Convention rights. It may also be noted here that the E.U. legislative process is subject to the European Convention on Human Rights by virtue of Art. 6 of the Treaty on European Union.
It may be asked whether the executive's discretion to bring enacted legislation into force, or rather any failure to do so, is subject to the Act; is this power covered by the words "make any primary legislation"? Section 21(1) of the Act includes within the definition of primary legislation an "order or other instrument made under primary legislation . . . to the extent to which it operates to bring" primary legislation into force; and the same is excluded from the definition of subordinate legislation. Accordingly, the effect of ss. 6(6)(b) and 21 is to exclude failures to bring primary legislation into force from the scope of s. 6 of the 1998 Act. *cf.* judicial review of the government's discretion on when (and if) to bring legislation into force: *R. v. Secretary of State for the Home Department, ex p. Fire Brigades Union* [1995] 2 A.C. 513 (exercise of prerogative power to legislate reviewable (and held abused) when effect is to surrender discretion to bring into force an Act of Parliament covering the same field).

[14] So far, it is not clear that E.C. law requires either national courts to order the enactment of implementing legislation or a finding of Parliamentary (as opposed to state) liability for legislative infractions of E.C. law. But see *R. v. Secretary of State for Employment, ex p. Equal Opportunities Commission* [1995] 1 A.C. 1: where primary legislation is found in breach of E.C. law, appropriate remedy is declaration to this effect; but in the same case in the Court of Appeal and Divisional Court, mandamus was sought (and refused, effectively in Scottish terms as incompetent) ordering the Secretary of State to introduce legislation to remedy violations of E.C. law: [1992] 1 All E.R. 545, *per* Nolan L.J. at 561 (DC); and [1993] 1 W.L.R. 872 (CA). See now *R. v. Secretary of State for Employment, ex p. Seymour Smith* [1997] 1 W.L.R. 473 (no right to mandamus against the state ordering that a directive be implemented). *cf. R. v. H.M. Treasury, ex p. Smedley* [1985] Q.B. 657 (Court of Appeal deciding that it has jurisdiction to grant a Declaration that draft subordinate legislation, if adopted, would violate E.C. law; but equally doubting

activities from section 6 is reinforced by section 6(3) defining the public authorities subject to the Act as excluding "either House of Parliament or a person exercising functions in connection with proceedings in Parliament".[15] But although section 6(6)(a) excludes the failure to make subordinate legislation from the definition of "unlawful act" in section 6(1), it is clear that once made subordinate legislation may be challenged as unlawful, subject to the general idea in the 1998 Act that removal of the breach of a Convention right by subordinate legislation is not prevented by primary legislation. However, the failure of the government to make a "remedial order" under section 10 of the Act to remedy any incompatibility in U.K. legislation declared by a U.K. court or found by the European Court of Human Rights is probably not an unlawful act for the purposes of the 1998 Act.[16]

The U.K. Parliament and the 1998 Act

6.46　　The 1998 Act excludes both Houses of Parliament and any "person exercising functions in connection with proceedings in Parliament" from the definition of public authority for the purposes of section 6.[17] Several points must be observed about this exclusion. First, by a rather convoluted exception to the exclusion, "the House of Lords in its judicial capacity" is included as a public authority.[18] It follows, therefore, that the Appellate Committee of the House of Lords and possibly also the Committee for Privileges of that House are to be regarded as public authorities under section 6. Secondly, the term "proceedings in Parliament" used in section 6(3) requires to be defined. Although there is a division of responsibility between Parliament and the courts in defining Parliament's privileges, it is for the courts to decide on the extent of Parliamentary privilege, how it affects those outside Parliament and what is covered within the term "proceedings in Parliament".[19] In one case brought by a Member of Parliament suing a television company for defamation, the Privy Council decided that the protection which Members of Parliament obtain from Parliament's privileges, and in particular the absolute privilege which speech in Parliament attracts from the rule in Article 9 of the Bill of Rights that proceedings in Parliament may not be "impeached or questioned in any court" outside Parliament, means

---

any power to order Parliament not to consider or enact subordinate legislation). For discussion, see Lewis, *Remedies and the Enforcement of European Community Law* (Sweet & Maxwell, London, 1996), pp. 83–90. For consideration of Parliament's liability under E.C. law for legislation violating E.C. law, see Convery, "State Liability in the United Kingdom After *Brasserie du Pêcheur*" (1997) 34 C.M.L.R. 603, esp. at 630–633; and Upton, "Crown liability in damages under Community Law", 1996 S.L.T. (News) 211. See further para. 5.51.

[15] But on problems defining "proceedings in Parliament" for this purpose, see para. 6.46 below.

[16] But such a failure may be challenged before the European Court of Human Rights: see para. 6.71.

[17] s. 6(3).

[18] In effect being treated as a court, courts being public authorities for the purposes of s. 6(1): see below. Strictly, of course, the Appellate Committee of the House of Lords is not a court but a committee of the House of Lords.

[19] *Stockdale v. Hansard* (1839) 9 A. & E. 1; *Clarke v. Bradlaugh* (1884) 12 Q.B.D. 271. On meaning of "proceedings in Parliament", see *Rost v. Edwards* [1990] 2 Q.B. 460 and *Prebble v. Television New Zealand Ltd* [1995] 1 A.C. 321. In the context of an inferior legislative body, see *Egan v. Willis* (1998) 73 A.L.J.R. 75 (HCA). A good discussion of the privileges of the U.K. Parliament is given in Bradley & Ewing, *Constitutional & Administrative Law* (12th ed., Longman, London, 1997), Chap. 11.

that the inability of a defendant to use proceedings in Parliament as part of a legal defence in court may require the whole defamation action to be stopped in the interests of justice.[20] It must be asked if this absolute protection for free speech in Parliament notwithstanding the nature of any injury or injustice caused to persons outside Parliament is compatible with Convention rights—in particular, the rights to a fair trial in Article 6 and to privacy in Article 8.[21] If the effect of section 6(3) is to exclude the jurisdiction of the U.K. courts to decide such matters, the European Court of Human Rights itself may be called on to do so. In any event, since section 6(3) means neither House of Parliament nor any person "exercising functions in connection with proceedings in Parliament" is a public authority, this exception to the guarantee of Convention rights should be construed narrowly, so that, for example, Parliament's dealings with its employees or with demonstrators outside Parliament are not "proceedings in Parliament" and therefore are acts covered by Convention rights. In other words, Parliament is not a public authority only when "exercising functions in connection with proceedings in Parliament".

Thirdly, the exclusion of the Houses of Parliament from the definition of public authorities in section 6 is only limited to this section. So, although what the Houses of Parliament and any person do as part of the legislative process cannot be regarded as an unlawful act under section 6(1), since the legislative process is fundamentally "proceedings in Parliament", the rest of the 1998 Act can still affect what Parliament does. In other words, the exclusion of Parliament from the definition of public authority in section 6 is without prejudice to other provisions of the 1998 Act: for example, sections 3, 4, 10 and 19. As discussed above, section 3 requires legislation to be interpreted so far as possible to be compatible with guaranteed Convention rights. It is clear, therefore, that section 3 affects the output of the legislative process by creating an interpretive obligation incumbent on everyone who may require to interpret and apply legislation.[22] Similarly, section 4 enables the superior courts to issue declarations of incompatibility where they find provisions in primary legislation or constrained secondary legislation contrary to Convention rights.[23] Although such declarations are non-binding,[24] the new jurisdiction to issue them touches on Parliament's activities. Further, since the exclusion of "proceedings in Parliament" is limited to

---

[20] *Prebble v. Television New Zealand Ltd* [1995] 1 A.C. 321. The Scotland Act 1998 s. 41 provides that proceedings of the Scottish Parliament are absolutely privileged for the purposes of the law of defamation. *Quaere* to what extent, being a provision in legislation, s. 41 must be construed so as to be consistent with Convention rights?

[21] *cf. De Lille v. Speaker of the National Assembly*, 1998 (3) S.A. 430 (where held that exercise of Parliamentary privilege in South African National Assembly was not immune from judicial review under Constitution of South Africa; Constitution is binding on Parliament and there could be no privilege inconsistent with the Constitution). See also *McNeill v. U.K.* (Application to European Human Rights Commission No. 35373/97): complaining of violation of Convention rights where M.P. makes defamatory statements in bad faith but in Parliament and so absolutely privileged.

[22] As discussed below, this obligation must also affect private persons who rely on legislation. The difficulty is determining what happens where a private party interprets legislation in a way that is incompatible with the Convention.

[23] The s. 4 declaration of incompatibility and its availablity are discussed in the preceding section of this Chapter: paras 6.34 *et seq.*

[24] Declarations of incompatibility are not binding on Parliament (s. 6(3)), nor on the parties to the proceedings in which the declaration is obtained (s. 4(6)(b)), nor on the government (s. 6(6)(b)).

section 6, judicial review of the power under section 10 is not clearly excluded thereby. Similarly, the power under section 19 to make a statement on the compatibility of a Bill with the Convention is imposed on a minister of the Crown in mandatory terms. Again, failure to make a statement may be reviewable, albeit not creating a statutory duty breach of which sounds in damages.[25]

Public Authorities

6.47   Section 6(1) of the 1998 Act provides that only the acts of public authorities are unlawful if incompatible with Convention rights. Section 6(3) defines public authority for the purposes of the section: "In this section 'public authority' includes–(a) a court or tribunal, and (b) any person certain of whose functions are functions of a public nature."[26] Importantly, however, section 6(5) provides: "In relation to a particular act, a person is not a public authority by virtue only of section 6(3)(b) if the nature of the act is private." Section 6 proceeds on the basis that there are obvious public authorities—for example, central and local government, the police and prisons—which do not have to be expressly included in the definition of "public authority".[27] But identifying every obvious "public authority" is not always a simple task.[28] The effect of section 6(5), however, is to make it a necessary one. This is because the acts of "obvious" public authorities will be unlawful if incompatible with Convention rights whatever the nature of the act: that is, irrespective of its private or public nature.[29] The focus here is the character of the body doing the act—whether it is an "obvious" public authority. But in the case of persons who are public authorities only by virtue of section 6(3)(b)—that is, because certain of their functions are of a public nature—their acts will be unlawful under section 6(1) only where the nature of the act is not private. Here the focus is on the character of the

---

[25] *cf. Mangawaro Enterprises v. Att.-Gen.* [1994] 2 N.Z.L.R. 451 (similar obligation in s. 7 of New Zealand Bill of Rights confers no right on the citizen; jurisdiction also excluded because power concerns proceedings in Parliament and protected by Art. 9 of Bill of Rights 1688); discussed by Bamforth, "Parliamentary Sovereignty and the Human Rights Act 1998" [1998] P.L. 572. However, there are other issues. First, standing: if an ordinary citizen has no title or interest under s. 19, does a Backbench M.P.? Secondly, as to Art. 9 of the Bill of Rights, the structure of the 1998 Act is different: "proceedings in Parliament" cannot be unlawful acts for the purposes of s. 6; but having confined the "proceedings in Parliament" exclusion to s. 6, it is arguable that Parliament does not intend the exclusion to apply to every provision in the Act. In particular, what gives Art. 9 of the Bill of Rights such an overarching effect that it can prevent judicial review of a discretion conferred, say, by s. 10, of the 1998 Act?

[26] As noted above, s. 6(3) goes on to exclude Parliament from the definition of "public authority".

[27] See the Government's White Paper preceding the Human Rights Bill, *Rights Brought Home*, Cm 3782 (HMSO, 1997), para. 2.2. See also the Lord Chancellor, Lord Irvine of Lairg, cited below. The Scottish Parliament and Scottish Executive must be obvious public authorities for the purposes of s. 6 of the Human Rights Act 1998. But since the Scotland Act 1998 makes express provision for their observation of Convention rights, it may be thought that s. 6 only has residual relevance for them: see further para. 7.33. Clearly, however, Scottish public bodies established by or otherwise operating under the Scottish Executive are directly covered by s. 6 of the Human Rights Act.

[28] See Sherlock, "The Applicability of the United Kingdom's Human Rights Bill: Identifying 'Public' Functions" [1998] 4 Eur. P.L. 593.

[29] See comments of the Lord Chancellor, Lord Irvine of Lairg, *Hansard*, H.L. Vol. 583, cols 810–812. (Nov. 24, 1997). The way s. 6(3) and (5) are drafted suggests that the public and private acts of courts and tribunals are caught by s. 6(1). But the application of s. 6 to courts is more complex and is discussed further below.

act once it is established that it is an act of a person certain of whose functions are "of a public nature". As the Lord Chancellor explained in the debates on the Bill in the House of Lords: "Section 6 accordingly distinguishes between obvious public authorities, all of whose acts are subject to Section 6, and bodies with mixed functions which are caught in relation to their public acts but not their private acts."[30]

If the distinctions between public bodies, public functions and private acts on which section 6 proceeds seem clear, they are amongst the hardest to draw with any consistency and predictability.[31] It may be that a workable approach can be found by reference to the acts which are or are not subject to the supervisory jurisdiction. The Scottish approach to the scope of judicial review is certainly more flexible than the English approach, indicating, perhaps, less difficulty with making bodies which perform "public functions" amenable to judicial review.[32] So, for example, judicial review of at least some acts and decisions of sporting regulatory bodies are subject to judicial review in Scotland. Whereas in *R. v. Disciplinary Committee of the Jockey Club, ex parte Aga Khan*,[33] the Court of Appeal held that the contractual nature of the relationship between the Jockey Club and one of its members meant that there was no "public law" element to make the club subject to judicial review, in *St Johnston Football Club Ltd v. Scottish Football Association*,[34] the Court of Session held that the Scottish Football Association was subject to the supervisory jurisdiction in Scotland.[35] But in so far as some bodies performing private acts, such as arbiters, are subject to judicial review, their acts may not be challengeable under the 1998 Act.[36] Equally, while "obvious" public bodies are amenable to judicial review for some purposes, it is clear that they are not for others: for example, their employment relationships.[37] Yet the 1998 Act would allow them to be challenged in relation to all their acts and decisions. This highlights the difficulty section 6 presents. While ascertaining the scope of judicial review may not be straightforward, it focuses on one question—namely is this a case amenable to judicial review. Section 6, however, presents three questions all of which involve matters of degree. The first is whether the body is an "obvious" public authority. If yes, all its acts are covered by the Act; if no, the second question is whether certain of the body's functions are of a public nature so as to make it a designated public authority; in which case, the third question is whether the nature of the latter's act is private. Only after the last question is answered affirmatively is the body not subject to the Act. Whatever the merits of

---

[30] *Hansard*, H.L. Vol. 583, col. 811. (Nov. 24, 1997). *cf. Eldridge v. Att.-Gen. of British Columbia* [1997] 3 S.C.R. 624, *per* La Forest J. at 660–662 speaking for a unanimous Supreme Court of Canada on the interpretation of s. 32 of the Canadian Charter of Rights and Freedoms (which defines the scope of the Charter), discussed further below.

[31] *cf.* Hogg, *Constitutional Law of Canada* (4th ed., Carswell, Toronto, 1997), at paras 34–16 *et seq.*

[32] But *cf.* Lord Woolf, "Droit Public–English Style" [1995] P.L. 57, esp. at 63 *et seq.*

[33] [1993] 1 W.L.R. 909.

[34] 1965 S.L.T. 171. For further discussion, see Chapter 8 on the scope of judicial review.

[35] *cf. Stevenage Borough Football Club Ltd v. The Football League Ltd* (1997) 9 Admin.L.R. 109 ("review" jurisdiction flowing from power of court in private law proceedings to "supervise" contracts in restraint of trade).

[36] Unless it can be said that the resolution of disputes by arbitration is so much a matter of general public interest as a proper method of settling points of difference between citizens as to make the arbiter's function a public one.

[37] See *West v. Secretary of State for Scotland*, 1992 S.C. 385; *cf. R. v. BBC, ex p. Lavelle* [1983] 1 W.L.R. 23.

the present Scottish approach to the scope of judicial review, it is hard to believe that a "public–private" distinction can be avoided under section 6 of the 1998 Act, if not in relation to the character of bodies *per se*, at least in relation to the nature of the acts of some "public" bodies.

"Obvious" public authorities

6.48 While many bodies obviously will be public authorities—for example, where they are properly to be identified as part of the Crown, or where they have been established by legislation[38]—experiences both from other areas of law and other jurisdictions suggest that there will often be difficult cases. At the margins, the difficult cases may fall to be treated as designated public authorities, that is, public authorities by virtue of section 6(3)(b) because certain of their functions are of a public nature. But the effect of section 6(5) means that the character of the challenged act as public or private will then be determinative. So, for example, acts done by obvious public authorities in the course of their private employment relationships will be challengeable as unlawful while similar acts done by designated public authorities will not. As the Lord Chancellor explained in the debates on the bill in the House of Lords:

> "In many cases it will be obvious to the courts that they are dealing with a public authority. In respect of government departments, for example, or police officers, or prison officers, or immigration officers, or local authorities, there can be no doubt that the body in question is a public authority. Any clear case of that kind comes in under s.6(1); and it is then unlawful for the authority to act in a way which is incompatible with one or more of the convention rights. In such cases, the prohibition applies in respect of all their acts, public and private. There is no exemption for private acts such as is conferred by s.6(5) in relation to s.6(3)(b)".[39]

How should the definition of "obvious" public authorities be approached? Although a variety of approaches seem to exist, they may all more or less be classified according to whether they focus on the institutional or structural nature of the body, or on the functions which the body performs.[40] Focusing on a body's institutional characteristics means asking how it was set up, who set it up, who pays for it and who controls it, in order to determine the extent of its links with government. While this suggests an attractive objective approach to identifying public bodies, it risks either being over-inclusive by taking in too many bodies simply by virtue of the smallest connection with government or under-inclusive by setting the requisite institutional nexus too high and generally allowing form to prevail over substance.[41] On the other hand, focusing on the functions of a body to determine whether they are sufficiently public can be subjective; the answer depends on temporal,

---

[38] That is, not "under legislation", which would technically include every company incorporated under the Companies legislation.

[39] *Hansard*, H.L. Vol. 583, col. 811 (Nov. 24, 1997).

[40] *cf.* Hogg, *Constitutional Law of Canada* (4th ed., Carswell, Toronto, 1997) at para. 34.16; and Gunther, *Constitutional Law* (12th ed., Foundation Press, New York, 1991), at pp. 890–891.

[41] Although deciding that a body is not an "obvious" public authority does not exclude it from the Act since it may be a designated public authority under s. 6(3)(b).

historical, social, cultural and political factors. So while a European would probably regard education and health care as public functions, an American might not; and a Scot might or might not. In any event, since the definition of public bodies by reference to their public functions is required under section 6(3)(b) of the Act, it seems preferable to define "obvious" public bodies by reference to their institutional or structural characteristics.

Designated public authorities: persons with public functions

Section 6(3)(b) includes within the definition of "public authority" **6.49** persons "certain of whose functions are functions of a public nature" but only if the nature of any challenged act is not private. In other words, some persons and bodies may rank as public authorities where only some of their functions are of a public nature but even then depending upon the nature of the particular act in question. The problem section 6(3)(b) raises is how to identify "functions of a public nature" and how to distinguish the acts of bodies performing such functions which are of a private nature. The Lord Chancellor explained the policy of section 6(3)(b) as follows:

> "[The section] . . . is there to include bodies which are not manifestly public authorities, but some of whose functions only are of a public nature. It is relevant to cases where the courts are not sure whether they are looking at a public authority in the full-blooded s.6(1) sense with regard to those bodies which fall into the grey area between public and private. The [Act] reflects the decision to include as 'public authorities' bodies which have some public functions and some private functions . . . Railtrack would fall into that category because it exercises public functions in its role as a safety regulator, but it is acting privately in its role as a property developer. A private security company would be exercising public functions in relation to the management of a contracted-out prison but would be acting privately when, for example, guarding commercial premises. Doctors in general practice would be public authorities in relation to their NHS functions, but not in relation to their private patients . . . In relation to employment matters, for example, I do not see a distinction between a private security company which has a contracted-out prison in its portfolio and one which does not. There is no reason to make the first company liable under s.6 in respect of its private acts and the second one not liable simply because the first company is also responsible for the management of a prison. As far as acts of a private nature are concerned, the two private security companies are indistinguishable; nor do I see a distinction in this area between Railtrack and other property developers or between doctors with NHS patients and those without".[42]

In regard to designated public authorities, therefore, section 6(3)(b) is intended to give the Convention rights vertical but not horizontal effects. In other words, the Convention rights can be relied on against the body *vis-à-vis* its public functions but not its private acts.[43] One commentator

---

[42] *Hansard*, H.L. Vol. 583, cols 811–812 (Nov. 24, 1997).
[43] The uncertainty of this kind of distinction is noted in the context of the scope of judicial review: para. 8.27.

on the Canadian experience has noted the difficulty of the distinction: "There is no principled way to classify the functions of public bodies into 'governmental' (or 'public') and 'commercial' (or 'private') categories. The only useful question is whether government has assumed control of the function".[44] Furthermore, it is not clear that the public–private discrimination in the application of Convention rights which section 6 entails is consistent with Article 14 of the Convention. It may not be easy to justify before the European Court of Human Rights that the guarantee of Convention rights depends, for example, on the status of an individual's employer, so that some individuals enjoy Convention rights and in identical (except for their private) circumstances others do not.[45] In any event, section 6 of the 1998 Act requires the courts to attempt classifying functions according to their public nature while distinguishing the public acts from the private acts of bodies which are public authorities only by virtue of section 6(3)(b).[46]

Defining public bodies and public functions

6.50   While a detailed comparative study is beyond the scope of the present book, some guidance may be available from situations where comparable problems have arisen. It is accordingly worth looking, albeit necessarily briefly, at some approaches to defining public bodies and public functions in other contexts and other jurisdictions.

Jurisprudence of the European Court of Human Rights

6.51   Since the intention of the 1998 Act is to give further effect to the European Convention, it is necessary to ask what the European Court of Human Rights has said about the scope of Convention rights. The Court has not approached the application of Convention rights in terms of a distinction between public and private bodies or an analysis of public functions. It must be recalled that as an international treaty the Convention focuses on breaches of the guaranteed rights by states.[47] When cases come before the Court it is a state which is the respondent and the Court's focus is on whether the facts disclose any act or omission which can be attributed to the state so as to put it in violation of Convention rights. Yet there are cases where the Court or the Commission have in substance found violations of Convention rights by public

---

[44] Hogg, *Constitutional Law of Canada* (4th ed., Carswell, Toronto, 1997), at para. 34.16.2, approving Supreme Court of Canada's approach to defining the scope of the Charter of Rights by focusing on the extent of government control over a body.

[45] *cf.* the jurisprudence of the European Court of Justice on the horizontal and vertical effects of directives: see, for example, Case 152/84 *Marshall v. Southampton and South-West Hampshire Area Health Authority* [1986] E.C.R. 723; and Case 106/89 *Marleasing SA v. La Comercial Internacional de Alimentacion SA* [1990] E.C.R. I-4135.

[46] The New Zealand Bill of Rights Act 1990, s. 3 also requires this task of New Zealand's courts: see Joseph, *Constitutional and Administrative Law in New Zealand* (Law Book Company, Sydney, 1993), Chap. 26; see also update on the New Zealand Bill of Rights by Joseph, "The New Zealand Bill of Rights" (1996) 7 *Public Law Review* 162. As this author cites, in *Smith v. Ministry of Transport* (1992) 8 C.R.N.Z. 621, hospital doctors were held to be performing public functions and therefore bound by the Bill of Rights when taking blood samples to determine the blood-alcohol levels of motorists. On this basis, the Lord Chancellor's example of NHS doctors being subject to the 1998 Act is valid, at least for some purposes (namely, carrying out functions, on detained suspects, perhaps under police supervision, the results of which may lead to criminal prosecution).

[47] See Art. 34 of the Convention; the Court only has jurisdiction over complaints alleging a breach of the Convention by one of the "High Contracting Parties".

bodies which are independent of the government.[48] Furthermore, the Court has found states to be responsible for violations of Convention rights which have emerged in the course of dealings between private parties. One of the leading cases is *X & Y v. Netherlands*,[49] where the Court found the state in breach of Article 8 of the Convention because its national law did not provide any criminal penalty for violations of an individual's privacy by another individual. But it is clear that in the context of private relations the Court will insist that the breach of Convention rights is not too remote from the state's responsibilities. So in *Botta v. Italy*,[50] where a disabled individual complained that the lack of facilities offered by private organisations for the use of disabled persons at a seaside resort violated the right to privacy guaranteed by Article 8 of the Convention, the Court decided that: "the right to gain access to the beach and the sea at a place distant from his normal place of residence . . . concerns interpersonal relations of such broad and indeterminate scope that there can be no conceivable direct link between measures the State was urged to take in order to make good the omissions of the private bathing establishments and the applicant's private life."[51] It is clear that omissions attributed to the state can found violations of Convention rights even where the matter arises in purely private relations.[52] Even if the state cannot be held directly responsible for a violation, the combined effect of Articles 1 and 13 of the Convention means that its failure to provide a remedy or otherwise deal with the problem can engage its own responsibility. Accordingly, the distinctions between public bodies, public functions and private acts are not central in Convention jurisprudence. Since section 7 of the 1998 Act provides that a person who is a "victim" of an act made unlawful by section 6 may bring legal proceedings against the responsible public authority, and section 7(7) effectively requires "victim" to be understood in the same way as it is under the Convention, it may be asked if the adoption of the Convention's approach to the definition of "victim" renders the complex public–private distinctions in section 6 necessary.[53]

English cases on "public bodies" and judicial review

Some of the relevant cases are mentioned in Chapter 8 (on the scope of judicial review).[54] One English case, *R. v. Panel on Takeovers and Mergers, ex parte Datafin*,[55] is, however, worth citing here. There the issue   **6.52**

---

[48] cf. *Young & James v. U.K.* (1977) 20 Yearbook of Eur. Convention on Human Rights 520 (acts of then nationalised British Rail in upholding a closed shop challengeable under Convention); and *X v. Ireland* (1971) 14 Yearbook of Eur. Convention on Human Rights 198. See also *Osman v. UK* (1999) E.H.R.R.

[49] (1986) 8 E.H.R.R. 235.

[50] (1998) 26 E.H.R.R. 241.

[51] ibid. at para. 35.

[52] See, for example, *Airey v. Ireland* (1980) 2 E.H.R.R. 305 and *Lopez Ostra v. Spain* (1995) 20 E.H.R.R. 277.

[53] By s. 7(1) and (7) of the 1998 Act, only a "victim" (as defined under Art. 34 of the Convention) can rely on Convention rights in proceedings before a U.K. court under s. 6(1): see the following part of this Chapter. cf. Professor Wade's views in "The United Kingdom's Bill of Rights", in Beatson *et al.*, *Constitutional Reform in the UK: Practice and Principles* (Hart Publishing, Oxford, 1998), at p. 64, arguing that emphasis on ss. 7 and 8 of the Act should be avoided so that the general law on breach of statutory duty can provide remedies as between private parties.

[54] See para. 8.27. For further discussion, see Bamforth, "The Public Law–Private Law Distinction: A Comparative and Philosophical Approach", in Leyland and Woods (eds), *Administrative Law Facing the Future* (Blackstone, 1997), Chap. 6.

[55] [1987] Q.B. 815.

was whether the Takeovers and Mergers panel was sufficiently "public" for its decisions to be subject to judicial review. Deciding that it was, the Court of Appeal was influenced by the panel's part in the government's regulatory framework for the City of London: although the panel was not set up by the government, it had been "incorporated" into the government's statutory regulatory framework, it comprised nomineees and representatives of the Bank of England and the Stock Exchange, and: "No one could have been in the least surprised if the panel had been instituted and operated under the direct authority of statute law".[56] Lord Donaldson M.R. was influenced by the panel's decisions indirectly affecting the rights of citizens, the panel's duty to act judicially and, although not established by statutory powers, "the bottom line being the statutory powers exercised by the Department of Trade and Industry and the Bank of England".[57] For Lloyd L.J., the panel had "a giant's strength" and the fact that it is "self-regulating . . . makes it not less but more appropriate that it should be subject to judicial review".[58] The source of the panel's powers not being found in statutory, or prerogative or common law powers could not be "the sole test whether a body is subject to judicial review".[59] Rather, "it is helpful to look not just at the source of the power but at the nature of the power. If the body in question is exercising public law functions, or if the exercise of its functions have public law consequences, then that may . . . be sufficient to bring the body within the reach of judicial review".[60] Nicholls L.J. emphasised the roles of the Bank of England and the Stock Exchange in the panel's functions and noted that the panel had responsibilities to assist the government in complying with E.C. law. Overall, the panel was performing "a public duty", namely "its public law task of spelling out standards and practices in the field of take-overs".[61]

Although the *ex parte Datafin* decision has been subjected to some criticism,[62] subsequent cases have confirmed the panel's susceptibility to judicial review.[63] Clearly, the approach of the Court of Appeal raises themes which are relevant in assessing the public nature of the functions performed by a body. Of particular relevance are whether a body is underpinned by statute, the strength of its powers and the sanctions it can impose, its place in a regulatory scheme, who its members are and who appoints them, and the nature and consequences of its decisions. In the last analysis, the courts should be attentive to the substance of public power irrespective of how it is dressed up. As Donaldson M.R. observed in *ex parte Datafin*: "I should be very disappointed if the courts could not recognise the realities of executive power and allowed their vision to be clouded by the subtlety and sometimes complexity of the way in which it can be exerted".[64]

---

[56] *ibid. per* Donaldson M.R. at 835. This point is used by Bingham M.R. in *R. v. Jockey Club Disciplinary Committee, ex p. Aga Khan* [1993] 1 W.L.R. 909 at 935 to suggest as an issue for the scope of judicial review whether, if a body did not exist in its (private) embodiment, the government would set it up.

[57] *ibid.* at 838.

[58] *ibid.* at 845.

[59] *ibid.* at 847.

[60] *ibid.*

[61] *ibid.* at 852.

[62] See Wade, "Beyond the Law: A British Innovation in Judicial Review" (1991) 43 Admin.L.R. 559.

[63] See *R. v. Panel on Takeovers and Mergers, ex p. Guinness plc* [1990] 1 Q.B. 146; and *R. v. Panel on Takeovers and Mergers, ex p. Fayed* (1992) 5 Admin.L.R. 337.

[64] [1987] Q.B. 815 at 839.

Public bodies and E.C. law

In E.C. law, the ECJ and national courts have had to decide whether **6.53**
bodies are "emanations of the state" for the purposes of being bound by
unimplemented directives, which, subject to certain conditions, only have
vertical direct effects.[65] In *Foster v. British Gas*,[66] the ECJ held that
British Gas when still a nationalised industry was an emanation of the
state.[67] In *Johnston v. Chief Constable of the Royal Ulster Constabulary*,[68]
the ECJ decided that the chief constable of a police force is an
emanation of the state. And in *National Union of Teachers v. Governing
Body of St Mary's Church of England (Aided) Junior School*,[69] the English
Court of Appeal held that the governing body of a voluntary aided
school is an emanation of the state for the purposes of the direct effect
of directives. In this case Schiemann L.J. said: "What emerges from the
case law is a number of indicia which point to the appropriateness of
treating the body in question as an emanation of the State, none of
which indicia is conclusive . . . the Community case law indicates that a
body may be an emanation of the State although it is not under the
control of central government".[70] As to the indicia, the ECJ itself has
explained: "A body, whatever its legal form, which has been made
responsible, pursuant to a measure adopted by the State, for providing a
public service under control of the State and has for that purpose special
powers beyond those which resulted from the normal rules applicable in
relations between individuals is included among the bodies against which
the provisions of a Directive capable of having direct effect may be
relied upon".[71] The ECJ's approach to providing tests for emanations of
the state has not always been clear,[72] which probably reflects the
difficulty of the task involved. While under section 6 of the 1998 Act
most of the difficulty will be focused on section 6(3)(b) and identifying
which persons certain of whose functions cause them to be a public
authority, the greater scope to challenge the acts of "obvious" public
authorities will make assessment of how close to the state a particular
body is significant.

Canadian Charter of Rights and Freedoms

There are several decisions of the Supreme Court of Canada on the **6.54**
application of the Canadian Charter of Rights and Freedoms which are
instructive in this country. Section 32 of the constitutional Charter

---

[65] The direct effect of directives is discussed in Chapter 5 (on judicial review and E.C.
law). Briefly, the ECJ has held that directives which a member state has not or not
properly implemented can in certain circumstances be relied on by individuals against the
state and emanations of the state in actions before national courts: Case 152/84 *Marshall v.
Southampton and South-West Hampshire Area Health Authority* [1986] E.C.R. 723. Directives do not have horizontal direct effects allowing one private individual to rely on
provisions in the unimplemented directive in a legal action against another private
individual.
[66] Case C–188/89 [1990] E.C.R. I-3133.
[67] *cf. Doughty v. Rolls Royce plc* [1992] I.R.L.R. 126.
[68] Case 222/84 [1986] E.C.R. 1651.
[69] [1997] I.R.L.R. 242.
[70] *ibid.* at 247–248.
[71] Case C–188/89 *Foster v. British Gas* [1990] E.C.R. I-3133, at para. 20 of the Court's
Judgment. But as Schiemann L.J. notes in *St Mary's School, supra*, this should not be
regarded as an exclusive "tripartite" formula.
[72] For discussion see Curtin, "The province of government: delimiting the direct effect
of directives in the common law context" (1990) 15 Eur. L.R. 195.

provides that it applies: "to the Parliament and government of Canada ... and to the legislature and government of each province". Section 32 has required the courts to decide if the acts and decisions of various bodies come within the scope of "government" or legislative action. While it is clear that once a body is held to be exercising statutory powers the Charter applies, more difficulty has been encountered with the identification of when bodies are part of "government" so as to be bound by Charter rights. A significant problem has been that section 32 does not expressly include a "public functions" basis for bodies to be bound by the Charter.[73] This has probably led to what has become a rather sophisticated case law. For example, in two cases a majority of the Supreme Court of Canada decided that neither a university nor a public hospital come within government or legislative action so as to allow these bodies' mandatory retirement policies to be challenged as violating the Charter's right to equality.[74] Although the relevant universities and hospital were established by statutes, received funding from the government, and were involved in the public function of providing tertiary education and health care, still the Supreme Court did not consider that they were bound by Charter rights when implementing their own employment policies. On the facts of the cases, neither the universities nor the hospital were to be considered as part of the "apparatus" of government, nor were they "implementing" government policies or acting in a government capacity when adopting the policies. In a companion case[75] in which the Court found that a college was "an emanation of government" and therefore bound by the Charter in implementing its employment policies, the Court explained the distinction in the following terms:

> "As its constituent Act makes clear, the college is a Crown agency established by the government to implement government policy. Though the government may choose to permit the college board to exercise a measure of discretion, the simple fact is that the board is not only appointed and removeable at pleasure by the government; the government may at all times by law direct its operation. Briefly stated, it is simply part of the apparatus of government both in form and in fact. In carrying out its functions, therefore, the college is performing acts of government ... Its status is wholly different from the universities in the companion cases ... which, though extensively regulated and funded by government, are essentially autonomous bodies."[76]

Commenting on these university, college and hospital cases, Professor Hogg has observed that: "Although the university and the hospital were

---

[73] *cf.* Anderson, "The Limits of Constitutional law: the Canadian Charter of Rights and Freedoms and the public–private divide" in Gearty and Tomkins (eds), *Understanding Human Rights* (1996).

[74] *McKinney v. University of Guelph* [1990] 3 S.C.R. 229; *Stoffman v. Vancouver General Hospital* [1990] 3 S.C.R. 483. See also *Lavigne v. OPSEU* [1991] 2 S.C.R. 211, where provincial governments exercised more control over the bodies being challenged allowing them to be regarded as part of the Crown and therefore "government" bound by Charter rights.

[75] *Douglas/Kwantlen Faculty Association v. Douglas College* [1990] 3 S.C.R. 570.

[76] *ibid.* per La Forest J. at 584–585.

both established and empowered by statute, the bodies were not possessed of powers any larger than those of a natural person."[77]

The Supreme Court of Canada has tended to emphasise the extent to which a body is linked to or controlled by government or is implementing government policies in deciding whether it is bound by Charter rights.[78] But once it is decided that a body is exercising statutory powers or is linked to government, the Charter applies to both its public and private activities.[79] It has, however, long been clear that attempting to define exactly when and where the Charter applies is impossible. In *McKinney v. University of Guelph*,[80] Sopinka and L'Heureux-Dube JJ. supported a "public functions" approach to at least some Charter cases, so that a body like a university could be subject to the Charter for some purposes and not others.[81] And although deciding that the university was not part of government, La Forest J. accepted that: "There may be situations in respect of specific activities where it can fairly be said that the decision is that of the government, or that the government sufficiently partakes in the decision as to make it an act of government."[82] These considerations have emerged more clearly in light of a recent decision of the Supreme Court in which it once more considers the extent to which the Charter can apply to a public hospital. In *Eldridge v. Attorney-General of British Columbia*,[83] a unanimous Supreme Court held that the Charter's equality rights did apply to a public hospital which discriminated against deaf people in the provision of medical services which it had been charged by the government to deliver to the public. Whereas in the earlier case the challenge concerned the hospital's employment policies, here the hospitals were providing "medically necessary services" to the public as part of a "specific government objective" which was part of a "comprehensive social programme", namely public health care established under legislation. Discussing the Court's approach to the application of the Charter, La Forest J. said:

> "It seems clear, then, that a private entity may be subject to the Charter in respect of certain inherently governmental actions. The factors that might serve to ground a finding that an activity engaged in by a private entity is "governmental" in nature do not readily admit of any *a priori* elucidation . . . [but] the Charter applies to private entities in so far as they act in furtherance of a specific governmental programme or policy. In these circumstances, while it is a private actor that actually implements the programme, it is government that retains responsibility for it . . . Just as governments are not permitted to escape Charter scrutiny by entering into commercial contracts or other 'private' arrangements, they should not be allowed to evade their constitutional responsibilities by

---

[77] Hogg, *Constitutional Law of Canada* (4th ed., Carswell, Toronto, 1997), at para. 34.12. As Professor Hogg observes, the difficulty of regarding establishment by or empowerment under statute as the applicable test for when a body is bound by Charter rights is that every private corporation is ultimately established under and derives some powers from the legislation under which it is incorporated.

[78] See Hogg, *supra*.

[79] See *Lavigne v. OPSEU* [1991] 2 S.C.R. 211, *per* La Forest J. at 314.

[80] [1990] 3 S.C.R. 229.

[81] *cf.* also the dissenting judgment of Wilson J. in *McKinney v. University of Guelph*, *supra* (supporting a governmental functions test for the Charter to apply).

[82] *ibid.* at 273–274.

[83] [1997] 3 S.C.R. 624.

delegating the implementation of their policies and programmes to private entities."[84]

Since the Charter of Rights refers only to "government" and does not expressly include a reference to "public functions", the Supreme Court has had to interpret "government" expansively. But as the cases above demonstrate, this has not caused it to accept that everything which may be designated "public" is subject to the Charter. In *Eldridge*, the Court clarified its approach:

> "First, the mere fact that an entity performs what may loosely be termed a 'public function', or the fact that a particular activity may be described as 'public' in nature, will not be sufficient to bring it within the purview of "government" [under the Charter] . . . The second important point concerns the precise manner in which the Charter may be held to apply to a private entity . . . First, it may be determined that the entity is itself "government" for the purposes of s.32 [of the Charter]. This involves an inquiry into whether the entity whose actions have given rise to the alleged Charter breach can, either by its very nature or in virtue of the degree of governmental control exercised over it, properly be characterised as "government" . . . In such cases, all of the activities of the entity will be subject to the Charter, regardless of whether the activity in which it is engaged could, if performed by a non-governmental actor, correctly be described as "private". Second, an entity may be found to attract Charter scrutiny with respect to a particular activity that can be ascribed to government. This demands an investigation not into the nature of the entity whose activity is impugned but rather into the nature of the activity itself. In such cases, in other words, one must scrutinize the quality of the act at issue, rather than the quality of the actor. If the act is truly "governmental" in nature–for example, the implementation of a specific statutory scheme or a government programme–the entity performing it will be subject to review under the Charter only in respect of that act, and not its other, private activities".[85]

It is likely that whatever may be the differences between section 6 of the 1998 Act and the Canadian Charter, the courts in the United Kingdom will be required to engage in some kind of analysis corresponding with that set out by the Supreme Court of Canada in *Eldridge*.[86] In particular, the extent to which a body is controlled by government, implements government policies, or is responsible for exercising statutory powers are factors which are relevant under section 6(1) and section 6(3)(b).[87]

Other systems

6.55 Experience in other systems with bills of rights will also be relevant. In particular, section 3 of the New Zealand Bill of Rights Act 1990 provides that it applies to acts done: "by the legislative, executive or judicial

---

[84] *ibid.* at 659–660.
[85] *ibid.* at 660–662.
[86] But for criticism of the Supreme Court of Canada's decision in *Eldridge*, see Hogg, *Constitutional Law of Canada* (4th ed., Carswell, Toronto, 1997) at paras 34.13 and 34.14.
[87] They are also relevant under the approach in *ex p. Datafin, supra.*

branches of the government of New Zealand; or by any person or body in the performance of any public function, power, or duty conferred or imposed on that person or body by or pursuant to law". So far, the Canadian experience has been influential in New Zealand both in regard to defining the legislative and executive branches and in relation to the identification of public functions.[88] Of special interest, however, is the application of the New Zealand Bill to the judiciary. The implications of this are considered below. In addition, decisions on the "state action" doctrine under the U.S. Bill of Rights provide a rich, although very intricate, source of material to be consulted. The U.S. Supreme Court has invariably held that the constitutional rights guaranteed in the Bill of Rights only protect against "state action".[89] But the Supreme Court has developed two lines of case law under which the concept of state action is extended beyond obvious governmental bodies to require nominally private bodies to comply with constitutional rights. The first line, most famously demonstrated by *Shelley v. Kraemer*,[90] concentrates on the link between particular bodies and government. The questions here focus on the "nexus" between the body and government: for example, whether the body is controlled or authorised by government so as to be deemed "governmental" for the purposes of the state action doctrine.[91] The search is essentially for indications of whether the government is "to some significant extent" implicated in the body's activities. So in *Shelley*, the Supreme Court found state action present when a state court adjudicating a dispute between private parties enforced a racially discriminatory restrictive covenant: "The judicial action . . . bears the clear and unmistakable imprimatur of the State".[92] Similarly, in *Burton v. Wilmington Parking Authority*,[93] a private restaurant which discriminated against a person on the ground of race was found to be engaged in "state action" because it was located in a car park which was owned and operated by the Wilmington Parking Authority, itself an agency of the State government: "The State has so far insinuated itself into a position of interdependence with [the restaurant] that it must be recognised as a joint participant in the challenged activity."[94]

The second line of cases focuses on the nature of the functions performed by a body to determine whether they are sufficiently public to

---

[88] See Joseph, *Constitutional and Administrative Law in New Zealand* (Law Book Company, Sydney, 1993), at pp. 852–855.

[89] *Civil Rights Cases* (1883) 109 U.S. 3. See Tribe, *American Constitutional Law* (2nd ed., Foundation Press, New York, 1988), Chap. 18; and Gunther, *Constitutional Law* (12th ed., Foundation Press, New York, 1991), Chap. 10, section 2. For a shorter, accessible introduction to state action doctrine under the U.S. Constitution, albeit focusing on the extent of constitutional rights in the private sector against race discrimination, see Abraham & Perry, *Freedom and the Court* (7th ed., OUP, Oxford, 1998), pp. 389–410.

[90] 334 U.S. 1 (1948).

[91] To this extent, therefore, the approach is similar to that adopted by the Supreme Court of Canada under the Charter: see *Eldridge, supra.*

[92] 334 U.S. 1, *per* Vinson C.J. at 20. Of course, this raises the important question of the extent to which courts are public authorities even when, as in *Shelley*, resolving disputes between private parties according to the common law: see below.

[93] 365 U.S. 715 (1961).

[94] *ibid. per* Clark J. But *cf. Moose Lodge No. 107 v. Irvis*, 407 U.S. 163 (1972) (private club which discriminates not engaging in state action by virtue of fact that it possesses a liquor licence granted by state); *Blum v. Yaretsky*, 457 U.S. 991 (1982) (privately owned nursing home receiving public money not engaged in state action for purposes of 14th Amendment); *Rendell-Baker v. Kohn*, 457 U.S. 830 (1982) (same conclusion *re* private school).

be considered "state action".[95] However, in recent times the Court has been much less enthusiastic about classifying functions as public or private, instead limiting the concept of "public functions" to powers which may be said to be "exclusively reserved to the State".[96] This will inevitably be rather few functions. Indeed, the reluctance to engage in defining "public functions" is shown in another area of the Court's jurisprudence. Whereas identifying "traditional government functions" was once thought to assist in delimiting the proper sphere of the two systems of government in the U.S. federation,[97] the Court eventually abandoned the task as unprincipled and subjective.[98]

Courts and Tribunals

6.56 Courts and tribunals are included within the definition of "public authority" by section 6(3)(a) of the 1998 Act.[99] The expression "court" is not defined in the Act. It should certainly cover any place where justice is judicially administered but it may extend further. The Court of Parliament is a court and the need to make an express exclusion of Parliament, other than its judicial activities, may suggest that other non-judicial courts may be included. A court should, however, require to have something of a public character to be included. So section 9(2) expressly provides that the Act does not increase the bodies which are subject to judicial review although they may be termed a court. As for tribunals, section 21(1) defines "tribunal" as meaning "any tribunal in which legal proceedings may be brought". That tends to suggest that it is only where there is a judicial function to be performed that a body can rank as a tribunal.[1] Will this allow the conduct and decisions of an arbitration to be challenged under the Act? While it is arguable that an arbitration involves a judicial function, it may be doubted if "legal proceedings" are technically brought before an arbitration.[2] More generally, the difficulty which section 6(3)(a) raises is whether the inclusion of courts and tribunals within the definition of public authority for the purposes of section 6(1) means that every "act" of a court is within the coverage of the Act. In particular, when a court "acts" to decide a case between two private parties, can its decision be challenged for violation

---

[95] The case usually cited as the first in this line is *Marsh v. Alabama*, 326 U.S. 501 (1946), but it is not wholly satisfactory: it concerned a state criminal prosecution, albeit for actions in a "private" town. See also *Amalgamated Food Employees Union v. Logan Valley Plaza Inc.*, 391 U.S. 308 (1968) (private shopping centre engaged in public functions and therefore bound to respect free speech rights of protesters), overruled by *Hudgens v. NLRB*, 424 U.S. 507 (1976) (private shopping centres not engaged in state action for free speech purposes).

[96] See *Jackson v. Metropolitan Edison Co.* 419 U.S. 345 (1974); *Flagg Brothers Inc. v. Brooks*, 436 U.S. 149 (1978); and *NCAA v. Tarkanian*, 488 U.S. 179 (1988).

[97] See *National League of Cities v. Usery*, 426 U.S. 833 (1976) and *Hodel v. Virginia Surface Mining & Reclamation Association*, 452 U.S. 264 (1981).

[98] See *Garcia v. San Antonio Metropolitan Transit Authority*, 469 U.S. 528 (1985). For discussion, see Tushnet, "Why the Supreme Court Overruled *National League of Cities*" (1994) 47 Vanderbilt Law Rev. 1623.

[99] *cf. Guilfoyle v. Home Office* (1981) 1 All E.R. 943 (deciding that proceedings before the European Court of Human Rights are legal proceedings because the Court exercises judicial functions, but proceedings in the European Commission of Human Rights are not because the Commission only reports on the facts and states an opinion; it does not exercise any judicial function).

[1] So form or nomenclature should not be definitive. Accordingly, the Children's Panel must be regarded as a tribunal.

[2] *cf.* definition of "legal proceedings" under English Arbitration Act 1996.

of Convention rights? That is, even where the Convention does not apply between private parties, is the effect of bringing a case to court to be to cause the Convention to apply?[3] If so, the Act's scope is increased significantly by virtue of courts being deemed public authorities and it may be asked what effect is to be left for section 6(5), which excludes private acts of designated public authorities from the scope of section 6. In the House of Lords, the Lord Chancellor said that: "it is right as a matter of principle for the courts to have a duty of acting compatibly with the convention not only in cases involving other public authorities but also in developing the common law in deciding cases between individuals. Why should they not? In preparing this bill, we have taken the view that it is the other course, that of excluding convention considerations altogether from cases between individuals, which would have to be justified".[4] While it is tempting to inquire into when it may properly be said that a court "acts", it is doubtful if such an approach will render anything but semantic distinctions.[5] The opportunity for human rights guarantees to apply between private parties has generated an enormous literature in several jurisdictions and only the briefest of mentions may be made of the issues here.[6]

Private Acts

It is possible that the inclusion of courts within the definition of public **6.57** authority under section 6 of the 1998 Act allows some scope for the Convention rights to apply to private activity.[7] But the extent to which human rights, at least those guaranteed in constitutional instruments, can apply in the private sector is controversial.[8] As a starting point, it is

---

[3] *cf. Shelley v. Kraemer*, 334 U.S. 1 (1948). For argument based on *Shelley* to support application of the New Zealand Bill of Rights, which expressly binds the "judicial branch", to private parties, see Butler, "The New Zealand Bill of Rights and private common law litigation" [1991] N.Z.L.J. 261; and *contra*, Joseph, *Constitutional and Administrative Law in New Zealand* (Law Book Company, Sydney, 1993), at p. 856. For the views of the Court of Appeal, see R. v. H [1994] 2 N.Z.L.R. 143; but *cf. Lange v. Atkinson* [1998] 4 B.H.R.C. 573.

[4] *Hansard*, H.L. Vol. 583, col 783 (Nov. 24, 1997). But see also the Lord Chancellor's comments during the bill's second reading at *Hansard*, Vol. 582, col. 1232 (Nov. 3, 1997): "Clause 6 does not impose any liability on organisations which have no public functions at all."

[5] In particular, it may be noted that for the purposes of judicial immunity, judges "act" when deciding cases between parties. See Wade & Ewing, *Constitutional and Administrative Law* (12th ed., Longman, London, 1997), at pp. 425–426.

[6] For a comprehensive discussion on human rights and the private sector, see Clapham, *Human Rights in the Private Sphere* (OUP, Oxford, 1993). For comparison between the U.S., Canada, Ireland and New Zealand, see the excellent article by Butler, "Constitutional Rights in Private Litigation: A Critique and Comparison" (1993) 22 Anglo-Am.L.R. 1.

[7] For discussion, see Wade, "Human Rights and the Judiciary" [1998] E.H.R.L.R. 520; Hunt, "The 'Horizontal Effect' of the Human Rights Act" [1998] P.L. 423; and Leigh, "Horizontal Rights, the Human Rights Act and Privacy: Lessons from the Commonwealth?" (1999) 48 I.C.L.Q. 57.

[8] As it is under many constitutional human rights laws. In contrast, human rights guarantees contained in ordinary statutes often apply to private persons and private activity—for example, the Sex Discrimination Act 1975 and the Race Relations Act 1976. The same is true in other systems whatever the scope of the constituional rights: consider, for example, in the USA the Civil Rights Act 1964, in Canada the various provincial Human Rights Acts and in New Zealand the Human Rights Act 1993. Many of the problems associated with human rights applying to private activity arise in the context of equality rights, such as the "equal protection of the laws" guarantee in the 14th

necessary to be clear about what is meant by Convention rights applying to private acts. In the modern world it is hard to isolate a situation which is completely private and some of the cases which are pointed to as "private" cases are in fact very much public ones. For example, in *Osman v. United Kingdom*[9] the European Court of Human Rights decided that the failure of English law to allow the plaintiff to sue the police in tort for their alleged negligence constituted a violation of the right to a fair trial guaranteed by Article 6 of the Convention. One view of this decision might be that it concerns the (private) law of negligence and that the Convention therefore applies as a higher standard against which the law of negligence must be measured. On a narrow and surely more correct analysis, however, the case concerns defects in the law of remedies against the police. As such it is very much a case concerning a public authority and therefore in no way exceptional, although possibly raising some more general questions about the general law of negligence. It would be strange, however, to argue that a case concerning the police and an individual is in any sense a private case.[10] Similarly, in *Lopez Ostra v. Spain*[11] the violation of Article 8 of the Convention which occurred between private parties could be attributed to the state because the private corporation which created the nuisance had received a subsidy out of public funds from a local government body. But this is not to say that there are no situations in which Convention rights can apply to purely private cases.[12]

Four observations in connection with this problem may be made. First, it is clear that section 6 of the 1998 Act covers all acts of "obvious" public authorities such as the central and local governments irrespective of whether those acts are private or public. Secondly, the private acts of persons who are only "public authorities" by virtue of section 6(3)(b) of the 1998 Act are expressly excluded from the Act by section 6(5). Although drawing the line between the public and private acts of designated public bodies is not easy, it is unavoidable under section 6(5) of the Act. Thirdly, whenever legislation applies in a case, the Convention rights are relevant since section 3 of the 1998 Act requires all legislation to be read and given effect so far as possible in a way which is compatible with the Convention rights. A private person cannot therefore come to court and expect to argue for legislation to be given a meaning which is incompatible with Convention rights. In other words, the obligation to read and give effect to legislation in a way which is compatible with Convention rights is addressed to everyone.[13] Section 3

Amendment to the U.S. Constitution and the equality rights in s. 15 of the Canadian Charter. Since the European Convention does not have an equivalent free-standing right to equality (*cf.* Art. 14 of the Convention), some of the problems relating to private activity may not arise here.

[9] [1998] E.H.R.L.R. 101.

[10] Excepting perhaps employment matters where the police force is an employer; but as an "obvious" public authority, the private acts of the police are reviewable for consistency with Convention rights.

[11] (1995) 20 E.H.R.R. 277.

[12] See Clapham, *Human Rights in the Private Sphere* (OUP, Oxford, 1993), Chap. 7.

[13] In the same way, the Canadian Charter of Rights and Freedoms allows challenge to legislation in cases arising between two private parties: see *Retail, Wholesale and Department Store Union, Local 580 v. Dolphin Delivery Ltd* [1986] 2 S.C.R. 573; and *Eldridge, supra*. But this is not so under all bills of rights: *cf. Tam Hing-yee v. Wu Tai-wai* [1992] 1 H.K.L.R. 185 (Hong Kong Bill of Rights Ordinance cannot be used to challenge legislation otherwise than in an action against the government). The fact that the 1998 Act

may be said to have vertical and horizontal effect, applying equally to legislation in cases between an individual and the government and between individuals.[14] Fourthly, under the Convention, albeit not under the 1998 Act, at least not in relation to failures by the U.K. Parliament to legislate, any violation of Convention rights occurring between private parties may be attributed to the state. That is, some failures to protect Convention rights in the context of private acts may be visited on a public authority. However, this still leaves the relationship between Convention rights and the common law.

The 1998 Act and the Common Law

Although the relationship between the 1998 Act and the common law is **6.58** complex, several principles are clear. First, it is clear that an "obvious" public authority cannot rely on the common law to act incompatibly with Convention rights.[15] Section 6 makes this unlawful. Secondly, a designated public authority must in the course of its public functions exercise its common law powers only in ways which are compatible with the Convention rights. But is a designated public authority free to conduct its private acts in accordance with the common law unhindered by Convention rights? And more generally, are all private persons who exercise common law rights and duties free from challenge on the grounds of Convention rights? The complex question, therefore, is deciding on the extent to which the 1998 Act and Convention rights apply to the common law as it operates between private parties. This will be relevant in judicial review in so far as any attempt is made to review the "private" acts of designated public bodies or any private person on the ground of violation of Convention rights. It is here that the inclusion of courts within the definition of public authority under section 6 is significant.

---

applies to all legislation does not necessarily mean that every case involving the interpretation of legislation between private parties is amenable to judicial review. Whether or not a case comes within the supervisory jurisdiction will still depend on the usual rules on the scope of judicial review, unless the courts accept that every civil case concerning Convention rights is by virtue of this fact amenable to judicial review.

[14] A good Canadian example of the implications of this conclusion is *Vriend v. Alberta* [1998] 1 S.C.R. 493. See also *Eldridge v. Att.-Gen. of British Columbia* [1997] 3 S.C.R. 624, at 644. It must be accepted, though, that the scheme of the 1998 Act means that if legislation is found to be incompatible with Convention rights in a case between two private parties, the party with the right under the incompatible legislation may prevail. Section 4 provides that a declaration of incompatibility does not affect "the validity, continuing operation or enforcement" of legislation. The losing party will be left to seek redress against the government, which remedy may have to be pursued before the European Court of Human Rights. Where the government remedies the legislative violation of Convention rights by means of a s. 10 remedial order, however, the state of play between the parties may change. Schedule 2, para. 1 allows such orders to have retrospective effect, so that the original winning party could become the losing party by virtue of a retrospective amendment to the incompatible legislation. It may be that this party will then expect to be compensated by the government for what might turn out to be interference with legal rights by retroactive legislation.

[15] *cf. RWDSU, Local 580 v. Dolphin Delivery* [1986] 2 S.C.R. 573, *per* McIntyre J. at 598–603, cited above. So, it follows that the Crown cannot exercise its prerogative powers inconsistently with Convention rights (*cf. Operation Dismantle v. The Queen* [1985] 1 S.C.R. 441) and no public authority can exercise common law (*e.g.* contract making) powers in a way which violates Convention rights (*cf. Douglas/Kwantlen Faculty Association. v. Douglas College* [1990] 3 S.C.R. 570). Similarly, exercises of prosecutorial discretion must come within the coverage of Convention rights (*cf. R. v. Swain* [1991] 1 S.C.R. 933: Charter applies to Crown's (common law) powers to call witnesses in a criminal trial).

The courts as public authorities

6.59   Some commentators have argued that the Convention rights will apply
to the common law and therefore indirectly to private parties by virtue
of courts and tribunals being included within the definition of public
authority under section 6(1).[16] The essence of this argument is that in
developing the common law courts must give effect to Convention rights.
They would be acting unlawfully if they decided cases, including those
between private parties, on the basis of judge-made common law rules
which were incompatible with Convention rights. In this way, it is
argued, the Convention rights will apply "indirectly" between private
parties. Support for this approach is often taken from some decisions of
the U.S. Supreme Court under the U.S. Bill of Rights. It has already
been noted that the Supreme Court has generally insisted on some
element of "state action" for the Bill of Rights to apply.[17] But the Court
has held that at least some constitutional rights can be violated by
private actors.[18] These cases, although few, have generated an extensive
literature and have caused some U.S. commentators to conclude that it
is not possible to find a principled basis on which to identify state
action.[19] It is tempting to conclude that in the United States, at least
historically, as much depends on the right which has allegedly been
violated as on the character or functional nature of the body violating.[20]
The difficult U.S. experience with race discrimination and the priority
which U.S. constitutional doctrine gives to freedom of speech often
provides the background for application of constitutional rights into the

---

[16] In particular, Wade, Hunt and Leigh, cited *supra*. See also Marshall, "Patriating
Rights - With Reservations: The Human Rights Bill 1998" in Beatson *et al.*, *Constitutional
Reform in the UK: Practice and Principles* (Hart Publishing, Oxford, 1998) at pp. 79–80 (a
contribution which contains many illuminating points on the effect which the 1998 Act may
have). Also Professor Basil Markesinis *Q.C.*, "Privacy, Freedom of Expression and the
Human Rights Bill; Lessons from Germany" (1999) 115 L.Q.R. 47.

[17] For criticism of this approach to the U.S. Constitution, see Sunstein, *The Partial
Constitution* (Harvard UP, Boston, 1993).

[18] In particular, consider *Shelley v. Kramer*, 334 U.S. 1 (1948) and *New York Times v.
Sullivan*, 376 U.S. 254 (1964). See also *American Federation of Labor v. Swing*, 312 U.S. 321
(1941). For criticism of Shelley, see Wechsler, "Toward Neutral Principles of Constitu-
tional Law" (1959) 73 Harv.L.R. 1 and Black, "Foreword: State 'Action'" (1967) 81
Harv.L.R. 69. It is probably now true that there is limited scope for most rights in the Bill
of Rights to apply in the private sector where there is no "significant" state involvement.
See (from an extensive list of possibilities) *Burton v. Wilmington Parking Authority*, 365
U.S. 715 (1961); *Jackson v. Metropolitan Edison Co.*, 419 U.S. 345 (1974); *Flagg Brothers
Inc. v. Brooks*, 436 U.S. 149 (1978); *Rendell-Baker v. Kohn*, 457 U.S. 830 (1982); and *NCAA
v. Tarkanian*, 488 U.S. 179 (1988), dealing with either the significance of the link between
private bodies and the state which is required to engage state action or the extent to which
performing "public functions" engages state action. But see also Tribe, *supra*, at 1711: "the
state 'acts' when its courts create and enforce common law rules", a statement not
immediately justifiable in light of Rehnquist J. (writing for a majority of the Court) in
Flagg Bros, supra: "[If] the mere denial of judicial relief is considered sufficient encouragement to make the State responsible for . . . private acts, all private deprivations of property
[justified under codified common law rules] would be converted into public acts whenever
the State, for whatever reason, denies [judicial] relief sought by the putative property
owner".

[19] See Tribe, *supra*.

[20] *cf.* Tribe, *supra*, at 1699 *et seq.*; and see dissent of Marshall J. in *Jackson v.
Metropolitan Edison Co.*, 419 U.S. 345 (1974).

private sector.[21] Accordingly, great care must be taken with arguments based on context-specific decisions of the U.S. Supreme Court under the U.S. Bill of Rights.

Indirect application

But this does not deny the "indirect" application of Convention rights to the conduct of private parties. One commentator has offered the example of the private club which excludes women[22]; assuming that a violation of her Convention rights is arguable, if the club is sued in delict for assault for physically ejecting a woman, the courts would be acting unlawfully under the Convention if they allowed the club to rely on any common law defence such as lawful ejection; otherwise the courts themselves would be acting incompatibly with the woman's Convention rights.[23] Sophisticated as the argument is, it begs the question about the scope which Parliament really intends the Convention rights to have. While it is uncontroversial that courts are part of the state and that they should act compatibly with Convention rights, including when deciding cases based on the common law, and also when such cases are between private parties,[24] to conclude that this means that private activity is thereby to be measured against Convention rights, however indirectly, is to detract from the Act's express application to the acts of public authorities and, in the case of designated public authorities, express exclusion of their private acts. In particular, it ignores the neutrality which certain common law rules have. For example, the law of defamation is not neutral; its purpose is to restrict freedom of speech; and so judicial development of the law of defamation and court orders under it to restrict speech are covered by Convention rights. In contrast, rules of contract law and property law are in substance neutral. They do not *per*

6.60

---

[21] This is certainly true with the two cases most frequently cited to support constitutional rights applying in the private sector, namely *Shelley v. Kraemer*, 334 U.S. 1 (1948) and *New York Times v. Sullivan*, 376 U.S. 254 (1964): in *Shelley*, the Supreme Court held that state action was satisfied by a state court enforcing a racially discriminatory restrictive covenant; while in *Sullivan* the issue was the compatibility of a state's law on defamation with the First Amendment's guarantee of freedom of speech. Since *Shelley*, however, the U.S. Congress has passed legislation prohibiting most forms of private racial discrimination; and the courts have stepped back from what is often claimed the logical deduction from *Shelley*—that all court action is state action: see *Flagg Bros Inc. v. Brooks, supra*. Certainly, as *Flagg Bros* shows, the Supreme Court has not accepted that private parties are bound by all the constitutional rights which are now guaranteed by virtue of their being incorporated into the "due process" clause of the 14th Amendment. So it may be that *Shelley* is explained by the courts extending constitutional rights in light of the legislature's (then) failure to deal effectively with the problem of racial discrimination. Similarly, *Sullivan* can be explained by the specific defamation context; the law of defamation is not "content neutral"; its purpose is to restrict the right to free speech; judicial development of the law of defamation therefore engages the right to freedom of speech; but it does not follow that all judicial decisions between private parties where neutral rules of law are in question engage constitutional rights—*cf. Washington v. Davis*, 426 U.S. 299 (1976).

[22] Hunt, "The 'Horizontal Effect' of the Human Rights Act" [1998] P.L. 423 at 442.

[23] The example also assumes that the police do not become involved. If they do, for example, by arresting the woman, the "private" aspects will fade away. *Quaere* whether, if the police refuse to become involved, the club and its members may have grounds to complain about a breach of their Art. 11 Convention right to freedom of association by virtue of the police's failure to act.

[24] *cf. Broome v. Cassell & Co. Ltd* [1972] A.C. 1027, *per* Lord Kilbrandon at 1133 (Convention relevant to law of defamation as it applies between private parties).

se violate Convention rights.[25] Rather, it is the use made of such rules by private individuals which may violate Convention rights. But the freedom of private individuals to decide the uses to which to put common law rights and powers is for better or worse fundamental and it is for the legislature to decide how to restrict this freedom in the interests of society.[26] Certainly, its failures to regulate in particular ways may engage the Convention rights, if not before national courts then before the European Court of Human Rights. But it is not apparent that Convention rights must apply by virtue only of one private party invoking the jurisdiction of a court to resolve a dispute with another private party which turns on the use made by one or other of them of substantively neutral common law rules. The balancing of interests which Convention rights requires is limited to balancing the interests of individuals against society, not the interests of individuals against other individuals. The courts may in their procedures require to comply with Convention rights, but it does not follow that the substance of their decisions in matters of private right or obligation must necessarily do so.

Indeed, even where human rights guarantees have been enacted expressly to bind the judiciary, as under the New Zealand Bill of Rights Act 1990, purely private activity has not been made subject to the human rights. The New Zealand courts have only acknowledged their obligation to develop the common law consistently with the guaranteed rights.[27] The Supreme Court of Canada has also accepted this obligation although the Canadian Charter does not expressly include courts within its scope of application.[28] Indeed, there is much in the Canadian approach to the application of the Charter to recommend it. In *Retail, Wholesale and Department Store Union v. Dolphin Delivery Ltd*,[29] the Supreme Court decided that the Charter did apply to courts and the common law but that it did not apply to private litigation. McIntyre J. explained the position in the following way:

> "Action by the executive or administrative branches of government will . . . be unconstitutional to the extent that it relies for authority or justification on a rule of the common law which constitutes or creates an infringement of a Charter right or freedom. In this way the Charter will apply to the common law, whether in public or private litigation. It will apply to the common law, however, only in so far as the common law is the basis of some governmental action which, it is alleged, infringes a guaranteed right or freedom . . . The courts are, of course, bound by the Charter as they are bound by all law. *It is their duty to apply the law, but in doing so they act as neutral*

---

[25] Indeed, private property rights and freedom of contract are expressly or implicitly protected by the Convention. There is nothing inherent in a private person's legal right to property or lawful exercise of a power to make contracts which violates Convention rights.

[26] As it has done in the U.K. by enacting the Race Relations Act 1976 and, to a lesser extent, the Sex Discrimination Act 1975.

[27] See *R. v. H* [1994] 2 N.Z.L.R. 143. *cf. Quilter v. Att.-Gen.* [1998] 1 N.Z.L.R. 523, discussed by Rishworth, "Reflections on the Bill of Rights after *Quilter v. Att.-Gen.* [1998] *N.Z. Law Review* 683; see also Butler, "Same-sex marriage and freedom from discrimination in New Zealand" [1998] P.L. 396.

[28] See Hogg, *Constitutional Law of Canada* (4th ed., Carswell, Toronto, 1997), Chap. 34.

[29] [1986] 2 S.C.R. 573 (where the Supreme Court decided that the Charter does not apply to a court issuing an injunction against secondary picketers of a private company on the basis of the tort of inducing breach of contract); *cf. Middlebrook Mushrooms v. TGWU* [1993] I.C.R. 612 (similar facts in England; Convention rights hardly discussed).

arbiters, not as contending parties involved in a dispute. To regard a court order as an element of governmental intervention necessary to invoke the Charter would ... widen the scope of Charter application to virtually all private litigation ... Where private party 'A' sues private party 'B' relying on the common law and where no act of government is relied upon to support the action, the Charter will not apply. I should make it clear, however, that this is a distinct issue from the question whether the judiciary ought to apply and develop the principles of the common law in a manner consistent with the fundamental values enshrined in the Constitution. The answer to this question must be in the affirmative. In this sense, then, the Charter is far from irrelevant to private litigants whose disputes fall to be decided at common law. But this is different from the proposition that one private party owes a constitutional duty to another."[30]

In other words, judicial "acts" to resolve disputes about the "acts" of private parties using neutral common law rules is an important stage removed from the acts of public authorities which are subject to Convention rights. Subsequent cases have clarified McIntyre J.'s approach in *Dolphin Delivery.*[31] In *R. v. Rahey,*[32] the Supreme Court decided that a judge violated the Charter right to trial within a reasonable time where he failed to reach a decision within a reasonable time: "the courts ... must themselves be subject to Charter scrutiny in the administration of their duties",[33] at least where "the court is acting on its own motion and not at the instance of any private party",[34] that is, when not resolving a "purely private dispute".[35] And in *Hill v. Church of Scientology,*[36] the Court confirmed that the common law must be developed in accordance with Charter values. In the context of a defamation case essentially between two private parties, Cory J. said:

"Private parties owe each other no constitutional duties and cannot found their action upon a Charter right. The party challenging the common law cannot allege that the common law violates a Charter *right* because, quite simply, the Charter rights do not exist in the absence of state action. The most that the private litigant can do is argue that the common law is inconsistent with Charter *values*. It is very important ... not to expand the application of the Charter

---

[30] at 598–603 (emphasis added).

[31] Although it has been criticised by scholars: see, for example, Slattery, "The Charter's Relevance to Private Litigation: Does Dolphin Deliver?" (1987) 32 McGill L.J. 905; and Hutchinson and Petter, "Private Rights/Public Wrongs: The Liberal Lie of the Charter" (1988) 38 U. of T.L.J. 278.

[32] [1987] 1 S.C.R. 588.

[33] *ibid. per* La Forest J. at 633.

[34] *BCGEU v. British Columbia* [1988] 2 S.C.R. 214, *per* Dickson C.J. at 244 (confirming approach in *R. v. Rahey, supra*).

[35] *ibid.* at 243. *cf.* position of Kentridge in "The Incorporation of the European Convention on Human Rights", in Beatson *et al., Constitutional Reform in the United Kingdom: Practice and Principles* (Hart Publishing, Oxford, 1998), at p. 70: "In my view [s. 6(3)(a)] means only that the courts in their own sphere must give effect to such fundamental rights as the right to a fair trial; and to more particular rights such as a right to an interpreter ... ".

[36] [1995] 2 S.C.R. 1130.

beyond that established by s.32(1), either by creating new causes of action, or by subjecting all court orders to Charter scrutiny."[37]

Cory J. (for a majority of the Court) held that where a private party challenges a common law rule as being inconsistent with the Charter in a case involving another private party, the party challenging: "should bear the onus of proving both that the common law fails to comply with Charter values and that, when these values are balanced, the common law should be modified".[38] This is different from the "ordinary situation" of an action against government, where the onus of establishing a conflict with rights is on the challenger but the onus of showing that the conflict is justified "in a free and democratic society" is on the government.[39] Rather, in an action between two private parties where common law rules are challenged: "It is up to the party challenging the common law to bear the burden of proving not only that the common law is inconsistent with Charter values but also that its provisions cannot be justified".[40]

It remains to be seen whether the courts in this country will approach in a similar way the potential for Convention rights to apply to the common law in cases between two private parties. In such cases, the burden of proving both that there is a conflict between the common law and Convention rights and that it cannot be justified by reference to proportionality and the United Kingdom's margin of appreciation will rest on the party challenging. In the end, however, the extent to which the 1998 Act can apply to the common law as it operates between private individuals is a value judgment for the courts. They must ask themselves, albeit bearing in mind the European Court's jurisprudence under the Convention, the extent to which, by enacting the 1998 Act, Parliament intends human rights "to restrain government action and to protect the individual" from public power,[41] or "to set up an alternative tort system" which "could strangle the operation of society".[42]

Finally, the relationship between the Convention rights, legislation of the Scottish Parliament and private activity raises further interesting issues which possess special interest for the Scottish courts. Since these pertain more generally to the relationship between Convention rights and the Scottish Parliament, the issues are discussed further in that context in Chapter 7.

VI REMEDIES UNDER THE HUMAN RIGHTS ACT 1998

Overview

6.61 Section 7(1) makes express provision for the raising of a claim that a public authority has acted, or is proposing to act, in a way which is made unlawful by section 6(1). Section 7(1) provides:

---

[37] *ibid.* at 1170 (emphasis in original). See also *R. v. Salituro* [1991] 3 S.C.R. 654, esp. Iacobucci J. at 670.

[38] *ibid.* at 271.

[39] That is, that the limit on Charter rights is justified under the general limitation clause in s. 1 of the Charter.

[40] [1995] 2 S.C.R. 1130 at 1172.

[41] *RWDSU v. Dolphin Delivery* [1986] 2 S.C.R. 573, *per* McIntyre J. at 595.

[42] *McKinney v. University of Guelph* [1990] 3 S.C.R. 229 *per* La Forest J. at 262, 263.

"A person who claims that a public authority has acted (or proposes to act) in a way which is made unlawful by section 6(1) may—

(a) bring proceedings against the authority under this Act in the appropriate court or tribunal, or

(b) rely on the Convention right or rights concerned in any legal proceedings,

but only if he is (or would be) a victim of the unlawful act."

Two opportunities are therefore provided to raise Convention rights. First, in terms of section 7(1)(a), a person may bring proceedings against the authority under the Act in the "appropriate court or tribunal", which section 7(2) provides will be determined in Scotland by rules to be made by the Secretary of State.[43] Such proceedings may only be brought against unlawful acts occurring after the 1998 Act enters into force.[44] Secondly, in terms of section 7(1)(b), a person may rely on Convention rights in any legal proceedings. By virtue of section 22(4), where a person relies on a Convention right in proceedings "brought by or at the instigation of a public authority", the Convention right may be relied on by way of defence whenever the act of the public authority took place. For this purpose, and this purpose alone, therefore, section 6(1) of the 1998 Act has retroactive effect. In both types of proceedings provided by section 7(1), however, only a person who is a "victim of the unlawful act" is entitled to raise the claim based on Convention rights.[45] In particular, while section 7(3) and (4) make clear that "proceedings" includes judicial review, this remedy is available against an act made unlawful by section 6(1) only at the instance of someone who is a victim of the unlawful act.

Proceedings under the 1998 Act

Section 7(5) of the 1998 Act provides a one-year time-limit within which proceedings must be brought. But this is without prejudice to any rule requiring proceedings to be brought within a shorter time-limit. The effect of these provisions on time-limits for bringing judicial review proceedings is considered further in Chapter 13 and reference is made to the discussion there.[46] Sections 8 and 9 of the 1998 Act make further

6.62

---

[43] See s. 7(9)(b). In England & Wales, the rules will be made by the Lord Chancellor or the Secretary of State and in Northern Ireland by the Northern Ireland Department. By s. 7(11) the appropriate rule-making minister may extend the jurisdiction of "a particular tribunal" to deal effectively with a violation of Convention rights under s. 6(1). It is not hard to see the government's concern not to be caught out by jurisdictional restrictions on the grounds which may be raised before and the remedial powers of certain tribunals as happened under E.C. law in relation to industrial tribunals: *cf.* Case C–271/91 *Marshall v. South West Hampshire Area Health Authority (No. 2)* [1993] E.C.R. I-4367.

[44] s. 22(4). But in Scotland, Convention rights have had effect by virtue of the Scotland Act 1998 in cases against the Scottish Executive since May 20, 1999 and in cases involving the Scottish Parliament since July 1, 1999. For further discussion of the relationship between the Human Rights Act 1998, Convention rights and the Scotland Act 1998, see paras 7.31 *et seq.*

[45] "Victim" is defined in s. 7(7) to have the same meaning as it has for the purposes of the Convention (under Art. 34 thereof): see below.

[46] But it should be noted here that where a challenge is brought under the Scotland Act 1998 against the Scottish Executive or Scottish Parliament on the grounds of Convention rights, the Scotland Act 1998 does not expressly provide a time-limit within which a "devolution issue" may be raised. Where the challenge is brought by way of judicial review in the Court of Session, it may be thought that the usual law in this context will apply: see Chap. 13.

provision regarding section 7 "proceedings" and these are discussed below. Importantly, however, section 11 expressly provides that sections 7 to 9 do not affect the right of any person to make any claim or bring any proceedings which he could make or bring apart from those sections. Section 11 further provides that a person may rely on a Convention right without prejudice to any other right or freedom conferred on him by or under any law having effect in any part of the United Kingdom. The guaranteed Convention rights should, therefore, be seen as additional to and in no way a substitution for any of the opportunities for judicial review under the general law outwith the scope of the 1998 Act.[47]

Locus standi: test for "victim"

6.63 By virtue of section 7(1) of the 1998 Act only a person who is or would be a "victim" of an act made unlawful by section 6(1) may rely on a Convention right.[48] In terms of section 7(4) of the Act, if the proceedings are raised by way of a petition for judicial review in Scotland, the applicant: "shall be taken to have title and interest to sue in relation to the unlawful act only if he is, or would be, a victim of that act".[49] The term "victim" is defined in section 7(7) by reference to Article 34 of the Convention: "For the purposes of this section, a person is a victim of an unlawful act only if he would be a victim for the purposes of Article 34 of the Convention if proceedings were brought in the European Court of Human Rights in respect of that act." Article 34 of the Convention provides: "The Court may receive applications from any person, non-governmental organisation or group of individuals claiming to be the victim of a violation by one of the High Contracting Parties [of a Convention right]." The Court and Commission's jurisprudence on Article 34 is therefore imported as the test for *locus standi* to rely on Convention rights and, in particular, as the test for title and interest in petitions for judicial review in respect of alleged unlawful acts under section 6. It may be that a consequence of the Act will be to bring different standing rules to bear on different aspects of the same case, with the usual rules of title and interest applying to the traditional grounds of judicial review and the "victim" test applying to the Convention grounds.

"Victim" in Convention jurisprudence

6.64 It is clear from both the Court's case law and the Commission's decisions on admissibility that there are limits to the concept of "victim" under Article 34 of the Convention.[50] While the term "person" can include both natural and legal persons,[51] including unincorporated associations,

---

[47] Or indeed of any other opportunities to rely on human rights which are part of the common law or which are contained in other international human rights treaties with which U.K. and Scottish legislation must be construed to comply.

[48] See also s. 100 of the Scotland Act 1998, applying the same "victim" test to challenges against the Scottish Parliament and Scottish Executive on the ground of violation of Convention rights contrary to that Act. See further, para. 7.33.

[49] On standing for the purposes of judicial review, see Chap. 10. Similarly, s. 7(3) provides that if the proceedings are brought in England and Wales "on an application for judicial review, the applicant is to be taken to have a sufficient interest in relation to the unlawful act only if he is, or would be, a victim of that act".

[50] A good discussion of standing under the Convention is given by Jacobs & White, *The European Convention on Human Rights* (2nd ed., OUP, 1996) at pp. 349–352.

[51] For examples of legal persons complaining of violations of their Convention rights see *Sunday Times v. U.K.* (1979–80) 2 E.H.R.R. 245; and *Pine Valley Developments Ltd v. Ireland* (1992) 14 E.H.R.R. 319. Also *F v. Switzerland* (1988) 10 E.H.R.R. 41; *Agrotexim v. Greece* (1996) 21 E.H.R.R. 250.

so that corporations and trade unions may be "victims", it is clear that Article 34 does not include representative actions within its scope, at least not unless a representative group can show that it is acting for specific individuals.[52] The "victim" must be directly affected by the act or omission in issue.[53] So where, for example, a welfare group seeks to challenge the act of a public authority on the ground that it violates the Convention rights of those it represents, it would not be able to proceed on the Convention points unless it specifies persons who would themselves be victims if the authority's act is found to be incompatible with the Convention.[54] Furthermore, it is clear that Article 34 does not include "governmental" organisations, so that the Scottish government cannot be a "victim" of a violation of Convention rights by the U.K. government (or vice versa). Where a child or disabled person is a victim, a parent or guardian is able to bring an application to the European Court on their behalf.[55] It must also be noted that the Court has held that a person may be a victim of a violation of Convention rights even where they are only a "potential" victim. In *Dudgeon v. United Kingdom*,[56] the applicant complained that the maintenance in force of laws prohibiting homosexual conduct was sufficient to violate his Article 8 right to privacy even without any criminal prosecution taken against him. Agreeing that he was a victim, the Court observed that: "In the personal circumstances of the applicant, the very existence of this legislation continuously and directly affects his private life".[57] The Court has increasingly adapted this formula into a general test to define who may claim to be a victim of a violation of Convention rights.[58] For example, in its recent decision in *Bowman v. United Kingdom*,[59] the Court said that even although the criminal prosecution against the applicant for violation of electoral law had been abandoned, the choice between modifying behaviour or risking future prosecution meant that she could "properly claim to have been directly affected by the law in question . . . and, therefore, to be the victim of a violation of the Convention".[60]

Locus standi and section 4 declarations of incompatibility

The test for "victim" under section 7 strictly only applies for the **6.65** purposes of relying on Convention rights against the acts of public authorities which are made unlawful by section 6(1). Section 7(1)

---

[52] See *Norris and National Gay Federation v. Ireland*, App. No. 10581 (1984) 44 D.R. 132; but *cf. Confederation des Syndicats medicaux français v. France*, App. No. 10983/84 (1986) 47 D.R. 225. For discussion of the problems the "victim" test might present for representative standing, see Marriott & Nicol, "The Human Rights Act, Representative Standing and the victim culture" [1998] E.H.R.L.R. 730. In Scotland, *cf. Scottish Old People's Welfare Council, Petitioners*, 1987 S.L.T. 179, discussed in Chap. 10 (on standing).

[53] See *Amuur v. France* (1996) 22 E.H.R.R. 535, para. 36.

[54] It may be that following developments in Canada, the introduction of human rights guarantees will cause the courts to expand the opportunities for representative groups to intervene in human rights cases as *amicus curiae* (that is, they will not be intervenors as such and will not become parties to the case). See, for example, Bryden, "Public Interest Intervention in the Courts" (1987) 66 Can. Bar Rev. 490.

[55] See, for example, *X and Y v. Netherlands* (1986) 8 E.H.R.R. 235. But in *A v. U.K.* (1998) 5 B.H.R.C. 137, a ten year old child brought the complaint.

[56] (1982) 4 E.H.R.R. 149. See also *Klass v. Germany* (1979–80) 2 E.H.R.R. 214.

[57] (1982) 4 E.H.R.R. 149 at para. 41.

[58] See *Norris v. Ireland* (1988) 13 E.H.R.R. 186 at para. 31.

[59] (1998) 4 B.H.R.C. 25.

[60] *ibid.* at para. 29.

expressly refers back to acts "made unlawful by section 6(1)". It may be suggested, therefore, that the "victim" qualification does not apply in proceedings the purpose of which is to obtain a declaration of incompatibility against legislation under section 4. Section 7(1) does not seem to cover such proceedings. For the purpose of such proceedings, the test for *locus standi* may be that which applies in judicial review generally.[61] So, for example, irrespective of whether the Court of Human Rights would regard it as a "victim" for the purposes of the Convention, a representative group which raised proceedings to obtain a declaration of incompatibility against a provision in primary legislation, the very existence of which it claimed violated one or more Convention rights of persons it was representing, may be considered as having *locus standi* for the purposes of section 4 but not of section 7.[62] Alternatively, independently of being a victim of a violation of Convention rights, an individual may be able to seek a declaration of incompatibility against the Lord Advocate or Attorney-General under section 4 where it is considered that a provision in incompatible legislation prevents success in future proceedings directly against a public authority.[63] Such examples may be considered far reaching but they are not clearly barred by the Act since section 7 is not coupled to section 4 in the way that it is to section 6.

Proceedings against the authority

6.66 The first of the two opportunities to raise Convention rights which are set out in section 7(1) is the bringing of proceedings against the authority under the Act.[64] The proceedings are to be taken in "the appropriate court or tribunal": that is, "such court or tribunal as may be determined in accordance with rules".[65] The proceedings may be by any form of legal process including a counterclaim or similar proceeding.[66] But special provision is made in section 9 for proceedings under section 7(1)(a) in respect of any act of a court or tribunal. This is considered below. It is clear from section 7(8) that criminal proceedings cannot be brought on the ground of a breach of the Convention rights since "nothing in this Act creates a criminal offence". So far as judicial review

---

[61] See Chap. 10.

[62] Because, in general, representative groups *per se* are not considered victims under Art. 34 of the Convention: *Norris & National Gay Federation v. Ireland*, App. 10581/83 (Commission decision of May 16, 1984). The example in the text draws on *Dudgeon v. U.K.* (1982) 4 E.H.R.R. 149 (where the very existence of a law in contravention of Convention rights was held sufficient to make Dudgeon a "victim") and *R. v. Secretary of State for Employment ex p. EOC* [1995] 1 A.C. 1 (EOC has standing to challenge primary legislation in violation of E.C. law for being discriminatory). But *cf. R. v. Secretary of State for Employment, ex p. Seymour-Smith* [1997] 1 W.L.R. 473.

[63] *cf. R. v. Secretary of State for Employment, ex p. Seymour-Smith* [1997] 1 W.L.R. 473 (employee of private sector employer cannot obtain a declaration against Secretary of State that legislation violates provision in an E.C. directive so as to remove obstacle posed by legislation to successful action against employer; directives do not have horizontal direct effect and cannot be given it "by an easy two stage process" (*per* Lord Hoffmann at 478)). But consider also *Vriend v. Alberta* [1998] 1 S.C.R. 493.

[64] s. 7(1)(a). Where the "authority" is the Scottish Parliament or Scottish Executive, then the provisions of the Scotland Act 1998 will apply and violation of Convention rights will be a "devolution issue" in terms of Sched. 6, para. 1 of the Scotland Act 1998: see further paras 7.04 and 31 *et seq.*

[65] Provision is made for the making of rules by s. 7(9) and in terms of s. 7(10) regard has to be had to s. 9 in the making of rules.

[66] s. 7(2).

is concerned, section 7(3) and (4) envisage judicial review as an avenue through which an alleged invasion of a Convention right will be explored, albeit subject to an applicant satisfying the requirement for standing of being a "victim" of the challenged act. It is clear from section 7(1)(a) that the proceedings brought by a person who claims to be a victim of an act made unlawful by section 6(1) must be brought against the responsible authority. So, for example, if the challenge concerns provisions in secondary legislation made by the U.K. government, proceedings against the unlawful act of making the secondary legislation may not be able to be brought under section 7(1)(a) against the Scottish authority which acts "to give effect to or enforce" the provisions.[67] But it may be that the Act will allow new remedies to be created so that, for example, although the public authority which enforces incompatible secondary legislation or otherwise acts unlawfully is not liable, the Crown may be made liable indirectly or vicariously.[68] It may be that such proceedings would properly fall under section 7(1)(b).

Reliance on the Convention in any proceedings: s. 7(1)(b)

The second of the two opportunities to raise Convention rights afforded   **6.67** by section 7(1) is the reliance on a Convention right in any legal proceedings.[69] The proceedings may be proceedings brought by or at the instigation of a public authority; or they may be an appeal against the decision of a court or tribunal.[70] But these are only examples of "any legal proceedings". Clearly, the proceedings may be of a civil or a criminal character. As noticed above, it must be stressed that while section 7(1)(b) applies to proceedings brought by or at the instigation of a public authority whenever the act in question took place, the section does not otherwise apply to an act committed before the coming into effect of section 7.[71] In other words, acts which occurred before the coming into effect of section 7 are immune from challenge on the ground of their having been unlawful under section 6(1) unless the proceedings are being brought by or at the instigation of a public authority.[72] While judicial review proceedings would be included within the scope of any legal proceedings under section 7(1)(b) it is more probable that they will fall under section 7(1)(a).

Acts of courts and tribunals

Special provision is made by section 9 of the Act in respect of   **6.68** proceedings against a public authority on the ground of an alleged unlawful act under section 6(1) where the proceedings are in respect of a judicial act.[73] The term "judicial act" is defined as meaning: "a judicial act of a court and includes an act done on the instructions, or on behalf of, a judge".[74] "Court" is expressly defined to include "a tribunal" and

---

[67] See s. 6(2)(b), discussed above.
[68] cf. *Simpson v. Att.-Gen. of New Zealand* [1994] 3 N.Z.L.R. 667 (*Baigent's* case), discussed below, para. 6.70.
[69] s. 7(1)(b).
[70] s. 7(6).
[71] s. 22(4).
[72] Of course, this does not prevent anyone taking a case to the European Court of Human Rights concerning alleged violations of Convention rights before the Act enters force.
[73] cf. *Dombo Beheer v. Netherlands* (1993) 18 E.H.R.R. 213.
[74] s. 9(5).

"judge" is defined to include "a member of a tribunal, a justice of the peace and a clerk or other officer entitled to exercise the jurisdiction of a court".[75] The term "judicial act" therefore seems wide enough to include acts of those who are charged with administrative responsibilities in relation to courts and tribunals.[76] However, section 9 imposes two restraints in respect of proceedings against a judicial act. First, the proceedings may be brought only by way of an appeal against the decision or on a petition for judicial review.[77] It is thought that this does not innovate upon the general rule that so long as an appeal is available judicial review will generally be excluded,[78] so that the course of an appeal is to take priority over the alternative of judicial review. Indeed it is expressly provided by section 9(2) that the preceding subsection does not affect any rule of law which prevents a court from being the subject of judicial review.[79] Secondly, it is declared by section 9(3) that damages may not be awarded in proceedings under the Act in respect of any "judicial act done in good faith" except so as to allow the victim to be compensated to the extent required by Article 5(5) of the Convention. This means that a person who has been the victim of an "arrest or detention" contrary to Article 5 as a result of a judicial act is entitled to damages. Equally, where the judicial act has been done in bad faith, section 9(3) is not a bar to bring proceedings for damages.[80] But by virtue of section 9(4) any award of damages based on an unlawful judicial act is to be made against the Crown. This has the effect therefore of excluding the personal liability of any person in relation to the exercise, or purported exercise, of the jurisdiction of a court or the administration of a court. While the effect of section 9 is intended to preserve judicial immunity, it remains to be seen how far it goes towards imposing a limit on the scope of challenge or remedy in cases of complaint for unlawful acts under section 6(1) in relation to courts and tribunals.

Judicial remedies

6.69 Section 8(1) provides that where a court or a tribunal[81] finds an act or a proposed act by a public authority to be unlawful under section 6(1): "it may grant such relief or remedy, or make such order, within its powers as it considers just and appropriate".[82] The wide discretion conferred on the courts clearly makes available the whole range of remedies which may be obtained in judicial review and which are discussed later in Part V.[83] In the House of Lords debates on the bill, the Lord Chancellor said

---

[75] *ibid.*

[76] For example, "judicial act" may include the acts of a trustee in bankruptcy: *cf. Harksen v. Lane NO & others*, 1998 (1) S.A. 300.

[77] s. 9(1).

[78] See Chap. 12.

[79] So, for example, this also means that Church of Scotland courts are not subject to judicial review in respect of their "judicial acts". See also s. 13.

[80] Including, it seems, against judicial acts done in bad faith by supreme court judges, who have so far been regarded as having absolute immunity for their judicial acts. See *Anderson v. Gorrie* [1895] 1 Q.B. 668 and *Sirros v. Moore* [1975] Q.B. 118; but *cf. Re McC (a minor)* [1985] A.C. 528.

[81] See s. 8(6) where "court" includes a tribunal.

[82] Interestingly, "powers" is used instead of "jurisdiction", which was used in drafts of the Bill. It may be that the difference is explained by s. 7(11), under which the "powers" of a tribunal may be expanded to enable it to deal effectively with violations of Convention rights.

[83] On remedies under the 1998 Act, see Feldman, "Remedies for violations of Convention rights under the Human Rights Act" [1998] E.H.R.L.R. 691.

that: "Section 8(1) . . . gives the courts ample scope for doing justice when unlawful acts are committed . . . Section 8(1) is of the widest amplitude."[84] In particular, the possibility provided by section 8(1) to proceed against "proposed" acts of public authorities means that interim remedies will be available against apprehended violations of Convention rights.[85] Section 8 does, however, provide some restraints in respect of the making of any award of damages for an act of a public authority which is found to be unlawful under section 6(1). First, such damages may only be awarded by a court or tribunal which has power to award damages, or to order the payment of compensation, in civil proceedings.[86] Secondly, no award of damages may be made unless certain preconditions are met. These are, first, that the court or tribunal must take account of all the circumstances: "including any other relief or remedy granted, or order made, in relation to the act in question by that or any other court [or tribunal], and the consequences of any decision of that or any other court [or tribunal] in respect of that act".[87] Thirdly, the court or tribunal must be satisfied in light of all the circumstances "that the award is necessary to afford just satisfaction to the person in whose favour it is made".[88] This last passage refers presumably to the making of an award rather than the quantification of it. In any event, in determining whether to award damages, and if so, how much to award, the court or tribunal is required to take into account the principles applied by the European Court of Human Rights in relation to an award of compensation under Article 41 of the Convention.[89] This is a significant restriction on the power to award damages. In general, awards of damages are not frequently made by the European Court and the levels of award tend to be lower than comparable awards in the United Kingdom.[90] Principles of modesty and restraint appear to be indicated. Indeed, in some cases the finding by the European Court of the fact of a violation may itself constitute sufficient "just satisfaction" and no compensatory award may be made.[91]

New means of relief

Although there is no suggestion that the remedies which are available in judicial review are in any way inadequate, it is possible that the 1998 Act will have the effect of introducing new means of relief for violations of Convention rights. It may be that violations of Convention rights will in some circumstances amount to a breach of statutory duty, just as in the **6.70**

---

[84] *Hansard*, H.L. Vol. 584, cols 1266–1267 (Jan. 19, 1998) (answering critics that not including Art. 13 of the Convention as one of the guaranteed Convention rights was not significant in light of s. 8(1)).

[85] *cf. Cruz Varen v. Sweden* (1992) 14 E.H.R.R. 1. See also *R. v. Ministry of Agriculture, Fisheries and Food, ex p. Monsanto plc* [1998] 4 All E.R. 321. But in Scotland, the approach once advanced in England in *American Cyanamid v. Ethicon Ltd* [1975] A.C. 396 to interim relief may require to be viewed with caution. See para. 25.29.

[86] s. 8(2).

[87] s. 9(3).

[88] *ibid.*

[89] s. 9(4).

[90] For a useful review of the European Court's damages awards see Mowbray, "The European Court of Human Rights' Approach to Just Satisfaction" [1997] P.L. 647. See also Amos, "Damages for breach of the Human Rights Act 1998" [1999] E.H.R.L.R. 178.

[91] See, for example, *McCann v. U.K.* (1995) 21 E.H.R.R. 97 (where the Court refused to award compensation for violation of Convention rights because the victims had been engaged in terrorist activities in Gibraltar).

context of E.C. law breach of statutory duty has developed to allow individuals to claim damages for violations of E.C. law.[92] Case law on remedies for violations of human rights in other jurisdictions points towards the development of new remedies. In *Maharaj v. Attorney-General of Trinidad and Tobago (No. 2)*,[93] the Privy Council decided that section 6(1) of the islands' Constitution, which provided that any person alleging violation of a guaranteed constitutional right may "without prejudice to any other action with respect to the same matter which is available . . . apply to the High Court for redress", established a new ground of "liability in the public law of the state". The result was a new civil remedy that sounded in damages. Similarly, the New Zealand Court of Appeal decided in *Simpson v. Attorney-General*[94] that the Bill of Rights Act 1990 impliedly created a new damages remedy available directly against the Crown for violation of guaranteed rights by its officers. Since this was a new, free standing, *sui generis* remedy and not a species of a tort action—in particular, it was not an example of breach of statutory duty—the Crown Proceedings Act did not apply and the Crown did not have the usual defences to tort liability available to it.[95] The Crown was directly, not vicariously, liable under the new public law remedy for "monetary compensation against the State for breach of the Bill of Rights". Although section 8 of the 1998 Act, unlike the New Zealand Bill of Rights, expressly empowers the court to "grant such relief or remedy . . . as it considers just and appropriate" for violations of Convention rights by public authorities, it also places some restrictions on the remedy of damages.[96] Nevertheless, the similarity between the New Zealand Bill and the 1998 Act is that both are ordinary enactments which do not have the formal status of higher constitutional law.[97] The *Simpson* case may therefore be used in the United Kingdom to argue for a new "public law liability" of the Crown for violations of the 1998 Act which are not otherwise remediable. This argument may have even greater force in Scotland where the Scottish government is

---

[92] Following the ECJ's decision in Cases C–6/90 and 9/90 *Francovich v. Italy* [1991] E.C.R. I-5357. But *cf. Garden Cottage Foods v. Milk Marketing Board* [1984] A.C. 130 and *Kirklees B.C. v. Wickes Building Supplies* [1993] A.C. 227. For discussion, see para. 5.51. Consider also the development of statutory tort/delicts under the Sex Discrimination Act 1975 and the Race Relations Act 1976; but on the limits on exemplary and aggravated damages in England, see *AB v. South-West Water Services* [1993] Q.B. 507.

[93] [1979] A.C. 385.

[94] [1994] 3 N.Z.L.R. 667, criticised by Smillie at (1995) 111 L.Q.R. 209; but see also response by Adrian Hunt at (1995) 111 L.Q.R. 565.

[95] So s. 2(5) of the Crown Proceedings Act 1947 (which is in similar terms to the equivalent New Zealand provision) would not prevent the development of an independent remedy against the Crown which is not based on delict.

[96] See ss. 8(3) and 8(4). *Quaere* whether the effect of s. 8 is to rule out the award of exemplary damages for violations of the Act in England. *cf. AB v. South-West Water Services* [1993] Q.B. 507 and *Meredith v. Ministry of Defence* [1995] I.R.L.R. 539 (no exemplary damages for "statutory tort" of violation of Sex Discrimination Act 1975).

[97] Jurisprudence in systems with a formal written constitution on the availability of damages against the state for violation of the constitution is mixed, *cf. Bivens v. Six Unknown Named Agents of Federal Bureaux of Narcotics*, 403 U.S. 388 (1971) (U.S. Supreme Court); *Kruger v. Commonwealth* (1997) 109 C.L.R. 1 (High Court of Australia); and *Nilabati Bahera v. State of Orissa AIR*, 1993 S.C. 1960 (Supreme Court of India).

challenged for violations of Convention rights since the rights effectively do have a higher, constitutional status in relation to Acts of the Scottish Parliament and acts and decisions of the Scottish Executive.[98]

VII THE UNITED KINGDOM AND THE STRASBOURG COURT

Continuing importance of the Convention institutions

It is important to understand that the institutional system established by **6.71** the European Convention on Human Rights continues to be important for the protection of Convention rights in the United Kingdom. Earlier in this chapter it was noted that the 1998 Act itself requires that national courts must take Convention jurisprudence into account when interpreting and applying the Convention rights as part of the law in the United Kingdom.[99] Accordingly, U.K. courts must pay attention to the development and elaboration of the Convention by the European Court of Human Rights in its case law. Furthermore, the Convention remains an international treaty binding on the United Kingdom and in so far as the 1998 Act or decisions under it do not correspond with the U.K. government's continuing international obligations under the Convention, recourse may still be had to the European Court of Human Rights in Strasbourg for a remedy. It is therefore important to say something about the Convention's own institutional system for the supervision and enforcement of Convention rights.

The Convention enforcement system before Protocol 11

Prior to Protocol 11 entering force, a complaint alleging violation of the **6.72** Convention first had to be made to the European Commission on Human Rights.[1] The Commission would apply the criteria required by Articles 26 and 27 of the Convention to decide whether the complaint was admissible.[2] If they decided that it was, an investigation into the complaint would begin. If the Commission concluded that the complaint disclosed a violation of the Convention, it would then undertake to reach a friendly settlement between the complainant and the state.[3] If a

---

[98] But *cf.* s. 100(3) of the Scotland Act 1998, limiting a court's jurisdiction to award damages for acts incompatible with Convention rights which are attributable to the Scottish Parliament or Executive to the powers conferred by s. 8 of the Human Rights Act 1998. Consider also the limitation on remedies available against the Scottish Parliament imposed by s. 40 of the Scotland Act 1998. It may also be noted that other remedies could develop in relation to Scottish legislation. For example, the courts may adopt an approach of "reading in", under which provisions have to be read into Acts of the Scottish Parliament so as to make them consistent with Convention rights: *cf. Vriend v. Alberta* [1998] 1 S.C.R. 493; and *Schachter v. Canada* [1992] 2 S.C.R. 679. See Childs, "Constitutional Review and Underinclusive Legislation" [1998] P.L. 647, and also para. 7.57.

[99] s. 2 of the 1998 Act. See part III above.

[1] Arts 24 and 25 of the original Convention before its amendment by Protocol 11.

[2] The criteria were that all domestic remedies had been exhausted and that no more than six months had elapsed between the final domestic decision and the complaint (Art. 26); and in the case of individual petitions (under Art. 25, on which see below), that the complaint was not anonymous, was not *res judicata* under the Convention or another international procedure, and was not "incompatible with the provisions of the present Convention, manifestly ill-founded, or an abuse" of the Convention's processes (Art. 27).

[3] Art. 30 of the original Convention. A Report of the Friendly Settlement had to be sent to the Committee of Ministers. It should be noted that until the case was referred to the Court, all the proceedings would have been conducted in secret (Art. 48 of the original Convention). This was meant to give an incentive to a state to reach a friendly settlement. On referral to the court, the proceedings would become public.

friendly settlement proved impossible, the Commission would report the case to the Council of Europe's Committee of Ministers with the opinion of the Commission on the question whether there had been a violation of the Convention.[4] It was possible for a case to end at this stage if the Committee of Ministers by a two-thirds majority found a violation of the Convention. Importantly, however, the Commission remained 'master of the instance' since the Convention allowed it or any state party to the Convention to refer the case to the European Court of Human Rights within three months of the Commission's decision.[5] The Court would then hear the case with the Commission pursuing the complaint and the state defending, the actual applicant taking the role of an observer, albeit with a right to be represented and heard.[6] The Court would finally decide *de novo* whether there had been a violation of the Convention and if so could award the victim "just satisfaction".[7]

Before the 11th Protocol entered force, the Commission could receive two types of complaint: interstate complaints under Article 24 where one state party complained of another state party's violation of the Convention; and individual petitions under Article 25 where the state complained against accepted the competence of the Commission to receive such individual petitions. The Court's jurisdiction over both types of complaint was not mandatory and had to be accepted by the relevant state under Article 46. In short, there were three levels of adherence to the Convention: the lowest level, which followed on ratification of the Convention, under which a state only allowed complaints made against it by another state to be heard by the Commission; an intermediate level under which a state expressly accepted the jurisdiction of the Court in such cases; and the highest level under which a state expressly accepted the jurisdiction of the Court and recognised the right of individuals to complain against it.

The 11th Protocol

6.73   The 11th Protocol to the Convention agreed at Strasbourg on May 11, 1994 and in force since November 1, 1998 radically alters the Convention's institutional system.[8] By virtue of Protocol 11, there is now only one level of adherence to the Convention, namely the highest level just mentioned with all state parties accepting both the jurisdiction of the Court over all complaints and the right of individual petition against state parties. Reflecting this enhancement of the Convention's institutional system, in place of the part-time Commission and Court there is

---

[4] Art. 31. Opinions of the Commission could be reached by a majority (Art. 34).

[5] Under Art. 5 of Protocol 9 to the Convention (in force since Oct. 1, 1994) an individual who had complained about a violation of the Convention against a State that had ratified the Protocol (which did not include the U.K.) had to obtain a copy of the Commission's Report and was entitled to refer the case to the Court, subject to satisfying a sort of leave requirement granted by a committee of three of the Court's judges. Protocol 9 heralds the more dramatic reforms of Protocol 11 and since Nov. 1, 1998 is superseded by Protocol 11.

[6] Rules of the European Court of Human Rights, rr. 38 and 39.

[7] Art. 50.

[8] For discussion of the 11th Protocol, see Schermers, "The Eleventh Protocol to the European Convention on Human Rights" (1994) 19 Eur.L.R. 367 and "Adaptation of the 11th Protocol to the European Convention on Human Rights" (1995) 20 Eur.L.R. 559.

now a single, permanent court staffed with full-time judges.[9] Subject to necessary transitional arrangements, the Commission and its role under the Convention is abolished.[10]

The new Convention machinery

The Convention now establishes the European Court of Human Rights **6.74** as the single institution charged with supervising and enforcing the Convention. The Court now performs all the preliminary work previously performed by the Commission, including attempts to reach a friendly settlement, while continuing to exercise its final decision-making powers on the merits of a complaint.[11] For these purposes, the Court now sits in three forms. To decide on the admissibility of individual applications under Article 34 it sits in committees of three judges[12]; it sits in chambers of seven judges where a committee of three cannot decide on admissibility in individual applications, to determine admissibility in all interstate cases under Article 33 and to determine the merits of both types of cases; finally it sits as a grand chamber of 17 judges where a chamber has transferred a complex case to the grand chamber under Article 30 or where the grand chamber acts as a sort of appeal court under Article 43. Accordingly, the Convention technically establishes both a first instance and an appellate procedure. In practice the bulk of the Court's work will fall to the chambers of seven judges with the grand chamber only convening occasionally.[13]

Criticism

The new processes introduced by Protocol 11 have been subject to **6.75** extensive criticism.[14] Although they are intended to underline the legal (rather than international political) nature of the Convention system, simplify the often tortuously long process of enforcing Convention rights

---

[9] Art. 19 of the Amended Convention, to which all subsequent citations are made. The appointment and tenure of the European Court of Human Rights judges is governed by Arts 21–24 of the Convention. Each state party to the Convention is entitled to a judge on the Court and the Council of Europe's Parliamentary Assembly elects the judges for renewable six-year terms from short lists submitted by the state party. According to Art. 21 the "judges shall be of high moral character and must either possess the qualifications required for appointment to high judicial office or be jurisconsults of recognised competence". The judges sit in their individual capacity, that is, not as representatives of their state, although this idea is somewhat compromised by Art. 27(2) allowing states "concerned" in the Case to have their national judge sit. The judges are required not to engage in activities inconsistent with their judicial office and they can only be removed by a two-thirds majority of all the judges of the Court. Section 18 of the Human Rights Act 1998 provides for the eligibility of the U.K. judge: All judges of the Supreme Court of Judicature and Circuit Judges in England & Wales, judges of the Court of Session and sheriffs in Scotland, and Judges of the Supreme Court and county courts of Northern Ireland are eligible: s. 18(2). While serving at the European Court of Human RIghts, they are not to count as part of the national judiciary: s. 18(4).

[10] Not to universal acclaim: see Schermers, *supra*.

[11] The Court can also give advisory opinions under Arts 47–49 of the Convention where requested to do so by the Committee of Ministers. The Court has also decided that its Rules allow it to award interim remedies, although these are "non-binding": *Cruz Varas v. Sweden* (1992) 14 E.H.R.R. 1.

[12] Art. 28. The new Procedure Rules are reproduced in (1999) 27 E.H.R.R. 125.

[13] It should be noted that the Committee of Ministers' role is now reduced to supervising compliance with the Court's judgments: Art. 46.

[14] See Schermers, *supra*.

in Strasbourg, reduce the backlog of cases,[15] and generally modernise a system that is some 50 years old, the compromises inherent in the new procedure are not ideal. For present purposes it may be noted that when the grand chamber hears appeals under Article 43, it could consist of at least two of the judges who sat in the chamber at first instance.[16] It may be questioned whether it is sufficient to leave this possible violation of natural justice to regulation by rules of the Court.

The United Kingdom before the European Court of Human Rights

6.76 Although the United Kingdom ratified the Convention in 1953, it took until 1966 for the U.K. government to accept the jurisdiction of the Court of Human Rights in cases brought by individuals against the United Kingdom.[17] Since 1966 the United Kingdom has not been a frequent defendant before the Court but when it has been its record has not been good. Several of the cases in which the United Kingdom has been found in violation of the Convention have become leading cases in the Convention's jurisprudence. Cases such as *Ireland v. United Kingdom*,[18] *Handyside v. United Kingdom*,[19] *Sunday Times v. United Kingdom*,[20] *Dudgeon v. United Kingdom*,[21] *Campbell & Cosans v. United Kingdom*[22] and *Soering v. United Kingdom*[23] are among the most significant cases the European Court of Human Rights has decided and all of them have had a considerable impact on U.K. law.

The European Court of Human Rights and the United Kingdom after the 1998 Act

6.77 Although the government's White Paper which preceded the Human Rights Act 1998 is entitled *Rights Brought Home*, the international character of the Convention is what remains significant. While the 1998 Act allows U.K. courts to protect guaranteed Convention rights in legal actions brought by individuals to enforce them, there are still restrictions on the remedies U.K. courts can award under the Act, notably where a provision in primary legislation is found to be incompatible with Convention rights and the government chooses not to remove the incompatibility. Where U.K. courts are unable to remedy violations of

---

[15] The number of cases decided by the Court has increased dramatically in recent years, partly as a result of new members of the Council of Europe accepting the Court's jurisdiction under the Convention and partly through increasing awareness of human rights and the Convention machinery. With the Court's responsibilities under the Convention now enhanced, it is likely that it will be called on even more.

[16] Namely the President of the Chamber and the national judge.

[17] See Lord Lester, "UK Acceptance of the Strasbourg Jurisdiction: What really went on in Whitehall in 1965?" [1998] P.L. 237. It is interesting to note that although there was some political controversy when the U.K. ratified the Convention in 1951, the decision to sign up to the individual petition procedure was taken without even a Cabinet decision. This is noted in an earlier article by Lester, "Fundamental Rights: the United Kingdom Isolated?" [1984] P.L. 46. See also Bradley, "The United Kingdom before the Strasbourg Court: 1975–1990", in Finnie *et al.*, *Edinburgh Essays in Public Law* (Edinburgh UP, 1991). The Annex to this essay contains a useful list of all the cases against the U.K. between 1975 (the date of the first case involving the U.K.) and 1990.

[18] (1978) 2 E.H.R.R. 25.

[19] (1976) 1 E.H.R.R. 737.

[20] (1979) 2 E.H.R.R. 245.

[21] (1982) 4 E.H.R.R. 149.

[22] (1982) 4 E.H.R.R. 293.

[23] (1989) 11 E.H.R.R. 439.

Convention rights, or where an unsuccessful plaintiff considers that U.K. courts have erred in applying the Convention and European Court jurisprudence, it is likely that cases will be taken to the European Court in Strasbourg. Indeed, given the manner in which Parliament has given effect to the Convention rights in U.K. law, together with the rights consciousness that the Act may raise, it should not be surprising if the European Court of Human Rights continues to hear many cases from the United Kingdom.

Taking a case to the European Court of Human Rights

Since November 1, 1998, following the entry into force of Protocol No. **6.78** 11 to the Convention, the only institution which exists to supervise and enforce the rights guaranteed under the Convention is the European Court of Human Rights. Several works discuss the procedures involved in bringing a case before the European Court and reference should be made to these when consideration is being given to taking a case to Strasbourg.[24] Briefly, Article 34 of the Convention (as amended) first requires the Court to decide on the admissibility of a case. For this purpose it will sit as a Court of three or seven judges. The admissibility criteria, which concern the Court's competence *ratione personae* and *ratione materiae*, are provided in Articles 26 and 27 of the Convention and must be satisfied before a case can proceed to the merits stage.[25] It is only at the merits stage that the Court will interpret and apply the Convention rights to decide if the facts established reveal a breach of the Convention. Most of the procedure before the Court will be written,[26] with oral argument not necessarily taking place in every case. Where oral argument is allowed in a case, it may be that there will only be one such opportunity, whether at the admissibility stage or at the merits stage. Oral argument will be very unlikely at both, meaning that advisers will have to decide where best to deploy their right of audience.

Since the European Court of Human Rights is an international court the jurisdiction of which depends on the Convention, which is an international treaty, the respondent in every case before the Court must be a member state of the Council of Europe.[27] Accordingly, irrespective of how the national case arises—whether as a result of an alleged violation by a court, a problem in primary legislation, a breach by the U.K. government, a breach by the Scottish government, or a breach by a private person—the respondent before the European Court of Human Rights will always be the U.K. government. What if the alleged violation of Convention rights essentially concerns measures taken by national authorities pursuant to E.C. law? This question raises intriguing issues

---

[24] See for example, Clements, Mole and Simmonds, *European Human Rights: Taking a Case Under the Convention* (2nd ed., Sweet & Maxwell, London, 1999); and Reid, *A Practitioner's Guide to the European Convention of Human Rights* (Sweet & Maxwell, London, 1998).

[25] The admissibility criteria were applied mostly by the Commission before Protocol No. 11 entered force. They are noted in summary in para. 6.72 at n. 2, *supra*. For a recent discussion of the requirement for admissibility that all domestic remedies be exhausted, see Bratza and Padfield, "Exhaustion of Domestic Remedies under the European Convention on Human Rights" (1998) *Judicial Review* 220.

[26] The languages of the Court being only English and French.

[27] So cases which come before the Privy Council involving states outside the Council of Europe do not give rise to Convention issues. It may, however, be asked whether the Privy Council is a "court" for the purposes of s. 6(1) so that its decisions in death penalty appeals raise any Protocol No. 6 issues.

about the relationship between the E.U. institutions and the Court of Human Rights and is considered next.

The Convention and the European Union

6.79 Can a complaint be made to the European Court of Human Rights about alleged violations of Convention rights by the European Community or by the member states when acting under or pursuant to E.C. law? As far as the E.U. institutions themselves are concerned, the Commission on Human Rights has answered in the negative, on the ground that the Convention organs have no jurisdiction *ratione personae* over E.U. institutions (because the European Community/European Union is not a state, albeit that the European Community has legal personality).[28] However, it is clear that this conclusion does not prevent the Court of Human Rights hearing a complaint against an E.U. state alleging that measures it has taken pursuant to E.C. law violate Convention rights.[29] From the standpoint of a national court faced with an apparent conflict between E.C. law and Convention rights, the task will be to reconcile the conflict or refer the point of E.C. law to the ECJ under Article 234 of the E.C. Treaty.[30] In any event, the problems associated with the relationship between the Convention and the European Union are alleviated by the development of fundamental human rights, including those guaranteed in the Convention, as part of E.U. and E.C. law.[31] As appropriate, both national courts and the E.C. courts will require to apply Convention rights as part of E.C. law.[32] But in so far as

---

[28] See *Melcher (M) v. Germany*, App. No. 13258/87, 64 D. & R. 138. See also *Gestra v. Italy*, App. No. 21072/92, 80B D. & R. 93 (inadmissibility of complaint about the application of the 1968 Brussels Jurisdiction & Judgments Convention).

[29] Unless, perhaps, a national court has referred the matter to the ECJ under Art. 234 of the E.C. Treaty, in which case Art. 27 of the Convention might exclude the Court of Human Rights' jurisdiction on the ground that the matter may be "substantially the same as . . . has already been submitted to another procedure of international supervision".

[30] *cf.* Lord Hope of Craighead, "Devolution and Human Rights" [1998] E.H.R.L.R. 367 at 373.

[31] First, Art. 6 of the Treaty on European Union binds the E.U. institutions to abide by the Convention and Art. 46(d) TEU gives the ECJ jurisdiction in accordance with the E.C. Treaty to supervise that they do so. Secondly, the ECJ has developed fundamental human rights as general principles of E.C. law: see, for example, Case 4/73 *Nold v. Commission* [1974] E.C.R. 491. In doing so, the ECJ has drawn on Convention rights, which may be said to be part of E.C. law to the extent that they are relevant to the scope of the E.C. (or more broadly E.U.): see Case 222/84 *Johnston v. Chief Constable of the RUC* [1986] E.C.R. 1651, esp. para. 18; Case C–13/94 *P v. S and Cornwall* [1996] E.C.R. I-2143; but *cf.* Case C–159/90 *SPUC v. Grogan* [1991] E.C.R. I-4685. Furthermore, where national measures fall within the scope of E.C. law (*e.g.* where national activities are covered by or national authorities are acting under E.C. law), the E.C. law fundamental rights will apply as part of national (constitutional) law: see Case C–260/89 *E.R.T v. DEP* [1991] E.C.R. I-2925. Nevertheless, the European Convention on Human Rights is not as such part of E.C. law, in particular because the E.C. has no competence to ratify it: see Opinion 2/94 [1996] E.C.R. I-1759.

[32] Chapter 5 of this book further discusses the protection of fundamental human rights as general principles of E.C. law and the scope which these E.C. law rights are capable of having in national law as grounds on which to challenge national measures. For more detailed discussion, see Craig & de Burca, *EU Law* (2nd ed., OUP, Oxford, 1998), Chap. 7; and see also de Burca, "Fundamental Human Rights and the Reach of EC Law" (1993) 13 O.J.L.S. 283. The enthusiasm of the ECJ for human rights is not always critically acclaimed: see Coppel and O'Neill, "The European Court of Justice: Taking Rights Seriously?" (1992) 12 L.S. 227; and *cf.* Weiler & Lockhart, "'Taking Rights Seriously' Seriously? The European Court and its Fundamental Rights Jurisprudence" (1995) 32 C.M.L.R. 51 and 579.

there are differences between human rights in E.C. law and as guaranteed under the Convention, it is possible that decisions of national courts applying E.C. law could be challenged in proceedings before the Court of Human Rights. It is to be hoped that the ECJ will ensure that there is equivalence between E.C. human rights and Convention human rights. Yet the very different roles, jurisdiction and purposes of the ECJ and Court of Human Rights seem to encourage scope for divergence.[33]

Effect of judgment of the Court of Human Rights

Although the European Court of Human Rights is not bound by its own **6.80** previous decisions, its practice is largely to follow them where appropriate. Certainly, some of its earlier decisions repeatedly feature in its case law and if not binding precedents in the common law sense, contain oft-quoted dicta that are classical in Convention jurisprudence.[34] But the flexibility of the doctrines of proportionality and margin of appreciation which the Court applies gives the balancing process in each case an individual quality. Moreover, the number of judges that may be involved in any case—17 in the Grand Chamber—adds a further element of unpredictability. Accordingly, the existence of a seemingly similar decision of the Court, perhaps from another country, should not necessarily preclude a case being taken to the Court. Of course, the more difficult issue is the extent to which a decision in favour of an individual against a state is binding on the state; in other words, is the United Kingdom bound to accept a decision of the European Court of Human Rights? As a matter of international law, the answer must be yes, subject to the right of the government to denounce the whole treaty or make a reservation or declaration effectively exempting it from the Court's decision or the relevant right in the Convention. As a matter of U.K. law, however, the government's failure to follow a decision of the European Court of Human Rights is not actionable or reviewable, at least not unless the matter is bound up with E.C. law, under which the government's discretion is more significantly constrained. In particular, it is worth noting again that decisions of the European Court of Human Rights are not binding on U.K. courts.[35] The 1998 Act instead requires that U.K. courts, so far as they consider them relevant, "must take into account" European Court of Human Rights decisions when "determining a question which has arisen in connection with a Convention right".[36] But it must be remembered that the European Court decisions interpreting the Convention themselves constitute international obligations binding on the United Kingdom, which in U.K. law means that all national laws must be interpreted consistently with them. This also means that although the 1998 Act does not give domestic effect to Article 13 of the Convention, which provides for the existence of an effective remedy in national law for Convention violations, U.K. courts must take account of what Article 13 requires as an international obligation binding on the

---

[33] See Craig & de Burca, *EU Law* (2nd ed., OUP, Oxford, 1998), at pp. 345–347, noting divergences in the human rights jurisprudence of the ECJ and Court of Human Rights.

[34] For example, on the doctrine of margin of appreciation, *Handyside v. U.K.* (1976) 1 E.H.R.R. 737 and *Dudgeon v. U.K.* (1981) 4 E.H.R.R. 149 are often cited.

[35] Unlike decisions of the European Court of Justice: European Communities Act 1972, s. 3. Of course, it may be that ECHR decisions become binding on U.K. courts by being permeated through E.C. law by the ECJ.

[36] Human Rights Act 1998, s. 2(1).

United Kingdom. While this means that the remedies provided by national law are not directly measureable against an effective remedies principle under the Convention in the same way as they are under E.C. law, the need to provide effective remedies for Convention violations is still a principle to which U.K. courts must have regard.

CHAPTER 7

THE SCOTLAND ACT 1998

I   INTRODUCTION
II   CHALLENGES TO THE SCOTTISH PARLIAMENT AND
     SCOTTISH LEGISLATION
III CHALLENGES TO THE EXECUTIVE
IV   E.U. LAW AND CONVENTION RIGHTS
V   FAILURES TO ACT AND OTHER QUESTIONS
VI   PROCEEDINGS AND REMEDIES

I   INTRODUCTION

The establishment of a Scottish Parliament by the Scotland Act 1998 is   **7.01**
an event of major importance in the history of Scotland and of great
significance for the constitutional law of the United Kingdom.[1] While the
Scotland Act 1998 may be seen as a further democratisation of executive
powers which have for many years been devolved to Scotland, the
establishment of a Scottish Parliament and a distinct Scottish Executive
takes devolution of government power within the United Kingdom to
new horizons.[2] The manner and nature of the arrangements for Scottish
devolution means that all of the effects of the creation of a Scottish
Parliament and a new Scottish Executive are difficult to predict.[3]
Nevertheless, it is clear that the Act presents several interesting opportunities for judicial review. First amongst these is the judicial review of
legislation passed by the Scottish Parliament which follows from the
limitations placed on the powers of the Parliament. The Scotland Act
1998 restricts the legislative competence of the Parliament in important
respects and in the event of dispute it will fall to the courts to decide
whether the Parliament has acted within its competence. So far as the
Scottish Parliament is concerned, the powers of the courts in this regard
will amount to a form of constitutional review of the exercise—or
proposed exercise—of its legislative powers. Secondly, the restrictions on
the powers of the Parliament also constitute restrictions on the powers
of the Scottish Executive, which will in addition be subject to the general
law when exercising its devolved powers. Accordingly, beyond the
significance and, in the United Kingdom, relative novelty of judicial

---

[1] The Scottish Parliament was formally established on July 1, 1999. The Scottish
Executive began exercising some devolved powers on May 20, 1999, and all of its devolved
powers on July 1, 1999.
[2] For views on the significance of legislative devolution, see Lord Steyn, "Incorporation
and Devolution—A Few Reflections on the Changing Scene" [1998] E.H.R.L.R. 153; Lord
Hope of Craighead, "Devolution and Human Rights" [1998] E.H.R.L.R. 367; and
Burrows, "Unfinished Business: The Scotland Act 1998" (1999) 62 M.L.R. 241. For
commentary on the Scotland Act 1998, see Himsworth and Munro, *Scotland Act 1998* (W.
Green, Edinburgh, 1999).
[3] For discussion of possible implications, see Hazell and O'Leary, "A Rolling Programme of Devolution: Slippery Slope or Safeguard of the Union?" in Hazell (ed.),
Constitutional Futures: A History of the Next Ten Years (OUP, Oxford, 1999), Chap. 3.

review of primary legislation.[4] the supervisory jurisdiction will be available to review the actings of the Scottish Executive not only to ensure conformity with the Scotland Act 1998 but also by reference to all the familiar grounds of judicial review. Thirdly, it follows from the Scotland Act 1998 that the Scottish Executive will have a relationship with the U.K. government which in significant respects is governed by law.[5] To some extent, this relationship will be similar to that between central or federal and state or regional governments in a federal state.[6] In the same way as disputes between different governments in a federal state often come to be resolved in the courts, both in and beyond disputes about legislative competence, it is possible that intergovernmental disputes between the Scottish Executive and U.K. government will be resolved in cases before U.K. courts, including judicial review cases in the Court of Session. These three matters for possible review—namely Acts of the Scottish Parliament, the acts and decisions of the Scottish Executive, and the resolution of intergovernmental disputes—are even in themselves sufficient to demonstrate the significance of the Scotland Act 1998 for judicial review both as it has traditionally been understood in Scotland and more broadly as a means for the constitutional supervision by the courts of legislative power.

The later parts of present chapter seek to provide an overview of some of the opportunities which the Scotland Act 1998 presents for judicial review. Part II focuses on the constitutional review which arises when challenges are made to Acts of the Scottish Parliament. Part III briefly identifies some special issues concerning judicial review of the Scottish Executive which follow from the provisions of the Scotland Act 1998, in addition to mentioning the scope for intergovernmental disputes to arise by way of judicial review. Part IV discusses the particular relationship between the Scottish Parliament and Executive and E.C. law and Convention rights, while Part V discusses "other questions" which may arise in terms of the residual category of "devolution issues" provided under the Scotland Act 1998.[7] Finally, Part VI touches upon some of the procedural and remedial issues which follow from the Act's provisions on the powers of the courts.

The Scotland Act 1998 and Devolution in the United Kingdom

7.02 The Scotland Act 1998 is one part of the U.K. devolution process which the Labour government elected in May 1997 has begun.[8] There is no doubt that the issues raised by the devolution arrangements for other

---

[4] In Scotland, Acts of the Scottish Parliament will *de facto* be primary legislation; in U.K. law, however, they will be secondary legislation, Acts of the U.K. Parliament remaining the only true form of primary legislation within the U.K.

[5] And concordats, the legal status and nature of which remain uncertain: see para. 7.46 below.

[6] Although it must be noted that the intention of the devolution arrangements is not to introduce federalism as such: see *Hansard*, H.L. Vol. 593, col. 1950.

[7] Sched. 6, para. 1(f).

[8] The U.K. devolution process may be viewed in the context of devolution of governmental power which has taken place in many European countries—in particular, Spain and Italy. Some aspects of the experience in other European countries may be instructive. For discussion, see Hopkins, "Regional Government in Western Europe" in Tindale, *The State and the Nations* (Institute for Public Policy Research, 1996), Chap. 2. On Italy, see also Rogoff, "Federalism in Italy and the Relevance of the American Experience" (1997) 12 Tulane Eur. & Civ. Law Forum 65.

parts of the United Kingdom, embodied in the Government of Wales Act 1998 and the Northern Ireland Act 1998, also present significant opportunities for judicial review.[9] The present discussion, however, is limited to looking at some of the implications for judicial review arising under the Scotland Act 1998. While comparison between the various Acts may be helpful in throwing light on the effect to be given to provisions in the others, the present chapter does not set out to compare the different legislation and focuses only on the implications of the Scotland Act 1998.[10] Equally, this chapter does not aspire to deal with all of the constitutional issues surrounding the Scotland Act 1998 or devolution more generally but aims only to identify some of the matters which are of interest to judicial review.[11]

Judicial review

It may be noted at the outset that in terms of section 126(4) of the Scotland Act 1998, references in the Act to "Scots private law" include "references to judicial review of administrative action". This classification requires further comment and is discussed later.[12] For present purposes, it should be stressed that judicial review must be understood as not only including judicial review of administrative action, but also the review of Acts of the Scottish Parliament which the Scotland Act 1998 establishes.[13] That is, there may be said to be at least two forms of judicial review which arise by virtue of the Scotland Act 1998. The first, judicial review of Acts of the Scottish Parliament, amounts to a form of constitutional review which may be exercised by any court or tribunal. It may or may not arise under the supervisory jurisdiction of the Court of Session and is not the exclusive province of the Court of Session's supervisory jurisdiction, although it may be that in practice this will be where many direct challenges to Acts of the Scottish Parliament are made.[14] The second is judicial review under the supervisory jurisdiction as it has traditionally been understood in Scotland.[15] Leaving aside whether this is properly to be characterised as "judicial review of

7.03

---

[9] For a discussion in a comparative context of judicial review under the Scotland Act 1998 and the Government of Wales Act 1998, see Craig and Walters, "The Courts, Devolution and Judicial Review" [1999] P.L. 274.

[10] For comparison between the Scotland Act 1998 and Northern Ireland Act 1998, see Hadfield, "The Nature of Devolution in Scotland and Northern Ireland: Key Issues of Responsibility and Control" (1999) 3 Edin.L.R. 3. On issues arising from devolution in Wales, see Williams, "Devolution: The Welsh Perspective" in Beatson *et al.* (eds), *Constitutional Reform in the UK: Practice and Principles* (Hart Publishing, Oxford, 1998).

[11] For further discussion, see Beatson *et al.* (eds), *Constitutional Reform in the UK: Practice and Principles* (1998), Chaps 1–5. For consideration of concerns about the involvement of the judiciary in political issues, see O'Neill, "The Scotland Act and the Government of Judges", 1999 S.L.T. (News) 61.

[12] See para. 7.47.

[13] By virtue of s.29 and Sched. 6, para. 1(a) of the Scotland Act 1998.

[14] Indeed, in Scotland it may be that the Scottish courts will decide that direct challenges to the legality of Acts of the Scottish Parliament must be brought by way of judicial review under the supervisory jurisdiction (posing a risk of procedural disputes similar to those presented by *O'Reilly v. Mackman* [1983] 2 A.C. 237 for judicial review in England & Wales). But it should be noted that challenges to Acts of the Scottish Parliament (and conduct of the Scottish Executive) may arise in cases elsewhere in the U.K. Parts III and IV of Sched. 6 provide for proceedings involving "devolution issues" which arise in other parts of the U.K.

[15] The scope and grounds of judicial review in this sense are the subjects of Parts III and IV of this book.

administrative action", in practice it may be thought that, just as in the past direct challenges to the lawfulness of executive actings have been made under the supervisory jurisdiction, similar challenges to conduct of the Scottish Executive will also be brought by way of judicial review under the Court of Session's supervisory jurisdiction. The only difference will be that in so far as such judicial review cases raise a "devolution issue", Schedule 6 to the Scotland Act 1998 will apply.

Devolution issues

7.04 The Scotland Act 1998 deals with legal questions which may arise under it by reference to what the Act terms "devolution issues". Schedule 6 to the Act[16] makes provision for the procedure by which the courts may deal with "devolution issues" and defines the term "devolution issue" in paragraph 1 of the Schedule by reference to six sub-paragraphs. These are as follows:

> "(a) a question whether an Act of the Scottish Parliament or any provisions of an Act of the Scottish Parliament is within the legislative competence of the Parliament,
>
> (b) a question whether any function (being a function which any person has purported, or is proposing, to exercise) is a function of the Scottish Ministers, the First Minister or the Lord Advocate,
>
> (c) a question whether the purported or proposed exercise of a function by a member of the Scottish Executive is, or would be, within devolved competence,
>
> (d) a question whether a purported or proposed exercise of a function by the Scottish Executive is, or would be, incompatible with any of the Convention rights or with Community law,
>
> (e) a question whether a failure to act by a member of the Scottish Executive is incompatible with any of the Convention rights or with Community law,
>
> (f) any other question about whether a function is exercisable within devolved competence or in or as regards Scotland and any other question arising by virtue of this Act about reserved matters."

Although this may not exhaust the legal issues which may arise under the Scotland Act 1998, it may be taken as a description of the greater part of the issues which are likely to arise and, in particular, which are of most interest to judicial review. The significance of the categorisation of "devolution issues" in Schedule 6, para. 1 lies in the procedural provisions which are set out in that Schedule—for example, in relation to the types of issues which may fall to be referred to the Judicial Committee of the Privy Council when they arise for decision in a case before the Court of Session. These procedural issues are touched upon later.[17] In the meantime, the six categories of "devolution issues" identified in Schedule 6, para. 1 provide a structure by which legal questions arising under the Scotland Act 1998 may usefully be examined.

---

[16] Made effective by s.98 of the Act.
[17] See part VI.

Interpretation of the Scotland Act 1998

A question arises about the extent to which interpretation of the **7.05** Scotland Act 1998 is to be approached on the basis that the Act is constitutional in nature, so that it is to receive a generous and purposive interpretation.[18] On the one hand it may be argued that the Act is an ordinary Act of the United Kingdom Parliament which expressly preserves the supremacy of that Parliament.[19] While it may be that the interpretation of Acts of Parliament is no longer approached with "the austerity of tabulated legalism",[20] the prolix nature of the legal code provided by the Scotland Act 1998 may be said to give a pre-eminence to the text and require the usual rules and canons of ordinary statutory interpretation.[21] But it may also be argued that the Scotland Act 1998 establishes a democratically elected Parliament and executive institutions. The Act puts in place a system of national political accountability under law. It gives the courts the power to set aside Acts of the Scottish Parliament and actings of the Scottish Executive on the grounds of inconsistency with the Act. These facts give the Act a character which is comparable with a written constitution.[22] It may be that these considerations support the view that the Scotland Act 1998 has a constitutional nature and is to be construed accordingly. This means that the Act is not to be "cut down" by a "narrow and technical construction" but is to receive a "large and liberal interpretation" which reflects its nature as a "living tree capable of growth and expansion within its natural limits"[23]; the Act should be interpreted by reference to its "great outlines and important objects" so that it may endure "for ages to come".[24]

II CHALLENGES TO THE SCOTTISH PARLIAMENT AND SCOTTISH LEGISLATION

The Scottish Parliament and the Courts

In general, the Scottish Parliament may be subject to legal challenges in **7.06**

---

[18] *cf.* Craig and Walters, "The Courts, Devolution and Judicial Review" [1999] P.L. 274 at 289–293.

[19] See s.28(7) of the Scotland Act 1998.

[20] *Minister of Home Affairs v. Fisher* [1980] AC 319 *per* Lord Wilberforce at 328.

[21] *cf. Amalgamated Society of Engineers v. Adelaide Steamship Co.* (1920) 28 C.L.R. 129 at 142–143 on interpretation of the Australian Constitution, which was established by the Commonwealth of Australia Constitution Act 1900.

[22] *cf.* Reed, "Devolution and the Judiciary" in Beatson *et al.* (eds), *Constitutional Reform in the UK: Practice and Principles* (1998), Chap. 2, at p. 23: "On an alternative approach the situation brought about by the Scotland Act, so far as devolved matters are concerned, may be regarded as the establishment of a Scottish constitution . . . whereby the Scotland Act, Community law and the ECHR have the status of a written constitution". See also Lord Hope of Craighead, "Judicial Aspects of Devolution", 1997 Hume Lecture; and "Devolution and Human Rights" [1998] E.H.R.L.R. 367, esp. at 373: "The system which will belong to us . . . will be almost indistinguishable from that which is known as constitutional sovereignty [where] . . . the constitution [that is, the Scotland Act 1998] is the supreme law".

[23] *Edwards v. Att.-Gen. of Canada* [1930] A.C. 124, *per* Lord Sankey at 136.

[24] *McCulloch v. Maryland*, 4 Wheat 316 (1819), *per* Marshall C.J. See also *New Zealand Maori Council v. Att.-Gen. of New Zealand* [1987] 1 N.Z.L.R. 641, esp. *per* Cooke P. at 655–663; and *Ng Ka Ling v. Director of Immigration* [1999] 1 HKLRD 315 at 339–340, *per* Li C.J. (on the approach to be taken in interpreting Hong Kong's new Basic Law).

two types of cases: first, where it is challenged as a body corporate[25] (for example, by one of its employees, or for some irregularity in its constitution or proceedings); and secondly, where its law-making competence is challenged.[26] While the two may overlap, as where it is argued that a law passed by the Parliament is invalid because of irregularity of proceedings, the first type of case does not present any special considerations for judicial review which require to be discussed at length. Whether or not the Parliament as a body corporate is to be subject to judicial review depends on the scope of the supervisory jurisdiction,[27] and several provisions in the Scotland Act 1998 specifically deal with irregularities in the constitution and proceedings of the Parliament.[28] But something more requires to be said about the second type of case, namely, where the legislative competence of the Parliament is challenged.

Before dealing with this important topic, it must be noticed that the Scotland Act 1998 provides a number of procedures which may contribute to reducing the number of challenges to the validity of Acts of the Parliament after they have been enacted. First, section 31 of the Scotland Act 1998 imposes obligations on the Scottish Executive and the Parliament's Presiding Officer to affirm that Bills introduced into the Parliament "would be within the legislative competence of the Parliament".[29] Secondly, section 33 of the Act allows the Advocate General for Scotland, the Lord Advocate and the Attorney-General to refer questions about the Parliament's legislative competence to pass a Bill or any provision in a Bill to the Judicial Committee of the Privy Council.[30] Accordingly, in any case where serious doubt arises about a Bill passed by the Scottish Parliament it may be set at rest by the pre-enactment scrutiny which section 33 provides in the form of a reference to the Judicial Committee of the Privy Council.[31] Thirdly, section 35 confers a

---

[25] See ss.21 and 40 of the Scotland Act 1998 (providing for proceedings by or against the Parliament to be taken by or against the "Parliamentary corporation", which is shorthand for the "Scottish Parliamentary Corporate Body").

[26] In which case a question may arise whether the proceedings should be raised against the Parliament or against the Lord Advocate, representing the Scottish Executive.

[27] Discussed in Part III of this book.

[28] But see para. 7.08 below.

[29] s.31(1) and (2). *cf.* s.19 of the Human Rights Act 1998.

[30] The Attorney-General is not defined: presumably it includes only the Attorney-General of England and Wales and not the Attorney-General of Northern Ireland: *cf.* s.100(2) of the Scotland Act 1998; but see also Sched. 6, para. 34 of the Act. The fact that s.33 allows the Advocate General and the Attorney-General to refer questions to the Judicial Committee of the Privy Council is curious: which law officer is principally responsible for advising the U.K. government on its interests in relation to the Scottish Parliament and Executive?

[31] See further para. 7.52 below. The pre-enactment judicial scrutiny of Bills passed by the Scottish Parliament provided for by s.33 may be compared with the powers of the French Conseil Constitutionnel (effectively the French Constitutional Court) under Art. 61 of the Constitution of the Fifth Republic (1958). In France, laws may ordinarily only be challenged before the Constitutional Council in the period between being passed by the National Assembly and being promulgated by the President of the Republic, and only at the instance of the President, the Prime Minister, the Presidents of the Assembly or the Senate, or at least 60 members of the Assembly or Senate. Once enacted (promulgated) they may not be challenged subsequently, in contrast, for example, to the position in the U.S. where the "cases and controversies" rule in Art. III of the Constitution means that the constitutionality of Acts of Congress (or state legislatures) are only challengeable in the context of actual cases at any time after enactment. Since s.33 is not exclusive, Acts of the Scottish Parliament are subject to pre-enactment scrutiny under s.33 and to challenge subsequently (and arguably both: to what extent will a decision of the Privy Council on a

power on the Secretary of State to make an order prohibiting a Bill from being submitted for Royal Assent in one or other of two situations.[32] The first is where he has reasonable grounds to believe that provisions of the Bill "would be incompatible with any international obligations or the interests of defence or national security".[33] The other is where the Bill contains provisions which make modifications of the law as it applies to reserved matters and which the Secretary of State has reasonable grounds to believe "would have an adverse effect on the operation of the law as it applies to reserved matters". Since any order made by the Secretary of State under section 35 must be based on the existence of "reasonable grounds",[34] it will be subject to judicial review, which may therefore cause the Judicial Committee of the Privy Council to become involved and thereby lead to what will in effect be a further opportunity for pre-enactment review of Bills passed by the Scottish Parliament. Taken together, therefore, these procedures amount to a set of pre-enactment safeguards designed to ensure that the Parliament only acts within its competence. However, it must also be acknowledged that the manner in which the competence of the Parliament is restricted by the Scotland Act 1998 may lead to difficulties all of which cannot be foreseen at the pre-enactment stage. Apart from problems associated with Convention rights and E.C. law,[35] problems may particularly arise in relation to the application of Schedules 4 and 5 to the Act, in relation to the treatment in Schedule 5 of the matters which are reserved to the U.K. Parliament and further to that in relation to whether a measure impermissibly touches on reserved matters.[36] Only time will tell how frequently the courts will be called on to review the Parliament's exercise of its legislative powers in cases arising after enactment of Acts of the Scottish Parliament.

Challenges Concerning Electoral Matters

It is unlikely that there will be much room for judicial review of matters related to the election of members of the Scottish Parliament. Section 12 of the Scotland Act 1998 enables statutory provision to be made about the conduct and questioning of elections. By virtue of section 12(5) of the Act, the procedure to be adopted will involve an application of the procedure under Part III of the Representation of the People Act 1983. Further, section 18 expressly provides for an application to the Court of Session for a declarator that a purported member of the Scottish Parliament is disqualified. But this is a common law action, following the ordinary procedure and not an application for judicial review.

7.07

---

s.33 reference render even the same substantive point *res judicata*?). For discussion of the French Constitutional Council's powers, see Bell, *French Constitutional Law* (Clarendon Press, Oxford, 1992), esp. pp. 30–33.

[32] s.35.

[33] "International obligations" is defined by s.126(10) to mean international obligations of the U.K. other than those arising under Community law or by virtue of the Convention rights.

[34] Which must be stated in reasons: s.35(2).

[35] Which are both dynamic and may change their demands after enactment of an Act of the Scottish Parliament.

[36] That is (i) whether the measure "relates to" reserved matters contrary to s.29(2)(b) and (3); (ii) whether it is inconsistent with s.29(4); and (iii) whether it violates the provisions in Sched. 4, and in particular, paras 2 and 3 of that Schedule. See further below, paras 7.11 *et seq.*

Challenges Based on Proceedings of the Parliament

7.08 The Scotland Act 1998 attempts to close off challenges to the Parliament and laws passed by it on the ground of irregularity of proceedings.[37] First, it is expressly provided that any vacancy in the membership of the Parliament is not to affect the validity of any of its proceedings.[38] Secondly, the Act provides that the validity of any proceedings of the Parliament is not to be affected by the disqualification of any person from being a member of the Parliament or from being a member for the constituency or region for which he purports to sit.[39] Thirdly, section 28(5) of the Act expressly provides that the validity of an Act of the Scottish Parliament "is not affected by any invalidity of the proceedings of the Parliament leading to its enactment." This last reference to any invalidity of the proceedings of the Parliament presumably is a reference to some failure to conform with the procedures for enactment, such as, for example, some failure to observe the Parliament's standing orders. The provision echoes the problems discussed elsewhere in relation to the possibility of challenge to Acts of the U.K. Parliament on the ground of irregularity of proceedings.[40] Nevertheless, the statutory source of the Scottish Parliament's authority allows some scope to question what amounts to "proceedings", in contrast to purported proceedings, not-withstanding the Act's attempts to prevent challenges based on irregularity in proceedings.[41] It may be, for example, that the statutory restraint placed upon challenge to Acts of the Scottish Parliament on the ground of failures in procedure will not foreclose challenge on grounds such as fraud or error, or conceivably human rights, given that the Scottish Parliament is a public authority for the purposes of section 6 of the Human Rights Act 1998 and that the Scotland Act 1998 itself must, in terms of section 3 of the Human Rights Act 1998, be read and given effect so as to be compatible with Convention rights. Much may depend on the extent to which the Parliament is to be considered as deserving of judicial deference to reflect its special constitutional nature. In any event, section 28(5) will only apply to a law which can qualify as an Act of the Scottish Parliament. Accordingly, if the measure is outwith the legislative competence of the Parliament as defined in section 29 of the Scotland Act 1998, a challenge would potentially be open on procedural grounds as well as the competency of its subject-matter.[42] Similar problems may arise in these regards in connection with concordats and these are noted later.[43]

---

[37] See ss.50 and 69(3) of the Act.

[38] s.1(4).

[39] s.17(5).

[40] cf. *British Railways Board v. Pickin* [1974] A.C. 765. See further, paras 4.32 and 9.10.

[41] On the reasoning of *Anisminic Ltd v. Foreign Compensation Commission* [1969] 2 A.C. 147. See Mullen and Prosser, "Devolution and Administrative Law" [1998] 4 Eur.P.L. 479, at 482.

[42] This touches on the question of judicial intervention in the Scottish Parliament's deliberation of a Bill, for example, where someone seeks an interdict against the Parliament to restrain it from considering a Bill which it has no competence to pass, or for threatened breach of its own procedures. This issue has arisen in several Australian cases, where the courts have generally denied, albeit not absolutely, a jurisdiction to intervene in the legislature's processes. See, for example, *McDonald v. Cain* [1953] V.L.R. 411; *Cormack v. Cope* (1974) 131 C.L.R. 432, esp. *per* Barwick C.J. at 454; and *Victoria v. Commonwealth* (1975) 134 C.L.R. 81. For discussion, see Hanks, *Constitutional Law in Australia* (2nd ed., Butterworths, 1996), pp. 148–157. cf. *Rediffusion (Hong Kong) Ltd v. Att.-Gen. of Hong Kong* [1970] A.C. 1136.

[43] See para. 7.46 below.

Limits on the Competence of the Scottish Parliament

The first of the "devolution issues" identified in Schedule 6, para. 1 of **7.09** the Scotland Act 1998 concerns: "a question whether an Act of the Scottish Parliament or any provisions of an Act of the Scottish Parliament is within the legislative competence of the Parliament".[44] The legislative competence of the Scottish Parliament is defined by sections 29 and 30 of the Act, along with Schedules 4 and 5 to the Act. Significantly, however, the limits on the Scottish Parliament's competence must also be read together with section 28(7) of the Act. Section 28 not only provides the power of the Scottish Parliament to make laws "to be known as Acts of the Scottish Parliament", but also provides that the Parliament's power to do so: "does not affect the power of the Parliament of the United Kingdom to make laws for Scotland".[45] It appears to follow from this provision that any clear conflict between an Act of the U.K. Parliament and an otherwise competent Act of the Scottish Parliament has to be resolved in favour of the U.K. Act.[46] In the event of such conflicts, which will only arise if the U.K. Act applies to Scotland,[47] it seems sensible to apply the rule of construction provided in section 101 of the Scotland Act 1998 and read the Scottish Act "as narrowly as is required" to avoid operational conflict with provisions in a U.K. Act.[48] Where conflicts between provisions in U.K. and Scottish Acts cannot be resolved, it may be that the Scottish provision is not *ultra vires* but only inapplicable in so far as the U.K. Act "pre-empts" it by covering the relevant (devolved) field.[49] In any event, it is to be hoped that in

---

[44] Sched. 6, para. 1(a).

[45] s.28(7).

[46] In the language of federalism, the U.K. Act will always "trump" the Scottish Act. This result follows independently of s.28(7) from the orthodox approach to the U.K. constitution under which the supremacy of the U.K. Parliament means that it cannot bind its successors. This leads to the doctrine of implied repeal: an inconsistent later enactment impliedly repeals an earlier one. Arguably, the effect of s.28(7) is wider than the doctrine of implied repeal. Not being qualified by words such as "in the future", s.28(7) may mean that U.K. Acts passed before the Scotland Act 1998, in addition to those expressly reserved by Scheds 4 and 5, will also "trump" inconsistent Acts of the Scottish Parliament. But since Scheds 4 and 5 to the Scotland Act 1998 make extensive provision for existing U.K. Acts which are reserved, and the purpose of the Scotland Act is to allow the Scottish Parliament what may be described as plenary power over U.K. enactments which are not reserved, it may be thought that the Parliament's power should not be further confined by existing U.K. enactments. The final provisions in the Scotland Act 1998 about the relationship between U.K. Acts and Scottish Acts may be compared with the earlier versions in Clause 28 of the Scotland Bill: for commentary, see Burrows, "Unfinished Business: The Scotland Act 1998" (1999) 62 M.L.R. 241 at 248–249.

[47] It is presumed that a public general statute applies to Scotland in the absence of any provision to the contrary.

[48] Similarly, ambiguities in U.K. legislation should be read down so as to avoid conflict with Scottish Acts. A somewhat fanciful example might be a Scottish Act requiring the Saltire to be flown "at all times" from all Scottish flagposts, while a later U.K. Act applying to Scotland requires the Union flag to be flown from all flagposts in the U.K. "on public holidays": operational conflict between the two Acts is avoided by requiring the Union flag to be flown according to the U.K. Act on public holidays and the Saltire to be flown at all other times.

[49] This is basically the position in the U.S., Australia and Canada where federal and state or provincial laws are found to overlap: see Hogg, *Constitutional Law in Canada* (4th ed., Carswell, Toronto, 1997), Chap. 16. But the operation of the doctrines of "pre-emption" (U.S.), "paramountcy" (Canada) and "inconsistency" (Australia) vary significantly between the three federal systems. For analysis of the Australian position, see Hanks, *Constitutional Law in Australia* (2nd ed., Butterworths, 1996), Chap. 8, esp. pp. 258 *et seq.*; and for the

practice such conflicts will be avoided by care on the part of the U.K. Parliament not to apply its enactments to Scotland outside the matters reserved to it by the Scotland Act 1998 and more generally by co-operation between the U.K. government and the Scottish Executive—for example, where it is thought desirable to have uniform legislation throughout the United Kingdom in an area devolved to the Scottish Parliament.[50]

It is now appropriate to turn to section 29 of the 1998 Act—section 29(1) provides that: "An Act of the Scottish Parliament is not law so far as any provision of the Act is outside the legislative competence of the Parliament".[51] Section 29(2) prescribes the five matters which the Act expressly provides as being beyond the Parliament's competence. Each of these five matters will now be examined in turn.

(a) Territorial limits

7.10 The first of the five specified limits on the competence of the Scottish Parliament is the making of a provision which: "would form part of the law of a country or territory other than Scotland, or confer or remove functions exercisable otherwise than in or as regards Scotland".[52] This necessary restriction on the scope of an Act of the Scottish Parliament to the territorial limits of Scotland is in itself straightforward.[53] "Scotland", as defined in section 126(1) of the Act, "includes so much of the internal waters and territorial sea of the United Kingdom as are adjacent to Scotland".[54] But problems could arise about the extraterritorial effects of legislation, where, for example, something is done in reliance on it which to some extent may be said to amount to enforcement of it extraterritorially. Jurisprudence in other contexts on the extraterritorial effects of legislation may be helpful in dealing with this restriction on the competence of the Scottish Parliament.[55]

U.S. position, see Tribe, *American Constitutional Law* (2nd ed., 1988), Chaps 5 and 6. Whether or not there is anything relevant in the comparative jurisprudence for the relationship between U.K. Acts and Acts of the Scottish Parliament will be for the courts, ultimately the Judicial Committee of the Privy Council, to decide. For more discussion of related problems in federal systems, see Wheare, *Federal Government* (4th ed., 1963) at pp. 70 *et seq.*

[50] See Scotland's Parliament, Cm 3658 (1997), para. 4.4, envisaging situations within devolved competence where it will be more "convenient" for U.K. legislation; and see also *Hansard*, H.L. Vol. 592, col. 791, discussing the possibility of a convention to develop whereby the U.K. Parliament would not "normally" legislate for devolved matters without the "consent of the Scottish Parliament" (or Executive?).

[51] What is to be understood by "not law" may be important. Does the term entail invalidity or only inapplicability? *cf.* s.102 of the Scotland Act 1998. See further, para. 7.56 below.

[52] s.29(2)(a). *cf.* s.3 of the Statute of Westminister.

[53] Although the implications for fishing matters proved troublesome during debates on the Scotland Bill in the House of Lords: see *Hansard*, H.L. Vol. 592, cols 835 *et seq.*

[54] See also ss.30(3) and 126(2) of the Act.

[55] The problems have particularly been discussed in Canada, in relation to legislation enacted in one province having effects in other provinces: see Hogg, *Constitutional Law of Canada* (4th ed., Carswell, Toronto, 1997), Chap. 13. In particular, see *Ladore v. Bennett* [1939] A.C. 468; *Interprovincial Co-operatives v. The Queen* [1976] 1 S.C.R. 477; and *The Queen v. Thomas Equipment* [1979] 2 S.C.R. 529. It may be that the approach required by s.29(3) of the Scotland Act 1998 for the purposes of clarifying s.29(2)(b), namely consideration of the "purpose of the provision, having regard (among other things) to its

(b) Reserved matters

The second limit specified by section 29(2) on the legislative competence **7.11** of the Scottish Parliament is that a provision in an Act of the Parliament will not be law so far as "it relates to reserved matters". This reflects the approach of the Scotland Act 1998, in contrast with the scheme for devolution in the Scotland Act 1978,[56] to allow in principle a plenary legislative competence to the new Parliament.[57] Under this approach, the Parliament's general competence is subject to defined exceptions, namely, the reserved matters and Schedule 4.[58] But the way in which the Act provides for the restrictions on the Parliament's competence in relation to reserved matters, while coherent, can only by described as complex. In particular, there is an interrelationship between section 29, section 30, Schedule 5 and Schedule 4, at least the second and third paragraphs of that Schedule,[59] the precise nature of which will only emerge through case law interpreting their effects. There is little doubt that such interpretation will have to be fine and delicate if the Scotland Act's scheme is to remain intelligible. The present discussion attempts only to identify the issues which may arise in the application of the restrictions on the Parliament's competence provided in section 29(2)(b) and Schedule 5, but as will become clear, this necessarily entails some overlap with analysis of section 29(2)(c) and Schedule 4.[60] As for section 30, it can be disposed of shortly. By virtue of section 30(2): "Her Majesty may by Order in Council make any modifications to Schedule 4 or 5 which She considers necessary or expedient." This includes the power to modify "any enactment", including the Scotland Act 1998 itself.[61] Accordingly, the legislative competence of the Parliament is alterable from time to time by Order in Council made under section 30.

For present purposes, four issues require attention: first, identification of the "reserved matters" and the law on reserved matters; secondly, definition of the expression "relates to", so as to clarify when a provision "relates to reserved matters"; thirdly, the relationship between the reserved matters and Scots law, modification of which is generally within the Scottish Parliament's competence; and fourthly, the extent of the Scottish Parliament's power to affect reserved matters and, in particular, the law on reserved matters.

---

effect in all the circumstances", will be useful too in the context of identifying impermissible extraterritorial effects of Scottish legislation: *cf. Ladore v. Bennett, supra.* More generally, the problem of extraterritorial effects has also been considered in E.C. law, in the context of the reach of Arts 81 and 82 (formerly 85 and 86) of the E.C. Treaty: see, for example, *ICI v. Commission* [1972] E.C.R. 619; *Ahlstrom v. Commission (Wood Pulp)* [1988] E.C.R. 5193; and for discussion and comparison with U.S. antitrust law, see Roth, "Reasonable Extraterritoriality: Correcting the 'Balance of Interests'" (1992) 41 I.C.L.Q. 245.

[56] For discussion of the Scotland Act 1978, see Mackay (ed.), *Scotland: The Framework for Change* (1979).

[57] That is, the Scottish Parliament has competence over all matters except those restricted to it by ss.29, 30, Scheds 4 and 5 of the Act; and subject also to s.28(7), as noted above.

[58] Which has effect by virtue of s.29(2)(c).

[59] But also para. 7 on restatements of the law. Schedule 4, para. 1 also lists enactments which are specifically protected from "modification" by the Scottish Parliament. They are, in other words, expressly reserved enactments which cannot be touched by the Scottish Parliament.

[60] Which are both briefly noted further in para. 7.20 below in regard to their own specific restraints on the Parliament's competence.

[61] s.30(4). s.30(3) also allows an Order in Council to increase or decrease the specification of "functions which are exerciseable in or as regards Scotland".

The Reserved Matters and the Law on Reserved Matters

7.12 Where a provision in an Act of the Scottish Parliament is challenged on the ground that it "relates to reserved matters", the starting point should be identification of what are the reserved matters. The "reserved matters" are defined at considerable length in Schedule 5 to the Act.[62] This schedule is of some complexity, including exceptions from particular reservations, and the detail of it is not appropriate for study in the present context. Mention may, however, be made, if only by way of example, of the general reservation provided in Part I of Schedule 5, reserving certain "aspects of the constitution",[63] namely the Crown, the Union of the Kingdoms of Scotland and England,[64] the Parliament of the United Kingdom, and the continued existence of the High Court of Justiciary and the Court of Session as courts of first instance and of appeal. But this general reservation is immediately followed by a list of qualifications to the reservation, excepting from its effect, for example, "Her Majesty's prerogative and other executive functions", at least so far as they are within devolved competence.[65] In turn, this approach of reservation and qualification is followed with the specific reservations listed in Part II of Schedule 5.

It may be that it will sometimes be obvious that a provision in an Act of the Scottish Parliament unlawfully "relates to reserved matters".[66] But the manner in which Schedule 5 deals with reserved matters means that even identifying such matters may not be straightforward. In particular, it must be noted that the "reserved matters" include "the law on reserved matters". But the law on reserved matters is never compendiously defined in the Act[67] and the concept sits somewhat ambiguously with the general competence of the Scottish Parliament over Scots law, some rules of which will clearly comprise "the law on reserved matters". Yet the relationship between Scots private law and Scots criminal law on the one hand and the law on reserved matters on the other is one of the linchpins of the Parliament's competence. The relationship is only understood in light of section 29(4), Schedule 4 and Schedule 5 taken together and is discussed further below. In the present context, it may be said that the difficulty raised by the specific reservations in Schedule 5 is in part caused by references to areas of governmental responsibility, such as home affairs or employment. More precisely, considerable use is made of the phrase "the subject-matter of" in the references to

---

[62] Which has effect by virtue of s.30(1). In addition to the General Reservations specified in Pt I of Sched. 5, Pt II specifies reservations by reference to 11 subject-matters, whose headings are broadly descriptive of areas of governmental activities, such as "Home Affairs", "Energy" and "Transport". Part III deals with Scottish and cross-border public bodies. But the "reserved matters" listed in Sched. 5 must also be understood along with Sched. 4: see below.

[63] Sched. 5, Pt I, para. 1.

[64] On which see further Sched. 4, para. 1(2)(a), placing beyond the reach of the Scottish Parliament the "freedom of trade" provisions in Arts 4 and 6 of the Acts of Union passed respectively by the Scottish and English Parliaments in implementation of the 1707 Treaty of Union; thus providing a sort of "interstate commerce clause" for the U.K.?

[65] See s.53(1) and (2). Similarly, Sched. 5, para. 7(1) reserves "international relations" (broadly defined) but does not reserve "observing and implementing international obligations" including E.U. law and the Convention rights (para. 7(2)).

[66] Leaving aside what is meant by "relates to", a provision which blatantly trenches on a reserved matter will clearly to that extent not be law. But this will surely be a rare occurrence.

[67] *cf.* Sched. 4, para. 2(2) providing a definition which only applies to para. 2 itself.

particular legislative provisions which are reserved or are to be excepted from a reservation.[68] While that phrase avoids the excessive restraint which would be involved in reference to the particular statutory measures themselves as they presently exist,[69] there may be an element of uncertainty and difficulty in defining with confidence the limits of what is comprehended in a particular "subject-matter". This difficulty will become greater after a subject-matter itself has undergone legislative amendment.[70] Even without amendment, however, rules of law may not be confined to the watertight compartments supposed by "subject-matters". It will, for example, not always be clear whether particular rules of law comprise a "subject-matter", as opposed to several subject-matters. An Act of the Scottish Parliament setting out to deal with the law on non-reserved matters may therefore unwittingly touch on the law on reserved matters.

"Relates to": The Effect of Section 29(3)

Once the contours of the reserved matter (or matters) in question are clarified, the next step in applying section 29(2)(b) must be to identify and consider the particular provision in the Act of the Scottish Parliament which is impugned so as to determine if it "relates to" reserved matters. It is clear that the phrase "relates to" is crucial to the scope of section 29(2)(b) as a restriction on the Scottish Parliament's competence. The phrase "relates to" will require careful interpretation. The Act provides some assistance in this regard by indicating how "relates to" is to be approached. Section 29(3) provides that: "For the purposes of this section, the question whether a provision of an Act of the Scottish Parliament relates to a reserved matter is to be determined, subject to subsection (4), by reference to the purpose of the provision, having regard (among other things) to its effect in all the circumstances."[71]

7.13

Pith and substance

In the debates on the Scotland Bill in the House of Lords, some discussion took place about how "relates to" in section 29(2)(b) is to be approached in light of section 29(3).[72] In particular, inspiration was drawn from the judicial interpretation of the Government of Ireland Act 1920 and therefore indirectly from the Canadian Constitution. In the context of the Government of Ireland Act 1920, where the critical phrase was "in respect of", the House of Lords decided that the competence of

7.14

---

[68] See, for example, Sched. 5, Pt II, C7 "Consumer protection"; E1, "Road transport"; and H1, "Employment and industrial relations".

[69] Which was one of the problems associated with the scheme for devolution provided by the Scotland Act 1978.

[70] Whether by the U.K. Parliament, or by the Scottish Parliament in relation to non-reserved aspects of the subject-matter, or by (or as a result of) E.C. legislation.

[71] s.29(4) applies to provisions in Acts of the Scottish Parliament modifying Scots law as it applies to reserved matters. Unless the purpose of such provisions is to ensure consistency in the law as it applies to reserved and non-reserved matters, they are to be treated as relating to reserved matters. See further para. 7.18 below.

[72] See, in particular, Lord Sewell, *Hansard*, H.L. Vol. 592, cols 818 *et seq.*

legislation enacted by the Northern Irish Parliament was to be determined by reference to its "pith and substance".[73] In *Gallagher v. Lynn*,[74] Lord Atkin said that: "It is well established that you are to look at . . . the 'pith and substance' of the legislation. If, on the view of the statute as a whole, you find the substance of the legislation is within the express powers, then it is not invalidated if incidentally it affects matters which are outside the authorised field."[75]

In *R.(Hume and Others) v. Londonderry Justices*,[76] however, the pith and substance test was rejected as the proper approach for the application of the phrase "in respect of". The Northern Ireland Court held that the legislative provisions there under challenge were in respect both of a legitimate matter (the preservation of law and order) and of an illegitimate matter (the actings of Her Majesty's forces on duty). That second matter was regarded not merely of incidental importance and the provisions were accordingly held to that extent to be *ultra vires*.

The "pith and substance" approach has its origins in the Privy Council's interpretation of the Canadian Constitution.[77] Sections 91 and 92 of the British North America Act, 1867[78] distribute legislative powers between the federal Parliament and the provincial legislatures in Canada.[79] While section 91 gives to the federal Parliament exclusive legislative authority over defined classes of subject, such as the regulation of trade and commerce,[80] and also residual legislative authority, this is all without prejudice to section 92 of the Act which confers exclusive legislative authority on the provincial legislatures to make laws "in relation to" enumerated subjects, such as "property and civil rights in the Province".[81] Where legislation of either the federal Parliament or the provincial legislatures is challenged as being *ultra vires*, the Privy Council established early on that what required to be considered in the application of the phrase "in relation to" was the "true nature and character of the legislation",[82] in other words, its "pith and substance".[83] But neither of these expressions readily explicates the task, which basically involves an examination of the challenged provision's purpose and effect:

---

[73] But the approach was criticised: see Calvert, *Constitutional Law in Northern Ireland* (Stevens, Belfast, 1968), pp. 187–196.

[74] [1937] A.C. 863.

[75] *ibid*. at 870. It may be observed that when *Gallagher v. Lynn* was decided the Privy Council was dealing with many cases from Canada (most notably the Labour Conventions case: *Att.-Gen. of Canada v. Att.-Gen. of Ontario* [1937] A.C. 326). It may be that these overly influenced the approach then taken to the Government of Ireland Act 1920.

[76] [1972] N.I. 91.

[77] The phrase "pith and substance" seems first to have been used by Lord Watson in *Union Colliery Co. of British Columbia v. Bryden* [1899] A.C. 580 at 587. The Judicial Committee of the Privy Council was Canada's highest appellate tribunal between 1867 and 1949, and made a distinctive contribution to the nature of Canadian federalism (although not always to universal acclaim: see, for example, Laskin, "Peace, Order and Good Government Re-examined" (1947) 25 Can. Bar Rev. 1054; but *cf.* Cairns, "The Judicial Committee and its Critics" (1971) 4 Can. J. of Pol. Science 301).

[78] 30 and 31 Vict. c.3. By virtue of the Canada Act 1982, c.11, the 1867 Act is now known in Canada as the Constitution Act, 1867.

[79] For discussion of Canadian federalism, see Hogg, *Constitutional Law of Canada* (4th ed., 1997), esp. Chaps 15 and 16.

[80] s.91(2).

[81] s.92(13).

[82] *Russell v. The Queen* (1882) 7 App.Cas. 829 at 839.

[83] A phrase still used by the Supreme Court of Canada: see, for example, *Whitbread v. Walley* [1990] 3 S.C.R. 1273 at 1286; but there seems not to be an exact French rendition of the phrase, beyond "caractère véritable"!

"There is no single test for a law's pith and substance. The approach must be flexible and a technical, formalistic approach is to be avoided ... While both the purpose and effect of the law are relevant considerations in the process of characterization ... it is often the case that the legislation's dominant purpose or aim is the key to constitutional validity."[84]

Effects

As to what is involved in considering a challenged provision's effects, a matter clearly made relevant by the terms of section 29(3) of the Scotland Act 1998, the Supreme Court of Canada has held that both "legal effect" and "practical effect" are relevant to the pith and substance test: "The analysis of pith and substance necessarily starts with looking at the legislation itself, in order to determine its legal effect. 'Legal effect' or 'strict legal operation' refers to how the legislation as a whole affects the rights and liabilities of those subject to its terms, and is determined from the terms of the legislation itself ... Legal effect is often a good indicator of the purpose of the legislation but is relevant in constitutional characterization even when it is not fully intended or appreciated by the enacting body."[85] The practical effect of challenged provisions basically concerns the legislation's "actual impact"—in other words, "the actual or predicted results of the legislation's operation and administration".[86] But in contrast to legal effect, practical effect is an unsure guide to the validity of legislation: "The difficulty with practical effect is that whereas in one context practical effect may reveal the true purpose of the legislation, in another context it may be incidental and entirely irrelevant even though it is drastic".[87] The main danger of practical effect is said to be that it takes the court closer to the "wisdom or efficacy of the statute" and the "court is not concerned with the wisdom of a statute".[88] Whether or not this is accepted,[89] in the Scottish context the practical effects of a challenged provision must still have some bearing on validity. Section 29(3) of the Scotland Act 1998 directs attention to "effect in all the circumstances" for the purposes of determining "relates to" in section 29(2)(b), and it would be surprising if this did not include practical effects. Clearly, however, the Canadian jurisprudence suggests that some caution may be required in the consideration of practical effect. **7.15**

The value of comparison

More generally, however, it is difficult to say how helpful comparison with judicial interpretation of the allocation of legislative powers in other systems will be. The main difficulty concerns the very specific provisions about competence in the Scotland Act 1998.[90] In particular, it is not **7.16**

---

[84] *R. v. Morgentaler* [1993] 3 S.C.R. 463, *per* Sopinka J. at 481–482. Cited in support of this approach is Rand J. in *Switzman v. Elbling* [1957] S.C.R. 285 at 302–303, who said that what must be looked at is "the true nature of the legislative act, its substance in purpose".

[85] *R. v. Morgentaler* [1993] 3 S.C.R. 463 at 482–483 (citations omitted).

[86] *ibid*. at 486.

[87] *ibid*.

[88] *ibid*. at 487–488.

[89] For critical commentary on the Supreme Court of Canada's federalism jurisprudence, see Monahan, *The Charter, Federalism and the Supreme Court of Canada* (Carswell, Toronto, 1987), esp. Chap. 7.

[90] In particular, the effect to be given to s.29(4) and Sched. 4, paras 2 and 3.

readily clear why the pith and substance test, invoking as it does the Canadian Constitution, appeared on the scene in the House of Lords debates on the Scotland Bill. Leaving aside its contested relevance to the Government of Ireland Act 1920, the Canadian Constitution's endeavour of defining exhaustively the exclusive competence of the federal Parliament and provincial legislatures is far removed from the scheme of the Scotland Act 1998, which gives a general, or residual, competence to the Scottish Parliament subject to reservation of matters to the U.K. Parliament. Accordingly, the extent to which Canadian jurisprudence is relevant to section 29(2)(b) and (3) of the Scotland Act 1998 may be questioned.[91] Indeed, it might be said that the Australian Constitution is more relevant.[92] Under the Australian Constitution, the states have residual legislative powers[93]; the Constitution confers some exclusive powers on the Commonwealth but the majority of legislative power is shared concurrently by the Commonwealth and the states. But section 109 of the Constitution provides that where a state law is inconsistent with a law of the Commonwealth, the latter shall prevail. At the risk of simplifying the Australian law, it may be said that the Australian High Court has interpreted section 109 to mean that where Commonwealth legislation is expressly or implicitly empowered by the Constitution and intends to "cover the field", there is no room left for state legislation, even if it is not inconsistent.[94] State legislative power is for most purposes removed by Commonwealth laws in areas of concurrent authority.[95] In so far as interpretation of the Australian Constitution has overwhelmingly favoured federal power, the Australian experience may not be an appropriate precedent for the Scotland Act 1998. But this at least serves to show that the extent to which other constitutional arrangements are relevant in the United Kingdom depends critically on their nature and purpose.

---

[91] For further discussion, see Craig and Walters, "The Courts, Devolution and Judicial Review" [1999] P.L. 274.

[92] Or, indeed, the U.S., or German or Indian constitutions. For a discussion of current trends in the law on US federalism, see Shapiro, *Federalism: A Dialogue* (Northwestern UP, 1995). On German federalism, see Blair, *Federalism and Judicial Review in West Germany* (Clarendon Press, Oxford, 1981); and Kommers, *The Constitutional Jurisprudence of the Federal Republic of Germany* (2nd ed., 1997).

[93] By virtue of s.107 of the Constitution.

[94] See the leading decisions in *Clyde Engineering Co. Ltd v. Cowburn* (1926) 37 C.L.R. 466; and *ex p. McLean* (1930) 43 C.L.R. 472, esp. *per* Dixon J. at 483. It may be noted that the Privy Council had almost no opportunity to contribute to interpretation of the Australian Constitution: in regard to what may be termed federalism disputes, the Constitution provided (in s.74) that appeals to the Privy Council from the High Court of Australia could only be with the latter's leave, which it only gave on one occasion (*Att.- Gen. of Australia v. Colonial Sugar Refining Co. Ltd* [1914] A.C. 237). Although appeals from Australian courts to the Privy Council have been abolished, ultimately by s.11 of the Australia Act 1986, appeals to the Privy Council in terms of s.74 of the Constitution theoretically remain. But the High Court has said it will not grant leave again: *Kirmani v. Captain Cook Cruises Pty Ltd (No. 2)* (1985) 159 C.L.R. 461.

[95] For discussion of federalism in Australia, see Hanks, *Constitutional Law in Australia* (2nd ed., Butterworths, 1996), Chap. 8; and Zines, *The High Court and the Constitution* (3rd ed., Butterworths, 1992), esp. at pp. 353 *et seq*. For comparison between Canada and Australia, see Gilbert, *Australian and Canadian Federalism, 1867–1984: A Study of Judicial Techniques* (1986), esp. Chaps 8 and 9.

Conclusion

It may be that the "pith and substance test" is intended to be applied to **7.17**
the phrase "relates to" in section 29(2)(b) of the Scotland Act.[96] But,
whatever may be the superficial similarity between "pith and substance"
and the reference to purpose and effects in section 29(3), it is not
immediately certain from the terms of section 29(3) taken as a whole,
not least its subjection to section 29(4), together more generally with the
effect to be given to Schedule 4, paras 2 and 3, that a "pith and
substance" approach is warranted. Indeed it may be noticed that in the
corresponding provision of the Northern Ireland Act 1998, section
6(2)(b), it is provided that a provision is outwith the legislative competence of the Assembly if "it deals with an excepted matter". It remains to
be seen whether the difference in language between the Scotland Act
and the Northern Ireland Act reflects a difference in meaning, and in
each case what the precise construction ought to be.

Scots law and Reserved Matters: Effect of Section 29(4)

A key problem for the competence of the Scottish Parliament is to what **7.18**
extent an Act of the Parliament the purpose of which does not relate to
reserved matters goes beyond competence because of its incidental effect
on reserved matters. Beyond section 29(3) of the Scotland Act 1998, the
Act deals with this problem by reference to the Parliament's competence
in relation to Scots law and the law on reserved matters. In effect, the
Scotland Act 1998 provides that the law on reserved matters is
reserved.[97] The Scottish Parliament has, in general, no power to "modify" it.[98] In contrast, Scots private law[99] and Scots criminal law[1] are not
reserved. The Scottish Parliament, again in general, has power to modify
them. But this apparently simple dichotomy hides great complexity.
First, the "the law on reserved matters" will inevitably include rules of
Scots law.[2] Therefore, some rules of Scots law are reserved by operation
of Schedules 4 and 5. Secondly, even where rules of Scots private law
and Scots criminal law do not form part of the law on reserved matters,
modifications of those rules may affect reserved matters or the law on
reserved matters. For example, a reform of the ordinary law of contract
may have some effect on reserved employment law. The Scotland Act
1998 attempts to deal with these difficulties in section 29(4) and
Schedule 4 to the Act. The Act deals distinctly with "modifications" by
the Parliament of the law on reserved matters, the subject of Schedule 4
and discussed further below, and "modifications" of Scots private law
and Scots criminal law as they "apply" to reserved matters, dealt with by
s.29(4). Section 29(4) provides that provisions which would "otherwise
not relate to reserved matters" but which make "modifications of Scots
private law, or Scots criminal law, as it applies to reserved matters", are:
"to be treated as relating to reserved matters, unless the purpose

---

[96] That was the intention as expressed by Lord Sewel on July 21, 1998 at the Committee
stage in the House of Lords, *Hansard*, H.L. Vol. 592, col. 818.
[97] See Sched. 4, para. 2(1).
[98] Modify includes "amend or repeal": s.126(1).
[99] Defined in s.126(4).
[1] Defined in s.126(5).
[2] See Sched. 4, para. 2(2) and (3).

of the provision is to make the law in question apply consistently to reserved matters and otherwise." Accordingly, even though a provision in an Act of the Scottish Parliament modifying Scots private law or Scots criminal law does not otherwise relate to reserved matters, section 29(4) means that it is to be treated as doing so unless its purpose is to make the law "apply consistently to reserved matters and otherwise". While section 29(4) appears only to apply to "modifications" of Scots private law and Scots criminal law, and not, for example, restatements of existing law,[3] its effect is clearly to expand the matters which are reserved and therefore beyond the competence of the Scottish Parliament. Beyond this, however, the effect of section 29(4) is less clear. For example, it may be questioned how different is the term "applies to reserved matters" from "relates to reserved matters"; or what is to be understood by "consistently" in this context. In relation to consistency consideration may have to be given to the direction in section 29(3) to "effect in all the circumstances", to the idea of proportionality expressed in Schedule 4, para. 3, or to the question whether the modification effected by a provision must also satisfy the conditions of Schedule 4. Such questions are not resolved by the Act and will depend on clarification in case law.

The Law on Reserved Matters: Effect of Schedule 4

7.19 As regards the relationship between the Scottish Parliament's competence and modifications of the law on reserved matters, consideration must be given to paragraphs 2 and 3 of Schedule 4.[4] Schedule 4, para. 2(1) provides the general rule that the Scottish Parliament cannot "modify" the law on reserved matters. For this purpose, paragraph 2(2) defines the law on reserved matters as meaning: "(a) any enactment the subject-matter of which is a reserved matter and which is comprised in an Act of Parliament or subordinate legislation under an Act of Parliament, and (b) any rule of law which is not contained in an enactment and the subject-matter of which is a reserved matter".[5] But in relation to rules of Scots private law and Scots criminal law which form part of the law on reserved matters, Schedule 4 para. 2(3) contains an important qualification the effect of which is to make some saving of the Scottish Parliament's competence to modify rules of Scots private law and Scots criminal law. Except where the rules in question are "special to a reserved matter", the Scottish Parliament has competence to modify the rules.[6] However, the Parliament's competence over the modification of Scots private law and Scots criminal law still remains subject to section 29(4), which, as noted above, restricts the Parliament's competence to modify Scots private law and Scots criminal law as they "apply" to reserved matters, unless the purpose of the modification is to make the law apply consistently to reserved matters and otherwise. Accord-

---

[3] On which see also Sched. 4, para. 7, in relation to restatements of the law on reserved matters.

[4] Sched. 4 applies as a restriction on the Scottish Parliament's competence by virtue of s.29(2)(c) of the Scotland Act 1998. It contains further restrictions on the Parliament's competence beyond "modifications" of the law on reserved matters: see para. 7.20 below.

[5] But "Act of Parliament" does not include the Scotland Act 1998 itself, which is for the most part put beyond the Scottish Parliament's competence by Sched. 4, para. 4, as it has effect by virtue of s.29(2)(c): see para. 7.20 below.

[6] Para. 2(3) also provides two specific reservations of rules of Scots law: see para. 2(3)(a) and (b).

ingly, the Parliament's powers over rules of Scots law which do not form part of the law on reserved matters because they are not "special" to reserved matters must still satisfy the conditions of section 29(4).

Significantly, however, Schedule 4 makes further provision for "incidental modifications" of the law on reserved matters. Schedule 4, para. 3(1) provides that the restriction on the Parliament's competence to modify the law on reserved matters does not apply to "modifications" which: "(a) are incidental to, or consequential on, provision made . . . which does not relate to reserved matters, and (b) do not have a greater effect on reserved matters than is necessary to give effect to the purpose of the provision".[7] On its terms, Schedule 4, para. 3 concerns only "modifications" of the law on reserved matters and not provisions passed by the Parliament which do not amount to modifications of the existing law, nor modifications of Scots private law or Scots criminal law as they apply to reserved matters.[8] But in so far as it applies, the effect of paragraph 3 is to introduce a form of proportionality test into the assessment of the incidental effects of otherwise competent enactments of the Scottish Parliament on reserved matters. Where such effects on reserved matters are proportionate in terms of paragraph 3(1)(b), the provision will not be treated as modifying the law on reserved matters. Equally, where the effects on reserved matters are disproportionate, it will be so treated. By virtue of paragraph 3, courts must weigh the purpose of a challenged provision (understood by reference to the Parliament's competence) against the nature and severity of its impact on reserved matters. In short, if the purpose is lawful and the effects not too bad by reference to the need to achieve the purpose, the provision will be competent. It may be that such an approach will come to be applicable generally in determining the proper scope of the Parliament's competence as it "relates" to reserved matters.[9]

It remains to be seen how all these somewhat convoluted provisions concerning the relationship between the competence of the Scottish Parliament and the reserved matters are going to be translated in practice. Without doubt, the whole work of the construction and application of the "reserved matters", and so of the devolved matters, will call for delicacy in handling and sensitivity in resolution.

(c) Section 29(2)(c) and Schedule 4 restrictions

Section 29(2)(c) provides that the Scottish Parliament has no competence to pass a law which "is in breach of the restrictions in Schedule 4". Schedule 4 contains restrictions on the Parliament's competence to "modify" specified enactments and the law on reserved matters. The impact of Schedule 4 as it applies to the law on reserved matters has already been discussed above in the context of the reserved matters.[10] In the present context, it may be noted that Schedule 4 denies competence to the Scottish Parliament to modify in whole or in part certain

7.20

---

[7] Which is to be determined only by reference to the Parliament's competence: para. 3(2).

[8] Which is governed by s.29(4), as explained above.

[9] *cf.* Craig and Walters, *supra*, who observe that the pith and substance test itself may be analogous to a proportionality test (certainly to the extent that it focuses on the effects of a challenged measure).

[10] See para. 7.19.

particular enactments, including aspects of Articles 4 and 6 of the Union with Scotland Act 1706 and Union with England Act 1707, the European Communities Act 1972, the Human Rights Act 1998, and the central aspects of the Scotland Act 1998 itself.[11] Section 126(1) of the Act defines "modify" as including amendments and repeals. But, in addition to the effect of paragraphs 2 and 3 of Schedule 4, the Schedule allows the Scottish Parliament some scope in relation to the law on reserved matters—for example, restating the law and repealing any "spent enactment".[12]

(d)   Convention rights and Community law

7.21   The fourth restriction on the competence of the Parliament is provided by section 29(2)(d): a provision is outside the competence of the Parliament so far as "it is incompatible with any of the Convention rights or with Community law". The implications of this restriction are considered later in the present chapter.[13]

(e)   The office of the Lord Advocate

7.22   The fifth restriction on the Parliament's competence is very particular. Section 29(2)(e) provides that the Parliament has no competence to: "remove the Lord Advocate from his position as head of the systems of criminal prosecution and investigation of deaths in Scotland". The Lord Advocate is one of the members of the Scottish Executive.[14] The unique constitutional position and more particularly the independence of the Lord Advocate in Scotland is of considerable importance.[15] Section 29(2)(e) seeks to preserve this by the protection of the office of Lord Advocate from legislation by the Scottish Parliament. The same purpose can be seen in other provisions of the Act, such as the Lord Advocate's immunity from Parliamentary investigation,[16] the special provisions for the appointment and removal of the Lord Advocate,[17] the securing of his exclusive right to exercise his functions,[18] and the restrictions on investigation of the Crown Office,[19] But, as noted elsewhere, what may formerly have been considered an immunity of the Lord Advocate from challenge in judicial review has to a significant extent been removed.[20]

Other Grounds of Challenge to Acts of the Scottish Parliament

7.23   While the "devolution issue" identified by Schedule 6, para. 1(a) concerns the competence of the Parliament to pass Acts, it may be that

---

[11] See Sched. 4, paras 1 and 4.
[12] See Sched. 4, paras 7 and 9. Restatement of the law on reserved matters will, however, relate to reserved matters: para. 7(2).
[13] See paras 7.31–7.38.
[14] s.44(1)(c) of the Scotland Act 1998.
[15] For discussion of the role of the Scottish law officers in relation to devolution, see Jamieson, "Devolution and the Scottish Law Officers", 1999 S.L.T. (News) 117.
[16] s.27(3).
[17] s.48(1)
[18] s.52(4).
[19] s.91(2) under reference to the Parliamentary Commissioner Act 1967.
[20] See para. 8.44.

grounds other than strict illegality will be available as grounds on which Acts of the Scottish Parliament are challengeable. It may be thought that the statutory source of the Parliament's authority means that the fairness or irrationality (or proportionality) of a measure might be open to question. But it is likely that occasion to resort to most other grounds of review will be rare. At least in regard to assessing the irrationality of Acts of the Scottish Parliament, respect will require to be given to the fact of their having been considered by the Scottish Parliament in a way corresponding to the approach which the courts take in relation to judicial review of subordinate legislation which has passed before the U.K. Parliament.[21] On this point, it will be interesting to see whether a similar approach is taken to subordinate legislation which has been approved by the Scottish Parliament. Proportionality, however, will be of particular relevance where Acts of the Scottish Parliament are challenged on the grounds of Convention rights or for violation of E.C. law.

Interpretation of Scottish Legislation

By virtue of section 101 of the Scotland Act 1998, an Act of the **7.24** Scottish Parliament or a Bill or any subordinate legislation made or confirmed or approved (or purporting to be so) "which could be read in such a way as to be outside competence": "is to be read as narrowly as is required for it to be within competence, if such a reading is possible, and is to have effect accordingly".[22] In this context "competence" is defined to mean, in relation to an Act or a Bill, "the legislative competence of the Parliament", and in relation to subordinate legislation, "the powers conferred by virtue of this Act".[23] Section 101 therefore provides a rule of interpretation which must be applied in the construction of all Acts of the Scottish Parliament. From the point of view of Convention rights, comparison may be made between section 101 and the different wording of section 3(1) of the Human Rights Act 1998. The latter provides: "So far as it is possible to do so, primary legislation and subordinate legislation must be read and given effect in a way which is compatible with the Convention rights." While the difference in wording between section 101 of the Scotland Act 1998 and section 3(1) of the Human Rights Act 1998 may be thought unhelpful in the context of Convention rights, it would be curious if significantly different approaches were to be applied to U.K. and Scottish legislation on account of the differences in wording.[24] Moreover, it is to be noticed that the definition of subordinate legislation in section 21(1) of the Human Rights Act 1998 includes Acts of the Scottish Parliament. So the interpretive obligation provided in section 3(1) of the Human Rights Act 1998 is presumably also to apply to Acts of the Scottish Parliament and no distinction in meaning and effect between the different expressions in the two Acts can be intended.

---

[21] *cf. Edinburgh D.C. v. Secretary of State for Scotland*, 1985 S.L.T. 551; and *Notts C.C. v. Secretary of State for the Environment* [1986] A.C. 240. See further paras 9.12 and 21.17.

[22] s.101(1) and (2).

[23] s.101(3)(a) and (b).

[24] For discussion of the effect of s.3(1) of the Human Rights Act 1998, see paras 6.30 *et seq*.

III CHALLENGES TO THE EXECUTIVE

The Scottish Administration

7.25 The Scottish Administration is the generic term for the devolved Scottish government.[25] As section 99(1) of the Scotland Act 1998 indicates, the Scottish Administration forms part of the Crown, in which capacity it may formally be referred to as "the Crown in right of the Scottish Administration". In contrast, the U.K. government is the "Crown in right of Her Majesty's Government in the United Kingdom". This serves to make clear that the Scottish Administration has its own personality and will be answerable in the courts for what it does in its own name. On the other hand, by virtue of its forming part of the Crown, the Scottish Administration will also enjoy all of the privileges and immunities of the Crown, such as the presumption of Crown immunity from statutes.[26]

The principal part of the Scottish Administration is the Scottish Executive which is established by section 44 of the Act and comprises the First Minister, such ministers as he may appoint under section 47 of the Act, the Lord Advocate and the Solicitor-General.[27] The Act refers collectively to the members of the Scottish Executive as "the Scottish Ministers", but it should be noted that the Scottish ministers are not as such ministers of the Crown.[28] Rather, the Act refers to ministers in the U.K. government as "Ministers of the Crown", although sometimes it refers specifically to the Secretary of State.[29] These distinctions between the U.K. government and the Scottish Administration are important to the scheme of executive devolution established by the Scotland Act 1998. They are interesting from a constitutional law viewpoint and certainly deserve further discussion in that context. In the present context, the main concern is with the limits on the powers of the Scottish Administration under the Scotland Act 1998.

Limits on the powers of the Scottish Administration

7.26 The limits which the Scotland Act 1998 imposes on the competence of the Scottish Parliament to make laws also constitute the principal limits on the authority of the Scottish Administration, and in particular, the Scottish Executive. Section 54 of the 1998 Act achieves this by providing that all exercises of devolved functions, including the making, confirming or approving of subordinate legislation, are subject to the same limits as apply to the legislative competence of the Scottish Parliament. The whole provisions relating to the competence of the Parliament accordingly are brought in to determine the competence not only of subordi-

---

[25] See s.126(6) and (7) of the Scotland Act 1998.

[26] In this regard, amendments have been made to the Crown Proceedings Act 1947 so as to extend its application to the Scottish Executive: see Sched. 8, para. 7 of the Scotland Act 1998. For further discussion of problems which may arise in the specific context of Crown immunity from statutes in light of devolution, see paras 4.49–4.50.

[27] s.44. In particular, it should be noted that the Scottish judiciary do not fall within the definition of the Scottish Administration, *cf. HMA v. Gourlay*, High Court of Justiciary, September 10, 1999, unreported.

[28] *cf.* s.44(3) and (4) of the Act.

[29] See, for example, ss.35 and 58 of the Act. References to the Secretary of State means any Secretary of State, that is, any member of the U.K. Cabinet who holds the office of Secretary of State: the office is theoretically one; see also the Interpretation Act 1978, Sched. 1.

nate legislation made under the Act but also the competence in general of the Scottish Executive and more broadly the Scottish Administration as a whole.

While the functions taken over by the Scottish ministers comprise the prerogative, executive and statutory functions of the ministers of the Crown so far as they are exercisable within devolved competence,[30] like much in the Scotland Act 1998, this general statement has to be qualified by reference to a number of exceptions. In effect, these constitute limits on the powers of the Scottish Executive and some of them may be mentioned here. First, in regard to cross-border public authorities,[31] such as, for example, the British Broadcasting Corporation, functions which are specifically exercisable by a minister of the Crown in relation to such bodies are not devolved to the Scottish ministers.[32] However, a minister of the Crown is required to consult the Scottish ministers before exercising certain functions in relation to a cross-border public authority, for example, where exercise of the function "might affect Scotland otherwise than wholly in relation to reserved matters".[33] This raises the prospect that a failure to consult could be open to challenge in judicial review. Reference may be made in this connection to consideration elsewhere on what is required by a duty to consult.[34] Secondly, among the functions of the Scottish Executive will be the making of subordinate legislation. The limits of devolved competence in this regard are expressly set out in section 54(2): it is outside devolved competence to make, confirm or approve subordinate legislation which would be outside the legislative competence of the Parliament if it was included in an Act of the Parliament. Thirdly, section 57(2) of the Scotland Act 1998 provides that no member of the Scottish Executive may act where the act is incompatible with any of the Convention rights or with Community law. However, section 57(3) provides an exception in relation to the Lord Advocate. The exception applies (a) where he is prosecuting any offence or (b) in his capacity as head of the system of criminal prosecution and investigation of deaths in Scotland; in these regards, the acts which are excepted from section 57(2) are acts which by virtue of sections 6(2) of the Human Rights Act 1998 are not unlawful in terms of section 6(1) of that Act— that is, in effect, where he is obliged by U.K. legislation so to act. Outwith this specific exception, however, it appears that the actings of the Lord Advocate, or any prosecutor acting under him, would be open to challenge on the grounds of Convention rights, for example, where a breach of Article 6(1) of the Convention is alleged.[35]

---

[30] s.53; but see s.57(1). Some flexibility is provided by s.63 of the Act, which provides that further provision for transfer of functions may be made by Order in Council.

[31] The definition of which is left to secondary legislation: see s.88(5); see also Sched. 5, Pt III, para. 3 of the Act.

[32] s.88(1).

[33] s.88(2).

[34] See paras 17.18 and 19.17.

[35] Further limitations on devolved competence include the retained functions of the Lord Advocate (s.53(2)); shared powers listed in s.56; and the implementation of obligations under Community law in terms of s.57(1), which in effect means that implementing E.C. law obligations is a responsibility shared between the U.K. government and the Scottish Executive. It may also be noted that while s.55(1) frees the Scottish Executive from the necessity of obtaining agreement from or consulting with any minister of the Crown, there is an express exception in s.55(2) in relation to the designation of enterprise zones.

Judicial review and the Scottish Executive

7.27   It is clear that the supervisory jurisdiction of the Court of Session in Scotland will be available to review the conduct of the Scottish Executive not only to ensure validity in terms of the Scotland Act 1998 but also more generally to ensure the legality and propriety of its conduct along the lines and on the grounds on which judicial review is traditionally available. The second and third of the "devolution issues" identified in Schedule 6, para. 1(b) and (c) point to two matters with which judicial review may particularly be concerned. The second of the devolution issues relates to functions which any person has purported, or is proposing, to exercise. The issue here is whether any such function is a function of the Scottish ministers, the First Minister or the Lord Advocate. Questions here will include the identification of functions as devolved or reserved functions and the identification of the person entitled to exercise a function. The devolution issue may be read as including consideration whether the function can be exercised by any of Scottish ministers, as well as consideration of which of them is the proper person to exercise the function. But as regards the former, the question whether the exercise of a function is within devolved competence expressly falls within the third of the devolution issues, and as regards the latter note should be taken of the express provision that statutory functions of the Scottish ministers shall be exercisable by any member of the Scottish Executive.[36] In addition, it must be noted that the Scotland Act 1998 specifically provides that the validity of any act of a member of the Scottish Executive or junior Scottish Minister[37] is not to be affected by any defect in his nomination by Parliament or, where Parliament has agreed to his appointment, any defect in such agreement.[38] As regards the third of the devolution issues, it is specifically concerned with the competence of a proposed or purported exercise of a function by a member of the Scottish Executive. The issue here is whether that exercise would be within devolved competence.[39] While the persons critically concerned are in substance the same as in the second devolution issue, the focus here is on the competence to exercise a function by reference to the distinction between devolved and reserved matters.

Subordinate legislation

7.28   The Scottish Executive is empowered to make subordinate legislation. Its powers in this regard may derive from the Scotland Act 1998 itself, from Acts passed by the Scottish Parliament and from "pre-commencement enactments" passed by the U.K. Parliament.[40] But the competence of the Scottish Executive to make subordinate legislation is to be determined by the same criteria which govern the competence of the Scottish Parliament.[41] As to the procedures governing the making of

---

[36] s.52(3). Consider also the relevance of the *Carltona* principle (derived from *Carltona Ltd v. Commissioners of Works* [1943] 2 All E.R. 560) in this context. For discussion of the principle, see de Smith, Woolf and Jowell, *Judicial Review of Administrative Action* (5th ed. Sweet & Maxwell, 1995), pp. 369–373.

[37] As defined in s.49.

[38] s.50.

[39] The limits of which are discussed in the preceding paragraphs.

[40] As defined by s.53(3) of the Scotland Act 1998.

[41] See s.54(2), noted above.

subordinate legislation, reference should be made to Schedule 7 to the Act which prescribes the procedure to be adopted for the passing of subordinate legislation under the various provisions of the Scotland Act 1998 which authorise such a course, and also to section 118, which makes provision for the procedure to be followed in relation to subordinate legislation under pre-commencement enactments. Judicial review will be available in relation to both matters of procedure as well as the legality (that is, competence) of the measure. In addition, subordinate legislation may also be challengeable on the other grounds of judicial review. But the reservations which are mentioned elsewhere on the availability of review where measures have undergone a Parliamentary scrutiny may require to be considered in the context of subordinate legislation under the Scotland Act.[42]

Public authorities

In addition to the Scottish Executive and more broadly the Scottish **7.29** Administration, a wide range of public authorities will exercise, or continue to exercise, authority in or as regards Scotland. Some of these authorities will be Scottish bodies—that is, in addition to bodies established by the Scottish Parliament, those established by or under U.K. legislation but exercising powers only, or mostly, in relation to Scotland—while others will be U.K. bodies or, in the terminology of the Act, "cross-border" public authorities.[43] As to any Scottish public authority, Schedule 5, Part III, para. 1 provides that such bodies are not reserved simply because some of their functions relate to reserved matters,[44] unless they are a "cross-border" public authority. In relation to Scottish public authorities, their conduct will be subject to the supervisory jurisdiction of the Court of Session according to the usual scope and grounds of that jurisdiction, and no more need be said about them here.[45] In relation to cross-border public authorities, the Scotland Act makes some provision for their relationship with the Scottish Executive.[46] As regards judicial review of their conduct in Scotland, the Court of Session should have jurisdiction in so far as their conduct has effect in Scotland, but there may be some doubt about the geographical reach of the Court of Session's supervisory jurisdiction in some cases.[47]

Judicial review, the Scottish Executive and the U.K. government

As far as the U.K. government is concerned, judicial review of acts and **7.30** decisions for which it is responsible will, of course, continue to be available in the Court of Session according to the ordinary law. The

---

[42] See paras 9.12 and 21.17.

[43] For a prescient discussion of some of the issues raised by devolution for regulatory bodies, see Reed, "Devolution and Regulatory Authorities", in Bates (ed.), *Devolution to Scotland: The Legal Aspects* (T&T Clark, Edinburgh, 1997).

[44] Such a body being referred to in the Act as a "Scottish public authority with mixed functions": Sched. 5, Pt III, para. 1(4); but see para. 1(2) and (3).

[45] It should be noticed, however, that challenge to such bodies on Convention grounds must be brought under s.6 of the Human Rights Act 1998 and not under the Scotland Act 1998, since the latter only allows of such challenge to be brought against the Parliament or the Scottish Executive.

[46] ss.88–90 and Sched. 5, Pt III.

[47] See *Bank of Scotland v. IMRO*, 1989 S.C. 107; *cf. Highland Regional Council v. Director of Passenger Rail Franchising*, 1996 S.L.T. 274. See para. 23.07 on jurisdiction.

respondent in judicial review proceedings involving the U.K. government may be the Advocate General for Scotland,[48] or the relevant U.K. government minister or government department.[49] Where conduct of the Scottish Executive is challenged in judicial review, it is likely that the respondent in some cases will be the Lord Advocate,[50] while in other cases it may be the relevant Scottish minister or department. Since the U.K. government as a whole embodies the Crown in right of the United Kingdom, and the Crown is domiciled everywhere in the United Kingdom,[51] the U.K. government should be judicially reviewable everywhere in the United Kingdom. Accordingly, where a person seeks to challenge an act or decision of the U.K. government, judicial review is competent in the Court of Session even if there is no particular Scottish element.[52] Equally, while the Scottish Executive and Scottish public authorities are primarily subject to judicial review in the Court of Session, since the Scottish Administration forms part of the Crown, it may be argued that it will be subject to judicial review everywhere in the United Kingdom, at least in so far as its acts and decisions have effects elsewhere in the United Kingdom.[53] In any event, Schedule 6 to the Scotland Act 1998 clearly envisages the possibility that devolution issues involving the Scottish Executive may arise before courts elsewhere in the United Kingdom.

One new type of case presented by the Scotland Act 1998 is the possibility of judicial review raised by one government challenging acts and decisions of another government. Such intergovernmental cases are an important part of constitutional litigation in many federal systems and, although the devolution arrangements do not amount as such to federalism, it is possible that there will be litigation involving the Scottish Administration and the U.K. government *inter se*. Such cases may be taken by or against the Lord Advocate on behalf of the Scottish Administration and by, but possibly not against, the Advocate General for Scotland on behalf of the U.K. government.[54] Alternatively, cases may involve the Attorney-General or the Secretary of State on behalf of

---

[48] In terms of s.1 and a new s.4A of the Crown Suits (Scotland) Act 1857 (c.44), amended by Sched. 8, para. 2 of the Scotland Act 1998.

[49] As, for example, in *Sokha v. Secretary of State for the Home Department*, 1992 S.L.T. 1049.

[50] Again in terms of the (amended) Crown Suits (Scotland) Act 1857, ss.1 and 4A. The Lord Advocate may be respondent both in cases challenging his own conduct and as a residual respondent in much the same way as the Attorney-General in England and Wales.

[51] By virtue of s.46 of the Civil Jurisdiction and Judgments Act 1982.

[52] For example, a decision of the Foreign and Commonwealth office such as that challenged in *R. v. Secretary of State for Foreign and Commonwealth Affairs, ex p. World Development Movement Ltd* [1995] 1 W.L.R. 386 (Pergau Dam case); *cf. Monckton v. Lord Advocate*.

[53] But see Poustie, "Sparring at oil rigs: Greenpeace, Brent Spar and Challenges to the Legality of Disposing of Disused oil rigs at sea", 1995 J.R. 542, discussing the unsuccessful attempt by Greenpeace to obtain judicial review of the Secretary of State for Scotland in the High Court in England (*R. v. Secretary of State for Scotland, ex p. Greenpeace*, unreported, *The Times*, May 24, 1995). The main ground of Greenpeace's failure was the bar imposed by the Acts of Union on the English courts hearing Scottish cases; leaving aside the historical question about whether the statutory creation which is the High Court of Judicature is a "court of Westminster Hall", it may be argued that decisions of any Secretary of State on behalf of the Crown are reviewable everywhere in the U.K., albeit (perhaps) subject to a principle of *forum non conveniens*.

[54] See Sched. 6, para. 4(1) and (2). Notwithstanding sub-para. (2), however, it may be that the Advocate General will become an appropriate respondent in some cases between the Scottish Executive and U.K. government.

the U.K. government. Without seeking to predict the types of cases which may arise, it is conceivable that cases could concern challenges by the Scottish Administration to actings of the U.K. government alleged to be *ultra vires*: for example, where an exercise of the power given to the Secretary of State under section 35 of the Scotland Act 1998 to prohibit the submission of a Bill for Royal Assent is challenged as having been exercised unlawfully; or where the Scottish Administration argues that the U.K. government has impinged on its powers, privileges, prerogatives or legitimate expectations (or vice versa); or where one government claims immunity from the laws passed by the Parliament of the other; or where the U.K. government challenges a failure to act by the Scottish Executive (or vice versa) (for example, for violation of E.C. law or Convention rights). It is possible that any of these issues could arise in judicial review in the Court of Session, thereby making judicial review a forum for constitutional litigation.

IV   E.U. LAW AND CONVENTION RIGHTS

Introduction

An important restriction on the powers of the Parliament and of the   **7.31** Scottish Executive is that they must be exercised consistently both with E.U. law and Convention Rights. The term used by the Scotland Act 1998 for "E.U. law" is "Community law", which is defined in section 126(9) as meaning: "(a) all those rights, powers, liabilities, obligations and restrictions from time to time created or arising by or under the Community Treaties, and (b) all those remedies and procedures from time to time provided for by or under the Community Treaties".[55] The "Convention rights" have the same meaning as defined by the Human Rights Act 1998.[56] While problems may well arise concerning the interrelationship between Community law and the Scotland Act 1998, it is the interplay between the Convention rights, the Human Rights Act 1998 and the Scotland Act 1998 which may occasion particular difficulty.

Community law

No law of the Scottish Parliament or conduct of the Scottish Executive   **7.32** can be valid if it is incompatible with Community law. Section 29(2)(d) makes this clear for the Parliament. As regards the Scottish Executive, it emerges from sections 53 and 57 of the Act that members of the Scottish Executive are required to observe and implement obligations of the United Kingdom arising under Community law. First, section 53 devolves to the Scottish ministers, "in so far as they are within devolved competence", a variety of governmental functions formerly exercisable by the U.K. government. Such functions clearly include the observation and implementation of Community law as it applies by virtue of the E.U. Treaties and the European Communities Act 1972.[57] Secondly, section

---

[55] The "Community Treaties" are defined by s.1(2) of the European Communities Act 1972 (as amended), an enactment which the Scottish Parliament has no competence to modify by virtue of s.29(2)(c) of and Sched. 4, para. 1(2)(c) to the Scotland Act 1998.

[56] Scotland Act 1998, s.126(1). See s.1 of the Human Rights Act 1998. The latter Act is also placed beyond the reach of modification by the Scottish Parliament by virtue of s.29(2)(c) of and Sched. 4, para. 1(2)(f) to the Scotland Act 1998.

[57] This is reinforced by Sched. 5, Pt I, para. 7(2) of the Scotland Act 1998.

57(2) provides that a member of the Scottish Executive has no power to make any subordinate legislation, or to do any other act, so far as the legislation or act is incompatible with Community law. But section 57(1) provides that: "Despite the transfer to the Scottish Ministers by virtue of section 53 of functions in relation to observing and implementing obligations under Community law, any function of a Minister of the Crown in relation to any matter shall continue to be exercisable by him as regards Scotland for the purposes specified in section 2(2) of the European Communities Act 1972." This appears to mean that the implementation of E.C. law in the United Kingdom is a responsibility shared between the U.K. government and the Scottish Executive or imposed upon both of them. In areas within devolved competence, obligations arising under E.C. law are primarily for the Scottish Executive to observe and implement.[58] In combination, however, sections 53 and 57 of the Act mean that there will be some obligations arising under E.C. law which will be for the U.K. government to implement while others will be for the Scottish Executive.[59] In so far as breach of E.C. law is attributable to the Scottish Executive, remedies, including judicial review, will lie against it.[60] Equally, the U.K. government will remain answerable in the courts for violations of E.C. law attributable to it.

Convention rights

7.33   Section 29(2) of the Scotland Act 1998 provides that no Act of the Scottish Parliament may be incompatible with the Convention Rights. Section 126(1) gives the Convention rights the same meaning as in the Human Rights Act 1998, namely Articles 2 to 12 of the European Convention on Human Rights, Articles 1 to 3 of the First Protocol and Articles 1 and 2 of the Sixth Protocol, as read with Articles 14 to 16 of the Convention. But unlike the approach taken in the Human Rights Act 1998 for challenge to U.K. primary legislation by way of a declaration of incompatibility,[61] the Scotland Act allows a direct challenge to the competence of Scottish legislation so as to establish its illegality.[62] As regards the conduct of the Executive, section 57(2) provides that a member of the Scottish Executive has no power to make any subordinate legislation, or to do any other act,[63] so far as the legislation or act is incompatible with any of the Convention rights. But section 57(3) provides that section 57(2) does not apply to an act of the Lord Advocate in prosecuting any offence or in his capacity as head of the systems of criminal prosecution and investigation of deaths in Scotland if

---

[58] This accords with the position as explained in the White Paper, *Scotland's Parliament*, (Cm 3658, July 1997), Chap. 8.

[59] In EC law, however, all of the E.C. obligations remain those of the U.K. At the E.U. level, the U.K. government is answerable not only for its own breaches of E.C. law but also for those of sub-national governments within the U.K.: see Case 103/88 *Costanzo (Fratelli) SpA v. Milano* [1989] E.C.R. 1839.

[60] Breach of E.C. law may arise by virtue of a failure to act: for example, failure to implement a directive timeously. In so far as the Scottish Executive (or conceivably the Scottish Parliament in its own right) is responsible for a failure to act which violates E.C. law, it may be liable thereunder. *cf.* Sched. 6, para. 1(e) (making a failure to act by a member of the Scottish Executive which is incompatible with Community law a "devolution issue").

[61] See paras 6.34 *et seq*.

[62] In consequence of s.29 of the Scotland Act 1998.

[63] By s.100(4) "act" in relation to the Scottish Executive includes a failure to act.

the act is not unlawful under section 6(1) of the Human Rights Act 1998 by virtue of section 6(2).[64] This serves to demonstrate what may be a complex interplay between the Scotland Act and the Human Rights Act the details of which will only be worked out in case law.[65] In particular, it may be asked whether section 57(3) is the limit of the benefit of section 6(2) of the Human Rights Act 1998 for the Scottish Executive.[66] If so, the Scottish Executive could be in a less favourable position in terms of section 6(2) than other public authorities.

By virtue of section 100(1) of the Scotland Act 1998, only those who are "victims" of a violation of Convention rights can complain of a violation by the Scottish Parliament or the Scottish Executive. But where a challenge is brought by the Lord Advocate, the Advocate General, the Attorney-General or the Attorney-General for Northern Ireland, the test for victim does not apply.[67] Section 100(1) defines "victim" by reference to Article 34 of the European Convention on Human Rights, which also applies in the same terms under section 7 of the Human Rights Act 1998. The test for victim under Article 34 of the Convention has already been discussed in the context of the Human Rights Act 1998.[68] It should be noted, however, that the victim test only applies in terms of section 100 of the Scotland Act 1998 in relation to challenges to the Scottish Parliament or Scottish Executive on the grounds of Convention rights. In relation to challenges on other grounds—for example, against the *vires* of an Act of the Scottish Parliament on the basis that it "relates to" reserved matters—the general rules of *locus standi* apply.[69]

Several issues arise concerning the relationship between Convention rights and legislation enacted by the Scottish Parliament and some of these may now be mentioned. In addition, it may be noted by way of introduction that Convention rights probably do not exhaust the human rights which the Scottish Parliament and Scottish Executive must observe. First, other human rights arise by virtue of international obligations incumbent on the United Kingdom: for example, under the United Nations International Covenant on Civil and Political Rights.[70] Such obligations require to be observed by the Scottish Parliament and Executive,[71] which may mean, for example, that legislation passed by the Parliament must be interpreted so as to conform with such international obligations. Secondly, some human rights may arguably be implied under the Scotland Act 1998 by virtue of the nature of the Act and its purpose in establishing democratic political institutions.[72]

---

[64] The effect of s.6(2) of the Human Rights Act 1998 is discussed at para. 6.44.

[65] See further, paras 7.34 *et seq.* below.

[66] For example, can the Scottish Executive or the broader Scottish Administration derive any benefit from s.6(2) of the Human Rights Act when "giving effect to" U.K. legislation?

[67] s.100(2). The inclusion of the Lord Advocate is interesting; s.100(2) may envisage inter-institutional litigation, for example, where the Lord Advocate brings proceedings (*e.g.* under s.33 of the Act) against the Scottish Parliament concerning an act (or failure to act) against Convention rights?

[68] See paras 6.63 *et seq.*

[69] Standing for the purposes of judicial review is discussed in Chap. 10.

[70] Cmnd 6702. For some other international human rights treaties which the U.K. has ratified, see para. 16.06.

[71] See Sched. 5, Pt I, para. 7(2) of the Scotland Act 1998.

[72] In so far as the Scotland Act establishes Scottish political institutions, it may be taken to imply some democratic political process rights in addition to Convention rights. This would involve interpreting the Scotland Act 1998 in a way similar to the High Court of Australia's interpretation of the Australian Commonwealth Constitution (which does not

Acts of the Scottish Parliament and Convention Rights

7.34 Mention has already been made of section 101 of the Scotland Act and section 3(1) of the Human Rights Act as regards interpretation of Acts of the Scottish Parliament.[73] It follows from section 101 of the Scotland Act that a court properly faced with a challenge to an Act of the Scottish Parliament on the ground that one of its provisions is in breach of one or more Convention rights must attempt to interpret the provision so as to be compatible with Convention rights. If this is impossible, section 29 of the Scotland Act means that the court is empowered to decide that the inconsistent provision is "not law".[74] The Scottish courts thus now possess the "awful responsibility" of judicial review familiar under some constitutions,[75] namely to determine the validity of legislation passed by a democratically elected legislature for compliance with human rights guarantees. In particular, when the challenge to an Act of the Scottish Parliament is based on violation of Convention rights, judicial review of the legislation may inevitably raise sensitive constitutional issues about judicial review and the role of the judiciary.[76] It may be, however, that the Scottish Parliament will be conceded a margin of appreciation by the courts so that the limitations which it chooses to impose on Convention rights can be more easily regarded as proportionate to the objectives they pursue and therefore justified in light of Scottish society's "pressing and substantial" concerns.[77]

Margin of Appreciation for the Scottish Parliament?

7.35 By virtue of section 29 of the Scotland Act 1998, an Act of the Scottish Parliament is "not law" to the extent that any of its provisions are incompatible with Convention rights. A court faced with such an incompatibility has the power to invalidate the law to the extent of the inconsistency.[78] Ultimately, it may be the Judicial Committee of the Privy Council which makes this decision but it may be asked whether courts at all levels should explicitly extend a form of margin of appreciation to the Scottish Parliament. Whether or not it is accepted that the doctrine of margin of appreciation is unsuitable in domestic litigation,[79] the sub-

---

have a bill of rights): consider *Nationwide News Party Ltd v. Wills* (1992) 177 C.L.R. 1; *Australian Capital Television Pty. Ltd v. Commonwealth* (1992) 177 C.L.R. 106; *Theophanous v. Herald and Weekly Times Ltd* (1994) 182 C.L.R. 104; and *Stephens v. Western Australian Newspapers Ltd* (1994) 182 C.L.R. 211. For discussion, see Mason "Courts, Constitutions and Fundamental Rights" in Rawlings (ed.), *Law, Society, and Economy*, Chap. 12 (Clarendon Press, Oxford, 1997). The Australian approach may be compared with the approach of the Supreme Court of Canada, which implied some human rights into the Canadian Constitution Act, 1867 (see *Re Alberta Legislation* (1938) 2 D.L.R. 81); now, of course, Canada has the Canadian Charter of Rights and Freedoms, which is entrenched in the Constitution Act, 1982 (under which the Canadian Constitution was finally made autochthonous through the authority of the Canada Act 1982 (1982 Statutes (U.K.) c.11) to which it is Sched. B).

[73] See para. 7.24.

[74] On the effect of such a decision, see para. 7.55 below.

[75] The quotation is from *McCulloch v. Maryland*, 4 Wheat 316 (1819), *per* Marshall C.J. at 400.

[76] These have been discussed in Chap. 4: see paras 4.20 *et seq.*

[77] *cf.* R. v. Oakes [1986] 1 S.C.R. 103 at 136. On the approaches to justification of limitations on human rights, see para. 6.20.

[78] But see s.102 of the Act, discussed at para. 7.56 below.

[79] *cf.* Laws, *"Wednesbury"*, in Forsyth & Hare (eds), *The Golden Metwand and the Crooked Cord* (OUP, Oxford, 1998), at p. 201.

stance of the doctrine is about judicial deference to legislative choices. National courts in other jurisdictions have adopted the substance of the margin of appreciation when reviewing legislative provisions for compatibility with human rights standards. In particular, the Supreme Court of Canada has said: "the courts must accord great deference to the legislature's choice because it is in the best position to make such a choice".[80] "When striking a balance between the claims of competing groups, the choice of means, like the choice of ends, frequently will require an assessment of conflicting scientific evidence and differing justified demands on scarce resources. Democratic institutions are meant to let us all share in the responsibility for these difficult choices. Thus, as courts review the results of [the] legislature's deliberations . . . they must be mindful of the legislature's representative function".[81]

The Privy Council has itself adopted the doctrine of margin of appreciation in deciding appeals from Hong Kong under the Hong Kong Bill of Rights. In *Ming Pao Newspapers Ltd v. Attorney-General of Hong Kong*,[82] Lord Jauncey of Tullichettle accepted that the Hong Kong legislature and courts enjoy a margin of appreciation when deciding on the "necessity" for limits on rights guaranteed in the Hong Kong Bill of Rights. Concluding that a limitation imposed on the right to freedom of expression was justified by reference to the "pressing social need" of preserving the integrity of investigations into corruption, Lord Jauncey said: "The European Court of Human Rights accepts that contracting states enjoy a margin of appreciation in determining what is necessary to achieve a legitimate aim . . . Given that local conditions of parties to the [ICCPR] are likely to vary far more widely than conditions in states . . . parties to the European Convention, their Lordships consider that the situation in Hong Kong must be of considerable importance in determining the proportionality of the means adopted to achieve the aim."[83] In the circumstances, the Hong Kong Legislative Council's margin of appreciation was not exceeded.[84]

It may be argued that the local conditions in the respective parts of the United Kingdom do not possess the degree of difference which may distinguish the local conditions in countries and territories from which appeals to the Privy Council are brought. The application of a margin of appreciation might be seen as only appropriate to an international tribunal so that it should have no place where the Convention rights are to be defined and applied within the territory of one state by its national courts. But the matter cannot perhaps be disposed of so readily within the United Kingdom where the distinct identity of the component parts has not only been long recognised but is now being fortified by devolution. In particular, the existence of the Scottish Parliament has its origins in differences, perceived or real, between Scotland and other parts of the United Kingdom. Accordingly, it may well be that the distinct power of the courts over Scottish legislation justifies extending a

---

[80] *Libman v. Att.-Gen. of Quebec* [1997] 3 S.C.R. 569 at 605–606.

[81] *Irwin Toy Ltd v. Att.-Gen. of Quebec* [1989] 1 S.C.R. 927 at 993. See also *R. v. Edwards Books & Art* [1986] 2 S.C.R. 713; *RJR-MacDonald Inc v. Att.-Gen. of Canada* [1995] 3 S.C.R. 199; and *Thomson Newspapers Ltd v. Att.-Gen. of Canada* [1998] 1 S.C.R. 877.

[82] [1996] A.C. 907.

[83] *ibid.* at 917–918.

[84] *cf. La Compagnie de Bel Ombre v. Mauritius* (Dec. 13, 1995, PCA 46/95, unreported appeal from Mauritius), where Lord Woolf accepts that the Board will in appropriate cases "extend a substantial margin of appreciation" to local courts and legislatures.

margin of appreciation to the Scottish Parliament. The Privy Council has accepted this doctrine when exercising its jurisdiction in human rights cases and the precedents exist to be drawn on when Scottish legislation is challenged on the ground of violation of Convention rights. In any event, as has been noted elsewhere,[85] the doctrine of margin of appreciation is linked to the strictness with which a court applies the principles of proportionality to assess the validity of limits on human rights. Even if the doctrine of a margin of appreciation is not expressly adopted, it is likely that it will apply in its substantial effect by virtue of the flexibility inherent in the application of the concept of proportionality.

Scottish Legislation, Convention Rights and Private Activity

7.36	An important question arising from the Human Rights Act 1998 is the extent to which the Convention rights apply to private activity.[86] Since the Scottish Parliament and Scottish Executive are obvious public authorities in terms of section 6 of the Human Rights Act, it follows that all of their acts,[87] both public and private, fall within the scope of Convention rights under that Act. But a difficult question arises where a provision in an Act of the Scottish Parliament is found to be *ultra vires* on the ground of incompatibility with Convention rights. The question is whether a private person who has relied on a Scottish Act which is later declared *ultra vires* may be found to have acted unlawfully by virtue of the unlawful Scottish legislation.[88] In other words, does a private person seeking to give effect to or enforce a provision in an Act of the Scottish Parliament act unlawfully if the Act is subsequently found to violate a Convention right? Could another private party who has been harmed seek judicial review or otherwise proceed against that person? If the answer is yes,[89] then the Convention rights potentially have greater scope to operate between private parties in Scotland by virtue of the Scotland Act 1998 than they do elsewhere in the United Kingdom by virtue of the Human Rights Act 1998.

In examining the problem it may be noted that all legislation must be interpreted and applied so far as possible to be consistent with Convention rights. This obligation applies to U.K. legislation and Scottish legislation,[90] and it is an obligation which also binds private persons.[91] But where U.K. primary legislation is declared incompatible with Convention rights under section 4 of the Human Rights Act 1998, its incompatibility does not affect the "validity, continuing operation, or enforcement" of the legislation. So, in an action between private parties, this means that the private party with the right to succeed under the incompatible legislation will prevail. Subject to any retroactive effect

---

[85] See para. 6.20.

[86] See paras 6.57 *et seq.*

[87] Including their failures to act: s.6(6) of the Human Rights Act 1998 applies to the Scottish Parliament and is therefore broader than s.100(4)(b) of the Scotland Act 1998, which applies only to failures to act attributable to the Scottish Executive.

[88] See Lord Reed, "Devolution and the Judiciary", in Beatson *et al.*, *Constitutional Reform in the UK: Practice and Principles* (Hart Publishing, 1998), at p. 27.

[89] As to the availability of judicial review against a purely private person in such a case, it is assumed that the Convention rights aspect is sufficient to bring the matter within the supervisory jurisdiction. In practice, this may not always be so.

[90] In terms of s.3 of the Human Rights Act 1998 and s.101(2) of the Scotland Act 1998. Section 3 of the Human Rights Act also applies to Acts of the Scottish Parliament (which are subordinate legislation for the purposes of the Human Rights Act: s.21(1)).

[91] See para. 6.57.

given to a Ministerial Order issued under section 10 of the Human Rights Act 1998 to remedy the incompatibility in legislation,[92] the other party will be left with a right against the U.K. government which might have to be pursued in Strasbourg. In Scotland, however, if the incompatibility is between an Act of the Scottish Parliament and Convention rights, one private party could be liable to another private party for relying on the *ultra vires* Scottish Act. On the other hand, it may be that it is properly the Scottish Executive which is liable and against which remedies, including judicial review, should be sought. It may be that the challenge should be directed at the act, or failure to act, of the Scottish Executive which has sponsored or tolerated Scottish legislation incompatible with Convention rights.[93] It would be curious if the Convention rights can have a greater impact between private parties in Scotland than they do elsewhere.[94] There is much to be said for private persons in Scotland not being exposed to any greater obligations under Convention rights than private persons elsewhere in the United Kingdom.[95]

It may be that section 102 of the Scotland Act 1998 will provide the solution under which private parties can be saved from liability *inter se* where Scottish legislation is declared *ultra vires*. This provision allows any court or tribunal which decides that an Act of the Scottish Parliament (or conduct of the Scottish Executive) is *ultra vires* to make an order: "(a) removing or limiting any retrospective effect of the decision, or (b) suspending the effect of the decision for any period and on any conditions to allow the defect to be corrected."[96] In exercising its discretion, the court or tribunal: "shall (among other things) have regard to the extent to which persons who are not parties to the proceedings would otherwise be adversely affected [by the finding of *ultra vires* legislation or executive conduct]."[97] Section 102 may allow a court to save a private party from liability under Convention rights which basically derives from an *ultra vires* Scottish Act. But among the "other things" to which the court or tribunal must have regard will be the Convention rights of those who may be affected by its exercise of discretion. Any discrimination in the guarantee of Convention rights which may be entailed will have to be balanced against Article 14 of the Convention to determine if any limitation of Convention rights is proportionate. Otherwise, the court or tribunal may itself act in violation of Convention rights.[98]

---

[92] In terms of Sched. 2, para. 1; but a retroactive order raises other difficult issues (such as compensation for the winner under the legislation but loser under the s.10 order).

[93] Under s.100(4), an "act" incompatible with Convention rights is defined as meaning "making any legislation" and "any other act or failure to act" when a member of the Scottish Executive is responsible for it.

[94] Leaving aside the possibility that either the Human Rights Act 1998 or the Scotland Act 1998 can create delictual liability under breach of statutory duty: *cf.* Wade "The United Kingdom's Bill of Rights", in Beatson *et al.*, *Constitutional Reform, supra*, at p. 64.

[95] This would appear consistent with the policy of the Scotland Act 1998, which seems to be to impose no greater obligations under Convention rights on the Scottish Executive than those possessed by the U.K. government (subject, of course, to matters of the legality of Acts of the Scottish Parliament). So s.100 of the Scotland Act 1998 provides that only a "victim"—defined identically under s.7 of the Human Rights Act 1998—can rely on violations of Convention rights in proceedings raised by private persons against the Scottish Parliament or Executive. But *cf.* s.57(3) of the Scotland Act: only the Lord Advocate has the benefit of s.6(2) of the Human Rights Act 1998; is this the limit of the relevance of s.6(2) for the Scottish Executive?

[96] Scotland Act 1998, s.102(2).

[97] s.102(3). See para. 7.56 below.

[98] And breach s.6(3) of the Human Rights Act 1998.

Convention Rights and Codification of the common law

7.37 One further issue may be raised concerning the potentially greater scope of Convention rights to apply to private activity in Scotland. Suppose the Scottish Parliament were to decide to codify areas of private law derived from the common law.[99] Would this have the effect of applying the Convention rights to the codified rules by virtue of their being contained in legislation? To this extent private activity formerly based on the common law may become affected by Convention rights by virtue of codification. Where this point has arisen under the U.S. Bill of Rights and the Canadian Charter of Rights, the U.S. and Canadian Supreme Courts have decided that codification of common law rules—or their provision in civil codes—did not in itself convert private actions based on the codified rules into challengeable state or government action.[1] It may be that a similar approach needs to be taken in Scotland. For example, the incompatibility between the codified rules and Convention rights should be treated solely as a *vires* matter for which the Scottish Parliament and Executive are liable.[2] That is, if the codifed common law rules violate Convention rights, the codifying Act will to the extent of its inconsistency be *ultra vires* by virtue of section 29 of the Scotland Act 1998. In this way, private parties' conduct may not be made subject to the Convention rights by virtue of the codification of common law rules. The Parliament's breach of Convention rights should not make a private person liable only through relying on or enforcing the incompatible codified common law rules against another private party. After all, under section 6(2) of the Human Rights Act 1998 a public authority might not be liable in similar circumstances.[3] It may be that, again, section 102 will allow this approach to be taken in Scotland in the context of the liability of private parties. The matter cannot be said to be neat and tidy but experience elsewhere shows that few implications of a "bill or rights" are.

The Scotland Act and the Human Rights Act

7.38 It is clear that the Human Rights Act 1998 also applies in its own terms to the Scottish Parliament and the Scottish Executive. First, both bodies are public authorities for the purposes of section 6 of the Human Rights Act. Secondly, for the purposes of the Human Rights Act, section 21(1) defines subordinate legislation as including Acts of the Scottish Parliament. Thirdly, the Scotland Act 1998 itself is subject to the interpretive rule provided by section 3 of the Human Rights Act. But all of this is in addition to the express provision which the Scotland Act 1998 makes in relation to the competence of the Scottish Parliament,[4]

---

[99] Codification of criminal law raises no "private" issues here: since it will be enforced by the state, it matters not in what form the criminal law is. But a failure to provide criminal penalties for some violations of Convention rights may engage the Convention: *cf. X and Y v. Netherlands* (1986) 8 E.H.R.R. 235. For further discussion, see Chapter 6.

[1] *Flagg Bros Inc. v. Brooks*, 436 U.S. 149 (1978), discussed by Brest, "State Action and Liberal [Theory]" (1982) 130 U.Penn.L.R. 1296; and *Tremblay v. Daigle* [1989] 2 S.C.R. 530, esp. at 571.

[2] Under s.100 of the Scotland Act 1998.

[3] At least when unavoidably acting under incompatible U.K. legislation. Whether the same is true in relation to public authorities' acts under Scottish legislation may raise the question whether Acts of the Scottish Parliament are "made under" the Scotland Act 1998 (that is, a piece of primary legislation passed by the U.K. Parliament) for the purposes of s.6(2) of the Human Rights Act 1998: see para. 6.44.

[4] s.29.

the powers of the Scottish Executive,[5] challenges against them on the ground of Convention rights[6] and the procedure for devolution issues contained in Schedule 6. Accordingly, there is some scope for overlap between the two Acts.[7] In regard to challenges to legislation of the Scottish Parliament and actings by the Scottish Executive, questions may arise about the propriety of proceeding under the provisions of one Act as opposed to the other. As long as the Human Rights Act 1998 is not in force, Convention rights issues involving the Scottish Parliament and Scottish Executive can only arise under the Scotland Act 1998. Since this has been in force since July 1, 1999, Convention rights have been available in cases arising under the Scotland Act. Once the Human Rights Act is in force, practical and procedural questions may arise about whether a challenge to the Scottish Parliament and Scottish Executive should be brought under the Scotland Act or directly under the Human Rights Act.[8] It may be thought that challenges to the Parliament or Executive on the grounds of violation of Convention rights should be taken under section 100 of the Scotland Act, since incompatibility with Convention rights is a "devolution issue" within Schedule 6 to the Act. Some support for this may be derived from noting that the Scotland Act 1998, being enacted some 10 days after the Human Rights Act 1998, is the later statement of the U.K. Parliament's will. Even so, the Convention rights in the Scotland Act 1998 must reflect the meaning which they have for the purposes of the Human Rights Act 1998. For example, it is the latter Act which provides for the use to be made by U.K. courts of the Convention jurisprudence.[9]

V FAILURES TO ACT AND OTHER QUESTIONS

Failures to Act

The fifth of the devolution issues identified by Schedule 6 to the **7.39** Scotland Act 1998 concerns whether a failure to act by a member of the Scottish Executive is incompatible with Convention rights or with Community law. Much of what has been noted already in relation to acts applies equally to failures to act. In the context of E.C. law, failures to act may include the failure properly to implement E.C. directives or otherwise give full and proper effect to all applicable E.C. law. Where such failure is properly attributable to the Scottish Parliament or Executive, they will be liable under E.C. law. As regards Convention rights, section 100(4) defines "act" for the purposes of section 100 as meaning "making any legislation" and "any other act or failure to act, if it is the act or failure of a member of the Scottish Executive". It is clear that failures to act may violate Convention rights,[10] so that the Conven-

---

[5] s.57.
[6] s.100.
[7] For a discussion of the issues, see Lord Hope of Craighead, "Devolution and Human Rights" [1998] E.H.R.L.R. 367.
[8] For example, proceedings under s.7(1)(a) of the Human Rights Act must by s.7(5) be brought within a year, unless the court grants an extension. But that time limit does not appear to apply to devolution issues arising under the Scotland Act. See Lord Reed, "Human Rights and Scotland" in Lord Lester and Pannick (eds), *Human Rights Law and Practice* (Butterworths, 1999).
[9] See s.2 of the Human Rights Act 1998.
[10] See para. 6.45.

tion rights will on occasion impose positive obligations on the Scottish Executive. But beyond the limits of section 100(4) of the Scotland Act 1998, it may be also that a failure to act which is attributable to the Parliament will violate Convention rights. Independently of any failure attributable to the Scottish Executive—for example, failing to introduce a Bill or have legislation repealed—a failure by the Scottish Parliament to legislate may be an unlawful failure to act contrary to section 6(1), taken with section 6(6) of the Human Rights Act 1998.

Other Questions

7.40 The sixth and last of the "devolution issues" listed in Schedule 6 is plainly designed to pick up any other question which might arise in relation to the extent of the devolved functions and powers. It covers "any other question about whether a function is exercisable within devolved competence or in or as regards Scotland and any other question arising by virtue of this Act about reserved matters."[11] But it is to be noted that this is all restricted to problems of competence, and, as has already been observed, opportunities for review may occur upon grounds other than competence, that is, to use the language adopted later in this book, legality. It is convenient at this stage to give some examples, albeit by no means exhaustive, of other issues where challenges, whether or not in respect of competence, may arise.

Standing orders

7.41 The proceedings of the Parliament are to be regulated by standing orders.[12] There are various provisions within the Act indicating some of the matters which may be the subject of standing orders.[13] The orders may be open to judicial review. For example in terms of paragraph 2 of Schedule 3 the standing orders may include provisions for withdrawing from a member of the Parliament his rights and privileges as a member. If a provision was made under that paragraph which took no account of the requirements of Article 6 of the European Convention on Human Rights, it may be that the validity of the order could be challenged.

Attendance orders

7.42 Provision is made by sections 23 to 27 for Parliament to call persons to attend to give evidence to the Parliament and to produce documents in their custody or control. Refusal in compliance is made a criminal offence by section 25. The limitations on the scope of the power set out in these sections could give rise to dispute and a resolution might be achieved by way of judicial review. In the event of criminal proceedings being taken then the absence of any obligation to comply with whatever the requirement was could be raised by way of defence.

Resolutions

7.43 Apart from legislation it will be competent for the Parliament to pass resolutions.[14] These will have to comply with the limits of the devolved matters, and could possibly be open to challenge on other grounds of review.

---

[11] Sched. 6, para. 1(f).
[12] s.22(1). See also Sched. 3.
[13] For example s.26(4), 27(1)(b) and 36, as well as Sched. 3.
[14] For example under s.81(5) the provisions for remuneration may be made by resolution.

Section 35 orders

In terms of section 35 it is provided that the Secretary of State may in **7.44** certain circumstances make an order prohibiting the Presiding Officer from submitting a Bill for Royal Assent.[15] The circumstances are where he has reasonable grounds to believe that the Bill would be incompatible with any international obligations or the interests of defence or national security, or that the modifications made by the Bill to the law on reserved matters would have an adverse effect on the law as it applies to reserved matters. The order must state the reasons for its being made,[16] and it requires to be made within certain time-limits.[17] Such an order could be challenged by way of judicial review if it failed to comply with the procedural requirements or if it could be claimed that the Secretary of State could have had no reasonable grounds for his belief. Dispute about such an order is one example of an issue which may not fall precisely within the definition of "Devolution Issues".

Section 58 orders

Section 58 contains provisions corresponding with those in section 35 but **7.45** aimed at actions to be taken by the Scottish Executive rather than proposed Acts of the Parliament. Under section 58 the Secretary of State may direct that proposed action[18] should not be taken, if he has reasonable grounds for believing that it would be incompatible with any international obligations. He may direct that action[19] shall be taken where he has reasonable grounds for believing that action by the Scottish Executive is required to give effect to any international obligations. Further the Secretary of State may revoke subordinate legislation which contains provisions which he has reasonable grounds to believe is incompatible with any international obligations or with the interests of defence or national security, and subordinate legislation which he has reasonable cause to believe modifies the law applying to reserved matters with an adverse effect on the law as it applies to reserved matters. The Secretary of State is expressly required to state the reasons for making any order under the section. These strong powers are at least in principle open to control by judicial review.

Concordats

Various working arrangements to facilitate the management of matters **7.46** of common concern between the Scottish Executive and U.K. government departments will be achieved by concordats. These are non-statutory arrangements which are not intended to be legally enforceable contracts. They will usually be between the two parties: the Scottish Executive and the U.K. government. But it is anticipated that some may be trilateral, involving such parties as the Meat and Livestock Commission or the British Waterways Board. Among the many things which they may cover, it has been said that likely topics include consultation

---

[15] Bills are proposed Acts of the Parliament: s.28(2).

[16] s.35(2).

[17] s.25(3).

[18] "Action" here includes making, confirming or approving subordinate legislation: s.58(3).

[19] "Action" here includes not only the making of subordinate legislation as in the previous footnote, but also introducing a Bill into the Parliament: s.58(3).

arrangements in relation to proposals for legislation, joint working
arrangements for liaison on E.U. and international matters, and consultation about appointments.[20] Concordats may not in themselves
necessarily be open to review, but an opportunity for review of a
concordat may arise if it were to exceed a proper construction of the
primary legislation.[21] But however that may be, they will be of significance in matters of review and while they are not legally contractual in
character, they may in effect be enforceable in an application for review
of an act or decision which has failed to comply with them. A concordat
may, for example, create a legitimate expectation of consultation, and so
in effect be enforced, not by either of the parties to the concordat, but by
a third party who was relying on its provisions being observed.

   One particular problem may arise in the event of a law being passed
contrary to the express provisions of a concordat. As has been noted, the
validity of an Act is not to be affected by any invalidity of the
proceedings of the Parliament leading to its enactment.[22] But if no
provision has been made requiring as a matter of procedure that
compliance with the concordat is required in the proceedings of the
Parliament leading up to the enactment of the law in question, it may
well be that a failure so to comply could provide grounds for a challenge
to the validity of the measure. If, for example, a concordat was to require
some process of consultation by a Scottish minister prior to the
enactment of the measure, and that requirement had not been fully
observed, there may be a question whether there was an invalidity
otherwise than in the proceedings of the Parliament, and so not affected
by section 28(5) of the Scotland Act 1998.

VI   PROCEEDINGS AND REMEDIES

Judicial review and the Scotland Act 1998

7.47   Section 126(4) of the Scotland Act 1998 provides that references in the
Act to "Scots private law" are to "the civil law of Scotland" and
expressly "include references to judicial review of administrative action".
Several questions arise from this characterisation of "judicial review" as
part of Scots private law. First, in light of the constitutional review of
Acts of the Scottish Parliament which arises under the Scotland Act
1998,[23] judicial review must be understood as including more than
"judicial review of administrative action". Where challenges to Acts of
the Scottish Parliament are brought by way of the judicial review
procedure (that is, under the supervisory jurisdiction of the Court of
Session), it is at least an understatement to describe the case as involving
judicial review of "administrative action". So it may be that judicial
review for the purposes of section 126(4) is to be understood as being
more limited than judicial review where at least some of the "devolution

---

[20] See the published "Guidance on Concordats Between the Scottish Executive and UK
Government Departments".
[21] See also para. 9.16.
[22] para. 7.08 above.
[23] By virtue of s.29, taken with Sched. 6, para. 1(a).

issues" defined in Schedule 6 to the Scotland Act 1998 arise.[24] Secondly, although judicial review of administrative action is certainly part of the civil law of Scotland,[25] it is somewhat strained, even in the Scottish context, to regard the remedy of judicial review as part of Scots private law.[26] The main, if not exclusive, purpose of the remedy is the supervision of defined authority to ensure that it is exercised lawfully and properly. Unlike "private law" cases, a judicial review case is not primarily concerned with the definition of rights and duties between persons *inter se*.[27] It may be that section 126(4) classifies judicial review as part of Scots private law only so as to clarify the legislative competence of the Scottish Parliament over it. Yet this leads to the third question. Since Scots private law is a devolved matter, subject to exceptions,[28] it follows that in general the subject-matter of judicial review of administrative action is substantially open to legislation by the Scottish Parliament. The Scottish Parliament may therefore be empowered to place the remedy of judicial review in Scotland on a statutory basis,[29] or more extensively reform the subject by, for example, defining the scope of the supervisory jurisdiction or codifying the grounds of judicial review.[30] But it may be argued that the nature of the supervisory jurisdiction of the Court of Session gives it a constitutional significance which puts it beyond the competence of the Scottish Parliament. Schedule 5, para. 1(f) provides that the "continued existence of the Court of Session" is an aspect of the constitution and is a reserved matter. The inherent nature of the Court of Session's supervisory jurisdiction should be considered a constitutional matter. On this basis, while the Scottish Parliament may provide for and regulate the jurisdiction as part of Scots private law, it has no competence to abolish the jurisdiction or affect it in such a way as would rob it of its essential aspects. In particular, in so far as judicial review is the most practicable means by which "devolution issues" can be raised in the Court of Session, the restrictions which Schedule 4 to the Scotland Act 1998 place on the Parliament's power to amend the Act indirectly amount to restraints on the Parliament's competence to legislate for judicial review.

---

[24] In particular, although the Scottish Parliament may have power to legislate on "judicial review of administrative action" as part of Scots private law, it appears from Sched. 4, para. 4 of the Scotland Act 1998 that the Scottish Parliament cannot amend the court's powers over "devolution issues" as defined in Sched. 6: see below.

[25] Although the High Court of Justiciary also possesses a supervisory jurisdiction: see para. 8.37.

[26] The classification sits uneasily with the English approach of defining the scope of judicial review by reference to matters of public law. But since this approach has not been adopted in Scotland, that is not in itself an issue. For a consideration of the public–private distinction in this context, see para. 8.27.

[27] *cf. R. v. Somerset C.C., ex p. Fewings* [1995] 1 All E.R. 513, *per* Laws J. at 524. For discussion of the (increasingly?) overlapping values of public law and private law, see Oliver, "The Underlying Values of Public and Private Law" in Taggart (ed.), *The Province of Administrative Law* (Hart Publishing, Oxford, 1997).

[28] See s.29(4), Sched. 4, para. 2 and Sched. 5 to the Scotland Act 1998.

[29] Which is basically the effect of s.31 of the Supreme Court Act 1981 in relation to the procedural aspects of judicial review in England and Wales. The same is true in many of the Canadian provinces (for example, Ontario).

[30] Which the Australian Administrative Decisions (Judicial Review) Act 1977 (Cth) attempted to do by codifying the grounds of judicial review available against federal "decisions or conduct" of "an administrative nature" made "under an enactment". Importantly, however, the Australian Act does not purport to provide an exclusive judicial review procedure, so that the prerogative writs continue to be available, for example, to seek review of the exercise of prerogative powers.

Devolution issues and judicial review

7.48   The six devolution issues listed by Schedule 6, para. 1 have been set out above.[31] But while the Act defines the devolution issues and expressly provides title for the Advocate General and the Lord Advocate to institute proceedings (without prejudice to the title of other persons), the Act is deliberately silent on the form of the proceedings. However, as has been noted throughout this chapter, the devolution issues concern matters which could arise in judicial review proceedings. Indeed, it has been said that most devolution issues are expected to be raised by way of judicial review in the Court of Session.[32] In this regard, however, it may be observed that Schedule 6, para. 2 of the Act provides that a devolution issue shall not be taken to arise where the court or tribunal before which a contention has been made in relation to a devolution issue considers it to be frivolous or vexatious. Such a conclusion, which would require to be expressed in the form of a decision, would presumably be open to appeal or, as appropriate, judicial review.

Devolution issues outside judicial review

7.49   A devolution issue could arise in the course of a wide variety of proceedings before courts and tribunals. Such proceedings will include proceedings under section 33 of the Scotland Act 1998, which provides for pre-enactment scrutiny of Bills passed by the Scottish Parliament. More generally and as has been observed elsewhere,[33] issues of excess of power in all its possible forms may arise in proceedings other than those of judicial review. The present book is not concerned directly with such other proceedings, although it must be accepted that the review of statutes passed by the Scottish Parliament is to be regarded as a form of constitutional judicial review even where it does not occur by virtue of the supervisory jurisdiction. In addition, it should also be noticed that Parliament has envisaged that devolution issues may arise in proceedings in England, Wales and Northern Ireland, no doubt including but not limited to judicial review, and special procedural provisions have been made for such cases.[34] But none of this interferes with the power of supervision which is expressed in Scotland by way of the remedy of reduction of an offending act or decision. This remedy should remain exclusive to the Court of Session.

Proceedings by the Advocate General or the Lord Advocate

7.50   Express provision is made to allow the Advocate General or the Lord Advocate to institute proceedings for the determination of a devolution issue and for the Lord Advocate to defend any proceedings instituted by the Advocate General.[35] But these provisions are without prejudice to the right of any other person to institute or defend proceedings involving a devolution issue.[36] While no form of process is prescribed for such

---

[31] See para. 7.04.
[32] Such was the expectation expressed by the Lord Advocate in the House of Lords on Nov. 2, 1998: *Hansard*, H.L. Vol. 594, col. 79.
[33] See para. 1.07.
[34] See Pts III and IV of Sched. 6 to the Act.
[35] Sched. 6, para. 4(1) and (2); but note that no express provision is made for the Advocate General to defend proceedings brought by the Lord Advocate.
[36] Sched. 6, para. 4(3).

proceedings, it is thought that a petition for judicial review would be appropriate in so far as the supervisory jurisdiction is being invoked. The proceedings then must be in the Court of Session.[37]

Proceedings by others

It is clear that the Advocate General and the Lord Advocate do not have **7.51** any exclusive right to initiate or to defend proceedings involving a devolution issue. The provisions empowering them to take proceedings is expressly said to be without prejudice to any power to institute or defend proceedings otherwise exercisable by any person.[38] But in any proceedings where a devolution issue arises before a court or a tribunal intimation of it must be given to the Advocate General and the Lord Advocate, unless they are already party to the proceedings.[39] They may then become party to the proceedings. This procedure will require to be followed where a devolution issue arises in an application for judicial review.

Preliminary proceedings

As noted above,[40] various provisions have been made to check the **7.52** competence of a proposed Act of the Scottish Parliament and proposed action of the Scottish Executive .[41] Section 31 of the Act makes provision not only for a member of the Scottish Executive on or before a Bill's introduction to the Parliament to affirm the Parliament's competence to pass the Bill, but also requires the Presiding Officer to decide whether the Bill is within the competence of the Parliament and state his decision.[42] Under section 33 of the Act, the Advocate General, the Lord Advocate or the Attorney-General may refer a question concerning the competence of a Bill to the Judicial Committee of the Privy Council.[43] In deciding whether or not to exercise this power, a degree of independence on the part of these law officers is called for. This raises the question of the extent to which a decision to exercise or not exercise the power under section 33 is reviewable and in turn the extent to which the decision of the Parliament's Presiding Officer is reviewable. This leads to the issue whether the Parliament's decision to deliberate a Bill is challengeable in judicial review at the instance of individuals or whether the effect of section 33 is to be that only the designated law officers can challenge the Parliament's competence before a Bill is enacted.[44] While

---

[37] See para. 8.04.
[38] Sched. 6, para. 4(3).
[39] para. 6.
[40] See para. 7.06.
[41] See ss.35 and 58 of the Scotland Act 1998.
[42] s.31(3).
[43] As noted earlier, the Secretary of State also has powers under s.35 to prohibit a Bill from being submitted for Royal Assent.
[44] The Secretary of State has power under s.35 of the Act to prohibit the submission of a Bill for Royal Assent. It may be noted that the English Bill of Rights 1689 expressly provided that "the freedom of speech and debates or proceedings in Parliament ought not to be impeached or questioned in any court or place out of Parliament", while the Scottish Claim of Right 1689 only declared that Parliaments ought to be allowed to sit and "the freedom of speech and debate secured to the members". These provisions do not of course apply to the Scottish Parliament. As is noted elsewhere there are some restraints on challenge to procedural matters in ss.1(4) and 17(5).

section 28(5) of the Act may protect the Parliament's Acts from challenge for invalidity in proceedings for their enactment, this does not foreclose pre-enactment challenge on the ground that the Parliament has no competence to enact the Bill. However, beyond section 33 (and section 35) of the Act, the policy reasons against challenge to the Parliament before a Bill is enacted are great. First, the Parliament may not in the end pass the Bill; secondly, the courts should be wary, not least on grounds of the separation of powers, from interfering in the deliberations of the Parliament; and thirdly, the possibility of subsequent challenge to the Act will be real and will generally provide a more concrete context in which the Act's legality can be measured.[45] More generally, assuming rules of standing can be satisfied, it is likely that pre-enactment challenges by individuals will be premature. It may be, however, that judicial reivew of a law officer's decision to refer (or not) under section 33 will be reviewable. In any event, the fact that no reference has been made under section 33 should not necessarily weigh in a challenge to the competence of an Act. Nor does the scrutiny of a Bill provided for by section 31 of the Act necessarily weigh heavily in subsequent consideration of its competence by the court.

References and appeals in devolution issues

7.53 Provisions are made in Schedule 6 to the Act for the reference of a devolution issue from tribunals or courts to the Inner House of the Court of Session or, in criminal matters. to the High Court of Justiciary.[46] Further provisions are made for reference and for appeal to the Judicial Committee of the Privy Council.[47] The reference procedure established by Schedule 6 raises several interesting issues. First, as to the Judicial Committee of the Privy Council, section 103 of the Scotland Act 1998 provides that its decision "shall be stated in open court and shall be binding in all legal proceedings" except those before the Committee itself. Section 103(2) makes specific provision on the persons who are eligible to sit on the Committee for the purposes of proceedings under the Act. Secondly, it is not clear if the Inner House of the Court of Session and the Judicial Committee of the Privy Council are required to hear and decide every case referred to them, or whether they may exercise a discretion to refuse to hear a case referred.[48] Thirdly, criteria

---

[45] *cf. Rediffusion (Hong Kong) Ltd v. Att.-Gen. of Hong Kong* [1970] A.C. 1136 (discussion of the competency of the court inquiring into the deliberative processes of the Legislative Council in Hong Kong). See also the Australian cases cited at para. 7.08.

[46] Sched. 6, paras 7–9.

[47] See the somewhat complex provisions of paras 8–13. Cases may come eventually to the Judicial Committee of the Privy Council or the House of Lords, but the latter may generally refer the case to the Privy Council under Sched. 6, para. 32. For the procedural rules see the Act of Sederunt (Devolution Issues Rules) 1999 (S.I. 1999 No. 1345), the Act of Sederunt (Proceedings for Determination of Devolution Issues Rules) 1999 (S.I. 1999 No. 1347), and the Act of Adjournal (Devolution Issues Rules) 1999. Rules have also been made for the procedure in and powers of the Privy Council: see The Judicial Committee (Devolution Issues) Rules Order 1999 and The Judicial Comittee (Powers in Devolution Cases) Order 1999. For a discussion of the role of the Judicial Committee of the Privy Council, see Lord Hope of Craighead, "The Judicial Committee of the Privy Council: Its Practice and Procedure" (1999) S.L.P.Q. 1.

[48] Comparison may be made in this regard with the powers of the Constitutional Court in Germany. Under the German Constitution, provision is made both for judicial referral to the Constitutional Court of constitutional law points arising in ordinary cases (see Art.

may need to be developed by reference to which tribunals and courts can decide in what circumstances they should refer a devolution issue to the Inner House, the High Court of Justiciary or, as appropriate, the Judicial Committee of the Privy Council.

Proceedings against the Parliament

Provision is made by section 40 of the Act for proceedings against the Parliament to be instituted against the Parliamentary corporation on behalf of the Parliament. By section 40(3) it is provided that: "In any proceedings against the Parliament, the court shall not make an order for suspension, interdict, reduction, or specific performance (or other like order) but may instead make a declarator." Accordingly, it would appear that in any proceedings brought against the Parliament where the competence of an Act is challenged, the court can go no further than declare the invalidity of the measure.[49] Presumably this applies also to proceedings brought in England, Wales or Northern Ireland under Parts III and IV of Schedule 6, since the application of section 40 is not limited to Scotland, provided that there was jurisdiction to grant such remedies in these other courts. There is a like restriction in the remedies which may be granted in any proceedings against any member of the Parliament, the Presiding Officer or a deputy, any member of the staff of the Parliament, or the Parliamentary corporation, if the effect of any of the remedies other than declarator would be to give a relief against the Parliament which could not have been given in proceedings against the Parliament.[50]

7.54

Effect of a decision that an Act of the Scottish Parliament is not law

Section 29(1) provides that an Act of the Scottish Parliament "is not law so far as any provision of the Act is outside the legislative competence of the Parliament". The words "not law" raise the questions whether a provision which breaches the Parliament's competence is invalid, or only inapplicable, and what retrospective effect a decision to this effect has. Similar difficulties arise in relation to acts and decisions of the Scottish Executive found to be *ultra vires*. In fact, the problem of what consequences are to follow in practice from a finding of *ultra vires*, which theoretically requires that the act or decision be void *ab initio*, may arise whenever a court invalidates a measure following a judicial review of its legality.[51] In essence, the problem is whether the *ultra vires*

7.55

100(1) of the Basic Law) and for individuals who have exhausted all their remedies to bring direct complaints to the Court where violation of constitutional rights is alleged. Possibly in light of the latter, the Constitutional Court has the power to reject a judicial referral as unfounded. For discussion of the German Constitutional Court, see Kommers, *The Federal Constitutional Court* (1994); and *The Constitutional Jurisprudence of the Federal Republic of Germany* (2nd ed., 1997).

[49] But it is not clear that all challenges to Acts of the Parliament will be brought against the Parliament; they could also be brought against the Executive. Indeed the effect of s.40(3) may be to encourage this, since more remedies may be available. The provisions of s.40 are of course subject to the overriding requirements of E.C. law and will require to be read subject to s.3 of the Human Rights Act 1998.

[50] s.40(4).

[51] See para. 14.15. In particular, see *Boddington v. British Transport Police* [1998] 2 W.L.R. 639; *R. v. Governor of Brockhill Prison, ex p. Evans (No. 2)* [1999] 2 Q.B. 1043; and *Percy v. Hall* [1996] 4 All E.R. 523.

measure is to be regarded as having attracted some valid consequences during the time before the court's decision when it was in force and normally presumptively valid. The problem is always difficult but clearly much more so when the measure invalidated is a provision in legislation of the most general application. Experience elsewhere suggests that an absolute rule of invalidity in relation to *ultra vires* primary legislation may not be practical.[52] For example, in *Norton v. Shelby County*,[53] the U.S. Supreme Court said: "An unconstitutional act is not a law; it confers no rights; it imposes no duties; it affords no protection; it creates no office; it is inoperative, as though it had never been passed." But in *Chicot County Drainage District v. Baxter State Bank*,[54] Chief Justice Hughes said that it is: "manifest from numerous decisions that an all-inclusive statement of a principle of absolute retroactive invalidity cannot be justified".

One solution to the problem is to give only prospective effect to a court decision that a law is invalid. That approach, once favoured by the U.S. Supreme Court,[55] has not met with much enthusiasm.[56] In Australia, where prospective overruling has been rejected,[57] section 109 of the Constitution provides that a state law inconsistent with a Commonwealth law is "invalid to the extent of the inconsistency". It has been laid down by the High Court of Australia that an inconsistent state law "remains valid though it is rendered inoperative to the extent of the inconsistency".[58] Although the Court does not adopt an inflexible rule of absolute invalidity where the Constitution is breached,[59] the High Court has held that acts done under a law later declared to be unconstitutional are not protected by the invalid law and can expose officials who relied on the law to delictual liability.[60] Similarly, in Canada, while the same conclusion of retroactive invalidity applies to a law found to be unconstitutional,[61] the Supreme Court has also indicated that some acts done under an "invalid" law will have valid effects.[62] Moreover, the Supreme Court has on occasion exercised a discretion to maintain in force rules of law which it has found to be unconstitutional, at least for a determinate period of time.[63] Although justified by exceptional circumstances, namely to prevent wholesale invalidity of the statute book of the province of Manitoba, the Supreme Court's decision provides an inter-

---

[52] For discussion of the position under E.C. law, see para. 5.69.

[53] 118 U.S. 425 (1886).

[54] 308 U.S. 371 (1940).

[55] See *Linkletter v. Walker*, 381 U.S. 618 (1965). Prospective overruling was the means by which the Warren court avoided re-opening possibly numerous criminal convictions following its decisions on the revised meanings of some rights in the U.S. Bill of Rights.

[56] Not even, in more recent times, in the U.S.: cf. *Griffith v. Kentucky*, 497 U.S. 314 (1987).

[57] See *Ha v. New South Wales* (1997) 189 C.L.R. 465.

[58] *Western Australia v. Commonwealth* (1995) 183 C.L.R. 373 at 465: there is no "absolute invalidity".

[59] See, for example, *Clayton v. Heffron* (1960) 105 C.L.R. 214, esp. at 246–248.

[60] See *James v. Commonwealth* (1939) 62 C.L.R. 339. This is, of course, the orthodox approach: the shield of the statute having been removed, liability depends on the ordinary law.

[61] For analysis of the Canadian position, see Hogg, *Constitutional Law in Canada* (4th ed., 1997), Chap. 55.

[62] See *Central Canada Potash Co. v. Government of Saskatchewan* [1979] 1 S.C.R. 42.

[63] See *Reference Re Manitoba Language Rights* [1985] 1 S.C.R. 721. See also *McDonald v. Att.-Gen. of Prince Edward Island* (1998) 155 D.L.R. (4th) 1. cf. *McGinty v. Western Australia* (1996) 186 C.L.R. 140, esp. at 215–216 and 223–224.

esting precedent on the court's powers to vary the effects of a decision that a law is invalid.[64] But there are no easy answers to the problems posed by a law's invalidity and in many cases a satisfactory solution will often rest with the law of restitution.[65] It is, however, important to note that, as is discussed in the next paragraph, section 102 of the Scotland Act 1998 expressly empowers courts and tribunals faced with an "invalid" provision in an Act of the Scottish Parliament to vary the effects of any decision in this regard.

The power of the court: section 102

As has already been noted in the context of Convention rights,[66] section 102 of the Scotland Act 1998 gives a particular power to courts and tribunals where they decide that a provision in an Act of the Scottish Parliament is not within the legislative competence of the Parliament or a member of the Scottish Executive does not have the power to make, confirm or approve a provision of subordinate legislation.[67] In such a case the court or tribunal, after giving intimation to the Lord Advocate and, where the issue is a devolution issue within the meaning of Schedule 6, to the appropriate law officer,[68] may make an order: "(a) removing or limiting any retrospective effect of the decision, or (b) suspending the effect of the decision for any period and on any conditions to allow the defect to be corrected."[69] This power is available to any court or tribunal in which the issue about a law's invalidity has arisen. Being a statutory power, section 102(2) does not affect the Court of Session's usual discretion when it exercises the supervisory jurisdiction. But the power conferred by section 102 may arise for consideration in applications for judicial review. As to the exercise of the power, section 102(3) provides: "In deciding whether to make an order under this section, the court or tribunal shall (among other things) have regard to the extent to which persons who are not parties to the proceedings would otherwise be adversely affected." While that is one specified consideration, it is clear that the court will require to have regard to all the circumstances in deciding whether and to what extent or in what manner the discretion conferred by section 102 ought properly to be exercised. The provision calls for a consideration of issues which may extend far beyond matters of law and involve matters of practical consequence and political intention on which the court will necessarily require to rely on the submissions put before it by the parties, and in particular, representations made on behalf of the administrative or governmental authority concerned. It may be noted, however, that any excess of legislative or executive power on the part of the Scottish Parliament or Executive may be remedied by subordinate legislation under section 107 of the Act.[70]

7.56

---

[64] Albeit with curious effects: for example, persons may still be convicted of crimes under the "invalid" law by virtue of its "validity" in terms of the court's decision: see *Bilodeau v. Att.-Gen. of Manitoba* [1986] 1 S.C.R. 449.

[65] See *Kleinwort Benson Ltd v. Lincoln City Council* [1998] 4 All E.R. 513, noted by Convery (1999) 3 Edin.L.R. 202.

[66] See para. 7.38.

[67] s.102. There is no corresponding power in the court under the Human Rights Act 1998.

[68] As defined in s.102(7).

[69] s.102(2).

[70] For an account of some of the factors bearing on a discretion to refuse relief, see *R. v. Monopolies and Mergers Commission, ex p. Argyll Group plc* [1986] 1 W.L.R. 763 at 774.

The power of the court: remedies

7.57 Where a court finds that a provision in an Act of the Scottish Parliament
is inconsistent with the Scotland Act 1998, only the inconsistent provision should be found to be "not law". The proper remedy may be one
of reduction or declarator. Questions may arise about the court's power
to sever repugnant provisions from those which are lawful.[71] Severing
provisions in legislation is an almost legislative function and courts
elsewhere with a similar constitutional jurisdiction have been cautious
about entering on this task.[72] The court must be careful not to change
the Act's overall effect through severance of unlawful provisions.[73]
Where an unlawful provision goes to the root of the Act, severance may
not be possible and a declarator may be the better judicial remedy,
thereby leaving the legislature to rectify the legislation. Alternatively, it
may be possible for the court to save a challenged provision by "reading
in" provisions. For example, where an Act of the Scottish Parliament is
deficient in some respect and thereby violates Convention rights, the
court may be able to "read in" provisions so as to make the Act
compatible. The danger again, even more so, is that the court treads on
the legislative function. But this has not stopped courts elsewhere from
cautiously exercising the power of reading in.[74] It is to be expected that
the Scottish courts will in appropriate cases and with all due care
exercise these various remedial powers so as to limit the effects of
successful challenges to Acts of the Scottish Parliament.

---

[71] But see s.40(3) and (4): where proceedings are against the Parliament, the court is
restricted to issuing a declarator. The effect of these provisions in Scotland may be to
direct challenges against Acts of the Parliament to the Lord Advocate.

[72] *cf. Schachter v. Canada* [1992] 2 S.C.R. 679.

[73] See *Wenn v. Att.-Gen. of Victoria* (1948) 77 C.L.R. 84, esp. *per* Dixon J. at 122.

[74] *cf. Vriend v. Alberta* [1998] 1 S.C.R. 493. For discussion, see Childs, "Constitutional
Review and Underinclusive Legislation" [1998] P.L. 647.

PART III

THE SCOPE OF JUDICIAL REVIEW

CHAPTER 8

THE SCOPE OF THE SUPERVISORY JURISDICTION

I   FIRST PRINCIPLES
II   THE SUBJECT-MATTER OF REVIEW
III   REMEDIES AS A GUIDE TO THE SCOPE OF REVIEW
IV   ATTEMPTS AT DEFINING THE SCOPE OF JUDICIAL REVIEW
V   CRIMINAL CASES
VI   CONCLUSION

Introduction

Any discussion of the supervisory jurisdiction requires a detailed exam- **8.01** ination of its scope and application.[1] As the practice of judicial review has increased in recent years, problems associated with the definition of its scope have arisen. Unfortunately the law on the scope of judicial review has acquired some complexity in both Scotland and England.[2] But if the fundamental purpose of judicial review is kept to the fore, it may be possible to devise a means whereby a definition of the scope of judicial review can be formulated in a structured manner. As was observed in Chapter 1, the fundamental purpose of the supervisory jurisdiction is the supervision of the exercise of lawful authority[3] so as to ensure that it is being exercised lawfully and properly.

This part of the book discusses the issues which are relevant to the scope of judicial review. The present chapter introduces general issues about the scope and availability of judicial review and seeks to ascertain the basis on which the courts decide in what circumstances, about which matters and against which bodies and persons judicial review is available. After setting out the "first principles" in light of which the proper scope of judicial review must be understood, it discusses some of the approaches which courts have taken to the scope of judicial review. It concludes with an attempted formulation of the position regarding the scope of judicial review which provides the basis for the subsequent chapters. In order, these deal with certain jurisdictional limitations on judicial review—that is, institutions and subject-matters over which judicial review is necessarily restricted[4]; the matter of standing to seek judicial review—that is, the conditions which a particular petitioner must

---

[1] The *nobile officium* of the Court of Session in Scotland is not exhausted by judicial review but in modern times judicial review must be regarded as the most important expression of it. The relationship between the *nobile officium* and judicial review is discussed in Chap. 2.

[2] *cf.* de Smith, Woolf and Jowell, *Judicial Review of Administrative Action* (5th ed., 1995), Chap. 3, for the development of the law in England and lamenting that in this area "there has been so much uncertainty" (at p. 156).

[3] On a strict view of ordinary language the word "authority" may more accurately represent the *vires* the exercise of which is supervised by the supreme court than the word "power", which in ordinary usage may extend to an illegitimate ability to compel obedience or compliance. But the use of the latter word is so well established in legal terminology that it may be regarded as acceptable in the present context.

[4] Chap. 9.

317

satisfy to obtain judicial review[5]; the exclusion of judicial review—for example, by virtue of the operation of privative clauses[6] or alternative remedies[7]; and certain further restrictions on judicial review, such as the time within which judicial review must be sought.[8] Throughout the discussion, however, two matters should be recalled. First, judicial review is a residual remedy. It must not normally be regarded as a remedy of first resort but rather, if not always a remedy of last resort, at least an exceptional remedy.[9] Secondly, as has been noted earlier,[10] cases which raise issues corresponding to the grounds of judicial review will often arise in proceedings outwith the supervisory jurisdiction. For example, a challenge to the legality of an exercise of authority may arise indirectly, as where a person's defence rests on the invalidity of official actions. Alternatively, there will be cases with constitutional significance—for example, involving E.C. law, human rights or devolution points—which will come before the court otherwise than under the judicial review procedure. While the supervisory jurisdiction may be the venue for the most significant cases in which the legality of legislation and other measures is reviewed on these grounds, the scope for constitutional judicial review on E.C. law, human rights and devolution grounds extends beyond the supervisory jurisdiction.[11]

I FIRST PRINCIPLES

8.02 Any attempt to identify the appropriate scope of judicial review is assisted by restating its first principles. It is therefore necessary to begin by recalling the fundamental purpose of judicial review, namely the supervision of the exercise of legal powers to ensure that they are exercised lawfully and properly.

The basic principles of judicial review in Scotland were formulated by Lord President Hope in *West v. Secretary of State for Scotland*[12]:

> "1. The Court of Session has power, in the exercise of its supervisory jurisdiction, to regulate the process by which decisions are taken by any person or body to whom a jurisdiction, power or authority has been delegated or entrusted by statute, agreement or any other instrument.
>
> 2. The sole purpose for which the supervisory jurisdiction may be exercised is to ensure that the person or body does not exceed or

---

[5] Chap. 10.

[6] Chap. 11.

[7] Chap. 12.

[8] Chap. 13.

[9] *cf. R. v. IRC, ex p. Preston* [1985] A.C. 835 at 852, where Lord Scarman describes judicial review as a "collateral" challenge as opposed to a statutory appeal, which is a "direct" challenge. In this context, Lord Scarman may be using "collateral" for "residual": the case concerned the circumstances in which a statutory appeal on point of law is to be preferred to proceedings by way of judicial review. See also *Chief Adjudication Officer v. Foster* [1993] A.C. 754. The interrelationship of statutory appeals and judicial review has been considered in Chap. 1.

[10] para. 1.07.

[11] The scope of what may be termed constitutional review, that is, where E.C. law, Convention rights or devolution issues are involved, and in particular, where the validity of primary legislation is challenged on these grounds, is considered in Part II of this book.

[12] 1992 S.C. 385.

abuse that jurisdiction, power or authority or fail to do what the jurisdiction power or authority requires".[13]

By "regulate the process by which decisions are taken", the Lord President explains that judicial review is about ensuring that those vested with legal powers exercise them and do so properly, that is, in accordance with law.[14] The existence of this supervisory jurisdiction is a prerequisite for the rule of law, limited government and the protection of human rights.[15]

Breadth of the jurisdiction

Baron Hume[16] said of the Court's power that it: "is very extensive indeed, and almost universal, and such as entitles them, in one shape or another to take cognisance of many matters which, in the first instance, cannot competently be brought before them". While the jurisdiction is not universal it is right at the outset to recognise that it is very wide and thus able to deal with very many kinds of cases where no other remedy is available.[17] The fact that the jurisdiction was acknowledged in such wide terms so long ago indicates its essential nature. That, in Baron Hume's words, it can encompass matters "which, in the first instance, cannot competently be brought before them" invites the suggestion that it is a jurisdiction having fundamentally a constitutional nature, perhaps implying that it cannot be taken away.[18]

8.03

---

[13] *ibid*. at 412.

[14] And "law" means not only the particular law conferring the decision-making power but also the broader legal rules concerning the proper exercise of decision-making and discretionary powers—for example, the principles of fairness. The grounds of judicial review are discussed in Part IV. One problem with the Lord President's formulation is that it does not seem to include judicial review of the exercise of prerogative powers. It is clear, however, that prerogative powers are reviewable in Scotland in the same way as they are in England & Wales: see *McDonald v. Secretary of State for Scotland*, 1996 S.L.T. 16.

[15] The constitutional dimensions of judicial review are discussed in Chap. 4. In this regard, however, one criticism of Lord President Hope's formulation of the scope of judicial review by reference to "tripartite" relationships is that it is not readily amenable to include judicial review of the exercise of prerogative powers: see Finney, "Triangles as Touchstones of Review" 1993 S.L.T.(News) 51. But it is apparent that exercises of prerogative powers are reviewable in Scotland, probably to the same extent as in England and Wales: see *McDonald v. Secretary of State for Scotland*, 1996 S.L.T. 16.

[16] *Lectures*, Stair ed., Vol. V, p. 270.

[17] And occasionally also where another remedy is available but for some reason not equivalent, inappropriate—or ineffective. See Chap. 12.

[18] Compare recent views in England, particularly from Lord Woolf M.R. and Sir John Laws, that the courts might refuse to recognise primary legislation abrogating the High Court's judicial review jurisdiction: see Lord Woolf, "Droit Public–English Style" [1995] P.L. 57, esp. at 67 *et seq*.; and Laws, "Law and Democracy" [1995] P.L. 72, esp. at 81 *et seq*.; but *cf.* Lord Irvine of Lairg, "Judges and Decision-makers: the Theory and Practice of Wednesbury Review" [1996] P.L. 590, at 76 *et seq*. On the fundamental nature of judicial review where human rights are concerned, see also: Laws, "Is the High Court the Guardian of Our Fundamental Constitutional Rights?" [1993] P.L. 59; Lord Browne-Wilkinson, "The Infiltration of a Bill of Rights" [1992] P.L. 397; and Allan, "Pragmatism and Theory in Public Law" (1988) 104 L.Q.R. 422. Traces of the sentiment that the court's supervisory power is fundamental may be observed in *MacCormick v. Lord Advocate*, 1953 S.C. 396 (that in the event of a fundamental violation of the 1707 Act of Union, the Court of Session might of necessity have to assume the jurisdiction of the Scottish Privy Council (with arguable implications for subsequent U.K. legislation)). For an instance of the English court defending the fundamental constitutional right of access to the courts, see *R. v. The Lord Chancellor, ex p. Witham* [1998] Q.B. 575 (Regulations increasing court fees

Availability of judicial review

8.04   The Court of Session, as the Supreme Court in Scotland,[19] has an exclusive jurisdiction to exercise judicial review in civil matters.[20] At an introductory level, whether a claim falls within that jurisdiction is to be determined by a consideration of the issues which are raised by the claim. Both the nature of the claim and the kind of remedy sought may assist in determining if the claim is properly susceptible to judicial review, but, "the final answer is to be found in a proper understanding of what the action is truly about".[21] To qualify for judicial review, the action must at a minimum truly be about a challenge to the exercise of powers which affect the rights or interests or legitimate expectations of a person.[22] The supervisory jurisdiction is, as its name implies, directed at providing a remedy for the improper exercise of power.

Limitations on the supervisory jurisdiction

8.05   The inherent limitations on the *nobile officium* of the Court of Session which have already been discussed in Chapter 3 also apply to that expression of it which is the supervisory jurisdiction, in other words, judicial review. Accordingly, in general the supervisory jurisdiction may only be exercised where there is no other remedy available. Secondly, Parliament's intention clearly expressed in primary legislation that a particular act or decision should be final may operate to exclude judicial review. Thirdly, the issue may not be one which the court is competent to review, where, for example, the matter raised is too uncertain, or has

---

declared unlawful in so far as they failed to take into account the position of those who lacked means but who would not qualify for legal aid); *cf. R. v. The Lord Chancellor, ex p. Lightfoot* [1998] 4 All E.R. 764, esp. *per* Laws J. at 771–774. *cf. Raymond v. Honey* [1983] 1 A.C. 1; and *R. v. Secretary of State for the Home Department, ex parte Leech (No. 2)* [1994] Q.B. 198. Consider also *R. v. Secretary of State for Social Security, ex p. Joint Council for the Welfare of Immigrants* [1997] 1 W.L.R. 275 and the Asylum and Immigration Act 1996, s. 9 overturning this decision; for reaction thereto see *e.g. R. v. Secretary of State for the Environment, ex p. Shelter and the Refugee Council* [1997] C.O.D. 49; *R. v. Hammersmith and Fulham LBC, ex p. M* (1997) 9 Admin.L.R. 504; and *R. v. Newham LBC, ex p. Gorenkin* [1997] C.O.D. 391.

[19] But not Scotland's supreme court which, in civil matters, is the House of Lords in London and in criminal matters is the High Court of Justiciary. By virtue of the Scotland Act 1998, in relation to some constitutional questions—for example, the validity of Acts of the Scottish Parliament—the Judicial Committee of the Privy Council is Scotland's supreme court, and comprehensively so: that is, in all cases whether civil or criminal.

[20] *Brown v. Hamilton D.C.*, 1983 S.C. (H.L.) 1. For a discussion of this case and its background, see Judge Edward, "Administrative Law in Scotland: The public law/private law distinction revisited" in Curtin & O'Keefe (eds), *Constitutional Adjudication in European Community and National Law* (Butterworths, 1992), Chap. 25. On the Court of Session's jurisdiction to exercise judicial review, see also *McDonald v. Secretary of State for Scotland*, 1996 S.L.T. 16. As to criminal cases, see *Reynolds v. Christie*, 1988 S.L.T. 68 and *K v. Scottish Legal Aid Board*, 1989 S.L.T. 617, and para. 8.40 below. It should, however, be noted that not all cases raising what may be thought to be judicial review issues—*e.g.* liability of the Crown in delict and breach of statutory duty—need to be brought in the Court of Session. Actions against the Crown may be raised in the sheriff court, subject to the Crown's right to remove them to the Court of Session: Crown Proceedings Act 1947 (10 & 11 Geo. 6, c. 44), s. 44. In addition, issues which could form the substance of an application for judicial review may arise collaterally: see para. 1.07. For an example, see *Boddington v. British Transport Police* [1999] 2 A.C. 637.

[21] *McDonald v. Secretary of State for Scotland (No. 2)*, 1996 S.L.T. 575 at 578.

[22] But perhaps not necessarily the actual applicant. Standing to bring judicial review applications is discussed in Chap. 10.

been raised too early or too late. Any of these factors may defeat judicial review and they are separately discussed in the following chapters.[23] These limitations on the power of the court have a variety of justifications. For the present it is sufficient to note the need for the efficient conduct of government and administration. This requires that there be some finality to decision making, that a degree of certainty exists enabling persons to rely on decisions being valid, and that decision-makers are not harried at every turn by challenges to their powers. The desirability of ensuring absolutely against any unfairness has to be balanced against the practical requisite of efficient administration. A utilitarian approach to balancing respect for individual rights against society's interest in efficient government is unavoidable. But in considering the competency of an application for judicial review—that is, the availability of judicial review in the circumstances of a particular case— regard may have to be had to the merits of the case as well as to the court's powers. As Baron Hume observed: "Jurisdiction or competency of review is often involved in and blended with the question on the merits".[24]

Further limitations on judicial review

In addition to the limitations arising out of the *nobile officium*, judicial **8.06** review possesses its own limitations. Most significantly, in contrast with an appeal procedure, judicial review (at least when not on human rights grounds) is solely concerned with the legality of a decision and not the merits of the case. Moreover, judicial review is limited in respect of the grounds on which it may be invoked.[25] And the supervisory jurisdiction of the Court of Session is limited territorially to Scotland, although difficult questions may arise about bodies which are not domiciled in Scotland and not part of the Crown but which exercise functions which have effects in Scotland.[26] The question arises, however, of whether there are further limitations on the exercise of judicial review. In particular, it may be asked how it is determined that cases are included within or excluded from the judicial review procedure and on what basis. This invites a consideration of the attempts to find some comprehensive definition of the category of cases over which the supervisory jurisdiction extends and whether there is any prospect of success in formulating a single comprehensive test.

---

[23] See Chap. 11 on exclusion clauses, Chap. 12 on alternative remedies, and Chap. 13 on the necessity for a real issue timeously raised.

[24] *Lectures*, Stair ed., Vol. V, p. 273.

[25] The grounds of judicial review are discussed in Part IV. But it may be noted here that the grounds of judicial review, unlike the categories of negligence, are not closed. There is great scope for their judicial development, reflecting the fact that they are not codified and are the result of common law development. Indeed, in the last 30 years the grounds of judicial review have expanded significantly and several newer grounds have appeared, not least human rights, protection of legitimate expectations and also proportionality.

[26] *cf. Bank of Scotland v. IMRO*, 1989 S.C. 107. Where a body is a tribunal in terms of the Civil Jurisdiction and Judgment Act 1982, the Court of Session's jurisdiction over the body is determined according to the common law (that is, jurisdiction exists if the tribunal is situated in Scotland). In other cases, the 1982 Act will apply. While the Act expressly provides (in s. 46) for the Crown to be treated as domiciled everywhere in the U.K. in respect of bodies not part of the Crown it may be necessary to establish jurisdiction by reference to the domicile or residence of the body or the locus of the wrong complained about. In addition, the plea of *forum non conveniens* may be made by a respondent otherwise subject to judicial review in the Court of Session. See also para. 23.07.

The relevance of the problem

8.07 It must be noticed that the question about the proper scope of judicial review should be one of procedural rather than substantive importance. The question whether or not a case falls within the scope of the supervisory jurisdiction relates only to the procedure to be followed in obtaining a remedy. Cases which are not amenable to judicial review may not necessarily go without a remedy. It is after all only the absence of another remedy which in general occasions recourse to the supervisory jurisdiction on the general principle recognised in all developed legal systems that no wrong should be without a remedy.[27] The question of the scope of judicial review should only be about determining whether a case falls within the scope of the procedural rule which prescribes the special procedure for cases of judicial review.[28] If the supervisory jurisdiction is defined so as to exclude certain types of case, in Scotland at least this should only mean that a remedy must be sought by the other forms of process, such as an ordinary action for reduction, declarator or interdict. While it may be convenient to use a single concept or label to identify the cases which may fall within the scope of judicial review, if such a course is to be adopted the concept or label must be chosen carefully and its significance must be fully appreciated, lest its substantive meaning in ordinary usage be taken unduly to circumscribe the limits of the supervisory jurisdiction. The experience in England throughout the development of judicial review warns against procedural terms and devices being allowed to dominate and overshadow the substance and purpose of judicial review. In this area more than most, procedure should not always be master.

II THE SUBJECT-MATTER OF REVIEW

Acts, failures to act and decisions

8.08 The next chapter discusses some particular limitations on the scope of judicial review in respect of its subject-matter. At this stage it may be noted that judicial review is available against both action and inaction.[29] A failure to perform a statutory duty or to do what ought to be done may be open to judicial review as much as a positive action. Most applications for judicial review in essence concern a decision taken by the individual or body against which the complaint is being made. For most purposes, therefore, judicial review is directed primarily at a decision rather than an act, although acts usually proceed upon decisions. However, there may be cases where judicial review is available absent any particular decision.[30] Often the matter is related to the

---

[27] Albeit that in a democratic society it must be accepted that the proper remedy will sometimes be political rather than one which the courts can grant.

[28] In Scotland, this is Chap. 58 of the Rules of Court.

[29] In this regard, compare Arts 230 and 232 of the E.C. Treaty, which give the ECJ (and the Court of First Instance) jurisdiction over cases against an E.U. institution based on its illegal actions (on the grounds specified in Article 230) or on its failure to act (for example, the European Commission's failure to act). The ECJ's jurisdiction in this regard is noted at para. 5–70.

[30] For example, where it might be possible to obtain an advisory declarator. Departmental circulars have also been subject to judicial review, arguably in circumstances that did not pose a live controversy: see *Gillick v. West Norfolk and Wisbech Area Health Authority* [1986] A.C. 112. But, as in *Gillick*, there should at least be a foreseeably live issue.

remedies available.[31] For example, interdict cannot be granted against a decision after it has been made but can be brought to stop the action following upon it—that is, to stop the decision being implemented.

Legality and substance in judicial review

It has already been noted that judicial review is classically concerned **8.09** with matters of legality and not with matters of substance.[32] It has long been recognised that the court must be careful to see that it does not intrude into areas where the discretion of the decision maker must be respected.[33] Where Parliament has conferred decision-making powers on a person, it has often been said that it is for the decision maker and not the courts to make the decision. The court's role in a judicial review case is to ensure that the decision is made lawfully and properly. In this regard, judicial review is often and necessarily distinguished from appeal.[34] Fundamental to the distinction between appeal and review is that in the latter: "it is not competent for the court to review the act or decision on its merits, nor may it substitute its own opinion for that of the person or body to whom the matter has been delegated or entrusted".[35] In the High Court of Australia, Mason J. summed up the position as follows:

"The limited role of a court reviewing the exercise of an administrative discretion must constantly be borne in mind. It is not the

---

[31] See Cane, *An Introduction to Administrative Law* (3rd ed., Clarendon Press, Oxford, 1996), at p. 23.

[32] At least in the U.K. see para. 1.04 above. This should be contrasted with the position in other systems. For example, in Germany, the federal administrative court (Bundesverwaltungsgericht) will exercise "review" of the merits of a challenged decision. Indeed, the fact that review of the merits takes place means that the court may in effect order what the right decision should be. This approach can mean that the court will consider any procedural irregularities in reaching the challenged decision as being remedied by its own review of the matter. For a discussion of administrative law in Germany and comparison with the powers of the ECJ, see Nolte, "General Principles of German and European Administrative Law—A Comparison in Historical Perspective" (1994) 57 M.L.R. 191. In common law systems, however, the merits of a decision are traditionally regarded as being beyond the purview of judicial review. But in Australia, Commonwealth law contains the Administrative Appeals Tribunal Act 1975 which establishes the Administrative Appeals Tribunal (AAT) and empowers it to review various administrative decisions on the merits. The AAT does not, however, have a general jurisdiction, its powers extending only to those decisions which statutes make subject to review by the AAT. AAT decisions themselves may be appealed to the Australian Federal Court but only on points of law, so that as far as the courts are concerned, merits review stops at the AAT. To some extent, the AAT is a general administrative tribunal which performs a role similar to that performed in the U.K. by various special tribunals. The creation of a general administrative tribunal was considered but rejected by the Justice—All Souls Report on Administrative Law (1988) at para. 9.77. Nevertheless, an interesting question remains about whether the traditional absence of merits review in an application for judicial review complies with Art. 6 of the European Convention on Human Rights (now made directly accessible in U.K. courts under the Human Rights Act 1998): *cf. Soering v. U.K.* (1989) 11 E.H.R.R. 439 and *Vilvarajah* (1992) 14 E.H.R.R. 248. See now *Lustig-Prean and Becket v. U.K., The Times,* October 11, 1999, unreported.

[33] *Guthrie v. Miller* (1827) 5S. 711.

[34] See *Chief Constable of North Wales Police v. Evans* [1982] 1 W.L.R. 1155, *per* Lord Brightman at 1173. See also *R. v. Entry Clearance Officer, ex p. Amin* [1983] 2 A.C. 818, *per* Lord Fraser at 829. The distinction is maintained elsewhere. See, for example, *Fraser v. State Services Commission* [1984] 1 N.Z.L.R. 116 (NZCA) and *Minister for Aboriginal Affairs v. Peko-Wallsend Ltd* (1986) 162 C.L.R. 24 (HCA).

[35] *West v. Secretary of State for Scotland,* 1992 S.C. 385, *per* Lord President Hope at 413.

function of the court to substitute its own decision for that of the administrator by exercising a discretion which the legislature has vested in the administrator. Its role is to set limits on the exercise of that discretion, and a decision made within those boundaries cannot be impugned."[36]

It was recognised at an early stage that where an inferior body has acted properly within the scope of its powers under the relevant statute the court may not intervene.[37] In *West v. Secretary of State for Scotland*,[38] a survey of the earlier cases demonstrated very clearly the consistent recognition of the power of the court to intervene only where inferior bodies had "been guilty of an excess of their jurisdiction, or have acted inconsistently with the authority with which they were invested".[39] There was no power in the court to intervene in the merits of the matter. In particular, in relation to discretionary decisions the court cannot interfere with the decision where it has been lawfully and properly reached.[40] As Lord Ackner observed in *R. v. Secretary of State for the Home Department, ex parte Brind*[41]: "Where Parliament has given to a minister or other person or body a discretion, the court's jurisdiction is limited, in the absence of a statutory right of appeal, to the supervision of the exercise of that discretionary power, so as to ensure that it has been exercised lawfully. It would be a wrongful usurpation of power by the judiciary to substitute its, the judicial view, on the merits and on that basis to quash the decision."[42]

In some cases, however, the distinction between the legality and the substance of a decision may become apparently fine. Four particular matters may be mentioned to illustrate how delicate the distinction can come to be. These are proportionality, irrationality and error as grounds of judicial review, and fourthly, the remedies available in judicial review.

Proportionality

8.10   Where an act or decision is challenged on the ground of proportionality, the merits of the case are unavoidably in question. Proportionality will often be an issue in cases presenting E.C. law issues and the human rights guaranteed by the Human Rights Act 1998. Where a case concerns an alleged breach of a guaranteed Convention right, the justification of any limit on the right entails the application of a test of proportionality.[43] That test requires the court to balance the means and ends involved in a decision in order to evaluate them for consistency with guaranteed Convention rights. The protection of human rights

---

[36] *Minister for Aboriginal Affairs v. Peko-Wallsend Ltd* (1986) 162 C.L.R. 24, at 40–41.

[37] *Dubs v. Police Commissioners of Crosshill* (1876) 3R. 758. For various statements of the grounds on which the court may intervene in exercise of its power of review, see Chap. 13.

[38] 1992 S.C. 385 at 395 *et seq.*

[39] Lord Chancellor Lyndhurst in *Campbell v.* Jones (1829) 3 W. & S. 441 at 448.

[40] See, for example, *Stewart v. Monklands D.C.*, 1987 S.L.T. 630.

[41] [1991] 1 A.C. 696.

[42] *ibid.* at 757. See also Lord Lowry at 765. For another affirmation of the impropriety of entering upon the merits of the decision, see *McDonald v. Secretary of State for Scotland*, 1996 S.L.T. 16.

[43] This holds whether the challenge is under s. 4 of the Human Rights Act 1998 in respect of an incompatibility of primary legislation with a Convention right or under ss. 6 and 7 of the Act in respect of an unlawful act of a public authority.

standards by the courts therefore makes some assessment of the merits of a challenged decision unavoidable.[44] Furthermore, even beyond the areas of human rights and E.C. law, proportionality may come to be more widely recognised and applied as a ground of judicial review.[45]

Irrationality

Beyond guaranteed Convention rights, it is clear that some of the **8.11** grounds of judicial review involve consideration of the reasons for a decision and it may be that this leads to a blurring of the borderline between appeal and review. In considering the legality or irrationality of a decision courts have not always abstained from entering into matters which might be seen as the merits of the case.[46] Judges have occasionally acknowledged that some of the grounds of review entail examining the merits of a decision. Lord Cooke of Thorndon once observed about one New Zealand Court of Appeal decision that: "The merits of the appellant's case and the grounds on which the Minister had dismissed her appeal . . . were seen as relevant in determining whether he had acted reasonably".[47]

While the irrationality of a discretionary decision is a ground of judicial review, describing the decision as irrational or unreasonable should be a comment on its legality or propriety and not its substance, which is for the decision maker. This ground of review has a residual quality about it, with a decision that risks being termed irrational usually having some other, narrower failure pointing to its unlawfulness.[48] As far as the scope of judicial review is concerned, although in the case of some grounds of review there are delicate boundaries to be drawn between the substance and the legality of the decision, the general principle holds firm; judicial review must focus on the legality and propriety of decisions, not on their merits.

---

[44] The implications for judicial review of the Human Rights Act 1998 are examined in Chap. 6 and the rights themselves are briefly discussed in Chap. 16. Legislation passed by both the U.K. and the Scottish Parliaments is challengeable in U.K. courts for inconsistency with guaranteed Convention rights; but whereas the remedy against incompatible U.K. primary legislation is initially a declaration of incompatibility, provisions in Acts of the Scottish Parliament found to be incompatible with Convention rights are "not law" and may be invalidated by the courts where the challenge is upheld. In such a case, therefore, the court is directly involved in measuring the choices made by an elected legislature against the values of human rights. See further paras 6–34 and 7–33.

[45] See Chap. 21. *cf.* The Rt Hon. The Lord Hoffmann, "A Sense of Proportion" in Andenas and Jacobs (eds), *European Community Law in the English Courts* (OUP, Oxford, 1998), Chap. 10.

[46] The often-quoted example is *Roberts v. Hopwood* [1925] A.C. 578, where Poplar Council's decision to pay low grade workers £4 per week under powers to pay such wages "as it thought fit" was held unlawful because the wages were deemed excessive. The statutory power had been used for a social purpose, condemned as inspired by "principles of socialist philanthropy", and the Council had failed to consider (and balance) its fiduciary obligations to the ratepayers. In a broad sense the Council had acted "unreasonably". For a similar controversy, see *Bromley LBC v. GLC* [1983] 1 A.C. 768 and compare *R. v. London Transport Executive, ex p. GLC* [1983] Q.B. 484. See further Chap. 21.

[47] Sir Robin Cooke, in Taggart (ed.), *Judicial Review of Administrative Action in the 1980s* (1986) at p. 10, commenting on *Daganayasi v. Minister of Immigration* [1980] 2 N.Z.L.R. 130 (NZCA) on which he sat.

[48] Indeed, according to Lord Greene M.R.'s formulation of the grounds of review of discretionary decisions, unreasonableness may be a residual ground: *Associated Provincial Picture Houses Ltd v. Wednesbury Corporation* [1948] 1 K.B. 223.

Error

8.12 As a ground of judicial review, some aspects of error present similar difficulties for the scope of review to those presented by irrationality.[49] As with irrationality, error as a ground of judicial review has the potential to address the actual decision reached. The extent to which a decision-maker acting "within jurisdiction" has "the power to go right and wrong" is one of the most difficult questions in a system of judicial review limited to ensuring legality and propriety in decision-making.[50] While it is attractive to say that the court's power of intervention is limited to errors which are classified as "jurisdictional" as opposed to "non-jurisdictional", case law reveals the complexity of the matter. This suggests that a more careful approach is required, for example, one which entails different thresholds for intervention, in other words, degrees of deference, depending on the type of decision-maker and the nature of the decision reviewed.[51]

Remedies

8.13 The limitation on the supervisory jurisdiction which restrains it from trespassing into the substance of a decision is the nature of the remedy available if the application for review is successful. In such a case, the court will not substitute its decision for that of the decision-maker but will reduce the challenged decision or will declare it invalid or order it not to be implemented. The matter will then be left to the decision-maker to reach a decision lawfully and properly. In this regard, the problem of the court entering upon the merits when supposedly exercising a limited review jurisdiction is not new. For example, in the context of the poor law in the middle of the nineteenth century the Court of Session sometimes took the view, albeit with a strong dissent from the minority, that they could pass judgment on the inadequacy of the quantum of a provision of aliment.[52] Such an approach might now perhaps be justified on the basis that the decision had been irrational. Even so, the court would not usually suggest what the proper solution to the case should be. The better (and older) view was that while the Court of Session could entertain a review on a question of the entitlement to parochial relief, the case should be remitted to the kirk session to adjust the quantum of aliment.[53] It is now well established that as regards the merits of a decision, the accepted course is to remit the matter back to

---

[49] Indeed, in the United States, references to the scope of judicial review in the context of administrative law generally concern the extent of the power of the court to review decisions for error: see Schwartz, *Administrative Law* (3rd ed., Little Brown, 1991), Chap. 10.

[50] In the U.K., the modern problems stem from the approach taken to the landmark House of Lords decision in *Anisminic v. Foreign Compensation Commission* [1947] 2 A.C. 147. In this case, Lord Reid draws a distinction between reviewable errors of law which cause a decision-maker to act without jurisdiction and non-reviewable errors of law which are made "within" jurisdiction. But the problem of distinguishing the different types of error of law, often associated with confusion about what is meant by "jurisdiction", has caused difficulty in several jurisdictions, including Scotland; and the trend in English law has been to abolish the distinction so as to make all errors of law reviewable, at least where they are made by a decision-maker which is not a court (and more arguably also not a tribunal). See further Chap. 22.

[51] See further para. 22–24.

[52] *Pryde v. Heritors and Kirk Session of Ceres* (1843) 5D. 552; *Halliday v. Balmaclellan Heritors* (1844) 6D. 1131.

[53] *Higgins v. Kirk Session of the Barony Parish of Glasgow* (1824) 3S. 168.

the empowered authority so that with the benefit of the guidance given by the court it can exercise its powers as it considers appropriate in accordance with the guidance.[54] The court will not itself in the ordinary case substitute a decision for one that it has found to be invalid. Thus, for example, it cannot usurp the functions of a discretionary authority by granting or renewing licences, instead leaving this to the authority which alone has the statutory power to do so.[55] Where a licensing decision has been successfully challenged, the court will quash the decision but will not grant a new licence since it has no power to do so.[56]

The flexibility and discretionary nature of remedies in judicial review allows the court to select the most appropriate remedy in light of all the circumstances. Rendering an impugned decision invalid is not the only option. So, again in the licensing context, the court can issue an order to the clerk of the licensing authority requiring corrections to a licence where an invalidity in a particular condition is identified.[57] In this way, the unlawful parts of the decision can be severed from the lawful parts, as long as severance does not result in a decision different in substance from that which the decision maker reached or had power to reach.[58]

III   REMEDIES AS A GUIDE TO THE SCOPE OF REVIEW

The nature of the remedy

It might be suggested that the particular remedy sought by an applicant **8.14** for judicial review may provide a proper basis for determining the availability of judicial review. But this approach to defining the scope of judicial review raises some difficulty. The remedies available in judicial review in Scotland are the nearly all the same civil remedies that are available generally in the Court of Session.[59] Scots law has never had special remedies peculiar to the supervisory jurisdiction, such as the prerogative orders in England & Wales, nor the specialised "Crown side proceedings" in the High Court in which key parts of what we now call judicial review took place. So the remedies sought in judicial review, including the most usual, declarator and reduction, are also available for cases outwith the scope of the supervisory jurisdiction. Two observations may then be made. The remedy of reduction may be sought in judicial review to quash a challenged decision; but simply because a reduction is being sought does not mean that the supervisory jurisdiction must be invoked.[60] Secondly, and correspondingly, the nature of the remedy sought does not indicate when it is appropriate to invoke the supervisory jurisdiction. This is a critical point since the Rules of the Court of Session provide that the application for judicial review procedure is exclusive: for example, where interdict is sought an ordinary action is incompetent if the case is truly one falling under the supervisory

---

[54] See, for example, *North-Eastern Ry v. North British Ry* (1897) 25 R. 333. See also in relation to reduction, para. 24.30: "Remit".

[55] See, for example, *Baillie v. Wilson*, 1917 S.C. 55.

[56] *Baillie v. Wilson*, 1917 S.C. 55.

[57] *Macbeth v. Ashley* (1874) 1R (H.L.) 14.

[58] On the remedy of severence, see *DPP v. Hutchinson* [1990] 2 A.C. 783, discussed in Lewis, *Judicial Remedies* (1992) at pp. 137–143.

[59] An exception is the statutory order for performance discussed in part II of Chap. 26.

[60] See *Bell v. Fiddes*, 1996 S.L.T. 51.

jurisdiction.[61] Equally, in a case properly for judicial review it should not be competent to seek interdict in the sheriff court—even if this has not always been recognised in practice.[62]

A problem may be thought to arise where all that is sought is an award of damages in an action against a public authority involving its *ultra vires* acts. Notwithstanding the exclusivity of the judicial review procedure, is it competent to proceed by way of an ordinary action to claim damages in such a case even though the substance of the matter could fall under the supervisory jurisdiction? It might be argued that the issue which is an essential ingredient for such a claim for damages, namely the legality of the act or omission by the public authority, is a matter to be determined by the supervisory jurisdiction. Rule of Court 58.4 expressly mentions damages as being among the remedies available in petitions for judicial review. So it might be suggested that all claims for damages against a public authority resting on their *ultra vires* acts must be made in a petition for judicial review.

It is thought, however, that the Rule of Court has no such intention. The power given in Rule 58.4 is simply for the convenience and economy where there is another principal remedy sought and an award of damages is an appropriate ancillary remedy. Even if the claim arises from an acting in excess of power which has to be established as part of the ingredients of the claim for damages, it is not appropriate to proceed by way of judicial review if the essence of the action is one of a claim for damages.[63] What is being exercised in such a case is the ordinary jurisdiction of the court to give a remedy by way of damages for the consequences of a wrongful act.[64] In substance the supervisory jurisdiction seeks to control the actings of public bodies. It is not primarily directed at providing compensatory remedies for their illegal behaviour, even although damages can incidentally be awarded. Thus where a petitioner had set out to seek a reduction but subsequently limited his claim to the remedies of declarator and damages, the court held that the case was still properly one for judicial review.[65] But where the only or the principal remedy sought was one of damages for negligence, the court decided that the matter should be pursued by way of an ordinary action for damages, not by a petition for judicial review.[66]

The problem of the remedy of damages exemplifies that the nature of the remedy is an unsure guide to the scope of judicial review.[67] In Scotland, the remedies available in judicial review are the same as those available in ordinary actions. The exclusivity of the judicial review procedure requires that the scope of judicial review is determined by

---

[61] See *Sleigh v. Edinburgh D.C.*, 1988 S.L.T. 253.

[62] See *McGowan v. City of Glasgow Friendly Society*, 1913 S.C. 991 and Lord Dunpark's comment thereon in *Brown v. Hamilton D.C.*, 1983 S.C.(H.L.) 1 at 28. See also the doubts expressed in *Bell v. The Trustees*, 1975 S.L.T. (Sh.Ct) 60.

[63] See, for example, *Tait v. Central Radio Taxis* (Tollcross) Ltd, 1989 S.L.T. 217.

[64] The case of *Gray v. Smart* (1892) 19 R. 692, where the pursuer sought damages for a breach of the statutory procedure for a sale under warrant as well as a reduction of the sale which had already taken place should probably be regarded as an ordinary action, not a case of judicial review.

[65] *Joobeen v. University of Stirling*, 1995 S.L.T. 120.

[66] *Shetland (1994) Ltd v. Secretary of State for Scotland*, 1996 S.L.T. 653 at 658.

[67] Equally, under the Human Rights Act 1998 damages is one of the remedies available for violation of Convention rights. Enforcement of Convention rights is not restricted to applications for judicial review so that simply because a human rights claim is involved does not mean that judicial review must be sought.

more than the type of remedy claimed. The choice of the precise remedy is no complete or conclusive ground for determining the scope of the supervisory jurisdiction.

The sheriff court and judicial review

As has already been noted, the remedy of judicial review is exclusive to **8.15** the Court of Session.[68] Accordingly, remedies that are available in the Court of Session and sheriff court—namely declarator, interdict and damages—will not be competent in the sheriff court if the matter is properly for judicial review.[69] However, the illegality of acts otherwise subject to judicial review may still come before the sheriff court, where, for example, a person seeks damages for a loss caused by an act of an authority beyond its powers. In the course of such a case the sheriff may have to decide whether the authority has acted unlawfully as a preliminary to giving a remedy in damages. This is an example of judicial review issues arising collaterally—that is, outside the judicial review procedure in the course of an ordinary action. Undoubtedly it is competent for the sheriff to rule on the *ultra vires* acts of a public authority in order to dispose of the action before the sheriff court. But in doing so, the sheriff is not exercising a power of review. The sheriff cannot instruct the decision maker on what the law requires, quash decisions which it has made, or stop it from taking steps beyond its powers. These remedial actions are exclusively for the Court of Session in the exercise of its supervisory jurisdiction in judicial review. While interdict and implement are within the remedies generally available in the sheriff court, they cannot be granted there if the substance of the case in which they are sought falls within the scope of the supervisory jurisdiction.[70] Further, it is not possible to confer jurisdiction on the sheriff by seeking a remedy that the sheriff court is competent to grant together with one that it is not. So if damages and reduction of a decision are sought, the proceedings must be brought in the Court of Session and where appropriate, by means of judicial review. It is thought that the permitting of reduction *ope exceptionis* in the sheriff court is a matter of procedural convenience and does not touch on the issue of jurisdiction, so that the availability of that procedure does not enable the sheriff to exercise a supervisory power nor affect the exclusive jurisdiction of the Court of Session on matters of judicial review.[71]

Questions of *vires* outwith review proceedings: collateral attack

As has been noticed earlier,[72] cases concerning the *vires* of a decision **8.16** maker may arise in proceedings outwith judicial review. The case of the ordinary action in the sheriff court for damages based on an unlawful act has just been mentioned. Another situation is where an accused person

---

[68] *Brown v. Hamilton D.C.*, 1983 S.C.(H.L.) 1. See *McDonald v. Secretary of State for Scotland (No. 2)*, 1996 S.L.T. 575. See para. 1.07.

[69] This has not always been observed in practice: for example, in *Shearer v. Hamilton* (1871) 9M. 456 an interdict was allowed in the sheriff court in a case of an alleged procedural failure.

[70] *Brown v. Hamilton D.C.*, 1983 S.C.(H.L.) 1.

[71] See *Dickson v. Murray* (1866) 4M. 797; *Donald v. Donald*, 1913 S.C. 274 at 278; *Docherty v. Norwich Union Fire Insurance Society*, 1974 S.C. 213 at 219.

[72] para. 8.01.

by way of a defence to a prosecution in the criminal courts argues that the law or decision under which he is being prosecuted is *ultra vires*.[73] That an act or decision is *ultra vires* has always been available as a defence in civil and criminal proceedings. Critically, however, in such proceedings the court does not quash the act or decision if it finds it *ultra vires*; this power is exclusively possessed by the Court of Session in the exercise of its supervisory jurisdiction.

The position is similar in England.[74] Immediately following the House of Lords' decision in *O'Reilly v. Mackman*,[75] which established the exclusivity of the English judicial review procedure where decisions are challenged on "public law" grounds, some uncertainty surrounded the circumstances in which a public authority's decision could be questioned outside judicial review proceedings.[76] The point is obviously of some importance. Does the exclusivity of the judicial review procedure provided under section 31 of the Supreme Court Act 1981 mean that all "public law" challenges to decisions must be made by way of judicial review? If so, a person who is sued in ordinary proceedings—for example, for a debt—cannot raise the legality of the circumstances of the debt, such as an *ultra vires* act or decision of the (public) creditor. The proper course might be for the court to sist the debt proceedings while the debtor takes the public law matters on judicial review, assuming that this is still possible.[77] The safeguards built into the judicial review procedure to protect public bodies from extravagant challenge to their powers (for example, the need for leave and the strict three-month time-limit) could be circumvented by the plaintiff's delays or freedom to choose the procedure. In *Cocks v. Thanet District Council*,[78] the House of Lords emphasised the exclusivity of judicial review by deciding that the plaintiff's ordinary action for a declaration and damages against the Council for alleged breach of its duties under the Housing (Homeless

---

[73] See the cases noted in para. 1.08.

[74] *cf. Wandsworth B.C. v. Winder* [1985] A.C. 461; and *Boddington v. British Transport Police* [1999] 2 A.C. 637.

[75] [1983] 2 A.C. 237.

[76] Before the procedural reforms introduced by Order 53 in 1977 and s. 31 of the Supreme Court Act 1981, there was no procedural obstacle to collateral attacks against decisions on "public law" grounds. Meanwhile, direct attacks on those decisions could be made either by seeking one of the prerogative orders (*e.g. R. v. Criminal Injuries Compensation Board, ex p. Lain* [1967] 2 Q.B. 864) or by raising an action for a declaration or injunction (*e.g. Ridge v. Baldwin* [1964] A.C. 40; and *Anisminic v. Foreign Compensation Commission* [1969] 2 A.C. 147). For a survey of the law before Order 53 came into effect in 1977, see the Law Commission's Report on Remedies in *Administrative Law*, Report No. 73 Cmnd. 6407 (1976), pp. 5–16. For the Law Commission's latest view of the law, see *Administrative Law: Judicial Review and Statutory Appeals*, Report No. 226 (1994), pp. 19–28.

[77] It may not be, since in England leave of the High Court must be obtained to bring an application for judicial review and there is a strict three-month time limit within which leave must be sought. For discussion on the Application for Judicial Review procedure in England & Wales, see Lewis, *Judicial Remedies in Public Law* (Sweet & Maxwell, London, 1992). There is also the danger of injustice to a plaintiff who is told to start again (if this is still possible) and bring the claim in a different type of proceedings since the proceedings chosen are inappropriate for the claim. But the House of Lords has been sensitive to this problem and stressed that the overriding concern of the court should be to avoid abuse of process: see *Mercury Communications Ltd v. Director General of Telecommunications* [1996] 1 W.L.R. 48. The problem will be removed following Lord Woolf's proposals in the English civil justice reforms that cases can transfer into and out of the application for judicial review procedure: see *Access to Justice Final Report* (1996), Chap. 18, paras 26 and 27.

[78] [1983] 2 A.C. 286 (decided on the same day as *O'Reilly v. Mackman*).

Persons) Act 1977 should have been brought in judicial review. Any private law right the plaintiff claimed depended first on establishing the *ultra vires* character of the Council's decision, which was a question solely for the judicial review procedure. In *Davey v. Spelthorne Borough Council*,[79] however, the plaintiff's damages action against the Council claiming that advice received by him from the Council had been negligent and therefore rendered an agreement between them based on the advice *ultra vires*, did not need to be brought by way of judicial review. The case was essentially a tort action, there was no "live issue" of public law raised and therefore the Council did not need the protections which the judicial review procedure afforded public bodies.

Several House of Lords decisions have had to explore the problem of indirect or collateral attack on public bodies' decisions. Most recently, in *Boddington v. British Transport Police*,[80] the House of Lords held that a person accused of a crime can plead as a defence to the charge any illegality in the act or decision, for example, a byelaw, on which the prosecution is based.[81] Similarly, in *Wandsworth London Borough Council v. Winder*,[82] the House of Lords held that procedural exclusivity for judicial review does not preclude a defendant sued by a public authority from challenging the legality of the authority's decisions by way of defence. Whereas in *Cocks* the plaintiff was bringing the public law points outside the judicial review procedure, in *Winder* the defendant was raising the points as a defence in an action raised against him by the Council. Furthermore, in *Roy v. Kensington and Chelsea and Westminster Family Practitioner Committee*,[83] the House of Lords effectively restricted the exclusivity rule established in *O'Reilly v. Mackman* to cases in which private rights are not in issue. So a doctor did not have to proceed by way of judicial review against his public employer even where the relevant "private rights" basically arose out of statutory provisions in a case against a public body.[84] But it is clear that the existence of "private rights" can prevent an applicant from obtaining judicial review. In *R. v. Secretary of State for Employment, ex parte EOC*,[85] the House of Lords held that an individual cannot seek judicial review against the Secretary of State on the basis of rights arising under an E.C. directive as against a private employer.[86]

So, too, in Scotland, the exclusivity of the judicial review procedure does not preclude judicial review issues arising outside judicial review. Where the substance of the action is a private right or the issue is raised as a properly pleaded defence, the exclusivity of judicial review is not a

---

[79] [1984] A.C. 262.

[80] [1998] 2 W.L.R. 639.

[81] The opportunity to do so will, however, always depend on the provisions in the relevant primary legislation. The House of Lords decision in *R. v. Wicks* [1998] A.C. 92 shows that there will be instances in which legislation prevents certain legality issues being taken later if they were not pursued in judicial review proceedings or under the statutory appeal scheme provided. For criticism of this decision, see Bradley, "Collateral challenge to enforcement decisions—a duty to apply for judicial review?" [1997] P.L. 365. Under the Human Rights Act 1998, it is likely that some of these issues may have to be considered in light of guaranteed Convention rights, in particular, the right in Art. 6 to a fair trial.

[82] [1985] A.C. 461.

[83] [1992] 1 A.C. 624.

[84] *cf. Watt v. Strathclyde Regional Council*, 1992 S.L.T. 324.

[85] [1995] 1 A.C. 1.

[86] See also *R. v. Secretary of State for Employment, ex parte Seymour-Smith* [1997] 1 W.L.R. 473.

ground for insisting that questions as to the legality of a decision maker's decision only be raised in judicial review. The exclusivity of the judicial review procedure relates to the power of the court and to the effect of the remedy which can be obtained. It affects neither the power of the court to exercise its ordinary jurisdiction in an ordinary action nor its power to hear a properly pleaded defence to a claim (or in the case of a criminal court, a criminal prosecution). It might perhaps be argued in light of the nature of judicial remedies in Scotland that the exclusivity of the judicial review procedure is unnecessarily troublesome and might be reconsidered. But the historical and theoretical considerations which reserve the supervisory jurisdiction to a supreme court, together with the practical advantages of a centralised adjudication in matters of validity of acts and decisions often of general application, may well be thought sufficient to justify exclusivity for the judicial review procedure.[87]

IV ATTEMPTS AT DEFINING THE SCOPE OF JUDICIAL REVIEW

Legal classifications

8.17 It is convenient for the purposes of studying and practising law to attempt some division of the subject into compartments. Hence, for example, the terms public law, private law, criminal law, international law and administrative law are found on the syllabus of law faculties and among the specialisms of lawyers. However, the separation of areas of law into compartments does not alter the reality that the law is a system and that the compartments frequently overlap. The law has the potential of extending over the whole range of human activity and the same activity may attract more than one area of the law.[88]

Civil and common law systems

8.18 Although classification is endemic, the labels attributed to the law's compartments tend to be imprecise. As new specialisations arise and new areas of law are developed, compartmentalisation increases and the preservation of a coherent system becomes more difficult. Maintaining a sense of the law's system—or the process of systematisation—is apparently more of a problem in common law systems than civil law systems.[89]

---

[87] It may be noted that in other jurisdictions, the problem of a distinct procedure for judicial review has caused some difficulty. In Australia and New Zealand, for example, the procedural reforms which introduced a judicial review procedure (in Australia, the Administrative Decisions (Judicial Review) Act 1977 and in New Zealand, the Judicature Amendment Act 1972) made judicial review available only in regard to "statutory powers of decision". Accordingly, the courts had to determine what was meant by this restriction. But in both countries, the judicial review procedure was not exclusive but complementary to the prerogative orders, which remain available to review other powers of decision, for example, those arising under prerogative powers.

[88] So in international private law, for example, the problem of characterisation is well known: in order to decide what the appropriate choice of law rules for a given matter are to be, the court must first decide what area of law the issue before it falls into. In the famous example, succession of a widow to her late husband's property can be regarded simultaneously as a matter for family law or for the law of property, both of which have different choice of law rules. Accordingly, the court must characterise the issue as relating to one or another area of law so as to determine the appropriate choice of law rule.

[89] At least from the difficulties it has had and is likely to continue having with defining the scope of judicial review, Scots law must for present purposes be counted among the common law systems.

There are many reasons for this but space prevents them being explored in detail here.[90] Among the reasons must be that in civil law systems scholars (and legislators) had a much greater influence on the law's development: "So Common Law comes from the court, Continental law from the study."[91] In any event, the civil law systems are certainly more accustomed to the classification of legal rules and remedies according to their relating to private law and public law.[92] In the classical civil law system there is a separate administrative court which deals with all cases against the administration.[93] While at least some civil law systems have confronted the problem of defining the scope of the powers of the separate administrative court, and although the boundary disputes have often been difficult,[94] many different institutional factors facilitate a public law–private law distinction in civil law systems.[95] Since traditional examinations of constitutional and administrative law in the United Kingdom have been notable by their absence of these institutional factors, such as a fully worked out concept of the state, the classification of laws, rights and remedies as pertaining to public law and private law is unusual here.[96]

The Emergence of Administrative Law

While criminal law and civil law form reasonably distinct categories, within the field of civil law there are various labels which, whatever their utility for particular purposes, do not have precise scope and may have **8.19**

---

[90] Many works on comparative law discuss the differences between the great legal traditions and their implications. For discussion, see Zweigert and Kotz (translated by Weir), *An Introduction to Comparative Law* (3rd ed., Oxford University Press, Oxford, 1998), particularly p. 67 *et seq.* The implications for public law of the systemic differences between the common law and civilian traditions have been explored by Allison, *A Continental Distinction in the Common Law* (Clarendon Press, Oxford, 1996).

[91] Zweigert and Kotz, *supra*, at p. 69.

[92] Most famously, the French Conseil d'Etat; but also elsewhere: for example, the Bundesverwaltungsgericht in Germany. Roman law itself accepted the distinction between public and private law: see Thomas, *Textbook of Roman Law* (1976), pp. 61–62; and Johnston, "The General Influence of Roman Institutions of State and Public law" in Carey Miller and Zimmermann (eds), *The Civlian Tradition and Scots Law* (Duckner and Humblot, Berlin, 1997).

[93] Most famously, the French Conseil d'Etat; but elsewhere, for example, the Bundesverwaltungsgericht in Germany.

[94] In France, jurisdictional conflicts between the Conseil d'Etat and the ordinary courts are resolved by the Tribunal des Conflits (which consists of an equal number of members of the Conseil d'Etat and the Cour de Cassation). But in Germany, there is no such separate tribunal to resolve conflicts and the matter is left to the Verwaltungsgericht itself (by way of interpretation of the Gerichtsverfassungsgesetz: that is, the administrative law code).

[95] For a comparison of the public law–private law distinction in France and under the English judicial review procedure, see Allison, *A Continental Distinction in the Common Law* (Clarendon Press, Oxford, 1996). Allison concludes that several institutional factors, notably a weak notion of separation of powers and no notion of the state, gives the public–private distinction no prospect of success in England. It may be assumed that the same is true in Scotland; but unlike England, Scotland shares some similarities with the Continent. Beyond historical reception of some rules of Roman law, Scotland has for long had a centralised system of criminal prosecution. That this did not develop into stronger notions of the state, and perhaps also a consciousness of a separate system of public law, should perhaps be explained by the Union. More specifically, it may be that (until J.D.B. Mitchell) Scots lawyers readily accepted Dicey's hostility to a separate system of administrative law, a point which raises interesting questions about Scots lawyers' historical attitudes (and the reasons for them) to Dicey's assertion of the superiority of the British constitutional model over the contintental, in particular, the French tradition.

[96] *cf. Davey v. Spelthorne B.C.*, [1984] A.C. 262, *per* Lord Wilberforce at 276.

different meanings from time to time. "Administrative law" itself, for example, in this country began as a label for the study of the structures and practical functions of local authorities. It included within its purview matters such as sewers, roads, parks, lighting and local taxation.[97] It is only since the Second World War, especially since the 1960s,[98] that administrative law has come to describe the control of statutory and other authorities by the courts.[99] In turn, the development of administrative law, and in particular that part of it relating to judicial review, has obscured the dividing line between administrative law and constitutional law. The older view that administrative law is constitutional law in action can no longer be said to be tenable. As must be inevitable under the United Kingdom's uncodified constitutional arrangements, characterising the exercise of the powers of the courts in relation to government as part of administrative law cannot disguise its enormous significance in constitutional law.[1] And so in more recent times, "public law" has come to be used to encompass both constitutional law and administrative law. Although the merging of the subjects is welcome in so far as it reveals what has been described as the bi-polar nature of sovereignty, at least that part of it concerning the powers of the courts,[2] it is not to be supposed that the term "public law", which in this context describes the area where particular remedies are available, is necessarily definitive of the boundaries judicial review. While in England public law has in some quarters come to be synonymous with judicial review, there are dangers inherent adopting the English terminology elsewhere. Even in England, the danger of the terminology is noticeable. The historical development of the remedies available in judicial review, especially the prerogative orders, continues to influence the law. The old prerogative orders were never united into a system of judicial control of decision-makers but retained their own particular rules which had to be satisfied before they could issue. Even under the new judicial review procedure in England,

---

[97] A study of the development of the substance of "Administrative Law" through the Calendars of the University of Edinburgh illustrates the point. See also Fraser, *Constitutional Law*, (2nd ed.) at p. 30.

[98] See, for example, Lord Reid's observation in *Ridge v. Baldwin* [1964] A.C. 40 at 77 (cited at para. 2.01 above).

[99] Of course, administrative law includes much more than judicial review and other legal actions against government in the courts. It includes other devices for redressing grievances against government and public bodies, such as the tribunals and inquiries system and the Ombudsman systems; beyond remedies for administrative action (and inaction), it includes government powers to make delegated legislation; the structure of government, both centrally and locally; regulation of private activities by public bodies; and special areas of regulatory activity such as planning law and immigration. But a comparison of studies on administrative law during the last 50 or so years reveals how judicial review has come to dominate the subject: compare, for example, Griffith and Street's first edition of *Administrative Law* (1951) with Craig's third edition of *Administrative Law* (1994).

[1] Consider, for example, *R. v. Secretary of State for the Home Department, ex p. Fire Brigades' Unions* [1995] 2 A.C. 513. And see Bradley, *Stair Encyclopaedia*, Vol. 1 para. 1. See also Sedley, "The Sound of Silence" (1994) L.Q.R.

[2] See Sir Stephen Sedley, "Human Rights: a Twenty-First Century Agenda" [1995] P.L. 386 at p. 389 and "The Sound of Silence: Constitutional Law without a Constitution" (1994) 110 L.Q.R. 270. *cf.* Hunt, "Constitutionalism and the Contractualisation of Government", Chap. 2 in Taggart (ed.), *The Province of Administrative Law* (Hart Publishing, Oxford, 1997). In this regard, several decisions of the New Zealand Court of Appeal extending the scope of judicial review to the decisions of private bodies which have significant implications for the public and society generally are instructive: see, *e.g. Finnigan v. NZRFU* [1985] 2 NZLR 181; and *Electoral Commission v. Cameron* [1997] 2 NZLR 421.

the former rules are still influential. Indeed, the effect of O'Reilly[3] was to require the scope of the prerogative orders to be considered before the remedies of declaration and injunction could be granted in judicial review. So these two remedies, greatly important in the development of the supervisory jurisdiction in England, in addition to having their own rules, must be understood in the context of judicial review against the purpose and function of the prerogative orders. But it may be questioned how far it is appropriate for the development of judicial review that it should be so closely tied to the restraints of procedure and forms of process.[4]

Judicial and Administrative

Character of the decision

Schemes of classification can be devised by reference to the character of the decision itself or the function of the decision maker. The nature or quality of the functions of an authority, either generally or in relation to some particular occasion, may be given a particular description to distinguish it from other kinds of function. Words such as legislative, administrative, ministerial, executive, judicial and quasi-judicial have at some time been used for this purpose. In the past such categorisation has played a critical part in the determination of the case as qualifying or not qualifying for review. However, as the law has developed and the grounds for review have become clarified, the significance and the usefulness of these classifications has diminished. Legislative and administrative acts may each be open to challenge on the ground of manifest unreasonableness. **8.20**

Judicial and administrative functions

The importance of the identification of a particular function as judicial (or as quasi-judicial) was of particular importance in England because if the proceedings were characterised as administrative and not judicial the writ of *certiorari* would not lie.[5] In Scotland distinctions were made between decisions of a judicial, or a legislative, or an administrative character.[6] On occasion the word "administrative" has been used to describe matters which are thought to be beyond judicial review. Thus Lord Stormonth-Darling observed in relation to a surcharge imposed by the Secretary of State on persons who had made payments out of county funds.[7] **8.21**

"It seems to me, therefore, we have no materials, and no jurisdiction to review what the minister has done in the exercise of a statutory duty which is partly, no doubt, judicial, but is also largely administrative".

In particular in the determination of the question whether in any given case the rules of natural justice do or do not apply it has sometimes been thought to be helpful to use such labels as "judicial" or "quasi-judicial" as opposed to "administrative" to identify the character of the body or its decision-making process, since the application of the rules of natural

---

[3] *O'Reilly v. Mackmann* [1983] 2 A.C. 237.
[4] *cf.* Judge Edward, supra, n. 20.
[5] *I.R. v. Barrs*, 1961 S.C.(H.L.) 22.
[6] As, for example, in *Dubs v. Police Commissioners of Crosshill* (1876) 3R. 758.
[7] *County Auditor of Lanark v. Lambie* (1905) 7F. 1049 at 1057.

justice is particularly appropriate where something at least of the elements of a judicial function are required to be exercised. On the other hand "a tribunal set up to decide administrative questions is under no obligation to hear evidence, and it may take a decision upon its own knowledge and experience".[8]

But while that distinction was at one time regarded as of particular importance for the success of judicial review, particularly on the ground of procedural failure, it was rejected in the landmark case of *Ridge v. Baldwin*[9] and since that time it has come to be recognised on both sides of the border that the distinction will not serve as a sound basis for the definition of the supervisory jurisdiction. As Sir William Wade put it,[10] the "judicial" fallacy was repudiated in *Ridge v. Baldwin*.[11] The distinction was probably the result of English decisions and the subtlety of the distinction leads to some uncertainty in its application. There is also the danger that by saying that a body is exercising a judicial function one is simply meaning that it has a duty to observe the rules of natural justice and so providing not a definition but merely a description, which is of little value in determining the susceptibility of the body to review. The term "quasi-judicial" had some currency in Scotland but is not now considered to be useful in the context of judicial review.[12] It is probably desirable to avoid its use.

Classification of functions in Scotland

8.22　It is not thought that an approach along the lines of such a classification is of assistance in the context of judicial review.[13] As Lord President Inglis observed long ago: "this Court has power to restrain administrative bodies as well as judicial bodies in the exercise of administrative functions".[14] Where a decision or action is administrative in character it has been considered that it is accordingly susceptible to judicial review[15]; and a decision of an administrative character which has adverse consequences for the petitioner may be treated as a sufficient qualification for an application for judicial review[16]; but that does not mean that that label sufficiently defines the scope of the supervisory jurisdiction. While it was argued in the case of *Blair v. Lochaber District Council*[17] that a criterion could be found in the classification of cases as administrative or judicial, either of which could involve the supervisory jurisdiction, and the word "administrative" was used as a means of exploring the nature of the dispute, it does not follow that such a criterion is useful as a general guide to the solution of the essential question. But while the

---

[8] *Glasgow and District Restaurateurs' and Hotel-keepers' Association v. Dollan*, 1941 S.C. 93, *per* Lord President Normand at 108. See also *Ramsay v. M'Laren*, 1936 S.L.T. 35, where nomination of an arbiter was held to be an entirely administrative task and not open to review.

[9] [1964] A.C. 40.

[10] *Administrative Law* (7th ed.), p. 511.

[11] [1964] A.C. 40.

[12] The inutility of the term was noted by J. Bennett-Miller in "The Place of the Quasi-judicial Decision in Scots Law", 1958 J.R. 39; for the past use of the term see Bradley, "Administrative Law", *Stair Encyclopaedia*, Vol, 1, para. 212.

[13] See J.D.B. Mitchell "Reflections on Law and Orders", 1958 J.R. 19.

[14] *Denny and Brothers v. Board of Trade* (1880) 7R. 1019 at 1023.

[15] *Bank of Scotland v. Investment Management Regulatory Organisation Ltd*, 1989 S.L.T. 432, *per* the Lord Ordinary at 437.

[16] *Darroch v. Strathclyde R.C.*, 1993 S.L.T. 1111.

[17] 1995 S.L.T. 409.

labels are useful as a descriptive shorthand they do not provide an analytic or determinative solution to the problem. Such an approach might well lead to the same kind of barren dispute as is invited by the use of the labels "private" and "public". The distinction between administrative and judicial decisions in matters of judicial review has been rejected in Scotland.[18] Indeed it has been regarded as appropriate to start by asking whether a decision can properly be described as administrative or judicial, because if it is, it is prima facie susceptible to judicial review.[19] So also a distinction between administrative and policy decisions on the one hand and executory or operative decisions on the other has been properly rejected as a sufficient guide for admissibility.[20]

Classification of functions in England

In England the distinction between judicial and administrative functions **8.23** has been discarded as a test for judicial review. As Lord Oliver of Aylmerton has observed,[21] ever since the decision of the House of Lords in *Ridge v. Baldwin*[22] "the susceptibility of a decision to the supervisory jurisdiction of the court does not rest upon some fancied distinction between decisions which are 'administrative' and decisions which are 'judicial' or 'quasi-judicial'. A domestic tribunal exercising a discretionary power must act fairly, whether the tribunal be described as judicial, quasi-judicial or administrative.[23] In *O'Reilly v. Mackman*[24] Lord Diplock referred to the long period over which the duty to act judicially gave rise to many attempts to draw subtle distinctions between decisions which were quasi-judicial and those which were administrative only and to the destruction of the relevance of such arguments by the decision in *Ridge v. Baldwin*. Under reference to the decisions of any body of persons having legal authority to determine questions affecting the common law or statutory rights or obligations of other persons he stated:

> "Wherever any person or body of persons has authority conferred by legislation to make decisions of the kind I have described, it is amenable to the remedy of an order to quash its decision either for error of law in reaching it or for failure to act fairly towards the person who will be adversely affected by the decision by failing to observe either one or other of the two fundamental rights accorded to him by the rules of natural justice or fairness, viz. to have afforded to him a reasonable opportunity of learning what is alleged against him and of putting forward his own case in answer to it, and to the absence of personal bias against him on the part of the person by whom the decision falls to be made".

The reality was expressed by Lord Lane,[25] that "there are degrees of judicial hearing, and those degrees run from the borders of pure

---

[18] *Brown v. Hamilton D.C.*, 1983 S.C. (H.L.) 1, where Lord Fraser of Tullybelton expressed the view (at 8) that "these 'subtle distinctions' are no longer relevant in England and it would be strange if they were to linger on in Scotland": *Connor v. Strathclyde R.C.*, 1986 S.L.T. 530.

[19] *Watt v. Strathclyde R.C.*, 1992 S.L.T. 324, *per* Lord President Hope at 329.

[20] *Stannifer Developments Ltd v. Glasgow Development Agency (No. 1)*, 1999 S.L.T. 430.

[21] *Leech v. Governor of Parkhurst* [1988] A.C. 533 at 573.

[22] [1964] A.C. 40.

[23] *Breen v. AEU* [1971] 2 Q.B. 175.

[24] [1983] 2 A.C. 237 at 279.

[25] *R. v. Commissioners for Racial Equality, ex p. Cottrell and Rothon* [1980] 1 W.L.R. 1580 at 1587.

administration to the borders of the full hearing of a criminal case or matter in the Crown Court. It does not profit one to try to pigeon-hole the particular set of circumstances either into the administrative pigeon-hole or into the judicial pigeon-hole. Each case will inevitably differ, and one must ask oneself what is the basic nature of the proceeding which was going on here."

Significance of the distinction

8.24   The distinction relates to the nature of the function, not to the character of the body. Broadly it may be said that a judicial function is one which deals with rights and legalities, while an administrative function is one which deals with policy and expediency. These functions carry with them distinctions in procedure. In the case of an administrative function the decision maker may be able to rely on his or her own practical experience and knowledge without hearing parties to an extent which would not be acceptable in the context of a judicial function. But in both cases the limits of the jurisdiction, power and authority have to be observed. The same body may at different times exercise each function. Thus a sheriff who has judicial functions may also have certain statutory functions which are administrative; one old example is the confirmation of byelaws.[26] The expression "quasi-judicial" should perhaps be avoided in so far as it imports the restrictive requirement of a judicial element into the test for the availability of judicial review. Correspondingly the idea of fairness, rather than that of natural justice, is now recognised as lying behind the standards of procedure which should be followed by a decision maker.[27]

Usefulness of the distinction

8.25   The distinction represented by the two words "judicial" and "administrative" is, however, not useless—at least as a method of distinguishing a difference of task. A judicial decision is one which has been reached in the application of the law to a given situation in the determination of the rights of parties. An administrative decision is one which has been reached after a consideration of matters of policy and expediency. Elements of discretion enter into both functions, more particularly into the latter. But the quality of the discretion and the grounds for a challenge of it may not coincide. The point was explored by Lord Fraser of Tullybelton in *G v. G*,[28] where his Lordship drew the distinction between appeals from a judicial discretion and challenges to an administrative discretion. He quoted an observation by Asquith L.J. in *Bellenden (formerly Satterthwaite) v. Satterthwaite*[29]: "We are here concerned with a judicial discretion, and it is of the essence of such a discretion that on the same evidence two different minds might reach widely different decisions without either being appealable. It is only where the decision exceeds the generous ambit within which reasonable disagreement is possible, and is, in fact, plainly wrong, that an appellate body is entitled to interfere." Respect has to be paid to the advantage which the original decision maker may have had in seeing and hearing

---

[26] *Glasgow Corporation v. Glasgow Churches' Council*, 1944 S.C. 97.
[27] See paras 17.05 and 18.01.
[28] [1985] 2 All E.R. 225.
[29] [1948] 1 All E.R. 343 at 345.

the witnesses, but beyond that the court may intervene more readily in a judicial context than it will in the field of administrative practice. The balancing of factors may be a matter wholly for the administrative decision maker, but if a court considers that a judge has given too much or too little weight to certain factors in reaching a judicial decision, the court may intervene.[30]

Relevance of the categorisation today

While it is no longer useful to categorise functions as judicial or **8.26** administrative in relation to the question of the availability of judicial review, the categorisation still has some value in determining the substance of the procedural requirements which a body may have to observe.[31] An analysis of the functions of the Secretary of State on dealing with a planning appeal may usefully proceed under reference to the administrative nature of the decision and the judicial qualities required of his procedure.[32] Furthermore, a distinction between acting in a judicial capacity and acting in an administrative capacity may be important for some purposes,[33] such as (in particular) whether a lower court has a privative jurisdiction or whether its decision is open to appeal,[34] or in defining the extent of a statutory discretion.[35] The distinction has been used for a variety of purposes.[36] Among these is the resolution of the question whether a right of appeal exists from a sheriff to the Court of Session.[37] It is accordingly worth noting some of the marks of a body exercising a judicial function, although these are not exhaustive or comprehensive and may even be consistent with the exercise of a non-judicial function. The marks of a body exercising a judicial function include the following[38]:

1. That the performance of it leads to a determination, particularly of an issue between opposing parties. Bodies which merely advise, deliberate, investigate or conciliate will not normally be judicial in character.

2. That a body has the trappings of a court, behaves like a court and follows the procedure of a court may well show its judicial character.

3. That a body is exercising an appellate function probably means that it is judicial.[39]

---

[30] *Re F. (a Minor) (Wardship: Appeal)* [1976] Fam. 238; [1976] 1 All E.R. 417, approved in G v. G, *supra*.

[31] It may be noted that "administrative matters" for the purposes of s. 16(1) of the Civil Jurisdiction and Judgments Act 1982 (c. 27) covers matters of "public law" and "private law" without distinction: *Bank of Scotland v. Investment Management Regulatory Organisation Ltd*, 1989 S.L.T. 432.

[32] *Strathclyde R.C. v. Secretary of State for Scotland*, 1991 S.L.T. 796.

[33] *Errington v. Wilson*, 1995 S.C. 550.

[34] *Rodenhurst v. Chief Constable of Grampian Police*, 1992 S.C. 1. See also *R. v. Cornwall Quarter Sessions, ex p. Kerley* [1956] 1 W.L.R. 906.

[35] *Strathclyde R.C.*, 1991 S.L.T. 796.

[36] For a summary of these see Bradley, "Administrative Law", *Stair Encyclopaedia*, Vol. 1 para. 209.

[37] *e.g. Rodenhurst v. Chief Constable, Grampian Police*, 1992 S.L.T. 104.

[38] Reference may usefully be made to the tests noted in de Smith, Woolf and Jowell, *Judicial Review of Administrative Action* (5th ed.), A-021.

[39] *Palmer v. Board of Management for Inverness Hospitals*, 1963 S.C. 311.

4. That it is called by name of a court or a tribunal may be an indication of its character, although the name "court" in Scotland is not infrequently used for a governing body which is not necessarily exercising a judicial function.

5. That it is structurally separate from the organisation which is primarily concerned with the matters with which it deals, and if it has members from outside that organisation it may well be judicial.[40]

6. If it interprets and applies the law it is likely to be judicial.

7. That it was set up under statute and the power to summon witnesses or call for documents may indicate a judicial function.

Public and Private

Public law and private law

8.27   A distinction has been developed in England between cases involving "public law" and cases involving "private law" with the remedy of judicial review being limited to the former category.[41] It was adopted in the cases of *O'Reilly v. Mackman*[42] and *Cocks v. Thanet District Council*[43] as a procedural distinction.[44] Thus in *R. v. East Berkshire Health Authority, ex parte Walsh*[45] the absence of statutory provisions which could "inject the element of public law necessary in this context to attract the remedies of administrative law" was held to distinguish the case from that of *Malloch v. Aberdeen Corporation*[46] and make the case inappropriate for judicial review. The classification was, as Lord Wilberforce explained, "a recent importation from the countries which, unlike our own, have separate systems concerning public law and private law."[47] The distinction has been authoritatively defined to the effect that public law enforces the proper performance by public bodies of the duties which they have to the public, while private law protects the private rights either of private individuals or public individuals.[48] But while such a classification may be convenient for some purposes, it is not sufficiently precise, at least in the Scottish context, as a workable distinction that can identify the occasions on which use is to be made of the special procedure for cases of judicial review without undue involvement of

---

[40] *Barrs v. British Wool Marketing Board*, 1957 S.C. 72. The case also illustrates factor 4.
[41] See Bradley, *Stair Encyclopaedia*, Vol. 1, para. 205.
[42] [1983] 2 A.C. 237.
[43] [1983] 2 A.C. 286.
[44] The refreshingly open description used by Lord Diplock in *O'Reilly* (at 279) is worth quoting where he spoke of those wishing "to challenge the lawfulness of a determination of a statutory tribunal or any other body of persons having legal authority to determine questions affecting the common law or statutory rights or obligations of other persons as individuals".
[45] [1985] 1 Q.B. 152. Leave to the House of Lords was refused: [1984] 1 W.L.R. 1357.
[46] 1971 S.C.(H.L.) 75.
[47] *Davy v. Spelthorne B.C.* [1984] A.C. 262 at 276.
[48] By The Rt Hon. Sir Harry Woolf (as he then was) [1986] P.L. 220 at 221. See also his account in The Hamlyn Lecture 1990, "Protection of the Public—A New Challenge".

procedural debate on the competency of the procedure selected.[49] The extent and degree to which the state may control or influence the operation of services provided for the benefit of the public may vary from time to time. Private bodies may take on duties to the public which may at other times or under other administrations be taken to be the responsibility of public bodies. The decision whether a body undertaking duties for the public benefit is or is not subject to "public law" for the purposes of judicial review may become narrow and difficult.[50] Furthermore, there are cases in Scotland where judicial review is plainly competent but where there is no element of "public law". The review of decisions of arbiters is the obvious example. Yet it was in the context of just such a case that it was long ago affirmed that review of arbitral proceedings was competent only in the Court of Session and that the sheriff court had no jurisdiction to deal with the matter, it being recognised that it fell under the same supereminent jurisdiction by which the supreme court reviews the actings of a wide variety of inferior bodies.[51]

Not now followed in Scotland

The Scottish courts flirted with this classification for a while; indeed in some cases it was adopted as a valid criterion for determining the competency of the application.[52] Particular recognition of it was given in the case of *Tehrani v. Argyll and Clyde Health Board (No. 2)*,[53] and in the cases following thereon consideration was given to the identification of a "public law" element.[54] However, the propriety of this classification came to be expressly doubted[55] and in the case of *West v. Secretary of State for Scotland*[56] it was authoritatively rejected. The use of the term "public" as a label to refer to the cases which are susceptible to judicial review may be convenient but it carries with it the great danger of a substantive analysis which may distort the true purpose and scope of judicial review. Certainly the word cannot be used in this context in the sense that it bears for the English practitioner, since it is now clear that the

8.28

---

[49] A distinction long ago attempted by Professor Holland between public law and private law was criticised by A.A. Mitchell in "Public Law and Private Law" (1905) 17 J.R. 30. Stair (*Inst.*, 1, 1, 23) distinguished public and private rights: "Public rights are those which concern the state of the Commonwealth: Private rights are the rights of persons and particular incorporations", but this has been described as an inaccurate distinction (Introduction to the edition by David M. Walker of *Stair's Institutions* (1981), p. 31. A discussion on the various meanings of the distinction is given by J.W. Jones, *Historical Introduction to the Theory of Law* (1940), Chap. 5. See also Judge David Edward, "Administrative Law in Scotland: The Public/Private Law Distinction revisited" in Curtis and O'Keefe (eds), *Constitutional Adjudication in E.C. and National Law* (1992).

[50] The danger of trying to identify a public law right was noted by the Justice All Souls Review of Administrative Law (1988), para. 6.20.

[51] *Forbes v. Underwood* (1886) 13R. 465. The Lord President (Inglis) spoke of arbiters as "public officers" (at 468) but it is apparent that he was not using the term "public" in the modern sense, but rather in the sense that the proper discharge of the arbitral function is a matter of public interest.

[52] *Connor v. Strathclyde R.C.*, 1986 S.L.T. 530 and *Safeway Food Stores Ltd v. Scottish Provident Institution*, 1989 S.L.T. 131, overruled by *West v. Secretary of State for Scotland*, 1992 S.L.T. 636.

[53] 1990 S.L.T. 118.

[54] *Criper v. The University of Edinburgh*, 1991 S.L.T. 129; *Kyle and Carrick D.C. v. A.R. Kerr and Sons*, 1992 S.L.T. 629; *Darroch v. Strathclyde R.C.*, 1993 S.L.T. 1111.

[55] *Watt v. Strathclyde R.C.*, 1992 S.L.T. 324. See comments by C.M.G. Himsworth "Public Employment and the Supervisory Jurisdiction", 1992 S.L.T. (News) 123.

[56] 1992 S.L.T. 636.

competency of application for judicial review in Scotland is not confined to those cases which English law has accepted as amenable to judicial review.[57] It may be that if the word is to be given any substantive meaning it should be understood as relating to all those matters and functions the fair and proper performance of which is of such interest to the public that they should be open to the supervision of the court.[58]

The risk of procedural dispute

8.29 A further danger in the selection of labels such as private and public is that there can develop a wasteful procedural wrangle about the classifying of particular cases, thereby adding to expense and not advancing the resolution of the substantive issue. The point is well illustrated in the English experience. In *Rye and others, Trustees of the Dennis Rye Pension Fund v. Sheffield City Council,*[59] which concerned a dispute about the payment of improvement grants for dwelling-houses, Lord Woolf M.R. began his judgment with these words:

> "This appeal raises yet again issues as to the relationship between public and private law proceedings. It illustrates the fact that, despite the hopes to the contrary, a very substantial volume of the resources of the parties and the courts are still being consumed to little or no purpose over largely tactical issues as to whether the correct procedure has been adopted. This appeal is the third court and the fourth hearing to consider the issue in the present proceedings. I have little doubt that the amount of the costs already incurred far exceeds the sum in issue in the proceedings but the parties and the courts have yet to turn their attention to the merits of the dispute."

The need for a single procedure and the problems of the public–private dichotomy as a measure of the procedural distinction have been discussed in England and even described as misguided.[60] It remains to be seen whether a reformulation of the test for the scope of Order 53 will be devised.[61] Be that as it may, in Scotland there may still on occasion remain a problem for the practitioner whether he should proceed by way of petition for judicial review or by ordinary action, which may sometimes lead to procedural dispute.

---

[57] *West v. Secretary of State for Scotland*, 1992 S.L.T. 636 at 650.

[58] cf. *R. v. Panel on Takeovers and Mergers, ex parte Datafin plc* [1987] Q.B. 815.

[59] July 31, 1997, unreported.

[60] See Wade and Forsyth, Administrative Law (7th ed.), pp. 667 and 684 *et seq.* The inadequacy of a public–private law test for judicial review and an argument that the decision in *Roy v. Kensington and Chelsea and Westminster Family Practitioner Committee* [1992] 1 All E.R. 705 makes the rule in *O'Reilly v. Mackman* virtually meaningless is considered by John Alder in "Hunting the Chimera—the end of *O'Reilly v. Mackman*" (1993) L.S. 183.

[61] See the article by Dawn Oliver on "Common Values in Public and Private Law and the Public/Private Divide" [1997] P.L. 630.

Public bodies and private bodies

The distinction between public and private law is linked with a distinc- **8.30**
tion between public and private bodies, but the classification in this
context is as imprecise as the attempt to classify laws in this way.[62] The
English court has sometimes endeavoured to find a distinguishing
characteristic for susceptibility to review by reference to the nature of
the body sought to be reviewed. Thus the question has been asked
whether the takeover panel,[63] or the Advertising Standards Agency,[64] had
a "public element", such as to render them susceptible to review.
Consideration has been given to such matters as whether the body was
exercising powers which the government might have assumed[65] or
whether the functions were governmental functions.[66] While issues of the
validity of the actings of bodies such as football clubs[67] on grounds of
natural justice, or a trade union on the ground of fairness,[68] or the
Jockey Club[69] on grounds of sexual discrimination, can be raised before
the English courts in ordinary actions, matters which lack the public
element cannot be raised by way of judicial review. The supervisory
jurisdiction in Scotland however readily extends to such "private" bodies
as football clubs,[70] although such an admission would involve a "quantum leap" for the English Court.[71] Decisions of a political party can be
reviewed in Scotland.[72] The actings of arbiters have long been open to
judicial review.[73] The scope of the supervisory jurisdiction of the Scottish
Court is not determined by considerations of the governmental or public
nature of the body in question. It extends equally to bodies of a domestic
or private character. It covers public tribunals and private arbitrations.
And the same grounds of review are available whether the decision-
making body is classified as public or as private.

---

[62] In *Ayr Harbour Trustees v. Oswald* (1883) 10R. 472, affirmed (1883) 10R.(H.L.) 85,
Lord President Inglis drew a distinction between trusts for the management and
improvement of a subject which is *inter res publicas* and which cannot be made the source
of profit or patrimonial interest and corporations constituted for the purpose of carrying
on a trade in the nature of a public utility. A discussion on "What a Public Body Is" by
A.D.D. can be found in (1901) 17 S.L.R. 238.

[63] *R. v. Takeover Panel, ex p. Datafin plc* [1987] Q.B. 815.

[64] *R. v. Advertising Standards Agency Ltd, ex p. Vernons Organisation plc* [1992] 1 W.L.R.
1289.

[65] *R. v. Chief Rabbi of the United Hebrew Congregations of Great Britain and the
Commonwealth, ex p. Watchmann* [1992] 1 W.L.R. 1036.

[66] *R. v. Disciplinary Committee of the Jockey Club, ex p. Aga Khan* [1993] 1 W.L.R. 909: *R.
v. Lloyds of London, ex p. Briggs* [1993] 1 Lloyd's Rep. 176 at 185.

[67] *Enderby Town Football Club Ltd v. Football Association Ltd* [1971] Ch. 591 (a tribunal
of the football association); *McInnes v. Onslow-Fane* [1978] 1 W.L.R. 1520 (the British
Boxing Board of Control).

[68] *Breen v. Amalgamated Engineering Union* [1971] Q.B. 175.

[69] *Nagle v. Feilden* [1966] 2 Q.B. 633.

[70] *e.g. St Johnston Football Club Ltd v. Scottish Football Association*, 1965 S.L.T. 171;
Ferguson, Petr, Feb. 1, 1996; *Dundee United Football Co. Ltd v. SFA and Scottish Football
League*, 1998 S.L.T. 1244.

[71] *R. v. Football Association Ltd, ex p. Football League Ltd* [1993] 2 All E.R. 833. See
Wade & Forsyth, *Administrative Law* (7th ed.), pp. 666–667.

[72] *Brown v. Executive Committee of Edinburgh Labour Party*, 1995 S.L.T. 985; *Lally v.
Labour Party*, Feb. 27, 1998.

[73] *e.g. Shanks & McEwan (Contractors) Ltd v. Mifflin Construction Ltd*, 1993 S.L.T. 1124.
On the propriety of arbitral decisions falling within judicial review regardless of any
public–private law distinction, see "Arbitration and Judicial Review", 1990 S.L.T. (News)
113.

Human rights and public functions

8.31 For the purposes of the Human Rights Act 1998 some definition will be required of the scope of the bodies to which the Act relates. Section 6 of the Act has adopted the language of public and private functions for the determination of the scope of activities to which the provisions of the Convention are to apply. It is thought that reference to older cases may be of less assistance in this matter of terminology. Thus, while public water trustees could be held not to be within the scope of the Public Authorities Protection Act 1893 as they were seen to be a commercial profit-making company,[74] it is unlikely that such a view would be taken today. It is suggested that a function is of a public nature when it is such that the general public would have an interest in securing that it is properly and validly performed.[75] It may then be that in this context, as may be the case more generally, the word "public" should be taken to mean those matters or functions the fair and proper conduct of which is of such general concern that they should fall under the supervision of the Court.[76]

The Tripartite Theory

The tripartite relationship

8.32 In the case of *West v. The Secretary of State for Scotland*,[77] the idea of a tripartite relationship was put forward as a significant element in all the cases of judicial review prior to the introduction of the expedited procedure under the former Rule of Court 260B. The essential feature of all the cases prior to the present century was said to be "the conferring, whether by statute or by private contract, of a decision making power or duty on a third party to whom the taking of the decision is entrusted but whose manner of decision making may be controlled by the court"[78] and that feature was also found to exist in the later cases. Indeed it was said that "the cases in which the exercise of the supervisory jurisdiction is appropriate involve a tri-partite relationship, between the person or body to whom it has been delegated or entrusted, the person or body by whom it has been delegated or entrusted and the person or persons in respect of or for whose benefit that jurisdiction, power or authority is to be exercised".[79]

---

[74] *Lanarkshire Upper Ward District Committee v. Airdrie, Coatbridge and District Water Trustees* (1906) 8F. 777.

[75] The definition advanced in de Smith, Woolf and Jowell, *Judicial Review of Administrative Action* (5th ed.), para. 3–024 looks to the aim of achieving a benefit for the public or a section of the public by a body which is accepted as having the authority to do so.

[76] For a discussion of the concept of "public interest cases", see Pleming, "The Contribution of Public Interest Litigation to the Jurisprudence of Judicial Review", in 1998 *Judicial Review* 63. It must, however, be recognised that such a test for defining "public body" is much broader than that which presently prevails in determining the scope of judicial review in England & Wales.

[77] 1992 S.C. 385.

[78] 1992 S.C. 385 at 400.

[79] *ibid.* at 413.

Not definitive

However, at least as a general test for the availability of the judicial **8.33** review procedure, the idea of tripartism came under some criticism.[80] In one case brought by a university student, while the court was able to identify a tripartite relationship it was observed that the test imposed an inflexible and over-formal restraint upon the jurisdiction of the court.[81] In another case also relating to a dispute between a student and the same university,[82] it was said that the concept should not be transformed into a technical test. In that case it was recognised that membership of such an institution could well produce situations in which judicial review was appropriate without the need to resort to a tripartite test, and as the particular problem involved a contractual dispute it was the ordinary jurisdiction of the court which was appropriate and not its supervisory jurisdiction. More recently it has been doubted whether in every case a tripartite relationship must exist.[83] In order to satisfy the concept Parliament has in some cases been brought in as one of the parties,[84] although that seems an unnecessary elaboration of the fact that a statutory power is being exercised.[85] It would certainly be unfortunate if an inability to find a tripartite relationship should lead to the exclusion of review even in cases where officials have acted without lawful authority, since ensuring that officials act within their powers might be thought to be of the essence of the supervisory jurisdiction.[86] While the concept of the tripartite relationship may be seen as descriptive of many cases where judicial review is competent, the formula should not be treated as definitive. The danger of the application of the tripartite formula is that it carries all of the rigidity which the public–private distinction has brought in England. Similarly, the source of the power the exercise of which is open to review will not serve as an adequate criterion of the scope of the supervisory jurisdiction. But the source of the power may have a bearing on the extent of the court's readiness to intervene in particular cases.

Employment cases

The problem of categorisation for the identification of the scope of **8.34** judicial review has arisen most sharply in cases involving contractual disputes, and most particularly disputes between employees and employers.[87] In England, in some cases judicial review has been held to be not available in disputed cases of employment on the ground that the

---

[80] *e.g.* by C.M.G. Himsworth in "Public Employment, the Supervisory Jurisdiction and Points West", 1992 S.L.T. (News) 257, and in "Further West? More Geometry of Judicial Review", 1995 S.L.T. (News) 127; W. Finnie "Triangles as Touchstones of Review", 1993 S.L.T. (News) 51; W.J. Wolfe, "The Scope of Judicial Review in Scots Law" [1992] P.L. 625.

[81] *Naik v. University of Stirling*, 1994 S.L.T. 449.

[82] *Joobeen v. University of Stirling*, 1995 S.L.T. 120 at 122.

[83] *McIntosh v. Aberdeenshire Council*, 1999 S.L.T. 93 at 97.

[84] *Joobeen v. University of Stirling, supra* at 122D; *Boyle v. Castlemilk East Housing Co-operative Ltd*, 1998 S.L.T. 56 at 59B.

[85] cf. *Boyle v. Castlemilk East Housing Co-operative Ltd, supra.*

[86] The rejection of review in *Importa Ltd v. Tayside R.C.*, 1994 G.W.D. 26–1542 may be seen primarily as based on the ground of the availability of an alternative remedy, although the thrust of the action does appear to have been aimed at the reduction of an acting by officials in excess of their powers.

[87] For a consideration of the situation of employment see G. Ian McPherson, "Judicial Review in Employment" (1992) 37 J.L.S.S. 314.

case did not have a public law character, even although the employer might be thought to be a public body carrying on a public function.[88] But, as has already been noted, that distinction has been rejected in Scotland. It was in the context of the problem of cases of employment that the idea of the tripartite relationship was conceived. In *Rooney v. Chief Constable of Strathclyde*[89] a tripartite analysis of the position of a police officer in relation to a chief constable and the Secretary of State was adopted in order to find a jurisdiction amenable to judicial review. The issue in the case was the validity of the exercise of the powers of a chief constable. In *Blair v. Lochaber District Council*[90] it was considered that the tripartite analysis was intended to cover all cases where there is a dispute between employee and employer but was not intended to serve as a general test for the availability of judicial review. The decision in that case that the petition was incompetent was based on the consideration that the true nature of the dispute was a contractual one. It is thought that the proper ground for exclusion of such questions is not to be found in a distinction between public and private functions nor in an application of a tripartite test, but in the consideration that in most cases the dispute is essentially on a matter of contract and an alternative remedy should lie in contract law. However, if the dispute between employer and employee affects others than the particular employee who has raised the point, judicial review may be available.[91] The insertion into the contract of employment of a standard circular issued by a government department may give the employee a right to have the procedural propriety of his dismissal reviewed.[92]

Cases not purely of employer and employee

8.35 But there can be cases where, in the context of employment law, review may be open. These will arise where there is a statutory power to dismiss.[93] As Lord Keith of Avonholm observed[94]: "Normally, and apart from the intervention of statute, there would never be a nullity in terminating an ordinary contract of master and servant." The significance of the intervention of statute is that it takes the case outside the pure consideration of master and servant. Lord Wilberforce later[95] identified the pure cases as those "in which there is no element of public employment or service, no support by statute, nothing in the nature of an office or a status which is capable of protection. If any of these elements exist, then in my opinion, whatever the terminology used, and even though in some *inter partes* aspects the relationship may be called that of master and servant, there may be essential procedural requirements to be observed, and failure to observe them may result in a dismissal being declared to be void." Thus where a schoolmaster who had a statutory right to a pension if dismissed without fault claimed that his dismissal had been brought about by oppression on the part of the School Board and by no fault on his part an action for declarator,

[88] *e.g. R. v. East Berkshire Health Authority, ex p. Walsh* [1985] 1 Q.B. 152.
[89] 1997 S.L.T. 1261.
[90] 1995 S.L.T. 407.
[91] *Watt v. Strathclyde R.C.*, 1992 S.L.T. 324; *Darroch v. Strathclyde R.C.*, 1993 S.L.T. 1111.
[92] *Palmer v. Inverness Hospitals Board*, 1963 S.C. 311.
[93] *e.g. Hanson v. Radcliffe Urban D.C.* [1922] 2 Ch. 490.
[94] *Vine v. National Dock Labour Board* [1957] A.C. 488 at 507.
[95] *Malloch v. Aberdeen Corporation*, 1971 S.C.(H.L.) 85 at 119.

payment and if necessary reduction was held competent.[96] In one case the court was prepared to determine the right of a prison governor to have his application to retire on the grounds of health referred to the Occupational Health Service in terms of his conditions of service as a matter of the construction of those terms.[97] In England the Court of Queen's Bench has always been able to correct any tribunal or body which has a power to remove persons from office if the essentials of justice have not been regarded.[98] In the field of employment care should be taken to see that the statutory remedies for unfair dismissal do not provide an alternative remedy excluding judicial review.

Contracts

The existence of a contractual relationship between the parties does not **8.36** necessarily exclude judicial review. A decision which is susceptible to judicial review may also constitute a failure to perform a contractual obligation or a breach of a contractual prohibition.[99] It may be implied that when a contract gives to one party an authority over another, that authority will only be exercised within the limits of the law, so that an excess of that limit may attract the supervisory jurisdiction. But such cases may rarely arise outside the field of appointment to an office. Where parties have agreed *inter se* to go to arbitration and have agreed on the identity of the arbiter, an application for review of his appointment may lie; the agreement is relevant as forming part of the substratum for a binding submission and so for the exercise of the arbiter's powers over which judicial review may operate; but agreement on the identity of the arbiter may exclude review of the arbiter's decision to accept office.[1] On the other hand, where the dispute is purely on the contract or the claim is for remedies arising out of the contract or a breach of it, then the matter is outwith the scope of judicial review. Where a developer entered into an agreement with a planning authority to preserve access to certain land adjoining the proposed development, it was held that judicial review was not available as a means of challenging a contractual agreement between the parties which had been acted upon.[2]

V CRIMINAL CASES

Suspension in criminal cases

Suspension has long been a remedy available in the High Court for cases **8.37** properly falling within the criminal jurisdiction of that Court. It is sought by means of the procedure of a Bill of Suspension. It is available where no other mode of appeal or review is open.[3] But as Lord Mackay observed in *Campbell v. Herron*[4]: "The existence of our power depends

---

[96] Marshall v. School Board of Ardrossan (1879) 7R. 359.
[97] Jackson v. Secretary of State for Scotland, 1992 S.L.T. 572.
[98] Osgood v. Nelson (1872) L.R. 5 H.L. 636 at 649.
[99] *Bank of Scotland v. IMRO*, 1989 S.L.T. 432, *per* Lord Cullen at 437. It was conceded in the Inner House that the petition for judicial review was competent.
[1] *Haden Young Ltd v. William McCrindle & Son Ltd*, 1994 S.L.T. 221.
[2] *McIntosh v. Aberdeenshire Council*, 1999 S.L.T. 93.
[3] Criminal Procedure (Scotland) Act 1995, s. 191.
[4] 1948 J.C. 127 at 135.

on defect of power below or on one of those errors of procedure which go to the vitals and fundamentals of a case".[5] In *Campbell v. Herron* the procurator-fiscal had sought to have a person committed to an asylum under section 15 of the Lunacy (Scotland) Act 1862 on the ground that he was "in a state threatening danger to the lieges". The legal nature of the proceeding was, as Lord Mackay observed, very far from being an ordinary criminal prosecution, but the matter was taken to the High Court.

Civil and criminal

8.38 There was, particularly in the nineteenth century, some uncertainty whether particular matters were properly to be raised for review in the Court of Session or the High Court. This point has already been noted in Chapter 2. In *Scott v. Muir and Annan*,[6] where the pursuer had been charged with a contravention of the Act 1621 c. 23 (an Act anent playing at cardes and dyce and horse-races), the Court of Session took the view that a reduction of proceedings on the summary complaint was incompetent as the proceedings were of a criminal nature. But where a penalty had been imposed on a failure to comply with a statutory provision relating to construction works the point was decided by the Court of Session even although the High Court of Justiciary had already determined it.[7]

Declarator of legality

8.39 There have been several cases where the English courts have granted a declarator that a course of action, particularly in the context of the medical treatment of patients, would be lawful. In *Airedale National Health Service Trust v. Bland*[8] declarations were made to the effect that all life-sustaining treatment might lawfully be discontinued in the case of a patient in a persistent vegetative state. In other English cases declaratory judgments have been used where consent has been required for medical treatment for persons unable to give a valid consent.[9] Scotland has, however, retained the ancient *pater patriae* jurisdiction which obviates the necessity to resort to a declarator as the only form of remedy. In the case of *Law Hospital National Health Service Trust v. The Lord Advocate*[10] a declarator of the lawfulness under civil law was allowed, if only to enable a remedy to be given in the existing process which was an action of declarator. But the proper course was recognised to be that of the granting of an authorisation of the proposed treatment or withdrawal of treatment. An alternative course which is open in Scotland where there is a requirement for continuing supervision is that of the appointment of a tutor dative.[11] In the *Airedale* case Sir Stephen

---

[5] Examples of the kinds of actings which are open to review in this way can be found in Walker's *Civil Remedies*, p. 212.

[6] (1868) 7M. 270. See *Rutherford v. Lord Advocate*, 1931 S.L.T. 405.

[7] *Glasgow City and District Ry v. Magistrates of Glasgow* (1884) 11R. 1110 and (1884) R.(J.) 43.

[8] [1963] A.C. 789.

[9] *e.g. Re F (Mental Patient: Sterilisation)* [1990] 2 A.C. 1; *Re R (A Minor) (Wardship: Consent to Treatment)* [1992] Fam. 11; *Frenchay Healthcare NHS Trust v. S* [1994] 1 W.L.R. 601.

[10] 1996 S.C. 301.

[11] See *Chapman, Petr*, 1992 S.L.T. 955; *Lawrence, Petr (sub nom. L v. L's Curator ad Litem)*, 1997 S.L.T. 167.

Brown, who granted the original declarations, stated that he did not consider it appropriate to make any declaration with regard to any possible consequences so far as the criminal law was concerned.[12] In the Court of Appeal and the House of Lords, however, the matter of lawfulness was extended so as to cover both the civil and the criminal law aspects of the problem. In *Attorney-General v. Able*[13] the English Court considered an application by the Attorney-General, who was seeking declarations raising questions whether certain conduct would amount to criminal offences, and refused to make any declaration, recognising the immense difficulty of framing a declaration defining *ab ante* the circumstances in which the conduct would be criminal. But it is not to be expected that the Lord Advocate in Scotland would seek the advice of Court of Session in that way.

High Court or Court of Session

In general in Scotland it can be said that the Court of Session will nowadays refrain from entering into matters which properly fall within the jurisdiction of the High Court and the latter will correspondingly respect the jurisdiction of the Court of Session. In *Cordiner, Petitioner* the Lord Justice-General Emslie[14] observed: "The Court of Session, however, as the supreme civil court of Scotland is wholly independent and separate from the High Court of Justiciary, and this Court has no jurisdiction to intervene in proceedings which are competently within the jurisdiction of that Court. The High Court and the Court of Session have different historical origins and functions, and their jurisdictions are independent and in no sense concurrent." In that case it was held incompetent to apply to the *nobile officium* of the High Court of Justiciary for interim liberation from prison in a matter of contempt of court which had occurred in the course of civil proceedings. Such a course would be an interference with the jurisdiction of the civil court and moreover the matter was susceptible of redress in the ordinary civil procedures of the Court of Session so that an extraordinary remedy was not called for. Thus, in *Reynolds v. Christie*[15] it was held that the supervisory jurisdiction of the Court of Session could not be invoked to challenge a refusal by a stipendiary magistrate to grant legal aid for the defence of a criminal prosecution.[16] But, while in general the distinction between the two jurisdictions is recognised, cases can occur where the borderline cannot easily be determined in absolute terms.

8.40

Incidental rulings

The civil court may of course be required to adjudicate upon matters of criminal law where they arise in a civil action incidentally to the seeking of civil remedy.[17] Thus interdict has been sought against the burning of heather contrary to the provisions of a penal statute.[18] Conduct such as careless driving may give rise to a civil claim for damages and also

8.41

---

[12] [1963] A.C. 789 at 805.
[13] [1984] 1 Q.B. 795.
[14] 1973 J.C. 16 at 18.
[15] 1988 S.L.T. 68.
[16] But compare *K v. Scottish Legal Aid Board*, 1989 S.L.T. 617, where the decision maker was a statutory body.
[17] *Morton v. Gardner* (1871) 9M. 548 at 551.
[18] *Watney v. Menzies* (1898) 6 S.L.T. 189; *Milburn v. Black*, 1920 2 S.L.T. 378.

constitute a statutory offence. Facts which might constitute common law crimes such as fraud or rape[19] may properly be explored in a civil action where a civil remedy is sought. But in these cases the inquiry into the crime by the civil court is incidental to the exercise of the civil jurisdiction.

Criminal and civil wrongs

8.42 Where the issue raised is one of the lawfulness of some particular actings equally as a matter of civil and of criminal law there may be grounds for admitting the competency of a declarator in the civil court. In *Southern Bowling Club Ltd v. Ross*[20] the pursuers sought a declarator that members of the Edinburgh police force were not entitled to enter the pusuers' club in disguise in circumstances where they had gone there to investigate the possibility of illegal trafficking in excisable liquor being carried on. The competency of the action was not challenged but it failed on relevancy. In *Glasgow City and District Railway Co. v. Magistrates of Glasgow*[20a] a declarator was held to be competent on the extent of a statutory obligation of repair where failure in the obligation involved a liability to a monetary penalty. A distinction might be drawn between a declarator of the lawfulness of conduct and a declarator of the unlawfulness of conduct. The latter at least may more obviously trench upon matters which properly fall within the scope of the jurisdiction of the criminal court. A declarator that the pursuer is entitled to take certain action, even if it involves, some consideration of the criminal as well as the civil law, may be competent in the civil court, where a plain declarator that certain conduct is contrary to the criminal law would be incompetent. At least where there is an alternative course open at civil law a declarator of the lawfulness of a proposed course of action under the criminal law will be refused.[20b]

Declarator on criminal issue *ab ante*

8.43 Where the matter is already the subject of proceedings in the criminal courts then it will be incompetent for the civil court to entertain a declarator on the same issue. Where the matter falls within the privative jurisdiction of the criminal courts a civil declarator will not lie.[20c] But where the issue is new and untested and no action has been embarked upon and no criminal proceedings taken, there may be cases where the civil court should give a ruling by way of declarator even although that ruling would be binding neither on the prosecuting authority nor on the criminal court.[21] It appears that in England in exceptional circumstances a declaration that particular behaviour does not constitute an offence may be granted.[22]

---

[19] *Black v. Duncan*, 1924 S.C. 738.
[20] (1902) 4F. 405.
[20a] (1884) 11R. 1110.
[20b] *Law Hospital NHS Trust v. Lord Advocate*, 1996 S.C. 301.
[20c] *Morton v. Gardner* (1871) 9M. 548.
[21] For the position in England, see Zamir & Woolf, *The Declaratory Judgment*, pp. 174–189.
[22] *Imperial Tobacco Ltd and Another v. Att.-Gen.* [1981] A.C. 718. The decision in *Royal College of Nursing v. DHSS* [1981] A.C. 800 is presumably an example.

Decisions to prosecute

In Scotland, the management of prosecutions is under the control of the **8.44**
Lord Advocate and his decision in such a matter was by a long tradition
not open to review. In *M'Bain v. Crichton*[23] the Lord Justice-General
(Clyde) affirmed the basic principle of the system of criminal administration in Scotland whereby the question of whether there is to be a public
prosecution is submitted to the impartial and skilled investigation of the
Lord Advocate and his department:

> "It is utterly inconsistent with such a system that the Courts should
> examine, as it was suggested it would be proper or competent for us
> to do, the reasons which have affected the Lord Advocate in
> deciding how to exercise his discretion, and it would be still more
> absurd for this Court to proceed to review their soundness."

However, this principle has now been breached by the Human Rights
Act 1998. It will now be competent to challenge any decisions by the
Lord Advocate on the raising or continuing or discontinuing of a
prosecution on the grounds of Convention rights.[24]

England

It was recognised in *Gouriet v. Union of Post Office Workers*[25] that the **8.45**
Attorney-General has an absolute and unfettered discretion to halt
prosecutions and his decision is not open to review. On the other hand,
it was also recognised that a private person could sue to prevent a public
wrong if he would sustain injury as a result of it. It was later held that in
rare cases the court could review a decision to prosecute a juvenile[26] and
further that a decision by the Revenue to prosecute an adult was open to
judicial review albeit in rare cases.[27] It is now apparent that the
prosecutional discretion of the DPP is susceptible to judicial review at
least on some grounds.[28] Moreover, there may be cases where a statute
expressly or by implication entitles a private person or body to enforce
the criminal law by civil action.

VI CONCLUSION

Scope of judicial review

If the supervisory jurisdiction of the Court of Session is to redress all **8.46**
wrongs where no other remedy exists it is inappropriate to define its
scope by reference to any rigid categorisation or analysis. It is certainly
easier to attempt to isolate the circumstances in which the jurisdiction is
not available even although no other remedy exists.[29] The range of

---

[23] 1961 J.C. 25 at 29.
[24] An amendment was proposed by the former Lord Advocate, Lord Mackay of
Drumadoon, to exclude review of decisions to prosecute, but the matter was not pressed:
Hansard, Vol. 583, col. 804.
[25] [1978] A.C. 435.
[26] *R. v. Chief Constable of the Kent County Constabulary, ex p. L.* [1993] 1 All E.R. 756.
[27] *R. v. IRC, ex p. Meas* [1993] 1 All E.R. 772.
[28] See *R. v. DPP, ex parte Chaudhary* [1995] 1 Cr. App. Rep. 136.
[29] See Chap. 9.

governmental and regulatory activity in modern society and the differing forms it takes make it unwise to confine the power of judicial review by the application of inflexible rules. In the past it was often the operation of such procedural rules that frustrated the remedy of judicial review— for example, by requiring that fair decision-making procedures were only required if the decision could be characterised as judicial. The move away from the classification of governmental powers as administrative, legislative and judicial as the threshold for deciding the competence of the court to exercise judicial review enabled the courts to develop judicial review as an effective remedy against all improper exercises of legal powers irrespective of the nature of the power. The position appears to be that neither by subject-matter, remedy, character nor function can any useful boundary be found for the scope of the supervisory jurisdiction.

Some definition can be found in the analysis of the context in which judicial review operates. It has to be predicated that there is a decision, made or about to be made, which is to be the subject of review. If the matter has only reached the stage of provisional thinking, judicial review will not lie.[30] Comments on the evidence to which the decision relates are not in themselves open to review.[31] The decision must have been one made by some person or body in the exercise of a power possessed by the person or body. In that sense it may be convenient to talk of "official" acts or omissions or of "official" bodies.[32] That power may originate in statute or contract or some other source. The challenge to be made has to be on the legality of the decision rather than its merits, so that in essence the allegation is being made that there has been an excess or abuse of power or a failure in duty on the part of the person or body possessing it.[33] The nature of the application made by the aggrieved party or of the remedy desired may serve to distinguish between cases which invoke the supervisory jurisdiction and those which do not. It is a matter of discovering what the action is truly about and the pleadings may make that clear.[34] Beyond that, the limitations which apply to the availability of the *nobile officium* and other limitations which are to be discussed in the following chapters provide sufficient definition of the extent of the equitable power of intervention. In particular, the absence of any alternative remedy will be found to provide one of the principal limitations on the scope of the supervisory jurisdiction, and it should serve to distinguish the troublesome cases of employment disputes where a contractual remedy is available from those (even in that field) where despite the existence of a contractual context the matter is open to judicial review. As will be seen in the subsequent chapters, the matter is not one where absolute boundaries can be drawn. But that is only to be expected in the context of a jurisdiction which is essentially of an equitable and supervisory character.

---

[30] *Hands v. Kyle and Carrick D.C.*, 1988 S.C.L.R. 470.

[31] *Smith v. Lord Advocate*, 1995 S.L.T. 379.

[32] This language was used in the Scottish Law Commission's Memorandum No. 14, paras 2.4 *et seq.*

[33] Thus judicial review is inappropriate for giving a remedy where a decree in absence has been granted as a result of the oversight of one party: *Bell v. Fiddes*, 1996 S.L.T. 51.

[34] *McDonald v. Secretary of State for Scotland (No. 2)*, 1996 S.L.T. 575.

A practical guide

The approach which has been suggested in the foregoing consideration **8.47** of the scope of review may be analysed into a number of progressive steps. First, the act or decision in question must be identified. Then it must be ascertained what the substance of the complaint about it is to be—is it essentially a challenge to its legality or propriety, in which case judicial review may be available, or is the intention to challenge it on its merits, or to let it lie but seek some redress by way of reparation? The latter will point away from an application to the supervisory jurisdiction. If the course is one which seeks to invoke that jurisdiction, the subject-matter of the act or decision must be considered to see that it does not lie outwith the scope of review. Then it must be confirmed that the complainer has *locus standi* to make the application. It must also be confirmed that the application is not shut out by any express finality clause or other exclusion and that either no alternative remedy is available[35] or, if there is such an alternative, there is good reason for seeking review. Finally, consideration will have to be given to the possible difficulties which may arise in respect of the timing of the application—is it too early or too late, or is there any problem of bar? These various considerations are considered in the following chapters and they are of course related to the competency, or availability, of an application. The whole matter of the strength of the merits of the complaint has yet to be assessed, as well as the possible remedies which might be sought. The remaining two Parts of the present book are taken up with these two matters in so far as they look to the grounds on which judicial review may be sought and the considerations of procedure and remedy.

The procedural significance

This chapter has been concerned with the common law jurisdiction of **8.48** the Court of Session with regard to the duties incumbent on those who possess certain powers. This jurisdiction is supervisory: its purpose is to supervise the extent and manner of the exercise of powers conferred by law. As has been explained, the significance of identifying the cases which fall within the supervisory jurisdiction is a procedural one, in respect that it is by reference to "the supervisory jurisdiction" that the Rules of Court identify the kinds of cases which are to proceed in accordance with the special procedure prescribed for such cases.[36] But disputes upon procedure should not be allowed to dominate the substantive opportunity for remedy which the supervisory jurisdiction affords.

---

[35] As, for example, being a matter of contractual dispute or otherwise falling into the kinds of case considered in Chaps 9 and 11.

[36] But Rule 58.3(1) expressly includes within the cases which are to be subject to the special procedure applications under s. 45(b) of the Court of Session Act 1988. Thus, procedurally such statutory applications are to be regarded as applications for judicial review, although they are founded on statutory provision and are not an aspect of the common law supervisory jurisdiction.

CHAPTER 9

JURISDICTIONAL LIMITATIONS

I   INTRODUCTION
II COURTS AND TRIBUNALS
III LEGISLATION
IV THE PUBLIC INTEREST

I   INTRODUCTION

Bodies susceptible to review

Considerable space could be taken up by listing the various bodies whose **9.01** decisions or actings have been the subject of judicial review,[1] but, as has already been indicated,[2] the nature of the body does not lead to a confident definition of the scope of the supervisory jurisdiction. Such a list is of as little value in defining the scope of the supervisory jurisdiction as a classification of functions.[3] The view has been expressed in England that "In a matter of jurisdiction it cannot be right to draw lines on a purely defensive basis and determine that the court has no jurisdiction over one matter which it ought properly to entertain for fear that acceptance of jurisdiction may set a precedent which will make it difficult to decline jurisdiction over other matters which it ought not to entertain".[4] In light of the difficulties in precisely defining the scope of judicial review, it is helpful at least to examine the issue from the obverse perspective, and to ask whether there is any body or any power which may not at all, or not in certain respects, be amenable to judicial review. No positive delineation of the scope of judicial review may usefully be found here but the extent to which there may be exceptions to the general availability of the jurisdiction as a source of ultimate redress deserves to be investigated.

Restraints on review

Judicial review proceeds on the broad principles that the rule of law **9.02** tolerates no excess of power and that it is the responsibility of the supreme court to supervise all those entrusted with power to secure that no such excess is committed. However, certain factors operate to restrain the generality of this responsibility. These restraints may be classified under three headings, of which the following may serve as a description. The first relates to bodies which themselves enjoy a supremacy in the law. The second relates to the law-giving function of Parliament in a

---

[1] *e.g.* Footnote to Rule of Court 58.3; *Stair Encyclopaedia*, Vol. 1, Cumulative Supplement, para. 234.

[2] para. 8.30.

[3] Chapter XXII of Burn-Murdoch on *Interdict* contains a useful survey of corporations and associations.

[4] *Leech v. Governor of Parkhurst Prison* [1988] 1 A.C. 533, *per* Lord Bridge of Harwich at 566.

democracy. The third relates to the overriding necessities of the public interest, which may operate to check the intervention of the court. These jurisdictional restraints on the court may not be absolute, but in practice they may be treated as being so. This chapter considers these three groups of limitations on the supervisory jurisdiction.

II COURTS, TRIBUNALS AND OTHER BODIES

Courts

9.03 The supervisory jurisdiction does not extend to the review of supreme courts. Lord Kinnear observed in *Moss' Empires v. Assessor for Glasgow*[5]: "Wherever any inferior tribunal or any administrative body has exceeded the powers conferred upon it by statute to the prejudice of the subject, the jurisdiction of the Court to set aside such excess of power as incompetent and illegal is not open to dispute", but he accepted that the Court would not interfere with a supreme tribunal, such as the Valuation Appeal Court or the Court of Justiciary or the Court of Teinds; "the Court will correct the proceedings, not of a supreme Court, but of an inferior Court, or, as I have said, of an administrative body, in so far as they are *ultra vires*". A decree by default in the Court of Session is open to reduction,[6] but that is by virtue of the ordinary jurisdiction of the Court and not the supervisory jurisdiction. A decree granted in the sheriff court is not open to judicial review where there is no excess of jurisdiction alleged,[7] but a decree of the sheriff court may be susceptible to review where the sheriff is acting in an administrative capacity and there is no alternative remedy provided by statute.[8] It has been accepted that a judicial review of a determination by a sheriff in a fatal accident inquiry is competent.[9] The validity of subordinate legislation made by the Supreme Court (as for example, by Act of Sederunt), is open to review.[10]

Specialist tribunals

9.04 While bodies which exercise a specialist jurisdiction will not on that account alone be immune from judicial review,[11] it must be observed that at least in respect of their procedure, and also in so far as grounds of challenge may touch upon the special areas with which they are concerned, some restraint may be exercised by the court in intervening out of respect for the expertise which such bodies possess. The work of the Parole Board may provide one example.[12] This may be seen as one particular aspect of the general approach by the court that it will not readily intervene in cases where the decision maker has a range of possible decisions open to it.[13]

---

[5] 1917 S.C.(H.L.) 1 at 6–7.
[6] Rules of Court, r. 20.1.4.
[7] *Bell v. Fiddes*, 1996 S.L.T. 51.
[8] See Macphail, *Sheriff Court Practice* (2nd ed.) paras 25.36 *et seq.*
[9] *Lothian R.C. v. Lord Advocate*, 1993 S.L.T. 1132.
[10] *Carron Co. v. Hislop*, 1931 S.C.(H.L.) 75.
[11] There may be a question whether a particular tribunal is a court in relation to matters of contempt: *Att.-Gen. v. British Broadcasting Corporation* [1980] 3 All E.R. 161.
[12] *McRae v. Parole Board for Scotland*, 1996 G.W.D. 14–852. It was observed by Lord Weir that a very strong case would have to be made out before intervention by judicial review would be justified.
[13] *R. v. Hillingdon LBC, ex p. Puhlhofer* [1986] A.C. 484.

Arbiters

In general the decisions of arbiters are open to review,[14] but, as has just **9.05** been noted, respect for a specialised expertise may impose some restraint on intervention. Challenge to an award may be made under the 25th Act of the Articles of Regulation 1695, which permitted reduction on the grounds only of corruption, bribery and falsehood—words which are to be understood in their ordinary meaning. But challenge is more usually based on grounds which are recognised at common law.[15] An invalidity in an arbitral award is strictly categorised as one of *ultra fines compromissi*, where the award has gone beyond the terms of the submission, or of *ultra vires* where the arbiter has acted in breach of some duty or obligation not contained within the terms of the submission. The *vires* of an arbiter will be determined by the provisions of the contract or statute under which he is acting. If an arbiter pronounces a decision or an order which goes beyond the scope of the matters submitted to him, the award may be reduced. Challenge can also be made at common law on such grounds as the failure of the award to exhaust the submission, the ambiguity or uncertainty of the award, the misconduct or the fraud of the arbiter, and the failure of the arbiter to deliver an award which complies with such procedural formalities as may be relevant to the case.[16] Thus, if he does not comply with the terms of the governing statutory provision the award is open to challenge.[17] If there is a severable part which alone goes beyond the submission then that part may be excised and reduced and the rest allowed to stand.[18] But where an invalid part is not severable the whole must fall. Error in a matter of law which was within the scope of the arbiter's jurisdiction has been held not to be a ground of challenge.[19] In *Mitchell v. Cable*,[20] Lord Jeffrey observed of an arbiter: "He may overlook or flagrantly misapply the most ordinary principle of law", but he added that "the true principle is this, that his decree-arbitral can stand only when he has done his duty fairly . . . that is equally, with both parties". Review can proceed on the ground of a breach of natural justice.[21] The court will not grant interdict to stop proceedings in a statutory arbitration unless there is a risk that the arbiter may exceed his jurisdiction.[22] It must be perfectly plain that the arbiter has no power such as he is invited to exercise.[23]

---

[14] *Kyle & Carrick D.C. v. A.R. Kerr & Sons*, 1992 S.L.T. 629. See generally, Walker, *Civil Remedies* pp. 239 *et seq.*

[15] For a more detailed study of this see Lord Hope's article "Arbitration" in the *Stair Encyclopaedia*, Reissue, paras 75 *et seq.*

[16] Express provision is made by ss.67 and 68 of the Arbitration Act 1996 in England for the grounds on which an award may be challenged. In arbitrations governed by the Uncitral Model Law on International Commercial Arbitration, implemented for Scotland by s.66 of the Law Reform (Miscellaneous Provisions) (Scotland) Act 1990, exclusive provision is made by Art. 34 for the setting aside of arbitral awards and intervention by a court is excluded by Art. 5 except where the law provides for it.

[17] Examples may be found in the valuation of sheep stock: *McIntyre v. Forbes*, 1939 S.L.T. 62; *Dunlop v. Mandell*, 1943 S.L.T. 286.

[18] *Miller & Son v. Oliver & Boyd* (1903) 6F. 77.

[19] *Brown v. Associated Fireclay Companies*, 1937 S.C.(H.L.) 42.

[20] (1848) 10D. 1297 at 1309.

[21] *Holmes Oil Co. v. Pumpherston Oil Co.* (1891) 18 R.(H.L.) 52; *Black v. John Williams & Co. (Wishaw)*, 1923 S.C. 510; *Fountain Forestry Holdings Ltd v. Sparkes*, 1989 S.L.T. 853.

[22] *Dunbarton Water Commissioners v. Lord Blantyre* (1884) 12 R. 115; *Glasgow Yoker and Clydebank Ry v. Ledgerwood* (1895) 23 R. 195.

[23] *Licences Insurance Corporation and Guarantee Fund Ltd v. W. and R.B. Shearer*, 1907 S.C. 10.

The Church of Scotland

9.06 The courts of the Church of Scotland possess an independent and supreme status whereby they enjoy an exclusive jurisdiction in matters of discipline or in matters of the internal regulation of procedure.[24] In such matters the Court of Session has no power to intervene. In *Lockhart v. Presbytery of Deer* Lord Ivory observed[25]:

> "This Court does not sit as a court of review over the Church Courts in ecclesiastical matters. We are asked to quash certain proceedings taken before the proper tribunal, the Ecclesiastical Court; and we are asked to to do so upon some such ground as this, that, being the supreme judicatory of the land, we have a control over all other judicatories and are bound to keep them within their proper forms of procedure.
>
> "Even taking the matter in that view, it is only as a supreme *civil* judicatory that the court can exercise these functions; and it is one of the inconveniences, if inconvenience it be, of having two independent and supreme judicatories in the same kingdom, that each is necessarily supreme within its own province, and is not, with reference to matters falling within that province, liable to any review whatever.
>
> "Even where the matter is properly within the province of the Civil Court, and where we are interfering with an inferior civil judicatory, whose jurisdiction in that particular matter has been declared exclusive, and not subject to review, our right to control its proceedings arises from the fact, that the inferior judicatory has exceeded its powers. We interfere, because the inferior court has gone beyond its province, and has, by doing so, lost the protection of the statute under which it possesses its exclusive jurisdiction.
>
> "I should no more think of disturbing a decision of the Supreme Ecclesiastical Court in an ecclesiastical matter, than I should of disturbing the decisions of the Courts of Justiciary or Exchequer in a matter falling within their respective provinces".

Thus, in relation to the established church the court will not interfere in a matter of ecclesiastical law and practice where the issue falls within the spiritual jurisdiction of the Church Courts.[26] The supremacy of the ecclesiastical courts of the Church of Scotland in ecclesiastical matters was more recently affirmed in *Logan v. Presbytery of Dunbarton*,[27] where the special position of the Church of Scotland was determined under reference to the inherent powers of that church which were recognised in but not conferred by the Church of Scotland Act 1921.[28] Ecclesiastical matters outwith a court proceeding may be immune to challenge, such as the decision to make an addition to a churchyard.[29]

---

[24] The courts of the Church of Scotland are the Kirk Session, the Presbytery, the Synod and the General Assembly. See Burn-Murdoch on *Interdict*, para. 204 for comment on some of the many 19th century cases on the church.

[25] (1851) 1D. 1296 at 1301.

[26] *Wight v. Presbytery of Dunkeld* (1879) 8M. 921.

[27] 1995 S.L.T. 1228.

[28] 11 & 12 Geo. 5, c.29.

[29] *Walker v. Presbytery of Arbroath* (1876) 4R.(H.L.) 1.

Other religious bodies

The acts and decisions of voluntary churches are subject to judicial **9.07** review in the same way as those of any other voluntary association. Although they may have elaborate constitutions. including mechanisms to secure compliance with their rules and ordinances, and even the provision of courts or tribunals, they do not enjoy any particular privilege or immunity. The judicatories of voluntary religious bodies have a privative jurisdiction within their own sphere in questions affecting their own members, but the court will intervene to secure that their proceedings are regular and in accordance with the law and constitution of the body.[30] Gross irregularity or abuse will justify intervention even if the letter of the constitution has been observed. As Lord President M'Neill observed in *M'Millan v. The Free Church*[31]:

> "If their byelaws, or constitution, or rules of government, are not contrary to law–are not illegal in themselves–the Court of law will not interfere between them and their members in the fair application and enforcement of such rules against parties who have chosen to enter the body, and to subject themselves to its laws. But if the office-bearers or the governing authorities of the body go altogether beyond the sphere of the constitution of the association– if they deal with a member in a way that they are not authorised by their constitution to deal with him–if they attempt to exercise over him a power or authority which he by becoming a member did not give them, and if by so acting they have done him injury, he will not be precluded from seeking redress, nor will the courts of law hold themselves precluded from giving him redress."

But in order to intervene it must be shown that there has not only been a breach of the constitution but some gross injustice or some invasion of civil right or interest. In *M'Donald v. Burns*[32] Lord Justice-Clerk Aitchison stated that the necessary preconditions for intervention were in general as follows:

> "(first) where the religious association through its agencies has acted clearly and demonstrably beyond its own constitution, and in a manner calculated to affect the civil rights and patrimonial interests of its members, and (secondly) where, although acting within its constitution, the procedure of its judicial or quasi-judicial tribunals has been marked by gross irregularity, such fundamental irregularity as would, in the case of an ordinary civil tribunal, be sufficient to vitiate the proceedings. But a mere irregularity is not enough. It must be so fundamental an irregularity that it goes beyond a mere matter of procedure, and becomes something so prejudicial to a fair and impartial investigation of the question to be decided as to amount to a denial of natural justice, as, for example, if a conviction of an ecclesiastical offence were to take place without an accusation being made, or without allowing the person accused to be heard in his defence. In short, the irregularity alleged must not be simply in

---

[30] See *M'Donald v. Burns*, 1940 S.C. 376, and cases cited there.
[31] (1859) 22D. 290 at 314.
[32] 1940 S.C. 376 at 383.

point of form, or a departure from prescribed regulation, but must go to the honesty and integrity of the proceedings complained of".

These principles apply to all religious bodies beyond the established church.[33]

Associations

9.08 The position of any voluntary association whose constitution binds its members as persons who have voluntarily undertaken to submit themselves to abide by its regulations is in principle the same as that which has been described in relation to voluntary churches. The rules of a trade union which are contrary to natural justice will be held to be invalid,[34] as will be the disciplinary proceedings of a club or an association, such as a football association,[35] or a political group.[36] At least in matters of procedure private tribunals or courts as well as arbitrations are treated with some respect and the court will not lightly interfere. But if there is a clear illegality, beyond a mere irregularity, and an invasion of civil rights and interests[37] or an extreme case of abuse, excess of power or irrationality,[38] the court will intervene to give a remedy. It is thought that the adoption of the form of an incorporated company is not a point of distinction from any other form of association in the present context. Acts in excess of statutory power by a railway company were subject to suspension and interdict under the supervisory jurisdiction.[39] Under modern company law there may be a sufficiency of statutory remedies which makes recourse to review less necessary.

The armed forces, prisons and schools

9.09 At least in the past there has been some reluctance on the part of the court to intervene in matters of the internal management of particular organisations which traditionally operated under their own regimes. It has long been held in England that the High Court has no jurisdiction to supervise the way discipline is enforced in the armed services.[40] A like view was once taken with regard to prison governors in relation to matters of discipline,[41] although the decision of a prison board of visitors on a disciplinary matter was held to be distinct from the disciplinary or managerial functions of a governor and to be susceptible to review.[42]

---

[33] English law has required to wrestle with the problem of the competency of judicial review of religious bodies by reference to the existence of an element of public law in the decision: *R. v. Chief Rabbi of the United Congregations of Great Britain and the Commonwealth, ex p. Wachmann* [1993] 2 All E.R. 249.

[34] e.g. *Edwards v. Society of Graphical and Allied Trades* [1971] 1 Ch. 354.

[35] *St. Johnstone Football Club Ltd v. Scottish Football Association*, 1965 S.L.T. 171. In that case Lord Kilbrandon pointed out under reference to *McDonald* (*cit. sup.*) that in cases of gross irregularity, such as a departure from the rules of natural justice, it was not necessary to show an interference with the civil rights or patrimonial interests of the complainer. See later (on *locus standi*) para. 10.21.

[36] e.g. *Brown v. Executive Committee of the Edinburgh Labour Party*, 1995 S.L.T. 985.

[37] *Oliver v. Skerret* (1896) 23 R. 468.

[38] *Shanks & McEwan (Contractors) Ltd v. Mifflin Construction Ltd*, 1993 S.L.T. 1124.

[39] *Ellis v. Invergarry and Fort Augustus Ry*, 1913 S.C. 849. See Burn-Murdoch on *Interdict*, p. 400.

[40] *R. v. Army Council, ex p. Ravenscroft* [1917] 2 K.B. 504. It may now be open to question how far this approach would be accepted today.

[41] *R. v. Deputy Governor of Camphill Prison, ex p. King* [1985] 1 Q.B. 735, overruled in *Leech v. Deputy Governor of Parkhurst Prison* [1988] 1 A.C. 533.

[42] *R. v. Board of Visitors of Hull Prison, ex p. St. Germain* [1979] Q.B. 425.

Eventually, in *Leech v. Deputy Governor of Parkhurst Prison*[43] the House of Lords affirmed that a prison governor's disciplinary adjudications were amenable to judicial review. The position regarding commanding officers and schoolmasters was left open; but it would seem difficult to draw any convincing distinction there. Decisions regarding prisoners may involve the exercise of a very wide discretion on the part of the Secretary of State and interference by the court in a matter such as a decision to transfer a prisoner may only be made in a rare and exceptional case.[44] For example, it will only be rarely that judicial review would be permitted of a decision on the transfer of a prisoner from one prison to another.[45] However, this is one area in which the Human Rights Act 1998 may encourage greater intervention by the Court.[46]

III LEGISLATION

Acts of Parliament

It was recognised by the Lord Advocate in the case of *MacCormack v.* **9.10** *Lord Advocate*[47] that the Parliament of Great Britain could not repeal or alter the fundamental and essential conditions of the Treaty of Union, that is to say those clauses which, unlike those which expressly reserve to the Parliament of Great Britain a power of subsequent modification, either contain no such power or emphatically exclude subsequent alteration by declaring that they are unalterable. But it is a distinct question whether the preservation of such fundamental provisions can be secured by the court. In *MacCormack* the distinction was drawn between matters concerning private right and matters concerning public right. In relation to the former the Lord President expressly reserved his opinion on the question whether a breach of the provisions relating expressly to the court and to the laws which concern private right would be determinable as a justiciable issue before the courts of Scotland or England. But so far as matters of public right were concerned he felt constrained to hold that it had not been shown that the Court of Session had authority to entertain such an issue. Lord Keith in *Gibson v. Lord Advocate*[48] followed this view, stating:

> "Like Lord President Cooper I prefer to reserve my opinion what the position would be if the United Kingdom Parliament passed an Act purporting to abolish the Court of Session or the Church of Scotland or to substitute English law for the whole body of Scots private law. I am, however, of opinion that the question whether a particular Act of the United Kingdom Parliament altering a particu-

---

[43] [1988] A.C. 533.

[44] *Thomson v. Secretary of State for Scotland*, 1989 S.C.L.R. 161.

[45] *Thomson, Petr*, 1989 S.L.T. 343. See J.J. Mcmanus, "Prisoners' Rights in Scotland; judicial review of allocation decisions" (1989) 149 SCOLAG 25.

[46] As examples of recent cases on courts-martial see *Findlay v. U.K.* (1997) 24 E.H.R.R. 221 (in the ECHR) and in relation to a question of abuse of process in relation to a court-martial, *R. v. Martin* [1998] 1 All E.R. 193 (in the House of Lords). On the problem of discharge from the armed services on account of sexual orientation see *R. v. Ministry of Defence, ex p. Smith* [1996] Q.B. 517.

[47] 1953 S.C. 396. In connection with the present discussion reference should also be made to the earlier chapter on the Constitution, para. 4.31.

[48] 1975 S.C. 136 at 144.

lar aspect of Scots private law is or is not for 'the evident utility' of the subjects within Scotland is not a justiciable issue in this Court . . . A general inquiry into the utility of specific legislative measures as regards the population generally is quite outside its competence".

The issue arose more recently in *Pringle, Petitioner*,[49] where the petitioner sought to invoke the *nobile officium* in order to be relieved of his liability to pay the community charge which had been recently introduced into Scotland a year before its introduction into England and Wales. He founded on Article IV of the Act of Union, claiming that the introduction of the charge into Scotland alone contravened the requirement of that Article in requiring the subjects of one part of the British Isles to pay a tax which was not levied on the subjects of the other part. The First Division held that it was incompetent to invoke the *nobile officium* in order to be relieved of a liability imposed by statute. It was not decided and did not have to be decided whether the new legislation could be struck down as contrary to the Act of Union. On that point the observations of the Lord President (Hope), who reserved his opinion on the matter, certainly did not exclude such a proposition and indeed on the contrary may be read as accepting the possibility provided that a detailed investigation of the different provisions for raising local taxation in the two countries justified such a course.

The question may be asked whether a Private Act of Parliament, or even a Public Act, might be challenged on the ground of fraudulent procedure.[50] But it was long ago held[51] that the court can only look to the parliamentary roll to see if an Act has passed both Houses of Parliament and received the Royal Assent, and that no court can inquire into the manner in which it was introduced, nor what passed in parliament during the various stages of its progress through both Houses. That the court cannot challenge the enactments of Parliament on the ground that Parliament was misled by fraud or otherwise was more recently affirmed in *Picken v. British Railways Board*.[52] It should also be noticed in the present context that legislation of the U.K. Parliament may be open to challenge on the ground of an incompatibility with E.C. law.[53] But in relation to the compatibility of an Act of the U.K. Parliament with the European Convention on Human Rights, the Human Rights Act 1998 only permits the court to declare an incompatibility and not reduce the offending legislation.[54]

Judicial review and parliament

9.11 Apart from the difficult constitutional problems which are raised, particularly in relation to the Treaties of Union, and apart also from the situation of conflict with E.C. law, the general constitutional position must be that courts in the United Kingdom do not have powers to review an Act of Parliament, declare it invalid or strike it down.[55] As

---

[49] 1991 S.L.T. 330.
[50] See J.W. Bridge, "Judicial Review of Private Legislation in the UK", 1973 J.R. 135.
[51] *Edinburgh & Dalkeith Ry v. Wauchope* (1842) 1 Bell 252.
[52] [1974] A.C. 765.
[53] *R. v. Secretary of State for Employment, ex p. Equal Opportunities Commission* [1995] 1 A.C. 1.
[54] See s.4 of the Human Rights Act 1998.
[55] *Pickin v. British Railways Board* [1974] A.C. 765.

Lord Reid observed in *Burmah Oil Co. (Burma Trading) Ltd v. Lord Advocate*[56]: "Since the seventeenth century we have lost the idea that our own sovereign, the king in Parliament, is under the law so that an Act of Parliament could be, in modern parlance, *ultra vires*". In light of there being no codified constitution in the United Kingdom, it is unsurprising that the courts have no such powers.[57] Yet beyond the bare question of a power to review the validity of Acts of Parliament, the matter is more complicated. First, as noted above, the courts give effect to the will of Parliament through the process of interpreting its enactments. Accordingly, their subordinacy is more apparent than real. Put shortly, Parliament's supremacy depends on its being able to express itself precisely. In reality, both the indeterminacy of language and the difficulties associated with determining the intention of a collective body such as a legislature make this practically impossible. Secondly, there may be a power to determine that an Act of Parliament is properly so called. Thirdly, the courts do have powers to review and invalidate subordinate legislation, not only on the narrow ground of incompatibility with the parent statute, but also on most of the wider grounds of judicial review, such as procedural impropriety and irrationality. In the generality it has to be recognised that the law courts and Parliament each have their own particular role to play in the constitution. "Collision between the two institutions is likely to impair their powers to vouchsafe those constitutional rights for which the citizens depend on them".[58] Lord Woolf M.R. has observed[59]: "Activities of government are the basic fare of judicial review. Activities of Parliament are not the basic fare of judicial review."

Subordinate legislation

Whatever may be the position regarding primary legislation, there is no **9.12** doubt that subordinate legislation is subject to review.[60] The question, however, arises whether or how far the courts may review subordinate legislation which has been approved by another body such as Parliament. In this connection regard must be had to the grounds on which it is sought to challenge the legislation. In one Scottish case the Crown accepted that where delegated legislation was subject to a negative resolution the court could entertain a challenge to its validity on the ground that the measure was beyond the scope of the enabling power.[61] In the later English case of *Hoffman-La Roche and Co. v. Secretary of State for Trade and Industry*[62] the fact that the order in question had been approved by both Houses of Parliament by the positive procedure did not prevent the court from declaring it invalid. The attack there made was based on alleged defects in the procedure which had been followed and on grounds of *ultra vires*. Where the attack is on the ground of

---

[56] 1964 S.C.(H.L.) 117 at 127.

[57] It should be noted that such powers are exceptional in most constitutional systems.

[58] *Pickin v. British Railways Board* [1974] A.C. 765, *per* Lord Simon of Glaisdale at 799.

[59] *R. v. Parliamentary Commissioner of Standards, ex p. Al Fayed* (1998) 1 All E.R. 93 at 96. An appeal to the House of Lords was refused on October 7, 1999.

[60] Orders made under the royal prerogative and certain subordinate legislation should be distinguished from statutory instruments as defined by the Statutory Instruments Act 1947, but all may be subject to review. For examples of challenges to ministerial orders and regulations see Gloag and Henderson, *The Law of Scotland* (10th ed.), para. 1.6. See also Bradley, *Stair Encyclopaedia*, Vol. 1, para. 298. See also on irrationality para. 21.17 below.

[61] *Glasgow Victoria Hospital v. Secretary of State for Scotland*, 1953 S.C. 279.

[62] [1975] A.C. 365.

irrationality the situation may be different. In *Rae v. Hamilton*[63] Lord McLaren, in holding that certain byelaws were not unreasonable, attached considerable weight to the fact that they had been approved by the Local Government Board as required by the relevant statute. Indeed he indicated that there was a presumption of reasonableness which arose when the byelaws had been approved by the statutory authority. The point was canvassed in Scotland in *City of Edinburgh D.C. v. Secretary of State for Scotland.*[64] In the Outer House Lord Jauncey held that where Parliament had reserved a control over subordinate legislation by requiring that such legislation was to be subject to its own approval, then the legislation could not be challenged as unreasonable or irrational. The courts[65] "can only hold to be *ultra vires* a statutory instrument which has been laid before and approved by Parliament where that instrument is patently defective in that it purports to do what is not authorised by the enabling statute or where the procedure followed in making that instrument departed from the requirements of the enabling statute". The decision that the instrument in question was not defective was upheld by the Second Division. There the view was taken that on the facts of the case none of the tests of illegality, irrationality or procedural impropriety were made out. The test of irrationality did not seem to be excluded as matter of principle. It was rather a matter of the extreme difficulty in conceiving of its application in the circumstances of a measure which was the expression of a decision on policy. Further support for the proposition that irrationality may rarely, if ever, be open as a ground for review where a Parliamentary approval is required may be found in *Nottinghamshire County Council v. Secretary of State for the Environment.*[66] It was there indicated that where executive power is only to be exercised with the consent and approval of one of the Houses of Parliament, courts could only interfere if the statute had been misconstrued or the minister had deceived the House. It was not for the judges to hold that the exercise was irrational; the matter was one of political judgment for the minister and for the House. There seems to be no reason to believe that there is any difference between English and Scottish law on the competency of challenging any subordinate legislation which requires to pass before Parliament.[67]

Acts of the Scottish Parliament

9.13 Judicial review of the Scottish Parliament and the Scottish government has been considered in Chapter 7. It may be noted in the present context that Acts of the Scottish Parliament will be open to review on the ground of their competence under the complex provisions of the Scotland Act 1998.

Prerogative

9.14 By prerogative power is meant the residue of discretionary power left in the hands of the Crown. The tendency of the older English cases was to regard powers exercised under the prerogative as immune from chal-

---

[63] (1904) 6F.(J.) 42.

[64] 1985 S.C. 261. For further discussion on this topic see C.M.G. Himsworth, "Defining the Boundaries of Judicial Review", 1985 S.L.T. (News) 369 and A.I.L. Campbell "Approval and Statutory Instruments", 1986 S.L.T. (News) 101.

[65] *Edinburgh D.C. v. Secretary of State for Scotland*, 1985 S.C. 261 at 275.

[66] [1986] A.C. 240.

[67] The position where subordinate legislation is declared to have effect as if enacted in an Act is considered later: see para. 11.20 (exclusion).

lenge in the courts,[68] but recently a wide range of prerogative powers have come to be recognised as open to review.[69] One example can be found in the original scheme for compensation for criminal injuries in which a Board was established under prerogative powers; it was held in England that the court had jurisdiction to review its proceedings.[70] Scotland may have taken a more robust view at least in an earlier period.[71] In *Officers of State for Scotland v. Lord Douglas*[72] the court reviewed a purported act of the royal prerogative, holding that the grant of an office with a salary by the late King George IV was *ultra vires*, since it was a grant which extended beyond his own lifetime and was a device to give the recipient a pension under the guise of a salary. Even the prerogative of mercy may now be open to review in England,[73] a point which has been expressly reserved in Scotland.[74] But it has been recognised in England that there are limits to the susceptibility to judicial review of actings under prerogative power. Powers relating to the making of treaties, the defence of the realm, the grant of honours, the dissolution of Parliament and the appointment of ministers are among matters which have been noted as not open to review.[75] A royal proclamation has been held not to support a claim that someone is acting under the prerogative and where the actings were beyond the authority's statutory and common law powers the court intervened.[76] The matter of remedies against the Crown is considered later.[77]

Orders in Council

As was held in the *GCHQ* case,[78] the mere fact that a minister's power **9.15** derived from a prerogative or common law source rather than a statutory one did not exclude his actions from judicial review. The justiciability of a prerogative act depended upon its subject matter. Accordingly an instrument purportedly made under an Order in Council was not immune from challenge. In *Griffin v. Lord Advocate*,[79] which concerned a claim for a naval pension, the view was taken that where an Order in Council imposed a duty on a government minister to carry out the provisions of it, the Order did not create rights in the eventual beneficiaries which can be enforced in the courts; the duty on the minister was a duty owed to the Crown and he acted solely as an agent of the Crown. Generally, however, Orders in Council proceeding under a statutory power will be open to review. Decisions made under Orders which derive from the prerogative power may be open to review, such as

---

[68] *Att.-Gen. v. De Keyser's Royal Hotel* [1920] A.C. 508.
[69] *R. v. Criminal Injuries Compensation Board, ex p. Lain* [1967] 2 Q.B. 864; *Civil Service Union v. Minister for Civil Service* [1985] 1 A.C. 374; see also *Laker Airways Ltd v. Department of Trade* [1977] Q.B. 643; see more generally de Smith, Woolf and Jowell, *Judicial Review of Administrative Action* (5th ed.), para. 6.046.
[70] *R. v. Criminal Injuries Compensation Board, ex p. Lain* [1967] 2 Q.B. 864.
[71] See para. 4.49 (in Constitution).
[72] (1838) 1D. 300.
[73] *R. v. Secretary of State for the Home Department, ex p. Bentley* [1994] Q.B. 349; but *cf. Recklay v. Minister of Public Safety and Immigration and Others (No. 2)* [1996] A.C. 527.
[74] *McDonald v. Secretary of State for Scotland*, 1996 S.L.T. 16.
[75] By Lord Roskill in *Council of Civil Service Unions v. Minister for the Civil Service* [1985] A.C. 374 at 418. His Lordship also mentioned the prerogative of mercy.
[76] *Grieve v. Edinburgh and District Water Trustees*, 1968 S.C. 700.
[77] para. 23.36.
[78] *Council of Civil Service Unions v. Minister for the Civil Service* [1985] A.C. 374.
[79] 1950 S.C. 448.

decisions of the Civil Service Appeal Board.[80] Review is also available where civil service regulations have not been observed.[81]

Conventions

9.16   It has already been noted that many of the U.K. constitution's values are contained in constitutional conventions.[82] In fact, most of the democratic aspects of the constitution are governed by convention.[83] Among these are the Monarch's powers in relation to Parliament and the principles associated with ministerial responsibility. Given the importance of conventions to the democratic character of the constitution, the question arises as to what role, if any, they have in judicial review. For example, if a minister refused to answer questions in Parliament and a majority in the House of Commons agreed not to censure the minister, could the decision not to answer questions be challenged by judicial review?[84] The consensus follows Dicey's view that conventions are not enforceable in the courts, although several commentators have explored what is meant by "enforceable".[85] Certainly, it cannot be said that conventions are irrelevant in the courts. While it is true that the values protected by conventions are often political, therefore rendering them non-justiciable, they form a significant part of the background against which legislation and government actions are examined. A like question may arise in relation to the concordats which may regulate matters between the Scottish Parliament and the U.K. Parliament, but, as has already been suggested, it may be that these would be open to review if they exceed a proper construction of the primary legislation.[86]

Ombudsmen

9.17   Decisions of the Parliamentary Commissioner for Administration are open to review.[87] But the Parliamentary Commissioner for Standards is immune from review.[88] The former considers the administration of government outside Parliament, but the latter is concerned with the proprieties of the activities of those who are engaged within Parliament. Thus a Local Commissioner for Administration is subject to the supervisory jurisdiction.[89]

---

[80] *e.g. R. v. Civil Service Appeal Board, ex p. Cunningham* [1991] 4 All E.R. 310.

[81] *Jackson v. Secretary of State for Scotland,* 1992 S.L.T. 572.

[82] See "Constitutional Law", *Stair Memorial Encyclopaedia,* Vol. 5; Wade & Ewing, *Administrative Law*; and on the relationship between law and convention, see Munro, "Law and Conventions" (1975) 91 L.Q.R. 218.

[83] The U.K. Constitution is not much different from other constitutions in this; the (codified) U.S. Constitution is also supplemented by conventions: see Mitchell, *supra* n. 1.

[84] Assuming, of course, that standing could be established, perhaps by an interested pressure group? Standing to bring an application for judicial review is discussed in Chapter 10.

[85] *cf.* Mitchell, *Constitutional Law* (2nd ed.) at pp. 29 *et seq.*

[86] see para. 7.46.

[87] *R. v. Parliamentary Commissioner for Administration, ex p. Dyer* [1994] 1 All E.R. 375.

[88] *R. v. Parliamentary Commissioner, ex p. Al Fayed* [1998] 1 All E.R. 93.

[89] *e.g. R. v. Local Commissioner for Administration for the North and East Area of England, ex p. Bradford Metropolitan City Council* [1979] 1 Q.B. 287. It has been held in England in *R. v. Insurance Ombudsman, ex p. Aegon Life Assurance Ltd* [1994] C.L.C. 88 that a decision of the insurance ombudsman is not subject to review, as not being a "public body", but it may be questioned whether a Scottish court would reach the same result. See the comment in de Smith, Woolf and Jowell, *Judicial Review of Administrative Action* (5th ed.), para. 3.051.

IV THE PUBLIC INTEREST

National security and public policy

In what may be an aspect of the consideration of prerogative powers **9.18** there may be cases where considerations of national security can override considerations of natural justice and bar a challenge which would otherwise have been open. Thus in *R. v. Secretary of State for Home Affairs, ex parte Hosenball*[90] the Secretary of State refused to provide a foreign journalist with the particulars of the allegations which he had to meet to resist a deportation order. It was held that since the Secretary of State had acted for reasons of public security the deportation order should not be questioned. In time of war national security may justify the withdrawing of details of the grounds for deportation of an alien.[91] But in other circumstances the risk to national security may have to be established before the court[92] and reasons may have to be disclosed for detention in order to meet the provisions of Article 5(1)(c) of the European Convention on Human Rights.[93] The principle that the Scottish court may override a ministerial objection to production of a document on grounds of public interest has long been recognised.[94] In the context of a public interest objection to the recovery of documents sought by an accused for the purposes of his defence to a criminal charge, it has been held that the court would require to decide whether the public interest in securing a fair trial required the production of the documents despite the objection.[95] In the *GCHQ* case the applicants failed because the requirements of national security were held to outweigh considerations of fairness. In *Chandler v. Director of Public Prosecutions* Lord Reid[96] declared it to be clear "that the disposition and armament of the armed forces are and for centuries have been within the exclusive discretion of the Crown and that no one can seek a legal remedy on the ground that such discretion has been wrongly exercised". But while national security may justify a withholding of reasons or confidential information[97] it may not avail against excess of power or bad faith.

Political issues

The exercise of government powers often concerns the most sensitive **9.19** political matters in the state. While the principle of legality requires that all government decisions are reviewable, a political constitution also requires the courts to accept that some subjects are exclusively for the politicians and not for the judges. Drawing the line between reviewable matters and non-reviewable matters is not an easy task for a legal system committed to the rule of law, but it is one that requires to be undertaken. The U.K. systems are not alone, although they may not be as experienced as others, in having to distinguish the reviewable from the non-reviewable in this area.

---

[90] [1977] 1 W.L.R. 766.
[91] *R. v. Secretary of State for the Home Department, ex p. Cheblack* [1991] 3 All E.R. 319.
[92] *R. v. Secretary of State for the Home Department, ex p. Ruddock* [1987] 2 All E.R. 518.
[93] *Fox v. U.K.* (1991) 13 E.H.R.R. 13.
[94] *Glasgow Corporation v. Central Land Board*, 1956 S.C.(H.L.) 1.
[95] *McLeod, Petr*, 1998 S.L.T. 233.
[96] [1964] A.C. 763 at 791.
[97] As in *R. v. Gaming Board, ex p. Benaim* [1970] 2 All E.R. 528.

In general, matters of political policy will be regarded as outwith the supervision of the court but matters of discretion in the implementation of policy will be open to review.[98] Public policy has generally been recognised by the courts as an area into which they should not enter.[99] Judges should rather be "trusted as interpreters of the law than as expounders of what is called public policy".[1] In *Nottinghamshire County Council v. Secretary of State for the Environment*[2] severe discouragement was given to the making of a challenge on a matter of the limits of public expenditure by local authorities and the incidence of the tax burden as between taxpayers and ratepayers. These were seen as matters for the Secretary of State and the House of Commons. In that case it was held that there was no ground for holding that the Secretary of State had acted in bad faith, or for an improper motive, or that his guidance "was so absurd that he must have taken leave of his senses". But while it is certainly to be recognised that the court will not lightly interfere with a minister's decision on a matter where the interests of various groups of the public require to be weighed and decision-making may require to be influenced by considerations of national policy of which the government must be the best judge, there is no absolute exclusion here of judicial review, albeit, as was recognised in the case, only in exceptional circumstances.[3] Matters of political judgment—for example in the fields of education or housing—are matters properly to be finally resolved by the appropriate authorities and not matters on which immediate recourse should necessarily be made to the courts.[4] Decisions on the level of fares to be charged for local public transport may be susceptible to review.[5] It is consistent with this respect for matters of policy that the court will only intervene in the case of statutory instruments which have been considered by Parliament where there is an illegality in the narrow sense of that word, or a defect in procedure.[6]

Acts of State

9.20 The exercise of the sovereign power abroad is immune from challenge. Thus acts done against an alien outside British territory which have been authorised or adopted by the Crown will not give rise to a remedy.[7] A wider view was taken in *Poll v. Lord Advocate*[8] where a German subject was refused a remedy for being prevented from landing fish at Aberdeen which he had caught outside territorial waters in breach of Scottish fishing laws. The prevention from landing had been authorised by the Secretary of State on behalf of Her Majesty. Nor will the annexation of foreign territory by conquest impose obligations enforceable in the courts of this country to honour liabilities earlier incurred by the

---

[98] *Padfield v. Minister of Agriculture, Fisheries and Food* [1968] A.C. 997.

[99] Public policy is "a very unruly horse, and when once you get astride of it you never know where it will carry you": Burrough J. in *Richardson v. Mellish*, 2 Bing. 252.

[1] In *Re Mirams* [1891] 1 Q.B. 594, *per* Cave J. at 595.

[2] [1986] A.C. 240 at 247.

[3] The intensity of judicial review may vary and there are some areas in which a judicial restraint on intervention is required. See later para. 14.13.

[4] In the context of homelessness, see *R. v. Hillingdon LBC ex p. Puhlhofer* [1986] A.C. 484, *per* Lord Brightman at 518.

[5] *Bromley LBC v. Greater London Council* [1983] A.C. 768.

[6] *City of Edinburgh D.C. v. Secretary of State for Scotland*, 1985 S.C. 261, see above, para. 9.12.

[7] *Buron v. Denman* (1848) 2 Ex. 167.

[8] (1899) 1F. 823.

conquered state.[9] The essential ingredient for the immunity of an Act of State appears to be that it was committed outside British territory.[10] Destruction of the property of a British subject in a Crown colony by virtue of the royal prerogative in time of war to prevent its use by the enemy has been held to admit of a remedy.[11]

---

[9] *West Rand Central Gold Mining Co. v. The King* [1905] 2 K.B. 391.
[10] See Wade and Forsyth, *Administrative Law* (7th ed.), p. 843.
[11] *Burmah Oil Co. (Burma Trading) Ltd v. Lord Advocate*, 1964 S.C.(H.L.) 117.

CHAPTER 10

LOCUS STANDI

I   GENERAL
II   TITLE AND INTEREST
III LOCUS STANDI IN JUDICIAL REVIEW

I   GENERAL

Introduction

In Scotland the usual terminology used for rules of standing is title and   **10.01**
interest to sue. The principle of standing, or *locus standi*, requires that
only those who are entitled to bring a claim to court may enforce that
claim before the court. Just as a pursuer in every action must establish
his *locus standi* to bring a legal claim before the competent court will
entertain the action, it is an essential prerequisite in an application for
judicial review that the applicant shows his *locus standi* to make the
application.[1] That is achieved by his making the relevant averments in
the first paragraph of the petition.[2] Form 58.6 in the Rules of Court
specifically requires a statement of the "title and interest"of the petitioner. In the context of human rights it should be noted that section 7 of
the Human Rights Act 1998 requires that only a "victim"of a breach of
Convention rights has standing to complain. This matter is discussed in
Chapter 6.[3]

Locus Standi and the Reality of the Issue

A distinction requires to be drawn between the requirement that the   **10.02**
person presenting the application for review has the *locus* to do so, and
the requirement that the issue which is raised in the application is a real
and practical one. It is possible to express the objection relative to the
latter consideration in terms of *locus standi*. Thus where the issue is too
remote and uncertain the incompetency of judicial review may be
expressed either as outwith the scope of judicial review or as one of no
interest to sue.[4] In the former case, where the issue is one of no interest
to anyone, the court will not entertain it because the court is concerned
to deal with matters of reality and substance and not hypothetical or
academic questions. In the latter case the issue may be a live one, but
while there may well be people with an interest to raise it, the pursuer is
not one of them. That issue is one of *locus standi*. It is thought to be

---

[1] For a discussion of recent developments in the law of standing for judicial review in
both Scotland and England, see Himsworth, "No Standing Still on Standing", in Leyland
and Woods (eds), *Administrative Law Facing the Future* (1997), Chap. 9.
[2] For an example of a failure to make a sufficient averment to constitute title to sue, see
Tait v. Earl of Lauderdale (1827) 5S. 330, where persons described as "servants" in the
locality were held to have no title, not being householders, to complain at the closure of a
road.
[3] See para. 6.63.
[4] *Moriarty v. City of Edinburgh District Licensing Board*, 1995 S.L.T. 40.

preferable to draw the distinction between these two situations. The point is noted later in the context of real issues.[5] Matters of *locus* may, however, arise on the assumption of a contingency. Thus, where it could not be predicated that a particular drainage scheme was necessarily in breach of the relevant statute it was held that the carrying out of the scheme could not properly be interdicted, but it was observed that if it did lead to the creation of a nuisance then those affected by it would have title and interest to complain about it.[6]

The Ordinary Rules

10.03 The Rule of Court which introduced the special procedure for judicial review did not innovate upon the existing rules governing the entitlement to raise or defend an action in the Court of Session. Accordingly the ordinary principles governing *locus standi* should apply to applications for judicial review. In Scotland the consideration of *locus standi* has traditionally been analysed into two ingredients, namely a title to sue and an interest to sue, with the requirement that a pursuer must qualify in both respects.[7] But it is questionable whether that two-fold analysis is always appropriate or helpful in the context of applications for judicial review. In practice a challenge to the *locus standi* of the pursuer is made by entering the formal plea "No title to sue"in the defences or answers to the claim. But that formulation is recognised in practice as covering both the element of title and that of interest so as to give notice of a challenge on either or both of those element.[8]

Facilitation and Restriction

10.04 Rules of standing may be viewed as facilitative and restrictive. On the one hand they prescribe the criteria of eligibility to bring legal actions and in this respect may operate widely for a broad class of claimants. On the other hand they also inevitably limit the scope to bring judicial proceedings by defining who may and who may not do so. This simultaneous function of the rules of standing may give rise to a particular tension in judicial review proceedings because of the potentially broad class of persons who may wish to resort to an application for judicial review to enforce public rights and duties. It has been the apparently limiting dimension of the rules of standing which have attracted particular attention where public rights and duties are in dispute. In particular the growth of interest groups may be thought to give rise to some particular problem or even to call for some development of the traditional rules of standing. But it should not be assumed that the Scottish rules are more restrictive than facilitative nor that they are incapable of adapting to the need to develop the full remedial potential of judicial review.[9]

---

[5] See later para. 13.02.
[6] *Steel v. Commissioners of Police of Gourock* (1872) 10M. 954.
[7] Maclaren, *Court of Session Practice*, pp. 188 *et seq.*
[8] *Agnew v. Laughlan*, 1948 S.C. 656 at 661.
[9] For an argument favouring a generous rule on standing, see Ian Cran, "Towards Good Administration - the Reform of Standing in Scots Law", 1995 J.R. 332.

II TITLE AND INTEREST

Title

The first of the two ingredients which is to be identified on the ordinary **10.05** approach to matters of *locus standi* is the possession of a title to sue. The classic description of title was formulated by Lord Dunedin in these words: "he must be party (using the word in its widest sense) to some legal relation which gives some right which the person against whom he raises the action either infringes or denies".[10] This has become the traditional starting point in Scots law for the consideration of title to sue. But Lord Dunedin expressly disowned the intention to formulate a definition and the statement is to be understood as descriptive without being definitive.[11] The legal relationship which provides the title may be of a contractual character or of a much wider and less formal kind. A right and a corresponding duty may arise at common law sufficient to create a title to sue. A sufficient mutuality of rights and obligations between co-feuars gives one a title to sue the other for enforcement of building restrictions in the property titles of each property.[12] The right which is infringed may be the counterpart of a duty created by statute. In that context questions may arise whether or not in relation to a particular statutory duty a particular individual can qualify a title to sue for the enforcement of that duty[13] or to claim damages in respect of a breach of it.[14] But in many cases the obligation to comply with the law carries with it a right on the part of anyone affected to challenge a failure in such compliance. Whether or not there is title can thus depend on the circumstances. The title to sue of a statutory body may depend upon its statutory powers. Thus a statutory body which had certain express powers of enforcement, but no power to resort to such common law remedies as an interdict, was held to have no title to sue such an action.[15] So also a local authority with statutory powers of administration was held to have no title to seek interdict against the discharge of refuse on the foreshore within the burgh.[16]

The *D. & J. Nicol* case

In the case of *D. & J. Nicol v. Trustees of the Harbour of Dundee*[17] the **10.06** Harbour Trustees were empowered by a local Act to operate ferries on the river Tay. They had more steamers than they needed at any one time to operate the ferries and decided to use the spare capacity to run river tours. D. & J. Nicol were competitors in the business of river tours and raised an action against the trustees complaining that they were acting *ultra vires* of the Act, because they had no authority to use steamers outside the ferry operation. On the preliminary issue of D. & J. Nicol's title to sue the House of Lords held that they had no title to sue as

---

[10] *D.&J. Nicol v. Trustees of the Harbour of Dundee*, 1915 S.C.(H.L.) 7 at 12.

[11] *Air 2000 Ltd v. Secretary of State for Transport (No. 2)*, 1990 S.L.T. 335 at 338.

[12] *Murray's Trustees v. Trustees for St Margaret's Convent* (1906) 8F. 1109.

[13] *Institute of Patent Agents v. Lockwood* (1894) 21R.(H.L.) 61; *Reid v. Mini-Cabs*, 1966 S.C. 137.

[14] e.g. *Pullar v. Window Clean Ltd*, 1956 S.C. 13, following, among other cases, *Cutler v. Wandsworth Stadium Ltd*, 1949 A.C. 398.

[15] *Tay District Fishery Board v. Robertson* (1887) 15 R. 40.

[16] *Magistrates of Buckhaven and Methil v. Wemyss Coal Co.*, 1932 S.C. 201.

[17] 1915 S.C.(H.L.) 7.

business competitors, but did have a title to sue as harbour ratepayers and as persons who might be qualified to vote in an election of the trustees or even be elected as trustees. The Trustees were seen to be trustees for those who were interested in the execution of their powers and who had contributed to the funds which they administered. The relevant "legal relation"with the Trustees which gave them title was the fiduciary duty of trust which the Trustees owed to them as harbour ratepayers under the statute The Lord Chancellor (Haldane) observed[18]: "it appears to me that their real case is that they are beneficially and individually interested in the administration of property and the execution of powers to be carried out in strict accordance with the terms and limits prescribed by the Act of Parliament, under which the incorporated trustees derive their capacity and the respondents their beneficial rights." Lord Dunedin referred to the examples of the existence of a legal relationship in the case of an owner vindicating or defending his property and the case where the relationship of contract gives one party a right to insist on performance by the other together with the exceptional case where one not a party to the conract may have title to sue for its enforcement, the case of the *jus quaesitum tertio*. He then passed to cases such as the one before him and observed[19]: "If any persons are in such a relation as to constitute them trustees, or if without being technically trustees, they have a fiduciary duty to others, those persons to whom they owe a fiduciary duty will have a title to sue to prevent the infringement of that duty. Infringement of duty may consist in wrong dealing with property."

The width of the definition

10.07   The decision that it was their capacity as harbour ratepayers which gave the title to sue opens up a wider class of pursuers, namely all Dundee harbour ratepayers, than the alternative approach of looking to the pursuers' capacity as competitors. Indeed the *locus* of the pursuers was sufficiently established by their qualification as harbour ratepayers without even the added element of the trade competition. Lord Dunedin, in disposing of the argument that the trade rivalry would provide title to sue, observed[20]: "In the phraseology of Scottish law, when a complainer can only say that he is a rival trader and nothing more, he qualifies an interest but no title". At the conclusion of his speech however he noted the circumstances of the case before him, namely the fact that the pursuers were harbour ratepayers and so members of the constituency erected to elect the trustees and were persons for whose benefit the harbour was kept up. He continued: "I cannot doubt that they have a title to prevent an *ultra vires* act of the appellants, which *ultra vires* act directly affects the property under their care. It is not only that loss of property through improper acting may have the effect of imposing heavier rates on the respondents in the future, but, in the words of Lord Johnston in the *Stirling County Council case*,[21] as they have contributed to the funds which bought the property, 'they have an interest in the administration of a ... fund to which they have contributed', and a title flowing from that position and interest. "The

---

[18] at 11.
[19] at 13.
[20] at 12.
[21] 1912 S.C. 1281 at 1293.

case thus supports a wide definition of the persons who may have at least a title to sue, even although the class may be restricted by the application of the further test of interest. Whether all ratepayers would also qualify an interest may be a distinct question, although it could be argued that all ratepayers would have an interest albeit not immediately of a pecuniary nature in securing that the trustees operated within the scope of their legal powers; and the final passage in Lord Dunedin's speech suggests that his Lordship was recognising that they had an interest as ratepayers and a title flowing from that interest. In the *Stirling County Council* case from which he took the quotation the plea was one of no title to sue but the substance of the argument was on the ground of an absence of any patrimonial interest. On this wide approach the court's task has been to ascertain whether there is a relevant "legal relation" between the pursuer and the defender. In applications for judicial review the question comes to be whether there is a relevant legal relation between the applicant and what in most cases will be a public authority, either a body or an individual. A legal connection has to be found between the applicant, the claim and the body or person against whom the claim is made.

Duties owed to the community

A statutory obligation on a public authority will often be found to entitle **10.08** members of the community to litigate in respect of it. But the matter depends upon a consideration of the particular statute. In *Adamson v. Edinburgh Street Tramways Co.*[22] two private individuals were held to be entitled to require a tramways company to carry out their statutory duty to install a passing place in the layout of a double line of tram rails where the footpath was less than a stated distance from the nearest rail. Although the local authority and others had a right to complain it was held that that did not exclude the right of the petitioners to do so. As members of the public they had a right to use the road. It is to be noticed that they had a particular interest in the matter as being omnibus and cab proprietors. but that did not seem to be relied upon as critical. Where a statute does not give a right of challenge to the public generally, it may give a right to particular persons or classes of people. In *Kershaw v. City of Glasgow District Council*[23] it was held that a statutory provision which bound the local authority in considering tenders for certain catering work not to act in a manner likely to have the effect of distorting competition had been intended to protect third party tenderers, and did not give any title to sue to the catering manager of the authority's own catering unit which had been operating as a direct labour organisation. But the ambit of the persons entitled to sue may extend beyond those who may be benefited by the public service. It has been held that performance of a statutory duty to lay main sewers to serve a private housing development can be enforced by the developer of the housing site.[24]

The *Independent Broadcasting Authority* case

In the case of *Wilson v. Independent Broadcasting Authority*[25] the question **10.09** was raised whether three members of the public who were entitled to vote in a referendum on the matter of devolution and were members of

---

[22] (1872) 10 M. 533.
[23] 1992 S.L.T. 71.
[24] *T. Docherty Ltd v. Monifieth Town Council*, 1970 S.C. 200.
[25] 1979 S.C. 351.

the "Labour Vote No Campaign", one being also a Scottish labour member of Parliament, were entitled to seek an interdict against the Independent Broadcasting Authority from putting out broadcasts which the petitioners alleged did not maintain a proper balance between the opposing views regarding the question which was the subject of the referendum. Section 2(2)(b) of the Independent Broadcasting Act 1973 imposed a duty on the Authority to "ensure that the programmes broadcast by [them] maintain . . . a proper balance". The petitioners argued that the political broadcasts to be transmitted by the Authority were *ultra vires* of their powers under that section, in respect that three of the four proposed broadcasts were to urge a "Yes" vote, and that was claimed to be a failure to observe a proper balance. The Authority challenged the petitioners' title and interest to sue. Lord Ross held that the petitioners had both title and interest. On the matter of title he observed[26]:

> "I regard it as significant that Parliament in the Act in question has laid duties on the respondents but has not provided any specific remedy for the breach of those duties. Who then can enforce those duties and take action if there is a breach? In particular, can a member of the public who is an ordinary voter do so?
>
> "In England it appears that proceedings of this kind might require the involvement of the Attorney-General, but no such rule applies in Scotland. In Scotland, I see no reason in principle why an individual should not sue in order to prevent a breach by a public body of a duty owed by that public body to the public. It may well be that the Lord Advocate could be a petitioner if the interests of the public as a whole were affected . . . but I see no reason why an individual should not sue provided always that the individual can qualify an interest."

It thus appears that the legal relation sufficient to constitute a title to sue where a breach of statutory duty is in question may encompass every member of the public. Indeed the position was expressed more generally in the petition of the *Scottish Old People's Welfare Council*[27] where the conclusion was drawn from the case of *Wilson* that "where there is a duty owed by a public body to the public, an individual member of the public has title to sue and if he also has an interest he will have the right to do so". Thus the view was expressed by the judge that under legislation which sought to provide benefit to all members of the public whenever particular conditions were satisfied, every member of the public would at least have a title to sue.

Interest

10.10 Lord Ardwall sought to explain the reasons for the requirement of interest in these words: "The grounds of this rule are (1) that the law courts of the country are not instituted for the purpose of deciding academic questions of law, but for settling disputes where any of the lieges has a real interest to have a question determined which involves

---

[26] at 356.
[27] 1987 S.L.T. 179 at 184. But see Professor Bradley's comments in "Applications for Judicial Review–the Scottish Model" [1987)] P.L. 313 at 319.

his pecuniary right or his status; and (2) that no person is entitled to subject another to the trouble and expense of litigation unless he has some real interest to enforce or protect."[28] Three comments fall to be made about this passage. In the first place the reference to "his pecuniary right or his status"should not be regarded as an exhaustive or complete definition. In the second place, while Lord Ardwall sought to distinguish title and interest in his judgment, when the case reached the Inner House, the First Division, reversing the Lord Ordinary, held that the pursuer had no interest to pursue the action and dealt with the question as being one of title to sue, because, as the Lord President observed, "a good title as next of kin to reduce a settlement is a title which is founded on interest". In the third place, at least the first of Lord Ardwall's two propositions fails to highlight the distinction already made between the nature of the case and the identity of the person raising it— that is, the distinction between the question whether the issue is a material one and the question whether the petitioner has an interest to sue. The principle that the courts will not entertain issues which are hypothetical or academic or remote is discussed later in this book.[29] In the present context the relevant question is not whether the issue matters, but whether it matters to the petitioner.

The *Scottish Old People's Welfare* case

The difficulty of defining with any precision what is required to constitute a sufficient interest in matters of judicial review was discussed in the case of the *Scottish Old People's Welfare Council* as follows: **10.11**

> "The interest must be such as to be seen as material or sufficient. The pursuit of an academic issue would not suffice, nor would an attempt to seek a general pronouncement of law on facts which were hypothetical. There must be a real issue. But the existence of a sufficient interest is essentially a matter depending upon the circumstances of the particular case. The variety of adjectives which are employed to describe the quality of interest required by the law reflects the difficulty of defining any single criterion."[30]

It is to be noted that this statement of the position has regard as much or even more to the nature of the issue as it does to the qualification of the person raising it. The petitioners in that case were held to have title to raise the application, because they were members of the public and the legislation in question sought to make benefit available to any member of the public who could qualify for it, but they failed to show a sufficient interest. But the reasoning which led to that result again went primarily on the nature of the issue raised. While it was said that the interest of the petitioners was too remote, the reason for that was that the construction of the regulations under which the benefit might be given was not yet a matter of real importance. No claims had been made by anyone. The implementation of the circular of which the petitioners were complaining was wholly in the future. It was still a matter of uncertainty whether the advice in the circular would ever have to be

---

[28] *Swanson v. Mason*, 1907 S.C. 426 at 429.
[29] See paras 13.02 *et seq.*
[30] 1987 S.L.T. 179 at 186.

followed. While in accordance with the terms of the plea on which the argument proceeded the issue was decided in terms of interest to sue it could well have been determined on the basis that the issue itself was not of sufficient immediacy or reality to render the matter open to judicial review.[31]

Kinds of interest

10.12   The consideration of interest as an ingredient in *locus standi* has been complicated by the use of a variety of different adjectives which have been on occasion used to describe its character. In the passage from the opinion of Lord Ardwall which has already been quoted, his Lordship referred to a real interest which involved "his pecuniary right to his status". But the use of that expression is not to be taken in any way definitively. A patrimonial interest, the interest of an owner in his own property, is clearly sufficient, such as the interest in enforcing building conditions in the title to one's property[32] or restrictive covenants.[33] Indeed the preservation of amenity[34] or a concern to preserve an aesthetic symmetry of a building[35] can provide a sufficient interest.[36] Moreover the interest may be small: "if there be a pecuniary or patrimonial interest, however small, depending on the determination of the question, the parties have a right to invoke the aid of a court of law to decide their difference".[37] Moreover the interest may be future or contingent.[38] It has been observed[39] that while in the case of building restrictions proprietary or patrimonial interests have most frequently been pleaded they are not the only interests which the law should recognise as warranting the imposition and maintenence of restrictive conditions upon the use of property. Accordingly even the use of the word "patrimonial" is not to be taken as definitive. In the case of *Gunstone v. Scottish Women's Amateur Athletic Association*[40] Lord Prosser observed: "I do not consider that out-of-date expressions such as 'patrimonial' are likely to be of much use as a test of true interests which the courts should protect; and if civil rights such as rights under contract are affected, I should regard little more as enough to show a true interest." Thus enforcement of the lawful provisions of a contract should constitute a sufficient interest for the innocent party.[41] Both pecuniary and patrimonial concerns are likely to involve considerations of the relationship between the parties which is properly a matter of title rather than interest.

---

[31] See para. 13.02 for this aspect of the competency of review.
[32] *Magistrates of Edinburgh v. Macfarlane* (1857) 20D. 156.
[33] *Ballachulish Slate Quarries Co. v. Grant* (1903) 5F. 1105.
[34] *Earl of Zetland v. Hislop* (1882) 9R.(H.L.) 40.
[35] *Stewart v. Bunten* (1878) 5R. 1108.
[36] It is respectfully suggested that the doubts expressed about the relevancy of amenity concerns in *Wilson v. Grampian R.C.*, 1993 S.L.T. 588 were misplaced.
[37] *Strang v. Stewart* (1864) 2M. 1015, *per* Lord Justice-Clerk Inglis at 1029.
[38] *Hannah v. Hannah's Trustees*, 1958 S.L.T.(Notes) 9, where a contingent beneficiary was held to have title to sue a reduction of a disposition by trustees.
[39] *Menzies v. Caledonian Canal Commissioners* (1900) 2F. 953, *per* Lord President Balfour at 962.
[40] 1987 S.L.T. 611 at 614.
[41] *Ballachulish Slate Quarries Co. Ltd v. Grant* (1903) 5F. 1105.

Material interest

A "true interest"may be defined as an interest in any right recognised by **10.13**
the law.[42] For that test to be satisfied the substance of the interest must
be such as the law will enforce and in particular it must be of a
sufficiently material or concrete character. Burn-Murdoch adopts that
terminology but a variety of similar expressions have been used to
describe this characteristic, such as substantial, sufficient, real, actual and
legitimate.[43] These words may hide the ambiguity which has already been
noted. In the first place they imply that the issue must be real and not
remote or hypothetical; but that is a matter of substance and not of
interest to sue. Pollution of a stream only becomes justiciable if it makes
the water unfit for its primary purpose.[44] A negative servitude will not be
enforced by interdict where there is no substantial interest to protect by
its enforcement because the feared invasion of rights is too remote.[45] In
a case of this category there will necessarily be no one with an interest
such as the court will recognise to raise it. As is later mentioned[46] the
courts are not concerned to deal with hypothetical, premature or
academic questions but only with live, practical questions. In the second
place the words may also imply that the matter is of reality to the
petitioner and not remote from him; but that is a matter of relationship
which may be as much a matter of title as of interest.The legality of the
dismissal of an official may not be raised by parties who only have an
indirect interest, when it is not known whether or not the official is
concerned to raise the issue or whether he is content to acquiesce in it
and he is not a party to the action.[47] Even where there is a live issue the
person raising it may not have the *locus* to do so. But where there is a
live issue and the applicant has a reasonable concern about it, that
should be sufficient to provide *locus standi*.[48]

Interest in the Independent Broadcasting Authority case

In the case of *Wilson v. Independent Broadcasting Authority*,[49] already **10.14**
discussed under reference to the matter of title, Lord Ross found that
the petitioners had averred a "sufficient interest"in three respects: first,
they were all persons entitled to vote in the referendum and the
referendum gave them the choice to say "Yes"or "No"; secondly, they
belonged to an organisation or group which apparently believed that the
question in the referendum should be answered in the negative; and
thirdly, it was implicit in the name of the organisation or group that the
petitioners wished to persuade other voters to vote in the negative. Lord
Ross rejected the contention put forward on behalf of the IBA that the
interest of the petitioners was too speculative to count. He accepted that
the broadcasts were likely to be influential upon the electorate in
Scotland, and if that was so he considered that the petitioners had "an
interest to see that the respondents do not act in breach of any statutory

---

[42] Mackay's *Manual of Practice*, p. 125.
[43] See Burn-Murdoch, *Interdict*, p. 57.
[44] *Duke of Buccleuch v. Cowan* (1866) 5M. 214.
[45] *Hood v. Traill* (1884) 12R. 362.
[46] para. 13.02.
[47] *Kilwinning Parish Council v. Board of Management of Cunninghame Combination Poorhouse*, 1909 S.C. 829.
[48] *Shaw v. Strathclyde R.C.*, 1988 S.L.T. 313.
[49] 1979 S.C. 351.

duties in relation to such programmes". The interest was said to be material and not abstract or inappreciable. Three observations may be made with regard to the factors on which Lord Ross proceeded. First, none of the factors that he listed involved any economic interest. As has already been noted it is not a prerequisite that the interest be economic. Secondly, the petitioners were members of a group but were suing as individuals and accordingly no issue arose regarding the propriety or otherwise of action being taken in the name of the group. But the fact that they were members of a group was regarded as being a relevant factor in affirming the interest of the individuals. Thirdly, while three factors were identified, in essence the interest lay in the desire to forward a campaign designed to promote the beliefs held by the petitioners and others in their group. It would appear that such an element may in itself be sufficient to constitute an interest for the purposes of *locus standi*.

Merger

10.15 Thus far the matter of *locus standi* has been considered in relation to the two elements of which it is traditionally conceived to comprise. But this analysis is by no means definite or constant. In the case of *Summerlee Iron Co. Ltd v. Lindsay* Lord Dunedin observed[50] that title and interest "although they are different often very much run into each other". He illustrated that by reference to a case[51] where it had been held that a particular statutory provision regarding the ventilation of buildings was intended to provide for the sanitary condition of the house itself and not to provide something for the benefit of the neighbours, and accordingly that a neighbour had, as Lord Dunedin put it, "either no title or no interest–I do not care which"to sue under that provision. Essentially in that case the defect was one of title to complain under the particular statutory provision. Lord Dunedin observed that the neighbour could not be heard as a sort of general protector of the public health and he could not show that it was anything to his house if his neighbour's house was badly ventilated internally. On the other hand, where the question is one such as building to an excessive height where you affect your neighbour far more than you affect yourself, then the neighbour may well have a title to found on the statutory provisions in that regard.

Simpson v. Edinburgh Corporation

10.16 In this case[52] the pursuer sought a declarator that certain grants of planning permission by the Corporation of the City of Edinburgh were *ultra vires* as being contrary to the local development plan. The defenders claimed that he had "no title *et separatim* no interest"to sue the action. They argued that the statutory provisions relevant to the grant gave the pusuer no right to enforce them. The Lord Ordinary held that the relevant legislation was not intended by Parliament to confer a separate right of action on an interested neighbour. He recorded that the pursuer had argued that he had a title to sue in virtue of the fact that his property would be injuriously affected by the grant of planning permission, that ownership of a house in the Square where the development

---

[50] 1907 S.C. 1161 at 1165.
[51] *Pitman v. Burnett's Trustees* (1882) 9R. 444.
[52] 1960 S.C. 313.

was to take place gave him sufficient interest to question a grant of planning permission to one of his neighbours in the Square and therefore that he had a title to insist in the action. But to that his Lordship said[53]: "I have no doubt that in certain circumstances, ownership of property may give a party an interest, but he must in my view in the present case qualify a patrimonial interest in the sense that some right of his, conferred by the Act of 1947, is being contravened."He then referred to the case of *Black v. Tennent*[54] where neighbouring proprietors had been held to have title to reduce an invalid grant of a public house licence, because they had a statutory right to object and had in fact unsuccessfully objected and continued: "The pursuer in the present case has no right under the Act of 1947 to object to the grant of planning permission. For the above reasons, I am unable to find any indication in the Act of 1947 that the pursuer has a title to enforce this aspect of planning control. I hold therefore that the pursuer has no title to sue."

In all of this it may be questioned whether the decision proceeded on a consideration of title, or of interest, or both. The Lord Ordinary accepted that ownership of property may confer an interest to sue but he required the pursuer to qualify "a patrimonial interest in the sense that some right of his, conferred by the Act of 1947, is being contravened." The pursuer had what might be regarded as a very good interest, namely the effect of the *ultra vires* actings on the value of his property. The passage in the opinion which has just been quoted suggests that there had to be some interest conferred by the statute. But it is rather in order to find a basis for a title to sue that the statute has to be examined. Yet on the matter of title it might be thought that the pursuer could have qualified a title as being a ratepayer of the local authority whose decision was being challenged. It can at least be said that there appears to be some merging if not confusion of title and interest in the case, and, as Professor Bradley[55] has recognised, it is not to be assumed that in all circumstances neighbours and third parties will have no title or interest to sue in respect of illegalities in the administration of planning law. The decision, however, still stands and has prompted doubts whether local taxpayers have title and interest to interdict a purchase of property by a local authority.[56] It has also been recognised that where a person has a commercial interest but no right has been infringed or denied he has no title to sue in respect of a grant of planning permission.[57]

Title and interest challenged on the same ground

In some cases the same ground is put forward both as a challenge on the title of the petitioner and as a challenge on his interest to sue. One example is the case of *Air 2000 Ltd. v. Secretary of State for Transport (No. 2)*.[58] An air traffic operator brought an application for judicial review arguing that two sets of regulations issued by the Secretary of State for Transport were *ultra vires* in respect that they did not come within the scope of section 31 of the Airports Act 1986. The regulations required carriers to make stops at Prestwick before commencing and

10.17

---

[53] at 317.
[54] (1899) 1F. 423.
[55] *Stair Memorial Encyclopaedia*, Vol. 1, para. 314.
[56] *Wilson v. Grampian R.C.*, 1993 S.L.T. 588.
[57] *Boundary Properties Ltd v. City of Edinburgh Council*, 1999 S.L.T. 127.
[58] 1990 S.L.T. 335.

after completing a transatlantic flight originating from or bound for Glasgow or Edinburgh. The applicant had a licence from the Civil Aviation Authority to operate flights from Glasgow to the United States of America, subject to the conditions in the regulations, and it intended to apply for licence to operate a route between Edinburgh and the United States of America. It was not disputed that the applicant had both title and interest to challenge the regulations so far as they related to Glasgow and Prestwick since it was already operating flights from Glasgow airport under the licence which it already held. But the Secretary of State challenged its title and interest to sue with respect to its proposed operations out of Edinburgh, arguing that there was no legal relation between the applicant and the Civil Aviation Authority or the Secretary of State because the applicant was only contemplating the possibility of making an application for a licence to fly between Edinburgh and the United States of America and had not yet made that application, and that the applicant for that very same reason had no interest to sue. On the matter of title the argument was that only when an application was made to the Civil Aviation Authority would a legal relationship with it be created giving a right which might then be infringed by the Secretary of State. The Lord Ordinary, however, found it unnecessary to explore the analysis which this argument invited because he was satisfied that "there is a relationship between the petitioner and the Secretary of State which suffices in the present case, whatever may be the position between the petitioner and the CAA. The petitioner is an established air traffic operator who uses the airports at Glasgow and Edinburgh and operates flights between Glasgow and the USA. The petitioner is one of those who may be closely affected by the performance of the Secretary of State's duties under section 31 in the conduct of its business". The petitioner had a legal relationship with the Secretary of State such as to give it a title to see that he properly performed his statutory duties and to challenge him if he did not. As regards the interest of the applicant, it was evident that the extra stop at Prestwick would involve extra cost and bring in no earnings. The argument that the applicant had not yet applied for a licence merged into an argument that the issue was not a real or immediate one, but the Lord Ordinary was satisfied that it was a matter of immediate and real concern to the petitioner in planning for the future operation of its business. That there was the one single ground of challenge which underlay the argument on title and on interest and on prematurity resulted in some merging of the considerations of title and interest. But the essential test for title to sue was still recognised in the consideration that the statutory scheme under which the Secretary of State was operating was one which gave the petitioner a right to complain about an unlawful acting. It was unnecessary to ascertain how many other people might also have qualified with a title to do so, and in particular to decide whether any individual member of the public could do so.

Interest amounting to title

10.18 It has been recognised that in some cases at least a sufficient interest may amount to a title. In one case a school board was held to have no title to call an outside body of trustees to account for an alleged maladministration of their trust because such a matter was outwith the scope of the statutory functions entrusted to the board; Lord Dunedin, however, observed that if they had had a sufficient interest he would have held that they would have had a title to sue, but the interest was too shadowy and remote.[59] Where an ice-cream vendor challenged the validity of certain conditions which the local authority proposed to insert into the licences which they would issue it was observed[60]: "It is quite a mistake to assume that this trader requires to postulate what he has not got, namely a licence, in order to find himself a title to sue. His title is his trade, which the respondents avow that they intend to interfere with by refusing to give the trader a licence except upon terms more onerous than the law allows." In *Doherty v. Norwich Union Fire Insurance Limited* it was stated that "in general a party with a pecuniary interest has a title to sue".[61] It was held in that case that motor insurers had a title to reduce a decree which had passed in absence against their insured because they were bound by statute to pay to the person entitled to the benefit of a judgment against the insured any sum payable thereunder in respect of the liability covered by the policy.

Title without Interest

From what has been already said it will be evident that there will be few cases where there will be a title but no interest. Examples can be found in the cases relating to servitudes and building restrictions[62] but at least where there is a real issue at stake it is not to be expected that examples should occur in the field of judicial review. **10.19**

Interest without Title

It has been said that "It is a general, and just short of a universal rule, that title to sue rests upon interest."[63] Interest without title is regarded by Maclaren[64] as relating to cases where there is no interest which the law recognises and for that reason no title. The question then comes to be whether there is an interest in any right recognised by law. Within limits the law respects the freedom of traders to compete. So the mere fact of competition in trade with another will not give a trader a title to sue the other, although he may have an interest to do so.[65] A beneficiary on an executry estate may be thought to have an interest to sue a debtor of the executry estate, but it is the executor who has the title to do that.[66] The unsuccessful candidate for a bursary which had been awarded to one whom he alleged was not an eligible candidate had no title to claim that he was in right of the bursary, since failing the winning candidate it could not be asserted that he would have won the award.[67] Beyond the content of the interest it must in its character be of materiality and substance and not remote or vague. This may be further analysed as a matter of the remoteness of the relationship of the parties or the speculative nature of the question. Where a woman had been found unconscious after having fallen or thrown herself out of a window and had been ordered to be **10.20**

---

[59] *School Boards of Dunlop and Stewarton v. Patrons of Cunninghame Graham Bursaries Endowment Fund*, 1910 S.C. 945.
[60] *Rossi v. Magistrates of Edinburgh*, (1904) 5F. 85, *per* Lord Roberston at 90.
[61] 1974 S.C. 213, *per* Lord Robertson at 220.
[62] *e.g. Maguire v. Burges*, 1909 S.C. 1283.
[63] *Pyper v. Christie* (1878) 6R. 143, *per* Lord Young at 14.
[64] *Court of Session Practice*, p. 191.
[65] *Reid v. Minicabs*, 1966 S.C. 137.
[66] *Morrison v. Morrison's Executrix*, 1912 S.C. 892.
[67] *M'Donald v. M'Coll* (1890) 17R. 951.

detained in an asylum where she died shortly thereafter without recovering consciousness, her husband was held to have no interest to reduce the order for her detention in the asylum. The order and the certificates on which it had been granted were spent and inoperative so that the pursuer had not made out "a case of such interest to have these documents reduced as would give him a good title to pursue the present action"; the husband could give no clear averments of prejudice caused by the death in the asylum and such prejudice as there was was "much too vague and remote to found such a patrimonial interest as might give the pursuer a sufficient title to insist on this action of reduction"; and the stigma on the deceased was not an actionable wrong on which a relative could claim damages, so that that did not assist in giving the pursuer "an interest and so a title to sue the present action".[68]

III　*LOCUS STANDI* IN JUDICIAL REVIEW

Title and Interest in Judicial Review

10.21　In matters of judicial review once title has been established and the issue between the parties is a real one the existence of a sufficient interest should almost invariably follow. Essentially judicial review is concerned with an alleged abuse (which includes excess) of power. If there exists a relationship of duty and right such as to give a title to sue, then in most cases anyone with a title should have a sufficient interest, without the need to explore these issues separately. It must be predicated in any case that there is a material issue to be resolved. Where the case concerns the exercise of statutory duties a consideration of the statute will identify the class of persons who may have a right, express or implied, to complain about any excess of statutory power. If the statute is one designed to benefit all members of the public, then any member of the public will have title to sue in respect of a failure to conform with the statute.[69] Where in a matter affecting some or all members of the public an authority is acting under common law powers, a consideration of those powers should enable the class of persons entitled to complain to be identified. Where the powers under which the particular person or body may be acting do not extend over members of the public or any class of them but only over the members of a particular organisation or group, or even the parties to a private arbitration, the extent of the legal relationship will be defined by the scope and extent of the power and rights of those involved. In whatever context the problem arises, whether it be in the public arena or a private setting, the extent of the legal relationship should also determine the extent of those having an interest in the matter to be reviewed. If the issue is a real and material one, then a person with title should generally be able to affirm an interest. Emphasis is now rightly laid on the matter of title although some formal recognition may still sometimes be paid to the idea of the duality of the requirement. An applicant for a licence may have an interest to complain of wrongful actings by the clerk to a licensing authority, and being qualified to make the application and hold a licence can claim a title to sue.[70] In the case of *St Johnstone Football Club v. The Scottish*

---

[68] *Agnew v. Laughlan*, 1948 S.C. 656. On the case of *injuria sine damnum*, see Walker on *Delict* (2nd ed.), pp. 40 and 463. That matter is not seen as one of title to sue.

[69] *Stirrat Park Hogg v. Dunbarton District Council*, 1996 S.L.T. 1113.

[70] *Tait v. City of Glasgow District Licensing Board*, 1987 S.L.T. 340.

Football Association Ltd[71] it was expressly affirmed that in cases of gross irregularity such as a departure from the rules of natural justice, an action would be entertained by the court whether or not the civil rights and patrimonial interests of its members had been interfered with by the proceedings complained of.

In cases relating to voluntary associations the court has been careful not to entertain actions which raise matters only of a social character and in that context has looked for the existence of a real or material interest, which (as has already been explained) need not be of a patrimonial nature. The interest in being protected against injustice should suffice.[72] The sufficiency of interest depends upon the circumstances and it is enough that the applicant has a reasonable concern in a live issue.[73] As is noted elsewhere, it is essential that there be a live issue.[74]

Purpose of the Rule in England

In the context of the English requirement for a sufficiency of interest in order to qualify for *locus standi* Lord Fraser of Tullybelton observed: "All are agreed that a direct financial interest or legal interest is not now required . . . There is also general agreement that a mere busybody does not have a sufficient interest. The difficulty is, in between those extremes, to distinguish between the desire of the busybody to interfere in other people's affairs and the interest of the person affected by or having a reasonable concern with the matter to which the application relates".[75] His Lordship answered that question by looking at the statute under which the duty arose to see whether it gave any express or implied right to persons in the position of the applicant to complain of the alleged unlawful act or omission. That is the question which in Scotland is considered under the aspect of title to sue. If the matter is of real and immediate significance such that it is not to be rejected as remote or hypothetical, then it is very unlikely that the applicant having title to sue will not have an interest to do so. **10.22**

The actio popularis

Although Lord Chancellor Cottenham once observed that "what is known under the denomination of a popular action forms no part of the law of Scotland"[76] the expression is well established in Scots law[77] and may cover any action where an individual in his capacity as a member of the public seeks to vindicate or defend a right which is said to be possessed by members of the public, such as in particular a public right of way. Maclaren[78] gives examples not only of actions to declare public rights of way but also of rights of market, of public navigation, of the use **10.23**

---

[71] 1965 S.L.T. 171.

[72] *Gunstone v. Scottish Women's Amateur Athletic Association*, 1987 S.L.T. 611.

[73] *Shaw v. Strathclyde R.C.*, 1988 S.C.L.R. 439.

[74] *Air 2000 Ltd v. Secretary of State for Transport (No. 2)*, 1990 S.L.T. 335; cf. *Moriarty v. City of Edinburgh District Licensing Board*, 1995 S.L.T. 40. See later para. 13.02.

[75] *R. v. IRC, ex p. National Federation of Self Employed and Small Businesses Ltd* [1982] A.C. 617 at 646.

[76] *Ewing v. Glasgow Commissioners of Police* (1839) M'L&R 847 at 860. But regard should be had to the previous meaning of the expression; Munro, "Standing in Judicial Review", 1995 S.L.T.(News) 279.

[77] *e.g.* Bell's *Dictionary*: 'Popular action'.

[78] *Court of Session Practice*, p. 226.

of common land and of the removal of public dangers or nuisance. Rights of ferry, of harbour, of pasturage and of grazings can be added to the list. One resident of a town may by this means seek to vindicate the rights of all the other residents. Sections of the public may thus enforce matters of public right in which they have a particular concern, as where several vegetable merchants of Edinburgh were held to have a title to sue the magistrates to enforce a right to hold markets.[79] Certainly a distinction has to be drawn between such matters of public right—that is, a matter of common right in which every member of the public may participate with everyone else—and matters of the rights of individuals which others may have but which are not held in common. But in so far as *locus standi* is concerned it is hard to see why, if an authority makes a decision which destroys a public right, a right such as would be open to a *popularis actio*, any member of the public should not have the right to challenge it.[80] In such a case *res judicata* should apply so as to exclude any reopening of the issue, but the procedure could still be by way of judicial review. In such a case intimation of the application should be made to the public. But limitations upon the scope of the *actio popularis* require to be observed. In *MacCormick v. Lord Advocate*[81] it was held that the question of the legality under the Treaty of Union of the Queen being proclaimed as Elizabeth the Second was outwith the scope of an *actio popularis* and that members of the Scottish public had no title to raise it. The Lord Ordinary held that there were no relevant averments that the real or personal rights of the petitioners would be infringed by the proposed proclamation and the Lord President (Cooper) observed[82]: "I cannot see how we could admit the title and interest of the present petitioners to raise the point in issue before the Court of Session without conceding a similar right to almost any opponent of almost any political action to which public opposition has arisen."

Res judicata

10.24 The decision in an *actio popularis* decided against one member of the public will be *res judicata* against all other members of the public.[83] But a formal decision on the existence of a discretionary power to restrain a right of market where the point had not been argued on appeal may not be *res judicata* against persons not parties to the action.[84] A decision on the legality of an assessment for rates given in an action by police commissioners against a county council was held not to be *res judicata* in an action against the county council brought by a ratepayer.[85] A final judgment on the existence of a right of way, not reached by compromise, is probably conclusive of the issue so that it cannot be reopened by other persons.[86]

---

[79] *Blackie v. Magistrates of Edinburgh* (1884) 8M. 1064.
[80] The point was raised but not answered in *Scottish Old People's Welfare Council, Petrs*, 1987 S.L.T. 179 at 184.
[81] 1953 S.C. 396.
[82] at 413.
[83] *Potter v. Hamilton* (1870) 8M. 1064, *per* Lord Benholme at 1069.
[84] *Magistrates of Edinburgh v. Blaikie* (1886) 13R.(H.L.) 78. Maclaren, *Court of Session Practice*, p. 397.
[85] *MacArthur v. Argyllshire County Council* (1898) 25R. 829.
[86] *Jenkins v. Robertson* (1864) 2M. 1162; (1867) 5M.(H.L.) 27. *Macfie v. Scottish Rights of Way and Recreation Society Ltd* (1884) 11R. 1094.

Individuals suing in public matters

The idea of a single member of the public raising an action to challenge **10.25** a matter which is of importance to the public in general or particularly to one section of the public is not unfamiliar in Scottish practice. A single ratepayer may challenge the legitimacy of the actings of his local authority, although many others than himself may be affected by the matter of which he complains and by the outcome of his challenge. The challenge to the legality of fluoridation of a water supply in *McColl v. Strathclyde Regional Council*[87] was mounted by a legally aided individual, although the matter was of concern to many of the local population. In such a case the decision will not technically be *res judicata* so far as any other member of the public is concerned, but the decision will for practical purposes probably be recognised as resolving the issue. An inhabitant of the burgh of Musselburgh, who was a burgess and a member of the Musselburgh Golf Club, was entitled to bring an interdict against the magistrates against their feuing off part of the links for building.[88] An inhabitant of a burgh may complain of a nuisance in the exercise by a statutory body of its statutory rights over a street in the burgh.[89] The legality of charging for inspection of a register which was to be "available for inspection by the public"can be challenged by any member of the public.[90]

Associations

The question whether a group of people who have come together into **10.26** some form of association which does not comprise a person in law is able to sue an action is, of course, a distinct question from whether such a group has *locus standi* for the purposes of judicial review. Unincorporated associations have no separate persona and in general may only engage in litigation through their authorised representatives.[91] Office bearers either appointed for the purpose or designated by the association's constitution will usually be recognised as the proper people to sue on behalf of the association.[92] But where individual members of an association sue as individuals and not as representatives of the association they may have a title as individuals to do so.[93] It has long been recognised that individuals may challenge the legality of actions in their own interest as distinct from acting on behalf of the public[94] and that a group of citizens may call on the magistrates to account for their administration.[95]

Groups of interested persons

An association of persons interested in protecting the rights of restaur- **10.27** ateurs and hotel keepers together with some individual holders of certificates for licensed premises have been accepted as entitled to

---

[87] 1973 S.L.T. 616.
[88] *Sanderson v. Lees* (1859) 22D. 24.
[89] *Ogston Aberdeen Tramways Co.* (1896) 24 R.(H.L.) 8.
[90] *Stirrat Park Hogg v. Dunbarton D.C.*, 1996 S.L.T. 1113.
[91] For an exception in the case of employers' associations and for trade unions, see the Act 1974 c.52 ss.2 and 3. Maxwell, *Practice of the Court of Session*, p. 144.
[92] Maclaren, *Court of Session Practice*, p. 253. *Renton Football Club v. McDowall* (1891) 18R. 670; *Pagan and Osborne v. Haig*, 1910 S.C. 341.
[93] *Cannon and Others v. Secretary of State*, 1964 S.L.T. 91; *Adam v. Secretary of State for Scotland*, 1958 S.C. 279.
[94] *Earl of Cassilis v. The Town of Wigton* (1750) M. 16122.
[95] *Anderson v. Magistrates of Renfrew* (1752) M. 16122.

challenge the validity of orders regulating the opening hours for licensed premises.[96] The title of The Incorporated Society of Law-Agents in Scotland to petition for the removal of a solicitor from the roll of law-agents was also accepted as sufficient.[97] A like view was taken where a petition was presented by the Faculty of Procurators of Glasgow and their principal officers.[98] Moreover, where a group of people come together to advance or protect some particular concern it should be competent for proceedings to be taken in the name of the group. In *Macfie v. Scottish Rights of Way and Recreation Society (Ltd)*[99] a limited company was allowed to be joined in an action representing the public interest in matters of rights of way. The action was an *actio popularis* and it was observed that a judgment against the society would be *res judicata* in a question with the public. In the *Scottish Old People's Welfare* case[1] it was held that the fact that the petitioner was an association was not in itself fatal to the matter of title, but the question whether it was acting in any representative capacity on behalf of the general public was doubted, but left open. A trade union has been held to have title to seek review of the legality of certain conditions which it was proposed should be inserted into the future employment contracts of staff.[2] However, in *PTOA Ltd v. Renfrew District Council*[3] it was held that an association of taxi operators had an interest but no title to challenge a policy decision relating to the geographical restrictions applicable to certain licences. The association had a statutory right to object to individual licence applications but it was considered that this was not sufficient to constitute a legal relationship with the authority.

Representative actions

10.28   In the *Scottish Old People's Welfare* case[4] the pursuer organisation included people who might as individuals have had a direct interest in the matter which was being challenged. The stage beyond that is the case where neither the body nor any of its individual members stand to gain any personal benefit by a successful challenge to the matter which is sought to be reviewed but where the body seeks to challenge something which is of direct personal interest to other people and so, if not representing those other people, at least seeks to present the case which they might present. That was the situation in the *Pergau Dam* case in England.[5] The applicant for judicial review there was a non-partisan

---

[96] *Glasgow and District Restaurateurs and Hotelkeepers' Association v. Dollan*, 1941 S.C. 93. For the *locus* of pressure groups in England, see *e.g. R. v. H.M. Inspectorate of Pollution, ex p. Greenpeace (No. 2)* [1994] 4 All E.R. 329; *R. v. Secretary of State for Foreign Affairs, ex p. World Development Movement Ltd* [1995] 1 All E.R. 611.

[97] *Incorporated Society of Law-Agents in Scotland v. Clark* (1886) 14R. 161.

[98] *Faculty of Procurators of Glasgow and Others v. Colquhoun* (1900) 2F. 1192.

[99] (1884) 11R. 1094.

[1] 1987 S.L.T. 179.

[2] *Educational Institute of Scotland v. Robert Gordon University*, 1996 G.W.D. 26–1511.

[3] 1997 S.L.T. 1112; see also *Inverness Taxi Owners and Drivers Association and Others v. Highland Council* 1999 G.W.D. 10–445.

[4] 1987 S.L.T. 179. It has been said that it is in respect of representative standing that the approach on *locus* standi in Scotland has been most obviously different from that in England: see Colin Munro, "Standing in Judicial Review", 1995 S.L.T. (News) 279. But it is also to be noted that both in England and in Scotland the *locus* to complain under s.7 of the Human Rights Act 1998 is given only to the "victim"; see para. 6.63.

[5] *R. v. Secretary of State for Foreign Affairs, ex p. World Development Movement Ltd* [1995] 1 All E.R. 611.

pressure group which had been in existence for 20 years with a large membership of considerable standing. It sought to improve the quality and quantity of British aid to other countries. It conducted research and analysis in relation to aid and it had an official consultative status with UNESCO. The matter which it was seeking to have reviewed was the legality of an exercise of powers given by the Overseas Development and Co-operation Act 1980 for the purposes of a grant of financial aid overseas. The high reputation and status of the body and the sincerity of its concern were clearly important elements in its *locus standi* being accepted. Its members were clearly not cranks, or busybodies or mischief makers. The court was also impressed by the consideration that but for them there would be nobody who could ensure that the statutory powers were being exercised legally. Furthermore its supporters had a direct interest in ensuring that funds furnished by the United Kingdom were used for genuine purposes. In the circumstances the court held that the body had a "sufficient interest"in the matter to make the application. In England the Child Poverty Action Group and the National Association of Citizens Advice Bureaux, both being bodies which play a prominent role in giving advice, guidance and assistance to claimants for supplementary benefit, have been enabled to apply for judicial review in a matter of concern to individual claimants for supplementary benefit.[6] As Lord Diplock observed in the *Fleet Street Casuals* case[7]: "It would, in my view, be a grave lacuna in our system of public law if a pressure group, like the federation, or even a single public-spirited taxpayer, were prevented by outdated technical rules of *locus standi* from bringing the matter to the attention of the court to vindicate the rule of law and get the conduct stopped. "He went on to observe that officers and departments of central government "are accountable to Parliament for what they do so far as regards efficiency and policy, and of that Parliament is the only judge; they are accountable to a court of justice for the lawfulness of what they do, and of that the court is the only judge". There is no reason to suppose that the Scottish court would not recognise the title of a responsible pressure group to pursue an application for judicial review where the statute giving the power, the exercise of which has given rise to the challenge, can be seen to give expressly or impliedly a real interest to the group to complain of an alleged unlawfulness.[8] The title and interest of a community council to challenge the administration by a local authority of common good property has been upheld where the community council existed to take action in the interests of the community which they represented.[9] It is also to be noted that it is open to the court at the stage of the First Order to order intimation to any interested parties,[10] and it would always be possible to enable an interest group to enter the proceedings by that route so that they could participate in the hearing.

---

[6] In *R. v. Secretary of State for Social Services, ex p. Child Poverty Action* [1990] 2 Q.B. 540, the point was not disputed but was expressly reserved. See also *R. v. Inspectorate of Pollution, ex p. Greenpeace Ltd (No. 2)* [1994)] 4 All E.R. 329.

[7] *R. v. IRC and National Federation of Self-Employed and Small Businesses Ltd* [1982] A.C. 617 at 644.

[8] See the discussion by Andrew D. Murray "Standing Up for the Scottish Public", 1997 J.R. 250.

[9] *Cockenzie and Port Seton Community Council v. East Lothian D.C.*, 1996 S.C.L.R. 209.

[10] See later para. 23.15

Locus standi of respondents

10.29 The title of anyone seeking to oppose an application for judicial review will rarely arise as a matter of dispute. Under Rule of Court 58.7 the First Order will specify the intimation, service and advertisement of the petition as may be necessary in the circumstances of the particular case. Those persons on whom service is made may be taken to have a sufficient interest in the proceedings as to be entitled to oppose them if they wish to do so. Anyone else may apply under Rule 58.8 to enter the process and it will be at that stage that any question regarding their entitlement to do so should be raised and resolved. Clearly anyone seeking to enter the process should be able to demonstrate that he has a real material interest in the issue raised in the application. Where the decision may be *res judicata* to all members of the public, as in an *actio popularis*, it is obviously of importance to secure that sufficient advertisement is given of the application so that all interested parties may be convened into the process.

Locus as a preliminary issue

10.30 It has been said that the matter of *locus standi* is logically prior to and conceptually distinct from the merits of the case.[11] It is then properly of a preliminary character and will usually fall to be dealt with prior to a consideration of the merits of the complaint.[12] But that is only a general rule since in some cases it may not be possible to resolve the point without inquiry into the merits.[13] The title of a respondent to defend may be bound up with the principal issue in the case.[14]

The Lord Advocate

10.31 It may be competent at common law for the Lord Advocate to bring a civil action in the public interest[15] but it is not a course which is followed in practice. The Lord Advocate may in certain circumstances apply for an order from the Court of Session for the specific performance by a local authority of a statutory duty.[16]

Examples of *locus standi* in judicial review

Objectors

10.32 Where under the relevant legislation an individual has a statutory right to object to an application for any form of licence or permission that should entitle him to challenge any abuse of power by the relevant authority in the granting of a such a licence or permission. On the other hand, where he has no statutory right to object, the requisite relationship

---

[11] *R. v. IRC, ex p. National Federation of Self-Employed and Small Businesses Ltd* [1982] A.C. 617, *per* Lord Fraser at 645; *Scottish Old People's Welfare Council, Petrs*, 1987 S.L.T. 179; *Matchett v. Dunfermline D.C.*, 1993 S.L.T. 537.

[12] *PTOA Ltd v. Renfrew D.C.*, 1997 S.L.T. 1112.

[13] *e.g. Baird & Co. v. Feuars of Kilsyth* (1878) 6 R. 116; *Gordon v. Kirkcaldy D.C.*, 1990 S.C. 107 at 118.

[14] *e.g. North British Ry v. Birrell's Trustees*, 1917 S.C. 33.

[15] *Magistrates of Buckhaven and Methil v. Wemyss Coal Co.*, 1932 S.C. 201 at 214.

[16] s.211 of the Local Government (Scotland) Act 1973.

on that basis will not exist and he will not be entitled to base his entitlement to challenge on that ground.[17] Where a person has a statutory right to object and does not exercise that right he may not be entitled to seek judicial review of the decision in the process in which he could have objected.[18] has been held to be the case even where the objector had been allowed to be heard by the licensing sub-committee despite his lack of entitlement.[19] Where a local authority had objected to the making of a grant of money for a forestry development it was held that they had title to challenge the grant as having a reasonable concern with a major project in their area which might affect its economy or amenity.[20]

Taxpayers

One taxpayer has no title to complain about the allegeldy illegal treatment given to another taxpayer, but if there was some exceptionally grave or widespread illegality on the part of the revenue then that might be a matter in relation to which any taxpayer might have *locus* to complain.[21]   **10.33**

Local authority taxpayers

While it was held in the past that ratepayers could not challenge an alleged misapplication of funds comprised in the common good,[22] a local ratepayer has a title to challenge unlawful or *ultra vires* acts of the local authority, particularly in matters of expenditure of funds raised by rating,[23] or to vindicate the customary rights of a burgh, or to prevent an *ultra vires* act directly affecting inalienable property.[24] Nor is the title to insist upon seeing local authority accounts affected by an express statutory power making the documentation available for inspection by "any person interested".[25] It is thought that the relationship between the payer of a local tax and the local authority to whom he pays it should be sufficient to entitle him to challenge any excess of the authority's powers.[26] It has been said that there is no logical difference between the position of a ratepayer and that of a taxpayer where each may reasonably assert that there is an unfairness in the administration of the respective systems.[27]   **10.34**

Companies

In *Nixon v. Edinburgh Northern Tramways Ltd*[28] it was held that a shareholder in a public company had no title to seek a reduction of an agreement allegedly made in contravention of an Act of Parliament.   **10.35**

---

[17] *Simpson v. Edinburgh Corporation*, 1960 S.C. 313. See the discussion of this case in para. 10.16.

[18] *Hollywood Bowl (Scotland) Ltd v. Horsburgh*, 1993 S.L.T. 241.

[19] *Matchett v. Dunfermline D.C.*, 1993 S.L.T. 537. See Bradley, *Stair Encyclopaedia*, Vol. 1, para. 313.

[20] *Kincardine and Deeside D.C. v. Forestry Commissioners*, 1992 S.L.T. 1180.

[21] *R. v. IRC and National Federation of Self-Employed and Small Businesses Ltd* [1982] A.C. 617; see *R. v. IRC* [1996] STC 681.

[22] *Conn v. Corporation of Renfrew* (1906) 8F. 905.

[23] *Stirling County Council v. Magistrates of Falkirk*, 1912 S.C. 1281: *Farquhar and Gill v. Magistrates of Aberdeen*, 1912 S.C. 1294.

[24] *Waddell v. Stewartry D.C.*, 1977 S.L.T.(Notes) 35.

[25] *Stirrat v. City of Edinburgh Council*, 1999 S.L.T. 274.

[26] It is respectfully suggested that the doubt expressed in *Wilson v. Grampian R.C.*, 1993 S.L.T. 588 is mistaken.

[27] *R. v. IRC, ex p. Federation of Self-Employed* [1980] 1 Q.B. 407 at 433.

[28] (1890) 18R. 264; (1893) 20R. (H.L.) 53.

Where it is alleged that a company has acted *ultra vires* it may be only a shareholder or debenture holder who may have a title to challenge such acting.[29] In general a statutory remedy will be available in case of allegedly *ultra vires* actings within companies incorporated under the Companies Acts, and that will exclude judicial review.

Trade competitors

10.36   In the *D. & J. Nicol* case the consideration of business competition was not regarded as relevant to constitute the legal relationship necessary to constitute title. The view taken was that there was no common law rule restricting competition, at least in the absence of conspiracy.[30] There may now be a question whether the court should absolutely exclude business competition as a source of a legal relationship. Unlawful competition may now give rise to remedies under statute or under E.C. law. There are various statutory and governmental controls over competition. It might now be arguable that the trustees were abusing their public monopoly in the ferry business and illegally subsidising their entry into the secondary river tour business.

---

[29] Burn-Murdoch on *Interdict*, p. 401.
[30] As to which see *Crofter Hand Woven Harris Tweed Co. v. Veitch*, 1942 S.C.(H.L.) 1.

CHAPTER 11

EXCLUSION CLAUSES

I   GENERAL
II   CONSTRUCTION OF EXCLUSION CLAUSES
III   OTHER FORMULAE

I   GENERAL

Introduction

This chapter is concerned with the attempts made expressly to exclude   **11.01**
review of some matter by the court.[1] Parliament has on occasion sought
to exclude recourse to the courts of law by providing that orders or
determinations made under particular statutory provisions shall not be
called into question in any court. "Statutory provisions which seek to
limit the ordinary jurisdiction of the court have a long history".[2] The
purpose of such provisions will usually be to secure certainty and finality
in administrative matters. Various formulations have been adopted to
secure this end, leading to such descriptive terms as "ouster clauses",
"exclusion clauses" or "finality clauses". From an early stage in the
development of judicial review, however, it came to be recognised that
such clauses should not readily exclude recourse to the supervisory
jurisdiction of the court. The attitude of the court over the last two or
three hundred years has been prompted by the idea that Parliament
should not be taken to have intended to exclude any remedy for actings
in excess of power. Accordingly, provisions for the exclusion of the court
have been construed so as to minimise their effect on judicial review.
Nor was the court alone in feeling anxiety about any significant exclusion
of their supervision. The use of such clauses was severely discouraged by
the Donoughmore Committee in 1932[3] and by the Franks Committee in
1957.[4] Following on the report of the latter committee Parliament
decided to embody in a statutory provision the established attitude of
the court. This was achieved by section 11(2) of the Tribunals and
Inquiries Act 1958[5] (now section 12(2) of the Tribunals and Inquiries
Act 1992[6]), which provides as respects Scotland that:

---

[1] Such an exclusion is to be contrasted with the purely procedural question whether a
challenge to the validity of a measure can be advanced in some other proceedings, such as
by way of a defence to a criminal charge, or must be raised by way of judicial review;
compare *R. v. Wicks* [1997] 2 All E.R. 801. The extent to which the courts recognise the
validity of an immunity from review imposed by Parliament raises consideration of the
doctrine of the separation of powers.

[2] *Anisminic v. Foreign Compensation Commission* [1969] 2 A.C. 147, *per* Lord Reid at
170.

[3] The Report of the Committee on Ministers' Powers, Cmd 4060 (1932), section II, para.
15 at p. 65.

[4] The Report of the Committee on Administrative Tribunals and Inquiries, Cmnd 218
(1956–57) para. 117.

[5] 6 & 7 Eliz. II, c.66.

[6] 1992 c.53.

"(a) any provision in an Act passed before 1st August 1958 that any order or determination shall not be called in question in any court, or

(b) any provision in such an Act which by similar words excludes any jurisdiction which the Court of Session would otherwise have to entertain an application for reduction or suspension of any order or determination, or otherwise to consider the validity of any order or determination,

shall not have effect so as to prevent the exercise of any such jurisdiction."

Subsection (3) of the section specifically excludes from its scope any order or determination of a court of law, as well as any cases where an Act makes special provision for application to the Court of Session within a time limited by the Act.[7] A corresponding provision was made for England,[8] but that related only to the remedies of certiorari and mandamus, as if those were the only remedies in judicial review proceedings. The provision for Scotland is framed in more comprehensive terms.

Tribunals and Inquiries Act 1992

11.02 Section 12(2) of the Tribunals and Inquiries Act 1992 operates so as to prevent the exclusion of opportunities for review, not to provide such opportunities where they do not otherwise exist. But in providing this prevention of exclusion the language which is used is, as has just been noticed, comprehensive. It relates not only to provisions that an order or determination is not to be called into question in any court but also to any provision which by similar words excludes the court's jurisdiction to consider its validity. This should catch all the various formulations which have been used to impose a finality or to oust recourse to the court. Four matters may be noted which do not fall within the scope of the provision. In the first place, the section deals with provisions which exclude review by the court, not with provisions which relate to statutory appeal procedures, either by excluding or by limiting them. Secondly, the express provision that the section is not to apply to any order or determination by a court of law leaves such orders and determinations open to protection by statutory finality or ouster clauses. Thirdly, the exclusion from review does not extend to cases where a special provision is made for appeal to the Court of Session within a specified time-limit. Finally, the section bears to relate only to provisions in Acts passed before August 1, 1958, or possibly also to provisions of Acts re-enacted in legislation after that date. While, however, it serves to encapsulate the essence of the law as it has been developed by the courts with regard to finality and ouster clauses its practical application may now be somewhat limited, since the use of exclusion clauses has diminished during the course of the twentieth century. But the law which has been developed over the years remains relevant to the admittedly more rare cases where exclusion clauses may still be used in statutes passed since August 1, 1958.[9]

---

[7] For the consideration of time-limits, see below paras 13.14 *et seq.*
[8] In s.11(1) of the 1958 Act, now s.12(1) of the 1992 Act.
[9] Lord Dunpark in *Watt v. Lord Advocate*, 1977 S.L.T. 130 at 134 regarded the failure to advance the date in the re-enactment of the provision in the Tribunals and Inquiries Act 1971 as an omission but it was clearly deliberate and may reflect the change in the frequency of such provisions.

England

In England it is well recognised that while a finality clause may prevent **11.03**
an appeal it will not be effective to stop an application for judicial
review.[10] It has even been held that where it is expressly provided that no
judgment of the county court is to be reversed by certiorari in any other
court, certiorari will lie if the judge has acted without jurisdiction.[11] The
approach to finality clauses in principle appears to be substantially the
same as in Scotland.

Finality not to be implied

In relation to all clauses of exclusion there is a clear presumption that **11.04**
the right to recourse at common law to the court is not to be denied. It is
indeed a matter of general principle that clear words in any statute are
required before the court will accept that its jurisdiction has been
excluded.[12] It has long been recognised that express provision is required
and that such an exclusion should not arise merely by implication.[13] An
exclusion must be expressed in positive and peremptory terms and be
free from all ambiguity if it is to oust the jurisdiction of the Court of
Session.[14] Thus where the statute requires an exercise of administrative
discretion and contains no machinery for review it should not be
concluded that the decision is immune from review.[15] The general rule is
that the court is bound to exercise jurisdiction unless the matter in
dispute is clearly referred to another body.[16] Provisions which merely
enable a dispute to be referred to arbitration will not suffice to exclude
the jurisdiction of the Court of Session,[17] and even where reference to
arbitration is mandatory that will not exclude review by the court where
what is complained of is something outwith the relevant statute.[18] As
Lord Justice-Clerk Macdonald observed in *Jeffray v. Angus*[19]:

> "Now, I think it cannot be disputed that the Supreme Court is open
> to every citizen who complains of wrong done in an inferior Court.
> The party called upon to resist an appeal in the Supreme Court can
> exclude the appeal only if he can show that by statutory enactment
> the power of review of the Supreme Court is excluded. There are of
> course many classes of proceedings the decisions in which have been
> declared to be final and not subject to review, but this cannot be
> done by implication. It must be by express exclusion."

Nor will it be readily held that the court's jurisdiction has been excluded
by any provision in delegated legislation. Where the Scottish Education

---

[10] See Wade and Forsyth, *Administrative Law* (7th ed.), p. 729.

[11] *R. v. Hurst, ex p. Smith* [1960] 2 Q.B. 133.

[12] *Brodie v. Kerr*, 1952 S.C. 216 at 224. See also *Ealing LBC v. Race Relations Board*
[1972] A.C. 342.

[13] *Guthrie v. Cowan*, Dec. 10, 1807, F.C.; *Anderson v. Campbell*, Feb. 28, 1811 F.C.;
(1818) 5Dow 412. It was held in the earlier case that an express exclusion of certiorari did
not exclude advocation.

[14] Hume, *Lectures*, p. 270.

[15] It may be doubted whether the decision in *County Auditor of Lanark v. Lambie* (1905)
7F. 1049, where the Secretary of State ordered a surcharge to be imposed upon certain
councillors without reasons and without redress, would be decided in the same way today.

[16] *Norfor v. Aberdeenshire Education Authority*, 1923 S.C. 881.

[17] *Lanark County Council v. East Kilbride Town Council*, 1967 S.C. 235 at 244.

[18] *Adamson and Others v. Edinburgh Street Tramways Co.* (1872) 10M. 533.

[19] 1909 S.C. 400 at 402.

Department was empowered by statute to make regulations respecting all necessary things preliminary or incidental to elections to a School Board, it was held that a regulation which declared that the decision of the returning officer on the validity of any nomination was to be final was *ultra vires*.[20]

Appeals from the sheriff court

11.05 The rule that exclusion cannot be implied but must be express appears to be an absolute rule so far as the supervisory jurisdiction is concerned. The position in relation to appeals from the sheriff court, as distinct from judicial review, is not so extreme. Certainly the cases indicate that exclusion in that context may be implied, at least if the implication is clear or necessary.[21] As a general rule, however, even in the matter of appeals from the sheriff, an express exclusion is necessary.[22] As has already been noticed, the Tribunals and Inquiries Act 1992 does not apply to decisions of a court of law, and so does not apply to decisions of the sheriff court.

II CONSTRUCTION OF EXCLUSION CLAUSES

Limited construction

11.06 Where there is express language the clause may fall to be given a limited construction so as not to exclude review. Exclusion clauses have always been strictly construed.[23] As Hume observed[24]: "It is obvious, that no special jurisdiction can be constituted absolute and uncontrollable judge of the extent and construction of its charter, and that in excluding the power of review, the Legislature must be held to speak with relation to those proceedings, that are done in pursuance, or in execution of the power granted by the Act." Thus even where the jurisdiction conferred on a body is expressly final and conclusive of challenge the court may review and correct an excess of power, such as its exercise by injurious and oppressive motives.[25] Thus in *Buchanan v. Towat*[26] where the Justices of the Peace were authorised "to hear and finally determine and adjudge all offences" under the Act Geo.1, c. 18 the court held that that did not mean that their determination was to be final but that the Justices were required to reach a conclusion. While review of decisions of the Dean of Guild in pursuance of the Glasgow Police Act 1866 was expressly excluded, it was held that this did not prevent review of what was regarded as a common law proceeding before the Dean of Guild.[27] A like view was taken, and an advocation held to be competent, where the decision complained of was at least as to one part of it not

---

[20] *Kerr v. Hood*, 1907 S.C. 895.

[21] *Arcari v. Dumbartonshire County Council*, 1948 S.C. 62 at 68; *Harper v. Inspector of Rutherglen* (1903) 6F. 23 at 25; *Rodenhurst v. Chief Constable of Grampian Police*, 1992 S.C. 1.

[22] *Marr and Sons v. Lindsay* (1881) 8R. 784. On finality clauses relating to decisions of the sheriff see Macphail, *Sheriff Court Practice* (2nd ed.), para. 25.32 and Muirhead, *Burgh Police Acts*, Vol. 2, p. 721.

[23] *Shivas* (1804) M. Jur.App. 21.

[24] *Lectures*, p. 271.

[25] *Dawson v. Allardyce*, Feb. 18, 1809, F.C.

[26] (1754) M. 7347.

[27] *Allan v. Whyte* (1890) 18R. 332.

appropriated to the statutory jurisdiction entrusted to the sheriff for final determination.[28] Where by statute certiorari was expressly excluded, it was held that advocation was nevertheless competent, the English form of practice being dissimilar to the corresponding processes in Scotland.[29] Where the decision of the returning officer on the validity of nominations for a School Board was made final, the view was expressed that that provision could not have been intended to exclude recourse to the court and that the intention was simply to secure that the electoral process was not stopped during its course.[30] In relation to the competency of an appeal from the sheriff to the sheriff principal, it has been held that a provision that the decision of the sheriff should be binding and conclusive and not open to appeal only applied to a decision on the merits, and not to a judgment which dismissed the action as incompetent.[31] In *Moss' Empires v. Assessor for Glasgow*[32] an entry in the valuation roll had been increased without the statutory notice having been given to the person affected. Section 30 of the Valuation of Lands (Scotland) Act 1874 provided that no valuation contained in the roll made up and authenticated in terms of the Act should be challengeable "by reason of any informality, or of any want of compliance with the provisions of this Act, in the proceedings for making up such valuation or valuation roll". But it was held that the failure to give notice was not a want of compliance with the provisions for making up the roll and that an action for reduction was competent. In *Anderson, Petitioner*,[33] however, it was held that a statutory provision whereby on the lodging of a stated case one appellant should be held to have abandoned "any other mode of appeal which might otherwise have been open to him" rendered an application to the *nobile officium* incompetent. A stated case had been lodged and taken to a conclusion, but it might be thought that even if appeal were excluded review was not.[34]

Matters prior to or subsequent to the statutory acting

A finality clause may be so construed as to confine it to matters other than that which is the subject of the particular challenge. Thus an issue not raised before the inferior body, and so not determined by them, may base a reduction of their order despite a finality clause; the decision may be final but an assumption on which it proceeded is not.[35] It was recognised in one case that the enlargement of holdings and the determination of fair rents is a matter for the Crofters Commission, but that, while they may have to determine questions of whether an individual is a crofter or not incidentally to their determination, their decision on that point is not final. It was observed that administrative bodies should not have an absolute and uncontrolled jurisdiction to determine matters of civil right.[36] A provision that any question arising out of the termination of a tenancy should be determined by arbitration did not stop the court from intervening where the issue was whether

11.07

---

[28] *Caledonian Ry v. Glasgow and Redburn Bridge Road Trustees* (1849) 12D. 399.
[29] *Guthrie v. Cowan* 1807 M. Jur.App., Pt I No. 17.
[30] *Kerr v. Hood*, 1907 S.C. 895.
[31] *Leitch v. Scottish Legal Burial Society* (1870) 9M. 40.
[32] 1917 S.C.(H.L.) 1.
[33] 1974 S.L.T. 239.
[34] See *L, Petr (No. 1)*, 1993 S.L.T. 1310.
[35] *Dalgleish v. Livingston* (1895) 22R. 646.
[36] *Sitwell v. Macleod* (1899) 1F. 950.

there had been a termination or not—a question precedent to any question for the arbiter.[37] So also a question of title to sue was held not to be excluded from the finality of a decision on the merits of a complaint to the sheriff.[38] However, a finality clause will not exclude recourse to the court where the error is not in the decree but in the proceedings following upon it.[39] And an express finality of proceedings "had or taken in pursuance of" the Act does not exclude an ordinary action to enforce rights arising under the Act.[40] Where, however, a sheriff granted an order requiring certain remedial works to be done to a house, but failed to specify a time for the performance of them, the express finality of the order as binding and conclusive on the parties rendered it later incompetent for the housing authority to seek an order from the court to enforce performance.[41]

Finality limited to the scope of the jurisdiction

11.08   The early small debt legislation envisaged review on the ground of "iniquity or oppression" and it was held that under such a provision it was insufficient to allege that the decision under challenge was wrong, without making any allegation of *malus animus*. That legislation was considered to have intended there to be an inexpensive and summary procedure and accordingly the scope of review permitted was deliberately limited.[42] On the other hand, where a wide jurisdiction is expressly given to the tribunal, the scope of the finality clause may be considerable. Thus where the power was given to determine "whether any compensation, and, if so, what amount, ought to be granted" and that jurisdiction was construed as including matters of entitlement to compensation as well as amount, the express finality of the inferior body was held to exclude the court from considering whether the pursuer was entitled to compensation.[43] In the case of *Simpson v. Harley*[44] it was held that the jurisdiction given to the sheriff under the General Road Act was wide enough to encompass any matter or thing committed to him under the Act so that the express finality of his judgment excluded review of an alleged error in the construction of the statute.

Actings under the statute expressly final

11.09   In some statutes the finality clause is expressly related to actings or orders or other things done under the statute in question. Finality in such cases will be limited by that definition and will not apply where the scope of the statutory jurisdiction has been exceeded. Where provision was made in the Nuisance Removal Act of 1848 to the effect that nothing done relating to the execution of that Act should be open to review, it was observed that while that might exclude review in matters of form and on the merits it would not bar a reduction where the proceedings were challenged as *ultra vires*.[45] Where a grocer and spirit

---

[37] *Donaldson's Hospital v. Esslemont*, 1925 S.C. 199; 1926 S.C. (H.L.) 68.
[38] *Erskine v. Kerr* (1857) 22D. 277.
[39] *Shiell v. Mossman* (1871) 10M. 58.
[40] *Edinburgh and Glasgow Ry v. Cadder Statute Labour Road Trustees* (1842) 5D. 218.
[41] *Magistrates of Kelso v. Alexander*, 1939 S.C. 78.
[42] *Sempill v. Alexander*, Jan. 19, 1810, F.C.
[43] *Alexander v. Angus Education Authority*, 1930 S.C. 1075.
[44] (1830) 8S. 977. The error was described as an "error of judgment". See later, para. 22.08.
[45] *Dunbar v. Levack* (1858) 20D. 538.

dealer was ordered to be instantly imprisoned failing payment of a fine although the relevant legislation allowed 14 days within which payment might be made, reduction of the sentence was held not to be excluded by a clause which excluded review of sentences granted "under the authority of the Act", as what had been done was not even colourably under that authority.[46]

Excess of jurisdiction

The approach considered in the preceding paragraph holds good even **11.10** where the finality clause does not expressly relate the finality to things done under the statute.[47] In *Grant v. Gordon*[48] Lord President Hope observed: "Where parties do not act within the provisions of the statute but go out of it, their actings are not covered by any peculiar privileges which the statute confers." As Lord Dunedin observed in *Caledonian Railway v. Glasgow Corporation*,[49]: "So long as the defenders keep within the lines prescribed by the statute, the Court will give effect to the finality clauses, and will not interfere by way of a declaratory finding or a reduction, but if under the name and guise of the statutory proceeding the defenders attempt to do something quite different from what the statute allows, then they are doing an *ultra vires* act, and no finality clause will or can protect their illegal acting from the restraint of the Supreme Court." Lord President Inglis has observed[50] that where proceedings are brought not as a process of review but to set aside as incompetent or illegal the proceedings of an inferior court "the jurisdiction of this Court to entertain such an action cannot be doubted, notwithstanding the entire prohibition of review of any kind". In the early case of *Patillo v. Maxwell*[51] the complainer stated that he was excluded from military service by being over the stated age and under the required height. The relevant statute provided that persons once listed were not to be taken out of His Majesty's service by any process other than for some criminal matter. But the court held that the statute did not exclude review where there was a very good reason shown and the Act forbade the enlistment of men of the age and height of the complainer. So also the court will intervene where there has been a failure to hear the interested parties,[52] or a failure to have a warrant of citation signed by the official specifically required by the statute to do so,[53] or a failure to comply with a statutory requirement to commit the evidence heard by the inferior body to writing.[54] So also where justices were held to have exceeded their jurisdiction in refusing to hear a case

---

[46] *M'Donald v. Dobbie* (1864) 2M. 407.

[47] In *Chivas v. Duke of Gordon and Others* (July 11, 1804, F.C.; M. Vol. 9 Jur.App., p. 21) a majority of the Court held that review of allegedly *ultra vires* actings was incompetent by virtue of a finality clause, but the decision was clearly influenced by the necessity of having an immediate effective militia at that time.

[48] (1833) 12S. 167 at 170.

[49] *Caledonian Ry v. Glasgow Corporation* (1905) 7F. 1020 at 1027.

[50] *Ashley v. Magistrates of Rothesay* (1873) 11M. 708 at 716; see also (1874) 1R.(H.L.) 14.

[51] (1797) M. 7386. Review failed in the earlier case of *Foote v. Marshall* (1778) M. 7385, in which the complainer had sought to found on the case of *Buchanan v. Towart* (1754) M. 7347; but in *Patillo* a particular point was made that that the complaint went to the jurisdiction of the authority. Review also failed in the case of *Robertson v. Justices of the Peace of Stirlingshire* (1744) M. 7340.

[52] *Lochgilphead School Board v. South Knapdale School Board* (1877) 4R. 389.

[53] *Forrest v. Harvey* (1845) 4 Bell's App. 197.

[54] *Brown v. Heritors of Kilberry* (1825) 4S. 174.

the court may intervene despite a statutory prohibition of recourse to a superior court.[55] A finality clause will not exclude the supervisory jurisdiction where there has been a breach of natural justice committed.[56] Nor will an improper exercise of a statutory discretion be barred by a finality clause.[57]

An invalid determination is no determination

11.11 One way of describing the same situation is to construe the finality clause as applying only to things done within the scope of the statutory power. Another way of expressing the position is to say that the decision can be regarded as a nullity. In *Manson v. Smith*[58] Lord Neaves said in relation to a small debt summons which had been signed by a sheriff-clerk, although it was raised at his instance as an individual, that the finality clause "refers only to proper causes, and this never became a true cause. It was no more a cause than if there had been no summons". A statutory finality clause will thus not protect a decision which has been reached by a breach of the proper procedure. In one case,[59] where a resolution by way of special order to adopt the General Police Act 1862 had been passed by the Commissioners of Police in the Burgh of Turiff without the local advertisement required by the statute, both it and a deliverance by the sheriff finding that the Act had been adopted were reduced by the Court of Session, although the Act provided that the sheriff's deliverance was to be final and "shall not be subject to be set aside, or reviewed, or affected by any Court or judicature, upon any ground or in any manner of way whatever". As Lord President Inglis observed[60] no resolution could be confirmed by the sheriff unless it was a resolution made and passed in terms of the statute and the special order would not be a special order unless the statutory provisions for advertisement had been complied with. In *Anisminic v. Foreign Compensation Commission*,[61] in relation to a clause which provided that a determination by the Commission of any application made to them under the Foreign Compensation Act 1950 "shall not be called in question in any Court of Law", Lord Reid observed: "I do not think it necessary or even reasonable to construe the word 'determination' as including everything which purports to be a determination but which is in fact no determination at all." In *Renfrewshire District Council v. McGourlick*[62] Lord McCluskey observed that a finality clause such as there was in the case before him "cannot oust the jurisdiction of the Court to determine whether or not what purports to be a decree or order made under the statute is truly a decree or order within the whole provisions of the statute".

Actings within jurisdiction

11.12 Where the inferior body has acted within its jurisdiction, a finality clause will bar review. But the question whether the decision was or was not within the jurisdiction can be a difficult one, and the problem also arises

---

[55] *Caledonian Ry v. Fleming* (1869) 7M. 554.
[56] *Smith and Tasker v. Robertson* (1827) 5S. 848; *cf Ridge v. Baldwin* [1964] A.C. 40.
[57] *Macbeth v. Ashley* (1874) 1R. (H.L.) 14.
[58] (1871) 9M. 492 at 497.
[59] *Stirling and Another v. Hutcheon and Others* (1874) 1R. 935.
[60] at 941.
[61] [1969] 2 A.C. 147, *per* Lord Reid at 170.
[62] 1987 S.L.T. 538 at 543.

as to who is to be the judge of the matter. This is one area where matters of the merits and the competency of an application for review may become involved together.[63] Thus reduction of a decree of the sheriff ordering under the Roads and Bridges (Scotland) Act 1878 that a party should pay for repairs caused by their having passed excessive weights along a road was refused, as it was held that the sheriff had acted within his jurisdiction in determining the matters of fact and law involved in the case.[64] Where justices were held to have acted within their powers in a matter of the provision of accommodation for a schoolmaster, the finality of their decision excluded access to the court.[65] In one case under the Bankruptcy (Scotland) Act 1856 the court refused to interfere with a decision that the trustee elected to act did not hold an interest opposed to the general interest of the creditors, that being a ground specified in the Act as being a disqualification. The court held that it was for the sheriff to consider and decide that point and as he had done so his decision was final.[66] So also where the sheriff acted within his jurisdiction in declaring the election of a trustee, review was held to be excluded by the finality clause.[67] But where the sheriff rejected a candidate for the trusteeship on a ground which was held to be unsound in law it was held that he had exceeded his jurisdiction and his decision could not stand, despite a finality clause.[68]

Finality where express remedy provided

Where there is not only a finality clause but an express remedy provided, **11.13** then recourse to the court may be effectively excluded.[69] This will particularly be the case where the statutory remedy has not been followed.[70] Where there is a finality clause and an express remedy provided by the statute on any of certain specified grounds which include grounds which might otherwise entitle recourse to the supervisory jurisdiction, review may be excluded. At an early period it was recognised that where a summary and economic course of remedy was provided which could sufficiently obviate the risk of wrong or abuse, the intention to exclude the court was the more evident.[71] The sheriff court small debt legislation has been recognised as being one example where review was excluded even on grounds of excess of jurisdiction,[72] although in *Campbell v. Young*[73] Lord President Hope observed: "Even when a statute debars any interference of the Court in the broadest terms, if the act be departed from, we have not hesitated to grant redress—as under the late Sheriff's Small Debt Act—Schoolmasters' Act, etc.; and though we would never trench on the power of review on the merits given to the Quarter Sessions, it is clear, when the act is so totally disregarded, we

---

[63] *Edinburgh and Glasgow Ry v. Earl of Hopetoun* (1840) 2D. 1255.
[64] *Milne & Co. v. Aberdeen District Committee* (1899) 2F. 220.
[65] *Heritors of Annan v. Herbertson* (1837) 15S. 645.
[66] *Grierson v. Ogilvy's Trustee*, 1908 S.C. 959.
[67] *Foulis v. Downie* (1871) 7M. 20.
[68] *Farquharson v. Sutherlands* (1888) 15R. 759; the matter had been raised by way of appeal to the Court of Session.
[69] *e.g. Balfour v. Malcolm* (1842) 1 Bell's App. 153.
[70] See *supra*, para. 12.07. Examples can be found in the early cases under the enlistment legislation such as *Imray v. Inverness Deputy Lieutenants*, Mar. 2, 1811, F.C.
[71] *Knowles v. Aberdeenshire Trustees* (1811) Hume's Dec. 207.
[72] *Caledonian Ry v. Fleming* (1869) 7M. 552, *per* Lord Justice-General Inglis at 556.
[73] (1835) 12S. 167 at 170.

are entitled to interfere". In that case it was held that there had not been merely a small irregularity, which might have been insufficient to warrant the interference of the court, but that the proceedings had been in no way under the Act. But suspension of a sheriff court small debt decree was held incompetent where in terms of section 30 of the Sheriff Court Small Debt Act[74] no such decree was to be subject to any form of review other than as was provided by the Act, and section 31 provided for an appeal to the next Circuit Court of Justiciary or the High Court in Edinburgh.[75] Furthermore, since the specified grounds for appeal in section 31 included "incompetency, including defect of jurisdiction" of the sheriff, a phrase which was taken to cover lack of jurisdiction, it was also held that the sheriff's decision on an objection that the alleged debtor did not reside within the sheriffdom could only be appealed to the next circuit court of justiciary and could not be reviewed by the Court of Session. The finality provision in section 30 related to any case "decided under the authority of this Act" and a case in which the sheriff decided the question of jurisdiction was such a case.[76] Where, however, the illegality is such as to vitiate the whole proceedings, as where a sheriff-clerk depute in that character signed a small debt summons at his instance as an individual, thereby committing a breach of natural justice, recourse to the Court of Session will not be excluded.[77] Where under the Burgh Police Acts appeal was allowed to Commissioners, whose decision was declared to be final, an appeal to the court under another section, applicable in the absence of any other provision in the statute, was held incompetent on the ground that the Commissioners had exercised their jurisdiction under the statute, and in choosing to go to them the appellants had submitted to a final decision.[78]

Fundamental nullity

11.14 Where excess of jurisdiction is alleged the existence of an express remedy and a finality clause may not exclude recourse to the court.[79] In one early case interdict against the erection of what was alleged to be an unauthorised toll-bar was held incompetent where a means of statutory redress against the erection of toll-bars was provided and the decision of the sheriff or justices in such a process was declared to be final.[80] In *Caledonian Railway v. Greenock and Wemyss Bay Railway*,[81] however, it was recognised that the statutory finality and the statutory appeal procedure did not exclude review where an excess of jurisdiction was alleged. In *Lord Advocate v. Police Commissioners of Perth*, where it was alleged that the works involving the discharge of sewage into the river Tay would pollute the water supply and were in violation of the respondents' statutory powers, recourse to the court was held competent, notwithstanding a provision for appeal to the sheriff. Lord Justice-Clerk Moncreiff observed: "A clause of finality cannot protect a Sheriff's

---

[74] 1 Vict. c.31.
[75] *Rankine v. Lang* (1843) 6D. 183.
[76] *Graham v. Mackay* (1845) 7D. 515; (1848) 6 Bell's App. 214.
[77] *Manson v. Smith* (1871) 9M. 492.
[78] *Brown v. Magistrates of Leith* (1896) 23R. 650.
[79] In *Key v. Stirling and Drymen Bridge Road Trustees* (1830) 9S. 167 the bill of suspension was passed to try the question, even although there was an express statutory remedy which was expressed to be final and conclusive and not subject to adjudication.
[80] *Wilson v. Leith Walk Trustees* (1831) 9S. 725.
[81] (1878) 5R. 995.

judgement, when, taking an erroneous view of a statute, he either refuses to sanction a lawful act or sanctions an unlawful one. It applies only to those matters of detail which concern the due and proper administration of the statute, and which are best disposed of by the sound discretion of a local Judge".[82] Where there is no express clause of finality, however, the existence of an express remedy may not suffice to exclude the court.[83]

Finality clauses and time-limits

In some cases there has been provided not only an alternative remedy **11.15** but a time-limit within which it is to be employed. The effect of that combination may be effectively to exclude judicial review. The matter is considered later in the context of time-limits.[84]

Finality of registers

In some instances rolls or registers have been decalared by statute to be **11.16** final or conclusive. But such finality is no bar to the intervention of the court upon such grounds as have already been discussed. Where a local statute provided that the local register of streets should fix conclusively the particulars of the streets entered therein, a clear indication was given that that would not prevent the court from interfering if an entry had been made *ultra vires*.[85] Valuation cases provide some particular examples of the treatment of a finality clause. Section 30 of the Lands Valuation (Scotland) Act 1854 Act provides that no valuation roll "which shall be made up and authenticated in terms of this Act and no valuation which shall be contained therein shall be challengeable or be capable of being set aside or rendered ineffectual by reason of any informality or any want of compliance with the provisions of the Act in the proceedings for making up such valuation or valuation roll". Where reduction was sought of an entry in the valuation roll which had been increased without notice of the change having been sent to the person affected in accordance with section 5 of the Act, it was held that the action was not barred by the provisions of section 30, on the reasoning that the failure to give notice was not a want of compliance with the provision for "making up" the roll.[86] In an earlier case[87] a finality clause was held not to prevent a remedy being given where subjects had been entered twice in the valuation roll and so liable to be assessed twice over, as the court regarded the matter as one of assessment and not of valuation. That distinction between the finality of the roll for valuation purposes but not for purposes of assessment has been recognised in other cases.[88] So also where an entry has been made unlawfully it will not be protected by any provision for finality.[89] On the other hand, where the legislation provided that the value in the valuation roll was to be deemed and taken to be the just amount of real rent for the purposes of

---

[82] (1869) 8M. 244 at 246.

[83] *Adamson and Others v. Edinburgh Street Tramways Co.* (1872) 10M. 533. The matter of the exhaustion of statutory remedies is considered in the following chapter.

[84] See para. 13.17.

[85] *Caledonian Ry v. Glasgow Corporation* (1905) 7F. 1020.

[86] *Moss Empires v. Assessor for Glasgow*, 1917 S.C. (H.L.) 1.

[87] *Sharp v. Latheron Parochial Board* (1883) 4R. 1163.

[88] See also on this point *Dante v. Assessor for Ayr*, 1922 S.C. 109 and *Distillers Co. v. Fife County Council*, 1925 S.C. (H.L.) 15.

[89] *Glasgow Corporation v. Assessor for Public Undertakings*, 1936 S.C. 754.

assessment for local taxation, the court held that they had no jurisdiction to review the process by which the entry in the roll had been reached, the figure in the roll being conclusive.[90] In one case where subjects had been entered in the roll of the Assessor for Public Undertakings and that entry had become by statute final it was held that an entry of the same subjects in the ordinary roll should be deleted, since the same subjects should not be exposed to double taxation.[91]

Modern practice

11.17 As was explained at the start of this chapter, exclusion clauses are not now often adopted by Parliament. When they are they will tend to be designed to make it clear that judicial review is intended to be absolutely excluded. But there must be sound reasons for permitting the possibility of error, injustice and illegality to be committed without redress. Conceivably in particular circumstances such a case may be found, but the court will require to be satisfied that such is the intention of Parliament. Certainly attempts to exclude the supervisory jurisdiction are likely nowadays to be framed in comprehensive terms. In section 44(2) of the British Nationality Act 1981 it was provided that: "The Secretary of State . . . shall not be required to assign any reason for the grant or refusal of any application under this Act the decision on which is at his discretion; and the decision of the Secretary of State . . . shall not be subject to appeal to, or review in, any court." However, it has been held by the Court of Appeal in England that the Secretary of State still had a duty to be fair, and that, in the absence of any information about what concerns the Secretary of State had had, the applicants had not received the fairness to which they were entitled in accordance with the rule of law.[92] Parliament has more recently sought to secure the exclusion of the court by bringing in reference to the jurisdiction of the tribunal. In the Interception of Communications Act 1985, section 7(8) provides: "The decisions of the Tribunal (including any decision as to their jurisdiction) shall not be subject to appeal or liable to be questioned in any court." In this context "decisions" may be thought to be intended to include purported decisions which are not decisions at all. But a construction which involves an approval by Parliament of an illegality is not one which may commend itself to any court of review.

Conclusion

11.18 The matter at the end of the day is one of the intention of the particular statutory provisions. This will involve consideration of the particular terms of the finality clause in relation to the particular point of the challenge, but above all it requires consideration of the scope of the jurisdiction intended to be conferred by Parliament. In constitutional terms the problem involves a reconciliation between the doctrine of the separation of powers and the basic principle of the rule of law.[93] It may be doubted whether it would ever now be held that Parliament would confer a jurisdiction to determine matters contrary to law, so that a finality clause is not likely to be intended to exclude review of, for

---

[90] *Magistrates of Glasgow v. Hall* (1887) 14R. 319.
[91] *John Menzies & Co. v. Assessor for Glasgow (Case 1)*, 1937 S.C. 263.
[92] *R. v. Secretary of State for the Home Department, ex p. Fayed* (1997) 1 All E.R. 228.
[93] See Chap. 4.

example, errors in the construction of legislation, or errors in the way the decision of an inferior body has been reached. Apart from the general presumption against the exclusion of review, the matter must depend upon the intention of the particular statute.

III OTHER FORMULAE

(a) Clauses of subjective opinion

Another formula of words which might seem to be designed to dis- **11.19**
courage intervention by the ordinary courts is that whereby an authority is entitled to act when "it is satisfied that" or "when it appears to it that" or when "in its opinion" a specified situation exists. A narrow view of this phraseology was taken in the case of *Holmes v. Secretary of State for Scotland*[94] an appeal against a compulsory purchase order. The Lord Justice-Clerk (Grant) observed[95] that it was for the Secretary of State to decide whether he was "satisfied", not for the court to say whether on the evidence and the facts before him he was entitled to be satisfied. The Secretary of State had not on a proper construction of the legislation exceeded his statutory power and he was entitled to confirm the order. Such a subjective approach was adopted in some of the earlier English cases.[96] In times of national emergency it may be appropriate to accept a construction of the language as conferring an absolute discretion on the executive. That may explain what Lord Reid in *Ridge v. Baldwin*[97] described as "the very peculiar decision of this House" in *Liversidge v. Anderson*.[98] But the trend of decision is away from any restrictive view of such phrases,[99] and they should now be seen as adding little if anything to the position which would hold without them, namely that no decision will usually be made unless the maker of it is satisfied that the proper circumstances exist for the making of it, and has applied his mind to the problem so as to arrive at an opinion upon it. But the point must turn as one of construction upon the particular context. In *Secretary of State for Education and Science v. Tameside Metropolitan Burgh Council*[1] the House of Lords decided that the words "if the Secretary of State is satisfied" in the Education Act 1944 did not confer an absolute discretion and that the court could inquire into a possible misdirection. In *Attorney-General v. Reynolds*[2] in the context of the Constitution of St Christopher, Nevis and Anguilla, the same phrase was also given a liberal construction, not as conferring dictatorial powers, but inferring that there were reasonable grounds for being satisfied on the matter in question and that the course decided upon was reasonably justifiable and necessary.

(b) "As if enacted . . ."

In some cases the empowering statute may expressly provide that an **11.20**
order made under it "shall have effect as if enacted in this Act". Opinions on the effect of such a provision were expressed in *Institute of*

---

[94] 1965 S.C. 1.
[95] at 9.
[96] *e.g. Robinson v. Minister of Town and Country Planning* [1947] K.B. 702.
[97] [1964] A.C. 40 at p. 73.
[98] [1942] A.C. 206.
[99] The development is discussed in Wade and Forsyth, *Administrative Law* (7th ed.), pp. 442 *et seq.*
[1] [1977] A.C. 1014.
[2] [1980] A.C. 637.

Patent Agents v. Lockwood,[3] where it was recognisd that the effect of such language was to make the rules made under the Act as effectual as if they were part of the statute itself, although they might have to be treated as subordinate to the provisions of the Act if any conflict was found to exist between them. But it was recognised that there was a difference between the rules and the statute in respect that, as Lord Herschell pointed out, that while "you may canvass a rule and determine whether or not it is within the power of those who made it, you cannot canvass in that way an Act of Parliament". Despite that, and in light of that decision, a majority of the First Division in *Glasgow Insurance Committee v. Scottish Insurance Commissioners*[4] took the view that where a statute authorised the making of regulations and provided that they should be laid before both Houses of Parliament and should have effect as if enacted in the Act unless annulled by Her Majesty in Council or by an address presented by either House of Parliament, their validity could not be challenged in a court of law even although they had not yet been laid before Parliament. The only method of review was that of the prescribed Parliamentary procedure. The point came later to be one on which opinions were reserved.[5] It was finally affirmed in *Minister of Health v. R., ex parte Yaffe*[6] that such a clause did not preclude the court from considering whether an order was or was not inconsistent with the provisions of the Act. This approach was followed in Scotland[7] and when in a subsequent Scottish case[8] the court raised the question the Solicitor-General conceded that the validity of the regulations which were there in issue could be subjected to consideration.

Present practice

11.21   The approach which was affirmed in the case of *Yaffe* is plainly in line with the developed attitude to legislative restraints on review. Regulations will only have effect as part of the empowering Act if they are truly regulations made under it. Their validity must still be open to question. But the particular question is now somewhat academic as the use of this particular formula has fallen into disuse. The point remains of interest in illustrating the principle. The adoption of the particular language is not now likely to be encountered.

(c)   Approval of subordinate legislation

11.22   The question arises whether, or how far, the courts may review subordinate legislation[9] which has been approved by another body. In *Rae v. Hamilton*[10] Lord McLaren, in holding that certain byelaws were not unreasonable, attached considerable weight to the fact that they had been approved by the Local Government Board as required by the

---

[3] [1894] A.C. 387.

[4] 1915 S.C. 504.

[5] *David Lawson Ltd v. Torrance*, 1929 J.C. 119. In that case and in *Hamilton v. Fife*, 1907 S.C.(J.) 79 the view was taken that a byelaw which was declared to have the force of an Act of Parliament could not be challenged merely on the ground of a procedural defect in the making or the passing of it.

[6] [1931] A.C. 494.

[7] *M'Ewen's Trustees v. Church of Scotland General Trustees*, 1940 S.L.T. 357.

[8] *Forster v. Polmaise Patent Fuel Co.*, 1947 J.C. 56.

[9] For the terminology and the kinds of subordinate legislation see Gloag and Henderson, *The Law of Scotland* (10th ed.), para. 1.6.

[10] (1904) 6F.(J.) 42.

relevant statute. Indeed he indicated that there was a presumption of reasonableness which arose when the byelaws had been approved by the statutory authority. In the English case of *Hoffman-La Roche and Co. v. Secretary of State for Trade and Industry*[11] the fact that the order in question had been approved by both Houses of Parliament did not prevent the court from declaring it invalid. The attack there made was based on alleged defects in the procedure which had been followed and on grounds of *ultra vires*. The point was canvassed in Scotland in *City of Edinburgh District Council v. Secretary of State for Scotland*.[12]
. In the Outer House Lord Jauncey held that where Parliament had reserved a control over subordinate legislation by requiring that such legislation was to be subject to its own approval, then the legislation could not be challenged as unreasonable or irrational. The courts[13] "can only hold to be *ultra vires* a statutory instrument which has been laid before and approved by Parliament where that instrument is patently defective in that it purports to do what is not authorised by the enabling statute or where the procedure followed in making that instrument departed from the requirements of the enabling statute". The decision that the instrument in question was not defective was upheld by the Second Division. There the view was taken that on the facts of the case none of the tests of illegality, irrationality or procedural impropriety were made out. The test of irrationality did not seem to be excluded as matter of principle. It was rather a matter of the extreme difficulty in conceiving of its application in the circumstances of a measure which was the expression of a decision on policy. Further support for the proposition that irrationality may rarely, if ever, be open as a ground for review where a Parliamentary approval is required may be found in *Nottinghamshire County Council v. Secretary of State*.[14] It was there indicated that where executive power is only to be exercised with the consent and approval of one of the Houses of Parliament, courts could only interfere if the statute had been misconstrued or the minister had deceived the House. It was not for the judges to hold that the exercise was irrational; the matter was one of political judgment for the Minister and for the House.[15]

---

[11] [1975] A.C. 365.
[12] 1985 S.C. 261. For further discussion on this topic see C.M.G. Himsworth, "Defining the Boundaries of Judicial Review", 1985 S.L.T. (News) 369 and A.I.L. Campbell, "Approval and Statutory Instruments", 1986 S.L.T. (News) 101.
[13] *Edinburgh D.C. v. Secretary of State for Scotland*, 1985 S.C. 261 at 275.
[14] [1986] A.C. 240.
[15] See the consideration of policy issues: para. 9.17.

CHAPTER 12

ALTERNATIVE REMEDIES

I   THE GENERAL RULE
II   EXCEPTIONS
III OTHER MATTERS

I THE GENERAL RULE

Introduction

As a general proposition it may be said that judicial review is not available **12.01** if there is an alternative means of relief open to the applicant. One example of such a case is where there is a contractual remedy open to the complainer.[1] But the matter of alternative remedies has usually arisen in relation to the provision of statutory remedies and it is with that problem that this chapter is particularly concerned. Where a particular remedy is provided the general rule is that it must first be pursued. This rule was recognised by Lord Kames[2] when he observed that "it is the province, one should imagine, of the sovereign, and supreme court, to redress wrongs of every kind, when a peculiar remedy is not provided". One may not neglect a statutory remedy and jump direct to the Court of Session.[3] Indeed, if the alternative statutory remedy is more suitable to the nature of the case and sufficiently obviates the risk of wrong or abuse, it may be exclusive or final.[4] The principle may be thus expressed in terms of an implied exclusion of the court, so that it can be said that where a statute provides an alternative method of review there is an implied exclusion of the jurisdiction of the Court of Session.[5] The rule has been held applicable not only to the cases of inferior courts and administrative bodies exercising statutory powers and duties, but also to disputes within the established church where the remedies open in the ecclesiastical courts have not been exhausted.[6] Review of an alleged failure to exercise a discretionary power should not lie where a statutory opportunity for redress exists.[7] The exclusion of the jurisdiction of the ordinary court by agreement or by statutory provision has long been a familiar feature of practice,[8] but an express provision or a clear implication must be found in the words of the statute before access to the court will be denied.[9] Moreover, the jurisdiction of the Court of Session may not be entirely ousted, at least for providing an operative order after the statutory procedure has been followed.[10]

---

[1] See para. 8.36.
[2] *Historical Law Tracts* (5th ed.), Book 2, Chap. 3, p. 341.
[3] *Knowles v. Aberdeen Trustees*, June 12, 1871; Hume, *Lectures*, Vol. V, p. 262.
[4] Hume, *Lectures*, Vol V, p. 274.
[5] Mackay, *Manual of Practice*, p. 92. *Green v. Lord Advocate*, 1918 S.C. 667.
[6] *Lang v. Presbytery of Irvine* (1864) 2M. 823.
[7] *Beckett v. Henderson* (1866) 1M.(H.L.) 6.
[8] *Brodie v. Ker*, 1952 S.C. 216 at 223.
[9] *Lanarkshire County Council v. East Kilbride Town Council*, 1967 S.C. 235 at 244; *Walker v. Strathclyde R.C.*, 1986 S.L.T. 523; *Pyx Granite Co. Ltd v. Minister of Housing and Local Government* [1960] A.C. 260.
[10] *Osborne v. British Coal Property*, 1995 S.L.T. 1349.

The Rules of Court

12.02 The point is reflected in the provisions of Rule of Court 58.3 (2), which states that "an application may not be made under paragraph (1) if that application is made, or could be made, by appeal or review under or by virtue of any enactment". Paragraph (1) requires any application to the supervisory jurisdiction to be made by petition for judicial review.[11] It is thought that this rule does not constitute any separate obstacle to recourse to judicial review where an alternative remedy exists, but only provides that alternative statutory remedies should be pursued under their own procedure rather than by the procedure for judicial review.[12] It should not exclude the established exceptions to the general rule.

England

12.03 In England, with its different history in the form and nature of the remedies available in judicial review, varying views have been taken. The cumbersome nature of the earlier writ of mandamus secured that it would not be granted where a more convenient remedy was available.[13] But more recent reforms in procedure have removed that objection. In general the older view in England was to the effect that an express statutory remedy was no bar to the pursuit of a common law remedy. But more recently the courts have expressed views to the contrary effect.[14] In *R. v. Inland Revenue Commissioners, ex parte Preston*[15] it was recognised that judicial review was not to be made available where an alternative remedy exists, at least in the absence of special circumstances. But Sir John Donaldson M.R. sought to represent the view in more modified terms by stating[16] that it "does not support the proposition that judicial review is not available where there is an alternative remedy by way of appeal. It asserts simply that the court, in the exercise of its discretion, will very rarely make this remedy available in these circumstances."

Equity

12.04 A corresponding approach has been advanced in Scotland as representing the sound basis for regarding the objection to an application for judicial review that an alternative remedy exists and has not been pursued. On this approach the matter should be seen as one of the equitable nature of the jurisdiction, so that the objection is regarded as a reason militating against the exercise of the supervisory jurisdiction, rather than one of a rule of strict law to which exceptions may be admitted.[17] The different analyses should not lead to a difference in the result and as a matter of form the traditional approach is adopted in the present chapter.

---

[11] The present formulation superseded a more elaborate version in Rule 260B(3) of the original rules on judicial review. For a discussion on the possible ambiguity of the rule, see Neil Collar "Judicial Review, The Significance of an Alternative Remedy" (1991) 36 J.L.S.S. 299 and 340.

[12] See *Simpson v. Inland Revenue*, 1992 S.L.T. 1069.

[13] *Re Nathan* [1884] 12 Q.B.D. 461.

[14] Wade & Forsyth, *Administrative Law* (7th ed.), p. 723.

[15] [1985] 1 A.C. 835 at 852.

[16] *R. v. Chief Constable, ex p. Calveley* [1986] 1 Q.B. 424 at 433.

[17] See *Ingle v. Ingle's Trustees*, 1999 S.L.T. 650 at 654. A stricter approach was, however, adopted in *Chowdry, Petr*, 1999 S.L.T. 697.

Special jurisdictions

The general principle in Scotland that judicial review is a remedy of last **12.05**
resort came, especially in the nineteenth century, to be developed
against the backgound of the specialised jurisdictions which were created
by Parliament for a variety of administrative purposes. The principle
then found expression in the recognition that where Parliament has
expressly created particular powers, obligations, rights, or liabilities and
has prescribed a particular machinery for their enforcement or control,
then in any question relating to such matters the statutory machinery
should be preferred for their resolution to a recourse to the common law
jurisdiction of the court. Where there is a new jurisdiction created it is
clear that parties must conform at least in the first instance to the
statutory appeal procedure and judicial review is premature and incompetent before that process has been followed through.[18] In one case Lord
Justice-Clerk Moncreiff recognised that where it was applicable the
principle was that "where a new and special jurisdiction is given to any
court the exercise of it must be regulated entirely by the conditions of
the statute under which it is conferred, and that in the general case
remedies which might have been competent in an ordinary civil process
are not to be presumed or inferred to be given by the particular
statute".[19] In an earlier case he observed[20]:

> "In the ordinary case, it would now, I think, be held that where
> statutory powers are given, and a statutory jurisdiction is set up, all
> other jurisdictions are excluded, and it appears to me that of late
> the views entertained on this point have been less strong than those
> expressed in the case of *Bremner*.[21] Accordingly, if, in the present
> case, it turns out on inquiry that the proposed operations are quite
> within the statute, I should be for refusing the note, as I consider
> that, in regard to questions arising in the administration of the
> statute and within its admitted scope, the Sheriff is the sole judge,
> and he is final.
>
> "If, however, the complainer's allegations be true, the proposed
> operations are admittedly outwith the statute, and *ultra vires*; and I
> know of no case in which the common law jurisdiction of the
> Supreme Court has been held to be excluded, where the act
> proposed to be done is prohibited by statute. It is quite true that the
> complainer might have got redress in a more summary form by
> going to the Sheriff. But what if his appeal had been dismissed? In
> that case, assuming the complainer's allegations to be true, the
> Sheriff would have sanctioned an illegal act, and the complainer
> would have been entitled to invoke the jurisdiction of the Supreme
> Court to give him a remedy."

In *British Railways Board v. Glasgow Corporation*[22] the view was taken
that the modern embodiment of an older legislative provision could still
rank as a new and special jurisdiction for the purposes of the rule and by

---

[18] *Alexander v. Seymour* (1828) 7S. 117; *Crawford v. Lennox* (1852) 14D. 1029.

[19] *Magistrate of Portobello v. Magistrate of Edinburgh* (1882) 10R. 130 at 137.

[20] *Lord Advocate v. Police Commissioners of Perth* (1869) 8M. 244 at 245–246.

[21] *Bremner v. Huntly Friendly Society*, Dec. 4, 1817, F.C. See below, para. 12.19
(exception (d)).

[22] 1976 S.C. 224 at 238.

"necessary implication" the jurisdiction of the Court of Session was thereby ousted. Where an applicant had commenced but not exhausted his statutory remedy, judicial review has been held to be incompetent.[23]

Other cases

12.06 But the rule is not confined to cases where a special jurisdiction has been created for the resolution of particular kinds of dispute. In one case it was held that since the opportunity was available to seek a stated case under section 3(1) of the Administration of Justice (Scotland) Act 1972 judicial review was not competent on the ground that review is available in limited circumstances where no other means of remedy exist.[24] Judicial review is not competent where the statutory remedy has been embarked upon, not only because judicial review is a remedy of last resort, but also because two actions on the same point cannot be simultaneously pursued.[25] On the other hand, the establishment of a special machinery for requiring employers to pay wages in accordance with a statutory scheme did not exclude the jurisdiction of the ordinary courts where an employee was seeking to enforce a common law right to wages.[26]

Remedy fenced with limitations

12.07 Where the statutory remedy is made subject to a time-limit and a finality clause judicial review will be more certainly excluded, and a failure to pursue the prescribed means of redress will leave the aggrieved complainer without redress. This matter is considered in the following chapter.[27]

Review of the sheriff court

12.08 Particular examples of the operation of the general principle can be found in the reduction of decrees of the sheriff court. But it must be remembered that reduction of such decrees does not necessarily involve an exercise of the supervisory jurisdiction, but may simply invoke the ordinary jurisdiction of the court.[28] Nevertheless, in light of the nature of the remedy of reduction, the same general principle applies. Thus, in general a decree granted in the sheriff court, from which a process of appeal is open under statutory provision, may not be challenged by reduction.[29] But that rule may not hold if there are exceptional circumstances justifiably excusing a party from failing to use the prescribed methods of redress.[30] Inadvertence and a failure to follow the proper procedural steps are not enough to warrant reduction,[31] nor will a failure

---

[23] *Nahar v. Strathclyde R.C.*, 1986 S.L.T. 570. For a consideration of the case see Steven L. Stuart, "Judial Review and Alternative Remedies", 1986 S.L.T. (News) 309.

[24] *O'Neill v. Scottish Joint Negotiating Committee for Teachers*, 1987 S.L.T. 648.

[25] *Strathclyde Buses Ltd v. Strathclyde R.C.*, 1994 S.L.T. 724.

[26] *Macdonald v. Singer Manufacturing Co.*, 1923 S.C. 551.

[27] See para. 13.17.

[28] *Bell v. Fiddes*, 1996 S.L.T. 51.

[29] *Philp v. Reid*, 1927 S.C. 224. See also *John Brown & Co. Ltd v. Orr*, 1910 S.C. 526, where the sheriff was regarded as performing a judicial act in statutory arbitration proceedings.

[30] *Mitchell Construction Co. (Scotland) Ltd v. Brands Transport and Demolition Ltd*, 1975 S.L.T.(Notes) 58; *J.&C. Black Ltd v. Alltransport International Group Ltd*, 1980 S.C. 75, which was not followed in *Kirkwood v. City of Glasgow D.C.*, 1988 S.L.T. 430.

[31] *Stewart v. Lothian Construction (Edinburgh) Ltd*, 1972 S.L.T.(Notes) 75.

to appeal in time.[32] But an error or ambiguity in the sheriff's interlocutor may suffice.[33] And where a decree had been allowed to be granted on grounds known by the pursuer to be false reduction should be available on the ground of fraud.[34]

Scope of the statutory remedy

In considering the applicability of the rule to any particular case, and in **12.09** particular in ascertaining whether an exception to the general rule exists, it is necessary at the outset to study the terms of the statutory remedy and the nature of the complaint.[35] The statute has to be construed against the general rule, but also having regard to the consideration that if the intention is to oust the jurisdiction of the court the ouster should be clear and unambiguous.[36] A statutory reference to a body for determination as to the due fulfilment or observance of a statutory obligation may be construed as covering matters of fact only, leaving an ordinary action competent for determining the legal question of the measure of the obligations.[37] Primarily the question in every case is whether the particular statutory provisions have the effect of superseding the jurisdiction of the court with reference to the complaint which is made. Where on a proper construction of the statutory means of appeal, it does not include the particular acting of which the complaint is made, then judicial review will be competent.[38] Where the statutory remedy is restricted to a breach of the statutory provisions, redress by a statutory appeal may fail to give relief to a complaint which is more widely based.[39] Review will also be available if the burden of the applicant's complaint is that he is not a person to whom the statutory machinery is available.[40] The terms of the statute providing for the remedy may be such as to allow argument that review is not excluded.[41]

Where the statutory machinery covers the complaint

In some cases the statutory jurisdiction may be wide enough to include **12.10** consideration of a ground of the complaint which may also lie as a ground for judicial review. Thus while allegations of *ultra vires* actings may in some cases enable an immediate application to the court, access to the court may be excluded where the statute in question has not only provided for a process for appeal but has included in that process the very matter which is sought to be challenged.[42] In *Crawford v. Lennox*[43] reduction on the ground of an impropriety in procedure was refused as the statutory form of redress had not been pursued. In *Graham v. Mackay*[44] the statute allowed appeal to the Court of Justiciary from the

---

[32] *Brennan v. Central SMT Co.*, 1947 S.L.T.(Notes) 4.
[33] *Matthewson v. Yeaman* (1900) 2F. 873.
[34] *Rowe v. Elliot*, 1973 S.L.T.(Notes) 41.
[35] *Mensah v. Secretary of State for the Home Department*, 1992 S.L.T. 177.
[36] *Kerr v. Hood*, 1907 S.C. 895 at 900.
[37] *Norfor v. Aberdeenshire Education Authority*, 1923 S.C. 881.
[38] *London and Clydesdale Estates v. Secretary of State for Scotland*, 1989 S.C.L.R. 195.
[39] *Hamilton v. Roxburghshire County Council*, 1970 S.C. 248.
[40] *Purves v. Edinburgh D.C.*, 1987 S.C.L.R. 164; the decision on the merits was reversed: 1987 S.C.L.R. 381.
[41] *Short's Trustee v. Keeper of the Registers of Scotland*, 1993 S.L.T. 1291.
[42] *Denny & Brothers v. Board of Trade* (1880) 7R. 1019.
[43] (1852) 14D. 1029.
[44] (1845) 7D. 515, affd (1848) 6 Bell 214, followed in *Lowden's Trustees. v. Patullo* (1846) 9D. 281 and *Crombie v. M'Ewan* (1864) 23D. 333.

decree of a sheriff on grounds which included "defect of jurisdiction of the sheriff". The defect in that case was very evident. The decree had been pronounced against one who was resident outwith the sheriffdom in which it had been pronounced. But the House of Lords affirmed that the Court of Session had no jurisdiction to interfere in the matter. A like view was taken where there had been an omission or irregularity in the citation of a summons[45] and where the sheriff had refused to hear evidence tendered to him.[46] In the early cases relating to the post-horse duties the statute provided in mandatory terms for appeal to the Quarter-sessions and expressly excluded any suspension or reduction or suchlike review of the determination of the justices; in these circumstances failure to use the statutory machinery was held to be fatal.[47] In *Alexander v. Seymour*[48] what was complained of was *ex facie* under the Act in question and the complainer was required at least in the first instance to use the statutory mechanism for redress. So also where it was considered that the statutory means of redress was sufficient in its jurisdiction to determine matters of competency recourse to the court was refused.[49]

Where the complaint is not covered by the statutory remedy

12.11 In some cases consideration of the statutory provisions and the substance and nature of the complaint may disclose that the complaint is outwith the scope of the statutory remedy. In such circumstances there should be no bar on an immediate application to the court, since it will then be clear that there is no alternative remedy available. It may be that the statutory jurisdiction is not privative.[50] The statutory procedure may not provide a remedy for the precise problem which has arisen.[51] So when elections could be challenged on certain specific grounds by a statutory procedure, a reduction on a ground not included in those grounds was held competent.[52] Where redress was available under the statute for complaints about orders or resolutions of the authority a complaint about the manner in which the work which had been ordered was carried out was held not to fall within the statutory process and so to be open to consideration by the ordinary court.[53] In *Adamson v. Edinburgh Street Tramways Co.*[54] a statutory provision requiring various differences to be settled by a referee was held not to cover a failure to provide a passing place in circumstances where the statute required one to be provided, and thus recourse to the ordinary court was available. Similarly a failure to pursue a statutory appeal was held not to preclude a defence to an action for payment where the case was not one to which the statutory

---

[45] *Lennon v. Tully* (1879) 6R. 1253.

[46] *Robertson v. Pringle* (1857) 14R. 474.

[47] *Cook v. Mill* (1823) 2S. 317, *Campbell v. Mill* (1823) 2S. 440; *Craigie v. Mill* (1826) 4S. 447; (1827) 2 W.&Sh. 642.

[48] (1828) 7S. 117.

[49] *Tarmac Econowaste Ltd v. Assessor for Edinburgh*, 1991 S.L.T. 77.

[50] *Bremner v. Huntly Friendly Society*. Dec 4, 1817, F.C.; *Lord Advocate v. Police Commissioners of Perth* (1869) 8M. 244.

[51] *Fraser v. M'Neill*, 1948 S.C. 517. In *Paterson*, 1984 S.L.T. 3 review was held competent where the legal validity of a decision in respect of an incorrect statutory reference was being challenged.

[52] *Kerr v. Hood*, 1907 S.C. 845.

[53] *Magistrates of Crieff v. Young* (1906) 8F. 48. The construction of the Act adopted in that case was disapproved in *Cumming v. Magistrate of Inverness*, 1953 S.C. 1.

[54] (1872) 10M. 533.

remedy was applicable.[55] Where what is sought is reparation for a breach of the statute, rather than a claim for damage arising from an act done under the powers of the statute, an ordinary action is competent.[56] Redress was able to be given against a double assessment to local rates where the error was treated as one of assessment and not of valuation, which would have required a remedy through the statutory procedure.[57] The existence of an alternative remedy has been held to be no bar to the making of an order to perform a statutory duty under section 91 of the Court of Session Act 1868.[58] Where the competency of the alternative remedy is under challenge, there may be no bar to judicial review.[59]

II EXCEPTIONS

Exceptions to the general rule

The rule that the statutory remedy ousts the jurisdiction of the court is, however, not absolute. As has already been noticed cases may occur where the statutory remedy does not cover the complaint in question. But those cases are not truly exceptions to the general rule. They do not fall within the scope of the rule at all. The true cases of exception are those where the remedy may be found both through the statutory machinery and by recourse to the supervisory jurisdiction. It is with such cases that this section is concerned.   **12.12**

Departing from the generality

In certain cases the existence of a statutory remedy will not be fatal to an application for review. These cases have sometimes been described as exceptional.[60] In *Cumming v. Magistrates of Inverness*, which concerned the erection of a bus shelter under provisions in the Burgh Police (Scotland) Act 1892, Lord President Cooper observed[61]:   **12.13**

> "The whole conception of the statute was that, apart from exceptional circumstances, a decision by a local authority in relation to an operation covered by section 110 (and many other sections) should not be reviewed in a common law Court by reference to common law considerations, but in the statutory appellate tribunal by reference to the widest administrative considerations, and with powers much ampler than those available to a common law court."

But to describe such cases as exceptional does not mean that they are to be regarded as particularly rare or highly special or unusual, but simply that they are departures from the generality of the position whereby the statute will usually be seen as intending that the resolution of disputes

---

[55] *Dundee Police Commissioners v. Mitchell* (1876) 3R. 762.

[56] *Colt v. Caledonian Ry* (1859) 21D. 1108; (1860) 3 Macq. 833.

[57] *Sharp v. Latheron Parochial Board* (1883) 10R. 1163; see, however, the comments on that decision in *Moss' Empires v. Assessor for Glasgow*, 1917 S.C.(H.L.) 1 at 11.

[58] *T. Docherty Ltd v. Town Council of Monifieth*, 1970 S.C. 200. The provision is now in s.45(b) of the Court of Session Act 1988.

[59] *Shanks & McEwan (Contractors) Ltd v. Mifflin Construction Ltd*, 1993 S.L.T. 1124.

[60] *Philp v. Reid*, 1927 S.C. 224; *Stornoway Town Council v. Macdonald*, 1971 S.C 78; *British Railways Board v. Glasgow Corporation*, 1976 S.C. 224.

[61] 1953 S.C. 1 at 6. Followed in *Stornoway Town Council v. Macdonald*, 1971 S.C. 78.

should be managed through the statutory machinery and not by the common law court.[62] The view that exceptions should only be allowed in the rarest of cases[63] may be open to misapplication. Certainly the presumed intention of Parliament that an express remedy should be preferred to any common law remedy is something to be respected[64] and the supervisory jurisdiction is in essence a source for remedy where no other remedy exists; nevertheless a slavish or technical approach to the matter is inappropriate. While the existence of exceptions to the general rule may be thought to give rise to some uncertainty in the scope of the supervisory jurisdiction,[65] it may have to be accepted that some lack of precise definition may be inevitable in what is essentially an equitable remedy.

Defining the exceptional

12.14 Divergent views have been adopted on the question whether exceptional circumstances may legitimately include other matters than those of a procedural nature.[66] It may be that a broader view is to be preferred by which the whole circumstances may properly be taken into account. On that approach it may be that the competency of the application may not always be open to resolution on a preliminary issue, but may require some understanding of the substance of the case. While there is no exhaustive categorisation of such cases, the following provide at least examples of the situations where exception may be admitted.

(a) Fundamental invalidity

12.15 Where a matter of fundamental invalidity is raised, application to the court may competently be made either before or after a statutory appeal and irrespective of the points taken in any such appeal.[67] The most obvious case is where it can be shown that the authority has acted beyond its powers, with the result that its whole actings are null and void. Such a case was *Sim v. Hodgert*[68] where justices purported to grant a decree of interdict in absence where the statute which determined their powers did not extend to the granting of interdicts, nor to granting decrees in absence. The court will thus intervene where there is a deviation from the statute not only in form but in substance[69] or where something has been done "quite different from what the statute allows",[70] or where the administrative body have acted wholly beyond their powers,[71] or where proceedings have been fundamentally null.[72] Where the whole basis of the proceedings can be seen to be a nullity, as

---

[62] *Cumming v. Magistrates of Inverness*, 1953 S.C. 1.

[63] See *Riverford Finance Ltd v. Kelly*, 1991 S.L.T. 300 and *Ingle v. Ingle's Trustee*, 1997 S.L.T. 160.

[64] Colin T. Reid, "Failure to Exhaust Statutory Remedies", 1984 J.R. 185.

[65] See Smith, "The Scope of Judicial Review Determined?", 1997 J.R. 122.

[66] *Alagon v. Secretary of State for the Home Department*, 1995 S.L.T. 381; *Sangha v. Secretary of State for the Home Department*, 1997 S.L.T. 545.

[67] *Mensah v. Secretary of State for the Home Department*, 1992 S.L.T 177.

[68] (1831) 9S. 507.

[69] *Campbell v. Young* (1835) 13S. 535.

[70] *Caledonian Ry v. Glasgow Corporation* (1905) 7F. 1020.

[71] *Abercromby v. Badenoch*, 1909 2 S.L.T. 114.

[72] *Perth General Station Committee v. Stewart*, 1924 S.C. 1004. For an example of grave oppression in the treatment of an alleged juvenile offender, see *Gray v. McGill* (1858) 3 Irv. 29.

for example where one acted as sheriff-clerk in his own case,[73] then the court will intervene even although the statute provides a remedy for incompetency, including defect of jurisdiction. The case must be one where reduction is necessary to produce substantial justice,[74] as where an immigrant had admittedly been wrongly deprived of entry clearance and could not renew her application as she was over the specified age.[75] Where there is an accumulation of grounds of challenge inviting the conclusion that the decision was fatally flawed, special circumstances may exist for an immediate recourse to judicial review.[76]

Mere irregularity not enough

Where the complaint is that there has been an irregularity which is not **12.16** so clearly wrong as to take the proceedings out of the statute altogether then the statutory means of appeal should be adopted in preference to the court.[77] "Where a statute provides another means of review, there is an implied exclusion of the jurisdiction of the Court of Session, except in cases of a palpable excess of jurisdiction",[78] as where it can be said that the proceedings were *funditus null*.[79] "Where a particular remedy is given in the form of appeal to one Court, it is not in the complainer's power to disregard that remedy, and to come here and obtain a suspension of proceedings on the very grounds on which suspension in another court might be asked. But if the complainer could have shown an excess of jurisdiction, he would have been entitled here to get the act done in excess of jurisdiction set aside".[80] The court will not intervene in the statutory process of appeal where the error alleged is not a "departure from the statute which stares you in the face" or so clearly wrong as to take the case out of the statute altogether. It is not every deviation which will infer a nullity. "You must bring forward something that strikes at the heart or brain and kills and vitiates the whole proceeding."[81] The determination of what is a fundamental nullity as opposed to a mere irregularity is not always an easy one to reach. The matter is one for the discretion of the court.[82]

(b) Equitable considerations

The court will also intervene in particular circumstances where it would **12.17** be inequitable to insist on resort to the statutory remedy. In *Matheson v. Yeaman*[83] reduction of a decree granted in the sheriff court was allowed where the decree contained an error which was highly prejudicial to the applicant but which he had reasonably not identified. In *British Railways Board v. Glasgow Corporation*[84] Lord Macdonald indicated that the court

---

[73] *Manson v. Smith* (1871) 9M. 492 (see Lord Benholme's dissent).
[74] *Bain v. Hugh L. S. McConnell Ltd*, 1991 S.L.T. 691.
[75] *Alagon v. Secretary of State for the Home Department*, 1995 S.L.T. 381. See Lord Marnoch's observations on this case in *Sangha v. Secretary of State for the Home Department*, 1997 S.L.T. 545.
[76] *Choi v. Secretary of State for the Home Department*, 1996 S.L.T. 590.
[77] *Campbell v. Strathern* (1848) 10D. 655.
[78] Mackay's *Manual of Practice*, p. 92.
[79] cf. *Tough's Trustees v. Edinburgh Parish Council*, 1918 S.C. 107.
[80] *M'Arthur v. Linton* (1864) 2M. 659, *per* Lord Justice-Clerk Inglis at 662.
[81] *Campbell v. Strathern* (1848)10D. 655.
[82] *Dumbarton Water Commissioners v. Lord Blantyre*, (1884) 12R. 115.
[83] (1900) 2F. 873; see *Philp v. Reid*, 1927 S.C 224.
[84] 1974 S.C. 261 at 268; 1976 S.C. 224 at 230 and 239.

could intervene where "the failure was due to ignorance owing to some irregularity of procedure on the part of the assessor or the rating authority, to the fact that resort to the statutory remedy would, in the particular circumstances, be otiose or to some other special reason." Lord Wheatley instanced averments of *ultra vires* or fraud as exceptional circumstances allowing access to the court. So, where the complainer has been prevented from pursuing a statutory appeal through a procedural irregularity on the part of the authority, he can seek review by the court.[85] Where the statutory appeal involved an application to magistrates who would, in the circumstances, be judges in their own cause an application for declarator and interdict at common law was allowed.[86]

(c) Practical considerations

12.18 Where the decision under challenge is of a general effect, such as one which affects the conditions of service of many members of a particular profession, judicial review may be competent despite the existence of an alternative remedy.[87] In *Edinburgh and Glasgow Railway v. Meek*[88] the majority of the court held that it was preferable to have one declarator *ab ante* than a series of separate actions by the railway company against 23 poor law authorities regarding the proper method of assessment of the railway for the purposes of the amounts to be paid in respect of each of the parishes through which the railway line extended. Where the statutory machinery for individual objections to the granting of taxi-cab licences was provided, it was considered that a challenge against a general decision in relation to a large number of future licences could competently be made matter for judicial review since the statutory procedure did not adequately cover such a situation.[89] Where a sheriff purported to change the effective date of a sequestration, reduction was held to be competent despite an alternative remedy; the court looked not only to the fact that the order was *ultra vires* and amounted to a miscarriage of justice, but also to the consequences to the creditors and the effect on the legitimacy of the actings of the trustee, if the later date which had been prescribed was to stand for the formal commencement of the sequestration.[90] In *Kennedy*[91] an attempt was made to bring under judicial review a sheriff's interlocutor in an appeal from a children's hearing, although the interlocutor was itself under appeal to the Court of Session under the statutory means of appeal. It was recognised that in special circumstances the court can entertain an application for review even although the statutory means of relief have not been exhausted. Lord Jauncey observed:

"If a body or an inferior court having pronounced a once-for-all order was then unable for a protracted period to implement the

---

[85] *Moss' Empires v. Assessor for Glasgow*, 1917 S.C. (H.L.)1; *Dante v. Assessor for Ayr*, 1922 S.C. 109, *per* Lord Blackburn at 114; also *London & Clydesdale Estates Ltd v. Aberdeen D.C.*, 1980 S.L.T. 81; *Bovis Homes (Scotland) Ltd v. Inverclyde D.C.*, 1982 S.L.T. 473. See *Mackinnon v. The Fairfield Shipbuilding and Engineering Co. Ltd*, 1921 2 S.L.T. 270.

[86] *Hope v. Corporation of Edinburgh* (1897) 5 S.L.T. 195.

[87] *Watt v. Strathclyde R.C.*, 1992 S.L.T. 324.

[88] (1849) 12D. 153.

[89] *City Cabs (Edinburgh) Ltd v. City of Edinburgh D.C.*, 1988 S.L.T. 184.

[90] *Accountant in Bankruptcy v. Allans of Gillock Ltd*, 1991 S.L.T. 765.

[91] 1988 S.C.L.R. 149.

necessary machinery for review of that order there might be circumstances in which the appellant could have recourse to the Court of Session for a common law remedy."[92]

That was, however, not the situation in that particular case since the hearing could properly review the case themselves without being fettered by the sheriff's earlier decision. So also where a dismissed schoolteacher had applied for a remedy to an industrial tribunal but had failed to exhaust that remedy, an application for judicial review was held incompetent.[93] The appropriate course in immigration cases is to seek judicial review of the decision of the Tribunal refusing leave to appeal, but a petition for review of the Adjudicator's dismissal was not rejected simply on the view that technically the remedy sought might not be the correct one, there being no possible prejudice to the respondent.[94] Where the scope of the alternative remedy is uncertain, review may be available.[95] The inadequacy of the statutory remedy in particular circumstances may be an exception which is open to development, but the court should be wary of trespassing on the jurisdiction of the alternative tribunal.[96]

(d) Where statutory remedy optional

Another case where the jurisdiction of the court is not ousted is where **12.19** the statutory means for redress are optional or are not wholly within the control of the complainer. Where the statute has provided in mandatory terms for the remedy to be taken, the common law jurisdiction will be excluded. Thus, where a statute provided that a person aggrieved by a sentence of a justice of the peace "shall and may" appeal to the quarter sessions a bill of suspension was held to be incompetent, since the suspender had not taken that course of appeal.[97] The words "shall and may" had already been construed as imperative.[98] In *Bremner v. Huntly Friendly Society*[99] the statutory remedy merely stated that "it may be lawful" to go to the Justices and that their judgment should be final. The majority of the court held that the statute should not be so construed as to give the justices an exclusive jurisdiction and that an action for damages was competent in the sheriff court. Where the remedy is purely permissive and is not exclusive of other remedies then an ordinary action will lie.[1] Where the applicant has only a subsidiary role in the statutory means of redress review may not be excluded. Thus where the statute allowed a remedy by way of complaint to the Secretary of State who might then order a defaulting authority to act it was held that the opportunity to complain to the Secretary of State did not exclude recourse to the court.[2]

---

[92] at 151.

[93] *Nahar v. Strathclyde R.C.*, 1986 S.L.T. 370. For comment on the case see S.L. Stuart, "Judicial Review and Alternative Remedies", 1986 S.L.T. (News) 309.

[94] *Ahmed v. Secretary of State for the Home Department*, 1992 S.L.T. 821.

[95] *Brown v. Executive Committee of Edinburgh District Labour Party*, 1995 S.L.T. 985.

[96] *Tarmac Econowaste v. Assessor for Lothian Region*, 1991 S.L.T. 77 at 79.

[97] *Craigie v. Mill* (1826) 4S. 447, affd (1827) 2 W. & Sh. 642.

[98] *Cook v. Mill* (1823) 2S. 317. (The case of *Aberdeenshire Trustees v. Knowles*, Hume's *Decisions* 262, sits uneasily here unless in that case "may" can be construed as "must".)

[99] Dec. 4, 1817, F.C.

[1] *Secretary of State for Scotland v. Fife County Council*, 1953 S.C.257.

[2] *Walker v. Strathclyde R.C. (No. 1)*, 1986 S.L.T. 523.

III OTHER MATTERS

Acquiescence

12.20 In some cases it has been observed that the complainer has acquiesced in the matter of which he makes his complaint. In *Dante v. Assessor for Ayr*[3] the pursuer had appealed to the valuation committee against the amount of the valuation of certain subjects but had not appealed against his being entered in the valuation roll as tenant and occupier. He departed from the appeal and sought a declarator that he was not the tenant or occupier and was not liable to be rated in respect of the subjects. The action was held to be incompetent. The Lord Justice-Clerk (Scott Dickson) observed:

> "A party complaining of what has been done under the statutory procedure, who has accepted and adopted what has been done, and has not availed himself of the statutory forms of review, is not entitled, after disregarding these opportunities of review or appeal, to have recourse to ordinary common law proceedings, and, in any event, is not entitled to do so without setting forth in his record a relevant case for so doing."[4]

In that case the opening up of the valuation roll was from a practical point of view undesirable. The inconvenience of opening up sequestration proceedings believed by the creditors to be final is a ground for holding a failure to take the statutory appeal within the permitted time-limit fatal to a reduction.[5] But while acquiescence may constitute a distinct ground of defence to an application for review, and is considered in the following chapter,[6] it should, as a matter of personal exception, be recognised as distinct from the point presently under discussion, which is one of the competency of invoking the supervisory jurisdiction. It may, however, be observed in the present context that it is all the more difficult to overcome the objection of a failure to take a statutory remedy where there has been long delay.[7]

Consequences of failure

12.21 Where the statutory machinery should have been used but has not been used then the complainer may well be left without remedy. This will clearly be the case if the time-limit for the statutory method of redress has expired. If there is doubt about the competency of resorting to the common law remedy it will be prudent first to attempt the statutory remedy.[8]

Where statutory remedy exhausted

12.22 Where the statute provides a mechanism for appeal and that course has been followed then judicial review may be open, provided, of course, that there is a ground for review, such as an excess of jurisdiction.[9] In

---

[3] 1922 S.C 109.
[4] at 121.
[5] *Baillie v. M'Gibbon* (1845) 8D. 10.
[6] See later, paras 13.23 *et seq.*
[7] *Crawford v. Lennox* (1852) 14D. 1029.
[8] *cf. Harvey's Trustees v. Harvey*, 1942 S.C. 582 at 586.
[9] *Abercromby v. Badenoch*, 1909 2 S.L.T. 114. In *Sharp v. Latheron Parochial Board* (1883) 10R. 1163 the finality of the valuation roll was held not to be an obstacle as the complaint was directed to the assessment not the valuation. See also *Watt v. Lord Advocate*, 1979 S.C. 120.

Mair v. Mill[10] the statutory appeal had been taken but a suspension was refused as incompetent because there was no allegation of an excess of power on the part of the justices of the peace or the quarter sessions. Where the statutory machinery expressly excludes a reduction then such an action will not be competent unless there is an allegation of actings in excess of jurisdiction.[11] Where a reduction was sought of a sheriff court decree by an unsuccessful claimant for damages, the reduction was refused because in the absence of a record of the proceedings it was impossible to hold that there had been a miscarriage of justice.[12] Viscount Dunedin[13] stated the general proposition that reduction is not competent "when other means of review are prescribed, and those means have either been utilised or the parties have failed to take advantage of them".

---

[10] (1822) 1S. 473.
[11] *Lundie v. Magistrate of Falkirk* (1890) 18R. 60.
[12] *Adair v. Colville & Sons*, 1926 S.C.(H.L.) 51.
[13] at 56.

CHAPTER 13

REALITY, PREMATURITY AND DELAY

I   REALITY
II PREMATURITY
III STATUTORY TIME-LIMITS
IV DELAY, ACQUIESCENCE AND PERSONAL BAR

Introduction

This chapter covers several distinct but related considerations, each of **13.01**
which may constitute a ground of objection to the presentation of an
application for judicial review. In the first place it is essential that the
issue raised be a real one. Even if it is real, the timing of the
presentation of an application for judicial review can be of importance in
determining its competence. It may fail because it is presented too early,
so that it will be rejected as premature. On the other hand delay may be
correspondingly fatal. A distinct but related ground for rejection may
exist in an acquiescence in the wrong which forms the subject-matter of
the complaint. All these can be seen as restraints on the scope of judicial
review or as grounds for a defence against an application.

I   REALITY

Necessity for a practical issue

The court will only consider live, practical questions, questions which are **13.02**
open to doubt and which require to be resolved, not questions which are
hypothetical or academic. This principle has been developed particularly
in the context of the action of declarator. The subject-matter of a
declarator must be directed at the establishment of "something of a
practical kind leading to patrimonial conclusions".[1] The action of
declarator "cannot be used for the mere purpose of declaring legal
propositions where no practical question or dispute lies beneath".[2] A
proposition which may be purely academic will not be allowed as a
matter for declarator.[3] The judges do not sit in court to decide
hypothetical questions[4] and if the question is merely theoretical the court
will not entertain it. As Lord Justice-Clerk Thomson observed: "Our
Courts have consistently acted on the view that it is their function in the
ordinary course of contentious litigation to decide only live, practical
questions, and that they have no concern with hypothetical, premature or
academic questions, nor do they exist to advise litigants as to the policy
which they should adopt in the ordering of their affairs. The Courts are
neither a debating club nor an advisory bureau."[5] On the other hand, "as

---

[1] *Officers of State v. Alexander* (1866) 4 M. 741, *per* Lord Neaves at 753.
[2] *North British Ry v. Birrell's Trustees*, 1918 S.C.(H.L.) 33, *per* Viscount Dunedin at 47.
[3] *Aberdeen Trades Council v. Shipconstructors and Shipwrights Association*, 1948 S.C. 94
at 103; 1949 S.C.(H.L.) 45 at 57.
[4] *Parochial Board of Bothwell v. Pearson* (1837) 11M. 399.
[5] *Macnaughton v. Macnaughton's Trustees*, 1953 S.C. 387, *per* Lord Justice-Clerk
Thomson at 392.

soon as a right which leads to actual consequence, either pecuniary or *in facto praestando*, is asserted and denied by the person against whom it is asserted, a declarator becomes available".[6] In the English case of *Russian Commercial and Industrial Bank v. British Bank for Foreign Trade Ltd*[7] Lord Dunedin observed:

> "The rules that have been elucidated by a long course of decisions in the Scottish Courts may be summarised thus: The question must be a real and not a theoretical question; the person raising it must have a real interest to raise it; he must be able to secure a proper contradictor, that is to say, some one presently existing who has a true interest to oppose the declaration sought."

That last observation reflects the distinction which should be made between the reality of the issue and the *locus standi* of the applicant. Where the issue is hypothetical or premature it may be considered that the applicant has no interest to sue[8] but it is thought preferable that the two matters should be kept distinct.[9] While in general the court will not be prepared to give an "advisory opinion", the existence of a real controversy may enable the required guidance to be given.[10] In England exceptions to the general rule have been identified in the case of "friendly" actions or where proceedings are instituted specifically as a test case[11] and possibly in matters of public law.[12]

Real issues

13.03   The issue must be a real one. Thus review was held to be incompetent in the case of a refusal of a licence for a performance on specific dates when those dates had passed and there was no averment of any future performance.[13] Nor will review be available where the dispute is not the legality of the decision but about its legal effect.[14] Judicial review is not available where there are no practical consequences to follow from success.[15] The view taken by a clerk to a licensing board has been accepted as a proper matter for review where the point was one of real doubt and the debate upon it was not academic.[16] But in an earlier case

---

[6] *Beardman & Co. v. Barry*, 1928 S.C.(H.L.) 47, *per* Viscount Dunedin at 52; *Turner's Trustees v. Turner*, 1943 S.C. 389.

[7] [1921] 1 A.C. 438 at 448. This approach has been found helpful in England: *Vine v. National Dock Labour Board* [1957] A.C. 488 at 500; *Re F* [1990] 2 A.C. 1 at 82.

[8] *Shaw v. Strathclyde R.C.*, 1988 S.L.T. 313.

[9] The point has been considered in the context of *locus standi* at para. 10.02.

[10] For a suggestion that the court might produce a constitutional response to an attempt by Parliament to pass a law which authorises a denial of fundamental freedoms, see Sir John Laws, "Judicial Remedies and the Constitution" (1994) 57 M.L.R.. 213. References to the Privy Council under the Scotland Act 1998 may come close to advisory opinions. See also *R. v. DPP, ex p. Merton LBC* (1999) C.O.D. 161.

[11] *Ainsbury v. Millington* (1987) 1 W.L.R. 379 at 381.

[12] See Lord Woolf, *Protection of the Public—A New Challenge* (1990) at 47–49. See also *R. v. Her Majesty's Treasury, ex p. Smedley* [1985] 1 Q.B. 657, and *R. v. Secretary of State for the Home Department, ex p. Salem* [1999] 1 A.C. 450.

[13] *Marco's Leisure Ltd v. West Lothian District Licensing Board*, 1994 S.L.T. 129.

[14] *Hands v. Kyle and Carrick D.c.*, 1989 S.L.T. 124.

[15] *Conway v. Secretary of State for Scotland*, 1996 S.L.T. 689. The applicant had already undergone his imprisonment but still had a real complaint about the loss of a period of remission and loss of wages.

[16] *First Leisure Trading Company v. City of Glasgow District Licensing Board*, 1996 S.L.T. 1018.

an attempt to challenge the practice of a clerk to a licensing authority regarding the receipt of applications for licences failed, because the date of the meeting to hear the application had passed and the practice might have changed for future applications.[17] Even where a second review of a prisoner's release date has been started, judicial review of the first recommendation may still be competent since the decision by the court may have a bearing on the making of the second recommendation.[18]

Future issues

Issues which may arise in the future provide a particular example of the   **13.04** problems of reality. In the past the court has been unwilling to determine questions regarding the validity of an action in advance of the action being taken.[19] Where the matter is one simply of a contingent eventuality and the court is being asked in effect to speculate and give advice on a future course of action the court has declined to do so.[20] The process of declarator is not intended "to declare remote and contingent or conditional rights, which nobody can well judge of through the long vista of future possibilities. Such actions should be reserved for the determination of matters of present and pressing controversy".[21] Where a scheme for benefit was challenged but the effect of its implementation so far as the complainer was concerned was unknown it was held that the issue was future and hypothetical.[22] The reality of the issue and more particularly the futurity of the issue may raise questions of prematurity, and that aspect of the matter is considered in the following section of this chapter.

Reality

Where there is a disputed matter of the construction of a deed and the   **13.05** practical choice between two courses of action depends upon the proper interpretation then the question may become a real and immediate one for decision by the court.[23] Where the nature of a beneficiary's interest is uncertain and forfeiture may follow on the adoption of an erroneous construction of it a declarator will lie to resolve the uncertainty and avoid the forfeiture which would be incurred by adopting the wrong course.[24] The validity of a form of licence which an authority proposed to issue has been challenged by declarator.[25]

Procedural detail

The court will not interfere where the complaint is directed to some   **13.06** minor technical matter which does not touch on the substantial rights of parties. But failure to observe statutory procedures may not generally be overlooked and will usually be fatal.[26] The Scottish court may be more

---

[17] *Moriarty v. City of Edinburgh District Licensing Board*, 1995 S.L.T. 40, distinguishing *Air 2000 Ltd v. Secretary of State for Transport (No. 2)*, 1990 S.L.T. 335.
[18] *Ritchie v. Secretary of State for Scotland*, 1999 S.L.T. 55.
[19] *Earl of Galloway v. Garlies* (1838) 12S. 1212, *per* Lord Medwyn at 1217.
[20] *Harveys v. Harvey's Trustees* (1860) 22D. 1310.
[21] *Magistrates of Edinburgh v. Warrender* (1863) 1M. 887, *per* Lord Neaves at 896.
[22] *Shaw v. Strathclyde R.C.*, 1987 S.C.L.R. 439.
[23] *Macnaughton v. Macnaughton's Trustees*, 1953 S.C. 387.
[24] *Chaplin's Trustees v. Hoile* (1890) 18R. 27.
[25] *Rossi v. Magistrates of Edinburgh* (1904) 7F.(H.L.) 85.
[26] *London & Clydeside Estates Ltd v. Aberdeen D.C.*, 1980 S.C.(H.L.) 1.

exact than the English courts to secure that the details of procedure have been observed, particularly in matters of criminal law.[27]

Identification of a practical issue

13.07 As Lord Justice-Clerk Thomson recognised in *Macnaughton v. Macnaughton's Trustees*,[28] it is not always easy to decide what is a live practical question. He considered that in the long run the decision must turn on the circumstances of the particular case in order to assess on the merits of each case the reality and immediacy of the issue which it seeks to raise. The court should hold the case to be incompetent unless satisfied that that is made out. No general rule can thus be prescribed to resolve the problem. The existence of serious controversy may render a future issue justiciable. Where the right of a party to a benefit under a settlement is challenged it may be determined by a declarator even if it is future and contingent.[29] But the competency of a declarator there depends upon the court being satisfied that all the persons with an interest in the fund which is in dispute are made parties to the action so that they will be bound by the decree.[30] The right of a neighbouring proprietor to object to a proposed grant by a railway company of a lease of surplus land for mining purposes has been resolved by declarator.[31] Even the potentiality for controversy may make a future issue justiciable. Where the extent of the jurisdiction of a water authority was open to challenge while a river flowed in a particular course and the river had changed to a course which did not give rise to challenge, a declarator was nevertheless granted because there was a real risk of the river reverting to the earlier course and the decision would settle the problem once and for all.[32] Where a right to relief against a possible future liability might be defeated by a statutory limitation of time it was held competent to obtain a declarator of the right to obtain an appropriate contribution from the authority against whom the right of relief was claimed.[33] Whether a proposed broadcast would constitute a contempt of court has been resolved in England on an injunction, although Viscount Dilhorne expressed reluctance to pronounce on "hypothetical questions".[34] Usually a declarator will only be granted if there is controversy about the right which is claimed; but it will not be granted to establish a truism.[35] A declarator that Orkney and Shetland formed an undivided shire, was held to be perfectly useless and unnecessary as being undisputed.[36] Where a declarator was sought to the effect that there were no rules and no agreement whereby a decision of a majority of the

---

[27] *cf. Jones v. Milne*, 1975 J.C. 16 and *R. v. Governor of Pentonville Prison, ex p. Osman (No. 3)* [1990] 1 All E.R. 999.

[28] 1953 S.C. 387 at 392.

[29] *Mackenzie's Trustees v. Mackenzie's Tutors* (1846) 8D. 964.

[30] *Allgemeine Deutsche Credit Anstalt v. Scottish Amicable Life Assurance Society*, 1908 S.C. 33.

[31] *North British Ry v. Birrell's Trustees*, 1918 S.C.(H.L.) 33.

[32] *Annandale and Eskdale D.C. v. The North-West Water Authority*, 1978 S.C. 187; *Smith v. McColl's Trustees*, 1910 S.C. 1121.

[33] *Central SMT Co. v. Lanarkshire County Council*; but *cf. Aberdeen Development Co. v. Mackie, Ramsay and Taylor*, 1977 S.L.T. 177.

[34] *Att.-Gen. v. BBC* [1981] A.C. 303 at 336; *cf. Royal College of Nursing of the U.K. v. Department of Health and Social Security* [1981] A.C. 800—a declaration sought in order to ascertain whether a particular course of procedure would be criminal.

[35] *Magistrates of Edinburgh v. Warrender* (1863) 1M. 887, *per* Lord Neaves at 896.

[36] *Gifford v. Trail* (1829) 7S. 854.

members of a trade union regarding working on May Day was binding on the minority, it appeared from the pleadings and the argument that that particular matter was not controversial, and it was held that a declarator in that regard was not a decree which according to Scottish law and practice could be granted.[37] A declarator of status may be granted where the circumstances warrant the course even although the action is undefended[38] but no declarator of right is in practice granted without there being a proper contradictor present.[39] A counterclaim for interdict of the activity which the pursuer claims in his declarator to be entitled to carry out will make it difficult for the defender to challenge the competency of the declarator on the ground that it is not necessary to resolve a live practical question between the parties.[40]

II PREMATURITY

General

The reluctance of the court to enter into a problem before it is clear that **13.08** the problem really exists can be expressed in terms of prematurity. Although the court will not entertain hypothetical questions, particular circumstances may justify the grant of a declarator in advance of the event.[41] Where there is a real uncertainty whether the wrong which is alleged is going to happen an application may be refused as premature.[42] The principle here is one inherent in the ordinary jurisdiction of the court. Whether public works will when completed create a nuisance is an issue which may have to be left until the works are completed.[43] Prematurity is a ground for refusing a declarator of rights under a policy of life insurance before it has matured.[44]

Alternative remedies

As has been discussed in the previous chapter, the existence of an **13.09** alternative remedy may exclude the availability of judicial review.[45] But this objection may also be expressed as one of prematurity. Where there is an alternative means of redress provided by statute which is still available and the applicant has not sought to use it the application may be refused *in hoc statu* as premature.[46] In *Caledonian Railway v. Glasgow Corporation*,[47] a declarator and reduction was sought in order to resolve an important question about the meaning of the word "width" in a

---

[37] *Drennan v. Associated Ironmoulders of Scotland*, 1921 S.C. 151.
[38] *Broit v. Broit*, 1972 S.C. 192.
[39] *Allgemeine Deutsche Credit Anstalt v. Scottish Amicable Life Assurance Society*, 1908 S.C. 33, *per* Lord Dunedin at 38.
[40] *McLean v. Marwhirn Developments Ltd*, 1976 S.L.T.(Notes) 47.
[41] See later on remedies, para 24.07.
[42] The identification of prematurity as against other objections to judicial review in England is discussed by Beatson, "The Need to Develop Principles of Prematurity and Ripeness for Review", (1998) 3 J.R. 79; see also the same writer in Forsyth and Hare (eds), *The Golden Metwand and the Crooked Cord* (1998) at p. 221.
[43] *Steel v. Commissioners of Police of Gourock* (1872) 10M. 954.
[44] *Allgemeine Deutsche Credit Anstalt v. Scottish Amicable Life Assurance Society*, 1908 S.C. 33.
[45] See Chap. 12.
[46] *Bellway Ltd v. Strathclyde R.C.*, 1980 S.L.T. 66. See 1926 S.L.T. 592.
[47] (1905) 5F. 1020.

statutory obligation to record the width of streets in Glasgow. A court of seven judges gave an opinion on the point but held that the action was premature as a statutory appeal to the sheriff was available and indeed had been sought. The court indicated that if the sheriff did not apply the view expressed by the court on the construction of the statute then the register would still be open to reduction, because no imprimatur of the sheriff could make *intra vires* what was an *ultra vires* act of the local authority. In *Cumming v. Magistrates of Inverness*[48] the court sisted the proceedings, which had in a sense gone completely off the rails, in order that the local authority could make a formal resolution and a statutory appeal could be taken. But in one case it was held to be sensible to decide in advance the assessable parts of a railway line which passed through a considerable number of different parishes, rather than waiting for the matter to be raised in separate proceedings in each parish, thus avoiding a large number of challenges by each of the local parish boards concerned.[49]

Statutory procedure pending

13.10   Reduction of the closure of a road may be premature before the statutory procedure for it has been completed and while a statutory remedy remains.[50] A like view was taken where a declarator was sought in the case of an allegedly erroneous entry in a register of streets where the register was not yet complete and was yet open to correction by the sheriff.[51] Where the question is one which falls to be determined by a particular body or official who would be bound by the decision of the Court of Session, the latter will not grant a declarator which would interfere with the powers and responsibilities of the other. Thus in *Callender's Cable and Construction Co. Ltd v. Corporation of Glasgow*[52] it was held incompetent to grant a declarator that a particular design of a damp course satisfied the provisions of a Glasgow byelaw since it was for the Master of Works and the Dean of Guild Court to decide in each case whether the damp course was of proper material. The declarator was drawn in such wide terms that it would determine the issue whenever material bearing the name given to it by the pursuers was used.[53]

Matter still *sub judice*

13.11   Where it is feared that a decision maker may exceed his jurisdiction but he has not yet entered upon the matter a challenge to his actings may be premature. Where an appeal was currently proceeding under the statutory process for appeal and no evident excess of jurisdiction had occurred such as could take the matter outside the scope of the statute the court refused to intervene.[54] A challenge to the procedure to be adopted by an advisory panel set up by a minister was held to be premature since it could not be assumed that the decision by the minister would be adverse to the applicant.[55] But where there is a real

---

[48] 1953 S.C. 1.
[49] *Edinburgh and Glasgow Ry v. Meek* (1894) 12D. 153.
[50] *Murray v. Stewart* (1831) 2D. 12.
[51] *Caledonian Ry v. Glasgow Corporation* (1905) 7F. 1020; 1907 S.C.(H.L.) 7.
[52] (1900) 2F. 397.
[53] See also *Todd v. Burnet* (1854) 16D. 794.
[54] *Magistrates of Arbroath v. Presbytery of Arbroath* (1883) 10R. 767.
[55] *Abbas v. Secretary of State for the Home Department*, 1993 S.L.T. 502.

anticipation that an authority will fail to consider a factor relevant to the decision the court may intervene even before the process leading up to the decision has formally commenced. Where the pleadings in an arbitration may go beyond the scope of the review it is premature to suspend the arbitration before the arbiter has decided to entertain such matters.[56] The court will only interdict an arbitration if the claim is clearly ill founded.[57]

Challenges to legislation

Difficult questions may arise in deciding the proper stage at which to launch a judicial challenge to proposed legislation. A government minister will generally have the power to present a Bill in Parliament and there would be little prospect of successfully challenging such a step. There is a risk that action in advance of the making of a governmental order will be treated as raising a hypothetical question and be rejected on that account.[58] Where there is an inquiry prior to or at the early stages of the legislative process, there may be room for a competent challenge. Interdict was granted against the holding of a provisional order inquiry where the proposed legislation appeared to be in part unlawful, and accordingly the inquiry into the whole of the proposed legislation could not proceed.[59] The opposite view was taken in *Ayr Town Council v. Secretary of State for Scotland*,[60] on the basis that the argument for stopping the inquiry rested on the assumption that the proposed legislation would be unlawful and that what was being sought was a hypothetical declarator. But that decision was coloured by the technical problem of the inability to seek interdict against the Crown. A statutory inquiry has been held to be *ultra vires* after its completion.[61] **13.12**

Drafts before Parliament

In *Glasgow Insurance Committee v. Scottish Insurance Commissioners*[62] it was held that regulations which required to be laid before Parliament and which were to have effect as if enacted in the principal Act unless annulled by His Majesty in Council or by an address presented by either House of Parliament, could not be challenged as *ultra vires* even before they had been laid before Parliament. The opposite result was reached in *R. v. Electricity Commissioners, ex parte London Electricity Joint Committee Company (1920) and Others*[63] and it is thought that the English view is to be preferred. The Scottish decision effectively removes any opportunity for challenging such proposed legislation, although there is no clear reason why all challenge should be excluded. If the view was correct any challenge may be either premature or too late. The English decision was followed and the *Glasgow Insurance* case was distinguished in *Bell v. Secretary of State for Scotland*[64] on the ground of the width of **13.13**

---

[56] *Bennets v. Bennet* (1903) 5F. 376.
[57] *Dumbarton Water Commissioners v. Lord Blantyre* (1884) 12R. 115.
[58] *Ayr Town Council v. Secretary of State for Scotland*, 1965 S.C. 394.
[59] *Russell v. Magistrates of Hamilton* (1897) 25R. 350.
[60] 1965 S.C. 394.
[61] *Magistrates of Ayr v. Lord Advocate*, 1950 S.C. 102 (an inquiry into the amalgamation of police forces).
[62] 1915 S.C. 504.
[63] [1924] 1 K.B. 171.
[64] 1933 S.L.T. 519.

the powers which had been granted to the insurance commissioners. It has been held in England that a draft order in Council may be reviewed for its legality.[65] Even where secondary legislation is subject to the affimative procedure and the appropriate resolution has been made, judicial review will still be open.[66] But where an order has been approved by both Houses of Parliament it will be very difficult to claim that it is irrational.[67]

III   STATUTORY TIME-LIMITS

Prescription

13.14   There is no specific statutory time-limit for the making of an application for judicial review, nor is it thought that there is any need for one.[68] The general statutory provisions for the prescription and limitation of actions is now to be found in the Prescription and Limitation (Scotland) Act 1973 as amended. That Act provides in section 6 for a five-year period of prescription for the enforcement of a number of specified obligations, but makes no express provision for applications for judicial review. It makes provision in section 2 for the exemption from challenge of positive servitudes and public rights of way once they have been possessed peaceably and without judicial interruption for 20 years. By section 7 it is provided that any obligation which is not covered by section 6 or by section 22A (which relates to certain obligations to make reparation for defective products) and is not one of the imprescriptible obligations listed in Schedule 3 shall be extinguished after a period of 20 years, if it has not during that period been the subject of a "relevant claim" as defined in section 9 or has not been "relevantly acknowledged" as defined in section 10. The likelihood of statutory provisions for limits of time coming into play in the context of applications for judicial review is relatively remote, with the exception of the limit of one year imposed by section 7 of the Human Rights Act 1998.[69]

Human rights

13.15   A time-limit has been prescribed for proceedings against a public authority on the ground of unlawful acting under section 6(1) of the Human Rights Act 1998. That limit applies to proceedings under section 7(1)(a) of the Act, that is, proceedings against a public authority on the ground that it has acted in breach of the Convention rights as defined in that Act. Section 7(1) requires that proceedings must be brought before the end of one year from the date on which the act complained of took place; but the period of one year may be extended to such longer period as the court or tribunal considers equitable having regard to all the circumstances. Proceedings for judicial review are in practice brought very shortly after the act or decision complained of and are unlikely to be raised after a year; but if such a case were to occur problems could obviously arise where the case was presented partly on grounds of a

---

[65] *R. v. H.M. Treasury, ex p. Smedley* [1985] 1 Q.B. 657.
[66] *Hoffman-La Roche v. Secretary of State for Trade and Industry* [1975] A.C. 295.
[67] *Nottinghamshire County Council v. Secretary of State for the Environment* [1986] 1 A.C. 240.
[68] "Judicial Review Research", 1996 S.L.T.(News) 165.
[69] See paras 6.62 and 13.15.

breach of Convention rights and partly on grounds which are recognised at common law, for example, if it was to be claimed that reasons should have been stated for a particular decision, that could be presented as a common law ground for review or as a breach of Article 6 of the European Convention. Presumably such problems could be remedied by an exercise of the power provided by section 7(5)(b) of the Human Rights Act. Section 7(5) preserves any stricter time-limit which may be imposed on the procedure in question, which safeguards the English three-month time-limit for judicial review.[70]

Ancillary claims

While the principal ground of attack in an application for judicial review **13.16** may thus be open at least under the statute for a long period some of the ancillary remedies which may be sought in the process may be subject to the five-year period laid down in section 6 of the Act. Rule of Court 58.4 empowers the court in exercising its supervisory jurisdiction on a petition for judicial review to make such order as it thinks fit, being an order that could be made if sought in any action or petition. This expressly includes orders for reduction, declarator, suspension, interdict, implement, restitution, and payment, whether of damages or otherwise. It may well be that some of the obligations which would lie behind the making of some of these orders would be obligations falling under one or other provision of the Act and so open to extinction after five years. A claim for damages may be one example.

Statutory time-limits and finality clauses

In some cases legislation may provide for a statutory means of appeal **13.17** saddled with a limitation on the time within which such an appeal may be brought and an express finality clause which seeks to oust the jurisdiction of the court. Cases of this kind may be seen as falling into a category where Parliament must have considered it to be in the public interest that if any challenge is to be made it must be made promptly. In one early example it was held that where parties had acted outwith the provisions of a statute neither a statutory time-limit on complaints nor a finality clause restrained the complainer from his remedy.[71] But in another case where an election had been held under royal warrant a statutory time-limit contained in the Act 16 Geo. 2 c. 11 was held to apply to it and that was held to exclude a common law remedy taken outwith the time-limit.[72] In *Heritors of Avondale v. Whitelaw*[73] a decision by the quarter sessions was reduced notwithstanding a finality clause, where they had entertained an appeal lodged outwith the statutory period for appealing. Section 12 of the Tribunals and Inquiries Act 1992 provides that statutory provisions passed prior to August 1, 1958 which provide that decisions are not to be called into question or which seek to exclude the jurisdiction of the Court of Session to review the decision are not to prevent the exercise of that jurisdiction; but section 12(3) provides that the section shall not apply to cases where there is a statutory time-limit within which applications to the Court of Session are

---

[70] Order 53, r. 4(1).
[71] *Grant v. Gordon* (1833) 12S. 167.
[72] *Tod v. Tod* (1827) 2 W & Sh. 542.
[73] (1864) 3M. 263.

to be made. Where a statutory right to compensation had been lost through the expiry of a statutory time-limit a decision to reject the claim was held to have been a valid administrative act.[74]

The question has arisen more recently particularly in relation to compulsory purchase orders. Under paragraph 15(1) of Schedule 1 to the Acquisition of Land (Authorisation Procedure) (Scotland) Act 1947 provision is made for a person who is aggrieved by a compulsory purchase order and who wishes to question its validity on certain specified grounds to apply to the Court of Session within six weeks of the publication of the notice of the confirmation or making of the order. Paragraph 16 provides that, subject to paragraph 15, a compulsory purchase order shall not, either before or after it has been confirmed, be questioned in any legal proceedings whatsoever. In the case of *Smith v. East Elloe Rural District Council*,[75] which related to similar provisions in other legislation, a declaration was sought that an order had been wrongfully made and in bad faith. The House of Lords held by a majority that paragraph 16 ousted a challenge even on the grounds of bad faith. The decision was commented upon but not overruled in the case of *Anisminic Ltd v. Foreign Compensation Commission*[76] and it was followed in Scotland in *Hamilton v. Secretary of State for Scotland*.[77] A similar view was expressed by Lord Dunpark in *Lithgow v. Secretary of State for Scotland*[78] in holding that a complaint of a breach of natural justice should qualify as a failure to act "within the powers" of the relevant legislation and so was subject to the time-limit there specified. In *Martin v. Bearsden and Milngavie District Council*[79] reduction was sought of a compulsory purchase order in respect of a small area of ground which had been included in the order, but in respect of which notice had not been served on the proprietors. It was held that the petition was incompetent by virtue of paragraph 16. The ground of challenge was one which fell expressly within the scope of paragraph 15, as being a challenge that a requirement of the Act had not been complied with, and the intention of paragraph 16 was said to be to exclude the kind of challenge for the making of which an express time-limit had been laid down. In relation to compulsory purchase orders it is the policy of Parliament that finality and security from challenge should be achieved in the public interest. In the context of a planning application it has been held that the effect of a statutory time-limit and an ouster clause limited the jurisdiction of the court so as to bar any challenge after the time-limit.[80] On the other hand, where the statutory procedure for appeal against an enforcement notice could not be timeously operated through a failure in service and by no fault of the person seeking to challenge it, it was held that it might still be challenged at common law; the failure in service rendered the notice a nullity.[81]

---

[74] *The Royal Bank of Scotland plc. v. Clydebank D.C.*, 1992 S.L.T. 350.
[75] [1956] A.C. 736.
[76] [1969] 2 A.C. 147 at 170, 200 and 210. For a discussion of this, see L.H. Leigh, "Time Limit Clauses and Jurisdictional Error" [1980] P.L. 34 and John Alder, "Time Limit Clauses and Conceptualism–A Reply" (1980) 43 M.L.R. 670.
[77] 1972 S.C. 72. Also in *R. v. Secretary of State for the Environment, ex p. Ostler* [1977] Q.B. 122.
[78] 1973 S.C. 1 at 9.
[79] 1987 S.L.T. 300.
[80] *Pollock v. Secretary of State for Scotland*, 1993 S.L.T. 1173.
[81] *McDaid v. Clydebank D.C.*, 1984 S.L.T. 162.

Statutory time-limit not observed

Judicial review will not provide a remedy where a statutory appeal has   **13.18**
been provided subject to a strict timetable which the would-be appellant
has failed to observe. In *Fenton, Petitioner*,[82] an accused person who had
failed to appeal against a refusal of his application for interim liberation
within the 24 hours prescribed by section 446(2) of the Criminal
Procedure (Scotland) Act 1975 applied to the *nobile officium* of the High
Court of Justiciary craving that he should be admitted to bail. The Court
recognised that the function of that power was to redress all wrongs for
which a particular remedy was not otherwise provided but held that it
was not for the court to exercise its power under the *nobile officium*
simply because an accused or his legal advisers had been mindless of a
statutory timetable.

Statutory time-limit not excluding review

Where a statute recognises or provides for a remedy but attaches a time-   **13.19**
limit to the availability of that remedy, review is not necessarily excluded
after the expiry of that time-limit. One clear example is where the statute
relates to actings done in execution of the Act or some such terminology
and the particular actings complained of do not fall under that description. Where it was provided that actions brought "on account of
anything done in the execution of" the Poor Law Amendment Act were
to be commenced within a period of three months, that was held not to
be applicable to a claim based on contract between an individual and the
Parochial Board. The clause was held to be applicable to other sorts of
things and not to an action for the implementation of a contract or a
declarator that a contract existed.[83] On the other hand, where an
irregularity was committed by a collector of poors'-rates in the execution
of his duties under the Poor Law Amendment Act, it was held that an
action of damages was incompetent because the Act required any action
to be commenced within three calendar months after the act committed
and notice in writing to be given to the defender at least one calendar
month before the commencement of the action, and the pursuer had not
given the due notice of his action.[84] Even where broad allegations of
illegality and oppression were made in the enforcement of the poor law
assessment, it has been held that the statutory remedy in the sheriff
court with its limitation in time was the proper course to be taken,
although if the matter had amounted to an abuse of the statutory powers
then a remedy might be open in the Court of Session.[85]

IV DELAY, ACQUIESCENCE AND PERSONAL BAR

Common law limits

The principal protection against stale claims is to be found not in any   **13.20**
statutory provision, but through the less rigid and more flexible medium
of the common law.[86] This section deals with three related concepts:

---

[82] 1982 S.L.T. 164.
[83] *Mackay v. Beattie* (1860) 22D. 1486; see also *Thompson v. Parochial Board of Inveresk*
(1871) 10M. 178.
[84] *Ferguson v. M'Ewen* (1852) 14D. 457.
[85] *M'Laren v. Steele* (1857) 20D. 48.
[86] On the desirability of including *mora* as a defence to a claim in administrative law, see
C.T. Reid, "Mora and Administrative Law", 1981 S.L.T.(News) 253.

delay, acquiescence and personal bar. As is noted later, the first two may be analysed as comprehended in the third. Moreover, the first two run with each other, reflecting a difference of emphasis rather than a difference of principle. Delay, in what is technically referred to as a plea of *mora*, provides a sufficient means of securing that only matters which are still of live and current dispute are open to review. The plea depends not simply on the passage of time but may merge with acquiescence. The plea is properly expressed by stating that the application "is barred by *mora*, taciturnity and acquiescence".[87] In the ordinary case the plea of *mora* involves not only delay, but such acquiescence as may amount to a bar on the action.[88] As Lord President Kinross observed in *Assets Co. Ltd v. Bain's Trustees*[89]: "It appears to me, however, that the plea of *mora* cannot be successfully maintained merely on account of the lapse of time but that the person stating it must also be able to show that his position has been materially altered, or that he has been materially prejudiced, by the delay alleged . . . I do not doubt that where, coupled with lapse of time, there have been actings or conduct fitted to mislead, or alter the position of the other party to the worse, the plea of *mora* may be sustained. But in order to lead to such a plea receiving effect, there must, in my judgment, have been excessive or unreasonable delay in asserting a known right coupled with a material alteration of circumstances, to the detriment of the other party." It is not, then, properly a preliminary plea in law since its application depends upon the facts and circumstances,[90] but rather a plea to the merits of the case.[91]

Delay in judicial review

13.21   While there is no formal time-limit for the presenting of an application for judicial review in Scotland, it is thought that the need for the provision of a rapid remedy in the cases to which the process is available may in principle justify the refusal of a petition on the ground of the passage of time where there is material delay and ascertainable prejudice.[92] As Lord Diplock observed in the case of *O'Reilly v. Mackman*[93]: "The public interest in good administration requires that the public authorities and third parties should not be kept in suspense as to the legal validity of a decision the authority has reached in purported exercise of decision making powers for any longer period than is absolutely necessary in fairness to the person affected by the decision." There may often occur cases where it is of practical importance for citizens to know where they stand and how they can order their affairs in the light of relevant decisions of a public authority.[94] The desirability of

---

[87] The subject of *mora* and in particular the decisions in *Hanlon v. Traffic Commissioners*, 1988 S.L.T. 802 and *Pickering v. Kyle and Carrick D.C.*, 1991 G.W.D. 7–361 are considered by Neil Collar in his articles, "Mora and Judicial Review", 1989 S.L.T.(News) 309 and 1992 S.L.T.(News) 335.

[88] *Stornoway Town Council v. Macdonald*, 1971 S.C. 78.

[89] (1904) 6F. 692 at 705.

[90] When the same case reached the House of Lords: (1907) 7F(H.L.) 104, *per* Lord Davey at 109.

[91] *Halley v. Watt*, 1956 S.C. 370.

[92] *Kwik Save Stores Ltd v. Secretary of State for Scotland*, 1999 S.L.T. 193.

[93] [1982] 3 All E.R. 1124 at 1131.

[94] See *R. v. Dairy Produce Quota Tribunal for England and Wales, ex p. Caswell* [1990] 2 A.C. 738 at 748. In England the delay is measured from the date when the grounds for action arose: *R. v. Secretary of State for Trade and Industry, ex p. Greenpeace* [1998] C.O.D. 59.

investigating an alleged unlawful acting may be outweighed by the impropriety of allowing a belated challenge to a decision which has been published and on which other people may have relied. Delay in bringing an application may strengthen the case for refusing it.[95]

Length of time

In *Colvin v. Johnston*, which concerned a claim for damages for breach of promise to marry in relation to which there was no statutory prescription, Lord M'Laren observed[96] that "in the absence of a settled period the law requires that the claim should be insisted in within a reasonable time. That time will depend on the nature of the action and the circumstances of the case." As Lord Prosser observed in *Hanlon v. Traffic Commissioner*: "The length of any delay before implications of acquiescence arise will be almost infinitely variable depending on the circumstances."[97] Failure to have recourse to a statutory method of redress against a closure of a road for 10 years where the road had been closed and the site disposed of prevented a reduction of the decision by the road trustees to close it.[98] Long delay may impose such a burden upon the party claiming that statutory procedure has not been complied with that proof of it may fail.[99] But even a considerable passage of time may not in particular circumstances prevent a claim.[1] In *Glasgow and District Restaurateurs' and Hotel-keepers' Association v. Dollan*[2] three licences were challenged, two relatively recent but one of some eight years' standing.

13.22

Acquiescence

Acquiescence is a branch of personal bar[3] and is essentially a matter of fact.[4] Where there has been inaction, the term acquiescence is strictly apposite. Where there has been action from which acceptance of a situation and the surrender of a right may be inferred, the more appropriate term is that of waiver, which is also a question of fact.[5] In such a case it is not necessary to plead prejudice.[6] In *Stornoway Town Council v. Macdonald*[7] a town council had resolved to make improvements to a private street and, in accordance with the statutory provisions relating to their power to do so, notified the proprietor of lands abutting on the street of their intentions and of his liability to pay for the work. He did not appeal against the decision and the work was carried out. It was held that he was "barred by acquiescence" from challenging the legality since the council had to his knowledge incurred expense in reliance on the resolution. Where citizens had accepted the repair of a street by a local authority as having been carried out in conformity with

13.23

---

[95] *Fife R.C. v. Scottish Legal Aid Board*, 1994 S.L.T. 96.

[96] (1890) 18 R. 115 at 118.

[97] 1988 S.L.T. 802 at 805.

[98] *Crawford v. Lennox* (1852) 14 D. 1029.

[99] *Scott v. Magistrates of Dunoon*, 1909 S.C. 1003.

[1] *Birrell v. Dundee Gaol Commissioners* (1859) 21 D. 640.

[2] 1941 S.C. 93.

[3] Burn-Murdoch on *Interdict*, para. 107.

[4] *Bicket v. Morris* (1866) 4 M.(H.L.) 44, *per* Lord Cranworth at 51.

[5] *Armia v. Daejan Developments Ltd*, 1979 S.C.(H.L.) 56.

[6] *Banks v. Mecca Bookmakers*, 1982 S.C. 7, a case of alleged waiver, pled also as acquiescence.

[7] 1971 S.C. 78; see Lord Avonside at 87.

certain statutory provisions they were barred from objecting to the assessment for the work on the ground that it was beyond the statutory power of the authority to do it.[8] In *Hanlon v. Traffic Commissioner*,[9] 96 holders of taxi operators' licences sought to challenge a decision of the traffic commissioner relating to a new scale of taxi fares. It was admitted that there had been a denial of natural justice but the petitioners were held to be barred by tacit acquiescence from making the challenge. They had been aware of the facts on which the decision had been made but only lodged their petition 10 months after the decision and some eight-and-a-half months after the new scale had been put into effect, with the taximeters being adapted and tested to comply with the new scale. Where a decree has been acted upon, review may be barred by acquiescence.[10] An attack on a planning agreement after seven years had elapsed and the agreement had been acted upon was held to render an application for judicial review incompetent on the grounds both of bar and the principles of good public administration.[11] It may be noted that acquiescence cannot enable a jurisdiction to be established where no jurisdiction exists. If magistrates assume a jurisdiction which they do not have, consent to the proceedings does not establish the jurisdiction.[12]

Acquiescence and change of position

13.24 Acquiescence usually entails more than mere silence.[13] Acquiescence involves an implied consent and the facts from which the consent is to be implied should be identified and set out in the pleadings. Such facts may be the allowance of works to proceed without objection. Thus where an authority had permitted part of a building to be constructed it was barred from objecting to its completion.[14] Acquiescence in a building which encroached onto a street may bar objection to further development within the area of the encroachment.[15] But a failure to object to one contravention of a building restriction may not bar an objection to another which is more injurious; acquiescence goes no further than the thing acquiesced in.[16] In *Atherton v. Strathclyde Regional Council*[17] delay by a contractor in applying for reinstatement on a list of approved contractors, during which time the lists had been reviewed, was held to be fatal to an application for reduction of the decision to remove the contractor. The question has been raised whether mere acquiescence without any alteration of position on the part of the respondents would suffice to constitute an acquiescence. In *Perfect Swivel Ltd v. City of Dundee District Licensing Board (No. 2)*[18] the Lord Ordinary reserved his opinion on the question but stated that the principles behind the rules governing judicial review in England were relevant considerations for a court in Scotland. In *Carlton v. Glasgow Caledonian University*[19] the same

---

[8] *Muirhead v. Martin* (1889) 17 R. 125.
[9] 1988 S.L.T. 802.
[10] *Ingle v. Ingle's Trustee*, 1997 S.L.T. 160.
[11] *McIntosh v. Aberdeenshire Council*, 1999 S.L.T. 93.
[12] *Forrest v. Harvey* (1845) 4 Bell's App. 197.
[13] *Cowan v. Lord Kinnaird* (1865) 4 M. 236 at 241.
[14] *Magistrates of Edinburgh v. Lord Advocate*, 1912 S.C. 1085, *per* Lord Johnston at 1094.
[15] *Duke of Buccleuch v. Magistrates of Edinburgh* (1865) 3 M. 528.
[16] *Mactaggart & Co. v. Roemmele*, 1907 S.C. 1318.
[17] 1995 S.L.T. 557.
[18] 1993 S.L.T. 112.
[19] 1994 S.L.T. 549.

Lord Ordinary again reserved his opinion on the point, but indicated some sympathy with the respondent's arguments that a delay of nearly two years during which time the body against which the complaint was made had changed from being a polytechnic to a university, succeeding to the rights, liabilities and obligations of the former institution, was fatal to the application for review of a decision of the polytechnic.

Personal bar

In a wide sense the idea of personal bar may comprehend a variety of **13.25** more particular expressions of the equitable principle which, correspond- ing to the concept of estoppel in English law, lies behind all its particular forms. Thus the pleas of *mora* and of acquiesence, themselves dis- tinguishable by the particular emphasis placed on the passage of time in the one case and an inference of consent in the other, may both be open to analysis as examples of personal bar. In the present context the term is used to cover what may more strictly be identified as personal bar by representation. The context in which this matter may arise is typically that where by way of defence an authority claims that the complainer is personally barred from pursuing his complaint, but the point may also arise as a counter presented by the complainer to a line of defence sought to be used by the authority. The principle here has been defined as follows: "Where A has by his words or conduct justified B in believing that a certain state of facts exists, and B has acted on such belief to his prejudice, A is not permitted to affirm against B that a different state of facts existed at the same time."[20] There must be a representation made to the other party.[21] The element of disadvantage is essential. Thus, where a local authority had removed certain barricades from a street they were held not barred from calling on the adjoining proprietors to pave it, since the removal had not prejudiced the proprietors but might even have benefited them.[22] Where a plea of bar is not available a ground of challenge may still be found in respect of the unfairness of an authority in taking particular action in circumstances where the com- plainer had been led to believe that such action would not be taken.[23]

Statutory rights and duties

Statutory rights and duties cannot be lost by prescription,[24] nor are **13.26** statutory powers lost by delay in their exercise, especially where there is no prejudice to those who are obliged to comply with its exercise.[25] Failure to perform a statutory duty does not constitute a bar on the proper performance of the duty so as to enable a statutory obligation to be avoided.[26] Nor does the failure of officials to act in the management of a trust bar their successors from so acting.[27] Officials have no power to waive the performance of a statutory duty and their department cannot be barred from enforcing the statutory provisions or from disputing the

---

[20] Lord Chancellor Birkenhead in *Gatty v. Maclaine*, 1921 S.C.(H.L.) 1 at 7.
[21] *Amour v. Scottish Milk Marketing Board*, 1938 S.C. 465.
[22] *Magistrates of Alloa v. Wilson*, 1913 S.C. 6.
[23] e.g. *R. v. Liverpool Corporation, ex p. Liverpool Taxi Fleet Operators' Association* [1972] 2 Q.B. 299; *Att.-Gen. of Hong Kong v. Ng Yuen Shiu* [1983] 2 A.C. 629.
[24] *Ellice's Trustees v. Commissioners of the Caledonian Canal* (1904) 6 F. 325.
[25] *Magistrates of Alloa v. Wilson*, 1913 S.C. 6.
[26] *Maritime Electric Co. v. General Dairies Ltd* [1937] A.C. 610.
[27] *Magistrates of Edinburgh v. M'Laren* (1881) 8 R.(H.L.) 140.

jurisdiction of a referee even although their officials have erroneously advised the complainer that the matter might be referred to a referee.[28] Where a government official has acted in excess of his powers the Crown is not barred from enforcing a statutory prohibition, nor does such acting entitle the subject to maintain that there has been no breach of the prohibition.[29] Where an authority had said that no planning permisson was necessary they were not barred from holding that there was a breach of planning law and taking steps for enforcement, since their decision to serve an enforcement notice was a matter of discretion to be exercised for the benefit of the public.[30] Nor can an authority be barred from their statutory duty to determine a planning application by the acts of one of their officers who has exceeded his powers.[31] Acts which are outwith an authority's power cannot give rise to a personal bar, since it is not possible to acquiesce in a fundamental nullity.[32]

---

[28] *Reid v. Department of Health for Scotland*, 1938 S.C. 601.
[29] *Howell v. Falmouth Boat Construction Co. Ltd* [1951] A.C. 837.
[30] *Southend-on-Sea Corporation v. Hodgson (Wickford) Ltd* [1962] 1 Q.B. 416.
[31] *Western Fish Products Ltd v. Penwith D.C.* [1981] 2 All E.R. 204.
[32] Rankine on *Personal Bar*, pp. 179 *et seq.*

PART IV

THE GROUNDS OF JUDICIAL REVIEW

CHAPTER 14

THE GROUNDS IN GENERAL

Introduction

In this part an account will be given of the grounds on which an **14.01**
application for judicial review may be made. There are certain general
observations which can conveniently be noted at the outset.

Scotland and England

It has long been recognised that the relevant principles regarding the **14.02**
grounds for judicial review are common both to Scottish and to English
law.[1] This, then, is an area in which recourse may be had to English
jurisprudence with confidence.[2] Indeed, given the volume of cases in
England the opportunities for development are greater there and it may
be all the more useful to look at English jurisprudence.

Fact and legality

As has already been noted judical review is concerned with the legality **14.03**
of decisions and acts and not with the merits of the case.[3] It has for a
long time been recognised that if redress is sought against the decision of
an administrative body the complainer must plead more than a contradiction of the factual finding on which the decision has proceeded.[4] Thus
in *Macdonald v. Secretary of State for Scotland*,[5] while it was recognised
that the court could review a decision by the Secretary of State exercising
his statutory power to refer any conviction or sentence to the High Court
of Justiciary for consideration, review was not available where no
impropriety of procedure was alleged and the decision was attacked only
on its merits. But that does not mean that the factual findings are simply
a context for argument in cases of judicial review. As will be seen, the
conclusions drawn from them may be explored as a matter of rationality,
their assessment may be analysed as a matter of proportionality and even
the establishment or the sufficiency of them may be considered in
questions of error. On the other hand, the court must refrain from going
so far as to enter into a consideration of the facts and form its own view
of them.[6] At the outset, however, in order to substantiate the grounds of

---

[1] *British Airports Authority and Others v. Secretary of State for Scotland*, 1979 S.C. 200. See
para. 2.02.
[2] General issues in relation to the grounds of judicial review are discussed by Fordham,
"Surveying the Grounds: Key Themes in Judicial Intervention", in Leyland and Woods,
Administrative Law Facing the Future (1997), Chap. 8. Reference may also be made to the
jurisprudence of other countries. See, for example, Philip A. Joseph, *Constitutional and
Administrative Law in New Zealand*; Margaret Allan, *Introduction to Australian Administrative Law*, and, for a recent account of the grounds for review in Canada, Costigan,
Introduction to Judicial Review in Canada (1998) 3 *Judicial Review* 102.
[3] See paras 1.04 and 8.06. For the distinction between fact and law, see para. 22.03.
(error).
[4] *Mackie v. Lord Advocate* (1898) 25R. 769.
[5] 1996 S.L.T. 16.
[6] *R. v. Secretary of State for Scotland*, 1999 S.L.T. 279.

a challenge a petitioner must be able to plead and prove the factual basis of his complaint. But in some cases the absence of the record of proceedings before the lower court may make it impossible for the court of review to decide whether or not there has been a miscarriage of justice.[7]

Classification

14.04   In a celebrated passage in his speech in the *GCHQ* case[8] Lord Diplock propounded a classification under three heads of the grounds upon which administrative action is subject to judicial review. The three-fold classification was quickly accepted as applicable in Scotland.[9] The first of these was "illegality" by which he meant "that the decision-maker must understand correctly the law that regulates his decision-making power and must give effect to it". The second was "irrationality" by which he meant what is referred to as "*Wednesbury* unreasonableness"—"a decison which is so outrageous in its defiance of logic or of accepted moral standards that no sensible person who had applied his mind to the question to be decided could have arrived at it". The third was "procedural impropriety", which covered a failure to observe basic rules of natural justice, a failure to act with procedural fairness to those who would be affected by the decison, and a failure to observe procedural rules laid down by statutory instrument. He also observed:

> "That is not to say that further development on a case by case basis may not in course of time add further grounds. I have in mind particularly the possible adoption in the future of the principle of 'proportionality' which is recognised in the administrative law of several of our fellow members of the European Economic Community".[10]

It is evident that Lord Diplock's threefold classification is not, and was not intended to be, exhaustive. Indeed it has been pointed out by Lord Scarman that Lord Greene's statement in the *Wednesbury* case was similarly not exhaustive. "The law has developed beyond the limits understood to apply for judicial review as practised by the courts in 1948. The ground upon which the Courts will review the exercise of an administrative discretion by a public officer is abuse of power".[11] He instanced as particular examples a mistake of law in construing the limits of the power, procedural irregularity, unreasonableness in the *Wednesbury* sense, or bad faith or improper motive in its exercise. He regarded Lord Diplock's formulation as valuable, already "classical", but certainly not exhaustive.[12]

Dangers

14.05   While the attempt to categorise and classify the various grounds has some use, it also carries with it some danger in giving the impression that a complete account of the grounds of review is being presented.

---

[7] *Adair v. Colville & Sons*, 1926 S.C.(H.L.) 51.

[8] *Council of Civil Service Unions v. Minister for Civil Service* [1985] 1 A.C. 374 at 410.

[9] *Edinburgh D.C. v. Secretary of State for Scotland*, 1985 S.C. 261.

[10] [1984] 3 All E.R. 935 at 950.

[11] *Nottinghamshire County Council v. Secretary of State for the Environment* [1986] 2 W.L.R. 1, *per* Lord Scarman at 6.

[12] See *R. v. Take-over Panel, ex p. Guiness plc* [1990] 1 Q.B. 146, *per* Lord Donaldson of Lymington M.R. at 160.

One difficulty with any classification is that the law is still developing. Any attempt at classification brings the risk that it will be regarded as exhaustive and so may introduce a rigidity in approach which is inappropriate to the basic ideas of fairness and justice which lie at the heart of the jurisdiction. Moreover, the attempt to formulate precise categories may be frustrated by the cross-flow of those basic ideas and the imprecision of the concepts usually used to identify one ground from another.

Statements of principle

In a number of cases general pronouncements have been made sum-marising what on a more particular analysis may be seen as several distinct grounds on which a challenge may be based for the purposes of judicial review. Such general pronouncements may be influenced by the context of the case in which they are made so that they may not always be, and often are not intended to be, comprehensive. For example, they may concentrate only on the grounds on which the exercise of a discretionary power may be attacked. They are, however, useful as providing a general view of the subject and some of them may conveniently be quoted at this stage.[13] **14.06**

Wednesbury

The *locus classicus* for an exposition of the leading principles is the judgment of Lord Greene M.R. in *Associated Provincial Picture Houses Ltd v. Wednesbury Corporation*.[14] It is useful to quote two extensive passages from Lord Greene's judgment[15]: **14.07**

"When an executive discretion is entrusted by Parliament to a body such as a local authority in this case, what appears to be an exercise of that discretion can only be challenged in the courts in a strictly limited class of case. As I have said, it must always be remembered that the court is not a court of appeal. When discretion of this kind is granted the law recognises certain principles upon which the discretion must be exercised, but within the four corners of those principles the discretion, in my opinion, is an absolute one, and cannot be questioned in any court of law. What then are those principles? They are well understood. They are principles which the court looks to in considering any question of discretion of this kind. The exercise of such a discretion must be a real exercise of the discretion. If, in the statute conferring the discretion, there is to be found expressly or by implication matters which the authority exercising the discretion ought to have regard to, then in exercising the discretion it must have regard to those matters. Conversely, if the nature of the subject-matter and the general interpretation of the Act make it clear that certain matters would not be germane to the matter in question, the authority must disregard those irrelevant collateral matters. There have been in the cases expressions used relating to the sort of things that authorities must not do, not

---

[13] A recent formulation was given in the House of Lords in *R. v. Secretary of State for Scotland*, 1999 S.L.T. 279 at 295.

[14] [1948] 1 K.B. 223.

[15] The first of these starts at [1948] 1 K.B. 223 at 228.

merely in cases under the Cinematograph Act, but, generally speaking, under other cases where the powers of local authorities came to be considered. I am not sure myself whether the permissible grounds of attack cannot be defined under a single head. It has been perhaps a little bit confusing to find a series of grounds set out. Bad faith, dishonesty—those of course, stand by themselves—unreasonableness, attention given to extraneous circumstances, disregard of public policy and things like that have all been referred to, according to the facts of individual cases, as being matters which are relevant to the question. If they cannot all be confined under one head, they at any rate, I think, overlap to a very great extent".

In conclusion he stated[16]:

"The court is entitled to investigate the action of the local authority with a view to seeing whether they have taken into account matters which they ought not to have taken into account, or, conversely, have refused to take into account or neglected to take into account matters which they ought to have taken into account. Once that question is answered in favour of the local authority it may still be possible to say that, although the local authority have kept within the four corners of the matters which they ought to consider, they have nevertheless come to a conclusion so unreasonable that no reasonable authority could ever have come to it. In such a case again, I think the Court can interfere."

The various grounds noticed in that judgment have been referred to as the "*Wednesbury* principles". More particularly one of the grounds, that of unreasonableness, has tended to be isolated as a distinct category of case, referred to as "irrationality" or "*Wednesbury* unreasonableness". But even here there is a looseness of language to be noticed. The taking of irrelevant considerations into account has been seen as within "unreasonableness".[17] Unreasonableness can be seen as covering such grounds as an improper purpose or bad faith. Lord Reid observed that the word "unreasonable" is not an apt description of an excess of power.[18] It may be that the phrase "*Wednesbury* unreasonableness" should be understood as referring only to irrationality. But whatever prominence is given to "Wednesbury unreasonableness" it is only one aspect of the various grounds which relate to those aspects of the validity of a decision which can be grouped under a general heading of fairness. It has also to be noted that Lord Greene was speaking in the context of the exercise of discretionary powers and did not attempt to categorise or group the various grounds which he identified. Indeed, he questioned whether the grounds could all be confined under one head, although it may be thought that the concept of excess of power may be sufficiently wide to embrace them all.

The Wordie Property case

14.08 A general statement propounded by Lord President Emslie in the course of his opinion in *Wordie Property Co. Ltd v. Secretary of State for Scotland*[19] has often been referred to as a convenient summary.

---

[16] *ibid.* at 233.
[17] *Malloch v. Aberdeen Corporation*, 1973 S.C. 227, *per* Lord Cameron at 267.
[18] *Westminster Bank v. Minister of Housing and Local Government* [1971] A.C. 508 at 530.
[19] 1984 S.L.T. 345 at 347.

"A decision of the Secretary of State acting within his statutory remit is ultra vires if he has improperly exercised the discretion confided to him. In particular it will be ultra vires if it is based on a material error of law going to the root of the question for determination. It will be ultra vires, too, if the Secretary of State has taken into account irrelevant considerations or has failed to take account of relevant and material considerations which ought to have been taken into account. Similarly it will fall to be quashed on that ground if, where it is one for which a factual basis is required, there is no proper basis in fact to support it. It will also fall to be quashed if it, or any condition imposed in relation to a grant of planning permission, is so unreasonable that no reasonable Secretary of State could have reached or imposed it. These propositions, and others which are not of relevance to the present appeals, are, it appears to me, amply vouched by many decided cases".

While the particular case concerned a matter of planning legislation the observations of the Lord President were of quite general application. They were indeed adopted a month later by the Lord Justice-Clerk (Wheatley) in a case relating to public passenger vehicle licensing.[20]

Other statements of principle

Two other quotations may be given. First, in *Ashbridge Investments Ltd v.*   **14.09**
Minister of Housing and Local Government, which concerned a statutory provision under which the court could only interfere if a minister had gone wider than the powers of the Act or if any requirement of the Act had not been complied with, Lord Denning observed[21]:

"Under that section it seems to me that the Court can interfere with the Minister's decision if he has acted on no evidence; or if he has come to a conclusion to which on the evidence he could not reasonably come; or if he has given a wrong interpretation to the words of the statute; or if he has taken into consideration matters which he ought not to have taken into account; or vice versa, or has otherwise gone wrong in law. It is identical with the position when the Court has power to interfere with the decision of a lower tribunal which has erred in point of law."

The second statement comes from the speech of Lord Reid in *Anisminic v. Foreign Compensation Commission*.[22] His Lordship was here speaking in the context of a decision-making body which has been entitled to enter upon a particular inquiry, that is to say, that it is acting within his jurisdiction in the narrow sense of that word.

"It may have given its decision in bad faith. It may have made a decision which it had no power to make. It may have failed in the course of the inquiry to comply with the requirements of natural justice. It may in perfect good faith have misconstrued the provisions giving it power to act so that it failed to deal with the

---

[20] *Strathclyde Passenger Executive v. McGill Bus Service Ltd*, 1984 S.L.T. 377 at 381.
[21] [1965] 1 W.L.R. 1320 at 1326.
[22] [1969] 2 A.C. 147 at 171.

question remitted to it and decided some question which was not remitted to it. It may have refused to take into account something which it was required to take into account. Or it may have based its decision on some matter which, under the provisions setting it up, it had no right to take into account. I do not intend this list to be exhaustive. But if it decides a question remitted to it for decision without committing any of these errors it is as much entitled to decide that question wrongly as it is to decide it rightly. I understand that some confusion has been caused by my having said in *Reg. v. Governor of Brixton Prison, Ex parte Armah* [1968] AC 192, 234 that if a tribunal has jurisdiction to go right it has jurisdiction to go wrong. So it has, if one uses 'jurisdiction' in the narrow original sense. If it is entitled to enter on the inquiry and does not do any of those things which I have mentioned in the course of the proceedings, then its decision is equally valid whether it is right or wrong subject only to the power of the court in certain circumstances to correct an error of law."

The grounds not exhaustive

14.10 The list of examples given by Lord Reid in the passage just quoted was expressly said not to be exhaustive. As the law develops new examples may be defined and new formulations devised of grounds which have in essence been recognised before. The consideration which now follows of particular grounds on which a challenge may be mounted should accordingly not be taken as final or definitive. As Lord President Hope observed in *West v. Secretary of State for Scotland*[23]: "The categories of what may amount to an excess or abuse of jurisdiction are not closed, and they are capable of being adapted in accordance with the development of administrative law".[24]

The grounds overlap

14.11 Furthermore, a hard and fast distinction between the grounds of challenge cannot always be precisely made. In many cases the same situation may well be open to more than one analysis. More than one ground may apply at the same time in any given case and in some cases the grounds will be found to shade into each other. On the ground that any power must impliedly be exercised with due regard to the standards of fairness it is possible to categorise a breach of the rules of natural justice as an *ultra vires* act. In one case where justices had wrongfully dismissed the informations it was held that the proper ground for quashing their decision was not that of natural justice but a nullity through failure to comply with their statutory duty.[25] Delegated legislation may be said to be *ultra vires* because it is unreasonable. While many of the grounds could be subsumed under the heading of abuse of power, that phrase may not be sufficiently precise or comprehensive to serve as a complete description. Some analysis of the principal elements is nevertheless worthwhile.

---

[23] 1992 S.C. 385 at 413.
[24] An argument for the adoption of the French idea of the neutrality of the public service to ease the problem of political disputes before the courts is presented by Ian Cram in "Public Authorities, Public protest and Judicial Review", 1995 S.L.T. (News) 213.
[25] *Re Harrington* [1984] 1 A.C. 743.

Categories of function

The significance, or the lack of significance, of a distinction between **14.12**
judicial and administrative functions has already been discussed.[26] A
distinction could be drawn between the kinds of decision where the
authority has a considerable discretion in deciding whether or not to
instruct a particular course of action and those kinds of decision where a
more precise application of a statutory provision calls for consideration
of the relevant law and the relevant facts with some restraint on the
width of the available discretion. But an element of what may be called a
discretion will rarely be totally absent. In relation to the application of
taxing statutes Lord Thankerton observed[27]:

> "It is often a delicate question as to how far the Courts are entitled
> to interfere with the exercise of such a discretionary power, but I
> apprehend, generally speaking, the Courts are not entitled to
> interfere unless either (a) the exercise of the discretion has not
> complied with the conditions provided by the statute for the
> exercise of the discretionary power, to which I shall refer as the
> statutory basis of the power, or (b) the power has not been
> exercised judicially. The first of these grounds involves a question of
> construction of the statutory provision, which is open to the Court
> on any appropriate occasion; the second ground will arise on a
> particular exercise of the discretionary power."

In the context of the actings of trustees it has been said that[28] "all
discretionary powers, without exception, must be used both reasonably
and according to law", which may stand as a concise statement of the
general position in judicial review. It is suggested, however, that there is
little purpose to be served in categorising the various kinds of decision
with a view to prescribing which grounds may be applicable to some or
other of them.

Intensity of review

The general point may be made at this stage that the grounds of review **14.13**
may be pressed to a greater or a lesser extent in light of the particular
circumstances of the case. But it is difficult to prescribe in advance the
degree of intensity to which review may be driven in relation to
particular kinds of decision and particular grounds on which review may
be based.[29] The concept is in substance an expression of the idea of a
margin of appreciation.[30] Particular areas of administrative activity may
be identified for the purposes of specialised study and the grounds of
review may be explored in the context of such activities.[31] But the

---

[26] para. 8.20 (scope).

[27] *Ross & Coulter v. Inland Revenue*, 1948 S.C.(H.L.) 1 at 16.

[28] *Board of Management for Dundee General Hospitals v. Bell's Trustees*, 1950 S.C. 406,
per Lord Russell at 427, quoting Lord President Clyde in *Donaldson's Hospital v.
Educational Endowment Commissioners*, 1932 S.C. 585 at 599.

[29] For the reticence of the court to interfere in certain areas of administrative discretion
see, for example, para. 9.09 (restraint—prisons). A useful collection of examples of judicial
restraint can be found in Fordham, *Judicial Review Handbook* (2nd ed.), section P13, pp.
157 *et seq.* See also para. 21.09 below.

[30] See in this connection Kennedy L.J. in *R. v. Chief Constable of Sussex, ex p. ITF* [1997]
2 All E.R. 65 at 80–81.

[31] For an account of the grounds of review in relation to planning matters, see Reed in
Gill (ed.), *Scottish Planning Encyclopaedia*, Vol. 1, paras A. 5030 *et seq.* See also Clarke
and Otton-Goulder in Black, Muchlinski and Walker (eds), *Commercial Regulation and
Judicial Review* (Hart Publishing, 1998).

intensity is a matter essentially of degree and circumstance, tailing off at the one extreme into the principle that the law will not be concerned with matters of trifling importance, where at least one clear dividing line in principle can be discerned. The present study attempts no separate analysis of intensity but reference is made to the matter in some of the particular contexts in which it may occur.[32]

Analysis

14.14 The scheme adopted for the consideration of the grounds of review contained in the following chapters proceeds by reference to the various aspects of the activity on which the authority may be engaged. First, consideration is given to the need to have the power to do whatever is sought to be done, that is, the legality of the act by reference to the power which is being invoked. Legality in this context includes not only the general sources of lawful power, but the particular statutory provisions whereby certain provisions of the European Convention on Human Rights have become accessible in the courts of the United Kingdom and also the matters of legality under E.C. law.[33] Secondly, on the assumption that there is a relevant power to be exercised, attention will be given to the way in which it is exercised; that includes the procedural matters laid down by statute or by the common law which may require to be observed as well as the restraints on the freedom to exercise powers, misuse of power and unfairness. Thirdly, consideration will be given to those grounds of challenge which relate more particularly to the decision itself, assuming it to have been made under a relevant power and in accordance with the proper procedures. These comprise matters of rationality, proportionality and error.

The effect of a successful challenge

14.15 In *Pollock v. Secretary of State for Scotland*[34] it was held[35] that where in an application for planning permission which had not been duly sent the parties had acted in good faith the decision of the reporter was at least voidable, but it was doubted that there was truly a distinction in administrative law between the concepts "void" and "voidable".[36] It is thought that while those expressions may be properly used in the context of contracts they should be regarded as inappropriate and misleading in the context of judicial review.[37] It was recognised in England in *Ridge v. Baldwin*[38] and in *Anisminic Ltd v. Foreign Compensation Commission*[39] that there are no degrees of nullity.[40] Thus a decision given without

---

[32] For a discussion of the ideas of higher and lower thresholds for irrationality and of "hard-edged review" see Lord Irvine of Lairg, "Judges and Decision-Makers: The Theory and Practice of Wednesbury Review" [1996] P.L. 59. See paras 17.000 and 18.000. See also *R. v. Monopolies and Mergers Commission, ex p. South Yorkshire Transport* [1993] 1 W.L.R. 23.

[33] These last matters have been considered in paras 5.52 *et seq*. and are not dealt with further in this Part of the book.

[34] 1993 S.L.T. 1173.

[35] Following *Lochore v. Moray D.C.*, 1992 S.L.T. 16.

[36] See *Martin v. Bearsden and Milngavie D.C.*, 1987 S.L.T. 300 at 304.

[37] *London & Clydeside Estates Ltd. v. City of Aberdeen D.C.*, 1980 S.C.(H.L.) 1 at 30 and 43; *Isaacs v. Robertson* [1985] 1 A.C. 97 at 103; *Merton v. Bearsden D.C.*, 1987 S.L.T. 300 at 307.

[38] [1964] A.C. 40.

[39] [1969] 2 A.C. 147 at 170.

[40] It has been suggested that the distinction should be between "lawful" and "unlawful" decisions; de Smith, Woolf and Jowell, *Judicial Review of Administrative Action* (5th ed.), para. 5.048.

regard to the principles of natural justice[41] or one given under a breach of statutory procedure[42] is not simply voidable, but void.

Reduction without prejudice to the past

If a decision or deed is reduced, the effect is retrospective in that it falls **14.16** to be treated as null from the start. It follows that reduction of the deed or decision will nullify anything which has followed on it. But this logical approach gives rise to considerable problems. Many things may have been done in reliance upon the validity of the decision and it seems unattractive to ignore the reality of history. But the question then sharply arises whether the court can consistently with the view that a decision is invalid nevertheless preserve it as a valid basis of rights in respect of some past period. The problem has been discussed recently in *Boddington v. British Transport Police*[43] without any agreed solution. The logic of the retrospective effect of a finding of nullity was recognised, but some solution was sought which could preserve the efficacy of acts prior to the ruling by the court on the validity of the act in question. In the circumstances it was not necessary to resolve the problem. The solution to it does not require a reopening of the old idea of voidable acts and decisions. In *Calvin v. Carr*[44] it was held that an appeal could be taken from a decision which was invalid, the decision being regarded as not totally void so as to be legally non-existent. In *Percy v. Hall*[45] the retrospective effect of the invalidity of a byelaw was recognised but it was thought that the police constables who sought to enforce what appeared to be a valid byelaw should have a good defence of lawful justification. However, the precise analysis of the status of an act or decision which is later found to be a nullity remains uncertain. It will be necessary before too long either to reconsider the retrospectivity of judicial decisions or to devise some satisfactory analysis of the extent to which the validity for some purposes of past actings may still be recognised where they have proceeded on what turns out to be a nullity.[46] A decision or a deed which could be open to reduction will require to be regarded as valid if no reduction is sought or if the attempt to reduce it fails: for example, on the ground of a lack of *locus standi* on the part of the applicant. The passage of time may also prevent a reduction and enable the deed or decision to stand as valid.[47] It may be noted that by virtue of section 102 of the Scotland Act 1998 where a court or tribunal decides that an Act of the Scottish Parliament or any

---

[41] *Ridge v. Baldwin* [1964] A.C. 40 at 80.
[42] *London & Clydesdale Estates Ltd v. Aberdeen D.C.*, 1980 S.C.(H.L.) 1.
[43] [1999] 2 A.C. 143, overruling *Bugg v. DPP* [1993] Q.B. 473. See also *R. v. Wicks* [1997] 2 All E.R. 801.
[44] [1980] A.C. 574.
[45] [1997] Q.B. 924.
[46] Reference may in the context of this problem be made to the law of restitution mentioned later, para. 26.23. The effect of *ultra vires* acts and decisions is discussed by Wade, "Unlawful Administrative Action; Void or Voidable" (1967) 83 L.Q.R. 499 and (1968) 84 L.Q.R. 95; see also Forsyth, "The metaphysic of Nullity—Invalidity, Conceptual Reasoning and the Rule of Law" in Forsyth and Hare (eds), *The Golden Metwand and the Crooked Cord* (1968). For a discussion of the problem from the viewpoint of New Zealand, see Philip A. Joseph, *Constitutional and Administrative Law in New Zealand* (1993) pp. 665 *et seq.* See also *Evans* [1982] 1 W.L.R. 1155 at 1175–1176 and *Reg. v. Governor of Brockhill Prison, ex p. Evans (No. 2)*, [1999] Q.B. 1043.
[47] See paras 13.20 *et seq.* (delay). For possible problems in the context of contract, see T.B. Smith, *A Short Commentary on the Law of Scotland*, p. 790.

subordinate legislation made by the Scottish ExecutIve is *ultra vires* the court or tribunal may remove or limit any retrospective effect of the decision or suspend its effect in order to allow the defect to be corrected.

In particular circumstances, such as the adjustment of a continuing liablity to a payment, such as teinds, the court has so designed its order as to preserve liabilities for past payments while reducing the authority for future payments.[48] Moreover, there is nothing to prevent the parties from agreeing as between themselves that notwithstanding the nullity matters may remain entire between them for the past, although of course such an agreement would not be binding on third parties. If it is otherwise desired to leave undisturbed actings which have taken place on the basis of the validity of the decision now impugned the appropriate remedy may be a declarator rather than a reduction, thereby enabling parties for the future to proceed upon a sound and legal footing. The court may not itself rewrite the decision which has been challenged but it may order the authority to make such specified corrections as may be necessary.[49]

---

[48] *Duncan v. Brown* (1882) 10R. 332; *Lord Elibank's Trustees v. Hope* (1891) 18R. 445.
[49] *e.g. Ashley v. Rothesay Magistrates* (1873) 11 M. 708.

CHAPTER 15

ILLEGALITY

I   GENERAL
II   THE POWER
III   THE PERSON ENTITLED TO EXERCISE THE POWER
IV   PARTICULAR EXAMPLES OF ILLEGALITY
V   DELEGATED LEGISLATION
VI   LICENCES AND PERMISSIONS

I   GENERAL

Introduction

It could be said that in one sense the sole ground of judicial review is **15.01** that of unlawfulness. All the particular respects in which decisions or actings can be challenged by way of judicial review may be seen as aspects of this basic ground. A like view could be taken with regard to the term *"ultra vires"*. In its widest sense the expression *ultra vires* may be interpreted as covering all forms of abuse or misuse of power as well as excess of power, and so indeed covering the whole field over which the supervisory jurisdiction extends. Such a usage can be justified on the basis that Parliament must be taken to have intended that all those to whom power is entrusted must be required to exercise that power fairly, reasonably, honestly and within the limits of the power.[1] Thus a statutory provision entitling challenge on the ground that a road scheme was "not within the purposes of the Act" has been held to include a challenge on the grounds of a breach of the rules of natural justice.[2] But while this wider sense of the words may reflect the basic idea which lies at the heart of all the particular grounds of review, it is of little utility for analysis or categorisation. In the narrow sense the expression *ultra vires* relates to a situation where someone has done something for the doing of which lawful authority is required and there is no, or no adequate, authority for it.[3] In the context of the present chapter it is in that more narrow sense that the words unlawful, illegal and *ultra vires* will be used.

Illegality and other grounds

The consideration of legality is properly the first of the various grounds **15.02** to be considered. If the decision is not made within the scope of the power which was purportedly being exercised, no other considerations need arise. On the other hand, if there was a sufficient power for the

---

[1] See the discussion in para. 4–15.

[2] *Lithgow v. Secretary of State for Scotland*, 1973 S.C. 1.

[3] As, for example, in *Peter Holmes & Son v. Secretary of State for Scotland*, 1965 S.C. 1. Lord Reid in *Anisminic Ltd v. Foreign Compensation Commission* [1969] 2 A.C. 147 at 171 referred to the narrow sense of "jurisdiction" as meaning that the tribunal was entitled to enter on the inquiry in question. In "Is the Ultra Vires Rule the Basis for Judicial Review?" [1987] P.L. 543, Dawn Oliver argues that *ultra vires* in the wider sense is not the basis for review.

making of the decision in question, the decision may be *intra vires* in the narrow sense of that expression but may still be open to challenge on one or other of the grounds to be considered in later chapters. But the distinction between illegality and other grounds for challenge may not be easily drawn. Problems closely related to considerations of illegality may arise in relation to the failure or refusal to exercise a power when it ought to be exercised or to the improper use of a power. Those matters are considered later under the heading of misuse of power. Again, an error of law may be seen as an illegality.[4] Whether the term "private street" includes exclusively an existing street or whether it can encompass other adjoining land may be seen as a matter of excess of power,[5] although it could also be considered as a matter of error of law. In the field of arbitration an arbiter will be acting illegally if he enters into a matter which is not within the terms of his remit[6] but that is distinct from his taking into account an irrelevant matter in the course of determining a matter which is within his remit.

The scope of illegality

15.03 In considering whether a particular decision is or is not illegal the practical consequences of the decision on other similar cases does not affect the issue.[7] All that matters are the terms of the particular statutory provision. But the consequences of the decision may have an effect on the choice of remedy to be given. The motive or object which the authority may have had in mind is of no consequence where the issue is one of alleged illegality. All that matters is whether there was a power which entitled that to be done which was done.

Illegality and discretion

15.04 A distinction may require to be observed between matters which are properly concerned with the scope of a power and matters which are concerned with the detail of its exercise. To take an example from Hume,[8] where the statute provides that toll gates are to be erected at least six miles apart along a road and they are erected at a distance less than that, the matter can be brought under review. On the other hand, if that minimum distance is observed the precise positioning of them may not be open to review, at least on the ground of illegality.

Protection of human rights

15.05 The passing of the Human Rights Act 1998 has introduced a significant statutory category of actings which may be challenged on the ground of illegality. In terms of section 6(1) of the Act it is unlawful for a public authority to act in a way which is incompatible with any of the rights and fundamental freedoms set out in the first Schedule to the Act, reproducing provisions of the European Convention on Human Rights and the First Protocol thereto. In so far as the matter is presented as one of unlawfulness it deserves mention in the present context; but the subject is of sufficient substance to warrant separate treatment and forms the subject of a separate chapter.

---

[4] *Highland Regional Council v. British Railways Board*, 1996 S.L.T. 274.
[5] *Greenock Corporation v. Bennett*, 1938 S.C. 563.
[6] *Glasgow City and District Ry v. Macgeorge* (1886) 13R. 609.
[7] *Gordon District Council v. Hay*, 1978 S.C. 327.
[8] *Lectures*, p. 273.

II THE POWER

Source

The source of the power will in most cases be statute, but it may also **15.06**
derive from contract[9] or some other source such as the royal prerogative.[10] The powers of any statutory corporation or authority are limited
by the statute which creates it.[11] Further powers may of course be added
to it at times subsequent to its creation by the authority which created it.
In any question of alleged *ultra vires* actings it is necessary first to
identify the powers under which the body or person is entitled to act and
more particularly any specific provisions under which he was purporting
to act.

Identification of the power

It will also be necessary to identify the power under which the acting in **15.07**
question is being taken. This matter becomes of particular importance
where there is more than one power available.[12] Where two distinct
statutory provisions may apply, the court may require to reconcile the
two[13] and decide whether one has or has not been impliedly repealed by
the other.[14] Where there are two distinct provisions in separate Acts,
each complete in itself, the authority may require to decide under which
provision they are going to proceed,[15] but there may be special circumstances where their choice could be challenged as unreasonable or as an
abuse of process.[16] Even if an authority has the power to perform some
particular act the actings may nevertheless be invalid if the authority
purports to proceed under another inadequate power. In this connection
no weight can be attached to such words of style as are often used in the
reference to the authorising legislation as "and all other powers enabling
him to act in that behalf", at least where the subordinate legislation is
expressed to be made under some specific power.[17] The authority must
act, and bear and be seen to be acting, under powers which are sufficient
for the particular occasion.

Construction of powers

All the recognised canons and guides to construction will require to be **15.08**
considered in ascertaining the extent and scope of the powers in
question.[18] Where the problem is one of construing the words of the
statute the general guidance afforded by the various recognised presumptions may be of assistance. It is, for example, a well-established
principle of law that a statute shall not be held to take away vested

---

[9] *West v. Secretary of State for Scotland*, 1992 S.C. 385 at 399 and 413.
[10] In *Leishmen v. Magistrates of Ayr*, Mar. 18, 1800, F.C., the Court held that even in an
emergency situation of food shortage a sheriff could not act at his own hand.
[11] Halsbury's *Laws of England*, (3rd ed.), Vol. 30, p. 686, para. 1324.
[12] *e.g. Brown v. Magistrates of Kirkcaldy* (1905) 8F. 77.
[13] *Hawick Orange Lodge v. Roxburgh D.C.*, 1980 S.C. 141.
[14] *Calder v. Alexander*, 1926 J.C. 51.
[15] *Montgomerie & Co. Ltd v. Haddington Corporation*, 1908 S.C.(H.L.) 6.
[16] *Westminster Bank v. Minister of Housing and Local Government* [1971] A.C. 508, *per*
Lord Reid at 530.
[17] *Forster v. Polmaise Patent Fuel Co.*, 1947 S.C. 56 at 60.
[18] Reference should be made to the standard textbooks for a detailed consideration of
statutory construction.

interests without compensation unless the intention to do so is expressed in clear and unambiguous terms.[19] Thus rights of property and rights to trade will not readily be assumed to have been taken away by statute. Where road trustees were empowered to take away for road works stones not required for the private use of the owner it was held that the statute must receive a reasonable interpretation, so as to avoid oppression to the private interest and enable the trustees to exercise their powers fairly.[20] Nor will it readily be concluded that the statute intends to invade public rights. In one case the court held that a footpath could not be closed up under a statutory provision authorising the shutting up of superfluous "roads".[21] But if the statute is sufficiently clear the intention to invade public rights will be recognised.[22] It will also be presumed that the legislation is not retrospective or retroactive.[23] Unless the contrary intention appears from the statute it will be taken not to intend to cause unfairness to those who would otherwise suffer in respect of past transactions.[24] Explicit legislative sanction would be required to make a new salary scheme retrospective in its effect so as to prejudice persons who are enjoying a salary under an existing scheme.[25] Under the Human Rights Act 1998, legislation will require to be read so far as possible as compatible with the Convention on Human Rights.[26] Clear words are required to overcome the various established presumptions. The whole scheme of the statute may require to be considered when deciding whether regulations made under it are or are not *ultra vires*.[27]

Construction of words

15.09   In general it is the meaning of the words used in the context of the statute which must be ascertained and if the words are plain and unambiguous they must receive effect. The particular language of the statute will require to be construed in a manner which is reasonable and fair for the practical operation of the provision in question and does not involve any stretching or straining of the words used. Three examples may be given. A power to lay water pipes in various places other than those which were not dedicated to public use was not sufficient to empower the suspending of pipes under a privately owned bridge which carried a public road across a railway.[28] A "street" for the purposes of the maintenance of streets under the Burgh Police Acts means an existing street not a proposed wider street.[29] A duty to provide whole-

---

[19] *Malloch v. Aberdeen Corporation*, 1973 S.C. 227 at 240 and 256.

[20] *Yeats v. Taylor* (1863) 1M. 221, *per* Lord President M'Neill at 224.

[21] *Pollock v. Thomson* (1958) 21D. 173, followed in *Lord Blantyre v. Dickson* (1885) 13R. 116.

[22] *Burnet v. Barclay*, 1955 J.C. 34.

[23] *Gardner v. Lucas* (1878) 5R.(H.L.) 105. The War Damage Act 1965 provides one blatant example of deliberate retrospective denial of rights.

[24] *Plewa v. Chief Adjudication Officer* [1995] 1 A.C. 249.

[25] *Coull v. Fife Education Authority*, 1925 S.C. 249 at 252.

[26] See s.3 of the Act. The decisions in *R. v. Home Secretary, ex p. Leech* [1994)] Q.B. 198 and *Leech v. Secretary of State for Scotland*, 1991 S.L.T. 910 reflect the former position. See, further, para. 6.16. The construction of the powers of Edinburgh University adopted by the majority of the court in *Jex-Blake v. Senatus of the University of Edinburgh* (1873) 11M. 784 would hardly be adopted today.

[27] *Forster v. Polmaise Patent Fuel Co.*, 1947 S.C. 56.

[28] *Magistrates of Glasgow v. Glasgow and South-Western Ry* (1895) 22R. (H.L.) 29.

[29] *Greenock Corporation v. Bennett*, 1938 S.C. 563. See also *Caledonian Ry v. Glasgow Corporation* (1905) 7F. 1020; 1907 S.C.(H.L.) 7.

some water has been held not to empower a local authority to improve dental health by the addition of fluoride.[30]

Discretionary powers

The word "may" usually falls to be construed as giving the authority a **15.10** choice whether or not to take the course it is empowered to take. But in the context of some statutes where "may", or other expressions such as "it shall be lawful", are used, the intention can be to impose an obligation to act rather than a discretion whether to act or not.[31] The matter is one for construction of the particular provision. Where the powers were to be exercised for the benefit of the public it was held that words which were permissive in form should be construed as imperative in effect.[32] Where the membership of a committee required to be set up under a statutory scheme was subject to certain express statutory qualifications a scheme which introduced further qualifications was held in that respect to be *ultra vires*.[33] Where the language is discretionary the scope of the discretion may only extend to taking the specified course or not, so that a third alternative is not admissible. In a report from the Solicitors' Discipline Committee it was provided that the court "may, if they shall think proper, thereupon cause such solicitor to be struck off the roll of solicitors". It was held that the only option available to the court was either to strike the solicitor off the roll or to take no action.[34]

Geographical extent of power

The jurisdiction of statutory bodies may be subject to a geographical **15.11** limitation. Local authorities will in general have no power to operate outwith the boundaries of their own areas. Thus harbour trustees having the statutory function of operating a ferry service were not entitled to use the boats for excursions beyond the limits within which they were authorised to sail.[35] An exemption from liability in byelaws concerning pilotage in the river Clyde was held not to extend to a collision occurring outwith the area over which the power to make the byelaws extended[36] and a power to make byelaws relating to incidents within a harbour or dock did not extend to operations in the navigable channel of the river.[37] Special provision for deviation may be made by statute. Where the limit permitted by statute is altered by even a small margin, a liability at least in damages will arise.[38]

Temporal extent of power

Whether a power can be exercised from time to time or on the other **15.12** hand is exhausted after it has been once exercised, will be a matter for the construction of the relevant statute. In one early case it was held that a statutory power to fix the situation of a schoolhouse where none had

---

[30] *McColl v. Strathclyde R.C.*, 1983 S.L.T. 636.
[31] *Fleming & Ferguson v. Magistrates of Paisley*, 1948 S.C. 547.
[32] *Gray v. St Andrews and Cupar District Committee of Fifeshire County Council*, 1911 S.C. 266.
[33] *Hunter v. Ayrshire County Council*, 1969 S.C. 45.
[34] *Solicitors' Discipline (Scotland) Committee v. B.*, 1942 S.C. 293.
[35] *D. & J. Nicol v. Dundee Harbour Trustees*, 1915 S.C.(H.L.) 7.
[36] *Steamship "Beechgrove" Co. v. Aktieselskabet "Fjord"*, 1916 S.C.(H.L.) 1.
[37] *Kerr v. Auld* (1899) 18R.(J.) 12.
[38] *Goldie v. Oswald* (1814) 2 DOW 534.

existed before could not be used later to make an alteration so as to
erect a new house in another part of the parish.[39]

Objects of the power

15.13 It is necessary that where a power is being exercised over persons, those
persons should be within the class of the persons over whom the power
may lawfully be exercised. This requirement may involve matters of
construction and application of the relevant legislation to the circumstances of the case. Thus, where the occupier of a smallholding was
found to be a sub-tenant and not a crofter, the power in the Crofters
Commission to determine fair rents of crofts was inapplicable.[40]

Incidental matters

15.14 The limits of a power, whether statutory or otherwise, will include not
only the express provisions as properly interpreted but also anything
which is fairly incidental to or consequential upon what is expressly
authorised.[41] The doctrine of *ultra vires* is to be reasonably, and not
unreasonably, construed and applied, so that "whatever may fairly be
regarded as incidental to, or consequential upon, those things which the
legislature has authorised, ought not (unless expressly prohibited) to be
held, by judicial construction, to be *ultra vires*".[42] In *D. & J. Nicol v.
Dundee Harbour Board Trustees* Lord Dunedin observed[43]: "'Incidental'
in my view means incidental to the main purposes of the business". But
while that includes powers reasonably incidental or consequential upon
the main purposes, it is not enough that they are merely sensible,
convenient or profitable, or simply consistent with or conducive to the
achievement of the main purposes.[44] It was held not to be an illegal use
of a country school to use it as a holiday camp in the summer for poor
children from Glasgow.[45] An arbiter has power to determine any
incidental questions which are necessary for the resolution of the
problem placed before him[46] and all matters necessary for deciding the
difference which is sent to arbitration should be decided in the arbitration.[47] Thus a power to determine just rebates from a charge included
the power to decide whether the charge was reasonable.[48] A power to
make regulations for written notice to be given of a decision to make a
deportation order has been held to cover the making of regulations
making notice unnecessary where the address of the person to whom it
should be directed was unknown.[49] A power of sale was not regarded as
incidental where a statutory port authority had been given certain
powers which omitted any mention of a power to sell.[50]

---

[39] *Dawson v. Allardyce*, Feb. 18, 1809, F.C.
[40] *Dalgleish v. Livingston* (1895) 22R. 646.
[41] For the position in statute law, see *Att.-Gen. General v. Great Eastern Ry* (1880) 5
App.Cas. 473 at 478.
[42] *Glasgow Corporation v. Flint*, 1966 S.C. 108, *per* Lord Wheatley at 129.
[43] 1915 S.C.(H.L.) 7 at 12.
[44] *Piggins & Rix Ltd v. Montrose Port Authority*, 1995 S.L.T. 418.
[45] *Hunter v. School Board of Lochgilphead* (1886) 14R. 135.
[46] *Bell v. Graham*, 1908 S.C. 1060.
[47] *Caledonian Ry v. Clyde Shipping Co.*, 1917 S.C. 107.
[48] *Cowan & Sons Ltd v. North British Ry* (1901) 4F. 334.
[49] *Singh v. Secretary of State for the Home Department*, 1990 S.L.T. 300.
[50] *Piggins & Rix Ltd v. Montrose Port Authority*, 1995 S.L.T. 418.

Connected but not incidental matters

But a distinction has to be made between matters which are incidental to **15.15** the authorised activity and matters which while they may be connected with it, are not simply another means of exercising the statutory power, but are so different as to go beyond and exceed it. Thus a statutory power to supply water was held not to entitle an authority to carry out plumbing work, even although the work was done at the request of the military authorities and was in accordance with a royal proclamation calling on the citizens to obey instructions given by the military.[51] The provision of medical "examination and supervision" was held not to include medical or dental treatment.[52] A power to assist students by various forms of payment was held not to include the power to assist them by making loans.[53] It is accordingly necessary to consider the statutory provision and ascertain from it the scope of the power. That should then determine the extent of the purpose of the legislation. Anything which is incidental to the express provision, which serves the purpose of the statutory provision as understood from its terms, may competently be undertaken. Anything which—even although it may serve the broad purpose which lies behind the statutory provision—is not within the main purpose of the power, will not be lawful.

Reconsideration

Whether an authority which has exercised a power is entitled to **15.16** reconsider the matter and make a fresh determination must depend primarily upon the terms of the relevant legislation. In some cases there may be an express provision in the statute entitling revocation.[54] Where a determination has to be made it will generally be the position that the matter may not be reopened and redetermined by the authority even with consent,[55] especially where third parties may be affected by the result of a rehearing.[56] If the party affected had acted on the determination a case of bar might arise.[57] In practice, if there has been no change of circumstances it might be difficult to justify a change in the decision, and such a course might open the way to a charge of unfairness or irrationality. Thus where an authority had decided to exercise a discretionary power to grant a gratuity of a single lump sum and paid it, it was held that they could not reverse that decision at a later date.[58] On the other hand, a power exercised for a future tract of time may be open to recall. If the authority discovers that the exercise of a discretionary power to issue a bus pass was based on a mistake on the facts, it may have a duty to reconsider the matter and withdraw a grant.[59] Where in such matters as salaries, where scales may be altered from time to time, changes can be introduced, although they will only be effective from the time fixed by the statutory procedures governing the making of the change.[60] Where the statutory scheme allows for review of the matter,

---

[51] *Grieve v. Edinburgh & District Water Trustees*, 1918 S.C. 700.
[52] *Glasgow School Board v. Allan*, 1913 S.C. 370.
[53] *Banffshire County Council v. Scottish Education Department*, 1934 S.C. 353.
[54] *e.g.* Town and Country Planning (Scotland) Act 1997 (c.8), s.65.
[55] *Matchett v. Dunfermline D.C.*, 1993 S.L.T. 537 at 541.
[56] *Smith v. Foster*, 1949 S.C. 269.
[57] *Re 56 Denton Road, Twickenham* [1953] 1 Ch. 51.
[58] *Campbell v. Glasgow Police Commissioners* (1895) 22R. 621.
[59] *Rootkin v. Kent County Council* (1981) 2 All E.R. 227.
[60] *Coull v. Fife Education Authority*, 1925 S.C. 240.

such as in the granting of periodical licences or the valuation of lands and heritages for rating purposes, then there is an obligation to consider the matter afresh, and the earlier decision may be of little or no relevance.

III THE PERSON ENTITLED TO EXERCISE THE POWER

Exercise by the wrong person

15.17 Even where the power may have been otherwise validly exercised, the exercise of it may be struck down on the ground that it was exercised by someone other than the person entitled to exercise it. Changes in local government legislation may give rise to problems on the transfer of functions which will depend upon the construction of the relevant statute.[61] After the functions of town councils as highway authorities had been transferred to county councils, it was held that the power to regulate traffic in a burgh remained with the magistrates, and accordingly that an order by the county council regulating the direction traffic was to move in a burgh was *ultra vires*.[62] In relation to the transfer of powers to the Secretary of State for Scotland the question arose whether regulations which had been made by a government minister and not by the Scottish Secretary applied to Scotland.[63] In another case an unsuccessful challenge was made of a deportation order on the ground that it should have been signed by the Secretary of State for Scotland and not the Home Secretary.[64] Problems may arise where the later legislation varies or extends the description of the persons entitled to exercise the power. Where an earlier statute gave one authority the exclusive power to regulate the sale of whisky, but a later statute gave a general power to another authority wide enough to cover sales of whisky, it was held that the latter authority was empowered to make regulations on such sales.[65] Where the issuing of instructions for a strike was committed by the rules of a union to a national executive council, it was held that a strike instructed by a special conference was *ultra vires*.[66] In the generality, no challenge will be allowed to the authority of any official as not being the holder of the office which he bears to hold.[67] But questions may arise in this context of the competency of delegation and of the powers of a delegate.

Delegation of power

15.18 Whether delegation is competent is a matter which calls for consideration of the relevant statutory powers. It is necessary to find an express provision or a necessary implication to justify it. The principle of *delegatus non potest delegare* is not to be taken to be an absolute rule. The nature of the function in question may be a factor to be taken into account in construing the power. Thus disciplinary functions have been found on a construction of the relevant provisions not to be open to

---

[61] *Tennent v. Magistrates of Partick* (1894) 21R. 735.
[62] *Fife County Council v. Lord Advocate*, 1950 S.C. 314.
[63] *Galloway v. Anderson*, 1928 J.C. 70.
[64] *Agee v. Lord Advocate*, 1977 S.L.T. (Notes) 54.
[65] *M'Inch v. Auld*, 1921 S.C. 13.
[66] *Paterson v. NALGO*, 1977 S.C. 345.
[67] *M'Arthur v. Linton* (1864) 2M. 661. Particular formalities may also be required: see para. 17.09.

delegation.[68] Delegation of a judicial function is less easy to establish than the delegation of an administrative function.[69] In such a context a provision for delegation must be clear and explicit.[70] In one case a prosecution failed because the solicitor appointed by the School Board to prosecute instructed an associate in his office to conduct the case but had no authority to delegate the task.[71] Where there is a power to delegate, consideration may also have to be given to the question whether the power has been exercised so as to effect a delegation of the power in question. It will be a matter of fact whether the necessary procedural step has been taken and a question of construction of the decision whether or to what extent the delegation has been effected.[72] It may be noted that a power to appoint committees or sub-committees may not infer a power to delegate the making of decisions.[73] An authority may instruct its staff to collect information necessary for the decision without delegating the task of making the decision.[74] A statutory power of delegation by ministers of the Crown was provided by the Civil Service (Management Functions) Act 1992.[75]

Delegation in local authorities

Provision is often made for delegation in local government legislation.[76] **15.19** But the relevant provisions and resolutions must be studied in order to ascertain the extent of any delegation. A delegation of the power to carry certain statutory powers into execution was held not to include the making of orders to repave a street, but only to see to the implementation of those orders.[77] The term "delegation" may be expressly defined to mean a remit to act on behalf of an authority without any transfer of the power or the duty of the authority, with the result that the statutory obligations remain on and can be enforced against the authority rather than the body to which the function has been "delegated".[78]

Devolution of power

A distinction should be observed between delegation and devolution. **15.20** While Parliament often provides for action to be taken by the Secretary of State it is well accepted that the power in question may validly be exercised by an official in his department. That need not be through a delegation of the minister's power but simply by a devolution of the power onto the official.[79] The principle was expounded by Lord Greene in *Carltona Ltd v. Commissioners of Works*[80] and is sometimes referred to as the *Carltona* principle.[81] While delegation requires the express

---

[68] *Vine v. National Dock Labour Board* [1957] A.C. 488.
[69] *Young v. Fife R.C.*, 1986 S.L.T. 331.
[70] *General Medical Council v. U.K. Dental Board* [1936] Ch. 41 at 49.
[71] *M'Murdo v. M'Cracken*, 1907 S.C.(J.) 1. See also *Thomson v. Scott* (1901) 3F.(J.) 79.
[72] *Pollock School v. Glasgow Town Clerk*, 1946 S.C. 373.
[73] *Thomson v. Dundee Police Commissioners* (1887) 15R. 164.
[74] *R. v. Race Relations Board ex p. Selvarajan* [1976] 1 All E.R. 12. *Young v. Fife R.C.*, 1986 S.L.T. 331.
[75] 1992 c.61.
[76] Examples can be found in the Local Government etc. (Scotland) Act 1994, Sched. 3, para. 12 (for residuary bodies) and Sched. 7, para. 18 (for a water and sewerage authority).
[77] *Thomas v. Elgin* (1856) 18D. 1204.
[78] *Lord Advocate v. Glasgow Corporation*, 1973 S.C.(H.L.) 1.
[79] *Re Golden Products* [1976] Ch. 300.
[80] [1943] 2 All E.R. 560.
[81] *e.g. R. v. Home Secretary, ex p. Oladehinde* [1991] 1 A.C. 254.

granting of the power to the delegate, settled procedure may be sufficient to support a devolution,[82] although devolution may also be achieved by an express authorisation.[83] The *Carltona* principle may also apply where a minister is required to take advice and the advice is given to an official with the relevant responsibilities.[84] Where there is a requirement for a ministerial consent, that may be presumed to have been given if the point is not challenged and proof may be held to be unnecessary. Where a prosecution required the consent of the Secretary of State it was held that evidence of the consent was incompetent and unnecessary, the statement by the Lord Advocate or his representative that it had been obtained being sufficient.[85] But where the Lord Advocate's concurrence, which was to be given "upon just cause shown only", was a statutory necessity for a special procedure for the reduction of letters-patent it was held that the signature of his first clerk was not sufficient.[86] Where provision is made that a signed certificate vouching some matter is to be conclusive evidence of the matter, investigation of the matter is excluded.[87]

Effect of illegal delegation

15.21   A purported exercise of power by a delegate where there was no power to delegate will be ineffective. If the power has been exercised by the correct body as an act of administration their decision should be valid and effective even although the purported delegate was also participating in it.[88]

IV   PARTICULAR EXAMPLES OF ILLEGALITY

Grounds for disciplinary action

15.22   Where a professional body has the power to remove names of practitioners from its register on specific grounds it may not remove a name on a ground not included within those which have been specified.[89] A committee authorised to deal with questions between a patient and his doctor in respect of treatment was held to have jurisdiction to deal with a complaint that the doctor had used insolent and abusive language.[90]

Imposition of charges

15.23   A harbour authority is not entitled to impose a special charge without express power to do so.[91] But there may be implied a power in an authority to levy sufficient funds to enable a statute to be workable.[92] Where assessments were to be applied in maintaining, keeping in repair and improving roads and bridges it was held that assessments could be

---

[82] *Dalziel School Board v. Scotch Education Department*, 1914 S.C. 234.
[83] *R. v. Home Secretary, ex p. Oladehinde[1991] 1 A.C. 254.*
[84] *Air 2000 Ltd v. Secretary of State for Transport (No. 2)*, 1990 S.L.T. 335 at 341.
[85] *Stevenson v. Roger*, 1915 J.C. 24.
[86] *Gillespie v. Young* (1861) 23D. 1357.
[87] *R. v. Clerkenwell Metropolitan Stipendiary Magistrate, ex p. DPP* [1984] 1 Q.B. 821.
[88] *School Board of Barvas v. Macgregor* (1891) 18R. 647.
[89] *Cheyne v. Architects' Registration Council*, 1943 S.C. 468.
[90] *Bennett v. Scottish Board of Health*, 1921 S.C. 772.
[91] *Somerville v. Leith Docks Commissioners*, 1908 S.C. 797.
[92] *Ferrier v. School Board of Parish of New Monkland* (1881) 9R. 30.

levied in order to accumulate funds for rebuilding a bridge.[93] Where a milk marketing board was entitled to require the payment of such contributions from producers as the Board considered necessary to cover the costs of operating the scheme it was held that they were not entitled to include in the costs the difference between the price which they received in the manufacturing market and the price which they would have received if the milk had been disposed of in the liquid market.[94] A power to regulate the use of parking places and to make provision as to the charges to be paid in connection with the use of a parking place was held not to enable the authority to state maximum charges in the order with the explanation that the actual charges would be displayed at the parking places.[95]

Charging of expenses

The payment of electioneering expenses out of the common good has **15.24** been held to be illegal.[96] The manufacturing of their own stationery by a local authority for their ordinary use and for carrying out their educational responsibilities has been held to be within the powers of the then current legislation.[97] In *Glasgow Corporation v. Flint*[98] it was held that the payment for home telephones for town councillors was not a legitimate charge on the funds raised by the levying of rates, but that such a charge against the common good was not contrary to the relevant statutory provisions and was legal. Silence on the matter of charging is not sufficient to satisfy "the rigorous test which has to be passed before a statutory power to charge can be held to exist by necessary implication".[99]

Local authorities holding land for public purposes

Where land is held for the public by a local or other public body the **15.25** rights of the public must be respected. Thus the local magistrates of the Burgh of Musselburgh were interdicted from granting a feu of part of the lands used for the ancient game of golf.[1] But a local authority which holds land for the public may not exclude an adjoining private proprietor from free access to the lands from his own property.[2] But the exercise of powers which the authority legally possesses comes to be a matter of discretion. As was observed in one case, "there is a large discretionary power in this Court to regulate the administration of the guardians of public property,–the managers of public property,–for the benefit of the community".[3] In that case the use of a school as a holiday camp for deprived children was recognised as being within the powers of the school board and it was believed that any challenge on the discretion to do so was not a matter to be raised in the sheriff court. The court will

---

[93] *British Fisheries Society v. Magistrates of Wick* (1872) 10M. 426.

[94] *Scottish Milk Marketing Board v. Ferrier*, 1936 S.C.(H.L.) 39. For another dispute on the contributions to a milk marketing board, see *Aberdeen and District Milk Marketing Board v. Mennie*, 1939 S.C. 232.

[95] *Freight Transport Association v. Lothian R.C.*, 1978 S.L.T. 14.

[96] *Kemp v. Glasgow Corporation*, 1920 S.C.(H.L.) 73.

[97] *Graham v. Glasgow Corporation*, 1036 S.C. 108.

[98] 1966 S.C. 108.

[99] *Stirrat Park Hogg v. Dunbarton D.C.*, 1996 S.L.T. 1113 at 1118.

[1] *Sanderson v. Lees* (1859) 22 D. 24.

[2] *Magistrates of Edinburgh v. Warrender* (1863) 1M. 887.

[3] *Hunter v. School Board of Lochgilphead* (1886) 14R. 135, *per* Lord Young at 140.

not intervene in the lawful exercise of a local authority's powers where there has been no abuse of power or of discretion.[4]

V DELEGATED LEGISLATION

General

15.26 Delegated or subordinate legislation constitutes one large category of case which illustrates the operation of the doctrine of *ultra vires*. In this context there is no discernible difference between the laws of Scotland and England. As Lord Robertson observed in *Da Prato v. Magistrates of Partick* with reference to the legality of byelaws.[5] "Questions of this kind have frequently arisen in the Scottish Courts and the principles upon which they proceed are identical with those upon which the Courts in this part of the country have proceeded". Challenge on grounds such as illegality or procedural deficiency will probably be more successful than those based on irrationality.[6] The legality of regulations depends upon the terms of the authorising statute and the nature of the regulations themselves.[7]

The scope of the power

15.27 Where the purported exercise of a power does not fall within the purpose for which the power was granted it may be invalid. In the early case of *Town of Perth v. Clunie*[8] the magistrates sought to stop Clunie who had a brewery near Perth from selling his locally brewed ale to the citizens by enacting a prohibition on the importation of ale. They sought to found *inter alia* on old statutory powers directed against the exercise of crafts in suburbs, but it was held that they had no power to enact the prohibition under those powers. Where a local authority had a power to make byelaws for the suppression of nuisances an enactment making it an offence to affix any bill or other notice to any of a variety of specified places without the consent of the owner or occupier was held to be *ultra vires*, since bill sticking could be but was not necessarily a nuisance and the power only allowed the authority to legislate against nuisances.[9] Where a regulation relating to arbitration between the landlord and tenant of an agricultural holding failed to meet the terms of the empowering legislation by not making the arbitration compulsory the regulation was held to be inept and a time-limit contained in the regulation did not operate so as the prevent the tenant raising a question which would otherwise have been excluded.[10] Rules which required all transatlantic flights to or from Glasgow or Edinburgh to stop at Prestwick airport were held not to fall within the scope of powers given to the Secretary of State to regulate the distribution of air traffic between airports in the United Kingdom.[11] Directions which constituted a general prohibition were held to be *ultra vires* when the statute was

---

[4] *Nicol v. Magistrates of Aberdeen* (1870) 9M. 306.
[5] 1907 S.C. (H.L.) 5 at 6.
[6] For challenge on the ground of irrationality, see paras 21.02 *et seq.*
[7] *Gordon D.C. v. Hay*, 1978 S.C. 327.
[8] (1752) Elchies, Burgh no. 34.
[9] *Eastburn v. Wood* (1892) 19R.(J.) 100.
[10] *M'Callum v. Buchanan-Smith*, 1951 S.C. 73.
[11] *Air 2000 Ltd v. Secretary of State for Transport*, 1989 S.L.T. 698.

intended to provide for measures to meet specific occasions.[12] Powers to give directions or orders or notices may not be sufficient to authorise matters of permanent regulation. For those the making of byelaws may be necessary.[13] A scheme for the discharge of a local authority's functions with regard to education was reduced where the composition of the sub-committees in the scheme failed to comply with the statutory provisions for its membership.[14] On the other hand, byelaws regulating the towing of vessels within a harbour were held to be *intra vires* on a proper construction of the empowering statute.[15] A power to make regulations providing for notice to be given to persons in respect of decisions taken in respect of them under the Immigration Act 1971 was held to include a power to provide for a dispensation of notice where the person's place of abode was unknown.[16] Regulations will not readily be held to be valid where they seek to exclude the jurisdiction of the Court of Session,[17]

Not meeting the power

Where an Act empowered regulations for requiring questions to be resolved by arbitration within a specified timetable, a regulation which stated a time for arbitration but did not require questions to be resolved by arbitration was held to be invalid.[18] A power to regulate places for bathing did not authorise a byelaw prohibiting bathing except at such places as the authority might appoint.[19] Power to make byelaws for regulating the carriage of heavy loads in particular situations cannot be used to make a general prohibition on such carriage.[20] On the other hand legislation passed for the preservation of amenity may entrust the authority with a wide discretion on the areas which they may regard as appropriate for protection and allow of a generous scope in the designation of the areas to which the byelaws should apply.[21] Domestic decisions must not of course exceed the provisions of European legislation.[22]

15.28

Lawful and unlawful acts

Subordinate legislation will be *ultra vires* if it is contrary to or repugnant to law. Byelaws which forbid the doing of something which is otherwise lawful but not obligatory or which require the doing of something which is lawful but not obligatory are valid.[23] On the other hand, byelaws which require the doing of something which is unlawful or which prohibit the doing of something which is by law obligatory will be invalid. The empowering Act may expressly provide that the subordinate legislation is to be of no effect if repugnant to the law of Scotland[24] but such a

15.29

---

[12] *Macdonald v. Mackenzie*, 1947 J.C. 122.
[13] *Baikie v. Charleson* (1901) 3F.(J.) 54.
[14] *Hunter v. Ayrshire County Council*, 1969 S.C. 45.
[15] *Peterhead Towage Services Ltd v. Peterhead Bay Authority*, 1992 S.L.T. 593.
[16] *Singh v. Secretary of State for the Home Department*, 1992 S.L.T. 200; 1993 S.L.T. 115.
[17] *Kerr v. Hood*, 1907 S.C. 895.
[18] *M'Callum v. Buchanan-Smith*, 1951 S.C. 73.
[19] *M'Gregor v. Disselduff*, 1907 S.C.(J.) 21.
[20] *Cadenhead v. Smart* (1894) 22 R.(J.) 1.
[21] *Robert Baird Ltd v. Glasgow Corporation*, 1935 S.C.(H.L.) 21.
[22] *Scottish Premier Meat Ltd v. Secretary of State for Scotland*, 1997 S.L.T. 1080, where the domestic legislation was upheld.
[23] *Rae v. Hamilton* (1904) 6F.(J.) 42.
[24] As, for example, in s.183 of the Public Health (Scotland) Act 1897.

provision will in any event be implied. But where the law does not
expressly declare something to be lawful or unlawful subordinate legislation may declare it to be unlawful.[25] That a matter is already unlawful at
common law does not prevent the matter being made a criminal offence
under subordinate legislation. Byelaws may validly be made which forbid
the doing of something which is already unlawful and impose a penalty
upon the doing of it.

Irrationality

15.30   Even where subordinate legislation has been made by the body entitled
to make it, deals with matter which is within the scope of the power,
satisfies the purpose of the statute and is not contrary to or repugnant to
law, it may nevertheless be invalid on the ground of irrationality. This
matter is considered in the context of irrationality in a later chapter.[26]

Uncertainty

15.31   In order to be valid the effect of the exercise of a power must be clear
and certain. This is particularly the case in matters of subordinate
legislation and of the imposition of conditions in the grants of licences or
permissions. Vagueness in the terms of what the authority has done may
well give opportunity for challenge. Excessive looseness in the framing of
a byelaw may cause it to be invalid as too wide and unreasonable.[27] A
byelaw which sought to control the use of flesh or offal as a fertilising
agent was held to be too vague for enforcement, since it failed to specify
any limit of time within which the material required to be ploughed into
the land.[28] To require the taking of reasonable care or reasonable
precautions has been held to be sufficiently precise for the basis of a
prosecution for breach of the provision of a statutory regulation.[29]
Where byelaws required the marking of boundaries for areas which were
to be prohibited to the public, the boundary fences had to coincide with
the area over which the prohibition was permitted to extend.[30] A
reference to organisations "describing themselves as 'republican clubs' or
any like organisations however described" was held not to be too vague
or uncertain to be effective.[31] On the basis that byelaws are to be
reasonably construed mere ambiguity may not suffice to establish an
invalidity.[32] It has been held that the expressions "near" and "reasonable
distance" are sufficiently precise in a provision intended to prevent dogs
from causing a nuisance.[33]

---

[25] *Gentel v. Rapps* [1902] 1 K.B. 161; *Ronaldson v. Williamson* (1911) 48 S.L.R. 983.
[26] See paras 21.02 *et seq.*
[27] *Eastburn v. Wood* (1892) 19R.(J.) 100.
[28] *Dunsmore v. Lindsay* (1903) 6F.(J.) 14.
[29] *Marshall v. Clark*, 1957 J.C. 68, overruling *Allan v. Howman*, 1918 J.C. 50 and *Morison v. Ross-Taylor*, 1948 J.C. 74.
[30] *Bugg v. DPP* [1993] Q.B. 473. The decision was overruled in *Boddington v. British Transport Police* [1998] 2 All E.R. 203 on the question whether the byelaw remained effective until quashed.
[31] *McEldowney v. Forde* [1971] A.C. 632.
[32] *Rutherford v. Somerville* (1904) 4F.(J.) 15.
[33] *Macpherson, Petr*, 1990 J.C. 5.

VI   LICENCES AND PERMISSIONS

The imposition of conditions

There are frequent occasions where in the granting of a licence or a **15.32** permission the authority may seek to impose conditions on the grant. Here again the scope of the power will require to be studied to ensure that the conditions are within the scope of the statutory power. Conditions which are more stringent than the statute allows will be invalid.[34] In the context of the imposition of conditions in grants of planning permission in the case of *Mixnam's Properties Ltd v. Chertsey Urban District Council*[35] Willmer L.J. gave a convenient summary of four respects in which the widest of powers must be limited: 1. The conditions must not be such as to effect a fundamental alteration in the general law relating to the rights of the person on whom they are imposed, unless the power is expressed in the clearest possible terms. 2. The power must be limited by reference to the subject-matter of the statute. 3. The conditions must not be unreasonable—*i.e.* such as Parliament cannot have intended should be imposed. 4. They may be void for uncertainty.[36]

The imposition of a restriction prohibiting the hiring of pleasure boats on Sundays was justified by the reduced availability of rescue facilities on Sundays, which indicated that the restriction had been legitimately imposed in terms of the governing statute for the safety of the lieges.[37] A condition on a grant of planning permission for a housing development requiring that the occupiers should be persons on the local authority's housing list with security of tenure for 10 years was held unreasonable and since the condition was fundamental to the grant the permission was quashed.[38] A condition in a grant of planning permission forbidding the extension of the service pipes to serve any other residential development except with the permissions of the planning and drainage authorities was held to be improper and unreasonable.[39]

---

[34] *Rossi v. Magistrates of Edinburgh* (1904) 7F.(H.L.) 85 (permitted hours for operation of a business); *Baker v. Glasgow D.C.*, 1981 S.C. 258 (resolution that licences should be non-transferable).

[35] [1965] A.C. 735; [1964] 1 Q.B. 214 at 226.

[36] See Young and Rowan-Robinson, *Scottish Planning Law and Procedure* (1985), p. 246, and the *Encyclopaedia of Planning Law* (Local Government Library), para. 1–106.

[37] *Blair v. Smith*, 1924 J.C. 24.

[38] *R. v. Hilllingdon LBC, ex p. Royco Homes Ltd* [1974] 1 Q.B. 720.

[39] *North East Fife D.C. v. Secretary of State for Scotland*, 1992 S.L.T. 373.

CHAPTER 16

THE SUBSTANCE OF HUMAN RIGHTS

I   INTRODUCTION
II THE RIGHTS
III GENERAL PROVISIONS

I INTRODUCTION

General

Following consideration of the ground of unlawfulness, it is appropriate   **16.01**
to turn to the particular form of unlawfulness which has been constituted
by the Human Rights Act 1988.[1] As has already been noted, that Act
allows for the making of a declaration of incompatibility by a court
where it determines that a provision of primary legislation is incompatible with one or more of the Convention rights as defined in the Act.[2]
Such a declaration may fall to be made by a court in the exercise of the
supervisory jurisdiction. Furthermore, and perhaps of even greater
relevance to judicial review, it is expressly provided by section 6 that it is
unlawful for a public authority to act in a way that is incompatible with
one or more of the Convention rights. The effect of that provision has
already been discussed. It remains to deal with the substantive grounds
in respect of which incompatibility may arise. The incompatibility in
question constitutes a new form of statutory illegality.

Outline

The subject is, however, one which deserves a substantial volume to   **16.02**
itself.[3] This chapter contains only a brief account of the rights set out in
the Schedule to the Act of 1998 with only a small selection of the many
reported cases decided in the European Court of Human Rights or
elsewhere. It is intended merely to serve as an introduction to a subject
well covered in numerous specialised textbooks and reference should be
made to such sources for further study.[4] The Human Rights Act is set
out in Appendix I to this book and reference should be made to the
Schedule to that Act for a reproduction of the relevant Convention

---

[1] At the time of writing it is believed that the Human Rights Act is not to come into
effect until late in 2000. Prior to that happening, the Convention rights will be accessible
through the Scotland Act 1998, so that challenges may be made under the Scotland Act on
human rights grounds even before the provisions of the Human Rights Act become
directly accessible, albeit only in respect of Scottish legislation and the actings of the
Scottish Executive and its emanations.

[2] para. 6.34.

[3] The view has been taken that even the word "right" may require analysis: *McInnes v.
Onslow-Kane* [1978] 1 W.L.R. 1520, *per* Megarry V.C. at 1528.

[4] See, for example, Jacobs & White, *The European Convention on Human Rights* (2nd
ed., Clarendon Press, Oxford, 1996); Harris, O'Boyle & Warbrick, *Law of the European
Convention on Human Rights* (Butterworths, London, 1995); Robertson & Merrills,
Human Rights in Europe (Manchester, 1993); Halsbury's *Laws of England*, Vol. 8(2);
Lester and Pannick, *Human Rights Law and Practice* (Butterworths, 1999).

rights which are now to be enforceable in the United Kingdom. In addition, it should be noted that the Convention rights do not purport to be an exhaustive catalogue of human rights and civil liberties.[5] Human rights which have developed at common law remain relevant,[6] as do human rights which are protected under E.C. law and in the various international human rights treaties which have been ratified by the United Kingdom but not implemented into national law by Act of Parliament.[7]

The incorporated rights

16.03   The rights guaranteed by the 1998 Act are those set out in Articles 2 to 12 and Article 14 of the Convention along with Articles 1 to 3 of the First Protocol and Articles 1 and 2 of the Sixth Protocol, all of which are to be "read with" Articles 16 to 18 of the Convention which serve as the Convention's interpretation clauses.[8] The Act refers to all of the guaranteed rights as "the Convention rights".[9] Importantly, however, the Act provides that the Convention rights are to have effect subject to any derogations and reservations made by the United Kingdom.[10] These derogations and reservations are explained in sections 14 to 17, which provide powers for giving effect in U.K. law to any future derogations or reservations made by the United Kingdom and for the alteration of any existing derogations and reservations. One derogation (from Article 5(3) of the Convention) and one reservation (from Article 2 of the First

---

[5] See s. 11 of the 1998 Act.

[6] See below, para. 16.06.

[7] For example, the Covenants noted below in n. 12. Of course, human rights which apply directly under the force of E.C. law are supreme; any national laws and administrative action (and, at least where E.C. law is directly applicable, private conduct) inconsistent with E.C. law must yield to the E.C. law right. It is probably the case that any conflict between E.C. law and the Human Rights Act 1998 must be resolved in favour of E.C. law (but see Art. 307 of the E.C. Treaty); although this raises the question of the extent to which fundamental human rights have an overriding constitutional force, even over and above E.C. law. This problem was highlighted in the relationship between E.C. law and German law: see Case 11/70 *Internationale Handelsgesellschaft GmbH v. Einfuhr und-Vorratstelle fur Getreide und Futtermittel*, [1970] E.C.R. 1125 and its consequences in Germany, discussed by Craig & de Burca, *EC Law* (Clarendon Press, Oxford, 1998) at pp. 260–263. In any event, the E.U. institutions are now bound by the European Convention, so the potential for any conflict should be limited: see Art. F (now 6) of the Treaty of European Union. The Convention rights are also part of E.C. law as general principles of law and as such bind the E.U. institutions and also the member states when they operate in the sphere of E.C. law, by, for example, giving effect to E.C. law (see, for example, Case C–260/89 *E.R.T v. Dimotiki Etairia Pliroforissis and Sotirios Kouvelas* [1991] E.C.R. I-2925, esp. para. 42 of ECJ Judgment). So this means, for example, that the Scottish Administration must comply with human rights guaranteed under E.C. law in addition to Convention rights (as must the U.K. government and Parliament, which are in a position inferior to E.C. law, their conduct inconsistent with E.C. law rights being invalid). But the Convention is not actually part of E.C. law since the Council of Ministers has no powers to ratify it (yet): see Opinion 2/94 [1996] 2 C.M.L.R. 265, esp. at 289. See generally Guild and Lesieur, *The European Court of Justice on the European Convention on Human Rights* (Kluwer Law International, 1998). It is also possible that some human rights may be implied under the Scotland Act 1998: see Chap. 7.

[8] 1998 Act, s. 1.

[9] s. 1(1).

[10] Reservations may be freely made by a state at the time when it ratifies an international treaty: see Art. 2.1(d) of the Vienna Convention on the Law of Treaties 1969. Derogations may be made subsequently in order to exclude obligations arising under the treaty, rather than denouncing it. The freedom to make reservations or derogations may be restricted by international law. For a full discussion reference should be made to Jennings & Watts, *Oppenheim's International Law* (9th ed., 1996) pp. 1240–1248.

Protocol) are recognised in sections 14(1) and 15(1) of the Act respectively and are set out in full in Parts 1 and 2 of Schedule 2.

Amendments to the Convention

The 1998 Act makes provision in subsections (4) to (6) of section 1 for **16.04** amendments to the definition of Convention rights to be made by order of the Secretary of State to reflect the effect in relation to the United Kingdom of a Protocol which the United Kingdom has ratified or has signed with a view to ratification. These powers allow further rights and freedoms which are added to the Convention by Protocol to be incorporated directly into U.K. law. However, the Act preserves the government's treaty-making prerogatives in relation to Protocols by providing that an order making amendments to the definition of Convention rights may not come into force before the Protocol is in force in relation to the United Kingdom. In other words, no amendment can be effective to incorporate a Protocol which the United Kingdom has not ratified or which has not yet entered force as an international obligation binding on the United Kingdom.

Convention articles not included

It may be noticed that Article 13 of the Convention has been omitted **16.05** from the list of Convention rights set out in the Schedule to the Act. That Article provides for a right to an effective remedy. Since the Act itself makes provision for remedies it was felt inappropriate for that Article to feature in the Schedule. But it will still be appropriate to refer to and consider the jurisprudence on Article 13 in the implementation of the 1998 Act. Article 15, which deals with derogations, is also omitted.

Convention rights not exhaustive

It has already been noted that the Act does not purport to be an **16.06** exhaustive catalogue of human rights and civil liberties.[11] The human rights standards which have developed at common law, both generally and in the context of judicial review, remain relevant as do the various international human rights treaties which the United Kingdom has ratified but which have not been implemented into domestic law.[12] Certain basic rights have long been recognised as part of the common law of Scotland, although they have not often been used as a basis for litigation. While their independent status is not to be forgotten it is thought that they might usefully be noticed in relation to the relevant Convention rights in so far as they may throw some light on the problems of application of the Convention rights in a national context.[13]

By way of illustration of past resort to matters of basic human right it may be noted that the court has recognised the right of an individual "to choose how to care for his own body".[14] The view has been taken that a

---

[11] para. 16–02.

[12] For example, the United Nations International Covenant on Civil and Political Rights 1966, the United Nations International Covenant on Economic, Social and Cultural Rights 1966, the United Nations Convention on the Elimination of all Forms of Discrimination Against Women 1979, and the United Nations Convention on the Rights of the Child 1989. For a consideration of the common law rights, see Fraser, *Constitutional Law* (2nd ed.), Pt VI and Mitchell, *Constitutional Law* (2nd ed.), Chap. 18.

[13] For accounts of the common law position see Fraser, *Constitutional Law* (2nd ed.), Pt VI and Mitchell, *Constitutional Law* (2nd ed.), Chap. 18.

[14] *McColl v. Strathclyde R.C.*, 1983 S.L.T. 616 at 623.

policy which ignored the humanitarian principle of respect for family life
would be unreasonable and subject to review by the court.[15] In *Leech v.
Secretary of State for Scotland*[16] it was recognised that the right of access
to the courts was a basic civil right and that it included the right of access
to a solicitor for confidential advice and assistance; but it was held that a
rule which entitled a prison governor to read and censor letters passing
between a prisoner and his solicitor but not to stop a letter inviting the
solicitor to come for an interview was not *ultra vires*. The view was taken
that confidentiality is not a basic civil right but was a matter concerned
with the recovery of documents in litigation.

Structure of the Articles

16.07 Some of the Articles—for example Article 3—are unqualified in their
terms so as to admit of no exception. Others—for example, Article 8—
have exceptions expressly built into them. All may be seen to be
restrained by Article 17 which strikes at any abuse of rights. It is
probably inappropriate to indulge in any too precise analysis of the
structures in approaching the application of the Convention. A balancing
of the relevant considerations may often be required, but a division of
the problem into distinct or successive stages may lead to undue
technicality.[17] On the other hand, it is proper to adopt an ordered and
methodical approach in considering the application of such particular
elements as constitute a qualification—for example, in Article 9, the
limitations "prescribed by law" and "necessary in a democratic society".
It may be noted that some of the Articles may involve the imposition of
positive obligations as well as what are primarily negative obligations;
and interests may be protected indirectly as well as directly by the
application of the Convention.

Democracy

16.08 Historically, there has been no need in the United Kingdom for the
courts to venture an attempt at what "democracy" or a "democratic
society" means in legal terms. Under the Human Rights Act 1998,
however, many of the guaranteed rights are subject to limitations to the
extent necessary in a democratic society.[18] The interpretation and
application of these guaranteed rights therefore requires consideration
of the nature of a "democratic society". Some assistance in this matter
can be derived from the decisions of the European Court of Human
Rights and also from decisions of the Privy Council. A review of judicial
explanations of what values democracy brings to a legal order indicates
that the word carries with it an overlay of the ideals of fairness and
equality which, while they may not be unique to a democratic system, are
inevitably part of its essential character. In particular, equality before the

---

[15] *Singh*, 1988 G.W.D. 32–1377.
[16] 1993 S.L.T. 365. But *cf . R. v. Secretary of State for the Home Department, ex p. Leech*
[1993] 4 All E.R. 539. In *Raymond v. Honey* 1983] 1 A.C. 1 the Privy Council held that the
stopping of letters from a prisoner to his solicitor regarding the prisoner's legal
proceedings was a contempt of court as being a denial of the prisoner's right of access to
the court.
[17] Compare the "two-stage" approach in Canada discussed in *Att.-Gen. of Hong-Kong v.
Lee Kwong-kut* [1993] A.C. 951.
[18] See Arts 8–11 of the European Convention on Human Rights, Sched. 1 to the Human
Rights Act 1998.

law—that is, that persons should be uniformly treated unless there is good reason to the contrary—is "one of the building blocks of democracy and necessarily permeates any democratic constitution".[19] But this does not mean that every democracy will apply the broader ideas which lie within the concept in precisely the same manner. Hence the key concept of margin of appreciation developed by the European Court of Human Rights under the European Convention.[20]

Several decisions of the Supreme Court of Canada are also instructive. This court has extensive experience interpreting section 1 of the Canadian Charter of Rights and Freedoms, which guarantees its rights "subject to such reasonable limits as are demonstrably justifiable in a free and democratic society". In *R v. Oakes* Dickson C.J. suggested as the central values[21]: "respect for the inherent dignity of the human person, commitment to social justice and equality, accommodation of a wide variety of beliefs, respect for cultural and group identity, and faith in social and political institutions which enhance the participation of individuals and groups in society". In so far as it can reasonably be accepted that these values are common to all societies worthy to be called "democratic", they should at the very least mean some priority must be given to human rights guaranteed by law. Accordingly, limits on rights should only be justifiable by reference to the most important social objectives. A court responsible for balancing human rights against reasons for limiting them should be concerned to establish that the limits are reasonable and no more than is necessary to achieve the important objective or objectives which they pursue.

II THE RIGHTS

The Right to Life (Article 2)

The right

This is expressed as an absolute right, admitting of no derogation. It **16.09** strikes at the intentional deprivation of life, so that operations, such as a vaccination programme which may carry with it a serious risk to life, should not constitute a violation.[22] It is not clear whether the medical termination of pregnancy would constitute a breach,[23] nor whether the legalisation of euthanasia could escape the application of the Article. The switching off of life support machines may also give rise to a problem here, but a solution might be found in the interplay between Articles 2 and 3 so as to permit the course in the case of a patient in a permanent vegetative state where the continued effort to preserve life could be seen as inhuman or degrading. The Article may impose an obligation on the state to provide machinery for the prevention of violations of Article 2, as may Articles 3, 5, and 8, but in the case of Article 2 at least the obligation only arises if the risk of violation is real and immediate. In *Osman v. United Kingdom*[24] the Commission held that

---

[19] *Matadeen v. M.G.C. Pointu and Others* [1998] 3 W.L.R. 18, *per* Lord Hoffmann at 26.
[20] Discussed in Chap. 6.
[21] [1986] 1 S.C.R. 103 at 136.
[22] *Association X v. U.K.* (1978) 14 D.R. 31.
[23] *X v. U.K.* (1980) 19 D.R. 244. See *Society for the Protection of Unborn Children (Ireland) Ltd (SPUC) v. Grogan* [1991] E.C.R. 4605.
[24] *Osman v. U.K.* [1998] E.H.R.L.R. 101. But there was a breach of Art. 6.

the risk posed by the schoolteacher who killed the Osmans was not such or so immediate that the police should have foreseen that the lives of the pupil and his father were in danger, so that there was no breach of Article 2.

The exceptions

16.10 The three exceptions set out in the second paragraph of Article 2 only apply where death results "from the use of force which is no more than is absolutely necessary" for the stated purposes. Considerations of necessity require the establishment of a pressing social need[25] and, so, an application of the doctrine of proportionality.[26] The test is described as a very strict and compelling one.[27]

Prohibition of Torture (Article 3)

16.11 It may be noted that this Article has no express qualifications and no express exceptions. But while it is absolute in its terms it will only apply to conduct which attains a minimum level of severity, assessed in light of all the circumstances, proved beyond reasonable doubt.[28] The circumstances include the duration of the treatment, its physical or mental effects and, in some cases, the sex, age and state of health of the victim. There must be a sufficiently serious degree of suffering on the part of the victim to meet the standard required by the Article and a sufficient level of humiliation and debasement. The assessment of that is necessarily a matter of circumstances, and in particular—for example, in the case of punishment—the nature and context of the punishment and the manner and method of its execution.[29]

Torture, treatment or punishment

16.12 While all these terms are used they are used in the alternative and little is to be gained by detailed analysis of the individual words. The first may carry a special stigma. The word is used to describe an aggravated form of inhuman treatment, usually carried out with some particular purpose, such as the obtaining of information or of a confession, or the infliction of punishment.[30] "Punishment" refers to conduct carried out for the particular purpose while the word "treatment" is perfectly general. In either case however the standard requires to be satisfied in respect of being inhuman or degrading. The brutality or the humiliation established in the circumstances must in either case be gross.

Examples

16.13 Several examples can be found in the various cases from the United Kingdom relating to corporal punishment.[31] Forcible imprisonment, even involving the necessary use of a straitjacket, may not fall within Article

---

[25] *Handyside v. U.K.* 1975 Series A, No. 24, para. 48: "necessity" is not synonymous with "indispensable", nor does it have the flexibility of such words as "advisable", "ordinary", "useful", "reasonable" or "desirable".

[26] *The Sunday Times v. U.K.* (1979) 2 E.H.R.R. 245.

[27] *Stewart v. U.K.* (1985) 7 E.H.R.R. 453, paras 16–18. See also *Andronicou and Constantinou v. Cyprus* (1998) 25 E.H.R.R. 491.

[28] *Ireland v. U.K.* (1979–80) 2 E.H.R.R. 25.

[29] *Tyrer v. U.K.* (1979–80) 2 E.H.R.R. 1, para. 30.

[30] *Denmark, Norway, Sweden and The Netherlands v. Greece (The Greek Case)* (1969) 12 Yearbook 186–510.

[31] *e.g. Costello-Roberts v. U.K.* , 1993 Series A, No. 247–C; *Campbell and Cosans v. U.K.* (1982) 4 E.H.R.R. 293; *Y v. U.K.* (1994) 17 E.H.R.R. 238.

3.[32] Nor may forcible feeding and medical treatment carried out on mental patients.[33] Close body searches of prisoners and confinement in isolation have been held not to amount to degrading treatment.[34] But violence in police custody over a considerable period of time may constitute a violation.[35] Expulsion from a country may involve treatment contrary to Article 3,[36] as may extradition[37] or the expulsion of asylum seekers.[38] Discrimination on the ground of race may constitute degrading treatment.[39]

Prohibition of Slavery and Forced Labour (Article 4)

Slavery or servitude

The prohibition here is absolute. But it is not likely to be invoked in judicial review proceedings. Slavery is the subject of international labour conventions[40] which have been ratified by the United Kingdom. **16.14**

Forced or compulsory labour

In the finding by a majority of the members of the Commission that an allegation of forced or compulsory labour was not established in the application *Iversen v. Norway*, some of the members who took the majority view identified two elements of forced or compulsory labour as follows: "first, that the work or service is performed by the worker against his will and, secondly, that the requirement that the work or service be performed is unjust or oppressive or the work or service itself involves avoidable hardship".[41] The former of these two is the principal consideration. The whole circumstances must be assessed including the burden of the obligation upon the particular complainant.[42] Consent should be no defence to a complaint under Article 4(2).[43] **16.15**

The exceptions. Four cases are expressly excluded from constituting "forced or compulsory labour". The first is work done in the ordinary course of detention or during conditional release. This includes work done under contract with private firms entered into by the prison authorities.[44] Under the second exception, that of military service, it has **16.16**

---

[32] *Ziedler-Kormann v. Federal Republic of Germany* (1968) 11 Yearbook 1020.

[33] *Herczegfalvy v. Austria* (1993) 15 E.H.R.R. 437.

[34] *McFeeley v. U.K.* (1981) 3 E.H.R.R. 161.

[35] *Tomasi v. France* (1993) 15 E.H.R.R. 1.

[36] *Amekrame v. U.K.* (1973) 44 C.D. 101.

[37] *Soering v. U.K.* (1989) 11 E.H.R.R. 439, paras 86–91. The applicant in that case, if extradited, might have been sentenced to death.

[38] *Vilvarajah v. U.K.* (1992) 14 E.H.R.R. 248 (where it was held that in the circumstances there was no violation of Art. 3).

[39] *East African Asians v. U.K.* (1973) 3 E.H.R.R. 76.

[40] These are Conventions agreed under the auspices of the International Labour Organisation; in particular, see the International Convention with the object of Securing the Abolition of Slavery and the Slave Trade, Geneva, 1926 (Cmd 2910), and the Supplementary Convention 1956 (Cmnd 257).

[41] *Iversen v. Norway* (1963) 6 Yearbook 278 at 328.

[42] *Van der Mussele v. Belgium* (1984) 6 E.H.R.R. 163, para. 37 (where a pupil advocate was required to represent clients without payment).

[43] *De Wilde, Ooms and Versyp v. Belgium (No. 1)* (1979–80) 1 E.H.R.R. 373, para. 65.

[44] *Twenty-One Detained Persons v. Federal Republic of Germany* (1968) 11 Yearbook 528. See also *Van Droogenbroeck v. Belgium* (1982) 4 E.H.R.R. 443 (work done by prisoners).

been held that the refusal of discharges for young recruits to the army and navy did not constitute forced or compulsory labour.[45] The third exception relates to services exacted in situations of emergency, and is unlikely to arise in the context of judicial review. The fourth exception relates to work or service forming part of normal civic obligations. The last phrase lacks precise definition, but an obligation on a lawyer to act unpaid for a poor person in criminal proceedings was considered not to fall within it.[46]

Common law

16.17 In one early case[47] regulations imposed by magistrates on the working practices of journeymen-tailors were seen to encroach on the liberty of the subject, but the court held that the encroachment was justified in relation to a trade which provided a commodity necessary for society and that some control was thereby permitted to the magistrates and justices of the peace "under review of the sovereign court".[48]

Liberty and Security (Article 5)

Deprivation of liberty

16.18 Whether a particular person has been deprived of his or her liberty or merely suffered a restriction on his liberty is a question of the degree and intensity of the restraints imposed, rather than the nature or substance of them: regard is to be had to such matters as the extent of the geographical limitation, the degree of supervision, the practicability of social contacts and the duration of the restraint.[49] A confinement to barracks may not constitute a deprivation, it being explained that account should be taken of a whole range of factors such as the nature, duration, effects and manner of execution of the penalty or the measure in question.[50] The return to custody of a prisoner sentenced to an indeterminate life sentence following on further offending during release on licence has been seen as connected with the original conviction where the object of the sentencing court was to secure continual supervision and the opportunity for release when such a course was safe, so that the return to prison was compatible with the original sentence and with Article 5(1).[51]

Security

16.19 Security of person in this context appears to mean little if anything more than liberty. It is with personal liberty that the Article is concerned and the additional reference to security disappears after the first sentence. The Article prescribes the sole circumstances in which deprivation of

---

[45] *W,X,Y and Z v. U.K.* (1968) 11 Yearbook 562.
[46] *Gussenbauer v. Austria* (1973) C.D. 41 and 94.
[47] *Tailors of Edinburgh v. Their Journeymen* (1762) M. 7682.
[48] It was the magistrates and the justices who had the power to make regulations, not the sheriff, the former being "more popular, more connected with, and supposed to be more kindly towards the inhabitants": *Incorporation of Tailors v. White* (1777) M. App. Jur., Pt I, No. 6.
[49] *Guzzardi v. Italy* (1980) 3 E.H.R.R. 333.
[50] *Engel v. The Netherlands* (1979–80) 1 E.H.R.R. 647, para. 59.
[51] *Weeks v. U.K.* (1988) 10 E.H.R.R. 293. But there was a breach of Art. 5(4).

liberty is permitted and continues with a detail of the rights of those arrested.

Lawful procedure

While the Article specified six exceptional cases in which persons may be **16.20** detained, it is necessary that in each case the detention is "in accordance with a procedure prescribed by law". This refers back to the particular domestic law. There must not only be a procedure laid down by law but that procedure must be followed in the particular case. Furthermore the procedure must be fair and proper.[52]

Arrest or detention

The six excepted cases are in summary as follows. **16.21**

(a) *Lawful detention after conviction.* The detention must be by a competent court, which need not be the sentencing court.[53]

(b) *Lawful arrest or detention after disobeying a court order or to secure fulfilment of an obligation.* The reference to obligation here is open to a wide construction, but the obligation must be a specific and concrete obligation.[54]

(c) *Lawful arrest or detention of a suspect or to prevent offending or flight.* In the case of a suspect the suspicion must satisfy the objective test of a reasonable suspicion.[55] In a complex case a considerable period of detention may be acceptable where there is a danger of absconding or re-offending.[56] The arrest and detention under this sub-paragraph must be, as the provision states, for the purpose of bringing the person before the competent legal authority, which must, in terms of Article 5(3), be achieved within a reasonable time.[57]

(d) *Detention of a minor for educational supervision or to bring him before the competent legal authority.* Placement in a children's home may fall within this exception.[58]

(e) *Lawful detention to prevent the spread of infection, or of persons of unsound mind, alcoholics, drug addicts or vagrants.* In the case of detention of the mentally ill a measure of discretion is permitted to the domestic authorities.[59] The opportunity of access to a court may be required.[60] Whether a person is a vagrant is a matter to be determined in accordance with the ordinary use of language and in light of the national law.[61]

(f) *Lawful arrest or detention of illegal immigrants or deportees.* Lawfulness here, as elsewhere, involves the absence of any arbitrary action, so that compliance with prescribed procedures is required.[62] The authorities must act with reasonable expedition in dealing with such cases.[63]

---

[52] *Winterwerp v. The Netherlands* (1979–80) 2 E.H.R.R. 387, para. 45.
[53] *X v. Federal Republic of Germany* (1963) 6 Yearbook 494.
[54] *Engel v. The Netherlands* (1979–80) 1 E.H.R.R. 647, para. 69.
[55] *Fox, Campbell and Hartley v. U.K.* (1991) 13 E.H.R.R. 157.
[56] *Matznetter v. Austria* (1979–80) 1 E.H.R.R. 198.
[57] *Lawless v. Ireland (No. 3)* (1979–80) 1 E.H.R.R. 15.
[58] *Family T v. Austria* (1990) 64 D.R. 176.
[59] *Winterwerp v. The Netherlands* (1979–80) 2 E.H.R.R. 387, para. 40.
[60] *Megyeri v. Germany* (1993) 15 E.H.R.R. 584.
[61] *De Wilde, Ooms and Versyp v. Belgium (No. 1)* (1979–80) 1 E.H.R.R. 373, p. 404.
[62] *Bazano v. France* (1987) 9 E.H.R.R. 297, para. 59.
[63] *Klompar v. Belgium* (1993) 16 E.H.R.R. 197: see *The Chahal Family v. U.K.* (1996) 23 E.H.R.R. 413.

Right to know reasons (Article 5(2))

16.22 Notification must be given under Article 5(2) in a language which the detained person understands, but it may be given in general terms.[64] It should be given reasonably promptly.[65]

Right to prompt hearing (Article 5(3))

16.23 Under Article 5(3) the person arrested or detained must be brought promptly[66] before a judge or other officer authorised by the law to exercise judicial power[67] and be entitled to trial within a reasonable time or to release pending trial. A high standard of promptness, verging on immediacy, is required here.[68] The requirement for a trial within a reasonable time has given rise to considerable case law for which reference should be made to the specialised textbooks. It may suffice to point out that release is not a simple alternative to trial within a reasonable time; that later obligation remains fundamental.[69]

Proceedings to determine lawfulness of detention, Article 5(4)

16.24 Article 5(4) entitles the detainee to take proceedings for a speedy decision on the lawfulness of his detention. What is required here is opportunity for review of the lawfulness of the detention,[70] that is to say, an independant inquiry whether the reasons for the original detention continue to subsist.[71] Since the necessity for detention may change through the passage of time, the detainee is entitled to take proceedings for a hearing at reasonable intervals.[72] A speedy disposal of the issue is required,[73] but the assessment of the precise time-limit depends upon the circumstances.[74] Difficulties may arise in the implementation of the requirement for speed in the case of mental patients.[75]

Compensation

16.25 Article 5(5) provides for an enforceable right to compensation for arrest or detention in contravention of the terms of the Article. Provision is made by section 8 of the 1998 Act for possible awards of damages. But the particular provision in Article 5(5) makes the matter one of an enforceable right.

Common law

16.26 It was long ago affirmed that slavery is inconsistent with the principles of Scottish law.[76] The common law has recognised the limitations on arrest, detention and imprisonment, and on the liability to be searched. These

---

[64] *Nielson v. Denmark* (1958–59) 2 Yearbook 412 at 462.

[65] *Fox, Campbell and Hartley v. U.K.* (1991) 13 E.H.R.R. 157, para. 40; *Murray v. U.K.* (1995) 19 E.H.R.R. 193, para. 72.

[66] Six days, let alone 15 days, is an excessive delay: *McGoff v. Sweden* (1986) 8 E.H.R.R. 246. Four-and-a-quarter days, and longer periods, were held excessive in *Brogan v. U.K.* (1989) 11 E.H.R.R. 117.

[67] For this, see *Pauwels v. Belgium* (1989) 11 E.H.R.R. 238.

[68] *Koster v. The Netherlands* (1992) 14 E.H.R.R. 396; *Brogan v. U.K.* (1989) 11 E.H.R.R. 117.

[69] *Wemhoff v. Germany* (1979–80) 1 E.H.R.R. 55, paras 4–5.

[70] *E v. Norway* , 1990 Series A, No. 181, para. 50.

[71] *X v. U.K.* 1982 4 E.H.R.R. 188, paras 58–61. See *Weekes v. U.K.* (1988) 10 E.H.R.R. 293.

[72] *Hussain v. U.K.* (1996) 22 E.H.R.R. 1.

[73] *Bezicheri v. Italy* (1990) 12 E.H.R.R. 210.

[74] *Sanchez-Reisse v. Switzerland* (1987) 9 E.H.R.R. 71.

[75] *Van der Leer v. The Netherlands* (1990) 12 E.H.R.R. 567.

[76] *Knight v. Wedderburn* (1778) M. 14545.

matters have been discussed in the undernoted textbook.[77] But habeas corpus has never been part of Scots common law.[78]

Fair Trial (Article 6)

The full terms of Article 6(1) are of considerable importance and reference should be made to Appendix 1 where they are reproduced in the Schedule to the Act of 1998. Inherent in the Article is the securing of an effective access to a court.[79]   **16.27**

Civil rights and obligations

It is with the determination of these, as well as of criminal charges, that Article 6 is concerned. The expression covers all proceedings the result of which is decisive for private rights and obligations irrespective of whether the parties are public or private[80]; thus the phrase may not be open to definition in terms appropriate to national systems.[81] While it is an autonomous concept, the content and effects of the right under national law have to be taken into account.[82] It is thought that it will encompass all the matters which are subject to the supervisory jurisdiction.[83] A claim for sickness benefit may be a matter of civil right,[84] as may be a compulsory purchase by a local authority of private property,[85] or a decision to sell liquor.[86] So also is the disputed right to repayment of a fine for overproduction of milk.[87] For a determination there must be a dispute, that is to say a genuine and serious dispute, on the rights or obligations.[88] The dispute may relate to the existence of a right or to its scope or the manner of its exercise.[89]   **16.28**

Criminal charges

The classification of a matter as a criminal charge involves an autonomous concept in which domestic law may not be completely conclusive; the Convention allows a distinction between criminal law and disciplinary law.[90] Disciplinary proceedings which may lead to a termination of a right to continue in a professional practice can be a civil proceeding.[91] It is "an official notification given to an individual by a   **16.29**

---

[77] Fraser, *Constitutional Law* , Chap. XVII.

[78] Habeas corpus procedure existed in the Exchequer Court, but even there it was not a remedy for wrongful imprisonment, but a means of compelling the appearance of an alleged debtor; McNeil, "Habeas Corpus in Scotland", 1960 S.L.T. (News) 46. Note should be made of the Act for Preventing Wrongous Imprisonment 1701 Will. I, c.6. See also para. 2.21.

[79] *Golder v. U.K.* (1975) 1 E.H.R.R. 524 at 536.

[80] *H v. France* (1990) 12 E.H.R.R. 74.

[81] *Ringeisen v. Austria* (1979–80) 1 E.H.R.R. 455, para. 94; *James v. U.K.* (1986) 8 E.H.R.R. 123.

[82] *Konig v. Federal Republic of Germany* (1979–80) 2 E.H.R.R. 170.

[83] For examples of matters which have fallen within the scope of Art. 6, see Jacobs and White, *The European Convention on Human Rights* (2nd ed.), p. 131. See also Richards "The Impact of Art. 6 of the ECHR on Judicial Review" (1999) 4 Jud. Rev. 106.

[84] *Feldbrugge v. The Netherlands* (1986) 8 E.H.R.R. 425.

[85] *Sporrong and Lonnroth v. Sweden* (1983) 5 E.H.R.R. 35.

[86] *Tre Traktorer Aktielbolag v. Sweden* (1991) 13 E.H.R.R. 309.

[87] *Procola v. Luxembourg* (1996) 22 E.H.R.R. 193.

[88] *Benthem v. The Netherlands* (1986) 8 E.H.R.R. 1, para. 33.

[89] *Balmer-Schafroth v. Switzerland* (1998) 25 E.H.R.R. 598.

[90] *Engel v. The Netherlands (No. 1)* (1979–80) 1 E.H.R.R. 647, para. 81.

[91] *Philis v. Greece (No. 2)* (1998) 25 E.H.R.R. 417.

competent authority of an allegation that he has committed a criminal offence".[92]

An independent and impartial tribunal

16.30 The tribunal must be established by law. There must be a real and evident absence of any bias. This will depend on such things as the manner of appointment of its members, the duration of their term of office, the existence of guarantees against outside pressures and whether it presents an appearance of independence.[93] There must be an objective impartiality and a structural independence.[94] Thus, even if he is in fact personally impartial, the appearance of a former member of the public prosecutor's department who may have had to deal with the case will be a breach of the Article if he sits as a judge in the trial.[95] But the making of pre-trial decisions by a judge will not disqualify him,[96] provided that he has not made extensive investigations.[97]

Fairness

16.31 Fairness involves, first, an equality of arms, that is to say that "each party must be afforded a reasonable opportunity to present his case–including his evidence–under conditions that do not place him at a substantial disadvantage *vis-à-vis* his opponent".[98] Application of a rule giving immunity to the police from liability for reparation in relation to operational decisions has been held to constitute a disproportionate restriction on the aggrieved person's right of access to a court.[99] Free legal advice may be required in order to secure fairness.[1] The obligation may extend in some circumstances to the provision of legal aid,[2] of an interpreter[3] and of legal representation.[4] In *Murray v. United Kingdom*[5] Article 6(1) was held to be applicable to the stages of a preliminary investigation by the police and the denial of access to a lawyer for the first 48 hours of the applicant's detention constituted a breach of the Article. Secondly each party must have the opportunity to have knowledge of and comment on the observations and evidence presented by the other party.[6] This may include the opportunity to recover by order of the court documentary material required for the defence of an accused person.[7] Thirdly, there should be a reasoned decision given by the tribunal.

---

[92] *Eckle v. Germany* (1983) 5 E.H.R.R. 1, para. 73.

[93] *Campbell and Fell v. U.K.* (1985) 7 E.H.R.R. 165, para. 78.

[94] In *Findlay v. U.K.* (1996) 21 E.H.R.R. C.D. 7 the link between the convening officer and the prosecution was enough to destroy independence.

[95] *Piersach v. Belgium* (1983) 5 E.H.R.R. 169.

[96] *Hauschildt v. Denmark* (1990) 12 E.H.R.R. 266.

[97] *De Cubber v. Belgium* (1985) 7 E.H.R.R. 236. Reference may be made to the discussion later on bias: paras 18.12 *et seq.* See also *Pullar v. U.K.* (1996) 22 E.H.R.R. 391 (juror employed by a key witness).

[98] *Dombo Beheer BV v. The Netherlands* (1994) 18 E.H.R.R. 213, para. 33.

[99] *Osman v. U.K.* [1998] E.H.R.L.R. 101; in the Commission.

[1] *Granger v. U.K.* (1990) 12 E.H.R.R. 469, para. 46–47. See para. 18–42 on legal assistance.

[2] *Maxwell v. U.K.* (1995) 19 E.H.R.R. 97.

[3] *Brozicek v. Italy* (1990) 12 E.H.R.R. 371.

[4] *Airey v. Ireland* (1979) 2 E.H.R.R. 305. See para. 18.42.

[5] (1996) 22 E.H.R.R. 29.

[6] *Ruiz-Mateos v. Spain* (1993) 16 E.H.R.R. 505, para. 63–68. See also *Unterpertinger v. Austria* (1991) 13 E.H.R.R. 175 (no cross-examination of evidence contained in witness statements); *Kotovski v. Netherlands* (1900) 12 E.H.R.R. 434 (anonymous witness).

[7] *Lamy v. Belgium* (1989) 11 E.H.R.R. 529; *McLeod, Petr*, 1998 S.L.T. 233.

Reasons

The obligation to give reasons which is recognised by the European **16.32**
Court of Human Rights,[8] is implied in Article 6(1) as an aspect of
fairness. But the substance of the reasons is a matter which depends on
the circumstances of the case.[9] Every point raised in argument need not
be included in the reasons.[10] The extent of the reasons must depend on
the nature of each case, but submissions which could be decisive of the
case should be included.[11] Moreover, in assessing the validity of the
proceedings under Article 6(1) account should be taken of the existence
of a right of appeal or even of the availability of judicial review. As was
recognised in *Bryan v. United Kingdom*,[12] even where there has been a
failure in compliance with Article 6(1) no violation can be found if the
proceedings are "subject to subsequent control by a judicial body that
has full jurisdiction and does provide the guarantees of Article 6 para 1".
If such an appeal or review is wide enough to make good any
deficiencies in the decision challenged in respect of a lack of reasons,
then while the obligation to give reasons remains, the result will not be
to invalidate the decision, because the proceedings viewed as a whole
may be regarded as fair. In one case it was observed that the court must
indicate with sufficient clarity the grounds on which they base their
decision so that the accused may usefully exercise the right of appeal
available to him.[13]

Public hearing

The hearing must not only be fair but must be public; the latter **16.33**
requirement is qualified by a list of exceptions, but the judgment must be
pronounced publicly. While a wide margin of appreciation may be
applied here, proceedings before an Appeals Council in private will
contravene the Article.[14] That confidential medical material will be
disclosed in a medical disciplinary proceeding has not justified a private
hearing.[15] The hearing must also be such as to explore the whole
substance of the decision. So a process of judicial review which does not
allow of an examination of the merits of the case[16] or a Court of
Cassation[17] will not meet the requirements of Article 6(1).

Reasonable time

The requirement that criminal proceedings be brought within a reason- **16.34**
able time is well established in Scotland, but in so far as the court has
accepted that the period may run from a date earlier than the bringing

---

[8] *Van der Hurk v. The Netherlands* (1994) 18 E.H.R.R. 481. See later paras 17.23 *et seq.*
and para. 18–52.
[9] *Helle v. Finland* (1998) 26 E.H.R.R. 159.
[10] *Van der Hurk v. Netherlands* (1994) 18 EHHR 481.
[11] *Hiro Balani v. Spain* (1995) 19 E.H.R.R. 566.
[12] (1995) 20 E.H.R.R. 342. The appeal there was only on a point of law, but that was
sufficient. See also *Wickramsinghe v. U.K.* , Application No. 31503/96 where appeal to the
Privy Council from a decision of the medical professional practice committee was
sufficient.
[13] *Hadjianasassiou v. Greece* (1993) 16 E.H.R.R. 219.
[14] *Albert and Le Compte v. Belgium* (1983) 5 E.H.R.R. 533, para. 37; *Stallinger and Kuso
v. Austria* (1998) 26 E.H.R.R. 81.
[15] *Diennet v. France* (1996) 21 E.H.R.R. 554.
[16] *Sporrong and Lonnroth v. Sweden* (1983) 5 E.H.R.R. 35.
[17] *Le Compte, Van Leuven and De Meyere v. Belgium* (1982) 4 E.H.R.R. 1.

of any charge[18] challenge may be available. But the Article applies to matters of civil right as well as criminal proceedings and it may be particularly in this context that problems may arise. Whether a delay is reasonable depends first on the ascertainment of the period and then on a consideration of all the circumstances.[19] The circumstances may include the complexity of the case, the conduct of the appellant and that of the relevant authorities, and the background to the matter.[20] The period starts to run from the date of the commencment of the proceedings, such as the filing of an application to set aside a decision[21] and it continues up until the decision which disposes of the dispute.[22] It may include the passage of several procedures where a succession of applications for redress have occurred.[23] A delay of over three years at one level of the court structure will probably be regarded as unreasonable.[24] Periods of between some four and six years were held unreasonable in complex cases of claims for damages for having contracted the Human Immunodeficiency Virus.[25] Only delay attributable to the state may justify a complaint of a failure to comply with a "reasonable time" requirement.[26] In criminal cases the date of arrest has been taken as the starting point,[27] and in the case of a retrial ordered by the court, the date of the order for the retrial.[28] A backlog of business will not serve to excuse unreasonable delays.[29]

Criminal trials

16.35 The presumption of innocence is affirmed in Article 6(2) and there follows a list of the minimum rights to which persons charged with criminal offences are entitled. A survey of these is beyond the scope of this summary and reference should be made to other works for discussion of them.

Retrospective Legislation (Article 7)

16.36 The provision that offences cannot be created with retrospective effect is unlikely to feature significantly in judicial review. If such a problem were to arise it should find a remedy within the ordinary civil or criminal process.[30]

---

[18] *e.g. Eckle v. Germany* (1983) 5 E.H.R.R. 1.

[19] *e.g. Silva Pontes v. Portugal* (1994) 18 E.H.R.R. 156.

[20] *H v. France* (1990) 12 E.H.R.R. 74; *Moreira de Azevedo v. Portugal* (1991) 13 E.H.R.R. 721, para. 71; *Milasi v. Italy* (1988) 10 E.H.R.R. 333.

[21] *De Moor v. Belgium* (1994) 18 E.H.R.R. 372. It may start before the issue of a writ; *Konig v. Federal Republic of Germany* (1978) 2 E.H.R.R. 170.

[22] *Guillemin v. France* (1998) 25 E.H.R.R. 435.

[23] *Darnell v. U.K.* (1994) 18 E.H.R.R. 205.

[24] *Zimmerman and Steiner v. Switzerland* (1984) 6 E.H.R.R. 17, para. 23.

[25] *A and Others v. Denmark* (1996) 22 E.H.R.R. 458.

[26] *Zimmerman , supra* , para. 24; *cf . Vernillo v. France* (1991) 13 E.H.R.R. 880.

[27] In *Mungroo v. The Queen* [1991] 1 W.L.R. 1351 the date of arrest was taken as the starting point and account was taken of the period before the accused was arrested.

[28] *Bell v. DPP* [1985] 1 A.C. 937 (a decision under the corresponding provisions of the Constitution of Jamaica).

[29] *Hentrich v. France* (1994) 18 E.H.R.R. 440, para. 61.

[30] For a discussion on the constitutionality of retrospective legislation see I.S. Dickinson, "Retrospective Legislation and the British Constitution" 1974 S.L.T. (News) 25. For an example, see *Welch v. U.K.* (1995) 20 E.H.R.R. 247.

Private and Family Life (Article 8)

Privacy

The right to private life extends beyond the right to live as one wishes, **16.37** protected from publicity, and comprises "to a certain degree, the right to establish and develop relationships with other human beings especially in the emotional field, for the development and fulfilment of one's own personality".[31] Private life may thus extend to activities of a professional or business nature.[32] Restraints on homosexual activity may breach the Article,[33] as may the failure to balance the interests of the individual against the general interest in the case of a transsexual.[34] The use of tape recordings of conversations and all the complex technology of communications may well give rise to new problems under the head of privacy. Phone-tapping requires to be controlled by express regulation so as to be in accordance with law.[35] Secret surveillance is only tolerable if it is strictly necessary for safeguarding democratic institutions and a balance has to be made between the right to privacy and the necessity for the surveillance in the interest of national security and the prevention of disorder or crime.[36] The common law has also recognised the need to protect privacy.[37]

Correspondence and records

Under Article 8 interference with written communications is prohibited. **16.38** The question whether the supervision of prisoners' correspondence can be defended under the exceptions set out in Article 8(2) depends upon whether the interference is necessary "having regard to the ordinary and reasonable requirements of imprisonment".[38] While it is recognised that some measure of control may be exercised by virtue of the exceptions "the resulting interference must not exceed what is required by the legitimate aim pursued".[39] In *Campbell v. United Kingdom*[40] the question was whether interference with communications between a prisoner and his solicitor was necessary in a democratic society. The Court saw no need to distinguish between different kinds of correspondence with lawyers—in principle all such private and confidential letters are protected by Article 8. In that case there was no pressing social need to open and read the letters. Article 8 also relates to official records relating to an applicant.[41]

Family life

Reference here should be made to the right to found a family contained **16.39** in Article 12. The concept of family embraces the interrelationships of parents and children and the links between them, even in the matter of

---

[31] *X v. Ireland* (1976) 5 D.R. 86.
[32] *Niemietz v. Germany* (1993) 16 E.H.R.R. 97.
[33] *Dudgeon v. U.K.* (1982) 4 E.H.R.R. 149. See also *Laskey and Others v. U.K.* (1997) 24 E.H.R.R. 39 and *Sutherland v. U.K.* [1998] E.H.R.L.R. 117.
[34] *R. v. France* (1993) 16 E.H.R.R. 1.
[35] *Malone v. U.K.* (1982) 4 E.H.R.R. 330 at 450.
[36] *Klass v. Germany* (1978) 2 E.H.R.R. 214. See also Art. 2.
[37] *e.g. Singh*, 1988 G.W.D. 32–1377.
[38] *Golder v. U.K.* (1979–80) 1 E.H.R.R. 524, para. 45. Also *Silver v. UK* (1983) 5 E.H.R.R. 347.
[39] *Pfeifer and Plankl v. Austria* (1992) 14 E.H.R.R. 692, para. 46; *cf . De Wilde, Ooms and Versyp v. Belgium* (1971) 1 E.H.R.R. 373.
[40] 1992 Series A, No. 223.
[41] *e.g. Gaskin v. U.K.* (1990) 12 E.H.R.R. 36.

name,[42] but is eventually a matter to be determined on the facts with regard being paid to the constancy of the relationship.[43] A deportation involving interference with the deportee's relationship with his parents, brothers and sisters has been held not to be "necessary in a democratic society".[44] But the importance of uniting a family may be outweighed by the State's right to control the settlement of non-nationals within its borders.[45] The concept is not limited to marriage-based relationships,[46] but extends to unmarried and engaged couples.[47] Despite the modern evolution in attitudes towards homosexuality, a stable homosexual relationship does not fall within the scope of the right to respect for family life, but is a matter affecting private life.[48] Access to children and questions regarding children in care fall within the Article.[49] Matters affecting family life may also arise in the context of immigration.[50]

Freedom of Thought, Conscience and Religion (Article 9)

16.40 The only limitations on the rights in Article 9 are set out in Article 9(2) and relate only to the freedom to manifest one's religion or beliefs.[51] Restraints imposed by the United Kingdom on the members of the Church of Scientology were held not to contravene Article 9,[52] but persistent evangelism amounting to improper proselytism by Jehovah's Witnesses was found to breach the rights protected by the Article.[53] It is also to be noted that a special provision was added to the Act in section 13, with a view to meeting the concerns expressed by certain religious bodies.[54]

Freedom of Expression (Article 10)

16.41 A wide variety of forms of expression are covered by this Article. It covers writings, broadcasting, films and all forms of artistic expression. It covers expression on political matters,[55] on commercial matters,[56] and expressions presented through the medium of art.[57] A refusal to grant a licence for a private radio station has been held to constitute a breach.[58] The right is not absolute, but is restricted by the limitations contained in Article 10(2).

---

[42] *Burghartz v. Switzerland* (1994) 18 E.H.R.R. 101.
[43] *Kroon v. Netherlands* (1995) 19 E.H.R.R. 263.
[44] *Moustaquim v. Belgium* (1991) 13 E.H.R.R. 802.
[45] *Gul v. Switzerland* (1996) 22 E.H.R.R. 93.
[46] *Keegan v. Ireland* (1994) 18 E.H.R.R. 342.
[47] *Wakeford v. U.K.* (1990) 66 D.R. 251.
[48] *S. v. U.K.* (1986) 47 D.R. 274 (No. 11716/85); see also *B v. U.K.* (1990) D.R. 278 (No. 16106/90), and Jane Liddy, "The Concept of Family Life under the ECHR" [1998] E.H.R.L.R. 15.
[49] *W v. U.K.* (1988) 10 E.H.R.R. 29; *Olssen v. Sweden* (1989) 11 E.H.R.R. 259.
[50] *e.g. Abdulaziz, Cabales and Balkandali v. U.K.* (1985) 7 E.H.R.R. 471.
[51] On this Art. see P.W. Edge, "Current Problems in Art. 9 of the European Convention on Human Rights", 1996 J.R. 42.
[52] *Church of X v. U.K.* (1969) 12 Yearbook 306.
[53] *Kokkimakis v. Greece* (1994) 17 E.H.R.R. 397.
[54] The question has been raised whether section 13 is compatible with the Convention rights.
[55] *Lingens v. Austria* (1986) 8 E.H.R.R. 407.
[56] *Markt Intern and Beermann v. Germany* (1990) 12 E.H.R.R. 161.
[57] *Muller and Others v. Switzerland* (1991) 13 E.H.R.R. 212, para. 27.
[58] *Radio ABC v. Austria* (1997) 25 E.H.R.R. 185.

Prescribed by law

To be effective the limitations must be "prescribed by law". The law may **16.42** be written or unwritten, but it must be adequately accessible. "The citizen must be able to have an indication that is adequate in the circumstances of the legal rules applicable to a given case" and it must also be of sufficient precision to enable the citizen to foresee to a reasonable standard the consequences which a given conduct may entail.[59] The law may be one which confers a discretion, provided that the scope of the discretion and the manner of its exercise could be clearly understood.[60]

Necessary in a democratic society

This test involves considerations of proportionality and a margin of **16.43** appreciation. "The notion of necessity implies that the interference corresponds to a pressing social need and, in particular, that it is proportionate to the legitimate aim pursued".[61] Different states may form different standards on such matters as obscenity and recognition should be given to that.[62] Pressing social need and the public interest in the freedom of expression have to be weighed in deciding whether the test is met.[63] A margin of appreciation is left to the member states.[64] The national court's asessment of the importance of the interests of national security may be allowed to outweigh the importance of free speech.[65] Insistence on the disclosure of a journalist's sources may, despite the state's margin of appreciation, in particular circumstances be held disproportionate to the legitimate aim pursued.[66]

Restriction on political activities of aliens

By virtue of Article 16 nothing in Article 10 is to prevent the imposition **16.44** by the state on the political activity of aliens. This provision relates also to Articles 11 and 14.

Common law

Freedom of discussion, which includes freedom of speech and freedom **16.45** of the press, is recognised as an essential element of a free society in Scots law.[67] It is subject to the restraints imposed by the law of defamation and by certain criminal sanctions where the right is abused. The matter is discussed in the undernoted work.[68]

Judicial remedies and freedom of expression

Section 12 has the effect of giving some priority in appropriate cases to **16.46** the Convention right to freedom of expression. First, in the absence of "compelling reasons", no *ex parte* order should be granted in civil

---

[59] *The Sunday Times v. U.K.* (1979–80) 2 E.H.R.R. 245, para. 49.
[60] *Brind v. U.K.* (1994) 77–A D.R. 42.
[61] *Olssen v. Sweden* (1989) 11 E.H.R.R. 259, para. 67.
[62] *Handyside v. U.K.* (1979–80) 1 E.H.R.R. 737 (the "Little Red Book"); *Muller and Others v. Switzerland* (1988) 13 E.H.R.R. 212.
[63] *The Sunday Times v. U.K.* (1979–80) 2 E.H.R.R. 243.
[64] *e.g. W v. U.K.* (1988) 10 E.H.R.R. 29, para. 60.
[65] *Observer and Guardian v. U.K.(1992) 14 E.H.R.R. 153 (the Spycatcher* case).
[66] *Goodwin v. U.K.* (1996) 22 E.H.R.R. 123. On the restriction on freedom of expression by state employees, see *De Freitas v. The Permanent Secretary of Ministry of Agriculture, Fisheries, Lands and Housing* [1998] 3 W.L.R. 675 (PC).
[67] See *Lord Advocate v. Scotsman Publications Ltd* , 1987 S.L.T. 705.
[68] Fraser, *Constitutional Law* (2nd ed.), Chap. XVIII.

proceedings which would affect the exercise of the right to freedom of expression. Secondly, no pre-publication restraints on freedom of expression are permitted in civil proceedings unless the court is satisfied that the applicant is likely to establish that publication should not be allowed. Thirdly, in relation to "journalistic, literary or artistic material (or to conduct connected with such material)", a court or tribunal must "have particular regard to the importance of" freedom of expression, to "any relevant privacy code", and to the extent to which: "(i) the material has, or is about to, become available to the public; or (ii) it is, or would be, in the public interest for the material to be published."[69] These provisions may have some relevance in a judicial review case where, for example, a public authority decides to exercise censorship powers and its decisions are challenged for violation of the right to freedom of expression guaranteed by Article 10 of the Convention. Similarly, the effect of section 13 of the 1998 Act is to give a priority to the Article 9 right to freedom of religion as it is exercised by a "religious organisation" where the latter's acts or decisions are challenged under the 1998 Act.

Freedom of Assembly and Association (Article 11)

Assembly

16.47 The right is one to a freedom of peaceful assembly. The right is "a fundamental right in a democratic society and, like the freedom of expression, is one of the foundations of such a society . . . As such this right covers both private meetings and meetings in public thoroughfares".[70] The right is exercised in particular by persons taking part in peaceful processions.[71] But again the right is subject to limitations. In relation to the phrase "necessary in a democratic society" in this context the court has said[72]: "The proportionality principle demands that a balance be struck between the requirements of the purposes listed in Article 11(2) and those of the free expresssion of opinions, by word, gesture or even silence by persons assembled on the streets or in other public places. The pursuit of a just balance must not result in *avocats* being discouraged for fear of disciplinary sanctions, from making clear their beliefs on such occasions".

Association

16.48 This includes freedom of the forming and joining associations,[73] but may not include any particular rights claimed by an association in relation to the state.[74] Trade unions are expressly included in the Article,[75] although compulsion to join a trade union may not always be contrary to the Convention.[76] But a lawful restriction may be made in the case of government servants by virtue of their being "members of the administration of the state".[77] Professional disciplinary bodies may not fall

---

[69] s.12(4).
[70] *Rassemblement Jurassien v. Switzerland* (1979) 17 D.R. 93 at 119.
[71] *Ezelin v. France* (1992) 14 E.H.R.R. 362, para. 37.
[72] *ibid* . para. 52. .
[73] *Young, James and Webster v. U.K.* (1982) 4 E.H.R.R. 38.
[74] *National Union of Belgian Police v. Belgium* (1975) 1 E.H.R.R. 578 (where a right to be consulted was claimed).
[75] *National Union of Belgian Police v. Belgium* (1979) 1 E.H.R.R. 578.
[76] *Gusafsson v. Sweden* (1996) 22 E.H.R.R. 409.
[77] *Council of Civil Service Unions v. U.K.* (1988) 10 E.H.R.R. 269.

within the Article as "associations",[78] but an association of taxi-drivers has been held to be included.[79]

Common law

The right to hold public meetings is recognised at common law as an **16.49** essential right for an effective democracy. It is subject to certain restraints with regard to the places in which the right may be exercised and the manner in which it is exercised. These restraints are either qualifications of the right itself or distinct limitations imposed by the criminal law. The matter is discussed in the undernoted work.[80] The problem of assemblies on the public highway has been discussed in *Director of Public Prosecutions v. Jones*.[81]

The Right to Marry (Article 12)

This right, with the right to found a family, is expressed without **16.50** qualification beyond that it be according to the national law. But it does not go so far as to require a state to accept for settlement into that state non-national spouses who happen to choose to set up their matrimonial residence there.[82] The right to marry refers to the traditional marriage between persons of the opposite biological sex.[83] The Article includes remarriage.[84]

Protection of Property

The peaceful enjoyment of his possessions is secured to every natural or **16.51** legal person by Article I of the First Protocol. This guarantees a right of property.[85] Possessions include moveables as well as heritage, incorporeals as well as corporeals. A vested right to an inheritance, but not a future prospective right, falls within the scope of property.[86] A breach occurs where the state has interfered with the peaceful enjoyment of property, or the state has deprived a person of free possession, or the state has imposed controls on possession.[87] The compulsory transfer of property in the pursuit of a legitimate social or economic policy, on which the view of the national legislature will be respected, may not constitute a breach of the provision.[88] But the suspension by government policy of the enforcement of decrees of eviction may be unfair to the landlord and constitute a breach of the provision.[89] At least in relation to private heritable property the common law has recognised a right to quiet enjoyment of it.[90] In relation to E.C. law it may be noted that in

---

[78] *Le Compte, Van Leuven and De Meyere v. Belgium* (1982) 4 E.H.R.R. 1.
[79] *Sigurdar A Sigurjonsson v. Iceland* (1993) 16 E.H.R.R. 462.
[80] Fraser, *Constitutional Law* (2nd ed.), Chap. XIX.
[81] House of Lords, Mar. 4, 1999, unreported.
[82] *Abdulaziz and Others v. U.K.* (1985) 7 E.H.R.R. 471, para. 68.
[83] *Rees v. U.K.* (1987) 9 E.H.R.R. 56, para. 49.
[84] *F. v. Switzerland* (1987) 10 E.H.R.R. 411.
[85] *Marckx v. Belgium* (1979–80) 2 E.H.R.R. 330, para. 63. On the taking of property without compensation in relation to the provisions of the Constitution of Mauritius, see *Société United Docks v. Government of Mauritius* [1985] 1 A.C. 585. But a modest scale of compensation may be justified on the nationalisation of an industry: *Lithgow v. U.K.* (1986) 8 E.H.R.R. 329; see also *The Holy Monasteries v. Greece* (1994) 20 E.H.R.R. 1.
[86] *Inze v. Austria* (1988) 10 E.H.R.R. 394.
[87] *Sporrong and Lonnroth v. Sweden* (1983) 5 E.H.R.R. 35.
[88] *James v. U.K.* (1986) 8 E.H.R.R. 123.
[89] *Scollo v. Italy* (1996) 22 E.H.R.R. 514.
[90] See Fraser, *Constitutional Law* (2nd ed.), pp. 283–285.

Booker Aquaculture Ltd v. Secretary of State for Scotland[91] it was held that interference with an individual's freedom of property (a fish farm) by an order for destruction which went beyond the relevant E.C. Directive and was excessive and unjustified in the circumstances, rendered the Secretary of State liable to compensate the owner of the fish farm.

Education

16.52 The right to education is secured by Article 2 of the First Protocol. But it does not extend to the necessary provision of education of a particular type or subject.[92] Regard must be had to the wishes of parents in respect of religious education, at least in state schools.[93] It has been held that compulsory sex education did not contravene Article 2.[94] The United Kingdom has made a reservation to this provision.[95] The convictions to which the Article refers are views of a certain level of cogency, seriousness, cohesion, and importance,[96] but it is a question of circumstances whether the act complained of is such as to offend the conviction.

Free Elections

16.53 The states members of the Convention undertake by Article 3 of the First Protocol to hold free elections at reasonable intervals by secret ballot. This provision has been regarded as of fundamental importance as securing the protection of rights and freedoms through an effective political democracy.[97] The state is entitled, however, to disenfranchise people so that the right to vote is not guaranteed.[98]

The Death Penalty

16.54 Articles 1 and 2 of the Sixth Protocol are concerned with the death penalty, and are mentioned here only for the sake of completeness.

III GENERAL PROVISIONS

Introduction

16.55 Articles 14 to 18 of the Convention set out certain provisions which are generally applicable to the rights and freedoms contained in the Convention and Protocols.

Prohibition of discrimination

16.56 Article 14 provides that the Convention rights are to be secured without discrimination "on any ground such as sex, race, colour, language, religion, political or other opinion, national or social origin, association

---

[91] (1999) 1 C.M.L.R. 35 (on appeal, the decision of the Inner House on August 12, 1999 has not yet been reported).

[92] *Belgian Linguistic Cases* (1979–80) 1 E.H.R.R. 241 and 252.

[93] *Larnell and Hardt v. Sweden* (1971) 14 Yearbook 676.

[94] *Kjeldsen and Others v. Denmark* (1979–80) 1 E.H.R.R. 711. See also *Valsamis v. Greece* (1996) 24 E.H.R.R. 294.

[95] See Schedule 2 to the Act.

[96] *Campbell and Cosans v. U.K.* (1982) 4 E.H.R.R. 293.

[97] *Mathieu-Mohin and Clefayt v. Belgium* (1988) 10 E.H.R.R. 1.

[98] *X v. Belgium* (1961) 4 Yearbook 324 at 338.

with a national minority, property, birth or other status". It is to be noticed that this provision does not give a distinct free-standing right to complain of discrimination, but is only related to the securing of the Convention rights, so that the discrimination is to be avoided in the context of the existence of those rights.[99] A difference in treatment is not in itself discriminatory where there is a reasonable and objective justification for it.[1]

Prohibition of abuse of rights

Article 15 permits certain derogations in time of war or other public **16.57** emergency,[2] and Article 16 permits certain restriction on the political activities of aliens. Article 17 expressly provides that nothing in the Convention is to be interpreted as implying that any state, group or person has any right to engage in any activity or perform any act aimed at the destruction of any of the Convention rights or at their limitation to a greater extent than is provided for in the Convention. The matter of interpretation of the Convention has been considered earlier[3] but it is proper to note in the present context this express provision to secure the full extent of the rights in question.

Limitation on use of restrictions on rights

A further restraint on any attempt to defeat the purpose of the **16.58** Convention is contained in Article 18 whereby the scope of application of the various restrictions in the Convention is expressly limited to the particular context in which they occur.

---

[99] *cf*. the position in Canada in *Att.-Gen. of Canada v. Lavell* (1974) S.C.R. 1349.
[1] *Belgian Linguistic Case (No. 2)* (1978) 1 E.H.R.R. 252.
[2] See *Ireland v. U.K.* (1978) 2 E.H.R.R. 25.
[3] paras 6.14 *et seq.*

CHAPTER 17

BREACH OF PRESCRIBED PROCEDURES

I INTRODUCTION

General

The grounds of review which relate to matters of procedural irregularity **17.01** are of considerable importance for the supervisory jurisdiction of the court in judicial review. The requirement for a due process is a basic element in the structure of a fair system of justice. At a minimum this involves that decision making be carried out in accordance with fair procedures. This means at least that decision makers must be impartial and that interested parties must be given some opportunity to present their case before a decision is made. But the range of failures which may fall within the scope of procedural irregularity is considerable, giving this ground of review a particular significance.

Statute and common law

The controls on procedure may find their origin in express provision or **17.02** in the common law. This chapter is concerned with the former. Prescribed rules of procedure are often provided under a statutory power but they may originate in other ways, as by the authority of an organisation which has the power to make rules for the management of its affairs. Thus, for example, failure to comply with the rules of a trade union can be fatal to the validity of union decisions.[1] For ease of terminology all such prescribed rules may be referred to as statutory. Where there are prescribed rules, however originating, the procedural obligations may be found in the express terms of the rules or by implication from the express terms as a matter of construction. Both of these are to be understood as comprised within the scope of the present chapter. The various rules with which this chapter is concerned are designed to apply in the particular specific fields for which they have been prescribed. But they will often comprise provisions of a common substance and provisions will often be found which correspond with the procedural requirements of the common law. That reflects one of the basic purposes which procedural rules should be designed to serve, namely to secure that the exercise of particular powers is restrained and controlled generally with a view to serving the interests of justice and

---

[1] *M'Gregor v. NALGO*, 1979 S.C. 401.

fairness. Thus notice may require to be given in advance of the exercise of certain powers and opportunity given for representations to be made by interested parties.

Problems may arise in defining the interrelationship between statutory rules and the rules of the common law. Often the statutory provision will be seen as an embodiment of a common law rule so that no practical distinction can be made between them. It may be difficult to resolve how far the statutory rules are intended to serve as a complete code or how far they may be supplemented by the common law rules; but it is not to be assumed that what Parliament has done is unfair, and if Parliament has deliberately omitted to provide for a hearing in particular circumstances then it may be assumed that Parliament did not consider that fairness required a hearing to be held.[2]

Familiarity

17.03 One reason for the concern taken by the law in this area of challenge may be strengthened by the familiarity which lawyers and judges have with matters of procedure. The standards of fair procedure do not only arise in applications for judicial review but apply throughout the law, in both civil and criminal litigation and in arbitration. The courts also may feel more comfortable with the application of proper procedures than with matters of irrationality or error where the area of challenge may begin to encroach on the merits of the matter and the law may hesitate to intrude.

Technicality

17.04 But the greater the disposition to develop an interest in matters of procedure the greater may be the technicality which is consequently created. That in turn may lead to a diminution of administrative efficiency. Thus a balance has to be struck whereby the essential element of fairness is preserved consistently with the smooth running of the administrative process. There can be no doubt but that the priority must be to secure that all matters are managed in a just and fair manner. There are advantages both to the private citizen and to the public official if that is achieved. But caution has to be observed in order to secure that procedure does not develop into any undue technicality or that by being developed for its own sake it becomes the master rather than the servant.

Fairness

17.05 Formal rules of procedure should be assumed to be fair until the contrary is shown.[3] Fairness ought to lie at the heart of all procedural rules, whether prescribed by authority or laid down in the common law. It is with that concept that judicial review is particularly concerned. Formal procedures must be exercised fairly and it is to the matter of fairness to which the court's attention should be directed. Thus, in order to obtain relief by way of judicial review it is not enough merely to identify some point of procedure which is open to criticism. "The courts will only interfere if a procedural impropriety results in a breach of the

---

[2] *Pearlberg v. Varty* [1972] 1 W.L.R. 534.
[3] *cf. Furnell v. Whangarei High School Board* [1973)] A.C. 660 at 681.

law which will most frequently be based on an allegation that the objectors were being treated unfairly".[4] A failure to call in one of two competing planning applications may in particular circumstances be unfair and open to reduction.[5] Where an application was so dealt with as to result in depriving a person of a right to object, the authority was held to have acted unfairly and the decision was reduced.[6]

II STATUTORY RULES OF PROCEDURE

Omnia rite acta praesumuntur

The presumption that statutory procedural formalities have been com-   **17.06** plied with can be rebutted, but the person alleging a failure in observance must be able to identify where the alleged defect lies. The presumption does not operate to overcome the lack of a valid power.[7] Where there has been a delay in making the challenge the presumption may be the more difficult to overcome and a greater onus may be imposed on the person making the challenge.[8] This will be especially the position where the state of affairs which is under challenge has existed and been acted upon for many years.[9]

Mandatory and directory requirements

Where the statutory procedure states that some course "shall" be   **17.07** followed, or some similar language is used, a question may arise whether the provision is mandatory, so that a failure to follow the course may be fatal, or merely directory, so that that consequence should not follow. This is a matter to be resolved on a sound construction of the relevant provision. The problem also arises, as a matter of construction, in connection with the substance of the power itself, and that is considered elsewhere.[10] The context in which the word "may" is used may disclose, perhaps by the proximity of contrasting language, that a discretionary meaning is intended..[11] The normal interpretation of the word "shall" is that it is mandatory.[12] Where a statute provided that before revoking an agricultural grant the Secretary of State "shall" give the applicant a statement of the reasons for revocation, allow him an opportunity of being heard by someone appointed by him and "shall" consider the report by such person and supply a copy of the report to the applicant, it was held that there was a mandatory requirement on the Secretary of State and, since he had failed to send a copy of the report to the applicant and so deprived him of any opportunity to make representations about it the decision was reduced.[13] Where "shall" is used, the

---

[4] *R. v. Secretary of State for Transport, ex p. Gwent County Council* [1988] 1 Q.B. 429, *per* Woolf L.J. at 435.

[5] *Lakin Ltd v. Secretary of State for Scotland*, 1988 S.L.T. 780; but compare *Narden Services Ltd v. Secretary of State for Scotland*, 1993 S.L.T. 871 and *Asda Stores Ltd v. Secretary of State for Scotland*, 1999 S.L.T. 503.

[6] *Lochore v. Moray D.C.*, 1992 S.L.T. 16.

[7] *Allied Breweries (U.K.) Ltd v. City of Glasgow District Licensing Board*, 1985 S.L.T. 302.

[8] *Scott v. Magistrates of Dunoon*, 1909 S.C. 1093.

[9] *Presbytery of Stirling v. Heritors of Larbert and Dunipace* (1902) 4F. 1048.

[10] See para. 15.10 in the context of illegality and para. 20.02 in the context of misuse of power.

[11] *Gordon D.C. v. Hay*, 1978 S.C. 327.

[12] *London and Clydeside Estates Ltd v. Aberdeen D.C.*, 1980 S.C.(H.L.) 1; *Jolly v. Hamilton D.C.*, 1992 S.L.T. 387.

[13] *Ryrie (Balingery) Wick v. Secretary of State for Scotland*, 1988 S.L.T. 806.

words "so far as reasonably practicable" will not readily be implied.[14] The word "will" may reflect a future certainty and so reflect a mandatory purpose.[15] Apart from the use of words such as "shall" or "will" the context and the related provisions may point to the solution. A sanction of nullity, or the absence of such a sanction, may indicate whether or not a failure in compliance is fatal[16] but a provision may still be mandatory if it is clear and precise but lacks any sanction.[17] In one case where an authority had prepared a scheme under statutory powers and had included in it a time-limit for the determination of the charges which they could subsequently levy, they were held to have created a mandatory provision such that they could no longer operate it after the time-limit had expired.[18] If a provision is seen on a construction of the Act to be a condition precedent to the exercise of the rights afforded then a mandatory construction will be intended.[19] In the context of valuation law it has been held that provisions regulating a right of appeal will usually be construed as directory and compliance is not an essential condition for the exercise of the appeal court's jurisdiction,[20] particularly where no one is prejudiced.[21] A failure to specify the particular amount which the appellant desired to have substituted in the valuation roll, as required by the statute, was held not to be fatal to an appeal proceeding.[22] But the application of the labels "mandatory" or "directory" to the particular provision may not be as important as the consequences of failing to comply with the provision, which may or may not be fatal.[23]

Identification of statutory procedure

17.08 Where more than one power is available for carrying out the particular matter the authority must be careful to see that the power or powers selected for the task are appropriate and that the procedure appropriate to the relevant power is then adopted.[24] In some cases the power to regulate particular matters may be found in more than one statutory provision and a more general power is not to be construed as excluding the substance of a more restricted power contained elsewhere in the same statute.[25] The statute may require careful construction in order for there to be confidence of the procedural steps necessary to achieve the desired purpose.[26] Where a statute requires the decision maker to "have regard" to some matter, such as advice from a particular source, that does not impose on him an obligation to be bound by that matter, so as to be required to follow the advice. He must apply his own mind and consider the matter himself; the decision must still be his own. On the other hand, if he is required to "act on" certain advice, then he must follow it.[27]

---

[14] *Grunwick Ltd v. Acas* [1978] A.C. 655.
[15] *Jackson v. Secretary of State for Scotland*, 1992 S.L.T. 572.
[16] *Wilson v. Stewart* (1853) 15D. 817.
[17] *Tullis v. Macdonald* (1847) 10D. 261 at 273.
[18] *Cullimore v. Lyme Regis Coroporation* [1962] 1 Q.B. 718.
[19] *Campbell v. Duke of Atholl* (1869) 8M. 308.
[20] *Maitland v. Assessor for Midlothian* (1888) 15R. 592 at 594.
[21] *National Commercial Bank of Scotland v. Assessor for Fife*, 1963 S.C. 197.
[22] *Ayrshire Education Authority v. Assessor of Irvine*, 1922 S.C. 435.
[23] *Johnston v. Secretary of State for Scotland*, 1992 S.L.T. 387.
[24] *Magistrates and Town Council of Edinburgh v. Paterson* (1880) 8R. 197.
[25] *Forster v. Polmaise Fuel Co.*, 1947 J.C. 56.
[26] e.g. *Metcalfe v. Cox* (1895) 22R.(H.L.) 13.
[27] *Hayman v. Lord Advocate*, 1951 S.C. 621.

The person exercising the power

The necessity to secure that the proper person is exercising a particular **17.09** power has already been noted.[28] But some formalities may be further required. If the person requires to be sworn before exercising the power a failure in that respect may be fatal.[29] It may be necessary to confirm that members of a tribunal are qualified to sit on it, since if they are not, the decision in which they participated may be reduced.[30] Where a clerk to a licensing board rejected an application as being lodged too late, it was held that the matter should have been placed before a licensing board to make the decision, since the clerk had no power to do so.[31] Legislation may give rise to problems of overlapping jurisdictions; as in one case where a question arose whether justices of the county had a concurrent jurisdiction with the magistrates of a burgh over an offence committed within the burgh.[32]

Opportunity for remedy

Where an authority is empowered to take action in some matter—as for **17.10** example, for the removal of a nuisance where the person primarily responsible has failed—the authority may be required before taking action itself to give the person primarily responsible an opportunity to take the necessary acts himself. In such a case a failure to give that opportunity may render the taking of the action by the authority unlawful and disentitle it from recovering the cost of the action which it has taken.[33] This holds good even when considerable delay may be incurred in identifying the person primarily responsible.[34]

Requirements for subordinate legislation

Local authority byelaws will usually require confirmation by the Secre- **17.11** tary of State before they come into force.[35] This will usually be an essential step so that failure to obtain it will be fatal to the validity of the measure. Confirmation is not a bar to a challenge to the validity of the measure.[36] Where the measure requires to be laid before Parliament regard may have to be had to the clause requiring that course. If it is designed only for the information of Parliament and not as a condition precedent to the validity of the measure, then the failure to lay it before Parliament may not be fatal to the validity of the measure.[37] In modern practice statutory instruments[38] laid before Parliament may be subject either to a negative resolution or to an affirmative resolution.[39] In the former case the instrument may be effective from the outset,[40] but the

---

[28] para. 15.17.
[29] *Winter v. Magistrates of Edinburgh* (1837) 16S. 276.
[30] *Blaik v. Anderson* (1899) 7 S.L.T. 299.
[31] *Tait v. City of Glasgow Licensing Board*, 1987 S.L.T. 340.
[32] *Tasker v. Simpson* (1904) 7F.(J.) 33.
[33] *Cadder Local Authority v. Lang* (1879) 6R. 1242.
[34] *United Kingdom Temperance and General Provident Institution v. Parochial Board of Cadder* (1877) 4R.(J.) 39.
[35] See Local Government (Scotland) Act 1973 (c.65), s.201.
[36] *Glasgow Corporation v. Glasgow Churches Council*, 1944 S.C. 97 at 125.
[37] *Hepburn v. Wilson* (1901) 4F.(J.) 18.
[38] Defined in the Statutory Instruments Act 1946 (9 & 10 Geo. 6, c.36), s.1.
[39] Statutory Instruments Act 1946, s.4.
[40] *ibid.* s.5(1): *Lafferty v. Caledonian Ry*, 1907 15 S.L.T. 411.

fact that the instrument has become final on the expiry of the time-limit for a negative resolution will not prevent a challenge to its validity either in respect of its content as being unlawful or in respect of the procedure followed prior to its being made.[41] In the latter case the effectiveness of the measure will depend upon the resolution being passed.[42]

Confirmation and laying before Parliament

17.12 Questions may arise whether challenge can be presented to subordinate legislation in advance of it being laid before Parliament, where that is a procedural necessity. Consideration has to be given to the relevant statutory provision but the requirement to lay subordinate legislation before Parliament may not necessarily be a condition precedent for the coming into force of the regulations,[43] so that a prosecution may proceed upon it. The effect of a provision that subordinate legislation is to have effect as if enacted in the Act has been considered earlier.[44] That a statutory instrument has not been issued by the Stationery Offfice is probably not fatal to its validity.[45]

III   INQUIRIES AND HEARINGS

Need for inquiry

17.13 In many cases the statute may require some form of inquiry to be held before a power is exercised. The language used to describe the inquiry may vary. The statute may refer simply to an "inquiry"[46] or to a "local inquiry".[47] Usage extends to such expressions as judicial inquiry, public inquiry, or public local inquiry. Terms descriptive of the subject-matter of the inquiry are also used in practice, such as a planning inquiry or a fatal accident inquiry. Inquiries may relate to a past incident or a future proposal. As matter of generality they require to be conducted in accordance with the prescribed procedure and will be susceptible to review in the event of a failure to do so. However, where an inquiry had been held and a final decision was held over, the failure to hold a continued inquiry, which was not a matter of particular statutory obligation, was held not to be fatal to the making of a final decision.[48] It is necessary at the outset to be sure that the appropriate powers are possessed before embarking on a procedure involving an inquiry. Where the court considered at least on a preliminary consideration that a matter fell outwith the scope of the authority's statutory powers and that a provisional order which they had sought would be *ultra vires* an interdict was granted against the holding of an inquiry into the order.[49]

---

[41] *Hoffman-La Roche v. Secretary for Trade and Industry* [1975] A.C. 295 at 365; *East Kilbride D.C. v. Secretary of State for Scotland*, 1995 S.L.T. 1238 at 1244.

[42] See, generally, Wade and Forsyth, *Administrative Law* (7th ed.), pp. 890 *et seq.* and Bradley, in *Stair Encyclopaedia*, Vol. 1, para. 300.

[43] *Hepburn v. Wilson* (1901) 4 F.(J.) 18.

[44] See para. 11.20.

[45] *R. v. Sheer Metalcraft Ltd* [1954] 1 Q.B. 586. See the Statutory Instruments Act 1946, s.3(2) for the failure in publication as a defence to criminal proceedings.

[46] For an English example, see s.81 of the Children Act 1989 (c.41).

[47] s.210(1) of the Local Government (Scotland) Act 1973 (c.65), for example, prescribed a local inquiry.

[48] *Dundee Combination Parish Council v. Secretary of State* (1901) 3F. 848.

[49] *Russell v. Magistrates of Hamilton* (1897) 25R. 350.

Where the Crown is involved and interdict is technically not competent different considerations may apply. In one case where declarator and not interdict had to be sought because the Crown was the respondent interim declarator was refused on the grounds that it would prejudge the issue and be hypothetical.[50]

The form of the inquiry

Where there is a requirement to hold an inquiry before determining a **17.14** particular matter it will be important to ascertain the nature of the inquiry intended by the provision and to hold the kind of inquiry which was intended. Where the Secretary of State was required to "hold a local inquiry" before making a scheme for the amalgamation of police forces, it was held that it was insufficient to hold a departmental inquiry in which evidence of objection to the scheme was heard, some questions were put by the Commissioner conducting the inquiry to representatives of the police inspectorate and the Scottish Home Department, but no cross-examination was allowed. What the legislation intended in that case was an independent investigation of the facts for the information and guidance of Parliament in its consideration of the proposed scheme.[51] Where the statute calls for a "local inquiry", the intention is that the inquiry should be held in a place where the people living in the locality are able to attend it and participate in it.[52] A public local inquiry is one where it is intended that the people most directly affected by the subject-matter of the inquiry or most closely interested in it should have the opportunity of expressing their view. A power to appoint someone to hold an inquiry has been held to include a power to appoint an assessor.[53]

Right to be heard

A requirement to hear interested persons before reaching a particular **17.15** decision may be expressly provided by statute, or may be implied. Thus a determination by the General Commissioners reached in the absence of an interested party was held invalid.[54] A duty to hear an applicant for a licence may exist even without an express requirement in the particular statutory provision under which the application is made.[55] Under the Licensing (Scotland) Act 1976 it was provided by section 15(1) that the board should not refuse a renewal or permanent transfer of a licence without hearing the applicant or his representative. Section 64, which dealt with applications for extensions of permitted hours, contained no such requirement. Other sections referred to hearings. It was held that in the absence of any express provision to the contrary the applicant had a right to be heard in an application under section 64 so that where the board had not heard him on a question of an extension of the permitted hours its decision was reduced as *ultra vires*.[56] A statutory right to be heard carries with it a right to hear the evidence brought to support a complaint and a right to reply to it.[57]

---

[50] *Ayr Town Council v. Secretary of State for Scotland*, 1965 S.C. 394. It may be doubtful whether such a result would be reached today.

[51] *Magistrates of Ayr v. Lord Advocate*, 1950 S.C. 102.

[52] *Bushel v. Secretary of State for the Environment* [1981] A.C. 75, *per* Lord Diplock at 94.

[53] *General Poster and Publicity Co. v. Secretary of State for Scotland*, 1960 S.C. 266.

[54] *Inland Revenue v. Barr*, 1956 S.C. 162.

[55] *Malloch v. Aberdeen Corporation*, 1971 S.C.(H.L.) 85 is an example.

[56] *CRS Leisure Ltd v. Dumbarton District Licensing Board*, 1989 S.C.L.R. 566.

[57] *Moore v. Clyde Pilotage Authority*, 1943 S.C. 457 at 464.

IV PRELIMINARY PROCEDURES

Notice of charge

17.16 In one case disciplinary regulations required that any member of a fire brigade who was charged with an offence should be given as soon as possible written information of the charge and copies of any documentary allegation on which the charge might be founded and any reports thereon. The written intimation of the charge and the reports founded on were given to the accused only four days before the hearing although the dates of the charges were about a month before. It was held that there had been a failure in compliance with the regulations and decisions of the tribunal which had heard the cases were irregular and fell to be reduced.[58] As that case illustrates, breaches of statutory procedure may also constitute a breach of the common law rules of fairness; but it is sufficient for the complainer to succeed on only one of these grounds.

Prior notice

17.17 The giving of prior notice of administrative procedures will usually be mandatory under the relevant legislation.[59] Thus notice was required to be given of an alteration made to the valuation roll.[60] Intimation to the parent of a mentally defective child was held to be necessary for a continuation of the child's detention.[61] Public notice or advertisement may be a requirement for the holding of particular statutory meetings, so that the failure to give proper public notice may be fatal to the validity of the proceedings.[62] Failure to carry out a statutory requirement of notice was held fatal to a claim by a local authority to have a private street converted into a public street.[63] Notice may also be required to be given of a right of appeal.[64] But notice of the alternative figure proposed to be entered in the valuation roll by an appellant may be directory only.[65] Notice of preliminary procedures may not be required to be given.[66]

Consultation and advice

17.18 There may be a procedural requirement for prior consultation. No such right appears to exist generally at common law, but the requirement may be express or implied in a statutory enactment.[67] Precisely who is entitled to be consulted may be a matter for the discretion of the authority and the court may not readily interfere with such a decision.[68] The timing of such consultation in relation to the particular action to be taken will depend upon the terms of the statutory provision and upon a correct construction of those terms.[69] The consultation must also be adequate to

---

[58] *M'Donald v. Lanarkshire Fire Brigade Joint Committee*, 1959 S.C. 141.
[59] *e.g. Midlothian County Council v. Oakbank Oil Co. Ltd* (1903) 5F. 700.
[60] *Moss' Empires Ltd v. Assessor for Glasgow*, 1917 S.C.(H.L.) 1.
[61] *Page v. General Board of Control for Scotland*, 1939 S.C. 182.
[62] *Stirling etc. v. Hutcheon etc.* (1874) 1R. 935; *Shearer v. Hamilton* (1871) 9M. 456.
[63] *Brown v. Corporation of Glasgow* (1903) 6F. 94.
[64] *London & Clydeside Estates Ltd v. Aberdeen D.C.*, 1980 S.C.(H.L.) 1.
[65] *Ayrshire Education Authority v. Assessor for Irvine*, 1922 S.C. 435, noted in para. 17.07.
[66] *Wiseman v. Boreman* [1971] A.C. 297.
[67] *cf. Re Findlay* [1985] 1 A.C. 318.
[68] *R. v. Post Office, ex p. Association of Scientific, Technical and Managerial Staffs* [1981] 1 All E.R. 139.
[69] *Easter Ross Land Use Committee v. Secretary of State for Scotland*, 1970 S.C. 182.

meet the terms of the statute. It will involve the making of a genuine invitation to advise[70] and a procedure of consultation which has been genuine and not such as could be described as a sham or a fiction.[71] Time accordingly has to be allowed for a reasonable opportunity for consultation and advice. In order to be satisfied that a requirement for consultation has been met, the substance and reality of what has occurred must be considered and a decision made whether there has been a proper opportunity for the expression of views and the tendering of advice.[72] But a meeting is not a necessary ingredient of the process of consultation, at least where there is no justification for expecting such a meeting.[73] In addition to any statutory obligation to consult, a duty to do so may arise at common law on the basis of a legitimate expectation, as is considered later.[74] Where there is a requirement to take advice, the advice may, subject to the particular statutory provisions, be informally given, and either orally or in writing, and need not necessarily be given in response to an express invitation.[75]

Procedure at hearings

The details of procedures to be followed may be prescribed by statute **17.19** and these must be observed. Thus, for example, provision may be made for a right of representation, or the denial of such a right.[76] Beyond what has been particularly prescribed, the rules of natural justice (which are considered in the following chapter) may require to be observed where they have not been expressly excluded by the terms of the relevant regulations.[77] It has been recognised that an investigation into the possible inability of a sheriff to continue in office requires to be conducted fairly.[78] But questions may arise as to the legitimacy of particular rules, especially in the context of human rights in light of the greater facility for access provided by the Human Rights Act 1998.

Intimation of objections

Statutory provisions may require the intimation of objections to a **17.20** proposal or an application, so that the proposer or applicant may have notice of the objections and be able to prepare a response. Where a licensing board took account of what was held to constitute an objection by the chief constable which had not been intimated in advance to the applicants, as required by section 64(7) of the Licensing (Scotland) Act 1976, the decision of the board was reduced.[79]

Evidential requirements

The procedures permitted by any statutory regulations may allow a very **17.21** considerable degree of informality in the conduct of hearings, but in some cases, especially where the person or property of the individual is

---

[70] *Agricultural, Horticultural and Forestry Industry Training Board v. Aylesbury Mushrooms Ltd* [1972] 1 All E.R. 280.
[71] *MacGillivray v. Johnston (No. 2)*, 1994 S.L.T. 1012 at 1022; *R. v. Secretary of State for Social Services, ex p. Association of Metropolitan Authorities* [1986] 1 All E.R. 164.
[72] *Rollo etc v. Minister of Town and Country Planning* [1947] 2 All E.R. 488.
[73] *MacGillivray v. Johnston (No. 2)*, 1994 S.L.T. 1012 at 1017.
[74] See Chap. 19.
[75] *Air 2000 Ltd v. Secretary of State for Transport (No. 2)*, 1990 S.L.T. 335.
[76] *e.g. Maynard v. Osmond* [1977] 1 Q.B. 240.
[77] It was held in *Kennedy*, 1986 S.L.T. 358 that reports might be withheld from the parents of children involved in children's panel hearings.
[78] *Stewart v. Secretary of State for Scotland*, 1996 S.L.T. 1203; 1998 S.L.T. 385.
[79] *Centralbite Ltd v. Kincardine and Deeside District Licensing Board*, 1989 S.C.L.R. 652.

affected, some particular evidential requirements may be imposed. Where a statute provided that orders might be made for the destruction of food unfit for consumption "if it appears to a justice of the peace on sworn information in writing" that it is so unfit, the taking of the information on a document not sworn and without the officer who presented it being put on oath before the justices was fatal to the decision.[80]

Time-limits

17.22 It is also to be noted that statutory procedures often involve observance of time-limits and a failure to comply with such requirements may be fatal.[81]

V DECISIONS

The giving of reasons

17.23 There is at present no general common law principle in Scotland or England requiring the giving of reasons for a decision,[82] but the obligation may be expressly prescribed by statutory provisions or may be a matter of implication on a proper construction of them. While statutory provision may be made in one context for the giving of reasons there may be no obligation to do so in the context of another section where no such express provision is made.[83] Section 10(1) of the Tribunals and Inquiries Act 1992[84] imposes a duty to furnish a statement, oral or written, of the reasons for a decision given by any of the tribunals specified in Schedule 1, or by any minister where there has been or could have been a statutory inquiry.[85] But this duty only exists under section 10(1) if a request to have the reasons stated has been made on or before the giving or notification of the decision. So also the statutory duty under section 18 of the Licensing (Scotland) Act 1976 was held to be a duty to provide reasons on request.[86] The duty to give reasons may be excluded by order of the Lord Chancellor and the Lord Advocate where it is unnecessary or impracticable to do so.[87] It is, however, not uncommon for procedural rules to require the giving of reasons whether or not a request for them is made. The obligation under section 10 is qualified by, among other reservations, the provisions in subsections (2) and (3) which allow for a refusal of the reasons on grounds of national security and for a refusal to provide the reasons to one not primarily concerned, where that is thought to be contrary to the interests of the person primarily

---

[80] *Stakis plc v. Boyd*, 1989 S.C.L.R. 290.

[81] *Steeples v. Derbyshire County Council* [1984] 3 All E.R. 468.

[82] See later, para. 18.52.

[83] As in the case of the Licensing (Scotland) Act 1976; *Purdon v. Glasgow District Licensing Board*, 1988 S.C.L.R. 466, following *R. v. Secretary of State for Social Services, ex p. Connolly* [1986] 1 W.L.R. 421 at 431; *Payne v. Lord Harwich of Greenock* [1981] 2 All E.R. 842.

[84] c.53.

[85] The requirement was introduced by the Tribunals and Inquiries Act 1958 (c.66), s.12, following on the Franks *Report on Administrative Tribunals and Inquiries*, Cmnd 218 (1957) and re-enacted in the Tribunals and Inquiries Act 1971 (c.62), s.12(1), now the Tribunals and Inquiries Act 1992 (c.53), s.10(1).

[86] *Bass Taverns Ltd v. Clydebank District Licensing Board*, 1995 S.L.T. 1275.

[87] see s.12(6).

concerned. Where the Act does not apply, the giving of reasons will be a matter for the terms of the relevant procedural rules. Where there is no provision in the rules requiring the giving of reasons but leaving the terms of the announcement of the decision to be a matter of discretion the decision cannot be successfully impugned on the ground that reasons should have been given.[88] Where a statutory form of procedure does not require grounds to be stated, non-disclosure of the grounds may not make the order inept[89]; but if reasons are given, even although there is no duty to do so, they may be subjected to scrutiny in review.[90] There is, however, as is noted later,[91] a growing recognition at common law of the necessity for reasons to be given. Where no grounds are given it may well prove more difficult to prevent a successful application for review.[92]

Decisions and reasons

The precise substance of the reasons required may depend upon the terms of the particular statutory provision. But the fundamental and elementary distinction must be observed between what is in substance nothing more than a statement of the decision itself and a statement which presents an explanation of the grounds and reasons on which that decision has been reached. That basic distinction is not infrequently ignored and what is presented as the reasons for a decision must at the outset of any potential challenge be examined to confirm that they do truly represent the ground for the decision as distinct from the decision itself. A quotation or a paraphrase of the language of the statutory provision in issue is not a statement of the reasons for a decision to apply it, but simply a restatement of the decision. Where the case is one of the application of a statutory provision to particular facts, the reason must explain why the provision does or does not apply to the particular case. The reasons must relate to the essence of the decision and not simply to anterior or procedural matters, such as a refusal to hear evidence.[93] Furthermore, where there is an obligation to find facts and to state reasons these two elements must be carefully distinguished from each other[94]; the part of the decision relating to the facts must contain the factual findings, stated as facts, which the decision maker has made and on which he has based his decision; the part relating to the reasons must set out the reasons for the decision based on those facts. Where a sheriff is required by statute to make findings in fact on certain matters, it is those findings which may be open to review rather than the comments which he may add regarding the evidence.[95]

17.24

Clarity

Where there is a requirement for reasons to be given, the statement of them must be plain and intelligible[96] and not confused and ambiguous.[97] Where regulations require a statement to be given of the reasons for a

17.25

---

[88] *Carr v. United Central Council for Nursing, Midwifery and Health Visiting*, 1989 S.L.T. 580. But the circumstances of the case may impose a duty to give reasons: *cf.* the circumstances in *Stefan v. General Medical Council* (1999) 1 W.L.R. 1293.

[89] *Kirkpatrick v. Town Council of Maxwelltown*, 1912 S.C. 288.

[90] *Asda Stores Ltd v. Secretary of State for Scotland*, 1997 S.L.T. 1286.

[91] See para. 18.52.

[92] *Purdon v. Glasgow District Licensing Board*, 1988 S.C.L.R. 466 at 469.

[93] *JAE (Glasgow) v. Glasgow District Licensing Board*, 1994 S.L.T. 1164.

[94] *Wordie Property Co. Ltd v. Secretary of State for Scotland*, 1984 S.L.T. 345.

[95] *Smith v. Lord Advocate*, 1995 S.L.T. 379.

[96] *Macleod v. Banff and Buchan District HBRB*, 1988 S.L.T. 753.

[97] *Brechin Golf and Squash Club v. Angus District Licensing Board*, 1995 S.L.T. 547.

decision and of the findings on material questions of fact, then proper and adequate reasons for the decision must be given which deal with the substantial questions in issue in an intelligible way. "The decision must, in short, leave the informed reader and the Court in no real and substantial doubt as to what the reasons for it were and what were the material considerations which were taken into account in reaching it."[98] Notes which record evidence and argument and do not even find facts are not reasons.[99] In *Albyn Properties Ltd v. Knox* in the context of a decision of a rent assessment committee the Lord President (Emslie) observed[1]:

> "The statutory obligation to give reasons is designed not merely to inform the parties of the result of the committee's deliberations but to make clear to them and to this Court the basis on which their decision was reached, and that they have reached their result in conformity with the requirements of the statutory provisions and the principles of natural justice. In order to make clear the basis of their decision a committee must state (i) what facts they found to be admitted or proved; (ii) whether and to what extent the submissions of parties were accepted as convincing or not: and (iii) by what method or methods of valuation applied to the facts found their determination was arrived at. In short they must explain how their figures of fair rent were fixed."

There is an obligation to set out clearly and separately the findings in matters of fact and the findings in matters of law.[2] The decision maker must make clear what his decisions are and what are his material considerations.[3] This may involve specifying what evidence is accepted and what is rejected, what is neither accepted nor rejected, what is irrelevant, and why any witness is disbelieved.[4] The reasons must show that the tribunal applied its mind to the matters which under the statute require to be taken into account.[5] Reasons should state positively the grounds on which the decision has been reached and not be expressed simply in negative terms.[6] In one case where a negative formulation had been presented the court allowed a fresh determination to be provided, stating the terms more fully and in positive terms.[7] Where an appeal tribunal is refusing an appeal, it may be sufficient to summarise or refer to the reasons given for the decision appealed against, which the appeal body is accepting as sound.[8] But where an appeal tribunal allows an appeal and differs from the reasoning of the lower body, it should explain what material factors it took into account and what conclusions it reached about them, including such matters as have been particularly recorded as having been raised at the hearing.[9] That an applicant for

---

[98] *Wordie Property Co. Ltd v. Secretary of State for Scotland*, 1948 S.L.T. 345, *per* Lord President Emslie at 348.

[99] *Glasgow Heritable Trust Ltd v. Donald*, 1977 S.C. 113.

[1] 1977 S.C. 108 at 112.

[2] *Greater Glasgow Health Board v. Pate*, 1983 S.L.T. 90 at 94.

[3] *Zia v. Secretary of State for the Home Department*, 1994 S.L.T. 288.

[4] *Singh v. Secretary of State for the Home Department*, 1988 S.L.T. 1370; see also *Mecheti v. Secretary of State for the Home Department*, 1996 S.C.L.R. 998.

[5] *Malcolm v. Tweedale District Housing Review Board*, 1994 S.L.T. 1212.

[6] *Brazier v. Minister of Pensions*, 1945 S.C. 359.

[7] *Calder v. Local Authority of Linlithgow* (1890) 18R. 48.

[8] *Ian Monachan (Central) Ltd, Petr*, 1991 S.L.T. 494.

[9] *Safeway Stores plc v. National Appeal Panel*, 1996 S.L.T. 235.

asylum is found not to be credible may properly be a determinative reason for refusing his application.[10] Disciplinary decisions, particularly where they are made by the Scottish Law Society, are expected to be clear and coherent.[11]

Brevity

The apparent demand for detail which is reflected in some of the cases **17.26** to which reference has just been made should not be taken as a universal requirement. The extent as well as the substance of the reasons must be determined by the circumstances of the case. A like view has been taken in the context of the obligation to state reasons in the context of Article 6(1) of the European Convention on Human Rights[12] and the jurisprudence of the European Court of Human Rights should be seen as providing at least the minimum requirement. While the statement of grounds must be intelligible and deal with the substantial points raised,[13] they may be stated briefly.[14] In relation to an award of compensation for the dismissal of an employee, Leggatt L.J. observed[15]: "Nothing more onerous is demanded of the board than a concise statement of the means by which they arrived at the figure awarded." Acceptance by a minister of the critical points in an inspector's report and his implied acceptance of the reasoning in the report may suffice for the giving of reasons.[16]

Discretion to decide in absence

A statutory tribunal may be given the power to determine a case without **17.27** the attendance of the applicant but that is a discretion which must be exercised with due regard to the circumstances of each case. A blanket decision to decline to hear the applicant in all cases will be an improper exercise of the the discretionary power.[17]

Deferment of decision

The relevant regulations may provide for deferments and for the date **17.28** and method of pronouncing decisions. But where there is no such express provision a duty to make a determination on an application for a licence or a permit will not prevent the authority deferring the decision, provided that there is good reason for the deferment and nothing in the statutory provisions to prevent such a course. A decision to delay the determination of an application for a permit to use amusement-with-prizes machines was held not to be an abrogation of the duty under the Gaming Act 1968 to determine the application where it was done to ascertain the fate of an appeal against a refusal to grant a public entertainment licence on the outcome of which the decision on the permit was considered to depend.[18]

---

[10] *François v. Secretary of State for the Home Department*, 1999 S.L.T. 79.
[11] *McKinsty v. Law Society of Scotland*, 1996 S.C.L.R. 421.
[12] See para. 61.32 and the cases cited there.
[13] *Re Poyser and Mills' Arbitration* [1964] 2 Q.B. 467.
[14] *Westminster Council v. Great Portland Estates plc* [1985] 1 A.C. 661 at 673.
[15] *R. v. Civil Service Appeal Board, ex p. Cunningham* [1991] 4 All E.R. 310 at 326.
[16] *Save Britain's Heritage v. Secretary of State for the Environment and Others* [1991] 2 All E.R. 10.
[17] *Bury v. Kilmarnock and Loudon District Licensing Board*, 1989 S.L.T. 110.
[18] *Noble Developments Ltd v. City of Glasgow D.C.*, 1989 S.C.L.R. 622.

VI FAILURE

Effect of failure

17.29 An order or decision will generally be presumed to be valid until the court finds otherwise. Failure to carry out a statutory procedure will generally lead to a quashing of the decision thereby reached.[19] The usual consequence of such a finding will be that the order or decision was never capable of having legal effect.[20] If the failure was such as to invalidate the decision then it will be void *ab initio*. Where a reporter failed to make the findings in fact which were required by the statutory rules of procedure for a planning appeal the decision taken by the Secretary of State following on the reporter's report was quashed.[21] A failure adequately to follow the preliminary steps of a statutory procedure can vitiate all that has followed on them so that the final steps may be reduced. An example may be taken from one of the older cases. The General Police and Improvement (Scotland) Act 1862 provided that where the Act was adopted in any burgh the meeting which adopted it should also fix the number of commissioners to carry the Act into operation. Having adopted the Act, the meeting failed to fix the number of commissioners. It was held that the Act had been validly adopted as the fixing of the number of commissioners was a separate matter from the adoption although the latter step required to be carried out at the meeting or at an adjourned meeting. But the subsequent attempt to elect commissioners at a later meeting and various steps which had followed on that were all held to be incompetent and were set aside. The situation consequently required a remedy through the extraordinary powers of the court or through legislation.[22] The impropriety of drawing a distinction between void and voidable decisions is considered elsewhere.[23] but as is there noted a problem still remains as to the possible efficacy for some purposes of a decision which is later quashed. But a void decision may still be susceptible of appeal.[24]

Failure to give reasons

17.30 A failure to give adequate reasons may require the decision to be reduced.[25] That may be analysed simply as a serious breach of the procedural rules, enough in itself to invalidate the decision; or it may be concluded from an inadequate statement of reasons that the decision-maker has omitted to take account of a material consideration, which on an alternative analysis can be seen as an error in law invalidating the decision.[26] Where the stated "reasons" are not clear, and do not deal with the provisions of the particular statutory tests which fall to be applied in the particular case, they will not be sufficient and it is not

---

[19] *e.g. Ross v. Findlater* (1826) 4S. 514.

[20] *Hoffman-La Roche Co. v. Secretary of State for Trade and Industry* [1975] A.C. 295 at 365.

[21] *J. & A. Kirkpatrick v. Lord Advocate*, 1967 S.C. 165, followed in *Paterson v. Secretary of State for Scotland*, 1971 S.C. 1.

[22] *Anderson v. Widnell* (1868) 7M. 81.

[23] See para. 14.15.

[24] *Calvin v. Carr* [1980] A.C. 574.

[25] *Alexander Russell Ltd v. Secretary of State for Scotland*, 1984 S.L.T. 81; *McLuskie v. City of Glasgow District Council*, 1993 S.C.L.R. 551; *Di Ciacca v. Lorn, Mid Argyll, Kintyre and Islay Divisional Licensing Board*, 1994 S.L.T. 1150.

[26] *Strathclyde Passenger Executive v. McGill Bus Services Ltd*, 1984 S.L.T. 377.

enough to explain or elaborate the reasons in the answers lodged to an application for judicial review.[27] The court may, however, remit a case back to the lower body in order to obtain an adequate statement of the reasons for the decision.[28]

The seriousness of the procedural deficiency

It is not every breach which will necesarily lead to an invalidity. The **17.31** point may depend upon the seriousness of the failure in procedure. Some procedural errors may be of such triviality as to have no effect on validity.[29] It must remain a question of the circumstances whether a procedural failure is of so little consequence that it may not affect the decision. In the context of the judgments of ecclesiastical bodies Lord Justice-Clerk Aitchison identifed two cases where the court would intervene[30]:

> "(first) where the religious association through its agencies has acted clearly and demonstrably beyond its own constitution and in a manner calculated to affect the civil rights and patrimonial interests of any of its members, and (secondly) where, although acting within its constitution, the procedure of its judicial or quasi-judicial tribunals has been marked with gross irregularity, such fundamental irregularity as would, in the course of an ordinary civil tribunal, be sufficient to vitiate the proceedings. But a mere irregularity in procedure is not enough. It must be so fundamental an irregularity that it goes far beyond a mere matter of procedure, and becomes something so prejudicial to a fair and impartial investigation of the question to be decided as to amount to a denial of natural justice, as, for example, if a conviction of an ecclesiastical offence were to take place without an accusation being made, or without allowing the person accused to be heard in his defence. In short, the irregularity alleged must not be simply a point of form, or a departure from prescribed regulation, but must go to the honesty and integrity of the proceedings complained of."

So also in an arbitration the Court will not lightly review matters of procedure, it being undesirable on general grounds to interfere, unless there is an excess or abuse of jurisdiction.[31] Minimal excesses may be ignored under the principle that the law is not concerned with trifling matters. Beyond that, an analysis under the concept of the intensity of review may be appropriate.[32]

Immaterial failure

Some examples may be taken from planning law to illustrate the **17.32** proposition that where the failure is not of material importance then it may not prove fatal. Thus, where a reporter had not made findings of

---

[27] *MacLeod v. Housing Benefit Review Board for Banff and Buchan District*, 1988 S.C.L.R. 165.
[28] *Safeway Stores plc v. National Appeal Board*, 1996 S.L.T. 235. See para. 24.30 on reduction.
[29] *Barrs v. British Wool Marketing Board*, 1957 S.C. 72, *per* Lord Sorn at 88.
[30] 1940 S.C. 376, at 383.
[31] *Shanks & McEwan (Contractors) Ltd v. Mifflin Construction Ltd*, 1993 S.L.T. 1124.
[32] See para. 14.13.

fact on every point which had been disputed but had made brief but sufficient findings in respect of the matters which had seemed to him of basic importance the decision by the Secretary of State based on the report was allowed to stand.[33] In *London & Clydeside Estates Ltd v. Aberdeen District Council*[34] the consequence of non-compliance with statutory requirements for the exercise of a statutory power was regarded by Lord Hailsham L.C. as a spectrum of possibilities ranging from a flagrant defiance of a fundamental obligation to a trivial defect; thus the circumstances have to be considered in deciding whether the failure is or is not fatal. A failure to give the reasons for every particular point raised at a hearing will not necessarily suffice for a successful challenge.[35] A failure in the service of an application for planning permission may not be sufficient to nullify the decision.[36] Under section 85(4)(a) of the Town and Country Planning (Scotland) Act 1972 the Secretary of State was given power to correct any error in an enforcement notice provided that the error was not "material". In one case an error in the date for appealing against the notice was held not to be material where it was plain from the form of the notice that it was erroneous.[37] A building warrant executed after the building in question was erected was held to be valid even although the warrant was not retrospective in its terms.[38]

Defect in form

17.33 Where precision is necessary a slip or a blunder in the form of the order made by the authority or the tribunal may be fatal to its validity. In one case long before the modern regime of planning legislation the order made by a disciplinary tribunal referred to the wrong statute as the relevant authority. The chairman corrected the order after it had been issued. It was held that the chairman had no power to make the alteration and that the statutory reference was a vitiating flaw but the reference was separable from the order and accordingly the validity of the order was otherwise able to stand as effective.[39] But some defects in matters of form may not be fatal. A condition added to the statutory form of licence as a footnote and not in the body of the text has been held effective.[40] But where a local authority issued a certificate of alternative development but omitted the obligatory statement of the rights of appeal it was held that the statutory time-limit on appeals did not apply and a finding was made that the appeal was timeous.[41]

---

[33] *London and Clydeside Properties Ltd v. City of Aberdeen D.C.*, 1983 S.C. 145.
[34] 1980 S.C.(H.L.) 1 at 30.
[35] *Re Poyser and Mills' Arbitration* [1964] 2 Q.B. 467 at 478.
[36] *Pollock v. Secretary of State for Scotland*, 1993 S.L.T. 1173.
[37] *John Clark (Specialist Cars) Ltd v. Secretary of State for Scotland*, 1990 S.C.L.R. 270.
[38] *Wilson & Sons v. Mackay's Trustees* (1895) 23R. 13.
[39] *Paterson v. Scottish Solicitors' Disciplinary Tribunal*, 1984 S.L.T. 3.
[40] *Black v. Magistrates of Grangemouth*, 1906 S.C. 218.
[41] *London and Clydeside Estates Co. v. Aberdeen D.C.*, 1977 S.L.T. 163.

CHAPTER 18

BREACH OF COMMON LAW PROCEDURES

I   INTRODUCTION
II   BIAS
III THE RIGHT TO BE HEARD
IV   THE CONDUCT OF THE HEARING
V   THE GIVING OF REASONS

I INTRODUCTION

Terminology

The term "procedural impropriety" became current in the 1980s to cover **18.01** breaches of natural justice and violations of the duty to act fairly. But the two concepts of natural justice and fairness may not be absolutely identical. The expression "natural justice" is used more exactly to refer to two long-established principles of fair practice: *nemo judex in sua causa* and *audi alteram partem*.[1] Underlying both of these principles is the requirement that justice must be seen to be done. But the term "natural justice" may be used more widely as representing not only the two principal expressions of it, but as referring to the basic concept on which they are founded, namely that of fairness. Thus it was said by Lord Morris of Borth y Gest that "natural justice is but fairness writ large and judicially".[2] Lord Justice Harman in *Ridge v. Baldwin*[3] observed that natural justice is, after all, only fair play in action. Lord President Hope in *Errington v. Wilson* expressed a like view: the duty to act fairly and the duty to act in accordance with the principles of natural justice "are different ways of expressing the same thing".[4] The expression "rules of natural justice" may be used, as Lloyd L.J. put it "compendiously, if misleadingly", to refer to the principles of fair procedure which the courts have developed over the years.[5] The phrase itself may not withstand close analysis.[6] "It has been pointed out many times that the word 'natural' adds nothing except perhaps a hint of nostalgia for the good old days when nasty things did not happen."[7] And in *McInnes v. Onslow-Fane*[8] Megarry V.-C. observed that "the further the situation is away from anything that resembles a judicial or quasi-judicial situation, and the further the question is removed from what may reasonably be called a justiciable question, the more appropriate it is to reject an expression which includes the word 'justice' and to use instead terms

---

[1] These principles have been otherwise expressed as impartiality and fairness: *Kanda v. Government of Malaya* [1962] A.C. 322 at 337.

[2] *Furnell v. Whangerei High School Board* [1973] A.C. 666 at 679.

[3] In the Court of Appeal [1963] 1 Q.B. 539 at 578.

[4] *Errington v. Wilson*, 1995 S.C. 550, *per* Lord President Hope at 555.

[5] *R. v. Panel on Take-overs and Mergers, ex p. Guiness plc* [1990] 1 Q.B. 146 at 184.

[6] For a discussion on the concept of natural justice, see J. Bennett-Miller, "Problems of Natural Justice", 1960 J.R. 29.

[7] Ormerod L.J. in *Norwest Holst v. Secretary of State for Trade* [1978] 1 Ch. 201 at 226.

[8] [1978] 1 W.L.R. 1520 at 1530.

such as 'fairness'". But despite the criticisms the label is a convenient one to use in relation to certain particular requirements of the common law which may apply to the composition of certain decision-making bodies, to the procedures they adopt and to the way in which they behave, that is to say the constitutional and procedural aspects of the task of decision-making.[9] The most common examples come from cases where there has been some unfairness in the conduct of the proceedings, such as may be prejudicial to one of the parties. It is of course competent to attack a decision both on a ground of a breach of natural justice and of a failure to comply with a statutory duty, even although only one ground may be successful.[10]

Procedural fairness

18.02 In the present context fairness is to be understood as applying solely to matters of procedure. While it may be strictly proper to speak of fairness rather than natural justice when considering the whole range of cases which may fall within the scope of the common law rules of procedure, the vagueness of the concept gives rise to the greater difficulty in determining in precisely what circumstances particular aspects of it are to apply.[11] In *R. v. Home Secretary, ex parte Doody* the House of Lords explored the procedural aspects attending a decision of the Home Secretary regarding the release of prisoners serving mandatory life sentences. Lord Mustill summarised the idea of procedural fairness as follows[12]:

> "(1)Where an Act of Parliament confers an administrative power there is a presumption that it will be exercised in a manner which is fair in all the circumstances. (2) The standards of fairness are not immutable. They may change with the passage of time, both in the general and in their application to decisions of a particular type. (3) The principles of fairness are not to be applied by rote identically in every situation. What fairness demands is dependent on the context of the decision, and this is to be taken into account in all its aspects. (4) An essential feature of the context is the statute which creates the discretion, as regards both its language and the shape of the legal and administrative system within which the decision is taken. (5) Fairness will very often require that a person who may be adversely affected by the decision will have an opportunity to make representations on his own behalf either before the decision is taken with a view to producing a favourable result; or after it is taken, with a view to procuring a modification, or both. (6) Since the person affected usually cannot make worthwhile representations without knowing what factors may weigh against his interests fairness will very often require that he is informed of the gist of the case which he has to answer."

Lord Woolf has added to this: "It is also a principle of our substantive law that when a decision is taken in a manner which breaches the

---

[9] *Errington v. Wilson*, 1995 S.C. 550 at 560.
[10] *R. v. Dorking Justices* [1984] 1 A.C. 743.
[11] See the discussion by Professor Bradley in the *Stair Encyclopaedia*, Vol. 1, para. 283.
[12] [1994] 2 A.C. 531 at 560. The passage was quoted and followed in *Ritchie v. Secretary of State for Scotland*, 1999 S.L.T. 55.

requirement that it should be taken fairly, in the absence of any alternative remedy, the member of the public who has been unfairly treated is entitled to a remedy from the High Court on an application for judicial review."[13] Fairness is not by itself a substantive ground for review, but must be seen in the context of procedure[14] or irrationality[15] or legitimate expectation.[16] Although the term "natural justice" should be reserved for the two situations which it has always been recognised to cover, the broader usage in practice cannot be ignored and in this chapter the two expressions are used interchangeably. There is probably little more to be gained from discussing the terminology.[17]

Administrative decisions and natural justice

As has already been discussed,[18] the principle of fairness embodied in **18.03** the rules of natural justice is not restricted to cases which can be categorised as judicial or quasi-judicial. Although it took time to be recognised, the principal significance of the decision of the House of Lords in *Ridge v. Baldwin*[19] was to undermine the distinction between judicial and administrative functions as a criterion for the availability of judicial review. It had, however, been accepted long before in *Board of Education v. Rice*[20] that departments or officers of state required to act fairly in making their decisions. It is now well settled that a duty to act fairly may arise in both administrative and judicial decisions.[21] As Lord Borth y Gest observed, natural justice is not "a leaven to be associated only with judicial and quasi-judicial occasions".[22] In *Lithgow v. Secretary of State for Scotland*[23] a question arose whether a decision of the Secretary of State under the Special Roads Act 1949, based on considerations which had not been expressed at a public inquiry, was "within the powers of this Act". In that case the Secretary of State was clearly acting in an executive capacity making a policy decision and not in a judicial capacity. Lord Dunpark accepted the argument that the phrase "within the powers of the Act" should be broadly construed so as to include the rules of natural justice. He stated[24]: "When Parliament confers powers upon a Minister to legislate on its behalf by way of statutory instrument, there is, in my opinion, an underlying assumption that the powers conferred will only be exercised in accordance with law ... If a Minister exercises a statutory power in a manner prohibited by common law, that, in my opinion, is just as much a non-exercise of his statutory powers as the purported exercise of non-existent powers." A similar view of the application of the rules of natural justice can be seen in the observation of Lord Diplock that "It has long been settled law that

---

[13] *R. v. Secretary of State, ex p. Fayed* [1997] 1 All E.R. 228 at 231.
[14] e.g. *Lochore v. Moray D.C.*, 1992 S.L.T. 16.
[15] *Shetland Lines (1984) Ltd v. Secretary of State for Scotland*, 1996 S.L.T. 653.
[16] Although legitimate expectation may relate to matters of substance as well as matters of procedure: see para. 19.16.
[17] *McInnes v. Onslow-Fane* [1978] 1 W.L.R. 1520 at 1530.
[18] para. 8.21.
[19] [1964] A.C. 40.
[20] [1911] A.C. 179 at 182.
[21] *Breen v. Amalgamated Engineering Union* [1971] 2 Q.B. 175; *R. v. Birmingham City Justices, ex p. Chris Foreign Foods (Wholesalers) Ltd* [1970] 1 W.L.R. 1428.
[22] *Furnell v. Whangarei High School Board* [1973] A.C. 660 at 679.
[23] 1973 S.C. 1.
[24] at 8.

a decision affecting the legal rights of an individual which is arrived at by a procedure which offends against the principles of natural justice is outside the jurisdiction of the decision-making authority".[25]

Application

18.04 So far as statutory rules of procedure are concerned there should be little difficulty in deciding whether they do or do not apply.[26] The problem in that context should be solved by reference to the particular statutory provisions. What is more difficult is to discover whether all or any of the common law rules apply. Here there is probably no single or comprehensive test available. It is very much a matter of considering the circumstances of the particular case. It is tempting to suppose that all decision making is subject to some of the principles of fairness. But it has to be recognised that there are limits on the scope of decisions which may be subject to judicial review, so that the precise limits cannot readily be defined simply in terms of a challenge on the ground of procedural impropriety.[27]

In *Errington v. Wilson*[28] the question was whether a justice, in hearing an application to have certain cheese condemned under certain food safety legislation, was entitled to deny the manufacturer any right to cross-examine the food authority's witnesses. In a petition for judicial review the food safety authority argued that the justice was acting in an administrative capacity under the Act and was not under a duty to observe the rules of natural justice but simply obliged to act fairly. It was held, however, that these concepts were inseparable. The court looked to the requirements of fairness in the whole circumstances of the case. It was observed[29] under reference to fairness and natural justice: "Just as those labels are useful in particular contexts to focus attention on particular areas of inquiry but may not be determinative, so also the categorisation of functions as administrative or judicial or quasi-judicial, while often useful as an element in the decision whether particular acts or omissions were or were not lawful as falling or not falling within the scope of what in the circumstances was required under the general principle of fairness, . . . should not be seen as determinative of that issue". It now seems that the focus is no longer on either the nature of the power or the nature of the decision maker, but on the procedures required by the circumstances of the case. The nature of the power and the nature of the decision maker remain relevant, at least in relation to the substance of the procedural rules, but the emphasis has shifted to the interests of the person affected by the decision and what those interests require of the proceedings.

Justice seen to be done

18.05 Where the ground for seeking judicial review is an alleged breach of the rules of natural justice it is irrelevant whether justice in fact has or has not been done. What matters is whether justice has been seen to be done. The basic principle was pronounced by Hewart C.J. in his

---

[25] *Att.-Gen. v. Ryan* [1980] A.C. 718 at 730.
[26] But see para. 17.07 on the matter of mandatory and directory requirements.
[27] See para. 9.08 above on Associations (Scope).
[28] 1995 S.C. 550.
[29] Lord Clyde at 560.

observation that "a long line of cases shows that it is not merely of some importance but is of fundamental importance that justice should not only be done, but should manifestly and undoubtedly be seen to be done".[30] In the case of *Barrs v. British Wool Marketing Board*[31] Lord President Clyde observed:

> "It is not a question of whether the tribunal has arrived at a fair result: for in most cases that would involve an examination into the merits of the case, upon which the tribunal is final. The question is whether the tribunal has dealt fairly and equally with the parties before it in arriving at that result. The test is not 'Has an unjust result been reached?' but 'Was there an opportunity afforded for injustice to be done?' If there was such an opportunity, the decision cannot stand. Hence if one party is allowed to give evidence, and this is denied to another, the decision would be reduced, not because the evidence led had convinced the tribunal, for this could hardly ever be established, but because the standards of fair play which underlie all such proceedings had not been satisfied".

It has been well recognised both in Scotland and in England that justice should not only be done, but should be seen to be done. This observation, on the one hand, makes it clear that the court should not be concerned with the merits of a decision but only with its legality in the sense of it having been reached in accordance with fair procedures. On the other hand, it states that the integrity of decisions, at least those to which the principles of natural justice apply, depends on a widespread faith in the process by which the decision is made. Arguably it is less important that justice be done and more important that an objective bystander may conclude that, whatever the decision, the procedures which have been followed allow justice to be done.

Exceptions

But there can be cases where the respondent may be allowed to submit **18.06** that the impropriety would in fact have made no difference to the result. The issue of causation might be opened up where the decision turned on a point of law on which in any event the petitioner had no case or where there were quite special circumstances relating to the involvement of an interested party.[32]

Duty or discretion

Where there is a duty to act fairly and fairness requires that something **18.07** should be done, it will be a breach of the duty to fail to do that thing.[33] Whether to do it or not will not be a matter to be left wholly to the discretion of the decision maker. The duty to act fairly does not entitle the decision maker to decide as matter of discretion what is or is not fair. Thus, for example, whether it is fair to allow cross-examination of witnesses, where it is not prescribed in any relevant procedural rules, is a

---

[30] *R. v. Sussex Justices, ex p. McCarthy* [1924] 1 K.B. 256 at 259.
[31] 1957 S.C. 72 at 82.
[32] Examples given by Lord Milligan in *Graham v. Ladeside of Kilbirnie Bowling Club*, 1990 S.C. 365.
[33] *Errington v. Wilson*, 1995 S.C. 550, *per* Lord President Hope at 555.

matter to be decided in the light of the circumstances; while the decision maker has a choice to make in allowing or refusing it, that choice is substantially governed by considerations of fairness and, if in the circumstances fairness requires cross-examination, a refusal to allow it will be subject to review, not as a matter of a wrong exercise of discretion, but as a possible breach of the rules of natural justice.

Merits and procedure

18.08   The distinction between doing justice and the role of the court in supervising decisions to ensure that justice is seen to be done hides a tension between merits-based and process-based review. For review on the ground of breach of the rules of natural justice to be truly effective, there has to be some connection between fair procedures and doing justice. One rationale for the principle of fairness has to be that better procedures make for better decisions. Thus the court's power to supervise procedures is not only directed to ensuring legality but is also justified by leading to better substantive decisions. Furthermore, the substance of a decision may also be relevant in assessing the procedures which may be required for a proper exercise of a decision-making power. Although the supervising court must always be conscious of the limits of its jurisdiction in cases where a decision is under challenge on the ground of an alleged procedural defect, it is nevertheless inappropriate for the court to ignore the merits completely. In many cases it may be necessary and proper to look at the substance of the decision so as to ascertain the propriety of the procedures used in reaching it. It is, for example, relevant and appropriate to take account of the relative seriousness of the decision in assessing the procedures adopted. A decision which involves a loss of life or liberty must require more exacting procedures than a licence application affecting a commercial business.[34]

Prejudice

18.09   A breach of the rules of natural justice involves an element of unfairness in procedure but it is not necessary for a successful case on an alleged breach of the rules of natural justice that the petitioner must plead that he or she has suffered actual prejudice by the breach.[35] The fact of the breach should be quite sufficient to establish prejudice, in so far as that element is relevant, without proof of any particular disadvantage suffered by the aggrieved party. On the other hand, it has been said that "a breach of procedure, whether called a breach of natural justice or an essential administrative fault, cannot give him a remedy in the Courts unless behind it there is something of substance which has been lost by the failure".[36] The proper view is probably that it is sufficient that the breach might have been prejudicial, but that the absence of any actual prejudice may affect the remedy to be given. In addition, considerations of the materiality of the defect may become relevant to the question whether the court should intervene at all in a matter which may lack

---

[34] See para. 14.13.
[35] The rubric in *Cigaro v. City of Glasgow District Licensing Authority*, 1982 S.C. 104 which records an observation to the contrary effect was held to be erroneous in *Errington v. Wilson*, 1995 S.C. 550.
[36] *Malloch v. Aberdeen Corporation*, 1971 S.C. (H.L.) 85, *per* Lord Wilberforce at 118.

sufficient reality. There is no place for an appeal to principles of natural justice if the decision is one which the decision maker is bound by law to pronounce; acceding to the plea in such circumstances would involve a breach of the law by those who have been entrusted with its administration.[37]

Correction

Where there is an appeal process available it may be that a breach of **18.10** natural justice can be cured through that process, particularly where that process involves a complete rehearing. This matter has been noted in the context of illegality.[38] But the matter admits of no absolute rule.[39] Where the possibility of cure cannot be confidently predicted, the decision should not be upheld.[40] Reference in this connection may be made to the significance of a right of appeal in relation to a failure to give reasons for a decision.[41] In general a tribunal may not alter a decision after it has been given, but it has been held in England that where there has been a procedural defect, such as a failure to receive a notice, the matter might be reopened provided that no one was prejudiced.[42]

The substance of natural justice and fairness

In the context of statutory rules of procedure it should be relatively easy **18.11** to identify the particular respect in which there has been a departure from the required procedure. So far as the common law rules are concerned, three distinct matters are now to be considered: first, in relation to the decision maker, the consideration of bias; secondly, in relation to the process of decision making, the matter of the need for and the substance of hearings; and thirdly, in relation to the decision itself, the necessity or otherwise for the giving of reasons.[43]

II BIAS

General

The identity of the individual making a decision may give rise to **18.12** unfairness, or the appearance of it.[44] Impartiality is a primary essential of the judicial function.[45] The rule "is founded in nature itself, that no man ought to be judge in his own cause".[46] The objection may arise from a variety of ways in which the decision maker is connected either with a party to the dispute or with the subject-matter of it. Stair instances the

---

[37] *Scott v. Aberdeen Corporation*, 1976 S.L.T. 141, *per* Lord Avonside at 147.
[38] para. 15.16 in relation to reconsideration.
[39] *Calvin v. Carr* [1980] A.C. 574.
[40] *Brown v. Executive Committee of Edinburgh Labour Party*, 1995 S.L.T. 985.
[41] Discussed later in para. 18.55. See also para. 16.32.
[42] *R. v. Kensington and Chelsea Rent Tribunal, ex p. Macfarlane* [1974] 1 W.L.R. 1486.
[43] Five principles were adopted by the Committee of Ministers on Sept. 28, 1977 in their resolution (77)31, (1977) 25 European Yearbook, namely a right to be heard, access to information, assistance and representation, the giving of a statement of reasons, and the giving of an indication of the remedies available in the case of an adverse decision.
[44] See, generally SN McMurtrie, "The Principles of *Nemo Iudex in Sua Causa* in Scots Law", 1996 J.R. 304.
[45] On the essential characteristics of a judge, see Balfour's *Practicks*, 280.
[46] Erskine, *Institutes*, 1, 2, 25.

considerations of the judge being in the prohibited degrees of affinity or consanguinity to either party, or as interested in the cause, or as having shown emnity against the party, or as having shown partiality.[47] The rule should apply in criminal cases as much as in civil cases[48] and it may extend beyond the identity of the actual decision maker to such persons as a medical referee sitting as an assessor.[49] The legislature can depart from the rule and appoint someone as a judge in a case in which the person may have a pecuniary interest, but clear words are required to achieve this.[50] The parties may, of course, agree that the judge may sit notwithstanding his interest, but the interest must first be disclosed and the parties given the opportunity to consider the position.

Forms of Bias

18.13 Bias may occur in a variety of forms. In some cases the judge may have an actual motivation to prefer one party to another, prompted by financial or other interest or simply by personal animosity. In the most crude form such cases are rare in practice. But the existence of an actual partiality may not always be evident. Moreover, the insidious nature of impartiality may not only render it hard for others to discover it but even conceal itself from the consciousness of the decision maker. The law accordingly operates to quash not only decisions made by one against whom an actual bias can be established, but also decisions made by persons whose relationship to the parties or to the matter in issue is such as to give rise to a potential impartiality and in addition decisions made by persons who by their behaviour give the impression that they are not impartial. Thus the proof of a potential impartiality or of an appearance of bias may be as fatal as an actual bias. That is nothing more than a reflection of the principle that justice should not only be done, but should manifestly and undoubtedly be seen to be done.[51] Thus the complaint of bias may operate whether or not there is in fact any partiality. The distinction between the situation where in a strict sense the judge is adjudicating in his own case and the situation where there are circumstances such as to make it improper for the judge to hear the case was explained in *R v. Bow Street Metropolitan Stipendiary Magistrate and Others, ex parte Pinochet Ugarte (No. 2)*[52] by Lord Browne-Wilkinson as follows:

> "The fundamental principle is that a man may not be judge in his own cause. This principle, as developed by the courts, has two very similar but not identical implications. First it may be applied literally: if a judge is in fact a party to the litigation or has a financial or proprietary interest in its outcome then he is indeed sitting as a judge in his own cause. In that case, the mere fact that he is a party to the action or has a financial or proprietary interest in its outcome is sufficient to cause his automatic disqualification.

---

[47] *Institutions*, 4, 1, 35 and 4, 39, 14.
[48] It is unlikely that the view taken in *Mackenzie v. Lang* (1874) 2R.(J.) 1 that it was indecorous but not incompetent for a magistrate to hear a case of theft of a firm's property where the magistrate was a partner of the firm would be followed today.
[49] *Glass v. Smith*, 1941 S.C. 54.
[50] *Jeffs v. New Zealand Dairy Production and Marketing Board* [1967] A.C. 551 at 565.
[51] *R. v. Sussex Justices, ex p. McCarthy* [1924] 1 K.B. 256, *per* Lord Hewart C.J. at 259.
[52] [1999] 1 All E.R. 577.

The second application of the principle is where the judge is not a party to the suit and does not have a financial interest in its outcome, but in some other way his conduct or behaviour may give rise to a suspicion that he is not impartial, for example because of his friendship with a party. This second type of case is not strictly speaking an application of the principle that a man must not be judge in his own cause, since the judge will not normally be himself benefiting, but providing a benefit for another by failing to be impartial."

His Lordship called the first application "automatic disqualification". The categorisation which is adopted in the following paragraphs seeks to distinguish between what may be seen as cases of potential bias, where the relationship between the decision maker and the particular case may involve his disqualification, and cases of what may be called apparent bias where the decision maker so conducts himself as to give such an appearance of impartiality as to constitute a disqualification.

(a) Potential bias

Pecuniary connection with a party

A pecuniary interest, however small, will in general be a ground for **18.14** disqualification.[53] But at least in civil cases the parties may by joint minute agree to waive the point.[54] The holding of stock in one of the parties to an arbitration will disqualify the arbiter and nullify his award.[55] An appointment by arbiters of an oversman with such an interest will be similarly fatal.[56] In *Dimes v. Proprietors of Grand Canal Junction Canal*[57] the Lord Chancellor was held to have been disqualified from sitting on an appeal where he had a substantial shareholding in the defendant. Lord Campbell stated[58]: "it is of the last importance that the maxim that no man is to be a judge in his own cause should be held sacred. And that is not to be confined to a cause in which he is a party, but applies to a cause in which he has an interest." By statute it is not a ground of declinature that a judge, whether of the Court of Session or in any of the inferior courts, is a partner in any joint stock company carrying on an assurance business which is party to the proceedings, nor that a judge is the holder, merely as a trustee, of stock or shares in a company which is a party to the proceedings.[59] Where magistrates have no individual or personal interest in the matter before them, but only an interest as magistrates, they were held not disqualified.[60]

Personal interest in the dispute

Even although he may have no connection with the parties a decision **18.15** maker may have an interest in the outcome of the dispute. In general no one should sit as a judge in a matter in which he has a substantial

---

[53] *Wildridge v. Anderson* (1897) 25R.(J.) 27 at 34. Lord Moncrieff formulated three rules on interest in a case: a pecuniary interest will disqualify; a non-pecuniary interest must be substantial if it is to disqualify; and an interest neither pecuniary nor substantial, not calculated to cause bias in the mind of the judge, will be disregarded.
[54] *Caledonian Ry v. Ramsay* (1897) 24R.(J.) 48.
[55] *Sellar v. Highland Ry*, 1919 S.C.(H.L.) 19.
[56] *Smith v. Liverpool and London and Globe Insurance Co.* (1887) 14R. 931.
[57] (1852) 3 H.L.Cas. 759.
[58] at 793.
[59] Court of Session Act 1868 (c.100), s.103.
[60] *Downie v. Fisherrow Harbour Commissioners* (1903) 5F.(J.) 101; (1903) 11 S.L.T. 250.

personal interest. In some cases Parliament may provide that a minister is to determine an issue in which his own department is an interested party. Where the identity of the person making the decision is not prescribed then any interest in the particular issue may involve disqualification. While by virtue of the matter of necessity[61] a person may not be formally disqualified from acting, nevertheless he must act objectively in reaching his decision. Members of a valuation committee should not sit where their own appeals are being considered.[62] In one case interdict was granted against a chief constable from himself conducting an inquiry into complaints which had been made against him.[63] Where a sheriff clerk depute who was in his private capacity suing for a business account signed the initiating summons as sheriff clerk, it was held that the proceedings were null.[64] Nor should someone sit as a member of a licensing authority to consider the licensing of premises in which he has a financial interest.[65] But a personal belief in the desirability or otherwise of particular kinds of administrative control should not necessarily constitute a disqualification from acting as a decision maker in those fields. Thus personal participation in work for the advancement of the cause of temperance does not necessarily disqualify one from sitting on or chairing a licensing court.[66]

Family relationships

18.16 Where the decision maker is related to one of the parties he should not act.[67] Declinature extends by statute to all judicatures in Scotland in the case of certain close relatives[68] and a breach of these provisions nullifies the proceedings[69] and cannot be waived.[70] But where one or both of the related parties is acting in his capacity as holder of an office then there may be no impropriety in them doing so even if they are related. Thus the view has been expressed that there is no impropriety in a member of a valuation committee sitting to hear an appeal although he was a brother of the assessor.[71] Nevertheless, the better course would be to decline.

---

[61] See para. 18.21.

[62] *Assessor for Lanarkshire v. O'Hara*, 1928 S.C. 391.

[63] *Lockhart v. Irving*, 1936 S.L.T. 567.

[64] *Manson v. Smith* (1871) 9M. 492; *Macbeth v. Innes* (1873) 11M. 404.

[65] *Ower v. Crichton* (1902) 10 S.L.T. 271; canvassing of other members of the tribunal is also improper: *Macdougall v. Miller* (1900) 8 S.L.T. 284.

[66] *Goodall v. Bilsland*, 1909 S.C. 1152; *M'Geehen v. Knox*, 1913 S.C. 688. It may be that a more strict view would now be taken.

[67] *Moncrieff v. Lord Moncrieff* (1904) 6F. 1021, where the Lord President was a brother-in-law of the appellant.

[68] Declinature Acts 1594 (c.22) and 1681 (c.79).

[69] *Ommanney v. A. Smith* (1851) 13D. 678.

[70] *Commissioners of Highland Roads and M'Neill v. Machray, Croall and Co.* (1858) 20D. 1165, where the Lord President was a brother of the only individual pursuer, who was suing as agent and had no personal interest.

[71] *McGilvray v. Oban Assessor*, 1916 S.C. 665. In *Low v. Kincardineshire Licensing Court*, 1974 S.L.T.(Sh. Ct) 54, the son of the clerk to the authority was depute-clerk and also a partner with his father in the same firm of solicitors. It was held that his acting for one party was not open to challenge since s.30(1) of the Licensing (Scotland) Act 1959 did not apply to the particular application which was being made, but the rules of natural justice were broken because the depute-clerk had retired with the court to consider the case. See also *R. v. Sussex Justices, ex p. McCarthy* [1924] 1 K.B. 256.

Official capacities

Where someone holds some particular office or appointment, the **18.17**
interest which he has by virtue of that office has not always been
regarded as a personal interest such as to disqualify him from acting as a
judge. Thus, where the connection of the judge with the subject-matter
of the case arises not out of some personal or pecuniary interest but
through his holding of an official position—as for example, where a
magistrate is an *ex officio* trustee of an institution the destruction of
whose property is the subject-matter of the case—there may be no
disqualification on him.[72] The competency of a judge to hear particular
disputes may be regulated by express statutory provision[73] and the
relevant statute may expressly make him the judge of disputes even
although he has an interest in an official capacity to secure enforcement
of the statute.[74] Thus the particular provisions under which the decision
maker is acting, whether contractual or statutory, may exclude considerations of bias[75]; but even in statutory procedures independence should be
expected of anyone appointed to conduct inquiries.[76] Where a university
was a party to a litigation the Chancellor was considered to be
disqualified from acting as a judge in the case, but a member of the
governing body was not.[77] Nor was the Chancellor disqualified from
sitting as a judge in a case concerning the validity of certain testamentary
writings under which bequests were made to the University of which he
was Chancellor.[78] Where an arbiter was appointed Dean of Guild it was
held that he was disqualified from continuing to act in an arbitration to
which the town council was a party.[79] A greater consciousness of matters
of human rights may nowadays require a stricter view to be taken on
official relationships than may have been accepted in the past. In the
second *Pinochet* case,[80] one member of the appellate committee of the
House of Lords was a director and chairperson of a charitable company
which had been incorporated to carry out some of the work of Amnesty
International Limited. The latter company was allowed to intervene in
the proceedings before the appellate committee and it was held that the
law lord's connection with the associated company was sufficient to give
an appearance of possible bias.

Where there may be a conflict of interest a person may not act in two
distinct official capacities, as where a law agent, who was acting for an
impoverished litigant, also acted as a reporter on the litigant's application for admission to the poor's roll in order to obtain legal assistance.[81] But where the function involved is not properly of a judicial
character, the rule may not apply. It has been held that there is no
impropriety in partners of the same firm of solicitors acting in the official
capacities of clerk of court and procurator fiscal in a trial before justices

---

[72] *Wildridge v. Anderson* (1897) 25R.(J.) 27.
[73] *e.g. Downie v. Fisherrow Harbour Commissioners* (1903) 5F.(J.) 101.
[74] *Martin v. Nicholson* (1920) 1 S.L.T. 67.
[75] *e.g. Franklin v. Minister of Town and Country Planning* [1948] A.C. 87.
[76] *University of Edinburgh v. Craik*, 1954 S.C. 190.
[77] *Jex-Blake v. Edinburgh University Senatus* (1873) 11M. 784.
[78] *Sibbald's Trustees v. Greig* (1872) 9M. 399.
[79] *Magistrates of Edinburgh v. Lownie* (1903) 5F. 711; but *cf. Phipps v. Edinburgh and Glasgow Ry* (1843) 5D. 1025.
[80] *R. v. Bow Street Metropolitan Stipendiary Magistrate and Others, ex parte Pinochet Ugarte (No. 2)* [1999] 1 All E.R. 577.
[81] *M'Kean v. Herbison*, 1913 S.C. 548.

of the peace.[82] It is perfectly proper for the Secretary of State for Scotland to appoint a reporter but reserve to himself the final decision and for him to differ from the reporter's view.[83]

Past involvement of the judge

18.18   It is inappropriate for a person to sit as a judge to determine the sentences for statutory offences committed by a company where he had earlier been dismissed from the employment of that company.[84] Where the judge has acted as counsel for one of the parties in the same dispute he should decline to sit.[85] Merely because he has acted in the past for one of the parties in other matters should not warrant declinature. Previous knowledge of a case obtained through judicial experience should not suffice as a disqualification. A sheriff is not disqualified from hearing an action for damages because he has presided over a fatal accident inquiry into the same matter.[86] But where members of a disciplinary tribunal had already, as members of the council of a voluntary association, considered the substance of the particular matter, interim interdict was pronounced on the basis that a reasonable man might well consider that the tribunal might be biased.[87] The discretion of a sheriff whether he should decline to hear a case on account of his having already heard a matter related to it will not lightly be interfered with.[88]

Interest disregarded

18.19   To make an effective challenge of a judge, it must be shown that the judge has "a substantial interest in the success of the cause, such an interest as would or might have a tendency to bias his judgment, or set up a prejudice against the accused".[89] Where the interest is neither substantial nor calculated to cause partiality in the mind of the judge it may be disregarded. A decision involving a possible increase in local taxation for which the judge, or a close relative of his, along with everyone else in the locality would be liable to pay is not a sufficient interest to warrant declinature.[90] Where one of the judges was a commissioner of supply he was held to be entitled to sit in proceedings brought against that body.[91] Persons exercising professional skills may be required to act in a capacity which requires them to act with a judicial impartiality even where they have some particular connection with the substance of the dispute, as for example an architect in a building

---

[82] *Laughland v. Galloway*, 1968 J.C. 26.

[83] *City of Glasgow D.C. v. Secretary of State for Scotland (No. 1)*, 1993 S.L.T. 198.

[84] *Harper of Oban (Engineering) Ltd v. Henderson*, 1989 S.L.T. 21; following *Bradford v. McLeod*, 1986 S.L.T. 244.

[85] *Free Church of Scotland v. McRae* (1905) 7F. 686. See also *M'Cardle v. M'Cardle's Judicial Factor* (1906) 7F. 419.

[86] *Black v. Scott Lithgow Ltd*, 1990 S.C. 322.

[87] *J.A. & D.S. Rennie v. Scottish Milk Records Association*, 1985 S.L.T. 272.

[88] *Dumfries and Galloway R.C. v. O*, 1994 S.C.L.R. 661. It may be noted that in *Henderson v. Maclellan* (1874) 1R. 920, a sheriff principal required to review a decision which he himself had given as sheriff-substitute.

[89] *Wildridge v. Anderson* (1897) 25R.(J.) 29, *per* Lord McLaren at 32.

[90] *Gray v. Fowlie* (1847) 9D. 811. The point is now covered for the Court of Session by s.4(1) of the Court of Session Act 1988 (c.36).

[91] *Lord Advocate v. Commissioners of Supply for the County of Edinburgh* (1861) 23D. 933.

contract. In one case a surveyor, who had been engaged to advise on the valuation of certain office premises, was held not to be disqualified from acting as arbiter in a dispute relating to the valuation of office premises situated on the floor above those; it was considered that his function in relation to the two valuations was distinct and the relevance of the one valuation to the other was not predictable before the arbitration.[92] In one case the purchase by a burgh of land which was owned to the extent of a one-half *pro indiviso* share by a member of the council was upheld although he had attended the meeting at which the motion to purchase was passed but was not present when the council confirmed the purchase.[93] A remote link, as where the chairman of the tribunal was a former partner of and currently a consultant to a firm of solicitors, two of the partners of which were brothers of the solicitor appearing for a party before the tribunal, will be disregarded.[94] A personal interest on the part of one member of a general meeting will not suffice where he has not influenced the other members.[95]

Bias in criminal courts and disciplinary tribunals

The principle that justice must be seen to be done will operate in **18.20** criminal proceedings. Thus, where justices had knowledge of further charges pending against an accused person but decided to hear the case themselves the conviction was quashed because of the appearance of bias which their conduct invited.[96] But while knowledge of potentially prejudicial material may be a ground for disqualification in a criminal court, the situation in internal disciplinary bodies may well be different. Members of a board of prison visitors will inevitably have considerable knowledge of the background of a prisoner charged with a disciplinary offence but such general background knowledge is not something which in that context would in the eyes of a fair-minded bystander amount to a necessary reason for the chairman of the board being disqualified from adjudicating on the disciplinary charge. It was so held where the chairman had been a member of a local review committee three weeks earlier which had considered an application by the prisoner for release on parole.[97] On the other hand, where members of the council of a voluntary association had already considered the material on which a disciplinary charge was to be brought against one of the members it was held that since the members of the disciplinary committee were members of the council there was a prima facie case of bias and interim interdict was granted against the proposed disciplinary proceedings.[98] And where councillors had voted for a motion critical of some of their colleagues on the council, they were interdicted from sitting on a disciplinary committee which was to consider their conduct.[99]

Grave public inconvenience

"Where the interest which is said to disqualify is not pecuniary, and is **18.21** neither substantial nor calculated to cause bias in the mind of the judge, it will be disregarded, particularly if to disqualify the judge would be

---

[92] *Grahame House Investments Ltd v. Secretary of State for the Environment*, 1985 S.L.T. 502.

[93] *Nicol v. Magistrates of Aberdeen* (1870) 9M. 306.

[94] *Smith v. East Dunbartonshire Council*, 1997 S.L.T. 997.

[95] *Anderson v. Manson*, 1909 S.C. 838.

[96] *R. v. Liverpool City Jusitices, ex p. Topping* [1983] 1 W.L.R. 119.

[97] *R. v. Board of Visitors of Frankland Prison, ex p. Lewis* [1986] 1 W.L.R. 130.

[98] *J.A. & D.S. Rennie v. Scottish Milk Records Association*, 1988 S.L.T. 272.

[99] *Brown v. Executive Committee of Edinburgh Labour Party*, 1995 S.L.T. 985.

productive of grave public inconvenience".[1] But the consideration of public inconvenience may come to justify persons acting as decision makers where their disqualification would lead to a breakdown in administration. Necessity may override considerations of bias and interest[2]; as, for example, where the declinatures, if sustained, would lead to the loss of a quorum.[3]

Waiver

18.22 A question arises whether a plea of bias may be overcome where the parties have agreed to waive the disqualification in full knowledge of it. Any objection to the judge must be raised at the outset of the proceedings.[4] English law recognises that waiver of statutory declinature provisions may be effective where the disqualification merely echoes the common law position.[5] Where the parties have agreed to the appointment of a particular person as arbiter one party may not later be able to object on the ground that the person was interested.[6] It is at least doubtful whether waiver should be available in the criminal courts as well as the civil courts.[7]

(b) Apparent bias

The appearance of bias

18.23 Even although there is no actual partiality exercised by a decision maker, any connection with one side in the dispute may be enough to disqualify the person from sitting or to render the decision open to reduction. "Even if he was as impartial as could be, nevertheless if right-minded persons would think that, in the circumstances, there was a real likelihood of bias on his part, then he should not sit."[8] The law of Scotland is the same as has been stated by Eve J. in *Law v. Chartered Institute of Patent Agents*[9] in these terms:

> "Each member of the Council in adjudicating on a complaint thereunder is performing a judicial duty, and he must bring to the discharge of that duty an unbiased and impartial mind. If he has a bias which renders him otherwise than an impartial judge he is disqualified from performing his duty. Nay more (so jealous is the policy of our law of the purity of the administration of justice), if there are circumstances so affecting a person acting in a judicial capacity as to be calculated to create in the mind of a reasonable

---

[1] *Wildridge v. Anderson* (1897) 25R.(J.) 27, *per* Lord Moncrieff at 34.

[2] *Macbeth v. Innes* (1873) 11M. 404 at 408; see Wade and Forsyth, *Administrative Law* (7th ed.), p. 477.

[3] *Douglas, Heron and Co. v. Grant* (1774) 1 Hailes 563. The court repelled the declinature in that case after examining the situation and finding that there would not be a quorum left if the declinatures were allowed.

[4] *Duke of Athole v. Robertson* (1869) 8M. 299.

[5] De Smith, Woolf and Jowell, *Judicial Review of Administrative Action* (5th ed.), p. 542.

[6] *Crawford Brothers v. Commissioners of Northern Lighthouses*, 1925 S.C.(H.L.) 22.

[7] It was doubted in *Caledonian Ry v. Ramsay* (1897) 24R.(J.) 48. For a recent review of the problem of waiver, see *Auckland Casino Ltd v. Casino Control Authority* [1995] 1 N.Z.L.R. 142.

[8] *Metropolitan Properties Co. (FGC) Ltd v. Lannon* [1969] 1 Q.B. 577 at 599.

[9] [1919] Ch. 276 at 289.

man a suspicion of that person's impartiality, those circumstances are themselves sufficient to disqualify although in fact no bias exists".

In one case the test was stated by Ackner L.J. as follows: "Would a reasonable or fair-minded person sitting in court and knowing all the relevant facts have a reasonable suspicion that a fair trial for the applicant was not possible?"[10] Similarly, Cross L.J. once observed[11]: "the question is not whether the tribunal will in fact be biased, but whether a reasonable man with no inside knowledge might well think that it might be biased."

In relation to this category of case there has been some debate on the formulation which expresses the test in the most appropriate words. In *Gough*[12] the test was preferred of a real danger of bias. That has been criticised on the grounds that it does not make it sufficiently clear that a possibility rather than a probability of bias may be fatal, that it stresses the danger rather than the appearance of bias, and that in removing any reference to the view of the reasonable third party it may prefer the court's view of the risk to the court's view of the public view of the risk. In *Webb v. The Queen*[13] the problem arose whether certain conduct on the part of a juror warranted the juror's disqualification. The court rejected the formulation proposed in *Gough* and preferred the greater latitude of the test of a reasonable apprehension or suspicion on the part of a fair-minded and informed member of the public that the juror or the jury would not discharge their task impartially. Such an approach may minimise the risk of unnecessary damage to the reputation of the person concerned and the embarrassment which a challenge on the ground of bias may understandably evoke. But it may be that the various differences in some at least of the terminology do not reflect a totally different approach in the substance of the matter.[14] The test which has been adopted in Scotland remains that of a suspicion of bias raised in the mind of a reasonable man.[15] That test has continued to be applied.[16]

Conduct during and outwith the hearing

Where someone acting in a judicial capacity expresses a view early in the proceedings favouring one side of the dispute there is a risk that he will appear to be biased. The use of language indicating a hostility to a particular party in the proceedings may be fatal to their validity.[17] But where there is a sufficient difference between the context in which earlier views were expressed and the matter which now arises for decision, review will be refused.[18] Expressions of opinion on the issue in the past will not suffice.[19] In the context of an arbiter nominated and

18.24

---

[10] *R. v. Liverpool City Justices, ex p. Topping* [1983] 1 W.L.R. 119 at 123.

[11] *Hannam v. Bradford Corporation* [1970] 1 W.L.R. 937 at 949.

[12] *R. v. Gough* [1993] A.C. 646 at 670.

[13] (1994) 181 C.L.R. 41.

[14] *Roylance v. The General Medical Council*, [1999] 3 W.L.R. 541.

[15] *Bradford v. McLeod*, 1986 S.L.T. 244. The Scottish position was referred to in *Re Pinochet*, Dec. 17, 1998, but in that case the House of Lords did not require to review the decision in *Gough*.

[16] *e.g. Doherty v. McGlennan*, 1997 S.L.T. 444; but the court's attention was not drawn to the case of *Gough*.

[17] *R. v. Inner West London Coroner, ex p. Dallaglio* [1994] 4 All E.R. 139.

[18] *London & Clydeside Estates v. Secretary of State*, 1987 S.L.T. 459.

[19] *Halliday v. Duke of Hamilton's Trustees* (1903) 5F. 800.

agreed to by the parties very specific averments of hostile actings are required before an arbiter can be disqualified.[20] It is not only conduct by the decision-making body during the course of the hearing which may give an evident indication of bias. Conduct outwith the hearing may be correspondingly fatal. Thus, where a sheriff had made a remark to a solicitor at a social function which was capable of being construed as displaying a bias against mineworkers it was held that the sheriff should have disqualified himself from hearing a case where the same solicitor was representing a mineworker charged with a summary offence.[21] It has been held that a sheriff should not hear a case in which the credibility of a party is in issue where earlier on the same day he has expressed a view on the credibility of that party in other proceedings.[22]

III THE RIGHT TO BE HEARD

Introduction

18.25 Two questions require to be distinguished. The first is whether before making a decision a decision maker is required to give any interested party an opportunity to present a view upon the matter. The second is what is the substance of that duty in the cases in which the duty arises. Some decisions may properly be made without the requirement of ascertaining anyone's view. The first problem then is to ascertain where the duty arises on the decision maker and a corresponding right to be heard arises in the interested party.

Right to a Hearing

18.26 A right to be heard may arise by express statutory provision. That matter has already been considered in the preceding chapter.[23] Alternatively, the right may arise by virtue of a legitimate expectation.[24] Beyond these two situations the question whether an individual has a right to be heard before a decision is made affecting his or her interests depends upon the circumstances of the case, although opinions may differ on what fairness requires in particular cases.[25] The basic position in the context of judicial proceedings was described by Lord Fraser of Tullybelton in these words[26]: "One of the principles of natural justice is that a person is entitled to adequate notice and opportunity to be heard before any judicial order is pronounced against him, so that he, or someone acting on his behalf, may make such representations, if any, as he sees fit. That is the rule of *audi alteram partem* which applies to all judicial proceedings, unless its application to a particular class of proceedings has been excluded by Parliament expressly or by necessary implication." Lord Denning expressed the view[27] that it was not possible "to lay down rigid rules as to when the principles of natural justice are to apply: nor as to

---

[20] *Scott v. Gerrard*, 1916 S.C. 793.

[21] *Bradford v. McLeod*, 1986 S.L.T. 244. See also *Doherty v. McGlennan*, 1997 S.L.T. 444.

[22] *McPherson v. Hamilton*, 1991 S.L.T. 611.

[23] See para. 17.15.

[24] See para. 19.18. See also *Stannifer Developments Ltd v. Glasgow Development Agency (No. 2)*, 1999 S.C. 156.

[25] *Breen v. AEU* [1971] 2 Q.B. 175.

[26] *Re Hamilton; Re Forrest* [1981] A.C. 1038 at 1045.

[27] *R. v. Gaming Board, ex p. Benaim* [1970] 2 Q.B. 417 at 430.

their scope and extent. Everything depends on the subject matter". It was stated in *Durayappah v. Fernando*[28] that "Outside well-known cases such as dismissal from office, deprivation of property and expulsion from clubs, there is a vast area where the principle can only be applied upon most general considerations". Three matters were identified which should be borne in mind when considering the possible application of the principle: "first, what is the nature of the property, the office held, status enjoyed or services to be performed by the complainant of injustice. Secondly, in what circumstances or upon what occasions is the person claiming to be entitled to exercise the measure of control entitled to intervene. Thirdly, when a right to intervene is proved, what sanctions in fact is the latter entitled to impose upon the other".

When the Right Arises

Where there is no statutory requirement for any hearing it has to be a **18.27** matter of circumstances whether any obligation lies on the decision maker to hear the parties, whether orally or in any other form. The guiding principle is that of fairness. One approach is to hold that the rules of natural justice will apply unless the circumstances are such as to indicate the contrary: the circumstances will include the person or body making the decision, the nature of the decision, the gravity of the matter in issue, and the terms of any provision governing the power to decide.[29] Some examples may now be given of the circumstances in which hearings may, and may not, be required.

Deprivation of property

In accordance with what may be referred to as the principle in *Cooper v.* **18.28** *Wandsworth Board of Works*[30] no man should be deprived of his property without having an opportunity of being heard. Where the decision involves such a consequence the duty to give an opportunity to the person affected will arise. In *Cooper* a local authority was held not to be entitled to exercise a statutory power to demolish a house, where notice of the intention to build had not been given, without giving to the person concerned an opportunity to be heard.[31] The position here is reinforced by the express provision on the protection of property contained in Article 1 of the First Protocol to the European Convention on Human Rights.[32]

Dismissals

Where the case is one of employment the matter will generally be **18.29** regulated by the law of contract and the correctness of the decision to terminate the contract will not depend on whether the employee has been heard in his own defence.[33] An officer holding office at pleasure has no right to a hearing before dismissal.[34] But where a person holds an

---

[28] [1967] 2 A.C. 337 at 349.
[29] *Galman v. National Association for Mental Health* [1971] 1 Ch. 317, *per* Megarry J. at 333.
[30] (1863) 14 C.B.N. S. 180.
[31] *Cooper v. Board of Works for the Wandsworth District* (1863) 14 C.B. (N.S.) 180.
[32] See para. 16.51.
[33] *Ridge v. Baldwin* [1964] A.C. 40 at 65.
[34] *Ridge v. Baldwin, supra.*

official position, of which Lord Reid in *Ridge v. Baldwin* gave several examples,[35] then the duty to hear him will arise.

Sanctions and matters of discipline

18.30   The exercise of powers which may affect the pocket or the position of the individual will generally give rise to the duty to hear a defence before determining the course to be taken with regard to the case. Where a body makes decisions which affect the rights of others or curtail their liberty they must act fairly.[36] Fairness in such a case will require the duty to hear such affected persons. Where an official position is at stake a hearing should be held, as for example in the case of a decision whether or not to endorse an election of a shop steward.[37]

Licences

18.31   Where a gaming board was to have regard only to certain specified matters in deciding whether to grant a certificate Lord Denning, M.R. observed[38]:

> "It follows, I think, that the board have a duty to act fairly. They must give the applicant an opportunity of satisfying them of the matters specified in the subsection. They must let him know what their impressions are so that he can disabuse them. But I do not think that they need quote chapter and verse against him as if they were dismissing him from an office, as in *Ridge v. Baldwin* [1964] AC 40; or depriving him of his property, as in *Cooper v. Wandsworth Board of Works* (1863) 14 C.B.N.S. 180. After all they are not charging him with doing anything wrong. They are simply inquiring as to his capability and diligence and are having regard to his character, reputation and financial standing".

In relation to licences it has been suggested that a hearing requires to be allowed where a licence earlier granted is being discontinued or forfeited, and also where a licence-holder seeks a renewal with a legitimate expectation that the renewal will be granted, but that no hearing is required where an application is made with no particular right or legitimate expectation to have it granted.[39]

Applications for naturalisation

18.32   In *R. v. Secretary of State for the Home Department, ex parte Fayed*[40] it was held that although there was no obligation to give reasons for refusing an application for British citizenship, the discretion required to be exercised reasonably and fairly. That meant that the Home Secretary was required in fairness to inform an applicant for naturalisation of any areas on which he was having concern before making his decision, so as to enable the applicant to make such representations as he could or, where matters were not being disclosed on grounds of public interest, to be

---

[35] *ibid.* at 66 *et seq.*
[36] *R. v. Commission for Racial Equality, ex p. Hillingdon LBC* [1982] A.C. 779 at 787.
[37] *Breen v. AEU* [1971] 2 Q.B. 175.
[38] *R. v. Gambling Board, ex p. Benain* [1970] 2 Q.B. 417 at 430.
[39] *McInnes v. Onslow-Fane* [1978] 3 All E.R. 211, *per* Megarry V.-C. at 218.
[40] [1997] 1 All E.R. 228.

enabled to challenge before the court the justification for the refusal to disclose.[41]

No Hearing Required

It is not in every case that fairness will require that the parties interested **18.33** in a decision must be allowed an oral hearing, or indeed any hearing, before a decision is made. Where there is no statutory obligation to hear parties the matter will depend upon the circumstances. The absence of any provision in a statute for a hearing may point to the absence of any requirement for one.[42] *In Lloyd v. McMahon*[43] where there was no statutory obligation, the parties had not requested a hearing and they had been able to make full written representations, it was held that the decision maker had not acted unfairly in not affording the parties an oral hearing. It has been held that approval by a central authority of a byelaw could be given without hearing objections.[44] The parties to an arbitration may agree not to have a hearing, but it is for them and not the arbiter to decide upon such a course[45] and the nature of the submission may make it plain whether or not a hearing is intended.[46]

Matters preliminary to a decision

Where matters have not yet reached the stage of starting upon the **18.34** decision-making process but the question has still to be resolved whether or not that process should be embarked upon, the rules of natural justice may be held not to apply. As Lord Reid once observed[47]: "Every public officer who has to decide whether to prosecute or raise proceedings ought first to decide whether there is a prima facie case, but no one supposes that justice requires that he should first seek the comments of the accused or the defendant on the material before him. So there is nothing inherently unjust in reaching such a decision in the absence of the other party." Thus a hearing may not be required where the only substance of the decision is whether or not action should be taken which, if taken, will involve a decision-making process, such as whether there is a prima facie case for a prosecution[48] or an investigation of a limited company.[49] Such preliminary considerations of the matter must be carried out fairly but will not require parties to be heard. The rules of natural justice were held not to apply to a company investigation ordered by the Board of Trade at a preliminary stage for the purposes of good administration.[50] In one case where it was a legislative function which was being performed, being neither administrative nor judicial, the rules of natural justice were held not to be applicable.[51] But where the actual process of decision-making is embarked upon a right to a hearing may arise. That requires consideration of the circumstances.

---

[41] See S.C. Smith, "The Comprehensive Approach to Fairness", 1997 S.L.T. (News) 265.
[42] *Kirkpatrick v. Town Council of Maxwelltown*, 1912 S.C. 258. For what is required of a hearing, see para. 18.37 *et seq.*
[43] [1987] 1 A.C. 627.
[44] *Scott v. Magistrates of Glasgow* (1899) 1F. 665; (1899) 1F(H.L.) 51.
[45] *Langmuir v. Sloan* (1840) 2D. 877.
[46] *Latta v. Macrae* (1852) 14D. 641.
[47] *Wiseman v. Borneman* [1971] A.C. 297 at 308.
[48] *Wiseman v. Borneman, supra; Furnell v. Whangerei High School Board* [1973] A.C. 660 at 681.
[49] *Norwest Holst Ltd v. Secretary of State for Trade* [1978] 1 Ch. 201.
[50] *ibid.*
[51] *Bates v. Hailsham* [1972] 1 W.L.R. 1373.

Public interest and national security

18.35 Considerations of national security may on occasion override the requirements of natural justice. Such has been the case in relation to the deportation of an alien[52] and the regulation of the conditions of service of civil servants.[53] In the public interest information may justifiably be withheld although its disclosure would otherwise be required under the principles of natural justice.[54]

Where a useless formality

18.36 If it can be shown that a hearing would in the circumstances have been a useless formality, because it would have made no difference whatever the complainer might have said, that may be a good answer to an argument that a hearing should have been permitted.[55] But such a situation may only rarely occur, since minds may often be induced to change where a case comes to be heard.[56] Where the submission is clearly without any conceivable merit, or seeks to persuade the authority to do something which it cannot lawfully do,[57] the refusal of a hearing may be justifiable.

IV   THE CONDUCT OF THE HEARING

Procedure

18.37 The procedure to be adopted to meet the requirements of natural justice depends substantially upon the facts and circumstances of each case.[58] The overriding principle in the absence of any statutory provision is that of fairness in the circumstances.[59] Statutory bodies may require to decide matters of law and matters of fact. As Lord Loreburn L.C. observed,[60] in doing either of these tasks "they must act in good faith and fairly listen to both sides, for that is a duty lying upon everyone who decides anything. But I do not think they are bound to treat such a question as though it were a trial. They have no power to administer an oath, and need not examine witnesses. They can obtain information in any way they think best, always giving a fair opportunity to those who are parties to the controversy for correcting or contradicting any relevant statement prejudicial to their view." The method for obtaining evidence and for receiving the views of interested parties may be regulated by the decision maker as he thinks fit, but always subject to the requirement to act fairly.[61] It may be sufficient for a reporter to report on all his findings but to leave the drawing of conclusions to the Secretary of State, provided that the whole process can be found to have been fair.[62] Fairness

---

[52] *R. v. Secretary of State for Home Affairs, ex p. Hosenball* [1977] 3 All E.R. 766. See M. Bovey, "Judicial Review of Immigration Cases: the Scottish Dimension" (1990) 35 J.L.S.S. 7.

[53] *Council of Civil Service Unions v. Minister for the Civil Service* [1985] A.C. 374.

[54] See Wade and Forsyth, *Administrative Law* (7th ed.), p. 855.

[55] *Malloch v. Aberdeen Corporation*, 1971 S.C.(H.L.) 85, *per* Lord Reid at 104.

[56] *R. v. Secretary of State for the Environment, ex p. Brent LBC* [1982] 1 Q.B. 593 at 646.

[57] *Scott v. Aberdeen Corporation*, 1976 S.L.T. 141 at 147.

[58] *University of Ceylon v. Fernando* [1960] 1 W.L.R. 223 at 231.

[59] *Bushell v. Secretary of State for the Environment* [1981] A.C. 75.

[60] *Board of Education v. Rice* [1911] A.C. 179 at 182.

[61] *Jeffe v. New Zealand Dairy Production and Marketing Board* [1967] A.C. 557.

[62] *R. v. Secretary of State for Transport* [1988] 1 Q.B. 429.

requires that the individual involved in the hearing should understand what is being said and done. An interpreter may thus be an essential requirement of fairness.[63]

Right to appear

There is a distinction to be made between a right to be heard and a right **18.38** to an oral hearing.[64] The latter may not be part of the former. The requirements of fairness may often be satisfied by the giving of a sufficient opportunity for written submissions without the need for anyone to appear at a formal hearing. A refusal of an oral hearing may well not contravene the rules of natural justice if there is no dispute about the facts and an opportunity has been given for the presentation of submissions in writing.[65] Where a decision is required of a group, such as a board, there is no general rule that they should hold an oral hearing, but it will usually be necessary that the group should meet to consider and determine the issue as a group rather than circulate papers and arrive at isolated conclusions.[66]

Notice of the proceedings

Even without any statutory provision fairness may demand that certain **18.39** things be done before a hearing commences. Built in to the right to be heard is the right to know when the opportunity of being heard will be afforded. It has long been recognised that a person is entitled to be given an opportunity to appear before a decision is pronounced against him.[67] In *Inland Revenue v. Barrs*[68] tax loss certificates granted by the general commissioners were quashed because the inspector of taxes had not been notified of their intention to determine the matter. A failure to notify a football club that the council of the association, of which it was a member, was considering confirming a decision of its executive committee to censure and fine the club, entitled the club to have the decision by the council declared *ultra vires*.[69] Where there is a right to be heard there should also be a right to notice of the date and place of the hearing. Where the tenant in a hearing before a rent assessment committee withdrew his objection and believed that the matter was then concluded, it was held that he was entitled to notice that the hearing would proceed and that the rent might be increased.[70] Moreover notice of a complaint must be given within sufficient time to enable the recipient to prepare his response.[71]

Notice of the issue and the evidence

It is also a necessary ingredient of the right to be heard, where it exists, **18.40** that the person affected should have notice of the issue which is to be determined, which includes any charge or complaint which is being

---

[63] *Liszewski v. Thomson*, 1942 J.C. 55.
[64] *Young v. Criminal Injuries Compensation Board*, 1997 S.L.T. 297 at 300.
[65] *Young, supra.* In *Local Government Board v. Arlidge* [1915] A.C. 120 an oral hearing was held not to have been required. In *Malloch v. Aberdeen Corporation*, 1971 S.C.(H.L.) 85 an oral hearing was required.
[66] *R. v. Army Board, ex p. Anderson* [1992] 1 Q.B. 169.
[67] *Earl of Roxburgh* (1663) M. 7328.
[68] 1961 S.C.(H.L.) 22.
[69] *St Johnson's Football Club v. Scottish Football Association*, 1965 S.L.T. 171.
[70] *Hanson v. Church Commissioners for England* [1978] 1 Q.B. 823.
[71] *Lanarkshire and Dunbartonshire Ry v. Main* (1894) 21 R. 1018; *M'Donald v. Lanarkshire Fire Brigade Joint Committee*, 1959 S.C. 141.

brought against him.[72] The sufficiency of the intimation will depend upon what is reasonable and fair in the circumstances.[73] Where a person is liable to be dismissed and is entitled to a hearing, he is entitled to know the substance of the case which is to be brought against him and he is entitled to know it in more detail than mere generalities.[74] Furthermore, decisions should not be allowed to be made upon material which has not been seen by the party affected.[75] A failure to disclose to a police inspector facing disciplinary proceedings a prejudicial report which was sent to the adjudicating officer was held to be a denial of natural justice.[76] A prisoner was held entitled to be informed of all the reports which were to be placed before the Parole Board for its consideration of his case.[77] It has also been held in England that where the Home Secretary is considering a referral of a conviction to the Court of Appeal, the victim of the possible miscarriage of justice may be entitled to see the information relating to his case before the decision on referral is made.[78] Notice need not be given of subsidiary material which may be before the tribunal and which is only of a general character and not such as to play any real part in the decision.[79] It is unfair for a tribunal to decide an application for a licence on a point not developed at the hearing without giving the applicant an opportunity to deal with it.[80]

Hearing must be fair

18.41 Where there is a duty to allow a hearing then the hearing must be fairly conducted, whatever particular form of procedure is adopted. Where there is evidence led, all the parties must have the opportunity of hearing it, which includes being present at any site inspection.[81] A tribunal may not "close its doors to justice" by declaring in advance that the conclusion of any hearing is foregone.[82] If the members of the decision-making body have already finally made up their minds before the hearing, the proceedings will be open to reduction; but the court will not entertain a mere speculation on that possibility if there is nothing to show that the hearing has been otherwise than fair.[83]

Representation

18.42 Representation is sometimes regulated by statutory provision[84] or by the rules of the particular domestic tribunal. In the context of a criminal offence Article 6(3) of the Convention on Human Rights provides for a

---

[72] *e.g. M'Donald v. Lanarkshire Fire Brigade Joint Committee*, 1959 S.C. 141, where the obligation was recognised both under regulation and (at 147) at common law.

[73] *Walker v. Arbroath Presbytery* (1876) 4R.(H.L.) 1.

[74] *McDonald v. Burns*, 1940 S.C. 376.

[75] *Wiseman v. Borneman* [1971] A.C. 297 at 309 and 320.

[76] *Kanda v. Government of Malaya* [1982] A.C. 322.

[77] *R. v. Parole Board, ex p. Wilson* [1992] Q.B. 740; see also *R. v. Home Secretary, ex p. Duggan* [1994] 3 All E.R. 277.

[78] *R. v. Home Secretary, ex p. Hickey (No. 2)* [1995] 1 W.L.R. 734.

[79] *Stewart v. Secretary of State for Scotland*, 1996 S.L.T. 1203; 1998 S.L.T. 385.

[80] *William Hill (Scotland) Ltd v. Kyle and Carrick District Licensing Board*, 1991 S.L.T. 559; *Tomkin v. City of Glasgow Licensing Board*, 1994 S.L.T. 34.

[81] *Drew v. Drew* (1855) 2 Macq. 1. The principle is recognised in criminal procedure: *Aitken v. Wood*, 1921 J.C. 84.

[82] *Sommerville v. Directors of the Edinburgh Assembly Rooms* (1899) 1F. 1091.

[83] *Leith Police Commissioners v. Spink* (1893) 1 S.L.T. 142.

[84] *e.g. Maynard v. Osmund* [1977] 1 Q.B. 240. See *Ceylon University v. Fernando* [1960] 1 All E.R. 631.

right to defend oneself through legal assistance.[85] But there is no common law right to have a representative acting for one[86] or to have legal representation in civil matters.[87] In the absence of any express provision a tribunal will have a discretion to allow or refuse a representative[88] and a minister setting up an advisory panel to hear complaints against deportation orders may reasonably decide in advance to exclude any legal representatives.[89] That there may be no legal representation before a tribunal does not mean that a law agent may not be employed to prepare and send in written representations to a body performing an administrative act.[90] Where a person has no representation, lay assistance in the presentation of a party's case should be permitted as part of the general obligation to secure fairness in the proceedings.[91] In one case where parties agreed to an informal arbitration the arbiter was held to be entitled to refuse to allow law agents to appear for the parties.[92]

Opportunity to comment

Where confirmation of a compulsory purchase order proceeded on an **18.43** important point which had not been canvassed at the inquiry but was included in the inspector's report as matter discovered at his inspection of the site, and no opportunity was given to the owners to challenge the point or to put forward an answer to it, the decision was quashed. It was held to be contrary to natural justice to confirm an order which might be shown to be erroneous on a matter to which the owners had had no opportunity to reply.[93] In *Tait v. Central Radio Taxis (Tollcross) Ltd*[94] a taxi driver was held entitled to damages for having been dismissed by a radio taxi company whose disciplinary tribunal had had before them material relating to the pursuer on which he had had no opportunity to comment. On the other hand, it has been held that the choice of an arbiter from a panel of names could not be challenged on the ground that one party did not have the opportunity of stating objections to the nomination.[95]

Right to submit argument and respond

Where the right to a hearing exists it is an essential that the party be **18.44** allowed both to present his case and to respond to any counter allegations or submissions.[96] It is "an elementary principle of natural

---

[85] See para. 16.31. The reference to criminal offences in the context of Article 6 has been strictly construed: *R. v. Board of Prisoners of H.M. Prison, The Maze, ex p. Hone* [1988] 1 A.C. 379 at 393. See, generally, S. Naismith, "European Court of Human Rights" (1995) 40 J.L.S.S. 32.

[86] *Enderby Town Football Club Ltd v. Football Association Ltd* [1971] 1 All E.R. 215.

[87] *Pett v. Greyhound Racing Association Ltd (No. 2)* [1970] 1 Q.B. 46.

[88] *Templeton v. Criminal Injuries Compensation Board*, 1997 S.L.T. 953. See also *R. v. Secretary of State for the Home Department, ex p. Tarrant* [1985] 1 Q.B. 251; *R. v. Board of Visitors of H.M. Prison, The Maze, ex p. Hone* [1988] 1 A.C. 379.

[89] *Abbas v. Secretary of State for the Home Department*, 1993 S.L.T. 502.

[90] *ibid.* at 503.

[91] *R. v. Leicester City Justices, ex p. Barrow* [1991] 2 Q.B. 260.

[92] *Paterson & Son v. Corporation of Glasgow* (1901) 3F(H.L.) 34.

[93] *Fairmount Investments Ltd v. Secretary of State for the Environment* [1976] 1 W.L.R. 1255.

[94] 1989 S.L.T. 217.

[95] *Ramsay v. McLaren*, 1936 S.L.T. 35. The judge held that the selection was an entirely administrative act and not quasi-judicial, a distinction not now recognised: see para. 8.21. The decision is now of doubtful validity.

[96] *R. v. Army Board, ex p. Anderson* [1992] 1 Q.B. 169.

justice" that a fair opportunity must be afforded to both parties to correct or contradict any relevant statement prejudicial to the contentions of either.[97] A right to be heard carries with it the right to hear the evidence brought against one, and the right to reply to it.[98] However, in the case of an emergency situation the risk of danger to the safety of property and persons may outweigh the duty of fairness to provide an opportunity to be heard.[99]

Right to lead evidence

18.45 In the generality of the matter the right to lead evidence may depend upon the nature and circumstances of the case. Where there is no statutory regulation on the point it is within the power of a decision-making body to decide whether or not they will allow evidence to be led or proceed simply on submission, provided always that both parties are afforded equal treatment.[1] Where there are disputed matters of fact evidence will normally be necessary.[2] The technical rules of evidence which apply in civil and criminal litigation form no part of the rules of natural justice.[3] What natural justice does require is firstly that the decision maker must base his findings on some material which tends logically to show the existence of facts consistent with the finding, and support the finding by reasoning which is not self-contradictory: and secondly, that the decision maker must listen fairly to any evidence which contradicts such findings and any rational argument against such findings, so that any proponent of a view contrary to those findings may have a fair opportunity of presenting all the material and submissions which might lead to the opposite result.[4] It may be unfair to reject unchallenged evidence without giving the party adducing it an opportunity to adduce support for it.[5] Associated with the right to lead evidence is the right to recover documentary material relevant to the presentation of the case. In criminal cases the accused may obtain an order from the court for the recovery of relevant documents to assist his case, if the court is satisfied that the order would serve a proper purpose and that the granting of it was in the interests of justice.[6]

Duty to hear both sides

18.46 Once it is evident that some form of hearing is required to be held before a decision is made then it is necessary that the hearing encompasses the views both of those supportive of and of those adverse to the proposal. Both sides should be allowed to be heard, both in civil

---

[97] *Inland Revenue v. Barrs*, 1959 S.C. 273 at 294; *Board of Education v. Rice* [1911] A.C. 179 at 182.
[98] *Moore v. Clyde Pilotage Authority*, 1943 S.C. 457 at 464.
[99] *R. v. Secretary of State for Transport, ex p. Pegasus Holidays (London) Ltd* [1989] 2 All E.R. 481.
[1] *Walsh v. Magistrates of Pollockshaws*, 1907 S.C.(H.L.) 1; *Cigaro Ltd v. City of Glasgow District Licensing Board*, 1982 S.C. 104 at 112; *R. v. Army Board, ex p. Anderson* [1992] 1 Q.B. 169 at 187; *JAE (Glasgow) Ltd v. City of Glasgow District Licensing Board*, 1994 S.L.T. 1164.
[2] *e.g. R. v. Board of Visitors of Hull Prison, ex p. St. Germain (No. 2)* [1979] 1 W.L.R. 1401; *cf. Reid & Son v. Sinclair Brothers* (1894) 22 R.(J.) 12.
[3] *R. v. Deputy Industrial Injuries Commissioner, ex p. Moore* [1965] 1 Q.B. 456.
[4] *Mahon v. Air New Zealand* [1984] A.C. 808 at 820.
[5] *Kriba v. Secretary of State for the Home Department*, 1998 S.L.T. 1113.
[6] *McLeod, Petr*, 1998 S.L.T. 233.

proceedings[7] and in criminal proceedings.[8] It is not fair for one party to be allowed to lead evidence and for the other to be denied the opportunity of doing so. Nor is it fair for an arbiter, having allowed further evidence to be obtained, to decide the case on the basis of the evidence favouring one party without having waited to hear the further evidence which might have favoured the other.[9] Where there is a hearing the decision maker must listen fairly to the contentions of all persons who are entitled to be represented at the hearing. Diplock L.J. has observed that that requires the person conducting the hearing, who was in the context in which he was considering the matter a deputy commissioner:

> "(a) to consider such 'evidence' relevant to the question to be decided as any person entitled to be represented wishes to put before him; (b) to inform every person represented of any 'evidence' which the deputy commissioner proposes to take into consideration, whether such 'evidence' be proffered by another person represented at the hearing, or is discovered by the deputy commissioner as a result of his own investigation; (c) to allow each person represented to comment upon such 'evidence' and, where the 'evidence' is given orally by witnesses, to put questions to those witnesses; and (d) to allow each person represented to address argument to him on the whole of the case."[10]

The imposition of a condition by a reporter on a grant of planning permission without giving the parties an opportunity to express their view on the substance of it has been held to be contrary to natural justice.[11] In an arbitration a refusal to hear relevant and proper evidence essential to the determination of the case may constitute misconduct,[12] but a refusal to hear irrelevant evidence does not infringe the principles of natural justice.[13]

Cross-examination

Where there is a duty to act fairly any form of oppressive conduct may **18.47** render the proceedings open to challenge. A refusal to allow cross-examination or to lead evidence has been held to constitute oppression.[14] Whether a party interested in a particular matter of inquiry is or is not entitled to cross-examine witnesses who give evidence at the inquiry may be evident or at least may be deduced from the terms of the statutory provisions regulating the inquiry. There is no general duty at common law to permit cross-examination and no presumption that cross-examination should be allowed. The existence of the duty will depend upon the circumstances. It is not necessarily unfair to refuse to allow the cross-examination of a witness who has given evidence at a local inquiry.

---

[7] *Barrs v. British Wool Marketing Board*, 1957 S.C. 72 at 82; *Inland Revenue v. Barrs*, 1961 S.C. (H.L.) 22.

[8] *M'Culloch v. M'Laughlin*, 1930 J.C. 8.

[9] *Mitchell v. Cable* (1848) 10D. 1297.

[10] *R. v. The Deputy Industrial Injuries Commissioner, ex p. Moore* [1965] 1 Q.B. 456.

[11] *Dumfriesshire D.C. v. Secretary of State for Scotland*, 1996 S.L.T. 89.

[12] *Holmes Oil Co. v. Pumpherston Oil Co.* (1891) 18R.(H.L.) 52 at 54.

[13] *Brown & Son v. Associated Fireclay Companies*, 1937 S.C.(H.L.) 42.

[14] *Cowe v. M'Dougall*, 1909 S.C.(J.) 1.

In *Bushell v. Secretary of State for the Environment*[15] an inquiry was attended by many people who wished to put forward certain views without the cost of legal representation and without the ability to attend throughout the whole course of the proceedings. Lord Diplock regarded it as unfair to "over-judicialise" such an inquiry by insisting on the observation of court procedures and observed[16]:

> "Whether fairness requires an inspector to permit a person who has made statements on matters of fact or opinion, whether expert or otherwise, to be cross-examined by a party to the enquiry who wishes to dispute a particular statement must depend on all the circumstances".

In *Errington v. Wilson*[17] it was held that a justice of the peace had acted unfairly in refusing cross-examination of witnesses led in a hearing under section 9 of the Food Safety Act 1990 in which the justice had decided that certain batches of cheese failed to comply with food safety requirements and ordered them to be disposed of or destroyed. The circumstances of the case involved the following factors: the statutory provisions required a hearing before a sheriff or a justice; the person in charge of the food was liable to prosecution under the Act and was entitled to be heard and to call witnesses; the justice or the sheriff might be the person sitting in the court in which any criminal prosecution might be brought against the person in charge of the food; an order made in the hearing could constitute sufficient evidence for the purpose of a criminal prosecution; the consequences of an adverse decision were of the gravest consequence for the manufacturer of the cheese; and the issue in the case was of some technical complexity and difficulty requiring the attendance of expert witnesses on each side. In these circumstances the justice was held to have acted unfairly in refusing to allow cross-examination. Merely to allow questions to be put through the justice was not a sufficient alternative for direct questioning by the representatives of the parties to the witnesses. In some circumstances that course may be appropriate and sufficient where direct questioning could lead to the proceedings becoming out of control.[18] But that course is not a proper substitute for direct cross-examination conducted by responsible counsel, particularly if it enables the person conducting the hearing to decide whether or not to ask a particular question.

Duty to hear the whole case

18.48   Where one member of a tribunal has not heard the whole of the case he should not take part in the decision and if he does the decision may be quashed.[19] In the case of *Goodall v. Billsland*[20] two members of a licensing appeal court arrived late after the hearing was well started. Both took part in the deliberations of the court and voted. The Lord President observed[21]: "If gentlemen happen to be late with their trains, or anything of that sort, the remedy is exceedingly simple. It is only for

---

[15] [1981] A.C. 75.
[16] 97E.
[17] 1995 S.C. 550.
[18] *e.g. R. v. Board of Visitors of Hull Prison, ex p. St Germain (No. 2)* [1979] 1 W.L.R. 1401.
[19] *M'Ara v. Carrick* (1821) 1S. 216 (Excise Ct); *Finlayson v. Balfour* (1847) 9D. 701 (justices of the peace); *M'Ghee v. Moncur* (1899) 5F. 594 (dean of guild court).
[20] 1909 S.C. 1152.
[21] at 1180.

the particular case that is going on and in that case if they have been absent they must say that they decline to vote; and if they do that, nobody will think that their mere presence beside their brethren will vitiate the determination to which their brethren come. But if they vote, and take part, consequently, in a total deliberation of the Court then I am clearly of the opinion that it does vitiate the whole proceedings."

Knowledge of decision maker

A tribunal is not entitled to proceed upon facts within the personal **18.49** knowledge of its members unless these are matters of public or general knowledge[22]: While a decision maker may be entitled to use the knowledge which his own experience or investigations have made available to him, he should not found on material facts which have not been disclosed to the parties, nor may he proceed to hear further evidence in private,[23] nor engage in a private inquiry[24] after the oral hearing without notifying the parties and enabling them to be further heard. If he has a particular expertise he may use that in assessing the evidence which he hears, but he should not proceed on matters of fact or opinion on which the parties have not had an opportunity to comment.[25] If there are matters which may be material to the decision which have not emerged at the hearing the decision maker must raise these with the parties for their comments. Such a course accords with fairness and may in practice cause the decision maker to revise his view about them. A decision based on a fact or facts within the knowledge of the decision maker but not disclosed to the parties for their comments is open to reduction as being contrary to natural justice.[26] A decision based on an opinion formed by an inspector on a site inspection on a point not raised in the inquiry has been quashed.[27] So also it is a breach of the principle of fairness that a decision maker should proceed upon facts obtained from one side after a hearing which conflict with those found at the hearing.[28] But a minister may take into acount departmental advice given after an inquiry without reopening the inquiry.[29] Where the decision maker has proceeded upon information which is confidential, such as personal references, it has been held that such material, being matter of opinion only, does not require to be disclosed to an applicant.[30] Mention has already been made of the right to have advance notice of the issue and the relevant evidence.

Timetables and ordering of hearings

Neither in the criminal context, nor it is thought in the civil context, is **18.50** there a common law right to have a trial conducted without unreasonable delay,[31] but if there is unfairness or actual prejudice then the right

---

[22] *Moyes v. Assessor for Perth*, 1912 S.C. 761; *Cotton v. Assessor for Dumbarton*, 1936 S.C. 279 (valuation committee); *Learmonth Property Investment Co. v. Aitken*, 1970 S.C. 223 (rent assessment committee).
[23] *R. v. Deputy Industrial Injuries Commissioner, ex p. Jones* [1962] 2 Q.B. 677.
[24] *Errington v. Minister of Health* [1935] 1 K.B. 249.
[25] *Taylor v. Minister of Pensions*, 1946 S.C. 49.
[26] *Freeland v. Glasgow District Licensing Board*, 1979 S.C. 226.
[27] *Fairmount Investment Ltd v. Secretary of State for the Environment* [1976] 2 All E.R. 865.
[28] *Hamilton v. Secretary of State for Scotland*, 1972 S.C. 72.
[29] *Bushell v. Secretary of State for the Environment* [1981] A.C. 75.
[30] *R. v. Joint Higher Committee on Surgical Training, ex p. Milner* (1995) 7 Admin. L.R. 454.
[31] For the position under the European Convention on Human Rights, see para. 16.34.

may arise on such grounds as those.[32] Thus, in England a criminal trial will not be stayed unless there is such prejudice as to make a fair trial impossible.[33] Regard should be had to all the circumstances, including the nature of the prosecution's case.[34] In one case where there was no statutory timetable but the matter required to be dealt with expeditiously, a hearing at a very few hours' notice was considered not to involve a breach of natural justice.[35] Under the older system for licensing, a licensing authority was held not to have acted improperly where it decided to grant all the unopposed applications before considering those which were opposed.[36] Mention has already been made of the possibility of deferment under statutory procedures.[37] Where there are no statutory provisions on deferment or adjournment the principle of fairness will decide whether or not an adjournment ought to be allowed.

Fairness in the process of determination

18.51 The making of a decision is not to be shared with anyone outside those who have the duty and responsibility for making it. They should not be assisted by third parties in reaching it and if they discuss and determine the issue among themselves they should do that outwith the presence of the parties or any third party. In *Barrs v. British Wool Marketing Board*[38] a wool producer appealed to a tribunal against a valuation of his wool made by an appraiser under a statutory scheme. The tribunal examined the wool in the presence of the original appraiser, another appraiser, a representative of the producer and the regional officer of the marketing board. When the tribunal retired to consider their decision the two appraisers and the regional officer retired with the tribunal but the representative of the producer was excluded. They decided to reduce the valuation to a figure lower than that fixed by the the appraiser but their decision was nevertheless quashed. A like view was taken where in an appeal for housing benefit the representative of one side remained in the same room as the tribunal while it formed its decision, although the other side's representative had left the room.[39] So also a conviction was quashed where the clerk to the justices in criminal proceedings was the solicitor acting in the civil claim against the accused arising out of the same incident and he retired with them while they considered the case.[40] Where a committee after a hearing, such as a hearing on the dismissal of a surgeon, reports its findings to a superior body for decision, it is unfair for one of the parties to be present while that body considers the report.[41] Fairness does not require that members of a tribunal consult with each other when they are all of the same opinion.[42] Where

---

[32] *Jago v. District Court of New South Wales* (1989) 63 A.J.L.R. 640.

[33] *Att.-Gen.'s Reference No. 1 of 1990* [1992] 1 Q.B. 630; *DPP v. Tokai* [1996] 3 W.L.R. 149. In Scotland statutory time-limits operate to restrain delay: see the Criminal Procedure (Scotland) Act 1995, s.65.

[34] *Att.-Gen. of Hong Kong v. Cheung Wai-Bun* [1994] 1 A.C. 1.

[35] *Stakis plc v. Boyd*, 1989 S.C.L.R. 290.

[36] *Goodall v. Shaw*, 1913 S.C. 630. Cases of this period in the development of licensing law were regarded as of little value in *Freeland v. Glasgow District Licensing Board*, 1979 S.C. 226 at 234.

[37] para. 17.29.

[38] 1957 S.C. 72.

[39] *McDonnell, Petr*, 1987 S.L.T. 486.

[40] *R. v. Sussex Justices*[1924] 1 K.B. 256.

[41] *Palmer v. Inverness Hospitals Board*, 1963 S.C. 311.

[42] *Howard v. Borneman (No. 2)* [1976] A.C. 301.

irrelevant and prejudicial material was put before a disciplinary tribunal and they were not instructed to disregard it, their decision was quashed on the ground that justice must be seen to be done.[43] But if a fair hearing has been provided, the decision maker is not obliged at common law to disclose what he is minded to decide so as to give a further opportunity for submissions on his state of mind.[44]

V THE GIVING OF REASONS

General

As has already been noted in the previous chapter,[45] there is no general common law obligation in Scotland, nor in England, to give reasons.[46] The giving of reasons may, as has also been noticed,[47] be a matter of statutory obligation and that obligation may be express or implied. In the latter case the obligation is spelled out as a matter of construction of the statutory provisions. But the obligation may also arise by the force of the common law. Here such statutory provisions as there may be relating to the nature, function and work of the decision maker, including any provisions regarding procedure, may be relevant in deciding whether in the particular context an obligation to state reasons may or may not arise. But even where assistance is found in the statutory provisions the duty, where it exists, is based not on an intention of the statute implied in its terms but on the common law on a principle of fairness. That the statutory provisions are silent on the matter does not mean that a common law obligation is excluded. As Lord Donaldson of Lymington observed in *R. v. Civil Service Commissioner, ex parte Cunningham*[48]: "I do not accept that, just because Parliament has ruled that some tribunals should be required to give reasons for their decisions, it follows that the common law is unable to impose a similar requirement upon other tribunals."

With the growth of administrative decision making there has come an increased concern for the giving of reasons for decisions. Its importance is such that it may come to be seen as a third limb of the rules of natural justice,[49] reasons a decision may more readily be open to the risk of being seen as arbitrary, and, if justice should not only be done but should also be seen to be done, a decision given without reasons may be more exposed to criticism and suspicion.[50] A recent discussion of the duty to give reasons can be found in *Stefan v. The General Medical Council*.[51]

18.52

---

[43] *Murphy v. General Teaching Council for Scotland*, 1997 S.L.T. 1152.
[44] *Hoffman-La Roche & Co. A.G. v. Secretary of State for Trade and Industry* [1975] A.C. 295 at 369.
[45] See the cases cited at para. 17.23.
[46] *Purdon v. City of Glasgow District Licensing Board*, 1989 S.L.T. 201; *Macpherson, Petr*, 1990 J.C. 5 at 13; *R. v. Secretary for Trade and Industry, ex p. Lonrho* [1989] 2 All E.R. 609; *R. v. Civil Service Appeal Board, ex p. Cunningham* [1991] 4 All E.R. 310 at 317; *Lawrie v. Commission for Local Authority Accounts*, 1994 S.L.T. 1185.
[47] para. 17.23.
[48] [1991] 4 All E.R. 310 at 318.
[49] It has been so seen in Canadian jurisprudence, David J. Mullan, *Administrative Law* (3rd ed.), p. 282, and in India, *Siemens Engineering and Manufacturing Co. of India Ltd v. Union of India and Another*, 1976 Supreme Court 1785, *per* Bhagevati J. at 1789.
[50] *R. v. Civil Service Appeal Board, ex p. Cunningham* [1991] 4 All E.R. 310 at 322. See also Professor Harold Potter, *The Quest of Justice* (1951), p. 13.
[51] [1999] 1 W.L.R. 1293.

The absence of reasons

18.53   The absence of reasons will not prevent the decision from being questioned.[52] Indeed, without reasons a complainer may require to take proceedings for judicial review in order to ascertain the reasons for the decision, since at that stage a full and fair disclosure must be made by the decision maker.[53] A decision without grounds may be open to attack on such a ground as irrationality and the view has been expressed that the taking, without giving reasons, of a course contrary to that to which all the prima facie reasons seem to point, may give rise to an inference that there was no good reason.[54] Thus, where no grounds are given it may well prove more difficult to prevent a successful application for review.[55] On the other hand, Lord Keith observed in *R. v. Secretary of State for Trade and Industry, ex parte Lonrho plc*[56]: "The absence of reasons for a decision where there is no duty to give them cannot of itself provide any support for the suggested irrationality of the decision. The only significance of the absence of reasons is that if all other known facts and circumstances appear to point overwhelmingly in favour of a different decision, the decision maker, who has given no reasons, cannot complain if the court draws the inference that he had no rational reasons for his decision."

The reasons for reasons

18.54   The advantages of the provision of reasons may be summarised as follows[57]: in improving the quality of decision making,[58] and so improving the machinery of government; in satisfying the parties affected by the decisions, enabling them to ascertain if there are grounds for appeal or convincing them of the soundness of the decision; in enabling a reviewing authority to understand the decision and identify any error; and in the public interest in giving confidence in the process of decision making. The advantages of a requirement for reasons lies not only in the general interest of fairness but in the more practical respects of encouraging decision makers to apply their minds with due concentration on the relevant issues and enabling the process of review to be more readily available where circumstances call for its exercise. As Lord Denning put it, the giving of reasons is "one of the fundamentals of good administration".[59] The arguments against the giving of reasons have also to be noted: the restraints on free discussion between decision makers, the burden of work, the delay and expense involved, the increase of "judicialisation" and a danger of excessive legalism which may create

---

[52] *Padfield v. Minister of Agriculture, Fisheries and Food* [1968] A.C. 997 at 1032.

[53] *R. v. Lancashire County Council ex p. Huddleston* [1986] 2 All E.R. 941.

[54] *Padfield, supra*, per Lord Pearce at 1053 and Lord Upjohn at 1061.

[55] *Purdon v. Glasgow District Licensing Board*, 1988 S.C.L.R. 466 at 469.

[56] [1989] 2 All E.R. 609 at 620. This view was adopted by Lord Denning in *Secretary of State for Employment v. ASLEF* (1972) 2 Q.B. 455 at 493; it was followed in *Bass Taverns Ltd v. Clydebank District Licensing Board*, 1995 S.L.T. 1275.

[57] A full discussion can be found in the report of the committee of the Justice-All Souls Review of Administrative Law in the United Kingdom, *Administrative Justice: Some Necessary Reforms* (1988), esp. at paras 3.117 *et seq.* See also De Smith, Woolf and Jowell, *Judicial Review of Administrative Action* (5th ed.), paras 9–042 *et seq.*

[58] On this, see also *Tramountana Armadon SA v. Atlantic Shipping Co. SA* [1978] 2 All E.R. 870 at 972; and Lord Woolf, 41st Hamlyn Lectures, *Protection of the Public–A New Challenge* (1990), p. 92.

[59] *Breen v. Amalgamated Engineering Society Union* [1971] 2 Q.B. 175 at 191.

an undue hazard for the decision maker[60]; the risk of an increase in challenges to decisions; and the fear that decision makers will resort to the use of forms of reasoning designed to preclude challenge and not reflecting the true or the complete reasoning.

Modern developments

In recent years the scope of the general principle has been gradually **18.55** restricted so that in time it may be declared that the cases where no reasons need be given will come to be the exceptions to a general, if not nearly absolute, rule. It has been thought in 1994 that this position was not far from being reached.[61] The tendency of policy generally at present is towards a greater openness or "transparency" in decision making.[62] This development may well be encouraged by the influence exerted by the European Court of Justice and the Court of Human Rights. The European Court of Justice long ago explained the necessity for the giving of reasons by the Commission as being the giving of an opportunity to the parties of defending their rights, the enabling of the exercise of its supervisory jurisdiction by the Court, and the informing of the member states and other interested nationals of the circumstances in which the Commission had applied the Treaty.[63] An express duty to give reasons for decisions is provided by Article 253 of the E.C. Treaty (formerly Article 190). In the context of Human Rights it is established that Article 6(1) of the Convention requires that reasons must be given for a decision. This enables an accused to exercise usefully the opportunities of appeal open to him, since a delay in providing reasons may constitute a breach of Article 6 as a denial of a fair trial.[64]

The passing of the Human Rights Act 1998 may accelerate the recognition of the necessity for giving reasons both in the context of the cases covered by Article 6(1) and other situations which may in principle be difficult to distinguish. It may well be thought that a blanket requirement that reasons must be given for all decisions of any kind in every circumstance would be extravagant, both in terms of economic administration and reasonableness. However, three observations may be made: first, while the obligation to give reasons may now become universal at least in matters of civil rights and obligations, the provision of a sufficient right of appeal may preserve the fairness of the whole procedure and so save the decision from invalidity, even where no grounds are given.[65] Secondly, and in any event, attention must be paid to the distinct but closely related matter of the substance of the reasons. In the jurisprudence of the European Court of Human Rights this essentially depends upon the circumstances of the case.[66] The universality of the obligation should not prove to be burdensome upon decision makers when in appropriate cases the briefest expression of the reasons will suffice. Thirdly, it may be that the development of the application of

---

[60] *Save Britain's Heritage v. Number 1 Poultry Ltd* [1991] 1 W.L.R. 153.

[61] See Munro,"The Duty to give Reasons for Decisions", 1994 S.L.T.(News) 5; also Colin T. Reid, "The Giving of Reasons", 1994 J.R. 324.

[62] *R. v. Secretary of State for the Home Department, ex p. Doody* [1994] 1 A.C. 531 at 561 and 566.

[63] Case 24/62 *Germany v. The Commission* [1963] E.C.R. 69.

[64] *Hadjianastassiou v. Greece* (1993) 16 E.H.R.R. 219. For the position under the ECHR, see para. 16.32.

[65] See *Stefan v. General Medical Council* [1999] 1 W.L.R. 1293.

[66] *e.g. Halle v. Finland* (1998) 26 E.H.R.R. 159, para. 55.

Article 6(1) of the European Convention on Human Rights may lead to the development of the distinction in the context of the giving of reasons between matters which do and matters which do not affect civil rights and obligations.[67] The common law may still retain a degree of flexibility outwith the cases where the Convention requires reasons to be given.

The test

18.56   That the function of the decision-making body or the nature of the issue is of an administrative character, as opposed to a judicial or "quasi-judicial" one is not determinative of a duty to give reasons.[68] But the fact that it is carrying out a judicial function is a consideration in favour of a requirement to give reasons.[69] The solution is to be found by a study of the whole circumstances, a consideration of the character of the decision-making body, the kind of decision it has to make and the framework in which it operates.[70] The principle is one of fairness, and fairness may require that reasons be given.[71] In general, as a matter of good practice, whether there is an obligation or not, it will be prudent for decision makers to give reasons, except in those cases where customarily reasons are never, or only exceptionally, given.

Examples

18.57   While the existence of an obligation to give reasons remains a matter of the circumstances of the particular case some guidance may be obtained from considering examples of situations where a requirement for reasons has been found to exist. In *R. v. Higher Education Funding Council, ex parte Institute of Dental Surgery*[72] it was recognised that two classes of case could be distinguished where reasons might in fairness be called for: one, on account of the nature of the process, and the other, on account of the existence of something peculiar to the decision itself. In the same case two examples were identified of situations where reasons ought in fairness to be given[73]: first, where the subject-matter is an interest highly regarded by the law, such as personal liberty, and second, where the decision appears aberrant. The following seven cases may be noted.

Where appeal or review available

18.58   It was recognised in *Cunningham*[74] that in some cases, such as that of justices in England, where there is a right of appeal to the Crown Court which hears the matter *de novo* and gives reasons for its decisions, a judicial decision may not require to be supported by reasons. Social Security Commissioners are not required to give reasons.[75] On the other hand, where appeal is available and there are no reasons given parties may be deprived of the opportunity of appealing.[76] But where there is no

---

[67] See para. 16.28.

[68] *R. v. Higher Funding Council, ex p. Institute of Dental Surgery* [1994] 1 All E.R. 651.

[69] *R. v. Civil Service Appeal Board, ex p. Cunningham* [1991] 4 All E.R. 310 at 323; followed in *R. v. Ministry of Defence, ex p. Murray* [1998] C.O.D. 134. See later para. 18.59.

[70] For an example, see *Stefan v. General Medical Council, supra*.

[71] *R. v. Civil Services Appeal Board, ex p. Cunningham* [1991] 4 All E.R. 310; *R. v. Home Secretary, ex p. Doody* [1994] A.C. 531 at 564.

[72] [1994] 1 All E.R. 651 at 667.

[73] *ibid.* at 671.

[74] *supra*, at 318.

[75] *R. v. Secretary of State for Social Services, ex p. Connolly* [1986] 1 W.L.R. 421.

[76] *Norton Tool Co. Ltd v. Tewson* [1972] I.C.R. 501, on the amount of compensation for unfair dismissal.

appeal in fact or in law outline reasons should be given sufficient to show to what the authority has directed its mind and whether the decision was lawful. Otherwise, as Lord Donaldson M.R. observed, the determining body would be reduced "to the status of a free-wheeling palm tree".[77] Furthermore, an obligation to give reasons may arise where there is a remedy available by judicial review.[78] In *R. v. Home Secretary, ex parte Doody*,[79] it was held that a person sentenced to life imprisonment was entitled to know the reasons for the decision determining the date for the first review of his sentence. In part the decision proceeded on the basis that fairness demanded that grounds be given. But the point was also made that without a statement of the reasons the prisoner had no means of ascertaining whether in the particular case the decision-making process had gone astray.[80] Thus, reasons may require to be given where there is a right of appeal or, whether or not there is a right of appeal, where there may be an opportunity for review, so as to enable the citizen to ascertain whether there are grounds for the intervention of the court. But the desirability of discovering whether grounds for appeal or review may exist cannot by itself be a general justification for requiring reasons to be given, otherwise the obligation would be virtually universal.[81] The better view is that the existence of a right of appeal strongly indicates an implied obligation to give reasons, but that the obligation depends on the particular circumstances of the decision being made.[82]

On a broader view of the whole problem, it may be thought that the existence of a right of appeal may itself be a justification in practice, although perhaps not in law, for not giving reasons for a decision. If the test is whether the whole proceedings are fair, the existence of a right of appeal, or even of review, may preserve the overall fairness of the proceedings and rescue the decision from any invalidity, provided that the scope of the appeal or the review is sufficient to cover the ground of complaint and will itself be explained by the giving of reasons.[83]

The nature of the function

In some circumstances, while there may be no formal requirement for the giving of reasons, that course may be regarded as necessary in particular circumstances in the interest of fairness. These circumstances may relate to the nature of the case in hand or the process which is being followed. Where a body is not a judicial body, is not carrying out a judicial function, but is acting in an administrative procedure rather than deciding an issue between parties, there may be no obligation to give reasons.[84] On the other hand, where the function is of a judicial character, such as the confirmation of an alderman by the Court of Aldermen in London, reasons may be required.[85] Where there are

18.59

---

[77] *R. v. Civil Service Appeal Board, ex p. Cunningham* [1991] 4 All E.R. 310 at 319.
[78] *ibid.* at 323; *R. v. Secretary of State for the Home Department, ex p. Doody* [1994] A.C. 531 at 565.
[79] [1994] 1 A.C. 531.
[80] *ibid.* at 565.
[81] *R. v. Higher Funding Council, ex p. Institute of Dental Surgery* [1994] 1 All E.R. 651 at p. 665.
[82] *Dundee United Football Co. Ltd v. Scottish Football Association*, 1998 S.L.T. 1244.
[83] See para. 18.10, para. 18.55 and para. 16.32. The thinking can be found in *Libman v. General Medical Council* [1972] A.C. 217 at 221, and in *R. v. Civil Service Appeal Board, ex p. Cunningham* [1991] 4 All E.R. 310 at 318.
[84] *Lawrie v. Commission for Local Authority Accounts*, 1994 S.L.T. 1185.
[85] *R. v. City of London, ex p. Matson* (1995) 94 L.G.R. 443.

executive or policy reasons in the matters of prison administration it may be inappropriate to require the reasons to be disclosed,[86] especially where there was no expectation for reasons to be given.[87] Where a body was regarded as carrying out a judicial function from which there was no appeal but where judicial review could lie it was held that the circumstances were such as to require reasons for the decison to be given.[88] Where an appeal body is reversing an earlier decision it should state sufficient reasons for doing so.[89] Where the function is of a legislative character the rules of natural justice may not apply.[90]

The subject-matter of the case

18.60 In matters affecting the liberty of the individual, or other matters of human rights, where in the circumstances the reasons may not be evident from the decision, reasons ought to be given.[91] On the other hand, a decision on research ratings may not require reasons to be given.[92] Where no right is being infringed there is no call to give reasons for a decision.[93] Thus, someone who holds an office at pleasure may be dismissed without reasons given.[94]

Departure from policy or precedent

18.61 Another situation where reasons may require to be given is where the decision is inconsistent with an existing policy and the divergence may thus call for explanation.[95] Again, where the absence of an explanation may lead to the conclusion that the particular decision is contrary to the policy and object of the relevant statute reasons ought to be given.[96] Where a decision is inconsistent with an earlier decision it may be proper to give an explanation for the difference.[97]

Where reason not obvious

18.62 In some cases the reason for the decision will be so obvious that it is unnecessary to state it. But in other cases it may be far from certain what the ground may be and in such a case it is fair that it should be stated. It has been said:

> "Where one gets a decision of a tribunal which either fails to set out the issue which the tribunal is determining either directly or by inference, or fails either directly or by inference to set out the basis on which it had reached its determination on that issue, then that is a matter which will be very closely regarded by this court, and in

---

[86] *Thomson, Petr*, 1989 S.L.T. 343.
[87] *Rea v. Parole Board*, 1993 S.L.T. 1074.
[88] *R. v. Civil Service Appeal Board, ex p. Cunningham* [1991] 4 All E.R. 310.
[89] *Safeway Stores Ltd v. National Appeals Panel*, 1996 S.C. 37. The matter was taken further in 1997 S.C. 189.
[90] *Bates v. Lord Hailsham* [1972] 1 W.L.R. 1372.
[91] *R. v. Secretary of State, ex p. Fayed* [1997] 1 All E.R. 228.
[92] *R. v. Higher Education Funding Council, ex p. Institute of Dental Surgery* [1994] 1 All E.R. 651.
[93] *Schmidt v. Secretary of State for Home Affairs* [1969] Ch. 149 at 173.
[94] *Ridge v. Baldwin* [1964] A.C. 40 at 65.
[95] *R. v. Mayor etc of Kensington and Chelsea, ex p. Grilla* (1996) 2 F.C.R. 56 at 67.
[96] *Padfield v. Minister of Agriculture, Fisheries and Food* [1968] A.C. 997 at 1032.
[97] *e.g.* in the context of planning, *North Wiltshire D.C. v. Secretary of State for the Environment and Others* [1992] 3 P.L.R. 113.

normal circumstances will result in the decision of the tribunal being quashed. The reason is this. A party appearing before a tribunal is entitled to know, either expressly stated by it or inferentially stated, what it is to which the tribunal is addressing its mind. In some cases it may be perfectly obvious without any express reference to it by the tribunal; in other cases it may not. Second, the appellant is entitled to know the basis of fact on which the conclusion has been reached. Once again in many cases it may be quite obvious without the necessity of expressly stating it, in other cases it may not".[98]

Inconsistent decisions

Where a decision is inconsistent with earlier decisions there may be a **18.63** requirement to explain the reason for the inconsistency. This problem has arisen in relation to planning decisions.[99] In the context of such situations as immigration, where there will be a considerable number of decisions being given by various authorities on the basis of the material which is respectively placed before them in different applications, inconsistencies may well arise and it may not be so critical to have any detailed reason for the difference of decision so long as the decision-maker is aware of the existence of the divergence of view.[1]

Legitimate expectation

Where there is a legitimate expectation that reasons will be given then **18.64** the obligation to give them will arise. Correspondingly where there was no legitimate expectation of a hearing there may be no breach of natural justice.[2] In one case it was been held that there was no general duty on prison authorities to give reasons for transferring a prisoner from one prison to another, although it was noted that no argument was presented to the effect that there may have been a legitimate expectation for reasons to be given for the transfer.[3] The concept of legitimate expectation may well be a useful basis for requiring reasons to be given.[4] The matter of legitimate expectation is considered more generally in a later chapter.[5]

Where reasons unnecessary

Where a body is engaged upon the carrying out of an administrative **18.65** procedure where there can be no real doubt regarding the basis on which its decision has been reached, there may be no duty to provide reasons.[6] Where an application is bound to fail there may be no need to give reasons.[7]

---

[98] *R. v. Immigration Appeal Tribunal, ex p. Khan* [1983] Q.B. 790, *per* Lord Lane C.J. at 794–795.

[99] *North Wiltshire District Council v. Secretary of State for the Environment* [1992] P.L.R. 113.

[1] *Sinathamby Kumar v. Secretary of State for the Home Department* (1996) Imm. A.R. 548.

[2] *Cinnamond and Others v. British Airports Authority* [1980] 1 W.L.R. 582.

[3] *Thomson v. Secretary of State for Scotland*, 1989 S.L.T. 343. In *Clyde Cablevision Ltd v. Cable Authority*, 1990 S.C.L.R. 35 it was held that there was no legitimate expectation that reasons would be given and no obligation to give reasons.

[4] Colin T. Reid, "An Expectation or an Explanation", 1990 S.L.T.(News) 133.

[5] See para. 19.01.

[6] *Lawrie v. Commission for Local Authority Accounts*, 1994 S.L.T. 1185.

[7] *Young v. Criminal Injuries Compensation Board*, 1997 S.L.T. 297.

Substance and nature of the reasons

18.66 The requirements regarding the substance and nature of reasons where they are given has already been considered in the context of statutory procedures and the same principles apply where there is an obligation to give reasons at common law.[8]

The effect of no reasons

18.67 Usually a breach of a duty to state reasons will prove fatal to the validity of the decision and it will be quashed.[9] But the court may in particular cases call for a statement, or a restatement of the reasons, from the decision maker and then determine the merits of the application. In one case the court ordered grounds for the decision to be explained and these, when given, were found to be conclusive of the decision.[10]

---

[8] See paras 17.24 *et seq.*

[9] See paras 17.30 *et seq.* for the position under the statutory obligation to give reasons. For the question of void or voidable decisions, see para. 14.15. See also, on reduction, para. 24.28.

[10] *Robb v. Logiealmond School Board* (1875) 2R. 698.

CHAPTER 19

LEGITIMATE EXPECTATION

I   INTRODUCTION
II   SOURCE OF THE EXPECTATION
III SUBSTANCE OF THE EXPECTATION

I INTRODUCTION

The idea of fairness lies behind many of the more particular grounds for **19.01**
judicial review. As has already been indicated the whole area of natural
justice is essentially an expression of the same concept. Illegality and
irrationality can be seen at least as allied with if not based on an idea of
fairness. It is through such particular expressions that the concept of
fairness can come to be explored and utilised. Taken by itself it may
prove too vague and uncertain a concept to be treated as a ground of
review in its own right rather than providing a basic idea on which more
precise grounds can be formulated. Unfairness is thus not a substantive
ground of review on its own; and while procedural unfairness may be
seen as an exception,[1] that too may be analysed as a particular
expression of the general concept, in so far as a breach of procedure is
only a ground of review if it results in unfairness.[2] "There is no general
rule that a body seeking to exercise a statutory power is under a duty to
act fairly."[3]

Forms of fairness

From what has been said it will be evident that there are few if any limits **19.02**
on what may fall within the scope of the idea of fairness for the purposes
of review. But it is necessary to find some forms of categorisation. These
may include the need to give notice, the need for a decision maker to be
impartial and the need for some form of hearing. Recently the concept
of legitimate expectation has become more prominent as a ground for
review.[4] It has been described as a valuable, developing doctrine which is
rooted in fairness.[5] But it is distinct in that it serves only to provide a
subjective explanation why a decision or acting is unfair. However, it is
of sufficient importance to justify a separate consideration in this
chapter.

Legitimate expectation and fairness

A decision or an action may be within the powers of the authority, may **19.03**
be carried out in accordance with such prescribed procedure as there
may be, may not be irrational, and yet may be unfair. One circumstance

---

[1] *Shetland Lines Ltd v. Secretary of State for Scotland*, 1996 S.L.T. 653.
[2] See para. 17.05. See also *Malloch v. Aberdeen Corporation*, 1971 S.C. (H.L.) 85, *per*
Lord Wilberforce at 122.
[3] *Stannifer Developments v. Glasgow Development Agency (No. 2)*, 1999 S.L.T. 459, *per*
Lord Justice-Clerk Cullen at 465.
[4] On the origins of legitimate expectation, see C.F. Forsyth, "The Provenance and
Protection of Legitimate Expectation" (1998) 47 C.L.J. 238.
[5] *R. v. IRC, ex p. MFK Underwriting* [1990] 1 W.L.R. 1545, *per* Bingham L.J. at 1569. For
a recent account of the idea, see G.J. Junor, "What Did You Expect?", 1998 S.L.T. (News)
123.

which may create that unfairness is where there is a threatened or actual disappointment of an expectation legitimately held. But this label merely identifies another particular situation in which unfairness may arise. "The doctrine of legitimate expectation in essence imports a duty to act fairly".[6] Bingham L.J. has said of the concept:

> "If a public authority so conducts itself as to create a legitimate expectation that a certain course will be followed it would often be unfair if the authority were permitted to follow a different course to the detriment of one who entertained the expectation, particularly if he acted on it. If in private law a body would be in breach of contract in so acting or estopped from so acting a public authority should generally be in no better position. The doctrine of legitimate expectation is rooted in fairness. But fairness is not a one-way street. It imports the notion of equitableness, of fair and open dealing, to which the authority is as much entitled as the citizen".[7]

The overlapping nature of the concepts is reflected in an observation by McNeill J.: "Whatever phrase be used – duty to act fairly, legitimate expectation, a right to be heard – it seems to me that natural justice entitles the payer at least to make representations to the effect that he should not pay the maximum, but some lesser sum."[8] The concept of legitimate expectation identifies a reason why in particular circumstances an act or an omission may be unfair. Thus it is not necessarily concerned with matters of legal rights or interests but extends to circumstances where a departure from an anticipated course, even if it is not a denial of a right, would nevertheless be unfair.

Reasonable or legitimate

19.04 While frequent use is made of the adjective "legitimate" in this context to describe the expectation, the more appropriate word may be "reasonable". It has been observed by Deans J. in the High Court of Australia,[9] where the notion is well established, that "the word 'legitimate' is prone to carry with it a suggestion of entitlement to the substance of the expectation whereas the true entitlement is to the observance of procedural fairness before the substance of the expectation is denied." He also pointed to the vagueness of the term which might give a misleading impression of the breadth of the concept. The importation of the qualification of reasonableness may give an appropriate degree of flexibility and relate the application of the concept to the particular statutory framework and the circumstances of the particular case. Lord Fraser of Tullybelton, who participated in many of the early decisions on the concept, used both terms, and in one case expressed the view of the Privy Council that "legitimate" falls to be read as meaning "reasonable".[10] "Accordingly 'legitimate expectations' in this context are capable

---

[6] *R. v. Secretary of State for the Home Department, ex p. Ruddock* [1987] 2 All E.R. 518, *per* Taylor L.J. at 531; see also *R. v. Secretary of State, ex p. U.S. Tobacco* [1992] 1 All E.R. 212 at 223.

[7] *R. v. Board of Inland Revenue, ex p. MFK Underwriting Agencies Ltd* [1990] 1 All E.R. 91 at 110.

[8] *R. v. Transport Secretary, ex p. GLC* [1986] Q.B. 556 at 587.

[9] *Haoucher v. Minister of State for Immigration and Ethnic Affairs* (1990) 93 A.L.R. 51 at 52.

[10] *Att.-Gen. of Hong Kong v. Ng Yuen Shiu* [1983] A.C. 629 at 636.

of including expectations which go beyond enforceable rights, provided they have some reasonable basis." On the other hand, Lord Diplock in the *GCHQ* case[11] expressed the view that it was preferable to use the term "legitimate expectation"

> "in order thereby to indicate that it has consequences to which effect will be given in public law, whereas an expectation or hope that some benefit or advantage would continue to be enjoyed, although it might well be entertained by a 'reasonable' man, would not necessarily have such consequences. The recent decision of this House in *In re Findlay*[12] presents an example of the latter kind of expectation. 'Reasonable' furthermore bears different meanings according to whether the context in which it is being used is that of private law or public law. To eliminate confusion it is best avoided in the latter."

This explanation of the word "legitimate" reveals that it is used simply to distinguish expectations which will lead to judicial review from those which will not. Since it is not every expectation which will found a challenge, it may be less helpful to use an adjective that merely describes the expectation without defining it. It might well be preferable to adopt the term "reasonable expectation" so as to reflect the basis on which relevant expectations may be distinguished from those which do not justify review. The basic principle is one of fairness and the term "reasonable" is apt to express that concept. But since the term "legitimate expectation" has become hallowed by usage it may be simplest to use that label to identify the category of cases which can conveniently be grouped together as a particular expression of the principle of fairness. Content can, however, be given to the adjective, whichever term is used. The expectation must arise in a reasonable or a legitimate way, and not have been manufactured by the claimant so as to enable him to qualify for a benefit in accordance with a prescribed policy, as where a person liable to deportation married and acquired a child and so sought leave to remain in the country on the ground that he now satisfied the usual requirement.[13]

Legitimate expectation as a ground for *locus standi*

In some cases the concept of legitimate expectation has been referred to **19.05** as giving the complainer the necessary *locus standi* to bring proceedings for judicial review. In one case in which a challenge was raised against the introduction of a new policy on the release of prisoners on parole, Lord Scarman observed[14]: "it is enough merely to note that a legitimate expectation can provide a sufficient interest to enable one who cannot point to the existence of a substantive right to obtain the leave of the court to apply for judicial review". But he went on to point out that in the circumstances of that case the most that the applicant could legitimately expect was that the case would be examined individually in the light of whatever the current policy might be, provided that that policy fell lawfully within the discretionary powers of the Secretary of

---

[11] [1985] 1 A.C. 374 at 408–409.
[12] [1985] A.C. 318.
[13] *Butt v. Secretary of State for the Home Department*, 1995 G.W.D. 16–905.
[14] *Re Findlay* [1985] A.C. 308 at 338.

State.[15] So also in *O'Reilly v. Mackman* Lord Diplock observed that a legitimate expectation by a prisoner that he would receive the maximum remission would give him an interest to challenge the legality of a disciplinary award which would be adverse to his expectation.[16] But it may not be useful to import the concept of legitimate expectation into the area of *locus standi*. The concept embodies the ingredient of interest which is an essential for *locus standi*; but the scope of its content in relation to the grounds of challenge in judicial review proceedings does not coincide with the requirements for *locus standi*. The concept is accordingly best restricted to the matter of the grounds of challenge.

Categorisation of legitimate expectation

19.06 In *R. v. Devon County Council, ex parte Baker*[17] Simon Brown L.J. identified in four broad categories various of the distinct senses in which the phrase "legitimate expectation" was currently used, describing them as follows:

> "(1) Sometimes the phrase is used to denote a substantive right, an entitlement that the claimant asserts cannot be denied him . . . the claimant's right will only be found established when there is a clear and unambiguous representation upon which it was reasonable for him to rely . . . (2) Perhaps more conventionally the concept of legitimate expectation is used to refer to the claimant's interest in some ultimate benefit which he hopes to retain (or, some would argue, attain). Here therefore it is the interest itself rather than the benefit that is the substance of the expectation . . . (3) Frequently, however, the concept of legitimate expectation is used to refer to the fair procedure itself . . . (4) The final category of legitimate expectation encompasses those cases in which it is held that a particular procedure, not otherwise required by law in the protection of an interest, must be followed consequent upon some promise or practice. Fairness requires that the public authority be held to it. The authority is bound by its assurance, whether expressly given by way of a promise or implied by way of established practice."

Legitimate expectation of fairness

19.07 The third of the categories listed above can be readily dealt with. Simon Brown L.J. commented[18] on it: "In other words it is contended that the claimant has a legitimate expectation that the public body will act fairly towards him." As was pointed out by Dawson J. in *Attorney-General for New South Wales v. Quin*,[19] this use of the term is superfluous and unhelpful: "it confuses the interest which is the basis of the requirement of procedural fairness with the requirement itself". Examples of the other three categories can be found in part III of the present chapter.

---

[15] A similar approach was adopted in *R. v. Secretary of State, ex p. Hargreaves* [1997] 1 All E.R. 397 at 413.

[16] [1983] 2 A.C. 237 at 275.

[17] [1995] 1 All E.R. 73 at 88. Reference may also be made to Paul Craig "Legitimate Expectations: a conceptual analysis" (1992) 108 L.Q.R. 79.

[18] *R. v. Devon County Council, ex p. Baker* [1995] 1 All E.R. 73 at 88.

[19] (1990) 93 A.L.R. 1 at 39.

Personal bar

Another analysis of the concept of legitimate expectation which has been **19.08** noticed in England is by reference to the principles of estoppel. In *R. v. Jockey Club, ex parte RAM Racecourses*[20] Stuart-Smith L.J. noted that the doctrine had many similarities with those principles and stated that the applicant had to prove five matters:

> "(1) A clear and unambiguous representation . . . (2) That since the applicant was not a person to whom any representation was directly made it was within the class of persons who are entitled to rely upon it; or at any rate that it was reasonable for the applicant to rely upon it without more . . . (3) That it did so rely upon it; (4) That it did so to its detriment. While in some cases it is not altogether clear that this is a necessary ingredient, since a public body is entitled to change its policy if it is acting in good faith, it is a necessary ingredient where, as here, an applicant is saying, 'You cannot alter your policy now in my case: it is too late'. (5) That there is no overriding interest arising from their duties and responsibilities for the proper conduct or due encouragement of horse-racing as required in their charter which entitled the Jockey Club to change their policy to the detriment of the applicant".

The first four of these were for the applicant to prove; the last was for the Jockey Club to establish. But legitimate expectation is not to be equated absolutely with personal bar. The unfairness may arise through a justifiable anticipation without proof of any actual reliance or of any change of position on the part of the complainer.

II SOURCE OF THE EXPECTATION

There must be a sufficient basis for the expectation; but it would be **19.09** inappropriate to attempt any comprehensive list of the sources from which a legitimate expectation may arise. It may have been sponsored by particular actings or representations or it may have come from practice or tacit understandings. Lord Fraser in the *CCSU* case observed[21]: "Legitimate, or reasonable, expectation may arise from an express promise given on behalf of a public authority or from the existence of a regular practice which the claimant can reasonably expect to continue." But it is not to be supposed that those two situations were intended to be an exhaustive list of the circumstances in which an expectation might arise, although they are at least the most obvious and the most common. But the expectation may arise out of the particular circumstances of the case, as where the withdrawal of an immigration permit before its due date may require an opportunity for the licensee to make representations on the matter.[22] Some particular sources may now be noted.

(a) Express representation

An authority may have given an express promise to an individual or a **19.10** group of individuals that an opportunity will be given for hearing their representations on some proposed course of action before a decision is

---

[20] [1993] 2 All E.R. 225 at 236.
[21] *Council of Civil Service Unions v. Minister for the Civil Service* [1985] A.C. 374 at 401.
[22] *Schmidt v. Secretary of State for Home Affairs* [1969] 2 Ch. 149 at 171.

made. A denial of that opportunity will constitute an unfairness by virtue of the representation and the consequent expectation, so as to entitle a challenge to be made to the decision. Where there has been some genuine misunderstanding about whether an express representation has or has not been made, it has been considered that the question then arising was whether a reasonable bystander would regard the promise as having been made.[23] Published criteria for the interception of private telephone communications have been held to create a legitimate expectation that they will be complied with.[24] But a recommendation by the parole board of a date for release on licence does not prevent a withdrawal of the recommendation on a change of circumstances.[25] The representation which founds the expectation must of course be made by someone with authority to make it, whether actual or ostensible.

(b) Contract

19.11 The representation may be embodied in some form of contractual arrangement. In one case the representation on which the applicants founded was embodied in a compact which as prisoners they had each signed and under which the prison promised to consider them for home leave subject to certain conditions.[26] If there is conduct equivalent to a breach of contract or a breach of representation, it may found an application for review.[27]

(c) Settled practice

19.12 Even although there has been no express statement or undertaking that a particular course will be followed, a settled practice of following a particular course may be sufficient to support a reasonable expectation that it will continue to be followed and give ground for complaint if on a particular occasion the course is departed from without warning. This is another illustration of the operation of the principle of fairness. The *GCHQ* case[28] provides a clear example. There had been a well-established practice of consultation between the officials of the Government Communications Headquarters and the representatives of the union to which the staff who worked there belonged. Following certain disruptive industrial action by the staff the minister instructed a variation of terms and conditions of service of the staff without consultation. It was held that the union and the members of staff would have had a legitimate expectation that the unions and the employees would be consulted before the instruction was issued. But while the decision-making process would in that respect have been unfair, the instruction was held to be valid on the ground that the decision not to consult in the circumstances had been based on considerations of national security and that these outweighed the expectation of consultation. So also the practice of allowing late claims for tax relief was sufficient to cut down a

---

[23] *R. v. Swale B.C. and Medway Ports Authority, ex p. RSPB* (1990) 2 Admin. L.R. 790. But reference to the reasonable man was discouraged in *R. v. Gough* [1993] A.C. 646; see para. 18.23 (bias, conduct).

[24] *R. v. Secretary of State for the Home Department, ex p. Ruddock* [1987] 2 All E.R. 518.

[25] *Rea v. Parole Board for Scotland*, 1993 S.L.T. 1074.

[26] *R. v. Secretary of State for the Home Department, ex p. Hargreaves etc.* [1997] 1 All E.R. 397.

[27] *R. v. IRC, ex p. Preston* [1985] A.C. 835 at 867.

[28] *Council of Civil Service Unions v. Minister for the Civil Service* [1985] A.C. 374.

refusal of a claim on the ground that it was too late.[29] A practice of hearing submissions only on contentious points may render it unfair for a licensing authority to refuse an application on a ground which, not having been put in issue, had not been covered by the submissions.[30] Where the prescribed procedures had in certain repects in relation to a resignation not been followed, it was held that that did not allow a legitimate expectation that the resignation could be withdrawn.[31]

(d) Expectation triggered by events

Here the expectation is not prompted by some representation or policy **19.13** but by particular events. An example can be found in *Schmidt v. Secretary of State for Home Affairs*[32] where it was said that a foreign alien who has leave to come to the United Kingdom for a limited period should be given an opportunity to make representations if his permit is to be revoked before the time-limit expires, because he would have a legitimate expectation of being allowed to stay for the permitted period. So also, where there was a general practice that a prisoner would be granted the maximum remission permitted by the prison rules if no disciplinary award had been made against him involving a forfeiture of remission, a prisoner would have a legitimate expectation of receiving the maximum remission in the absence of any such award.[33]

Representation must be clear

It is well established that a representation can only be relied upon as the **19.14** basis for a reasonable expectation if it is clear and unambiguous.[34] Thus in the case cited, a promise given to a prisoner that he would be considered for home leave after serving one-third of his sentence was not a sufficiently clear representation to enable him to challenge a change of the period from one-third to one-half of the sentence. The most that he could expect was a consideration of his case in the light of whatever policy the Secretary of State saw fit lawfully to adopt. In the context of an assurance given by the Inland Revenue of the treatment which would be given to the index-linked element of the gain in the value of certain bonds for tax purposes, it was observed that it would not be fair to hold the revenue bound by "anything less than a clear, unambiguous and unqualified representation".[35] But the categories of unfairness are not closed and in particular circumstances, as has been already seen, settled practice may suffice.[36]

Recipient of the representation

In the usual case the person who is applying for review will be the person **19.15** or one of the persons to whom the representation was made. But it is not essential that that should be established. It will be sufficient if he is within the class of persons who are entitled to rely upon it, or in any

[29] *R. v. CIR, ex p. Unilever plc* [1996] STC 681.
[30] *Perfect Leisure v. City of Edinburgh District Licensing Board*, 1996 S.L.T. 1267.
[31] *Rooney v. Chief Constable, Strathclyde Police*, 1997 S.L.T. 1261.
[32] [1969] 2 Ch. 149.
[33] *O'Reilly v. Mackman* [1983] 2 A.C. 237 at 275.
[34] *R, v. Secretary of State, ex p. Hargreaves* [1997] 1 All E.R. 397 at 413.
[35] *R. v. Board of Inland Revenue, ex p. MFK Ltd* [1990] 1 All E.R. 91, *per* Bingham L.J. at 111.
[36] *R. v. IRC, ex p. Unilever plc* [1996] STC 681.

event that it is reasonable for him to rely upon it.[37] Thus, where a statement was made on behalf of the Governor of Hong Kong that each illegal immigrant from Macau would be interviewed and his case treated on its merits, an illegal immigrant successfully challenged the execution of a removal order made against him in the absence of his having been given an opportunity to be heard. "When a public authority has promised to follow a certain procedure, it is in the interest of good administration that it should act fairly and should implement its promise, so long as implementation does not interfere with its statutory duty."[38]

III SUBSTANCE OF THE EXPECTATION

Procedure and substance

19.16 The concept of legitimate expectation was seen at first as an expression of fairness in the context of procedural matters. But it has come to be extended to matters relating to the substance of the decision under review. The dividing line is not a difficult one to cross. In *R. v. Secretary of State for the Home Department, ex parte Khan*[39] it was not only the procedure to be followed but the criteria to be applied which could be said to have been legitimately expected to be followed. Furthermore, as that case also illustrates, the problem can be viewed as one of the rationality of the substance of the decision so as further to cloud the distinction between procedure and substance. The development of legitimate expectation should not go so far as to obtrude on the proper jurisdiction of the authority.[40] Most of the cases which fall within the category of legitimate expectation have been claims of a right to be heard.[41] But while the complaint will in many cases be related to matters of procedure the concept has developed to cover an expectation of matters of substance. It may relate to any benefit or advantage.[42]

Consultation

19.17 Whether there is or is not a duty of consultation is a matter of circumstances. Failure to consult interested parties before the making of an order or a regulation may give grounds for challenge. In some cases an express provision is made requiring some particular consultation to be carried out before a particular power is exercised. In such cases the question may arise whether the requirement is mandatory or directory. If it is the former opportunity for challenge may exist if the requirement has not been fulfilled.[43] But even where there is no express requirement for consultation there may be a legitimate expectation of consultation. The right to be heard which may arise from the existence of a legitimate expectation requires that the authority should be fair and open with the consultees and give them the opportunity to respond to the considera-

---

[37] *R. v. Jockey Club, ex p. RAM Racecourses* [1993] 2 All E.R. 225 at 236.

[38] *Att.-Gen. of Hong Kong v. Ng Yuen Shiu* [1983] A.C. 629, *per* Lord Fraser of Tullybelton at 638.

[39] [1985] 1 All E.R. 40.

[40] *R. v. Secretary of State for the Home Department, ex p. Ruddock* [1987] 1 W.L.R. 1482; see *R. v. IRC, ex p. Matrix Securities* 1994] 1 W.L.R. 570.

[41] *CCSU v. Minister for the Civil Service* [1985] A.C. 374, *per* Lord Roskill at 415.

[42] *ibid., per* Lord Diplock at 408.

[43] *e.g. R. v. Social Service Secretary, ex p. AMA* [1986] 1 W.L.R. 1.

tions supporting the view to which they are opposed. This may arise from an express promise given on behalf of the authority or from a regular practice which the claimant can reasonably expect to continue.[44] The practice of providing free transport for schoolchildren may create a legitimate expectation for consultation prior to any change of policy.[45] In the *GCHQ* case it was held that the appellants would have had a legitimate expectation that they would be consulted before a variation in the terms and conditions of their service was affected and in that respect the instruction purporting to make the variation was amenable to judicial review. Whether such a right to be heard or consulted exists is a matter to be determined in the circumstances of the case if it is not expressly prescribed by statute, but it may depend upon the "scale" or "context" of particular decisions.[46] In *Connor v. Strathclyde Regional Council*[47] an unsuccessful applicant for a post as assistant head teacher at a school was held to have had a legitimate expectation of appearance before a selection board. In *Lakin v. Secretary of State for Scotland*[48] a decision which had the effect of depriving the petitioner of a legitimate expectation of having their appeal determined at a public local inquiry was quashed.[49] In *R. v. Secretary of State, ex parte U.S. Tobacco*[50] it was held that the applicants had no legitimate expectation that they would be permitted to continue marketing snuff on the basis of procedures which had been agreed in the past with the government, that is to say that there was no legitimate expectation that the Secretary of State would not change his policy, but that it was not fair for the Secretary of State to introduce a total change of policy involving a ban on production without disclosing to them the scientific advice on which the decision to make the ban was based and giving them the opportunity to respond to it. But where neither the statutory provisions nor any information or guidance given by the statutory authority disclose an obligation to raise with the applicant any matters which might operate towards a refusal of a licence sought, where there is no undertaking given and no practice to support such consultation, there is no right to be informed of such matters before the decision is taken.[51]

Emergency situations

In some cases an authority may require to act at short notice in situations of emergency for the protection of members of the public or particular groups of people and it may be impracticable to consult with interested persons before taking action. In such cases a failure in prior consultation may not provide a ground for challenge. But there may be a requirement for a body which has the duty to act fairly to provide procedures to enable representations to be made for the immediate setting aside of a decision so reached or for an appeal against it. It was **19.18**

---

[44] The matter is explored by Lord Diplock in *O'Reilly v. Mackman* [1983] 2 A.C. 237. See also *Att.-Gen. of Hong-Kong v. Ng Yuen Shiu* [1983] 2 A.C. 629.

[45] *R. v. Rochdale Metropolitan Borough Council, ex p. Schemet* [1994] E.L.R. 89.

[46] *Re Westminster City Council* [1986] 2 W.L.R. 807.

[47] 1986 S.L.T. 530. In respect of its dependence upon a "public law" element the case is to that extent unsound.

[48] 1988 S.L.T. 780.

[49] 1986 S.L.T. 530.

[50] [1992] 1 All E.R. 212.

[51] *Clyde Cablevision v. Cable Authority*, 1990 S.C.L.R. 28.

so held in relation to a self-regulating organisation for life assurance and unit trust business.[52]

Expectation of a hearing

19.19 It is a matter of the particular circumstances whether, in fairness to the party concerned, a hearing should or need not be held. It has been held that it was open to a committee to refuse to endorse the election of shop steward where they had acted in good faith and consonantly with their responsibilities.[53] Where the circumstances are such that it would be unfair to deprive someone of a hearing before an administrative decision is reached which touches his interests, then he may be regarded as having a reasonable expectation that he will be afforded the opportunity of a hearing and have a legitimate ground for complaint if he is not given that opportunity.[54] Thus, where the Secretary of State proceeded to consider the merits of two competing planning applications before calling in one of them, the developers were deprived of the legitimate expectation of having their appeal determined at a public inquiry.[55] The mere fact that a hearing might affect the outcome of the decision-making process is not sufficient to support a case that there is a duty to allow a hearing. There must be a legitimate expectation of the opportunity to create the duty to provide it. Where there is a long history of enjoyment of a licence to engage in trade in particular premises carried on peacefully and responsibly, a refusal to allow a continuance of the trade will be unfair without the opportunity of a hearing. But where the permission has been abused and the trade has been carried on in a manner contrary to the standards required by the owner of the lands then there may be no duty to hold a hearing because in such circumstances there would be no expectation of it.[56]

Reasons for a decision

19.20 The occasions where a duty to give reasons may arise at common law have already been discussed. As was there noticed,[57] one element in the case for a requirement for reasons in particular cases may be that of a legitimate expectation.

Representations on policy

19.21 In *R. v. Liverpool Corporation, ex parte Taxi Fleet*[58] an undertaking was given by a local authority that the number of taxi licences would not be increased until certain proposed private legislation had been enacted and come into force. The authority thereafter resolved on an increase. The authority had a statutory power to regulate the number of taxicabs and matters of policy in that regard were of course matters for them to determine. But they had to act fairly in the exercise of that power and it was held that the authority had acted wrongly and that the resolution should not be put into effect. Lord Denning M.R. observed:

---

[52] *R. v. Life Assurance and Unit Trust Regulatory Organisation Ltd, ex p. Ross* [1993] 1 All E.R. 545.

[53] *Breen v. Amalgamated Engineering Union* [1971] 2 Q.B. 175.

[54] *Rea v. Parole Board for Scotland*, 1993 S.L.T. 1074.

[55] *Lakin v. Secretary of State for Scotland*, 1988 S.L.T. 780, distinguished in *Asda Stores Ltd v. Secretary of State for Scotland*, 1999 S.L.T. 503.

[56] *Cinnamond and Others v. British Airports Authority* [1980] 2 All E.R. 368.

[57] See para. 18.52 *et seq.*

[58] [1972] 2 Q.B. 299, *per* Lord Denning at 308.

"So long as the performance of the undertaking is compatible with their public duty, they must honour it. And I should have thought that the undertaking was so compatible. At any rate they ought not to depart from it except after the most serious consideration and hearing what the other party has to say: and then only if they are satisfied that the overriding public interest requires it. The public interest may be better served by honouring their undertaking than by breaking it."

Representations on procedure

So also where a policy was published stating the criteria and procedure **19.22** which had to be satisfied for allowing a child from abroad to enter the United Kingdom for the purpose of adoption it was held that the Secretary of State had acted unfairly in applying different criteria and a different procedure; his refusal of an entry clearance was accordingly quashed. The applicant for review had had a reasonable expectation that the procedure in the circular would be followed and that if the Secretary of State was satisfied that the criteria were met an entry clearance certificate would be granted.[59] So also a police constable was held entitled to expect that the procedures recommended in a manual of procedure would be followed by the chief constable.[60]

Changes in policy

It is not necessarily to be expected that policies will remain unaltered; **19.23** indeed it is more reasonable to anticipate that from time to time policies will be changed.[61] There can then be no necessary expectation that an existing policy will be applied. As Lord Diplock observed in relation to the policy regarding retirement dates of certain civil servants[62]:

"Administrative policies may change with changing circumstances, including changes in the political complexion of governments. The liberty to make changes is something that is inherent in our constitutional form of government. When a change in administrative policy takes place and is communicated in a departmental circular to, among others, those employees in the category whose age at which they would be compulsorily retired was stated in a previous circular to be a higher age than 60 years, any reasonable expectations that may have been aroused in them by any previous circular are destroyed and are replaced by such other reasonable expectations as to the earliest date at which they can be compelled to retire if the administrative policy announced in the new circular is applied to them."

It may not be unfair to make changes in a policy even where people have acted in reliance upon it.[63] But the expectation should be that any change would be made by reference to the public interest.

---

[59] *R. v. Secretary of State for the Home Department, ex p. Khan* [1985] 1 All E.R. 40.

[60] *Rooney v. Chief Constable, Strathclyde Police*, 1996 G.W.D. 39–2235.

[61] On the effect of a change in policy, see Paul Craig's paper in Chap. 3 Andenas (ed.), *English Public Law and the Common Law of Europe*.

[62] *Hughes v. Department of Health and Social Security* [1985] A.C. 776.

[63] *R. v. Ministry of Agriculture, Fisheries and Food, ex p. Hamble (Offshore) Fisheries Ltd* [1995] 2 All E.R. 714. The idea expressed by Sedley J. that the court could consider the substance of the decision in order to see whether it was fair not to accommodate reasonable expectations which the policy would thwart was rejected in *R. v. Secretary of State, ex p. Hargreaves* [1994] 1 W.L.R. 74. See also *R. v. Secretary of State for Transport, ex p. Richmond LBC* [1994] 1 W.L.R. 74.

Expectation under policy

19.24   Since policies may change, the expectation which may legitimately be
held in relation to any given policy may only be that the individual's case
will be considered under whatever policy is currently in force, and not
that he will be entitled to the benefit afforded by the current policy. Thus
a prisoner may not be able to claim an expectation that he will be given
parole,[64] or that he will be given home leave,[65] but only that his case will
be considered under the current policy on the matter.

Legitimate expectation of a substantive decision

19.25   In this context the expectation is not related to the procedures by which
some right or interest is sought but to the benefit itself.[66] The expectation here is usually derived from some representation or policy. If an
authority goes back on a representation which it has given to the
prejudice of the citizen a remedy may lie.[67] An interesting example is
provided in *R. v. Secretary of State for the Home Department, ex parte Fire
Brigades Union*,[68] where Lord Browne-Wilkinson said that the expectation that a statutory scheme for compensation would be brought into
force could found a legitimate expectation for the purposes of judicial
review.[69] In the earlier case of *HTV Ltd v. Price Commission*, Lord
Denning M.R. observed[70]:

> "It has been often said, I know, that a public body, which is
> entrusted by Parliament with the exercise of powers for the public
> good, cannot fetter itself in the exercise of them. It cannot be
> estopped from doing its public duty. But that is subject to the
> qualification that it must not misuse its powers; and it is a misuse of
> power for it to act unfairly or unjustly towards a private citizen
> when there is no overriding public interest to warrant it. So when an
> army officer was told that his disability was accepted as attributable
> to war service, and he acted on it by not getting his own medical
> opinion, the Minister was not allowed to go back on it.[71] And where
> an owner who was about to build on his land, was told that no
> planning permission was required, and he acted on it by erecting the
> building the Minister was not allowed to go back on it[72]: Very
> recently where a man was issued with a television licence for a year,
> then, although the Minister had power to revoke it, it was held that

---

[64] *Findlay v. Secretary of State for the Home Department* [1985] A.C. 318.

[65] *R. v. Secretary of State for the Home Department, ex p. Hargreaves etc.* [1997] 1 All E.R.
397.

[66] The High Court of Australia in *Minister for Immigration and Ethnic Affairs v. Teoh*
(1995) 183 C.L.R. 273 has extended the concept of legitimate expectation to include an
expectation that a ratified but unimplemented international treaty would be taken into
account in the exercise of statutory powers. For criticism of this decision, see Taggart,
"Legitimate Expectation and Treaties in the High Court of Australia" (1996) 112 L.Q.R.
50. But see *Tavita v. Minister of Immigration* [1994] 2 N.Z.L.R. 257 and *R. v. Secretary of
State for the Home Department, ex p. Mohammed Hussain Ahmed*, July 30, 1999, CA,
unreported.

[67] *R. v. IRC, ex p. Preston* [1985] 1 A.C. 835.

[68] [1995] 2 A.C. 513.

[69] at 553. But see Lord Keith of Kinkel at 545.

[70] [1976] I.C.R. 170 at 185.

[71] *Roberston v. Minister of Pensions* [1949] 1 Q.B. 227.

[72] *Wells v. Minister of Housing and Local Government* [1967] 1 W.L.R. 1000 and *Lever
Finance Ltd v. Westminster (City) LBC* [1971] 1 Q.B. 222.

it would be a misuse of that power if he revoked it without giving reasons or for no good reason; see *Congreve v. Home Office* [1976] 2 WLR 291."

In matters of licensing, where the grant is one of a privilege rather than a right, there will in general be no legitimate expectation that a licence will be granted. The only expectation will be that the application will be considered fairly.[73] But where a licence has been held for a long time it is to be expected that it will not be taken away without a hearing; and where there is a long practice of granting licences in particular circumstances, a hearing should be held if there is an intention to refuse it.

In one case in Scotland,[74] albeit an action for damages where the damages sought were for wrongful detention, Lord Morton of Shuna founded upon the pursuer's legitimate expectation of release as an ingredient in finding a relevant case of actings contrary to natural justice. Otherwise, the approach in Scotland regarding a legitimate expectation of a substantial benefit has been a cautious one, permitting an authority to depart from an assurance which it has given on a matter of substance, and requiring the application of a test of irrationality to such a departure.[75] It remains to be seen whether a bolder approach will develop.

---

[73] *McInnes v. Onslow-Fane* [1978] 3 All E.R. 211.
[74] *Walsh v. Secretary of State for Scotland*, 1990 S.L.T. 526.
[75] *McPhee v. North Lanarkshire Council*, 1998 S.L.T. 1317.

CHAPTER 20

MISUSE OF POWER

I   INTRODUCTION
II   DISHONESTY
III FAILURE TO USE POWER
IV POLICIES
V   ABUSE OF PROCESS

I INTRODUCTION

General

Even although a person or body has acted *intra vires* in the narrow sense **20.01** of those words and has complied with any procedural rules applicable to the decision-making process, whether under statute or at common law, the decision may still be open to challenge if the power, albeit discretionary, has been exercised improperly. It has to be remembered that the supervisory jurisdiction is not an appellate jurisdiction.[1] It does not allow the court to interfere with a discretionary decision which has been legally and properly reached. The court may not substitute its own decision because it prefers a different construction of the facts or because the result is not one which the court would have reached. But if the power has been exercised with an improper motive or in a manner which is inconsistent with honesty and fair dealing then the court may interfere. That means that powers must not be exercised capriciously or arbitrarily, but responsibly and with a due regard to the purposes and objects for which the powers have been granted. Where the power has been exercised with a reason, but the reason is such as no reasonable authority would have exercised, then review may be admitted on the ground of irrationality. But where the power is exercised for no reason at all, then it may be open to challenge on the ground of an arbitrary acting. Where it is not only inexpedient, but "so obviously and absolutely inexpedient – it may be so plainly done not in the interests of the community, but for some other and unworthy purpose"[2] the court may intervene. Powers must be exercised "without favouritism, caprice or corruption".[3] It is with such cases that this chapter is concerned.

While in principle any exercise of a power may be open to challenge on the ground of a misuse of the power, bad faith or an improper motive will only rarely arise in relation to the making of subordinate legislation[4] or in the application of statutory powers to particular situations. The challenge is more likely to arise in matters of a discretionary nature where there may be a choice of courses, all lawful, open to the authority. In the latter situation the discretion is limited by considerations of

---

[1] See para. 1.03.
[2] *Nicol v. Magistrates of Aberdeen* (1870) 9 M. 306 at 308.
[3] *Perth School Board v. Henderson*, 1917 S.C. 253 at 259.
[4] *East Kilbride D.C. v. Secretary of State for Scotland*, 1995 S.L.T. 1238.

reason and justice. "It is to be, not arbitrary, vague and fanciful, but legal and regular".[5] The extent of a discretionary power must be determined by the terms by which it was created. But to talk of an "unfettered" power may be misleading because it will always be subject to the control of the court. As Lord Denning put it, "The discretion of a statutory body is never unfettered".[6]

Discretionary and obligatory powers

20.02 The problem of determining whether powers are mandatory or discretionary has already been noted in the context of matters of procedure.[7] In the present context it arises in connection with the substance of the matter with which the power is concerned. The problem is one of construction. The use of the word "may" or equivalent expressions should usually be understood as intending a discretion to act. But in some cases it falls to be construed as imposing an obligation. The question must be resolved "from the context, from the particular provisions, or from the general scope and objects of the enactment conferring the power".[8] The juxtaposition of the words "shall" and "may" in the legislation may indicate that the words are respectively to bear their usual meanings.[9] As a very general rule, where "the thing to be done is for the public benefit or in advancement of public justice" the power may be intended to be obligatory in its exercise.[10] Thus, where a power was given for the benefit of the public to widen a road to a stated width, the provision was held to be obligatory in character.[11] In one case the filling of vacancies in a body of police commissioners was a matter of public duty, and mandatory, although the matter was expressed as one that "it shall be lawful" for the authority to perform.[12] On the other hand, the addition to such a phrase of such words as "if they see fit" may confirm that the expression "it shall be lawful" is to bear its ordinary meaning as a discretion.[13] Another guide towards resolving the problem is to ascertain whether a right ordinarily exists or has been conferred by the statute to support the power and indicate that an obligation is intended.

> "When a party can point to having a legal right, either personal or in which he is entitled to benefit as a member of a class or as one of the public, and the object of the power is to bring into effect, to fulfil or complete that right, or to use Lord Blackburn's words, 'to effectnate it', he can rely on the words, although permissive in form, being given a compulsive force."[14]

---

[5] Lord Halsbury L.C. in *Sharpe v. Wakefield* [1891] A.C. 173 at 179, quoted in *Walsh v. Magistrates of Pollockshaws* (1905) 7 F. 1009 at 1017, where it was recognised that an arbitrary exercise of discretion can be seen as an excess of power in a wide sense of that expression.

[6] *Breen v. Amalgamated Engineering Union* [1971] 2 Q.B. 175 at 190.

[7] para. 17.07. See also para. 15.10.

[8] Lord Selborne in *Julius v. Bishop of Oxford* (1850) 5 App.Cas. 214; see also *Fleming and Ferguson Ltd v. Magistrates of Paisley*, 1948 S.C. 547.

[9] *Gordon D.C. v. Hay*, 1978 S.C. 327.

[10] *R. v. Tithe Commissioners* (1849) 14 Q.B. 459, *per* Coleridge L.J. at 474.

[11] *Walkinshaw v. Orr* (1860) 22 D. 627, discussed in *Gray v. St Andrews and Cupar District Committee of Fifeshire County Council*, 1911 S.C. 266, *cf. Beckett v. Campbell and Hutcheson* (1864) 2 M. 482 (1866) 4 M.(H.L.) 6.

[12] *Sime v. Coghill* (1877) 5 R. 132 at 136.

[13] *Sinclair v. Moulin School Board*, 1908 S.C. 772.

[14] *Monaghan v. Glasgow Corporation*, 1955 S.C. 80, *per* Lord Carmont at 89, quoted in *Black v. Glasgow Corporation*, 1958 S.C. 260 at 269.

As Lord Blackburn stated in *Julius v. Bishop of Oxford*[15]: "if the object of giving the power is to enable the donee to effectuate a right, then it is the duty of the donee of the powers to exercise the power when those who have the right call upon him to do so." Thus the existence of a legal right of safe passage will require an imperative construction to be given to a provision expressed in permissive terms.[16] But a mere reference to the expediency of the exercise of the power is not sufficient to establish an obligation.[17] Where no legal right exists and none has been created by the statute then the ordinary permissive meaning of the language may be required.[18]

Fairness

The principle of fairness which runs as a common thread through so much of the various grounds for review finds its expression in the present context on the necessity for powers to be exercised reasonably. On this use of language abuse of power can be seen as one aspect of unfairness. A duty of fairness was held in the *Self-Employed* case[19] to be owed by the Inland Revenue Commissioners to each individual taxpayer. But in *R. v. IRC, ex parte Preston*[20] what the commissioners had determined to be fair was held not to be open to challenge without the taxpayer establishing that they had failed to discharge their statutory duty towards him or that they had abused their powers or had acted *ultra vires*. Conduct equivalent to a breach of contract or a breach of representation might enable an unfairness in the purported exercise of a power to rank as an abuse or excess of power. Where a grant had been guaranteed but there was no record of the receipt of the application, an insistence on compliance with a closing date which could not then be complied with was held to be unreasonable.[21] Where it is desired to reduce the total number of public-house licences in an area it may be preferable to consider all the licences in the area and determine which should be granted, rather than grant all those which are unopposed and consider reduction only from the number of those which are opposed.[22]

20.03

II DISHONESTY

(a) Bad faith or dishonesty

Examples of decisions taken in bad faith or dishonesty are happily not numerous. In the particular context of statutory instruments it has been recognised that a challenge on the grounds of bad faith or improper motive arises only rarely.[23] A decree obtained by fraud may be susceptible to reduction on the ground of fraud.[24] In *Innes v. Royal Burgh of*

20.04

---

[15] (1850) 5 App.Cas. 214 at 243.
[16] *Black v. Glasgow Corporation*, 1958 S.C. 260.
[17] *Renfrew County Council v. Orphan Homes of Scotland* (1899) 1 F. 186.
[18] *Degan v. Dundee Corporation*, 1940 S.C. 457.
[19] *Inland Revenue Commissioners v. National Federation of Self-Employed and Small Businesses Ltd* [1982] A.C. 617.
[20] [1985] 1 A.C. 835.
[21] *Woods v. Secretary of State for Scotland*, 1991 S.L.T. 197.
[22] *Goodall v. Shaw*, 1913 S.C. 630.
[23] *East Kilbride D.C. v. Secretary of State for Scotland*, 1995 S.L.T. 1238.
[24] *Smith v. Kirkwood* (1897) 24 R. 872.

Kirkcaldy[25] a decision to reduce the rents of certain council houses was successfully attacked on the ground that it had not been made with an honest consideration of the circumstances by councillors whose minds had already been made up before they came to exercise their discretion. In the course of his opinion Lord Cameron stated[26]:

> "In my opinion counsel for the defenders' argument goes too far when it seeks to deny any right to a ratepayer to challenge acts or decisions which are prima facie *intra vires* of local authorities. I think that if it can be shown that an authority clothed with discretionary power, has exercised it for reasons which are corrupt or wholly unrelated to the matters in issue or for purposes entirely dissociated from the function or duty in respect of which the power is exercised, then the exercise of the power can be restrained. Equally, if it can be shown that an authority or a majority of its members has deliberately closed its mind to matters which in the exercise of its discretion it would require to take into account, so also in that case its action or position can be subject to successful challenge on record. This, of course, is something very different from mere disagreement with the grounds of action taken by an authority acting prima facie *intra vires*, grounds which are objected to for personal or political reasons, or because it is felt that the grounds, though proper for consideration, appear to the party aggrieved to be of insufficient weight to warrant the decision arrived at".

The exercise of a statutory power carried out on legitimate grounds within the scope of the statute may not be open to review even if the exercise has been accompanied by feelings of malice.[27] It has been said that malice in the performance of a statutory duty was irrelevant where a public duty was being performed. "If the thing ought to be done, the circumstance that the person who did it has the greatest rancour and hatred against the object of that resolution will not make the resolution invalid if it is well founded in itself."[28] Allegations of *mala fides* or of malice are not lightly to be made and accordingly require specific averments with a plea-in-law to support them.[29] Lack of good faith, or dishonesty, "involves a grave charge".[30] Similarly averments of fraud must be specific in order to be relevant.[31]

(b)   Ulterior motive

20.05   This ground of challenge is an aspect of abuse of power. It should be distinguished from the taking into account of an irrelevant consideration in the reaching of a decision, which should be seen as an aspect of error

---

[25] 1963 S.L.T. 325.

[26] at 328.

[27] *Macfarlane v. Mochrum School Board* (1875) 3 R. 88 at 101; *Robson v. School Board of Hawick* (1900) 2 F. 411 at 418.

[28] *Macfarlane v. Mochrum School Board, supra,* at 101. The opinion whether a case of oppression could be made out against a public board in the execution of a public duty was reserved.

[29] *Macaulay v. North Uist School Board* (1887) 15 R. 99; *Elder v. Ross and Cromarty Licensing Board,* 1990 S.C.L.R. 1 at 8.

[30] *Cannock Chase D.C. v. Kelly* (1978) 1 All E.R. 152, *per* Megaw L.J. at 156.

[31] *Milne & Co. v. Aberdeen District Committee* (1899) 2 F. 220 at 228.

and is considered in that context later. Where a power is exercised to achieve indirectly what cannot be achieved by a direct and legitimate means a challenge may be open. A warrant to search granted for the execution of a criminal investigation cannot be properly used for a totally different purpose.[32] Power to require land for the remodelling of a city may not be used to acquire land for the ulterior object of profiting from its increased value.[33] In *Ashley v. Magistrates of Rothesay*[34] the magistrates had power to vary the statutory opening hours of public houses in localities. But, with a view to achieving a general reduction in closing hours throughout the burgh, they proceeded to define a locality in the burgh for the varied hours by drawing a line which included in the area affected by the variation all the public houses in the burgh, leaving as a locality unaffected by the variation an area which had no public houses in it. The Lord Chancellor observed: "If under pretence of exercising a discretion the Magistrates sought to subvert and change the general rule laid down by the legislature this House would discountenance and prevent the exercise of a power which was used in that way"; Lord Chelmsford observed: "The law will not allow that to be done indirectly which cannot lawfully be done directly: and therefore I have no doubt whatever that this was *ultra vires* of the magistrates of the Burgh". So also a power to have private streets reconstructed could not be used to enable a new thoroughfare to be constructed over both the private street and adjoining land.[35] Whether the supply of houses for those inadequately housed was a purpose falling within the scope of the Defence (General) Regulations 1939 was held to be a political matter outwith the control of the court but it was held relevant for a challenge of a decision to requisition certain houses used by a fee-paying school to aver that the determination had been made without any impartial consideration but capriciously and as part of a political campaign to suppress fee-paying schools.[36] Further examples can be found where the ulterior motive was to compel Sunday observance[37] or where the improvement of dental health was sought under the guise of making water more wholesome[38] or where the true motive of a decentralisation arrangement was to evade a prohibition of covenant schemes for general capital expenditure.[39] On the other hand, a power to regulate traffic was held to be sufficiently wide in its terms to prohibit a procession, even although the authority's concern included considerations of religious tolerance and civil disorder.[40] However, it was on the ground of illegality and not on the ground of an ulterior purpose that the court held invalid a decision to organise a railway service so that for practical purposes it was serving no useful ends in order to avoid formal closure procedures.[41]

---

[32] *William Reid* (1765) M. 7361, where a power to search for smuggled goods was used to discover a secret process. The main point in the argument was whether the matter should be pursued in the Exchequer Court.

[33] *Municipal Council of Sydney v. Campbell* [1925] A.C. 338.

[34] (1873) 11 M. 708; (1894) 1 R.(H.L.) 14 (reported as *Macbeth v. Ashley*), *per* the Lord Chancellor at 18 and Lord Chelmsford at 20.

[35] *Glasgow Corporation v. Bennett*, 1948 S.C. 563.

[36] *Pollock School v. Glasgow Town Clerk*, 1946 S.C. 373.

[37] *Blair v. Smith*, 1924 J.C. 24; *Western Isles Islands Council v. Caledonian MacBrayne Ltd*, 1990 S.L.T. (Sh.Ct) 97 (a case of confirmation of byelaws).

[38] *McColl v. Strathclyde R.C.*, 1983 S.L.T. 616.

[39] *Sleigh v. City of Edinburgh D.C.*, 1988 S.L.T. 253.

[40] *Hawick Orange Lodge v. Roxburgh D.C.*, 1980 S.C. 141.

[41] *Highland R.C. v. British Railways Board*, 1996 S.L.T. 274.

In presenting a challenge on the ground of an ulterior motive difficulties of proof may well arise. While minutes of the critical meetings and the evidence of those involved may be necessary, care must be taken to see that where the decision has been one taken by a group rather than a single individual the motive which inspired the group is identified and not simply the motives of some particular individuals. Where the decision maker is motivated by more than one purpose and the purposes can be disentangled, the validity of the decision can be sustained on the basis of such one or more of the purposes as are lawful even although other purposes are unlawful. But where the purposes cannot be disentangled and the decision has been substantially influenced by an unlawful purpose then the decision will be altogether invalid.[42]

Examples in planning law

20.06 Examples can also be found in planning law. In *Pyx Granite Co. Ltd v. Ministry of Housing and Local Government*, Lord Denning observed[43]: "Although the planning Authorities are given very wide powers to impose 'such conditions as they think fit' nevertheless the law says that these conditions to be valid must fairly and reasonably relate to the permitted development. The planning authority are not at liberty to use their powers for an ulterior object, however desirable that object may seem to them to be in the public interest." Thus, where planning permission to develop ground for industrial purposes was granted with a condition requiring a road to be built which would then become a public highway without cost to the local authority, that was held to be *ultra vires* in respect that it sought to achieve an ulterior purpose beyond the scope of the permission.[44] So also a grant of planning permission for residential development subject to a condition that the developer would provide houses for people waiting for council houses was quashed.[45]

Examples in licensing

20.07 In one case the authority empowered to issue licences to taxicab operators resolved to issue 50 new licences with a condition that they should not be transferable. The licences could be granted subject to such terms and conditions as were specified in the licence, but one of the relevant byelaws permitted the magistrates in their discretion to transfer a licence on the death, retiral or resignation of the holder. It was held that the condition was unlawful since it was in conflict with the intention that the licences should be transferable. The court held that the objective sought by the authority should be achieved by legislation and not by the device of imposing the proposed condition.[46] A condition prohibiting the sale of ice cream on Sundays was held to be unlawful in a licence authorising the sale of ice cream. It was a restraint on a common law

---

[42] *R. v. Lewisham LBC, ex p. Shell U.K. Ltd* [1988] All E.R. 938. See para. 24.29 on the separability of invalid parts.

[43] [1958] 1 Q.B. 554 at 572; [1960] A.C. 260. The passage was approved in *Fawcett Properties v. Buckinghamshire County Council* [1961] A.C. 636.

[44] *Hall & Co. Ltd v. Shoreham by Sea UDC* [1964] 1 W.L.R. 240. See also *British Airports Authority v. Secretary of State for Scotland*, 1979 S.C. 200.

[45] *R. v. Hillingdon LBC, ex p. Royco Homes Ltd* [1974] Q.B. 720. See also *North-East Fife D.C. v. Secretary of State for Scotland*, 1990 S.C.L.R. 647.

[46] *Baker v. City of Glasgow D.C.*, 1981 S.L.T. 320.

right of all subjects to open a shop and sell what they please subject to legislative restriction.[47]

(c) Oppression

In any circumstances where there is a duty to act fairly any form of **20.08** oppressive conduct may render the proceedings open to challenge. In the context of an Act which empowered road trustees to take unwanted stones from private land Lord President Colonsay observed: "That statute must receive a reasonable interpretation. On the one hand it must be interpreted in such a way as not to be unreasonably oppressive; and if the road trustees inflict injury, by the exercise of their rights in a nimious manner, there are undoubted powers in the court to restrain them. On the other hand, where the powers of the road trustees are fairly exercised, they are not to be interfered with."[48] A refusal to allow cross-examination or to lead evidence has been held to constitute oppression.[49] Where a local authority imposed restraints on the activities of a football club after three members of the club had played in South Africa it was held that, while they had a power to consider the best interests of race relations under section 71 of the Race Relations Act 1976 in exercising their power of the management of recreation grounds their decision to ban the club from using the ground fell to be quashed. The decision was held to be irrational, unfair and a misuse of a statutory power.[50] In periods of emergency finer points of humanity may require to be ignored, as where orders for the billeting of soldiers extended to the soldiers being quartered in the houses of unmarried women.[51] Interference with a prisoner's correspondence may be the breach of a "constitutional right".[52]

III   FAILURE TO USE POWER

Three forms of deficiency may be identified here: a failure or refusal to **20.09** act, an abrogation of power and a divestiture of power.

(a) Failure to act

Certain statutes make express provision for the Secretary of State to **20.10** intervene where a local authority has failed to perform a statutory duty.[53] But quite apart from such provisions it is recognised at common law that an authority is not allowed to refuse to exercise a discretionary power which it has a duty to exercise.[54] A refusal to exercise a jurisdiction when

---

[47] *Rossi v. Magistrates of Edinburgh* (1904) 7 F.(H.L.) 85.

[48] *Yeats v. Taylor* (1863) 1 M. 221 at 224. See also *Mercer Henderson's Trustees v. Dunfermline District Committee of the County Council of Fife* (1899) 2 F. 164.

[49] *Cowe v. M'Dougall*, 1909 S.C. (J.) 1. See para. 18.47 on cross-examination.

[50] *Wheeler v. Leicester City Council* [1985] 1 A.C. 1054.

[51] *Boswell v. Magistrates of Cupar*, July 10, 1804, F.C.

[52] *R. v. Secretary of State for the Home Department, ex p. Leech* [1994] Q.B. 198 at 210; but the court there did not agree with the Scottish decision in *Leech v. Secretary of State for Scotland*, 1991 S.L.T. 910.

[53] *e.g.* Local Government (Scotland) Act 1973 (c. 65), s. 211; Town and Country Planning (Scotland) Act 1997 (c. 8), s. 47(2); Education (Scotland) Act 1962 (c. 47), s. 71. See *Lord Advocate v. Glasgow Corporation*, 1973 S.C. (H.L.) 1.

[54] See *Ferguson v. Earl of Kinnoul* (1842) 1 Bell 662. For the same idea operating in a statutory context, see *Bovis Homes (Scotland) Ltd*, 1982 S.L.T. 473.

it is competent to do so may constitute an abuse which the court will review.[55] In the early case of *Fraser v. Burnett and Others*,[56] a jury had awarded a nil figure of compensation for a compulsory acquisition of land because they considered that the proprietor had received a benefit from the loss of the land. The court saw the jury's finding that no compensation was due as a refusal to obey the statute which required the loss to be ascertained and quantified, and considered that it could interfere with the jury's verdict as in a case of excess of power. In *Padfield v. Minister of Agriculture, Fisheries and Food*[57] the relevant Act provided for the making of an investigation into complaints about the operation of milk marketing schemes. The minister had a discretion to refer a complaint to a committee of investigation. The House of Lords held that in the circumstances of the case the refusal of the minister to refer the complaint in question had the effect of frustrating the purpose of the Act. A limitation on the granting of taxi licences to a fixed number which prevented consideration of individual applications has been held invalid.[58]

Method of exercise

20.11 There is a distinction to be made between the duty to exercise the power and the discretion to exercise it in a particular way. Provided the duty is exercised, the failure to take a particular course in the exercise of a discretionary power will not be open to challenge as a failure in duty,[59] although the exercise of the discretion may be subject to attack on such grounds as irrationality. And provided the authority has applied its mind to the propriety of exercising the power it may not be faulted if it decides not to exercise the power, although again such a decision may be challenged on grounds of irrationality. In matters of public administration, such as the lighting of streets, absolute compliance is not to be expected, so that the failure of a lamp is not necessarily a breach of a statutory obligation to light[60]; nor is a roads authority expected always to keep all roads absolutely clear of snow.[61]

Part performance

20.12 The court may, however, intervene where there has been a total failure in performance; and they may review cases where there has been an incomplete performance. In one case, where the duty was one of taking certain steps "so far as practicable" the court was prepared to decide whether that duty had been performed.[62]

(b) Abrogation

20.13 It has already been noted that in general a decision-making power vested in one person may not be delegated to another.[63] In addition to that, where one body has been entrusted with a discretion it may not act

---

[55] *Caledonian Ry v. Fleming* (1869) 7 M. 554.
[56] 1806 Hume 256. For the sequel, see 257. Also *Young v. Mrs Milne*, June 28, 1814, F.C. and *Heritors of Corstorphine v. Daniel Ramsay*, Mar. 10, 1812, F.C.
[57] [1968] A.C. 997.
[58] *Aitken v. City of Glasgow D.C.*, 1988 S.C.L.R. 287.
[59] *Beckett v. Hutchison* (1866) 4 M. (H.L.) 6.
[60] *Keogh v. Magistrates of Edinburgh*, 1926 S.C. 814.
[61] *Cameron v. Inverness County Council*, 1935 S.C. 493.
[62] *Adams v. Secretary of State for Scotland*, 1958 S.C. 279.
[63] para. 15.18.

under the direction of another body or abrogate what is its own responsibility by acting under the influence of another. Where a minister dismissed a planning appeal purely on account of certain objections put forward by another minister, his decision was quashed, since he had in effect delegated the decision to the other minister.[64]

(c) Divestiture

An authority may not effectively bind itself not to exercise a discretion so **20.14** as to divest itself of the powers with which it has been entrusted. In *Ayr Harbour Trustees v. Oswald*[65] the view was taken that Parliamentary Commissioners who were managing a harbour for the public could not bind their successors to a restricted use of certain lands which they sought to acquire. The terms of the statutory provisions under which any particular body may be acting is, of course, of critical importance in determining the extent of the body's powers; but in the generality where a discretionary power has been granted it must be respected. A licensing authority may not exercise its power so as to deny all material effect to its duties under the empowering legislation.[66] A minister who is empowered by Parliament to bring into effect a scheme which it has approved may not by a pretended exercise of prerogative power introduce an alternative scheme whereby he debars himself from exercising the power entrusted to him by Parliament.[67]

IV POLICIES

Creating policy

A body which has to exercise a discretion may not fetter its discretion by **20.15** creating rules of policy which prevent the proper exercise of the discretion in individual cases. The adoption and the recognition of principles and policies is undoubtedly a perfectly proper course, and indeed is necessary and useful in any coherent system of administration. Where a statutory body requires under a discretionary power to consider numerous applications, there is no objection to it formulating and adopting a general policy as guidance in the performance of its functions. The legitimacy of adopting a policy in the exercise of an administrative discretion has been recognised by the courts.[68] Indeed, it has been said that an administrative function necessarily involves questions of policy.[69] Policy may grow up through the development of a practice over a considerable period without any formal establishment of the practice as a policy, and compliance with such practice will be defensible provided it does not become a matter of slavish adherence and a blind belief that things must always be done in that particular way. It has been thought that if a general rule had been adopted by the Keeper of the Register to refuse for registration deeds which did not

---

[64] *Lavender and Son v. Minister of Housing* [1970] 1 W.L.R. 1231.
[65] (1883) 10 R. 472.
[66] *Gerry Cottle's Circus Ltd v. City of Edinburgh D.C.*, 1990 S.L.T. 235.
[67] *R. v. Secretary for the Home Department, ex p. Fire Brigades Union* [1995] 2 All E.R. 244.
[68] *Re Findlay* [1985] 1 A.C. 318, *per* Lord Scarman at 335.
[69] *General Poster and Publicity Co. v. Secretary of State for Scotland*, 1960 S.C. 296, *per* Lord Justice-Clerk Thomson at 275.

conform with the statutory requirements for conveyances, that would probably not be open to challenge.[70] Policy may be adopted in a variety of different fields. In the execution of public works, such as the provision of electricity supplies, a policy of laying cables under footpaths and verges rather than under the carriageways was regarded as within the proper exercise of the discretionary powers of the electricity authority, so that their repositioning became "necessary" for the purposes of a statutory obligation to pay for the cost of repositioning when the road authority proposed to widen the street.[71] The law regarding the adoption and use of policies in this context is the same in Scotland and England.[72] The restraint on the adoption of policies does not mean that an authority is not entitled to enter into a long-term contract.[73]

Essentials

20.16   Policies should be consistent with the relevant statutory provisions. They should be reasonable, in the sense of not being arbitrary, frivolous or vexatious, and if the policy is otherwise sound it is no valid ground of objection that it may have been prompted by declarations of the policy of the central government.[74] It should not exclude the exercise of the authority's discretion. A decision which is made simply in the hidebound furtherance of a policy is improper.[75] The individual circumstances of each application must still be considered whatever the policy may be. A policy of restricting licensing hours to 2.00 a.m. to avert public disorder and violence can be applied provided that individual exceptions can be admitted.[76] A policy of not encouraging promotion to the office of chief constable from the members of the local force has been held to be a proper exercise of administrative discretion and not so restrictive as to frustrate the proper exercise of the discretionary power of appointment.[77] The imposition of a rigid and restrictive condition in all licences for the operation of taxicabs has been held to be inconsistent with the proper exercise of a discretion.[78] Where there are no circumstances sufficient to take the case out of the general policy and where the authority have taken into account all the relevant circumstances a decision which accords with the policy will not be open to reduction.[79] If there are no special circumstances which might take the case outside the policy then it may be lawfully applied.

Form

20.17   What is in truth a declaration of policy may sometimes appear in the shape of a resolution, or a circular, or in some other such form. Policy may be declared in an election manifesto.[80] It will be necessary in every case to ascertain the true character of the statement in order to discover

---

[70] *Macdonald v. Keeper of the General Register of Sasines*, 1914 S.C. 854 at 858.
[71] *Magistrates of Paisley v. South of Scotland Electricity Board*, 1956 S.C. 502.
[72] *Elder v. Ross and Cromarty Licensing Board*, 1990 S.L.T. 307 at 311.
[73] *Birkdale District Electric Supply Co. Ltd v. Corporation of Southport* [1926] A.C. 355.
[74] *Malloch v. Aberdeen Corporation*, 1973 S.C. 227 at 268.
[75] *Centralbite Ltd v. Kincardine and Deeside District Licensing Board*, 1989 S.C.L.R. 652, where the authority was held not to have fallen into such error.
[76] *Cinderella's Rockafella's Ltd v. Glasgow District Licensing Board*, 1994 S.C.L.R. 591.
[77] *Magistrates of Kilmarnock v. Secretary of State for Scotland*, 1961 S.C. 350.
[78] *Holt v. Watson*, 1983 S.L.T. 588.
[79] *Semple v. Glasgow District Licensing Board*, 1990 S.C.L.R. 73.
[80] *Bromley LBC v. Greater London Council* [1983] A.C. 768.

whether or not it is such as to destroy a free exercise of a discretionary power or whether it is in reality a statement of general guidance which leaves the discretion essentially intact. If it falls to be construed as limiting the scope of the statutory discretion it will be invalid.[81] "If a discretion is to be narrowed, that must be done by statute; the tribunal has no power to give its decisions the force of statute."[82]

Nature of policy

In its nature a policy is guidance rather than regulation, and so even if **20.18** there is statutory authority for the making of rules and regulations for the conduct of the authority which may require ministerial approval a policy does not have the status that requires such procedure.[83] The policy must be based on grounds relating to and consistent with and not destructive of the statutory provisions under which the discretion is to be exercised. Where the statutory provisions require consideration to be given to circumstances in a locality a policy may properly be made to cover a larger area than any particular locality, although in considering each individual case regard will require to be had to the local conditions relevant to that case. It is not necessary for the competency of the formulation and adoption of a policy that the relevant statute should refer to any policy and the authority is entitled to change the policy from time to time, provided that the changes are not such as to amount to a perversity or unreasonableness. The policy must not be so rigidly formulated that if applied the statutory authority will be disabled from exercising the discretion entrusted to it.[84] Indeed, it may well be desirable to take such a course so as to obtain some consistency in dealing with applications of a similar character and so carry out their duties in a reasonable and proper manner. Thus, for example, it was held to be proper for justices to agree that as a general rule they would look with disfavour on applications by holders of restricted licences for their replacement by full licences[85] or again for justices to use their local knowledge of the risks of anti-social behaviour to restrict the permitted hours on the renewal of music and dancing licences.[86] Furthermore, there is nothing wrong in the publication of such a policy; that step may indeed be conducive to good administration.[87] A policy in appointment of officers may be expressed as a preference for those with a particular qualification, or a rule of practice which leaves an unfettered discretion to depart from it.[88]

Application of policy

But where there is a discretionary power to be exercised the principles **20.19** and policies are not to be regarded as binding to the extent of foreclosing a free exercise of the power. This applies both to the exercise

---

[81] *M'Lean v. Paterson*, 1939 J.C. 52 at 58.
[82] *Merchandise Transport Ltd v. British Transport Commission* [1962] 2 Q.B. 173, *per* Devlin L.J. at 193.
[83] *Clark v. Board of Supervision* (1873) 1 R. 261.
[84] *Elder v. Ross and Cromarty District Licensing Board*, 1990 S.C.L.R. 1 provides authority for much of the foregoing.
[85] *R. v. Torquay Licensing Justices, ex p. Brockman* [1951] 2 K.B. 784.
[86] *R. v. Torbay Licensing Justices, ex p. White* [1980] 2 All E.R. 25.
[87] *Elder v. Ross and Cromarty District Licensing Board*, 1990 S.L.T. 307.
[88] *Magistrates of Kilmarnock v. Secretary of State*, 1961 S.C. 350.

of their powers by such bodies as licensing authorities and to central or local government officials exercising discretionary powers as, for example, in the making of grants. In one such case Lord Reid observed[89]:

> "The general rule is that anyone who has to exercise a statutory discretion must not 'shut his ears to an application' . . . I do not think that there is any great difference between a policy and a rule. There may be cases where an officer or an authority ought to listen to a substantial argument reasonably presented urging a change of policy. What the authority must not do is to refuse to listen at all. But a Ministry or large authority may have had to deal already with a multitude of similar applications and then they will almost certainly have evolved a policy so precise that it could well be called a rule. There can be no objection to that, provided the authority is always willing to listen to anyone with something new to say".

That an application conflicts with the policy is no proper ground for refusing to consider the circumstances of the case. A blanket decision not to consider licence applications unless the applicant was present, without regard to the question whether his presence was necessary for deciding the application, has been held to be unreasonable.[90] While it is perfectly proper to have a policy, it must not be allowed to rule the case and exclude a genuine consideration of the particular application.[91] Thus, where a policy based on the view that performances by animals were evils in themselves influenced a refusal of a licence for a circus entertainment, the decision was held to be bad.[92] If the authority has applied a policy decision without exercising its discretion, the decision will not stand.[93] Nor is an exercise of discretion to be carried out "by seeking to apply labels or generalities" (such as a categorisation of landlords as "vigilant estate managers" or "lethargic rent collectors"), but by a consideration of the particular circumstances of the case under consideration.[94] Thus the application of a predetermined tariff is no proper exercise of a discretion in criminal sentencing,[95] nor is an undiscriminating flat increase on the valuation of dwelling-houses the exercise of a proper judicial function by a valuation committee.[96] Furthermore, the authority must apply any policy fairly and even-handedly, so that while absolute uniformity of all decisions is not essential a significant inconsistency, particularly if unexplained, will open the way to review.[97] But if an authority states that it has not applied a blanket policy the court cannot interfere without making an investigation of the facts behind such an assertion.[98] Where the authority has looked at the particular circumstances and found no reason to depart from the general policy the decision may stand.[99] But even where a policy still

---

[89] *British Oxygen Co. v. Board of Trade* [1991] A.C. 610 at 625.
[90] *Bury v. Kilmarnock and Loudon District Licensing Board*, 1989 S.L.T. 110.
[91] *Centralbite Ltd v. Kincardine and Deeside District Licensing Board*, 1989 S.C.L.R. 652.
[92] *Gerry Cottle's Circus Ltd v. City of Edinburgh D.C.*, 1990 S.L.T. 235.
[93] *Sagnata Investments Ltd v. Norwich Corporation* [1971] 2 Q.B. 614.
[94] *M'Callum v. Arthur*, 1955 S.C. 188, per Lord President Clyde at 197.
[95] *Sopwith v. Cruickshank*, 1959 J.C. 78.
[96] *Naismith v. Assessor for Renfrewshire*, 1921 S.C. 615.
[97] *Cashley v. City of Dundee D.C.*, 1994 S.C.L.R. 6.
[98] *Gerry Cottle's Circus Ltd v. City of Edinburgh D.C.*, 1990 S.L.T. 235.
[99] *R. v. Torquay Licensing Justices, ex p. Brockman* [1951] 2 K.B. 784.

enables an authority to make exceptions to it, the authority may be entitled to refuse to make any exceptions.[1]

Change of policy

It is reasonable and proper to make changes of policy from time to time. **20.20** Considerations here may arise of the necessity for consultation, a matter already noted in the context of legitimate expectation.[2] The adoption of a new policy that is reasonable will be valid provided that it does not exclude the consideration of exceptional cases which may fall outside it.[3] A policy which introduces limitations which go beyond the statement of the policy to Parliament is open to challenge, as where the policy envisaged early judicial consultation on the proper basic period for imprisonment for a life prisoner and the minister introduced a rule of practice whereby the consultation was deferred.[4]

V ABUSE OF PROCESS

General

An abuse of process in this context means the taking of any form of legal **20.21** process in circumstances where it is unfair to do so. The process may be by way of civil action or proceeding or by way of criminal prosecution. Lord Lowry has defined an abuse of process in the context of criminal proceedings as "something so unfair and wrong that the court should not allow a prosecutor to proceed with what is in all respects a regular proceeding".[5]

Criminal prosecutions

In England the concept of abuse of process was at one time thought to **20.22** be confined to cases where there had been undue delay in the proceedings or where there had been manipulation or misuse of the rules of procedure.[6] But the concept has been extended. In *Hunter v. Chief Constable of West Midland Police*[7] Lord Diplock referred to "the inherent power which any court of justice must possess to prevent misuse of its procedure in a way which, although not inconsistent with the literal application of its procedural rules, would nevertheless be manifestly unfair to a party to litigation before it, or would otherwise bring the administration of justice into disrepute among right-thinking people. The circumstances in which abuse of process can arise are very varied." Two categories of case were distinguished in *Schlesinger*[8]: "The first was where there had been prejudice to a defendant or a fair trial could not be had. The second was where the conduct of the prosecution had been such as to justify a stay regardless of whether a fair trial might still be possible".

---

[1] *Malloch v. Aberdeen Corporation*, 1973 S.C. 227, *per* Lord Keith at 247.
[2] See para. 19.17.
[3] *Re Findlay* [1985] 1 A.C. 318.
[4] *R. v. Secretary of State for the Home Office, ex p. Handscomb* (1988) 86 Cr.App.R. 59.
[5] *Hui Chi-ming v. R.* [1992] 1 A.C. 34 at 57.
[6] *R. v. Croydon Justices, ex p. Dean* [1993] Q.B. 769 at 777.
[7] [1982] A.C. 529 at 536.
[8] [1995] Crim.L.R. 137 at 138.

Where a youth of 17 years had for some weeks been regarded as a witness for the prosecution in proceedings against others for a murder and had been given some representation or promise in good faith from the police that he would not be prosecuted for the destruction of a car which he admitted he had carried out with the intention of impeding the apprehension of the murderers, it was held that it was an abuse of process to raise a prosecution against him.[9] It would be possible to classify the case as an example of the unfairness of a breach of an undertaking. Alternatively, it could be analysed as an example of a legitimate expectation that he would not be prosecuted. But a breach of a promise not to prosecute does not necessarily make a prosecution an abuse; it may do so if circumstances have changed.[10]

Witness

20.23 Where a witness had been assured by the Independent Commission Against Corruption in Hong Kong that he would not be required to give evidence, a subpoena served on him and his conviction for contempt of court were set aside as an abuse of process. McMulli V.-P. observed: "there is a clear public interest to be observed in holding officials of the state to promises made by them in full understanding of what is entailed by the bargain".[11]

Delay

20.24 Undue delay by the tax authority causing loss to the taxpayer may constitute a ground for review if established.[12] In England a criminal prosecution may in exceptional circumstances be stayed.[13] The question is whether in all the circumstances the situation created by the delay is such as to make it unfair for a criminal trial to be held.[14]

Pre-trial impropriety

20.25 In *Sinclair v. H.M. Advocate*[15] the accused complained that he had been illegally apprehended abroad and brought back in custody to Scotland to be tried for certain criminal offences. He was detained in Glasgow on a regular warrant pending his trial. It was held that irregularities in bringing him to the United Kingdom did not justify a suspension of the warrants which had been issued for his apprehension and detention. The criminal proceedings were not to be stopped on account of any irregularities committed abroad. Lord M'Laren observed[16]: "In a case of substantial infringement of right this Court will always give redress, but the public interest in the punishment of crime is not to be prejudiced by irregularities on the part of inferior officers of the law in relation to the prisoner's aprehension and detention". There is thus a balance to be struck between fairness to the accused and the public interest in the prosecution of allegedly criminal behaviour. The approach adopted in

---

[9] *R. v. Croydon Justices, ex p. Dean, supra.*
[10] *Townsley, Dearsley and Bretscher* [1997] 2 Crim.L.R. 540.
[11] *Chiu piu-wing v. Att.-Gen.* (1984) H.K.L.R. 411 at 417.
[12] *R. v. IRC, ex p. Preston* [1985] 1 A.C. 835.
[13] *Att.-Gen's Reference (No. 1 of 1990)* [1992] 1 Q.B. 630.
[14] See *Att.-Gen. of Hong Kong v. Cheung* [1994] 1 A.C. 1.
[15] (1890) 17 R. (J.) 38.
[16] at 44.

Sinclair was later followed in England.[17] More recently, however, the issue has been reconsidered by the House of Lords, and it now appears that in the interests of fairness the attempt to prosecute one who has been unlawfully brought within the jurisdiction of the court for the purpose of pursuing a prosecution will now be treated with greater circumspection. In *R. v. Horseferry Road Magistrates' Court, ex parte Bennett*,[18] judicial review was sought of the decision of the magistrates to refuse an adjournment which had been sought to enable the applicant to challenge the jurisdiction of the court. The defendant in criminal proceedings in England had been forcibly returned to England from South Africa through an alleged collusion between the police forces of the two countries. It was held that the High Court had the power in the exercise of its supervisory jurisdiction to inquire into the circumstances under which a person has been brought within the jurisdiction and to stay the proceedings if satisfied that there had been a disregard of extradition procedures. In that case Lord Griffiths observed[19]:

"In the present case there is no suggestion that it would have been unfair to try him if he had been returned to this country through extradition procedures. If the court is to have the power to interfere with the prosecution in the present circumstances it must be because the judiciary accept a responsibility for the maintenance of the rule of law that embraces a willingness to oversee executive action and to refuse to countenance behaviour that threatens either basic human rights or the rule of law."

Thereafter the Divisional Court, having heard evidence, quashed the committal for the trial. However, the problem then came before the Scottish High Court of Justiciary because a warrant had also been issued in Scotland for his arrest on certain charges of fraud. Bennett sought by a petition to have the warrant suspended. The High Court, contrary to the view reached in the Divisional Court, held that Bennett had not been the victim of a collusive agreement between the British and South African police. The Lord Advocate had certainly not been involved in any such arrangements and there was nothing oppressive or illegal in the enforcement of the Scottish warrant.[20] Thereafter the Divisional Court held that it had no jurisdiction to entertain an application in England for judicial review of the decision to execute the warrant in Scotland.[21] While the decision in *Sinclair* was distinguished by the High Court in Scotland, its authority has clearly been shaken and it may well be that the Scottish Court would now incline towards the approach adopted by the House of Lords in *Bennett*.

---

[17] *R. v. Plymouth Justices, ex p. Driver* [1986] 1 Q.B. 95; contrary decisions were there held to have been made *per incuriam*.

[18] [1993] 3 W.L.R. 90.

[19] at 104.

[20] *Bennett, Petr*, 1994 S.C.C.R. 902.

[21] See the Commentary in 1994 S.C.C.R. 923.

CHAPTER 21

IRRATIONALITY AND PROPORTIONALITY

I   INTRODUCTION
II   IRRATIONALITY
III   PROPORTIONALITY

I   INTRODUCTION

Irrationality, often, if misleadingly, referred to as *"Wednesbury* unrea- **21.01**
sonableness",[1] is one of the most familiar grounds of judicial review.
Although the exercise of power on irrational grounds is often treated as
a specific example of misuse of powers, irrationality is now well
established as an independent ground of review.[2] Proportionality as a
ground of review is, as will be seen, closely related to irrationality.[3] Not
only does proportionality share with irrationality the potential to bring
judicial review overtly into the merits of a decision, but also, as the
courts have acknowledged that the level or intensity of review required
by irrationality varies depending on the nature of the particular decision
and the rights and interests which it affects. Whilst the enactment of the
Human Rights Act 1998 means that proportionality is likely to become
an independent ground of review, certainly in cases with human rights
implications, it has long been clear that proportionality is a general
principle of E.C. law and therefore already a ground of judicial review in
that context, namely where a court considers a challenge to national
measures which fall within the scope of E.C. law on the ground of their
inconsistency with applicable E.C. law. More generally, the principle of
proportionality has already been considered briefly[4] in the contexts of
E.C. law and human rights, but, at least at this stage of the development
of the grounds of judicial review, it is appropriate to combine the two
grounds of irrationality and proportionality in the same chapter.

II   IRRATIONALITY

Analysis

The ground of irrationality may often overlap with other grounds. **21.02**
Alleged defects in procedure may be challenged on the ground of
irrationality.[5] Some grounds of challenge may be analysed under the

---

[1] See paras 14.07 and 21.04.
[2] See, for example, *Council of Civil Service Unions v. Minister for the Civil Service* [1985]
A.C. 374 (hereafter *GCHQ*) *per* Lord Diplock at 410–411, who first used the term
irrationality as the equivalent for the "unreasonableness" ground of review articulated by
Lord Greene M.R. in *Associated Provincial Picture Houses Ltd v. Wednesbury Corporation*
[1948] K.B. 223.
[3] Technically, of course, the ground of review is that of disproportionality, but the term
"proportionality" is universally used. See generally, Jowell and Lester, "Proportionality:
Neither Novel nor Dangerous" in Jowell and Oliver (eds), *New Directions in Judicial
Review* (Stevens, London, 1988).
[4] See paras 5.41 and 6.20.
[5] *Asda Stores Ltd v. Secretary of State for Scotland*, 1999 S.L.T. 503.

heads of irrationality or error. Irrationality and error often overlap. For example, when a decision is challenged on the ground that it is based on factual errors, the court may approach the issues by asking whether the decision maker's assessment of and conclusions from the facts are irrational.[6] In *James Aitken & Sons (Meat Producers) v. City of Edinburgh District Council*,[7] a failure to take into account a material consideration was seen as unreasonable, although perhaps that failure may also be treated as an error of law.[8] Furthermore, a departure from what is rational may be treated as an illegality, as where an excessive expenditure was regarded as unreasonable and illegal.[9] But none of this detracts from irrationality as an independent ground of review.

Fact and law

21.03   However, it has to be noticed that where an act or decision is challenged on the ground of its irrationality, the discussion of the issues more patently involves a consideration of the merits of the decision. Review for irrationality requires the court to define the limits of the actual decisions which a decision maker may reach and it may require the court to go over the ground traversed by the decision maker. Accordingly, in so far as review for irrationality requires this, the purpose and function of judicial review must be preserved as distinct from any appeal on the merits or any reassessment of the substance of the decision.[10] The characterisation of a decision as unreasonable or irrational requires finding that it is one which "no reasonable decision-maker properly instructed could have reached". One way in which the limits of judicial review may be preserved is to formulate the test for irrationality in strict terms. But, while all the grounds of review may raise the question of the appropriate intensity of review, irrationality and error, in light of their being concerned with the substance of decisions, present this question most acutely. The standard required to meet irrationality is not a universal one and must vary with the circumstances so that what is irrational for one decision maker may not be for another. In other words, the approach to irrationality will require deference in some cases and stricter scrutiny in other cases.

Terminology

21.04   The word "unreasonableness" is open to construction, but it should not be allowed to cover disputes about whether a decision is merely wise or unwise.[11] The difficulty is that, as with "fairness", the term "unreasonableness" has an ordinary usage which is quite different from its technical meaning as a ground of judicial review. Indeed, the difficulty is greater with unreasonableness: whereas it is possible, if not always

---

   [6] *cf. Edwards v. Bairstow* [1956] A.C. 14.
   [7] 1990 S.L.T. 241, followed in *Trusthouse Forte (U.K.) Ltd v. Perth and Kinross D.C.*, 1990 S.L.T. 737.
   [8] *Ettrick & Lauderdale D.C. v. Secretary of State for Scotland*, 1995 S.L.T. 996.
   [9] *Roberts v. Hopwood* [1925] A.C. 578 (where the characterisation of the Council's decision as "unreasonable" came close to review of the decision on its merits).
   [10] *McTear v. Scottish Legal Aid Board*, 1997 S.L.T. 109, where the decision was held neither perverse nor unreasonable.
   [11] This point has long been accepted: see Muirhead, *Municipal and Police Government in Scotland* (3rd ed.), p. 666. See also *Shetland Line (1984) Ltd v. Secretary of State for Scotland*, 1996 S.L.T. 653 (noting that substantive unfairness is not a ground of review and cannot be made so by being raised under irrationality).

convincing, to distinguish the procedural from the substantive in relation to fairness, it is much harder to do so when the ground of review is whether a challenged decision is itself, in its result, "unreasonable". Historically, the ground of review is that of "unreasonableness" in the sense expressed by Lord Greene M.R. in the *Wednesbury* case, namely that the authority has "come to a conclusion so unreasonable that no reasonable authority could have come to it".[12] However, the term "*Wednesbury* unreasonableness" is misleading because it is capable of including most of the grounds of review which relate to misuse of powers. Indeed, Lord Greene M.R.'s discussion of "unreasonableness" may be taken to suggest that it is one instance of misuse of powers. In any event, subsequent cases have made clear that Lord Greene M.R.'s dictum on unreasonableness is independent of the other grounds of review and focuses on the actual decision itself. But, as Lord Reid observed in *Westminster Bank v. Beverley Borough Council*,[13] the word "unreasonable" as used in the *Wednesbury* case requires a little expansion: "The decision of any authority can be attacked on the ground that it is in excess of its powers. The word 'unreasonable' is not at all an apt description of action in excess of power, and it is not a very satisfactory description of action in abuse of power."[14] In the present work, the use of the term "irrationality" is preferred. Irrationality indicates that this ground of review involves review of more than the purposes for which and the procedures by which a decision was reached, although it is still concerned with defining what the legal powers of the decision maker are. In this regard, irrationality expresses more adequately the standard which normally has to be achieved if a successful challenge is to be made on this ground.

Defining irrationality

Lord Diplock has observed: "In public law 'unreasonable' as descriptive **21.05** of the way in which a public authority has purported to exercise a discretion vested in it by statute has become a term of legal art. To fall within this expression it must be conduct which no sensible authority acting with the due appreciation of its responsibilities would have decided to adopt."[15] In the *Wednesbury* case itself, Lord Greene M.R. pointed to the example given by Warrington L.J. in *Short v. Poole Corporation*[16] of the red-haired teacher dismissed because she had red hair. Such a decision would be "something so absurd that no sensible person could ever dream that it lay within the powers of the authority".[17] In an early Scottish case it was said that the acts of a local authority with which the court could interfere included acts "such as are manifestly inexpedient and improper as to go beyond the bounds of fair administration".[18] And in *Kruse v. Johnson*,[19] Lord Russell C.J. explored what it means to say that a byelaw is "unreasonable": "But unreasonable in what sense? If, for instance, they were found to be partial and unequal in their

---

[12] [1948] 1 K.B. 223 at 234.
[13] [1971] A.C. 508.
[14] *ibid.* at 530.
[15] *Secretary of State for Education v. Tameside B.C.* [1977] A.C. 1014 at 1064.
[16] [1926] Ch. 66 at 90–91.
[17] [1948] 1 K.B. 223 at 229.
[18] *Nicol etc. v. Magistrates of Aberdeen* (1870) 9 M. 306, *per* Lord Kinloch at 313.
[19] [1898] 2 Q.B. 91.

operation as between classes; if they were manifestly unjust; if they disclosed bad faith; if they involved such oppressive or gratuitous interference with the rights of those subject to them as could find no justification in the minds of reasonable men, the court might well say, 'Parliament never intended to give authority to make such rules; they are unreasonable and ultra vires'."[20] Lord Russell's dictum presents many of the issues which continue to inform irrationality: the extent to which inequality of treatment may raise irrationality; whether injustice suggests irrationality; the relevance of the motives for a decision in showing irrationality; and the extent to which a decision interferes with the rights of others beyond acceptable standards, which in turn raises the overlap between irrationality and the the balancing process required by proportionality.[21] In modern times, the meaning of irrationality has been put in various ways. In the *GCHQ* case,[22] where Lord Diplock first adopted irrationality as the term for "*Wednesbury* unreasonableness", his Lordship defined the concept in strong terms: "It applies to a decision which is so outrageous in its defiance of logic or of accepted moral standards that no sensible person who had applied his mind to the question to be decided could have arrived at".[23] In another case, Lord Scarman considered that a decision vitiated by irrationality meant that it was "so absurd that he [the minister] must have taken leave of his senses".[24] In *R. v. Hillingdon London Borough Council, ex parte Puhlhofer*,[25] Lord Brightman considered that irrationality meant that a decision was "perverse" and demonstrated "unreasonableness verging on an absurdity".[26] Lord Lowry has given a possibly more restrained definition: "so unreasonable that no statutory authority/public officer acting reasonably could have come to it".[27]

While there are many words and expressions which may be used to explain irrationality, there may be dangers in seeking to find other words to define or even use other words to describe it. Descriptive phrases may readily bear an element of expressive intensity which adds unnecessary colour to what ought to be a single concept, although the precise application of the concept may vary in accordance with the particular circumstances of particular cases. Perhaps the most that needs to be said is that the concept of irrationality draws on the fundamental values of the legal system and of society. As Lord Diplock observed in *GCHQ*: "Whether a decision falls within [irrationality] is a question that judges by their training and experience should be well-equipped to answer, or else there would be something badly wrong with our judicial system."[28] The judge must, however, recall that it is a supervisory jurisdiction which is being exercised and that the decision is not being considered on its merits. A court has no power to invalidate a decision simply on the

---

[20] *ibid.* at 99–100.
[21] Traditionally, the unusually severe consequences of a decision have not of themselves led to the decision being considered irrational: *Purdon v. Glasgow District Licensing Board*, 1988 S.C.L.R. 466. But as proportionality develops as a ground of review, severe consequences will have to be considered as part of the balancing process.
[22] *Council of Civil Service Unions v. Minister for the Civil Service* [1985] A.C. 374.
[23] *ibid.* at 410.
[24] *Nottinghamshire County Council v. Secretary of State for the Environment* [1986] A.C. 240 at 247.
[25] [1986] A.C. 484.
[26] *ibid.* at 518.
[27] *Champion v. Chief Constable of the Gwent Constabulary* [1990] 1 W.L.R. 1 at 16.
[28] [1985] A.C. 374 at 410.

ground of irrationality because it exhibits "eccentric principles of socialist philanthropy" or "a feminist ambition to secure the equality of the sexes".[29] Rather, the judge must ask whether the challenged decision: "looked at objectively, [is] so devoid of any plausible justification that no reasonable body of persons could have reached [it]".[30]

The spectrum of decisions

While it may be difficult to affirm that the task is wholly objective, it must be accepted that all the modern statements on irrationality identify it as requiring a high standard of perversity—or absurdity—for its satisfaction. In *Puhlhofer*,[31] the just conceivable was seen as the limit before perversity was reached. This invites a formulation of irrationality in terms of whether the authority was entitled to reach its decision rather than to concentrate on the extremes of all possible cases.[32] As Lord Hailsham L.C. explained in *Re W (an infant)*[33]: "Not every reasonable exercise of judgment is right, and not every mistaken exercise of judgment is unreasonable. There is a band of decisions within which no court should seek to replace the individual's judgment with his own".[34] More recently, this approach to irrationality has been expressed as requiring it to be shown: "that the decision is unreasonable in the sense that it is beyond the range of responses open to a reasonable decision-maker".[35] This approach makes clear that whatever definition of irrationality is preferred, it is a matter of degree. There is a spectrum of irrationality and only a judge can decide whether a particular decision falls inside or outside the range of decisions which a decision maker's finite legal powers permit to be made. A balancing process is involved and it is now clear that the standard connoted by irrationality varies according to the circumstances of particular cases.

21.06

The standard to be applied

It follows from the terms in which irrationality has been expressed that the standard is an exacting one.[36] This means that there is a heavy burden on an applicant to establish irrationality.[37] Lord Scarman has written that the standard required to meet irrationality makes it a "rare

21.07

---

[29] *Roberts v. Hopwood* [1925] A.C. 578, *per* Lord Atkinson at 594; for discussion and criticism of this decision, see Keith-Lucas, "Popularism" [1962] P.L. 52.

[30] *Bromley LBC v. Greater London Council* [1983] 1 A.C. 768, *per* Lord Diplock at 821. This case, known at the time as the "Fair Fares" case, concerned an attempt by the GLC to use its spending powers to enable money raised by local rates to subsidise fares on London Transport. The tense political atmosphere led to the decision becoming a 1980s version of *Roberts v. Hopwood*, a development partially helped by the Court of Appeal's decision articulating "*Wednesbury* unreasonableness" in terms which effectively amounted to a review of the GLC's decisions on the merits. The House of Lords' decision properly focused on the extent to which the GLC was using its powers for their proper purposes, so that the decision is not really an irrationality decision at all.

[31] *supra*.

[32] *cf. Stewart v. Monklands D.C.*, 1989 S.C.L.R. 45.

[33] [1971] A.C. 682.

[34] *ibid.* at 700.

[35] *R. v. Ministry of Defence, ex p. Smith* [1996] Q.B. 517 at 554.

[36] *K v. Scottish Legal Aid Board*, 1989 S.L.T. 617 at 620; *Venter v. Scottish Legal Aid Board*, 1993 S.L.T. 147.

[37] See *Purdon v. City of Glasgow Licensing Board*, 1989 S.L.T. 201; and *City of Edinburgh D.C. v. Secretary of State for Scotland*, 1985 S.L.T. 551, *per* Lord Jauncey at 556. In relation to the review of subordinate legislation on the ground of irrationality, see below.

bird which is not to be allowed any very extensive flight".[38] In Lord Greene M.R.'s words in *Wednesbury* itself, showing unreasonableness "would require something overwhelming".[39] But in practice what constitutes irrationality, while susceptible to various linguistic formulations, is eventually a matter of assessment of the decision in the circumstances. On this approach some distinction might be made between the various kinds of occasion on which decisions may require to be made, such as, for example, whether the decision is one of determining a general policy, or whether it involves the application of funds to some particular project, or whether it is for the granting or refusing of some particular application, or whether it concerns matters which have human rights implications. In deciding whether in particular circumstances the decision is or is not open to challenge on the ground of irrationality regard has to be had to the nature of the subject-matter and the character of the decision in order to give proper regard to the situation facing the decision maker and proper respect to the various considerations which he is necessarily in the best position to assess. Respect always requires to be given to the special knowledge of the circumstances which the decision maker may have, whether it be an acquaintance with particualar conditions in a locality or matters requiring an expert appraisal of the technicalities of the case.[40] But beyond that the court must be entitled, as Lord Bridge of Harwich has observed, "to subject an administrative decision to the more rigorous examination, to ensure that it is in no way flawed, according to the gravity of the issue which the decision determines".[41]

The context

21.08 The court must review a decision against the background of the material available to the decision maker at the time of the decision and not by reference to subsequent events.[42] In a developing situation, however, it may be unrealistic to ignore changes which have occurred since the decision was made.[43] More generally, the court must preserve and respect a degree of appreciation of the decision maker's task and, while concentrating on matters of legality and propriety, avoid assuming the mantle of the decision maker's responsibilities. A pragmatic and functional approach requires to be adopted in which the jurisdiction of the

---

[38] Lord Scarman, "The Development of Administrative Law: Obstacles and Opportunities" [1990] P.L. 490 at 492.

[39] [1948] 1 K.B. 223 at 230.

[40] But the court will interfere with a decision in an arbitration on a procedural matter if it is unreasonable: *Shanks & McEwan (Contractors) Ltd v. Mifflin Construction Ltd*, 1993 S.L.T. 1125.

[41] *R. v. Secretary of State for the Home Department, ex p. Bugdaycay* [1987] 1 A.C. 514 at 531. See also *R. v. Secretary of State for the Home Department, ex p. Brind* [1991] 1 A.C. 696; *R. v. Secretary of State for the Home Department, ex p. MacQuillan* [1995] 4 All E.R. 400; *R. v. The Lord Chancellor, ex p. Maxwell* [1997] 1 W.L.R. 104; *R. v. Radio Authority ex p. Bull* [1997] 3 W.L.R. 1094; and (significantly, since it concerned subordinate legislation) *R. v. Secretary of State for Social Security, ex p. Joint Council for the Welfare of Immigrants* [1997] 1 W.L.R. 275. *Cf. R. v. Secretary of State for the Environment, ex p. Hammersmith and Fulham LBC* [1991] 1 A.C. 521; *R. v. Chief Constable of Sussex, ex p. International Traders' Ferry Ltd* [1997] 2 All E.R. 65; and *R. v. Secretary of State for the Home Department, ex p. Launder* [1997] 1 W.L.R. 839. See also now *Lustig-Prean und Becket v. U.K., The Times,* October 11, 1999.

[42] *Shetland Line (1984) Ltd v. Secretary of State for Scotland*, 1996 S.L.T. 653 at 658.

[43] See, for example, *R. v. Secretary of State for the Home Department, ex p. Launder* [1997] 3 All E.R. 961.

decision making body is understood in light of a consideration of all the circumstances and, where appropriate, all due deference given to it.[44] For example, due deference requires to be given in cases where the decision making body has a particular specialised expertise and long experience in dealing with particular issues. So, for example, in the context of medical treatment the court may review matters relating to the legality of a health authority's decision but not the priority to be given to the allocation of funds.[45]

The intensity of review

This approach has implications both for the substance and the definition of a challenge on the ground of irrationality. As has been mentioned earlier,[46] and as has also been indicated in the foregoing paragraphs, the intensity which the court will apply in judicial review may vary from case to case depending upon the subject-matter. It may be that "tiers of scrutiny" are required to allow review for irrationality to respect the responsibilities of the decision maker. A balancing process may be required under which the importance of the right or interest affected must be balanced against the nature of the decision and the decision-making process.[47] As the right or interest becomes more important, the court's review becomes more stringent.[48] Such an approach clearly merges with the concept of proportionality and it is no accident that it is in human rights cases that the courts have suggested that a more searching or "anxious" scrutiny is appropriate in review on grounds of irrationality.[49] Indeed, in such cases, it may be that a decision violating fundamental human rights can only be supported where there are

21.09

---

[44] An instructive approach that seeks to balance the court's judicial review power with an appreciation of the responsibilities of the decision-maker and the context and circumstances in which the decision must be taken is provided in the Supreme Court of Canada's recent decisions in administrative law: see, for example, *Bell Canada v. Canadian Radio-Television and Telecommunications Commission* [1989] 1 S.C.R. 1722; *United Brotherhood of Carpenters and Joiners of America, Local 579 v. Bradco Construction* [1993] 2 S.C.R. 316; *Pezim v. British Columbia (Superintendent of Brokers)* [1994] 2 S.C.R. 557. But for criticism of the balancing approach and its roots in a continuing distinction between jurisdictional and non-jurisdictional errors of law (following the Supreme Court's decision in *Canadian Union of Public Employees, Local 953 v. New Brunswick Liquor Corporation* [1979] 2 S.C.R. 227), see Dyzenhaus, "The Politics of Deference: Judicial Review and Democracy" in Taggart (ed.), *The Province of Administrative Law* (Hart, Oxford, 1997). As a general matter, many Canadian judicial review cases involve challenges to the decisions of statutory labour arbitrations. *Bradco*, for example, concerns the Court's powers over such labour arbitrations, a context that in most societies will always be sensitive and invite considerable deference to decision makers. Nevertheless, beyond the particularities of the Canadian law, the approach itself deserves some consideration: for further comparison, see Craig, *Administrative Law* (3rd ed., 1994) at pp. 375 *et seq.*

[45] *R. v. Cambridge Health Authority, ex p. B* [1995] 2 All E.R. 129.

[46] para. 14.13.

[47] As noted, such a balancing approach is evident in Canada. But it is not without its critics: see Dyzenhaus, *supra.*

[48] There is already arguably some evidence of this being the approach: *R. v. Ministry of Defence, ex p Smith* [1996] Q.B. 517, esp. *per* Bingham M.R. at 554–555. See also *Kriba v. Secretary of State for the Home Department*, 1998 S.L.T. 1113, *per* Lord Hamilton at 1116 and *R. v. Lord Saville, ex p. A, The Times*, July 29, 1999 (C.A.). But see the views of Lord Irvine of Lairg against different levels of scrutiny being part of the *Wednesbury* unreasonableness test: "Judges and Decision-Makers: The Theory and Practice of Wednesbury Review" [1996] P.L. 59.

[49] It may be that the Human Rights Act 1998, under which the courts must adopt proportionality tests to examine alleged breaches of human rights, will slow down the development of tiers of scrutiny in rationality review beyond the sphere of human rights.

rational reasons for it, which is a qualitatively different inquiry from that involved in deciding if the decision is irrational.

Some specific examples may now briefly be noticed:

Matters of policy

21.10   Sir Thomas Bingham has observed[50]: "The greater the policy content of a decision, and the more remote the subject matter of a decision from ordinary judicial experience, the more hesitant the court must necessarily be in holding a decision to be irrational. That is good law and, like most good law, common sense. Where decisions of a policy-laden, esoteric or security-based nature are in issue, even greater caution than normal must be shown in applying the test, but the test itself is sufficiently flexible to cover all situations." In the construction of a policy the court will also take a deferential approach.[51]

Financial administration

21.11   In matters of public financial administration where a course of action has been approved by Parliament review by the court on the ground of irrationality will, as has already been noticed, usually be inappropriate.[52] Political judgments subject to approval by the House of Commons, such as the determination of what is an excessive expenditure by a local authority, are only open to challenge on the grounds of bad faith, improper motive or manifest absurdity.[53] But even short of such cases, where the decision is one involving an exercise of discretion in regard to the raising of taxes or the allocation of public funds or other resources, the court should not readily intervene. Good public administration may require speed, decisiveness and finality as well as an objective assessment of the public interest, and the courts may not be well placed in every situation to achieve such an assessment.[54] For example, the legal aid board may be entitled to take into account the risk of hazarding a substantial sum of public money on a case with only limited prospects of a worthwhile return.[55] On the other hand, where a decision is partial or unequal in its operation as between different persons or groups of persons within its scope, the decision may be unlawful as being unreasonable or unfair. Failure to balance fairly the interests of ratepayers and transport users and casting an unfair burden on the ratepayers may be a breach of fiduciary duty, unjust and unreasonable. Thus, in *Bromley London Borough Council v. Greater London Council*,[56] it was held to be beyond the powers given under the Transport (London) Act 1969 for the Greater London Council to reduce fares on public transport and levy a supplementary rate to cover the cost.

Parole board

21.12   It was observed by Lord Weir that in challenging the reasonableness of a decision of the parole board, where fairness to the individual concerned has to be balanced against the safety of the public and there are anxious,

---

[50] *R. v. MOD, ex p. Smith* [1996] Q.B. 517 at 556.

[51] Maurici, "The Meaning of Policy: A Question for the Court?" (1998) 85, 3 Jud.Rev.

[52] *Nottinghamshire County Council v. Secretary of State for the Environment* [1986] A.C. 240. See paras 9.12 and 9.19 in Illegality. See also *City of Edinburgh D.C. v. Secretary of State for Scotland*, 1985 S.L.T. 551.

[53] *R. v. Secretary of State for the Environment, ex p. Hammersmith LBC* [1991] A.C. 521.

[54] See *R. v. Monopolies and Mergers Commission, ex p. Argyll Group plc* [1986] 1 W.L.R. 763 at 774.

[55] *McTear v. Scottish Legal Aid Board*, 1977 S.L.T. 108.

[56] [1983] A.C. 768.

difficult and heavy responsibilities to be discharged, "a very strong case has to be made out before intervention by judicial review is justified".[57]

Human rights

Where matters of human rights are in issue the court will be more **21.13** anxious to scrutinise the circumstances before determining a question of reasonableness. Thus, in the case of an asylum seeker it was said that "where the result of a flawed decision may imperil life or liberty a special responsibility lies on the court in the examination of the decision-making process".[58] In the same case[59] Lord Bridge of Harwich said: "The most fundamental of all human rights is the individual's right to life and, when an administrative decision under challenge is said to be one which may put the applicant's life at risk, the basis of the decision must surely call for the most anxious scrutiny." In *R. v. Home Secretary, ex parte Brind*,[60] the House of Lords while applying a test of reasonableness recognised that any restriction of the right of freedom of expression could only be justified by an important competing public interest. In *R. v. Ministry of Defence, ex parte Smith*[61] the observation was accepted that "in judging whether the decision-maker has exceeded the margin of appreciation the human rights context is important. The more substantial the interference with human rights, the more the court will require by way of justification before it is satisfied that the decision is reasonable" in the sense of not being beyond the range of responses open to a reasonable decision maker. The examination and reading of a prisoner's correspondence with his solicitor, while held justifiable in Scotland on the ground of his qualified right to confidential consultation with his solicitor in the prison,[62] has been held in England to be objectionable as a breach of his basic rights[63] and in a Scottish case was held by the Court of Human Rights to be in breach of Article 8 of the Convention.[64] But in considering the propriety of interim liberation of an illegal immigrant the power of the court has been said to be wider than its general power to review administrative acts.[65]

Grants of licences

Where a licensing board had two applications from the same applicant it **21.14** was held that their refusal of the first one did not mean that their grant of the second was irrational.[66] It was held not to be irrational for an extension of permitted hours to be refused due to a change of policy although such grants had been regularly made in the past.[67]

---

[57] *McRae v. Parole Board for Scotland*, 1997 S.L.T. 97 at 101.
[58] *R. v. Home Secretary, ex p. Bugdaycay* [1987] 1 A.C. 514, *per* Lord Templeman at 537.
[59] at 531.
[60] [1991] 1 A.C. 696.
[61] [1996] Q.B. 517 at 554; 1 All E.R. 257 at 263.
[62] *Leech v. Secretary of State for Scotland*, 1991 S.L.T. 910.
[63] *R. v. Home Secretary, ex p. Leech* [1994] Q.B. 198.
[64] *Campbell v. U.K.* (1992) 15 E.H.R.R. 137.
[65] *Singh v. Secretary of State for the Home Department*, 1993 S.L.T. 950.
[66] *Ladbroke Racing Ltd v. William Hill (Scotland) Ltd*, 1995 S.L.T. 134.
[67] *Bass Taverns Ltd v. Clydebank District Licensing Board*, 1995 S.L.T. 1275.

Financial awards

21.15 The court always felt itself able to intervene where an award had been made for the support of the poor which had been elusory. Following from that, it has gone further and reviewed an award as inadequate.[68] In England the court has held an award of compensation on a dismissal as so low as to be unreasonable.[69]

Planning conditions

21.16 Considerations of unreasonableness have arisen in connection with the conditions attached to grants of planning permission. In one case[70] power was given to impose conditions on a grant of planning permission "for regulating the development for use of any land under the control of the applicant . . . so far as appears to the local planning authority to be expedient for the purpose of or in connection with the development authorised by the permission". It was held among other things that a condition seeking to control the direction of take-off and landing of aircraft was *ultra vires* as unreasonable, and a condition restricting operating hours of helicopters where in fact the land was not used for helicopters was *ultra vires* as not reasonably related to the development. It is not unreasonable to impose a condition to the effect that no development should start until another event should occur.[71] But apart from irrationality, and perhaps proportionality, matters of planning judgment are within the exclusive province of the planning authority or the Secretary of State. The courts are only concerned with the legality of the decision.[72]

Subordinate legislation

21.17 As was indicated earlier,[73] and as has been recognised for a long time,[74] subordinate legislation may be invalid on the ground of irrationality. But it has been said in the context of byelaws designed in the public interest to preserve amenity that unreasonableness "is something which can never be made out except upon a case of great strength and clearness"[75] and, indeed, generally the court will be slow to hold byelaws void for unreasonableness.[76] A byelaw which restrains the liberty of the subject and constitutes a new offence with the sanction of a penalty will be subjected to particular scrutiny.[77] Approval by a confirming authority may raise a presumption of reasonableness[78] and the difficulty may

---

[68] *Pryde v. Heritors and Kirk-Session of Ceres* (1843) 5D. 552; esp. *per* Lord President Boyle at 567. Also *Fraser v. Burnett and Others*, 1806 Hume 256.

[69] *R. v. Civil Service Appeal Board, ex p. Cunningham* [1991] 4 All E.R. 310.

[70] *British Airports Authority v. Secretary of State for Scotland*, 1979 S.L.T. 197.

[71] *Grampian R.C. v. City of Aberdeen D.C.*, 1984 S.L.T. 197.

[72] *Tesco Stores v. Secretary of State* [1995] 2 All E.R. 636 at 657.

[73] See para. 9.12.

[74] See James Muirhead, *Municipal and Police Government in Scotland* (3rd ed., 1924), p. 665.

[75] *Robert Baird Ltd v. Glasgow Corporation*, 1935 S.C.(H.L.) 21, *per* Lord Tomlin at 27. For an example of an unsuccessful attempt to challenge a byelaw as unreasonable, see *De Prato v. Magistrates of Partick*, 1907 S.C.(H.L.) 5.

[76] *Drummond v. Pendreich*, 1972 J.C. 27 at 34.

[77] *Scottish General Transport Co. v. Glasgow Corporation*, 1928 S.C. 248 at 255: it was held that a power to regulate traffic by fixing points of departure did not extend to a prohibition on traffic.

[78] *Rae v. Hamilton* (1904) 6 F.(J.) 42.

become insuperable where it has been laid before the House of Commons and been considered there[79] or expressly or impliedly approved by Parliament. In that context the test of manifest absurdity comprised in the ground of reasonableness can only be satisfied in extreme and extraordinary circumstances, and the only grounds available are that the instrument was not authorised by the empowering statute or that the proper procedure has not been followed.[80]

Proof of irrationality

In most cases the substance of the decision against the background of **21.18** the circumstances of the case will provide the material on which the decision for or against rationality will fall to be made. In some cases other material may be available. The time taken to arrive at a decision may in an appropriate case lead to an inference that a discretion could not have been reasonably exercised, but this may depend upon the number and complexity of the issues involved and the extent to which they had been canvassed and explored in discussion before the body which required to make the determination.[81]

Examples of rational decisions

From what has already been said a finding that a decision is reasonable **21.19** will depend eventually on its particular circumstances. The subject-matter of such decisions has included the granting of taxi drivers' licences,[82] the granting of legal aid,[83] the renewal of detention orders under the Mental Health Act,[84] the making of planning decisions,[85] the decision whether a person was homeless,[86] and the determination of the fitness of a person responsible for the day-to-day running of a public house.[87] A decision to grant a second application for a betting shop licence and to refuse an earlier application which had been returned after an appeal for reconsideration was held not unreasonable.[88] Where a byelaw made by a company which operated trams and buses required that at the point where in the course of a journey passengers changed from the one form of conveyance to the other they had to get off the bus and go into an office to have their tickets stamped it was held that the provision was reasonable.[89]

---

[79] See *City of Edinburgh D.C. v. Secretary of State for Scotland*, 1985 S.L.T. 551, considered in *Chief Adjudication Officer v. Foster*] [1993] A.C. 754 as going further than English law had gone. See also *Nottinghamshire County Council v. Secretary of State for the Environment* [1986] 1 A.C. 240, *per* Lord Scarman at 250. In *Crichton v. Forfar County Road Trustees* (1886) 13 R.(J.) 99, Lord McLaren questioned whether the court could ever intervene where byelaws had been confirmed by the Secretary of State. The *City of Edinburgh* case was discussed by Himsworth in "Defining the Boundaries of Judicial Review", 1985 S.L.T. (News) 369 and by Campbell in "Approval and Statutory Instruments", 1986 S.L.T. (News) 101. See also para. 9.12, *supra*.

[80] *East Kilbride D.C. v. Secretary of State for Scotland*, 1995 S.L.T. 1238.

[81] *R.W. Cairns Ltd v. Busby East Kirk Session*, 1985 S.L.T. 493.

[82] *Monklands District Independent Taxi Owners Association v. Monklands D.C. (No. 2)*, 1997 S.L.T. 7.

[83] *K v. Scottish Legal Aid Board*, 1989 S.L.T. 617; *McTear v. Scottish Legal Aid Board*, 1997 S.L.T. 108.

[84] *K v. Murphy*, 1997 S.L.T. 248.

[85] *Bonnar v. West Lothian D.C.*, 1997 S.L.T. 398.

[86] *McAlinden v. Bearsden and Milngavie D.C.*, 1986 S.L.T. 191.

[87] *J. & J. Inns Ltd v. Angus District Licensing Board*, 1992 S.L.T. 930.

[88] *Ladbroke Racing (Strathclyde) Ltd v. William Hill (Scotland) Ltd*, 1995 S.L.T. 134.

[89] *Apthorpe v. Edinburgh Street Tramways Co.* (1882) 10 R. 344.

Examples of irrational decisions

21.20 A decision that a local authority had acted in a manner having the effect
of restricting, distorting or preventing competition was held to be
unreasonable.[90] A decision by a Valuation Appeal Committee refusing to
refer a complex case to the Lands Tribunal was held to be a defiance of
logic.[91] Where no rational basis was discoverable between the permission
for public entertainments performed by some types of animals and those
performed by others, review was allowed.[92] A decision that a person was
not "vulnerable" in the context of homelessness has been held in the
circumstances to be irrational.[93] It has also been held to be unreasonable
for a planning authority to grant a second application for a housing
development when the first one was still under appeal and its outcome
could not be taken into account.[94] A condition in a planning permission
requiring the developer to build a road which would then be dedicated
to public use was held to be irrational.[95] A rigid insistence on adherence
to a stipulated closing date for applications which had no statutory force
has been held unreasonable.[96] And rigidly to apply a set period of times
in order to satisfy a qualification of having a family connection with a
district was held to be treating guidance as if it was a rule.[97] To reach
opposite conclusions on the same facts may be a mark of perversity, but
where the decisions in question can be sufficiently distinguished—that is
to say where a reasonable authority could distinguish them—then the
decision may be regarded as a reasonable one.[98] Where there is an
explanation available for a discrepancy between one decision and a later
one in the same case the discrepancy will not be sufficient to condemn
the later decision as irrational.[99] Consistency in decision making is
generally a feature of good administration, but a departure from
consistency may well be open to justification.

III PROPORTIONALITY

Definition

21.21 In a strict sense this ground of review should be labelled "Disproportionality". But the use of the term "Proportionality" is now so well
established that its continued use is amply warranted. Proportionality
connotes that the means determined upon for achieving some object
ought to be sufficient and not excessive for the purpose of achieving that
object. The idea of proportionality is well established in E.C. law[1] and in

---

[90] *Ettrick and Lauderdale D.C. v. Secretary of State for Scotland*, 1995 S.L.T. 996.
[91] *Civil Aviation Authority v. Argyll and Bute Valuation Committee*, 1988 S.L.T. 119.
[92] *Gerry Cottle's Circus Ltd v. City of Edinburgh D.C.*, 1990 S.L.T. 235.
[93] *Kelly v. Monklands D.C.*, 1986 S.L.T. 169.
[94] *James Aitken & Sons (Meat Producers) v. City of Edinburgh D.C.*, 1990 S.L.T. 241,
followed in *Trusthouse Forte (U.K.) Ltd v. Perth and Kinross D.C.*, 1990 S.L.T. 737. Both
decisions were distinguished in *Henderson v. Argyll and Bute Council*, 1998 S.L.T. 1224.
[95] *Hall v. Shoreham by Sea UDC* [1969] 1 W.L.R. 240; see the consideration of this case
in *Tesco Stores Ltd v. Secretary of State for the Environment* [1995] 1 W.L.R. 759.
[96] *Woods v. Secretary of State for Scotland*, 1991 S.L.T. 197.
[97] *McMillan v. Kyle and Carrick D.C.*, 1995 S.C.L.R. 365; the case may be seen either as
one of error or of irrationality.
[98] *Semple v. Glasgow District Licensing Board*, 1990 S.C.L.R. 73.
[99] *R. v. Secretary of State for the Home Department, ex p. Pierson* [1996] 1 All E.R. 837.
[1] See para. 5.41. For discussion of proportionality in E.C. law, see Ellis (ed.), *The
Principle of Proportionality in the Laws of Europe* (Hart Publishing, 1999).

the jurisprudence of human rights.[2] Where alternative means for achieving the objective are available, the least onerous should be adopted and the disadvantages caused must not be disproportionate to the aims pursued.[3] The approach requires consideration of the appropriateness and the necessity of the proposed measure, and a balancing of the opposing benefits and disadvantages involved. It thus involves a measure of discretion. But it should be noted that, in the European jurisprudence, only if the decision is found to be manifestly inappropriate should the court intervene.[4] In relation to the application of the concept of proportionality, regard has also to be had to the propriety of a margin of appreciation, which operates as a restraint upon too rigorous an application of the principle. In other words, proportionality is a flexible concept which may be applied anxiously or deferentially according to the circumstances.

Proportionality and irrationality

The concept of proportionality can be seen as one expression of the ground of review which is known as irrationality, providing one example of the respect in which a decision may be found to be invalid as being irrational. On that approach proportionality can be accepted without difficulty as part of one of the well-recognised grounds of review and some of the decisions which have been made on the formula of irrationality could doubtless be analysed as examples of proportionality on that approach.[5] But it is arguable that proportionality is to be distinguished from irrationality as a ground of review, imposing a more intense scrutiny of the decision in issue so as to challenge its justification by a standard more rigorous than one of reference to a reasonable decision maker. **21.22**

Reluctance to extend the idea

The distinction was considered by the House of Lords in *R. v. The Home Secretary, ex parte Brind*.[6] The test of proportionality requires a balancing of the reasons for and against the decision. That involves an investigation of the merits of the decision and the courts have always regarded the merits as being beyond their concern in judicial review. The House of Lords plainly discouraged the introduction of the ground of proportionality at least in the case before them. Lord Lowry listed the reasons why proportionality should not be recognised as a ground for review. These were, first, that it would be an abuse of the supervisory jurisdiction to interfere with those to whom Parliament has entrusted the making of the decision; secondly, the judges do not possess the knowledge or experience to weigh delicately balanced administrative considerations; **21.23**

---

[2] An example can be found in *Dudgeon v. U.K. Bela Muhle* (1982) 4 E.H.R.R. 149. See also *Ming Pao Newspapers Ltd v. Att.-Gen. of Hong Kong* [1996] A.C. 907. The matter is touched on in para. 6.20 above on Human Rights.

[3] Case C–331/88 *R. v. Minister of Agriculture, Fisheries and Food, ex p. Fedesa* [1990] E.C.R. 1–4023.

[4] *e.g. ibid.*

[5] See Lord Hoffmann, "A Sense of Proportion" in Andenas and Jacobs (eds), *European Law in the English Courts*. See also Jowell and Lester, "Proportionality: Neither Novel nor Dangerous" in Jowell and Oliver (eds), *New Directions in Judicial Review* (Stevens, London, 1988).

[6] [1991] A.C. 696.

thirdly, to allow a challenge on this ground would jeopardise stability and relative certainty; and fourthly, delay, expense and uncertainty would be involved through the consequential increase in judicial review applications. Lord Templeman, however, observed[7]:

> "The subject matter and date of the *Wednesbury* principles cannot in my opinion make it either necessary or appropriate for the courts to judge the validity of an interference with human rights by asking themselves whether the Home Secretary has acted irrationally or perversely. It seems to me that the courts cannot escape from asking themselves whether a reasonable Secretary of State, on the material before him, could reasonably conclude that the interference with freedom of expression which he determined to impose was justifiable. In terms of the Convention, as construed by the European Court, the interference with freedom of expression must be necesary and proportionate to the damage which the restriction is designed to prevent."

Matters of substance

21.24 An assessment of a decision on the grounds of proportionality runs very close to a review of the decision on its merits, a danger of which the courts have been aware.[8] Some kinds of decisions require to be made by politicians rather than judges. In the context of the problem of the early release of prisoners it was observed that "neither the board nor the judiciary can be as close, or as sensitive, to public opinion as a minister responsible to Parliament and to the electorate. He has to judge the public acceptability of early release and to determine the policies needed to maintain public confidence in the system of criminal justice."[9] Thus the court in matters of judicial review must be wary lest it trespasses onto ground which must be the preserve of the executive. The suggestion that a minister's policy objectives and reasoning were an important element of the forensic exercise and that a consideration of fairness extended to a consideration of the omission of some element from a revised policy was rejected: "On matters of substance (as contrasted with procedure) *Wednesbury* provides the correct test".[10] However, the court has intervened where it considered that the authority had failed to achieve the proper balance between the interests of ratepayers and transport users[11] and in undertaking the weighing of the necessity for the making of an administrative order the court may be seen to be applying a test of proportionality as distinct from reasonableness.[12]

Application

21.25 While there may be dangers in the loss of flexibility in attempting to analyse successive steps which an application of the idea of proportionality may involve, some stages in the process may be noticed. First,

---

[7] at 751.
[8] *R. v. Barnsley Metropolitan B.C., ex p. Hook* [1976] 3 All E.R. 452; *Chief Constable of the North Wales Police v. Evans* [1982] 3 All E.R. 141.
[9] *Findlay v. Secretary of State for the Home Department* [1985] A.C. 318, *per* Lord Scarman at 333.
[10] *R. v. Secretary of State, ex p. Hargreaves* [1997] 1 All E.R. 397, *per* Hirst L.J. at 412.
[11] *Bromley LBC v. Greater London Council* [1983] 1 A.C. 768.
[12] *R. v. Secretary of State for the Home Department, ex p. Leech* [1994] Q.B. 198.

the objective of the decision under review must be identified and assessment made of its importance and seriousness. The severity of its effects and the extent to which it may invade fundamental rights and freedoms should be considered. Secondly, the means proposed to achieve the objective need to be identified. The connection between the means and the objective should be considered, with a view to the effectiveness, sufficiency and reasonableness of the means. Finally, an appraisal has to be made of the relationship between the objective and the means, so as to weigh the one against the other and see if a sufficient balance exists. But while these elements in the exercise can be so analysed, the process should not be approached in a mechanical way, but broadly and flexibly with an eye to the basic principle of fairness. An example of the application of the principle in Canada may be found in *Thomson Newspapers v. Canada*.[13] The sections of the majority judgment in that case reflect the successive stages of the process as applied in that case: the legislative objective, whether the objective was pressing and substantial, a rational connection, minimal impairment to freedom, and proportionality between the deleterious effects and the benefits.

Future extension

The passing of the Human Rights Act 1998, which enables alleged **21.26** contraventions of the European Convention on Human Rights to be raised directly in the national courts in the United Kingdom, will however bring with it the necessity (at least in that context) of applying the concept of proportionality. For example, the evaluation of compliance with Article 10 involves a balancing of the right to free expression against the qualifications of the right there set out.[14] It may no longer be sufficient to adopt the approach followed by Lord Bridge of Harwich in *R. v. Secretary of State for the Home Office, ex parte Brind*[15] of leaving aside the question whether the particular competing public interest justifies the particular restriction which has been imposed and asking simply whether a reasonable minister could on the material before him reasonably decide to do as he has done. The balancing will now itself be open to review.[16] Lord Goff of Chievely has equated the provisions of Article 10 with the common law. "It is established in the jurisprudence of the European Court of Human Rights that the word 'necessary' in this context implies the existence of a pressing social need, and that interference with freedom of expression should be no more than is proportionate to the legitimate aim pursued. I have no reason to believe that English law, as applied in the courts, leads to any different conclusion."[17] The admission of proportionality in the context of human rights will make it impossible to resist its appearance generally as a ground of review and it remains to be seen whether the limits will still be set in terms of "*Wednesbury* unreasonableness". The application of E.C. law also invites recourse to considerations of proportionality.[18]

---

[13] (1998) 1 S.C.R. 877. The case concerned a statutory provision banning for a specified period before an election day the broadcasting of the results of opinion surveys of how the electors would vote. The ban was held to infringe the right to freedom of expression.

[14] As in *The Sunday Times v. U.K.* (1979) 2 E.H.R.R. 245.

[15] [1991] 1 A.C. 696 at 749.

[16] As it was in, *e.g.*, *The Sunday Times v. U.K.*, *supra*.

[17] *Att.-Gen. v. Guardian Newspapers (No. 2)* [1990] 1 A.C. 109 at 283–284.

[18] See, for example, *Torfaen B.C. v. B & Q plc* [1990] 1 All E.R. 129; *NALGO v. Secretary of State for the Environment* [1992] T.L.R. 576.

CHAPTER 22

ERROR

I INTRODUCTION
II ERROR IN CONTEXT
III ERROR BEFORE *ANISMINIC*
IV *ANISMINIC* AND AFTER
V ERROR TODAY

I INTRODUCTION

In a general sense, the exercise of a power may be said to be erroneous if **22.01** it is vitiated on any of the grounds which have been discussed in the foregoing chapters. So where a power has been exceeded or where the proper procedure has not been followed or where the exercise of a power has been irrational in its purpose or result, an error in a general sense may be said to have occurred. Beyond all of that, however, an exercise of power may also be flawed where it has in a narrower sense "gone wrong". For example, a decision maker otherwise acting lawfully and properly may err and reach a wrong decision by misconstruing a statutory provision, thereby denying a claim which should have been upheld. In such a case the error is of a kind distinct from those identified by the other grounds of review. Thus, in the present context it can be assumed that the authority has the necessary power,[1] that the proper procedure has been observed, that there has been no misuse of power and that the result is not irrational. Nevertheless, the decision may yet be open to challenge on the ground that it is wrong. This chapter is concerned with the problem of the kind of error which may warrant intervention in judicial review.

As a ground of review, error in the narrow sense of a decision maker with power acting properly but still "going wrong" presents several difficulties. The first is identification of the error. The challengeable error will usually lie in a decision and may be identified in any record of a decision, such as a circular.[2] But there may be no record or no reasons. Secondly, there is the problem of classifying errors as relating to fact or law. Thereafter, the major problem concerns the proper scope of judicial review for errors made by decision makers. In this regard, if on the one hand all errors are reviewable, the scope of review will be wide and the area exclusively for the decision maker commensurately narrow. On the other hand, only some errors may be reviewable, in which case the task is to identify which those may be. Is it, for example, only those which are "jurisdictional" or "collateral" or in some sense crucial to the decision? In turn, this raises a question about the extent to which Parliament may limit or exclude the jurisdiction of the courts to review decisions for errors and particularly errors of law. This question has overshadowed the

---

[1] That is, jurisdiction in the "narrow sense" according to Lord Reid's analysis in *Anisminic v. Foreign Compensation Commission* [1969] 2 A.C. 147 at 171.
[2] *Scottish Old People's Welfare Council, Petr*, 1987 S.L.T. 179.

more recent development of error of law as a ground of judicial review. Before considering further the emergence of error as a ground of review it is necessary to place error in the context of the other grounds of judicial review.

II ERROR IN CONTEXT

Interference in the merits

22.02 Athough the court in exercising the supervisory jurisdiction does not take on the task of the decision maker, many of the grounds of judicial review go beyond matters of method and procedure in the decision-making process and take account of the decision itself. One obvious example is review on the ground of irrationality of the decision, but the risk of interference in the merits is also presented by review for error. Where the challenge to a decision is that it is vitiated by an error in the narrow sense of a mistake as to the facts or law on which it is based, the court may be involved in assessing whether the actual decision reached is right or wrong. Yet if a decision maker has the power to make a decision, should this include the power to make a decision which a court of review might consider to be wrong? If so, should there be any limit on the kind or extent of error which is to be allowed? The problem is that two competing interests arise: the need to allow the decision-making body to exercise the powers entrusted to it; and the duty of the court to ensure that the law is observed. Often the resolution of these two interests may be readily achieved, as where the decision-making body was biased or reached its decision in bad faith. But with error, particularly error of law, the resolution is not so clear. It can be recognised that there are some matters—for example, matters of policy, or the assessment of the weight to be given to particular considerations in the reaching of a decision—which are best left to the decision-making body itself to resolve and which are therefore beyond the power of the court to assess.[3] But the rule of law requires that the court have the final say on what is to be the meaning and effect of the law, including rules of law which the decision maker has the power to apply.

Fact and law

22.03 A distinction between matters of fact and matters of law might be suggested as a guide to the boundary which marks the limit of the court's supervisory power. But this seemingly simple distinction has for long caused difficulty.[4] The twofold distinction is in practice often unclear and inadequate. Not infrequently resort has to be had to a hybrid category of case referred to as one of mixed fact and law. The need for such a category in itself suggests that this means of distinction is unpromising. The case of *M'Millan v. Barclay, Curle & Co. Ltd*[5] may serve as an

---

[3] *McTear v. Scottish Legal Aid Board*, 1995 S.L.T. 108, *cf. Minister for Aboriginal Affairs v. Peko-Walsend Ltd* (1996) 162 C.L.R. 241, *per* Mason C.J. at 42.

[4] See, for example, Wilson, "A Note on Fact and Law" (1963) 26 M.L.R. 609; and "Questions of Degree" (1969) 32 M.L.R. 361; Mureinik, "The Application of the Rules: Law or Fact?" (1982) 98 L.Q.R. 587. See also the observations by Lord Reid in *Griffiths v. J.P. Harrison (Watford) Ltd* [1963] A.C. 1 at 15; and in *Cozens v. Brutus* [1973] A.C. 854 at 861. For a recent discussion of the problem see Endicott, "Questions of Law" (1998) 114 L.Q.R. 292.

[5] (1899) 2 F. 91.

example. The question in this case was whether a dock two miles from a shipbuilding yard was "near the yard" for the purposes of the Workmen's Compensation Act 1897. This was regarded by two of the judges as a question of fact, while Lord M'Laren saw some element of law in the construction of the phrase. The case demonstrates the particular difficulty in determining whether the application of a statutory provision to particular facts is a matter of law or of fact.[6] The expressions "error of law" and "error of fact" may become dangerously close to becoming labels to represent reviewable and non-reviewable errors, whereas a distinction between matters of fact and matters of law does not define the area of justiciability with sufficient precision.

The decision in *Edwards v. Bairstow*

In *Edwards v. Bairstow*,[7] the House of Lords set aside the conclusion **22.04** which had been reached on the facts by the general commissioners. There was debate about whether the situation should be analysed in the way in which the Scottish courts had been accustomed, namely by regarding the question as one of law, or of mixed fact and law, or alternatively by the course of regarding the matter as one of fact, but holding that the commissioners had acted without any evidence or upon a view of the facts which could not reasonably be entertained. The House of Lords preferred the latter analysis. An inference of fact could thus be challenged as a matter of law. Lord Radcliffe observed:

> "If the case contains anything *ex facie* which is bad law and which bears upon the determination, it is, obviously, erroneous in point of law. But, without any such misconception appearing *ex facie*, it may be that the facts found are such that no person acting judicially and properly instructed as to the relevant law could have come to the determination under appeal. In those circumstances, too, the court must intervene. It has no option but to assume that there has been some misconception of the law and that this has been responsible for the determination. So there, too, there has been error in point of law. I do not think it much matters whether this state of affairs is described as one in which there is no evidence to support the determination or as one in which the evidence is inconsistent with and contradictory of the determination, or as one in which the true and only reasonable conclusion contradicts the determination."[8]

It was the third and last of these alternatives which provided the preferred formulation in the decision.

Matters of law

Parliament often creates a right of appeal on points of law to the Court **22.05** of Session in Scotland, with equivalent provisions in England, when it establishes an administrative scheme.[9] Such a general right of appeal to

---

[6] Whether a person was unable to pay school fees was a question of fact: *Fairbairn v. Sanderson* (1885) 13 R. 81; whether a boxroom was "a habitable home" was a question of fact: *Ferguson v. Secretary of State for Social Services*, 1989 S.L.T. 117; whether waste was "household waste" or "trade waste" was in the opinion of Lord Cullen not a matter of law but one for the local authority to determine, in the opinions of Lord Ross and Lord McCluskey a matter of law and in the opinion of Lord Dunpark a matter of mixed fact and law: *Gordon v. Kirkcaldy D.C.*, 1990 S.L.T. 644.

[7] [1956] A.C. 14.

[8] *ibid.* at 36.

[9] *e.g.* Social Security Administration Act 1992, Pt II.

the Supreme Court is conferred by section 13(1) of the Tribunals and Inquiries Act 1971 from the tribunals listed in Schedule 1 to that Act. The statutory right of appeal may be on point of law,[10] or on the ground that the body has erred in law,[11] or in some such phrase which indicates an apparently identifiable category of error. But it does not follow that matters of fact are excluded from such a category. Certainly matters of "mixed fact and law" are included. As was observed by Lord Johnston:

> "A question of pure law is not very likely to occur, though it may do so. But a question of law arising on ascertained facts, as, for instance, what is the sense or meaning of the statute when applied to a specific set of circumstances, that is to say, a mixed question of fact and law, is open to review. It is for the Land Court to ascertain the facts, but their legal deduction from these is not final and may be reviewed . . . But here I would add two things–(1st) that by no conceivable stretch of their functions can the Land Court make that a question of fact, by calling it a fact, which is not a question of fact but of law or of mixed fact and law; and (2nd) that neither can they make that a fact, by calling it a fact, which is not a reasonable conclusion in fact from the facts which they say has been established before them."[12]

In describing the substance of a question of law in the context of the statutory grounds for appeal against a decision of an employment appeal tribunal, Lord President Emslie instanced a misdirection in law, entertainment of the wrong issue, a misapprehension or misconstruction of the evidence, the taking into account of matters irrelevant to the decision, or an irrational result.[13]

Jurisdictional and non-jurisdictional errors

22.06 Both errors of law and errors of fact may be classifed as relating to the jurisdiction of the decision maker or as having been made "within jurisdiction", that is, in the course of making the decision. But the distinction between jurisdictional and non-jurisdictional errors, particularly errors of law, has been a cause of some complexity in many legal systems. Some of the difficulty arises from the ambiguity of the word "jurisdiction", a point to which Lord Reid referred in *Anisminic v. Foreign Compensation Commission*.[14] The greater difficulty, however, is that the distinction is not secure so as to be predictable. The problem is that everything done in pursuance—or purported pursuance—of a defined authority is potentially "jurisdictional". Even where the decision-making power exists, it may be interpreted wrongly so as to assume or

---

[10] *e.g.* Social Security Administration Act 1992, s. 24, from the Social Security Commissioners to the Court of Session.

[11] *e.g.* Licensing (Scotland) Act 1976, from a licensing board to a sheriff. In *Chief Adjudication Officer v. Foster* [1993] A.C. 754 an excess of power in the making of regulations was held to fall within a ground of appeal that a decision was "erroneous in point of law".

[12] *Malcolm v. M'Dougall*, 1915 S.C. 283 at 292. His dissent on the particular circumstances does not touch on his general observation.

[13] *Melan v. Hector Powis Ltd*, 1981 S.L.T. 74 at 76; see also Lord Fraser of Tullybelton at 79.

[14] [1969] 2 A.C. 147 at 171. For discussion of the problems associated with "jurisdiction", see Lord Cooke of Thorndon, "The Liberation of English Public Law" in *Turning Points of the Common Law* (Sweet & Maxwell, London, 1997).

deny power improperly; terms to be applied in the course of the decision may be applied wrongly so as to reach a decision which there was no power, that is, "jurisdiction", to reach; and the consequence of violation of all the grounds of review, including those made in the course of a decision which the decision maker had power to reach at the outset of the inquiry, is to render the decision void. These considerations have caused the courts in England for most purposes to abandon the distinction between jurisdictional and non-jurisdictional errors. In Scotland, however, the distinction continues to be referred to as an indication of the scope of the court's power to review errors of law.

Error and other grounds

The interplay between the different grounds of challenge bedevils any **22.07** attempt to produce neat compartments and categories. The conclusion mistakenly drawn from primary facts can be classified as an example of irrationality. It can also be described as an error of law, to distinguish it from those matters of fact which are beyond the purview of the court. On the other hand, there are legitimate grounds of challenge that consist of a misunderstanding or a misapplication of the law which fall short of the standard of being irrational. It is with all these sorts of cases that the present chapter is primarily concerned, even although it may also encompass cases which may additionally fall within other grounds of review, and in particular the ground of irrationality which, like error, touches closely upon the substance of the decision whose validity is in issue. That there may be no easy dichotomy between errors of fact and errors of law does not prevent the use of the expression "error of law" as a convenient label to categorise those particular aspects of the substance of a decision which are open to judicial review.

III   ERROR BEFORE *ANISMINIC*

Jurisdiction

The Scottish cases have tended to discuss issues of error in terms of *vires* **22.08** or jurisdiction, rather than the susceptibility of administrative decisions to review for errors of law *per se*.[15] From an early stage it was recognised that an appeal tribunal has no jurisdiction to uphold an illegality, even although that involved the court of review considering the original issue and deciding whether the appeal body had formed a correct view of it. If it had not, then it had overstepped the limits of its jurisdiction and the court could interfere. An example can be found in the case of *Lord Prestongrange v. Justices of the Peace of Haddington*.[16] In that case a question arose as to whether certain road trustees had abused their powers in entering into a transaction with a local landowner regarding the payment of tolls for the passage of coal and salt. A complaint was made to the justices, who were authorised to hear and finally determine any complaint without further or other appeal. They held that the transaction was void as an abuse of the powers given to the trustees. The

---

[15] *e.g. Magistrates of Perth v. Trustees on the Road from Queensferry to Perth* (1756) Kilkerran's Notes, 5 Brown's Supp. 318; *Baillie v. McGibbon* (1845) 8 D. 10; *Milne and Co. v. Aberdeen District Council of the County of Aberdeen* (1899) 2 F. 220 at 230; *Caledonian Ry v. Glasgow Corporation* (1905) 7 F. 1020 at 1027.

[16] (1756)M. 7350.

matter came to the court by way of a suspension and a preliminary point was argued that the suspension was incompetent, as the justices' decision was final and not to be reviewed. The report of the case continues:

> "But this by an obvious distinction received a satisfactory answer. The Justices of the Peace with respect to all matters trusted by the statute to their cognisance are final. But if they exceed their bounds and find that to be an abuse which, in reality, is no abuse, they so far assume a jurisdiction which they have not, and their proceedings must be null as *ultra vires*. If then it be contended that the transaction made with the suspender is an abuse the Court is bound to take cognisance in order to determine the preliminary point with respect to the jurisdiction of the justices. If it shall appear to the Court that the transaction . . . is no abuse, it must follow, of course, that the justices have assumed a jurisdiction which the statute has not bestowed upon them, and their sentence is void. But if on the other hand the transaction be found an abuse, the justices are, by the statute, empowered to redress the wrong, and their sentence in that view is final however iniquitous it may be in any other respect."

The court held that the transaction was an abuse and so they had no power to interfere. The issue into which the court required to go was whether or not the justices had erred in holding that the trustees had abused their powers.

The distinction between what is within and what is not within the jurisdiction of a tribunal was also recognised in the case of *Countess of Loudon v. The Trustees on the High Roads in Ayrshire*,[17] which concerned a decision by road trustees, upheld by the quarter session, to close a road. The road had been held in some earlier proceedings in 1782 to have been of importance to the public. The decision of the quarter session was stated by statute to be "final and conclusive". The Court of Session held that:

> "the judgments of Quarter Sessions were not liable to review in such points as fixing the line of road, or the position of the toll-bars, which were discretionary in their nature, and in the exercise of the powers exclusively committed to the trustees. But it was on the other hand agreed, that a right to review, in case of the smallest excess of power, was essential, and was not excluded by the words of the act. It could not be supposed, [it was observed,] that the trustees or Justices were meant themselves to be the sole and exclusive judges of the extent of their own powers, or that such a jurisdiction, which might even be held to be in some measure unconstitutional, was intended to be given. In this way, the question of competency came to be blended with the question of the merits; and with respect to this last, the Court were clear, that the trustees had done wrong, in shutting up a road as a by-road, which had, by the judgment of the supreme Court, been found a public and useful road to the country; and that as in doing so, they had exceeded their powers, their judgment was liable to review".

It may be observed that the *ratio* of the decision could be found on the ground of irrationality, or indeed of error in law, although it was expressed in terms of illegality.

---

[17] (1793)M. 7398 at 7400.

The approach to error based on considerations of jurisdiction, which was recognised in the eighteenth century, was developed in the following century. In one case of a prosecution for payment of toll-duties it was alleged that the sheriff had made an erroneous construction of the statute in holding that certain loads of dung were being "carried for sale" and so were outwith an exemption from the toll.[18] A question of the competency of a suspension of the sheriff's decision arose. The Lord Ordinary expressed the view[19] that the matter would depend on the merits of the construction adopted by the sheriff, involving a question as to the powers of the sheriff to make an erroneous construction of the statute. But the Lord Justice-Clerk (Boyle) took a robust view that the judgment of the sheriff was under the statute final on the point and that the alleged excess of power was "merely an error of judgment".[20] Such language and such an approach was, however, rejected in *Dunbar v. Levack*[21] where the Lord Justice-Clerk (Hope) observed:

> "It is in vain to meet such cases by the answer, that after all it is only an error of judgment on the merits, if the party proceeded against is not within the provisions of the statute, or if the case is not one to which the statute applies. The answer might be equally stated as to every case in which the judgment of an inferior tribunal is in excess of jurisdiction. There must generally have been a judgment, express or implied, of the inferior tribunal on the matter, which creates the excess or want of jurisdiction. But jurisdiction cannot be created or obviated by treating the matter as an error of judgment. Jurisdiction there must be, else the deliverance or act of the inferior tribunal cannot be supported."

Finality clauses

In many of the early cases there was a purported restraint on the **22.09** intervention of the court through the means of a finality clause. It has already been observed that there is a long tradition of attempts by Parliament to protect decisions from review by the ordinary courts.[22] The empowering statute may provide for no appeal or only for a limited appeal not extending to the tribunal's error. Alternatively and more importantly in the present context the statute may exclude recourse to the ordinary courts by some statutory formula designed to achieve that purpose.[23] Such clauses may be made to apply irrespective of the existence of a specially prescribed appeal mechanism and they have given rise to considerable argument on the power of the Supreme Court to intervene where it may be thought that the decision of some inferior body was erroneous. The modern development of judicial review in cases of error on a point of law is materially coloured by the judicial approach to finality clauses and this area of law has been rendered somewhat intricate as a result of the careful attempts by the courts to overcome

---

[18] *Simpson v. Harley* (1830) 8 S. 977.
[19] He decided the case on a point of time-bar.
[20] A like argument was presented in *Heritors of Annan v. Herbertson* (1837) 15 S. 645.
[21] (1858) 20 D. 538 at 542.
[22] See para. 11.01. As was explained in para. 11.02, the use of such clauses became ineffective for legislation passed prior to Aug. 1, 1958 in terms of the Tribunals and Inquiries Act 1958 (6 & 7 Eliz. II, c. 66).
[23] For the effect of the various formulations devised by Parliament, see Chap. 11.

Parliament's efforts to exclude judicial review from certain administrative schemes. Finality clauses have played a significant part in the development of the court's approach to error and in particular to the idea of error within and without jurisdiction.[24] The point can be traced in some of the early cases.

The effect of finality clauses

22.10   At one time the existence of a finality clause invited the conclusion that the court should not interfere even where there was an error of law involved.[25] But, as has been explained earlier, the court came to construe finality clauses in a way which eventually deprived them of their effect. The *coup de grâce* was administered in the *Anisminic* case[26] but the approach had been settled long before. Before the end of the nineteenth century it was recognised that an error of law should not be allowed to escape review through the existence of a finality clause. In *Caledonian Railway v. Glasgow Corporation*,[27] a seven-judge case, the Lord President (Dunedin) stated: "So long as the defenders keep within the lines prescribed by the statute, the Court will give effect to the finality clause, and will not interfere by way of a declaratory finding or a reduction, but if under the name and guise of statutory proceeding the defenders attempt to do something quite different from what the statute allows, then they are doing an *ultra vires* act, and no finality clause will or can protect their illegal acting from the restraint of the Supreme Court." In that case the challenge was against a register of streets required to be prepared by the Glasgow Corporation. There required to be entered in the register among other details of each street "the width". What had been entered was not the actual width (which in some cases could vary substantially along the length of the street) but a figure representing the ideal width. The court held that that was erroneous since the actual width should be entered and that there was a relevant ground for challenge, although in the circumstances the action was premature. The error was thus an error of law. In *Lord Advocate v. Police Commissioners of Perth* Lord Justice Clerk Moncreiff observed[28]: "A clause of finality cannot protect a Sheriff's judgment, when, taking an erroneous view of a statute, he either refuses to sanction a lawful act or sanctions an unlawful one. It applies only to those matters of detail which concern the due and proper administration of the statute, and which are best disposed of by the sound discretion of a local judge." In *Dalgeish v. Livingston*[29] Lord Rutherford-Clark doubted whether a decision of the Crofters Commission to the effect that the defenders were crofters would be caught by a statutory finality clause "for I am not willing to construe the Act as giving to a commission which is not a Court of law the power of deciding important legal questions without any review". In some cases of finality clauses the issue of competency and the issue on the merits are involved together[30] but it appears that an error of law was not necessarily excluded for review by a finality clause.

---

[24] In *O'Reilly v. Mackman* [1983] 2 A.C. 237 at 278, Lord Diplock recognised that it was a finality clause which "provided the occasion for the landmark decision of this House in *Anisminic Ltd v. Foreign Compensation Commission* [1969] 2 A.C. 147".

[25] *e.g. Milne & Co. v. Aberdeen District Committee* (1899) 2 F. 220.

[26] *Anisminic Ltd v. Foreign Exchange Compensation Committee* [1969] 2 A.C. 147.

[27] (1905) 7 F. 1020 at 1027; affd 1907 S.C.(H.L.) 8.

[28] *Lord Advocate v. Police Commissioners of Perth* (1869) 8 M. 244 at 246, described by Lord Ormidale in *Dante v. Assessor for Ayr*, 1922 S.C. 109 at 128 as a very special case.

[29] (1895) 22 R. 646 at 658.

[30] *e.g. Edinburgh and Glasgow Ry v. Earl of Hopetoun* (1840) 2 D. 1255.

Error in discretionary decisions

Where there is a discretion in the decision maker, and particularly where **22.11** two or more possible answers to a problem may be open, none of which may constitute an error of law, the court may hesitate to interfere. In such cases the ground for challenge would require to be on considerations of rationality rather than considerations of error. In this connection a distinction came to be drawn between existing jurisdictions and those which had been specially created for a particular purpose. In *Guthrie v. Miller*[31] the proprietor of villas which were beyond the limit of the area which the local authority had been able to afford to light sought to be exempt from local charges on the ground that they received no benefit. Lord Alloway observed: "The great distinction is, that when this court has[32] previous jurisdiction, it requires express terms to exclude. But when there is no previous and radical jurisdiction, and the jurisdiction is created by statute, the question comes to be determined on this ground, Have the parties intrusted with powers exceeded them? For while they keep within the bounds of the statute, which commits them to a discretionary power, unless excess of that power is pointed out, this Court cannot well interfere." In *Bremner v. Huntly Friendly Society*[33] the Lord Justice-Clerk observed that "it would have been the duty of the legislature, in creating a new jurisdiction, to have declared it exclusive if they meant so. But there are no such words in the statute, but merely the general clause, 'that it may be lawful' to go before the Justices, and that parties having gone to that court, the judgment should be final". The authority of a body constituted for the carrying out of particular purposes is limited to the terms of those purposes and the court will intervene to secure that they keep within those limits.[34]

Special jurisdictions

The idea came to be recognised that a particular restraint should be **22.12** exercised by the court in relation to the decisions of bodies which had been specially created to carry out some particular function. Decisions by such bodies in matters which may readily allow of alternative answers leave little room for a challenge on the ground that they are erroneous in law. The more likely opportunity for challenge would occur if the extremes are reached where the ground of rationality may arise. Thus, for example, in *Milne & Co v. Aberdeen District Committee*[35] the view was expressed that the court could not interfere with a decision made by a sheriff in exercising a summary and final decision on a matter of the recovery of extraordinary expenses incurred by a roads authority in repairing damage due to excessive weight passing along the road. In the more recent case of *O'Neill v. Scottish Joint Negotiating Committee for Teaching Staff*[36] the committee were held entitled to hold that the "full salary" to which a teacher was entitled during maternity leave meant her salary after deduction of maternity benefit. In *Leith Police Commissioners v. Campbell*[37] the decision of a sheriff on a statutory appeal that a

---

[31] (1827) 5 S. 711.
[32] The text says "no" but this must be a textual error. *Cf.* the quotation at (1866) 5 M. 252.
[33] Dec. 4, 1817, F.C.
[34] *Shand v. Henderson* (1814) 2 Dow 519.
[35] (1899) 2 F. 220.
[36] 1987 S.C.L.R. 275.
[37] (1868) 5 M. 247.

particular street was a public and not a private street was held not open to challenge where he had not exceeded his jurisdiction and his decision was expressly final and conclusive. The Lord Justice-Clerk observed:

> "it is important to consider whether this Court had jurisdiction in the subject of the action antecedent to the statute or not, for if the Court had jurisdiction, it is difficult to oust its jurisdiction; but if it had not, it is more easily to be inferred that the statute was intended to give the Sheriff a privative jurisdiction. Now the subject of this action is entirely a matter of burgh police, with which this court never had anything to do, and this statute has, I think, for its object to introduce a procedure very summary and final."

In *Don Brothers, Buist & Co. Ltd v. Scottish Insurance Commissioners*[38] the insurance commissioners were expressly charged with the duty of determining the rate of contributions to be paid for the purpose of national insurance. These varied under the statute according to the rate of remuneration for "a working day". The employee in question worked ten hours for five days and five hours on a sixth day. The problem was whether the rate was to taken on the basis of a ten-hour working day or as an average working day taking all six days into account. This was held in light of the terms of the statute to be a matter for the commissioners. The Lord President stated that "when the Act of Parliament said that they were to fix 'the rates of contributions payable in respect of an employed contributor by the employer and the contributor respectively', it handed over to the Insurance Commissioners a question which may be a question of pure fact, but may be of fact and of law also in so far as a question of construction is always a question of law."

Arbitrations

22.13　The approach adopted in that case was the same as that adopted in *Holmes Oil Company v. Pumpherston Oil Company*,[39] where an arbiter had erred in law but the court could not interfere since the parties had entrusted the determination of the issue to him. Arbitrations provide an example of a situation where the parties have entrusted to the tribunal the determination of all kinds of questions including questions of law. A determination by an arbiter as to the admissibility of evidence is not open to review where he has acted within the scope of the submission, even if the decision is erroneous in law.[40] If an arbiter directs himself properly he is entitled to err in law, provided that the error does not relate to the determination of his jurisdiction.[41] In such cases the merits of the decision involve or indeed may consist solely of a matter of law, but the court is not entitled to enter into the merits of the decision.[42]

A wider view

22.14　The generality of the extent of the supervisory jurisdiction, which had been formulated by Lord Kames,[43] was clearly recognised by Lord Shaw of Dunfermline in *Moss' Empires v. Assessor for Glasgow*[44] when he

---

[38] 1913 S.C. 607.
[39] (1891) 18 R.(H.L.) 52.
[40] *ibid.*
[41] *O'Neill v. Scottish Joint Negotiating Committee*, 1987 S.C.L.R. 275.
[42] For review of arbitral decisions, see para. 9.05.
[43] See para. 2.18, *supra.*
[44] 1917 S.C.(H.L.) 1 at 11.

stated: "It is within the jurisdiction of the Court of Session to keep inferior judicatories and administrative bodies right, in the sense of compelling them to obey those conditions without the fulfilment of which they have no powers whatsoever. It is within the power of the Court of Session to do that, but it is not within the power or function of the Court of Session itself to do work set by the legislature to be performed by those administrative bodies or inferior judicatories themselves." The approach which has generally been taken in the twentieth century has been to regard neither the fact that the body was created for some particular function nor the existence of any finality clause as a reason for excluding the exercise of the supervisory jurisdiction. Moreover, even if the initial approach is one of defining the jurisdiction of the decision-making body, it is not readily to be concluded that the jurisdiction is intended to include a freedom to err in matters of law. On the other hand, the cases where the court has refrained from interfering can be seen now as examples of the operation of the idea of a relative intensity of review which has been noted earlier.[45] The refusal of the court to intervene in such cases is not to be ascribed to a lack of jurisdiction but to a sensitivity in the exercise of the jurisdiction.

English law

It is instructive at this stage to step aside to the development of English **22.15** law on the present subject. In England the primary remedy in matters of what is now called judicial review has from an early stage been that of certiorari.[46] It has always been possible to obtain certiorari on the ground of error on the face of the record.[47] Although dormant for about a hundred years[48] the existence of the remedy was confirmed by the Court of Appeal in 1951.[49] By means of this remedy the High Court was able to quash a tribunal decision where an error of law was manifest on the record of the case. The scope of the remedy has widened over the years. At one time it was seen as restricted to cases where the tribunal owed a duty to act judicially,[50] but that limitation was destroyed by the decision in *Ridge v. Baldwin*.[51] Furthermore, the earlier narrow conception of the record as being limited to the pleadings and the actual decision gave way to a recognition that the record included all the proceedings, including not only the reasons for the decision[52] but the evidence.[53] It is important to note in relation to error on the face of the record that certiorari issued to all errors of law which appeared on the face of the record

---

[45] Para. 14.13.

[46] A history of declarations in England, including the influence of the Scottish practice, is given in De Smith, Woolf and Jewel, *Judicial Review of Administrative Action* (5th ed.), paras 14–155 *et seq.* See also on History, para. 2.02. See also Zamir and Woolf, The Declaratory Judgment (2nd ed., Sweet & Maxwell, 1993).

[47] Something of the same idea can be found in Lord M'Laren's opinion in *Milne & Co v. Aberdeen District Committee* (1899) 2 F. 220 at 230. English law was imposed on the Scottish Exchequer Court: see History, para. 2.21.

[48] See Wade and Forsyth, *Administrative Law* (7th ed.), p. 309.

[49] *R. v. Northumberland Compensation Appeal Tribunal, ex p. Shaw* [1952] 1 K.B. 338.

[50] *R. v. Electricity Commissioners, ex p. London Electricity Joint Committee Co. (1920) Ltd* [1924] 1 K.B. 171.

[51] [1964] A.C. 40. See *O'Reilly v. Mackman* [1983] 2 A.C. 237 at 279.

[52] *R. v. Knightsbridge Crown Court, ex p. International Sporting Club (London) Ltd* [1982] Q.B. 304.

[53] *R. v. Certsey Justices, ex p. Franks* [1962] 1 Q.B. 152.

whether or not it affected the jurisdiction of the tribunal.[54] Lord Griffiths described the position as follows[55]:

> "In the case of bodies other than courts, in so far as they are required to apply the law they are required to apply the law correctly. If they apply the law incorrectly they have not performed their duty correctly and judicial review is available to correct their error of law so that they may make their decision upon a proper understanding of the law.
>
> "In the case of inferior courts, that is, courts of a lower status than the high court, such as justices of the peace, it was recognised that their learning and understanding of the law might sometimes be imperfect and require correction by the High Court and so the rule evolved that certiorari was available to correct an error of law of an inferior court."

Jurisdictional error

22.16	Apart from error on the face of the record, the English courts also developed the concept of jurisdictional error which allowed of judicial intervention. The distinction was recognised between cases where a body was given the power to make decisions in certain circumstances and cases where additionally it was given the power to determine whether those circumstances in fact existed.[56] In a case falling into the former category the court could intervene on the ground that there had been an excess of jurisdiction in respect of the collateral issue as to whether the facts precedent to the exercise of the power existed, even although the substance of the decision was immune from review.[57] In the latter kind of case the decision maker's jurisdiction will have been entrusted to the decision maker to determine, a situation which the court has always been reluctant to accept.[58] While the court could intervene in a case of jurisdictional error, it could not review a decision made within jurisdiction even although it was erroneous in law.[59]

Finality clauses in England

22.17	In England as in Scotland, Parliament has in the past not infrequently sought to exclude recourse to the court either by providing a finality clause in the empowering statute or by expressly excluding judicial review of the tribunal's decision. It was recognised that such clauses excluded any appeal[60] and could oust the ordinary court.[61] But as had occurred in Scotland, the courts came to subject finality clauses to close scrutiny and apply a narrow construction to them.[62]

---

[54] Wade & Forsyth, *Administrative Law* (7th ed.), p. 306.
[55] *R. v. Hull University Visitor, ex p. Page* [1993] A.C. 682 at 693.
[56] *R. v. Income Tax Special Purpose Commissioners* (1888) 21 Q.B.D. 313.
[57] *R. v. Fulham etc Rent Tribunal ex p. Zerek* [1951] 2 K.B. 1 at 6.
[58] *R. v. Shoreditch Assessment Committee, ex p. Morgan* [1910] 2 K.B. 859.
[59] *R. v. Northumberland Compensation Appeal Tribunal, ex p. Shaw* [1952] 1 K.B. 338.
[60] *Westminster Corporation v. Gordon Hotels Ltd* [1908] A.C. 142.
[61] *Smith v. East Elloe Rural D.C.* [1956] A.C. 736.
[62] *e.g. R. v. Medical Appeal Tribunal, ex p. Gilmour* [1957] 1 Q.B. 574.

IV *ANISMINIC* AND AFTER

The *Anisminic* Case

A notable step forward was taken in the case of *Anisminic Ltd v. Foreign* **22.18**
Compensation Commission.[63] In that case Anisminic successfully challenged the validity of a decision by the Foreign Compensation Commission. Anisminic had made a claim for compensation for loss of property
in Egypt during the Suez affair. The Commission rejected the claim on
the ground that Anisminic's assets had been acquired by an Egyptian
company ("T.E.D.O.") and in terms of the relevant Order in Council
any "successor in title" to the British claimant had to be of British
nationality. It was held by the House of Lords that that was an erroneous
interpretation of the Order in Council, since the Egyptian company was
not Anisminic's "successor in title". But the Foreign Compensation Act
1950 excluded the power of the High Court to review errors of law made
within the jurisdiction of the Commission. However, the House of Lords
held (by a majority) that the error in interpretation had made the
Commission take into account an irrelevant factor (the nationality of the
Egyptian company), that it had exceeded its jurisdiction and the decision
was a nullity. Lord Morris of Borth y Gest, who dissented, took the view
that where there was an express ouster of review the scope of review was
then limited to errors which affected the jurisdiction of the inferior
tribunal. But Lord Pearce observed[64]: "Further it is assumed, unless
special provisions provide otherwise, that the tribunal will make its
inquiry and decision according to the law of the land. For that reason the
courts will intervene when it is manifest from the record that the tribunal
though keeping within its mandated area of jurisdiction, comes to an
erroneous decision through an error of law. In such a case the courts
have intervened to correct the error".

Lord Reid observed that when it is said that it is only where a tribunal
acts without jurisdiction that its decision is a nullity, the word "jurisdiction" was being used in a very wide sense. He took the view that the
word "jurisdiction" should be used in the narrow and original sense of
the tribunal being entitled to enter on the inquiry in question. His
Lordship continued:

> "But there are many cases where, although the tribunal had
> jurisdiction to enter on the inquiry, it has done or has failed to do
> something in the course of the inquiry which is of such a nature that
> its decision is a nullity. It may have given its decision in bad faith. It
> may have made a decision which it had no power to make. It may
> have failed in the course of the inquiry to comply with the
> requirements of natural justice. It may in perfect good faith have
> misconstrued the provisions giving it power to act so that it failed to
> deal with the question remitted to it and decided some question
> which was not remitted to it. It may have refused to take into
> account something which it was required to take into account. Or it
> may have based its decision on some matter which, under the
> provisions setting it up, it had no right to take into account. I do not
> intend this list to be exhaustive. But if it decides a question remitted

---

[63] [1969] 2 A.C. 147.
[64] *ibid*. at p. 195.

to it for decision without committing any of these errors it is as much entitled to decide that question wrongly as it is to decide it rightly. I understand that some confusion has been caused by my having said in *Reg. v. Governor of Brixton Prison, Ex parte Armah* [1968] AC 192, 234 that if a tribunal has jurisdiction to go right it has jurisdiction to go wrong. So it has, if one uses 'jurisdiction' in the narrow original sense. If it is entitled to enter on the inquiry and does not do any of those things which I have mentioned in the course of the proceedings, then its decision is equally valid whether it is right or wrong subject only to the power of the court in certain circumstances to correct an error of law".[65]

As regards the particular case he said[66]:

"It cannot be for the Commission to determine the limits of its powers. Of course if one party submits to a tribunal that its powers are wider than in fact they are, then the tribunal must deal with that submission. But if they reach a wrong conclusion as to the width of their powers, the court must be able to to correct that–not because the tribunal has made an error of law, but because as a result of making an error of law they have dealt with and based their decision on a matter with which, on a true submission of their powers, they had no right to deal. If they base their decision on some matter which is not prescribed for their adjudication, they are doing something which they have no right to do and, if the view which I expressed earlier is right, their decision is a nullity. So the question is whether on a true construction of the Order the applicants did or did not have to prove anything with regard to successors in title. If the Commission were entitled to enter on the inquiry whether the applicants had a successor in title, then their decision as to whether T.E.D.O. was their successor in title would I think be unassailable whether it was right or wrong: it would be a decision on a matter remitted to them for their decision."

While he recognises that a tribunal may have a jurisdiction to err, it is thought that such an "error" will be found in practice to be in respect of a particular matter of fact and not an error of law.

After *Anisminic*

22.19   The effect of the decision in *Anisminic* remained for a time in some uncertainty. It had been held that where a tribunal makes a decision under an error of law which went to its jurisdiction it was acting *ultra vires* and the decision could be quashed by the court. The House of Lords had decided that the essential response to a statutory clause ousting the jurisdiction of the court is that unless Parliament has said otherwise the ouster clause is only effective in protecting the tribunal's decision when that decision was made within the tribunal's jurisdiction. Thus where the tribunal makes an error of law which affects its jurisdiction it acts *ultra vires* and the court is entitled to quash the decision. But the difficulty remained of characterising which errors would go to jurisdiction and which would not.

---

[65] *ibid*. at 171. The passage has also been quoted in para. 14.09.
[66] *ibid*. at 174.

The effect of *Anisminic*

The courts in England then proceeded to develop the law towards the **22.20** abolition of a distinction between errors which did and errors which did not go to jurisdiction. In *Pearlman v. Keepers and Governors of Harrow School*, Lord Denning M.R. observed[67] that the fine distinction between error within and error outwith jurisdiction was being eroded and suggested that the distinction should be discarded. The distinction was so fine that the court had a choice before it whether it wished to interfere with the decision under review. As he put it "no court or tribunal has any jurisdiction to make an error of law on which the decision of the case depends". Lord Diplock in *Re Racal Communications Ltd* observed: "The breakthrough made by *Anisminic* was that, as respects administrative tribunals and authorities, the old distinction between errors of law that went to jurisdiction and errors of law that did not was for practical purposes abolished."[68] He added: "Any error of law that could be shown to have been made by them in the course of reaching their decision on matters of fact or of administrative policy would result in their having asked themselves the wrong question with the result that the decision which they reached would be a nullity." But other judges in that case and in *South East Asia Fire Bricks v. Non-Metallic etc. Union*[69] held to the traditional view that where there was an error of law not affecting jurisdiction, review was not available. Lord Diplock repeated his view in *O'Reilly v. Mackman*[70] saying that the speech of Lord Reid had "liberated English public law from the fetters that the court had theretofore imposed upon themselves so far as determinations of inferior courts and statutory tribunals were concerned by drawing esoteric distinctions between errors of law committed by such tribunals that went to their jurisdiction, and errors of law committed by them within their jurisdiction. The breakthrough that the *Anisminic* case made was the recognition by the majority of this House that if a tribunal whose jurisdiction was limited by statute or subordinate legislation mistook the law applicable to the facts as it had found them, it must have asked itself the wrong question, i.e. one into which it was not empowered to inquire and it had no jurisdiction to determine. Its purported 'determination', not being a 'determination' within the empowering legislation, was accordingly a nullity."

These views were eventually to prevail. The House of Lords eventually accepted in *R. v. The Lord President of the Privy Council, ex parte Page*[71] that *Anisminic* must finally be taken to have destroyed the distinction between errors of law going to jurisdiction and errors of law within jurisdiction.[72] Thus a position has been reached where all errors of law take a tribunal outside its jurisdiction and an administrative body which makes an error of law in the course of its decision acts *ultra vires*. In that case Lord Browne-Wilkinson observed: "in general any error of law made by an administrative tribunal or inferior court in reaching its

---

[67] [1979] Q.B. 56 at 70. The question in the case was whether a central heating installation fell within a statutory reference to "structural addition . . . or alteration".

[68] [1981] A.C. 374 at 383.

[69] [1981] A.C. 363.

[70] [1983] 2 A.C. 237 at 278.

[71] [1993] A.C. 682.

[72] *per* Lord Browne-Wilkinson at 701–702, Lord Slynn of Hadley at 706 and Lord Griffiths at 693.

decision can be quashed for error of law". It should be noted that the generality of the proposition is limited by the consideration that the error must be one in the reaching of the decision.[73]

Scottish Law after *Anisminic*

22.21   Although there was no question about the relevance of the decision in *Anisminic* to the law of Scotland, no immediate occasion arose in Scotland for a consideration of its effect.[74] The problem of error within and without jurisdiction did eventually come to be explored in the case of *Watt v. Lord Advocate*.[75] The question was whether a storeman was "directly interested in the trade dispute which caused the stoppage of work" and so disqualified from receiving unemployment benefit. The storeman sought reduction of a decision of a national insurance commissioner who held that he was directly interested in the trade dispute and so was not entitled to the benefit. In the Outer House Lord Dunpark took the *ratio* of *Anisminic* from the speech of Lord Wilberforce; this was to the effect that the commission had acted outside its powers by seeking to impose a condition which was not warranted by the relevant Order in Council and had made no determination of that which it alone could determine. He adopted the language of Lord Pearce[76] and held that in the case before him the commissioner had asked the right question. But he also explored and sought to illustrate the distinction between intra vires and ultra vires errors, using the language of "doing wrong" and "going wrong" to make the point. He drew a distinction between misconstruction of the nature or limits of the statutory duty and misapplication of the statute to the relevant facts[77]:

> "The former is an ultra vires error in respect that the inferior court has wrongly defined the nature or limits of its statutory duty and, by doing something which the statute did not authorise, or by not doing something which the statute required it to do, has not acted in accordance with its statutory powers. In the latter case, the court has performed its statutory function in the manner laid down by the statute, and, acting within its statutory powers, has produced the wrong answer to a question of mixed fact and law. So long as the court asks the right question, it does not, in my opinion, necessarily make an ultra vires error by producing the wrong answer. The distinction is between "doing wrong" which is *ultra vires*, and "going wrong", which is intra vires."

But Lord Dunpark also suggested that the distinction between error going to jurisdiction and error within jurisdiction was more apparent

---

[73] The distinction between illegality by proceeding on *ultra vires* regulations and erroneously construing *intra vires* regulations was regarded by Lord Keith of Kinkel and Lord Jauncey of Tullichettle as a distinction without a difference in *Woolwich Equitable Building Society v. Inland Revenue Commissioners* [1993] A.C. 93 at 161 and 196.

[74] It was distinguished by Lord Kissen in *Hamilton v. Secretary of State for Scotland*, 1972 S.C. substantially on the ground of the difference in the provisions excluding review. The point had been discussed prior to the decision: *e.g.* Sheriff Middleton in 1958 Jur.Rev. 183, Prof. J.D.B. Mitchell in 1959 Jur.Rev. 197, and in the Scottish Law Commission's Memorandum No. 14, App. II.

[75] In the Outer House, 1977 S.L.T. 130; in the Inner House, 1979 S.C. 120.

[76] [1969] 2 A.C. at 196; *cf.* Lord Reid at 174 and Lord Pearson at 223; the phrase was criticised by Lord Wilberforce at 210.

[77] 1977 S.L.T. at 135.

than real. The particular decision in the case was reversed in the Inner House where it was held that the commissioner had misconstrued the only question which he required to answer so that his decision was *ultra vires* and fell to be reduced.

Intra vires error

In the course of his opinion in *Watt*, although he accepted that it was **22.22** unnecessary for him to express a view on the point, the Lord President (Emslie) expressed the view that the Court of Session had never had power to correct an *intra vires* error of law made by a statutory tribunal or authority exercising statutory jurisdiction.[78] But the general statement may be too widely framed. His Lordship referred to the observation of Lord Justice-Clerk Moncreiff in *Lord Advocate v. Police Commissioners of Perth etc.*,[79] a case which was earlier described[80] as very special, where he stated at the outset of his opinion: "In the ordinary case, it would now, I think, be held that where statutory powers are given, and a statutory jurisdiction is set up, all other jurisdictions are excluded." The case concerned the competency of a suspension of certain proposed operations by Police Commissioners allegedly in violation of the statute under which they were bound to act. The statute provided for appeal to the sheriff. But the action of suspension in the Court of Session was held competent because illegality was alleged. Lord Justice-Clerk Moncreiff observed: "I know of no case in which the common law jurisdiction of the Supreme Court has been held to be excluded, where the act proposed to be done is prohibited by statute". In his opening sentence in the context of the case he was propounding the general proposition that where a statutory remedy has been provided it must, at least in the first instance, be pursued. On that point there can be no doubt. The supervisory jurisdiction is usually only available where no other remedy exists. However, as he explained in that case, in a matter of alleged illegality the right of recourse to the Supreme Court would remain despite a decision to the contrary by the sheriff even although his judgment was expressed to be final. The observations do not, however, seem to define the extent of the errors which the supervisory jurisdiction may correct. Nor do they seem to support the exclusion of the National Insurance Commissioner from review as was suggested in *Watt v. Lord Advocate*.[81]

After *Watt*

The observations in *Watt* which suggested a limitation on the jurisdiction **22.23** of the Scottish court have been kept alive both in argument[82] and decision.[83] Following on the *Anisminic* case there was some recognition

---

[78] His Lordship saw this as a difference between Scottish and English law, but it has been argued that the alleged difference would probably have little practical effect: Robert Reed, "Judicial Review of Errors of Law", 1979 S.L.T. (News) 241.

[79] (1869) 8 M. 244. The case is also noted in para. 22.10.

[80] By Lord Ormidale in *Dante v. Assessor for Ayr*, 1922 S.C. 109 at 128.

[81] 1979 S.C. 120 at 131.

[82] *e.g. CAA v. Argyll and Bute Valuation Committee*, 1988 S.L.T. 119; *Gordon v. Kirkcaldy D.C.*, 1989 S.C.L.R. 90.

[83] *e.g. O'Neill v. Scottish Joint Negotiating Committee*, 1987 S.L.T. 648. It may be questioned whether the understanding expressed in the case to the effect that Lord Diplock in the *GCHQ* case (*Council of Civil Service Unions v. Minister for the Civil Service* [1985] A.C. 374) was intending to recognise the immunity of *intra vires* error is correct.

in Scotland that an error of law may involve the asking and answering of the wrong question[84] even in statutory appeals,[85] and that approach opens the way to a more general challenge on the ground of error of law. But the view that any tribunal has a jurisdiction to commit errors of law continues to be recognised.[86] The decision in *Anisminic* was plainly recognised in *Watt* as applicable in Scotland, and there can be no reason to doubt but that the significance of the case as it came to be recognised in England applies to Scotland. It has for a long time been understood that no difference exists between the grounds for review in Scotland and in England.[87] It is thought that there is no deficiency in Scots law as was conceived in *Watt* but that such "error" as a tribunal may be permitted to make is not truly an error of law.[88] The doubts which Lord Dunpark expressed in *Watt* about the validity of any distinction between *intra vires* and *ultra vires* error have been shown to be entirely justified in the more recent understanding of *Anisminic* and the unreality of the distinction can now be more confidently affirmed. Attempts to develop the distinction between errors lead to the uncertainty of conflicting decisions. Without it the court may remain as the final arbiter on what the law means. It may be that with the decreasing use of finality clauses the point may tend to become less critical, but there is room for clarification of the position.

Conclusion

22.24   The versatility of the word "jurisdiction" which was noted as a potential source for misunderstanding has more recently been identified and illuminated by Lord Cooke of Thornden, who suggested that its popularity and convenience might be partly due to its very ambiguity.[89] Quite apart from the way in which the law has been developing it may be desirable to use the word with care, and perhaps even better to avoid it if possible. The position seems now to have been reached where an error in point of law may be seen as a free-standing ground of review in its own right. The problem is not now one to be approached by consideration of the *vires* or jurisdiction of the body whose decision is under challenge. A failure to understand the law becomes an excess of power without the necessity of exploring the *vires* of the decision maker.[90] But a general proposition that the court can intervene in judicial review to correct any error of law is too wide.[91] In the first place the error must be one which affected the decision. An error in some subsidiary or incidental matter, not affecting the decision, may be of no consequence. But beyond that, and more importantly, there may still be situations where the court may not intervene. These will require to be justified by

---

[84] *e.g. Wincentzen v. Monklands D.C.*, 1988 S.L.T. 259 and 847.

[85] *e.g. City of Glasgow D.C. v. Secretary of State*, 1985 S.L.T. 19.

[86] It is suggested that while in the circumstances the result in *Rae v. Criminal Injuries Compensation Board*, 1997 S.L.T. 291 could be jusitified, the approach adopted by the court is open to question.

[87] See para. 14.02.

[88] An argument for the availability of a defence of *intra vires* error is given by Peter M. Gilmour in "Judicial Review of Errors of Law", 1993 S.L.T.(News) 371.

[89] *R. v. Bedwellty Justices, ex p. Williams* [1996] 3 W.L.R. 361 at 367.

[90] See Lord President Hope in *West v. Secretary of State for Scotland*, 1992 S.C. 385 at 413. It may then be inappropriate to construe that passage as meaning a failure of such a kind as to entail an excess or abuse of jurisdiction as was suggested in *Shanks & McEwan (Contractors) Ltd v. Mifflin Construction Ltd*, 1993 S.L.T. 1124 at 1130.

[91] Professor Walker, *Civil Remedies*, p. 166.

the particular terms of the relevant legislation or the particular nature of the body or decision in question. An example may be found in the case of *R. v. Hull University Visitor, ex parte Page* where errors of fact or of law could be recognised as within the particular function of the body there concerned.[92] The general rule thus gives way where the point is one which Parliament should be taken either expressly or impliedly to have left to the decision-making body to the exclusion of the court or where the character of the decision-making body is such as to require such a particular degree of respect as to warrant its immunity from review on the ground of error of law.[93] These cases will be found usually in the context of tribunals and other bodies which are called upon to determine issues put before them for decision, rather than in the context of authorities who are exercising purely discretionary powers. That distinction is considered further in the next part of this chapter.

V ERROR TODAY

Decision making

It remains to explore the extent to which in practice error may be a **22.25** ground for challenge of an administrative decision. For this purpose some analysis is required of the process of decision making. In the generality the process may to a greater or lesser extent in particular cases involve an exercise of a discretion on the part of the decision maker. At one extreme the matter may be purely for his own discretion whether a particular course of action should or should not be taken—as, for example, where in the application of a statutory measure the authority is given a discretion in deciding whether or not the statute should be applied to given facts or where a grant or an approval for action should be given in relation to particular circumstances. At the other extreme the question may be whether the facts found by him fall within the terms of some statutory provision. In such a case, if the question is whether they do or do not so fall, and not whether they should or should not so fall, the decision is not one which admits of any real discretion on his part, whereby he could freely apply his own preference. The existence of a discretionary element in the making of certain decisions has been noted earlier in this chapter.[94]

Discretion

Where a decision is wholly a matter of discretion but the decision maker **22.26** has erred in his understanding of the relevant law, the decision should be open to challenge. It is not to be assumed that wholly discretionary decisions may properly be made in the face of the empowering legisla-

---

[92] Also referred to as *R. v. Lord President of the Privy Council, ex p. Page* [1993] A.C. 682.

[93] Note may be made of the position in Australia: for example, *Craig v. South Australia* (1995) 184 C.L.R. 163 and in Canada: for example, *Canadian Union of Public Employees, Local 953 v. New Brunswick Liquor Corporation* [1979] 2 S.C.R. 227 (in both countries, the distinction between "jurisdictional" and "non-jurisdictional" errors of law as articulated in *Anisminic* continuing to apply, at least for some purposes). If the approach was to be that all errors of law are reviewable, the distinction between legality and merits would no longer hold where a decision was challenged on the ground of error of law. *Cf. Minister for Immigration and Ethnic Affairs v. Eshetu* (1999) 73 A.L.J.R. 746.

[94] para. 22.11.

tion. But where the task is not one of determining an issue between parties but purely one of exercising a discretionary power, the grounds for challenge may be most appropriately analysed in terms of procedural error or of irrationality. Where the task is to apply a statutory provision to particular facts, cases may arise where the decision maker may have a choice between several alternative solutions. In such a case the decision will fall to be tested by reference to the ground of rationality in respect that the application of the law, correctly construed, to the facts, correctly determined, was perverse. An exercise of judgment will be called for and the decision will not be open to challenge unless it falls into the category of irrational or perverse decisions. Thus in one case while the court was able to provide guidance on the meaning of the word "substantial" there remained the question whether a particular area was a "substantial part of the United Kingdom".[95]

Decisions of courts and tribunals

22.27 In the context of inferior courts and tribunals the supervisory jurisdiction should be readily available to correct errors of law. It is not lightly to be supposed that bodies set up to determine issues brought before them for decision are free to pronounce conclusions which have been reached through some error of law. But some decision-making bodies may be entitled by their nature finally to resolve matters of law[96] and in other cases Parliament may succeed in excluding a decision from review. But some very clear and doubtless elaborate provision would require to be expressed in the legislation if such a result was to be intended.[97] In addition to, or alternatively to, a challenge on the ground of error in law it is to be remembered that challenge may also lie on other grounds such as irrationality. To reach opposite conclusions on the same facts may be a mark of perversity, but where the decisions in question can be sufficiently distinguished, that is to say whether a reasonable authority could distinguish them, then the decision may be regarded as a reasonable one.[98] The view was expressed by Lord Denning M.R.[99] that while the courts should intervene where a matter of law of general application was involved the tribunals should be left to interpret the legislation "in a broad reasonable way, according to the spirit and not the letter". While it is certainly desirable to avoid an accumulation of applications for review on any and every point of statutory construction,[1] applications should not be excluded simply because the decision is a reasonable interpretation of the Act, if it is nevertheless unsound in law.

---

[95] *R. v. Monopolies and Mergers Commission, ex p. South Yorkshire Transport Ltd* (1993) 1 W.L.R. 23.

[96] In England such a view may be taken with regard to courts of law: *R. v. Hull University Visitor, ex p. Page* [1993] A.C. 682 at 693 and 703.

[97] On the exclusion of review by finality clauses, see Chap. 11.

[98] *Semple v. Glasgow District Licensing Board*, 1990 S.C.L.R. 73. If an immigration adjudicator is satisfied on the material before him that a particular country is a safe third country although he is aware that there are other decisions to the contrary effect, he is not required to explore those inconsistent decisions in detail but is entitled to hold to his own conclusion: *Sinathamby Kumar v. Secretary of State for the Home Department* (1996) Imm. Ar. 548. Reasons should be given for departing from an inconsistent planning decision: *North Wiltshire D.C. v. Secretary of State for the Environment* [1992] P.L.R. 113.

[99] *R. v. Preston Appeal Tribunal, ex p. Moore* [1975] All E.R. 807 at 813.

[1] *R. v. Hillingdon LBC, ex p. Puhlhofer* (1986) A.C. 484, *per* Lord Brightman at 518.

The elements

In the account which now follows of some of the particular instances **22.28** which may occur by way of error of law it is largely but not wholly in the context of inferior courts and tribunals that such examples are likely to arise. Three critical stages in the process of decision making may be identified. First, the decision maker must determine his jurisdiction. Secondly, he must ascertain the factual circumstances by reference to which the decision is to be made. Thirdly, the decision maker has to reach a particular determination. This again may necessitate regard being had to such provisions of law as are related to the task. This may overlap with the considerations applied in stage one and involve little more than an appreciation of the express terms of the statutory power under which he is acting. It may involve a study of the terms of a statutory provision which he requires to apply. Each of these stages may give occasion for error.

(a) Error in determining jurisdiction

The first thing of which a decision maker must assure himself is that he **22.29** has the jurisdiction to consider the particular matter which is before him.[2] Thus an arbiter must first decide whether he has jurisdiction before he proceeds to consider the case.[3] He is not the final judge of his own jurisdiction,[4] although in some cases the decision-maker may have a degree of discretion in the settlement of his jurisdiction such as may exclude the jurisdiction of the court.[5] A power to decide the just rebates to be made from rates for railway services was held to include the ability to decide whether the charges for the railway services were reasonable.[6] The question whether a congenital deficiency was an injury for the purposes of a claim to the Criminal Injuries Compensation Board required to be resolved in order to determine whether the Board had jurisdiction.[7] The decision maker must understand not only the nature and limits of his jurisdiction, but also any rules which require to be observed in the exercise of his power.[8] If he mistakenly construes the basis on which his decision is to be made, or has not exercised a discretion judicially, his decision will be open to review.[9] If he mistakenly regards guidance as if it was a peremptory rule the decision may be reduced.[10] This initial stage includes the consideration whether the power is being exercised by the proper person, a matter which has been considered earlier in the context of illegality.[11]

(b) Error in ascertaining the facts

Without prejudice to the basic rule that the merits of the decision are for **22.30** the decision-making body, there are a number of respects in which the decision may be vitiated in connection with the initial responsibility of

---

[2] The danger of using the word "jurisdiction" has already been pointed out. That a decision maker has jurisdiction to determine his jurisdiction provides an example of the flexibility of the word.

[3] *Christison's Trustees v. Callender-Brodie* (1906) 8 F. 928 at 931.

[4] *Donaldson's Hospital v. Esslemont*, 1925 S.C. 199 at 205.

[5] *M'Ewen's Trustees v. Church of Scotland Trustees*, 1940 S.L.T. 357.

[6] *Cowan & Son Ltd v. North British Ry*, (1901) 4 F. 334.

[7] *P's Curator Bonis v. Criminal Injuries Compensation Board*, 1997 S.L.T. 1180.

[8] *Milton v. Argyll and Clyde Health Board*, 1997 S.L.T. 565.

[9] *Sinclair-Lockhart's Trustees v. Central Land Board*, 1951 S.C. 258 at 269.

[10] *Abdadoa v. Secretary of State for the Home Department*, 1999 S.L.T. 229.

[11] para. 15.17.

the body in properly ascertaining the factual situation in which the decision is to be made. These respects may be categorised as errors of law. The examples which follow are not to be understood as necessarily exhaustive. Care must, however, be taken to secure that the court does not set about the task of finding matters of fact, but keeps within the limit of correcting error in the process adopted by the decision maker in the finding of the facts. It is with such matters as procedure, sufficiency, construction, inference, and application that the court is concerned. Where a tribunal with a specialised expertise has assessed the evidence before it and reached a view on a matter of fact it may well be immune from review if no error of law is identified.[12] It may be noted that an error in the facts material to the decision where the decision maker had the opportunity to ascertain the truth prior to making the decision may constitute an irrationality.[13]

22.31 *(i) Absence of evidence* If a decision has been reached on the basis of some fact which should have been supported by evidence and for which no evidence has been presented the decision will be open to review. Where there is an onus placed on one party to establish a particular proposition and no material has been presented to prove that proposition, a tribunal will not be entitled to find that the onus has been discharged.[14] If all the evidence on which a tribunal has proceeded is incompetent then its decision is open to review (notwithstanding a finality clause).[15] But the absence of evidence must be distinguished from the assessment of evidence. The latter aspect may raise more directly considerations of rationality as a ground of challenge.

22.32 *(ii) Whether the finding can be supported by the evidence* As has already been noticed[16] considerations of error and of rationality may merge. In the context of the Workmen's Compensation Act 1906 appeal was limited to questions of law, but that was recognised to include the question whether the findings could be supported upon the evidence submitted. In one such case it was observed: "The criterion is whether anyone could reasonably have come to that conclusion. It has been said more than once that this criterion is, if not exactly the same, at least strictly analogous to the criterion we are in use to apply when we are asked to direct a new trial on the ground that the verdict of the jury is contrary to the evidence. It is not a question of whether the decision is right or wrong, but a question of whether there was evidence led upon which the decision can be supported."[17] Lord Fraser of Tullybelton has observed[18] that "an immigration officer is only entitled to order the detention and removal of a person who has entered the country by virtue of an *ex facie* valid permission if the person is an illegal entrant. That is a 'precedent fact' which has to be established. It is not enough that the immigration officer reasonably believes him to be an illegal entrant if the evidence does not justify his belief. Accordingly the duty of the court

---

[12] *Irving v. Minister of Pensions*, 1945 S.C. 21.
[13] *Ettrick and Lauderdale District Council v. Secretary of State for Scotland*, 1995 S.L.T. 996; *Shetland Line (1984) Ltd v. Secretary of State for Scotland*, 1996 S.L.T. 653.
[14] *Mitchell v. Minister of Pensions*, 1945 S.C. 131.
[15] *Cullen & Flynn v. Linton* (1872) 1 M. 120 at 123.
[16] para. 21.02.
[17] *Eamon v. Dalziel & Co.*, 1912 S.C. 966, *per* Lord President Dunedin at 968.
[18] *R. v. Home Secretary ex p. Khawaja* [1984] 1 A.C. 74 at 97.

must go beyond inquiring only whether he had reasonable grounds for his belief." But that does not mean the determination of the facts is not properly a matter for the immigration officer and the Secretary of State.[19] So also it has been recognised that in a stated case under the Income Tax Acts the court may always review a finding in fact on the ground that there was no evidence to support it.[20] Whether someone is intentionally homeless may be classed as a question of fact, but the ground for challenge may be whether the authority were entitled to reach the decision which they reached.[21] There is no logical distinction between a decision which is based solely on inadmissible evidence and one which is based solely on evidence which is not reasonably capable of supporting it.[22]

(iii) No factual basis Where a factual basis for a decision is required **22.33**
and there is no proper factual basis established, the decision will be open to challenge. In some cases there may be a formal requirement for the making of findings in fact, and the absence of such findings may then be fatal to the decision.[23] But when it cannot be said that there is no evidence to support the decision, the correctness of the decision cannot be challenged as a matter of law.[24] A tribunal may, to some degree noted,[25] proceed upon its own knowledge and experience[26] and to the extent that it can do so a sufficient factual basis for the decision may thereby be found.

(iv) Incorrect material fact This ground figures in certain statutory **22.34**
contexts as a ground for appeal: as, for example, in the Licensing (Scotland) Act 1976. In the context of judicial review it will not suffice simply to claim that something which has been found as a primary fact is incorrect. There may be an opportunity for challenge if there has been an error of law in the finding of the fact, or if the procedure whereby the fact was found was incorrect. There may also be room for challenge in relation to secondary facts, that is to say facts and conclusions which have been derived from primary facts. The inference by which the finding has been reached may be perverse. If an authority draws an inference as a factual basis for its decision and the inference is not one which no authority could reasonably draw, the decision may be immune from challenge.[27] The evaluation of evidence in the sense of deciding the weight to be given to conflicting factors is very much a matter for the decision-making body, but it may be going too far to say that an "erroneous evaluation of the evidence by a tribunal of fact, however gross," is not an error of law, since a gross error may well be an example of irrational or perverse judgment.[28]

---

[19] *R. v. Home Secretary, ex p. Bugdaycay* [1987] A.C. 514 at 522. *Cf. Minister for Aboriginal Affairs v. Peko-Wallsend Ltd* (1986) 162 C.L.R. 24, *per* Mason C.J. at 42.

[20] *Inland Revenue v. Fraser*, 1942 S.C. 493 at 497.

[21] *Stewart v. Monklands D.C.*, 1987 S.L.T. 620.

[22] *R. v. Bedwelly Justices, ex p. Williams* [1996] 3 W.L.R. 361 at 371.

[23] *Wordie Property Co. Ltd v. Secretary of State for Scotland*, 1984 S.L.T. 345. *Cf. London & Clydeside Properties Ltd v. City of Aberdeen D.C.*, 1984 S.L.T. 50.

[24] *Nelson v. Allan Brothers & Co. (U.K.) Ltd*, 1913 S.C. 1003.

[25] see para. 18.48.

[26] *Glasgow and District Restaurateurs' and Hotelkeepers' Association v. Dollan*, 1941 S.C. 93 at 108.

[27] *Mecca Leisure Ltd v. City of Glasgow D.C.*, 1987 S.C.L.R. 26.

[28] *Rae v. Criminal Injuries Compensation Board*, 1997 S.L.T. 291 at 296.

22.35 *(v) Failure to take account of relevant considerations* Where an authority has failed to take into account considerations that are relevant to the decision which is to be made the decision may be open to challenge. A failure to take account of the nature of alternative accommodation may be fatal to a decision on the assessment of housing benefit.[29] Where a sheriff in confirming a resolution on the prescribing of boundaries failed to take into account matters relating to the number of houses and the amount of the population involved it was held that he had erred. He was bound by the statute to hear all interested parties and these reasonable grounds of objection had been raised before him.[30] An order prohibiting freshwater fish farming on a loch was declared invalid since the Secretary of State had failed to have regard to the fact that the appellants' operations were statutorily excempt.[31] So also the failure to consider certain rents in the locality as required by the statute for the fixing of local authority housing rents was a fatal omission.[32] In one case[33] a housing association had appealed to the Secretary of State against a deemed refusal of planning permission for a housing development. Before the result was known they lodged a second application which was granted ten days before the reporter issued his decision dismissing the appeal on the first application. The petitioners had objected to the second application and sought judicial review. It was held that it was unreasonable on the *Wednesbury* standard for the district council to have disposed of the second application while the first was undecided, because the outcome of the appeal on the first application was a material consideration which they should have taken into account. Where relevant material had been considered only by a licensing authority's officials and had not been placed before the authority itself, it was held that the authority had failed to take account of all relevant considerations.[34] On the other hand, a decision maker cannot be faulted for not taking account of a consideration which has not been raised at all.[35]

22.36 *(vi) Account taken of irrelevant considerations* Where parochial relief was refused on the ground that the applicant was a native of Ireland, it was held that consideration should have been given to his residence rather than his place of birth.[36] Where a statutory test is laid down—for example, social considerations in the locality—a decision which satisfies that test and applies a test which is irrelevant to the question, such as the condition of the premises, will be invalid.[37] In matters of licensing it is not relevant to have concern regarding the number of other applications which might be made, since each one has to be considered on its own merits.[38] A refusal to act for an irrelevant reason is open to challenge.[39]

22.37 *(vii) Misunderstanding or ignorance of an established and relevant fact* The fact may be physical, that is to say something which existed or

---

[29] *Malcolm v. Tweeddale District Housing Benefit Review Board*, 1994 S.L.T. 1212.

[30] *White v. Magistrates of Rutherglen* (1897) 24 R. 446.

[31] *North Uist Fisheries Ltd v. Secretary of State for Scotland*, 1992 S.L.T. 333.

[32] *Dundee Corporation v. Secretary of State for Scotland*, 1941 S.C. 120.

[33] *James Aitken & Sons (Meat Producers) Ltd v. City of Edinburgh D.C.*, 1990 S.L.T. 241, followed in *Trusthouse Forte Ltd v. Perth and Kinross D.C.*, 1990 S.L.T. 737.

[34] *City Cabs (Edinburgh) Ltd v. City of Edinburgh D.C.*, 1988 S.L.T. 184.

[35] *Tayside R.C. v. Secretary of State for Scotland*, 1996 S.L.T. 473.

[36] *Higgins v. Heritors and Kirk Session of the Barony Parish of Glasgow* (1824) 3S. 239.

[37] *Bantop Ltd v. Glasgow District Licensing Board*, 1989 S.C.L.R. 731.

[38] *Centralbite Ltd v. Kincardine and Deeside District Licensing Board*, 1988 S.C.L.R. 652.

[39] *Heritors of Corstorphine v. Ramsay*, Mar. 10, 1812, F.C.

occurred or did not, or it may be mental, that is to say, an opinion. Thus, if a minister acted under the mistaken belief that a particular state of affairs which was material for the exercise of his statutory power existed and it did not exist, or if contrary to the understanding of the decision maker there was a respectable body of professional or expert opinion which was available to him, the decision may be open to challenge.[40] The view has been expressed that where a minister in reliance on a report which he has instructed, has failed to take into account the true facts, a remedy should be available to a person who has suffered as a result of the minister's decision, proceeding as it did on an inaccurate factual basis.[41]

(c) Errors in exercising the power

In what has been analysed as the third stage in a decision-making **22.38** process the authority may be required to direct himself correctly on the relevant law. It is to be assumed that under stage one he has correctly identified a particular power which he is entitled to exercise. He has also ascertained the relevant facts in accordance with stage two. The relevant statutory provision which is to be applied in the particular matter has been ascertained. The problem remains of its application. Here the decision maker may be found to have proceeded on some erroneous understanding of the rights of parties or in some other respect mistaken the ordinary law, and in such a case review will be open.[42] In addition, matters of construction of the statutory provisions may arise, and there is room for reviewable error in the proper interpretation of them. The circumstances in which such problems may arise are many and varied. Where the question is within arguable limits one of degree, the court will be disinclined to interfere.[43] Three groups of examples in relation to statutory provisions may be noted.

(i) Matters of procedure

(i) Matters of procedure Where letters of appeal had been sent on **22.39** January 26, and so were presumed under section 7 of the Interpretation Act 1978 to have arrived on January 27, but which did not actually arrive until January 28 and 29, the question arose whether that satisfied a requirement that they were appeals "made up to and including 27 January". It was held that the reality rebutted the presumption of arrival and that the appeal was made when the letters were received, not when they were sent. The case was presented on the question whether the Secretary of State had been entitled to reject the appeal as out of time, but can be analysed more particularly as a case of alleged error.[44] Where the price at which milk was to be sold by a milk marketing board for the manufacture of butter fell to be fixed and certified by auditors in accordance with a formula which related to "the average gross realised price per cwt. of the board's milk salted butters" it was held by the Inner House that the auditors' certificates should be reduced on the ground

---

[40] *Secretary of State for Education and Science v. Tameside Metropolitan B.C.* [1977] A.C. 1014 AT 1030. See the discussion of this in Wade and Forsyth, *Administrative Law* (7th ed.), p. 316, where a strong argument is presented for the recognition of broad and simple rules of review whereby erroneous and decisive facts may enable a decision to be quashed.

[41] *Daganayasi v. Minister of Immigration* [1980] 2 N.Z.L.R. 130, *per* Cooke J. at 145–149.

[42] *North-Eastern Ry v. North British Ry* (1897) 25R. 333.

[43] *Inland Revenue v. Livingston*, 1927 S.C. 251 at 258; *Inland Revenue v. Fraser*, 1942 S.C. 493 at 497.

[44] *Adam v. Secretary of State*, 1987 S.C.L.R. 697.

that they had erroneously construed and applied the formula.[45] In the preparation of a register of streets the view was expressed that the width of the street to be entered in the register should be the actual width and not an ideal width fixed with a view to future improvement.[46] Where tests were prescribed for assessing the levels of rentals those tests must be properly understood and applied.[47]

22.40 *(ii) Extent of power* The extent of a statutory power to deposit earth in the building of a railway has been held to be open to review.[48] A detention authorised on the day after the expiry of a period of detention was a detention "immediately after the expiry" of that period and so was in breach of section 26 of the Mental Health (Scotland) Act 1984.[49] A duty to provide premises and facilities "for the purposes of the district court" was held to include a duty to provide cell accommodation.[50] In *Gordon v. Kirkcaldy District Council*,[51] a local authority was empowered by statute to charge for the collection and disposal of trade waste, but not of household waste. Both of those expressions were defined by the statute and the definition of the latter term included the expression "dwelling-house". It was held that whether or not particular premises constituted a "dwelling-house" and whether waste was "household waste" or "trade waste" were questions which the court in review could consider and answer. They were not matters which were left to the discretion of local authorities to determine.

22.41 *(iii) Qualification under statutory provision* In the construction of a local authority's housing policy the term "applicants" was held to include those who gave up a tenancy as well as those who had not yet obtained one.[52] The question has arisen as matter of law whether there was a continuing causal connection between an abandonment of a tenancy and a present homelessness so as to render a person still intentionally homeless.[53] In one case a determination had to be made on the construction of the phrase "a substantial part of the United Kingdom".[54] The construction of the expression "housing benefit" as a pure question of law has been held to be within the scope of judicial review.[55] Whether an institution qualified as a "ragged school" for an exemption from rates is a matter of law.[56] In *Malcolm v. McDougall*[57] it was held that the Land Court were warranted in concluding that a plot of ground and a thatched cottage were a "holding" for the purposes of the Small Landholders (Scotland) Act 1911. There is also a question of law open in regard to particular activities, such as whether for the purposes of a pension a fireman playing badminton while on stand-by duty was injured "in the

---

[45] 1972 S.L.T. 137; 1975 S.L.T. 39, affd in House of Lords at 76. There was no finality clause.

[46] *Caledonian Ry v. Glasgow Corporation* (1905) 7 F. 1020; 1907 S.C.(H.L.) 7.

[47] *MacLeod v. Banff and Buchan District Housing Benefit Review Board*, 1988 S.L.T. 763.

[48] *Edinburgh and Glasgow Ry Co. v. Earl of Hopetoun* (1840) 2 D. 1155.

[49] *R, Petr*, 1990 S.C.L.R. 757.

[50] *Strathclyde R.C. v. City of Glasgow D.C.*, 1989 S.L.T. 235.

[51] 1990 S.C. 107.

[52] *Lennox v. Hamilton D.C.*, 1990 S.C.L.R. 514.

[53] *Hynds v. Midlothian County Council*, 1986 S.L.T. 54—the claim failed.

[54] *Stagecoach Holdings plc v. Secretary of State for Trade*, 1997 S.L.T. 940.

[55] *Andrew v. City of Glasgow D.C.*, 1996 S.L.T. 814.

[56] *Renfrewshire County Council v. Trustees of Orphan Homes of Scotland* (1898) 1F. 186.

[57] 1916 S.C. 283.

execution of his duties" as a fireman,[58] or whether the extraction and stockpiling of timber was included in the term "forestry",[59] or whether an accident was one "arising out of and in the course of the employment",[60] or whether a person had failed "grossly and without reasonable excuse" to perform a duty,[61] or whether there was "special cause" for not endorsing a driving licence.[62] On the other hand, it was held in one case that the question whether use had been made of "insulting words" was a matter of fact: Lord Reid observed that "The meaning of an ordinary word of the English language is not a question of law. The proper construction of a statute is a question of law."[63] The matters considered in this context may be described as an asking of the wrong question in so far as the key lies in the correct understanding of the statutory meaning. Thus in deciding whether a person is vulnerable for the purposes of the housing of homeless persons it has been held that to ask whether a person was at great risk was to ask the wrong question because the test of vulnerability required a comparative assessment.[64]

Errors and ambiguities in decree

Where there is an error or an ambiguity in the terms of the order made **22.42** by an inferior body a reduction will be competent. Thus, where an order by a sheriff was found to be in wider terms than it should consistently with his decision have been, it was held that it could competently be reduced, even although it had not been made the subject of appeal to the Court of Session.[65] Where an order was pronounced requiring a tenant to restock his farm but erroneously omitting any prescription of the time by which that was to be done the order fell to be reduced.[66]

Effect of error

In many cases the discovery of an error will lead to the quashing of the **22.43** decision. But circumstances may occur where a decision has been reached on a ground erroneous in law, but which is still correct on a proper understanding of the law. In such a case the decision should not be regarded as a nullity unless there are compelling reasons for doing so. A decision by the Secretary of State that planning permission was not required was sustained as sound in law, although the grounds on which the Secretary of State had reached the decision were in law erroneous.[67]

---

[58] *Waldie v. Glasgow Corporation*, 1954 S.C. 47.
[59] *Farleyer Estate v. Secretary of State for Scotland*, 1992 S.L.T. 476.
[60] *Durham v. Brown Bros Ltd* (1898) 1 F. 279.
[61] *Campbell v. Jameson* (1877) 4 R.(J.) 17.
[62] *Muir v. Sutherland*, 1940 S.C. 66.
[63] *Cozens v. Brutus* [1973] A.C. 854 at 861. The question whether a statutory expression is to bear the meaning of an ordinary word in the English language is a question of law.
[64] *Wilson v. Nithsdale District Council*, 1992 S.L.T. 1131. In that case the decision was held erroneous but not perverse; in *Kelly v. Monklands D.C.*, 1986 S.L.T. 169 a decision on vulnerability was held to be unreasonable.
[65] *Mathewson v. Yeaman* (1900) 2 F. 873.
[66] *Macdonald v. Mackessock* (1888) 16 R. 168.
[67] *Glasgow D.C. v. Secretary of State for Scotland*, 1980 S.C. 150.

PART V

PROCEDURE AND REMEDIES

CHAPTER 23

PRACTICE AND PROCEDURE

I   COMPETENCY AND JURISDICTION
II PROCEDURE
III REMEDIES

I COMPETENCY AND JURISDICTION

History

Prior to the introduction of the present procedure for judicial review in **23.01**
1985 the usual procedure for obtaining review of decisions and actings of
administrative bodies was to seek the ordinary remedies of reduction,
declarator, suspension or interdict, or some combination of these in the
ordinary way in which such actions were raised in the Court of Session.
A more particular remedy was also available under section 91 of the
Court of Session Act 1868, subsequently re-enacted in section 45 of the
Court of Session Act 1988, whereby application could be made by
summary petition not only for the restoration of possession of property
of which the applicant had been violently or fraudulently deprived but
for an order for the specific performance of any statutory duty.[1] The
history leading up to the introduction of the present procedure has
already been mentioned in Chapter 2. Judicial review is only available in
the Court of Session, not the sheriff court.

Present Procedure

As has already been noted, in 1985 a new procedure was introduced by **23.02**
Act of Sederunt[2] inserting a new rule 260B into the Rules of the Court
of Session. The Act of Sederunt came into effect on April 30, 1985. The
new rule prescribed an expeditious and flexible procedure for applications for judicial review. These were described in the original formulation of the rule as applications "to the supervisory jurisdiction of the
Court which immediately before the coming into operation of this rule
would have been made by way of summons or petition". In the current
revised version of the Rules of Court the relevant provisions are
comprised in Chapter 58, and in this version the provisions are simply
made applicable to "an application to the supervisory jurisdiction of the
court".[3]

Application of the procedure

The expression "the supervisory jurisdiction" has already been consid- **23.03**
ered.[4] For the purposes of the procedure for judicial review "the Court"
to which the rule refers is the Court of Session so that matters of

---

[1] The process has only seldom been used since its introduction and, as is noted later, it is
now expressly included within the scope of the new procedure for judicial review.
Particular provision has sometimes been made by statute for the Court of Session to
review an alleged failure by a statutory authority to perform its duty: see MacLaren's *Court
of Session Practice*, p. 120.

[2] Act of Sederunt (Rules of Court Amendment No. 2) (Judicial Review) 1985.

[3] Rules of the Court of Session ("RCS"), r. 58.1(1).

[4] See para. 1.02.

criminal business, which are the preserve of the High Court of Justiciary, do not fall within the scope of judicial review procedure.[5] Rule 58.3.(1), which requires that applications to the supervisory jurisdiction shall be made by petition for judicial review, however, expressly "includes" within the supervisory jurisdiction applications for the specific performance of a statutory duty under section 45(b) of the Court of Session Act 1988. That section empowers the Court to order the specific performance of any statutory duty and thus creates a statutory jurisdiction in the Court to do so. Such an order is thus not an exercise of the common law supervisory jurisdiction but for convenience is brought within the procedural provisions of Chapter 58 of the Rules by including it within that jurisdiction.[6] While applications for the restoration of property under the provisions of section 45(a) of the Act of 1988 are not brought within the scope of Chapter 58 since it was not considered appropriate to do so,[7] it is thought that the remedy thereby provided would be among the remedies obtainable under an application for judicial review in light of the wide terms of rule 58.4(b),[8] although there would probably be few cases in which occasion would arise for the affording of such a remedy.

Exclusions

23.04 Rule 58.3 expressly excludes from its scope any application which is made or could be made by appeal or review under or by virtue of any enactment.[9] This is essentially a restatement of the principle that an application to the supervisory jurisdiction is not open if an alternative remedy exists and has not been exhausted. But as has already been stated that principle is not an absolute one.[10] It is thought that despite the absolute language of rule 58.3(2) it is not intended to exclude the availability of judicial review in the exceptional cases in which that course may be held to be competent notwithstanding a failure to exhaust a statutory remedy.[11]

Mandatory nature of the procedure

23.05 Rule 58.3(1) is in mandatory terms so that any application which falls within the scope of the rule will be treated as incompetent if attempted by any other procedure. Correspondingly, applications which do not invoke the supervisory jurisdiction should be regarded as incompetent if brought as applications under the rule.[12] In the case of *Sleigh v. City of Edinburgh District Council*[13] local authority councillors had presented an ordinary petition for interdict against the local authority to prevent the making of a scheme which they alleged was illegal. Interim interdict was

---

[5] *Reynolds v. Christie*, 1988 S.L.T. 68. For review of criminal matters, see paras 8.37 *et seq.*
[6] The consequence presumably is that matters which may not be within what is usually regarded as matters of administrative law, such as the enforcement of health and safety legislation, will require to proceed by way of "judicial review".
[7] See the note to para. 58.3.4. of the Rules of Court in the *Parliament House Book*.
[8] See para. 26.25.
[9] In terms of r. 58.3(2).
[10] See para. 12.12.
[11] *cf.*, however, the view taken in St Clair and Davidson, *Judicial Review in Scotland*, para. 3.21. See also Lord Davidson's observations in relation to the former rule 260B(3) in *Nahar v. Strathclyde R.C.*, 1986 S.L.T. 570.
[12] *Bell v. Fiddes*, 1996 S.L.T. 51.
[13] 1988 S.L.T. 253.

pronounced, but thereafter the local authority rescinded its resolution to make the scheme, the interdict was recalled by consent, and both parties sought their expenses. At the hearing of the motion for expenses it was held that the petition was incompetent and that the matter should have been raised by way of an application for judicial review. The view was also expressed that it would not have been competent for the petitioners to have amended the petition so as to convert it into an application for judicial review, a procedure which was markedly distinct from the ordinary petition procedure. However a fresh application in the correct form could easily and rapidly have been presented and the respondents were not prejudiced by the adoption of the wrong form of process. The petitioners were found entitled to one half of their expenses.

Nominated judges

Several individual judges of the Outer House of the Court of Session are expressly nominated by the Lord President under the terms of rule 58.5 for the hearing of applications for judicial review. The purpose of the rule is to have such applications dealt with by judges who are experienced in the substance and procedure of such cases. Provision is, however, made for the the hearing of such cases by any other judge of the court, including the vacation judge, if none of the nominated judges are available.[14] The participation of the judge in an application for review is more positive than the traditional role.[15] Indeed, judicial initiatives and control of the procedural detail may be a significant factor in securing expeditious disposal of applications.

23.06

Jurisdiction

The jurisdiction of the Court of Sesson to entertain any application to it is generally determined by the provisions of the Civil Jurisdiction and Judgments Act 1982.[16] By section 16 and Schedule 4 provision is made for the determination of the jurisdiction of the courts within the United Kingdom among themselves. By section 20 and Schedule 8 provision is made for the rules on jurisdiction in Scotland. One exception, however, must be noted and that is with regard to reviews of tribunals, which are expressly excepted from Schedules 4 and 8.[17] In the case of a review of a tribunal decision the jurisdiction of the Court of Session will rest on the common law basis of the tribunal being situated in Scotland.[18] Where the Act of 1982 applies the general rule is that the Court of Session will have jurisdiction where the respondent is domiciled in Scotland.[19] Rule 2 of Schedule 8 also provides for certain special jurisdictions in Scotland. Thus in proceedings for interdict, if the wrong is likely to be committed

23.07

---

[14] RCS r. 58.5. The powers of the vacation judge are, however, limited: see RCS, r. 11.1. Nominated or other judges may accordingly have to be found in vacation for an urgent hearing on the merits of a case.

[15] Lord Justice-Clerk Thomson in *Thomson v. Glasgow Corporation*, 1961 S.L.T. 237 at 246, compared judges with referees at boxing contests, seeing that the rules are kept and counting the points.

[16] c.27. For a full consideration of these provisions reference should be made to the current textbooks, such as Anton & Beaumont, *Civil Jurisdiction in Scotland* and Briggs and Rees, *Civil Jurisdiction and Judgments*.

[17] By Sched. 5, para. 4 and Sched. 9, para. 12.

[18] Maclaren, *Court of Session Practice*, pp. 118–119.

[19] Sched. 4, Art. 2; Sched. 8, r. 1.

in Scotland, the Court of Session will have jurisdiction.[20] Where the proceedings have as their object a decision of an organ of a legal person, the Court of Session will have jurisdiction if the place where the legal person has its seat is in Scotland.[21] In *Bank of Scotland v. IMRO*[22] it was held that in a matter relating to the performance of certain rules of an organisation the case fell under rule 2(10) rather than rule 2(2), which related to the performance of contracts, with the result that the Court of Session had no jurisdiction since the seat of the organisation was in England.[23] Rule 2(13) gives the Court of Session jurisdiction in proceedings concerning an arbitration conducted in Scotland or where Scots law governs the procedure. The power to sist or dismiss on the ground of *forum non conveniens* is expressly preserved by the Act.[24]

II PROCEDURE

Form

23.08 An application for judicial review must be made by way of a Petition.[25] The form of the application is, in terms of Rule 58.6, to be that set out in Form 58.6 appended to the Rules of Court. This provides a layout of several numbered paragraphs. The first sets out the designation of the petitioner and his or her title and interest. It also sets out the designation and relation of the respondent to the matter to be reviewed. It also specifies such other persons as may have an interest in the application. The second paragraph details the act, decision or omission to be reviewed. As has already been observed, where the issue is as to the effect of a decision, not as to the validity of the decision, judicial review is not competent.[26] The third states the remedies sought by the petitioner but also asks for the court to pronounce such further order, decrees or orders (including an order for expenses) as the court may consider just and reasonable in the circumstances of the case. This provision reflects the principle that the court is not bound to grant all or any of the remedies sought by the petitioner in the event of finding that the application is well founded on its merits. But on the other hand the court should not compel a petitioner to accept a remedy not sought and not desired by him.[27] The fourth paragraph sets out the grounds for challenging the matter which is sought to be reviewed. The fifth allows for a short statement of the facts in support of the grounds of challenge. These may be set out in one or more paragraphs as may be appropriate. The final paragraph or paragraphs are designed to set out the legal argument with reference to enactments or judicial authority on which it is intended to rely. As is noted later, the pleadings will be given a more liberal construction than that traditionally given to pleadings in an

---

[20] But the interdict may be enforced by another state party to the Brussels Convention with regard to future conduct outwith Scotland: *Barratt International Resorts Ltd v. Martin*, 1994 S.L.T. 434 at 437L.
[21] Sched. 8, r. 2(12).
[22] 1959 S.C. 107.
[23] For a critical account of the case, see A. Mennie, "Jurisdiction and Competency in Proceedings for Judicial Review", 1990 S.L.T. (News) 1.
[24] s.49(1); *e.g. Sokha v. Secretary of State for the Home Department*, 1992 S.L.T. 1049.
[25] RCS, r. 14.2.
[26] *Hands v. Kyle and Carrick D.C.*, 1989 S.L.T. 124. See para. 13.03.
[27] *Mecca Leisure Ltd. v. City of Glasgow Licensing Board*, 1987 S.L.T. 483. See para. 23.33.

ordinary action in the Court of Session.[28] There follows provision for the stating of one or more pleas-in-law. By a plea-in-law is meant a distinct legal proposition applicable to the facts in the case.[29] It should accordingly focus the essence of each ground on which the challenge is being presented. The petition is signed by counsel or such other person as may have right of audience in the Court of Session, that is to say a practising member of the Faculty of Advocates or a person having a right of audience before the court under Part II of the Law Reform (Miscellaneous Provisions) (Scotland) Act 1990 in respect of applications for judicial review.[30]

Schedules for service

The petition concludes with two schedules, one listing the respondents **23.09** and any interested parties on whom service of the petition is sought either in common form or by advertisement respectively, and the other specifying any documents, and the person who has possession or control over such documents, being documents not within his possession or control but ones upon which he is founding in the application.[31] These may be documents held or controlled by the respondent or by some other person. In practice, completion of the former schedule is universal but the latter is seldom used. Where judicial review is sought of the decision of an adjudicator appointed under section 12 of the Immigration Act 1971 the Home Secretary and not the adjudicator should be called as the respondent but the petition should be intimated to the adjudicator as a person who may have an interest.[32]

Lodging the application

The petition duly completed requires to be lodged in the Petition **23.10** Department. Together with the petition the petitioner is required to lodge all relevant documents in his possession and within his control.[33] It is to be noted that the rule requires the lodging of all the documents which the petitioner has relevant to the application and not just those on which he may be founding in the petition or to which he may be referring in body of the pleadings. It is not anticipated that there should be opportunity or necessity for any further disclosure so far as his archives are concerned. The documents lodged will usually include the written communication or other record of the decision which is under challenge, a copy of which the petitioner will have been able to obtain, if indeed it has not been specifically sent to him by the respondent.[34] Cases may, however, occur where the documents held by or available to the petitioner do not disclose the decision, act or omission in question and the basis on which it is to be challenged and, where that is not apparent

---

[28] See para. 23.19 (Pleadings).

[29] *J. and R. Young and Co. v. Graham* (1860) 23D. 36.

[30] RCS, r. 1.3(1). For the position of party litigants, see RCS, r. 4.2.5. The original provision enabled a petition to be signed by the applicant's counsel or solicitor, the width of which secured an avoidance of delay; 1985 SCOLAG at 121–122.

[31] See RCS, r. 58.6(3).

[32] Practice Note No. 1 of 1992.

[33] RCS, r. 58.6.

[34] Where a decree is to be reduced, an extract of it should be produced: *Scouller v. McLaughlan* (1864) 2M. 955; *Miller & Son v. Oliver & Boyd* (1901) 9 S.L.T. 287. For reduction, see para. 24.21.

from the documents lodged with the petition, the petitioner is required
to lodge an affidavit stating the terms of the decision, act or omission
and the basis of the petitioner's complaint against it.[35] Where the
petitioner founds on a document which is not within his possession or
control he is, as has already been stated in the previous paragraph,
required to specify the document and the person who possesses it or has
control over it in a schedule to the petition. Where such a document is
held by any party who appears in the petition process he may seek an
order from the court under rule 58.9(2)(b)(vii) for that party to lodge the
document within such period as the court shall specify, but that order
can only be sought and granted at the first hearing of the petition, not at
the time of the first order.[36] Apart from that it is open to a petitioner to
recover such a document from any person, whether or not that person is
the respondent or a possible party in the petition, by applying to the
court by separate application for an order under section 1 of the
Administration of Justice (Scotland) Act 1972, and he may make such an
application at any time after or even before the presentation of the
petition.

Hearing for first order

23.11 On the lodging of the petition and the accompanying papers the petition
requires to be brought forthwith to a Lord Ordinary for a first order.
The judge will usually be one of the judges nominated by the Lord
President under rule 58.5 for the hearing of applications for judicial
review, but if such a judge is not available then any other judge of the
court, including the vacation judge, may under that rule deal with it. The
judge may deal with the petition in court or in chambers. The petition
does not appear in the motion roll. The attendance of counsel at the
stage of the first order is appropriate, particularly where the case raises a
question of general interest affecting other persons than the particular
applicant or respondent and particular consideration has to be given to
the extent of intimation, service and advertisement of the application.[37]
In such cases counsel's advice on that matter may well be sought. It is
open to the court with the agreement of parties to dispense with
intimation and service and with any first hearing, and then deal with the
whole application by argument at a mutually agreed date.[38]

Caveats

23.12 Not infrequently the respondent will have lodged a caveat in anticipation
of an application for judicial review.[39] Indeed, local authorities and
agencies or departments of central government may well keep a caveat
in force against the possibility of any petition being raised against them
of which they wish to have forewarning.[40] The caveat is a document
lodged in the petition department requiring that notice be given to the
person specified in it of any application made to the court for certain

---

[35] RCS, r. 58.6(4).

[36] *Kelly, Petr*, 1985 S.C. 333.

[37] *Sutherland D.C. v. Secretary of State for Scotland*, 1988 G.W.D. 4–167.

[38] e.g. *Stewart v. Monklands D.C.*, 1987 S.C.L.R. 45 (the point is not covered in the report
in 1987 S.L.T. 630).

[39] For further detail on caveats, see Chap. 5 of the Rules of Court.

[40] A caveat will remain in force for a year after it is lodged and may be renewed
annually: RCS, r. 5.2(2).

specified kinds of order. These include various kinds of interim order which could be sought at the stage of the first order in proceedings for judicial review. The caveat may be general so as to apply to any of the orders against which a caveat may be lodged, or particular so as to apply only to an order of a specified kind. The lodging of a caveat has the effect that no such order as is covered by it should be pronounced before the person on whose behalf it has been lodged has had an opportunity of being heard on the matter. In the context of judicial review a caveat may not under the present Rules of Court now be lodged simply against an application for an order for service and intimation of the petition.[41] But it will be available where the petitioner seeks an interim order at the stage of the first order. There can be practical advantages in having a representation by the respondents at the stage of the first order and this can sometimes be arranged between the parties. Apart from that it will only be in the event of a caveat having been lodged and an interim order covered by it being sought that an appearance on behalf of the respondents can be expected.

Devolution issues

Issues regarding the extent and the exercise of devolved powers to Scotland may arise in applications for judicial review. They may be raised by the Advocate General or the Lord Advocate.[42] Corresponding issues may be raised under the Northern Ireland Act 1998 and the Government of Wales Act 1998. The raising of such issues and the consequent need for intimation are covered by the Rules of Court, Chapter 25A,[43] to which reference should be made.

23.13

Granting and refusing a first order

The first order will specify (i) such intimation, service and advertisement as may be necessary, (ii) any documents to be served with the petition, and (iii) a date for the first hearing. It may also include any interim order which the petitioner may seek at that stage. The judge is not bound to grant the order or any part of it. Rule 58.7 expressly provides that having heard counsel or other person having right of audience, the Lord Ordinary "may" grant such an order. While there is, in distinction from the English practice, no requirement for leave to make an application for judicial review, it is open to the judge after reading the petition and hearing the petitioner's representative to refuse to grant even an order for service and dismiss the application there and then.[44]

23.14

Orders for intimation and service

In the usual case the first order will include an order for service on the respondent and for intimation to any parties listed in the Schedule to the petition as having an interest in it. If the respondent is already present at

23.15

---

[41] Formerly a caveat could be used to give warning of any First Order: *Kelly v. Monklands D.C.*, 1986 S.L.T. 165. Under the present terms of RCS, r. 5.1 this is not now possible; see the notes to that rule in the *Parliament House Book*.

[42] Scotland Act 1998, Sched. 6, para. 4.

[43] Introduced by the Act of Sederunt (Devolution Issues Rules) 1999 (S.I. 1999 No. 1345) (see 1999 S.L.T. (News) 196). See also the Act of Adjournal (Devolution Issues Rules) 1999 (S.I. 1999 No. 1282), amending the Criminal Procedure Rules 1996 (1999 S.L.T. (News) 183).

[44] *e.g. Sokha v. Secretary of State for the Home Department*, 1992 S.L.T. 1049; *Butt v. Secretary of State for the Home Department*, 1995 G.W.D. 16–905. This echoes the practice of the former Bill Chamber: see para. 2.23 (History).

the time of the first order, service on him may be dispensed with and that course is usually taken with his consent in the interest of speed and economy. Intimation on the walls of the court remains as a formal method of public intimation of the raising of any petition, including petitions for judicial review.[45] But while in the case of other kinds of petitions circumstances may justify dispensing with such a course[46] such circumstances are not likely to apply in cases of judicial review and in practice intimation on the walls will be ordered. In addition to that, where the subject-matter of the application has a particular importance either to some locality or more generally, the court may order intimation in one or more newspapers having a circulation appropriate to the circumstances. All such public advertisement enables anyone with a legitimate interest in the subject-matter of the application to enter the process and be heard upon it. The court may well wish to consider whether intimation should be made to any body or association which is concerned with the subject-matter of the application, so that the views of interest groups may be available at the hearing. In practice it is not often that there is any necessity for the serving of any documents with the petition, although provision is expressly made for that in rule 58.7. The critical documents in the case, including the statement of the decision or order which is under challenge, will almost certainly already be within the archives of the respondent and an order for the service of documents is rarely if ever made.

Date for first hearing

23.16 It is to be noted that in relation to the inclusion in the first order of the specification of a date for the first hearing rule 58.7 requires that that date shall be "a date not earlier than 7 days after the expiry of the period specified for intimation and service". It is understood that the intention of the rule is that the court should keep control of the process and not simply grant an order for service and intimation which in the absence of any limit in time could be delayed in its execution by the petitioner. By requiring the specification of a period for service and intimation—that is a period within which service and intimation are to be carried out—the court can ensure that it keeps control of the procedure and that the processing of the application is not subject to any delay on the petitioner's part. The first order should on this approach specify a period within which service and intimation is to be made by the petitioner. In practice a period of two or three days should be sufficient for this purpose and that should be specified in the interlocutor embodying the first order. The order will then also specify the date for the first hearing. This requires, as has just been noted, to be not earlier than seven days after the period specified for intimation and service. In practice the date is initially left blank in the interlocutor when signed by the Lord Ordinary and is completed later, as soon as a date has been fixed by the Keeper of the Rolls for the first hearing often after consultation with the parties. A full copy of the petition is required by the Keeper's Office for the fixing of dates of hearings.[47] The date will usually be arranged as expeditiously as may be practicable after the expiry of the seven-day period.

---

[45] See RCS, r. 14.7.
[46] *e.g. Lowe, Petr*, 1920 S.C. 351.
[47] Practice Note No. 3 of 1996.

Interim orders

So far as any interim orders are concerned, these may be granted with or **23.17** without an appearance by the respondent, except that where a caveat has been lodged covering the interim order which is being sought, the order may not be granted without intimation of the application to the person having the protection of the caveat and the giving to him of an opportunity to be heard upon it. The broad purpose of an interim order will usually be to preserve the present state of affairs from change pending resolution of the challenge presented in the petition. Obvious examples are the ordering of the provision of temporary accommodation pending the resolution of a dispute in cases of alleged homelessness or an interdict against the carrying into effect of an administrative decision the validity of which is challenged. In practice, where the respondent is present at the stage of the first order an undertaking will often be given whereby the petitioner's position can be safeguarded until the petition is disposed of.

Answers

No express provision is made in rule 58.7 for the lodging of answers to **23.18** the petition to be covered in the first order. Express provision is made in rule 58.9(2)(b)(iv) for an order to be made at the stage of the first hearing for answers to be lodged within such period as the court may specify. Prior to that stage, rule 58.8(1)(b) provides that "a person to whom intimation of the first hearing has been made and who intends to appear . . . may lodge answers". It would appear that the original intention was that the stage of the first order would simply achieve the initiation of the process and that the first hearing would deal with subsequent procedure in anticipation of a determination of the case at the second hearing. Provision was, however, made for the determination of the petition at the stage of the first hearing and as practice has developed the first hearing has come in the vast majority of cases to be the occasion for the discussion and determination of the merits of the whole case. Where that has for any reason not proved practicable—for example, where some further information is required and cannot immediately be obtained and the hearing cannot usefully proceed at once—the usual course is to continue the first hearing to another date under rule 58.9(2)(b)(i). The course which has thus been adopted in practice secures that an even simpler and more expeditious completion of the process has been achieved than that originally envisaged. This does, however, give rise to a problem regarding the lodging of answers, the availability of which is always desirable and the absence of which can give rise to considerable inconvenience at the stage when the merits of the petition are under consideration. While it may be possible to resolve a pure question of the competency of an application without answers having been lodged, such a course may well be unsatisfactory and, at least where it is intended to refer to matters of fact, answers ought to be available so that factual issues which may exist can be identified or agreement reached on the factual background.[48] In these circumstances it is considered to be appropriate at least to signal the desirability of having answers available in time for the first hearing by making reference in the first order to the lodging of answers in slightly more

---

[48] *Blair v. Lochaber D.C.*, 1995 S.L.T. 407.

positive terms than rule 58.8(1)(b). Since that rule requires anyone intending to appear to intimate his intention to do so to the petitioner's agent and to the Keeper of the Rolls not less than 48 hours before the date of the hearing, and in practice that injunction is reproduced in the usual form of the first order, it may be useful to add to it an injunction that such a person should also lodge answers "if so advised" within the same limit of time. In practice answers are usually lodged by respondents in time for the first hearing but the importance of that being done is sufficient to justify the earliest formal indication that that should be done.

Pleading

23.19 The degree of precision and detail which has traditionally characterised pleadings in the generality of other forms of action in Scotland is not to be looked for in applications for judicial review. As has been noted, the Rules provide the outline of what is required in the petition, but the factual history should be set out succinctly, and the grounds of attack do not need to be elaborated in any full written argument. The critical matters of fact, as well as the respects in which the decision or actings are challenged, should be set out with sufficient clarity to give the respondent fair notice of the case which is being presented against him. A brief statement of the basis for the challenge together with a note of the relevant judicial authorities will usually give the respondent sufficient notice of the case which is to be presented against him. But the pleadings will be given a more liberal construction than that which has traditionally been given to pleadings in an ordinary action in the Court of Session.[49] Correspondingly, in the answers a less formal approach than is usual in the case of defences to an ordinary action is acceptable. The pleadings in cases of judicial review should not be subjected to any narrow or meticulous construction.[50] In practice some adjustment of the petition or the answers, or both, may be made by the parties prior to the first hearing. While such a course may be advantageous in helping to focus issues and clarify facts, it should be accommodated within the existing timetable and, bearing in mind the latitude allowed to pleadings in judicial review, should not be allowed to extend to unnecessary elaboration.

Notice of appearance

23.20 During the period between the first order and the first hearing the respondents and any interested parties on whom the petition has been served have the opportunity of deciding whether they wish to appear at the first hearing and if they do wish to do so then they are required to give the intimation mentioned in the preceding paragraph to the petitioner's agent and to the Keeper of the Rolls within the specified time-limit. They should not only, as has been mentioned, lodge answers to the petition, but also intimate such answers to the petitioner and to the other parties who may be appearing. The purpose of answers is to give notice of the position of the respondent with regard to the allegations made by the petitioner. Thus they should serve to focus any

---

[49] *City Cabs (Edinburgh) Ltd. v. City of Edinburgh D.C.*, 1988 S.L.T. 184.
[50] *Mecca Bookmakers (Scotland) Ltd. v. East Lothian District Licensing Board*, 1988 S.L.T. 520, *per* Lord Jauncey at 522.

points of fact on which there is dispute or, as is often the case, recognise that there is no material divergence on the factual background, and to enable the points of law to be identified on which the merits of the petition will essentially fall to be decided. The form of the answers should be in numbered paragraphs corresponding to the numbered paragraphs in the petition, together with appropriate pleas-in-law.[51] In addition to the answers, in terms of Rule 58.8(1)(b), there must also be lodged "any relevant documents". This provision echoes the obligation on the petitioner to lodge with the petition all relevant documents within his possession or control.[52] These two provisions should secure that all documentation founded on or referred to in the petition or the answers, as well as all other documentation relevant to the determination of the matter raised in the petition, is available in the process before the first hearing. So far as any other person is concerned, on whom the petition has not been served but who wishes to enter the process, he may apply by motion to the court for leave to do so. In order that the motion can be considered, the person should explain his title and interest to enter the process. If the motion is granted the provisions regarding intimation of his intention to appear and the lodging of answers contained in rule 58.8(1) will then apply to him as they apply to the persons specified for service in the first order.[53]

The first hearing

The next and often the final stage of the procedure is the first hearing. **23.21** At the outset the judge is required to satisfy himself that the petitioner has duly complied with the terms of the first order made under Rule 58.7.[54] Evidence of any service, intimation and advertisement should be among his papers and confirmation can be obtained from counsel appearing at the hearing that any other particulars in the first order have been carried out. By confirming that the terms of the order have been carried out assurance can be obtained that the opportunity has been given for all interested persons to enter the process if they wish to do so. Thereafter the judge must hear the parties.[55] As mentioned above, the original intention of the draftsman of the rules appears to have been that the first hearing should be an occasion for resolving any preliminary and procedural details in anticipation of a second hearing which would be the occasion for a final disposal of the case. But in practice the first hearing has come to be the stage at which the majority of cases are finally resolved. In some cases it may be that a decision can be reached in principle which will effectively resolve the dispute, and if the question in controversy can be determined, either by a formal finding by the court or more simply by the issuing of the court's opinion on the point, then the petition may be continued in order to enable the parties to consider their positions and resolve the particular matter by consent and achieve an agreed course for the determination of the petition.[56]

---

[51] RCS, r. 18,3.
[52] RCS, r. 58.6(2). See para. 23.10. Confidential documents may be lodged in a sealed packet; and a motion may then be enrolled for the court to allow it to be opened and the document made available under RCS, r. 35.8.
[53] RCS, r. 58.8(2).
[54] RCS, r. 58.9(1)(a).
[55] RCS, r. 58.9(1)(b).
[56] *e.g. Lennox v. Hamilton D.C.*, 1990 S.C.L.R. 514.

Continuation

23.22 Problems may, however, arise which call for a more extended procedure and in those cases the first hearing will simply be concerned with such procedural matters, with the final hearing being deferred either by a continuation of the first hearing or by the ordering of a second hearing as the judge may consider appropriate in the circumstances. If the petition is not determined at the first hearing the judge is entitled to make such order for further procedure as he thinks fit. Rule 58.9(2)(b) lists some particular matters which he may so order in particular circumstances. Thus he may adjourn or continue the first hearing to another date, a course which would obviously be appropriate where there are some procedural matters outstanding which require to be resolved before the case can be determined. It may be that it appears at the first hearing that the petition should be served on someone who was not mentioned at the stage of the granting of the first order and the judge may order service to be made on such a person. He is also entitled to make any interim order, although since most petitions are disposed of at the first hearing and, if the case is one which calls for an interim order, it will probaby have been sought and, if appropriate, allowed at the stage of the first order, this will not be a frequent course. The rule also provides for the ordering of answers to be lodged within a specified time but, as has been mentioned already it is preferable and indeed usual in practice for answers to have been lodged in advance of the first hearing.

Further orders

23.23 The judge is also expressly authorised at the stage of the first hearing to make orders designed to clarify points of uncertainty so as to focus the questions in controversy. Thus he may order further specification in the petition or the answers in relation to such matters as he may specify. He may also order that any fact founded on by a party at the hearing is to be supported by evidence on affidavit to be lodged within such period as he may specify. He may also order any party who appears to lodge such documents relating to the petition as he may specify within a specified period. Furthermore, he may appoint a reporter to report to him on such matters of fact as he may specify.[57] Finally, at least so far as the particular orders listed in rule 58.9(2)(b) are concerned, the judge may order a second hearing on such issues as he shall specify.

Questions of fact

23.24 The terms of the answers will disclose the extent of any dispute on matters of fact which there may be between the parties. In many cases the differences, if indeed there are any at all, will not be of such significance as to prevent the petition being determined without them being formally resolved. In practice, apparent points of difference can often be resolved during the course of the first hearing by concession or oral agreement. Further facts may thus be presented by counsel at the bar without the need for any formal proof.[58] If evidence is thought to be

---

[57] The initiative here is with the judge and it is for him to decide what he considers is useful for the resolution of the dispute.

[58] *e.g. CRS Leisure Ltd. v. Dumbarton District Licensing Board*, 1989 S.C.L.R. 566.

appropriate or necessary by the judge or any party this can be provided by way of affidavit. In this context an affidavit includes affirmation and a statutory or other declaration and it must be sworn or affirmed before a notary public or other competent authority,[59] such as a justice of the peace, a sheriff, or a judge. It should be sworn or affirmed and signed by the person giving it and also by the person before whom it is taken. As has been noticed already,[60] rule 58.6 expressly provides for the lodging of an affidavit stating the terms of the decision, act or omission which is complained of and the basis of the complaint, and rule 58.9(2)(b) empowers the judge to order any fact founded on by a party at the first hearing to be supported by evidence on affidavit. This form of presenting evidence is adopted in the interests of speed and economy. Where it is used to vouch matters of fact it should be given by a person with direct knowledge of the facts and preferably by the person with the closest and best knowledge of them. The substance of the material contained in an affidavit may be of crucial significance in the case.[61] Another method of resolving matters of fact which may be adopted is the appointment by the judge of a reporter with the express instruction to investigate and report to the judge on such particular matters as the judge may specify. This is not a power of which any significant use has been made. In so far as matters of fact require a formal resolution, resort will usually be had to proof if affidavit evidence is not considered to be sufficient or satisfactory.

The second hearing

After the first hearing and any continuation of it the Rules allow for the holding of a second hearing as one of the courses which may be ordered at the first hearing. Where this is ordered the Keeper of the Rolls is required to fix a date for the second hearing as soon as is reasonably practicable.[62] The Rules provide that this is to be done in consultation with the Lord Ordinary and the parties. Various procedural steps may be taken in anticipation of the second hearing, with a view to securing that all relevant material will be available before the court on that occasion. Orders may have already been made at the first hearing to that end under rule 58.9(2)(b). Subject to the terms of any such orders, the parties are required under rule 58.10(2) to lodge not less than seven days before the date of the second hearing all documents and affidavits to be founded on by them at that hearing, together with copies for the use of the court. Beyond that, the judge, if he considers that particular information is necessary for the proper disposal of the petition at the hearing, may at any time before the date of it have the petition put out on the By Order roll for that purpose.[63] The Rules plainly envisage that the judge will be keeping a close eye on the documentation as the preparation goes forward between the first and the second hearing and that the papers will be available to him as and when they are lodged so that he can form a view on the sufficiency of the material for the disposal of the case. If the case is put out on the By Order roll on his initiative at this stage, the judge is expressly empowered at the hearing on that roll to

23.25

---

[59] RCS, r. 1.3(2).
[60] para 23.10.
[61] *e.g. Lakin v. Secretary of State for Scotland*, 1988 S.L.T. 780.
[62] RCS, r. 58.10(1).
[63] RCS, r. 58.10(3).

make such order as he thinks fit, having regard to all the circumstances, including an order appointing a commissioner to recover a document or to take the evidence of a witness.[64] Resort to these provisions has, however, seldom (if ever) had to be made. Where a second hearing is held the Lord Ordinary has power to adjourn the hearing, to continue it for such further procedure as he thinks fit, or to determine the petition.

Decision

23.26 The determination of the case will be given by the judge, if not immediately after the termination of the hearing at which the substance of the dispute has been argued, at least within a short time thereafter. Usually a written opinion will be issued. If the application is unsuccessful it may simply be refused. It is not usual in practice formally to sustain any pleas-in-law tabled by the respondent in his answers. In terms of Rule of Court 68.4(a) the court may grant or refuse any part of the petition, with or without conditions. Where the application is successful the formal order will prescribe the particular remedy or remedies which the court considers appropriate in the circumstances. Where the decision under challenge is correct, although given for the wrong reason, it is proper to refuse to quash it, even where the respondent admits that the reasoning was wrong and presents a quite different justification for it.[65]

Reclaiming

23.27 If either party is dissatisfied with the decision of the Lord Ordinary they may appeal to the Inner House of the Court of Session by marking a reclaiming motion under Rule of Court 38.6. An interlocutor, that is to say a decree of the court, determining an application for judicial review may be reclaimed against without leave within 21 days after it has been pronounced.[66] Interlocutors which may be pronounced during the course of the proceedings which do not determine the application may be reclaimed against only with the leave of the Lord Ordinary within 14 days after the date on which the interlocutor was pronounced.[67] Reclaiming motions against interlocutors in applications for judicial review are given a particular priority so as to ensure that the matter may be expeditiously resolved. Appeal may further be taken from the Inner House to the House of Lords. The procedural details of reclaiming and appeal, which are common to applications for judicial review and other forms of action, lie outwith the scope of the present work, as also are the procedural details for reference of devolution issues.[68]

Fees and expenses

23.28 Court fees are required to be paid for the lodging of the process documents and for the hearings in court, all as regulated by the current Court of Session Fees Order.[69] Expenses may be awarded in applications

---

[64] RCS, r. 58.10(4).

[65] *Andrew v. City of Glasgow D.C.* 1996 S.L.T. 814; see later on reduction.

[66] RCS, r. 38.3(2).

[67] RCS, r. 38.4(4).

[68] See Rules of Court Chap. 25A and the Judicial Committee (Devolution Issues) Rules Order 1999 (S.I. 1999 No. 665), and the Judicial Committee (Powers in Devolution Cases) Order 1999 (S.I. 1999 No. 1320).

[69] This can be conveniently found in the *Parliament House Book*.

for judicial review; and in exceptional cases, as when an authority has behaved in a vexatious way, it may be proper to make an award.[70] A similar approach has been adopted in valuation appeals.[71]

III REMEDIES

Introduction

In terms of Rule of Court 58.4(b) the court in exercising its supervisory **23.29** jurisdiction on a petition for judicial review may "make such order as it thinks fit, whether or not such order was sought in the petition, being an order that could be made if sought in any action or petition, including an order for reduction, declarator, suspension, interdict, implement, restitution, payment (whether of damages or otherwise) and any interim order". This wide provision, reflecting the essentially flexible nature of the whole procedure, calls for some particular comments. The first point is that the power to grant a remedy is not expressly confined to cases where the petitioner has been successful. There may be situations where it could be appropriate to grant a declarator affirming the position taken up by the respondent, and such a course appears to be open under the provisions of the rule.

The basis for a remedy

Secondly, it has to be remembered that the rule is only of procedural **23.30** significance. It does not in itself authorise any particular remedy. The rule "provides no remedy or relief which did not already exist".[72] The right to any remedy remains based on the principles of the ordinary law. Thus, for example, the power to make an award of damages contained in rule 58.4 does not innovate upon the ordinary legal requirements which have to be satisfied before an award of damages can properly be made. The remedies themselves are not unique to judicial review and it is accordingly inappropriate in the context of Scots law to adopt the English expression of "public law remedies".[73] The development of judicial review in England has been based upon remedies rather than, as has been the case in Scotland, principle.[74]

Equity

Thirdly, it should be noticed that the Scottish courts have never **23.31** recognised the distinction, which has played so significant a part in the development of English law and practice, between equity and the common law.[75] The distinction is reflected in the different approaches adopted towards the granting of such remedies as interdict and perfor-

---

[70] *Liddall v. Ballingry Parish Church* (1908) 16 S.L.T. 258. In England, where costs may follow the event, "pre-emptive cost" orders may be sought, where the court grants an order early in the process that no order for costs against the applicant will be made irrespective of the outcome: *R. v. Lord Chancellor, ex p. Child Poverty Action Group* [1998] 2 All E.R. 755. Awards for expenses are often not pursued: see Mullen and others, "Judicial Review in Scotland" (1997) 2 S.L.P.Q. 1 at p. 16.

[71] See Armour on *Valuation* (5th ed.), para. 5–61.

[72] *O'Neill v. Scottish Joint Negotiating Committee for Teachers*, 1987 S.C.CR. 275 at 277.

[73] As was done in *Connor v. Strathclyde R.C.*, 1986 S.L.T. 530.

[74] *West v. Secretary of State for Scotland*, 1992 S.C. 385, *per* Lord President Hope at 409.

[75] *Allen v. M'Combie's Trustees*, 1909 S.C. 710, *per* Lord President Dunedin at 716.

mance, even although the end result in any given case may be the same.[76] Thus in England injunction is primarily a discretionary remedy,[77] as also is the remedy of specific performance.[78] But in Scotland the basic position is that (apart from cases of interim orders) where operations have been found to be unlawful the wronged party has a definite right to an interdict[79] or an order for performance. However, particularly where the case involves a public authority (indeed it may be said in all cases where judicial review may arise), the element of discretion in granting such remedies as interdict or specific performance is undoubtedly present and may significantly qualify any legal right to the particular remedy. In matters of public right raised in an *actio popularis* the court may in the interests of the community refrain from enforcing the right and prefer some alternative solution in the exercise of an equitable discretion.[80] In *Grahame v. Magistrates of Kirkcaldy*, in which an inhabitant sought to interdict the magistrates from building upon lands held by them as a bleaching ground and recreation ground for the inhabitants, interdict was refused. Lord Chancellor Selborne observed[81]: "In Scotland the legal and equitable jurisdictions have always been united, and the natural result of that union is that strict legal rights ought not, in such a case as the present, to be enforced without regard to the discretion which from the nature of the subject matter, and of the interest of all those concerned in it, ought to be exercised in a court of equity." Lord Watson stressed the rarity of the court declining upon equitable grounds to enforce an admittedly legal right, requiring the existence of extraordinary circumstances and some very cogent reason for justifying the adoption of it. But where the court is dealing with a responsible public authority who can be trusted to comply with the findings of the court the discretion to withhold interdict may more easily be exercised.[82]

Discretion in the court

23.32 The fourth observation relates closely to the third. In terms of the rule, the court "may" grant any of the remedies. There is thus built in to the procedure a discretion to grant or refuse any particular remedy. That means that as a matter of procedure the court has a discretion whether or not in a current process of judicial review it will or will not grant any particular form of remedy. It is thought that a refusal to grant a particular remedy as a matter of discretion should not exclude or bar a separate action being subsequently raised for a specific remedy under the ordinary jurisdiction of the court. The decision whether or not to grant a particular remedy, such as damages, in the same process of judicial review could be influenced by considerations of procedural convenience,

---

[76] *Co-operative Insurance Society Ltd v. Argyll Stores (Holdings) Ltd* [1998] A.C. 1.

[77] *Colls v. Home and Colonial Stores Ltd* [1904] A.C. 179 at 192.

[78] *Co-operative Insurance Society Ltd v. Argyll Stores (Holdings) Ltd* [1997] 3 All E.R 934; compare *Co-operative Wholesale Society Ltd v. Saxone Ltd*, 1997 S.L.T. 1052.

[79] *Clippens Oil Co. Ltd v. Edinburgh and District Water Trustees* (1897) 25R. 370 at 382; *Wilson v. Pottinger*, 1908 S.C. 580; *Ferguson v. Tennant*, 1978 S.C.(H.L.) 19 at 47 and 52; *McIntyre v. Sheridan*, 1997 G.W.D. 20–933.

[80] *Grahame v. Magistrates of Kirkcaldy* (1882) 9R(H.L.) 91; *Macdonald v. Magistrates of Arbroath*, 1916 2 S.L.T. 303.

[81] (1882) 9R(H.L.) 96 at 97.

[82] *Scottish General Transport Co. Ltd. v. Glasgow Corporation*, 1928 S.C. 248. See *Perth General Station Committee v. Ross* (1897) 24R.(H.L.) 44 and *David Colville & Sons Ltd v. Dalziel Parish Church*, 1927 S.L.T. 118.

such as the sufficiency of the pleadings where some complex issue consequential upon the result of the petition arises. But matters of prescription and limitation might also have to be taken into account. On the other hand, while the rule is discretionary in its terms the intention of it should be that every possible remedy should be available in the one process so that no ancillary litigation should be necessary. The court should be encouraged to grant all the relief which the parties require in the same process.

Choice of order

Fifthly, and consistently with what has just been said, in deciding what remedy to give, the court should allow parties an opportunity to express their view on the propriety of any remedy, at least where it is one which the applicant has not expressly sought in his application. The court should not compel an applicant to accept a remedy which he has neither sought nor desired.[83]

23.33

The rule not comprehensive

Finally, the list of remedies set out in the rule should not be regarded as comprehensive. The remedies listed in the rule are stated as examples included in the remedies which may be granted. Any order not included in the list may be granted, provided it is an order which could be made if sought in any action or petition. One such order would be a remit to the determining body so that it can reconsider the case. This again stresses the point that the rule is not introducing new substantial remedies, but is only regulating procedure.

23.34

Particular remedies

Some consideration is given to the principal remedies in the next three chapters. It should, however, be stressed that little more than an outline is given and that for a more comprehensive examination reference should be made to the various specialised textbooks. In the present context regard is had particularly to remedies in relation to matters of judicial review, although many of the points to be made are of more general significance and can usefully be illustrated by examples from other situations where such remedies are also available.

23.35

Remedies against the Crown

The position of the Crown has already been considered in relation to the constitutional context of judicial review.[84] Particular problems may arise in relation to interdict. As has already been noted,[85] the Scottish Supreme Court did not suffer the restraint which prevented the English courts from proceeding against the Crown. Proceedings could not, however, be brought in any inferior court, so that interdict against the Crown in the Dean of Guild Court was incompetent.[86] Thus, on occasion interdict was granted against the Crown[87] or a minister.[88] On the other

23.36

---

[83] *Mecca Leisure Ltd v. City of Glasgow D.C.*, 1987 S.C.L.R. 26.
[84] paras 4.39 *et seq.*
[85] para. 2.11.
[86] *Somerville v. Lord Advocate* (1893) 20R. 105.
[87] *Green v. Lord Advocate*, 1918 S.C. 667.
[88] *Bell v. Secretary of State for Scotland*, 1933 S.L.T. 519.

hand, the Crown could not be sued for damages in respect of the "torts" or wrongful acts of its officers,[89] although debate continued on the scope of what was comprised in the Crown for this purpose.[90] However, this freedom came to be restricted by Parliament in terms of the Crown Proceedings Act 1947, section 21(1)(a), whereby neither interdict nor specific performance could be granted against the Crown, a declarator being available in place of such remedies. This has been taken to extend to interim interdict.[91] However, rules of national law must give way to the requirements of Community law and if the restraint on seeking an interim remedy against the Crown is the only obstacle to the granting of relief in a case concerning Community law, then that rule must be set aside.[92] On that approach an order *ad factum praestandum* has been granted against an officer of the Crown.[93] A health board does not fall within section 21 of the Crown Proceedings Act 1947 and so may competently be interdicted; it was observed that the purpose of the Act was to make it easier rather than more difficult for a subject to sue the Crown.[94] The matter of public interest immunity has been considered in relation to the constitutional context of judicial review.[95] It may be noted that under the Scotland Act 1998 the definition of "officer" includes a member of the Scottish Executive.[96]

Statutory orders for performance

23.37　The remedy available under statute for ordering the performance of a statutory duty is considered later.[97] In *Carlton Hotel Co v. Lord Advocate*,[98] Lord Salvesen expressed the opinion that an order for specific performance under what was then section 91 of the Court of Session Act 1868 could competently be pronounced against the Crown. A question arises here regarding the effect of the Crown Proceedings Act 1947. That Act prohibits the granting of interdict against the Crown.[99] The Act also deals with specific performance, the English equivalent of implement, but there is no mention of section 91 of the Act of 1868 (now section 45(b) of the Court of Session Act 1988). There is thus a probability that the statutory remedy, which is distinct in its nature and origin from implement, should be available as a remedy against the Crown.

---

[89] *Wilson v. 1st Edinburgh City Royal Garrison Artillery Volunteers* (1904) 7F. 168. The immunity of the Crown's servants from liability for negligence was affirmed in *Macgregor v. Lord Advocate*, 1921 S.C. 847 at 853.

[90] A medical board was not regarded as falling within the scope of the Crown in *Smith v. Lord Advocate*, 1932 S.L.T. 374.

[91] *McDonald v. Secretary of State for Scotland*, 1994 S.L.T. 692. See I.S. Dickinson, "Interim Relief Against the Crown–An Update", 1989 S.L.T. (News) 365; "The Scope for Interim Relief Against Ministers of the Crown", 1993 S.L.T. (News) 311, and "Still No Interdicts Against the Crown", 1994 S.L.T.(News) 217. It has been suggested that the decision in *McDonald* may now have to be reconsidered: Christine Boch, "Interim Remedies Against the Crown Revisited", 1997 S.L.T. News 165.

[92] *R. v. Secretary of State for Transport, ex p. Factortame (No. 2)* [1991] A.C. 603. See J. Algazy, "The Crown, Interim Relief and EEC Law" (1991) 141 N.L.J. 1303.

[93] *Miller & Bryce v. Keeper of the Registers of Scotland*, 1997 S.L.T. 1000.

[94] *British Medical Association v. Greater Glasgow Health Board*, 1989 S.C.(H.L.) 65.

[95] See para. 4.52.

[96] Sched. 8, para. 7(2)(b).

[97] paras 26.10 *et seq.*

[98] 1921 S.C. 237 at 249.

[99] s.21(2) as applied by s.43(a).

England

After much doubt injunctions, including interim injunctions, are now **23.38** available in England against the Crown and its officers in judicial review proceedings, both where E.C. law is involved and generally.[1] Although it had been held that section 21 of the Crown Proceedings Act 1947 prevented injunctions against the Crown and its officers,[2] and although the House of Lords had previously reached the same conclusion,[3] in *M v. Home Office* the House of Lords decided that the Supreme Court Act 1981, which placed the new judicial review procedure on a statutory footing, meant that injunctions are available against the Crown and ministers in the same way as they are against other respondents in judicial review proceedings.[4] However, by virtue of section 21 of the Crown Proceedings Act 1947, it remains the law that injunction is not available against the Crown and its officers outside judicial review proceedings, that is, in "civil proceedings", and the decision in *Re M* is not binding in Scotland since it is mainly based on the provisions of the Supreme Court Act 1981 which only applies in England and Wales.[5]

The Scottish Parliament

Mention has already been made of the procedural provisions for dealing **23.39** with devolution issues under the Scotland Act 1998 and the persons against whom proceedings for review may be taken.[6] The Scotland Act 1998 provides for the taking of proceedings against the Parliamentary corporation on behalf of the Parliament.[7] Section 40(3), however, imposes restraints upon the remedies which may be given in proceedings against the Parliament. The court is not to "make any order for

---

[1] *M. v. Home Office (Re M)* [1994] 2 A.C. 377. De Smith, *Judicial Review*, p. 719 notes that in practice injunctions against the Crown and its officers will be rare and will amount to "no more than a peremptory declaration". In *M*, the older tradition, shaken by *R. v. Secretary of State for Transport, ex p. Factortame* [1990] 2 A.C. 85, was reaffirmed; injunctions are available against ministers of the Crown in judicial review proceedings in England and Wales although they are by virtue of the Crown Proceedings Act 1947, s.21 not available against the Crown directly. In Scotland, however, the 19th century conflation of the Crown with all its officers still seems to mean that (except in any matter involving E.C. law) interdicts are not available against the Crown or its ministers: see the foregoing paragraph, *McDonald v. Secretary of State for Scotland*, 1994 S.L.T. 692. See Edwards, "Interdict and the Crown in Scotland" (1995) 111 L.Q.R. 34.

[2] *Merricks v. Heathcoat-Amory* [1955] Ch. 567; *cf. R. v. Secretary of State for the Home Department, ex p. Herbage* [1987] Q.B. 872, *per* Hodgson J. at 884; and *R. v. Licensing Authority, ex p. Smith Kline & French Laboratories Ltd. (No. 2)* [1990] Q.B. 574 (both holding that injunctions are available against officers of the Crown; both overruled in *Factortame (No. 1)* [1990] 2 A.C. 85).

[3] *Factortame v. Secretary of State for Transport* [1990] 2 A.C. 85 (known as *Factortame No. 1*).

[4] See n. 1 to para. 23.38, *supra*.

[5] In *McDonald v. Secretary of State for Scotland*, 1994 S.L.T. 692 an argument was presented to the effect that proceedings for judicial review did not fall within "civil proceedings" within the meaning of s.21. The Lord Justice-Clerk (Ross) observed (698) that there were formidable difficulties in the way of such a submission, but the point was not decided and remains open for determination.

[6] See paras 7.47 *et seq.* and the Act of Sederunt (Devolution Issues Rules) 1999 (S.I. 1999 No. 1345) (1999 S.L.T. (News) 196) (introducing Chap. 25A to the Rules of Court), the Act of Sederunt (Proceedings for Determination of Devolution Issues Rules) 1999 (S.I. 1999 No. 1347) (1999 S.L.T. (News) 204), and the Act of Adjournal (Devolution Issues Rules) (S.I. 1999 No. 1282) (1999 S.L.T. (News) 183), amending the Criminal Procedure Rules.

[7] s.40(1) of the Scotland Act 1998.

suspension, interdict, reduction, or specific performance (or other like order) but may instead make a declarator". A corresponding provision is made by section 40(3) in respect of proceedings against any member of the Parliament, the Presiding Officer or a deputy, any member of the staff of the Parliament or the Parliamentary corporation, where the effect of any such order would be to give relief against the Parliament which could not have been given in proceedings against the Parliament. Where a declarator is granted it is to be expected that the appropriate remedy will be forthcoming, albeit not by virtue of a directly enforceable order.

CHAPTER 24

DECLARATOR AND REDUCTION

I   DECLARATOR
II   REDUCTION

General

The two remedies most closely associated nowadays with the supervisory **24.01**
jurisdiction may reasonably be said to be those of declarator and
reduction. While both are available and used in a wide variety of other
contexts, the remedy of declarator has a particular utility in enabling a
judicial statement of the unlawfulness of actings which are challenged
under the supervisory jurisdiction; and the remedy of reduction is the
essential method of cancelling a decision which has been the subject of a
successful application for review.

I   DECLARATOR

Introduction

The ability of the supreme court in Scotland to pronounce a declarator, **24.02**
or declaration, is of considerable antiquity. It took the place of the
ancient brieve of right[1] which used to be tried by jury. After the
institution of the College of Justice in 1532 the system of civil juries was
discontinued and the procedure of seeking a declarator by way of a
summons came to be established. In developing this practice the court
was no doubt influenced both by the existing procedures of the Court of
the Official[2] and the traditions of practice in France.[3] Examples of
decrees of declarator being pronounced can be found in the early reports
of cases coming before the newly constituted court in the sixteenth
century.[4] Actions of declarator formed one of the three groups of actions
identified by Viscount Stair, the others being petitory and possessory
actions. He stated[5]: "Declaratory actions are those, wherein the right of
the pursuer is craved to be declared, but nothing is claimed to be done
by the defender." The process of declarator was said by Lord Gifford to
be "deeply rooted in the law of Scotland and in the practice of its
Supreme Court".[6]

Effect

A declarator does not confer any new right but simply declares the **24.03**
existence of a right. As Erskine put it: "A declaratory action is that in
which some right, either of property or of servitude, or some inferior

---

[1] Stair, *Institutes* 4, 4, 1; see also 4, 3, 47.
[2] See Vol. 34 of the Stair Society publications: *The Court of the Official.*
[3] See the article by R.S., "The Scotch Action of Declarator" (1849) 41 *The Law
Magazine* 173 at 180–181.
[4] *e.g.* Lord Borthwick (1541)M. 3407.
[5] Stair, *Institutes*, 4, 3, 47.
[6] *Fleming v. Fraser's Trustees* (1879) 6R. 588 at 596.

right, is sought to be declared in favour of the pursuer, but where nothing is demanded to be paid or performed by the defender."[7] It may be a right which has come into being at some time in the past, so that in that respect the declarator may be to an extent retrospective. On the other hand, in some cases, such as a delarator of marriage or a declarator of irritancy, the formal existence of the right may be dated from the date of the declarator. The declarator will often suffice by itself to enable parties to proceed lawfully and properly without the need for any more positive remedy. But where an unlawful decision has been made it may often be undesirable to dispose of it by a reduction rather than let it stand.[8] The matter is very much one of practice in the particular circumstances of each case.

Value

24.04 The value and convenience of a declarator has been recognised throughout the centuries of its use in Scotland. The process was described by Lord Jeffrey as "the triumph and pride of our judicial system."[9] When the case of *Earl of Mansfield v. Stewart* reached the House of Lords, Lord Brougham observed[10]: "My Lords, I cannot close my observations in this case without once more expressing my great envy, as an English lawyer, of the Scotch jurisprudence, and of those who enjoy under it the security and the various facilities and conveniences which they have from that most beneficial and most admirably-contrived form of proceeding, called a declaratory action". It was through the efforts of Lord Brougham and others that statutory reforms were introduced in England during the latter part of the nineteenth century to develop the availability of a declaratory relief in that country.[11]

Wide application

24.05 Lord Dunedin observed that "one great merit of the Scottish action of declarator is its elasticity".[12] As Lord Stair put it, the action may be pursued for instructing and clearing any kind of right relating to liberty, dominion or obligation.[13] Thus in the exercise of the ordinary jurisdiction of the Court of Session a declarator has been used in a very wide range of cases. These include matters of status, such as declarators of marriage,[14] or of membership of an association,[15] matters of succession, such as the validity of a will,[16] matters of trust administration, such as whether a renunciation granted by a beneficiary was valid,[17] matters of property, such as the existence of a public right of way,[18] and matters of

---

[7] Erskine, *Institutes*, 4, 1, 46.
[8] See para. 24.26.
[9] *Edinburgh & Glasgow Ry Co. v. Meek* (1849) 12D. 153 at 162.
[10] (1846) 5 Bell's App. 139 at 160.
[11] For the history of the remedy in England, see Zamir & Woolf on *The Declaratory Judgment*, (2nd ed.), 1993. Provision was made in England for declaratory relief by the Chancery Act 1850 and the Chancery Procedure Act 1852.
[12] *North British Ry v. Birrell's Trustees*, 1918 S.C.(H.L.) 33 at 47.
[13] *Institutes*, 4, 3, 47.
[14] This has been and still to an extent is of particular value in the cases of the irregular forms of marriage recognised under Scots law: *e.g. Petrie v. Petrie*, 1922 S.C. 360.
[15] *e.g. Martin v. Scottish Transport and General Workers Union* 1952 S.C.(H.L.) 1.
[16] *e.g. Chisholm v. Chisholm*, 1949 S.C. 434.
[17] *Douglas-Hamilton v. Duke and Duchess of Hamilton's Trustees*, 1961 S.C. 205.
[18] *Norrie v. Kirriemuir Magistrates*, 1945 S.C. 302.

contract, such as whether or not a contract has been concluded.[19] Very many examples over a wide range of matters can be found in the reported cases.

Declarators of status

Matters of status, including the holding of a particular office, may **24.06** consequentially involve matters of right. A declarator of status may be granted where there is a practical utility in the granting of it.[20] In this context there may be no necessity for there to be a contradictor and, for example, actions for declarator of marriage or of nullity of marriage may often proceed as undefended actions. Where someone has been divorced in a foreign country and wishes to have that divorce recognised in Scotland a declarator may be granted although the action is not defended and there are no consequential orders sought.[21] Where the issue is one concerning the membership of a body or the holding of some office there will probably be a fairly evident purpose to be served by the obtaining of the declarator. In one case the pursuer sought a declarator that he was a member of a trade union and the reduction of a resolution which had purported to terminate it.[22] In another case a member of the body known as Jehovah's Witnesses, who was claiming exemption from national service, sought a declarator that he was a "regular minister of a religious denomination".[23] Where there is no purpose beyond the use of the declarator as evidence in proceedings before some other court or tribunal the decree may be refused.[24] A declarator that a pursuer is entitled to a particular military rank has been refused.[25]

Availability in judicial review

Declarators are of particular value in cases of judicial review. The **24.07** remedy is available to declare any of the many forms of unlawfulness which may be established on any of the various grounds for judicial review which have already been considered.[26] Thus, for example, it may be used to declare the limits of supply of a water board,[27] the legality of a particular procedure,[28] whether resolutions for the increase of rents of houses owned by a housing association were *ultra vires*,[29] or whether toll moneys had been properly applied.[30] The subject-matter with which it may be concerned thus includes the legality, possibly including legality under the criminal law, of actings past, continuing or future.[31] Even if no

---

[19] *Low v. Thomson*, 1978 S.C. 343.

[20] *Broit v. Broit*, 1972 S.C. 193.

[21] *e.g. Galbraith v. Galbraith*, 1971 S.C. 65, where decree of divorce was sought as an alternative; *Bain v. Bain*, 1971 S.C. 146. In *Di Rollo v. Di Rollo*, 1959 S.C. 75 the pursuer sought divorce or declarator that the marriage had been annulled.

[22] *Martin v. Scottish Transport and General Workers Union*, 1952 S.C.(H.L.) 1. See also *Berry v. Transport and General Workers Union*, 1933 S.N. 110.

[23] *Walsh v. Lord Advocate*, 1956 S.C.(H.L.) 126.

[24] See paras 13.02 *et seq.* on the need for a proper purpose.

[25] *Smith v. Lord Advocate* (1897) 25R. 112.

[26] See Chaps 14–22.

[27] *Grangemouth v. Stirlingshire and Falkirk Water Board*, 1963 S.C.(H.L.) 49.

[28] *Magistrates of Ayr v. Lord Advocate*, 1950 S.C. 102.

[29] *Midlothian County Council v. Scottish Special Housing Association*, 1959 S.C. 8.

[30] *Guild v. Scott*, Dec. 21, 1809, *Faculty Decisions* 469, where the declarator was expressed as a finding. Further examples may be found in the Law Commission Memorandum No. 14 (1971), para. 7.3.

[31] See para. 8.39 for a consideration of the declarator of criminal actings.

stronger form of order is required a declarator will always be available to express the substance of the court's view and it can readily be fortified by an additional order such as interdict or performance or reduction. Correspondingly, it is susceptible to the defences which have been considered as restraints on the availability of judicial review.[32] As Lord Dunedin once observed of the action of declarator[33]: "The rules that have been elucidated by a long course of decisions in the Scottish Courts may be summarised thus: The question must be a real and not a theoretical question: the person raising it must have a real interest to raise it; he must be able to secure a proper contradictor, that is to say, someone presently existing who has a true interest to oppose the declaration sought." Of particular importance in relation to declarator is the necessity for a real issue, a point which has been considered earlier.[34] Examples can be found in relation to the construction of statutes.

Declarators on the meaning or validity of statutes

24.08 Since a declarator will not be granted to affirm a general proposition about which there is no dispute, it is not competent to seek a declarator of a proposition already clearly laid down in an Act of Parliament. But where the language of the statute is ambiguous and there is a real interest in having the meaning declared, a declarator may competently be granted.[35] While it is not competent to seek a declarator in the abstract as to the meaning of an Act of Parliament, where the question concerns the application of a statute to particular circumstances, then the matter can be made the subject of a declarator, even although a general question of construction may be involved in the determination of the issue. Thus the question whether a particular street was a public or a private street within the terms of a statute,[36] and what was meant by the "width" of a street for the purposes of a register of streets under a statutory provision,[37] have been held to be competent matters for a declarator. Questions of the liability to local rates of bodies claiming to be of a charitable character for that purpose have been determined by actions for declarator[38] and, with the possible exception of cases where there is only a minor detail in dispute,[39] the action can be used in advance of any formal demand for the tax being made.[40] In *Hogg* (the case just referred to), Lord Young observed[41]: "A question of liability, on the one hand, or exemption from liability on the other, to pay a continuing money payment, whether that liability depends on the application of statute law or of common law to the facts of a particular case, may always be raised in a declarator." In *Lord Advocate v.*

---

[32] The restraints on the scope of review have been considered particularly in Chaps 9–13.

[33] *Russian Commercial and Industrial Bank v. British Bank for Foreign Trade Ltd* [1921] 2 A.C. 438 at 448, quoted by Lord Goff of Chieveley in *Re F (Mental Patient: Sterilisation)* [1990] 2 A.C. 1 at 82.

[34] See paras 13.02 *et seq.*

[35] Mackay's *Manual of Practice*, p. 376.

[36] *Leith Police Commissioners v. Campbell* (1866) 5M. 247; the action was held incompetent for other reasons.

[37] *Caledonian Ry v. Glasgow Corporation* (1905) 7F. 1020.

[38] *Cowan v. Gordon* (1868) 6M. 1018; *Belhaven-Westbourne Church v. Glasgow Corporation*, 1965 S.C.(H.L.) 1; *Scottish Burial Reform and Cremation Society v. Glasgow Corporation*, 1967 S.C.(H.L.) 116.

[39] *Edinburgh and Glasgow Ry v. Meek* (1849) 12D. 153, *per* Lord Fullerton at 159.

[40] *Hogg v. Parochial Board of Auchtermuchty* (1850) 7R. 986.

[41] *ibid.* at 992.

Dumbarton District Council[42] a negative declarator was sought to the effect that certain sections of the Roads (Scotland) Act 1984 had no application to certain works carried out by or on behalf of the Crown.

Uses of declarator

It is expressly provided by section 21 of the Crown Proceedings Act **24.09** 1947, as applied to Scotland by section 43, that where an interdict might otherwise have been granted in proceedings against the Crown, the court may instead grant a declarator of the rights of the parties.[43] But even in cases where no such formal prohibition lies on the granting of an interdict there are often cases where it is not necessary nor desirable to grant a more potent remedy, such as a reduction or an interdict, and the parties can proceed to resolve the practical aspects of their dispute themselves once their respective rights or obligations have been clarified and made the subject of a declarator. It is often useful in any event to preface other conclusions with a declarator, in order to focus the issue in dispute and enable it to be determined as a distinct matter in addition to any other consequential remedy.

Bare declarators

In ordinary civil actions a declarator will frequently be found along with **24.10** another conclusion or conclusions, such as a reduction or an interdict. In such a context it serves to bring into focus the precise issue on which some other conclusion may depend. It is always competent to include a declarator along with petitory, reductive or possessory conclusions, which will enable effect to be given to the rights so declared, and in some cases in ordinary actions it is necessary to preface the other conclusions with a declarator.[44] But a declaratory conclusion may competently stand by itself, provided that it has a legal consequence and a practical effect.[45] Where a declarator would not be abstract or hypothetical but would decide a live practical question, it can competently be granted by itself, particularly where it resolves a problem which is at the root of the controversy between the parties.[46] But where no consequent right flows from the declarator, it will be incompetent, as where a declarator was sought on the method to be adopted in determining a development charge which had already been decided by the body responsible.[47] In the context of judicial review a bare declarator is often a convenient remedy to be granted since the parties are simply concerned to have a judicial resolution of the point in issue and there is no practical necessity for an executive conclusion. A bare declarator which challenges the legality of an electricity tariff[48] or affirms the correct construction of a statutory provision on which the calculation of a due payment requires to be made[49] has been recognised as competent. In proceedings against the

---

[42] 1990 S.C.(H.L.) 1.
[43] See para. 23.36.
[44] Maclaren, *Court of Session Practice*, pp. 647–648.
[45] See the consideration of real issues in paras 13.02 *et seq.*
[46] *Unigate Foods v. Scottish Milk Marketing Board*, 1975 S.C.(H.L.) 75, *per* Lord Fraser at 110.
[47] *Sinclair-Lockhart's Trustees v. Central Land Board*, 1950 S.L.T. 283, affd 1951 S.C. 258.
[48] *British Oxygen Co. Ltd v. South-West Scotland Electricity Board*, 1958 S.C. 53, 1959 S.C.(H.L.) 17.
[49] *Unigate Foods Ltd v. The Scottish Milk Marketing Board, supra.*

Crown where, as has been mentioned above, a declaratory order may be competent, the question whether a bare declarator is competent has been raised but not determined.[50] If it is competent to declare an Act of Parliament invalid, that could be done by a bare declarator.[51] Such a course may be appropriate where proceedings are instituted for the resolution of a devolution issue under Schedule 6 to the Scotland Act 1998.[52]

Negative declarators

24.11   A declarator in negative terms, asserting a negative, may competently be granted. The negative may be implicit in the wording, such as a declarator that a marriage is null or that a byelaw is *ultra vires*, or it may be express in the terms of the declarator, such as a declarator that an alleged right of way does not exist,[53] or that the defender had no right of ferry,[54] or that the defender was not entitled to erect a particular building,[55] or that a hotelier had no right to enter a railway station without the leave of a railway company,[56] or that under particular statutory provisions a valuation of a railway entered in the valuation roll was not the value for the purposes of local rates,[57] or that the insertion of a condition in a licence was not *ultra vires*,[58] or that certain persons had no right or title to object to the granting of a lease.[59]

Interim declarator

24.12   In *Ayr Town Council v. Secretary of State for Scotland*[60] the pursuer sought a declarator to the effect that an order which the Secretary of State proposed to make under the Water (Scotland) Act 1946 was *ultra vires* and a second declarator that it was the duty of the Secretary of State to refrain from causing a local inquiry to be held into the order. The pursuer moved for an interim decree to be granted in terms of the second declarator, and also an interim interdict against the reporter appointed by the Secretary of State from holding the inquiry. Lord Fraser expressed no opinion on the general question whether an interim declarator could ever be granted.[61] He refused to grant the interim declarator on the ground that he could only grant it on the assumption that the first conclusion (the declarator that the Secretary of State had acted *ultra vires*), was well founded and that the averments relating to it were correct; the declarator which he was being asked to grant was accordingly hypothetical, and the Crown Proceedings Act 1947 did not entitle him to make a hypothetical order of the rights of parties. In

---

[50] *Griffin v. Lord Advocate*, 1950 S.C. 448.
[51] *Gibson v. Lord Advocate*, 1975 S.C. 136.
[52] For devolution issues, see para. 7.04.
[53] *Hope v. Gemmill* (1898) 1F. 74.
[54] *Tay Ferry Trustees v. Edinburgh, Perth and District Ry* (1851) 14D. 103.
[55] *Midlothian County Council v. Musselburgh Co-operative Society*, 1960 S.C. 177.
[56] *Perth General Station Commissioners v. Ross* (1897) 24R.(H.L.) 44.
[57] *West Highland Ry v. County Council of Inverness* (1904) 6F. 1052.
[58] *Rossi v. Magistrates of Edinburgh* (1903) 5F. 480.
[59] *North British Ry v. Birrell's Trustees*, 1918 S.C.(H.L.) 33.
[60] 1965 S.C. 394.
[61] It may be noted that in his work on *Constitutional Law* (1948), p. 166, W.I.R. Fraser (as he then was) wrote, in the context of interdict against the Crown, that "Presumably it will be possible in future to obtain an interim declaratory order, corresponding to an interim interdict, for these purposes".

holding that the Act did not allow him to make an order without prejudging the issue in the case, he followed the approach taken in an earlier case by Lord Strachan.[62] While the English courts have denied the competency of an interim declarator as being a contradiction in terms,[63] arguments have been presented to the opposite effect.[64] The point is still open in Scottish practice and, while the occasions for requiring to use such a remedy may be rare, it is for serious consideration whether such an interim form of relief should not be available, particularly in cases of judicial review against the Crown.[65]

Rights not facts

A declarator is properly an affirmation of the existence or non-existence **24.13** of a right. It should accordingly be more than a mere finding of some particular matter or matters of fact. A declarator will not be granted to declare an abstract fact, such as that a person is a trustee, without any conclusion resulting from that.[66] Similarly, a declarator that the land-holders of Shetland exercised the privilege of freeholders in the election of members of Parliament was held incompetent as a declarator of a fact.[67] But it is competent to express in a declarator matters of fact which have been established and which constitute the basis for the consequential declaration of the matter of right which the pursuer seeks to have affirmed or a more positive order proceeding upon the rights arising from the declared facts. Thus in *Highland Regional Council v. British Railways Board*[68] a reduction of a decision to close a railway line was prefaced by a declarator that a proposal to withdraw a sleeper service constituted a proposal to discontinue all passenger services over certain sections of the line.

Need for precision

The wording of a declarator must be precise and unambiguous. A **24.14** declarator in terms which are vague or ambiguous will not be granted.[69] Care accordingly has to be taken in the formulation of the declarator appropriate to the circumstances of the case, particularly where it forms the basis for an interdict, breach of which may have quasi-criminal consequences.

---

[62] *Robertson v. Lord Advocate*, Mar. 25, 1950. The opinion is printed at the end of the report of the *Ayr Town Council* case. For remedies against the Crown, see para. 23.36.

[63] *International General Electric Company of New York Ltd v. Commissioners of Customs and Excise* [1962] 2 Ch. 784, approving *Underhill v. Ministry of Food* [1950] 1 All E.R. 591; also *R. v. I.R.C. ex p. Rossminster* [1980] A.C. 1014.

[64] See Zamir & Woolf. *The Declaratory Judgment* (1993), pp. 81–86. The view has been expressed that the English courts have the jurisdiction to grant an interlocutory declaration and an express provision for an interim declaration has been proposed: De Smith, Woolf and Jowell, *Judicial Review of Administrative Action* (5th ed.), para. 18–016, first cum. supp. para. 18–015.

[65] The decision of the Israel Supreme Court affirming the competency of an interim declaration in *Yotvin Engineers and Constructors Ltd v. State of Israel* 34 P.D.(2) 344, set out in the Appendix to Zamir & Woolf, is of interest in this question.

[66] *Lyle v. Balfour* (1830) 9S. 22.

[67] *Gifford v. Trail* (1829) 7S. 854.

[68] 1996 S.L.T. 274.

[69] *Aberdeen Development Co. v. Mackie, Ramsay and Taylor*, 1977 S.L.T. 177.

Need for a particular consequence

24.15 A declarator must be related to the particular facts of the particular issue. A declarator "not with reference to any particular case, but in general" is incompetent.[70] Thus a statement of the legal relations in general between innkeepers and travellers will not be a competent matter for a declarator.[71] A declarator will not be granted of abstract principles with no immediate effect on the parties.[72]

Need for proper purpose

24.16 A declarator will not be granted simply in order that it may be used as evidence in some other court or tribunal and which does not finally settle anything so far as the pursuer is concerned. Thus in *Menzies v. M'Kenna*[73] a declarator that the pursuer was the heir of a certain deceased person was refused as incompetent because the only purpose of the action was to use the decree as evidence before the Privy Council in support of the pursuer's claim to be placed on the Roll of Baronets.

Declarator in the sheriff court

24.17 It was provided by section 5(1) of the Sheriff Courts Act 1907 that the jurisdiction of the sheriff should extend to and include actions of declarator, subject to certain exceptions more recently restricted to declarations of marriage or of nullity of marriage.[74] But apart from these statutory restrictions, it is well established that the section did not confer a new jurisdiction on the sheriff court, but simply added to the forms of procedure which could be available there.[75] Matters which fall within the scope of the supervisory jurisdiction of the Court of Session accordingly cannot be made the subject of a declarator in the sheriff court. Care then has to be taken to secure that, even although the form of action may be competent in the sheriff court, the substance of the matter is not one falling within the exclusive jurisdiction of the Court of Session.[76]

II REDUCTION

Nature of the remedy

24.18 Stair said of reduction that it was "peculiar to this nation, and is a more absolute security of men's rights than any form of process in Roman law or in any neighbouring nation".[77] He recognised a distinction between reduction of decrees and reductions of other rights[78] and in relation to the latter treated the remedy of reduction as a negative declaration of a right, and so considered that they were to be classified as declaratory

---

[70] *Callender's Cable and Construction Co. Ltd v. Corporation of Glasgow* (1902) 2F. 397, *per* Lord Adam at 401.
[71] *Rothfield v. North British Ry*, 1920 S.C. 805.
[72] *Griffin v. Lord Advocate*, 1950 S.C. 448.
[73] 1914 S.C. 272.
[74] The amendment was made by the Law Reform (Parent and Child) (Scotland) Act 1986, Sched. 2.
[75] *Brown v. Hamilton D.C.*, 1983 S.C.(H.L.) 1, *per* Lord Fraser at 45.
[76] *e.g. McDonald v. Secretary of State for Scotland (No. 2)*, 1996 S.L.T. 575.
[77] *Institutes*, 4, 20, 8.
[78] For the history of reduction, see Walker, *History*, Vol. IV, p. 592.

actions.[79] In relation to rights founded on deeds, while a declarator may affirm a right, a reduction reduces and annuls a pretended right by reducing the writ which is necessary for the right. Erskine[80] identified a distinct category of rescissory actions which he defined as "those which our law has established for the voiding of deeds, services, decrees, or other writings, or of illegal acts done by any body-corporate or society of men, ex. gr. the election of magistrates or other public officers". This distinction between reduction generally and reduction of decrees as a means of review is important in the present context. It is reflected in the approach taken by Erskine[81] and is recognised by writers on matters of practice[82] and in case law.[83] Reduction of decrees may or may not involve an exercise of the supervisory jurisdiction.[84] Reduction of a sheriff court decree on the ground of *ultra vires* would involve the supervisory jurisdiction, since a question of the extent of the power of the court is involved. But reduction of an otherwise competent decree of the court on the ground of a mistake by one of the parties to the case is a matter for the ordinary, and not the supervisory, jurisdiction.[85] In relation to reductions of rights a further distinction of procedural significance also used to be recognised between what was known as a simple reduction and a reduction-improbation.[86] The latter term referred to cases where falsehood and forgery were alleged and were dealt with in the Bill Chamber. However, the difference in procedure fell into disuse and is no longer recognised. The closest corresponding English remedy is that of certiorari.[87]

Availability

In *Adair v. Colville & Sons*[88] Viscount Dunedin observed: **24.19**

> "I shall not attempt, for I think such attempt would end in failure, to define categorically the cases in which reduction is competent. One obvious instance would be where a judgment has been obtained by reason of some fraud practised on the court; but, generally speaking, it is certainly not competent when other means of review are prescribed, and these means have either been utilised or the parties have failed to take advantage of them . . . it is not possible to set right by the form of reduction what could have been set right by appeal."

Reduction of a decree pronounced by a justice of the peace has been held not to be available where the decree had not been extracted: the

---

[79] Stair, *Institutes*, 4, 20, 2.
[80] *Institutes*, 4, 1, 18.
[81] *Institutes*, 4, 3, 8.
[82] *e.g.* Mackay's *Manual of Practice*, p. 391; Maclaren's *Court of Session Practice*, pp 82–84 and 675.
[83] *J and J v. C's Tutor*, 1948 S.C. 636 at 645.
[84] *Gilmour Transport Sevices Ltd v. Renfrew D.C.*, 1982 S.L.T. 290 at 291.
[85] *Bell v. Fiddes*, 1996 S.L.T. 51.
[86] Stair, *Institutes*, 4, 20, 3 *et seq.*
[87] In *R. v. East Berkshire Health Authority, ex p. Walshe* [1985] Q.B. 152, Sir John Donaldson M.R. observed (at 162) that the Scottish procedure of reduction was "akin to certiorari, but it is available whether or not the claim involves 'public' or 'administrative' law". See Loewensohn (1942) 58 S.L.R. 4 for a comparative law study.
[88] 1926 S.C.(H.L.) 51 at 56.

case was one in which the value of the cause was such as to exclude advocation but suspension was available.[89] It was observed by Lord Deas[90] that "Laying aside the case in which review is altogether excluded, I have always understood that while reduction is the appropriate method of reviewing a final judgment where no other remedy is competent, and in certain other cases where another remedy is competent, these other cases must be brought within one or other of the two categories, viz., either, 1st, where the judgment has been extracted, or 2nd, where it is a judgment which falls to be executed without extract."[91] Reduction is not barred by an earlier process of suspension in the same matter, the latter not constituting *res judicata*.[92] But where the statute anticipated that a reduction *ex post facto* should be the proper form of remedy an interim interdict was refused.[93] Reduction cannot be granted *ad interim*.

As a mode of review

24.20   In *Mathewson v. Yeaman* Lord Traynor observed[94]: "the right of review by reduction is a common law right which has existed for a very long time, and is a mode of review which cannot be taken away except by statutory enactment". As was recognised in that case, reduction may be used where there has been an error in the writing out of the sheriff's interlocutor but should not be used to review the merits of the dispute.[95] Reduction is of the essence of the process of judicial review and while in particular cases it may not turn out to be the decree actually awarded on success, it will very often be the principal remedy sought.

Production

24.21   In an ordinary action of reduction the document to be reduced has first to be produced. If the document is in the possession of the defender the pursuer will seek production as well as reduction of the document. If it is in the possession of the pursuer he will produce it with the summons.[96] In an ordinary action production may be deferred in light of any objection tabled by the defender, but beyond that a failure in production of the document may lead to the pursuer obtaining decree by default.[97] In an application for judicial review, however, production does not feature as a distinct stage in the process. The resolution or determination which is under challenge will in ordinary course be lodged at the outset of the process or at least lodged after its recovery by the petitioner.[98] The petitioner will usually have a copy of it and will lodge it with the application and if an original or more formal version is required

---

[89] *Scoular v. M'Laughlan* (1864) 2M. 955.

[90] at 962.

[91] Any alternative remedy should be pursued before resort is had to reduction, even where the reduction falls under the ordinary and not the supervisory jurisdiction: *J&C Blach (Haulage) Ltd v. Alltransport International Group Ltd*, 1980 S.C. 57 (reduction of a decree by default through oversight).

[92] *Caledonian Ry v. Lockhart* (1855) 17D. 775.

[93] *Anderson v. Kirkintilloch Magistrates*, 1948 S.C. 27.

[94] (1900) 2F. 873 at 881.

[95] For a consideration of reduction of sheriff court decrees, see Macphail, *Sheriff Court Practice* (2nd ed.), para. 18.05.

[96] See RCS, r. 53.5.

[97] RCS, r. 53.4.2.

[98] See the preceding chapter on procedure: para. 23.10.

then it may be ordered to be lodged during the early stages of the procedure.

Reduction in judicial review

In the context of judicial review the focus of the challenge is usually **24.22** directed upon a decision of some kind. The decisions will in most cases be written or recorded in writing, and any distinction between decrees, resolutions or actings should not be of consequence. There must be something to reduce. An invalid and ineffective decree is a fit subject for reduction, even although it could be said that in such a case, since nothing effective has been done, there is nothing to review.[99] Moreover, the invalidity is not such as to render the decision incapable of appeal so that if there is an appeal available a decision which is invalid and ineffective may quite properly be the subject of the appeal, a point which has been recognised in England[1] as well as Scotland.[2] The essential ground on which reduction will be granted will be the invalidity of the decision in question, and that invalidity may be in respect of any of the various grounds which have been canvassed in earlier chapters of this book.[3] An action for reduction, rather than an application to the supervisory jurisdiction, is the proper course where a decree in absence has been granted by an oversight.[4]

Examples of reduction of determinations

Some examples of the kinds of decisions which are open to reduction **24.23** may be given.[5] They include decisions by licensing authorities to grant or refuse licence, such as a licensing appeal court,[6] decisions of a disciplinary tribunal,[7] a decision by a valuation tribunal,[8] decisions by a committee regarding inclusion on an official list of opticians,[9] a decision by a board to dismiss a doctor,[10] a resolution of an education committee to dismiss a teacher and the consequent notice of dismissal.[11]

Reduction of deeds in review

While in most cases a challenge in judicial review will be brought against **24.24** a determination which may or may not have been recorded in writing, it may be desirable on occasion to reduce a written record. In some cases the pursuer has concluded "if necessary, for reduction of certain Minutes relating to the decision complained of".[12] In one case reduction was sought "if necessary" of an entry in the register of public streets.[13] The

---

[99] *Perth General Station Commissioners v. Stewart*, 1924 S.C. 1004 at 1014.
[1] *Calvin v. Carr* [1980] A.C. 574.
[2] *London and Clydeside Estates Ltd v. Aberdeen D.C.*, 1980 S.C. (H.L.) 1 at 35 and 44.
[3] See Chaps 14–22.
[4] *Bell v. Fiddes*, 1996 S.L.T. 51.
[5] For a further list of examples, see Bradley in *Stair Encyclopaedia*, Vol. 1, para. 325, n. 3, and, more generally, Murral and Wolffe in *Stair Encyclopaedia*, Vol. 13, paras 37–42. See also the Scottish Law Commission Memorandum No. 14 (1971): "Remedies in Administrative Law".
[6] *Goodall v. Bilsland*, 1909 S.C. 1152.
[7] *M'Donald v. Lanarkshire Fire Brigade Joint Committee*, 1959 S.C. 141.
[8] *Barrs v. Wool Marketing Board*, 1957 S.C. 72.
[9] *Hayman v. Lord Advocate*, 1951 S.C. 621.
[10] *Palmer v. Inverness Hospitals Board*, 1963 S.C. 311.
[11] *Malloch v. Aberdeen Corporation*, 1971 S.C. (H.L.) 85.
[12] e.g. *Marshall v. School Board of Ardrossan* (1879) 7R. 359.
[13] *Caledonian Ry v. Glasgow Corporation* (1905) 7F. 1020.

validity of byelaws has been tested by an action for reduction,[14] as has an interlocutor refusing confirmation of a byelaw.[15] An entry in the valuation roll has been held subject to reduction in somewhat special circumstances.[16] Reduction has been granted of a certificate of alternative development.[17]

Exclusion

24.25 In accordance with what has earlier been stated reduction will not be available where there is an alternative statutory remedy,[18] or where judicial review is otherwise not open. Reduction will in general be refused where the remedy of an appeal is available and has not been pursued,[19] particularly where there is a finality clause.[20] It is a matter of statutory construction whether an alternative remedy is available.[21] Reduction is not an alternative option to an appeal where an appeal is available.[22] The right of reduction is not to be taken away by implication. Express statutory provision is required to exclude it.[23] Acquiescence may bar a reduction[24] and reduction will be inappropriate when the decision is spent.[25] These matters have all been considered in an earlier chapter.[26]

Necessity for reduction

24.26 In some circumstances it may be necessary for a reduction to be awarded so as to enable a fresh decision to be issued. Where a certificate of alternative development was sought and was held to be invalid, it was reduced and the local authority was declared bound to grant a fresh certificate and ordered to do so.[27] So also in *Ferguson v. Malcolm*[28] it was held proper for the pursuer to seek reduction of a warrant to levy a sum of poor's rates, a deposition of search, a certificate of non-payment and a warrant of imprisonment, which he claimed were illegal or false. On the other hand, where an election had by an earlier process already been held to be void, no decree of reduction was regarded as necessary in order for an appointment of interim managers to be made.[29] Where no evident decision or resolution has been taken but a challenge is made to allegedly unlawful actings, a declarator alone may be appropriate.[30] Where the validity of an election to the board of management of a

---

[14] *Scott v. Glasgow Corporation* (1899) 1F.(H.L.) 51; *Da Prato v. Magistrates of Partick*, 1907 S.C.(H.L.) 5.

[15] *Glasgow Corporation v. Glasgow Churches' Council*, 1944 S.C. 97.

[16] *Moss' Empires v. Assessor for Glasgow*, 1917 S.C.(H.L.) 1.

[17] *London and Clydeside Estates Ltd v. Aberdeen D.C.*, 1980 S.C.(H.L.) 1.

[18] *Hamilton v. Secretary of State for Scotland*, 1972 S.C. 72. See generally Chap. 12.

[19] *Baillie v. M'Gibbon* (1845) 8D. 10.

[20] See para. 11.13.

[21] *e.g. Thomson v. Inveresk Parochial Board* (1871) 10M. 178.

[22] *Philp v. Reid*, 1927 S.C. 224.

[23] *Mathewson v. Yeaman* (1900) 2F. 873.

[24] *Crawford v. Lennox* (1852) 14D. 1029. But *cf. Birrell v. Dundee Gaol Commissioners* (1859) 21D. 640, and *Glasgow and District Restaurateurs and Hotelkeepers' Association v. Dollan*, 1941 S.C. 93.

[25] *Shetland Lines (1984) Ltd v. Secretary of State for Scotland*, 1996 S.L.T. 653.

[26] See Chap. 13.

[27] *London and Clydeside Estates Ltd v. Aberdeen D.C.*, 1980 S.C.(H.L.) 1.

[28] (1850) 12D. 732.

[29] *Kidd v. Young* (1853) 15D. 555.

[30] *Pollock v. Thomson* (1858) 21D. 173; see also *Abercromby v. Badenoch*, 1909 2 S.L.T. 114.

friendly society was challenged it was held unnecessary to reduce the minutes relative to the election, since a declarator and interdict would suffice.[31] In general, if a lesser remedy will suffice that is to be preferred.[32] It is eventually a matter for the court to decide whether the circumstances call for a reduction to be pronounced or whether some lesser step will suffice.[33] A declarator may well be sufficient to resolve the rights and duties of the parties and there may be no practical need for any formal reduction to be pronounced. Where the court considers that the authority arrived at the correct result although for the wrong reason, it may refuse to grant a reduction.[34] Similarly, where reduction would serve no purpose, it may be refused.[35] Where a reduction is granted a declarator of the effect of the reduction is not appropriate.[36]

Bare reduction

A decree of reduction may be combined with other conclusions, perhaps **24.27** most frequently a declarator of the rights of the parties on which the reduction should follow. The final decree may have been preceded by an interim interdict to preserve the position pending a final determination. But it is not necessary to add any further order to a reduction. It can stand without a declarator or without any petitory conclusion.[37] Where, however, a claim for interdict and for damages was not insisted upon the court refused to grant the only remaining claim for reduction, on the ground that in the circumstances it would lead to no result.[38] It is a matter of the circumstances of the case whether any additional order is required and in the context of judicial review, if a reduction is appropriate, it may well stand alone.

Effect of reduction

As has already been noticed[39] there are no degrees of nullity, and the **24.28** expressions "void" and "voidable" should be regarded as inappropriate and misleading in the context of judicial review. Where a decision or deed is reduced the effect is in general retrospective, in that it falls to be regarded as null from the start. The particular problem which may then arise about the validity of actings which have taken place on the basis that the decision was valid has been discussed earlier.[40]

Partial reduction

As distinct from the problem which has just been mentioned, where **24.29** some part of a decision or deed has not been challenged, or has survived challenge, it may be possible by severing one part of the decision or deed

---

[31] *M'Gowan v. City of Glasgow Friendly Society*, 1918 S.C. 991. The case was raised in the sheriff court, although it should not have been since it was one properly falling under the supervisory jurisdiction of the Court of Session.

[32] Thomson and Middleton's *Manual of Court of Session Practice*, p. 141.

[33] *Jex-Blake v. Edinburgh University Senatus* (1873) 11M. 784.

[34] *Andrew v. City of Glasgow D.C.*, 1996 S.L.T. 814, following *Glasgow D.C. v. Secretary of State for Scotland*, 1980 S.C. 150.

[35] *Dillon v. Secretary of State for the Home Department*, 1997 S.L.T. 842.

[36] *CRS Leisure Ltd v. Dumbarton District Licensing Board*, 1980 S.C.L.R. 566.

[37] *Ferguson v. Malcolm* (1850) 12D. 732.

[38] *Skerret v. Oliver* (1850) 23R. 468.

[39] See para. 14.15.

[40] See para. 14.16.

from another to reduce some part or parts and preserve the rest. Whether this is possible or not will depend upon whether or not the whole can be divided so as to enable that which is sound to remain entire. If the matter is not divisible, then the whole will fall to be reduced. In general, it will not often be possible to treat the invalid part as separable so that there can be identified a coherent and independent balance. Thus where lands are conveyed under one contract in one disposition and for one price a reduction excepting a part of them will not be allowed.[41] Where among the subjects transferred by an order by statutory commissioners to the General Trustees of the Church of Scotland was a field to which the minister claimed title, it was held that the order could not be reduced in part only.[42] The same principle has been applied to arbitration awards. Where an arbiter's award contained a distinct head which went beyond the terms of the reference to him a separation of the invalid part was found to be possible.[43] So also where an arbiter awarded a larger sum than had been claimed a reduction was granted to the extent of the excess.[44] But where the invalid element in the award is dependent upon other parts of the award, then it cannot be treated as separable.[45] Where part of the determination by a sheriff in a fatal accident inquiry was successfully challenged, a separation was found to be possible, so that only the offending passages were reduced.[46] Where the invalidity in a grant relates to the essence of the grant itself, then it will not be separable and the whole will fall.[47] On the other hand, where several reasons have been given for a decision, only one of which is bad, the decision may stand on the basis of the other reasons, if they are by themselves sufficient to support it.[48] But that approach may not be available where the grounds are stated cumulatively.[49] In relation to permissions and licences to which some invalid conditions have been attached the matter may turn upon the number and importance of the conditions which are found to be invalid. Generally the reduction of a condition will invalidate the whole grant[50] and the whole may well require to be reduced if the condition is inseparable. Thus, a statutory sanction granted for the business of glue-making was held wholly reducible because an invalid condition restricting the raw materials to hide clippings only was inseparable from the grant.[51] But reduction of a relatively few unimportant conditions in a grant of planning permission may not invalidate the whole.[52] Where the court was acting under a statutory power which only entitled it to quash a decision, it was held

---

[41] *Whyte v. Forbes* (1896) 17R. 895.

[42] *M'Ewen's Trustees v. Church of Scotland General Trustees*, 1940 S.L.T. 357.

[43] *Cox Bros. v. Binning* (1867) 6M. 161.

[44] *Adams v. Great North of Scotland Ry* (1889) 16R. 843.

[45] *Mitchell v. Cable* (1848) 10D. 1297; *Miller & Sons v. Oliver and Boyd* (1903) 6F. 77.

[46] *Lothian R.C. v. Lord Advocate*, 1993 S.L.T. 1132, where a part of the determination which attributed the cause of a road accident to a blocking of the road by the local authority was severable; *Smith v. Lord Advocate*, 1995 S.L.T. 179, where such of the criticism as was directed at two doctors considered together when they should have been considered separately was found separable.

[47] *John Durney & Son v. Calder District Committee* (1904) 7F. 239.

[48] *e.g. R. v. Broadcasting Complaints Commission, ex p. Owen* [1985] 1 Q.B. 1153.

[49] *Pirie v. Aberdeen D.C.*, 1993 S.L.T. 1155.

[50] *Pyx Granite Co.Ltd v. Ministry of Housing and Local Government* [1958] 1 Q.B. 554; *Hall & Co. v. Shoreham by Sea UDC* [1964] 1 All E.R. 1.

[51] *John Thorney & Son v. Calder District Committee of Midlothian County Council* (1904) 7F. 239.

[52] *Fawcett Properties Ltd v. Buckinghamshire County Council* [1961] A.C. 636.

that, although the invalidity lay in certain conditions of the planning permission, the whole had to be quashed.[53]

Remit

Where a decision has been reduced on judicial review the court will not **24.30** usually have the necessary jurisdiction to make the order which the authority should have made. In such a case the proper course is for the court to remit the matter back to the proper authority to make the appropriate order. Thus the court has ordered a licensing board to reconvene and consider a licensing application afresh.[54] A reduction of a decision may have the effect of a remit. Where the decision of an adjudicator was found to be flawed and a tribunal had refused leave to appeal, a reduction of the latter decision by itself enabled the tribunal to recall the adjudicator's decision and consider the whole matter afresh.[55]

---

[53] *British Airports Authority v. Secretary of State for Scotland*, 1979 S.C. 200.
[54] *Barntop Ltd v. Glasgow District Licensing Board*, 1989 S.C.L.R. 173.
[55] *Zia v. Secretary of State for the Home Department*, 1994 S.L.T. 288; *cf. Ahmed v. Secretary of State for the Home Department*, 1992 S.L.T. 821.

CHAPTER 25

SUSPENSION AND INTERDICT

I   SUSPENSION
II INTERDICT

Introduction

This chapter covers two remedies of a negative character. While in **25.01** practice they have come in many instances to be taken together, they are properly distinct remedies in their own particular right and deserve to be treated distinctly. Suspension as a process of review is to be distinguished from suspension as a process of staying diligence. In the latter context it is to be associated with interdict or with liberation.[1] Interdict alone was always possible but in practice was never heard of in the Bill Chamber.[2]

I   SUSPENSION

Nature and origin

In Stair's words suspension signifies a stopping of execution.[3] As a form **25.02** of process it dates back to the to the infancy of Scottish jurisprudence.[4] It was intended as an immediate remedy; the grounds for it required to be immediately verifiable. The process was introduced by the court for the benefit of those who had a decree against them pronounced in their absence or were subjected to summary charges, but it came also to be available against all decrees, even in defended actions.[5] Procedurally, suspension was a remedy proper to the Bill Chamber.[6]

As a form of review

Suspension was originally directed at decrees, serving to prevent their **25.03** being carried into execution.[7] This developed into a distinct purpose in the staying of legal diligence, available both in respect of the enforcement of decrees of the court and in respect of the enforcement of decrees of registration, proceeding upon bonds or bills or other obligations which had been registered for execution. Thus Lord President Normand described suspension as "an equitable remedy available to a complainant either against a charge served upon him or against the threat of a charge".[8] But it came also to serve as a means of reviewing

---

[1] Maclaren, *Court of Session Practice*, p. 641.
[2] Maclaren, *Bill Chamber Practice*, p. 49.
[3] *Institutes*, 4, 52, 2.
[4] Burn-Murdoch on *Interdict*, p. 6. See also Walker, *History*, Vol. IV, p. 590.
[5] Stair, *Institutes*, 4, 52, 11 *et seq.*
[6] An account of suspension of decrees in the Bill Chamber is given by Maclaren, *Bill Chamber Practice*, pp. 80–93.
[7] *e.g. Broomfield v. Hately* (1585) M. 15135; Balfour's *Practicks*, II, 393.
[8] *Richmond Park Laundry Co. v. Lawson*, 1944 S.C. 445 at 454.

the judgment whose execution was being stopped. As Lord Traynor observed in *Lamb v. Thompson*[9]: "Suspension is a mode of obtaining review of an inferior court judgment of very ancient standing, and was distinctly recognised as being so in the Act of 1838. It is competent now as it was then." Where under the Judicature Act 1825 it was provided that suspension should be the only method of application to the Court of Session against a decree of removing, appeal was held to be incompetent.[10]

Development

25.04 It appears that in the eighteenth century the process of suspension came to be extended to all forms of wrongful action.[11] Later Erskine[12] was able to say: "Where there is no decree there may be a suspension, though not in the strict acceptation of that word; for suspension is a process authorised by law, for putting a stop not only to the execution of iniquitous decrees, but to all encroachments either on property or possession, and, in general, to every unlawful proceeding. Thus a building, or the exercise of any illegal power which one assumes to himself, is a proper subject of suspension". This extended use is recognised in Mackay's *Manual of Practice*.[13] While it came to be often linked with interdict, suspension by itself remained a competent method for testing the validity of decisions of an inferior judicatory or the extent of its jurisdiction.

Appeals and suspensions

25.05 The development of procedures for appeal from inferior courts naturally required that a priority should be given to such procedures, and in general review was left to be available only where no other remedy was available. Thus a suspension as a means of review is not competent where a remedy by way of appeal is available.[14] In *Smith v. Kirkwood*[15] Lord M'Laren expressly questioned how far suspension was competent in view of the radical changes introduced by the Court of Session Act 1868. But it has remained as a remedy available in the context of review of administrative and other bodies and has been so recognised in legislation. Under section 239(4) of the Town and Country Planning (Scotland) Act 1997[16] provision is made for the suspension of the operation of an order pending an appeal. Suspension is expressly mentioned along with reduction in section 12(2) of the Tribunals and Inquiries Act 1992[17] as being a remedy in connection with the validity of any order or determination. It is also expressly identified in the Court of Session Act 1986 as available for the suspension of decrees of the Court of Session granted in absence.[18] While it was described in 1948 as obsolescent, it has regained a new lease of life in the later years of the twentieth century.[19]

---

[9] (1901) 4 F. 88 at 92.
[10] *Campbell's Trustees v. O'Neill*, 1910 S.C. 188; *Mackay v. Menzies*, 1937 S.C. 691.
[11] The history is traced by Burn-Murdoch on *Interdict*, para. 6.
[12] *Institutes*, 4, 3, 20.
[13] p. 420.
[14] Mackay's *Manual of Practice*, p. 615.
[15] (1897) 24 R. 872 at 874.
[16] c. 8.
[17] c. 53.
[18] Court of Session Act 1986, s. 34.
[19] *J and J v. C's Tutor*, 1948 S.C. 636, *per* Lord President Cooper at 643; Maxwell, *Practice of the Court of Session*, p. 579.

Suspension today

The separate purposes of a suspension are still to be distinguished today. **25.06**
A suspension of a charge following on a decree does no more than
suspend diligence on the decree. On the other hand, suspension as a
form of review of a decree challenges the decree itself.[20] Consistently
with general principle[21] suspension for the former purpose can be
obtained in the sheriff court within the limitations laid down by statute.[22]
But where what is sought is the review of a decree the suspension must
be sought in the Supreme Court and cannot competently be obtained in
the sheriff court.[23] It is, as has been noted,[24] expressly mentioned in Rule
of Court 58.4, and it has met with some increased favour as a remedy in
practice.

Effect

The effect of a suspension, if it is granted, is simply to stop the **25.07**
proceedings complained of. It is retrospective in its effect. It does not
prevent a repetition or a continuation of those proceedings. If a
prohibition is required against future actings, that would have to be
achieved by way of interdict. A permanent suspension will have the
substantial effect of a reduction.[25]

Suspension of charges

This is less likely to occur in the context of judicial review,[26] but it may **25.08**
be noted that the grounds for the remedy in relation to charges
correspond with those generally recognised in judicial review. Any error
or omission of an important particular will in general be fatal to the
validity of a charge and render it liable to suspension.[27] Suspension of a
charge is available where there is a fundamental nullity in the proceedings,[28] where the charge threatened a sanction beyond what was competent,[29] or where the decree has been satisfied or, in the case of a
threatened charge proceeding on a Court of Session decree, where the
debtor was willing to pay or consign the sum in question in return for an
assignation.[30] Where a charge is threatened or where at least it has not
been followed up by poinding or imprisonment, a simple suspension
should lie.

---

[20] *cf. Macdonald v. Denoon*, 1929 S.C. 172.
[21] See para. 1.07.
[22] Sheriff Courts (Scotland) Act 1907 s. 5(3), as amended by the Law Reform
(Miscellaneous Provisions) (Scotland) Act 1980, s. 15(a) and Sched. 3.
[23] *Blandford v. Corsock Church of Scotland*, 1950 S.L.T. (Sh.Ct) 37; *Lamont v. Hall*, 1964
S.L.T. (Sh.Ct) 25.
[24] para 23.29.
[25] Stair noted certain differences between the two processes: *Institutes*, 4, 52, 3.
[26] A more extensive discussion can be found in Walker, *Civil Remedies*, pp. 199 *et seq.*
See also Maclaren, *Bill Chamber Practice*, Chap. II and Thompson & Middleton, *Court of
Session Practice*, pp. 287 *et seq.*
[27] Graham-Stewart on *Diligence*, pp. 279 and 291.
[28] *Manson v. Smith* (1871) 9 M. 492.
[29] *Mackay v. Parish Council of Risolis* (1899) 1F. 521. In *Macdonald v. Denoon*, 1929 S.C.
172, suspension of a charge following on a decree for aliment and a warrant for
imprisonment were suspended on the ground that the sheriff had no jurisdiction to grant
them.
[30] *Paul v. Henderson* (1867) 5 M. 1120.

Availability of suspension in judicial review

25.09 Suspension should be available as a remedy where any decision of a body subject to judicial review has been given unlawfully. On the basis that extrinsic matter could not be introduced in a suspension it was held that a challenge to a decree on the ground of fraud could not competently be brought by way of suspension; a reduction would be the only way of upsetting the decree on that ground.[31] But it may be that such a view would not now be accepted in the context of judicial review. Where the procedure in an inferior court has been contrary to the relevant statute a decree later obtained for the expenses of the successful party in the earlier action was suspended, since the inferior court was purporting to act beyond its jurisdiction.[32] It may be noted that suspension has been used to challenge the validity of an English decree on the ground of want of jurisdiction.[33] Suspension has been granted of a purported planning permission.[34]

Suspension of Court of Session decrees

25.10 Suspension of a decree granted by the Court of Session is incompetent where the decree is a decree *in foro*.[35] The ordinary and proper practice where objection is taken to an Outer House decree is to take a reclaiming motion and, on the principle that alternative remedies must be exhausted, where that course is available or through inadvertence has not been timeously adopted, suspension is incompetent.[36] Where an appeal has been taken and failed, the appellant cannot then fall back on a suspension.[37] Where a party claims that a litigation has been carried on without his knowledge or authority, his remedy against a decree is not a suspension but a reduction.[38] But suspension has been granted in somewhat special circumstances where all that was sought was to prevent execution pending an action of reduction without any review of the decree.[39] Suspension may also be sought where the diligence has been irregular. Under statutory provision a suspension can be obtained of a decree in absence, not being a decree *in foro*.[40]

Decrees of sheriff courts

25.11 In accordance with the principle that review will only lie when any other means of redress have been exhausted, suspension of a sheriff court decree will not be competent where there is provision available for appeal and that opportunity has not been taken, or has been taken and has failed. But where it is too late for appeal or extract has been issued suspension may be available[41] even on grounds which could have been stated before a decree by default has been obtained.[42] Where appeal has

---

[31] *Smith v. Kirkwood* (1897) 24 R. 872.
[32] *Miller v. M'Callum* (1840) 3 D. 65.
[33] *M'Queen v. M'Queen*, 1920 2 S.L.T. 405.
[34] *J. Aitken & Sons (Meat Producers) Ltd v. City of Edinburgh D.C.*, 1989 S.C.L.R. 674.
[35] *Macpherson v. Graham* (1863) 1 M. 973. Maclaren, *Bill Chamber Practice*, p. 80.
[36] *Lumsdaine v. Australian Company* (1834) 13 S 215; *Maule v. Tainsh* (1879) 6R. 44.
[37] *Lamb v. Thompson* (1901) 4 F. 88, *per* Lord Moncreiff at 92.
[38] *Young v. List and M'Hardie* (1863) 24 D. 587.
[39] *M'Carroll v. M'Kinstery*, 1923 S.C. 94.
[40] Court of Session Act 1988, s. 34. *Lowson v. Cooper or Reid* (1861) 23 D. 1089.
[41] *Turner v. Gray* (1824) 3 S 165.
[42] *Lamb v. Thompson* (1901) 4 F. 88.

been taken but with a failure to follow through the required procedure so that the sheriff court decree has become final by default, resort may not then be had to suspension.[43] A suspension of a decree in absence is competent where the inferior court has exceeded its jurisdiction[44]; but if the lower court has exceeded its jurisdiction suspension will lie even in a defended decree.[45] And this will hold even where the appellate jurisdiction of the Court of Session is excluded by statute.[46] In proceedings for suspension of a sheriff court decree the court may regulate all matters relating to interim possession.[47] The court must remit the case to the sheriff with instructions, but only after hearing counsel or receiving a written answer from the respondent.[48] But while suspension may be competent at common law, it should only be sought by way of judicial review if the case falls properly within the scope of the supervisory jurisdiction.[49]

Suspension excluded

In accordance with the general rule already discussed suspension will not   **25.12**
be available where there is an alternative statutory remedy which has not been used,[50] or is in course of being used.[51] But in *Sharp v. Latheron Parochial Board*[52] the court held that a duplication of an entry in the valuation roll was a matter of assessment and not of valuation and so could be remedied by a suspension of a distress warrant for rates and a perpetual interdict without requiring recourse to the statutory remedies for altering the valuation roll. Prematurity will be a bar to a suspension, as where the court would be interfering with the pursuit of a statutory complaint.[53] Acquiescence may also be a defence to a suspension. Where the suspender has acquiesced in the decree which he seeks to suspend, suspension will be refused.[54] But where a suspension is stopped by acquiescence, a declarator may still be available.[55] Where the proceedings in the inferior court had been defended, suspension would not be granted on a ground which could competently have been presented to that court but which was omitted.[56] If the decree has been implemented, as where execution has taken place, suspension will not be competent.[57] Where the matter complained of is a *fait accompli* suspension will not be competent. In *Lord Provost of Glasgow etc. v. Abbey*[58] suspension and interdict of the actings of one who had been elected a General Commissioner of Police was held to be incompetent because he had been sworn into his office and had acted as Comissioner for some

---

[43] *Watt Bros & Co. v. Foyn* (1870) 7 R. 126.
[44] *Lindsay v. Barr* (1826) 4 S 748.
[45] *Bruce v. Irvine* (1835) 13 S 437.
[46] *Campbell v. Brown* (1829) 3 W.&Sh. 441; *Miller v. McCallum* (1840) 3 D. 65.
[47] 1988 Court of Session Act (c. 36), s. 35(1).
[48] s. 35(2).
[49] cf. *Bell v. Fiddes*, 1996 S.L.T. 51, for the position in reduction.
[50] *Mackenzie v. Maclennan*, 1916 S.C. 617; see *West Highland Ry v. Grant* (1902) 10 S.L.T. 413.
[51] *Magistrates of Arbroath v. Presbytery of Arbroath* (1883) 10 R. 767.
[52] (1883) 10 R. 116.
[53] *Lowson v. Police Commissioners of Forfar* (1877) 4 R.(J.) 35.
[54] *Ewing v. Cheape* (1835) 13 S. 515; *Wotherspoon v. Winning* (1849) 11 D. 371.
[55] *Buchanan v. Glasgow Corporation Waterworks Commissioners* (1869) 7 M. 853.
[56] *Rennie v. James*, 1908 S.C. 681.
[57] *Macintosh etc. v. Robertson* (1830) 9 S. 75; *M'Dougall v. Galt* (1863) 1 M. 1012.
[58] (1825) 4 S. 246.

months. But an interdict was granted to prevent him destroying the written votes and other documents relating to the election. Nor is a suspension and interdict the proper process for challenging the legality of the making of a larger assessment than was necessary for the current maintanance of roads and bridges with a view to accumulating funds for the rebuilding of a bridge which had become ruinous.[59] On the other hand, where the decree is alternate and one part has been obtempered, suspension may lie. It was so held in a charge on a decree for adherence and aliment where the husband averred that he was willing to adhere.[60] Since the theoretical basis for the suspension of a decree is that a charge may follow on the decree it is not competent to suspend a decree of absolvitor.[61]

Interim suspension

25.13 It is competent for an interim suspension to be granted with or without an interim interdict or an interim liberation.[62] As in the case of interdict, the court must be satisfied that the applicant has a prima facie case for the remedy and also that the balance of convenience favours the making of an interim order. An interim suspension and an interim interdict were granted in *Brown v. Executive Committee of the Edinburgh Labour Party*[63] in respect of disciplinary proceedings taken against certain local councillors, thereby enabling them to stand for election. Where interim suspension is granted and is not earlier recalled it will continue during the subsequent procedure in the application until a final decision is given.[64]

Caution or consignation

25.14 Caution was formerly required in ordinary petitions for suspension, as a means of securing to the creditor that the suspender would pay the sum charged and the expenses of the process of suspension. But this is now a matter for the discretion of the court.[65] In matters of judicial review such a question might arise in connection with the making of an interim order, but since in any event these considerations are more appropriate to the suspension of a charge they are unlikely to occur in review. Correspondingly, while the court may order consignation of the sum for which the suspender has been charged, this is not likely to arise in an application for judicial review. Consignation of a sum to cover the expenses as well as the sum charged for would require to be specifically ordered as the latter does not usually cover the former.[66]

Suspension and other remedies

25.15 Suspension is often coupled with interdict so as to prevent repetition or continuation of the acts complained of, but it can properly stand by itself. Where a charge has been followed by imprisonment then a

---

[59] *British Fisheries Society v. Magistrates of Wick* (1872) 10 M. 426.

[60] *Brown v. Brown*, 1971 S.C. 22.

[61] *M'Gregor v. Lord Strathallan* (1862) 24 D. 1006; Mackay, *Practice*, 2. 484.

[62] It was allowed in an ordinary action in *Gilmont Transport Services Ltd v. Renfrew D.C.*, 1982 S.L.T. 290.

[63] 1995 S.L.T. 985.

[64] On the enlarged relief available for enforcement of Community rights, see Lane "Interim Suspension of Acts of Parliament" (1990) 35 J.L.S.S. 310.

[65] Rules of Court of Session, r. 60.2.2.

[66] *Peddie v. Davidson* (1856) 18 D. 85.

suspension and liberation should be sought. Various combinations of suspension with interdict and liberation may be appropriate in particular circumstances.

II INTERDICT

Nature

Interdict is an order designed to prevent the commission of a threatened **25.16** wrong or the continuance of current wrongdoing.[67] "Broadly speaking, interdict is granted against a wrong which is in the course of being committed or where there is reasonable ground for apprehending that a wrong is intended to be committed."[68] It is a preventive proceeding, not a remedy for a wrong which has been done.[69] It is analgous to the English remedy of injunction, both being remedies *in personam*.[70] It has been described as a quasi-criminal process, in that if the party interdicted fails to observe the interdict he is liable to be brought to court and punished as well as made liable in expenses.[71] But interdict is granted at the risk of him who seeks it, and if he was not entitled to the interdict he may be liable in damages.[72]

Origin

Although it was referred to in 1849 as "the old Scotch remedy",[73] **25.17** interdict appears to have developed particularly during the eighteenth century from the old process of suspension.[74] For a considerable period suspension and interdict went together as associated remedies, but in time interdict alone came to be recognised as sufficient to stop wrongs which were in course of being committed as well as wrongs which were apprehended. It is still competent to grant interdict in isolation.[75] The combined remedy of suspension and interdict should only be granted where there is both an illegality to be suspended and a continuing or apprehended future wrongdoing.

Sheriff court

Interdict has for a long time been competent in the sheriff court but that **25.18** court may not trespass upon the supervisory jurisdiction which is exclusive to the Court of Session.[76] In the past the distinction has not always been carefully observed.[77]

Equity

The place of equity in Scottish law has been already discussed under the **25.19** general heading of remedies.[78] In the present context a distinction may be noted between the grant of interdict *ad interim* and perpetual

---

[67] For a recent study, see Scott Robinson, *The Law of Interdict* (2nd ed., 1994).

[68] *Inverurie Magistrates v. Sorrie*, 1956 S.C. 175, *per* Lord Justice-Clerk Thomson at 179.

[69] *Earl of Breadalbane v. Jamieson* (1877) 4 R. 667, *per* Lord President Inglis at 671.

[70] *Borrows v. Colquhoun* (1864) 1 Macq. 691 at 696.

[71] *Kelso School Board v. Hunter* (1874) 2 R. 228, *per* Lord Deas at 231.

[72] *Fife v. Orr* (1895) 23 R. 8.

[73] *National Exchange Co. of Glasgow v. Glasgow etc. Ry* (1849) 11 D. 571, *per* Lord Justice-Clerk Hope at 575.

[74] Burn-Murdoch on *Interdict*, p. 6.

[75] *Exchange Telegraph Co. Ltd v. White*, 1961 S.L.T. 104.

[76] Burn-Murdoch on *Interdict*, p. 25.

[77] *e.g. Kelso School Board v. Hunter* (1874) 2 R. 228.

[78] See para. 23.31.

interdict. The former is very much a matter of discretion in the particular circumstances, but in relation to the latter consideration of strict legal right may more sharply arise. On the strict view, the fact that the granting of interdict will cause loss to the person interdicted out of all proportion to any advantage to the person whose rights have been invaded is not a ground for refraining from granting interdict.[79] In matters of real injury to private property, such as damage to land by the working of minerals, the right to interdict may be strictly enforced, even although the result is to prevent the minerals being used.[80] In one such case it was observed: "For the Court to abstain from enforcing a right, because that enforcement would cause great inconvenience or pecuniary loss to somebody else, is a doctrine which is quite unknown to the law of Scotland."[81] On the other hand, the court has also recognised that an element of discretion is available. In *White v. Dickson* Lord Justice-Clerk Moncreiff observed[82]: "The question of granting an interdict is always a matter for the discretion of the Court."[83] While observations can be found which suggest that interdict is essentially a discretionary remedy[84] the better view appears to be that the remedy is one of right, subject to a discretion to withhold it.[85] Exceptionally interdict may be withheld and another course taken, such as a declarator. Here the court will have careful regard to the consequences of a grant of interdict both on the legitimate interests of the party to be interdicted and upon the public interest.[86] Lord M'Laren stated in *Clippens Oil Co. v. Edinburgh & District Water Trustees*,[87] in reference to the power to adopt such alternative solutions: "I think, on consideration of the cases where this power has been exercised, it will be found that they all belong to one or other of two categories, viz., either (1) that the granting of immediate interdict would be attended with consequences to the rights of the respondent as injurious, or possibly more so, than the wrong that was complained of; or (2) again, because the effect of an immediate interdict would be to cause some great and immediate public inconvenience." Beyond what has been stated, such questions as the balance of convenience or loss will not prevent a final grant of interdict against illegal actings.[88] The position appears to be that considerations of equity and discretion will be permitted in light of the particular subject-matter of the case. Thus, in matters of nuisance remedial measures may be permitted in place of interdict.[89] In *Webster v. Lord Advocate*[90] the Lord Ordinary suspended the operation of the interdict for six months in order to enable steps to be taken to mitigate the nuisance of the noise of

---

[79] *Bank of Scotland v. Stewart* (1891) 18 R. 957.

[80] *Shotts Iron Co. v. Inglis* (1882) 9 R.(H.L.) 78 at 88.

[81] *Bank of Scotland v. Stewart* (1891) 18 R. 957, *per* Lord President Inglis at 971.

[82] (1881) 8 R. 896 at 901.

[83] See also Lord Young in *Macleod v. Davidson* (1886) 24 S.L.R. 69 and Lord Deas in *Kelso School Board v. Hunter* (1874) 2 R. 228.

[84] *e.g.* Lord Deas in *Kelso School Board v. Hunter* (1874) 2 R. 228 that interdict is not granted as a matter of right "but only in the exercise of a sound judicial discretion".

[85] Burn-Murdoch on *Interdict*, p. 103.

[86] *Ben Nevis Distillery (Fort William) Ltd v. North British Aluminium Co.*, 1948 S.C. 592 at 598.

[87] (1848) 25 R. 373 at 383.

[88] *Ferguson v. Tennant* 1978 S.C. (H.L.) 19, *per* Lord Justice-Clerk Wheatley at 47.

[89] *Duke of Richmond v. Burgh of Lossiemouth* (1904) 12 S.L.T. 166; *M'Ewen v. Steedman & M'Alister*, 1913 S.C. 761.

[90] 1984 S.L.T. 13; 1985 S.L.T. 361.

the construction work in connection with preparations for the Edinburgh Military Tattoo. And in a matrimonial case Lord President Dunedin stated[91]: "I do not think that this Court is ever bound to exercise an equitable jurisdiction (which it always does when it deals with interdict) without being sure that the result of its own judgment is not necessarily to cause another wrong". But in the context of judicial review the court has in any event an overriding discretion.[92]

Deferment of interdict

The court may in appropriate cases defer the making of a perpetual **25.20** order of interdict so as to allow an alternative solution to be found. Thus, if the wrong in question is remediable the court may refuse interdict *in hoc statu*, or simply continue the case[93] or continue an interim interdict with a remit to an expert,[94] or continue the interim order so that an opportunity can be given for preventative measures to be devised and effected.[95] One practice is to appoint the respondents, preferably within a limited period, to lodge a minute stating the steps which they would propose to take to overcome the point of objection.[96] Another course is to grant decree but suspend the operation of the interdict for a prescribed period of time to enable alternative action to be taken whereby the cause of the complaint may be obviated.[97]

Grounds for interdict in judicial review

All the grounds for review which have already been canvassed may **25.21** justify the granting of interdict in their particular circumstances. In *Campbell's Trustees v. Police Commissioners of Leith*[98] the Lord Chancellor, Lord Hatherley, observed of public bodies that "In all matters regarding their jurisdiction they are, of course, allowed to exercise those powers according to their judgment and discretion; but when they exceed those powers, they are immediately arrested by interdict or by injunction, it not being a sufficient answer on their part to say, 'You have your remedy at law'."

Availability

In order to justify the granting of an interdict it must be shown that a **25.22** wrong is being committed or that there are reasonable grounds for fearing that a wrong is about to be committed.[99] Thus it cannot be granted, for example, against the police to stop action which they have a legal right to do,[1] nor to stop construction works being carried out within

---

[91] *MacLure v. MacLure*, 1911 S.C. 200 at 206.
[92] See para. 23.32.
[93] *Duke of Buccleuch v. Cowan* (1873) 11 M. 675.
[94] *Fraser's Trustees v. Cran* (1877) 4 R. 794; (1877) 5 R. 290; (1879) 6 R. 451.
[95] *Fleming v. Gemmill*, 1908 S.C. 340.
[96] *Gavin v. Ayrshire County Council*, 1950 S.C. 197.
[97] *Webster v. Lord Advocate*, 1984 S.L.T. 13.
[98] (1870) L.R. 2 Sc. & Div. 1 HL.
[99] *Hay's Trustees v. Young* (1877) 4 R. 398, *per* Lord Ormidale at 401 quoting Sheriff-substitute Dickson: "Interdict is a remedy, by decree of Court, either against a wrong in course of being done, or against an apprehended violation of a party's rights, only to be awarded on evidence of the wrong, or on reasonable grounds of apprehension that such violation is intended".
[1] *Southern Bowling Club Ltd v. Ross* (1902) 4 F. 405.

the terms of a statutory power,[2] nor where a stop notice was validly issued.[3] Interdict is not available against actings in performance of a statutory duty,[4] nor against actings which are authorised by statute.[5] Interdict was held not to be available where a statute provided for a remedy by way of reduction.[6] Nor is interdict a competent process for testing the legality of past acts of financial administration.[7] Where there is a prima facie case for an arbitration it will not be interdicted.[8] In cases of alleged trespass, interdict will not usually be granted where the alleged wrongdoing has been carried out in good faith,[9] or with the permission of the tenant of the land, where no threat exists to the interests of the proprietor.[10] It is also necessary that the rights and duties of the parties should be precise and clear.[11]

Examples

25.23 The following may be cited as examples of the some of the many situations of alleged unlawful behaviour in which interdict has been sought: the implementing of an unlawful resolution,[12] the distribution of a newspaper in breach of electoral legislation,[13] the sale of railway property in excess of a statutory power,[14] the operation of pleasure cruises by harbour trustees,[15] the requisition of houses allegedly in bad faith,[16] the undertaking of public works[17] or a compulsory taking of lands[18] without compliance with the proper preliminary procedure, the creation of more damage than the statute permitted in the carrying on of works,[19] the addition of fluoride to a water supply in excess of statutory power,[20] the assessment of land beyond the boundary of a local authority,[21] an assessment to rates unlawfully levied,[22] and to water rates for buildings in respect of which rates were not due,[23] where a statutory arbiter acts beyond his powers,[24] the following up of a petition for a Provisional Order,[25] or the arranging for a public local inquiry,[26] but not

---

[2] *Douglas v. Dundee Railway Co.* (1827) 6 S. 329; *Edinburgh Street Tramways Co. v. A. & C. Black* (1873) 11 M. (H.L.) 57.
[3] *Central R.C. v. Clackmannan D.C.*, 1983 S.L.T. 666; *Earl Car Sales (Edinburgh) Ltd v. Edinburgh D.C.*, 1984 S.L.T. 8.
[4] *Thomson v. Thomson & Co.* (1902) 4 F. 930.
[5] *Shepherd v. Menzies* (1900) 2 F. 443.
[6] *Anderson v. Kirkintilloch Magistrates*, 1948 S.C. 27.
[7] *British Fisheries Society v. Magistrates of Wick* (1872) 10 M. 426.
[8] *Glasgow, Yoker and Clydebank Ry v. Lidgerwood* (1895) 23 R. 195.
[9] *Hay's Trustees v. Young* (1877) 4 R. 398.
[10] *Steuart v. Stephen* (1877) 4 R. 873.
[11] *Kelso School Board v. Hunter* (1874) 2 R. 228.
[12] *Meek v. Lothian R.C.*, 1980 S.L.T. (Notes) 61.
[13] *Meek v. Lothian R.C.*, 1982 S.C. 84.
[14] *Ellice v. Invergarry and Fort William Ry*, 1913 S.C. 849.
[15] *D. & J. Nicol v. Dundee Harbour Trustees*, 1915 S.C. (H.L.) 7.
[16] *Pollock School v. Glasgow Town Clerk*, 1946 S.C. 373.
[17] *Campbell v. Leith Police Commissioners* (1870) 8 M. (H.L.) 194.
[18] *M'Callum v. Glasgow District Subway Co.* (1895) 3 S.L.T. 194.
[19] *Gillespie v. Luca & Aird* (1893) 20 R. 1035.
[20] *McColl v. Strathclyde R.C.*, 1983 S.L.T. 616.
[21] *Hope v. Corporation of the City of Edinburgh* (1897) 5 S.L.T. 195.
[22] *Stirling County Council v. Magistrates of Falkirk*, 1912 S.C. 1281.
[23] *Distillers Co. v. Fife County Council*, 1925 S.C. (H.L.) 15.
[24] *Wm McCoard & Son v. Glasgow Corporation*, 1935 S.L.T. 117.
[25] *Russell v. Hamilton Magistrates* (1897) 25 R. 350.
[26] *Ayr Magistrates v. Lord Advocate*, 1950 S.C. 102.

an application to Parliament for special powers,[27] in relation to the membership of a governing body,[28] or of a local authority,[29] or of the staff of a university,[30] or the holding of senior post in a hospital[31] or a school,[32] against the closure of a school,[33] to secure impartiality in the organising of party political broadcasts,[34] or publications by a local authority[35] at times of election, and to prohibit the unauthorised use of confidential information.[36]

Negative interdict

Where the substance of what is sought is to interdict someone from not **25.24** doing something, interdict will not be granted.[37] A negative interdict is not competent. Thus an interdict to stop a tenant from ceasing to occupy and use commercial premises was refused as incompetent[38] as was an attempt to interdict a local authority from stopping payment of housing benefits.[39] No juggling with words or the use of double negatives should be allowed to cloak what is in substance a positive order.[40] But the point can be a fine one. Interdict has been granted against the taking of steps towards the closure of a school,[41] or against the withdrawal of a railway service,[42] thereby achieving the positive result of the continuance of the activity. A more direct solution may be to seek an order for specific relief under sections 45 or 46 of the Court of Session Act 1988.[43]

Past wrongs and completed acts

Since interdict looks to the future an interdict cannot be granted in **25.25** respect of a wrong which has already been completed.[44] But evidence of past wrongdoing may support an argument that a further wrong is threatened, although the mere fact that a wrong has been done does not necessarily point to a risk of repetition.[45] Where the wrongful act is approaching completion—as, for example, in building operations where some work has yet to be done—interdict will be available, if the application is timeously presented.[46] Interdict may be refused where the

---

[27] *Wedderburn v. Scottish Central Ry* (1848) 10 D. 1317.
[28] *Brown v. Edinburgh University Court*, 1973 S.L.T.(Notes) 55.
[29] *Gilmour v. Craig* (1852) 14 D. 521.
[30] *Lawson v. Senatus Academicus of St Andrews University* (1898) 5 S.L.T. 269.
[31] *Adams v. Secretary of State for Scotland*, 1958 S.C. 279.
[32] *Trapp v. Aberdeenshire County Council*, 1960 S.C. 302.
[33] *Deane v. Lothian D.C.*, 1986 S.L.T. 22.
[34] *Wilson v. IBA* 1979 S.C. 351.
[35] *Meek v. Lothian R.C.*, 1983 S.L.T. 494.
[36] *Levin v. Farmers Supply Association of Scotland and Another*, 1973 S.L.T. (Notes) 43.
[37] *Wemyss v. Ardrossan Harbour Co.* (1893) 20 R. 500.
[38] *Grosvenor Development (Scotland) plc v. Argyll Stores Ltd*, 1987 S.L.T. 738; *Church Commissioners of England v. Abbey National plc*, 1994 S.C. 651. See also *Retail Park Investment v. Royal Bank of Scotland*, 1995 S.L.T. 1156; 1996 S.C. 227. The matter is discussed by N.R. Whitty in "Positive and Negative Interdicts" (1990) 35 J.L.S.S. 453 and 510.
[39] *Edinburgh Property Management Association v. Edinburgh D.C.*, 1987 G.W.D. 38–1348.
[40] Burn-Murdoch on *Interdict*, para. 192.
[41] *Deane v. Lothian R.C.*, 1986 S.L.T. 274.
[42] *Highland R.C. v. British Railways Board*, 1996 S.L.T. 274.
[43] See para 26.10.
[44] *Dick v. Thom* (1829) 8 S. 232; *Glen v. Caledonian Ry* (1868) 6 M. 797 at 799; *Caledonian Ry v. Magistrates of Aberdeen* (1905) 13 S.L.T. 109.
[45] *Hay's Trustees v. Young* (1877) 4 R. 398.
[46] *Lowson's Trustees v. Crammond* (1864) 3 M. 53.

building is practically complete.[47] Where the wrongful act is complete, consequential actings which are harmless in themselves will not justify interdict.[48] Where works have been allowed to be installed contrary to the empowering statute the proper remedy may be a decree of declarator and removal.[49]

Interdict excluded

25.26   In general the various grounds for the exclusion of judicial review apply to interdict. Thus, in accordance with the general principle which has been already discussed, interdict should not be available where there is a prescribed statutory remedy available.[50] Moreover, where a statute provides for penalties for a breach of regulations or byelaws a statutory body which has been set up to enforce such provisions is not entitled to resort to interdict to enforce them.[51] Considerations of prematurity, delay and acquiescence arise particularly in connection with this form of remedy. Interdict was refused where it was premature.[52] Undue delay may disable an applicant from obtaining an interdict, whether interim[53] or final. Where a wrong has been acquiesced in, interdict will not be granted.[54] Delay which has led to a change in circumstances may well have a significance in the granting or withholding of interim or perpetual interdict. Nor will interdict be granted where the order would achieve no purpose, such as an interdict against a person in respect of the actings of others over whom he had no control.[55]

Continuing acts

25.27   In some circumstances the wrongdoing may extend beyond the initial wrongful act so as to enable interdict to be granted for the continuing operations which originated in the initial act. Thus one who has wrongfully entered on land and ploughed it can be interdicted from taking possession of the land and ploughing it.[56] So also the continued actings of a company on a contract which was entered into *ultra vires* have been the subject of interdict.[57]

Threat of appreciable wrong

25.28   It must be clearly established that an invasion of a legal right is definitely apprehended before interdict will be granted.[58] The threatened invasion must also be immediate, otherwise an interdict would be premature.[59] It

---

[47] *Heriot's Trust v. Carter* (1903) 10 S.L.T. 514.
[48] *Edgar v. Glasgow Friendly Society*, 1914 2 S.L.T. 408.
[49] *Buchanan v. Glasgow Corporation Waterworks Commissioners* (1868) 7 M. 853.
[50] *e.g. Green v. Lord Advocate*, 1918 S.C. 667; *Anderson v. Kirkintilloch Magistrates*, 1948 S.C. 27; *Hamilton v. Lanarkshire County Council*, 1971 S.L.T. (Notes) 12. In the special circumstances of *Cumming v. Inverness Magistrates*, 1953 S.C. 1 the action was sisted in the anticipation that the statutory process could be followed. See para. 13.09.
[51] *Magistrates of Buckhaven and Methil v. Wemyss Coal Co.*, 1932 S.C. 201.
[52] *Anderson v. Kirkintilloch Magistrates*, 1948 S.C. 271; *Hamilton v. Lanarkshire County Council*, 1971 S.L.T. (Notes) 12.
[53] *Ayala v. Dowell* (1893) 1 S.L.T. 374.
[54] *Hoyle v. Shaws Water Co.* (1854) 17 D. 83.
[55] *Butler v. Registrar-General for Scotland*, 1962 S.L.T. (Notes) 12.
[56] *Wallace-James v. Montgomerie & Co. Ltd* (1899) 2 F. 107.
[57] *Symington v. Wilsons and Union Tube Co. Ltd* (1904) 11 S.L.T. 589.
[58] *Earl of Crawford v. Paton*, 1911 S.C. 1017.
[59] *Caledonian Ry. v. Glasgow Magistrates* (1897) 25 R. 74.

cannot be sought to protect a contingent right.[60] Moreover, the threat must be of an appreciable wrong. Where the alleged wrong is minimal the court will not usually be prepared to grant an interdict. In the case of *Winans v. Macrae*[61] interdict was refused where a pet lamb had strayed onto an extensive area of deer forest. Lord Young observed that no appreciable harm was threatened. The wrong in question must be substantial and the risk of it must be real. As Lord Guthrie observed in *Hay's Trustees v. Young*[62]: "But interdict is never granted as a matter of course, and ought not to be applied for or granted without strong, or, at least, reasonable grounds."

Interim interdict

Interdict *ad interim* is frequently granted to preserve the status quo, pending the resolution of a dispute on the rights of parties. There is statutory authority for it to be granted on the motion of any party in any cause containing a conclusion for interdict,[63] and in the particular context of applications for judicial review it may be granted at the stage of the first order,[64] or at any later stage. The court may wait for answers to be lodged before deciding whether to grant or refuse an interim order, so that consideration can be given to the written response to the application and enable a more mature consideration to be given to the issue.[65] If a caveat has been lodged the matter may be resolved at the stage of the first order. The hearing on an application for interim interdict, particularly where all parties are represented and present argument, may well be determinative of the whole dispute, even although the merits do not require to be finally resolved at that stage.

25.29

Requirements for an interim order

The applicant must first satisfy the court that he has a prima facie case.[66] The question then is one for the discretion of the court to assess on the balance of convenience whether an interim order should or should not be made.[67] Since the matter is one primarily of discretion an appeal court can only interfere if it can be shown that the judge has in some way erred in law.[68] It is essential for the judge to understand the nature of the dispute.[69] The court may recall an interim interdict.

25.30

Factors affecting the balance of convenience

While the matters which may influence the court in deciding whether or not to make an interim order are necessarily related to the circumstances of the particular case and do not admit of any exhaustive summary, the

25.31

---

[60] *Hood v. Traill* (1884) 12 R. 362.
[61] (1885) 12 R. 1051.
[62] (1877) 4 R. 398 at 402.
[63] Administration of Justice (Scotland) Act 1933 (c. 41), s. 6; Court of Session Act 1988 (c. 36), s.47.
[64] See para. 23.17 (procedure).
[65] *Gauldie v. Magistrates of Arbroath*, 1936 S.C. 861.
[66] In England the test was said in *American Cyanamid v. Ethicon Ltd* [1975] A.C. 396 to be one of a serious issue to be tried, but at least in cases of judicial review, where leave is required, the former test of a prima facie case continues to be applied.
[67] *National Dock Labour Board v. Sheppard (Group) Ltd*, 1989 S.L.T. 661.
[68] *Hay v. Hay*, 1968 S.C. 179 at 184.
[69] *Scottish Milk Marketing Board v. Paris*, 1935 S.C. 287 at 296.

following factors may be noted as among the more common considerations.

(a) *Preservation of the status quo*: it has long been recognised that interdict will readily be granted to prevent an inversion of possession pending the resolution of the rights of parties.[70] This has extended to a recognition that the status quo should in general be preserved.[71] It may sometimes be considered that innovating on the status quo may do more harm than good.[72]

(b) *Where there is a threat of irreparable harm either to public or to private interests*, such as the destruction of a public building,[73] the carrying on of quarrying operations in a royal park,[74] or the flooding of mineral workings,[75] interim interdict will be more readily granted.

(c) *The immediacy of the threatened wrong may operate to justify interim interdict*, as where an imminent broadcast is to be made,[76] or an imminent publication contrary to law[77]; but on the other hand, the fact that there is no immediacy for the performance of the actions complained of may justify an interim order on the ground that postponement will not cause any hardship.[78]

(d) *The extent of the expenditure involved*: in deciding that interim interdict was appropriate in the case of *Adams v. Magistrates of Glasgow*,[79] Lord President Inglis said: "In the next place, these operations involve considerable expense . . . If the operations had been carried so far that the greater part of this sum had been expended, and only a small part remained to be laid out in completing the works, that would have influenced me a great deal. But that is not the case, for it has been explained that not more than one-fifth of the whole amount has been expended."

(e) *A breach of natural justice would occur if interdict is not granted*, as where a chief constable was proceeding to investigate complaints in which he was personally involved.[80]

(f) *The strength of the applicant's case on the merits*: while the court is not required at the stage of making an interim order to form a concluded view on the merits of the application, the relative strength or weakness of the case may weigh in the balance in deciding whether an interim order should be made.[81] Where it appears that there are grounds for challenging the competency of the application,[82] that may militate against making an interim order.

(g) *The interest of the public and of public administration*: public interest and public convenience may require to prevail over private

---

[70] *Borrows v. Colquhoun* (1854) 1 Macq. 691.

[71] *e.g. Wilson v. Scottish Typographical Association*, 1910 2 S.L.T. 269; *Innes v. Royal Burgh of Kirkcaldy*, 1963 S.L.T. 325.

[72] *Brown v. Edinburgh University Court*, 1973 S.L.T. (Notes) 55.

[73] *Crawford v. Magistrates of Paisley* (1870) 7 M. 693.

[74] *Earl of Haddington v. Duff* (1826) 4 S. 830.

[75] *Baird v. Monkland Iron and Steel Co.* (1862) 24 D. 1418.

[76] *Waddell v. BBC*, 1973 S.L.T. 246; *Wilson v. IBA*, 1979 S.C. 351.

[77] *Meek v. Lothian R.C.*, 1982 S.C. 84.

[78] *Adams v. Magistrates of Glasgow* (1868) 40 Sc.Jur. 524 at 525.

[79] *ibid.*

[80] *Lockhart v. Irving*, 1936 S.L.T. 567.

[81] *NWL Ltd v. Woods* [1979] 1 W.L.R. 1294, *per* Lord Fraser of Tullybelton at 1310; *Toynar Ltd v. Whitbread & Co. Ltd*, 1988 S.L.T. 433.

[82] That is, that it falls outwith the scope of judicial review in any of the various respects considered in Part II.

convenience in the decision whether or not to grant an interim interdict. "There is a material difference between a case in which the ordinary civil rights of two subjects come into conflict and a case in which the executive administration of a statutory authority, established by Act of Parliament for the purpose of controlling a particular department of trade, is obstructed by a person trading in that department."[83] The continuity of the conduct of public works is not lightly to be interrupted.[84]

Refusal of interim interdict on conditions

In some cases, particularly where considerations of public interest point **25.32** to the desirability of allowing activities to proceed, the court may prescribe particular conditions on which it will be prepared to refrain from granting an interdict. Thus security by way of caution may be required by the court as a condition of not granting interim interdict in order to secure that if the operations complained of cause damage to the applicant there may be security available for compensation.[85] In one case conditions directed to the minimisation of damage and nuisance were imposed.[86] Undertakings to keep accounts may be required.[87] Where the respondent is a responsible public body the court may well be prepared to refuse or recall interdict on an appropriate undertaking being presented by the respondent.[88]

Grant of interim interdict on conditions

Correspondingly, caution, or security, may be required as a condition of **25.33** granting interdict to guard against the risk of loss caused by the interdicting of the respondent's actings.[89] Consignation may in an appropriate case be an alternative to caution.[90] Special undertakings may be given or special arrangements entered into as a condition of the interdict being granted. A requirement to keep accounts may be imposed on the complainer in the granting of interdict.[91]

The respondent

An interdict may bind persons not individually named but sufficiently **25.34** described in the decree, such as anyone "acting on behalf" of the respondent. An interdict against a corporate body binds the individual members of it.[92]

The Crown

The particular matter of interdict against the Crown has been considered **25.35** earlier and reference should be made to the undernoted paragraphs.[93]

---

[83] *Scottish Milk Marketing Board v. Paris*, 1935 S.C. 297, *per* Lord President Clyde at 298.
[84] *Trainer v. Renfrewshire Upper District Committee*, 1907 S.C. 1117 at 1120.
[85] *Fergusson-Buchanan v. County Council of Dumbartonshire*, 1924 S.C. 42.
[86] *Forth Yacht Marina Ltd v. Forth Road Bridge Joint Board*, 1984 S.L.T. 177.
[87] Especially in cases of infringement of intellectual property rights.
[88] *e.g. Mutter v. Fyfe* (1848) 11 D. 303.
[89] *Williams and Son v. Fairbairn* (1899) 1 F. 944. The matter of caution is discussed more fully in Burn-Murdoch, *Interdict*, pp. 141 *et seq.*
[90] *Sharp v. Latheron Parochial Board* (1883) 10 R. 1163.
[91] *Monkland Canal Co. v. Dixon* (1822) 1 S. 412.
[92] *R. v. Poplar B.C. (No. 2)* [1922] 1 K.B. 95.
[93] para. 23.36.

Precision

25.36 Since the consequences of a failure to comply with an interdict may be penal it is essential that the terms of the decree, and accordingly of the prayer, should be precise and clear. The defender must be enabled to know, and know exactly, what he may do without incurring the penalties which attach to a breach of the order.[94] The decree must be in itself clear and definite; uncertainty cannot be resolved by reference to the terms of the application.[95] "It must be in terms so plain that he who runs may read".[96] Further, and for the same reason, an interdict "must be directed against some specific act which is alleged to be in contravention of the statute, and not merely against anything which is contrary to the statute".[97] It must go no further than is necessary to curb the illegal actings complained of.[98] It is also necessary that the respondent should be correctly designated. A significant error in the designation may invalidate the application,[99] although a trifling misnomer or misdescription may be ignored as immaterial.[1]

Breach

25.37 A breach of interdict involves an interference with the administration of the law and an impeding of the course of justice. "It is not the dignity of the Court which is offended—a petty and misleading view of the issues involved—it is the fundamental supremacy of the law which is challenged."[2] As such it calls for punishment as a contempt of court. Detail of the procedure is considered in the undernoted texts.[3]

---

[94] *Perth General Station Committee v. Ross* (1896) 23 R. 885 at 894.
[95] *Cairns v. Lee* (1892) 20 R. 16.
[96] *Kelso School Board v. Hunter* (1874) 2 R. 229, *per* Lord Deas at 232.
[97] *Fleming v. Liddesdale District Committee* (1897) 24 R. 281, *per* Lord M'Laren at 283.
[98] *Murdoch v. Murdoch*, 1973 S.L.T. (Notes) 13, *per* Lord President Emslie at 13.
[99] *Overseas League v. Taylor*, 1951 S.C. 105.
[1] *Anderson v. Stoddart*, 1923 S.C. 755.
[2] *Johnson v. Grant*, 1923 S.C. 789, *per* Lord President Clyde at 790.
[3] *Stair Encyclopaedia*, Vol. 5, para 322; Maxwell, *Practice*, p. 520; *Gribben v. Gribben*, 1976 S.L.T. 266 (the standard of proof is beyond reasonable doubt).

CHAPTER 26

POSITIVE REMEDIES

I SPECIFIC PERFORMANCE
II THE STATUTORY ORDER FOR PERFORMANCE
III LIBERATION
IV PAYMENT AND RESTITUTION
V DAMAGES

Introduction

This chapter deals with various remedies of a positive character whereby **26.01** different forms of relief may be afforded. These should not be regarded as exhaustive of the courses which the court may adopt and they may, of course, be combined with some or other of the remedies already considered.

I SPECIFIC PERFORMANCE

Basis

By a decree of specific performance the court orders the respondent to **26.02** perform some act which he is under a legal duty to perform. The remedy is variously referred to as an order for specific implement, or an order *ad factum praestandum*. The duty may have originated in the common law, or by contract, or by statute. In England an obligation *ad factum praestandum* may be enforced by the equitable remedy of specific performance.[1] The prerogative order of mandamus is available as a discretionary remedy in England for compelling the performance of a public duty.

In judicial review

It has long been recognised that by virtue of its supereminent jurisdiction **26.03** the Court of Session has the power to order an inferior judge of any kind, or any public officer, such as a statutory commissioner or trustee, to perform his duty.[2] In practice the granting of a formal order may not be necessary, since performance will not be in issue once the obligation to perform, which will often be the point of dispute, has been resolved. Where an arbiter had accepted a submission to act as arbiter, but then sought to renounce it on the ground that he could not afford the time, he was held bound to carry out the arbitration, but the remedy sought and granted was one of declarator.[3] However, where there was a dispute as to which of two officials had the duty of making out and delivering a public house certificate, an action for performance against both of them was pursued to resolve the issue.[4]

---

[1] Bell's *Principles*, para. 29. *Halsbury's Laws*, Vol. 44(1), para. 801.
[2] *Forbes v. Underwood* (1886) 13R. 465 at 467–478.
[3] *Marshall v. Edinburgh and Glasgow Ry* (1853) 1D. 603.
[4] *Kerr v. Marwick and Gray* (1901) 3F. 670.

Jurisdiction

26.04 Consistently with principle the remedy in the context of judicial review is only available in the Court of Session, although orders for performance may otherwise be granted in the sheriff court. In *Brown v. Hamilton District Council*[5] the pursuer sought a declarator in the sheriff court that he was entitled to accommodation under the Housing (Homeless Persons) Act 1977 and an order ordaining the defenders to provide him with suitable accommodation. The action was held to be incompetent.

Availability

26.05 Where on any of the grounds on which judicial review may proceed it is found that an authority has failed to do something which it ought to do, an order for performance may be the appropriate remedy.[6] In one case an order was granted for the destruction of illegally obtained fingerprints.[7] In many cases, however, as was indicated in the preceding paragraph, it may be sufficient simply to grant a declarator of the obligation in dispute, since once the issue is resolved the authority will be willing to carry out its obligation without the necessity of any formal order. The remedy will be excluded by any of the grounds which bar judicial review.[8] Where a procedure was available to resolve a dispute about the form of a stated case in a matter of an agricultural tenancy, recourse to an action for an order for a stated case was held to be incompetent.[9]

Interim orders

26.06 It is competent to grant an interim order for performance.[10] Where there is a prima facie case of a failure to perform a statutory duty and a justification for immediate performance in the circumstances of the case, an interim order may provide a just relief pending a final resolution of the dispute.

Sanction

26.07 Failure to comply with an order for performance may lead to an order for the imprisonment of the party so failing, not as a matter of criminal prosecution, but by virtue of the court's inherent power to ordain performance.[11]

Equity

26.08 The extent of a discretion in granting an order for performance, and the distinction in this regard between Scottish and English law, has already been considered.[12] Where performance would involve exceptional hardship or be otherwise unjust an alternative remedy may be appropriate.

---

[5] 1983 S.C.(H.L.) 1.
[6] Early examples can be found in *Heritors of Corstorphine v. Ramsay*, Mar. 10, 1812, F.C.; *Moderator of Presbytery of Caithness v. Heritors of Reay* (1773) M. 7449.
[7] *Adamson v. Martin*, 1916 S.C. 319.
[8] See Chaps 14–22.
[9] *Forsyth-Grant v. Salmon and Gordon*, 1961 S.C. 54.
[10] *Scottish Flavour Ltd v. Watson*, 1982 S.L.T. 78 (a contract of sale).
[11] *Wilson v. M'Kellar* (1896) 24R 254.
[12] See para. 23.31.

Need for precision

Since a failure to comply with the decree may attract penal consequences **26.09**
it is essential that the order be drawn in clear, precise and unambiguous
terms.[13] The terms must be such as to leave the respondent in no doubt
as to the precise action which he is required to take. In general, and
particularly in the context of contractual relationships, the precision
must extend not only to the substance of the action in question but also
to the time and place for its performance.[14] It must be "absolutely
precise in every particular, both as to time and to place".[15] It must also
give the respondent a sufficient time for the performance of the act in
question, but if he fails to set about the performance he cannot be heard
to complain that the time was too short.[16] In one case where the erection
of buildings was required to be carried out, being an operation more
extensive than a single act, it was considered that the word "forthwith"
was too uncertain to be appropriate and performance was ordered within
one year.[17] But that is not to say that the court must dictate precisely
how a statutory authority is to perform its duty. If there is a statutory
duty to provide accommodation for the applicant it is not for the Court
necessarily to specify precisely where that accommodation is to be. It is
sufficient that the authority is left in no doubt about its obligation to
provide accommodation at such place and for such period as may be
within the provisions of the statute.[18]

II THE STATUTORY ORDER FOR PERFORMANCE

Introduction

By section 91 of the Court of Session Act 1868 there was introduced into **26.10**
Scotland a statutory remedy whereby upon application by summary
petition the court could order the specific performance of any statutory
duty subject to such conditions and penalties in the event of the order
not being implemented as the court might consider proper. The current
provision is to be found in section 45(b) of the Court of Session Act
1988.[19] In terms of Rule of Court 58.3(1) applications under section
45(b) are expressly included within the applications to the supervisory
jurisdiction of the court, and so require to be made by petition for
judicial review. The source of the jursidiction exercised by the court in
relation to such applications is, however, statutory and not the common
law supervisory power. The statutory provision may be compared with
the English remedy of mandamus,[20] but it has been held both in an early
case,[21] where two individuals complained of a failure to construct a
passing-place in the layout of a tramway, and, more recently,[22] in relation

---

[13] *Middleton v. Leslie* (1892) 19R 801 at 802.
[14] *Munro v. Liquidator of Balnagowan Estates*, 1949 S.C. 49, *per* Lord President Cooper
at 55.
[15] *ibid.*
[16] *M'Kellar v. Dallas's Ltd*, 1929 S.C. 503.
[17] *Middleton v. Leslie* (1892) 19R. 801.
[18] *cf.* para. 26.16.
[19] c.36. Special relief may also be granted under s.46, including reinstatement in a
possessory right. Orders for interim possession may be granted at any stage in any case in
dependence before the Court: Court of Session Act 1988, s.47(2).
[20] *Sons of Temperance Friendly Society*, 1926 S.C. 418 at 426.
[21] *Adamson v. Edinburgh Street Tramways Co.* (1872) 10M. 533.
[22] *Docherty v. Monifieth Town Council*, 1970 S.C. 200.

to the provision of a sewer, that unlike that remedy an application may be made under the statute even although another remedy is available. In that respect the Scottish remedy is, by virtue of its statutory character, an exception to the principle which applies generally to judicial review. Though the provision has been on the statute book for a considerable period, it is a remedy which has only rarely been adopted. Its advantage as a remedy in administrative matters is shown by the use which was made of it as a means of obtaining an expeditious solution to grievances arising under the Housing (Homeless Persons) Act 1977 before the introduction of the special procedure for judicial review.[23]

Jurisdiction

26.11   Just as the common law remedy of implement is not competent in the sheriff court, so also the statutory remedy is only competent in the Court of Session. As has been noted above,[24] the sheriff court does not have the jurisdiction to grant an order for specific performance by a local authority of its statutory duty.

Availability

26.12   It is, of course, essential that the respondent should be under a statutory duty to take certain action, and not merely be entitled to act under a statutory power, before the remedy can be given.[25] The duty may be created by a public general statute or a local and personal statute. But the duty must be clear and definite.[26] There must be a sufficiently precise duty expressed in the statute for the application to be competent, so that the application will fail if there is no express statutory duty at which an allegation of failure in performance can be directed.[27] In one case an attempt was made unsuccessfully to order a local authority to provide housing for a homeless person.[28] It may be a fine question whether in some cases an order for performance is at common law or under the statute. Where an application to a licensing board had been wrongly rejected by the clerk, the court under the common law power ordered the board to meet and deal with the application.[29]

Title

26.13   This matter has been discussed more fully in the chapter on *locus standi*.[30] But it may be observed in the present context that the statutory remedy may be sought by anyone to whom the particular statutory duty was owed. That may involve the members of some particular group of persons or it may extend to any member of the public. In *Adamson v. Edinburgh Street Tramways Co.*[31] the petitioners were held to have title as citizens and as omnibus and cab proprietors.

---

[23] *e.g. Galbraith v. Midlothian D.C.*, 1979 SCOLAG 122; *Mackenzie v. West Lothian D.C.*, 1979 SCOLAG 123.

[24] para. 26.04.

[25] An example can be found in the case of *Fleming & Ferguson v. Paisley Magistrates*, 1948 S.C. 547 where a decree at common law was sought.

[26] *Annan v. Leith Licensing Authority* (1901) 9 S.L.T. 63.

[27] *Carlton Hotel Co. v. Lord Advocate*, 1921 S.C. 237.

[28] *Mackenzie v. West Lothian D.C.*, 1979 S.C. 433.

[29] *Tait v. Horsburgh*, 1987 S.C.L.R. 310.

[30] Chap. 10.

[31] (1872) 10M. 533.

Crown

Consideration has earlier been given to the matter of remedies against **26.14** the Crown.[32] As has been there suggested, the statutory remedy presently under discussion should be available as a remedy against the Crown.

Respondents

The statutory remedy has been used in the context of matters which may **26.15** be classified as private as well as those of a more public character. In *Sons of Temperance Friendly Society (Leishman v. Scott)*[33] it was used to order a friendly society to perform its statutory duty of granting a certificate recognising the secession of the Scottish branch of a society registered in England and so enabling the Scottish branch to be registered as a society in its own right. In *Docherty v. Monifieth Town Council*[34] the local authority were ordered to lay the sewers necessary for the draining of a private housing development. In two cases, *Macandrew, Petr*,[35] and the later case of *Langlands v. Manson*,[36] a valuation committees were ordered to state a case for appeal to the Lands Valuation Appeal Court where in breach of their statutory duty they had failed to do so.

Precision

As has been stated in relation to implement, a high degree of precision is **26.16** called for in any order for performance at common law, and also in the case of interdict.[37] In the making of orders under the statute, however, it is thought that a corresponding degree of precision is not necessary, in particular with regard to the particular way in which the duty is to be performed.[38] As has been noted, the duty set out in the statute must be clear and precise, but provided that a precise duty exists the order for performance may not require to be in detailed terms.

III LIBERATION

Nature

A decree ordering liberation is available as a civil remedy, appropriate in **26.17** a case of wrongful or illegal imprisonment. Often the remedy sought has been one of suspension and liberation, the former order suspending the proceedings on the ground of some irregularity and the latter order restoring the complainer to his liberty. As Lord Fullerton observed[39]: "A bill of liberation is only a pro forma bill, the success of which depends on the merits, which must first be decided in the suspension."

History

The power to imprison for debt was substantially reduced by the Debtors **26.18** (Scotland) Act 1880 and the Debtors (Scotland) Act 1987. The few cases where imprisonment may be ordered for a failure to comply with a court

---

[32] para. 23.37.
[33] 1926 S.C. 418.
[34] 1970 S.C. 200.
[35] 1925 S.L.T. 18.
[36] 1962 S.C. 493.
[37] *e.g. Webster v. Lord Advocate*, 1985 S.L.T. 361.
[38] *Walker v. Strathclyde R.C.*, 1986 S.L.T. 523.
[39] *Barr v. Wotherspoon* (1850) 13D. 305 at 311.

order or for contempt of court will almost always occur in circumstances where a remedy will lie by recourse to the court which ordered the imprisonment. The opportunities for invoking the remedy of liberation in such a context will not now be frequent. The most usual context in which liberation at present arises in judicial review is that of immigration.

Civil or criminal

26.19 A question may arise whether liberation is to be sought in the Court of Session or in the High Court as a criminal matter. In *Campbell v. Herron*[40] an application to commit a person to a lunatic asylum was presented in the High Court. So also in respect of proceedings in contempt of court committed in the course of sequestration proceedings resort has been had to the High Court. In *Graham v. Robert Younger Ltd,*[41] the Lord Justice-Clerk (Thomson) observed that there had been no challenge to the jurisdiction of the High Court to entertain the bill and the competence of that course appeared to be affirmed by *MacLeod v. Speirs.*[42] On the other hand, as a matter of long practice appeals in cases of breach of interdict in sheriff court processes have been treated as civil matters and brought in the Court of Session.[43] Appeal to the Inner House of the Court of Session is in those cases competent.[44] Where imprisonment has been instructed in the course of the processing of immigrants and asylum seekers the matter is clearly of a civil nature, arising out of an administrative act, and the Court of Session is the proper forum for review.

Interim liberation

26.20 Interim liberation may be granted to give the complainer his liberty pending the resolution of the substantial ground for the application. Statutory authority is given for the grant of interim liberation on motion by any party.[45] It is in this connection that liberation is regularly sought as a remedy in applications for judicial review in cases where immigrants have been imprisoned by the Secretary of State pending disposal of their applications for residence or asylum.[46] Interim liberation is not infrequently allowed in practice, subject to conditions such as a substantial deposit of bail money and an obligation on the applicant to report to a local police station at prescribed times and dates. But while the court will lean towards the granting of liberty, the grounds for granting liberation are no wider than the grounds generally available under the supervisory jurisdiction.[47]

Speed

26.21 Applications for liberation or interim liberation are matters which by their nature call for a considerable degree of expedition in their processing. Where there are grounds for giving the applicant his liberty

---

[40] 1948 J.C. 127.

[41] 1955 J.C. 28 at 33.

[42] (1884) 11R.(J.) 26.

[43] *Stark's Trustees v. Duncan* (1906) 8F. 429.

[44] *Maclachlan v. Bruce*, 1912 S.C. 440; *Caledonian Ry v. Hamilton* (1850) 7 Bell's App. 272.

[45] Court of Session Act 1988 (c.36), s. 47(1); Administration of Justice (Scotland) Act 1933 (c.41), s.6(7).

[46] *e.g. Sokha v. Secretary of State for the Home Department*, 1992 S.L.T. 1049. See also Bovey "Judicial Review of Immigration Cases" 1990 35 J.L.S.S. 7.

[47] *Singh v. Secretary of State for the Home Department*, 1993 S.L.T. 950.

the application should not be delayed in its presentation and a due priority should be given in the hearing of it.[48]

IV PAYMENT AND RESTITUTION

Payment

Cases may occur where on the resolution of a challenge to the validity of **26.22** some decision the petitioner is consequentially able to affirm some contractual or statutory right to a payment which has been withheld pending the dispute. The obligation may be enforced incidentally to the order pronounced in the proceedings for review.

Principle of restitution

Under the general principle that *nemo debet locupletari aliena jactura* **26.23** Scots law allows a remedy by way of restitution or recovery where one person has unjustly benefited by another's loss.[49] More particularly, the term repetition is used where what is sought is the recovery of money paid, where, for one reason or another, it is unjust that the recipient should keep it. This includes the case where money has been paid in the erroneous belief that it was due. Recompense is the term used where actings have been carried out without the intention of donation to the benefit of another person. Restitution refers to the recovery of goods. There is, however, some flexibility in the use of these labels for the various forms of recovery which the law permits and the terminology used in English practice may not necessarily be the same.

Application

Where a charge has been made which is found to be *ultra vires*, the **26.24** successful party may recover the excess payments which he has made by virtue of the unlawful charge. Such a result followed from the finding that a tariff for the supply of electricity was contrary to the statutory requirement of avoiding any undue discrimination.[50] The availability of the equitable remedy of recompense depends critically on the circumstances of each case and accordingly may require to be determined only after proof of the facts.[51] But if work has been done for the applicant's own purposes, the claim will not lie.[52] An action on recompense is not open where an alternative remedy exists and has not been pursued,[53] but that is in any event a precondition for recourse to the supervisory jurisdiction. Payments made in error can be recovered whether the error is one of fact or of law.[54] Under the earlier understanding of the law, error in the construction of a private contract was treated as an error of

---

[48] Graham-Stewart on *Diligence*, pp. 759–760. The matter now involves consideration of human rights: see para. 16.23.

[49] Reference may be made to the *Stair Encyclopaedia*, Vol. 15 paras 10 *et seq.* and W. Stewart, *The Law of Restitution in Scotland* (1992).

[50] *British Oxygen Co. v. South of Scotland Electricity Board*, 1959 S.C.(H.L.) 17.

[51] *Lawrence Building Co. Ltd v. Lanark County Council*, 1979 S.L.T. 1.

[52] *Site Preparations Ltd v. Secretary of State for Scotland*, 1975 S.L.T.(Notes) 41.

[53] *Varney (Scotland) Ltd v. Lanark Town Council*, 1974 S.C. 245; *City of Glasgow D.C. v. Morrison McChlery & Co.*, 1985 S.C. 52.

[54] *Morgan Guaranty Trust Co. of New York v. Lothian R.C.*, 1995 S.L.T. 299. See also *Woolwich Building Society v. IRC* [1993] A.C. 70.

fact[55] but error in construing a formula prescribed by a statutory body was not.[56]

Restoration

26.25 While it is not likely to occur in the context of judicial review note may be made of the provision contained in section 45(a) of the Court of Session Act 1988[57] for the restoration of possession of any real or personal property, the possession of which the petitioner may have been violently or fraudulently deprived. It may be observed that the original text of rule 260B in the earlier version of the Rules of Court brought the whole of what was then section 91 of the Court of Session Act 1868 within the umbrella of judicial review. Now, however, the current edition in Chapter 58.3 of the Rules of Court only refers to section 45(b) of the Court of Sesson Act 1988, that is orders for specific performance of a statutory duty, to the exclusion of orders for the restoration of possession. But while the latter do not require to be pursued through the procedure of judicial review, it is thought that it would be competent in such an application to grant this remedy as being an order which "could be made if sought in any action or petition" within the meaning of that phrase in rule 58.4(b).

Reinstatement and specific relief

26.26 Similarly it is thought that an order under section 46 of the Court of Session Act 1988 for the performance of an act necessary to reinstate a petitioner in his possessory right could be granted in a process of judicial review. Of possibly greater value, however, may be the order for specific relief which is available under the same section. An order for the demolition of walls which blocked a right of access has been granted under this section[58] and it may well be a useful remedy in judicial review, particularly where interdict is not available.

V DAMAGES

Introduction

26.27 The Rule of Court includes damages among the list of remedies which the court may grant in an application for judicial review. But the rule is, as has been explained,[59] of procedural significance only. It has not innovated on the law so as to introduce a ground for damages which has not existed before. Accordingly, damages may only be claimed or awarded if there can be shown to be a ground entitling the applicant to such an award under the ordinary law.[60] The problems associated with claims against the Crown are dealt with elsewhere.[61] A detailed account of the law relating to damages is inappropriate in the present context and in the following paragraphes only a brief outline is attempted. In

---

[55] *British Hydro-Carbon Chemicals and BTC, Petrs*, 1961 S.L.T. 280.
[56] *Unigate Foods Ltd v. Scottish Milk Marketing Board*, 1972 S.L.T. 137.
[57] c.36.
[58] *Five Oaks Properties Ltd, v. Granite House Ltd*, 1994 S.C.L.R. 740.
[59] para. 23.30.
[60] The position in England was reviewed in *X (Minors) v. Bedfordshire County Council* [1995] 2 A.C. 633.
[61] para. 23.36.

general a successful challenge by way of judicial review does not necessarily lead to any entitlement to damages.[62]

Statutory authority and nuisance

Where acts have been carried out under and within the limit of statutory **26.28** power, any damage inevitably arising from those acts may be redressed by such compensation, if any, as is afforded by the statute which authorised the work.[63] Where the exercise of a statutory power inevitably creates a nuisance, so that the nuisance is the necessary result of the implementation of the statute, no action will lie.[64] But "the party executing the work must use all care and diligence to avoid creating a nuisance, and will escape liability only if he proved that he has done so and that the nuisance could not be avoided."[65] The empowering statute may even expressly prohibit the creation of a nuisance.[66] A company with a statutory right to operate a tramway service was held not to be entitled to create a nuisance by removing snow from the tramlines to the side of the road and scattering salt on the lines.[67] The alteration of a city sewage system to the prejudice of private fishing interests by way of pollution has been interdicted at common law.[68] Whether or not a defence of statutory immunity is available is a matter of construction of the legislation.[69] Various statutes make provision for compensation in relation to the particular matters which they authorise, and these also may require construction by the court.[70] Provisions for compulsory purchase are an obvious example.[71] Clear words in a statute are required before it will be construed as empowering the deprivation of rights without compensation. Protection of private property is also secured by the provisions of Article I of the First Protocol to the European Convention on Human Rights.[72] There is also a right to compensation at common law where a private citizen is deprived of his property through an exercise of the Crown's prerogative power in the public interest.[73]

Negligence

Even if damage done under the authority of statutory power will not **26.29** admit of a remedy on the ground of nuisance, it may allow of a claim under the ordinary law of negligence, if it is done negligently.[74] Issues of

---

[62] In England it has been laid down that "a breach of a public law right by itself gives right to no claim for damages": *X (Minors) v. Bedfordshire County Council, supra, per* Lord Browne-Wilkinson at 730. For recent discussion, see Thomson, "Delictual Liability of State Agencies—Further Confusion", 1999 S.L.T. (News) 245.

[63] *e.g. Davie v. Magistrates of Edinburgh*, 1951 S.C. 720.

[64] *Managers of the Metropolitan Asylum District v. Hill* (1881) 6 App.Cas. 193; *Dormer v. Newcastle-upon-Tyne Corporation* [1940] 2 K.B. 204.

[65] Lord Keith in *Rae v. Musselburgh Town Council*, 1973 S.C. 291 at 296; *Manchester Corporation v. Farnworth* [1930] A.C. 171.

[66] *e.g. Adam and Another v. Commissioner of Police of Alloa* (1874) 2R 143.

[67] *Ogston v. Aberdeen Tramway Co.* (1896) 24 R.(H.L.) 8.

[68] *Moncreiffe v. Perth Police Commissioners* (1886) 13R 921.

[69] *e.g. Allen v. Gulf Oil Refining Ltd* [1981] A.C. 1001.

[70] *Steel-Maitland v. British Airways Board*, 1981 S.L.T. 110 (statutory compensation for nuisance and trespass).

[71] In *Stirling v. North of Scotland Hydro-Electric Board*, 1975 S.L.T. 26 it was held that the damages due under a statutory scheme were such damages as would have afforded a ground of action without any such scheme.

[72] Human Rights Act 1998, Sched. 1, Pt II. See para. 16.51.

[73] *Burmah Oil Co. (Burma Trading) Ltd v. Lord Advocate*, 1964 S.C.(H.L.) 117.

[74] *Geddis v. Proprietors of Bann Reservoir* (1878) 3 App.Cas. 430 at 455; *Rae v. Musselburgh Town Council*, 1973 S.C. 291.

the negligent, as distinct from the unlawful, actings of an authority are unlikely to arise in the context of judicial review.[75] If an authority was acting not only unlawfully but also negligently, the latter issue and the matter of damages should probably be raised in an ordinary action, and certainly should be if the purpose of the action is to obtain damages rather than to stop or reduce the allegedly illegal action. Thus if personal injury has been caused through the acts or omissions of a public authority, the proper remedy is by an action for reparation and not an application for judicial review. The general principle is that where an authority has been negligent, that is to say has acted in breach of a duty of reasonable care owed to the injured party, a claim for damages should lie. Even although actings are authorised by legislation, if the execution of what the legislature has authorised is negligently managed, an action may lie.[76] But the mere assertion of the careless exercise of a statutory power or duty, such as negligence in the exercise of a statutory duty involving considerations of policy, is not enough; there must be a duty of care owed to the injured party.[77] Critical questions in that context may be whether such a duty exists and whether public policy requires an immunity from liability,[78] or whether it is just and reasonable for liability to be imposed.[79] A local authority has no liability for economic loss incurred by the owners or occupiers of houses by reason of their approving building plans on negligent advice.[80] Damages may be due in respect of loss caused by reliance on a negligent statement by an employee of an authority.[81]

Breach of statutory duty

26.30 The failure by an authority to perform a statutory duty which has caused injury to a third party may entitle that third party to claim damages for that injury. The question will depend primarily on the provisions of the statute under which the authority has acted.[82] If the nature of the duty in question is directed to the benefit of the citizen or some particular class of citizens then the intention may be that a breach of the statute should permit a claim for damages. That intention may be the more evident if the statute provides no measures of its own for enforcement by penalty or some other machinery for redress. It had been recognised in England[83] as well as Scotland that a breach of the provisions of the Housing (Homeless Persons) Act 1977[84] might give rise to a claim for damages. In *Mallon v. Monklands District Council*[85] a decision that the petitioner did not have a priority need for the purposes of that Act, which was reduced as unreasonable,[86] was held to have caused her a minor psychiatric illness for which she was awarded £100. However, in

---

[75] On negligence generally, reference may be made to Walker on *Delict*.

[76] *Geddis v. Proprietors of Bann Reservoir, supra*, at 455–456.

[77] *X (Minors) v. Bedfordshire County Council* [1995] 2 A.C. 633.

[78] *e.g. Home Office v. Dorset Yacht Co. Ltd* [1970] A.C. 1004.

[79] *Peabody Fund v. Sir Lindsay Parkinson* [1985] A.C. 210.

[80] *Murphy v. Brentwood D.C.* [1991] 1 A.C. 398, overruling *Anns v. Merton LBC* [1978] A.C. 728.

[81] *Minister of Housing and Local Government v. Sharp* [1970] 2 Q.B. 223.

[82] *Cutler v. Wandsworth Stadium* [1949] A.C. 398. A wider approach was adopted in earlier cases such as *Ferguson v. Earl of Kinnoul* (1842) 9 Cl.& F. 251.

[83] *Thornton v. Kirklees Metropolitan B.C.* [1979] 1 Q.B. 626.

[84] See now the Housing Act 1985 (c.68) and the Housing (Scotland) Act 1987 (c.26).

[85] 1986 S.L.T. 345.

[86] *sub. nom. Kelly v. Monklands D.C.*, 1986 S.L.T. 169.

O'Rourke v. Camden London Borough Council[87] the House of Lords has held that Parliament had not intended that a failure in the duty under section 63 of the Housing Act in England to provide housing accommodation for homeless persons should create a right to claim damages and the Scottish position may accordingly require to be reconsidered. The basis for a claim to damages is that as a matter of policy Parliament intended in the particular legislation that an action for damages should lie in the event of a breach of its provisions.[88] That a statute prescribes a penalty for a failure in compliance may not exclude a common law claim for damages for private injury.[89]

Excess of statutory authority

Actings without statutory authority may give rise to a potential claim for damages in the event of injury[90] or injurious affection[91] being caused thereby. Where the liberty of an individual, or a person's property rights, are infringed, a claim for damages may lie. In one case a magistrate was held liable in damages for imposing a sentence of imprisonment in excess of his statutory powers[92] and a case was held to be relevant where property had been seized on a warrant but retained by a procurator fiscal for a period longer than that authorised by the statute.[93] But a mere excess of power through an honest error will not found a claim for damages[94] and the improper exercise of power does not give rise to a civil liability.[95] There are policy reasons in the interest of expeditious administration that a Minister should not be liable in negligence in respect of a misconstruction of a statute and a consequent *ultra vires* act.[96] The fact that a resolution is void may not by itself be a ground for damages.[97]   **26.31**

Discretionary decisions

Where an authority is empowered but not obliged to carry out some function, such as the provision of street lighting, so that they have a discretion whether or not to light some particular street, a mere failure to provide lighting will by itself not give rise to a liability to make reparation to someone who has been injured because of the absence of lighting.[98] The proper exercise of a statutory discretion does not provide   **26.32**

---

[87] [1997] 3 All E.R. 23.

[88] Difficult questions may arise in connection with the failure to exercise a power and in particular whether there may be a duty to exercise the power; see the comments on *East Suffolk Rivers Catchment Board v. Kent* [1941] A.C. 74 in *Clerk & Lindsell on Torts* (17th ed.), para. 7–103, but see also *Stovin v. Wise* [1996] 2 A.C. 923.

[89] *Clyde v. Glasgow City and District Ry* (1885) 12R. 1215; see 3 Dow 380.

[90] e.g. *Edwards v. Parochial Board of Kinloss* (1891) 18R. 867, where the defenders were unable to claim the statutory protection of having acted in bona fide execution of the Act.

[91] e.g. *Sinclair v. Lanarkshire Middle Ward District Committee*, 1907 S.C. 285.

[92] *M'Creadie v. Thomson*, 1907 S.C. 1176. Cf. *M'Phee v. Macfarlane's Executor*, 1933 S.C. 163. Under s.170 of the Criminal Procedure (Scotland) Act 1995 (c.46), the pursuer must show *inter alia* that the act was done with malice and without probable cause. See Renton & Brown's *Criminal Procedure* (6th ed.), para. 27–05. Inferior judges did not possess the absolute privilege enjoyed by Supreme Court judges and sheriffs.

[93] *Bell v. McGlennan*, 1992 S.C. 41.

[94] *Bourgoin SA v. Ministry of Agriculture, Fisheries and Food* [1986] 1 Q.B. 716.

[95] *Lonrho plc v. Tebbit* [1991] 4 All E.R. 973 at 980.

[96] *Rowling v. Takaro Properties Ltd* [1998] A.C. 473 at 502.

[97] *Dunlop v. Woollahra Municipal Council* [1982] A.C. 158.

[98] *Sheppard v. Glossop Corporation* [1921] 3 K.B. 132.

a basis for a claim for damages. On the other hand, where there has been an abuse of or an excess of statutory power liability may arise.[99] In *Stovin v. Wise*[1] Lord Hoffmann observed:

> "The fact that Parliament has conferred a discretion must be some indication that the policy of the Act conferring the power was not to create a right to compensation. I think the minimum preconditions for basing a duty upon a statutory power, if it can be done at all, are, first, that it would in the circumstances have been irrational not to have exercised the power, so that there was a public law duty to act, and secondly, there are exceptional grounds for holding that the policy of the statute requires compensation to be paid to persons who suffer loss because the power was not exercised."

Thus, if the exercise, or the non-exercise, of a discretionary power, which has injured a third party, has been improper—as, for example, being outwith the authority of the statute or not made in good faith in the interests of the public, then a liability may arise to make reparation to the third party.[2] The effects of a decision will not be open to a remedy in damages unless there has been a misfeasance or abuse of power amounting to bad faith.[3] Further, an error of judgment in the manner in which a discretionary power is exercised will not be sufficient to give rise to a claim for damages by someone who has sustained injury as a result of the exercise of the power.[4] In the making of decisions on a matter of policy it is necesary to allege bad faith.[5] Such decisions are, in the public interest, entitled to some degree of immunity from claims for damages. Negligence in the making of a discretionary decision without any element of bad faith will not give rise to a claim for damages. On a more exact analysis the liability will not arise during the discretionary stage of the exercise of a power, that is while there is a choice of courses open to the authority, but once the executive stage has begun, where the matter has become one for action, then liability may arise.[6] A decision reached by a process of honest judgment should not be open to challenge on the ground of negligence.[7] "The process whereby the decision-making body gathers information and comes to a decision cannot be the subject of an action in negligence."[8]

---

[99] *Home Office v. Dorset Yacht Co. Ltd* [1970] A.C. 1004, *per* Lord Reid at 1031.

[1] [1996] A.C. 923 at 953. See also *Hill v. Chief Constable of West Yorkshire* [1989] 1 A.C. 53. The law here may be affected by the outcome in *Osman v. U.K.* [1998] E.H.R.L.R. 101.

[2] *Hallett v. Nicholson*, 1979 S.C. 1 at 9.

[3] *Shetland Line (1982) Ltd v. Secretary of State for Scotland*, 1996 S.L.T. 653.

[4] *Bonthrone v. Secretary of State for Scotland*, 1987 S.L.T. 34. While the case followed *Anns v. Merton LBC* [1978] A.C. 728 which was overruled by *Murphy v. Brentwood D.C.*, [1991] 1 A.C. 398, it is thought that the decision is not affected.

[5] *Ross v. Secretary of State for Scotland*, 1990 S.L.T. 13; but it has been said that the court cannot adjudicate on matters of policy: *X(Minors) v. Bedfordshire County Council* [1995] 2 A.C. 633, *per* Lord Browne-Wilkinson at 738.

[6] *Bonthrone v. Secretary of State for Scotland*, *supra*. See Lord Wilberforce's observations in *Anns v. Merton LBC supra*, at 754. The distinction has been regarded as an inadequate test for determining the existence of a duty of care: *Stovin v. Wise* [1996] A.C. 923. For a discussion of negligent omissions see Jane Convery "Public or Private? Duty of Care in a Statutory Framework" (1997) 60 M.L.R. 559.

[7] *Everett v. Griffiths* [1921] 1 A.C. 631; *cf. West Wiltshire D.C. v. Garland* [1995] 2 All E.R. 17.

[8] Lord Woolf M.R. in *W v. Home Office* [1997] Imm.A.R. 302.

Misuse of power

Beyond the kind of case already considered there can be cases where a **26.33** public body has misused its power and the applicant has suffered loss thereby.[9] In *Micosta SA v. Shetland Islands Council*[10] Lord Ross concluded from a survey of English and Scottish authorities that "deliberate misuse of statutory powers by a public body would be actionable under the law of Scotland at the instance of a third party who has suffered loss and damage in consequence of the misuse of statutory powers, provided that there was proof of malice or proof that the action has been taken by the public authority in the full knowledge that it did not possess the power which it purported to exercise." Thus, where the respondent is found to have acted with malice or bad faith, or otherwise with some dishonest motive, an entitlement to damages may arise where it would not otherwise have done.[11] But even actings conceived to be in the public interest may be challenged. In the Canadian case of *Roncarelli v. Duplessis*[12] the plaintiff was awarded damages against the President personally where he had knowingly acted without authority in instructing that a licence be withdrawn from the plaintiff.[13]

Damages and E.C. law

The European Court of Justice has held that member states may be **26.34** liable in damages for violations of E.C. law which cause loss to others. In *Francovich and Bonifaci v. Italian Republic*,[14] the court held that a member state which fails to implement an E.C. directive in defiance of its E.C. obligations is liable for losses caused to individuals as a result of the non-implementation. In that case, the unimplemented directive required the payment of wages to employees from a state-created guarantee fund in the event of the bankruptcy of their employers. Even though the directive did not have direct effect, the Court held that the employees could sue the Italian government for damages in the Italian courts. The remedy was based on Article 10 (formerly 5) of the E.C. Treaty and was to be provided according to the conditions imposed by national law for similar actions against the state arising under national law. But the Court made clear that national law had to provide such a remedy and could not impose conditions on its availability which make the remedy virtually impossible or excessively difficult.

In subsequent cases, the Court has further clarified the nature of the damages remedy and its extent. First, the remedy applies in all cases where a person is responsible for a violation of E.C. law which has direct effect. Secondly, in the case of a member state found to be in violation of E.C. law, damages may be recovered from the state irrespective of whether the provision in E.C. law has direct effect and irrespective of the particular organ or agency of the state which was responsible for the breach. The state for this purpose is widely defined. It includes the executive, the legislature and the judiciary and bodies outside the immediate structure of government to an extent not yet precisely defined.[15] Clearly, however, the U.K. state includes the Scottish Parlia-

---

[9] *Dawson v. Allardyce*, Feb. 18, 1809, F.C.
[10] 1986 S.L.T. 193 at 198.
[11] *Watt v. Thomson* (1870) 8M.(H.L.) 77; *Robertson v. Keith*, 1936 S.C. 29.
[12] (1959) 16 D.L.R. (2d) 689.
[13] See also *Bourgoin SA v. Ministry of Agriculture, Fisheries and Food* [1988] Q.B. 716.
[14] [1991] E.C.R. 1–5357.
[15] *cf.* Case C–188/89 *Foster v. British Gas plc* [1990] E.C.R. 1–3312.

ment and Executive. Thirdly, the damages remedy is available where the breach is of a provision of E.C. law intended to confer rights on individuals, is of a sufficiently serious nature and has caused the damage in question.[16] Non-implementation of a directive by its due date may be the classic example of a sufficiently serious breach of E.C. law.

The state may not take advantage of its own failure to implement E.C. directives. Where a directive has not been implemented, the state may be held liable in damages for loss sustained by a citizen, including loss caused by the failure of a private person to observe the directive. But where the problem is the incorrect implementation of a directive, the state will only be liable to individuals injured by the inadequacy where it is shown that the state was at fault. So, where losses arise from primary legislation found to be inconsistent with E.C. law, the state will only be liable where it is shown that Parliament has manifestly and gravely disregarded the limits of its discretion under E.C. law. But this does not necessarily mean that it acted intentionally or negligently.[17]

In addition to the damages remedy, E.C. law is relevant generally in relation to compensatory remedies for violations of rights created by E.C. law. This follows from the principle of E.C. law that national law must ensure the full effectiveness of rights conferred by E.C. law. Accordingly, where a directive has direct effect its provisions will override domestic legislation of a remedial nature which fails to satisfy E.C. law's requirement of the need for adequate remedies. Thus, in *Marshall v. Southampton and South-West Hampshire Area Health Authority (No. 2)*,[18] a victim of sexual discrimination contrary to the Equal Treatment directive was held to be entitled to found on the directive and to receive full compensation despite a limitation on the amount available under the relevant domestic legislation. The award comprised a sum for financial loss, for interest and a sum of £1,000 as compensation for injury to feelings.

Human rights

26.35 Express provision is made in the Human Rights Act 1998 for the award of damages for the unlawful acts of a public authority[19] and for arrest or detention in contravention of Article 5 of the Convention.[20] The court is expressly required by section 8(4) of the Act to take account of the principles applied by the Court of Human Rights in awarding compensation. As has already been noted in Chapter 6, the court exercises a due restraint both in the awarding of compensation and in the amount of any award made.

The Scotland Act 1998

26.36 It is unlikely that in the generality of the matter the Scotland Act will give rise to any particular problems with regard to damages. Where potential for such a claim arises the principles noted in this chapter

---

[16] Cases C–46 & 48/93, *Brasserie de Pêcheur SA v. Germany*; *R. v. Secretary of State for Transport, ex p. Factortame Ltd* [1996] E.C.R. 1–1029. The decision gives some guidance on the quantification of damages. There was no sufficiently serious breach in Case C–392/93, *R. v. H.M. Treasury, ex p. British Telecommunications plc* [1996] E.C.R. 1–1631, nor in *R. v. Ministry of Agriculture, Fisheries and Food, ex p. Lay and Gage* [1998] C.O.D. 387.

[17] *R. v. Secretary of State for Transport, ex p. Factortame Ltd* [1998] C.O.D. 381; in the House of Lords, July 1999.

[18] Case C–271/91 [1993] E.C.R. I–4367.

[19] s.8. For a recent discussion see Merris Amos, "Damages for breach of the Human Rights Act 1998" [1999] 2 E.H.R.L.R. 178.

[20] s.9. See the earlier discussion at para. 6.69.

should apply. But difficult questions may arise where legislation has been set aside with some consequential loss or damage.

APPENDICES

APPENDIX

APPENDIX 1

HUMAN RIGHTS ACT 1998

(1998 c. 42)

ARRANGEMENT OF SECTIONS

Introduction

681

SCHEDULES

An Act to give further effect to rights and freedoms guaranteed under the European Convention on Human Rights; to make provision with respect to holders of certain judicial offices who become judges of the European Court of Human Rights; and for connected purposes.   [9th November 1998]

BE IT ENACTED by the Queen's most Excellent Majesty, by and with the advice and consent of the Lords Spiritual and Temporal, and Commons, in this present Parliament assembled, and by the authority of the same, as follows:-

Introduction

The Convention Rights

1.–(1) In this Act "the Convention rights" means the rights and fundamental freedoms set out in—

    (a) Articles 2 to 12 and 14 of the Convention,
    (b) Articles 1 to 3 of the First Protocol, and
    (c) Articles 1 and 2 of the Sixth Protocol,
        as read with Articles 16 to 18 of the Convention.

(2) Those Articles are to have effect for the purposes of this Act subject to any designated derogation or reservation (as to which see sections 14 and 15).

(3) The Articles are set out in Schedule 1.

(4) The Secretary of State may by order make such amendments to this Act as he considers appropriate to reflect the effect, in relation to the United Kingdom, of a protocol.

(5) In subsection (4) "protocol" means a protocol to the Convention—

    (a) which the United Kingdom has ratified; or
    (b) which the United Kingdom has signed with a view to ratification.

(6) No amendment may be made by an order under subsection (4) so as to come into force before the protocol concerned is in force in relation to the United Kingdom.

Interpretation of Convention rights

2.–(1) A court or tribunal determining a question which has arisen in connection with a Convention right must take into account any—

    (a) judgment, decision, declaration or advisory opinion of the European Court of Human Rights,
    (b) opinion of the Commission given in a report adopted under Article 31 of the Convention,
    (c) decision of the Commission in connection with Article 26 or 27(2) of the Convention, or
    (d) decision of the Committee of Ministers taken under Article 46 of the Convention,

whenever made or given, so far as, in the opinion of the court or tribunal, it is relevant to the proceedings in which that question has arisen.

(2) Evidence of any judgment, decision, declaration or opinion of which account may have to be taken under this section is to be given in proceedings before any court or tribunal in such manner as may be provided by rules.

(3) In this section "rules" means rules of court or, in the case of proceedings before a tribunal, rules made for the purposes of this section—

(a) by the Lord Chancellor or the Secretary of State, in relation to any proceedings outside Scotland;

(b) by the Secretary of State, in relation to proceedings in Scotland; or

(c) by a Northern Ireland department, in relation to proceedings before a tribunal in Northern Ireland—

    (i) which deals with transferred matters; and

    (ii) for which no rules made under paragraph (a) are in force.

Legislation

Interpretation of legislation

3.–(1) So far as it is possible to do so, primary legislation and subordinate legislation must be read and given effect in a way which is compatible with the Convention rights.

(2) This section—

(a) applies to primary legislation and subordinate legislation whenever enacted;

(b) does not affect the validity, continuing operation or enforcement of any incompatible primary legislation; and

(c) does not affect the validity, continuing operation or enforcement of any incompatible subordinate legislation if (disregarding any possibility of revocation) primary legislation prevents removal of the incompatibility.

Declaration of incompatibility

4.–(1) Subsection (2) applies in any proceedings in which a court determines whether a provision of primary legislation is compatible with a Convention right.

(2) If the court is satisfied that the provision is incompatible with a Convention right, it may make a declaration of that incompatibility.

(3) Subsection (4) applies in any proceedings in which a court determines whether a provision of subordinate legislation, made in the exercise of a power conferred by primary legislation, is compatible with a Convention right.

(4) If the court is satisfied—

(a) that the provision is incompatible with a Convention right, and

(b) that (disregarding any possibility of revocation) the primary legislation concerned prevents removal of the incompatibility,

it may make a declaration of that incompatibility.

(5) In this section "court" means—

(a) the House of Lords;

(b) the Judicial Committee of the Privy Council;

(c) the Courts-Martial Appeal Court;

(d) in Scotland, the High Court of Justiciary sitting otherwise than as a trial court or the Court of Session;

(e) in England and Wales or Northern Ireland, the High Court or the Court of Appeal.

(6) A declaration under this section ("a declaration of incompatibility")—

(a) does not affect the validity, continuing operation or enforcement of the provision in respect of which it is given; and

(b) is not binding on the parties to the proceedings in which it is made.

Right of Crown to intervene

5.–(1) Where a court is considering whether to make a declaration of incompatibility, the Crown is entitled to notice in accordance with rules of court.

(2) In any case to which subsection (1) applies—

(a) a Minister of the Crown (or a person nominated by him),

(b) a member of the Scottish Executive,

(c) a Northern Ireland Minister,

(d) a Northern Ireland department,

is entitled, on giving notice in accordance with rules of court, to be joined as a party to the proceedings.

(3) Notice under subsection (2) may be given at any time during the proceedings.

(4) A person who has been made a party to criminal proceedings (other than in Scotland) as the result of a notice under subsection (2) may, with leave, appeal to the House of Lords against any declaration of incompatibility made in the proceedings.

(5) In subsection (4)—

"criminal proceedings" includes all proceedings before the Courts-Martial Appeal Court; and

"leave" means leave granted by the court making the declaration of incompatibility or by the House of Lords.

Public authorities

Acts of public authorities

6.–(1) It is unlawful for a public authority to act in a way which is incompatible with a Convention right.

(2) Subsection (1) does not apply to an act if—

(a) as the result of one or more provisions of primary legislation, the authority could not have acted differently; or

(b) in the case of one or more provisions of, or made under, primary legislation which cannot be read or given effect in a way which is compatible with the Convention rights, the authority was acting so as to give effect to or enforce those provisions.

(3) In this section "public authority" includes—

(a) a court or tribunal, and

(b) any person certain of whose functions are functions of a public nature,

but does not include either House of Parliament or a person exercising functions in connection with proceedings in Parliament.

(4) In subsection (3) "Parliament" does not include the House of Lords in its judicial capacity.

(5) In relation to a particular act, a person is not a public authority by virtue only of subsection (3)(b) if the nature of the act is private.

(6) "An act" includes a failure to act but does not include a failure to—

(a) introduce in, or lay before, Parliament a proposal for legislation; or

(b) make any primary legislation or remedial order.

Proceedings

7.–(1) A person who claims that a public authority has acted (or proposes to act) in a way which is made unlawful by section 6(1) may—

(a) bring proceedings against the authority under this Act in the appropriate court or tribunal, or

(b) rely on the Convention right or rights concerned in any legal proceedings,

but only if he is (or would be) a victim of the unlawful act.

(2) In subsection (1)(a) "appropriate court or tribunal" means such court or tribunal as may be determined in accordance with rules; and proceedings against an authority include a counterclaim or similar proceeding.

(3) If the proceedings are brought on an application for judicial review, the applicant is to be taken to have a sufficient interest in relation to the unlawful act only if he is, or would be, a victim of that act.

(4) If the proceedings are made by way of a petition for judicial review in Scotland, the applicant shall be taken to have title and interest to sue in relation to the unlawful act only if he is, or would be, a victim of that act.

(5) Proceedings under subsection (1)(a) must be brought before the end of—

(a) the period of one year beginning with the date on which the act complained of took place; or

(b) such longer period as the court or tribunal considers equitable having regard to all the circumstances,

but that is subject to any rule imposing a stricter time limit in relation to the procedure in question.

(6) In subsection (1)(b) "legal proceedings" includes—
    (a) proceedings brought by or at the instigation of a public authority; and
    (b) an appeal against the decision of a court or tribunal.

(7) For the purposes of this section, a person is a victim of an unlawful act only if he would be a victim for the purposes of Article 34 of the Convention if proceedings were brought in the European Court of Human Rights in respect of that act.

(8) Nothing in this Act creates a criminal offence.

(9) In this section "rules" means—
    (a) in relation to proceedings before a court or tribunal outside Scotland, rules made by the Lord Chancellor or the Secretary of State for the purposes of this section or rules of court,
    (b) in relation to proceedings before a court or tribunal in Scotland, rules made by the Secretary of State for those purposes,
    (c) in relation to proceedings before a tribunal in Northern Ireland—
        (i) which deals with transferred matters; and
        (ii) for which no rules made under paragraph (a) are in force,
        rules made by a Northern Ireland department for those purposes,
and includes provision made by order under section 1 of the Courts and Legal Services Act 1990.

(10) In making rules, regard must be had to section 9.

(11) The Minister who has power to make rules in relation to a particular tribunal may, to the extent he considers it necessary to ensure that the tribunal can provide an appropriate remedy in relation to an act (or proposed act) of a public authority which is (or would be) unlawful as a result of section 6(1), by order add to—
    (a) the relief or remedies which the tribunal may grant; or
    (b) the grounds on which it may grant any of them.

(12) An order made under subsection (11) may contain such incidental, supplemental, consequential or transitional provision as the Minister making it considers appropriate.

(13) "The Minister" includes the Northern Ireland department concerned.

Judicial remedies

8.–(1) In relation to any act (or proposed act) of a public authority which the court finds is (or would be) unlawful, it may grant such relief or remedy, or make such order, within its powers as it considers just and appropriate.

(2) But damages may be awarded only by a court which has power to award damages, or to order the payment of compensation, in civil proceedings.

(3) No award of damages is to be made unless, taking account of all the circumstances of the case, including—
    (a) any other relief or remedy granted, or order made, in relation to the act in question (by that or any other court), and
    (b) the consequences of any decision (of that or any other court) in respect of that act,
the court is satisfied that the award is necessary to afford just satisfaction to the person in whose favour it is made.

(4) In determining—
    (a) whether to award damages, or
    (b) the amount of an award,
the court must take into account the principles applied by the European Court of Human Rights in relation to the award of compensation under Article 41 of the Convention.

(5) A public authority against which damages are awarded is to be treated—
    (a) in Scotland, for the purposes of section 3 of the Law Reform (Miscellaneous Provisions) (Scotland) Act 1940 as if the award were made in an action of damages in which the authority has been found liable in respect of loss or damage to the person to whom the award is made;
    (b) for the purposes of the Civil Liability (Contribution) Act 1978 as liable in respect of damage suffered by the person to whom the award is made.

(6) In this section—
"court" includes a tribunal;
"damages" means damages for an unlawful act of a public authority; and
"unlawful" means unlawful under section 6(1).

Judicial acts
9.–(1) Proceedings under section 7(1)(a) in respect of a judicial act may be brought only—
(a) by exercising a right of appeal;
(b) on an application (in Scotland a petition) for judicial review; or
(c) in such other forum as may be prescribed by rules.
(2) That does not affect any rule of law which prevents a court from being the subject of judicial review.
(3) In proceedings under this Act in respect of a judicial act done in good faith, damages may not be awarded otherwise than to compensate a person to the extent required by Article 5(5) of the Convention.
(4) An award of damages permitted by subsection (3) is to be made against the Crown; but no award may be made unless the appropriate person, if not a party to the proceedings, is joined.
(5) In this section—
"appropriate person" means the Minister responsible for the court concerned, or a person or government department nominated by him;
"court" includes a tribunal;
"judge" includes a member of a tribunal, a justice of the peace and a clerk or other officer entitled to exercise the jurisdiction of a court;
"judicial act" means a judicial act of a court and includes an act done on the instructions, or on behalf, of a judge; and
"rules" has the same meaning as in section 7(9).

Remedial action

Power to take remedial action
10.–(1) This section applies if—
(a) a provision of legislation has been declared under section 4 to be incompatible with a Convention right and, if an appeal lies—
(i) all persons who may appeal have stated in writing that they do not intend to do so;
(ii) the time for bringing an appeal has expired and no appeal has been brought within that time; or
(iii) an appeal brought within that time has been determined or abandoned; or
(b) it appears to a Minister of the Crown or Her Majesty in Council that, having regard to a finding of the European Court of Human Rights made after the coming into force of this section in proceedings against the United Kingdom, a provision of legislation is incompatible with an obligation of the United Kingdom arising from the Convention.
(2) If a Minister of the Crown considers that there are compelling reasons for proceeding under this section, he may by order make such amendments to the legislation as he considers necessary to remove the incompatibility.
(3) If, in the case of subordinate legislation, a Minister of the Crown considers—
(a) that it is necessary to amend the primary legislation under which the subordinate legislation in question was made, in order to enable the incompatibility to be removed, and
(b) that there are compelling reasons for proceeding under this section,
he may by order make such amendments to the primary legislation as he considers necessary.
(4) This section also applies where the provision in question is in subordinate legislation and has been quashed, or declared invalid, by reason of incompatibility with a Convention right and the Minister proposes to proceed under paragraph 2(b) of Schedule 2.

(5) If the legislation is an Order in Council, the power conferred by subsection (2) or (3) is exercisable by Her Majesty in Council.

(6) In this section "legislation" does not include a Measure of the Church Assembly or of the General Synod of the Church of England.

(7) Schedule 2 makes further provision about remedial orders.

Other rights and proceedings

Safeguard for existing human rights
11. A person's reliance on a Convention right does not restrict—
   (a) any other right or freedom conferred on him by or under any law having effect in any part of the United Kingdom; or
   (b) his right to make any claim or bring any proceedings which he could make or bring apart from sections 7 to 9.

Freedom of expression
12.–(1) This section applies if a court is considering whether to grant any relief which, if granted, might affect the exercise of the Convention right to freedom of expression.

(2) If the person against whom the application for relief is made ("the respondent") is neither present nor represented, no such relief is to be granted unless the court is satisfied—
   (a) that the applicant has taken all practicable steps to notify the respondent; or
   (b) that there are compelling reasons why the respondent should not be notified.

(3) No such relief is to be granted so as to restrain publication before trial unless the court is satisfied that the applicant is likely to establish that publication should not be allowed.

(4) The court must have particular regard to the importance of the Convention right to freedom of expression and, where the proceedings relate to material which the respondent claims, or which appears to the court, to be journalistic, literary or artistic material (or to conduct connected with such material), to—
   (a) the extent to which—
      (i) the material has, or is about to, become available to the public; or
      (ii) it is, or would be, in the public interest for the material to be published;
   (b) any relevant privacy code.

(5) In this section—
"court" includes a tribunal; and
"relief" includes any remedy or order (other than in criminal proceedings).

Freedom of thought, conscience and religion
13.–(1) If a court's determination of any question arising under this Act might affect the exercise by a religious organisation (itself or its members collectively) of the Convention right to freedom of thought, conscience and religion, it must have particular regard to the importance of that right.

(2) In this section "court" includes a tribunal.

Derogations and reservations

Derogations
14.–(1) In this Act "designated derogation" means—
   (a) the United Kingdom's derogation from Article 5(3) of the Convention; and
   (b) any derogation by the United Kingdom from an Article of the Convention, or of any protocol to the Convention, which is designated for the purposes of this Act in an order made by the Secretary of State.

(2) The derogation referred to in subsection (1)(a) is set out in Part I of Schedule 3.

(3) If a designated derogation is amended or replaced it ceases to be a designated derogation.

(4) But subsection (3) does not prevent the Secretary of State from exercising his power under subsection (1)(b) to make a fresh designation order in respect of the Article concerned.

(5) The Secretary of State must by order make such amendments to Schedule 3 as he considers appropriate to reflect—

    (a) any designation order; or

    (b) the effect of subsection (3).

(6) A designation order may be made in anticipation of the making by the United Kingdom of a proposed derogation.

Reservations

15.–(1) In this Act "designated reservation" means—

    (a) the United Kingdom's reservation to Article 2 of the First Protocol to the Convention; and

    (b) any other reservation by the United Kingdom to an Article of the Convention, or of any protocol to the Convention, which is designated for the purposes of this Act in an order made by the Secretary of State.

(2) The text of the reservation referred to in subsection (1)(a) is set out in Part II of Schedule 3.

(3) If a designated reservation is withdrawn wholly or in part it ceases to be a designated reservation.

(4) But subsection (3) does not prevent the Secretary of State from exercising his power under subsection (1)(b) to make a fresh designation order in respect of the Article concerned.

(5) The Secretary of State must by order make such amendments to this Act as he considers appropriate to reflect—

    (a) any designation order; or

    (b) the effect of subsection (3).

Period for which designated derogations have effect

16.–(1) If it has not already been withdrawn by the United Kingdom, a designated derogation ceases to have effect for the purposes of this Act—

    (a) in the case of the derogation referred to in section 14(1)(a), at the end of the period of five years beginning with the date on which section 1(2) came into force;

    (b) in the case of any other derogation, at the end of the period of five years beginning with the date on which the order designating it was made.

(2) At any time before the period—

    (a) fixed by subsection (1)(a) or (b), or

    (b) extended by an order under this subsection,

comes to an end, the Secretary of State may by order extend it by a further period of five years.

(3) An order under section 14(1)(b) ceases to have effect at the end of the period for consideration, unless a resolution has been passed by each House approving the order.

(4) Subsection (3) does not affect—

    (a) anything done in reliance on the order; or

    (b) the power to make a fresh order under section 14(1)(b).

(5) In subsection (3) "period for consideration" means the period of forty days beginning with the day on which the order was made.

(6) In calculating the period for consideration, no account is to be taken of any time during which—

    (a) Parliament is dissolved or prorogued; or

    (b) both Houses are adjourned for more than four days.

(7) If a designated derogation is withdrawn by the United Kingdom, the Secretary of State must by order make such amendments to this Act as he considers are required to reflect that withdrawal.

Periodic review of designated reservations

17.–(1) The appropriate Minister must review the designated reservation referred to in section 15(1)(a)—

(a) before the end of the period of five years beginning with the date on which section 1(2) came into force; and

(b) if that designation is still in force, before the end of the period of five years beginning with the date on which the last report relating to it was laid under subsection (3).

(2) The appropriate Minister must review each of the other designated reservations (if any)—

(a) before the end of the period of five years beginning with the date on which the order designating the reservation first came into force; and

(b) if the designation is still in force, before the end of the period of five years beginning with the date on which the last report relating to it was laid under subsection (3).

(3) The Minister conducting a review under this section must prepare a report on the result of the review and lay a copy of it before each House of Parliament.

Judges of the European Court of Human Rights

Appointment to European Court of Human Rights

18.–(1) In this section "judicial office" means the office of—

(a) Lord Justice of Appeal, Justice of the High Court or Circuit judge, in England and Wales;

(b) judge of the Court of Session or sheriff, in Scotland;

(c) Lord Justice of Appeal, judge of the High Court or county court judge, in Northern Ireland.

(2) The holder of a judicial office may become a judge of the European Court of Human Rights ("the Court") without being required to relinquish his office.

(3) But he is not required to perform the duties of his judicial office while he is a judge of the Court.

(4) In respect of any period during which he is a judge of the Court—

(a) a Lord Justice of Appeal or Justice of the High Court is not to count as a judge of the relevant court for the purposes of section 2(1) or 4(1) of the Supreme Court Act 1981 (maximum number of judges) nor as a judge of the Supreme Court for the purposes of section 12(1) to (6) of that Act (salaries etc.);

(b) a judge of the Court of Session is not to count as a judge of that court for the purposes of section 1(1) of the Court of Session Act 1988 (maximum number of judges) or of section 9(1)(c) of the Administration of Justice Act 1973 ("the 1973 Act") (salaries etc.);

(c) a Lord Justice of Appeal or judge of the High Court in Northern Ireland is not to count as a judge of the relevant court for the purposes of section 2(1) or 3(1) of the Judicature (Northern Ireland) Act 1978 (maximum number of judges) nor as a judge of the Supreme Court of Northern Ireland for the purposes of section 9(1)(d) of the 1973 Act (salaries etc.);

(d) a Circuit judge is not to count as such for the purposes of section 18 of the Courts Act 1971 (salaries etc.);

(e) a sheriff is not to count as such for the purposes of section 14 of the Sheriff Courts (Scotland) Act 1907 (salaries etc.);

(f) a county court judge of Northern Ireland is not to count as such for the purposes of section 106 of the County Courts Act Northern Ireland) 1959 (salaries etc.).

(5) If a sheriff principal is appointed a judge of the Court, section 11(1) of the Sheriff Courts (Scotland) Act 1971 (temporary appointment of sheriff principal) applies, while he holds that appointment, as if his office is vacant.

(6) Schedule 4 makes provision about judicial pensions in relation to the holder of a judicial office who serves as a judge of the Court.

(7) The Lord Chancellor or the Secretary of State may by order make such transitional provision (including, in particular, provision for a temporary increase

in the maximum number of judges) as he considers appropriate in relation to any holder of a judicial office who has completed his service as a judge of the Court.

Parliamentary procedure

Statements of compatibility

19.–(1) A Minister of the Crown in charge of a Bill in either House of Parliament must, before Second Reading of the Bill—

(a) make a statement to the effect that in his view the provisions of the Bill are compatible with the Convention rights ("a statement of compatibility"); or

(b) make a statement to the effect that although he is unable to make a statement of compatibility the government nevertheless wishes the House to proceed with the Bill.

(2) The statement must be in writing and be published in such manner as the Minister making it considers appropriate.

Supplemental

Orders etc. under this Act

20.–(1) Any power of a Minister of the Crown to make an order under this Act is exercisable by statutory instrument.

(2) The power of the Lord Chancellor or the Secretary of State to make rules (other than rules of court) under section 2(3) or 7(9) is exercisable by statutory instrument.

(3) Any statutory instrument made under section 14, 15 or 16(7) must be laid before Parliament.

(4) No order may be made by the Lord Chancellor or the Secretary of State under section 1(4), 7(11) or 16(2) unless a draft of the order has been laid before, and approved by, each House of Parliament.

(5) Any statutory instrument made under section 18(7) or Schedule 4, or to which subsection (2) applies, shall be subject to annulment in pursuance of a resolution of either House of Parliament.

(6) The power of a Northern Ireland department to make—

(a) rules under section 2(3)(c) or 7(9)(c), or

(b) an order under section 7(11),

is exercisable by statutory rule for the purposes of the Statutory Rules (Northern Ireland) Order 1979.

(7) Any rules made under section 2(3)(c) or 7(9)(c) shall be subject to negative resolution; and section 41(6) of the Interpretation Act Northern Ireland) 1954 (meaning of "subject to negative resolution") shall apply as if the power to make the rules were conferred by an Act of the Northern Ireland Assembly.

(8) No order may be made by a Northern Ireland department under section 7(11) unless a draft of the order has been laid before, and approved by, the Northern Ireland Assembly.

Interpretation, etc.

21.–(1) In this Act—

"amend" includes repeal and apply (with or without modifications);

"the appropriate Minister" means the Minister of the Crown having charge of the appropriate authorised government department (within the meaning of the Crown Proceedings Act 1947);

"the Commission" means the European Commission of Human Rights;

"the Convention" means the Convention for the Protection of Human Rights and Fundamental Freedoms, agreed by the Council of Europe at Rome on 4th November 1950 as it has effect for the time being in relation to the United Kingdom;

"declaration of incompatibility" means a declaration under section 4;

"Minister of the Crown" has the same meaning as in the Ministers of the Crown Act 1975;

"Northern Ireland Minister" includes the First Minister and the deputy First Minister in Northern Ireland;

"primary legislation" means any—

(a) public general Act;

(b) local and personal Act;

(c) private Act;

(d) Measure of the Church Assembly;

(e) Measure of the General Synod of the Church of England;

(f) Order in Council—

    (i) made in exercise of Her Majesty's Royal Prerogative;

    (ii) made under section 38(1)(a) of the Northern Ireland Constitution Act 1973 or the corresponding provision of the Northern Ireland Act 1998; or

    (iii) amending an Act of a kind mentioned in paragraph (a), (b) or (c);

and includes an order or other instrument made under primary legislation (otherwise than by the National Assembly for Wales, a member of the Scottish Executive, a Northern Ireland Minister or a Northern Ireland department) to the extent to which it operates to bring one or more provisions of that legislation into force or amends any primary legislation;

"the First Protocol" means the protocol to the Convention agreed at Paris on 20th March 1952;

"the Sixth Protocol" means the protocol to the Convention agreed at Strasbourg on 28th April 1983;

"the Eleventh Protocol" means the protocol to the Convention (restructuring the control machinery established by the Convention) agreed at Strasbourg on 11th May 1994;

"remedial order" means an order under section 10;

"subordinate legislation" means any—

(a) Order in Council other than one—

    (i) made in exercise of Her Majesty's Royal Prerogative;

    (ii) made under section 38(1)(a) of the Northern Ireland Constitution Act 1973 or the corresponding provision of the Northern Ireland Act 1998; or

    (iii) amending an Act of a kind mentioned in the definition of primary legislation;

(b) Act of the Scottish Parliament;

(c) Act of the Parliament of Northern Ireland;

(d) Measure of the Assembly established under section 1 of the Northern Ireland Assembly Act 1973;

(e) Act of the Northern Ireland Assembly;

(f) order, rules, regulations, scheme, warrant, byelaw or other instrument made under primary legislation (except to the extent to which it operates to bring one or more provisions of that legislation into force or amends any primary legislation);

(g) order, rules, regulations, scheme, warrant, byelaw or other instrument made under legislation mentioned in paragraph (b), (c), (d) or (e) or made under an Order in Council applying only to Northern Ireland;

(h) order, rules, regulations, scheme, warrant, byelaw or other instrument made by a member of the Scottish Executive, a Northern Ireland Minister or a Northern Ireland department in exercise of prerogative or other executive functions of Her Majesty which are exercisable by such a person on behalf of Her Majesty;

"transferred matters" has the same meaning as in the Northern Ireland Act 1998; and

"tribunal" means any tribunal in which legal proceedings may be brought.

(2) The references in paragraphs (b) and (c) of section 2(1) to Articles are to Articles of the Convention as they had effect immediately before the coming into force of the Eleventh Protocol.

(3) The reference in paragraph (d) of section 2(1) to Article 46 includes a reference to Articles 32 and 54 of the Convention as they had effect immediately before the coming into force of the Eleventh Protocol.

(4) The references in section 2(1) to a report or decision of the Commission or a decision of the Committee of Ministers include references to a report or decision made as provided by paragraphs 3, 4 and 6 of Article 5 of the Eleventh Protocol (transitional provisions).

(5) Any liability under the Army Act 1955, the Air Force Act 1955 or the Naval Discipline Act 1957 to suffer death for an offence is replaced by a liability to imprisonment for life or any less punishment authorised by those Acts; and those Acts shall accordingly have effect with the necessary modifications.

Short title, commencement, application and extent

22.–(1) This Act may be cited as the Human Rights Act 1998.

(2) Sections 18, 20 and 21(5) and this section come into force on the passing of this Act.

(3) The other provisions of this Act come into force on such day as the Secretary of State may by order appoint; and different days may be appointed for different purposes.

(4) Paragraph (b) of subsection (1) of section 7 applies to proceedings brought by or at the instigation of a public authority whenever the act in question took place; but otherwise that subsection does not apply to an act taking place before the coming into force of that section.

(5) This Act binds the Crown.

(6) This Act extends to Northern Ireland.

(7) Section 21(5), so far as it relates to any provision contained in the Army Act 1955, the Air Force Act 1955 or the Naval Discipline Act 1957, extends to any place to which that provision extends.

SCHEDULES

Schedule 1

THE ARTICLES
PART I
THE CONVENTION

RIGHTS AND FREEDOMS

ARTICLE 2

RIGHT TO LIFE

1. Everyone's right to life shall be protected by law. No one shall be deprived of his life intentionally save in the execution of a sentence of a court following his conviction of a crime for which this penalty is provided by law.

2. Deprivation of life shall not be regarded as inflicted in contravention of this Article when it results from the use of force which is no more than absolutely necessary:

    (a) in defence of any person from unlawful violence;
    (b) in order to effect a lawful arrest or to prevent the escape of a person lawfully detained;
    (c) in action lawfully taken for the purpose of quelling a riot or insurrection.

ARTICLE 3

PROHIBITION OF TORTURE

No one shall be subjected to torture or to inhuman or degrading treatment or punishment.

ARTICLE 4

PROHIBITION OF SLAVERY AND FORCED LABOUR

1. No one shall be held in slavery or servitude.

2. No one shall be required to perform forced or compulsory labour.

3. For the purpose of this Article the term "forced or compulsory labour" shall not include:

(a) any work required to be done in the ordinary course of detention imposed according to the provisions of Article 5 of this Convention or during conditional release from such detention;

(b) any service of a military character or, in case of conscientious objectors in countries where they are recognised, service exacted instead of compulsory military service;

(c) any service exacted in case of an emergency or calamity threatening the life or well-being of the community;

(d) any work or service which forms part of normal civic obligations.

ARTICLE 5

RIGHT TO LIBERTY AND SECURITY

1. Everyone has the right to liberty and security of person. No one shall be deprived of his liberty save in the following cases and in accordance with a procedure prescribed by law:

(a) the lawful detention of a person after conviction by a competent court;

(b) the lawful arrest or detention of a person for non-compliance with the lawful order of a court or in order to secure the fulfilment of any obligation prescribed by law;

(c) the lawful arrest or detention of a person effected for the purpose of bringing him before the competent legal authority on reasonable suspicion of having committed an offence or when it is reasonably considered necessary to prevent his committing an offence or fleeing after having done so;

(d) the detention of a minor by lawful order for the purpose of educational supervision or his lawful detention for the purpose of bringing him before the competent legal authority;

(e) the lawful detention of persons for the prevention of the spreading of infectious diseases, of persons of unsound mind, alcoholics or drug addicts or vagrants;

(f) the lawful arrest or detention of a person to prevent his effecting an unauthorised entry into the country or of a person against whom action is being taken with a view to deportation or extradition.

2. Everyone who is arrested shall be informed promptly, in a language which he understands, of the reasons for his arrest and of any charge against him.

3. Everyone arrested or detained in accordance with the provisions of paragraph 1(c) of this Article shall be brought promptly before a judge or other officer authorised by law to exercise judicial power and shall be entitled to trial within a reasonable time or to release pending trial. Release may be conditioned by guarantees to appear for trial.

4. Everyone who is deprived of his liberty by arrest or detention shall be entitled to take proceedings by which the lawfulness of his detention shall be decided speedily by a court and his release ordered if the detention is not lawful.

5. Everyone who has been the victim of arrest or detention in contravention of the provisions of this Article shall have an enforceable right to compensation.

ARTICLE 6

RIGHT TO A FAIR TRIAL

1. In the determination of his civil rights and obligations or of any criminal charge against him, everyone is entitled to a fair and public hearing within a reasonable time by an independent and impartial tribunal established by law. Judgment shall be pronounced publicly but the press and public may be excluded from all or part of the trial in the interest of morals, public order or national security in a democratic society, where the interests of juveniles or the protection of the private life of the parties so require, or to the extent strictly necessary in the opinion of the court in special circumstances where publicity would prejudice the interests of justice.

2. Everyone charged with a criminal offence shall be presumed innocent until proved guilty according to law.

3. Everyone charged with a criminal offence has the following minimum rights:

(a) to be informed promptly, in a language which he understands and in detail, of the nature and cause of the accusation against him;

(b) to have adequate time and facilities for the preparation of his defence;

(c) to defend himself in person or through legal assistance of his own choosing or, if he has not sufficient means to pay for legal assistance, to be given it free when the interests of justice so require;

(d) to examine or have examined witnesses against him and to obtain the attendance and examination of witnesses on his behalf under the same conditions as witnesses against him;

(e) to have the free assistance of an interpreter if he cannot understand or speak the language used in court.

ARTICLE 7

NO PUNISHMENT WITHOUT LAW

1. No one shall be held guilty of any criminal offence on account of any act or omission which did not constitute a criminal offence under national or international law at the time when it was committed. Nor shall a heavier penalty be imposed than the one that was applicable at the time the criminal offence was committed.

2. This Article shall not prejudice the trial and punishment of any person for any act or omission which, at the time when it was committed, was criminal according to the general principles of law recognised by civilised nations.

ARTICLE 8

RIGHT TO RESPECT FOR PRIVATE AND FAMILY LIFE

1. Everyone has the right to respect for his private and family life, his home and his correspondence.

2. There shall be no interference by a public authority with the exercise of this right except such as is in accordance with the law and is necessary in a democratic society in the interests of national security, public safety or the economic well-being of the country, for the prevention of disorder or crime, for the protection of health or morals, or for the protection of the rights and freedoms of others.

ARTICLE 9

FREEDOM OF THOUGHT, CONSCIENCE AND RELIGION

1. Everyone has the right to freedom of thought, conscience and religion; this right includes freedom to change his religion or belief and freedom, either alone or in community with others and in public or private, to manifest his religion or belief, in worship, teaching, practice and observance.

2. Freedom to manifest one's religion or beliefs shall be subject only to such limitations as are prescribed by law and are necessary in a democratic society in the interests of public safety, for the protection of public order, health or morals, or for the protection of the rights and freedoms of others.

ARTICLE 10

FREEDOM OF EXPRESSION

1. Everyone has the right to freedom of expression. This right shall include freedom to hold opinions and to receive and impart information and ideas without interference by public authority and regardless of frontiers. This Article shall not prevent States from requiring the licensing of broadcasting, television or cinema enterprises.

2. The exercise of these freedoms, since it carries with it duties and responsibilities, may be subject to such formalities, conditions, restrictions or penalties as are prescribed by law and are necessary in a democratic society, in the interests of national security, territorial integrity or public safety, for the prevention of disorder or crime, for the protection of health or morals, for the protection of the reputation or rights of others, for preventing the disclosure of information received in confidence, or for maintaining the authority and impartiality of the judiciary.

ARTICLE 11

FREEDOM OF ASSEMBLY AND ASSOCIATION

1. Everyone has the right to freedom of peaceful assembly and to freedom of association with others, including the right to form and to join trade unions for the protection of his interests.

2. No restrictions shall be placed on the exercise of these rights other than such as are prescribed by law and are necessary in a democratic society in the interests of national security or public safety, for the prevention of disorder or crime, for the protection of health or morals or for the protection of the rights and freedoms of others. This Article shall not prevent the imposition of lawful restrictions on the exercise of these rights by members of the armed forces, of the police or of the administration of the State.

ARTICLE 12

RIGHT TO MARRY

Men and women of marriageable age have the right to marry and to found a family, according to the national laws governing the exercise of this right.

ARTICLE 14

PROHIBITION OF DISCRIMINATION

The enjoyment of the rights and freedoms set forth in this Convention shall be secured without discrimination on any ground such as sex, race, colour, language, religion, political or other opinion, national or social origin, association with a national minority, property, birth or other status.

ARTICLE 16

RESTRICTIONS ON POLITICAL ACTIVITY OF ALIENS

Nothing in Articles 10, 11 and 14 shall be regarded as preventing the High Contracting Parties from imposing restrictions on the political activity of aliens.

ARTICLE 17

PROHIBITION OF ABUSE OF RIGHTS

Nothing in this Convention may be interpreted as implying for any State, group or person any right to engage in any activity or perform any act aimed at the destruction of any of the rights and freedoms set forth herein or at their limitation to a greater extent than is provided for in the Convention.

ARTICLE 18

LIMITATION ON USE OF RESTRICTIONS ON RIGHTS

The restrictions permitted under this Convention to the said rights and freedoms shall not be applied for any purpose other than those for which they have been prescribed.

PART II

THE FIRST PROTOCOL

ARTICLE 1

PROTECTION OF PROPERTY

Every natural or legal person is entitled to the peaceful enjoyment of his possessions. No one shall be deprived of his possessions except in the public interest and subject to the conditions provided for by law and by the general principles of international law. The preceding provisions shall not, however, in any way impair the right of a State to enforce such laws as it deems necessary to control the use of property in accordance with the general interest or to secure the payment of taxes or other contributions or penalties.

ARTICLE 2

RIGHT TO EDUCATION

No person shall be denied the right to education. In the exercise of any functions which it assumes in relation to education and to teaching, the State shall respect the right of parents to ensure such education and teaching in conformity with their own religious and philosophical convictions.

ARTICLE 3

RIGHT TO FREE ELECTIONS

The High Contracting Parties undertake to hold free elections at reasonable intervals by secret ballot, under conditions which will ensure the free expression of the opinion of the people in the choice of the legislature.

PART III

THE SIXTH PROTOCOL

ARTICLE 1

ABOLITION OF THE DEATH PENALTY

The death penalty shall be abolished. No one shall be condemned to such penalty or executed.

ARTICLE 2

DEATH PENALTY IN TIME OF WAR

A State may make provision in its law for the death penalty in respect of acts committed in time of war or of imminent threat of war; such penalty shall be applied only in the instances laid down in the law and in accordance with its provisions. The State shall communicate to the Secretary General of the Council of Europe the relevant provisions of that law.

Schedule 2

REMEDIAL ORDERS

Orders

1.–(1) A remedial order may—
    (a) contain such incidental, supplemental, consequential or transitional provision as the person making it considers appropriate;
    (b) be made so as to have effect from a date earlier than that on which it is made;
    (c) make provision for the delegation of specific functions;
    (d) make different provision for different cases.
(2) The power conferred by sub-paragraph (1)(a) includes—
    (a) power to amend primary legislation (including primary legislation other than that which contains the incompatible provision); and
    (b) power to amend or revoke subordinate legislation (including subordinate legislation other than that which contains the incompatible provision).
(3) A remedial order may be made so as to have the same extent as the legislation which it affects.
(4) No person is to be guilty of an offence solely as a result of the retrospective effect of a remedial order.

Procedure

2. No remedial order may be made unless—
    (a) a draft of the order has been approved by a resolution of each House of Parliament made after the end of the period of 60 days beginning with the day on which the draft was laid; or
    (b) it is declared in the order that it appears to the person making it that, because of the urgency of the matter, it is necessary to make the order without a draft being so approved.

Orders laid in draft

3.–(1) No draft may be laid under paragraph 2(a) unless—
    (a) the person proposing to make the order has laid before Parliament a document which contains a draft of the proposed order and the required information; and
    (b) the period of 60 days, beginning with the day on which the document required by this sub-paragraph was laid, has ended.
(2) If representations have been made during that period, the draft laid under paragraph 2(a) must be accompanied by a statement containing—
    (a) a summary of the representations; and
    (b) if, as a result of the representations, the proposed order has been changed, details of the changes.

Urgent cases

4.–(1) If a remedial order ("the original order") is made without being approved in draft, the person making it must lay it before Parliament, accompanied by the required information, after it is made.
(2) If representations have been made during the period of 60 days beginning with the day on which the original order was made, the person making it must (after the end of that period) lay before Parliament a statement containing—
    (a) a summary of the representations; and
    (b) if, as a result of the representations, he considers it appropriate to make changes to the original order, details of the changes.
(3) If sub-paragraph (2)(b) applies, the person making the statement must—
    (a) make a further remedial order replacing the original order; and
    (b) lay the replacement order before Parliament.
(4) If, at the end of the period of 120 days beginning with the day on which the original order was made, a resolution has not been passed by each House approving the original or replacement order, the order ceases to have effect (but without that affecting anything previously done under either order or the power to make a fresh remedial order).

Definitions

5. In this Schedule—
    "representations" means representations about a remedial order (or proposed remedial order) made to the person making (or proposing to make) it and includes any relevant Parliamentary report or resolution; and
    "required information" means—
    (a) an explanation of the incompatibility which the order (or proposed order) seeks to remove, including particulars of the relevant declaration, finding or order; and
    (b) a statement of the reasons for proceeding under section 10 and for making an order in those terms.

Calculating periods

6. In calculating any period for the purposes of this Schedule, no account is to be taken of any time during which—
    (a) Parliament is dissolved or prorogued; or
    (b) both Houses are adjourned for more than four days.

Schedule 3

DEROGATION AND RESERVATION

PART I

DEROGATION

The 1988 notification

The United Kingdom Permanent Representative to the Council of Europe presents his compliments to the Secretary General of the Council, and has the honour to convey the following information in order to ensure compliance with the obligations of Her Majesty's Government in the United Kingdom under Article 15(3) of the Convention for the Protection of Human Rights and Fundamental Freedoms signed at Rome on 4 November 1950.

There have been in the United Kingdom in recent years campaigns of organised terrorism connected with the affairs of Northern Ireland which have manifested themselves in activities which have included repeated murder, attempted murder, maiming, intimidation and violent civil disturbance and in bombing and fire raising which have resulted in death, injury and widespread destruction of property. As a result, a public emergency within the meaning of Article 15(1) of the Convention exists in the United Kingdom.

The Government found it necessary in 1974 to introduce and since then, in cases concerning persons reasonably suspected of involvement in terrorism connected with the affairs of Northern Ireland, or of certain offences under the legislation, who have been detained for 48 hours, to exercise powers enabling further detention without charge, for periods of up to five days, on the authority of the Secretary of State. These powers are at present to be found in Section 12 of the Prevention of Terrorism (Temporary Provisions) Act 1984, Article 9 of the Prevention of Terrorism (Supplemental Temporary Provisions) Order 1984 and Article 10 of the Prevention of Terrorism (Supplemental Temporary Provisions) (Northern Ireland) Order 1984.

Section 12 of the Prevention of Terrorism (Temporary Provisions) Act 1984 provides for a person whom a constable has arrested on reasonable grounds of suspecting him to be guilty of an offence under Section 1, 9 or 10 of the Act, or to be or to have been involved in terrorism connected with the affairs of Northern Ireland, to be detained in right of the arrest for up to 48 hours and thereafter, where the Secretary of State extends the detention period, for up to a further five days. Section 12 substantially re-enacted Section 12 of the Prevention of Terrorism (Temporary Provisions) Act 1976 which, in turn, substantially re-enacted Section 7 of the Prevention of Terrorism (Temporary Provisions) Act 1974.

Article 10 of the Prevention of Terrorism (Supplemental Temporary Provisions) (Northern Ireland) Order 1984 (SI 1984/417) and Article 9 of the Prevention of Terrorism (Supplemental Temporary Provisions) Order 1984 (SI 1984/418) were both made under Sections 13 and 14 of and Schedule 3 to the 1984 Act and substantially re-enacted powers of detention in Orders made under the 1974 and 1976 Acts. A person who is being examined under Article 4 of either Order on his arrival in, or on seeking to leave, Northern Ireland or Great Britain for the purpose of determining whether he is or has been involved in terrorism connected with the affairs of Northern Ireland, or whether there are grounds for suspecting that he has committed an offence under Section 9 of the 1984 Act, may be detained under Article 9 or 10, as appropriate, pending the conclusion of his examination. The period of this examination may exceed 12 hours if an examining officer has reasonable grounds for suspecting him to be or to have been involved in acts of terrorism connected with the affairs of Northern Ireland.

Where such a person is detained under the said Article 9 or 10 he may be detained for up to 48 hours on the authority of an examining officer and thereafter, where the Secretary of State extends the detention period, for up to a further five days.

In its judgment of 29 November 1988 in the Case of *Brogan and Others*, the European Court of Human Rights held that there had been a violation of Article 5(3) in respect of each of the applicants, all of whom had been detained under Section 12 of the 1984 Act. The Court held that even the shortest of the four periods of detention concerned, namely four days and six hours, fell outside the constraints as to time permitted by the first part of Article 5(3). In addition, the Court held that there had been a violation of Article 5(5) in the case of each applicant. Following this judgment, the Secretary of State for the Home Department informed Parliament on 6 December 1988 that, against the background of the terrorist campaign, and the over-riding need to bring terrorists to justice, the Government did not believe that the maximum period of detention should be reduced. He informed Parliament that the Government were examining the matter with a view to responding to the judgment. On 22 December 1988, the Secretary of State further informed Parliament that it remained the Government's wish, if it could be achieved, to find a judicial process under which extended detention might be reviewed and where appropriate authorised by a judge or other judicial officer. But a further period of reflection and consultation was necessary before the Government could bring forward a firm and final view.

Since the judgment of 29 November 1988 as well as previously, the Government have found it necessary to continue to exercise, in relation to terrorism connected with the affairs of Northern Ireland, the powers described above enabling further detention without charge for periods of up to 5 days, on the authority of the Secretary of State, to the extent strictly required by the exigencies of the situation to enable necessary enquiries and investigations properly to be completed in order to decide whether criminal proceedings should be instituted. To the extent that the exercise of these powers may be inconsistent with the obligations imposed by the Convention the Government has availed itself of the right of derogation conferred by Article 15(1) of the Convention and will continue to do so until further notice.

Dated 23 December 1988.

The 1989 notification

The United Kingdom Permanent Representative to the Council of Europe presents his compliments to the Secretary General of the Council, and has the honour to convey the following information.

In his communication to the Secretary General of 23 December 1988, reference was made to the introduction and exercise of certain powers under section 12 of the Prevention of Terrorism (Temporary Provisions) Act 1984, Article 9 of the Prevention of Terrorism (Supplemental Temporary Provisions) Order 1984 and Article 10 of the Prevention of Terrorism (Supplemental Temporary Provisions) (Northern Ireland) Order 1984.

These provisions have been replaced by section 14 of and paragraph 6 of Schedule 5 to the Prevention of Terrorism (Temporary Provisions) Act 1989, which make comparable provision. They came into force on 22 March 1989. A copy of these provisions is enclosed. The United Kingdom Permanent Representative avails himself of this opportunity to renew to the Secretary General the assurance of his highest consideration.

23 March 1989.

PART II

RESERVATION

At the time of signing the present (First) Protocol, I declare that, in view of certain provisions of the Education Acts in the United Kingdom, the principle affirmed in the second sentence of Article 2 is accepted by the United Kingdom only so far as it is compatible with the provision of efficient instruction and training, and the avoidance of unreasonable public expenditure.

Dated 20 March 1952

Made by the United Kingdom Permanent Representative to the Council of Europe.

Schedule 4

JUDICIAL PENSIONS

Duty to make orders about pensions

1.–(1) The appropriate Minister must by order make provision with respect to pensions payable to or in respect of any holder of a judicial office who serves as an ECHR judge.

(2) A pensions order must include such provision as the Minister making it considers is necessary to secure that—

   (a) an ECHR judge who was, immediately before his appointment as an ECHR judge, a member of a judicial pension scheme is entitled to remain as a member of that scheme;

   (b) the terms on which he remains a member of the scheme are those which would have been applicable had he not been appointed as an ECHR judge; and

   (c) entitlement to benefits payable in accordance with the scheme continues to be determined as if, while serving as an ECHR judge, his salary was that which would (but for section 18(4)) have been payable to him in respect of his continuing service as the holder of his judicial office.

Contributions

2. A pensions order may, in particular, make provision—
    (a) for any contributions which are payable by a person who remains a member of a scheme as a result of the order, and which would otherwise be payable by deduction from his salary, to be made otherwise than by deduction from his salary as an ECHR judge; and
    (b) for such contributions to be collected in such manner as may be determined by the administrators of the scheme.

Amendments of other enactments

3. A pensions order may amend any provision of, or made under, a pensions Act in such manner and to such extent as the Minister making the order considers necessary or expedient to ensure the proper administration of any scheme to which it relates.

Definitions

4. In this Schedule—
"appropriate Minister" means—
    (a) in relation to any judicial office whose jurisdiction is exercisable exclusively in relation to Scotland, the Secretary of State; and
    (b) otherwise, the Lord Chancellor;
"ECHR judge" means the holder of a judicial office who is serving as a judge of the Court;
"judicial pension scheme" means a scheme established by and in accordance with a pensions Act;
"pensions Act" means—
    (a) the County Courts Act Northern Ireland) 1959;
    (b) the Sheriffs' Pensions (Scotland) Act 1961;
    (c) the Judicial Pensions Act 1981; or
    (d) the Judicial Pensions and Retirement Act 1993; and
"pensions order" means an order made under paragraph 1.

ACT OF SEDERUNT (RULES OF THE COURT OF SESSION)

(S.I. 1994 No. 1443)

CHAPTER 58

APPLICATIONS FOR JUDICIAL REVIEW

Application and interpretation of this Chapter

58.1.—(1) This Chapter applies to an application to the supervisory jurisdiction of the court.

(2) In this Chapter—
"the first hearing" means a hearing under rule 58.9;
"the second hearing" means a hearing under rule 58.10.

Disapplication of certain rules to this Chapter

58.2. The following rules shall not apply to a petition to which this Chapter applies:
rule 14.4 (form of petitions),
rule 14.5 (first order in petitions),
rule 14.9 (unopposed petitions).

Applications for judicial review

58.3.—(1) Subject to paragraph (2), an application to the supervisory jurisdiction of the court, including an application under section 45(b) of the Act of 1988 (specific performance of statutory duty), shall be made by petition for judicial review.

(2) An application may not be made under paragraph (1) if that application is made, or could be made, by appeal or review under or by virtue of any enactment.

Powers of court in judicial review

58.4. The court, in exercising its supervisory jurisdiction on a petition for judicial review, may—
(a) grant or refuse any part of the petition, with or without conditions;
(b) make such order in relation to the decision in question as it thinks fit, whether or not such order was sought in the petition, being an order that could be made if sought in any action or petition, including an order for reduction, declarator, suspension, interdict, implement, restitution, payment (whether of damages or otherwise) and any interim order;
(c) subject to the provisions of this Chapter, make such order in relation to procedure as it thinks fit.

Nominated judge

58.5. A petition for judicial review shall be heard by a judge nominated by the Lord President for the purposes of this Chapter or, where such a judge is not available, any other judge of the court (including the vacation judge).

Form of petition

58.6.—(1) A petition for judicial review shall be in Form 58.6.

(2) The petitioner shall lodge with the petition all relevant documents in his possession and within his control.

(3) Where the petitioner founds in the petition on a document not in his possession or within his control, he shall append to the petition a schedule

specifying the document and the person who possesses or has control over the document.

(4) Where the decision, act or omission in question and the basis on which it is complained of is not apparent from the documents lodged with the petition, an affidavit shall be lodged stating the terms of the decision, act or omission and the basis on which it it complained of.

First order

58.7. On being lodged, the petition shall, without appearing in the Motion Roll, be presented forthwith to the Lord Ordinary in court or in chambers for—
    (a) an order specifying—
          (i) such intimation, service and advertisement as may be necessary;
         (ii) any documents to be served with the petition;
        (iii) a date for the first hearing, being a date not earlier than seven days after the expiry of the period specified for intimation and service; or
    (b) any interim order;
and, having heard counsel or other person having a right of audience, the Lord Ordinary may grant such an order.

Compearing parties

58.8.—(1) A person to whom intimation of the first hearing has been made and who intends to appear—
    (a) shall intimate his intention to do so to—
          (i) the agent for the petitioner, and
         (ii) the Keeper of the Rolls,
        not less than 48 hours before the date of the hearing; and
    (b) may lodge answers and any relevant documents.

(2) Any person not specified in the first order made under rule 58.7 as a person on whom service requires to be made may apply by motion for leave to enter the process; and if the motion is granted, the provisions of this Chapter shall apply to that person as they apply to a person specified in the first order.

First hearing

58.9.—(1) At the first hearing, the Lord Ordinary shall—
    (a) satisfy himself that the petitioner has duly complied with the first order made under rule 58.7; and
    (b) hear the parties.
(2) After hearing the parties, the Lord Ordinary may—
    (a) determine the petition; or
    (b) make such order for further procedure as he thinks fit, and in particular may—
          (i) adjourn or continue the first hearing to another date;
         (ii) order service on a person not specified in the first order made under rule 58.7;
        (iii) make any interim order;
        (iv) order answers to be lodged within such period as he shall specify;
        (v) order further specification in the petition or answers in relation to such matters as he shall specify:
       (vi) order any fact founded on by a party at the hearing to be supported by evidence on affidavit to be lodged within such period as he shall specify;
      (vii) order any party who appears to lodge such documents relating to tbe petition within such period as the Lord Ordinary shall specify;
     (viii) appoint a reporter to report to him on such matters of fact as the Lord Ordinary shall specify; or
      (ix) order a second hearing on such issues as he shall specify.

Second hearing

58.10.—(1) Where the Lord Ordinary orders a second hearing under rule 58.9(2)(b)(ix), the Keeper of the Rolls shall, in consultation with the Lord

Ordinary and the parties, fix a date for the second hearing as soon as reasonably practicable.

(2) Subject to the terms of any order for further procedure made under rule 58.9(2)(b), the parties shall, not less than seven days before the date of the second hearing, lodge all documents and affidavits to be founded on by them at the second hearing with copies for use by the court.

(3) At any time before the date of the second hearing, the Lord Ordinary may cause the petition to be put out for hearing on the By Order Roll for the purpose of obtaining such information from the parties as he considers necessary for the proper disposal of the petition at the hearing.

(4) At a hearing on the By Order Roll under paragraph (3), the Lord Ordinary may make such order as he thinks fit, having regard to all the circumstances, including an order appointing a commissioner to recover a document or take the evidence of a witness.

(5) At the second hearing, the Lord Ordinary may—
    (a) adjourn the hearing;
    (b) continue the hearing for such further procedure as he thinks fit; or
    (c) determine the petition.

INDEX